GNP and Expenditure Components (Billions of 1982 Dollars)

YEAR	GROSS NATIONAL PRODUCT (billions of 1982 dollars)	PERSONAL CONSUMPTION EXPENDITURES (billions of 1982 dollars)	GROSS PRIVATE DOMESTIC INVESTMENT (billions of 1982 dollars)	GOVERNMENT EXPENDITURES (billions of 1982 dollars)	NET EXPORTS (billions of 1982 dollars)
1929	709.6	471.4	139.2	94.2	4.7
1933	498.5	378.7	22.7	98.5	−1.4
1939	716.6	480.5	86.0	144.1	6.1
1940	772.9	502.6	111.8	150.2	8.2
1941	909.4	531.1	138.8	235.6	3.9
1942	1,080.3	527.6	76.7	483.7	−7.7
1943	1,276.2	539.9	50.4	708.9	−23.0
1944	1,380.6	557.1	56.4	790.8	−23.8
1945	1,354.8	592.7	76.5	704.5	−18.9
1946	1,096.9	655.0	178.1	236.9	27.0
1947	1,066.7	666.6	177.9	179.8	42.4
1948	1,108.7	681.8	208.2	199.5	19.2
1949	1,109.0	695.4	168.8	226.0	18.8
1950	1,203.7	733.2	234.9	230.8	4.7
1951	1,328.2	748.7	235.2	329.7	14.6
1952	1,380.0	771.4	211.8	389.9	6.9
1953	1,435.3	802.5	216.6	419.0	−2.7
1954	1,416.2	822.7	212.6	378.4	2.5
1955	1,494.9	873.8	259.8	361.3	.0
1956	1,525.6	899.8	257.8	363.7	4.3
1957	1,551.1	919.7	243.4	381.1	7.0
1958	1,539.2	932.9	221.4	395.3	−10.3
1959	1,629.1	979.4	270.3	397.7	−18.2
1960	1,665.3	1,005.1	260.5	403.7	−4.0
1961	1,708.7	1,025.2	259.1	427.1	−2.7
1962	1,799.4	1,069.0	288.6	449.4	−7.5
1963	1,873.3	1,108.4	307.1	459.8	−1.9
1964	1,973.3	1,170.6	325.9	470.8	5.9
1965	2,087.6	1,236.4	367.0	487.0	−2.7
1966	2,208.3	1,298.9	390.5	532.6	−13.7
1967	2,271.4	1,337.7	374.4	576.2	−16.9
1968	2,365.6	1,405.9	391.8	597.6	−29.7
1969	2,423.3	1,456.7	410.3	591.2	−34.9
1970	2,416.2	1,492.0	381.5	572.6	−30.0
1971	2,484.8	1,538.8	419.3	566.5	−39.8
1972	2,608.5	1,621.9	465.4	570.7	−49.4
1973	2,744.1	1,689.6	520.8	565.3	−31.5
1974	2,729.3	1,674.0	481.3	573.2	.8
1975	2,695.0	1,711.9	383.3	580.9	18.9
1976	2,826.7	1,803.9	453.5	580.3	−11.0
1977	2,958.6	1,883.8	521.3	589.1	−35.5
1978	3,115.2	1,961.0	576.9	604.1	−26.8
1979	3,192.4	2,004.4	575.2	609.1	3.6
1980	3,187.1	2,000.4	509.3	620.5	57.0
1981	3,248.8	2,024.2	545.5	629.7	49.4
1982	3,166.0	2,050.7	447.3	641.7	26.3
1983	3,279.1	2,146.0	504.0	649.0	−19.9
1984	3,501.4	2,249.3	658.4	677.7	−84.0
1985	3,618.7	2,354.8	637.0	731.2	−104.3
1986	3,717.9	2,446.4	639.6	761.6	−129.7
1987	3,845.3	2,515.8	669.0	779.1	−118.5
1988	4,016.9	2,606.5	705.7	780.5	−75.9
1989	4,117.7	2,656.8	716.9	798.1	−54.1
1990	4,155.8	2,682.2	690.3	820.8	−37.5

SOURCE: Council of Economic Advisers, *Economic Report of the President, 1991* (Washington, D.C.: U.S. Government Printing Office, 1991).

ECONOMICS

ECONOMICS

SECOND EDITION

ROGER A. ARNOLD

CALIFORNIA STATE UNIVERSITY, SAN MARCOS

WEST PUBLISHING COMPANY

ST. PAUL   NEW YORK   LOS ANGELES   SAN FRANCISCO

TO
SHEILA, DANIEL, AND DAVID

Production Credits
Production, Prepress, Printing, and
Binding by West Publishing Company
Copy Editing: Elaine Levin
Composition: Parkwood Composition Service
Indexing: Pat Lewis

Photo Credits
All photographs are supplied courtesy of the
individual economists featured in the interviews.

Acknowledgments
15 Friedman, Milton, "The Methodology of Positive Economics," *Essays in Positive Economics.* (Chicago: The University of Chicago Press, 1953), p. 15. Reprinted with permission. **95** Leijonhufvud, Axel. "Effective Demand Failures," *Swedish Journal of Economics* 75 (1973), p. 28. Reprinted with permission. **478** Samuelson, Paul. "Proof That Properly Discounted Present Values of Assets Vibrate Randomly." Copyright 1973. Reprinted from *The Bell Journal of Economics* with permission of the RAND Corporation. **566** Posner, Richard, A. "Theories of Regulation." Copyright 1974. Reprinted from *The Bell Journal of Economics* with permission of the RAND Corporation. **670** Friedman, Milton. *Capitalism and Freedom.* (Chicago: The University of Chicago Press, 1952), p. 191. Reprinted with permission **723, top:** Buchanan, James. *The Limits of Liberty, between Anarchy and Leviathan.* (Chicago: The University of Chicago Press, 1975), p. 149. Reprinted with permission. **724** From the song *Elected* by Alice Cooper. Reprinted with permission. **825–826** Smith, Adam. *The Theory of Moral Sentiments.* (Oxford: Oxford University Press, 1976), p. 234. Reprinted with permission. Material from *The New Palgrave: A Dictionary of Economics* reprinted with permission from Macmillan Press Ltd.

Library of Congress Cataloging-in-Publication Data

Arnold, Roger A.
  Economics / Roger A. Arnold.—2nd ed.
    p. cm.
  Includes bibliography references and index.
  ISBN 0-314-88424-6
  1. Economics.   I. Title.
HB171.5.A695 1992
330—dc20

91-37237
CIP ∞

CONTENTS IN BRIEF

MICROECONOMICS   409

■

THE WORLD ECONOMY   737

■

CONTENTS

ECONOMICS IN OUR TIMES
■
Economic Growth: An Expanding PPF Ends the Political Tug-of-War, for a While   40

ECONOMICS IN OUR TIMES
■
Interview: Vernon Smith   65

CONTENTS
■
x

ECONOMICS IN OUR TIMES
■
**What Does Price Have to Do with
Being Late to Class?** 84

MACROECONOMICS 89
■

CONTENTS
■

ECONOMICS IN OUR TIMES
■
The Underground Economy 119

ECONOMICS IN OUR TIMES
■
**No Communication with the
Outside World: The BEA at
Work 125**

ECONOMICS IN OUR TIMES
■
**How Do You Know if You're
Beating Inflation or If Inflation is
Beating You?**

ECONOMICS IN OUR TIMES
■
**Can Economics Pick the
Winner? 143**

ECONOMICS IN OUR TIMES
■
**How Does Foreign Buying of U.S.
Goods Affect the U.S. Price Level,
Real GNP, and Unemployment
Rate? 169**

ECONOMICS IN OUR TIMES
■
Interview: George Akerlof 187

CONTENTS
■
xiii

ECONOMICS IN OUR TIMES
■

**What Caused the Great
Depression? A Keynesian
Answer   207**

ECONOMICS IN OUR TIMES
■

**Interview: Paul A.
Samuelson   210**

CONTENTS
■
xiv

ECONOMICS IN OUR TIMES
■
**A Lot of Finger Pointing Goes on
During a Rapid Inflation   292**

ECONOMICS IN OUR TIMES
■
**Does Dog Racing Cause
Continued Inflation?   294**

ECONOMICS IN OUR TIMES
■
**Does the Fed Think in Terms of
MV = PQ?   307**

CONTENTS
■

ECONOMICS IN OUR TIMES
■

**If Cars Get More Miles Per
Gallon, Will There Be More or
Less Car Pollution? 451**

CONTENTS
■
xx

ECONOMICS IN OUR TIMES
■
Interview: George Stigler   526

ECONOMICS IN OUR TIMES
■
Interview: Gordon Tullock   544

ECONOMICS IN OUR TIMES
■
**If the Tax Is Divided Equally,
Why Do I Pay It All? 595**

ECONOMICS IN OUR TIMES
■
**College Sports and the
NCAA 612**

CONTENTS
■
xxiv

ECONOMICS IN OUR TIMES
■
How Much Is That Medical Degree Worth? 62

ECONOMICS IN OUR TIMES
■
Stories from Down on the Farm 646

THE WORLD ECONOMY   737
■

CONTENTS
■

In the second edition of *Economics*, I have tried to retain the strengths of the first edition, eliminate any weaknesses, and continue in my endeavor to write a text that is both exciting and pedagogically sound. It is a cliche, perhaps, but nevertheless true: one of the major motivating factors for my writing a principles text is to convey to students the excitement, richness, and power of economic analysis that I, and thousands of economics professors across the country, experience daily.

The second edition of *Economics* is a cleaner, better organized, more innovative text than the first edition. I have listened to the constructive comments of numerous reviewers and colleagues, hundreds of students, the editorial staff of West Publishing Company, and the little voice inside of me, to write a book that I trust you will find worth your time.

ORGANIZATION OF THE SECOND EDITION

Section I. Economics: The Science of Scarcity.   This book is organized into four sections. Section I discusses the key concepts and tools in economics. Two of the four chapters are devoted to supply-and-demand analysis. Upon completion of this section, the student should have a solid understanding of the economic way of thinking.

Section II. Macroeconomics.   The organization of macroeconomics is different than in the first edition. Adopters of the second edition will find a smoother macroeconomics to teach. First, a new introductory chapter, Chapter 5, introduces the student to the key players in macroeconomics (consumers, businesses, government, foreigners, the Fed, and so on) and presents an organizational scheme that can be used as he or she reads the 13 remaining macroeconomic chapters.

Overall, macroeconomics is presented in terms of major topics. The first topic is macroeconomic measurements. Gross national product (GNP), real GNP, price indices, and unemployment and employment rates are discussed. The second topic is theory and fiscal policy. Here the origins of Keynesian theory, both old and new Keynesian theory, and fiscal policy are discussed. The third topic is theory, money, and policy. Money and banking, the Federal Reserve System, classical and monetarist theory, inflation, and monetary policy are discussed. The fourth topic is theory, expectations, and policy. Phillips curve analysis, job search theory, new classical theory, adaptive and rational expectations, business cycles, and monetary and fiscal policy are discussed. There are other items discussed under each of the four major topics, but the major ones have been noted here. Also, the defining framework of the macroeconomics section is the aggregate demand-aggregate supply (AD-AS) framework, although the income-expenditure (I-E) framework and $MV = PQ$ framework are used, too.

Three Organizational Categories.   Offices can be cluttered without file cabinets and bookshelves, and minds can be cluttered without methods of organizing information. The macroeconomics student is better able to understand all the information that comes her way in a macroeconomics course if she has a way of "processing" and "filing" the information as it is obtained. With this in mind, three organizational categories have been developed for the student studying macroeconomics. (See Chapter 5 for a complete discussion of the three organizational categories.) The first organizational category is the P-Q category, where P stands for the price level and Q stands for real GNP. The student learns that P and Q are two very important variables in macroeconomics and that much of what he or she studies is either directly or indirectly related to these variables. For example, GNP is P times Q, inflation is a rising P, deflation is a falling P, economic growth is related to an increasing Q, a recessionary gap is the condition in the economy when Q is below its natural level, the business cycle consists of recurrent swings (up and down) in Q, and so on. Seeing topics in terms of either directly or indirectly relating to P and/or Q helps the student to see the common denominator of much that is discussed in macroeconomics.

The second organizational category is the *inherently stable-inherently unstable* category. The student learns that much of the debate in macroeconomics centers around whether or not the economy is self-equilibrating, or self-regulating, and inherently stable. There are those economists who believe that it is (e.g., monetarists and new classical economists), and those economists that do not (e.g., Keynesians). The view of the economy an economist has is implicit in the theory in which he believes is true and in his policy proposals. The uses of this category are numerous for the student. For example, upon learning, say, that Keynesians believe the economy is inherently unstable, the student is led to ask: But why do Keynesians believe the economy is inherently unstable? This brings the student to a discussion of inflexible wages, monopoly elements in the economy, and more.

The third organizational category is the *effective-ineffective* category. Here the words *effective* and *ineffective* describe fiscal and monetary policy. The student learns that an economist can take one of several positions within this category. She can believe that monetary policy is effective and fiscal policy is not, or that fiscal policy is effective and monetary policy is not, or that neither is effective, and so on. Also, the student learns that one's view of the economy (as being inherently stable or inherently unstable) also is tied to whether or not one advocates trying to use policy to stabilize the economy.

In short, the three categories are there to help the student categorize and organize the many details he is asked to learn. They are there to help him keep the big picture, or the fundamental issues, of macroeconomics in front of him as proceeds to work through the technical aspects of macroeconomic problems, theories, and policies.

International Coverage in Macroeconomics. Every author of a principles text says that it is imperative to integrate international economics into macroeconomics, and every author is correct. But it is important *how* it is integrated. Is it integrated to such an extent that domestic macroeconomic issues take second place? Is it integrated to such an extent that the macroeconomics course is a completely new course to teach? Is it integrated in a non-substantive way, such as throwing in, here and there, a phrase or two that mentions, say, the international value of the dollar? I have tried to integrate international economics into macroeconomics in, what I consider, a substantive, complete, but not overtaxing way. Mainly, it has been added to the theoretical and policy discussions in the text. To cite only three of the many examples, there is a theoretical discussion of the relationship between the budget deficit and the trade deficit, and a policy discussion of both fiscal and monetary policy in an open economy.

Section III. Microeconomics. Readers of the second edition will find the chapter organization of microeconomics the same as in the first edition—with one important change. Chapter 19, the first microeconomics chapter in the text, briefly discusses the players in microeconomics—consumers, firms, factor owners, and government—so that students know right away who and what is involved. Then it develops a "microeconomics mindset" the student can use to organize, categorize, and understand the myriad topics in microeconomics as he proceeds to read on. The "mindset" came by asking this question: What is microeconomics about? Here is my three-part answer.

First, the student learns that microeconomics is about consumers, firms, and factor owners sharing a reality: each has an objective, each faces constraints, and each has to make choices. Objectives-Constraints-Choices. For example, consumers' objective is to maximize utility, and they are constrained by their limited incomes and by the positive prices for each good. Given limited purchasing ability, the consumer will attempt to gain as much utility as possible from each dollar spent. In practice, this is done by *choosing* marginal analysis in making consumption decisions—by comparing additional (marginal) benefits and additional (marginal) costs of each purchase. In short, the trilogy of objectives-constraints-choices gives our microeconomic discussion of consumers focus. The student quickly sees the key elements around which the whole discussion takes place.

Second, students learn that microeconomics is about the interaction between consumers and firms, and between firms and factor owners, in market settings. In short, microeconomics is about markets. Once the student understands this, and realizes that much of what she learns has to do with the interactions of economic agents, we can go on to specify different types of market settings—e.g., perfectly competitive, monopolistic, and so on.

Third, microeconomics is about the workings of markets with and without government intervention. The student is instructed to examine both the *purpose* and the *effects* of government's involvement in markets. The *effects*, in particular, can be related to the objectives, constraints, and choices of consumers, firms, and factor owners. To illustrate, suppose government decides to tax firms. We would want to know how the tax affects the objectives, constraints, and choices of the firm, and then how the (perhaps) changed behavior on one side of the market (supply side) affects overall market outcomes.

In conclusion, the microeconomics mindset the student carries through his learning microeconomics includes the following points:

- Microeconomics is about consumers, firms, and factor owners.
- Consumers, firms and factor owners each have objectives.
- They try to achieve their objectives in the face of certain constraints.
- Because they try to achieve objectives in a world of constraints, they are forced to make choices.
- They make their choices in a certain way: by weighing additional benefits and additional costs.
- Consumers and firms, and firms and factor owners, interact in market settings. In any market, there is always something being bought and something being sold.
- There exist different types of market settings.
- Government can affect the behavior of consumers, firms, and factor owners, and thus affect overall market outcomes.

The Power of Microeconomics. I believe that microeconomic tools are the most powerful tools of analysis in the social sciences. From my reading and study, I do not believe that the fields of sociology, political science, or psychology have tools of analysis that come even close to the power of the *economist's microeconomic* tools. However, I also believe that college students are usually unaware of this—sometimes even after having taken an economics course or two. With this in mind, I have tried to sharpen the presentation of microeconomics in this edition, and mainly to apply microeconomic tools in a way that will catch the student's attention. I believe that microeconomic tools not only are powerful enough to tell students about costs, production, firms, market structures and so on, but are also powerful enough to help students gain insights into why they have the number of friends they have (why not more?), why they sometimes get bored, why they chose the major that they did, and why they are sometimes late for class, among other things. My deepest feeling is that unless we use the microeconomics tools we have at our disposal to excite students, they will continue to think that microeconomics is simply about the supply and demand for cars, or about the costs of a firm, and so on. Nobel Laureate James Buchanan once wrote that what a science [such as economics] does, or should do, is simply to allow the average man . . . to command the heights of genius. I rewrote the microeconomics section of the first edition of *Economics* with this statement in mind. I want students to come into the microeconomics principles class with nothing but their notebooks, pens, and an open mind, and I want them to leave feeling like they have found gold.

THINKING LIKE AN ECONOMIST: A NEW FEATURE
■

The authors of principles books are quick to point out that their books teach students how to think like an economist—but they never tell us how they accomplish this feat. Supposedly, students will read the book and simply figure out how economists think. It is true that some students do pick up how economists think by using this method, but too many do not. I believe that it is the author's responsibility to explicitly point out, where possible, how economists think. I have done this throughout this book, at appropriate places. These places are easily identifiable throughout the text.

ECONOMICS IN OUR TIMES: APPLICATIONS
■

Gary Becker, in his interview in this book, said that the way to give students a good feel for economics is to show them "how to use it to understand the world about them." I believe Becker is exactly right. In the classroom, I have found that students get unusually excited over economics when I use it to provide them with insights into their world. After all, the student is rational; raise the benefits of learning economics relative to the costs, and he will want to learn more economics. I have tried to make the applications in this book as exciting and relevant to the student as I could. Some people may feel that a few of the applications are a little offbeat, and are not ordinary. Well, I hope so. I don't think that we have to continually use the same old applications to illustrate economic analysis to our students. We can break out of the mold sometimes, get a little daring, and just have some fun.

INTERSPERSED QUESTIONS: ANTICIPATING WHAT THE READER WANTS TO ASK
■

Often when I read books I wish the author were around so that now and then I could ask a question. I think students feel the same way when they are reading an economics textbook such as this one. That is why I have interspersed throughout the text questions that the reader might have come up with as he or she is reading along. Then, I have answered these questions.

INTERVIEWS: SOME NEW, MANY UPDATED
■

It is one thing to have the author of a text discuss monetarism, and it is quite another to read what Milton Friedman has to say about it. It is one thing to have the author of a text discuss Phillips curve analysis, and it is quite another to have Robert Solow discuss it. There are 21 interviews with well-known economists in this text. The economists interviewed include Gary Becker, Paul Samuelson, Alice Rivlin, Milton Friedman, Allan Meltzer, Robert Solow, Thomas Sargent, George Akerlof, George Stigler, Gordon Tullock, William Baumol, Charles Plosser, John Kenneth Galbraith, Walter Williams, Murray Weidenbaum, Harold Demsetz, James Buchanan, Lester Thurow, Irma Adelman, Allen Kneese, and Vernon Smith. Many of the interviews are new and many are updated from the first edition.

INTERNATIONAL COVERAGE
■

With international economic news making front-page headlines, it is imperative to present students with a book that clearly identifies how international economic events affect the U.S. economy and how U.S. economic events affect the world economy. This edition of *Economics* has international economics thoroughly integrated throughout, but especially in the macroeconomics part of the book.

A MODERN BOOK
■

The second edition of *Economics* continues in the tradition of the first edition: to present the reader with a truly modern book. Topics added to the second edition include experimental economics, environmental economics, an expanded and updated discussion of new Keynesian economics, economic changes in Eastern Europe and the Soviet Union, and the Japanese economy, among others.

SUPPLEMENTS: PRINTED, COMPUTERIZED, AND LASER TECHNOLOGY
■

The supplements that go along with this book include:

■ Study Guides
■ MicroGuide Computerized Study Guide
■ Instructor's Manual
■ Enrichment Lectures
■ Test Bank (over 6,000 questions)
■ WestTest Microcomputer Testing
■ Study Wizard Software Package (Computer Software for Microeconomics and Macroeconomics)
■ Transparencies
■ Video disc/Videotape

Study Guide. The Study Guide was principally written by Thomas Wyrick of Southwest Missouri State University. Each chapter explains, reviews, and tests the student on important facts, concepts, and diagrams found in corresponding chapters in this book. Chapter parts include an introduction to and purpose of each chapter, a review of concepts from earlier chapters, a fill-in-the-blank review of concepts to be learned, and problems and exercises. I wrote the self-test that ends each chapter. The Study Guide also comes in microeconomics and macroeconomics splits.

MicroGuide Computerized Study Guide.   The computerized study guide allows students to sit at the computer and quiz themselves on text material chapter by chapter. The questions are taken from the printed study guide. Students can choose any chapter or combination of chapters and the program will provide multiple-choice, true/false, matching, and fill-in-the-blank questions. Special features include: feedback on the correct answer and page-referencing to the main text, grading at the end of each session, the option to print quiz questions and results. MicroGuide is available for IBM PCs/compatibles with 512K or Macintoshes with Hypercard.

Instructor's Manual.   The Instructor's Manual was written by Keith A. Rowley, formerly of Baylor University. It offers detailed lecture assistance for this book. Chapter parts include an overview of each text chapter, a list of chapter objectives, a list of key terms, a detailed chapter outline with lecture notes, and answers to end-of-chapter questions.

Enrichment Lectures.   Twenty-five lectures with accompanying transparencies are included in the supplement package. The lectures are on current topics of high interest to instructors and students alike. The lectures were prepared by Keith Rowley and Thomas Wyrick.

Test Bank.   The double-size test bank contains more than 6,000 test questions. Approximately 1,000 questions are new, with special emphasis on graphing-related problems. The test bank was prepared by Patricia Freeman of University of Southern Louisiana and Dusan Stojanovic of Washington University.

WestTest Microcomputer Testing.   The new WestTest 2.0 testing system for either IBM PCs and compatibles or Macintoshes allows you to choose, create, edit, store, and print exams and answer keys. The system is menu-driven with a new desktop format and the options of using keystrokes or a mouse, accelerators, and function keys.

The New Economics Study Wizard 2.0 Software Packages.   There are two software packages—one for microeconomics and one for macroeconomics. The software packages were developed by Dennis Muraoka of California State University at Long Beach. Each software package has the following components: a graphics tutorial that is animated and annotated and contains a quiz on the graphs; terms and definitions in the form of a game; and a quiz that provides a review for the exam. Hardware requirements: IBM PC/compatibles, DOS 2.0 or higher with minimum 256K available in RAM. Graphics tutorials require CGA, EGA, or VGA with color monitor. At the end of each chapter in the text, students will find questions and problems. A few of the questions and problems have a logo next to them, indicating that the material in these questions and problems can be used in conjunction with the software package.

Transparencies. 150 transparencies (many in color) of key exhibits in the text are available for classroom use.

Video Disc/Videotape. I am excited about the fact that the second edition of *Economics* comes with a supplement like this one. Laser technology now makes it possible, with a touch of a button, to access key diagrams from the text. Not only that but the illustrations are presented in such a way that students can clearly and in proper time sequence see how the diagrams are built. Suppose the instructor wants to show students the intricacies of supply-and-demand analysis. He or she pushes the button, and there is a demand curve. Push the button again, and a supply curve appears. Push again, and the equilibrium point is identified. Push again, there is equilibrium price. And so on. For students this is a way to understand diagrams by seeing how they are built. For instructors, this is a way to offer step-by-step explanations and diagrammatics with simply a push of a button.

The new video disc also makes it possible to access footage from the popular Economics U$A* series which was funded by the Annenberg/CPB project. This is a way to bring real-world economic events (sights, sounds, and analysis) into the classroom. Economics has never been more real and relevant to students. (All the video segments which appear on the disc are also available on videotape presented as clips in the same order in which they appear on the disc.)

In Appreciation

■

This book could not have been written and published without the generous and expert assistance of many people. A deep debt of gratitude is owed to the reviewers of the first edition, the reviewers of the second edition, and the numerous persons who have offered constructive comments and suggestions on one or both of the editions.

First Edition Reviewers and Others I Wish to Thank

Jack Adams
University of Arkansas, Little Rock

William Askwig
University of Southern Colorado

Michael Babcock
Kansas State University

Dan Barszcz
College of DuPage, Illinois

Robert Berry
Miami University, Ohio

George Bohler
Florida Junior College

Tom Bonsor
Eastern Washington University

Michael D. Brendler
Louisiana State University

Baird Brock
Central Missouri State University

Kathleen Bromley
Monroe Community College, New York

Kathleen Brook
New Mexico State University

Douglas Brown
Georgetown University

Ernest Buchholz
Santa Monica Community College, California

Gary Burbridge
Grand Rapids Junior College, Michigan

Maureen Burton
California State Polytechnic University, Pomona

Carol Carnes
Kansas State University

Paul Coomes
University of Louisville, Kentucky

Eleanor Craig
University of Delaware

Diane Cunningham
Glendale Community College, California

Wilford Cummings
Grosmont College, California

Douglas C. Darran
University of South Carolina

Edward Day
University of Central Florida

Johan Deprez
University of Tennessee

James Dietz
California State University, Fullerton

Stuart Dorsey
University of West Virginia

Richard Douglas
Bowling Green State University, Ohio

Natalia Drury
Northern Virginia Community College

Lu Ann Duffus
California State University, Hayward

John Eckalbar
California State University, Chico

*Economics U$A was produced by Educational Film Center. Copyright © 1986 by Educational Film Center.

John Elliott
University of Southern California

Charles Fischer
Pittsburg State University, Kansas

John Gemello
San Francisco State University

Carl Guelzo
*Cantonsville Community College,
Maryland*

Jan Hansen
University of Wisconsin, Eau Claire

John Henderson
Georgia State University

Ken Howard
East Texas Baptist University

Mark Karscig
Central Missouri State University

Stanley Keil
Ball State University, Indiana

Richard Kieffer
State University of New York, Buffalo

Gene Kimmett
William Rainey Harper College, Illinois

Luther Lawson
University of North Carolina

Frank Leori
College of San Mateo, California

Kenneth Long
New River Community College, Virginia

Michael Magura
University of Toledo, Ohio

Bruce McCrea
Lansing Community College, Michigan

Gerald McDougall
Wichita State University, Kansas

Kevin McGee
University of Wisconsin, Oshkosh

Francois Melese
Auburn University, Alabama

Herbert Miliken
American River College, California

Richard Miller
Pennsylvania State University

Ernest Moser
Northeast Louisiana University

Farhang Niroomand
University of Southern Mississippi

Eliot Orton
New Mexico State University

Marty Perline
Wichita State University, Kansas

Harold Petersen
Boston College

Douglas Poe
University of Texas, Austin

Joseph Rezny
St. Louis Community College, Missouri

Terry Ridgway
University of Nevada, Las Vegas

Thomas Romans
State University of New York, Buffalo

Robert Ross
Bloomsburg State College, Pennsylvania

Keith A. Rowley
Baylor University, Texas

Anandi Sahu
Oakland University, Michigan

Richard Scoggins
California State University, Long Beach

Alan Sleeman
Western Washington University

John Sondey
University of Idaho

Shahram Shafiee
North Harris County College, Texas

Paul Seidenstat
Temple University, Pennsylvania

Robert W. Thomas
Iowa State University

Roger Trenary
Kansas State University

Richard L. Tontz
California State University, Northridge

Bruce Vanderporten
Loyola University, Illinois

Richard O. Welch
University of Texas at San Antonio

Thomas Weiss
University of Kansas

Donald A. Wells
University of Arizona

John Wight
University of Richmond, Virginia

Thomas Wyrick
Southwest Missouri State University

Second Edition Reviewers and Others I Wish to Thank

Scott Bloom
North Dakota State University

Thomas Carroll
University of Nevada, Las Vegas

Larry Cox
Southwest Missouri State University

Diane Cunningham
Los Angeles Valley College

Emit Deal
Macon College

Charles Van Eaton
Hillsdale College

Michael Fabritius
University of Mary Hardin Baylor

Frederick Fagal
Marywood College

Ralph Fowler
Diablo Valley College

Bob Gillette
Texas A&M University

Lynn Gillette
Indiana University, Indianapolis

Simon Hakim
Temple University

Lewis Karstensson
University of Nevada, Las Vegas

Abraham Kidane
*California State University, Dominguez
Hills*

W. Barbara Killen
University of Minnesota

J. David Lages
Southwest Missouri State University

Anthony Lee
Austin Community College

Marjory Mabery
Delaware County Community College

Bernard Malamud
University of Nevada, Las Vegas

Michael Marlowe
*California Polytechnic State University,
San Louis Obisto*

Phil J. McLewin
Ramapo College of New Jersey

Tina Quinn
Arkansas State University

Terry Ridgway
University of Nevada, Las Vegas

Paul Snoonian
University of Lowell

Paul Taube
Pan American University

Roger Trenary
Kansas State University

Mark Wheeler
Bowling Green State University

Thomas Wyrick
Southwest Missouri State University

I offer my sincerest thanks to the twenty-one (21) economists who appear in the interviews in this book. Each was generous with his or her time, genuinely interested in reaching students, and always gracious. Their contributions have greatly added to the range and richness of views found in this book.

I offer my sincerest gratitude to Thomas Wyrick (Southwest Missouri State University), who, besides writing the study guide, read the entire manuscript and provided detailed comments and invaluable suggestions. My thanks to Keith Rowley (formerly of Baylor University), who wrote the instructor's manual and enrichment lectures. My heartfelt appreciation to Patricia Freeman (University of Southwestern Louisiana) who wrote questions for and organized the test bank and to Dusan Stojanovic (Washington University) who wrote questions for the test bank.

My deepest debt of gratitude goes to Clyde Perlee, Jr., editor-in-chief of West's college division. He continues to be my inspiration for writing the best book I know how to write. He is one of those persons who you know has made your life better just by being who he is. I am extremely fortunate that he is my editor and my friend. My many thanks to Bill Stryker, production editor, who has the ability to produce a book that is better than an author has a right to hope for. My belief—that he is the best at what he does—continues to be confirmed. I am also grateful to Theresa O'Dell, developmental editor. She worked hard and capably supervising all the details of the supplement package and she continues to make working on this project fun.

My thanks also go to Kristin J. McCarthy and Ellen Stanton for their work on the marketing program and to Beth Hoeppner for her work on the video disc. In addition, my gratitude to Elaine Levin for her excellent copy-editing.

My deepest appreciation goes to my wife, Sheila. She is always there with her support, encouragement, understanding, and love. Finally, I want to thank my two sons: Daniel, who is four years old, and David, who is 17 months old. Watching them, in everything they do, from sleeping to tearing the house apart, is one of the great pleasures of life.

Suggested Course Outlines

This book is intended for the two-semester sequence in macroeconomics and microeconomics that is taught at colleges and universities. The book is available in a combined macro-micro hardbound volume and two paperback split versions, titled *Macroeconomics* and *Microeconomics.* The combined macro-micro hardbound volume can be used for a one-semester course that covers both macroeconomics and microeconomics. The suggested outlines (listed below) for one-semester, one-quarter, and combined macro-micro courses reflect the author's preferences only. Instructors may want to design courses with different emphases.

Suggested One-Semester and One-Quarter Course Outlines

CHAPTERS	MACRO EMPHASIS	MICRO EMPHASIS	COMBINED MACRO-MICRO
1 What Economics Is About	• •	• •	• •
2 Fundamentals of Economic Thinking: Within the Production Possibilities Framework	•	• •	
3 Supply, Demand, and Price: Theory	• •	• •	• •
4 Supply, Demand, and Price: Applications		•	
5 An Introduction to Macroeconomics	• •		• •
6 Measuring GNP	• •		• •
7 Measuring the Price Level, Real GNP, and Unemployment	• •		• •
8 The Aggregate Demand-Aggregate Supply Framework	• •		• •
9 Keynesian Theory: Emphasis on Unemployment	• •		• •
10 Fiscal Policy	• •		•
11 Money and Banking	• •		• •
12 The Federal Reserve System	• •		• •
13 Inflation	• •		• •
14 Classical and Monetarist Theory: Emphasis on the Price Level and GNP	• •		•
15 Monetary Policy	• •		•
16 Job Search Theory, Phillips Curve Analysis, and New Classical Theory: Enter Expectations	• •		
17 Business Cycles: Theories of Economic Expansion and Contraction	• •		
18 Budget Deficits and the National Debt	•		
19 An Introduction to Microeconomics		• •	• •
20 The Logic of Consumer Choice		• •	• •
21 Elasticity		• •	• •
22 The Firm		• •	
23 Production and Costs		• •	• •
24 Perfect Competition		• •	• •
25 Monopoly		• •	• •
26 Monopolistic Competition and Oligopoly		• •	• •
27 Factor Markets: With Emphasis on the Labor Market		• •	•
28 Wages, Unions, and Labor		•	
29 Interest, Rent, and Profit		•	
30 Agriculture: Problems and Policies		•	
31 The Distribution of Income and Poverty		•	
32 Antitrust, Business Regulation, and Deregulation		•	
33 Market Failure: Externalities, The Environment, and Public Goods		• •	•
34 Public Choice: Economic Theory Applied to Politics		•	
35 International Trade	• •	• •	• •
36 International Finance	•		
37 Economic Growth and Development	•		
38 Alternative Economic Systems: Theory, Practice, and Evolutionary Aspects	•	•	•

• One-Semester Course   • One-Quarter course

AN INTRODUCTION TO ECONOMICS

PART

I

ECONOMICS: THE SCIENCE OF SCARCITY

CHAPTER

1

WHAT ECONOMICS IS ABOUT

WHAT THIS CHAPTER IS ABOUT

We begin this chapter by answering some of the questions you may have about the study of economics. Next, we discuss what many economists consider to be the most important concept in economics—scarcity. Then, we discuss the role and nature of theory in economics and the scientific way of thinking. Finally, we discuss the several categories into which economics can be divided.

Scarcity is the basic economic problem that all individuals and societies face.

■

Scarcity
The condition where our wants are greater than the limited resources available to satisfy those wants.

Economics
The science of scarcity: the science of how individuals and societies deal with the fact that wants are greater than the limited resources available to satisfy those wants.

Economic Analysis
The process of applying economic tools and the economic way of thinking to real-world problems.

Here are the answers to five questions about economics that students are likely to ask.

What Is Economics?

Without matter and motion, there would be no physics; without living things, there would be no biology; and without **scarcity,** there would be no economics.

Scarcity is the condition where our wants are greater than the limited resources available to satisfy those wants. Scarcity is the basic economic problem that all individuals and societies face.

Since there would be no economics without scarcity, **economics** is defined as the *science of scarcity.* Specifically, *it is the science of how individuals and societies deal with the fact that wants are greater than the limited resources available to satisfy those wants.*

What Do Economists Study?

Economists study markets, prices, costs, production, inflation, unemployment, interest rates, business cycles, budget deficits, trade deficits, exchange rates, and so on. These are many of the subjects discussed in this book.

But economists increasingly study other areas of human activity as well—such things as crime, family relationships, war, politics, psychology, the law, and much more.[1]

Economists today do not have a preconceived notion of what they should and should not study. They may simply observe the world until something captures their attention or piques their curiosity. They then apply **economic analysis**— composed of the tools of economics and the economic way of thinking—to whatever it is that they are interested in.

This may seem like an odd way to proceed. Some noneconomists think it would be better if economists decided on the 30 or so topics they feel they are best equipped to study and then study these and no more. But economists believe this approach grossly underestimates the power of economic analysis. Although economists do not believe that economics can explain everything about the world, they do believe it can explain much about it. An objective of this text is to show you that economic analysis is more powerful at explaining your world to you than you may have believed was possible.

What Is the Economic Way of Thinking?

In general, the economic way of thinking refers to the way economists view, interpret, and analyze the world. Consider an analogy from the field of architecture. Suppose you see a skyscraper in New York City. To your untrained eye, you see only a building that rises high into the sky. An architect sees much more. She sees a certain form and style; she secs the way that geometric shapes have come together to create an atmosphere and a mood. She sees things that others are blind to.

So it is with the economist. In a grocery store you may see shelves of food and drink. An economist sees more. He sees buyers and sellers having come together to determine what goods will be produced and at what prices the goods will be

[1]The subjects listed in this paragraph are not usually covered in a principles of economics course.

sold; he sees costs and production. He sees buyers and sellers trying to make themselves better off; he sees profit and loss. The economist sees the *process* that has resulted in the shelves of food and drink in much the same way that the architect sees the process of the creation of the skyscraper.

Why Study Economics?

Not everyone studies economics for the same reasons. Some people study it because of its relevance to problem solving in the real world. For example, the economist Alfred Marshall (1842–1924) was greatly concerned with poverty, which he believed was at the root of many social problems. He hoped that the study of economics would enable him to better understand the causes of poverty and to find a solution to it.

Some people study economics because of its explanatory and predictive power. For them, economics answers many of their questions—it explains why things are as they are and it predicts what is likely to happen under certain conditions. This can be a heady experience. The economist Paul Samuelson (b. 1915) said that setting out to explore the exciting world of economics for the first time is a unique thrill. Many undergraduate economics students agree.

Other people study economics because of their desire to learn about certain ideas that have shaped the world. The economist John Maynard Keynes (1883–1946) said that "the ideas of economists and political philosophers, both when they are right and when they are wrong, are more powerful than is commonly understood. Indeed, the world is ruled by little else. Practical men, who believe themselves to be quite exempt from any intellectual influences, are usually slaves of some defunct economist."

In this text, we hope to show you that your study of economics can enrich and broaden your life and provide you with much stimulating thought along the way.

Why Study Economics in the 1990s?

An understanding of economics is your ticket to some of the most exciting events in the world.

Many of the big news stories of the early 1990s were economics stories. For example, in 1990, the eyes of the world turned to the Soviet Union and many Eastern European nations as they began to move away from a highly controlled economy to one that placed greater emphasis on individual initiative and market forces.

In 1990, Iraq moved into Kuwait and the world began to worry about the future oil supply. In the United States, economists and others wondered how a sharp rise in the price of oil would affect the U.S. economy. Would it mean higher prices, a cutback in production, and an increase in unemployment?

In 1991, an unsuccessful coup attempt against Soviet President Mikhail Gorbachev resulted in his banning many of his colleagues from rule, forming a political alliance with Russian President and economic reform advocate, Boris Yeltsin, and resuming the move towards greater economic and political freedom. The world watched as a once tightly closed command-economy nation opened itself, albeit shakily at times, to the forces of democracy and free enterprise. The stage was set for the unfolding of an economic and political event that would have repercussions throughout the world and had the potential to change the character of the world economy.

> *The one language that bids to become universal is the language of economics.*
>
> ■

In 1992, many European nations moved toward further economic integration in what has been termed a "United States of Europe." In the United States and Japan, people wondered what a United States of Europe would mean in terms of international trade (Will an economically united Europe promote or retard international trade?), international competitiveness, domestic jobs, and much more.

In the United States, in 1990, the longest peacetime economic expansion in U.S. history halted. People worried about the oncoming economic recession. They asked, how long will the recession last, how deep will it be, how high will unemployment rise, and what will it mean to U.S. competitiveness in the world?

The days when the people of different nations could live lives isolated from one another are gone forever. The world is getting smaller, but individuals' consciousness of global events and their impact is increasing. We think the catalyst for this increased international awareness is economic in nature. Americans are interested in the Japanese because Japanese economic decisions affect American lives. The Japanese are interested in Europe because European economic unification affects Japan.

The one language that bids to become universal is the language of economics. The American businessperson may not speak Japanese, and the Japanese businessperson may not speak English, but both of them know the language of supply and demand, profits, production, costs, international trade, and competition. Both of them know the language of economics. It is becoming an increasingly important language for you to know, too.

SCARCITY, CHOICE, AND OPPORTUNITY COST
■

In this section, we discuss the basics of economics, which include scarcity, choice, and opportunity cost. We look at several questions. What are the consequences of scarcity? What is the relationship between scarcity and choice? And what is the relationship between choice and opportunity cost?

Scarcity

Good
Anything from which individuals receive utility or satisfaction.

Bad
Anything from which individuals receive disutility or dissatisfaction.

Utility
The satisfaction one receives (from the consumption of a good).

Disutility
The dissatisfaction one receives (from the consumption of a bad).

Free Good
A good where the amount available is greater than the amount people want at zero price.

Economic Good
A scarce good. A good where the amount available is less than people would want if it were given away at zero price.

As noted earlier, *scarcity* is the condition where our wants outstrip the limited resources available to satisfy those wants. Bluntly put, given the unlimited wants of people, there is never enough.

But never enough of what? Do we mean that there are never enough resources to produce *everything* in the world—from computers to pollution? Might there be too much of some things—pollution, for example? Economists break down "things" into two categories: **goods** and **bads.** A good is anything from which individuals receive **utility** or satisfaction. A bad is anything from which individuals receive **disutility** or dissatisfaction. Goods are such things as clothing, education, leisure time, food, television sets, and houses. Bads are such things as pollution and garbage.

The category *goods* is broken down further into **free goods** and **economic goods.** A free good is a good sufficiently available from nature to satisfy all possible desires. More formally, a free good is a good where the amount available is greater than the amount people want at zero price. An example would be clean air before the days of air pollution or sunshine in a sunny climate (such as in Phoenix, Arizona.)

An economic good is scarce: It is a good for which the quantity available is less than people would want if it were given away at zero price. For example, a car is an economic, or scarce, good. Even if cars were given away at zero price, still people would want more cars than there would be cars available.

So when we ask, Never enough of *what?* the answer is that there are never enough resources to produce enough *economic goods* to satisfy peoples' unlimited wants. This is the **economic problem** in a nutshell. It is a problem for people in the United States, the Soviet Union, France, Brazil, or any other place in the world.

Question:

It was stated earlier that "clean air before air pollution" is an example of a free good. Does this mean than clean air today is not a free good? People don't pay for the air they breathe today; doesn't it follow that it must be a free good?

Answer:

Consider the air in Los Angeles County today. Some of the air is dirty, some is very dirty, some is clean. For example, the air in Malibu is relatively clean compared with the air in Pasadena and Riverside. The people who live in Malibu are "buying" clean air by paying a higher price for Malibu property—that is, the price of clean air in Malibu is included in the purchase price of Malibu property. Stated differently, people are prepared to pay a higher price for Malibu property than Riverside property because Malibu residents have relatively clean air.

Before pollution, when all air was equally clean, individuals would not have paid for clean air either directly or indirectly through the purchase price of property. But now that Malibu has an environmental advantage, property values have risen there relative to Pasadena and Riverside. We conclude that (1) a free good at one time may be an economic good at another, and (2) people may pay for something even if there is no explicit charge.

To understand that people may pay for something even if there is no explicit charge for it is to think like an economist. As we explained, individuals who purchase homes in Malibu "pay" for the relatively clean air although they are not explicitly charged for it. An understanding of this point prevents us from incorrectly thinking that they are getting something for nothing.

THINKING LIKE AN ECONOMIST

Scarcity Implies Choice

Because scarcity exists, people must make **choices,** that is, they must select among restricted alternatives. The logic is straightforward: Because of scarcity, because our infinite wants bump up against limited resources, some wants must go unsatisfied. We must therefore choose which wants we will satisfy and which we will not. For example, Valerie wants a one-month vacation in Hawaii, new clothes, and a down payment for a car. She cannot satisfy all her wants; she chooses the one-month vacation in Hawaii.

We are always either making choices or living the consequences of choices we have made. At this moment you are living the consequence of a choice you made earlier. That choice was to read this chapter. You could have been doing something else. Daily, you make choices about what to buy, how much to buy, what to do, and so on. There is no way to avoid making choices because (you guessed it) there is no way to avoid scarcity.

Consider how choice operates in the following scenario: Three U.S. senators are having a discussion. "We need more schools," says the senator from Florida.

What Does Scarcity Have to Do with the Number of Friends You Have?

At first glance, scarcity and the number of friends you have probably seem unrelated. But scarcity implies choice, and choice implies opportunity cost; thus if a person incurs an opportunity cost when he or she makes a friend, the link between the number of friends a person has and scarcity is established.

But does a person incur an opportunity cost when he or she makes a friend? The answer is yes. First, you have to meet someone (could you be doing something else?), you have to talk to this person (could you be doing something else?), you may have to drive over to this person's house for a party (could you be doing something else?), you may have to invite this person over to your house for dinner (could you be doing something else?), you have to be there for this person when he or she needs your help (could you be doing something else?). In short, making friends comes at a cost. (It comes with benefits, too.)

Now the higher the opportunity cost of making friends, the fewer friends you will have, all other things held constant. For example, the average five-year-old may say she has 10 friends and that she plays with each of them every week. The average 40-year-old may say he has four friends and that he talks to, or gets together with, maybe one or two every two weeks. Are adults less friendly than children, or do adults simply face higher opportunity costs of making friends than children do? We suggest it is the latter. An adult who spent as much time a week making and keeping friends as a child does would

have to forfeit the opportunity to work at a job and earn an income.

Pursuing the analysis, would there be any difference between the number of friends a person would have in a large city than in a small town? In large cities there are museums, plays, numerous restaurants, great libraries, concerts, sports events, and usually better opportunities to earn a large income than exist in small towns. There are more things competing for a person's time in a large city than in a small town. We conclude that the opportunity cost of making friends is higher in a large city than in a small town and that the "average" person will have fewer friends in a large city than in a small town. Perhaps this is why large cities are so often said to be cold and impersonal and small towns are said to be friendly.

"Indeed we do," says the senator from South Carolina, "but not at the expense of a stronger national defense. First we must rebuild our defenses, and then later we will build more schools."

"You are both misguided," says the senator from Kansas. "What we need to do first is to take better care of the unfortunate among us: the old, the sick, and the poor."

Words to this effect are spoken daily in the U.S. Congress, on college campuses, in state legislatures, in homes, and on news programs. You may not have paid much attention to such talk, viewing it as simply part of life. People always disagree, don't they?

Notice, though, that the disagreements concern choices. The senator from Florida chooses education over national defense and other options. The senator from South Carolina chooses national defense over education and other things. The senator from Kansas chooses helping the poor over education, defense, and other things. They are involved in a political tug-of-war because not all the senators can get what they want. More resources for education mean fewer resources for defense. Why? The answer is: *scarcity*.

Choice and Opportunity Cost

Choices imply opportunities or alternatives forfeited. For example, when you chose to read this chapter, you forfeited the opportunity to do something else—

watch television, talk on the telephone, or sleep. The most highly valued opportunity or alternative forfeited when a choice is made is known as **opportunity cost.** If watching television is what you would have done had you not chosen to read this chapter—if it was your *next best alternative*—then the opportunity cost of reading this chapter is watching television.

Opportunity Cost
The most highly valued opportunity or alternative forfeited when a choice is made.

Can you make a choice without incurring a cost? (Economists often leave off the word *opportunity* before the word *cost*. We occasionally follow this accepted practice.) Can you choose to attend class tomorrow without giving something up? Can you choose to buy a Toyota without giving up the opportunity to buy a Ford? Can the United States choose to build more roads without giving up the opportunity to build more schools? The answer to all these questions is no. To capture the idea that there are always opportunity costs to making choices, economists say *"there is no such thing as a free lunch."*

Economics has the ability to make the invisible visible. Consider how the three words "no free lunch" can do this.

Suppose the federal government builds a new interstate highway system. It hires thousands of people to work on the project. The newspapers in the towns the interstate highway passes through report on all the increased job activity. It looks as if there are more people working on road construction and no fewer people than formerly working at anything else; it looks as if there are more highways and nothing less of anything else (no fewer cameras, cars, computers, and so on). But say the words "no free lunch" and see if the picture changes.

"No free lunch" reminds us that something must have been given up to build the new interstate highway system. First, the taxpayers give up dollars, so we add taxpayers to our picture.

But what specifically did the taxpayers give up by paying taxes? They gave up the opportunity to buy more clothes, cars, books, and so on. So we add to our picture all the goods and services that would have been produced and consumed had the highway not been built. And if, say, more clothes would have been produced had the highway not been built, it follows that more people would have worked in the clothing industry than worked in it when the highway system was built. We add them to our picture. When we remind ourselves that there is no such thing as a free lunch, we begin to see things that *might have been*. And that, we think, is something worth seeing.

> Economists understand that "there is no such thing as a free lunch." Obtaining any desirable good or service requires giving up the opportunity to have others. A consequence of this way of thinking is the ability to see things that might have been.

Opportunity Cost and Behavior

Look around your class. Are there any rock stars between the ages of 18 and 25 in the class? Any movie stars? Any fashion models? Probably not. The reason is that, for these people, the opportunity cost of attending college is much higher than it is for most 18-to-25-year-olds.

What do you give up to go to college? Most people say the tuition money. If you pay $1,000 a semester for eight semesters, this is $8,000. But, of course, as long as you could be earning income working at a job, this $8,000 is not the full cost of your attending college. For example, if you weren't in college you might be working at a full-time job earning $25,000 annually. Certainly, this $25,000, or at least a part of it if you are currently working part-time, is forfeited because you attend college. It is part of the cost of your attending college.

Even if the tuition cost is the same for everyone who attends your college, the opportunity cost of attending is not the same for everyone. What would an 18-year-old rock star be forfeiting in unearned income if he decided to attend your college? What would a 17-year-old top fashion model be giving up in income? Such persons rarely attend college—although the tuition cost would be easy for them to pay—because of the relatively high opportunity costs. They might say that they "can't afford to attend college." This doesn't mean that they can't afford the tuition, but that they don't want to do without the large income they would earn if they do not attend college. An economist would put it this way: The benefits of attending college are outweighed by the costs.

Let us consider another example. Two economists at Michigan State University, Daniel Hamermesh and Jeff Biddle, have found that people reduce their sleep time (up to the biological limit) the higher their wages. For example, if the wages of an average worker are doubled, that person will spend approximately 20 minutes less in bed. The reason has to do with opportunity cost: The higher one's wages, the higher the opportunity cost of not working. "Not working" takes into account sleeping, since sleeping is one of the things people do when they are not working. In short, higher wages come with higher opportunity costs of sleeping and it turns out that people end up sleeping less.

THE NATURE AND ROLE OF THEORY

Economics is a field replete with theories. In this section, we explain why and how theories are used in economics.

Why Build Theories?

Economists build theories in order to explain and predict real-world events. Not only do economists build theories, but you do, too. Almost anytime you want to explain something to yourself or to others—for example, why you prefer to read fiction than nonfiction, why your brother got a divorce, why you consistently gain weight during the holiday season—you build a theory. In seeking an explanation, you are not doing anything different from the economist who wants to explain the behavior of, say, consumers, or the sociologist who wants to explain the behavior of adult males reared in slums.

What Is a Theory?

Theory
An abstract representation of the real world designed with the intent to better understand that world.

A **theory** is an abstract representation of the real world designed to better understand that world. It is built on the factors, or variables, that the theorist believes are most important to explain and predict the phenomenon under consideration. Thus, the essence of good theory building is separating the wheat from the chaff.

For example, suppose a criminologist's objective is to explain why some people turn to crime. Before actually building the theory, she considers a number of variables that may explain why some people turn to crime. These variables include (1) the ease or difficulty of getting a gun, (2) parental childrearing practices, (3) the neighborhood a person grew up in, (4) whether a person was abused as a child, (5) family education, (6) the type of friends a person has, (7) a person's IQ, (8) climate, and (9) a person's diet.

The criminologist may think that some of these variables greatly affect the chance that a person will become a criminal, whereas some affect it only slightly, and others do not affect it at all. A theory emphasizes only those variables that the theorist believes are the main or critical variables that explain an event. The process of focusing on a limited number of variables to explain or predict an event is called **abstraction.** Thus, if the criminologist in our example thinks that parental childrearing practices and family education are likely to explain much more about criminal behavior than the other variables, her (abstract) theory will emphasize these two variables only. Such variables as IQ, climate, and a person's diet will be ignored by her theory.

"Leaving certain variables out," or a greater degree of abstraction, is sometimes the best thing to do even when you are not building theories. Suppose you are walking across campus and someone asks you how to get to the president's office. How much detail would you give? We expect that it would be just enough to get the person from where she is to where she wants to go. You might say, "Go straight until you come to the big red building, turn right, walk about 100 yards, and then turn left. The president's office is in the circular building."

You would probably not say, "Go straight for 556 yards, during which time you will pass the English building, in which Dr. Quirk teaches English 101 in Room 156, and the music building, which, by the way, was constructed in 1899 . . . and on and on.

The simple, direct set of instructions leaves out certain information, such as where Dr. Quirk teaches English and when the music building was constructed. But if the objective is to get the person to the president's office rather than to give a tour of the campus, this information is unnecessary. Too much information simply clutters and makes accomplishing the objective at hand more difficult.

Abstraction
The process (used in building a theory) of focusing on a limited number of variables to explain or predict an event.

Question:

Suppose a person criticizes a theory because it doesn't consider all the variables that might explain the phenomenon it seeks to explain. Is this a weak or strong criticism of the theory?

Answer:

It is a weak criticism. No theory considers all the variables that might explain a given phenomenon. All theories are abstractions from reality. But it doesn't follow that (abstract) theories *cannot* explain reality. The objective in theory building is to ignore those variables that are essentially irrelevant to the case at hand, so that it becomes easier to isolate the important variables that the untrained observer would probably miss.

Building and Testing a Theory

There is a procedure to do scientific work—whether in biology, chemistry, or economics. We outline this approach next.

1. Decide on what it is you want to explain or predict. For example, you may want to explain or predict interest rates, the exchange rate between the U.S. dollar and the Japanese yen, and so on.

2. Identify the variables that you believe are important to what you want to explain or predict. Variables are magnitudes that can change. For example, price is a variable. One day the price of a good may be $10 and a week later it may be $12.

An economist who wants to explain or predict the buying behavior of consumers may build his "theory of buying behavior" on the variable *price*.

3. State the assumptions of the theory. An assumption is a critical or key element of a theory. It is a statement that one *supposes* to be true. The difference between an assumption and a fact is that a fact represents objective truth. It is a fact that you are reading this book this moment; no one doubts this. With an assumption, objective truth does not necessarily exist; there is room for doubt. An economist may make the assumption that the only motive that the owners of business firms have is to earn as much money as possible—that is, to maximize their profits. But, of course, this may not be the truth. The owners of business firms may not be *only* motivated by profits, or they may not be motivated by profits at all. We discuss how important the realism of assumptions is to a theory in the next section.

4. State the hypothesis. A hypothesis is a conditional statement specifying how two variables relate. Typically, hypotheses follow the "if–then" form: For example, *if* you smoke cigarettes, *then* you will increase the probability of getting lung cancer. In effect, the hypothesis is a *prediction* as to what will happen to one thing as something else changes.

5. Test the theory by comparing its predictions against real-world events. Suppose the theory predicts that, as taxes are raised, there will be less investment and lower economic growth. We then look at the data on investment and economic growth to see if the evidence fails to reject the theory that produced that specific prediction.

6. If the evidence fails to reject the theory, then no further action is necessary, although it is a good idea to continue to examine the theory closely. If a theory predicts that, say, orange prices will rise within two weeks of a cold snap in Florida, and this actually happens, then the evidence fails to reject the theory.

7. If the evidence rejects the theory, then either formulate a new theory, or amend the old theory in terms of its variables, assumptions, and hypotheses. For example, if a theory predicts that interest rates will rise within two months of an increase in the money supply, and this does not happen, then it is time to either formulate a new theory or amend the old theory.

Question:

In the preceding points 5 and 6, the phrase "fails to reject" was used instead of the word "prove." Why not simply say that "we look at the data to see if the evidence proves the theory," instead of saying "we look at the data to see if the evidence fails to reject the theory"?

Answer:

The following example explains why. Suppose a theory predicts that all swans are white. Researchers go out into the field and record the color of all the swans they see. Every swan they see is white. The evidence does not prove the theory is correct because there may be swans that are not white that the researchers did not see. How can the researchers be certain they saw all the swans? Thus, it is more accurate to say that the evidence *fails to reject* the theory than to say it *proves* the theory. (See Exhibit 1–1 for a schematic summary of the scientific process.)

How Do We Judge Theories?

Many people think the assumptions in many theories are unrealistic. In fact, countless jokes have been made about economists theorizing on the basis of unrealistic assumptions.

EXHIBIT 1–1
Building and Testing a Theory

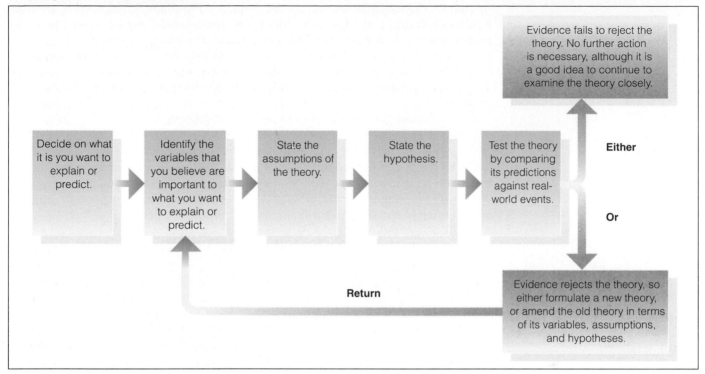

In one of the more popular jokes, a physicist, a chemist, and an economist are shipwrecked on a desert island. A few days pass and a can of beans is washed up on the shore.

The physicist, explaining to the others how the can may be opened, says, "I've calculated that the terminal velocity of this can thrown to a height of 27 feet is 204 feet per second. If we place a rock under the can, the impact will burst the seams without splattering the beans."

The chemist says, "That's risky since we can't be sure we will throw the can to exactly 27 feet high. Here's a better idea. We can start a fire and heat the can over it for 88 seconds. According to my calculations, the heat should just burst the seams."

The economist thinks about it a minute and then says, "Both of your methods for opening the can may work, but they are too complicated. My approach is much simpler. Assume a can opener."

Are there unrealistic assumptions in economics? The answer is yes, but many economists maintain that arguing about assumptions is a waste of time ("My assumptions are more nearly realistic than yours") because *a theory is better judged by its predictive power than by its assumptions.* In short, the better the theory predicts, the better the theory—no matter the degree of realism of its assumptions. Economist Milton Friedman argues that

> the relevant question to ask about the "assumptions" of a theory is not whether they are descriptively "realistic," for they never are, but whether they are sufficiently good approximations for the purpose in hand. And this question can be answered only by seeing whether the theory works, which means whether it yields sufficiently accurate predictions.[2]

[2]Milton Friedman, "The Methodology of Positive Economics in *Essays in Positive Economics* (Chicago: The University of Chicago Press, 1953), p. 15. Reprinted with permission.

To illustrate, Friedman cites Newton's law of falling bodies, which assumes, unrealistically, that bodies fall in a vacuum. Does the theory predict well, even though it is based on an unrealistic assumption? For many falling bodies, such as a rubber ball dropped off a roof, it does. Friedman would argue that the theory is useful because it predicts well for numerous falling bodies, even though in the real world bodies do not always fall in a vacuum. We could say that for many falling bodies it is *as if* they were falling in a vacuum. Friedman would say that the assumption of a vacuum is a "sufficiently good approximation for the purpose in hand."

The Friedman position can be summarized as follows: If the theory works, if the evidence fails to reject the theory, then it is a good and useful theory, and the assumptions of the theory, no matter what anyone might think of them, are a sufficiently good approximation for the purpose in hand. Some economists accept Friedman's position, along with all its implications.[3] Other economists, many of them well respected, do not. As you will soon find out, there are not only numerous theories in economics, but there are also numerous debates.

SCIENTIFIC THINKING

◼

The economic way of thinking is a subset of the scientific way of thinking. In this section, we discuss a few of the fundamentals of scientific thinking. The topics include the association–causation issue, the fallacy of composition, and the *ceteris paribus* condition. The first two topics describe obstacles to thinking scientifically, whereas the third is an important component of scientifically describing relationships between things.

The Association–Causation Issue

Association is one thing, causation is another. A problem arises when we confuse the two.

Two events are associated if they are linked or connected in some way. For example, suppose you wash your car at 10:00 A.M. and at 10:30 A.M. it starts to rain. Since it rains shortly after you wash your car, the two events are associated (linked, connected) in time. Does it follow that the first event (your washing the car) *caused* the second event (the rain)? The answer is no. *Association is not causation.* If A occurs before B, it does not necessarily follow that A is the cause and B the effect.

In the car–rain example it is obvious that association was not causation, but consider a case where it is not as apparent. Suppose Jones tells you that the U.S. trade deficit got bigger in January and 11 months later economic activity had turned down. She then states that the first event (the growing trade deficit) caused the second event (the downturn in economic activity). You may be tempted to accept this as truth. But, of course, a simple statement of cause and effect is not enough to establish cause and effect. Without any evidence, we can't be certain that we haven't stumbled onto a disguised version of the car–rain example.

Question:

If two events are associated, can one of the events be the cause of the other?

[3]All parts of this position are not original with Friedman. However, he is given credit for refining the position and arguing its merits.

Answer:

Yes. For example, suppose that on Monday evening James comes into close contact with a person who has the measles. A few days later he comes down with the measles. The two events are associated, and it is the case that the first event (coming into close contact with a person who has the measles) is the cause of the second event (coming down with the measles). So there can be causation where there is association. The main point, though, is that causation doesn't necessarily follow association.

The Fallacy of Composition

The **fallacy of composition** is the erroneous view that what is good or true for the individual is *necessarily* good or true for the group. In fact, what is good for the individual may be good for the group, but not necessarily. For example, John stands up at a soccer game and sees the game better. Does it follow that if *everyone* stands up at the soccer game *everyone* will see better? No. Mary moves to the suburbs because she dislikes crowds in the city. Does it follow that if *everyone* moves from the city to the suburbs for the same reason as Mary *everyone* will be better off? No. Bob does his holiday shopping early so he can beat the crowds. Does it follow that if *everyone* does his holiday shopping early that *everyone* can beat the crowds? No.

The Ceteris Paribus Condition: Taking One Thing at a Time

Ceteris Paribus is a Latin term that means "all other things held constant." Individuals use the term when they are trying to separate out effects. To illustrate, assume that both good nutrition and moderate exercise *increase* the number of years people live and that bad nutrition and little-to-no exercise *decrease* the number of years people live. Suppose now that a person eats well. Will he or she live longer or not? We would answer, "If a person eats well, that person will live longer, *ceteris paribus.* We add the condition that "all other things are held constant" because, as we have already pointed out, another factor, little-to-no exercise, can decrease the number of years a person lives. Thus, a person who eats well but doesn't exercise may end up living a shorter life. If this were the case, would it mean that good nutrition does not increase the number of years a person lives? Not at all. It would only mean that the lack of exercise reduced the person's life by more than the good nutrition added to it, *making it appear as if* good nutrition does not increase the number of years a person lives. To convey the correct relationship between good nutrition and years lived, we must use the *ceteris paribus* condition.

ECONOMIC CATEGORIES

■

Economics is sometimes broken down into different categories, according to the type of questions economists ask. Four common economic categories include positive economics, normative economics, macroeconomics, and microeconomics. We discuss each in turn.

Positive and Normative Economics

Positive economics attempts to determine *what is.* **Normative economics** addresses *what should be.* Essentially, positive economics deals with *cause–effect relation-*

Interview: Gary Becker

Gary Becker has been described as "one of the most original minds in modern economics" and as an "economic imperialist" because of his work in extending the economic way of thinking into traditionally non-economic areas. He is currently at the University of Chicago.

How and when did you first come to the realization that economic theory could be used to analyze behavior outside the marketplace? And was it a gradual realization, or did it occur suddenly?

It was gradual on my part. A couple of things I did early in my career involved applications outside the traditional areas. One was on racial discrimination. No economist had been looking at that problem although it has been a major social problem. About the same time I did a shorter piece on the application of economic thinking to political behavior. Then I worked on such topics as human capital, population, and allocation of time. Only gradually did I begin to see that the economic way of thinking provided a unified way to approach many subjects in the social sciences.

Is there a difference between the way an economist thinks about problems and the way, say, a sociologist does? For example, would the economist and the sociologist approach the problem of welfare in a different way?

The economist instinctively thinks in terms of the paradigm of rationality. Specifically, economists assume that people are maximizing, say, utility or profit. From here they reason that people respond to changes in prices and costs. For example, the economist will argue that if you increase welfare benefits, this will increase the number of people who will go on welfare. And in turn this will have other effects. It will increase the birth rates of unmarried

mothers, and so on. This is the economist's line of attack.

Many sociologists deemphasize the importance of the assumption of rationality. They look more at social or aggregate influences on people. They might ask questions such as, Does what other people are doing influence what I want to do? How does peer pressure operate on people? In short, sociologists will stress the social structure and social forces, and economists will stress individual variables. Both are relevant and both should be merged and in some of my recent work I am trying to do this.

Along the same lines, it appears that the tools of economics have been applied to areas in sociology but that the reverse is not true to any great extent. Is this correct?

On the whole you are correct, but things are beginning to change. The influence of some sociologists is being felt in economics in regard to bringing in more social influences on individual behavior. As I mentioned, economists have been lax in not paying attention to this. We all live in society and we all are greatly influenced by what people around us are doing. The question is how to analyze this. We are learning now how to do so, and in recent years

economists have written papers examining how social forces influence different phenomena—such as underclass behavior. I have a paper coming out on restaurant prices that addresses why restaurants may not raise prices even in the face of excess demand.

Do you think the tools of economics can explain things in psychology—such as phobias, neurosis, and so on.

I believe some of those things can be illuminated with the tools of economics. For example, drug addiction and other addictive behavior is usually thought of as simply a psychological or biological problem, but there is a very important economic component there. The economic component helps us to understand how people get addicted, and how the addiction might change when various life events, employment, or prices change. So, yes, in many areas of psychology the economic way of thinking has value. And some psychologists use very similar ways of thinking to analyze behavior.

You are actively involved in economics research. What questions are you currently trying to answer?

I am working on problems of habitual and addictive behavior—drugs and alcohol. But also ordinary habits, too. For example, we may get accustomed to a particular view or a standard of living as a habit. I am also trying to analyze in a systematic manner how social factors influence behavior. For example, if other people like to go to a restaurant that might influence whether I go. Or if other people in my neighborhood are going to college, or if their children are going to college, this might influence my own behavior or my family's behavior. These are some of the types of issues I am currently working on.

What are the consequences of economic

illiteracy on the individual's level? on society's level?

Economic literacy helps people make better decisions for themselves. Consider a simple problem like buying a house. Economics helps people understand mortgages and interest rates. It helps them understand how mortgage rates will be affected if there is inflation. There are many circumstances under which individuals would benefit significantly if they had greater command of very simple tools of economic analysis.

On the social level it has important consequences for how voters or citizens react to different policy proposals. For example, economists are quick to point out the undesirable effects of rent controls. However rent controls exist in some places of the U.S.—such as New York City and Berkeley, California. There are many reasons for this—pressure groups supporting certain policies and so on. But it also comes down to what the average citizen is going to support and vote for. Economic literacy would help enormously in evaluating these and many other policy proposals. So at a social level it is very important to upgrade economic literacy as it would improve policies—although it is important to remind ourselves that illiteracy is not the only reason we get most of these policies.

What do you predict will be a major economic problem the United States will have to face in the mid-1990s?

I think that the quality of our human capital, especially at the elementary and high school levels, has deteriorated quite a bit lately. We are educating a lot of people but we are educating them poorly. This deterioration in human capital is also showing up in the data. For example, the earnings of high school graduates has declined in real terms in the past decade. This is something of great concern. Not only on the domestic front, but in the international arena as well, since international com-

petition is becoming more and more important. The issue of how we go about increasing the quality of our human capital is very serious and surely it will be with us to the end of this century.

What got you interested in economics?

I got interested when I was an undergraduate in college. I came into college with a strong interest in mathematics, and at the same time with a strong commitment to do something to help society. I learned in the first economics course I took that economics could deal rigourously, a la mathematics, with social problems. That stimulated me because in economics I saw that I could combine both the mathematics and my desire to do something to help society. There was a rigor in economics, a theoretical framework of analysis, that I found very appealing.

What do you think a good principles of economics text should do?

I think it should put less emphasis on dotting all the i's and crossing all the t's of formal theory, and try to give the reader a good feel for economics and how to use it to understand the world about him or her. I find that this is the way to stimulate graduate students and it is even truer of undergraduate students. A textbook should help students interpret the economic and social world.

Suppose you could ask a student who had just completed a microeconomics principles course only one or two questions in order to determine if he or she understood the way economists think. What would the question(s) be and how would you answer it (them)?

I was recently in Moscow and I was asked by the Vice Dean of Moscow State University to interview some of their students who would come to the University of Chicago to do graduate work. I only had an hour to interview six students so I had to be very quick. I was told what courses they had had, and so I decided to ask them one or two

microeconomic questions. My questions were simple ones: First, What determines a shortage in a competitive market? Second, What does your answer imply about black market prices? The answers are that a shortage is caused by preventing prices from equilibrating, and black market prices tend to exceed what market prices would be in a competitive market because supply is restricted. Some of them did quite well and some did not do well. But those would be two of the questions I would ask and there is nothing fancy about them. But the way they answered told me if someone had learned by rote, or had learned to think like an economist.

What persons have had the greatest influence on your thinking and how would you summarize what you learned from each of them?

The four most influential economists were Milton Friedman, T. W. Schultz, H. G. Lewis, who were all teachers of mine at the University of Chicago, and George Stigler, who came to Chicago after I left, but who I have had as a colleague for many years now.

I learned many things from all of them. Milton Friedman was my teacher in the first year and he solidified my belief that economics is not for playing games but that it is a powerful tool for understanding the world. All the others stressed the same thing. Lewis taught me that labor economics didn't simply have to be institutional, that it could rely on economic analysis—which labor economics had not done up until that point. Ted Schultz put stress on looking at the big picture—economic development, human capital and many other areas. George Stigler has taught me many things about industrial organization and the value of economics in understanding regulation and other problems. From all of them I got some things in common, yet each had unique insights. I feel enormously indebted that I was fortunate enough to study in one way or another with such people.

19

ships that can be tested. Normative economics, however, deals with *value judgments* and *opinions* that cannot be tested.

Many topics in economics can be discussed within both a positive and a normative framework. Consider the minimum wage. An economist practicing positive economics would want to know the effect of the minimum wage on, say, teenage unemployment. An economist practicing normative economics would address issues that directly or indirectly relate to whether the minimum wage should exist.

This book mainly deals with positive economics. For the most part, we discuss the economic world as it is, not the way someone might think it should be. As you read, there are two points to keep in mind. First, although we have taken pains to keep our discussions within the boundaries of positive economics, at times we may operate perilously close to the normative border. If, here and there, we drop a value judgment into the discussion, recognize it for what it is. It would be wrong for you to accept as true something that we simply state as an opinion. Second, keep in mind that, no matter what your normative objectives, positive economics can shed some light on how they might be accomplished.

For example, suppose you believe that absolute poverty *should* be eliminated and the unemployment rate *should* be lowered. No doubt you have ideas as to how these goals can be accomplished. But are they correct? For example, will a greater redistribution of income eliminate absolute poverty? Will lowering taxes lower the unemployment rate? There is no guarantee that the means you *think* will bring about certain ends will do so. This is where sound positive economics can help. It helps us see *what is.* As someone once said, It is not enough to want to do good, it is important also to know how to do good.

Macroeconomics and Microeconomics

It has been said that the tools of microeconomics are microscopes, the tools of macroeconomics telescopes. Macroeconomics stands back from the trees in order to see the forest. Microeconomics gets up close and examines the tree itself, its bark, its limbs, and the soil in which it grows. **Microeconomics** is the branch of economics that deals with human behavior and choices as they relate to relatively small units—the individual, the firm, the industry, a single market. **Macroeconomics** is the branch of economics that deals with human behavior and choices as they relate to the entire economy. In microeconomics economists discuss a single price; in macroeconomics they discuss the price level. Microeconomics deals with the demand for a particular good or service; macroeconomics deals with aggregate or total demand for goods and services. Microeconomics examines how a tax change affects a single firm's output; macroeconomics looks at how a tax change affects the entire economy's output.

Microeconomics
The branch of economics that deals with human behavior and choices as they relate to relatively small units—the individual, the firm, the industry, a single market.

Macroeconomics
The branch of economics that deals with human behavior and choices as they relate to the entire economy.

CHAPTER SUMMARY

Economics

■ Economics is the science of scarcity: It is the science of how individuals and societies deal with the fact that wants are greater than the limited resources available to satisfy those wants.

Goods and Bads

■ A good is anything from which individuals receive utility or satisfaction. A bad is anything from which individuals receive disutility or dissatisfaction.
■ Economists usually speak of two types of goods: economic goods and free goods. A free good is a good where the amount available is greater than the amount people want at zero price. An economic good is scarce: It is a good where the quantity available is less than people would want if it were given away at zero price.

Scarcity, Choice, Opportunity Cost

■ Scarcity implies choice. In a world of limited resources, we must choose which wants will be satisfied and which will go unsatisfied.
■ Choice implies opportunity cost. Opportunity cost is the most highly valued opportunity or alternative forfeited when a choice is made. Cost implies sacrifice and can have both a money and a nonmoney dimension.

Theory

■ Economists build theories in order to explain and predict real-world events. Theories are necessarily abstractions from, as opposed to descriptions of, the real world.
■ All theories abstract from reality; they focus on the critical variables that the theorist believes explain and predict the phenomenon at hand.

Here are the steps in building and testing a theory:

1. Decide on what it is you want to explain or predict.
2. Identify the variables that you believe are relevant to what you want to explain or predict.
3. State the assumptions of the theory.
4. State the hypothesis.
5. Test the theory by comparing its predictions against real-world events.
6. If the evidence fails to reject the theory, then no further action is necessary, although it is a good idea to continue to examine the theory closely.
7. If the evidence rejects the theory, then either formulate an entirely new theory, or amend the old theory in terms of its variables, assumptions, and hypotheses.

■ Economists commonly judge a theory according to how well is predicts, not the degree of realism of its assumptions.

Scientific Thinking

■ Association is one thing, causation is another. Simply because two events are associated (in time, for example), it does not necessarily follow that one is the cause and the other is the effect.
■ The fallacy of composition is the erroneous view that what is good or true for the individual is necessarily good or true for the group.
■ *Ceteris paribus* is a Latin term that means "all other things held constant." The *ceteris paribus* condition is used to separate out effects.

Economic Categories

■ Positive economics attempts to determine *what is;* normative economics addresses *what should be.*

■ Microeconomics deals with human behavior and choices as they relate to relatively small units—the individual, the firm, the industry, a single market. Macroeconomics deals with human behavior and choices as they relate to the entire economy.

Key Terms and Concepts

Scarcity	Free Good	Fallacy of Composition
Economics	Economic Good	*Ceteris Paribus*
Economic Analysis	Economic Problem	Positive Economics
Good	Choice	Normative Economics
Bad	Opportunity Cost	Microeconomics
Utility	Theory	Macroeconomics
Disutility	Abstraction	

QUESTIONS AND PROBLEMS

1. Give two examples for each of the following: (a) a free good, (b) an economic good, (c) a bad.

2. The United States is considered a rich country because Americans have an abundance of goods and services to choose from. How can there be scarcity in a land of abundance?

3. Explain the links between scarcity, choice, and opportunity cost.

4. If someone were to say that there is zero opportunity cost to your doing homework, what would this mean?

5. Give an example that illustrates that a person can incur a cost without spending dollars.

6. Which of the following statements would Milton Friedman agree with and why?

Statement 1: The theory does not work because its assumptions are false.
Statement 2: The assumptions are false because the theory does not work.

7. Do a simple exercise that will help you understand the concept of opportunity cost. On one side of a sheet of paper, list all the goods you buy and the activities you undertake in a single day. On the other side, note the opportunity cost of each purchase or activity.

8. Discuss the opportunity costs of attending college for four years. Is college more or less costly than you thought it was? Explain.

9. How would your life be different if you didn't live in a world characterized by scarcity?

10. Explain the relationship between changes in opportunity costs and changes in behavior.

11. Think of a few examples that illustrate that association is not causation.

12. Think of a few examples that illustrate the fallacy of composition.

13. Some employees remark that they receive free health insurance from their employers. Is this truly free health insurance?

APPENDIX A

WORKING WITH GRAPHS

A picture is worth a thousand words. With this familiar saying in mind, economists construct their graphs. A few lines, some curves, a few points, and much can be conveyed.

HOW TO READ GRAPHS

Most graphs look like one-half of a picture frame with something inside. For example, take a look at Exhibit 1A–1a. It has two axes: the vertical axis and the horizontal axis. On the vertical axis we have written "Y" and on the horizontal

EXHIBIT 1A–1
A Downward-Sloping Line: What It Says, How to Calculate Its Slope

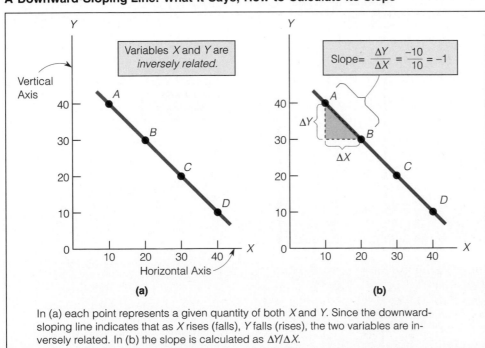

In (a) each point represents a given quantity of both X and Y. Since the downward-sloping line indicates that as X rises (falls), Y falls (rises), the two variables are inversely related. In (b) the slope is calculated as ΔY/ΔX.

axis "X". As we move up the vertical axis and to the right on the horizontal axis, the numbers become larger.

Inside the area marked off by the two axes is a downward-sloping line with four points, *A, B, C,* and *D.* Each point corresponds to so much *X* and so much *Y.* For example, point *A* corresponds to *10X* and *40Y* and *B* corresponds to *20X* and *30Y.* The downward-sloping line indicates the relationship between the two variables. It tells us that as *X* rises, *Y* falls; and as *X* falls, *Y* rises. If one variable goes up as the other goes down, the two variables are **inversely related.**

Consider now the lines in Exhibit 1A–2. In (a) *X* and *Y* move in the same direction: As *X* rises, *Y* rises; as *X* falls, *Y* falls. The two variables are **directly re-**

Inversely Related
Two variables are inversely related if they move in opposite directions.

EXHIBIT 1A–2
Different Relationships

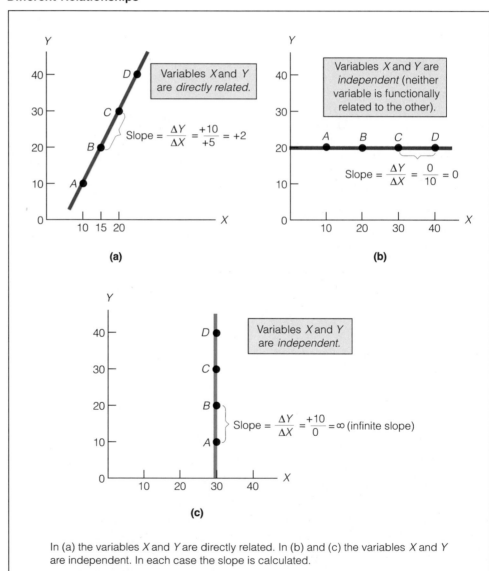

In (a) the variables *X* and *Y* are directly related. In (b) and (c) the variables *X* and *Y* are independent. In each case the slope is calculated.

lated.[1] In (b) as X increases, Y does not change. The two variables are **independent.** In (c) as Y increases, X does not change. Again the two variables are *independent.*

SLOPE OF THE LINE

■

It is often not only important to know *how* two variables are related but also to know *how much* one variable changes as the other variable changes. To find out, we need only calculate the **slope** of the line. The slope is the ratio of the change in the variable on the vertical axis to the change in the variable on the horizontal axis. For example, if Y is on the vertical axis and X on the horizontal axis, the slope is equal to $\Delta Y/\Delta X$. (The symbol "Δ" means "change in.")

$$\text{Slope} = \frac{\Delta Y}{\Delta X}$$

Suppose we calculate the slope between point A and B in Exhibit 1A–1b. The change in Y is equal to -10 (from 40 down to 30); the change in X is equal to $+10$ (from 10 up to 20). The slope therefore is $-10/+10 = -1$.[2] We have also calculated the slopes of the lines in Exhibit 1A–2.

THE SLOPE OF A CURVE

■

Economic graphs use both lines and curves. The slope of a curve is not constant throughout as it is for a straight line. The slope of a curve varies from one point to another.

Calculating the slope of a curve at a given point requires two steps as illustrated for point A in Exhibit 1A–3. First, draw a line tangent to the point (a tangent line is one that just touches the curve but does not cross it). Second, pick any two points on the tangent line and determine the slope. In Exhibit 1A–3 the slope of the line between points B and C is $+.67$. It follows that the slope of the curve at point A (and only at point $A)$ is $+.67$.

THE 45° LINE

■

Economists sometimes make use of the *45° line.* This is a straight line that bisects the right angle formed by the intersection of the vertical and horizontal axes. (See Exhibit 1A–4.) As a result, the 45° line divides the space enclosed by the two axes into *two equal parts.* We have illustrated this by shading the two equal parts in different colors. The major characteristic of the 45° line is that any point that lies on it is equidistant from both the horizontal and vertical axes. For example, point A is exactly as far from the horizontal axis as it is from the vertical axis. It follows that point A represents as much X as it does Y. Specifically, in the exhibit we see that point A represents 20 units of X and 20 units of Y.

---

[1]Instead of the term *inversely related,* some economists speak of two variables that move in opposite directions as being *negatively related.* Inversely related = negatively related. Similarly, instead of the term *directly related,* some economists speak of two variables that move in the same direction as being *positively related.* Directly related = positively related.
[2]A minus sign before the number signifies that the two variables, X and Y, are *inversely related.* A plus sign signifies that the two variables are *directly related.*

Directly Related
Two variables are directly related if they move in the same direction.

Independent
Two variables are independent if as one changes, the other does not.

Slope
The ratio of the change in the variable on the vertical axis to the change in the variable on the horizontal axis.

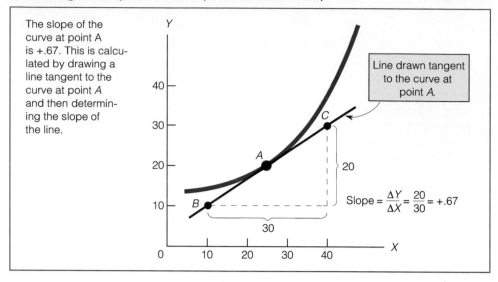

The slope of the curve at point A is +.67. This is calculated by drawing a line tangent to the curve at point *A* and then determining the slope of the line.

Line drawn tangent to the curve at point *A*.

$$\text{Slope} = \frac{\Delta Y}{\Delta X} = \frac{20}{30} = +.67$$

PIE CHARTS

In numerous places in this text you will come across a *pie chart.* A pie chart is a convenient way to represent the different parts of something which when added together equal the whole. Suppose we consider a typical 24-hour weekday for Charles Myers. On a typical weekday, Charles spends 8 hours sleeping, 4 hours taking classes at the university, 4 hours working at his parttime job, 2 hours doing homework, 1 hour eating, 2 hours watching television, and 3 hours doing really nothing (we'll call it "hanging around"). It is easy to represent the breakdown of a typical weekday for Charles in pie chart form. We have done this in Exhibit 1A–5. As you will notice, pie charts give you a quick visual message as to rough percentage breakdowns and relative relationships. For example, in Exhibit 1A–5

EXHIBIT 1A–4
The 45° Line

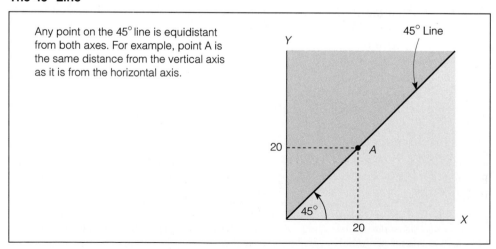

Any point on the 45° line is equidistant from both axes. For example, point A is the same distance from the vertical axis as it is from the horizontal axis.

45° Line

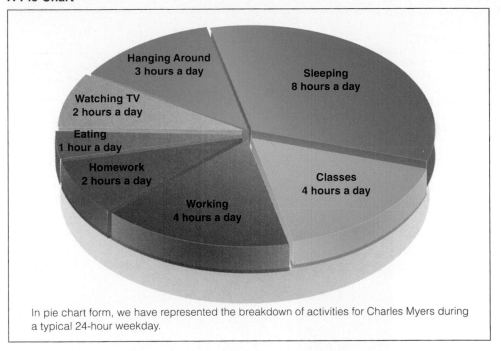

In pie chart form, we have represented the breakdown of activities for Charles Myers during a typical 24-hour weekday.

it is easy to see that Charles spends twice as much time working as doing homework.

BAR GRAPHS

The bar graph is another visual aid that economists use to convey relative relationships. For example, suppose we wanted to represent the **gross national product** (GNP) for different countries in a single year, say, 1988. Gross national product is the total market value of all final goods and services produced annually in an economy. In a bar chart we not only can note the actual GNP for each country but also provide a quick picture of the relative relationships between the GNPs of different countries. For instance, in Exhibit 1A–6 it is easy to see that the GNP of Japan was slightly over three times the GNP of France in 1988.

Gross National Product
The total market value of all final goods and services produced annually in an economy.

LINE GRAPHS

Sometimes information is best and most easily displayed in a line graph. Line graphs are particularly useful when illustrating changes in a variable over some time period. Suppose we want to illustrate the variations in "average points per game" for a college basketball team in different years. As you can see from Exhibit 1A–7a, the basketball team has been on a roller coaster during the years 1977–90. Perhaps the message that is transmitted here is that there is a lack of consistency in the performance of the team from one year to the next.

Suppose now we were to plot the data presented in (a) of Exhibit 1A–7 in (b) of the exhibit, except this time we use a different measurement scale on the vertical axis. As you can see, there appears much less variation in the performance of the

EXHIBIT 1A–6
A Bar Graph

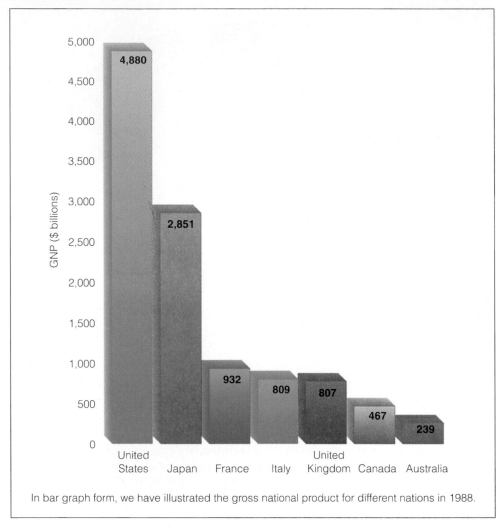

In bar graph form, we have illustrated the gross national product for different nations in 1988.

SOURCE: U.S. Bureau of the Census, Statistical Abstract of the United States, 1990 (Washington, D.C.: U.S. Government Printing Office, 1990).

basketball team than appeared in (a). In fact, we could choose some scale such that if we were to plot the data we would end up with close to a straight line. Our point is simple: Data plotted in line graph form may convey different messages depending on the measurement scale used.

Sometimes economists will present two line graphs in one exhibit. This is usually done when someone either (1) wants to draw attention to the relationship between the two variables, or (2) the difference between the two variables is noteworthy. In Exhibit 1A–8, we use line graphs to note the variation and trend in federal government expenditures and tax receipts for the years 1975–90 and to draw attention to what has been happening to the "gap" between the two. Since, for the years noted, expenditures were greater than receipts, the "gap" is the **budget deficit.** (If expenditures are greater than receipts, there is a budget deficit; if expenditures are less than receipts, there is a budget surplus.)

Budget Deficit
Occurs when government expenditures outstrip tax receipts.

EXHIBIT 1A–7
The Two Line Graphs Plot the Same Data

Year	Average Points per Game
1977	50
1978	40
1979	59
1980	51
1981	60
1982	50
1983	75
1984	63
1985	60
1986	71
1987	61
1988	55
1989	70
1990	64

In (a) we plot the average points per game for a college basketball team in different years. The variation between the years is pronounced. In panel (b) we plot the same data as were plotted in (a) and there appears much less variation in the performance of the team than appeared in (a).

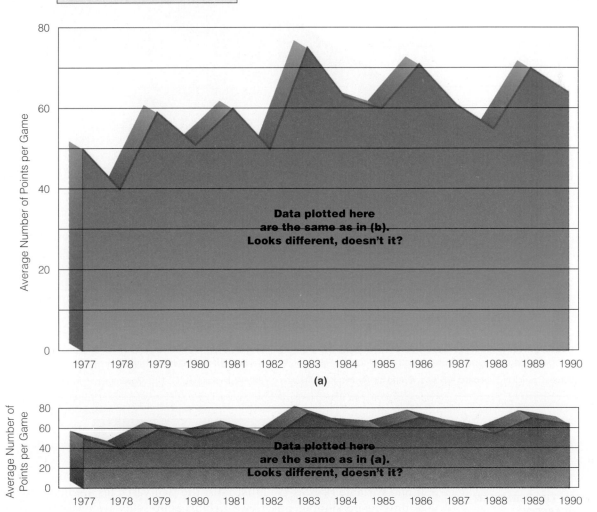

(a)

(b)

EXHIBIT 1A–8
Federal Government Expenditures and Tax Receipts, 1975–90.

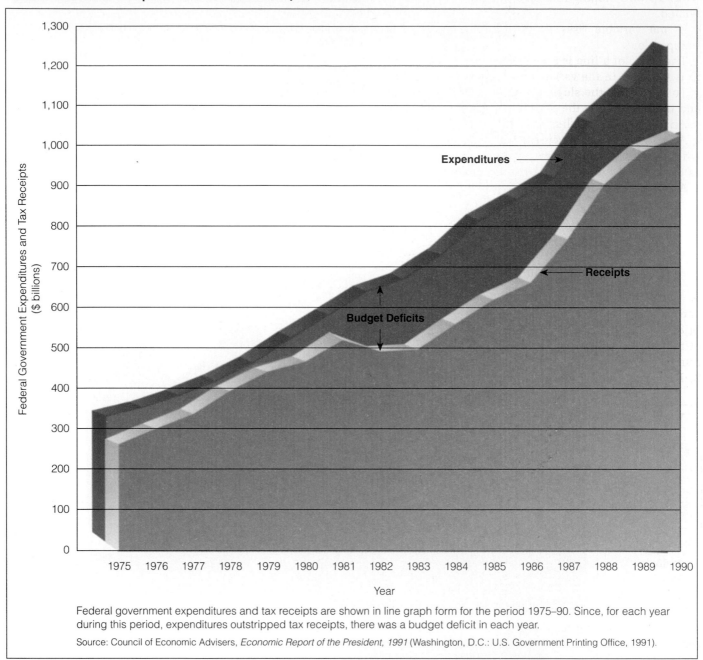

Federal government expenditures and tax receipts are shown in line graph form for the period 1975–90. Since, for each year during this period, expenditures outstripped tax receipts, there was a budget deficit in each year.

Source: Council of Economic Advisers, *Economic Report of the President, 1991* (Washington, D.C.: U.S. Government Printing Office, 1991).

APPENDIX SUMMARY

■ If one variable rises as the other falls, the two variables are inversely related.
■ A downward-sloping line (left to right) represents two variables that are inversely related.

- If one variable rises as the other rises, the two variables are directly related.
- An upward-sloping line (left to right) represents two variables that are directly related.
- If one variable rises as the other remains constant, the two variables are independent.
- The slope of a line is the ratio of the change in the variable on the vertical axis to the change in the variable on the horizontal axis.
- To determine the slope of a point on a curve, draw a line tangent to the point and then determine the slope of the line.
- Any point on a 45° line is equidistant from the two axes.
- A pie chart is a convenient way to represent the different parts of something which when added together equal the whole. A pie chart gives a visual message as to rough percentage breakdowns and relative relationships.
- A bar graph is a convenient way to represent relative relationships.

QUESTIONS AND PROBLEMS

1. What type of relationship would you expect between the following: (a) hot dogs and hot dog buns, (b) the price of winter coats and sales of winter coats, (c) the price of personal computers and the production of personal computers, (d) sales of toothbrushes and sales of cat food, (e) number of children in a family and the number of toys in a family.

2. Represent the following data in bar graph form.

Year	U.S. Money Supply ($ Billions)
1980	408.9
1981	436.5
1982	474.5
1983	521.2
1984	552.1
1985	620.1
1986	724.7
1987	750.4
1988	787.5
1989	794.8
1990	825.5

3. Plot the following data and specify the type of relationship between the two variables. (Place "price" on the vertical axis and "quantity demanded" on the horizontal axis.)

Price of Apples ($)	Quantity Demanded of Apples
0.25	1000
0.50	800
0.70	700
0.95	500
1.00	400
1.10	350

4. In Exhibit 1A–1a, determine the slope between points B and C.

5. In Exhibit 1A–2a, determine the slope between points A and B.

6. What is the special characteristic of a 45° line?

7. What is the slope of a 45° line?

8. When would it be preferable to illustrate data using a pie chart instead of a bar chart?

9. Plot the following data and specify the type of relationship between the two variables. (Place "price" on the vertical axis and "quantity supplied" on the horizontal axis.)

Price of Apples ($)	Quantity Supplied of Apples
0.25	350
0.50	400
0.70	500
0.95	700
1.00	800
1.10	1000

2

FUNDAMENTALS OF ECONOMIC THINKING
WITHIN THE PRODUCTION POSSIBILITIES FRONTIER (PPF) FRAMEWORK

WHAT THIS CHAPTER IS ABOUT

In economics, there are frameworks that provide the "environment" within which certain topics are discussed. Probably the best-known framework in economics is the supply-and-demand framework (see Chapter 3). Here, we introduce you to the production possibilities frontier framework (the PPF framework). Within it, we discuss a few key economic concepts. Then we describe the efficiency criterion, a tool that economists can use to evaluate policies. Finally, we look at three economic questions that every society must answer.

THE PRODUCTION POSSIBILITIES FRONTIER FRAMEWORK

■

In this section, we begin by defining the four categories of resources and developing the *production possibilities frontier framework* (the PPF framework). Next, we use the framework to discuss and illustrate the key economic concepts of scarcity, choice, opportunity cost and the law of increasing costs, economic growth, efficiency and inefficiency, and unemployed resources.

Resources

Goods are produced with *resources* (sometimes resources are referred to as *inputs* or *factors of production*). Economists commonly divide resources into four categories: **land, labor, capital,** and **entrepreneurship.** *Land* includes all natural resources, such as minerals, forests, water, and unimproved land. *Labor* refers to the physical and mental talents that people contribute to the production process. *Capital* consists of produced goods that can be used as inputs for further production, such things as machinery, tools, computers, trucks, buildings, and factories. *Entrepreneurship* refers to the particular talent that some people have for organizing the resources of land, labor, and capital into the production of goods and to the search for new business opportunities and the development of new ways of doing things.

The Production Possibilities Frontier

The **production possibilities frontier (PPF)** represents the possible combinations of two goods that an economy can produce in a certain period of time, under the conditions of a given state of **technology,** no unemployed resources, and efficient production. Within this context, there can exist (1) constant opportunity costs between the two goods or (2) changing opportunity costs between the two goods. We discuss each in turn.

Constant Opportunity Costs between Goods: The Case of the Straight-Line Production Possibilities Frontier. Assume three things: (1) Only two goods can be produced in an economy, computers and television sets. (2) The opportunity cost of 1 television set is 1 computer. (3) The opportunity cost between television sets and computers is *constant* as more of one good is produced.

In Exhibit 2–1a, we have identified six combinations of computers and television sets that can be produced. For example, combination *A* is 50,000 computers and 0 television sets; combination *B* is 40,000 computers and 10,000 television sets, and so on.[1] We plotted these six combinations of computers and television sets in Exhibit 2–1b. Each combination represents a different point. For example, the combination of 50,000 computers and 0 television sets is represented by point *A*. The line that connects the points *A–F* is called the production possibilities frontier.

Notice that the production possibilities frontier is a straight line. This is because the opportunity cost of producing computers and television sets is constant. For example, if the economy were to move from point *A* to *B*, or from *B* to *C*, and so on, the opportunity cost of each good would remain constant at 1 for 1. For example, at point *A*, 50,000 computers and 0 television sets are produced. At *B*,

[1]If zero television sets are produced, which is the case for combination A, we are implicitly assuming that zero resources are used in the production of television sets.

Land
All natural resources, such as minerals, forests, water, and unimproved land.

Labor
The physical and mental talents people contribute to the production process.

Capital
Produced goods that can be used as inputs for further production, such things as machinery, tools, computers, trucks, buildings, and factories.

Entrepreneurship
The particular talent that some people have for organizing the resources of land, labor, and capital into the production of goods, seeking new business opportunities, and developing new ways of doing things.

Production Possibilities Frontier
Represents the possible combinations of two goods that an economy can produce in a certain period of time, under the conditions of a given state of technology, no unemployed resources, and efficient production.

Technology
The body of skills and knowledge concerning the use of resources in production. An advance in technology commonly refers to the ability to produce more output with a fixed amount of resources or the ability to produce the same output with fewer resources.

EXHIBIT 2–1
Production Possibilities Frontier (Constant Opportunity Costs)

COMBINATION	COMPUTERS	AND	TELEVISION SETS	POINT IN PANEL (b)
	(number of units per year)			
A	50,000	and	0	A
B	40,000	and	10,000	B
C	30,000	and	20,000	C
D	20,000	and	30,000	D
E	10,000	and	40,000	E
F	0	and	50,000	F

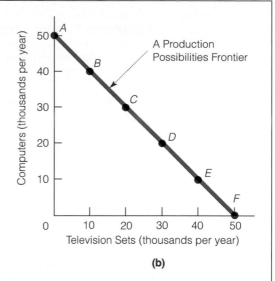

(a)

We assume that the opportunity cost of producing either good does not change as more of the other good is produced. Under the conditions of a given state of technology, no unemployed resources, and efficient production, the economy can produce

(b)

any of the six combinations of computers and television sets in panel (a). We have plotted these combinations in panel (b). The line connecting these points is a production possibilities frontier.

40,000 computers and 10,000 television sets are produced. We conclude that for every 1 computer not produced, 1 television set is produced.

Changing Opportunity Costs between Goods: The Case of the Bowed Outward (Concave) Production Possibilities Frontier. Assume two things: (1) Only two goods can be produced in the economy, computers and television sets. (2) The opportunity cost between computers and television sets changes as more of one good is produced.

In Exhibit 2–2a, we have identified four combinations of computers and television sets that can be produced. For example, combination A is 50,000 computers and 0 television sets; combination B is 40,000 computers and 20,000 television sets; and so on. We plotted these four combinations of computers and television sets in Exhibit 2–2b. Each combination represents a different point. The curved line that connects the points A–D is called the production possibilities frontier.

Notice that the production possibilities frontier is bowed outward, or *concave.* This is because the opportunity cost of television sets changes (increases) as more sets are produced. For example, when the economy moves from producing 0 television sets to 20,000 television sets, the opportunity cost comes in the form of 10,000 fewer computers (computer production falls by 10,000, from 50,000 to 40,000). This means for every 1 television set produced, ½ computer is not produced; thus, the opportunity cost of 1 television set is ½ computer.

Notice, though, that when the economy moves from producing 20,000 television sets to producing 40,000 television sets, the opportunity cost comes in the form of 15,000 fewer computers (computer production falls by 15,000, from 40,000 to 25,000). This means for every 1 television set produced, ¾ computer is not produced. In short, the opportunity cost of producing television sets increases as more television sets are produced.

EXHIBIT 2–2
Production Possibilities Frontier (Changing Opportunity Costs)

COMBINATION	COMPUTERS	AND	TELEVISION SETS	POINT IN PANEL (b)
	(number of units per year)			
A	50,000	and	0	A
B	40,000	and	20,000	B
C	25,000	and	40,000	C
D	0	and	60,000	D

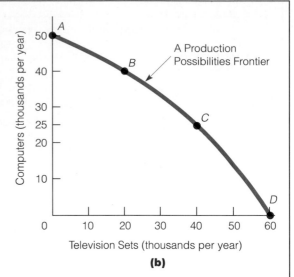

(a)

(b)

We assume that the opportunity costs change as more of one good is produced. Under the conditions of a given state of technology, no unemployed resources, and efficient production, the economy can produce any of the four combinations of computers and television sets in panel (a). We have plotted these combinations in panel (b). The curve connecting these points is a production possibilities frontier.

Scarcity

Recall from Chapter 1 that scarcity is the condition where wants outstrip the resources available to satisfy those wants. The finiteness of resources is graphically portrayed by the production possibilities frontier itself (Exhibit 2–3). The frontier tells us, "At this point in time, that's as far as society can go. It is limited to choosing any combination of two goods on the frontier or below it."

The frontier separates two regions: (1) an **attainable region,** which consists of the points on the PPF and all points below it, and (2) an **unattainable region,** which consists of the points above the PPF. Scarcity implies that some things are attainable and some things are unattainable.

Attainable Region
Includes those points on and below the production possibilities frontier.

Unattainable Region
Includes those points above the production possibilities frontier.

Choice

Choice is visible in Exhibit 2–3 once we realize that an economy can operate at only one point at a time. For example, an economy cannot operate at points A *and* B in Exhibit 2–3, producing 10 apples and 6 potatoes *and* producing 9½ apples and 7 potatoes, too. It must *choose* one.

Opportunity Cost

Opportunity cost becomes visible as we move from one point to another. Suppose we are at point *D* in Exhibit 2–3 and choose to move to point *E*. At *D* the economy produces 11 potatoes and 5 apples. At *E* it produces 12 potatoes and 3 apples. In moving from *D* to *E*, what is the opportunity cost of the addition (the 12th) potato? It is what must be forfeited to obtain that potato—which is 2 apples.

EXHIBIT 2–3
Economic Concepts within a PPF Framework

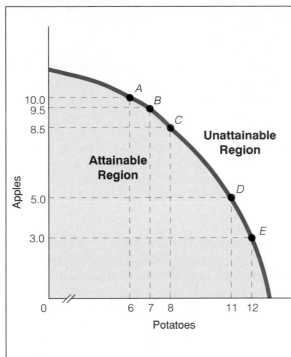

Within the production possibilities frontier framework, we illustrate four economic concepts: scarcity, choice, opportunity cost, and the law of increasing opportunity costs. First, the finiteness of resources implicit in the condition of *scarcity* is illustrated by the *PPF* itself. Second, since the economy can operate at only one of many points, it must make a *choice*. Third, *opportunity cost* is illustrated by a movement from point *D* to point *E*: to produce the 12th potato, the cost is 2 apples. Fourth, the law *of increasing opportunity costs* is illustrated as we move down the *PPF* from point *A* to *B* to *C* and so on. As the economy produces more potatoes, the cost in terms of forfeited apple production rises. (Note: We have not identified the "time period" of production on either the vertical or horizontal axis, as we did in Exhibits 2–1 and 2–2. Within the *PPF*-framework, this is implicit.)

Law of Increasing Opportunity Costs. A resource is *specialized* if it is better suited to the production of one good than others. A resource is *nonspecialized* if it is equally suited to the production of all goods.

When resources are specialized, increased production of one good comes at increased opportunity costs. This is the **law of increasing opportunity costs,** which is illustrated in Exhibit 2–3. Notice that moving from the production of 6 to 7 potatoes (point *A* to *B)* requires giving up ½ apple. Moving from 7 to 8 potatoes (point *B* to *C)* requires giving up 1 apple, however. And moving from 11 to 12 potatoes (point *D* to *E)* requires giving up 2 apples. We conclude that as more potatoes are produced, the opportunity cost of producing potatoes rises: hence, the law of increasing opportunity costs.

It is easy to see that increasing costs give the production possibilities frontier its curvature. But since a production possibilities frontier need not be curved, but can be a straight line, increasing costs need not occur.

Are most production possibilities frontiers curved? Do increasing costs occur often? The answer is yes. The reason is that most resources are simply better suited for the production of some goods than others. For example, some land is better suited for the production of wheat than corn. Some individuals are better suited for producing cars than tomatoes. Also, in the early stages of the production of a good, it is likely that the resources best suited to its production are used and that as production increases, more and more less-well-suited resources are used.

Consider the production of houses. In the early stages of house production, no doubt the persons most skilled at house building are employed. If house production increases, though, less skilled individuals will enter the house-building in-

Law of Increasing Opportunity Costs
As more of a good is produced, the higher the opportunity costs of producing that good.

EXHIBIT 2–4
Economic Growth within a PPF Framework

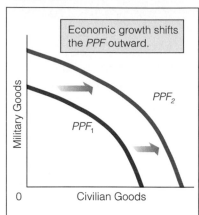

Economic growth refers to an increase in the productive capabilities of an economy, resulting in a shift outward in the production possibilities frontier.

Efficiency
In terms of production, the condition where the maximum output is produced with given resources and technology. Efficiency implies the impossibility of gains in one area without losses in another.

Inefficiency
In terms of production, the condition where less than the maximum output is produced with given resources and technology. Inefficiency implies the possibility of gains in one area without losses in another.

dustry. Where three skilled house builders could build a house in a month, as many as seven unskilled builders may be required to build it in the same time.

Economic Growth

Economic growth refers to the increased productive capabilities of an economy; it is illustrated by a shift outward in the production possibilities frontier. Two major factors that affect economic growth are (1) an increase in the quantity of resources and (2) an advance in technology.

An Increase in the Quantity of Resources. With an increase in the quantity of resources (say, through a new discovery of resources), it is possible to produce a greater quantity of output. In Exhibit 2–4, an increase in the quantity of resources makes it possible to produce more military goods and more civilian goods, thus shifting the PPF outward from PPF_1 to PPF_2.

An Advance in Technology. Earlier we defined technology as the body of skills and knowledge concerning the use of resources in production. An advance in technology commonly refers to the ability to produce more output with a fixed quantity of resources or the ability to produce the same output with a smaller quantity of resources.

Suppose there is an advance in technology such that more military goods and more civilian goods can be produced with the same quantity of resources. As a result, the PPF shifts outward in Exhibit 2–4 from PPF_1 to PPF_2. The outcome is the same as in the first condition, increasing the quantity of resources.

Efficiency

Economists speak about different types of **efficiency.** Here we discuss *efficiency in production* (productive efficiency). We say that the economy is *efficient* if it is producing the maximum output with given resources and technology. In Exhibit 2–5, points *A, B, C, D,* and *E* are all efficient points. Notice that each point lies *on* the production possibilities frontier instead of below it; each point represents the *outer limit of the attainable region.* In other words, we are getting the most (in terms of output) out of what we have (in terms of available resources and technology).

It follows that the economy is exhibiting **inefficiency** if it is producing less than the maximum output with given resources and technology. In Exhibit 2–5, point *F* is an inefficient point. It lies below the production possibilities frontier; it is *below the outer limit of the attainable region.* In other words, we could do better with what we have.

Consider another way of viewing efficiency and inefficiency. Start at efficient point *A* in Exhibit 2–5 and move to efficient point *B.* We go from a position of more television sets (55,000) and fewer cars (5,000) to a position of fewer television sets (50,000) and more cars (15,000). Move now from point *B* back to *A.* We go from a position of fewer television sets (50,000) and more cars (15,000) to a position of more television sets (55,000) and fewer cars (5,000). Notice that if we start at an efficient point—such as *A* or *B*—it is impossible to get more of one good without getting less of another good. Once again, we can move from *A* to *B* and get more cars, but not without getting fewer television sets. *Efficiency implies that gains are impossible in one area without losses in another.* This is common sense. If efficiency exists, we already are getting the most we can out of what we have; therefore we cannot do better in one area (getting more of one good) without necessarily doing worse in another (getting less of another good).

Now consider inefficient point *F*, a point at which the economy is *not* producing the maximum output with given resources and technology. Move from point *F* to *C*. We get more television sets and no fewer cars. What if we move from *F* to *D*? We get more television sets and more cars. Finally, move from *F* to *E*. We get more cars and no fewer television sets. We can only conclude that moving from *F* can give us more of at least one good and no less of another good. (Moving from *F* to *D*, we got more of both goods.) *Inefficiency implies that gains are possible in one area without losses in another.* This is also common sense. If inefficiency exists, we are *not* getting the most out of what we have; therefore we can do better in one area without necessarily doing worse in another.

Efficiency implies that gains are impossible in one area without losses in another. Inefficiency implies that gains are possible in one area without losses in another.

Question:

Suppose we move from point F *to* B. *More television sets are produced but fewer cars—in other words, more of one good but less of another. Doesn't this mean* F *is an efficient point although it was labeled an inefficient point?*

Answer:

Efficiency implies that gains are impossible in one area without losses in another. Point *F* does not fit this definition, since from *F* we *could* move to *C, D,* or *E*—all these moves are possible—and get gains in one area without getting losses in another. It follows that *F* is an inefficient point. Simply because a move from *F* to

EXHIBIT 2–5
Efficiency, Inefficiency, and Unemployed Resources within a PPF Framework

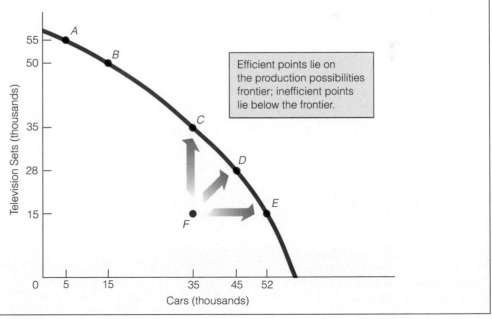

Points *A, B, C, D,* and *E* are efficient points. They lie on the production possibilities frontier. It is *impossible* to move away from these points and get more of one good without getting less of another good. Point *F* is an inefficient point. It lies below the production possibilities frontier. It is *possible* to move away from it and get more of (at least) one good and no less of another. At efficient points, all resources are being used in the production of goods. At inefficient points, some resources are not being used to produce goods, that is, there are some unemployed resources.

Efficient points lie on the production possibilities frontier; inefficient points lie below the frontier.

39

Economic Growth: An Expanding PPF Ends the Political Tug-of-War, for a While

Liberals and conservatives of both political parties often pull in different economic directions. To illustrate, suppose we are currently at point A in Exhibit 2–6, with X_2 of good X and Y_2 of good Y. Conservatives prefer C to A and thus try to convince the liberals and the rest of the nation to move to C. The liberals, however, prefer B to A and try to convince the conservatives and the rest of the nation to move to B. Thus, we have a political tug-of-war.

Is there a way that both groups can get what they want? There is, but the production possibilities frontier must shift outward from PPF_1 to PPF_2. This can occur if there is economic growth. With a new production possibilities frontier, PPF_2, point D represents the quantity of X that the conservatives want and the quantity of Y that the liberals want. At point D, conservatives have X_3 units of good X, which is what they would have had at C; and liberals have Y_3 units of good Y, which is what they would have had at B. Through economic growth, both conservatives and liberals can get what they want; the political tug-of-war will cease, at least for a while.

We say "for a while" because even at point D there is scarcity: The wants of liberals and conservatives are both greater than the resources available to satisfy those wants. Starting at point D, liberals might push for a movement up the production possibilities frontier and conservatives for a movement down it.

A question to think about: Would you expect to see more intense political battles in a growing economy or in a stagnant economy, *ceteris paribus*? Why?

EXHIBIT 2–6
Economic Growth Ends Political Battles, for a While

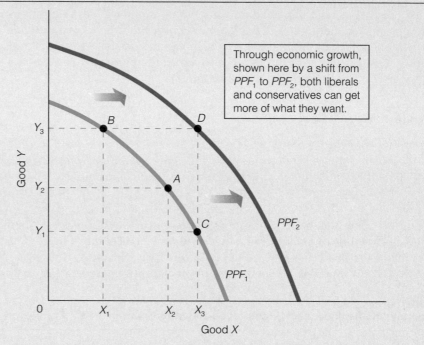

Through economic growth, shown here by a shift from PPF_1 to PPF_2, both liberals and conservatives can get more of what they want.

The economy is at point A, but conservatives want to be at C and liberals want to be at B. As a result, there is a political tug-of-war. Both conservatives and liberals can get the quantity of the good they want through economic growth. This is represented by point D on PPF_2.

B brings gains in one area and losses in another, it does not necessarily follow that a move from *F* to some other point would always bring the same results. In short, as long as it is *possible* to move from *F* to some point and get gains in one area without getting losses in another, then *F* is an inefficient point.

Unemployed Resources

When the economy exhibits inefficiency, it is not producing the maximum output with the available resources and technology. One reason may be that it is not using all its resources—that is, some of its resources are unemployed, such as at point *F* in Exhibit 2–5.

When the economy exhibits efficiency, it is producing the maximum output with the available resources and technology. This means it is using all its resources to produce goods—all its resources are employed, none are unemployed. At the efficient points *A–E* in Exhibit 2–5, there are no unemployed resources.

The Efficiency Criterion

Besides evaluating production, economists also evaluate policies, programs, and institutions in terms of efficiency. Here they employ the **efficiency criterion,** which, broadly speaking, addresses the question of whether an alternative arrangement of resources or goods exists that can make at least one person better off without making anyone else worse off.

Efficiency Criterion
Addresses the question of whether an alternative arrangement exists that can make at least one person better off without making anyone else worse off.

Suppose it is wartime and the government rations gasoline. The rationing scheme works this way: (1) Each person is given 10 ration tickets per week. (2) Each ticket permits the holder to buy 1 gallon of gasoline. (3) People are prohibited from selling their ration tickets. Is this gasoline rationing system efficient or inefficient?

Consider Johnson and Brown. Johnson is a traveling salesman who usually buys 50 gallons of gasoline a week. Brown is a writer, who usually works at home and buys 3 gallons of gasoline a week. Currently Brown uses 3 of his 10 (rationed) gallons of gasoline for work purposes and he uses the remaining 7 gallons for simply leisure driving. Since Brown places a low priority on leisure driving, he agrees to illegally sell Johnson seven ration tickets at a price of $1 per ticket.

Who is better off? Who is worse off? Both Johnson and Brown expect to be better off (they wouldn't have traded otherwise), and it appears that no one is worse off. We conclude that the specific gasoline rationing system—where buying and selling rationing tickets is prohibited—is an inefficient system. An alternative system used by Johnson and Brown, in which ration tickets are bought and sold, helps at least one person (in this example it helped two) and makes no one worse off.

Question:

A legal gasoline rationing system has been labeled inefficient, and it is strongly implied that an illegal gasoline rationing system is preferable to it. Is this the type of conclusion that we want?

Answer:

When we do positive economic analysis, there is no specific type of conclusion that we want. The question is simply whether an alternative arrangement would permit a more highly valued use of the nation's resources than rationing.

THREE ECONOMIC QUESTIONS EVERY SOCIETY MUST ANSWER

■

These are the economic questions that every society must answer.

First, **What goods will be produced?** We know that in a world of efficiently utilized scarce resources, more of one good necessarily means less of something else. Should we have more cars and fewer subways or more subways and fewer cars. More generally, should we have more military goods and fewer civilian goods?

Second, once it has been decided which goods will be produced, **How will the goods be produced?** For example, will farmers using modern tractors produce food, or will farmers using primitive tools produce it? Will the food be produced on private farms, where production decisions are made by individual farmers, or will it be produced on collective farms, where production decisions are made by government bureaucrats?

Third, **For whom will the goods be produced?** Will it be anyone who is able and willing to pay the prices for the goods, or will government decide who will have the goods?

In the late-1980s and early-1990s, numerous socialist societies began to look at different answers (from those formerly held to) for some or all of the questions. The Soviet Union, the People's Republic of China, and the nations of Eastern Europe commenced, to different degrees, to allow the market forces of supply and demand to play a larger role in everyday economic affairs. We shall see just how the market forces of supply and demand operate in Chapters 3 and 4.

The layperson looks at nations and sees differences. For example, people speak French in France and English in the United States; the crime rate is higher in the United States than it is in England; and so on. The economist looks at nations and sees similarities. For example, the United States has to decide which goods to produce and so does China. The economist sees similarities because scarcity—the defining feature of economics—and its consequences are common to all nations—the United States, France, China, and so on. The English language may "disappear" at a nation's border, but scarcity doesn't.

Resources

■ Economists divide resources into four categories: land, labor, capital, and entrepreneurship.

■ Land includes all natural resources, such as minerals, forests, water, and unimproved land.

■ Labor refers to the physical and mental talents that people contribute to the production process.

■ Capital consists of produced goods that can be used as inputs for further production, such things as machinery, tools, computers, trucks, buildings, and factories.

■ Entrepreneurship refers to the particular talent that some people have for organizing the resources of land, labor, and capital into the production of goods and to the search for new business opportunities and the development of new ways of doing things.

The Production Possibilities Frontier

■ The production possibilities frontier (PPF) represents the possible combinations of two goods that an economy can produce in a certain period of time, under the conditions of a given state of technology, no unemployed resources, and efficient production.

Economic Concepts within a PPF Framework

■ The finiteness of resources implicit in the scarcity condition is represented by the production possibilities frontier itself. The frontier separates what is attainable from what is unattainable.
■ Choice is visible in the PPF framework once we realize that society cannot operate at more than one point at a time: thus, it must choose.
■ Opportunity cost is visible in the PPF framework when we move from one point on the PPF to another point on the PPF.
■ A curved (bowed outward) PPF illustrates the law of increasing costs: Increased production of one good comes at increased opportunity costs.
■ Economic growth is illustrated by a shift outward in the PPF. Two major factors that affect economic growth are (1) an increase in the quantity of resources and (2) an advance in technology.

Efficiency and Inefficiency

■ All points on the production possibilities frontier are efficient points; all points below it are inefficient.
■ Efficiency implies that gains are impossible in one area without losses in another. Inefficiency implies that gains are possible in one area without losses in another.
■ When the economy is efficient, it is employing all its resources. When the economy is inefficient, some resources are unemployed.

The Efficiency Criterion

■ Economists sometimes use the efficiency criterion to evaluate policies, programs, and institutions. The efficiency criterion addresses the question of whether an alternative arrangement exists that can make at least one person better off without making anyone else worse off. If the answer is no, then the (existing) policy–program–institution is said to be efficient. If the answer is yes—that is, if an alternative exists that can make at least one person better off without making anyone else worse off—then the (existing) policy–program–institution is inefficient.

Three Economic Questions

■ Every society must answer three economic questions: (1) What goods will be produced? (2) How will the goods be produced? (3) For whom will the goods be produced?

Key Terms and Concepts

Land

Labor

Capital

Entrepreneurship

Production Possibilities
  Frontier

Technology

Attainable Region

Unattainable Region

Law of Increasing
  Opportunity Costs

Efficiency

Inefficiency

Efficiency Criterion

QUESTIONS AND PROBLEMS

1. How would each of the following affect the U.S. production possibilities frontier: (a) an increase in the number of illegal aliens entering the country; (b) a war; (c) the discovery of a new oil field; (d) a decrease in the unemployment rate; (e) a law that requires individuals to enter lines of work for which they are not suited?

2. Suppose the economy can produce cars and computers only. Write out six attainable combinations of the two goods, holding the opportunity cost (between the two goods) constant at something other than 1 for 1. Draw the production possibilities frontier.

3. Suppose the economy can produce cars and computers only. Write out six attainable combinations of the two goods in which you represent the law of increasing opportunity costs. Draw the production possibilities frontier.

4. Explain how the following can be represented in a production possibilities framework: the finiteness of resources implicit in the scarcity condition, choice, and opportunity cost.

5. What condition must hold before the production possibilities frontier is bowed outward? a straight line?

6. Within the PPF framework, explain each of the following: (a) a disagreement between a person who favors more domestic welfare spending and one who favors more national defense spending; (b) an increase in the population; and (c) a technological change that makes resources less specialized.

7. Some people have said that the Central Intelligence Agency (CIA) regularly estimates (a) the total quantity of output produced in the Soviet Union and (b) the total quantity of civilian goods produced in the Soviet Union. Of what interest would this data, or the information that perhaps could be deduced from it, be to the CIA? (Hint: Think in terms of a PPF).

8. Suppose the United States can produce the following efficient combinations of cars and tanks.

	Possible Combinations				
	A	B	C	D	E
Cars (in millions)	0	10	20	30	40
Tanks (in thousands)	60	55	45	30	0

a. Are there constant or increasing opportunity costs associated with tank production?

b. Draw the production possibilities frontier based on the data in the table.

c. Suppose there is a change in technology that allows the United States to produce more tanks with the same resources, but does not allow it to produce more cars with the same resources. Draw and label the new PPF in relation to the old PPF.

9. Suppose a nation's PPF shifts inward as its population grows. What happens, on average, to the material standard of living of the people? Explain your answer.

10. "A nation may be able to live beyond its means, but the world cannot." Do you agree or disagree? Explain your answer.

3

SUPPLY, DEMAND, AND PRICE: THEORY

WHAT THIS CHAPTER IS ABOUT

Psychologists sometimes play a game called *word association* to learn more about their patients. The psychologist says a word, and the patient says the first word that comes into his or her head. Morning, night. Girl, boy. Sunrise, sunset. If the patient were an economist and the psychologist said "supply," the economist would undoubtedly answer "demand." To economists, supply and demand go together. (Thomas Carlyle, the historian and philosopher, said that "it is easy to train economists. Just teach a parrot to say 'Supply and Demand.'" Not funny, Carlyle.) Supply and demand have been called the "bread and butter" of economics. In this chapter, we discuss them, first separately and then together.

46

DEMAND

■

A **market** is any arrangement by which people exchange goods and services. There are two sides to a market: a buying side and a selling side. *Demand* is relevant to the buying side, *supply* is relevant to the selling side. We start with a discussion of demand.

About Demand

The word **demand** has a specific meaning in economics. It refers to (1) the willingness and ability of buyers to purchase different quantities of a good (2) at different prices (3) during a specific time period (per day, week, and so on).[1]

There is no demand, and a person is not a buyer, unless there is both willingness and ability to buy. For example, Josie may be willing to buy the computer but be unable to pay the price; Tanya may be able but unwilling. Neither Josie nor Tanya demand a computer.

If you think that people will buy more units of a good at lower than higher prices, you instinctively understand the **law of demand,** which holds that *as the price of a good rises, the quantity demanded of the good falls, and as the price of a good falls, the quantity demanded of the good rises, ceteris paribus.* Simply put, the law of demand states that the price of a good and the quantity demanded of the good are inversely related, *ceteris paribus:*

$$P\uparrow \qquad Q_d\downarrow$$
$$P\downarrow \qquad Q_d\uparrow \qquad ceteris\ paribus$$

where P = price, and Q_d = quantity demanded.

Quantity demanded is the number of units of a good that individuals are *willing* and *able to buy* at a particular price during some time period. For example, suppose individuals are willing and able to buy 100 TV dinners per week at the price of $4 per unit. One hundred units is therefore the quantity demanded of TV dinners at $4.

Question:

If a person is willing and able to buy a particular car at $40,000, will she actually make this purchase?

Answer:

Not necessarily. Willingness and ability to buy refers to the buyer, but it takes both a buyer *and* a seller before an exchange can be made. A person may be willing and able to buy a particular car for $40,000, but that car may not currently exist, or it may exist and a seller may not be willing to sell it for $40,000.

Market
Any arrangement by which people exchange goods and services.

Demand
The willingness and ability of buyers to purchase different quantities of a good at different prices during a specific time period.

Law of Demand
As the price of a good rises, the quantity demanded of the good falls, and as the price of a good falls, the quantity demanded of the good rises, *ceteris paribus.*

When Bill says, "The more money a person has, the more expensive cars—Porsches, Corvettes, Jaguars, and so on—he will buy," he is *not* thinking like an economist. An economist knows that the ability to buy something does not necessarily imply the willingness to buy it.

THINKING LIKE
AN ECONOMIST

[1]Demand takes into account *services* as well as goods. Goods are tangible and include such things as shirts, books, and television sets. Services are intangible and include such things as dental care, medical care, and an economics lecture. To simplify the discussion, however, we refer to only *goods.*

From the Law of Demand to a Demand Schedule to a Demand Curve

Demand Schedule
The numerical tabulation of the quantity demanded of a good at different prices.

(Downward-sloping) Demand Curve
The graphical representation of the law of demand.

A **demand schedule** is one way of representing the inverse relationship between price and quantity demanded specified by the law of demand. It is the numerical tabulation of the quantity demanded of a good at different prices. A demand schedule for good X is illustrated in Exhibit 3–1a.

In Exhibit 3–1b, the four price–quantity combinations are plotted and the points connected, giving us a **(downward-sloping) demand curve.** A (downward-sloping) demand curve is the graphical representation of the inverse relationship between price and quantity demanded specified by the law of demand. In short, the demand curve is a picture of the law of demand.

The Market Demand Curve

An *individual demand curve* represents the price–quantity combinations for a single buyer. A *market demand curve* represents the price–quantity combinations for all buyers of a particular good. For example, we could speak about Jones's demand for honey. Here an individual demand curve would be relevant. Or we could speak about all buyers' demand for honey. Here a market demand curve would be relevant.

In Exhibit 3–2, we have derived a market demand curve by "summing up" the individual demand curves. A demand schedule for Jones, Smith, and "all other buyers" is shown in (a). The market demand schedule is then obtained by adding up the quantity demanded by each party at each price. In (b) the data points are plotted, giving us a market demand curve.

How Much of a Good Buyers Are Willing to Buy Depends on Price, Among Other Things

How many car stereos are people willing to buy? How many 16-year-olds on summer vacation are local businesses willing to hire? Are people willing to buy 5,000

EXHIBIT 3–1
Demand Schedule and Demand Curve

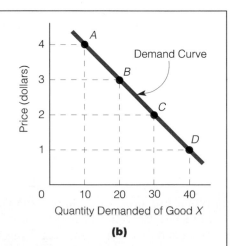

PRICE (dollars)	**QUANTITY DEMANDED**	**POINT IN PANEL (b)**
4	10	A
3	20	B
2	30	C
1	40	D

(a)

(b)

(a) A demand schedule for good X. (b) A demand curve, obtained by plotting the different price–quantity combinations and connecting the points. On a demand curve the price (in dollars) represents price per unit of the good; and the quantity demanded, on the horizontal axis, is always relevant for a specific time period (a week, a month, and so on).

car stereos and hire 3,300 16-year-olds? Is there one specific number in each case? No. People might be willing to buy anywhere from 0 to 50,000 car stereos. It depends on the price of car stereos. At $50 they will probably buy more car stereos than at $200.

This is an obvious point, perhaps. But think of how often we mistakenly believe that the quantity demanded of a good is independent of the price of the good. For example, some people often speak as if there are a fixed number of jobs in the United States. You might have heard someone say, "We've got to protect U.S. jobs from foreign competition, because if foreign firms outcompete U.S. firms, U.S. workers will lose their jobs, and it is unlikely they will find work elsewhere because there are *only so many jobs*."

But it is not true that there are only so many jobs. There are only so many jobs at a *particular wage rate* (just as people are willing to buy only so many car stereos

EXHIBIT 3–2
Deriving a Market Demand Schedule and Market Demand Curve

In (a), the market demand schedule is derived by adding up the quantity demanded by each party at each price. In (b), the data points are plotted, giving us a market demand curve. Only two points on the market demand curve are noted.

PRICE	Quantity Demanded			
	JONES	SMITH	OTHER BUYERS	ALL BUYERS
$15	1	2	20	23
14	2	3	45	50
13	3	4	70	77
12	4	5	100	109
11	5	6	130	141
10	6	7	160	173

(a)

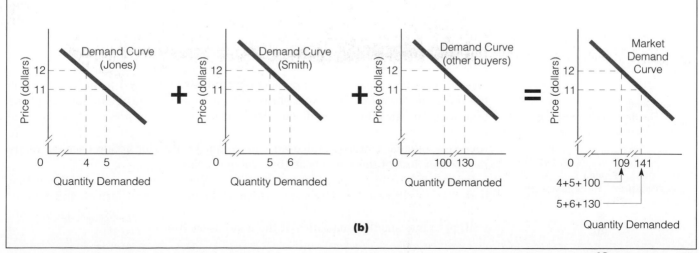

(b)

at a particular price). The lower the wage rate, the greater the quantity demanded of labor, and the more jobs there are, *ceteris paribus*.

Question:

The history department at the university has hired additional history professors during the past five years, even though salaries have stayed constant. The additional professors were hired because of an increase in student enrollment. Doesn't this indicate that the number of jobs in the history department depends on how many students want to take history classes, not on the salaries of history professors?

Answer:

Recall that how much of a good people are willing to buy depends on price, *among other things.* Student enrollment is one of the *other things.* But simply because student enrollment affects the number of job openings for history professors, it does not follow that professors' salaries do not.

Look at it this way. Suppose *all other things* (student enrollment and so forth) are held constant while history professors' salaries go down. What would the university do? It might hire more history professors and have smaller classes (classes averaging 30 students instead of 40 students, for example). Now suppose salaries rise. What would the university do? It might not be as willing to grant permanent positions to its history faculty, and it probably will have bigger history classes.

Factors That Can Cause the Demand Curve to Shift

We constructed the demand schedule in Exhibit 3–1a and plotted the demand curve in (b) with the condition that all other things are held constant. But what if any of those other things change? Obviously, the demand schedule will change, and the demand curve will shift. Here we discuss what these other things are and how changes in them can affect (shift) the demand curve.

Income. As a person's income rises, he or she *can* buy more of any particular good (say, blue jeans) at given prices. But the ability to buy more blue jeans does not necessarily imply the willingness to do so.

Let's consider two cases. First, suppose a person's income increases and she buys more blue jeans. In this case, the demand curve for blue jeans shifts rightward, or, as economists also say, the demand for blue jeans increases. In this case, blue jeans are a **normal good.** The demand for a normal good rises as income rises and falls as income falls. The demand for a normal good and income are directly related.

Now suppose a person's income increases and she buys fewer jeans. In this case, the demand curve for blue jeans shifts leftward, or demand decreases; this time blue jeans are an **inferior good.** The demand for an inferior good falls as income rises and rises as income falls. The demand for an inferior good and income are inversely related. Hotdogs and used cars might be inferior goods because many people buy less of these goods as their incomes rise.

Exhibit 3–3a illustrates a rightward shift in the demand curve (implying that people are willing to buy larger quantities of the good at each price), and Exhibit 3–3b illustrates a leftward shift in the demand curve (implying that people are willing to buy smaller quantities of the good at each price).

Normal Good
A good the demand for which rises (falls) as income rises (falls).

Inferior Good
A good the demand for which falls (rises) as income rises (falls).

Preferences. Peoples' preferences affect the amount of a good they are willing to buy at a particular price. A change in preferences in favor of a good shifts the demand curve rightward. A change in preferences away from the good shifts the demand curve leftward. For example, if people begin to favor spy novels to a greater degree than previously, the demand for spy novels increases, and the demand curve shifts rightward.

Prices of Related Goods. There are two types of related goods: **substitutes** and **complements.** Two goods are substitutes if they satisfy similar needs or desires. With substitutes, the demand for one rises as the price of the other rises, and the demand for one falls as the price of the other falls. For example, for many people Coca-Cola is a substitute for Pepsi-Cola; thus, higher Coca-Cola prices will increase the demand for Pepsi-Cola as people substitute Pepsi for the higher priced Coke (Exhibit 3–4a). Other examples of substitutes include coffee and tea, corn chips and potato chips, two brands of margarine, and foreign and domestic cars.

Two goods are complements if they are consumed jointly. For example, tennis rackets and tennis balls are used together to play tennis. With complements, the demand for one rises when the price of the other falls and the demand for one falls as the price of the other rises. For example, as the price of tennis rackets rises, the demand for tennis balls falls, as Exhibit 3–4b shows. Other examples of complements include cars and tires, shirts and trousers, lightbulbs and lamps, and golf clubs and golf balls.

Number of Buyers. The demand for a good in a particular area is related to the number of buyers in the market area. The more buyers, the higher the demand; the

EXHIBIT 3–3
Shifts in the Demand Curve

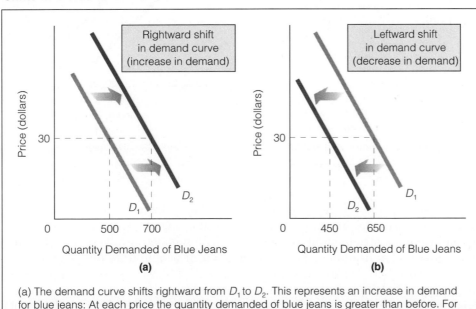

(a) The demand curve shifts rightward from D_1 to D_2. This represents an increase in demand for blue jeans: At each price the quantity demanded of blue jeans is greater than before. For example, 700 units instead of 500 is the quantity demanded at $30. (b) The demand curve shifts leftward from D_1 to D_2. This represents a decrease in demand for blue jeans: At each price the quantity demanded of blue jeans is less. For example, 450 units instead of 650 is the quantity demanded at $30.

EXHIBIT 3–4
Substitutes and Complements

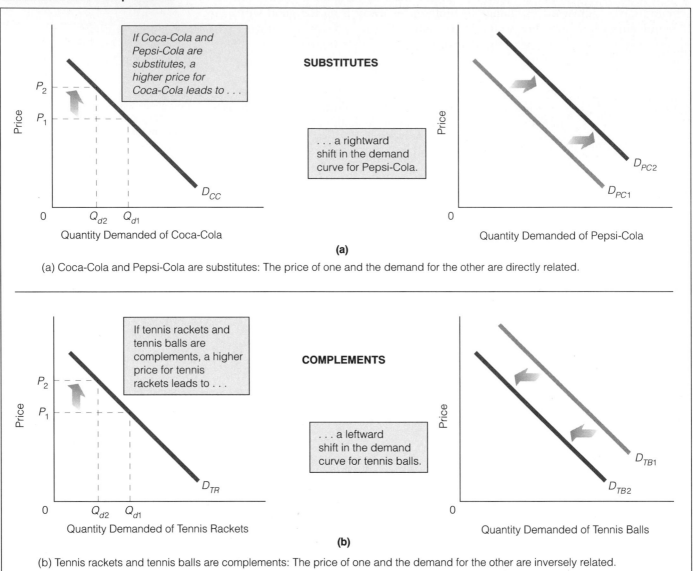

SUBSTITUTES

If Coca-Cola and Pepsi-Cola are substitutes, a higher price for Coca-Cola leads to . . .

. . . a rightward shift in the demand curve for Pepsi-Cola.

(a)

(a) Coca-Cola and Pepsi-Cola are substitutes: The price of one and the demand for the other are directly related.

COMPLEMENTS

If tennis rackets and tennis balls are complements, a higher price for tennis rackets leads to . . .

. . . a leftward shift in the demand curve for tennis balls.

(b)

(b) Tennis rackets and tennis balls are complements: The price of one and the demand for the other are inversely related.

fewer buyers, the lower the demand. The number of buyers may increase owing to a higher birthrate, increased immigration, the migration of people from one region of the country to another, and so on. The number of buyers may decrease owing to a higher deathrate, war, the migration of people from one region of the country to another, and so on.

Expectations of Future Price. Buyers who expect the price of cars to be higher next month may buy cars now, increasing the current demand for cars. Buyers who expect the price of cars to be lower next month may put off buying cars now, decreasing the current demand for cars and increasing the future demand for cars.

A Change in Quantity Demanded versus a Change in Demand

A *change in demand* refers to a shift in the demand curve, as illustrated in Exhibit 3–5a. For example, saying that the demand for apples has increased is the same as saying that the demand curve for apples has shifted rightward. As we have seen, the factors that can change demand (shift the demand curve) include income, preferences, prices of related goods, number of buyers, and expectations of (future) price.

A *change in quantity demanded* refers to a movement along a demand curve as in Exhibit 3–5b. What can cause a change in the quantity demanded of a good? A change in the price of the good, or (its) **own price.** For example, a change in the price of computers brings about a change in the quantity demanded of computers.

It is important to distinguish between a *change in demand* (shift in the demand curve) and a *change in quantity demanded* (movement along a demand curve), as the following exercise illustrates.[2]

[2]Note to students: Economics professors are sticklers when it comes to your knowing the difference between a change in demand and a change in quantity demanded. Consequently, you can expect a question or two that relate to the difference on the next test. A typical true-or-false question might be, "A rise in the price of oranges will lead to a fall in the demand for oranges, *ceteris paribus.*" The correct answer is False. A rise in the price of oranges will lead to a fall in the *quantity demanded* of oranges, *ceteris paribus.* Remember, own price directly changes quantity demanded.

A change in demand refers to a shift in the demand curve; a change in quantity demanded refers to a movement along a demand curve.

Own Price
The price of a good. For example, if the price of oranges is $1, this is (its) own price.

EXHIBIT 3–5
A Change in Demand versus a Change in Quantity Demand

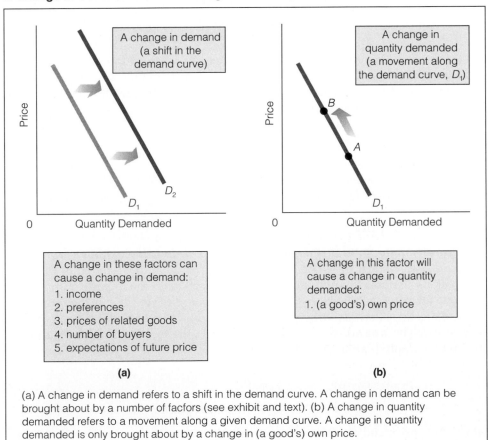

(a) A change in demand refers to a shift in the demand curve. A change in demand can be brought about by a number of facfors (see exhibit and text). (b) A change in quantity demanded refers to a movement along a given demand curve. A change in quantity demanded is only brought about by a change in (a good's) own price.

An Exercise: Learning to Keep the Law of Demand Straight

Your friend says, "I've noticed that the price of dining out at restaurants has gone up. I've also noticed that more people are dining out at restaurants. But the law of demand predicts the opposite. It holds that if the price of a good rises, less of that good will be consumed. Obviously, the law of demand must be wrong."

Suppose we accept as truth that the price of dining out at restaurants has gone up and that more people are eating out at restaurants. Does it follow that the law of demand does not hold? Not at all. The inverse relationship between price and quantity demanded holds if *all other things are held constant.* What your friend has observed is a case where all other things were not constant.

To illustrate, consider Exhibit 3–6a. Your friend may initially have observed two points, *A* and *B,* where *B* represents a higher price and a greater consumption of meals than *A.* From this he concluded that people buy more restaurant meals at higher prices than lower prices. In short, your friend sees the demand curve as upward sloping as in Exhibit 3–6b.

But the important point is that the 14 million meals consumed at point *B* is *not the result of a higher price but the result of a higher demand curve,* as in Exhibit 3–6c. In short, the consumption of meals has increased from 10 million to 14 million because the demand curve has shifted rightward from D_1 to D_2 (owing perhaps to a rise in incomes or a change in preferences), not because price has increased from \$10 to \$15 (as your friend mistakenly thought was the case).

SUPPLY
■

We turn now to the other side of the market: supply. Using a format similar to our discussion of demand, we first define the law of supply, then discuss the factors that can cause the supply curve to shift. Finally, we distinguish between a change in quantity supplied and a change in supply.

What Is Supply?

The word **supply** has a specific meaning in economics. It refers to (1) the willingness and ability of sellers to produce and offer to sell different quantities of a good (2) at different prices (3) during a specific time period (per day, week, and so on).

The Law of Supply

The **law of supply** states that *as the price of a good rises, the quantity supplied of the good rises, and as the price of a good falls, the quantity supplied of the good falls, ceteris paribus.* Simply put, the price of a good and the quantity supplied of the good are directly related, *ceteris paribus.*[3] *(Quantity supplied* is the number of units of a good sellers are willing and able to produce and offer to sell at a particular price.) The *upward-sloping* **supply curve** is the graphical representation of the law of supply (Exhibit 3–7).

The law of supply can be summarized as

$$P\uparrow \qquad Q_s\uparrow$$
$$P\downarrow \qquad Q_s\downarrow \qquad ceteris\ paribus$$

where P = price and Q_s = quantity supplied.

[3]The law of supply, like the law of demand, holds for services as well as goods.

Supply
The willingness and ability of sellers to produce and offer to sell different quantities of a good at different prices during a specific time period.

Law of Supply
As the price of a good rises, the quantity supplied of the good rises, and as the price of a good falls, the quantity supplied of the good falls, *ceteris paribus.*

(Upward-sloping) Supply Curve
The graphical representation of the law of supply.

EXHIBIT 3–6
Keeping the Law of Demand Straight

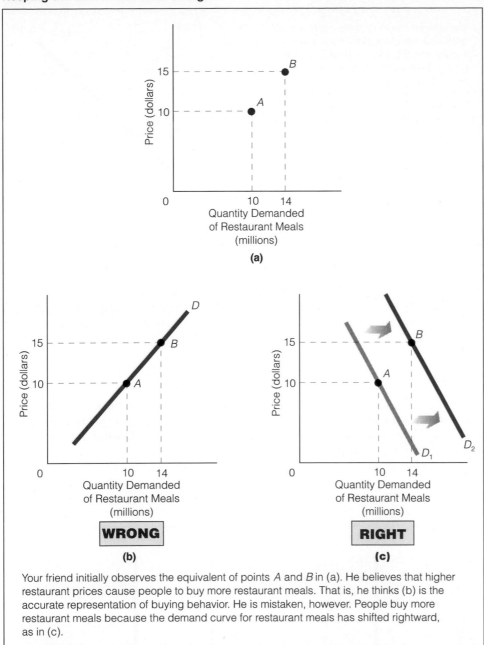

Your friend initially observes the equivalent of points *A* and *B* in (a). He believes that higher restaurant prices cause people to buy more restaurant meals. That is, he thinks (b) is the accurate representation of buying behavior. He is mistaken, however. People buy more restaurant meals because the demand curve for restaurant meals has shifted rightward, as in (c).

The law of supply holds for the production of most goods. It does not hold when there is *no time to produce more units of a good*. For example, a theater in Atlanta is sold out for tonight's play. Even if ticket prices were to increase from $30 to $40, there would be no additional seats in the theater. There is no time to produce more seats. The supply curve for theater seats is illustrated in Exhibit 3–8a. It is fixed at the number of seats in the theater, 500.[4]

[4]The vertical supply curve is said to be *perfectly inelastic*.

EXHIBIT 3–7
A Supply Curve

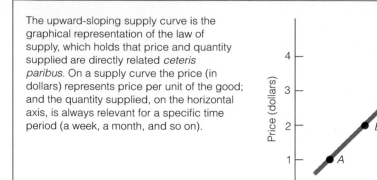

The upward-sloping supply curve is the graphical representation of the law of supply, which holds that price and quantity supplied are directly related *ceteris paribus*. On a supply curve the price (in dollars) represents price per unit of the good; and the quantity supplied, on the horizontal axis, is always relevant for a specific time period (a week, a month, and so on).

The law of supply also does not hold *for goods that cannot be produced over any period of time*. For example, since the violin maker Antonio Stradivari died in 1737, a rise in the price of Stradivarius violins does not affect the number of Stradivarius violins supplied, as Exhibit 3–8b illustrates.

Question:

The law of supply holds that price and quantity supplied are directly related. The upward-sloping supply curve is the graphical representation of this law. But then, what do the vertical supply curves in panels (a) and (b) of Exhibit 3–8 represent? It can't be the law of supply.

EXHIBIT 3–8
Supply Curves When There Is No Time to Produce More or No More Can Be Produced

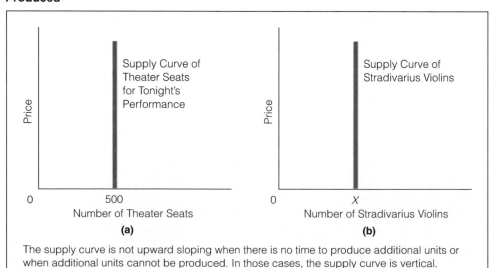

The supply curve is not upward sloping when there is no time to produce additional units or when additional units cannot be produced. In those cases, the supply curve is vertical.

Answer:

They represent an independent relationship between price and quantity supplied.

Why Most Supply Curves Are Upward Sloping

Most supply curves are upward sloping. The fundamental reason for this involves the *law of diminishing marginal returns,* which we discuss at length in Chapter 23. Here, it suffices to say that an upward-sloping supply curve reflects the fact that, under certain conditions, a higher price is an incentive to producers to produce more of a good. This incentive comes in the form of higher profits. For example, if the price of computers rises, and all other things (for example, per-unit costs) are held constant, computer companies will earn higher profits per computer, which encourages them to increase the quantity of computers they supply to the market.

Generally, though, producing more of good does not come with constant per-unit costs. As we learned in Chapter 2, the law of increasing costs is usually operable. The law states that increased production of a good comes at increased opportunity costs. Thus, an upward-sloping supply curve reflects the fact that per-unit production costs rise when more units of a good are produced, so a higher price is necessary to elicit more output.

The Market Supply Curve

An *individual supply curve* represents the price–quantity combinations for a single seller. The *market supply curve* represents the price–quantity combinations for all sellers of a particular good. In Exhibit 3–9, we have derived a market supply curve by "summing up" the individual supply curves. In (a) a **supply schedule,** the numerical tabulation of the quantity supplied of a good at different prices, is given for Brown, Alberts, and "all other suppliers." The market supply schedule is then obtained by adding up the quantity supplied by each party at each price, *ceteris paribus.* In (b), the data points are plotted, giving us a market supply curve.

Supply Schedule
The numerical tabulation of the quantity supplied of a good at different prices.

Factors That Can Cause the Supply Curve to Shift

The supply curve in Exhibit 3–7 is based on the condition that all other things are held constant. But what if any of these other things change? Obviously, the supply curve will shift rightward or leftward, as in Exhibit 3–10. Here we discuss what these other things are and how changes in them can affect (shift) the supply curve.

Prices of Relevant Resources.   Resources are necessary to produce goods. For example, wood is necessary to produce doors. If the price of wood falls, the supply curve of doors shifts rightward; if the price of wood rises, the supply curve of wood shifts leftward. Another example: Farmland, fertilizer, and tractors are necessary to produce corn. A fall in the price of one of these resources decreases the per-unit cost of producing corn, and therefore increases the quantity of corn that farmers will be willing and able to sell at each price; it shifts the supply curve of corn rightward. A rise in the price of one of these resources increases the per unit cost of producing corn and shifts the supply curve leftward.

Technology.   In Chapter 2, we defined *technology* as the body of skills and knowledge relevant to the use of inputs or resources in production. We also said that an advance in technology refers to the ability to generate more output with a fixed amount of resources, thus reducing per-unit production costs. If this occurs, the quantity supplied of a good at each price increases. Why? The reason is that lower costs increase profitability and therefore provide producers with an incentive to produce more. For example, if corn growers develop a way to grow more corn using the same amount of water and other resources, it follows that per-unit production costs fall, profitability increases, and growers will want to grow and sell more corn at each price. The supply curve of corn shifts rightward.

Number of Sellers. If more sellers begin producing a particular good, perhaps because of high profits, the supply curve shifts rightward. If some sellers stop producing a particular good, perhaps because of losses, the supply curve shifts leftward.

EXHIBIT 3–9
Deriving a Market Supply Schedule and Market Supply Curve

(a) The market supply schedule is derived by adding up the quantity supplied by each party at each price. (b) The data points are plotted, giving us a market supply curve. Only two points on the market supply curve are noted.

	Quantity Supplied			
PRICE	BROWN	ALBERTS	OTHER SUPPLIERS	ALL SUPPLIERS
$10	1	2	96	99
11	2	3	98	103
12	3	4	102	109
13	4	5	106	115
14	5	6	108	119
15	6	7	110	123

(a)

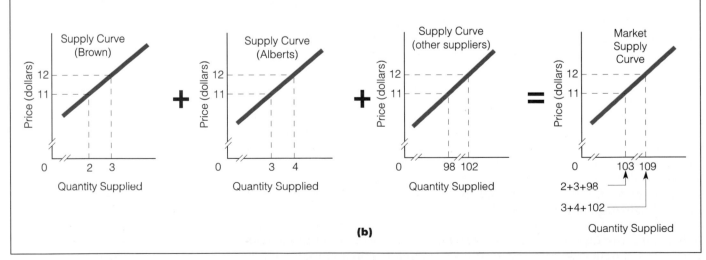

(b)

EXHIBIT 3–10
Shifts in the Supply Curve

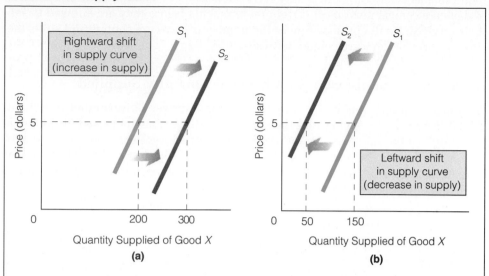

(a) The supply curve shifts rightward from S_1 to S_2. This represents an increase in the supply of good X: At each price the quantity supplied of good X is greater. For example, 300 units instead of 200 is the quantity supplied at $5. (b) The supply curve shifts leftward from S_1 to S_2. This represents a decrease in the supply of good X: At each price the quantity supplied of good X is less. For example, 50 units instead of 150 is the quantity supplied at $5.

Expectations of Future Price. If the price of a good is expected to be higher in the future, producers may hold back some of the product today (if possible—for example, perishables cannot be held back) to have more to sell at the higher future price. Therefore, the current supply curve shifts leftward. For example, if oil producers expect the price of oil to be higher next year, some may hold oil off the market this year to be able to sell it next year. Similarly, if they expect the price of oil to be lower next year, they might pump more oil this year than previously planned.

Taxes and Subsidies. Some taxes increase per-unit costs. Suppose a shoe manufacturer must pay a $2 tax per pair of shoes produced. This would lead to a leftward shift in the supply curve, indicating that the manufacturer would want to produce and offer to sell fewer pairs of shoes at each price. If the tax is eliminated, the supply curve would shift rightward.

Subsidies have the opposite effect. Suppose the government subsidizes the production of corn. It promises to pay corn farmers $2 for every bushel of corn they produce. Because of the subsidy, the quantity supplied of corn is greater at each price, and the supply curve of corn shifts rightward. Removal of the subsidy shifts the supply curve of corn leftward. A rough rule of thumb is that we get more of what we subsidize and less of what we tax.

Government Restrictions. Sometimes government acts to reduce supply. Consider a U.S. import quota on Japanese television sets. An import quota, or quantitative restriction on foreign goods, reduces the supply of Japanese television sets. It shifts the supply curve leftward. The elimination of the import quota allows the supply of Japanese television sets in the United States to shift rightward.

Licensure has a similar effect. With licensure, individuals must meet certain requirements before they can legally carry out a task. For example, owner-operators of day-care centers must meet certain requirements before they are allowed to sell their services. No doubt this reduces the number of day-care centers and shifts the supply curve of day-care centers leftward.

A Change in Supply versus a Change in Quantity Supplied

A *change in supply* refers to a shift in the supply curve, as illustrated in Exhibit 3–11a. For example, saying that the supply of oranges has increased is the same as saying that the supply curve for oranges has shifted rightward. As we discussed earlier, the factors that can change supply (shift the supply curve) include prices of relevant resources, technology, number of sellers, expectations of future price, taxes and subsidies, and government restrictions.

A *change in quantity supplied* refers to a movement along a supply curve as in Exhibit 3–11b. What can cause a change in the quantity supplied of a good? The answer is a change in the price of the good, or own price.

EXHIBIT 3–11
A Change in Supply versus a Change in Quantity Supplied

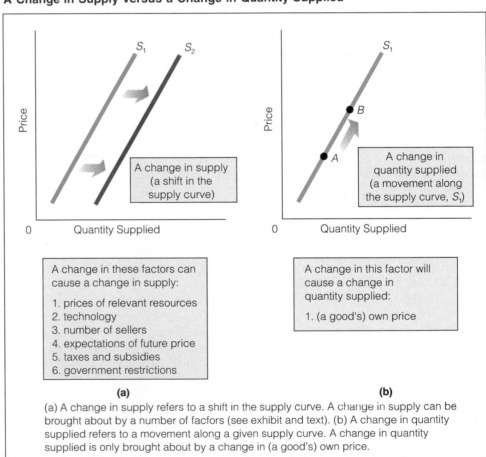

(a) A change in supply refers to a shift in the supply curve. A change in supply can be brought about by a number of factors (see exhibit and text). (b) A change in quantity supplied refers to a movement along a given supply curve. A change in quantity supplied is only brought about by a change in (a good's) own price.

THE MARKET: PUTTING SUPPLY AND DEMAND TOGETHER

■

The English economist Alfred Marshall (1842–1924) compared supply and demand to the two blades of a pair of scissors. It is impossible to say which blade does the actual cutting. In the same way, it is impossible to say whether demand or supply is responsible for the market price we observe: Price is determined by both sides of the market.

Supply and Demand at Work at an Auction

Think of yourself at an auction where bushels of corn are bought and sold. In this auction, the auctioneer will adjust the corn price to sell all the corn offered for sale. The supply curve of corn is vertical as is Exhibit 3–12. It cuts the horizontal axis at 40,000 bushels; that is, quantity supplied is 40,000 bushels. The demand curve for corn is downward sloping. Furthermore, suppose each potential buyer of corn is sitting in front of a computer that registers the number of bushels he or she wants to buy. For example, if Nancy Bernstein wants to buy 5,000 bushels of corn, she simply types the number "5,000" into her computer.

The auction begins. (Follow along in Exhibit 3–12 as we relay to you what is happening at the auction.) The auctioneer calls out the price:

$6.00. The potential buyers think for a second, and then each registers the number of bushels he or she wants to buy at that price. The total is 10,000 bushels, which is the quantity demanded of corn at $6.00. The auctioneer, realizing that 30,000 bushels of corn ($40,000 - 10,000 = 30,000$) will go unsold at this price, decides to lower the price per bushel to:

$5.00. The quantity demanded increases to 20,000 bushels, but still the quantity supplied of corn at this price is greater than the quantity demanded. The auctioneer calls out:

EXHIBIT 3–12
Supply and Demand at Work at an Auction

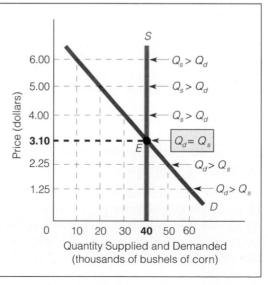

Q_d = quantity demanded; Q_s = quantity supplied. The auctioneer calls out different prices, and buyers record how much they are willing to buy. At prices $6.00, $5.00, and $4.00, quantity supplied is greater than quantity demanded. At prices $1.25 and $2.25, quantity demanded is greater than quantity supplied. At $3.10, quantity demanded equals quantity supplied.

- $4.00. The quantity demand increases to 30,000 bushels, but the quantity supplied at $4.00 is greater than the quantity demanded. The auctioneer drops the price down to:
- $1.25. At this price, the quantity demanded jumps to 60,000 bushels and is greater than quantity supplied by 20,000 bushels. The auctioneer calls out a higher price:
- $2.25. The quantity demanded drops to 50,000 bushels, but still buyers want to buy more corn at this price than there is corn to be sold. The auctioneer calls out:
- $3.10. At this price, the quantity demanded of corn is 40,000 bushels, and the quantity supplied of corn is 40,000 bushels. The auction stops. The 40,000 bushels of corn are bought and sold at $3.10 per bushel.

Learning the Language of Supply and Demand: A Few Important Terms

Surplus (Excess Supply)
A condition in which quantity supplied is greater than quantity demanded. Surpluses only occur at prices above equilibrium price.

If quantity supplied is greater than quantity demanded, a **surplus** or **excess supply** exists. If quantity demanded is greater than quantity supplied, a **shortage** or **excess demand** exists. In Exhibit 3–12, a surplus exists at $6.00, $5.00, and $4.00. A shortage exists at $1.25 and $2.25. The price at which quantity demanded equals quantity supplied is the **equilibrium price** or **market-clearing price.** In our example, $3.10 is the equilibrium price. The quantity that corresponds to the equilibrium price is the **equilibrium quantity.** In our example, it is 40,000 bushels of corn. Any price at which quantity demanded is not equal to quantity supplied is a **disequilibrium price.** A market that exhibits either a surplus ($Q_s > Q_d$) or a shortage ($Q_d > Q_s$) is said to be in **disequilibrium.** A market in which quantity demanded equals quantity supplied ($Q_d = Q_s$) is said to be in **equilibrium.** *Equilibrium* is identified by the letter "E" in Exhibit 3–12.

Shortage (Excess Demand)
A condition in which quantity demanded is greater than quantity supplied. Shortages only occur at prices below equilibrium price.

Equilibrium Price (Market-clearing Price)
The price at which quantity demanded of the good equals quantity supplied.

Equilibrium Quantity
The quantity that corresponds to equilibrium price. The quantity at which the amount of the good buyers are willing and able to buy equals the amount sellers are willing and able to sell, and both equal the amount actually bought and sold.

Disequilibrium Price
A price other than equilibrium price. A price at which quantity demanded does not equal quantity supplied.

Question:

Some people use the words shortage *and* scarcity *as synonyms. Do they refer to the same thing?*

Answer:

No. Scarcity is the condition where wants are greater than the resources available to satisfy those wants. Shortage is the condition where quantity demanded is greater than quantity supplied. A shortage occurs at *some* prices: specifically, at any disequilibrium price that is *below* equilibrium price (for example, $2.25 in Exhibit 3–12). Scarcity occurs at *all* prices. Even at equilibrium price ($3.10 in Exhibit 3–12), where quantity demanded equals quantity supplied, scarcity exists.

Disequilibrium
A state of either surplus or shortage in a market.

Equilibrium
Equilibrium means "at rest." Equilibrium is the price–quantity combination in a market from which there is no tendency for buyers or sellers to move away. Graphically, equilibrium is the intersection point of the supply and demand curves.

Moving to Equilibrium: What Happens to Price When There Is a Surplus or a Shortage?

What did the auctioneer do when the price was $6.00 and there was a surplus of corn? He lowered the price. What did the auctioneer do when the price was $2.25 and there was a shortage of corn? He raised the price. The behavior of the auctioneer can be summarized this way: If a surplus exists, lower price; if a shortage exists, raise price. This is how the auctioneer moved the corn market into equilibrium.

Not all markets have auctioneers. (When was the last time you saw an auctioneer in the grocery store?) But many markets act *as if* an auctioneer were calling out higher and lower prices until equilibrium price is reached. In many real-world auctioneerless markets, prices fall when there is a surplus and rise when there is a shortage. Why?

Why Does Price Fall When There Is A Surplus? With a surplus, suppliers will not be able to sell all they had hoped to sell at a particular price. As a result, their inventories grow beyond the level they hold in preparation for demand changes. Sellers will want to reduce their inventories. Some will lower prices to do so; some will cut back on production; others will do a little of both. As we show in Exhibit 3–13, there is a tendency for price and output to fall until equilibrium is achieved.

Why Does Price Rise When There Is A Shortage? With a shortage, buyers will not be able to buy all they had hoped to buy. Some buyers will bid up the price to get sellers to sell to them instead of to other buyers. Some sellers, seeing buyers clamor for the goods, will realize that they can raise the price on the goods they have for sale. Higher prices will also call forth added output. Thus, there is a tendency for price and output to rise until equilibrium is achieved (see Exhibit 3–13).

Not all markets have auctioneers, but many markets act as if an auctioneer were calling out higher and lower prices until equilibrium price is reached.

EXHIBIT 3–13
Moving to Equilibrium

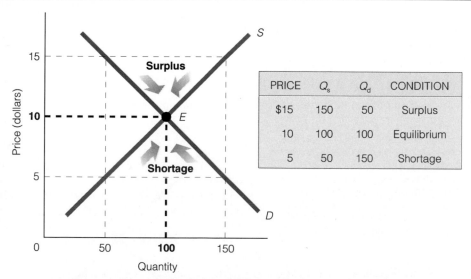

PRICE	Q_s	Q_d	CONDITION
$15	150	50	Surplus
10	100	100	Equilibrium
5	50	150	Shortage

If there is a surplus, sellers' inventories rise above the level they hold in preparation for demand changes. Sellers will want to reduce their inventories. As a result, price and output fall until equilibrium is achieved. If there is a shortage, some buyers will bid up price to get sellers to sell to them instead of to other buyers. Some sellers will realize they can raise the price on the goods they have for sale. Higher prices will call forth added output. Price and output rise until equilibrium is achieved. (Note: Recall that price, on the vertical axis, is price per unit of the good; and quantity, on the horizontal axis, is for a specific time period. In this text we do not specify this on the axes themselves, but consider it to be understood.)

Moving to Equilibrium: Maximum and Minimum Prices

Our discussion of surpluses and shortages has illustrated how a market moves to equilibrium, but there is another way to show this. Exhibit 3–14 depicts the market for good X. Look at the first unit of good X. What is the *maximum price buyers would be willing and able to pay for it?* The answer is $7. This can be seen by following the dotted line up from the first unit of the good to the demand curve.

What is the *minimum price sellers need to receive before they would be willing and able to produce and offer to sell* this unit of good X? It is $1. This can be seen by following the dotted line up from the first unit to the supply curve. Since the maximum price buyers are willing and able to pay is greater than the minimum price sellers need to receive, we can be sure that the first unit of good X will be exchanged.

What happens to the second unit? Here the maximum price buyers are willing and able to pay is $6, and the minimum price sellers need to receive is $2. We can be sure that the second unit of good X will be exchanged. In fact, we can be sure exchange will occur as long as the maximum price buyers are willing and able to pay is greater than the minimum price sellers need to receive. The exhibit shows that a total of four units of good X will be exchanged. The fifth unit will not be exchanged because the maximum price buyers are willing and able to pay ($3) is less than the minimum price suppliers need to receive ($5).

In the process just described, buyers and sellers exchange money for goods as long as both benefit from the exchange. The market converges on a quantity of 4 units of good X and a $4 price per unit. This is equilibrium. This way of explaining the movement to equilibrium illustrates two points that were hidden from view when we discussed it in term of surpluses and shortages: (1) *At equilibrium, all the mutually beneficial gains from the exchange have been obtained.* (2) *At equilibrium price, maximum price (for the buyer) and minimum price (for the seller) are the same.*

EXHIBIT 3–14
Moving to Equilibrium in Terms of Maximum and Minimum Prices

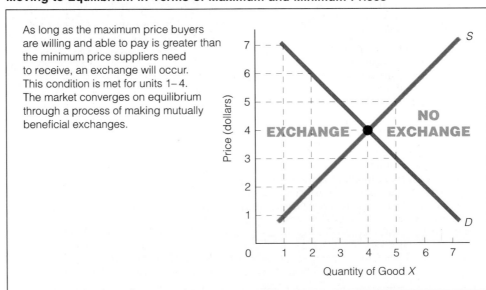

As long as the maximum price buyers are willing and able to pay is greater than the minimum price suppliers need to receive, an exchange will occur. This condition is met for units 1– 4. The market converges on equilibrium through a process of making mutually beneficial exchanges.

Interview: Vernon Smith

On the blackboard, the economics instructor draws a downward-sloping demand curve. She then draws an upward-sloping supply curve. A small dot is placed at the intersection of the two curves. "This is the equilibrium point," the instructor says. The instructor then identifies equilibrium price—the price at which quantity demanded equals quantity supplied. "This is how many markets work," the instructor comments. "Supply and demand determine price." But is this right? Do supply and demand determine price? They do on the blackboard, but do they in real life, too?

Some economists have begun to study economic behavior and test economic theories under *laboratory conditions*. This new area of research is called *experimental economics*. One of the pioneers in this area is Vernon L. Smith. Professor Smith is at the University of Arizona, Tucson.

What is experimental economics?

There are two kinds of experiments in economics: field and laboratory experiments. In field experiments the investigator seeks to measure the demand, supply or incentive response of subjects in a particular institutional setting in the economy. For example, proposals to introduce peak load pricing rules into the pricing of electric power, or to modify welfare or unemployment insurance programs to include incentive payments for seeking employment, have been evaluated by comparing the responses of samples of households with and without the proposed incentives.

Laboratory experiments are used to study the performance of markets using reward motivated subjects under controlled laboratory conditions. Every laboratory experiment has three elements.

(1) A value/cost *environment*. Thus buyers are assigned redemption values, and sellers costs, for units of an abstract commodity to be exchanged. This environment defines the conditions of demand and supply in a competitive market experiment or the market structure of an oligopoly experiment. Buyers are paid in cash the difference between the assigned (demand) values and the prices at which they buy; sellers receive the difference between selling price and assigned unit costs. Thus, buyers are motivated to buy as cheaply as they can, and sellers to sell as high as they can. This control over the supply/demand environment distinguishes the laboratory from the field experiment.

(2) An *institution,* defining the rules of communication or message transfer among market participants. It is these rules that determine the incentives and strategies of market participants. For example, in a progressive auction buyers announce bids in sequence until there is only one outstanding bid, which is declared the winner. In a stock ex-

change buyers freely announce bids to buy, sellers announce offers to sell, and contracts for exchange occur whenever a bid or an offer is accepted. In retail markets, sellers post take-it-or-leave-it price offers, and buyers accept or reject units at these prices.

(3) The *behavior* of the participants. Elements (1) and (2) are controlled by the experimenter, who then observes (3).

Among the many objectives of an experiment are to use observations for the following. (a) Test a received theory. (b) Discriminate among theories. (c) Evaluate policy proposals. (d) Compare environments. (e) Compare institutions. (f) Evaluate new institutional designs using the laboratory as a testbed.

In your experiments, have you found that supply and demand forces work like economists say they work?

Generally, yes. But there are many features of these forces that are not adequately addressed in traditional theory. For example, there are variations in the speed of a market's response to these forces depending upon the trading institutions: posted price and sealed-bid auction markets do not respond as quickly as the open outcry double (two-sided) auction used in commodity and stock exchanges. In the case of the double auction institution the forces of supply and demand actually work *better* than economists have said they do. Thus convergence to the supply and demand equilibrium occurs quickly even when numbers are very small—2 to 4 buyers and as many sellers are usually sufficient to guarantee the predicted supply and demand equilibrium. If anything, traditional economics has underestimated the power of supply and demand under some institutional implementations.

What are a few of the questions you have answered using experimental methods?

(1) A key contestable market hypothesis: If entry and exit are free will competitive pricing result even where costs show increasing returns to scale and the industry can support only one firm? In research conducted by R. Mark Issac (University of Arizona) and myself we have experimental results that are consistent with this hypothesis.

(2) Do laboratory stock markets support the hypothesis that asset market prices reflect the underlying fundamental value of the asset; that is, are expectations rational in such markets? Work with a number of coauthors using software developed by Arlington Williams (Indiana University) provides only weak support for this hypothesis. In asset markets current demand depends strongly on the expectations of the participants. If the participants have bullish expectations that prices will rise yielding capital gains, this fact alone can cause rising prices (expectations are self-fulfilling). In experimental markets with fundamental value known by all trades (the dividend structure is common information), we observe large departures of asset prices from asset value (price booms, followed by crashes), but this discrepancy is reduced when the same subjects return for a second experiment, and is largely eliminated when they return for a third. Eventually, in a stationary environment, subjects come to have common rational expectations by learning that sustainable profits cannot be made at prices that depart from fundamental value.

(3) Do market regulations or restraints sometimes perversely affect the competitive performance of markets? Yes. For example in pioneering work by R. Mark Issac and Charles Plott (Cal Tech) it has been shown that price ceilings, even when they are not binding (are above

the equilibrium supply and demand price) tend to depress prices in double auction markets. This is because the price controls interfere with the institutional dynamics of trade by restricting the strategies of sellers more severely than buyers. Consequently, convergence is slower and more erratic than in unrestrained markets. In collaboration with Don Coursey (Washington University, St. Louis) we have found that these results extend to posted price markets.

What questions are you currently trying to answer?

(1) Can some of the discrepancies between the predictions of standard theory and experimental observations be explained or modelled by introducing decision cost; that is, by hypothesizing that there is an effort cost (of thinking, analyzing and deciding) to be weighed against value in choosing a best response?

(2) Are subjects more likely to engage in self-interested behavior at the expense of an opponent, when they feel that any advantage they enjoy has been earned, and is therefore justified? This question is central to the role of "property rights" in markets. The pioneers in this research were Elizabeth Hoffman (University of Arizona) and Matthew Spitzer (USC).

(3) How can the computer make possible new forms of exchange? With my colleague, Stephen Rassenti, and Kevin McCabe (University of Minnesota) we are studying new "smart" computer assisted market institutions. In these institutions a computer helps coordinate technologically interdependent markets by applying algorithms for maximizing the gains from exchange to the bids and offers of decentralized agents. For example, we are applying such computerized trading institutions to pricing and allocation among producers, wholesalers and transporters in complex natural gas pipeline networks. This market

combines the information advantages of decentralized ownership with the coordination advantages of central (computerized) pricing.

Have you ever been surprised by one of your research findings?

Many times. My education left me completely unprepared for the discovery that quite small numbers can yield competitive equilibrium outcomes under double auction trading rules. The finding that price controls affect market dynamics, even though they are nonbinding at the static equilibrium was a surprise; although a study of experimental data has made it entirely understandable. I was also surprised to find it so easy to observe stock market price bubbles in the laboratory.

What impact has experimental economics had on the economics profession? Do you think a larger percentage of the profession will be experimental economists in the next two decades?

I first began doing experiments, as classroom exercises, at Purdue University, in early 1956. At about this same time Reinhard Seltan ran some oligopoly experiments in Germany. But the output of research papers was modest until about the mid-1970s when Charles Plott and I, and soon many others, became much more active in experimentation. Interest and research accelerated greatly in the 1980s. The University of Arizona has had a computerized laboratory for experimental economics since 1976, but there are now many more laboratories: Cal Tech, Texas A&M, Indiana University, University of Houston, University of Pittsburgh, Virginia Commonwealth University, Carnegie-Mellon University, University of Michigan, University of Iowa, New York University, University of Colorado, in German and British universities, and others in the making. This growth in experimental economics laboratories suggests a larger percentage of economists may be experimentalists in the next two decades. Professional and foundation support has been excellent.

What got you interested in economics?

My father's influence (he was a tool and die maker) started me in science and engineering at Cal Tech, but my mother, who was active in socialist politics, probably accounts for the great interest I found in economics when I took my first introductory course. Although I completed my BS degree at Cal Tech, I went on to graduate study in economics at the University of Kansas and Harvard. But it was my experimental subjects who taught me that markets work, under weaker conditions than were traditionally thought to be necessary, and are much more trustworthy in promoting efficient allocations than are the central planning and regulation systems of government. But government is important in defining and enforcing property rights and fostering free institutions of exchange.

Changes in Equilibrium Price and Quantity

Equilibrium price and quantity are determined by supply and demand. Anytime either demand or supply changes or both change, equilibrium price and quantity change. Exhibit 3–15 illustrates 14 different cases where this occurs. Cases (a)–(d) illustrate the four basic changes in supply and demand, where either supply *or* demand changes. Cases (e)–(n) are combinations of (a)–(d), where both supply *and* demand change.

- (a) Demand rises (the demand curve shifts rightward), and supply is constant (the supply curve does not move). Equilibrium price rises, equilibrium quantity rises, too.
- (b) Demand falls, supply is constant. Equilibrium price falls, equilibrium quantity falls.
- (c) Supply rises, demand is constant. Equilibrium price falls, equilibrium quantity rises.
- (d) Supply falls, demand is constant. Equilibrium price rises, equilibrium quantity falls.
- (e) Demand rises and supply falls by an equal amount. Equilibrium price rises, equilibrium quantity is constant.
- (f) Demand falls and supply rises by an equal amount. Equilibrium price falls, equilibrium quantity is constant.
- (g) Demand rises by a greater amount than supply falls. Equilibrium price and quantity rise.
- (h) Demand rises by a lesser amount than supply falls. Equilibrium price rises, equilibrium quantity falls.
- (i) Demand falls by a greater amount than supply rises. Equilibrium price and quantity fall.
- (j) Demand falls by a lesser amount than supply rises. Equilibrium price falls, equilibrium quantity rises.
- (k) Demand rises by a greater amount than supply rises. Equilibrium price and quantity rise.
- (l) Demand rises by a lesser amount than supply rises. Equilibrium price falls, equilibrium quantity rises.
- (m) Demand falls by a greater amount than supply falls. Equilibrium price and quantity fall.
- (n) Demand falls by a lesser amount than supply falls. Equilibrium price rises, equilibrium quantity falls.

EXHIBIT 3–15
Equilibrium Price and Quantity Effects of Supply-Curve and Demand-Curve Shifts

The exhibit illustrates the effects on equilibrium price and quantity of a change in demand, a change in supply, or a change in both. Below each diagram the condition leading to the effects are noted, using the following symbols: (1) a bar over a letter means *constant* (thus, $\overline{S}$ means that supply is constant);

(2) a downward-pointing arrow ($\downarrow$) indicates a fall; (3) an upward-pointing arrow ($\uparrow$) indicates a rise. A rise (fall) in demand is the same as a rightward (leftward) shift in the demand curve. A rise (fall) in supply is the same as a rightward (leftward) shift in the supply curve.

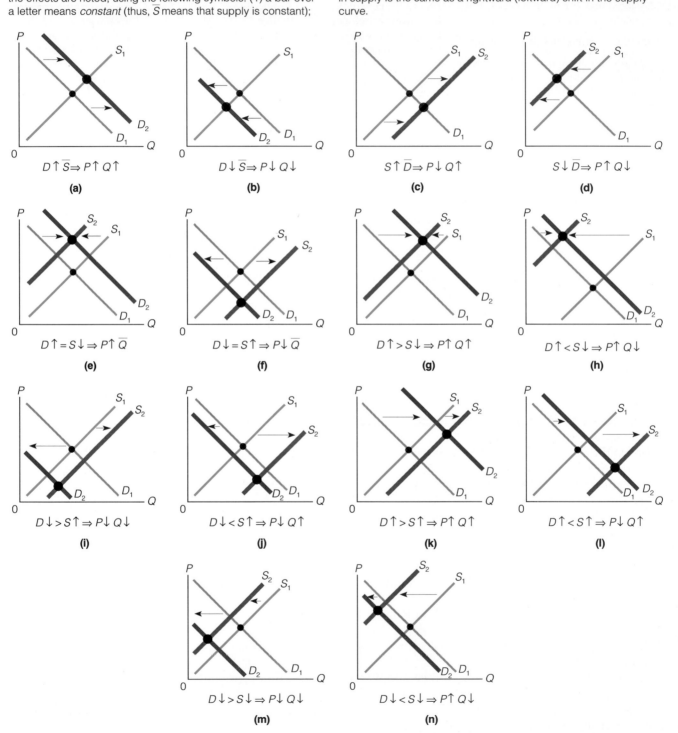

$$D\uparrow\overline{S}\Rightarrow P\uparrow Q\uparrow$$

(a)

$$D\downarrow\overline{S}\Rightarrow P\downarrow Q\downarrow$$

(b)

$$S\uparrow\overline{D}\Rightarrow P\downarrow Q\uparrow$$

(c)

$$S\downarrow\overline{D}\Rightarrow P\uparrow Q\downarrow$$

(d)

$$D\uparrow=S\downarrow\Rightarrow P\uparrow\overline{Q}$$

(e)

$$D\downarrow=S\uparrow\Rightarrow P\downarrow\overline{Q}$$

(f)

$$D\uparrow>S\downarrow\Rightarrow P\uparrow Q\uparrow$$

(g)

$$D\uparrow<S\downarrow\Rightarrow P\uparrow Q\downarrow$$

(h)

$$D\downarrow>S\uparrow\Rightarrow P\downarrow Q\downarrow$$

(i)

$$D\downarrow<S\uparrow\Rightarrow P\downarrow Q\uparrow$$

(j)

$$D\uparrow>S\uparrow\Rightarrow P\uparrow Q\uparrow$$

(k)

$$D\uparrow<S\uparrow\Rightarrow P\downarrow Q\uparrow$$

(l)

$$D\downarrow>S\downarrow\Rightarrow P\downarrow Q\downarrow$$

(m)

$$D\downarrow<S\downarrow\Rightarrow P\uparrow Q\downarrow$$

(n)

Absolute and Relative Prices

The **absolute price** of a good is its price in money terms. For example, the absolute price of a car might be $20,000. The **relative price** of a good is its price in terms of another good (not in terms of money). Suppose the absolute price of a car is $20,000 and the absolute price of a computer is $2,000. The relative price of the car (in terms of computers) is 10 computers. A person necessarily gives up the opportunity to buy 10 computers when he or she buys a car.

What happens to the relative price of a good as its absolute price increases (decreases) *ceteris paribus.* Suppose the absolute price of the car rises to $22,000. The relative price of the car rises to 11 computers. If the absolute price of the car falls to $18,000, the relative price of the car falls to 9 computers. We conclude that as the absolute price of a good rises, the relative price of the good rises; as the absolute price of a good falls, the relative price of a good falls, *ceteris paribus.* (If we had omitted *"ceteris paribus,"* the statement would not necessarily be true.)

Absolute Price
The price of a good in money terms.

Relative Price
The price of a good in terms of another good.

Question:

Is it possible for the absolute price of a good to rise while its relative price falls?

Answer:

Yes. Suppose there are two goods, houses and cars, whose absolute prices are $100,000 and $20,000, respectively. The relative price of 1 house is 5 cars. Now suppose the absolute price of houses rises to $120,000 and the absolute price of cars rises to $30,000. This is a 20 percent increase in the absolute price of houses and a 50 percent increase in the absolute price of cars. Now the relative price of a house is 4 cars. We conclude that even though the absolute price of houses has increased (from $100,000 to $120,000), its relative price has decreased (from 5 to 4 cars). This is because the absolute price of cars increased by a greater percentage than the absolute price of houses.

Using Relative Price to Think Like An Economist

Let us use relative price to think through a problem. Suppose that both high-quality and medium-quality apples are grown in the state of Washington. Their prices are 10 cents and 5 cents, respectively. The cost of transportation to New York City per apple, regardless of quality, is 5 cents. In New York City, a high-quality apple is 15 cents and a medium-quality apple is 10 cents. In which place, Washington or New York, would you predict that *relatively* more high-quality apples are consumed, *ceteris paribus?*

An economist would predict that relatively more high-quality apples would be consumed in the place where high-quality apples are relatively cheaper. And this is in New York.

The relative price of a high-quality apple in Washington is 2 medium-quality apples; the relative price of a high-quality apple in New York is 1.5 medium-quality apples. We show the simple arithmetic here.

Washington

1 high-quality apple = 10 cents
1 medium-quality apple = 5 cents
1 high-quality apple = 2 medium-quality apples

New York

1 high-quality apple = 15 cents
1 medium-quality apple = 10 cents
1 high-quality apple = 1.5 medium-quality apples

Question:

If the higher the price of a good, the lower the quantity demanded of that good, why do New Yorkers buy more high-quality apples than Washingtonians when New Yorkers pay 15 cents per high-quality apple and Washingtonians pay 10 cents per high-quality apple?

Answer:

We did not say that New Yorkers buy *more* high-quality apples than Washingtonians, but that New Yorkers buy *relatively more* high-quality apples than Washingtonians. There is a difference between *more* and *relatively more. More* indicates a larger absolute number; *relatively more* indicates a greater share of the total.

To illustrate, let's say that Washingtonians buy 10,000 high-quality apples and 30,000 medium-quality apples, and New Yorkers buy 5,000 high-quality apples and 7,500 medium-quality apples. Washingtonians buy *more* high-quality apples, but New Yorkers buy *relatively more* high-quality apples. Of all the apples New Yorkers buy, 40 percent are high-quality apples (5,000 is 40 percent of 12,500). Of all the apples Washingtonians buy, 25 percent are high-quality apples (10,000 is 25 percent of 40,000).

The apple example illustrates that relative price, *not* absolute price, is what matters in predicting consumer behavior. In fact, people only care about absolute price to the degree that it relates to relative price. For example, if Jackie's college tuition rises from $35 to $70 a credit, *ceteris paribus,* this means she *forfeits more of other things*—more movies on Friday, more dinners out, more new clothes—as a result, it is this forfeiture of other things that matters to Jackie; it is the relative price of her education that matters to her.

Demand

- The law of demand states that as the price of a good rises, the quantity demanded of the good falls, and as the price of a good falls, the quantity demanded of the good rises, *ceteris paribus*. The law of demand holds that price and quantity demanded are inversely related.
- Quantity demanded is the total number of units of a good that buyers are willing and able to buy at a particular price.
- A (downward-sloping) demand curve is the graphical representation of the law of demand.
- Factors that can shift the demand curve include income, preferences, prices of related goods (substitutes and complements), number of buyers, and expectations of future price.

■ A change in quantity demanded is directly brought about by a change in a good's own price.

Supply

■ The law of supply states that as the price of a good rises, the quantity supplied of the good rises, and as the price of a good falls, the quantity supplied of the good falls, *ceteris paribus.* The law of supply asserts that price and quantity supplied are directly related.
■ The law of supply does not hold when there is no time to produce more units of a good, or for goods that cannot be produced (over any period of time).
■ The upward-sloping supply curve is the graphical representation of the law of supply. More generally, a supply curve (no matter how it slopes) represents the relationship between price and quantity supplied.
■ Factors that can shift the supply curve include prices of relevant resources, technology, number of sellers, expectations of future price, taxes and subsidies, and government restrictions.
■ A change in quantity supplied is directly brought about by a change in a good's own price.

The Market

■ Both demand and supply establish equilibrium price and quantity.
■ A surplus exists in a market if, at some price, quantity supplied is greater than quantity demanded. A shortage exists if, at some price, quantity demanded is greater than quantity supplied.

Absolute and Relative Prices

■ The absolute price of a good is its price in money terms. The relative price of a good is its price in terms of another good.
■ As the absolute price of a good rises, its relative price may rise or fall. What happens depends on the percentage increase in the absolute price of other goods. For example, if the absolute price of apples rises by a greater percentage than the absolute price of oranges, the relative price of oranges falls, even though its absolute price has risen.

Key Terms and Concepts

Market	Complements	Equilibrium Price (Market-clearing Price)
Demand	Own Price	
Law of Demand	Supply	Equilibrium Quantity
Demand Schedule	Law of Supply	Disequilibrium Price
Demand Curve	Supply Curve	Disequilibrium
Normal Good	Supply Schedule	Equilibrium
Inferior Good	Surplus (Excess Supply)	Absolute Price
Substitutes	Shortage (Excess Demand)	Relative Price

1. True or false? As the price of oranges rises, the demand for oranges falls, *ceteris paribus.* Explain your answer.

2. "The price of a bushel of wheat was $3.00 last month and is $3.70 today. The demand curve for wheat must have shifted rightward between last month and today." Discuss.

3. "Some goods are bought largely because they have 'snob appeal.' For example, the residents of Palm Beach gain prestige by buying expensive items. In fact, they won't buy some items unless they are expensive. The law of demand, which holds that people buy more at lower prices than higher prices, obviously doesn't hold for Palm Beachers. In short, the following rule applies in Palm Beach: high prices, buy; low prices, don't buy." Discuss.

4. "The price of T-shirts keeps rising and rising, and people keep buying more and more. T-shirts must have an upward-sloping demand curve." Identify the error.

 5. "Demand is more important to the determination of price than supply." Discuss.

 6. Predict what would happen to the equilibrium price of marijuana if it were legalized.

7. Compare the ratings for television shows with prices for goods. How are ratings like prices? How are ratings different from prices? (Hint: How does rising demand for a particular television show manifest itself?)

8. In this chapter, we showed that because the relative price of high-quality apples is lower in New York than in Washington State, New Yorkers consume relatively more high-quality apples. Apply this principle in different areas. For example, ask yourself if you would consume relatively more expensive meals on vacation in Mexico than at home. (Hint: Might there be a transportation cost of going on vacation that is analogous to the transport cost of moving apples from Washington State to New York?)

9. Discuss whether you think the law of demand holds for criminal activity? Do potential criminals "buy" less (more) crime, the higher (lower) the "price" of crime, *ceteris paribus?* Explain your answer.

10. Many movie theaters charge a lower admission price for the first show on weekday afternoons than for a weeknight or weekend show. Explain why.

11. The current price for good X is $10, the quantity demanded is 150 and the quantity supplied is 190. For every one dollar decrease in price, quantity supplied falls by 5 units and quantity demanded rises by 7 units. What is the equilibrium price and quantity of good X?

12. In year 1 the price of a television set is $400 and the price of a computer is $2,000. In year 2 the price of a television set is $450 and the price of a computer is $2,100. What is the relative price of a television in both years? What is the relative price of a computer in both years?

4

SUPPLY, DEMAND, AND PRICE: APPLICATIONS

WHAT THIS CHAPTER IS ABOUT

Price has two tasks: It is a rationing device and a transmitter of information. We begin this chapter with a discussion of these two tasks. Next, we discuss what happens when price controls prevent price from performing its two tasks. Finally, we give some real-world examples of supply, demand, and price at work.

Price serves as a rationing device.

Rationing Device
Something that is used to decide who gets what of available goods and resources. Price is a rationing device.

Price as a Rationing Device

Because scarcity exists, a *rationing device* is needed to determine who gets what of the available limited resources and goods. Price serves as a rationing device. It rations *scarce resources* to those producers who pay the price for the resources. It rations *scarce goods* to those buyers who pay the price for the goods. It is as simple as this: Pay the price, and the resources or goods are yours. Don't pay the price, and they aren't.

Resources and goods do not have to be rationed by price. They could be rationed by *political power, ethnic background, physical appearance, religion, favoritism, brute force,* or on a *first-come-first-served* basis, to name only a few possibilities. All these are means that could be used to decide who gets what. Therefore, all could be rationing devices.

Consider a world where brute force is the only rationing device. There the only way you could get what you want is by physically taking it from someone else. Of course, other people would be trying to take things away from you. Suppose you build a canoe to go fishing in, but your next-door neighbor, a burly fellow, hits you over the head and takes the canoe. He gets what he wants, not by paying a price, but through brute force. The strongest persons most willing to use their muscle to get what they want would rule. How would you fare in this world?

Consider a world where religion backed up by the power of the state is used as a rationing device. If you want a car, or food, or an education, you must be a member of the "right" religion as determined by the persons that rule.[1]

Consider a world where ethnic background is used as a rationing device. Who gets what is decided by whether a person is the "right" ethnic background.[2]

Question:

Clearly, rationing devices such as brute force, religion, and ethnic background work to the disadvantage of the weak and people of the "wrong" religion and ethnic background. But price as a rationing device also works to the disadvantage of some people: specifically, the poor. Isn't this correct?

Answer:

Undoubtedly, if price is the rationing device, poor people will not be able to buy some goods that rich people can buy. It is similar, in this sense, to using ethnic background as the rationing device and prohibiting the Chinese, for example, from buying some goods that the non-Chinese can buy. However, a poor person can sometimes earn the income to pay the price, but a Chinese person can never change his or her ethnic background. There are thousands of examples of poor people becoming rich people, but there is not one example of a Chinese person becoming English, Spanish, or French.

[1]Even recently, in some countries religion has been used to ration goods. For example, in Ayatollah Khomeini's Iran, buying many goods was illegal unless you were a Moslem. Members of the Baha'i and Jewish faiths were discriminated against in this regard.
[2]There are numerous cases throughout history where persons of a particular ethnic background could not legally buy certain goods. In the United States, the most notable example is that blacks were at one time prohibited from buying food in "white" restaurants.

Finally, we need to understand that no matter what rationing device is used, it will be of greater benefit to some people than others. This is a consequence of living in a world of inherently unequal individuals.

Follow-up Question:

Why not use need *as the rationing device?*

Answer:

There are problems here. First, who would determine which groups are in need? Republicans? Democrats? Social workers? Second, what is it that people really need? We might agree that all people need a certain amount of food, water, clothing, and shelter. But what else? Do people need television sets, VCRs, trips to Aspen in the winter, personal computers, and so forth? Third, if need were the rationing device, would there be an incentive to work? With price as a rationing device, people have to produce goods and services to earn the income necessary to buy goods. If they could obtain these goods and services without working—by simply expressing a "need"—would anything be produced? Would anyone actually work under such a system?

Price as a Transmitter of Information

On the surface, price is a number with a dollar sign ($) in front of it. Below the surface, price is a transmitter of information, much as telephones, letters, and smoke signals are transmitters of information. To illustrate, consider the following set of events.

On Saturday, Noelle walks into a local grocery store and purchases a half-gallon of orange juice for $2.50. On Sunday, unknown to her, a cold spell hits Florida and wipes out one-quarter of the orange crop. The cold spell shifts the supply curve of oranges leftward and leads to a rise in the equilibrium price of oranges. Higher orange prices shift the supply curve of orange juice leftward and drive up its equilibrium price. Next Saturday, Noelle returns to the grocery store and notices that the price of a half-gallon of orange juice is $3.50. She decides to buy a quart of orange juice for $1.75 instead of a half-gallon for $3.50. (Her demand curve for orange juice is downward sloping; she buys less at higher prices than at lower prices.)

What kind of information does price transmit? By moving up and down, it transmits information on the *relative scarcity* of a good. The higher price for orange juice is saying (once we translate its message into English): "There has been a cold spell in Florida resulting in less orange juice. The gap between people's wants for orange juice and the amount of orange juice available to satisfy those wants has widened."

Notice, too, that because Noelle directly responded to the higher price of orange juice by cutting back on her consumption, she indirectly responded to the information of the increased relative scarcity of orange juice, even without being informed about Florida weather conditions. Because the price increase has encouraged Noelle to help conserve orange juice, it has worked to promote social cooperation.

PRICE CONTROLS
■

Price is not always permitted to be a rationing device and transmitter of information. Sometimes it is controlled. There are two types of price controls: price ceilings and price floors. In our discussion of price controls, we use the word *price* in the generic sense. It refers to the price of an apple, for example, the price of labor (wage), the price of credit (interest rate), and the price of a rental unit (rent).

Price Ceiling: Definition and Effects

Price Ceiling
A government-mandated maximum price above which legal trades cannot be made.

A **price ceiling** is a government-mandated maximum price above which legal trades cannot be made. For example, suppose the government mandates that the maximum price at which good *X* can be bought and sold is $8. It follows that $8 is a price ceiling. If $8 is below the equilibrium price of good *X,* as in Exhibit 4–1, any or all of the following effects may arise.[3]

Shortages. At the $12 equilibrium price in Exhibit 4–1, the quantity demanded of good *X* (150) is equal to the quantity supplied (150). At the $8 price ceiling, a

[3]If a price ceiling is above the equilibrium price (say, $8 is the price ceiling and $4 is the equilibrium price), it has no effects. Usually, however, a price ceiling is below the equilibrium price.
The price ceiling effects we discuss here hold for a particular market structure and not necessarily for all market structures. The relevant market structure is usually referred to as a perfectly competitive market, a price-taker market, or a perfect market. No matter what the term, we are assuming enough buyers and sellers so that no single buyer or seller can influence price.

EXHIBIT 4–1
A Price Ceiling

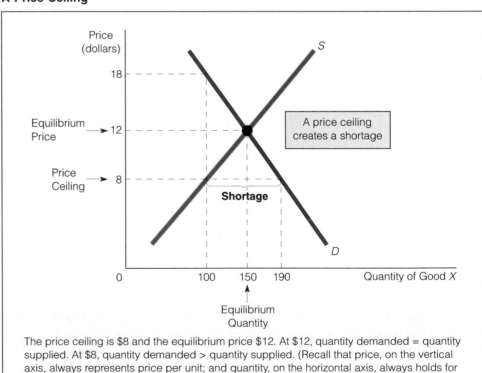

The price ceiling is $8 and the equilibrium price $12. At $12, quantity demanded = quantity supplied. At $8, quantity demanded > quantity supplied. (Recall that price, on the vertical axis, always represents price per unit; and quantity, on the horizontal axis, always holds for a specific time period.)

shortage exists: The quantity demanded (190) is greater than the quantity supplied (100). In Chapter 3, we learned that when a shortage exists, there is a tendency for price and output to rise to equilibrium. But when a price ceiling exists, this tendency cannot be realized since it is unlawful to trade at the equilibrium price.

Fewer Exchanges. At equilibrium price, 150 units of goods X are bought and sold. At the price ceiling in Exhibit 4–1, 100 units of good X are bought and sold. (Buyers would prefer to buy 190 units, but only 100 are supplied.) We conclude that price ceilings cause fewer exchanges to be made.

Nonprice Rationing Devices. If an equilibrium price of $12 *fully* rationed good X before the price ceiling was imposed, it follows that a (lower) price of $8 can only partly ration it. In short, price ceilings prevent price from rising to the level sufficient to ration goods fully. What then helps price do what it once did alone? The answer is some other (nonprice) rationing device, such as first-come-first-served (FCFS).

In Exhibit 4–1, 100 units of good X will be sold at $8 although buyers are willing to buy 190 units at this price. What happens? Possibly, good X will be sold on a FCFS basis for $8 per unit. In other words, to buy good X a person needs not only to pay $8 per unit but also to be one of the first persons in line.

Black Market. A black market is an illegal market. There are principally two varieties: one in which illegal goods are bought and sold (for example, cocaine in this country) and one in which goods are bought and sold at illegal prices (for example, buying and selling goods above a price ceiling). The latter type of black market is relevant here. Buyers and sellers will regularly get around a price ceiling by making their exchanges "under the table." For example, some buyers of good X may offer some sellers more than $8 per unit in order to buy the good. No doubt some sellers will accept the offers.

Black Market
An illegal market. There are two varieties: one in which illegal goods are bought and sold and one in which goods are bought and sold at illegal prices.

Question:

Why would some buyers offer more then $8 per unit when they can buy good X for $8?

Answer:

Not all buyers can buy the amount of good X they want at $8. As Exhibit 4–1 shows, there is a shortage: Buyers are willing to buy 190 units at $8, but sellers are only willing to sell 100 units. In short, 90 fewer units will be sold than buyers would like to buy. Some buyers will go unsatisfied. How, then, does any *one* buyer make it more likely that sellers will sell to him or her instead of to someone else? The answer is by offering to pay a higher price. Since it is illegal to pay a higher price, however, the transaction must be made "under the table." It is a black market transaction.

Tie-in Sales. In Exhibit 4–1, what is the maximum price buyers would be willing and able to pay per unit for 100 units of good X? As we can see, it is $18. The maximum *legal* price, however, is $8. This difference between the two prices often prompts a **tie-in sale,** a sale whereby one good can be purchased *only if* another good is also purchased. For example, if Ralph's Gas Station only sells gasoline to customers if they buy a car wash, the two goods are linked together in a tie-in sale.

Tie-in Sale
A sale whereby one good can be purchased only if another good is also purchased.

Suppose that the sellers of good X in Exhibit 4–1 also sell good Y. They might offer to sell buyers good X at $8 only if the buyers agree to buy good Y at, say, $10. We choose $10 as the price for good Y because that is the difference between the maximum per-unit price buyers are willing and able to pay for 100 units of good X (specifically, $18) and the maximum legal price ($8).

In New York City and other communities with rent-control laws, tie-in sales sometimes result from rent ceilings on apartments. Occasionally, in order to rent an apartment, an individual must agree to buy the furniture in the apartment.

> Economists understand that government policy sometimes has unintended effects. For example, a price ceiling policy that may be intended to lower prices for the poor ends up causing shortages, the use of nonprice rationing devices, black markets, and tie-in sales. It is not clear that once we consider both the price ceiling *and* its effects that the poor are helped. The economist knows that wanting to do good (for others) is not sufficient. It is important to know *how* to do good, too.

Do Buyers Prefer Lower Prices to Higher Prices?

"Of course," someone might say, "buyers prefer lower prices to higher prices. What buyer in his right mind would want to pay a higher price for anything?" But wait a minute. Price ceilings are often lower than equilibrium prices. Does it follow that buyers prefer price ceilings to equilibrium prices? Not necessarily. As explained earlier, price ceilings have effects that equilibrium prices do not: shortages, use of first-come-first-served as a rationing device, tie-in sales, and so on. It could be that a buyer would prefer to pay a higher price (an equilibrium price) and avoid the effects of a price ceiling than pay a lower price and have to deal with them. All we can say for certain is that *if all other things are held constant,* buyers prefer lower prices to higher prices. As in many cases, the *ceteris paribus* condition makes all the difference.

Price Ceilings and False Information

Let's go back to the orange juice example we discussed previously. Suppose there is a price ceiling on orange juice at $2.50 per half-gallon, which happens to be the equilibrium price of orange juice before the cold spell in Florida. Further, suppose the price ceiling is maintained even after the cold spell and subsequent fall in the supply of orange juice. Price is not permitted to rise to its new equilibrium level, $3.50, even though the supply curve of orange juice has shifted leftward. Can the information about the increased relative scarcity of orange juice (due to the cold spell) get through to orange juice buyers? No. Since price is prohibited from rising, it obviously cannot transmit this information. As far as buyers are concerned, nothing has changed, and they mistakenly think that they can go on drinking orange juice at the same rate as before. But this is a delusion. One way or the other, some people must curtail their consumption of orange juice, now that fewer oranges are available.

The lesson is simple. Price ceilings (below equilibrium price) distort the flow of accurate information to buyers. Buyers end up thinking that reality is something other than it is; they base their buying expectations on false information. Problems follow, buyers soon feel the unintended, unexpected, and undesirable effects of price ceilings.

Price Floor: Definition and Effects

A **price floor** is a government-mandated minimum price below which legal trades cannot be made. For example, suppose the government mandates that the minimum price at which good X can be sold is $20. It follows that $20 is a price floor (Exhibit 4–2). If the price floor is above the equilibrium price, the two following effects arise.[4]

Surpluses. At the $15 equilibrium price in Exhibit 4–2, the quantity demanded of good X (130) is equal to the quantity supplied (130). At the $20 price floor, a surplus exists; the quantity supplied (180) is greater than the quantity demanded (90). In Chapter 3, we learned that a surplus is a temporary state of affairs. When a surplus exists, there is a tendency for price and output to fall to equilibrium. But when a price floor exists, this tendency cannot be realized since it is unlawful to trade at the equilibrium price.

Fewer Exchanges. At equilibrium price in Exhibit 4–2, 130 units of good X are bought and sold. At the price floor, 90 units are bought and sold. (Sellers want to sell 180 units, but buyers buy only 90.) We conclude that price floors cause fewer exchanges to be made.

Two Cases of Price Floors

We turn now to two real-world examples of price floors. The first is *agricultural price supports;* the second is the *minimum wage law.*

[4]If a price floor is below the equilibrium price (say, $20 is the price floor and $25 is the equilibrium price), it has no effects. Usually, however, a price floor is above the equilibrium price.
As with price ceilings, the price floor effects we discuss here hold for a perfectly competitive market. See footnote 3.

Price Floor
A government-mandated minimum price below which legal trades cannot be made.

EXHIBIT 4–2
A Price Floor

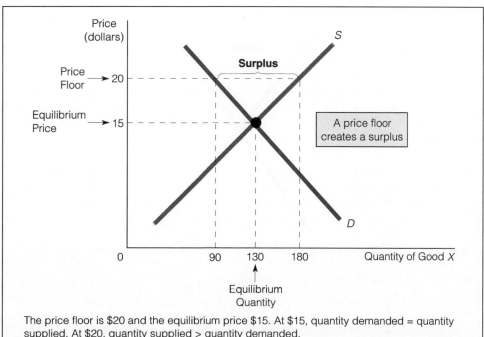

The price floor is $20 and the equilibrium price $15. At $15, quantity demanded = quantity supplied. At $20, quantity supplied > quantity demanded.

Price Support
The minimum price government determines farmers will receive for their products. Not all agricultural products have price supports.

Case 1: Agricultural Price Supports. A price support (in agriculture) is an example of a price floor. It is a government-guaranteed minimum price. Some of the agricultural products that either have or have had price supports include wheat, cotton, feed grains, dairy products, peanuts, and tobacco. Suppose the price support for wheat is set above the equilibrium price at $6 per bushel, as in Exhibit 4–3. At this price, quantity supplied is greater than quantity demanded and there is a surplus of wheat. Also, the number of bushels of wheat bought by *private citizens* is less (10) at the price support (price floor) than at equilibrium price (18).[5] We would expect wheat buyers to dislike the price support program since they end up paying higher than equilibrium price for the wheat they buy.

What happens to the surplus? Under supply-and-demand conditions, farmers could get rid of the surplus of wheat by lowering price. But, of course, there is no need to lower price. The price is supported by *government,* which buys the surplus at the price support. Since the government's purchase of surplus wheat needs to be stored, it sometimes must pay huge storage costs. For example, in the 1950s and early 1960s, storage costs for wheat rose rapidly, reaching over $1 million per day at one period. For the taxpayers who ultimately had to pay the bill, this was not a happy state of affairs.

Thus, the effects of agricultural price supports are (1) a surplus, (2) fewer exchanges (less wheat bought by private citizens), (3) higher prices paid by consumers of wheat, and (4) government purchase and storage of the surplus wheat (for which taxpayers end up paying).[6]

[5]We specify *private citizens* here because some of the wheat crop is purchased by the government.
[6]For more on agriculture and government policies that affect this industry, see Chapter 30.

EXHIBIT 4–3
Effects of an Agricultural Price Support

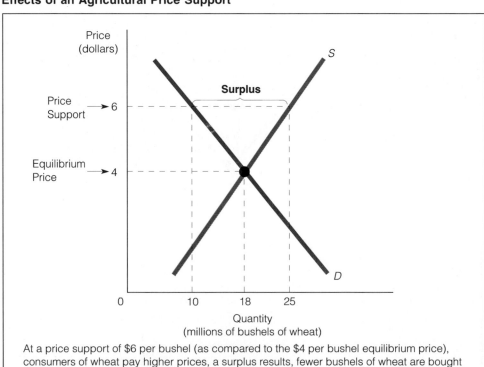

At a price support of $6 per bushel (as compared to the $4 per bushel equilibrium price), consumers of wheat pay higher prices, a surplus results, fewer bushels of wheat are bought by private citizens, and government buys and stores the surplus (which taxpayers pay for).

Case 2: The Minimum Wage Law. The *minimum wage* is a price floor—a government-mandated minimum price for labor. It affects the market for unskilled labor. In Exhibit 4–4, the minimum wage is $4.25 an hour and the equilibrium wage is $3.25. At the equilibrium wage, N_1 workers are employed. At the higher minimum wage, N_3 workers want to work, but only N_2 actually do work. There is a surplus of workers equal to $N_3 - N_2$ in this unskilled labor market. In addition, fewer workers are working at the minimum wage (N_2) than at the equilibrium wage (N_1). Overall, the effects of the minimum wage are (1) a surplus of unskilled workers and (2) fewer workers employed.[7]

Question:

Isn't the minimum wage necessary to guarantee everybody a decent wage? If the minimum wage didn't exist, wouldn't employers hire workers for next to nothing?

Answer:

Employers may want to hire workers for "next to nothing," but the wages workers receive depend on the demand for and supply of labor. In other words, employers

[7]We remind the reader that the effects of the minimum wage are determined for a perfectly competitive (price-taker or perfect) market.

EXHIBIT 4–4
Effects of the Minimum Wage

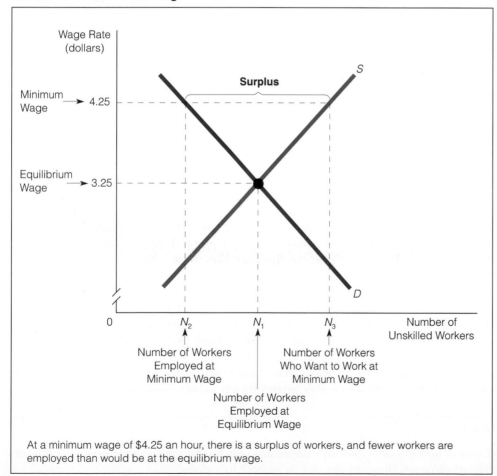

At a minimum wage of $4.25 an hour, there is a surplus of workers, and fewer workers are employed than would be at the equilibrium wage.

do not set wages at whatever level they like: In a competitive market setting, the forces of supply and demand determine equilibrium wages.

As to the minimum wage guaranteeing a decent wage, suppose Johnny Bates, a 17-year-old in Chicago, finds that his labor is worth $3.25 an hour to employers. If the government mandates that Johnny must be paid $4.25 an hour ($1 more an hour than he's currently worth to employers), no employer will hire him. So the minimum wage does not guarantee Johnny a decent wage; in fact, it may guarantee him no wage.

APPLICATIONS OF SUPPLY AND DEMAND

Do the tools of supply and demand help us to understand more about the real world? We think they do, and we hope you agree. But if, by chance, you remain an unbeliever, then this section is for you. In it we present more applications of supply and demand. They all illustrate how price serves as a rationing device.

Freeway Congestion

What does a traffic jam on a busy freeway in any large city have to do with supply and demand? Actually, it has quite a bit to do with supply and demand. Look at it this way: There is a demand for driving on the freeway and a supply of freeway space. The supply of freeway space is fixed (freeways do not expand and contract over a day, week, or month). The demand, however, fluctuates. Sometimes it is higher than at other times. For example, we would expect the demand for driving on the freeway to be higher at 8 A.M. (rush hour) than at 11 P.M. But even though this may be the case, the money price for driving on the freeway is always the same—always zero. A zero money price means that no tolls are paid to drive on the freeway.

Exhibit 4–5 shows two demand curves for driving on the freeway: $D_{8A.M.}$ and $D_{11P.M.}$ We have assumed the demand at 8 A.M. is greater than at 11 P.M. We have also assumed that at $D_{11P.M.}$ and zero money price the freeway market clears: Quantity demanded of freeway space equals quantity supplied of freeway space. At the higher demand, $D_{8A.M.}$, however, this is not the case. At zero money price, a shortage of freeway space exists: The quantity demanded of freeway space is greater than the quantity supplied of freeway space. The shortage appears in the form of freeway congestion, bumper-to-bumper traffic. One way to eliminate the shortage is through an increase in the money price of driving on the freeway at 8 A.M. For example, as Exhibit 4–5 shows, a toll of 70 cents would clear the freeway market at 8 A.M.

If charging different prices (tolls) at different times of the day on freeways sounds like an unusual idea, consider how Miami Beach hotels price their rooms. They charge different prices for their rooms at different times of the year. During the winter months when the demand for vacationing in Miami Beach is high, the hotels charge higher prices than when the demand is (relatively) low. If different prices were charged for freeway space at different times of the day, freeway space would be rationed the same way Miami Beach hotel rooms are rationed.

EXHIBIT 4–5
Freeway Congestion and Supply and Demand

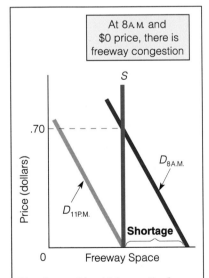

The demand for driving on the freeway is higher at 8A.M. than at 11P.M. At zero money price and $D_{11P.M.}$, the freeway market clears. At zero money price and $D_{8A.M.}$, there is a shortage of freeway space, which shows up as freeway congestion. At a price (toll) of 70 cents, the shortage is eliminated and freeway congestion disappears.

82

Question:

If this is correct, and freeway congestion can be eliminated by charging different tolls at different times of the day, why isn't this done?

Answer:

First, simply because a certain action will eliminate a problem, it does not necessarily follow that it is desirable to carry out that action. A system of tolls will reduce, if not eliminate, freeway congestion, but it may not be worth the cost to build and staff the toll booths. As technology for monitoring usage and billing improves, however, it's possible that we'll institute such a system. In some places in Hong Kong, this has already been done.

Second, freeways are "owned" by the taxpayers and managed by government, not privately owned and managed. The present owner–management team (taxpayers and government officials) is less likely to propose and implement a toll system than a privately owned and managed team that seeks to maximize profits.

Finally, some people argue that rationing freeway space by money price would hurt the poor by making it more expensive for them to get to work and to travel; a few traffic jams are preferable.

Tipping at a Las Vegas Show

To get a good seat at a Las Vegas show, you have to tip (in advance) the person who seats you. Tourists in Las Vegas usually complain, "I don't know why I have to pay that guy $10 to walk me to my seat. It is ridiculous." But is it? Supply and demand explain what is going on.

In Las Vegas, all tickets for the same show sell for the same price (unlike tickets for a play in New York, say, where some tickets sell for higher prices than others). There are no seat assignments, however; buying a ticket guarantees you a seat, but it could be *any* seat from a good seat, center stage, to a bad seat, far in the back.

The show, therefore, has two markets: a market for good seats and a market for bad seats. In each market there is a demand for and a supply of seats. The bad

EXHIBIT 4–6
Good and Bad Seats at a Las Vegas Show

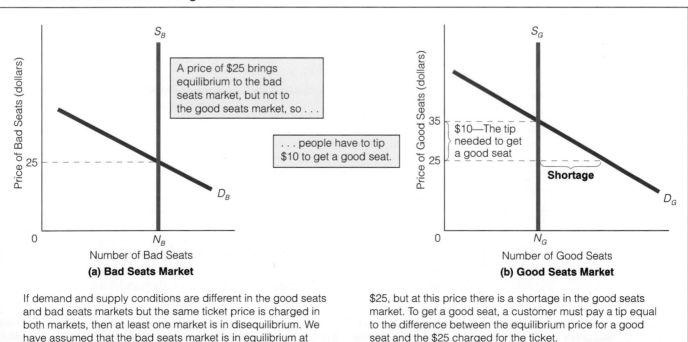

(a) Bad Seats Market

(b) Good Seats Market

If demand and supply conditions are different in the good seats and bad seats markets but the same ticket price is charged in both markets, then at least one market is in disequilibrium. We have assumed that the bad seats market is in equilibrium at $25, but at this price there is a shortage in the good seats market. To get a good seat, a customer must pay a tip equal to the difference between the equilibrium price for a good seat and the $25 charged for the ticket.

What Does Price Have to Do with Being Late to Class?

Class starts at 10 o'clock in the morning. At 10:09, Pam Ferrario walks in late. She apologizes to the instructor, saying, "I've been on campus for 20 minutes, but I couldn't find a parking space." Her classmates nod, knowing full well what she is talking about. Here at the university, especially between the hours of 8 A.M. and 2 P.M., parking spaces are hard to come by.

This scene is replayed every day at many universities and colleges across the country. Students are late for class because on many days there isn't a parking space to be found.

What can be done about this? Students could start for class earlier. Suppose you have a class at 10 A.M., and you live in an apartment 5 miles from the campus. If you are lucky enough to find an open parking space as soon as you enter the campus parking lot, then you need only leave home at 9:35. However, you can't count on such good luck, so you'd better leave at 9:15, just to be on the safe side.

Who pays for the shortage of parking spaces under this scheme? The student does. He or she doesn't pay in money but in time.

Or, if you choose not to leave home earlier, then you might pay in being late to class, as we saw earlier.

Are there alternatives to the pay-in-time and pay-in-being-late-to-class schemes for rationing campus parking spots? Some economists have suggested a pay-in-price scheme. For example, the university could install meters in the parking lot and raise the fee high enough so that between the hours of 8 A.M. and 2 P.M., the quantity demanded for parking spaces equals the quantity supplied.

Such suggestions are sometimes criticized because students must pay the fee, no matter how high, in order to attend classes. Well, that's not exactly true. Parking off campus and using public transportation are sometimes alternatives. But this is not really the main point. The issue isn't paying or not paying, but choosing the form in which payment is made—dollar price, time, or being late for class.

Some economists have taken the pay-in-price scheme farther and have argued that parking spots should be auctioned on a yearly basis. In other words, a student would rent a parking spot for a year. This way the student would always know that a parking spot would be open when he or she arrived at the campus. People who parked in someone else's spot would be ticketed by campus police.

Additionally, under this scheme, a student who rented a parking spot and chose not to use it between certain hours of the day could rent it out to someone else during this period. So we would expect to see notices like this on campus billboards:

Parking Spot for Rent

Near Arts Building and Student Union. Ideal for liberal arts students. Available on a 2–12 hour basis between 12 noon and 12 midnight. Rate: 50 cents per hour. Call 471-3564.

The argument is often heard that allocating campus parking spots according to price may be all right for rich and middle-income students, but that it hurts poor students. This is not a trivial argument, but it is often misleading. Poor students are not necessarily students without an income; they are simply students with relatively lower incomes than others. Poor students may choose to rearrange their purchases and buy more of one thing (a parking spot) and less of another (clothes, entertainment, and so on). We shouldn't jump to the conclusion that the poor would always prefer a nonmoney rationing scheme to a money rationing scheme.

Give price rationing for campus parking spots some thought. Consider what you believe to be its advantages and disadvantages. Perhaps the next time you're late for class and your instructor looks at you disapprovingly, you might say, "Is it my fault that we don't ration campus parking spots by price?"

seats market is shown in Exhibit 4–6a, the good seats market in Exhibit 4–6b. Notice that the demand is greater for good seats than bad seats (as we would expect).[8]

Normally, different market conditions (different demand and supply curves)

[8]We have drawn a vertical supply curve in both the good seats and bad seats markets. We are assuming here that the time period under consideration is so short that the quantity supplied of both good seats and bad seats cannot change even if price does. However, even with an upward-sloping supply curve in each market, the analysis is the same.

would bring about different equilibrium prices. The (manager of the) show, however, sells all tickets for the same price, $25. This is the equilibrium price in the bad seats market, but, as Exhibit 4–6b shows, it is a disequilibrium price (below equilibrium price) in the good seats market. The results is a shortage of good seats.

How are the "too few" good seats rationed? That is done by price in the form of a tie-in sale. To get a good seat, it is necessary to tip (in advance) the person who decides where you will sit. First tip the person who does the seating, then get a good seat (assuming, of course, you tipped enough). The necessary tip to get a good seat is equal to the difference between the equilibrium price for a good seat and the $25 charged. In Exhibit 4–6, we have assumed the equilibrium price is $35; thus, the tip is $10.

GPAs, ACTs, and SATs

In many colleges and universities, students pay less than the equilibrium tuition (price) to attend. Usually, the student pays part of the price of his or her education (by way of tuition payments), and taxpayers and private donors pay part (by way of tax payments and charitable donations, respectively). To illustrate, suppose the student at University X pays the tuition, T_1 (Exhibit 4–7a). As we can see, this is below the equilibrium tuition, T_E. At T_1, the number of students who want to

EXHIBIT 4–7
University Admissions

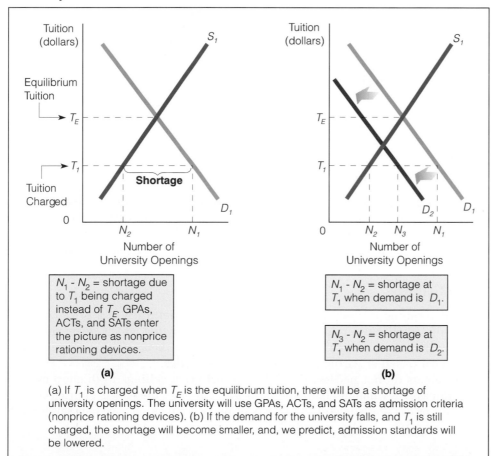

$N_1 - N_2$ = shortage due to T_1 being charged instead of T_E. GPAs, ACTs, and SATs enter the picture as nonprice rationing devices.

$N_1 - N_2$ = shortage at T_1 when demand is D_1.

$N_3 - N_2$ = shortage at T_1 when demand is D_2.

(a)

(b)

(a) If T_1 is charged when T_E is the equilibrium tuition, there will be a shortage of university openings. The university will use GPAs, ACTs, and SATs as admission criteria (nonprice rationing devices). (b) If the demand for the university falls, and T_1 is still charged, the shortage will become smaller, and, we predict, admission standards will be lowered.

CHAPTER 4
SUPPLY, DEMAND, AND PRICE:
APPLICATIONS

■

85

attend the university (N_1) is greater than the number of openings at the university (N_2): that is, quantity demanded is greater than quantity supplied. A shortage of university space exists. The university receives more applications for admission to the freshman class than there are places. Something has to be done. But what? The way the university rations its openings is by some combination of money price and other selected nonprice rationing devices. The student must pay the tuition, or have someone else pay it, *and* meet the standards of the nonprice rationing devices, which usually include such things as GPAs (grade point average), ACTs (American College Test), and SATs (Scholastic Aptitude Test).

Question:

Suppose the demand for University X falls, but tuition T_1 is still charged. Would admission requirements be reduced?

Answer:

The theory predicts that admission requirements would be reduced. To illustrate, suppose the demand for university openings falls from D_1 to D_2, as in Exhibit 4–7b. The shortage of university openings falls from $N_1 - N_2$ to $N_3 - N_2$. As the shortage falls, the GPA, ACT, and SAT requirements do not need to be as stringent as before. We would predict that if the demand for University X falls, university admission standards would be reduced, *ceteris paribus.*

CHAPTER SUMMARY

Price as a Rationing Device

■ Scarcity implies the need for a rationing device. Possible rationing devices include price, political power, first-come-first-served, ethnic background, physical appearance, religion, favoritism, and brute force.

Price as a Transmitter of Information

■ In a market in which price is permitted to rise and fall according to supply and demand, price transmits information on the relative scarcity of a good. A higher (lower) price informs us that the gap between people's wants and the amount of resources or goods available to satisfy those wants has widened (narrowed).

Price Ceilings

■ A price ceiling is a government-mandated maximum price. If a price ceiling is below the equilibrium price, some or all of the following effects arise: shortages, fewer exchanges, nonprice rationing devices, black markets (of the variety in which it is illegal to sell at particular prices), and tie-in sales.
■ Consumers do not necessarily prefer (lower) price ceilings to (higher) equilibrium prices. They may prefer higher prices and none of the effects of price ceilings to lower prices and some of the effects of price ceilings. All we can say for sure is that consumers prefer lower to higher prices, *ceteris paribus.*

■ Freely flexible prices (prices that are allowed to respond to the forces of supply and demand) transmit accurate information about relative scarcities. Controlled prices transmit inaccurate or false information about relative scarcities.

Price Floors

■ A price floor is a government-mandated minimum price. If a price floor is above the equilibrium price, the following effects arise: surpluses and fewer exchanges.
■ Both agricultural price supports and the minimum wage are examples of price floors. The effects of agricultural price supports are surpluses, fewer exchanges, higher prices for consumers, and government purchase and storage (or other disposal) of the surplus (that is, taxpayers pay). The effects of the minimum wage are a surplus (of unskilled labor) and fewer workers employed.

Key Terms and Concepts

Rationing Device	Black Market	Price Floor
Price Ceiling	Tie-in Sale	Price Support

QUESTIONS AND PROBLEMS

1. "If price were outlawed as the rationing device used in markets, there would be no need for another rationing device to take its place. We would have reached utopia." Discuss.
2. Many of the proponents of price ceilings argue that government-mandated maximum prices simply reduce producers' profits and do not affect the quantity supplied of a good on the market. What must the supply curve look like before a price ceiling does not affect quantity supplied?
3. The minimum wage hurts some unskilled workers because it prices them out of the labor market. For example, if the minimum wage is $4.25 per hour, and employers are only willing to pay a person $2.90 per hour, that person cannot legally be hired. Since the minimum wage largely applies to unskilled workers, would you expect all unskilled workers to be against the minimum wage?
4. Some people argue that the minimum wage, by pricing many unskilled teenagers out of the labor market, causes these individuals to turn to selling drugs. After all, if a person can't get a job legally, he or she will get one illegally. The alternative is to starve. Other people disagree. They state that some teenagers would still sell drugs even if all could be hired at the minimum wage—because of the monetary difference between clerking for $4.25 an hour and selling drugs for hundreds of dollars a week. What do you think?
5. What kind of information does price transmit?
6. Suppose the price of IBM stock rises by $2 a share. Does the price rise transmit any information to you? What does it say?
7. Should grades in an economics class be "rationed" according to money price instead of how well a student does on the exams? If they were, and potential employers learned of this, what effect might this have on the value of your college degree?

8. The money price of driving on a freeway is always the same—zero. Is the (opportunity) cost always the same and zero, too? Explain your answer.

9. Think about ticket scalpers at a rock concert, a baseball game, or an opera. Might they exist because the tickets to these events were originally sold for less than the equilibrium price? Why? In what way is a ticket scalper like and unlike your retail grocer, who buys food from a wholesaler and turns around and sells it to you?

10. How might we go about determining the equilibrium toll on a freeway at a particular time of day?

MACROECONOMICS

PART

II

MACROECONOMIC FUNDAMENTALS

5

AN INTRODUCTION TO MACROECONOMICS

WHAT THIS CHAPTER IS ABOUT

This chapter is a preview of later macroeconomics chapters. First, it presents a way to categorize much of what you will learn in macroeconomics. Second, it describes the major players in the macroeconomic arena. Third, it discusses some of the facts and questions macroeconomists find interesting. Fourth, it provides a roadmap to our study of macroeconomics.

THREE MACROECONOMIC ORGANIZATIONAL CATEGORIES

Macroeconomics is the branch of economics that deals with human behavior and choices as they relate to highly aggregated markets (such as the goods and services market) or the entire economy. The subject matter in macroeconomics includes (1) macroeconomic problems, (2) macroeconomic theories, (3) macroeconomic policies and, (4) different views of how the economy works. To help you categorize what you learn in macroeconomics, we develop three macroeconomic organizational categories. We call these categories (1) the P–Q category, (2) the inherently stable–inherently unstable category, and (3) the effective–ineffective category.

The *P–Q* Category

Macroeconomics has two major variables—the **price level** and **real GNP.** The price level is the weighted average of the prices paid for goods and services. Real GNP is the total market value of the entire output produced annually in an economy, adjusted for price changes. We discuss both the price level and real GNP in depth in Chapter 7, but for now you may simply want to view the price level as an average price and real GNP as the quantity of output produced.

The symbol we use for the price level is P; the symbol we use for the real GNP is Q. Thus, we can talk about the P–Q category.

Here is a list of topics in macroeconomics. Notice how each of the topics is defined, or partly defined, by price level (P), real GNP (Q), or both.

Gross national product (GNP). P times Q.
Real GNP. Q.
Price level. P.
Unemployment. Changes in unemployment are related to changes in Q.
Inflation. A rising P.
Deflation. A falling P.
Economic growth. Related to increasing Q.
Stagflation. A rising P combined with rising unemployment.
Business cycle. Recurrent swings (up and down) in Q, among other things.
Recessionary gap. The condition of the economy when Q is below its natural level.
Inflationary gap. The condition of the economy when Q is above its natural level.
Fiscal policy. Concerned with stabilizing P, achieving low unemployment (which is related to Q), and promoting economic growth (which is also related to Q), among other things.
Monetary policy. Concerned with stabilizing P, achieving low unemployment (which is related to Q), and promoting economic growth (which is also related to Q), among other things.

Question:

How should the P–Q category be used by a student of macroeconomics?

Answer:

When the student comes across a macroeconomics topic, she should ask herself if it relates directly or indirectly to either P, Q, or both. In many cases, she will see

---

Macroeconomics has two major variables— the price level (P) and real GNP (Q).

Macroeconomics
The branch of economics that deals with human behavior and choices as they relate to highly aggregated markets (such as the goods and services market) or the entire economy.

Price Level
The weighted average of the prices of all goods and services.

Real GNP
The value of the entire output produced annually in an economy, adjusted for price changes. It also can be defined as GNP (gross national product) valued in prices prevailing in the base year.

that it does. This realization helps the student to see the *common denominator* of much that is discussed in macroeconomics.

Some economists argue that the economy is inherently stable and others argue that it is inherently unstable.

The Inherently Stable–Inherently Unstable Category

In Chapter 3, we showed that an unhampered market tends toward equilibrium. If price is above its equilibrium level, a surplus develops and price falls. If price is below its equilibrium level, a shortage develops and price rises. A market is self-equilibrating, or self-regulating, and inherently stable. No one directs it to equilibrium, the point at which quantity supplied equals quantity demanded. It moves there under its own forces.

Does the same hold true for the economy? Does the economy as a whole tend toward equilibrium and stability? Economists are divided. Some argue that it does, and some argue that it does not.

Consider the Great Depression of the 1930s. During this period in U.S. history, unemployment skyrocketed, the production of goods and services plummeted (*Q* fell), prices fell (*P* fell), banks closed, savings were lost, and companies went bankrupt. What does this period indicate about the inherent properties of a market economy? Some observers argue that the Great Depression is proof of the *inherent instability* of a market (or capitalist) economy, and demonstrates that natural economic forces, if left to themselves, may bring on human suffering.

Other observers see things differently. They argue that left to itself, the economy would never have nosedived into the Great Depression. The Depression, they believe, was largely caused and made worse by government tampering with the *inherently stable,* self-equilibrating, and wealth-producing properties of a market economy.

Which came first? Did the market economy turn down under the weight of its own forces, producing massive unemployment, with government later stepping in to restrain the destructive market forces? Or was the market economy pushed into depression, and held there, by government economic tampering? The answer largely depends on how the inherent properties of a market economy are viewed. As economist Axel Leijonhufvud notes:

> The central issue in macroeconomic theory is—once again—the extent to which the economy, or at least its market sectors, may properly be regarded as a self-regulating system. . . . How well or badly, do its "automatic" mechanisms perform?[1]

Question:

It sounds as if one person simply "views the economy" one way and another person simply views it another way—much as one person likes chocolate ice cream and another person likes vanilla. Is there more to it than preference or likes and dislikes?

Answer:

Yes. A person may come to hold a particular view of things in a number of different ways: through his or her reading of the facts, through a leap of faith, and so on. But we are not focusing our attention on the course one travels to come to a particular view of the economy, only on the view itself. Furthermore, we believe that a difference in views can and does generate debate, which is valuable. The interviews with economists in this text present a number of views.

[1]Axel Leijonhufvud, "Effective Demand Failures," *Swedish Journal of Economics* 75 (1973): 28.

The effectiveness of fiscal and monetary policy is a key issue of economic debate.

■

Fiscal Policy
Changes in government expenditures and taxation in an effort to achieve particular macroeconomic goals, such as low unemployment, stable prices, economic growth, and so on.

Monetary Policy
The deliberate control of the money supply and credit conditions in an effort to achieve particular macroeconomic goals, such as low unemployment, stable prices, economic growth, and so on.

Follow-up Question:

Can't positive economic analysis settle all debates?

Answer:

There are times when positive economic analysis may not be enough to settle debates. Deep-seated differences in the way people view the world may cause them to view the same facts in a different light.

The Effective–Ineffective Category

Here the words *effective* and *ineffective* describe **fiscal policy** and **monetary policy**. Fiscal policy relates to changes in government expenditures and taxation in an effort to achieve particular macroeconomic goals, such as low unemployment, stable prices, economic growth, and so on. Monetary policy refers to the deliberate control of the money supply and credit conditions in an effort to achieve the same macroeconomic goals.

An economist can take one of several positions within the effective–ineffective category. She can believe that fiscal and monetary policy are always effective (at meeting their goals), or that both fiscal and monetary policy are ineffective, or that fiscal policy is effective and monetary policy is ineffective, and so on.

Often, an economist's position on the effectiveness–ineffectiveness of policy is implicit in his or her view of how the economy works—that is, whether the economy is inherently stable or unstable.

Question:

How should the effective–ineffective category be used by a student of macroeconomics?

Answer:

The effective–ineffective category is sometimes useful in turning the implicit into the explicit, or pushing what is below the surface up to the surface. For example, a student may read what economist Jones says on, say, unemployment and inflation without being aware of the common thread that runs between the two topics. At times like this, he should ask himself if and how what is being said either supports or invalidates a particular position on policy. For example, does what economist Jones says support the position that fiscal policy is effective at achieving the macroeconomic goal of low unemployment?

A Final Word on the Three Organizational Categories

One or more of the three macroeconomic organizational categories can be used in much of what we discuss in macroeconomics. They are there to help you categorize and organize the many details you will be asked to learn. Moreover, they are there to help you keep the big picture, or the fundamental issues, of macroeconomics in front of you as you proceed to work through the technical aspects of macroeconomic problems, theories, and policies.

THE MACROECONOMIC PLAYERS

■

The principal players in macroeconomics are (1) households, (2) businesses, (3) government at all levels, (4) the federal government, in particular the president of the United States, the U.S. Congress, and the U.S. Treasury, (5) foreigners as buyers of U.S. goods, (6) Americans as buyers of foreign goods, and (7) the Federal Reserve System. We briefly discuss each of them in turn. You will learn much more about each in subsequent chapters.

Households

Economists usually divide the economy into four sectors: the household sector, the business sector, the government sector, and the foreign sector. The household sector consists of persons like you and your family. These are people who buy consumer goods—such goods as television sets, carpets, lamps, cars, refrigerators, toothpaste, and much more. Household expenditures are referred to as **consumption.** The total amount of, and changes in, consumption may influence economic events.

Consumption
Household spending on consumer goods.

Businesses

Gross private domestic investment, (or simply **investment**) is the sum of all purchases made by businesses on newly produced capital goods plus changes in business inventories. It also includes expenditures on new residential housing. The total amount of, and changes in, investment may influence economic events.

Gross Private Domestic Investment, or Investment
The sum of all purchases of newly produced capital goods plus changes in business inventories. It also includes expenditures on new residential housing.

Government at All Levels

Expenditures made by government at all levels—local, state, and federal—are referred to as **government expenditures,** or **government spending.** The total amount of, and changes in, government expenditures may influence economic events.

Government Expenditures, or Government Spending
The total dollar amounts spent by federal, state, and local governments on final goods and services.

The Federal Government

The federal government—in particular, the president of the United States, the U.S. Congress, and the U.S. Treasury—is important to the working of the economy. Together, the president and the Congress decide on matters of government spending and taxation—that is, *fiscal policy.* The U.S. Treasury is important because it finances federal budget deficits. The actions of these three institutions may influence economic events.

Foreigners as Buyers of U.S. Goods

Foreigners buy goods produced by Americans. The total foreign spending on domestic (U.S.) goods is called **exports.** How much foreigners spend on American goods may influence economic events in the United States.

Exports
Total foreign spending on domestic (U.S.) goods.

Americans as Buyers of Imported Goods

Americans buy goods from the residents of foreign nations. The total domestic (U.S.) spending on foreign goods is called **imports.** How much Americans spend on foreign goods may influence economic events in the United States.

Imports
Total domestic (U.S.) spending on foreign goods.

The Federal Reserve System

The **Federal Reserve System,** popularly called **the Fed,** is the central bank of the United States. Its principal components are the Board of Governors, which is the

The Federal Reserve System (the Fed)
The central bank of the United States; its primary duty is to control the money supply.

97

governing body of the Federal Reserve System, the 12 Federal Reserve District Banks, and the approximately 6,000 member commercial banks. The primary duty of the Federal Reserve System is to control the money supply, or implement *monetary policy*. You will learn in later chapters that the Fed can increase and decrease the money supply and that such actions may influence economic events.

A FEW FACTS AND QUESTIONS IN MACROECONOMICS
■

An economist, like any scientist attempting to understand the world, deals with facts. Facts are often interesting in themselves, but they usually don't stand alone. Facts often lead to questions.

What follows are some macroeconomic facts and some of the questions economists have asked about those facts. Together, the facts and the questions define some of the issues of macroeconomics and ultimately lead to the development of theories (to explain the facts and predict what will happen) and policies.

The Price Level

Exhibit 5–1 shows the price level in the United States for the years 1800–1990. As you can see, the price level went up in some years and down in other years. This fact leads us to ask, What causes the price level to rise? to fall?

EXHIBIT 5–1
The Price Level, 1800–1990

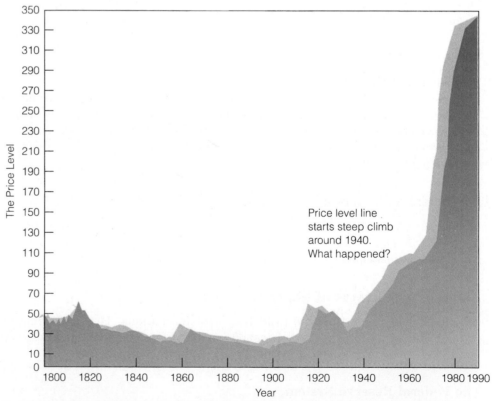

Price level line starts steep climb around 1940. What happened?

SOURCE: U.S. Bureau of the Census, *Historical Statistics of the United States* (Washington, D.C.: U.S. Government Printing Office, 1960); Council of Economic Advisers, *Economic Report of the President, 1991* (Washington, D.C.: U.S. Government Printing Office, 1991).

The Unemployment Rate

Exhibit 5–2 shows the unemployment rate in the United States for the years 1800–1990. We notice an unusually high unemployment rate during the Great Depression years (1929–33). Overall, we notice that the unemployment rate rises in some years and falls in other years. The facts lead us to ask, What caused the skyrocketing unemployment rate during the Great Depression? What causes the unemployment rate to rise? to fall?

Unemployment and Inflation

Over the short run, there sometimes is a **trade-off** between unemployment and inflation. A trade-off exists between unemployment and inflation if as one rises the other falls, that is, they move in opposite directions, or are *inversely related*.[2]

Trade-off
A situation in which the attainment of something desirable necessarily implies the loss of something else desirable.

[2]We remind the reader that if two variables move in the same direction, they are *directly related;* if they move in the opposite directions, they are *inversely related*. See Chapter 1, Appendix A.

EXHIBIT 5–2
The Unemployment Rate, 1990–1990

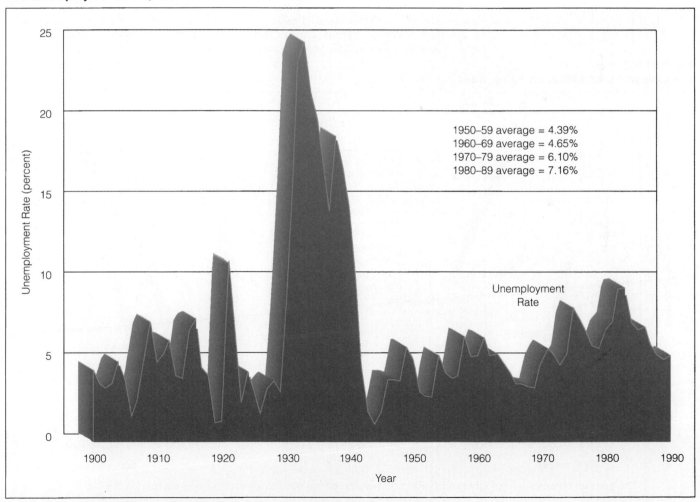

1950–59 average = 4.39%
1960–69 average = 4.65%
1970–79 average = 6.10%
1980–89 average = 7.16%

SOURCE: U.S. Bureau of the Census, *Historical Statistics of the United States* (Washington, D.C.: U.S. Government Printing Office, 1960); Council of Economic Advisers, *Economic Report of the President, 1991* (Washington, D.C.: Government Printing Office, 1991).

For example, in 1965, the unemployment rate was 4.5 percent and the inflation rate was 1.6 percent. One year later, in 1966, the unemployment had dropped to 3.8 percent, but the inflation rate had risen to 2.8 percent.

The same trade-off between inflation and unemployment existed between 1972 and 1973, 1976 and 1977, 1981 and 1982, 1986 and 1987, to name only four other sets of years. Exhibit 5–3a illustrates the inflation and unemployment rates for *selected years only.*

If we look at periods longer than one year, however, such as 1966 to 1970, 1972 to 1977, or 1973 to 1981 (Exhibit 5–3b), we notice that inflation and unemployment didn't move in the *opposite* direction, they moved in the *same* direction. For example, both inflation and unemployment were higher in 1970 than 1966. In short, there was no trade-off. We ask, Why is there sometimes a trade-off between inflation and unemployment over the short run? Why isn't there a trade-off in the long run?

Inflation and Interest Rates

High inflation rates are associated with high interest rates, and low inflation rates are associated with low interest rates[3] (Exhibit 5–4). This apparent relationship raises several questions: Do high inflation rates cause high interest rates? Or do

[3]The interest rate we are talking about here is the *nominal* (or *market*) interest rate, as measured by three-month U.S. Treasury bill rate. In a later chapter, you will learn that economists sometimes distinguish between the nominal interest rate and the real interest rate.

EXHIBIT 5–3
Unemployment and Inflation Rates, Selected Years

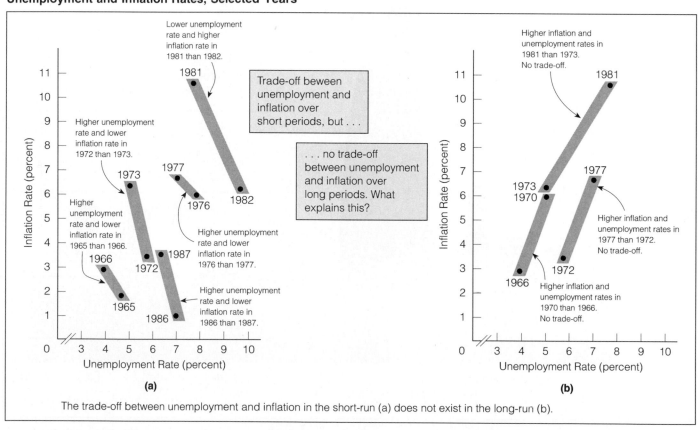

The trade-off between unemployment and inflation in the short-run (a) does not exist in the long-run (b).

Source: Council of Economic Advisers, *Economic Report of the President, 1991* (Washington, D.C.: U.S. Government Printing Office, 1991).

EXHIBIT 5–4
Inflation and Interest Rates, 1960–90

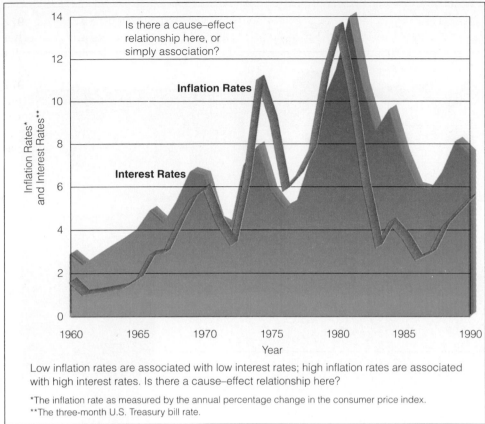

Is there a cause–effect relationship here, or simply association?

Inflation Rates

Interest Rates

Inflation Rates* and Interest Rates** (y-axis)

Year (x-axis)

Low inflation rates are associated with low interest rates; high inflation rates are associated with high interest rates. Is there a cause–effect relationship here?

*The inflation rate as measured by the annual percentage change in the consumer price index.
**The three-month U.S. Treasury bill rate.

SOURCE: Council of Economic Advisers, *Economic Report of the President, 1991* (Washington, D.C.: U.S. Government Printing Office, 1991).

high interest rates cause high inflation rates? Or is neither the cause nor the effect of the other?

Budget Deficits and Surpluses

Between 1946 and 1969, a run of federal government **budget deficits** was usually followed fairly closely by a run of federal **budget surpluses** (Exhibit 5–5). Beginning in 1970, however, a budget deficit has occurred each year. This raises the questions, What happened in or around the 1960s and 1970s to change things? What is the effect of budget deficits on the economy?

Recessions and Politics

Between the end of the Civil War in 1865 and 1990, the United States experienced 28 **recessions.** The most severe downturn in economic activity occurred during the years of the Great Depression. Some people have argued that the economic hardships encountered during this time led to major political changes. In particular, they mention the New Deal of President Franklin D. Roosevelt with its political restructuring of social and economic institutions. This raises the questions, Were these major political developments merely coincidental to the Great Depres-

Budget deficit
Occurs when government expenditures (*G*) are greater than tax receipts (*T*): $G > T$.

Budget surplus
Occurs when government expenditures (*G*) are less than tax receipts (*T*): $G < T$.

Recession
A decline in real GNP (real output) that lasts for two consecutive quarters (six months) or more.

101

EXHIBIT 5–5
The Status of the Federal Budget, 1946–90

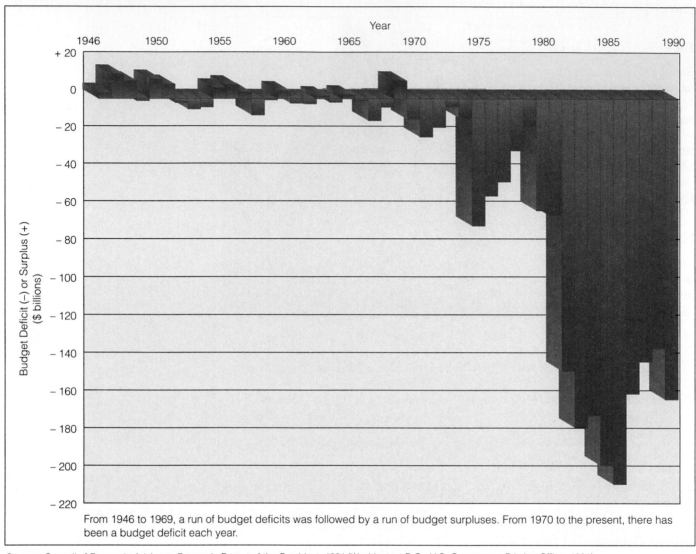

From 1946 to 1969, a run of budget deficits was followed by a run of budget surpluses. From 1970 to the present, there has been a budget deficit each year.

SOURCE: Council of Economic Advisers, *Economic Report of the President, 1991* (Washington, D.C.: U.S. Government Printing Office, 1991).

sion, or were they a consequence of it? More generally, what is the relationship between economic events and political change? Finally, what causes recessions?

Business Cycles

Over long periods, the U.S. economy has fluctuated between expansionary and contractionary phases in economic activity, like a roller coaster. The roller coaster rises to the top, and then it comes down, then it goes up again, and then down. These upward and downward fluctuations in economic activity are referred to as **business cycles.** There are four stages to a business cycle: (1) the *expansion,* (2) the *peak* of the expansion, (3) the *contraction,* and (4) the *trough* or bottom of the contraction. The typical business cycle—from the beginning of the expansion through the trough of the contraction—is approximately four to five years, although

Business cycle
Recurrent swings in general economic activity, usually measured in terms of the unemployment rate and real GNP.

102

a few have been shorter and some longer. This pattern leads to a question: Why doesn't economic activity stay on a steady course instead of moving upward and downward in a seemingly endless cycle?

Deficits and Inflation Rates

Some economists argue that bigger budget deficits (as a percentage of total output) cause higher inflation rates. They point to the periods 1961–65, 1966–70, 1971–75, and 1976–80 as evidence. In each of these five-year periods, as the average annual deficit grew, the average annual inflation rate rose.

But other economists argue that bigger budget deficits do not cause higher inflation rates. They cite the 1981–85 period, in which the average annual deficit grew and the average annual inflation rate fell.

The evidence is mixed bag. Is there a cause–effective relationship between deficits and inflation or not? Under what conditions might there be?

Net Exports

For most of this century, United States exports were greater than its imports—that is, **net exports** (or the difference between exports and imports) were positive. Beginning in 1983, though, the situation began to reverse (see Exhibit 5–6). This raises the question, How has this turnabout affected the U.S. economy?

Net Exports
Exports − imports.

A ROADMAP TO MACROECONOMICS
■

When beginning a long trip by car, it is customary to have a roadmap in front of you so that you know where you are going and what you can expect along the way. Similarly, when beginning a course of study, such as macroeconomics, it is nice to have a roadmap in front of you to know where you are headed and what you will learn on the way. Let's now outline our roadmap to learning macroeconomics. (As you follow the roadmap, note the times our discussion relates either directly or indirectly to P, the price level, or Q, real GNP).

In Chapter 6, we discuss a key economic measurement, **gross national product (GNP).** Gross national product is the total market value of all final goods and services produced annually in an economy. In P–Q terms, GNP is P times Q. For example, if a tiny economy produces, say, only 12 oranges the whole year, and the price of each orange is $2, then the GNP for the economy is $2 times 12 oranges, or $24.

In Chapter 7, we take the two components of GNP—P and Q—and look at each separately. We study the price level, then we study real GNP. Finally, we discuss unemployment, which is related to changes in real GNP.

In Chapter 8, we develop a framework of analysis, called the aggregate demand–aggregate supply framework (*AD–AS* framework), in which we can graphically represent changes in the key variables we have studied up to this point—that is, changes in GNP, the price level, real GNP, and to a lesser extent, unemployment. Chapter 8 puts into pictures much of what we have been discussing in Chapters 6 and 7.

Next, we begin our discussion of economic theory. The theory we discuss in Chapter 9 emphasizes unemployment. In Chapter 10, we discuss fiscal policy, in particular, how it may be used to deal with unemployment.

Gross national product (GNP)
The total market value of all final goods and services produced annually in an economy.

EXHIBIT 5–6
Net Exports, 1970–1990

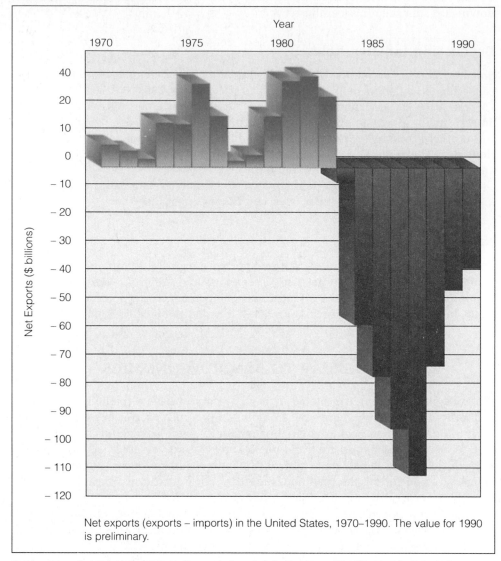

Net exports (exports – imports) in the United States, 1970–1990. The value for 1990 is preliminary.

SOURCE: Council of Economic Advisers, *Economic Report of the President, 1991* (Washington, D.C.: U.S. Government Printing Office, 1991).

Chapters 11–15 introduce money into the macroeconomics picture. Chapters 11 and 12 deal with money and banking and the Federal Reserve System, respectively.

In Chapter 13, we discuss a major macroeconomic problem, inflation, in terms of the *AD–AS* framework developed earlier.

In Chapter 14, we turn again to economic theory and discuss a theory that emphasizes the price level and a theory that emphasizes GNP.

In Chapter 15, our focus is monetary policy, in particular, how it may be used to deal with inflation and unemployment.

In Chapter 16, both inflation and unemployment is our theme. We introduce the important concept of expectations to the macroeconomics discussion, as well as a new macroeconomic theory.

In Chapter 17, we bring together a number of points developed in earlier chapters and discuss them within the context of business cycle theory.

In our last macroeconomics chapter, Chapter 18, we discuss budget deficits and debt, two topics of current interest.

Familiarity Does Not Equal Knowledge

As you study macroeconomics, we urge you to be open minded. Partly because economics is, in part or wholly, the subject of so many stories reported in magazines and newspapers, on the radio and television, laypersons often think they know more about it than they really do. In other words, familiarity with, not knowledge of, economics sometimes prompts people to hold ideas that may not be correct. Perhaps you already have some ideas about the causes of high inflation rates or high unemployment rates. Maybe your ideas are correct, and maybe not. Whatever mindset you bring to the study of macroeconomics, we hope you will be open to new ideas. This does not mean that you should accept everything you read in this text or everything your economics professor tells you. Both the text and the professor need to be questioned (undoubtedly, at times your professor will question the text). But remember that just as you question the text and the professor, you should question your own preconceived ideas, too. Your attitude is as important to understanding the subject as reading the text and taking notes.

CHAPTER SUMMARY

Three Macroeconomic Organizational Categories

■ The *P–Q* category: Macroeconomics emphasizes two major economic variables—the price level (*P*), the weighted average of prices paid for goods and services, and real GNP (*Q*), the total market value of economic output, adjusted for price changes. Many of the topics discussed in macroeconomics are directly or indirectly related to *P, Q,* or both.

■ The inherently stable–inherently unstable category: Some economists view the economy as self-equilibrating, or inherently stable, and some view it as inherently unstable (and therefore in need of manipulation).

■ The effective–ineffective category: Some economists believe that macroeconomic policy, such as fiscal policy, is effective at accomplishing its goals; some economists believe it is ineffective.

Macroeconomic Players

■ The key macroeconomic players are (1) households, (2) businesses, (3) government at all levels, (4) the federal government, in particular the president of the United States, the U.S. Congress, and the U.S. Treasury, (5) foreigners as buyers of U.S. goods, (6) Americans as buyers of foreign goods, and (7) the Federal Reserve System.

Facts and Questions

■ Economists often proceed from facts to questions to theories. For example, an economist might note that the price level was stable over one period of time and rising over another. He might then ask, Why? What factors affect the price level?

Naturally, the economist tries to find an answer. At this level of analysis, theories are formed, explanations offered, predictions made, and later, policies suggested. ■ Macroeconomic facts and questions relate to some of the following topics: the price level, unemployment, inflation, interest rates, budget deficits, recessions, and business cycles.

Key Terms and Concepts

Macroeconomics

Price Level

Real GNP

Fiscal Policy

Monetary Policy

Consumption

Gross Private Domestic
   Investment
   (Investment)

Government
   Expenditures

Exports

Imports

Federal Reserve System
   (the Fed)

Trade-Off

Budget Deficit

Budget Surplus

Recession

Business Cycle

Net Exports

Gross National Product

QUESTIONS AND PROBLEMS

1. Explain how each of the following is related to *P, Q,* or both: (a) inflation, (b) unemployment, (c) stagflation, (d) monetary policy, (e) fiscal policy.

2. What does it mean to say a person believes the economy is inherently unstable? inherently stable?

3. Suppose economist Jones says that fiscal policy is ineffective. Ineffective at what?

4. What is the Fed and what is its primary duty?

5. What is the difference between monetary policy and fiscal policy?

6. According to economist Axel Leijonhufvud, what is the central issue in macroeconomic theory?

7. Some persons are likely to argue that since the data show rising inflation rates and rising budget deficits over some time periods, and falling inflation rates and rising budget deficits over other time periods, there is obviously no connection between deficits and interest rates. What might be incorrect about this conclusion?

8. In the text, it was noted that economists do not all share the same view as to the inherent nature of a market economy. With this point in mind, what differences of opinion might arise concerning the business cycle?

9. What explanations can you offer for the seesaw movement between budget surpluses and deficits before 1969 and the record of annual budget deficits afterward?

10. Important economic, social, and political developments have sometimes been linked to major economic woes. In the 1970s, the United States incurred high inflation rates relative to its economic past. Can you name any institutional changes that may have resulted from this bout with inflation?

11. "Economists disagree on macroeconomic policies; therefore, we may conclude that some economists are not as smart as other economists." Discuss.

12. To familiarize yourself with some of the macroeconomic topics that are discussed in the following chapters, read some recent back issues of the *Wall Street Journal.* Discuss some of the macroeconomic questions you would like to have answered that were not brought up in this chapter.

13. Make a list of the major macroeconomic problems of the day as conveyed to you through news magazines, newspapers, and television news programs. What are some of the economic policies that are currently being implemented to deal with the problems?

MEASURING GNP

WHAT THIS CHAPTER IS ABOUT

In a way, economists are like doctors. Just as the doctor wants to measure aspects of a patient's physiology to see how the patient is doing, the economist wants to measure the economy to see how it is doing. To find out, the economist must make use of macroeconomic measurements. A key macroeconomic measurement is gross national product (GNP), which is the major topic of this chapter.

FOUR ECONOMIC SECTORS AND FOUR TYPES OF EXPENDITURES

■

As stated in Chapter 5, economists divide the economy into four sectors: the *house-hold sector,* the *business sector,* the *government sector,* and the *foreign sector.* Each of these sectors makes expenditures. The expenditures of the household sector are called *consumption;* the expenditures of the business sector are called *gross private domestic investment,* or simply *investment;* the expenditures of the government sector are called *government expenditures* and the expenditures of the foreign sector are called *net exports.* We discuss each type of expenditure next.

Household Sector: Consumption

Consumption expenditures (*C*) include (1) spending on durable goods, (2) spending on nondurable goods, and (3) spending on services.

Durable goods are goods that are expected to last for more than a year, such as a refrigerator, oven, or car. *Nondurable goods* are goods that are not expected to last for more than a year, such as food. *Services* are intangible items such as lawn care, car repair, and entertainment. In 1990, consumption was $3,658 billion.

Business Sector: Gross Private Domestic Investment

Gross private domestic investment (usually denoted by *I,* for *investment*) is the sum of (1) the purchases of newly produced capital goods, sometimes referred to as **fixed investment**[1], and (2) changes in business inventories, sometimes referred to as **inventory investment.** For example, if business spent $500 billion on newly produced capital goods, and its inventories increased by $150 billion, then (gross private domestic) investment would equal $650 billion. In 1990, investment was $745 billion.

Fixed Investment
Business purchases of capital goods, such as machinery and factories, and consumer purchases of new residential housing.

Inventory Investment
Changes in the stock of unsold goods.

Government Sector: Government Expenditures

Government expenditures (*G*) consist of the total dollar amounts spent by federal, state, and local governments on final goods and services. Government **transfer payments,** which are payments to persons that are not made in return for goods and services currently supplied, are not included in government expenditures. Social Security benefits and welfare payments are two examples of transfer payments, since neither is a payment for current productive efforts.[2] In 1990, government expenditures were $1,098 billion.

Transfer Payments
Payments that are not made in return for goods and services currently supplied.

Foreign Sector: Net Exports

Net exports is equal to exports (*X*) minus imports (*M*). Net exports can be positive or negative. If positive, then exports are greater than imports; if negative, then imports are greater than exports. In 1990, net exports were −$38 billion.

[1]Fixed investment also includes new residential housing. Government statisticians include consumer expenditures on new residential housing in gross private domestic investment because they believe that a new house is an investment good that will provide a stream of services far into the future.
[2]Specifically, Social Security and welfare payments are examples of *government transfer payments.* Beside government transfer payments, there are personal and business transfer payments. For now, we are only concerned with government transfer payments.

Economists divide the economy into four sectors: household, business, government, and foreign.

■

Business firms are sellers in goods and services markets and buyers in factor (resource) markets.

■

The Spending Stream, Injections, and Leakages

In this section we discuss the spending stream, injections, and leakages.

The Spending Stream. Consider an economy with only two sectors: a household sector and a business sector. Since there is no government sector, there are no taxes to be paid. And since there is no foreign sector, (U.S.) business firms do not sell export goods and (U.S.) households do not buy import goods.

In this two-sector economy, business firms do two things: They sell goods and services to households, and they purchase the factors of production (land, labor, capital, and entrepreneurship) from households. In short, business firms are *sellers* in the goods and services markets, and they are *buyers* in factor (resource) markets.

Similarly, households do two things: They buy goods and services from business firms, and they sell factors (resources) to firms. In short, they are *buyers* in the goods and services markets, and they are *sellers* in factor (resource) markets.

We start with two conditions: (1) Business firms sell everything they produce. (2) Households spend their entire income on goods and services as soon as they receive it. For example, suppose the entire output of business firms consists of 1,000 units of X, where each unit of X is sold for $4. Households spend $4,000 ($4 × 1,000 units) to purchase the 1,000 units of X. The $4,000 the business firms receive goes for the factors (resources) they buy. The payment to labor is called *wages;* the payment to land is called *rent;* the payment to capital is called *interest;* and the payment to entrepreneurship is called *profits.*

As you can see, the $4,000 is being passed around from one sector to the other. The household sector, in its role as buyer of goods and services, pays the $4,000 to business firms. Business firms, in their role as seller of goods and services, receive the $4,000 in payment for the goods and services they sell to households.

But then the business firms, in their role as buyers of factors (resources), pay out the $4,000 to households. Households, in their role as sellers of factors (such as labor) receive the $4,000 in payment for the factors they sell to business firms.

The process of passing the $4,000 from the household sector to the business sector and then from the business sector to the household sector, over and over again, describes a *spending stream.* For now, think of a spending stream as you would a real stream (of water). Water flows from one place to another in a real stream, and dollars flow from one sector to another in a spending stream.

Leakages and Injections. As in a real stream, the water level can rise or fall. If there is a heavy rain, the water level in the stream will rise. If there is a drought, the water level in the stream will fall.

Similarly, in the spending stream, its level of spending can rise or fall. To illustrate, let's return to our spending stream of $4,000 at the point where business firms are paying the $4,000 to households for factors purchased. The household sector now has the $4,000 in its possession. Suppose that instead of spending the entire $4,000 on goods and services produced by the business sector, households decide to spend only $3,000 on consumer goods. They decide to save $1,000. What happens to the spending in the spending stream? It falls, much like the water level in a real stream might fall. The spending stream now only has $3,000 in it instead of $4,000. In our example, *saving* is considered a **leakage:** A leakage is an outflow or withdrawal of expenditures from the spending stream. Stated differently, any part of income that does not go to purchase (U.S.) goods and services is considered a leakage.

The households that saved the $1,000 placed it in the **credit market.** A credit market is a market that channels funds from savers (lenders) to borrowers. Suppose

Leakage
An outflow or withdrawal of expenditures from the spending stream. Any part of income that does not go to purchase (U.S.) goods and services is considered a leakage.

Credit Market
A market that channels funds from savers (lenders) to borrowers.

now that business firms borrow the $1,000 that households saved and use it to purchase a new capital good. Notice what business firms are doing: They are *buying* a capital good, which is an investment expenditure. Up until this time, all that business firms have done is (1) sell goods and services in the goods and services markets and (2) buy factors in factor markets. Now, to this list we add (3) buy a good in the goods and services markets.

How does this investment expenditure by business firms (in the goods and services markets) affect the spending stream? We left the spending stream when it was down to $3,000. The $1,000 purchase by business firms is an **injection,** or an inflow of expenditures, into the spending stream. Any expenditures on (U.S.) goods and services besides consumption expenditures is considered an injection. As a result of this $1,000 injection, the spending stream rises to $4,000.

Let us summarize a few key points.

1. The spending stream (initially) consists of the consumption expenditures of the household sector, wherein households spend their entire income on consumer goods.
2. The spending stream can rise or fall depending on whether there are injections into, or leakages out of, the spending stream.
3. Saving is a leakage; investment is an injection.

Types of Injections and Leakages.   In our example earlier, saving was a leakage and investment was an injection. What are other injections and leakages?

We remind ourselves that any expenditure on (U.S.) goods and services besides consumption expenditures is considered an injection. For example, as we saw earlier, investment spending is an injection. But so are government spending and foreign spending on U.S. goods and services (exports).

We remind ourselves that any part of income that does not go to purchase (U.S.) goods and services is considered a leakage. For example, as we saw earlier, saving is a leakage. But so are taxes (when people pay taxes they can't use those funds to buy U.S. goods and services) and the spending that Americans do when they buy foreign goods (imports).

In summary, investment expenditures, government expenditures, and exports are injections. Saving, taxes, and imports are leakages.

Total Expenditures.   The sum of the expenditures on goods and services made by the different sectors of the economy comprise *total expenditures.* For example, if the four sectors of the economy together spend $5 trillion on goods and services, then total expenditures equal $5 trillion.

Sum of the expenditures made by the
four sectors of the economy =
Total Expenditures

A Four-Sector Economy

Many of the key activities that take place in an economy can be seen with the help of a *circular-flow diagram,* such as the one in Exhibit 6–1. This is a circular-flow diagram of a four-sector economy. Consider what is happening in each sector.

Household Sector.   First, households are making consumption expenditures on U.S. goods and services. As you can see in Exhibit 6–1, the "consumption expenditures arrow" flows into U.S. goods and services markets.

Households are buyers in goods and services markets and sellers in factor (resource) markets.

Injection
Any expenditure on (U.S.) goods and services besides consumption expenditures is considered an injection. In short, any nonconsumption expenditure.

EXHIBIT 6–1
The Circular-Flow Diagram of a Four-Sector Economy

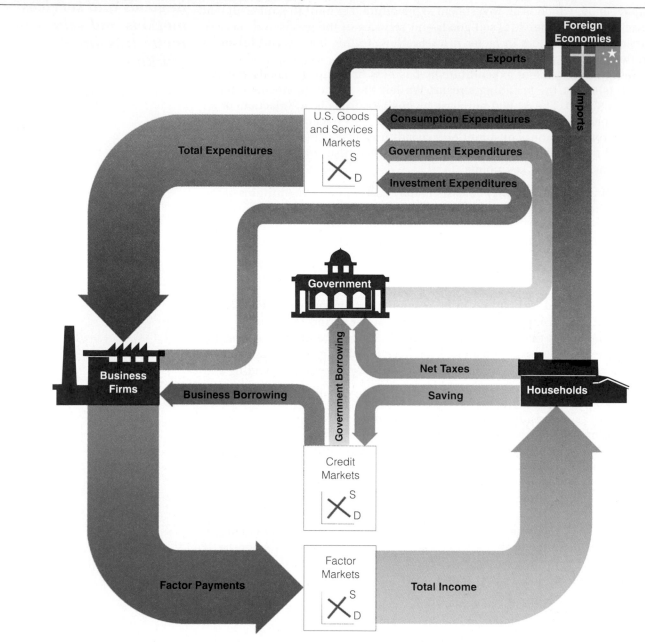

The circular-flow diagram shows the economic activities of the four sectors of the economy. Households (1) make consumption expenditures, (2) save, (3) pay net taxes, and (4) buy imported goods. Businesses (1) borrow funds and (2) make investment expenditures. Government (1) borrows funds (2) collects net taxes and (3) makes expenditures. Foreigners (1) buy American goods. (In the exhibit, we have simplified things by assuming that only households buy imported goods. In the real world, households, businesses, and government buy imported goods. If we modified the diagram to take this into account, the investment expenditures and government expenditures arrows would flow into foreign economies as well as into the U.S. goods and services markets. Also, in the real world, foreigners are lenders in the U.S. credit market. We have not shown this in the exhibit.)

Second, households are saving. As we learned earlier, saving is a leakage—it does not go to buy goods and services. (Notice that the "saving arrow" *does not* flow into goods and services markets.) Saving finds its way into a credit market, which channels funds from savers (or lenders) to borrowers.

Third, households are paying **net taxes**. Net taxes is equal to taxes minus transfer payments. Earlier, we defined *transfer payments* as payments to persons that are not made in return for goods and services currently supplied, for example, a Social Security payment to a retired person. What happens is that taxes flow from households to government, and transfer payments flow from government to households. Net taxes is simply the difference between the two.

Fourth, households are buying imported goods. We discuss this later.

Net Taxes
Taxes minus transfer payments.

Business Sector.   First, business firms borrow funds in the credit market (see the "business borrowing arrow" in Exhibit 6–1). Second, businesses use the borrowed funds, and perhaps some nonborrowed funds, too, to buy new capital goods. The purchase of new capital goods is investment. Notice that the "investment expenditures arrow" flows into U.S. goods and services markets.

Government Sector.   The government is involved in three activities: First, it collects net taxes from the household sector; second, it borrows funds in the credit market; and third, it uses borrowed and perhaps nonborrowed funds to purchase goods and services. Notice that the "government expenditures arrow" flows into the U.S. goods and services markets.

Foreign Sector.   In Exhibit 6–1, we see that two things are going on in the foreign sector. First, U.S. households are buying imported goods from foreigners. This is a leakage from the U.S. spending stream, since the money spent on imported goods is spent in foreign goods and services markets, not U.S. goods and services markets. (Notice that the "imports arrow" does not flow into the U.S. goods and services markets.)

Second, foreigners are buying U.S. exported goods. This is an injection into the U.S. spending stream, since the money spent on exported goods does go into U.S. goods and services markets. (Notice that the "exports arrow" does flow into the U.S. goods and services market.)[3]

Economists are keenly aware of the constraints that operate in different areas of human activity. They use their knowledge of these constraints to gain insights into the workings of the economy. Here is an illustration, in two steps.

Step 1: The Constraint. In Exhibit 6–1, we showed that the household sector places its savings in the credit market and that both the business and government sectors borrow funds in the credit market. It follows that the total amount of funds that business and government borrow *cannot be greater* than the total amount of funds that households save. Simply put, business and government borrowing is *constrained* by household saving.

Step 2: The Insight. With the knowledge of this constraint, we can see how government actions may affect the economy. For example, the principal reason government borrows funds is because it must finance budget deficits, and

---

[3]A third thing that is happening in the foreign sector is that foreign funds are coming into the credit market. We have ignored this fact to keep the analysis relatively simple at this stage.

the larger the deficits, the more funds that are borrowed. But funds the government borrows cannot be borrowed by business, too. And the less business borrows, the smaller investment spending will be. Insight: Deficits, originating in the government sector, *may reduce* the amount of investment spending in the economy.[4]

Where Do Total Expenditures Go?

Where do the dollars that flow into U.S. goods and services markets go? In Exhibit 6–1, we see that total expenditures end up in business firms (the "total expenditure arrow" flows out of goods and services markets and into business firms).

But what do the business firms do with the expenditures made by the four sectors of the economy? Recall that business firms do not produce goods and services out of thin air. It takes factors of production, or resources—*land, labor, capital, and entrepreneurship*—to produce goods and services. Each of these factors receives a payment for its use: *wages* (to labor), *rent,* (to land), *interest* (to capital), and *profits* (to entrepreneurship).

So, ultimately, the total expenditures received by business firms end up as factor payments. For example, let's say that total expenditures equal $40 billion. Some of the $40 billion will go to pay for labor, some will go to pay for land, some will go to pay for capital goods, and some will go to pay for entrepreneurship. The sum of the factor payments—that is, wages + rents + interest + profits—will equal total expenditures.

Total expenditures = Sum of factor payments

With this in mind, consider Exhibit 6–1 again. Notice that total expenditures flow into business firms (purple arrow) and factor payments flow out of business firms (dark blue arrow). Factor payments are made in factor (or resource) markets—such as the labor market, the capital goods market, and so on. The recipients of the factor payments are members of the household sector. The factor payments that households receive are considered *income.* Therefore, we conclude that the sum of the factor payments is equal to total income.

Sum of factor payments = Total income

Key Points Concerning a Four-Sector Economy

Let us review some key points.

1. In a four-sector economy, total expenditures is the sum of the expenditures made by the four sectors of the economy.

Sum of the expenditures made by the four sectors of the economy =
Total expenditures

2. Business firms receive total expenditures. This total dollar amount is used to make factor payments to labor (wages), land (rent), capital (interest), and entrepreneurship (profits). Therefore,

Total expenditures = Sum of factor payments

[4]We say "may reduce" the amount of investment spending in the economy because some economists argue that as the government finances the deficit, citizens perceive higher taxes in the future and thus save more today in order to pay the higher taxes tomorrow. If this happens, the pool of funds firms at their disposal to borrow from grows. Much more will be said about this in a later chapter.

3. The recipients of the factor payments consider the payments to be income. Therefore,

Sum of factor payments = Total income

4. Since *total expenditures* = sum of factor payments (point 2), and the sum of factor payments = *total income* (point 3), it follows that

Total expenditures = Total income

Later, we will see that economists measure the gross national product (GNP) in two ways: by the *expenditure approach* and by the *income approach*. For now, we simply note that the two ways to measure GNP will give us the same dollar figure, since, as we have just learned in point 4, *total expenditures* equal *total income*.

GROSS NATIONAL PRODUCT
■

In Chapter 5, we said that much of what economists discuss in macroeconomics has to do with the price level, (*P*), real GNP (*Q*), or both. Gross national product (GNP) has to do with both, since it is the product of *P* times *Q*. In Exhibit 6–2, you see GNP figures for selected nations.

GNP Is a Flow Variable

Gross national product is *the total market value of all final goods and services produced annually in an economy*. For example, suppose we deal with a one-good economy: Here, only 10 units of one good are produced and each unit sells for $4. The GNP of the one-good economy is $40—or the *price* of each unit of the good *times* the *quantity*. If we move to a large economy, where there are thousands of goods produced and thousands of different prices, GNP is the price level (*P*) *times* real GNP (*Q*).

GNP is a **flow variable** as opposed to a **stock variable.** A flow variable is a variable that can only be meaningfully measured over a period of time. For example, if someone were to ask you your income, it would be important to specify your income over *some time period*—a week, or a month, or a year. If you simply stated your income as, say, $4,000, it would not be clear if you were talking about $4,000 a year, $4,000 a month, or $4,000 a week, since some people fall into each of these three categories.

A stock variable is one that can be meaningfully measured at a moment in time. The U.S. money supply is a stock variable. If someone were to ask how much the money supply is, it would not be necessary to specify a time period. We would not say that the money supply is $800 billion a week, or a month, or a year. We would simply say that the money supply is $800 billion, period.

The Common Denominator in GNP

How can different goods, such as bicycles, radios, and carpets, be added together to form a meaningful measurement? After all, all goods are not measured in the same units. Some are measured in pounds, others in feet and inches, and so on. All goods, however, are sold for dollar price, which serves as a common denominator. In the definition of GNP, the words *total market value* refer to *total dollar value at current prices*. For this reason, economists sometimes refer to GNP more

Gross National Product (GNP)
The total market value of all final goods and services produced annually in an economy.

Flow Variable
A variable that can only be meaningfully measured over a period of time. GNP is a flow variable.

Stock Variable
A variable that can be meaningfully measured at a moment in time. For example, the nation's money supply is a stock variable.

EXHIBIT 6–2
GNP in Selected Nations, 1987 (in billions)

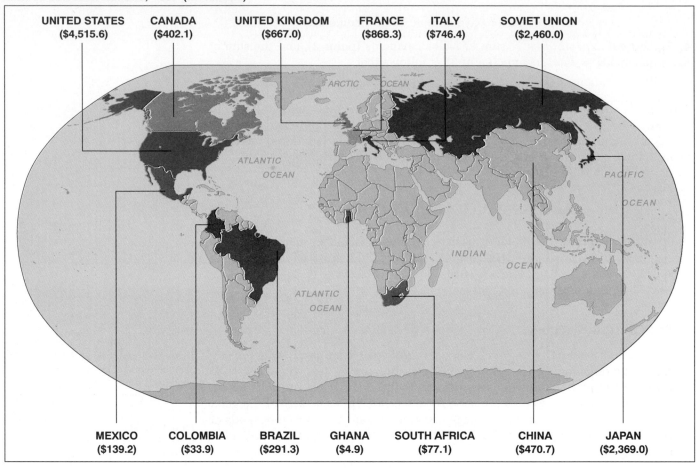

UNITED STATES ($4,515.6)   CANADA ($402.1)   UNITED KINGDOM ($667.0)   FRANCE ($868.3)   ITALY ($746.4)   SOVIET UNION ($2,460.0)

MEXICO ($139.2)   COLOMBIA ($33.9)   BRAZIL ($291.3)   GHANA ($4.9)   SOUTH AFRICA ($77.1)   CHINA ($470.7)   JAPAN ($2,369.0)

SOURCES: U.S. Bureau of the Census, *Statistical Abstract of the United States,* 1990 (Washington, D.C.: U.S. Government Printing Office, 1990), and Council of Economic Advisers, *Economic Report of the President, 1991* (Washington, D.C.: U.S. Government Printing Office, 1991).

Nominal GNP
The value of final goods and services produced in a given year in that year's prevailing market prices. The terms GNP, nominal GNP, and current-dollar GNP are used interchangeably.

specifically as *current-dollar GNP* or **nominal GNP.** In this text, GNP refers to current-dollar or nominal GNP.

Why calculate GNP? Is it so important to have a measurement of the total value of all final goods and services produced annually in a nation's economy? Many economists argue that measuring GNP gives economists and governmental policy makers a "fix" on the economy that they would not otherwise have and without which they could not formulate appropriate economic policies as easily or as precisely.

Why Measure Final Goods?

Final Good
A good in the hands of its final user.

Intermediate Good
A good that is an input in the production of a final good.

The words **final goods** in the definition of GNP mean a good in the hands of its final or ultimate user. In contrast, an **intermediate good** has not reached its final user. For example, the car that you buy is a final good. In producing the car, the car company had to purchase such things as steel, glass, rubber, plastic, and so

116

on. These goods are called intermediate goods: They are inputs in the production of the final good—the car.

Gross national product takes into account (measures the value of) only final goods (and services). The reason is that the national income accountants who calculate GNP do not want to count the same goods more than once. They do not want to commit the error of **double counting.**

To illustrate, suppose a book is a final good and that intermediate goods paper, ink, and glue go together to make it. Let us also suppose that the final good, the book, is sold for $20 and that intermediate goods paper, ink, and glue are sold for $10, $6, and $4, respectively.

If we were to count the market value of the book *and* the market value of each of the intermediate goods, we would be counting the intermediate goods twice.

Doing this (which is wrong, but not so easy to see as wrong)

(1)

Market value of book	$20
Market value of paper	10
Market value of ink	6
Market value of glue	4
	$40

is the same as doing this (which is obviously wrong):

(2)

Market value of paper	$10
Market value of ink	6
Market value of glue	4
Market value of paper	10
Market value of ink	6
Market value of glue	4
	$40

It is clear in (2) that we are counting the intermediate goods *twice.* It is not so clear that we are doing this in (1), *but we are.* Since the market value of the book is the sum of the market values of paper, ink, and glue, the total in (1) equals the total in (2). To avoid double counting, national income accountants compute GNP by counting the total market value of *only final goods and services* produced annually in an economy. In our example, this would be the market value of the book ($20).

What GNP Omits

Some exchanges that take place in an economy are omitted from the GNP measurement. As the following list indicates, these range from sales of used cars to illegal drug deals.

Certain Nonmarket Goods and Services. If a family hires a person through the classified section of the newspaper to cook and clean, the service is counted in GNP. If a family member performs the same tasks, however, their services will not be counted in GNP. The difference is that, in the first case, a service is actually bought and sold for a price in a market setting, and in the other, it is not.

There are, however, some nonmarket goods that GNP does not omit. For example, the market value of food produced on a farm but consumed by the farm family is estimated, and this *imputed value* is part of GNP.

Underground Economy
Unreported exchanges that take place outside the normal recorded market channels. Some underground activities deal with illegal goods; others deal with legal goods and tax evasion.

Underground Activities, Both Legal and Illegal.   The **underground economy** consists of unreported exchanges that take place outside the normal recorded market channels.[5] Some underground activities deal with illegal goods (such as cocaine), and others deal with legal goods and tax evasion.

Illegal goods and services are not counted in GNP because no record exists of such transactions. There are no written records of illegal drug sales, illegal gambling, and prostitution. Neither are there written records of some legal activities that individuals want to keep from government notice. For example, a gardener might agree to do some gardening work only on the condition that he is paid in cash. Obviously, it is not illegal for a person to buy or sell gardening services, but still the transaction might not be recorded if one or both of the parties does not want it to be. Why might the gardener want to be paid in cash? Perhaps he doesn't want to pay taxes on the income received—an objective more easily accomplished if there is no written record of the income being generated.

Sales of Used Goods.   GNP is a measurement of current production (that is, occurring during the current year). A used car sale, for example, does not enter into the current year statistics because the car was counted when it was originally produced.

Financial Transactions.   The trading of stocks and bonds is not counted in GNP because it does not represent the production of new assets, but simply the trading of assets (stocks or bonds for money).

Government Transfer Payments.   Government transfer payments—such as Social Security benefits and veterans' benefits—are not counted in GNP because they do not represent a payment to individuals for current production.

Leisure.   Leisure is a good, in much the same way that cars, houses, and shoes are goods. More new cars, houses, and shoes get counted in GNP, but more leisure does not because it is too difficult to quantify. In this century in the United States, the length of the work week has fallen—indicating to us that the leisure time individuals have to consume has increased—but GNP computations do not take this into account.

Bads Generated in the Production of Goods.   Economic growth often comes with certain *bads.* For example, producing more cars, furniture, and steel often generates more air and water pollution—considered bads by most people. (Remember from Chapter 1 that a bad is anything from which individuals receive disutility.) GNP counts the additional goods and services, but it does not net out the additional air and water pollution, thus overstating, some economists argue, our overall economic welfare.

[5]Other adjectives beside *underground* have been used to describe the type of economy we are discussing: subterranean, irregular, hidden, unrecorded, unofficial, concealed, parallel, informal, unobserved, submerged, shadow, cash, clandestine, moonlight, twilight, second, counter, the back door, and off the books.

The Underground Economy

Economists estimate that the underground economy in the United States is larger than the economies of many countries—within the range of 5 to 12 percent of GNP. If we settle on 8 percent as a reasonable estimate, then this amounts to $437 billion in 1990. This is larger than the GNP of Belgium, Denmark, Greece, Ireland, Luxembourg, Portugal, Spain, Austria, Finland, Norway, Sweden, Switzerland, Turkey, Australia, New Zealand, and many more countries.

In a study conducted by the U.S. Department of Commerce, the United States was estimated to have a larger underground economy (relative to its GNP) than Switzerland and Japan, but smaller than Sweden, Norway, Canada, and Italy. Some economists argue that the relative size of the underground economy grows when the tax burden becomes heavier, *ceteris paribus.*

How do economists judge the size of the underground economy, which, after all, is not visible? Their estimates are based on the assumption that there is a strong association between the amount of cash (relative to checks) individuals use in making their exchanges and the amount of underground economic activity. Since underground economic activity is based on cash, some economists argue that the more cash that is demanded relative to other forms of making monetary payment, the larger the relative size of the underground economy. For example, in recent years most banks in the Miami area have witnessed a huge increase in the use of cash, which likely indicates an increase in the underground illicit drug trade.

If the underground economy is between 5 and 12 percent of GNP, then official economic statistics both overstate and understate the economic truth. For example, growth rates in GNP understate the growth of the overall economy, and unemployment rates certainly overstate the true unemployment rate.

Question:

Suppose a radio is produced during this year but is not sold to any customer. Is the radio counted as part of GNP?

Answer:

Yes, it is. To illustrate, suppose a firm produces 10,000 radios this year, but only sells 9,000 radios. The remaining 1,000 radios become part of inventory, and are considered, by national income accountants, to have been "bought" by the firm that produced them.

Our definition of *investment* includes (1) the purchases of new capital goods *and* (2) changes in inventory. In other words, the radio that is produced but not sold is added to inventory and is considered to be a part of investment. If the radio is sold next year, it will not be counted again in GNP since it was produced the year before and thus no longer represents current production.

Follow-up Question:

Suppose someone reads in the newspaper that investment in the United States is up from last year. Is this good for the economy?

Answer:

The article in the newspaper does not specify if investment is up because business firms are buying more new capital goods or because consumers are buying fewer goods than expected and consequently inventories are rising (much to the dismay

CHAPTER 6
MEASURING GNP

■

119

of business firms). To answer the question, we need to know not only that investment is up, buy *why* it is up.

GNP: Is It a Measurement of Happiness of Well-Being?

Are the persons in a country with a higher GNP, or higher per capita GNP, better off or happier than the persons in a country with a lower GNP, or lower per capita GNP? We cannot answer that question because well-being and happiness are subjective. A person with more goods may be happier than a person with fewer goods, but possibly not. For all we know, the person with fewer goods, but a lot of leisure, little air pollution, and a relaxed way of life, may be much happier than the person with many goods, little leisure, and a polluted, stressful environment.

We make this point to warn against reading too much into GNP figures. GNP figures are useful for obtaining an estimate of the productive capabilities of an economy, but they are not necessarily a measurement of happiness or well-being.

TWO WAYS OF MEASURING GNP
■

Gross national product is measured by the Bureau of Economic Analysis (BEA), which is a division of the U.S. Department of Commerce. The BEA uses two approaches to measure GNP: the *expenditure approach* and the *income approach*. Exhibit 6–3 provides an overview of each approach.

EXHIBIT 6–3
Two Approaches to Measuring GNP

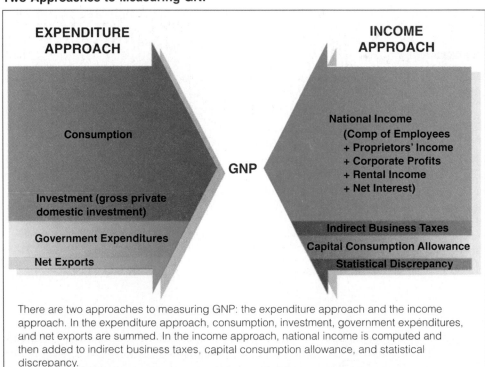

There are two approaches to measuring GNP: the expenditure approach and the income approach. In the expenditure approach, consumption, investment, government expenditures, and net exports are summed. In the income approach, national income is computed and then added to indirect business taxes, capital consumption allowance, and statistical discrepancy.

The Expenditure Approach

The expenditure approach to measuring GNP sums the expenditures made by the four sectors of the economy. This may give you reason to pause, since the definition of GNP on page 115 did not mention expenditures. Rather, GNP was defined as the total market value of all final goods and services *produced* annually in an economy.

The discrepancy is cleared up quickly once we remember that national income accountants assume that anything that is produced but not sold (to consumers) is "bought" by the firm that produced it. In other words, if something is produced but not sold it goes into business inventory and is considered investment. Thus, we can measure GNP by summing the expenditures made by the four sectors of the economy. GNP equals consumption (C) plus investment (I) plus government expenditures (G) plus net exports ($X - M$) (Exhibit 6–4).

$$GNP = C + I + G + (X - M)$$

Question:

In recent years, there has been added interest in international economic events. How do residents in foreign nations affect the U.S. GNP?

Answer:

One way is through the net exports component of GNP. Suppose foreigners increase their purchases of American exports. In the GNP equation—GNP = $C + I + G + (X - M)$—exports (X) rise, and this increases U.S. GNP, *ceteris paribus.* On the other hand, if foreigners decrease their purchases of American exports, U.S. GNP falls, *ceteris paribus.* In general, whether we are talking about the interna-

EXHIBIT 6–4
Components of GNP (Expenditure Approach)

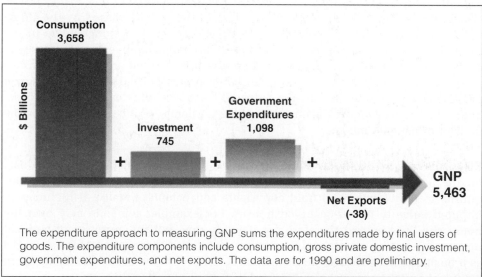

The expenditure approach to measuring GNP sums the expenditures made by final users of goods. The expenditure components include consumption, gross private domestic investment, government expenditures, and net exports. The data are for 1990 and are preliminary.

Source: Council of Economic Advisers, *Economic Report of the President,* 1991 (Washington, D.C.: U.S. Government Printing Office, 1991).

tional economic arena or the domestic economic arena, anything that raises (lowers) *C, I, G,* or *X* will raise (lower) GNP; anything that raises (lowers) *M* will lower (raise) GNP.[6]

The Income Approach

The second approach to measuring GNP is the income approach, which has two steps: First, we add up the payments to the factors of production, which gives us **national income (NI).** Second, we adjust national income for indirect business taxes, a capital consumption allowance (or depreciation), and a statistical discrepancy. (We define these terms in our discussion.)

Factor payments include wages, rents, interest, and profits. Note, though, that national income accountants have fancier terms for factor payments than wages, rent, interest, and profits. They are compensation to employees, proprietors' income, corporate profits, rental income of persons, and net interest.

Compensation of Employees. Compensation of employees consists of wages and salaries paid to employees plus employers' contributions to Social Security and employee benefit plans, as well as the monetary value of fringe benefits, tips, and paid vacations. Compensation of employees is the largest component of national income. In 1990, it accounted for 73.4 percent of national income. Note that compensation of employees is not 73.4 percent of GNP because national income does not equal GNP.

Proprietors' Income. Proprietors' income includes all forms of income earned by self-employed individuals and the owners of unincorporated businesses, including unincorporated farmers. Included in farm income is an estimate of the value of the food grown and consumed on farms. In 1990, proprietors' income accounted for 8 percent of national income.

Corporate Profits. Corporate profits include all the income earned by the stockholders of corporations. Some of the profits are paid out to stockholders in the form of dividends, some are kept within the firm to finance investments (these are called undistributed profits or retained earnings), and some are used to pay corporate profits taxes. (The portion of corporate profits that goes to pay corporate profits taxes is counted as income "earned" by households even though households do not receive the income.) In 1990, corporate profits accounted for 6.9 percent of national income.

Rental Income (of Persons). Rental income is the income received by individuals for the use of their nonmonetary assets (land, houses, offices). It also includes returns to individuals who hold copyrights and patents. Finally, it includes an imputed value to owner-occupied houses. For example, someone may own the house she lives in, and therefore not pay any rent, but for purposes of national income accounting a rental value is imputed. In short, homeownership is viewed as a business that produces a service that is sold to the owner of the business. In 1990, net rental income accounted for 1.1 percent of national income.

National Income
The sum of the payments to suppliers of the factors of production. It is equal to the compensation of employees + proprietors' income + corporate profits + rental income of persons + net interest.

[6]For information on how exports and imports affect real GNP, see the Economics In Our Times in Chapter 8.

Net Interest.   This is the interest income received by U.S. households and government minus the interest they paid out. In 1990, it was 10.6 percent of national income.

National Income and GNP: A Slight Modification

In the circular-flow diagram in Exhibit 6–1, total expenditures equalled total income. We would expect, then, that GNP, equal to the sum of the expenditures made by the four sectors of the economy, would equal national income. This is not the case, however. For example, GNP in 1990 was $5463 billion and national income was $4417.5 billion. This is because there are two nonincome expense items—indirect business taxes and the capital consumption allowance—that are not paid to factor owners, plus a relatively minor statistical discrepancy. If we add the two nonincome expense items and the statistical discrepancy to national income, the sum equals GNP.

Indirect Business Taxes.   The main items that comprise indirect business taxes include excise taxes, sales taxes, and property taxes. These taxes are not part of national income because they are not considered a payment to any factor of production. (Recall that national income is the sum of factor payments.) They are, however, included in total expenditures, and therefore are picked up in the expenditure approach to measuring GNP. Therefore, we must add indirect business taxes to national income in order to move closer to comparable approaches to measuring GNP.

Question:

Earlier, it was noted that corporate profits taxes are considered a factor payment. Now, we learn sales taxes are not considered a factor payment. Why is one tax considered a factor payment whereas the other is not?

Answer:

National income accountants consider corporate profits taxes to be income "earned" by households, even though they are not directly received as income by households. Therefore, corporate profits taxes are included in national income. A sales tax, however, is not considered to be income earned by anyone. Therefore, it is not considered a factor payment and is not included in national income.

Capital Consumption Allowance.   Some capital goods are used up in the production process through natural wear, obsolescence, or accidental destruction (for example, the machinery that breaks down and no longer works). The cost to replace these capital goods is called the **capital consumption allowance,** or **depreciation.** Replacing depreciated capital does not actually represent new production; therefore, we reduce the value of total production by this amount to show net production for the year (see the discussion of net national product in the next section). For our purposes here, however, capital consumption is added to national income in order to move us closer to GNP.

Capital Consumption Allowance or Depreciation
The estimated amount of capital goods used up in production through natural wear, obsolescence, and accidental destruction.

Statistical Discrepancy.   GNP and national income are measured using different sets of data. Hence, statistical discrepancies or pure measurement errors often occur and must be accounted for in the national income accounts.

The Income and Expenditure Approaches Compared

Exhibit 6–5 illustrates the income approach to measuring GNP for 1990. GNP equals national income (the sum of compensation of employees, proprietors' income, corporate profits, rental income, and net interest) + indirect business taxes + capital consumption allowance + statistical discrepancy. Compare Exhibit 6–5 with Exhibit 6–4, which illustrates the expenditure approach to measuring GNP. You will see that we get the same dollar amount.

OTHER NATIONAL INCOME ACCOUNTING MEASUREMENTS
■

Besides gross national product (GNP) and national income(NI), three other national income accounting measurements are important. They are net national product, personal income, and disposable income. The five measurements—gross national product, national income, net national product, personal income, and disposable income—are often used interchangeably as measurements of the output produced and income earned in an economy.

Net National Product

If we use the expenditure approach to measuring GNP, we add consumption, investment, government expenditures, and net exports. Investment (or, more specifically, gross private domestic investment) includes fixed investment and inventory

EXHIBIT 6–5
Components of GNP (Income Approach)

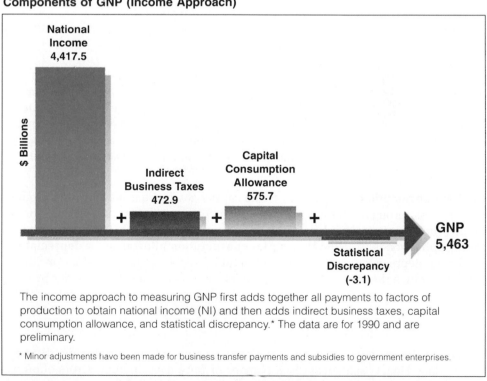

The income approach to measuring GNP first adds together all payments to factors of production to obtain national income (NI) and then adds indirect business taxes, capital consumption allowance, and statistical discrepancy.* The data are for 1990 and are preliminary.

* Minor adjustments have been made for business transfer payments and subsidies to government enterprises.

SOURCE: Council of Economic Advisers, *Economic Report of the President,* 1991 (Washington, D.C.: U.S. Government Printing Office, 1991).

No Communication with the Outside World: The BEA at Work

When the economists at the Bureau of Economic Analysis sit down to measure GNP, they are beginning a lengthy—and secret—procedure. Two main teams of economists and statisticians do the job. One team measures GNP using the income approach; the other team measures GNP using the expenditure approach.

Initially, each team works independently of the other. Within both teams are subteams of economists and statisticians who compute the individual items. One subteam might be computing consumption, another subteam might be computing investment, and so on. On the morning before the day the GNP figures are officially released to the public, both teams come together in a conference room in order to sum the figures and check each other's work. For example, the consumption figures are added to the investment figures and so on, and the income-approach team checks to see if its figure for GNP is equal to the figure computed by the expenditure-approach team. If they find discrepancies, they are worked through.

During this time, no one is allowed in or out of the room—except to go to the restroom, but then they must make their visits in pairs. Also, no phone calls—in or out—are allowed.

Absolute secrecy is the rule. Secrecy is important because a leak of the GNP figure could give some people an advantage over others in the bond market, futures markets, and so on.

When the work has been completed (usually late at night), each person in the room is sworn to secrecy. One person takes the GNP figure to the chairman of the Council of Economic Advisers. The chairman then gives the GNP figure to the president of the United States. The next morning, the secretary of the Commerce Department releases the GNP figure to the press.

---

investment. Some of the fixed investment, however, simply goes to replace worn-out or obsolete capital goods. It does not go for new goods. In short, gross private domestic investment contains within it the capital consumption allowance. If we subtract the capital consumption allowance from GNP, we are left with **net national product (NNP)**.[7] NNP measures the total value of new goods available in the economy in a given year, after worn-out capital goods have been replaced. According to Exhibit 6–5, in 1990 the capital consumption allowance was $575.7 billion and GNP was $5,463 billion. It follows that net national product was the difference between the two, or $4,887.3 billion.

$$NNP = GNP - \text{capital consumption allowance}$$

Net National Product (NNP)
GNP minus the capital consumption allowance.

Personal Income

Not all income earned is received, and not all income received is earned. An example of "income earned but not received" is undistributed profits. Undistributed profits are earned by stockholders but are not received by them. Instead, they are usually reinvested by the corporation. An example of "income received but not earned" is Social Security benefits.

Personal income (PI) is the amount of income that individuals actually receive. It is equal to national income minus such major earned-but-not-received items such as undistributed corporate profits, social insurance taxes (Social Security con-

Personal Income (PI)
The amount of income that individuals actually receive. It is equal to national income minus undistributed corporate profits, social insurance taxes, and corporate profits taxes, plus transfer payments.

[7]If we subtract the capital consumption allowance from gross private domestic investment, we are left with *net private domestic investment*. Instead of saying that net national product (NNP) = gross national product − capital consumption allowance, we could say that NNP = consumption + net private domestic investment + government expenditures + net exports.

125

tributions), and corporate profits taxes plus transfer payments (which are received but not earned).[8] In 1990, personal income was $4,645.6 billion.

$$PI = NI - \text{undistributed corporate profits} - \text{social insurance taxes} - \text{corporate profits taxes} + \text{transfer payments}$$

Disposable Income

The portion of personal income that can be used for consumption or saving is referred to as **disposable income (DI).** It is equal to personal income minus personal taxes (especially income taxes). Sometimes disposable income is referred to as spendable income or take-home pay. In 1990, disposable income was $3,945.8 billion.

$$DI = \text{personal income} - \text{personal taxes}$$

Per-Capita Macroeconomic Measurements

Often economists prefer to work with per-capita economic measurements rather than totals. Any of the five macroeconomic measurements we have discussed—GNP, NNP, NI, PI, or DI—can be converted to a per-capita measurement by dividing by population. For example, if we take the total disposable income in 1990, $3,945.8 billion, and divide it equally among the approximately 251 million people in the United States in 1990, per-capita disposable income would be approximately $15,717. Some economists suggest this is a better measure of the "well-being" of citizens than total disposable income because it adjusts for the number of people who will live on the $3,945.8 billion.

CHAPTER SUMMARY

Types of Expenditures

■ There are four sectors in the economy: household, business, government, and foreign. Each sector makes expenditures. The expenditures of the household sector are called *consumption;* the expenditures of the business sector are called *gross private domestic investment,* or simply, *investment;* the expenditures of the government sector are called *government expenditures;* the expenditures of the foreign sector are called *net exports.*

■ Consumption expenditures include spending on durable goods, nondurable goods, and services.

■ Investment is the sum of the purchases of newly produced capital goods and changes in business inventories. It also includes expenditures on new residential housing.

■ Government expenditures consist of the total dollar amount spent by federal, state, and local governments on final goods and services. Government expenditures do not include transfer payments.

[8]In footnote 2, we gave examples of government transfer payments (Social Security payments, welfare payments) and also noted that government transfer payments are not the only kind of transfer payment. In our definition of personal income, we use the term *transfer payments* to include all varieties.

■ Net exports is the total foreign spending on domestic goods minus the total domestic spending on foreign goods, or exports minus imports.

■ The sum of the expenditures on goods and services made by the different sectors of the economy equals *total expenditures.*

Total Expenditures, the Sum of Factor Payments, and Total Income

■ Business firms *sell* final goods and services and *buy* factors of production (or resources). As sellers, business firms receive the total expenditures made in an economy. As buyers, they pay out the total expenditures in the form of factor payments (payments for land, labor, capital, and entrepreneurship). The recipients of the factor payments consider the payments income. We conclude that total expenditures = sum of factor payments = total income.

Gross National Product

■ Gross national product (GNP) is the total market value of all final goods and services produced annually in an economy. The words *total market value* refer to total dollar value at current prices. Therefore, we can speak of current-dollar or nominal GNP.

■ To avoid the problem of double counting, only final goods and services are counted in GNP.

■ GNP omits certain nonmarket goods and services, both legal and illegal underground activities, the sale of used goods, financial transactions, and transfer payments. GNP is not adjusted for the amount of leisure people consume (even though leisure is a good) or for the bads (like pollution) that sometimes accompany production.

Measuring GNP

■ GNP can be measured in two ways: by the expenditure approach and by the income approach. In the expenditure approach, expenditures of different sectors of the economy are summed. These expenditures are consumption, investment, government expenditures, and net exports.

$$GNP = C + I + G + (X - M)$$

■ In the income approach, national income (NI) is calculated and then added to indirect business taxes, capital consumption allowance, and statistical discrepancy.

$$GNP = NI + \text{indirect business taxes} + \text{capital consumption allowance} + \text{statistical discrepancy}$$

Measurements Other Than GNP

■ Net national product (NNP) equals gross national product (GNP) minus capital consumption allowance.

$$NNP = GNP - \text{capital consumption allowance}$$

■ National income (NI) equals the sum of factor payments.

$$NI = \text{compensation of employees} + \text{proprietors' income} + \text{corporate profits} + \text{rental income} + \text{net interest}$$

- Personal income (PI) equals national income (NI) minus undistributed profits, social security insurance taxes, and corporate profits taxes plus transfer payments.

$$PI = NI - \text{undistributed profits} - \text{social insurance taxes} - \text{corporate profits}$$
$$\text{taxes} + \text{transfer payments}$$

- Disposable income (DI) equals personal income (PI) minus personal taxes.

$$DI = PI - \text{personal taxes}$$

Key Terms and Concepts

Fixed Investment	Gross National Product	Underground Economy
Inventory Investment	Flow Variable	National Income
Transfer Payments	Stock Variable	Capital Consumption Allowance (Depreciation)
Leakage	Nominal GNP	
Credit Market	Final Good	Net National Product
Injection	Intermediate Good	Personal Income
Net Taxes	Double Counting	Disposable Income

QUESTIONS AND PROBLEMS

1. "I just heard on the news that GNP is higher this year than it was last year. This means that we're better off this year than last year." Comment.

2. Which of the following are included in the calculation of this year's GNP? (a) Twelve-year-old Johnny mowing his family's lawn; (b) Dave Malone buying a used car; (c) Barbara Wilson buying a bond issued by General Motors; (d) Ed Ferguson's receipt of a Social Security payment; (e) the illegal drug transaction at the corner of Elm and Fifth.

3. Discuss the problems you see in comparing the GNP of one country, say, the United States, with the GNP of another country, say, the People's Republic of China.

4. The manuscript for this book was typed by the author. Had he hired someone to do the typing, GNP would have been higher than it was. What other activities would increase GNP if they were done differently? What activities would decrease GNP if they were done differently?

5. What do you think the growth in the underground economy is dependent on? Explain your answer.

6. Using the following data, calculate the following: (a) gross national product (GNP); (b) net national product (NNP); (c) national income (NI); (d) personal income (PI); (e) disposable income (DI); (f) saving (S). All numbers are in billions of dollars.

Consumption	1,732.0
Investment	445.3
Government expenditures	530.3
Net exports	32.1
Capital consumption allowance	303.8

Indirect business taxes	213.3
Statistical discrepancy	4.9
Social insurance taxes	216.5
Transfer payments	405.6
Undistributed profits	91.0
Corporate profits taxes	77.7
Personal taxes	340.0
Dividends	0.0

7. How would an increase in social insurance taxes (Social Security contributions) affect gross national product? How would an increase affect net national product? How would it affect personal income?

8. Is it possible for personal income to rise as disposable income falls?

9. A business firm produces a good this year that it doesn't sell. As a result, the good is added to its inventory. How does this inventory good find its way into GNP?

10. Identify each of the following as an *injection* or a *leakage:* (a) saving, (b) investment expenditures, (c) imports, (d) taxes, (e) government expenditures, (f) exports.

11. Suppose the household sector saves $100 billion this year and the business sector borrows $100 billion to spend on the purchase of new capital goods. This is an example of a leakage (saving) being equally offset by an injection (investment). Give two other examples of a leakage being equally offset by an injection.

12. In Exhibit 6–1, we showed both the business and government sectors borrowing funds in the credit markets. Government borrows largely to finance budget deficits, which exist if government spends more than its tax receipts. Business borrows largely to purchase new capital goods. Suppose government increases its borrowing because of bigger budget deficits. How might government's action affect business borrowing to purchase new capital goods?

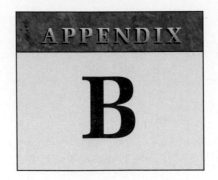

APPENDIX B

THE TWIN DEFICITS: BUDGET AND TRADE

A federal budget deficit exists if government expenditures (G) are greater than tax receipts (T): $G > T$. A trade deficit exists if imports (M) are greater than exports (X): $M > X$. In this appendix, we examine the link between the two deficits.

We start with what we know about GNP. Roughly speaking, GNP equals disposable income (DI) plus taxes (T).[1]

$$\text{GNP} = DI + T \tag{1}$$

Now one can do two things with disposable income, consume (C) it or save (S) it. Thus:

$$DI = C + S \tag{2}$$

Combining equations (1) and (2), we have

$$\text{GNP} = C + S + T \tag{3}$$

In this chapter, one of the ways we defined GNP was

$$\text{GNP} = C + I + G + (X - M) \tag{4}$$

In short, equations (3) and (4) are two different ways of expressing GNP. Since they are equal,

$$C + I + G + (X - M) = C + S + T \tag{5}$$

If we subtract C from both sides, we have

$$I + G + (X - M) = S + T \tag{6}$$

Rearranging the terms in a way that is appropriate to macroeconomic and international economic analysis, we have

$$G - T = (S - I) - (X - M) \tag{7}$$

[1]We say "roughly speaking" because this is not exactly correct. For our purposes here, however, a simplified version is sufficient and does not lead to any loss in content. For the precise definitions of GNP, DI, and many other macroeconomic measurements, see this chapter.

If $G > T$, such that there is a budget deficit, and $M > X$, such that there is a trade deficit, then the equation says

$$\text{Budget deficit} = (S - I) + \text{trade deficit} \qquad (8)$$

You might wonder why we changed the minus $(-)$ sign in equation (7) to a plus sign $(+)$ in equation (8). This is because if $M > X$, then net exports, or the difference between X and M, is negative. On the right side of equation (7), we would have $(S - I) -$ (negative net exports). But a negative times a negative is a plus. So this can be rewritten as $(S - I) +$ trade deficit.[2] In other words, then, equation (8) says that the *budget deficit equals the amount of saving over investment plus the trade deficit.*

For example, if the budget deficit is $200 billion, and saving is greater than investment by $40 billion, it follows that the trade deficit is $160 billion. Put this way, it is easy to see the link between the budget deficit and the trade deficit. For instance, if the budget deficit rises, say, from $200 billion to $210 billion, and the difference between S and I remains constant, then the trade deficit rises.[3] This tells us that one way to reduce the trade deficit is to reduce the budget deficit.

APPENDIX SUMMARY

- A budget deficit exists if government expenditures are greater than tax receipts.
- A trade deficit exists if imports are greater than exports.
- The link between the budget deficit and the trade deficit is: Budget deficit = $(S - I)$ + trade deficit, where S = saving and I = investment. For example, if the budget deficit is $200 billion, and saving is greater than investment by $40 billion, it follows that the trade deficit is $160 billion.
- Assuming that the difference between saving and investment remains constant, one way to reduce the trade deficit is to reduce the budget deficit.

QUESTIONS AND PROBLEMS

1. Explain why the budget deficit equals the difference between saving and investment plus the trade deficit.
2. Suppose the budget deficit is $200 billion, saving is $660 billion, and investment is $630 billion. How much money is the American public providing to finance the U.S. budget deficit? Where does the remainder come from? (As you think about this question, keep in mind that the budget deficit = $(S - I)$ + trade deficit.)
3. Explain why $C + I + G + (X - M) = C + S + T$.

---

[2]Try this numerical example. Let $G = \$100$, $T = \$50$, $S = \$40$, $I = \$20$, $X = \$10$, and $M = \$40$. Substituting into the equation $G - T = (S - I) - (X - M)$, we get $\$100 - \$50 = (\$40 - \$20) - (\$10 - \$40)$, or $\$50 = (\$20) - (-\$30)$. This $-\$30$ is negative net exports. Instead of *subtracting* a negative $30 from $20, we are simply *adding* a positive $30 to $20. As you can see, the results are the same; that is, $\$20 - (-\$30) = \$50 = \$20 + \$30$.
[3]This explanation of the link between budget and trade deficits is mechanical. The economics of *why* there is a link between the two deficits depends on such things as the balance of payments, the causes of currency appreciation, the link between budget deficits and real interest rates, and more.

MEASURING THE PRICE LEVEL, REAL GNP, AND UNEMPLOYMENT

WHAT THIS CHAPTER IS ABOUT

In the last chapter, we discussed how to measure gross national product (GNP), which, in our *P–Q* terminology, is *P times Q.* In this chapter, we discuss how to measure the price level, *P;* real GNP, *Q;* and the unemployment rate, which is related to changes in real GNP.

THE PRICE LEVEL

In Chapter 5, we defined the *price level* as the weighted average of the prices of all goods and services. Economists measure the price level by constructing a **price index.** There are two major price indices: the *consumer price index (CPI)* and the *GNP deflator.* We discuss both in this section.

Consumer Price Index

The most widely cited price index is the **consumer price index (CPI).** The CPI is calculated by the Bureau of Labor Statistics through its sampling of thousands of households and businesses. When a news report says that the "cost of living" increased by, say, 7 percent, it is usually referring to the CPI.[1]

The CPI is based on a representative group of goods and services purchased by a typical household.[2] This representative group of goods is called the *market basket.* To simplify, let's say that the market basket is made up of only three goods instead of the many goods it actually contains. Our market basket will consist of 10 pens, 5 shirts, and 3 pairs of shoes.

To calculate the CPI, we must first calculate the total dollar expenditure of the market basket in two years: the current year and the **base year.** The base year is a benchmark year that serves as a basis of comparison for prices in other years.

In Exhibit 7–1, by multiplying the quantity of each good in the market basket (column 2) by the current-year price of each good (column 3) the current-year expenditure on each good is computed (column 4). By adding the dollar amounts in column 4, the total dollar expenditure on the market basket in the current year is obtained. This amount is $167. To find the total expenditure on the market basket in the base year, we multiply the quantity of each good in the market basket (column 2) times base-year price (column 5) and then sum the figures in column 6. This gives us $67.

To find the CPI for the current year, we use the formula:

$$\text{CPI}_{\text{current year}} = \frac{\text{Total dollar expenditure on market basket in current year}}{\text{Total dollar expenditure on market basket in base year}} \times 100$$

Plugging in the numbers, we see that the CPI for the current year is 249.

$$\text{CPI}_{\text{current year}} = \$167/\$67 \times 100 = 249$$

Question:

What does the CPI in the base year equal?

Answer:

When the base year *is* the current year, the numerator—total dollar expenditure on market basket in current year—turns out to be the same as the denominator—total dollar expenditure on market basket in base year. Dividing the numerator ($67 in our example in Exhibit 7–1) by the denominator ($67) gives us 1. When we multiply 1 times 100, we get 100. The CPI in the base year is 100.

[1] While changes in the CPI are often used to compute the change in the "cost of living," one's cost of living usually takes into account more than is measured by the CPI. For example, the CPI does not include taxes, yet taxes are a part of most person's cost of living.

[2] Notice that when we discuss the CPI we are only talking about goods and services that the household sector buys. The purchases of other sectors of the economy are not taken into account.

Price Index
A measure of the price level.

Consumer Price Index
The most widely cited index number for the price level; the weighted average of prices of a specific set of goods and services purchased by a typical household.

Base Year
The year chosen as a point of reference or comparison for prices in other years; a benchmark year.

EXHIBIT 7–1
Computing the Consumer Price Index

This exhibit uses hypothetical data to show how the CPI is computed. To find the "total dollar expenditure on the market basket in the current year," we multiply the quantities of goods in the market basket times current-year prices and sum. This gives us $167. To find the "total dollar expenditure on the market basket in the base year," we multiply the quantities of goods in the market basket times base-year prices and sum. This gives us $67. We then divide $167 by $67 and multiply times 100.

(1) GOODS IN MARKET BASKET	(2) MARKET BASKET	(3) CURRENT- YEAR PRICES	(4) CURRENT- YEAR EXPENDITURES (2) x (3)	(5) BASE- YEAR PRICES	(6) BASE- YEAR EXPENDITURES (2) x (5)
Pens	10 pens	$ .70	$ 7.00	$ .20	$ 2.00
Shirts	5 shirts	14.00	70.00	7.00	35.00
Shoes	3 pairs of shoes	30.00	90.00	10.00	30.00
Totals			**$167.00**		**$67.00**
			Total dollar expenditure on market basket in current year		Total dollar expenditure on market basket in base year

$$\text{CPI}_{\text{current year}} = \frac{\text{Total dollar expenditure on market basket in current year}}{\text{Total dollar expenditure on market basket in base year}} \times 100$$

$$= \frac{\$167}{\$67} \times 100$$

$$= 249$$

The consumer price index in 1988 for selected nations is noted in Exhibit 7–3; also noted is the average annual inflation rate of the selected nations during the period 1980–88.

Percentage Change in the CPI and Your Cost of Living

EXHIBIT 7–2
CPI, 1980–1990

Year	Consumer Price Index (1982–84 = 100)
1980	82.4
1981	90.9
1982	96.5
1983	99.6
1984	103.9
1985	107.6
1986	109.6
1987	113.6
1988	118.3
1989	124.0
1990	130.7

$$\frac{96.5+99.6+103.9}{3}=100$$

SOURCE: Council of Economic Advisers, *Economic Report of the President*, 1991 (Washington, D.C.: U.S. Government Printing Office, 1991).

Suppose we learn that prices, as measured by the CPI, have risen 10 percent over the last year. Does this mean that your cost of living has risen by 10 percent? Not necessarily. Your cost of living may have risen by 10 percent, less than 10 percent, or more than 10 percent. The reason is that you may or may not have bought the bundle of goods that is in the market basket that is used to compute the CPI.

For example, suppose that the market basket contains 4 units of good A (4A), 3B, and 17C. Your market basket might contain 3A, 3B, 15C, and 2D. In short, your bundle of goods—*your* market basket—is not the same bundle of goods that is in *the* market basket, so the change in the prices you pay for goods will be different from the change in the prices that people pay for goods in the typical market basket.

GNP Deflator

The CPI measures the price level of those goods and services households purchase for their consumption. Households, however, are not the only ones that purchase goods and services. Business firms, government, and foreigners purchase goods, too. The **GNP deflator** is the weighted average of prices of all goods and services produced in an economy and purchased by households, firms, government, and foreigners.

The GNP deflator is calculated much the same way that the CPI is calculated, except that with the GNP deflator, we take into account all goods and services produced. To illustrate, consider Exhibit 7–4.

We have assumed that in a tiny economy in the current year, four goods are produced: pens, shirts, shoes, and bricks (column 1). Column 2 lists the quantity of each good produced in the current year, and column 3 lists the price of each good in the current year. In column 4, we multiply *current-year quantities* times *current-year prices.* When we sum column 4, we get $199, which represents the

A 6 percent rise in the CPI is not necessarily a 6 percent rise in your cost of living.

GNP Deflator
The weighted average of prices of all goods and services produced in an economy.

EXHIBIT 7–3
Consumer Price Index for Selected Nations, 1988

In the exhibit, 1982–84 = 100. The first number in parentheses under the name of the nation is the CPI for 1988; the second number is the average annual inflation rate for the period 1980–88. For example, in the United States in 1988, CPI = 118.3. The average annual inflation rate in the United States during the period 1980–88 was 3.9 percent.

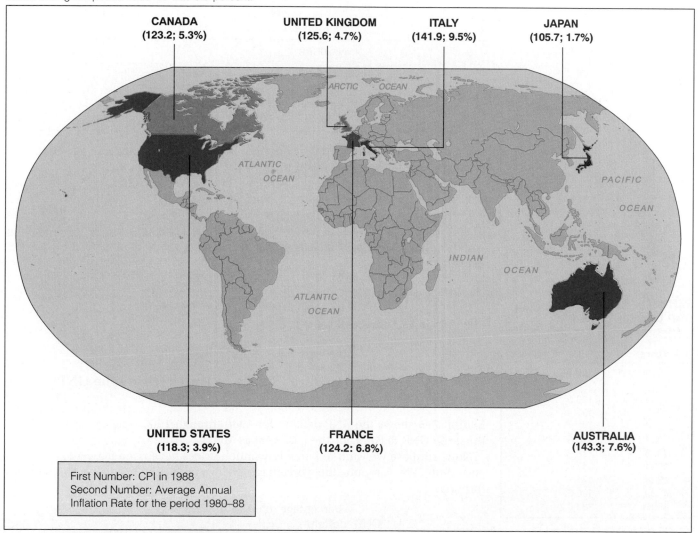

CANADA
(123.2; 5.3%)

UNITED KINGDOM
(125.6; 4.7%)

ITALY
(141.9; 9.5%)

JAPAN
(105.7; 1.7%)

UNITED STATES
(118.3; 3.9%)

FRANCE
(124.2; 6.8%)

AUSTRALIA
(143.3; 7.6%)

First Number: CPI in 1988
Second Number: Average Annual
Inflation Rate for the period 1980–88

SOURCE: U.S. Bureau of the Census, *Statistical Abstract of the United States,* 1990 (Washington, D.C.: U.S. Government Printing Office, 1990).

EXHIBIT 7–4
Computing the GNP Deflator
This exhibit uses hypothetical data to show how the GNP deflator is computed. To find nominal GNP, we multiply current-year quantities times current-year prices and sum. To find real GNP, we multiply current-year quantities times base-year prices and sum. We find the GNP deflator by dividing nominal GNP by real GNP and multiplying times 100.

(1) GOODS	(2) CURRENT-YEAR QUANTITIES	(3) CURRENT-YEAR PRICES	(4) CURRENT-YEAR EXPENDITURES AT CURRENT PRICES (2) x (3)	(5) BASE-YEAR PRICES	(6) CURRENT-YEAR EXPENDITURES AT BASE-YEAR PRICES (2) x (5)
Pens	10	$ .70	$ 7.00	$ .20	$ 2.00
Shirts	5	14.00	70.00	7.00	35.00
Shoes	3	30.00	90.00	10.00	30.00
Bricks	8	4.00	32.00	2.00	16.00
Totals			**$199.00** Nominal GNP$_{current\ year}$		**$83.00** Real GNP$_{current\ year}$

$$\text{GNP deflator}_{current\ year} = \frac{\text{Nominal GNP}_{current\ year}}{\text{Real GNP}_{current\ year}} \times 100$$

$$= \frac{\$199}{\$83} \times 100$$

$$= 239.7$$

value of the total output produced by the economy in the current year at *current prices*. In other words, $199 is the nominal GNP of the economy.[3]

Next, we want to calculate the value of the total output produced by the economy in the current year at *base-year prices*. To do this, we multiply the *current quantities* (column 2) times *base-year prices* (column 5) and then sum the figures in column 6. When we sum column 6, we get $83. (This is called *real GNP*, about which more will be said shortly.) The formula we use to calculate the GNP deflator is:

$$\text{GNP deflator}_{current\ year} = \frac{\text{Nominal GNP}_{current\ year}}{\text{Real GNP}_{current\ year}} \times 100$$

Plugging in the numbers, we get:

$$\text{GNP deflator}_{current\ year} = 199/83 \times 100 = 239.7$$

How to Compute Percentage Change in Prices (Using the GNP Deflator)

Exhibit 7–5 shows the GNP deflator for 1980 through 1900. The base year is 1982; thus, the GNP deflator for the base year is 100.

Now, suppose we want to know how much prices have risen between, say, 1983 and 1986. We compute the percentage change in prices by using this general formula:

$$\text{Percentage change in prices} = \frac{\text{GNP deflator}_{later\ year} - \text{GNP}_{earlier\ year}}{\text{GNP deflator}_{earlier\ year}} \times 100$$

[3]Recall from Chapter 6 that the terms *GNP, nominal GNP,* and *current-dollar GNP* are interchangeable.

EXHIBIT 7–5
GNP Deflator, 1980–1990

Year	GNP Deflator (1982 = 100)
1980	85.7
1981	94.0
1982	100.0
1983	103.9
1984	107.7
1985	110.9
1986	113.8
1987	117.4
1988	121.3
1989	126.3
1990	131.5

SOURCE: Council of Economic Advisers, *Economic Report of the President,* 1991 (Washington, D.C.: U.S. Government Printing Office, 1991).

In our example, the GNP deflator for the later year (1986) is 113.8, and the GNP deflator in the earlier year (1983) is 103.9. Plugging the numbers into the formula we get:

$$\text{Percentage change in prices} = \frac{113.8 - 103.9}{103.9} \times 100 = 9.5$$

REAL GNP

■

In the last section, we described how the price level (P) is measured. In this section, we look at real GNP (Q). *Real GNP*—how much is it, how much has it changed, is it headed up or down, and so on—is central to our discussion in later chapters. For example, later we will learn that changes in real GNP affect the unemployment rate and that the roller coaster ride real GNP sometimes finds itself on constitutes the business cycle.

Real GNP: A Simple Example

Suppose in year 1, in a tiny economy, only one unit of a good is produced and sold for $10. The GNP of the economy is $10, or price ($10) *times* quantity (1). In Year 2, the GNP rises to $40.

$$\text{Year 1: GNP} = \$10$$
$$\text{Year 2: GNP} = \$40$$

Would you know *why* GNP is higher in the second year? The answer should be "no." You wouldn't know if GNP was higher in the second year because price was higher ($40 instead of $10), or because quantity was higher (4 units instead of 1 unit), or because both price *and* quantity were higher ($20 and 2 units).

This is the same problem that economists have when they look at (nominal) GNP figures. For example, the GNP figures for 1985 and 1986 were $4,014.9 and $4,231.6, respectively. A simple look at the two figures does not tell us if the higher figure in 1986 is due to (1) more output having been produced in 1986 than 1985, (2) higher prices in 1986 than 1985, or (3) more output produced in 1986 than 1985 *and* higher prices in 1986 than in 1985, and so on.

A more meaningful measurement than GNP is *real GNP*. **Real GNP** is GNP valued in base year prices or GNP adjusted for price changes. For example, in 1985, real GNP was $3,618.7 billion, and in 1986 real GNP was $3,717.9 billion. Do we know why the 1986 real GNP is higher than the 1985 real GNP? The answer is "yes." Look at it this way: (1) Since real GNP is *GNP valued in base-year prices,* this means that (2) the output produced in 1985 and the output produced in 1986 are *both* valued in base-year prices; therefore, (3) the only way the dollar figure for 1986 could be higher than the dollar figure for 1985 is if more output was produced in 1986 than 1985.

We conclude that a comparison of GNP figures does not tell us why the GNP is higher or lower in one year than in another year. But a comparison of real GNP figures does. If the real GNP figure is lower in year 1 than in year 2, it is because less output was produced in year 1 than in year 2. If the real GNP figure is higher in year 1 than in year 2, it is because more output was produced in year 1 than in year 2.

Real GNP
GNP (output) valued in base year prices.

How Do You Know If You're Beating Inflation or If Inflation Is Beating You?

The **(annual) inflation rate** is defined as the annual percentage increase in some price index—such as the CPI or GNP deflator. For example, if we want to use the CPI to measure the annual inflation rate, we would use this formula:

(Annual) inflation rate

$$= \frac{CPI_{given\ year} - CPI_{previous\ year}}{CPI_{previous\ year}} \times 100$$

Suppose the CPI in year 1 is 100 and the CPI in year 2 is 110. Prices are 10 percent higher in year 2 than in year 1 (110 − 100/100 × 100 = 10 percent). The inflation rate in year 2 is 10 percent.

If prices, on average, are 10 percent higher in year 2 than in year 1, this means that each dollar a person has in his or her possession in year 2 has lost 10 percent of its value as compared with year 1. Look at this way. Dollars are used to *buy* goods and services for which people pay *prices.* Thus, if prices, on average, are 10 percent higher, each dollar buys 10 percent fewer goods and services than it did before prices increased. Or, stated differently, what $1,000 could buy in year 1 will take $1,100 to buy in year 2.

Whether a person is (1) keeping up with, (2) not keeping up with, or (3) more than keeping up with inflation depends on whether his or her income is (a) rising by the same per-centage as, (b) a lesser percentage than, or (c) a greater percentage than the inflation rate, respectively. Another way to look at this is to compute and compare a person's **real income** in different years. Real income is a person's **(money) income** adjusted for any change in prices. Real income is computed the following way:

Real income$_{given\ year}$

$$= \frac{(Money)\ income_{given\ year}}{CPI_{given\ year}} \times 100$$

Let's consider three cases.

Case 1. Keeping Up with Inflation: Real Income Stays Constant. Jim earns $50,000 in year 1 and $55,000 in year 2. The CPI in year 1 is 100 and in year 2 it is 110. Jim's income has risen by 10 percent ($55,000 − $50,000/$50,000 × 100 = 10 percent), and the inflation rate is 10 percent (110 − 100/100 × 100 = 10 percent). Since Jim's income has risen by the *same percentage* as the inflation rate, he has kept up with inflation, or, in other words, his *real income* is the same in the two years. In year 1, it is $50,000 ($50,000/100 × 100 = $50,000), and in year 2 it is $50,000 ($55,000/110 × 100 = $50,000).

Case 2. Not Keeping Up with Inflation: Real Income Falls. Karen earns $50,000 in year 1 and $52,000 in year 2. The CPI in year 1 is 100 and in year 2 it is 110. Karen's income has risen by 4 percent and the inflation rate is 10 percent. Since her income has risen by a *lesser percentage* than the inflation rate, she has not kept up with inflation. Karen's real income has fallen from $50,000 in year 1 to $47,272 in year 2.[4]

Case 3: More Than Keeping Up With Inflation: Real Income Rises. Carl earns $50,000 in year 1 and $60,000 in year 2. The CPI in year 1 is 100 and in year 2 it is 110. Carl's income has risen by 20 percent and the inflation rate is 10 percent. Since his income has risen by a *greater percentage* than the inflation rate, he has more than kept up with inflation. Carl's real income has risen from $50,000 in year 1 to $54,545 in year 2.[5]

[4]Real income$_{year\ 1}$ $= \dfrac{\$50,000}{100} \times 100$

$= \$50,000.$

Real income$_{year\ 2}$ $= \dfrac{\$52,000}{110} \times 100$

$= \$47,272.$

[5]Real income$_{year\ 1}$ $= \dfrac{\$50,000}{100} \times 100$

$= \$50,000.$

Real income$_{year\ 2}$ $= \dfrac{\$60,000}{110} \times 100$

$= \$54,545.$

THINKING LIKE AN ECONOMIST

Comparing one thing with something else can be extremely useful. For example, in each of the three cases noted in the Economics in Our Times above, we compared the percentage change in a person's (money) income with the *inflation rate.* Through this comparison, we learned something that we could not have learned had we looked at either factor alone: We learned how a person fared under inflation. Making comparisons is part of the economic way of thinking.

How To Measure Real GNP

Real GNP is measured by multiplying the current-year quantity of each final good and service produced times its *base-year price* and then summing. We did this in Exhibit 7–4 (page 136) for our four-good economy. The quantities of each good produced are listed in column 2. The base-year prices for these goods are noted in column 5. By multiplying the current-year quantity for each good by its base-year price, we get the current-year expenditure at base-year prices in column 6. Summing the figures in column 6 gives us real GNP.

Real GNP is also computed this way:

$$\text{Real GNP}_{\text{given year}} = \frac{\text{Nominal GNP}_{\text{given year}}}{\text{GNP deflator}_{\text{given year}}} \times 100$$

For example, if nominal GNP in year 1 is $4,000 billion, and the GNP deflator that year is 115, then real GNP is $3,478 billion, expressed in base year prices.

$$\text{Real GNP}_{\text{year 1}} = \frac{\$4,000 \text{ billion}}{115} \times 100 = \$3,478 \text{ billion}$$

Real Income
Income that has been adjusted for price changes.

(Money) Income
The current-dollar amount of a person's income.

(Annual) Inflation Rate
The annual percentage change in some price index—such as the CPI or GNP deflator.

MEASURING UNEMPLOYMENT

Every month, the Bureau of Census surveys 60,000 households to gather information on labor market activities. Later, the Bureau of Labor Statistics (BLS) processes this information and derives the number of Americans unemployed. We explain the details in the following sections.

Who Are the Unemployed?

The total population of the United States can be broken down into two broad groups (Exhibit 7–6). One group consists of persons who are (1) under 16 years of age, (2) in the armed forces, or (3) institutionalized—that is, they are in a prison, mental institution, or home for the aged. The second group, which consists of all others in the total population, is called the *noninstitutional adult civilian population.*

We can take the noninstitutional adult civilian population, in turn, and break it down into two groups: The first consists of those persons *not in the labor force;* the second consists of those persons in the *civilian labor force.*[6] Those persons *not in the labor force* are persons who are neither working nor looking for work. For example, persons who are retired, engaged in own-home housework, or who choose not to work fall into this category.

Persons in the civilian labor force fall into one of two categories: *employed* or *unemployed.* A person is employed if he or she

1. Did at least one hour of work as a paid employee during the survey week.
2. Worked in his or her own business or profession.
3. Worked at least 15 hours per week as an "unpaid" worker on a family-owned farm or business.
4. Was temporarily absent from work for reasons of illness, vacation, strike, or bad weather.

[6]Although our definition of the "civilian labor force" excludes persons in the armed forces, some recent measures of the labor force include them. If we add members of the armed forces residing in the United States, we then speak about the "labor force" instead of the civilian labor force.

EXHIBIT 7–6
Breakdown of the U.S. Population and the Labor Force
In 1990, the noninstitutional adult civilian population consisted of 188 million people; the civilian labor force was 124.7 million people, of whom 117.9 million were employed and 6.8 million were unemployed.

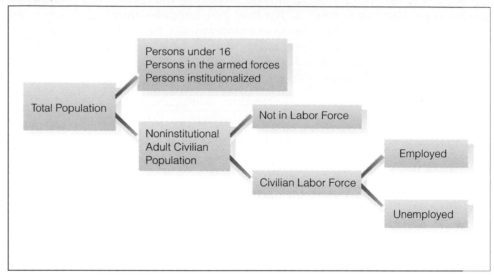

A person is unemployed if he or she

1. Did not work during the survey week, actively looked for work within the past four weeks, and is currently available for work.
2. Is waiting to be called back to a job from which he or she has been laid off.
3. Is waiting to report to a job within 30 days.

Question:

Suppose a person has been unsuccessfully searching for work for 15 months. He finally gives up his search. For the past 7 months he simply has been sitting at home. Is this person considered to be unemployed?

Answer:

No, this person is considered to be a *discouraged worker,* not an unemployed worker. To be unemployed, a person must meet three conditions: (1) not have worked during the survey week, (2) be available to work, and (3) actively have looked for work within the past four weeks. The person here definitely meets condition (1), probably meets condition (2), but he fails to meet condition (3).

Follow-up Question:

What category in Exhibit 7–6 does a discouraged worker fit into?

Answer:

He or she fits into the category of *not in the labor force.* In short, unemployed persons are in the *civilian labor force,* and discouraged workers are *not in the labor force.*

The Unemployment and Employment Rates

The unemployment and employment rates are both measures of the health of the economy. The **unemployment rate** is the percentage of the civilian labor force that is unemployed. It is equal to the number of persons unemployed divided by the number of persons in the civilian labor force. (Exhibit 7–7 gives the unemployment rate in the United States for the period 1980–1990.)

$$\text{Unemployment rate (U)} = \frac{\text{Number of persons unemployed}}{\text{Number of persons in the civilian labor force}}$$

The **employment rate** is the percentage of the noninstitutional adult civilian population that is employed. It is equal to the number of persons employed divided by the number of persons in the noninstitutional adult civilian population.

$$\text{Employment rate (E)} = \frac{\text{Number of persons employed}}{\substack{\text{Number of persons in the noninstitutional} \\ \text{adult civilian population}}}$$

It is important to notice that the denominator in the unemployment rate is different from the denominator in the employment rate. (See Exhibit 7–7 for the employment rate in the United States for the period 1980–1990.)

Economists usually point to three reasons why the commonly used unemployment rate may not be as accurate a measure of the health of the economy as the employment rate.

First, the unemployment rate can increase *even without a slowdown in the economy.* It increases simply if more individuals wish to become members of the civilian labor force. Suppose 1,000 persons currently not in the labor force decide to join the civilian labor force. Furthermore, suppose that 400 of them become employed, and 600 of them are unemployed.

What happens to the unemployment rate? The denominator increases by 1,000 and the numerator increases by 600. If the percentage change in the numerator is greater than the percentage change in the denominator, the unemployment rate increases.

What happens to the employment rate? The numerator increases by 400, but the denominator stays the same, and therefore the employment rate increases at the same time that the unemployment rate increases.

Unemployment Rate
The percentage of the civilian labor force that is unemployed: Unemployment rate = number of unemployed persons/number of persons in the civilian labor force.

Employment Rate
The percentage of the noninstitutional adult civilian population that is employed: Employment rate = number of persons employed/number of persons in the noninstitutional adult civilian population.

EXHIBIT 7–7
The Unemployment and Employment Rates, 1980–90*
*The sum of the unemployment and employment rates do not equal 100 percent.

Year	Unemployment Rate (percent)	Employment Rate (percent)
1980	7.1	59.2
1981	7.6	59.0
1982	9.7	57.8
1983	9.6	57.9
1984	7.5	59.5
1985	7.2	60.1
1986	7.0	60.7
1987	6.2	61.5
1988	5.5	62.3
1989	5.3	63.0
1990	5.5	62.7

SOURCE: Council of Economic Advisers, *Economic Report of the President, 1991* (Washington, D.C.: U.S. Government Printing Office, 1991).

The unemployment rate plus the employment rate does not equal 100 percent.

■

Second, some economists argue that the unemployment rate is *higher* than it would be if the "welfare incentive" were taken into account. The welfare incentive exists because, to qualify for certain welfare programs, a person must be declared unemployed. In short, there is an incentive to become unemployed. The welfare incentive does not affect the employment rate because neither the number of persons employed (numerator) nor the noninstitutional adult civilian population (denominator) changes as a result of it.

Third, other economists argue that the unemployment rate is *lower* than it would be if the "discouraged worker effect" were taken into account. Earlier, we noted that discouraged workers are classified as "not in the labor force." Economists who think it more accurate to place discouraged workers in the category of the unemployed naturally argue that the unemployment rate is lower than it would be if they were. People who quit actively searching for work before finding work reduce the unemployment rate, even though nothing in the economy may have changed. They do not affect the employment rate, however.

Question:

If the unemployment rate is 10 percent, does it follow that the employment rate is 90 percent?

Answer:

No. Remember that the denominator in the employment rate (number of persons in the noninstitutional adult civilian population) is not the same as the denominator in the unemployment rate (number of persons in the civilian labor force). For this reason, it does not follow that if the unemployment rate is 10 percent, the employment rate is 90 percent. Also, a quick look at Exhibit 7–7 shows that the unemployment rate plus the employment rate does not equal 100 percent.

ECONOMIC STATISTICS IN POLITICS
■

Adding the inflation rate to the unemployment rate gives us what economists commonly call the *discomfort index.* In 1976, Jimmy Carter, running against Gerald Ford for the presidency of the United States, renamed the discomfort index the *misery index,* and then used the existing relatively high misery index in his campaign against Ford. Carter said that the misery index was higher under Ford than it had been under the preceding five presidents. Many political observers believe that Carter's effective use of the misery index helped him win the election.

Then in 1980, Ronald Reagan, running for the presidency against Jimmy Carter, used the same measure against him, with equal success. The misery index seems to be an easy way to focus voters' attention on a president's economic record.

Question:

If the state of the economy matters so much to the way people vote in a presidential election, why is it that in many presidential elections, the state of the economy is hardly discussed relative to such things as foreign policy, abortion, the crime rate, and so on. Aren't these the issues that matter to the American voter?

Can Economics Pick the Winner?

The political use that has been made of the discomfort, or misery, index shows that the state of the economy can have an impact on how people vote. In fact, many economists and political observers believe that the state of the economy is a *major factor* that voters take into account when they are deciding how they will cast their ballot in a presidential election.

Most studies indicate that the unemployment rate and the inflation rate (the two components of the misery index) do not predict the winners of presidential elections as well as (1) the recent change in real GNP (which is related to changes in the unemployment rate) and (2) the infla-

tion rate in the year preceding the election.

If the economy is growing, as evidenced in real GNP, and inflation is low, then voters tend to vote for the person representing the incumbent party. If the economy is slowing, or has turned down, and inflation is high, then voters tend to vote against the person representing the incumbent party. This means that *voters largely vote their pocketbooks*. If growth is rapid and inflation is low, then their pocketbooks are full and they are happy. A vote for the incumbent party is a vote to keep the good times rolling. If growth is weak or nonexistent and inflation is high,

then pocketbooks are sagging and people are unhappy. A vote against the incumbent party is a vote to throw out the rascals who did this to us.

One model that has impressive results in using economic data to predict elections is the DRI (Data Resources, Inc.) model, named after an economics forecasting firm. The model correctly predicted the winner of the last 11 presidential elections. Also, its forecast of the percentage of the vote received by the winner is close to the actual percentage of the vote received by the winner.

Answer:

They probably matter, but the real question is *how much* they matter. Also, simply because one issue (say, foreign policy) may get more media attention in a presidential race than the state of the economy, it does not necessarily follow that foreign policy is more important to voters than the state of the economy.

But the main point is this: Economic models have used "recent changes in real GNP" and "inflation rate" as factors to predict presidential elections. And so far, these models have consistently predicted presidential winners and (close to) the percentage of the vote they receive. There is no guarantee, though, that these models will continue to make accurate predictions, since it is possible that pocketbook issues may become less important in the future.

CHAPTER SUMMARY

Consumer Price Index

■ The CPI is the most widely cited index number for the price level; it is the weighted average of prices of a specific set of goods and services purchased by a typical household. To calculate the CPI for the current year, use this formula:

$$CPI_{current\ year} = \frac{Total\ dollar\ expenditure\ on\ market\ basket\ in\ current\ year}{Total\ dollar\ expenditure\ on\ market\ basket\ in\ base\ year} \times 100$$

GNP Deflator

■ The GNP deflator is a weighted average of prices of all goods and services produced in an economy and purchased by households, firms, government, and foreigners. To calculate the GNP deflator for the current year, use this formula:

$$\text{GNP deflator}_{\text{current year}} = \frac{\text{Nominal GNP}_{\text{current year}}}{\text{Real GNP}_{\text{current year}}} \times 100$$

Percentage Change in Prices

■ To find the percentage change in prices using the CPI, use this formula:

$$\text{Percentage change in prices} = \frac{\text{CPI}_{\text{later year}} - \text{CPI}_{\text{earlier year}}}{\text{CPI}_{\text{earlier year}}} \times 100$$

■ To find the percentage change in prices using the GNP deflator, use this formula:

$$\text{Percentage change in prices} =$$
$$\frac{\text{GNP deflator}_{\text{later year}} - \text{GNP deflator}_{\text{earlier year}}}{\text{GNP deflator}_{\text{earlier year}}} \times 100$$

Inflation Rate

■ To compute the (annual) inflation rate, use this formula:

$$\text{(Annual) inflation rate} = \frac{\text{CPI}_{\text{given year}} - \text{CPI}_{\text{previous year}}}{\text{CPI}_{\text{previous year}}} \times 100$$

Real Income

■ Real income is (money) income adjusted for any change in prices. To compute real income in a given year, use this formula:

$$\text{Real Income}_{\text{given year}} = \frac{\text{(Money) income}_{\text{given year}}}{\text{CPI}_{\text{given year}}} \times 100$$

Real GNP

■ Real GNP is GNP valued in base year prices and adjusted for price changes. To compute real GNP in a given year, use this formula:

$$\text{Real GNP}_{\text{given year}} = \frac{\text{Nominal GNP}_{\text{given year}}}{\text{GNP deflator}_{\text{given year}}} \times 100$$

The Unemployed, Unemployment, and Employment Rates

■ A person is unemployed if he or she (1) did not work during the survey week, actively looked for work during the past four weeks, and is currently available for work; (2) is waiting to be called back to a job from which he or she has been laid off; or (3) is waiting to report to a job within 30 days.

■ A discouraged worker is classified as "not in the labor force," not as "unemployed." A discouraged worker is a person who is available for work and who has looked for work, but is currently no longer looking.

■ The unemployment rate is equal to the number of unemployed persons divided

by the civilian labor force. The employment rate is equal to the number of employed persons divided by the noninstitutional adult civilian population.
■ Some economists maintain that the employment rate is a better measure of the health of the economy than the unemployment rate. They argue that the unemployment rate may increase even if there is no slowdown in the economy. In addition, it is sometimes argued that the unemployment rate is higher than it would be otherwise because individuals cannot qualify for certain welfare benefits unless they are unemployed. At the same time, it can also be argued that the unemployment rate is lower than it would be if the "discouraged worker effect" were taken into account.

Key Terms and Concepts

Price Index	Base year	Real Income
Consumer Price Index (CPI)	GNP Deflator	(Money) Income
	Real GNP	Unemployment Rate
	(Annual) Inflation Rate	Employment Rate

QUESTIONS AND PROBLEMS

1. Assume the market basket contains 10X, 20Y, and 45Z. The current-year prices for goods X, Y, and Z are $1, $4, and $6, respectively. The base-year prices are $1, $3, and $5, respectively. What is the CPI in the current year?
2. If the total dollar expenditures on the market basket in the current year is $400, and the total dollar expenditures on the market basket in the base year is $360, what is the CPI in the current year? in the base year?
3. Using Exhibit 7–2, compute the percentage change in prices between (a) 1980 and 1981, (b) 1983 and 1987, and (c) 1984 and 1986.
4. What is the difference(s) between the CPI and the GNP deflator?
5. Using Exhibit 7–5, compute the percentage change in prices between (a) 1983 and 1984, (b) 1985 and 1987, and (c) 1983 and 1984.
6. In 1980 U.S. GNP was $2,732.0 billion and real GNP was $3,187.1 billion. How is it possible for real GNP to be greater than GNP?
7. Suppose Stephanie's (money) income in 1985, 1986, and 1987 is $30,000, $35,000, and $40,000, respectively. Using the data in Exhibit 7–2, compute Stephanie's real income in each of these years.
8. Using the hypothetical data in the following table, calculate real GNP for the years noted. (GNP and real GNP are in billions of dollars.)

Year	Nominal GNP	GNP defaltor	Real GNP
1	$4,989	121	?
2	4,886	122	?
3	5,221	143	?
4	5,333	155	?

9. Economists prefer to compare real GNP figures for different years instead of (nominal) GNP figures. Why?

10. John earned $45,000 in year 1 and $55,000 in year 2. It follows that John is better off in terms of the quantity of goods and services he can buy in year 2 than year 1. Comment.

11. Which of the following persons would be included in the civilian labor force: (a) a farmer working on his own farm, (b) a 14-year-old boy looking for a summer job, (c) a 57-year-old man who was laid off 18 months ago and has quit looking for work because he thinks he doesn't have the skills to fill any of the jobs he would want, (d) a full-time college student, (e) a person working 37 hours a week as a sales clerk in a department store at the local mall, (f) a person fired from work yesterday?

12. Is it possible for the unemployment rate to fall when the number of persons unemployed is rising? Explain your answer.

13. Some economists speak of the *underemployed*—persons who are working at jobs beneath their education and skills. For example, a person with a Ph.D. in English literature may drive a taxi in Washington, D.C. because he can't find other work. Do you think the problem of the underemployed is as serious as the problem of the unemployed? Why?

14. What is wrong with saying that an unemployed person is a person who is not working?

15. Here are some data: noninstitutional adult civilian population = 100 million persons; civilian labor force = 87 million persons; total population = 240 million persons; employed persons = 45 million persons. Calculate the following: (a) unemployment rate, (b) employment rate, (c) number of persons not in the labor force, and (d) number of discouraged workers.

16. Why is it that the sum of the unemployment and employment rates does not equal 100 percent?

17. "Models that use "recent changes in real GNP" and "inflation rate" to predict presidential election winners have high predictive power; therefore, nothing beyond these two factors matters when it comes down to how people vote in presidential elections." Discuss.

THE AGGREGATE DEMAND— AGGREGATE SUPPLY FRAMEWORK

WHAT THIS CHAPTER IS ABOUT

In order to see changes in GNP ($P \times Q$), the price level (P), and real GNP (Q), we need a new framework. This is the aggregate demand—aggregate supply (*AD–AS*) framework, which we develop in this chapter. We first discuss aggregate demand, next aggregate supply, and then the two sides of the economy together. In examining aggregate demand, we derive the aggregate demand curve and briefly discuss shifts in it. Then we apply the same procedure to aggregate supply, and look at short-run and long-run aggregate supply curves as well. The latter are particularly important to our discussions of macroeconomic theory and policy debates in later chapters.

AGGREGATE DEMAND

■

EXHIBIT 8–1
The Aggregate Demand Curve

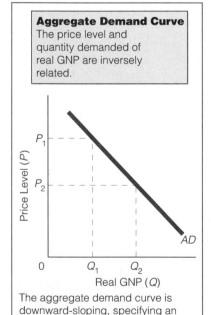

Aggregate Demand Curve
The price level and quantity demanded of real GNP are inversely related.

The aggregate demand curve is downward-sloping, specifying an inverse relationship between the price level and the quantity demanded of real GNP.

148

Just as there are two sides to a market, there are two sides to an economy—a demand side and a supply side. Aggregate demand relates to the demand side, and aggregate supply relates to the supply side. In this section, we discuss aggregate demand and develop an aggregate demand curve.

The Aggregate Demand Curve

Take a look at Exhibit 8–1. On the vertical axis is the *price level.* In the last chapter, we discussed two measures of the price level—the CPI and the GNP deflator. Think of the price level in the exhibit as the GNP deflator. As we move up the vertical axis, the price level rises; as we move down the vertical axis, the price level falls.

On the horizontal axis is *real GNP.* As we move to the right on the horizontal axis, real GNP rises; as we move to the left on the horizontal axis, real GNP falls.

Now take a look at the curve drawn in the space between the two axes. This is an **aggregate demand (*AD*) curve.** The *AD* curve shows the quantity demanded of real GNP at different price levels, *ceteris paribus.* Notice that the higher price level (P_1) corresponds to a lower quantity demanded of real GNP (Q_1), and the lower price level (P_2) corresponds to a higher quantity demanded of real GNP (Q_2). In short, the price level and the quantity demanded of real GNP are inversely related.

Why Does the Aggregate Demand Curve Slope Downward?

The downward-sloping *AD* curve is the graphical representation of the inverse relationship between the price level and the quantity demanded of real GNP. So when we ask, Why does the AD curve slope downward? we are essentially asking, Why is there an inverse relationship between the price level and the quantity demanded of real GNP? The answer leads us to the topics of (1) the real balance effect, (2) the interest rate effect, and (3) the international trade effect.

Real Balance Effect. The **real balance effect** states that the inverse relationship between the price level and the quantity demanded of real GNP is established through changes in the value of person's **monetary wealth,** or *money holdings.*

To illustrate, start with a person who has $50,000 in cash. Now suppose the price level rises. As this happens, the **purchasing power** of the $50,000 falls. That is, the $50,000 that once could buy, say, 100 television sets at $500 each, can now buy 80 sets at $625 each.

A decrease in the purchasing power of the person's $50,000 is identical to saying that his monetary wealth has decreased. (After all, isn't the $50,000 less valuable when it can buy less than when it can buy more?) And as he becomes less wealthy, he buys fewer goods.

In summary, a *rise in the price level* causes purchasing power to fall, which decreases a person's monetary wealth. As people become less wealthy, *the quantity demanded of real GNP falls.*

Now suppose the price level falls. As this happens, the purchasing power of the person's $50,000 rises. That is, the $50,000 that once could buy 100 television sets at $500 each, can now buy 125 sets at $400 each. An increase in the purchasing power of the person's $50,000 is identical to saying that his monetary wealth has increased. And as he becomes wealthier, he buys more goods.

In summary, *a fall in the price level* causes purchasing power to rise, which increases a person's monetary wealth. As people become wealthier, the *quantity demanded of real GNP rises.*

Interest Rate Effect. The **interest rate effect** states that the inverse relationship between the price level and the quantity demanded of real GNP is established through changes in household and business spending that is sensitive to changes in interest rates.

Let's consider a person who buys a fixed bundle of goods (food, clothing, and shelter) each week. Now suppose the price level rises. This reduces the purchasing power of the person's money. With less purchasing power (per dollar), she will have to acquire *more money* in order to buy her fixed bundle of goods. In her attempt to acquire more money, she goes to a bank and requests a loan. In terms of simple supply-and-demand analysis, the *demand for credit* increases. Subsequently, the price of credit, which is the *interest rate,* rises.[1] As the interest rate rises, households borrow less to finance, say, automobile purchases, and firms borrow less to finance new capital goods spending. Thus, the quantity demanded of real GNP falls.

If the price level falls, the purchasing power of a person's money increases. With more purchasing power (per dollar), she can purchase her fixed bundle of goods with *less money.* What does she do with (part of) this gain in her financial wealth? She saves it. In terms of simple supply-and-demand analysis, the *supply of credit* increases. Subsequently, the interest rate drops. As the interest rate drops, households and businesses borrow more and so they end up buying more goods. Thus, the quantity demanded of real GNP rises.

The International Trade Effect. The **international trade effect** states that the inverse relationship between the price level and the quantity demanded of real GNP is established through foreign sector spending, which includes U.S. spending on foreign goods (imports) and foreign spending on U.S. goods (exports).

Suppose the price level in the United States rises. As this happens, U.S. goods become relatively more expensive than foreign goods. As a result, both Americans and foreigners buy fewer U.S. goods. The quantity demanded of (U.S.) real GNP falls.

Now suppose the price level in the United States falls. As this happens, U.S. goods become relatively cheaper than foreign goods. As a result, both Americans and foreigners buy more U.S. goods. The quantity demanded of (U.S.) real GNP rises.

For a review of the three effects—real balance, interest rate, and international trade—see Exhibit 8–2.

A Change in the Quantity Demanded of Real GNP versus a Change in Aggregate Demand

In Chapter 3, we learned that there is a difference between a *change in quantity demanded* and a *change in demand.* Similarly, there is a difference between *a change in the quantity demanded of real GNP* and *a change in aggregate demand* (or what amounts to the same thing, a *change in the demand for real GNP).*

We know that a change in the quantity demanded of real GNP is brought about by a change in the price level. As the price level falls (rises), the quantity demanded of real GNP rises (falls), *ceteris paribus.* In Exhibit 8–3a, a change in the quantity demanded of real GNP is represented as a movement from one point (A) on AD_1 to another point (B) on AD_1.

---

[1]In the credit market, there is a demand for, and a supply of, credit. The price of credit is the interest rate. As in other markets, when the demand for credit rises, the price of credit (interest rate) rises; when the supply of credit rises, the price of credit (interest rate) falls.

EXHIBIT 8–2
Why the Aggregate Demand Curve Is Downward Sloping

This exhibit outlines the three effects that explain why the *AD* curve is downward sloping. Each effect relates to a change in the price level leading to a change in the quantity demanded of real GNP.

Type of Effect	How It Works	Graphical Representation of What Happens
Real Balance Effect	***Price level rises*** → purchasing power falls → monetary wealth falls → **buy fewer goods.** ***Price level falls*** → purchasing power rises → monetary wealth rises → **buy more goods.**	
Interest Rate Effect	***Price level rises*** → purchasing power falls → borrow money in order to continue to buy fixed bundle of goods → demand for credit rises → interest rate rises → businesses and households borrow less at higher interest rate → **buy fewer goods.** ***Price level falls*** → purchasing power rises → less money needed to buy fixed bundle of goods → save more → supply of credit rises → interest rate falls → businesses and households borrow more at lower interest rate → **buy more goods.**	
International Trade Effect	**Price level in U.S. rises** relative to foreign price levels → U.S. goods relatively more expensive than foreign goods → both Americans and foreigners **buy fewer U.S. goods**. **Price level in U.S. falls** relative to foreign price levels → U.S. goods relatively less expensive than foreign goods → both Americans and foreigners **buy more U.S. goods**.	

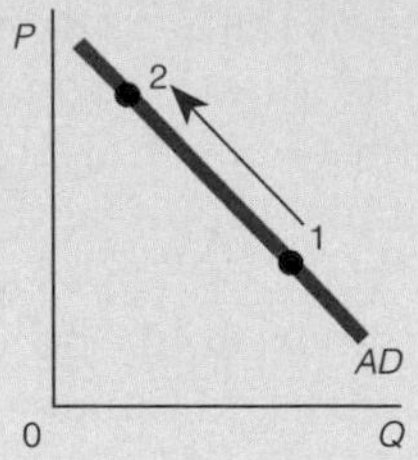

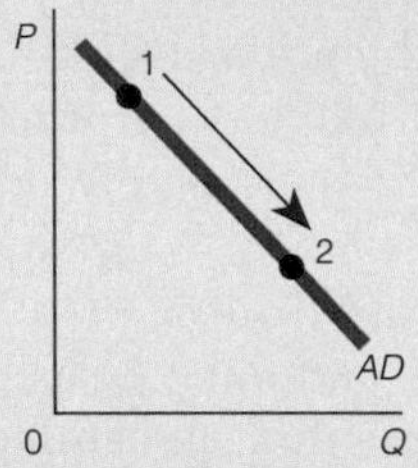

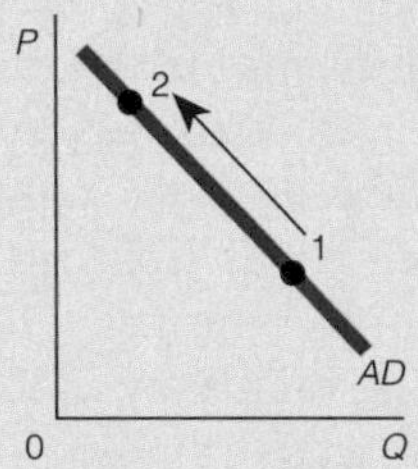

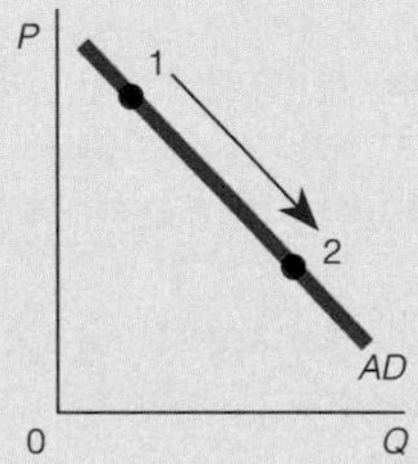

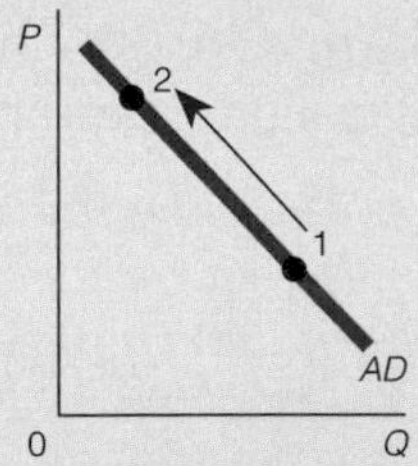

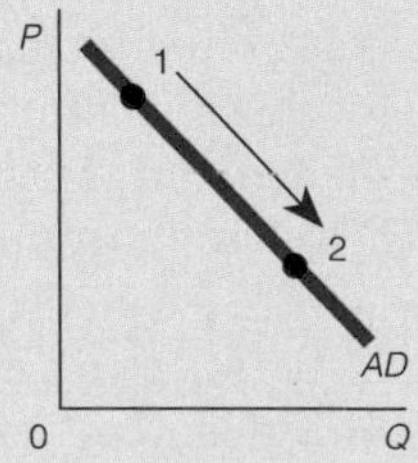

150

EXHIBIT 8–3

EXHIBIT 8–3
A Change in the Quantity Demanded of Real GNP versus a Change in Aggregate Demand

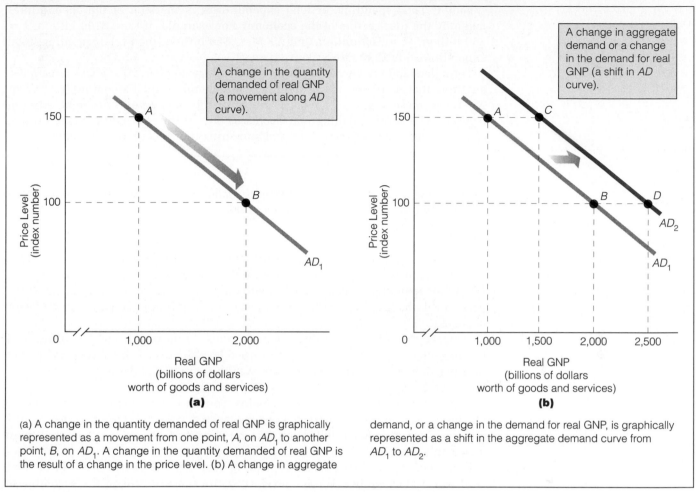

(a) A change in the quantity demanded of real GNP is graphically represented as a movement from one point, *A*, on *AD*₁ to another point, *B*, on *AD*₁. A change in the quantity demanded of real GNP is the result of a change in the price level. (b) A change in aggregate demand, or a change in the demand for real GNP, is graphically represented as a shift in the aggregate demand curve from *AD*₁ to *AD*₂.

A change in aggregate demand, or a change in the demand for real GNP, is represented in Exhibit 8–3b as a shift in the aggregate demand curve from AD_1 to AD_2. Notice that with a shift in the aggregate demand curve, the quantity demanded of real GNP changes even though the *price level remains constant*. For example, at a price level (index number) of 150, the quantity demanded of real GNP is $1,000 billion on AD_1 in Exhibit 8–3b. But at the same price level (150), the quantity demanded of real GNP is $1,500 billion on AD_2.

Changes in Aggregate Demand

Here are some facts established in earlier chapters:

Fact 1: There are four sectors in the economy: household, business, government, and foreign.

Fact 2: Each of these four sectors buys some of the real GNP produced in this country.

Fact 3: The expenditures (on real GNP) made by the household sector are called *consumption* (*C*); the expenditures made by the business sector are called *investment* (*I*); the expenditures made by the government sector are called *government*

CHAPTER 8
THE AGGREGATE DEMAND—
AGGREGATE SUPPLY FRAMEWORK
■

expenditures (G); and the expenditures made by the foreign sector are called *net exports (X − M)*.

Fact 4: Total spending, or total expenditures, is the sum of the expenditures made by the four sectors of the economy. For example, if C = $100 billion, I = $50 billion, G = $60 billion, and $X − M$ = $20 billion, then total spending (total expenditures) is $230 billion.

To understand changes in aggregate demand, remember: *At a given price level,* anything that increases any of the four components of total spending (*C, I, G,* or *X − M*), increases aggregate demand and shifts the *AD* curve to the right. Also, *at a given price level,* anything that decreases any of the four components of total spending decreases aggregate demand and shifts the *AD* curve to the left.

Question:

In reminding the reader that total spending changed at a given price level, why is it important to specify at a given price level?

Answer:

We specify *at a given price level* because the expenditures of persons may change for more than one reason. Consider an individual's purchases of goods and services. Her spending, or *consumption,* will change for one of two reasons: (1) if the price level changes or (2) if the price level is constant and some nonprice factor changes.

Suppose the price level falls, *ceteris paribus.* From our discussion of the real balance effect, we learned that a lower price level increases the purchasing power of a person's money, so her monetary wealth increases and she ends up buying more goods and services.

Suppose now the price level remains constant and some nonprice factor changes; for example, the person's income taxes decrease, *ceteris paribus.* As this happens, her disposable (after-tax) income rises and she ends up buying more goods and services.

Here, then, are two cases where spending changes. The causal factor in the first case was a "change in the price level" and the causal factor in the second case was a "change in income taxes."

Economists distinguish between changes in spending according to whether the price level is constant or not. In general, a change in the price level changes the *quantity demanded of real GNP.* And a change in a nonprice factor—such as income taxes in our example—changes *aggregate demand* or the *demand for real GNP.*

Question:

What is the difference between total spending *or* total expenditures *and* aggregate demand? *Sometimes they sound as if they are the same thing?*

Answer:

Total expenditures refers to the sum of the expenditures made by the four sectors of the economy at a given price level—that is, the sum of consumption, investment, government expenditures, and net exports. This sum is a specific dollar amount, say, $4 trillion.

Aggregate demand is not a specific dollar amount; instead, it is a *schedule* consisting of the different amounts of real GNP that households, businesses, government, and foreigners are willing and able to buy at different price levels. For instance, a given aggregate demand may specify that the four sectors of the economy are willing and able to buy $3 trillion worth of goods and services at a price level (CPI) of 112, *and* $3.3 trillion worth of goods and services at a price level of 105, and so on. Simply put, think of aggregate demand as consisting of *different* dollar amounts of real GNP that the four sectors of the economy are willing and able to purchase at different price levels.[2]

Shifts in the Aggregate Demand Curve: A Brief Comment

It is customary at this point to list and explain some of the (nonprice) factors that can change aggregate demand and thereby shift the AD curve. We have chosen not to follow custom. We owe you a reason as to why. The major reason is that much of the controversy and debate that takes place in macroeconomics is focused on aggregate demand. Our objective in this text is to convey the full specifics of this debate, and this requires us to discuss the factors that influence aggregate demand in their proper context, giving attention to arguments and counterarguments. For example, when we discuss government expenditures we begin by showing that an increase in government expenditures can shift the AD curve to the right and that a decrease in government expenditures can shift the AD curve to the left. But also related to increases in government expenditures are the questions of how the expenditures are financed (through taxes or borrowed funds?) and the degree of *crowding out*—that is, the degree to which, say, consumer expenditures fall as government expenditures rise. At this point, you perhaps do not know the important details of these issues, and that makes our point. We feel it better to wait until we have fully explained these issues before we discuss government expenditures and its effect on aggregate demand.

For now, we leave you with the general statement regarding aggregate demand that we made earlier:

At a given price level, anything that increases any of the four components of total spending (C, I, G, or net exports), increases aggregate demand and shifts the AD curve to the right. Also, *at a given price level,* anything that decreases any of the four components of total spending, decreases aggregate demand and shifts the AD curve to the left.

AGGREGATE SUPPLY

■

In this section, we first talk about what the aggregate supply curve is and what factors can shift it. Then we distinguish between the short-run and long-run aggregate supply curves.

The Short-Run Aggregate Supply Curve

A **short-run aggregate supply (SRAS) curve** is illustrated in Exhibit 8–4. It shows the real GNP producers will offer for sale at different price levels, *ceteris paribus.* Notice that the SRAS curve is upward sloping, indicating a direct relationship between the price level and the quantity supplied of real GNP. It is likely that the direct relationship between these two variables will hold *for a while.*

[2]We see this when we look at the aggregate demand (*AD*) curve, which shows the quantity demanded of real GNP at different price levels: so much quantity demanded at P_1, so much quantity demanded at P_2, and so on.

Short-Run Aggregate Supply (SRAS) Curve
Shows the real GNP producers will offer for sale at different price levels, *ceteris paribus.*

EXHIBIT 8–4
The Short-Run Aggregate
Supply Curve

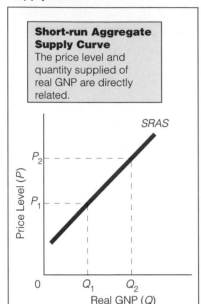

Short-run Aggregate Supply Curve
The price level and quantity supplied of real GNP are directly related.

The short-run aggregate supply curve is upward-sloping, specifying a direct relationship between the price level and the quantity supplied of real GNP.

To explain why, consider firms that produce goods. Each firm's profit per unit is equal to price per unit minus cost per unit (profit per unit = price per unit − cost per unit). If price rises while costs per unit stay constant, there will be greater profit in producing goods, and it is likely firms will produce more. If price falls while costs per unit stay constant, there will be less profit in producing goods, and it is likely firms will produce less. The response is summarized in the upward-sloping SRAS curve.

We offer one proviso. In the preceding example, *prices changed* and *unit production costs remained constant.* It is unlikely that this configuration between prices and costs would last for more than a few months. Initially, an increase in the price of goods might occur without any increase in unit production costs; for example, labor costs may remain constant owing to existing labor contracts. But eventually costs adjust upward. In other words, the aggregate supply curve in Exhibit 8–4, which represents a direct relationship between the price level and quantity supplied of real GNP, holds for a configuration of prices and costs (specifically, rising or falling prices and constant costs) that is only temporary. This is why economists refer to this curve as the *short-run* aggregate supply curve.

Shifts in the Short-Run Aggregate Supply Curve

The factors that can shift the short-run aggregate supply curve include the wage rate, prices of nonlabor inputs, productivity, and supply shocks. In a later chapter, we add inflation expectations to this list.

The Wage Rate. Changes in the wage rate have a major impact on the position of the SRAS curve, since wage costs are usually a firm's major cost item. The impact of a rise or fall in equilibrium wage rates can be understood in terms of the equation given earlier: profit per unit = price per unit − cost per unit. Higher wage rates mean higher costs and, at constant prices, translate into lower profits and a reduction in the number of goods managers of firms will want to produce. Lower wage rates mean lower costs and, at constant prices, translate into higher profits and an increase in the number of goods managers will decide to produce.

The impact of higher and lower equilibrium wages is shown in Exhibit 8–5. We start with $SRAS_1$. At the given price level, *P,* real GNP is Q_1. Next, we introduce higher wage rates. As we just mentioned, this reduces a firm's profits at a given price level; consequently, there is a reduction in production. In the diagram, we move from Q_1 to Q_2, which at the given price level corresponds to point *B*. Point *B* represents a point on a new aggregate supply curve ($SRAS_2$). We see that a rise in equilibrium wage rates leads to a leftward shift in the aggregate supply curve. The steps are simply reversed for a fall in equilibrium wage rates.

Prices of Nonlabor Inputs. There are other inputs in the production process besides labor. Changes in their prices affect the SRAS curve in the same way as wage–rate changes. An increase in the price of a nonlabor input (say, oil) shifts the SRAS curve leftward; a decrease in the price of a nonlabor input shifts the SRAS curve rightward.

Productivity. Productivity describes the output produced per unit of input employed over some period of time. For example, consider the input labor. Increases in labor productivity cause the SRAS curve to shift rightward; decreases in labor productivity cause the SRAS curve to shift leftward. A host of factors lead to increased labor productivity, including a more educated labor force, a larger stock of capital goods, technological changes, and improved management techniques.

EXHIBIT 8–5
Wage Rates and a Shift in the Short-Run Aggregate Supply Curve

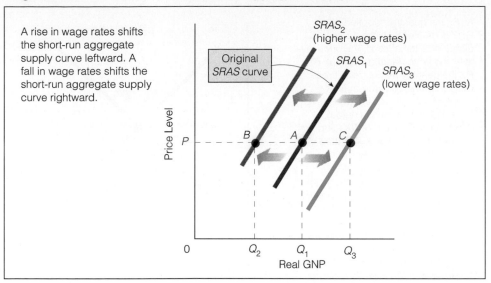

A rise in wage rates shifts the short-run aggregate supply curve leftward. A fall in wage rates shifts the short-run aggregate supply curve rightward.

Supply Shocks. Major natural or institutional changes on the supply side of the economy that affect aggregate supply are referred to as *supply shocks.* Bad weather that wipes out a large part of the midwestern wheat crop would be considered a supply shock. So would a major cutback in the supply of oil coming to the United States from the Middle East. Supply shocks are of two varieties. There are *adverse supply shocks* (examples just given), which shift the *SRAS* curve leftward, and *beneficial supply shocks,* which shift it rightward. Examples of the latter include a major oil discovery and unusually good weather leading to the increased production of a food staple. These supply shocks are reflected in resource or input prices.

Short-Run Equilibrium: Putting *AD* and *SRAS* Together

It is time to put the two sides of the economy together. Exhibit 8–6 shows an aggregate demand (*AD*) curve and a short-run aggregate supply (*SRAS*) curve. We consider the "quantity demanded of real GNP" and the "quantity supplied of real GNP" at three different price levels: P_1, P_2, and P_E.

At P_1, the quantity supplied of real GNP (Q_2) is greater than the quantity demanded (Q_1). There is surplus of goods. As a result, the price level drops and firms decrease output and consumers increase consumption. Why do consumers increase consumption as the price level drops? (Hint: Think of the real balance effect.)

At P_2, the quantity supplied of real GNP (Q_1) is less than the quantity demanded of real GNP (Q_2). There is a shortage of goods. As a result, the price level rises, firms increase output, and consumers decrease consumption. In instances of both surplus and shortage, economic forces are moving the economy toward P_E, where the quantity demanded of real GNP equals the (short-run) quantity supplied of real GNP. This is the point of **short-run equilibrium.** P_E is the short-run equilibrium price level; Q_E is the short-run equilibrium real GNP.

A change in either aggregate demand, short-run aggregate supply, or both will obviously affect the price level and/or real GNP. For example, an increase in aggregate demand raises the equilibrium price level and, in the short run, real GNP

Short-Run Equilibrium
In the economy, the condition that exists when the quantity demanded of real GNP equals the (short-run) quantity supplied of real GNP. This condition is met where the aggregate demand curve intersects the short-run aggregate supply curve.

155

EXHIBIT 8–6
Short-Run Equilibrium

At P_1, the quantity supplied of real GNP is greater than the quantity demanded. As a result, the price level falls and firms decrease output. At P_2, the quantity demanded of real GNP is greater than the quantity supplied. As a result, the price level rises and firms increase output. Short-run equilibrium occurs at point E, where the quantity demanded of real GNP equals the (short-run) quantity supplied. This is at the intersection of the aggregate demand (AD) curve and the short-run aggregate supply ($SRAS$) curve. (Note: Although real world AD and $SRAS$ curves can, and likely do, have some curvature to them, we have drawn both as straight lines. This does not affect the analysis. Whenever the analysis is not disturbed, we follow suit throughout the text.)

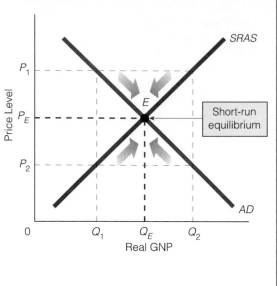

(Exhibit 8–7a). An increase in short-run aggregate supply lowers the equilibrium price level and raises real GNP (Exhibit 8–7b). A decrease in short-run aggregate supply raises the equilibrium price level and lowers real GNP (Exhibit 8–7c).

THE LONG-RUN AGGREGATE SUPPLY CURVE

In this section, we discuss the long-run aggregate supply ($LRAS$) curve and long-run equilibrium. To understand why the $LRAS$ curve looks the way it does, we need to take a short detour through some issues related to unemployment.

Frictional Unemployment

Every day, demand conditions change in some markets, causing qualified individuals with transferable skills to leave some jobs and move to others. To illustrate, suppose there are two computer firms, A and B. For some reason, the demand for firm A's computers falls, and the demand for firm B's computers rises. Consequently, firm A produces fewer computers. With fewer computers being produced, firm A doesn't need as many employees, so it fires some employees. Firm B ends up producing more computers. With more computers being produced, firm B hires additional employees.

The employees fired from firm A have skills that they can transfer to firm B—after all, both firms produce computers. However, it takes time for persons to transfer from one firm to another. During this time, they are said to be *frictionally unemployed;* and the unemployment owing to the natural "frictions" of the economy, caused by changing market conditions and represented by qualified individuals with transferable skills who change jobs, is called **frictional unemployment.** We use the symbol U_F to designate the frictional unemployment rate.

Frictional Unemployment
The unemployment due to the natural "frictions" of the economy, caused by changing market conditions and represented by qualified individuals with transferable skills who change jobs.

EXHIBIT 8–7
Changes in Short-Run Equilibrium

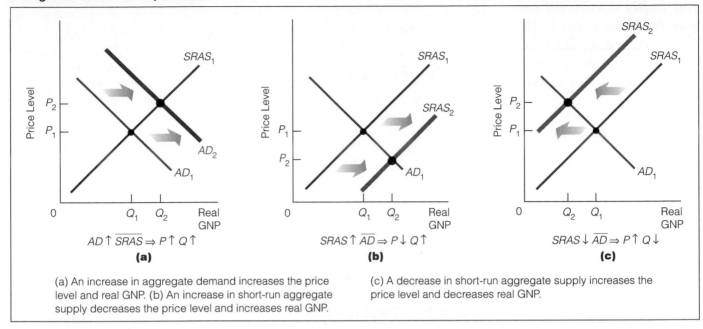

(a) An increase in aggregate demand increases the price level and real GNP. (b) An increase in short-run aggregate supply decreases the price level and increases real GNP.

(c) A decrease in short-run aggregate supply increases the price level and decreases real GNP.

In a dynamic, changing economy like ours, there will always be frictional unemployment. Many economists believe that the basic cause of frictional unemployment is imperfect or incomplete information, which prevents individuals from leaving one job and finding another instantly.

Consider the situation where there are 1,000 job vacancies and 1,000 persons with the qualifications to fill the jobs. Will there be some unemployment? It is likely that there will be, because not every one of the 1,000 job seekers will know where an available job is, nor will all employers give the job to the first applicant who knocks on the door (employers don't know if "better" applicants are around the corner). Matching qualified workers with jobs takes time.

Structural Unemployment

Structural unemployment is unemployment due to structural changes in the economy that eliminate some jobs and create others for which the unemployed are unqualified. Most economists argue that structural unemployment is largely the consequence of automation (labor-saving devices) and long-lasting shifts in demand. The major difference between the frictionally unemployed and the structurally unemployed is that the latter do not have transferable skills. Their choice is between prolonged unemployment and retraining. For example, suppose there is a pool of unemployed automobile workers and a rising demand for computer analysts. If the automobile workers do not currently have the skills necessary to become computer analysts, they are structurally unemployed. We shall use the symbol U_S to designate the structural unemployment rate.

Natural Unemployment

If we add the frictional unemployment rate to the structural unemployment rate we get the **natural unemployment rate** (or natural rate of unemployment). We shall

Structural Unemployment
Unemployment due to structural changes in the economy that eliminate some jobs and create others for which the unemployed are unqualified.

Natural Unemployment Rate
Unemployment caused by frictional and structural factors in the economy. Natural unemployment rate = frictional unemployment rate + structural unemployment rate. For some economists, this is the unemployment rate toward which the economy tends to return; it is the long-run average unemployment rate.

157

Full employment does not imply a zero (0) unemployment rate. Full employment exists when the economy is operating at its natural unemployment rate.

■

Full Employment
The condition that exists when the unemployment rate is equal to the natural unemployment rate.

Cyclical Unemployment Rate
The difference between the unemployment rate and the natural unemployment rate.

use the symbol U_N to designate the natural unemployment rate. Currently most economists' estimate of the natural unemployment rate is between 4.0 and 6.5 percent.

$$U_N = U_F + U_S$$

The (Actual) Unemployment Rate

Neither TV news reporters nor newspaper journalists cite the frictional, structural, or natural unemployment rates. You will not hear a newscaster say, "Today in Washington the frictional unemployment rate was reported to be 3 percent." Instead, she might say, "Today in Washington the unemployment rate was reported to be 6.9 percent." Notice there is no adjective before the word *unemployment*.

Recall that we measure the unemployment rate as follows:

$$\text{Unemployment rate } (U) = \frac{\text{Number of persons unemployed}}{\text{Number of persons in the civilian labor force}^3}$$

Suppose the unemployment rate (U) is computed to be 7 percent. This, then, is the unemployment rate that *actually* exists in the economy. Soon, we examine the (actual) unemployment rate in relation to the natural unemployment rate.

What Is Full Employment?

What do you think of when you hear the term *full employment?* Most people think full employment only exists if the (actual) unemployment rate is zero. But full employment of this type does not exist in a dynamic, changing economy, owing to *frictional* and *structural* changes that continually occur. In fact, it is *natural* for some unemployment to exist—some *natural* unemployment, that is. For this reason, economists do not equate **full employment** with a zero (0) unemployment rate. Instead, for economists, *full employment* exists when the economy is operating at its natural unemployment rate. For example, if the natural unemployment rate is 5 percent, then full employment exists when the unemployment rate (in the economy) is 5 percent.

Question:

In other words, the economy can be operating at full employment and some people will be unemployed. Is this correct?

Answer:

Yes, that is correct.

Cyclical Unemployment

The unemployment rate that exists in the economy is not always at its natural rate. The difference between the existing unemployment rate and the natural unemployment rate is the **cyclical unemployment rate** (U_C).

$$U_C - U - U_N$$

---

[3]The "number of persons in the civilian labor force" excludes persons in the armed forces. If we add members of the armed forces residing in the United States, we would then speak about the "number of persons in the *labor force*."

When the unemployment rate (U) that exists in the economy is greater than the natural unemployment rate (U_N), the cyclical unemployment rate (U_C) is *positive*. For example, if $U = 8$ percent, and $U_N = 6$ percent, then $U_C = 2$ percent.

When the unemployment rate that exists in the economy is less than the natural unemployment rate, the cyclical unemployment rate is *negative*. For example, if $U = 4$ percent and $U_N = 6$ percent, then $U_C = -2$ percent.

Changes in Real GNP and Changes in the Unemployment Rate

There is always some unemployment rate (U) in the economy. And no matter what the unemployment rate is—5 percent, 6 percent, whatever—there is always some real GNP (Q) that is being produced at that unemployment rate.

All other things held constant, we expect a *higher real GNP* level to be associated with a *lower unemployment rate* and a *lower real GNP* level to be associated with a *higher unemployment rate.* In other words, real GNP and the unemployment rate are *inversely related*—as one goes up, the other goes down.

But why? The reason is that more workers are needed to produce more output and fewer workers are needed to produce less output, *ceteris paribus.* Since more workers are needed to produce more output (more real GNP), fewer persons remain unemployed and the unemployment rate drops, *ceteris paribus.* Since fewer workers are needed to produce less output, more persons are unemployed and the unemployment rate rises, *ceteris paribus.*

Ceteris Paribus Makes All the Difference

Here are some real-world data. In 1980, real GNP was $3,187.1 billion and the unemployment rate was 7.1 percent. In 1981, real GNP had risen to $3,248.8 billion and the unemployment rate had risen to 7.6 percent. The data show that real GNP and the unemployment rate are *directly* related, not *inversely* related as we just stated. What is wrong?

Recall that the inverse relationship between real GNP and the unemployment rate is conditioned by *ceteris paribus*—all other things held constant. To illustrate, let's first measure the unemployment rate, which is equal to the number of persons unemployed divided by the number of persons in the civilian labor force. For example, if there are 100,000 unemployed persons and the civilian labor force is 1 million persons, the unemployment rate is 10 percent. Let's say that at this 10 percent unemployment rate, real GNP is $500 billion.

Now suppose real GNP rises to $520 billion. *All other things held constant,* we would expect the unemployment rate to drop. But suppose all other things are not constant. Suppose that as the number of persons unemployed falls to 98,000, the civilian labor force does not stay constant at 1 million persons, but falls to 900,000 persons. When we divide the number of persons unemployed (98,000) by the civilian labor force (900,000) we get an unemployment rate of 10.9 percent. In other words, we witness a *rising* real GNP (from $500 to $520 billion) associated with a *rising* unemployment rate (from 10 to 10.9 percent).

Does this then mean that a *falling* real GNP will be associated with a *falling* unemployment rate? Not necessarily. For example, real GNP in 1981 was $3,248.8 billion and the unemployment rate was 7.6 percent. In 1982, real GNP had *fallen* to $3,166.0 billion and the unemployment rate had *risen* to 9.7 percent.

The *ceteris paribus* condition makes all the difference. So a higher real GNP is associated with a lower unemployment rate, and a lower real GNP is associated with a higher unemployment rate, as long as we add *ceteris paribus.*

The economy is always in one of three states: (1) producing Q_N, (2) producing less than Q_N, or (3) producing more than Q_N.

■

Natural Real GNP
The real GNP that is being produced at the natural unemployment rate.

Suppose the economy is currently operating at its natural unemployment rate (U_N). The real GNP that is produced when the economy is at the natural unemployment rate is called **natural real GNP.** We use the symbol Q_N to represent natural real GNP. At U_N, the economy is producing Q_N.

Three States of the Economy

The economy is always in one of three economic states. Before we outline them, we review four symbols: Q = real GNP being produced in the economy, Q_N = natural real GNP, U = unemployment rate that exists in the economy, and U_N = natural unemployment rate. The three economic environments include:

1. $Q = Q_N$. The real GNP being produced in the economy is equal to the natural real GNP. When this occurs, it follows that the unemployment rate in the economy (U) equals the natural unemployment rate (U_N). When the economy is in this situation, it is said to be in *long-run equilibrium:*

$$Q = Q_N$$
$$\text{and}$$
$$U = U_N$$

Recessionary Gap
The condition where the real GNP the economy is producing is less than the natural real GNP, and the unemployment rate that exists is greater than the natural unemployment rate.

2. $Q < Q_N$. The real GNP being produced in the economy is less than the natural real GNP. When this occurs, it follows that the unemployment rate in the economy is greater than the natural unemployment rate. When the economy is in this situation, it is said to be in a **recessionary gap:**

$$Q < Q_N$$
$$\text{and}$$
$$U > U_N$$

Why is it the case that if $Q < Q_N$, it follows that $U > U_N$? The reason is that fewer workers are needed to produce less output than more output, *ceteris paribus.* Since Q is less than Q_N in our example, fewer workers are needed to produce Q than Q_N; thus, more workers are unemployed at Q than at Q_N.

Inflationary Gap
The condition where the real GNP the economy is producing is greater than the natural real GNP, and the unemployment rate that exists is less than the natural unemployment rate.

3. $Q > Q_N$. The real GNP being produced in the economy is greater than the natural real GNP. When this occurs, it follows that the unemployment rate in the economy is less than the natural unemployment rate. When the economy is in this situation, it is said to be in an **inflationary gap:**

$$Q > Q_N$$
$$\text{and}$$
$$U < U_N$$

Why is it the case that if $Q > Q_N$, it follows that $U < U_N$? The reason is that more workers are needed to produce more output than less output, *ceteris paribus.* Since $Q > Q_N$ in our example, more workers are needed to produced Q than Q_N; thus, fewer workers are unemployed at Q than at Q_N. (See Exhibits 8–8 and columns 1–3 in Exhibit 8–9 for a quick review of these points.)

Let's take a close look at column 4 of Exhibit 8–9, a graphical representation of the three states of the economy. The large black dot in each diagram represents the current position of the economy.

The first diagram shows the economy in long-run equilibrium ($Q = Q_N$). The second diagram shows the economy in a recessionary gap ($Q < Q_N$). The third

EXHIBIT 8–8
The Unemployment Rate and the Natural Unemployment Rate

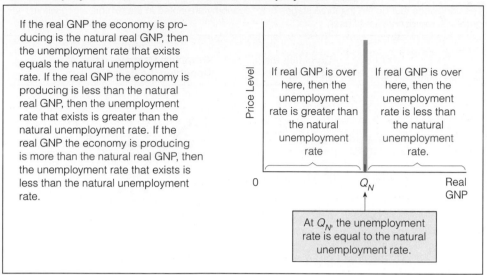

If the real GNP the economy is producing is the natural real GNP, then the unemployment rate that exists equals the natural unemployment rate. If the real GNP the economy is producing is less than the natural real GNP, then the unemployment rate that exists is greater than the natural unemployment rate. If the real GNP the economy is producing is more than the natural real GNP, then the unemployment rate that exists is less than the natural unemployment rate.

If real GNP is over here, then the unemployment rate is greater than the natural unemployment rate

If real GNP is over here, then the unemployment rate is less than the natural unemployment rate.

At Q_N, the unemployment rate is equal to the natural unemployment rate.

diagram shows the economy in an inflationary gap ($Q > Q_N$). We will use similar graphs representing the three states of an economy throughout the text.

Inverse Relationship between Real GNP and the Unemployment Rate

Remember, if the economy is producing a real GNP level greater than the natural real GNP, the unemployment rate is lower than the natural unemployment rate; and if the economy is producing a real GNP level less than the natural real GNP, the unemployment rate is greater than the natural unemployment rate. Exhibit 8–10 will help you keep this in mind.

In Exhibit 8–10, we have added an additional horizontal axis to the standard *AD–AS* diagram. The first horizontal axis is the "real GNP" axis; the second horizontal axis is the "unemployment rate" axis. What is important is to notice that the origin (0) for real GNP is on the *far left,* and the origin for the unemployment rate is on the *far right.* This means that as we move *rightward* along the real GNP axis, real GNP gets larger. And as we move *leftward* along the unemployment rate axis, the unemployment rate gets larger.[4]

The juxtaposition of the origins of the two axes is necessary in order that we maintain the inverse relationship between real GNP and the unemployment rate. That is, as real GNP grows, the unemployment rate falls; and as real GNP declines, the unemployment rate rises.

Now let us look at the three states of the economy in terms of Exhibit 8–10. First, suppose the economy is in long-run equilibrium producing Q_N. If we look directly below Q_N, we notice that the natural unemployment rate (U_N) corresponds to it.

[4]The way the two horizontal axes are drawn (one under the other) may suggest that a 1 percent change in real GNP (Q) will bring about a 1 percent change in the unemployment rate (U). We state emphatically that this need not be the case. Furthermore, according to Okun's law (named after Arthur Okun who was a member of President John Kennedy's Council of Economic Advisers) it *is not* the case. Okun's law holds that for every 3 percent that real GNP rises above (falls below) its natural level, the unemployment rate falls below (rises above) its natural level by 1 percent. That is, a 3 percent increase in real GNP above its natural level will decrease the unemployment rate by 1 percent below its natural level.

EXHIBIT 8–9
Three States of the Economy

The conditions that define the three stages of an economy are noted in the exhibit, along with a graphical representation of each.

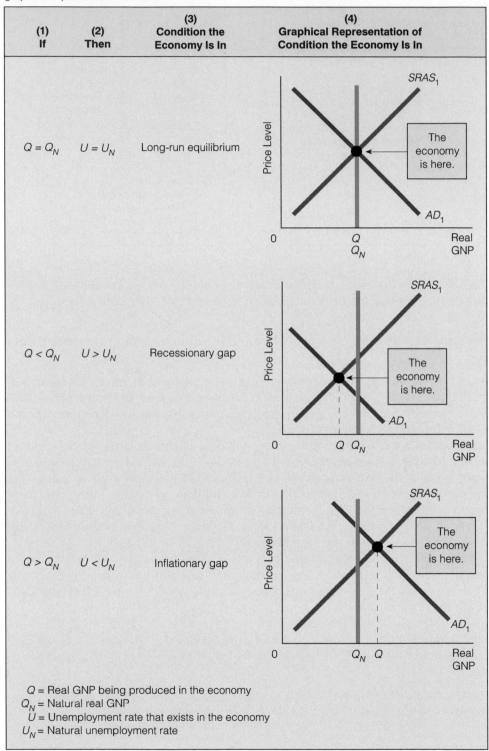

(1) If	(2) Then	(3) Condition the Economy Is In	(4) Graphical Representation of Condition the Economy Is In
$Q = Q_N$	$U = U_N$	Long-run equilibrium	
$Q < Q_N$	$U > U_N$	Recessionary gap	
$Q > Q_N$	$U < U_N$	Inflationary gap	

Q = Real GNP being produced in the economy
Q_N = Natural real GNP
U = Unemployment rate that exists in the economy
U_N = Natural unemployment rate

EXHIBIT 8–10
A Diagram With Two Horizontal Axes

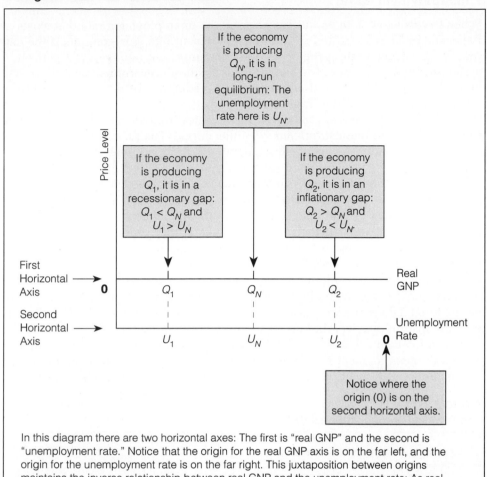

In this diagram there are two horizontal axes: The first is "real GNP" and the second is "unemployment rate." Notice that the origin for the real GNP axis is on the far left, and the origin for the unemployment rate is on the far right. This juxtaposition between origins maintains the inverse relationship between real GNP and the unemployment rate: As real GNP rises, the unemployment rate falls, and as real GNP falls, the unemployment rate rises.

Now suppose the economy produces Q_1. Since Q_1 is less than Q_N, we know the economy is in a recessionary gap. The unemployment rate that corresponds to Q_1 is U_1. Is the natural unemployment rate higher or lower than U_1? A quick look at the second horizontal axis tells us that U_1 lies farther away from the origin than U_N, so U_1 is greater than U_N.

Next, suppose the economy produces Q_2. Since Q_2 is greater than Q_N, we know the economy is in an inflationary gap. The unemployment rate that corresponds to Q_2 is U_2. Is the natural unemployment rate higher or lower than U_2? A quick look at the second horizontal axis tells us that U_2 lies closer to the origin than U_N, so U_2 is less than U_N.

Although, throughout this text, we draw the standard *AD–AS* diagram with one horizontal axis (real GNP) and one vertical axis (price level), the two-horizontal-axes diagram in Exhibit 8–10 may clarify the relationship between different unemployment rates in the different states of the economy.

How Can the Unemployment Rate Be Less Than the Natural Unemployment Rate?

When the economy is in an inflationary gap, the unemployment rate that exists in the economy is less than the natural unemployment rate. For example, if the natural unemployment rate is 6 percent, the unemployment rate is, say, 4 percent.

But how can the economy do better than the natural unemployment rate, which, after all, is equated with full employment? To explain, we need to make use of two production possibilities frontiers.

In Exhibit 8–11, the two production possibilities frontiers are the *physical PPF* (purple curve) and the *institutional PPF* (blue curve). The physical PPF illustrates different combinations of goods the economy can produce given the physical constraints of (1) finite resources and (2) the current state of technology. The institutional PPF illustrates different combinations of goods the economy can produce given the physical constraints of (1) finite resources, (2) the current state of technology, and (3) any institutional constraints. Broadly defined, an institutional constraint is anything that prevents economic agents from producing the maximum real GNP physically possible. For example, the minimum wage law, which is an institutional constraint, specifies that workers must be paid a wage rate at least equal to the legislated minimum wage. One effect of this is that those unskilled persons whose value to employers falls below the legislated minimum wage will not be hired. Fewer workers means less output produced, *ceteris paribus.* (This is why the institutional *PPF* lies closer to the origin than the physical *PPF.)*

Within the confines of society's physical *and* institutional constraints, there is a natural unemployment rate. This state of affairs is represented by any point on the institutional *PPF.* In the exhibit, points *A, B,* and *C* are all such points.

EXHIBIT 8–11
The Physical and Institutional PPFs

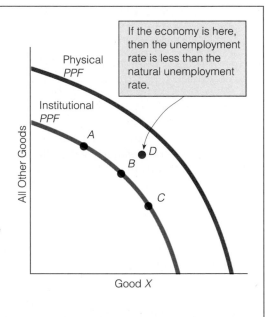

A society has both a physical *PPF* and an institutional *PPF.* The physical *PPF* illustrates different combinations of goods the economy can produce given the physical constraints of 1) finite resources and 2) the current state of technology. The institutional *PPF* illustrates different combinations of goods the economy can produce given the physical constraints of 1) finite resources, 2) the current state of technology, and 3) any institutional constraints. The economy is at the natural unemployment rate if it is located on its institutional *PPF,* such as at points *A, B,* or *C.* An economy can never operate beyond its physical PPF, but it is possible for it to operate beyond its institutional *PPF,* since institutional constraints are not always equally effective. If the economy does operate beyond its institutional *PPF,* such as at point *D,* then the unemployment rate that exists in the economy is lower than the natural unemployment rate.

If the economy is here, then the unemployment rate is less than the natural unemployment rate.

Physical PPF

Institutional PPF

All Other Goods

Good X

A

B

C

D

An economy can never operate beyond its physical *PPF,* but it is possible for it to operate beyond its institutional *PPF.* For example, suppose inflation reduces the purchasing power of the minimum wage, thus reducing or eliminating the constraining properties of the minimum wage law on the unskilled labor market.[5] This would make one of society's institutional constraints ineffective, allowing the economy to temporarily move beyond the institutional constraint.

Logic dictates that if the economy is operating at the natural unemployment rate when it is located *on* its institutional PPF, then it must be operating at an unemployment rate lower than the natural rate when it is located *beyond* its institutional PPF (but below its physical PPF). Because society's institutional constraints are not always equally effective, it is possible for an economy to be operating at an unemployment rate below the natural rate.

RECESSIONARY AND INFLATIONARY GAPS

∎

In this section, we first discuss what happens when the economy is in a recessionary gap, then what happens when the economy is in an inflationary gap.

What Happens If the Economy Is in a Recessionary Gap?

Some economists contend that if the economy is in a recessionary gap, it can, under its own forces, eliminate that gap smoothly and quickly. In other words, the economy can heal itself. We explain the process.

In Exhibit 8–12a, the quantity supplied of real GNP in the short run (Q_1) is equal to the quantity demanded of real GNP (Q_1). The economy is in short-run equilibrium at point *E.* And since the real GNP the economy produces (Q_1) is *less than* natural real GNP (Q_N), the economy is in a recessionary gap. (Yes, it is possible for the economy to be in a recessionary gap *and* in short-run equilibrium, too.)

In a recessionary gap, the unemployment rate is *greater than* the natural unemployment rate. Consequently, as old wage bargains expire, firms end up paying workers lower wage rates. This is because unemployment is relatively high: The number of job seekers is high compared with the number of jobs to be filled.[6]

Exhibit 8–12b shows what happens. As wage rates fall (costs fall), the *SRAS* curve shifts rightward from $SRAS_1$ ultimately to $SRAS_2$. As a result of the increase in short-run aggregate supply, the price level falls. As the price level falls, the quantity demanded of real GNP rises owing to the real balance, interest rate, and international trade effects. As we learned earlier, when the price level falls, we move from one point on the aggregate demand curve to another point on the same curve. In Exhibit 8–12b, this is a movement down the AD_1 curve from point *E* to point *E'.*

As long as the economy's real GNP is less than Q_N, the price level will continue to fall.

Ultimately, the economy moves to long-run equilibrium at point *E',* corresponding to P_2 and Q_N.

---

[5]Inflation reduces the real (inflation-adjusted) minimum wage. If the minimum wage rate is $5 and the price level is 1, the real minimum wage rate is $5 (or $5 divided by the price level, 1). If the price level rises to 2, then the real minimum wage rate falls to $2.50 (which is $5 divided by the price level, 2). The lower the real minimum wage, the greater the number of unskilled workers that employers will hire, because the demand curve for unskilled labor is downward sloping.

[6]In this discussion of the economy eliminating a recessionary gap, we have emphasized wages adjusting. Besides wages, other input prices may adjust as well.

EXHIBIT 8-12
A Recessionary Gap and Its Automatic Removal

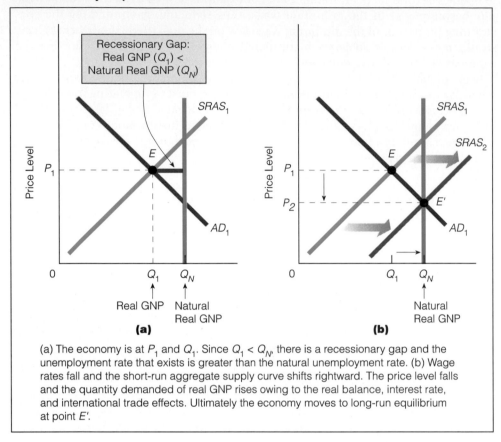

(a) The economy is at P_1 and Q_1. Since $Q_1 < Q_N$, there is a recessionary gap and the unemployment rate that exists is greater than the natural unemployment rate. (b) Wage rates fall and the short-run aggregate supply curve shifts rightward. The price level falls and the quantity demanded of real GNP rises owing to the real balance, interest rate, and international trade effects. Ultimately the economy moves to long-run equilibrium at point E'.

What Happens If the Economy Is in an Inflationary Gap?

Some economists contend that if the economy is in an inflationary gap, it can, under its own forces, eliminate that gap smoothly and quickly. In other words, the economy can heal itself. We explain the process.

In Exhibit 8–13a, the quantity supplied of real GNP in the short run (Q_1) is equal to the quantity demanded of real GNP (Q_1). The economy is in short-run equilibrium at point E. And since the real GNP the economy produces (Q_1) is *greater than* natural real GNP (Q_N), the economy is in an inflationary gap.

In an inflationary gap, the unemployment rate is *less than* the natural unemployment rate. Consequently, as old wage bargains expire, firms end up paying workers higher wage rates. This is because unemployment is relatively low: The number of job seekers is low compared with the number of jobs to be filled.[7]

Exhibit 8–13b shows what happens. As wages rates rise (costs rise), the SRAS curve shifts leftward from $SRAS_1$ ultimately to $SRAS_2$. As a result of the decrease in short-run aggregate supply, the price level rises. As the price level rises, the quantity demanded of real GNP falls owing to the real balance, interest rate, and international trade effects. As we learned earlier, when the price level rises, we

[7]In this discussion of the economy eliminating an inflationary gap, we have emphasized wages adjusting. Besides wages, other input prices may adjust as well.

EXHIBIT 8–13
An Inflationary Gap and Its Automatic Removal

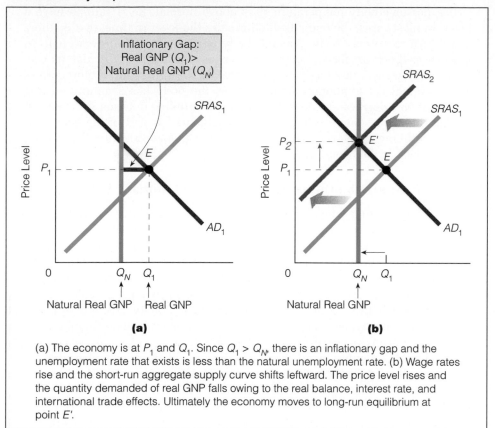

(a)

(b)

(a) The economy is at P_1 and Q_1. Since $Q_1 > Q_N$, there is an inflationary gap and the unemployment rate that exists is less than the natural unemployment rate. (b) Wage rates rise and the short-run aggregate supply curve shifts leftward. The price level rises and the quantity demanded of real GNP falls owing to the real balance, interest rate, and international trade effects. Ultimately the economy moves to long-run equilibrium at point E'.

move from one point on the aggregate demand curve to another point on the same curve. In Exhibit 8–13b, this is a movement up the AD_1 curve from point E to point E'.

As long as the economy's real GNP is greater than Q_N, the price level will continue to rise.

Ultimately the economy moves to long-run equilibrium at point E', corresponding to P_2 and Q_N.

Economists, like other scientists, are often interested in knowing whether there is a natural resting place for the phenomena they are studying. For example, think of a natural resting place for a ball thrown high into the air. The natural resting place for it is the ground. Gravity pulls the ball downward. Think of a natural resting place for a competitive market. It is where the quantity demanded of a good equals the quantity supplied of the good. Markets are "at rest" when they are in equilibrium.

Macroeconomists want to know if there is a natural resting place for the economy. Some economists think there is. They think the natural resting place for the economy is where natural real GNP is being produced and the natural unemployment rate exists. Economists who believe that the economy can eliminate both recessionary and inflationary gaps smoothly and quickly

THINKING LIKE
AN ECONOMIST

CHAPTER 8
THE AGGREGATE DEMAND—
AGGREGATE SUPPLY FRAMEWORK
■

167

by itself, and thus return to its natural state, may use the analogy of a person's normal body temperature, which is 98.6 degrees.

If a person's body temperature rises above normal, he is said to have a fever. In most cases, the body itself eliminates the fever in time; that is, there is a return to normal. If the person's body temperature is below normal, in most cases this is an aberration and in time his temperature will edge its way back up to normal. In short, a temperature below normal and a temperature above normal are temporary states. Just as the body has a natural resting place—at 98.6 degrees—so does the economy. Thinking in terms of a "natural resting place," an "equilibrium," or a "benchmark" is part of the economic way of thinking. However, not all economists agree as to where the natural resting place of the economy is.

A Different Analysis of Recessionary and Inflationary Gaps

It may not be true that when either a recessionary or an inflationary gap exists, the economy will move *smoothly and quickly* to the natural real GNP level. Some economists argue that (1) there is no guarantee that the economy will in all cases automatically work itself out of a recessionary or inflationary gap; and (2) even in those instances when the economy does automatically work toward long-run equilibrium, it may take too long for the economy to reach its natural real GNP level.

Another point is this. In our discussion of a recessionary gap, we argued that because the unemployment rate is greater than the natural unemployment, when old wage bargains expire, employers will be able to pay workers lower wage rates because unemployment is relatively high. Because of the lower wage rates, the *SRAS* curve shifts rightward—thus moving the economy towards its natural real GNP level.

Now some economists would say that *wages are not likely to fall when the unemployment rate is greater than the natural unemployment rate.* They argue that wage rates are often sticky or inflexible in the downward direction. If this is correct, consider how it changes our analysis. If the economy is in a recessionary gap, and wage rates are inflexible in the downward direction, then even though the unemployment rate is greater than the natural unemployment rate, wage rates will not fall. But if wage rates do not fall, the *SRAS* curve will not shift rightward. And if the *SRAS* curve does not shift rightward, the economy will not automatically move toward its natural real GNP level. We conclude, then, that the economy may not always be able to automatically eliminate a recessionary gap by itself. Instead, the economy may get *stuck* in a recessionary gap.

These issues are explored in greater detail in the forthcoming theory chapters.

The Long-Run Aggregate Supply Curve

The possibility of automatic adjustments in the economy gives rise to the concept of the **long-run aggregate supply (*LRAS*) curve.** The *LRAS* curve shows the real GNP the economy is prepared to supply at different price levels, assuming wage rates and all other input prices have fully adjusted to eliminate a recessionary or inflationary gap.

As we described earlier, if wage rates and other prices are flexible, there is a tendency for an economy in either a recessionary or inflationary gap to settle down eventually at its natural real GNP level. It follows that the vertical (green) line locked in on natural real GNP, Q_N, in Exhibits 8–12 and 8–13 is the *LRAS* curve. It also follows that **long-run equilibrium** is at the intersection of the *AD* curve and

Long-Run Aggregate Supply Curve
The long-run aggregate supply curve shows the real GNP the economy is prepared to supply at different price levels, assuming wage rates and all other input prices have fully adjusted to eliminate a recessionary or inflationary gap.

Long-Run Equilibrium
The condition that exists in the economy when the real GNP being produced equals the natural real GNP and the unemployment rate that exists equals the natural unemployment rate. In long-run equilibrium, the quantity demanded of real GNP equals the (long-run) quantity supplied of real GNP. This condition is met at the intersection of the aggregate demand curve and the long-run aggregate supply curve.

168

How Does Foreign Buying of U.S. Goods Affect the U.S. Price Level, Real GNP, and Unemployment Rate?

"At a given price level, anything that increases any of the four components of total spending (*C, I, G,* or net exports—$X-M$), increases aggregate demand and shifts the *AD* curve to the right. Also, *at a given price level,* anything that decreases any of the four components of total spending decreases aggregate demand and shifts the *AD* curve to the left."

Also, "anything that shifts the *AD* curve also changes the price level and real GNP in the short run. For example, if the *AD* curve shifts rightward, the price level and real GNP rise."

Let us put these two pieces of knowledge together in two examples to show how the residents of foreign nations can affect the U.S. real GNP, price level, and unemployment rate in the short run.

Example 1: Suppose foreigners begin to buy more U.S. goods, so exports (*X*) increase, *ceteris paribus.*[8]

[8]In this text, we assume that if the physical quantity of U.S. goods purchased by foreigners rises (falls) that exports (*X*) rise (fall). Remember, exports do not refer to the physical goods themselves, but to the total foreign spending on domestic goods. Exports is a dollar amount.

This causes U.S. net exports ($X-M$) to increase. And if U.S. net exports increase, the *AD* curve shifts rightward. Essentially, people (consisting of Americans and foreigners, too) are collectively buying more U.S. real GNP at a given price level.

As a result of a rightward shift in the *AD* curve, the price level and real GNP in the United States rise in the short run. Finally, if real GNP rises, the U.S. unemployment rate falls (Exhibit 8–14).

Example 2: Suppose foreigners begin to buy fewer U.S. goods, so exports (*X*) decrease, *ceteris paribus.*

EXHIBIT 8–14
A Foreign–U.S. Economic Link

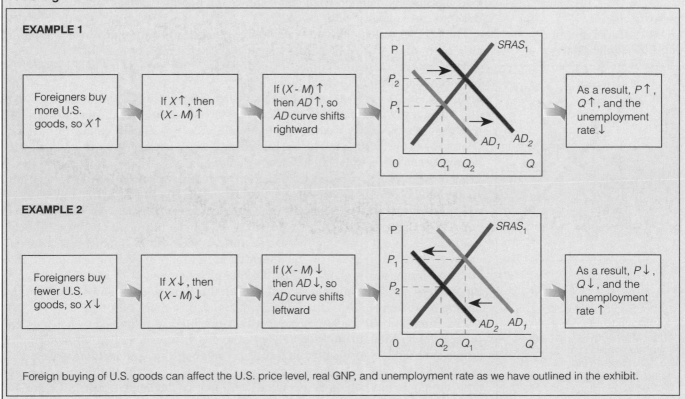

Foreign buying of U.S. goods can affect the U.S. price level, real GNP, and unemployment rate as we have outlined in the exhibit.

This causes U.S. net exports $(X-M)$ to decrease. And if U.S. net exports decrease, the *AD* curve shifts leftward. As a result, the price level and real GNP in the United States fall in the short run. Finally, if real GNP falls, the U.S. unemployment rate rises (Exhibit 8–14).

So far, then, we know this: Anything that affects foreign buying of U.S. goods affects (1) U.S. net exports, and thus (2) the *AD* curve in the United States, and consequently (3) the price level, real GNP, and unemployment rate in the United States.

In other words, there is an economic link between what happens in foreign nations and what happens in the United States.

the *LRAS* curve. Recall that short-run equilibrium is at the intersection of the *AD* curve and the *SRAS* curve. Both the long-run and short-run equilibrium positions, as well as the *LRAS* curve, are represented in Exhibit 8–15. (In Exhibit 8–15, does a recessionary or inflationary gap exist in the short run? The answer is an inflationary gap.)

CHAPTER SUMMARY

Aggregate Demand

EXHIBIT 8–15
The LRAS Curve and Short- and Long-Run Equilibrium

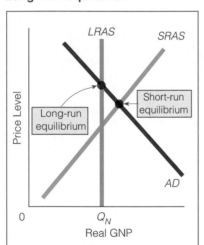

Short-run equilibrium exists at the point where the *AD* curve and the *SRAS* curve intersect. Long-run equilibrium exists at the point where the *AD* curve and the *LRAS* curve intersect. The *LRAS* curve is a vertical line at natural real GNP, Q_N.

■ The aggregate demand (*AD*) curve shows the quantity demanded of real GNP at different price levels, *ceteris paribus*.
■ The aggregate demand curve slopes downward, indicating an inverse relationship between the price level and the quantity demanded of real GNP.
■ The aggregate demand curve slopes downward because of the real balance, interest rate, and international trade effects.
■ The real balance effect states that the inverse relationship between the price level and the quantity demanded of real GNP is established through changes in the value of a person's monetary wealth or money holdings. Specifically, a fall in the price level causes purchasing power to rise, or increases a person's monetary wealth. As people become wealthier, the quantity demanded of real GNP rises. A rise in the price level causes purchasing power to fall, or reduces a person's monetary wealth. As people become less wealthy, the quantity demanded of real GNP falls.
■ The interest rate effect states that the inverse relationship between the price level and the quantity demanded of real GNP is established through changes in household and business spending that is sensitive to changes in interest rates. Specifically, as the interest rate rises, businesses and households borrow less and so they end up buying fewer goods. Thus, the quantity demanded of real GNP falls. As the interest rate falls, businesses and households borrow more and so they end up buying more goods. Thus, the quantity demanded of real GNP rises.
■ The international trade effect states that the inverse relationship between the price level and the quantity demanded of real GNP is established through foreign sector spending. Specifically, as the price level in the United States rises, U.S. goods become relatively more expensive than foreign goods and both Americans and foreigners buy fewer U.S. goods. The quantity demanded of (U.S.) real GNP falls. As the price level in the United States falls, U.S. goods become relatively

less expensive than foreign goods and both Americans and foreigners buy more U.S. goods. The quantity demanded of (U.S.) real GNP rises.

■ At a give price level, anything that increases any of the four components of total spending (consumption, investment, government expenditures, or net exports) increases aggregate demand and shifts the *AD* curve to the right. At a given price level, anything that decreases any of the four components of total spending decreases aggregate demand and shifts the *AD* curve to the left.

Short-Run Aggregate Supply

■ The short-run aggregate supply (*SRAS*) curve shows the real GNP that producers will offer for sale at different price levels, *ceteris paribus.*

■ The *SRAS* curve is upward sloping, indicating a direct relationship between the price level and the quantity supplied of real GNP.

■ A decrease in wage rates, a decrease in the price of nonlabor inputs, an increase in productivity, and a beneficial supply shock all shift the *SRAS* curve to the right. An increase in wage rates, an increase in the price of nonlabor inputs, a decrease in productivity, and an adverse supply shock all shift the *SRAS* curve to the left.

Short-Run Analysis in the *AD–AS* Framework

■ Diagrammatically, short-run equilibrium exists at the intersection of the *AD* and *SRAS* curves. A shift in either or both of these curves can change the price level and real GNP.

Natural Unemployment Rate and Natural Real GNP

■ The natural unemployment rate equals the frictional unemployment rate plus the structural unemployment rate.

■ Natural real GNP is the level of real GNP that is produced when the economy is operating at the natural unemployment rate.

Three Economic States

■ The economy is always in one of three economic states: (1) long-run equilibrium, (2) a recessionary gap, or (3) an inflationary gap.

■ In long-run equilibrium, the real GNP that the economy is producing is equal to the natural real GNP. Also, the unemployment rate that exists in the economy is equal to the natural unemployment rate.

■ In a recessionary gap, the real GNP that the economy is producing is less than the natural real GNP. Also, the unemployment rate that exists in the economy is greater than the natural unemployment rate.

■ In an inflationary gap, the real GNP that the economy is producing is greater than the natural real GNP. Also, the unemployment rate that exists in the economy is less than the natural unemployment rate.

One View of the Economy

■ Some economists contend that the economy can eliminate both recessionary and inflationary gaps smoothly and quickly by itself. They say the economy works this way: First, assume the economy is in a recessionary gap. The unemployment rate is greater than the natural unemployment rate. As old wage bargains expire, wage rates fall. This shifts the *SRAS* curve to the right and brings down the price level. As the price level drops, the quantity demanded of real GNP rises. Ultimately, the economy moves to long-run equilibrium where the real GNP the economy produces equals the natural real GNP.

■ Now assume the economy is in an inflationary gap. The unemployment rate is less than the natural unemployment rate. As old wage bargains expire, wage rates rise. This shifts the *SRAS* curve to the left and increases the price level. As the price level rises, the quantity demanded of real GNP falls. Ultimately, the economy moves to long-run equilibrium where the real GNP the economy produces equals the natural real GNP.

Another View of the Economy

■ Some economists argue that (1) there is no guarantee that the economy will in all cases automatically work itself out of a recessionary or inflationary gap; and (2) even in those instances when the economy does automatically work toward long-run equilibrium, it may take too long for the economy to reach its natural real GNP level.

■ Some economists argue that when the economy is in a recessionary gap, and the unemployment rate is greater than the natural rate, wage rates may be inflexible downward and thus not adjust to eliminate the recessionary gap. According to these economists, the economy may get stuck in a recessionary gap.

Long-Run Analysis in the *AD–AS* Framework

■ The long-run aggregate supply (*LRAS*) curve shows the real GNP the economy is prepared to supply at different price levels, assuming wage rates and other input prices have fully adjusted to eliminate a recessionary or inflationary gap.

■ Diagrammatically, long-run equilibrium is at the intersection of the *AD* and *LRAS* curves.

Key Terms and Concepts

Aggregate Demand (AD) Curve	Short-Run Equilibrium	Cyclical Unemployment Rate
Real Balance Effect	Frictional Unemployment	Natural Real GNP
Monetary Wealth	Structural Unemployment	Recessionary Gap
Purchasing Power		Inflationary Gap
Interest Rate Effect	Natural Unemployment Rate	Long-Run Equilibrium
International Trade Effect	Full Employment	Long-Run Aggregate Supply (LRAS) Curve
Short-Run Aggregate Supply (SRAS) Curve		

1. Is aggregate demand a specific dollar amount? For example, is it correct to say that aggregate demand is, say, $1 trillion this year?

2. In the short run, what is the impact on the price level and real GNP of each of the following:

a. an increase in consumption brought about by something other than a change in the price level

b. a decrease in exports brought about by something other than a change in the price level

c. an increase in imports brought about by something other than a change in the price level

d. an increase in investment brought about by something other than a change in the price level

e. a fall in wage rates

f. an adverse supply shock

g. a decline in productivity

h. a beneficial supply shock

i. a fall in nonlabor input prices

j. a rise in nonlabor input prices

3. What does it mean to say that the economy can get "stuck" in a recessionary gap?

4. Why might the natural rate of unemployment be 5 percent in one country and 2 percent in another?

5. Within the *AD–AS* framework, note at least three areas where debates among economists may arise.

6. If real GNP is less than natural real GNP, it follows that the unemployment rate that exists in the economy is greater than the natural rate of unemployment. Explain why.

7. One of the assumptions in an economic theory we discuss in Chapter 14 (the strict quantity theory of money) is that real GNP is constant in the short run. Draw the short-run aggregate supply curve that corresponds to this assumption.

8. Why do you think some positive natural rate of unemployment is always likely to exist?

9. What might government do to shift the long-run aggregate supply curve leftward? What might it do to shift it rightward?

10. If the economy is operating at a point on its short-run aggregate supply curve that is below natural real GNP, where is the economy in terms of its production possibilities frontier? Explain your answer. (You may need to review the material on the production possibilities frontier in Chapter 2).

11. Diagrammatically represent an economy in a recessionary gap. Next, explain the process of how the economy eliminates the gap by itself.

12. Diagrammatically represent an economy in an inflationary gap. Next, explain the process of how the economy eliminates the gap by itself.

13. Are the real balance, interest rate, and international trade effects relevant to a change in quantity demanded of real GNP or to a change in aggregate demand? Explain your answer.

14. What effect do the economic actions of the Japanese, English, Germans, and French (to name the residents of a few foreign nations) have on the U.S. real GNP?

15. Can an economy be in long-run equilibrium and in an inflationary gap, too? Can an economy be in short-run equilibrium and in an inflationary gap, too? Explain your answers.

16. Consider the following data:

Price Level	Quantity Demanded of Real GNP	Quantity Supplied of Real GNP in the Short Run	Quantity Supplied of Real GNP in the Long Run
		(billions of 1982 dollars)	
100	4,800	3,700	4,400
105	4,600	3,900	4,400
110	4,500	4,200	4,400

a. At a price level of 110, is the economy in short-run equilibrium? Explain your answer.

b. At a price level of 105, is the economy in long-run equilibrium? Explain your answer.

c. Will the price level in long-run equilibrium be greater than, less than, or equal to 110? Explain your answer.

PART

III

MACROECONOMIC THEORY AND FISCAL POLICY

KEYNESIAN THEORY: EMPHASIS ON UNEMPLOYMENT

WHAT THIS CHAPTER IS ABOUT

In the course of studying macroeconomics, you will learn about four theories, or schools of thought. In this chapter we first discuss classical theory and then Keynesian theory, which was born out of a major economic event—the Great Depression.

A Refresher on Theory and a Note on Labels

The role of theory in economics can be summarized in the following three statements.

1. The purpose of a theory is to better understand the world. It is built on the critical variables that (the theorist believes) explain and predict the phenomenon under consideration.
2. The process of focusing on a limited number of variables to explain or predict an event is called abstraction.
3. A theory is better judged by its predictions than by its assumptions.

No doubt there will be times in your reading when you will say, "This theory is too abstract," or "This theory doesn't take enough into consideration," or "I don't understand why the theory assumes what it does." We urge you to resist the natural temptation to judge theories without a fair hearing. Remember, *all* theories are abstract and *all* theories make assumptions, and it is better to judge a theory by how well it predicts than by its assumptions, level of abstraction, or anything else.

Theories have names, or labels. Four macroeconomic theories or schools of thought are called *classical, Keynesian, monetarist,* and *new classical.* Once you know the names, there is the temptation to ask, Which theory is correct? You may even think, Why can't economists just tell us which theory is correct and ignore all the rest? Wouldn't this save time? Wouldn't it be less confusing?

Well, maybe, except that economists do not agree about which theory is correct. Also, *the objective at hand is to teach economics—not a particular view of the economy and not just one theory.* If economics seems a little messier than mathematics, engineering, or biology, that is not necessarily bad, and it doesn't necessarily mean that economics is any less of a science. It may simply suggest that the answers to economic questions are not as forthcoming as they are in some other disciplines.

There is plenty of time for you to decide which theory is correct, or which theory is wrong, or which theory is right or wrong under certain conditions. For now, we simply want to learn what each theory says.

Also, as you read, keep in mind that the economic labels *classical, Keynesian, monetarist,* and *new classical* are sometimes used differently from, say, religious or ethnic labels. For example, when a person says he is Asian, he not only tells you what he is, but what he is not (he is not African-American, Hispanic, and so on). Or when someone calls herself a Buddhist, she is not only telling you what she is, but she is also telling you what she is not. This kind of label is exclusive: Being one thing excludes a person from being something else.

Economic labels are not as rigid. It is possible for an economist to describe himself as "largely a monetarist," but "with Keynesian tendencies *at times,* or *under certain conditions.*" We offer a medical analogy.

Dr. Diane Newcombe is a physician. She believes that about 90 percent of the time the body has sufficient healing powers to cure itself. But 10 percent of the time, it does not. For example, it can cure a cold, but probably not some types of cancer. If someone were to label Dr. Newcombe as a believer in the healing properties of the body, this is largely true, but still it may be slightly misleading since she is not a believer in the healing properties of the body under all conditions or at all times.

Similarly, when we use the labels *classical, Keynesian, monetarist,* and *new classical,* we are talking about the essence of the particular macroeconomic theory.

We remind ourselves that economists and others may choose a small portion from one and much from another.

Also, each of the four theories is changing in small, but occasionally far-reaching, ways. For example, Keynesian theory today has more of a micro foundation, or incentive-based aspect to it, than it did 15 years ago.

Finally, as you read about the different macroeconomic theories, try to place these ideas in the three macroeconomic categories: the P–Q category, the inherently stable–inherently unstable category, and the effective–ineffective category. We are ready to show you how. We start with classical theory.

THE CLASSICAL THEORY

In this section, we present the classical theory as it relates to unemployment and production. This discussion is important for three reasons.

First, it gives us knowledge of an important school of economics, the classical school. This school includes among its members such famous economists of the past as Adam Smith, Jean Baptiste Say, Jeremy Bentham, David Ricardo, and John Stuart Mill.

Second, classical theory provides the backdrop for the development of Keynesian theory.

Third, classical theory makes up a large part of the intellectual heritage of monetarism and the new classical school of economics, which we discuss in later chapters. Neither development can be fully understood without knowing something about the classical theory on which they are based.

Classical Theory On Production, Unemployment, and Demand and Supply in the Macroeconomy

Here is what classical theory has to say on some topics.

1. On Production. The economy is always close to or on its production possibilities frontier. This means that the economy is always close to or at the point of producing natural real GNP (Q_N) or the full-employment real GNP (Q_F).[1] Another way to say this is that the economy is always on or near its *LRAS* curve.

2. On Unemployment. The economy is always close to or at full employment, or the natural unemployment rate. This follows from (1), since if the economy is producing natural real GNP, it does so at the natural unemployment rate.

3. On Demand and Supply in the Macroeconomy. Whatever real GNP is produced and supplied will be demanded.

Overall, the classical economists believed that the economy is a self-adjusting mechanism that stabilizes itself at full-employment output, or natural real GNP. This position is based on (1) Say's law, (2) interest rate flexibility, and (3) wage–price flexibility.

Say's Law

The nineteenth-century French economist Jean Baptiste Say is credited with expounding the principle that has come to be known as **Say's law:** Supply creates its own demand. Say's basic idea is most easily understood in terms of a barter

Say's Law
Supply creates its own demand. Production creates demand sufficient to purchase all goods produced.

[1]Recall from Chapter 8 that if the economy is operating on its (institutional) production possibilities frontier (PPF) it is at the natural unemployment rate producing natural real GNP.

179

economy. Consider a person baking bread to trade; he is a supplier of bread. Why does he do what he does? According to Say, the baker works at his trade because he plans to demand other goods. As he is baking his bread, the baker is thinking of the goods and services he will obtain in exchange for it. Thus, his act of supplying bread is linked to his demand for other goods. Supply creates its own demand.

If the supplying of some goods is simultaneously the demanding of other goods, then Say's law implies that there cannot be either (1) a general overproduction of goods (where total supply in the economy is greater than total demand) or (2) a general underproduction of goods (where total demand is greater than total supply).

Now suppose the baker is baking bread in a money economy. Does Say's law hold? Over a period of time, the baker earns an income as a result of his supplying bread. But what does he do with his income? For one thing, he buys goods and services. However, his demand for goods and services does not necessarily match the income that he generates through his actions as a supplier of bread. It is possible that the baker spends less than his full income because he engages in saving. Noting this, we might think that Say's law does not hold in a money economy since the act of supplying goods and services, and thus earning income, need not create an equal amount of demand. The classical economists disagreed. They argued that even in a money economy, where individuals sometimes spend less than their full incomes, Say's law still holds. Their argument was partly based on the assumption of interest rate flexibility.

Interest Rate Flexibility

As we noted in Chapter 6, saving is a leakage and investment is an injection. For Say's law to hold in a money economy, funds saved (leaked) must give rise to an equal amount of funds invested (injected); that is, what leaves the spending stream through one door must enter through another door. If not, then leakages may be greater than injections, and thus some of the income earned from supplying goods may not be used to demand goods (goodbye Say's law). As a result, there will be an overproduction of goods.

The classical economists argued that saving is matched by an equal amount of investment because of interest rate flexibility in the credit market. To understand their argument, take a look at Exhibit 9–1, where I represents investment and S represents saving. First, notice that I_1 is downward sloping, indicating an inverse relationship between the amount of funds firms invest and the interest rate (i). The reason for this is straightforward. The interest rate is the cost of borrowing funds, so therefore the higher the interest rate, the fewer funds firms borrow and invest; and the lower the interest rate, the more funds firms borrow and invest.

Notice that S_1 is upward sloping, indicating a direct relationship between the amount of funds households save and the interest rate. The reason is that the higher the interest rate, the higher the reward for saving (or the higher the opportunity cost of consuming), and therefore the fewer funds will be consumed and the more funds will be saved. Market-equilibrating forces move the credit market to interest rate i_1 and equilibrium point E_1, where the number of dollars households save ($100,000) equals the number of dollars firms invest ($100,000).

Suppose now that saving increases at each interest rate. We represent this by a rightward shift in our saving curve from S_1 to S_2. The classical economists believed that an increase in saving (leakages) will put downward pressure on the interest rate, moving it to i_2, thereby increasing the number of dollars firms invest. Ulti-

EXHIBIT 9–1
The Classical View of the Credit Market

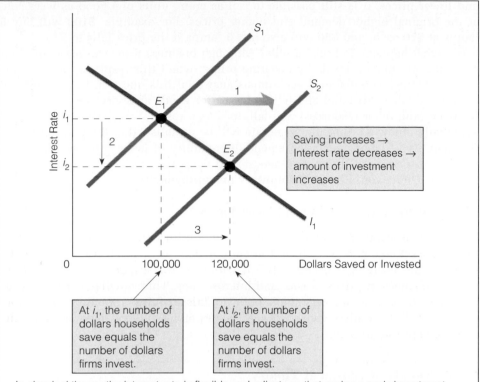

At i_1, the number of dollars households save equals the number of dollars firms invest.

At i_2, the number of dollars households save equals the number of dollars firms invest.

In classical theory, the interest rate is flexible and adjusts so that saving equals investment. Thus, if saving increases and the saving curve shifts rightward from S_1 to S_2 (arrow 1), the increase in saving eventually puts pressure on the interest rate and moves it downward from i_1 to i_2 (arrow 2). A new equilibrium is established at E_2 (arrow 3), where once again the amount households save equals the amount firms invest.

mately, the number of dollars households save ($120,000) will once again equal the number of dollars firms invest ($120,000). Interest rate flexibility ensures that saving equals investment, so that leakages equal injections. (What goes out one door comes in the other door.) In short, changes in the interest rate uphold Say's law in a money economy where there is saving.

Wage–Price Flexibility

According to the classical economists, *even if* interest rate adjustments do not equate saving and investment in a reasonable time, other prices in other markets will adjust in a way that ensures there will be no general overproduction of goods—at least not for long.

Specifically, classical economists assumed that *prices in goods and services markets and prices in labor markets (wages) will adjust in accordance with the laws of supply and demand.* For example, suppose households temporarily save more than firms are willing to invest and, consequently, total spending in the economy decreases. According to classical theory, real GNP will not fall and the unemployment rate will not rise *as long as* the prices of goods *quickly adjusted downward,* which classical economists believed would occur.

Classical economists believed that as demand falls, competing producers of goods will lower their prices to rid themselves of surpluses. With lower demand and lower prices, it is still possible to sell as many units of a good as were sold at the original higher demand and higher prices. For example, $100 will buy 5 lamps at $20 each, and $50 will also buy 5 lamps if the price falls to $10.

But what happens to firms' profits? Although business firms can maintain their sales and production levels by lowering prices, won't this result in lower profits or even losses? The classical economists answered this question by arguing that because of falling demand and falling prices for goods and services, the demand for labor (and other resources) will fall, too. As a result, wage rates will fall, and eventually a new equilibrium wage rate will be established at the point at which the quantity of labor demanded equals the quantity of labor supplied. All those who want to work at the market-determined wage rate will have an opportunity to do so: There would be no **involuntary unemployment.**

Involuntary Unemployment
A condition where people who want to work at the market-determined wage rate cannot find work at this wage rate.

Classical Economic Policy: Laissez-Faire

The classical economists believed in the self-equilibrating, stabilizing properties of the market economy. For them, full-employment, or natural, real GNP was the norm. If the economy became "ill," it certainly was capable of healing itself through changes in prices, wages, and interest rates. This view led classical economists to advocate a macroeconomic policy of **laissez-faire,** or noninterference. As the classical economists viewed things, government did not have an economic management role to play.

Laissez-faire
A public policy of not interfering with market activities.

Major Tenets of Classical Theory

The P–Q Category. Classical economists believed that the economy is always close to or at the point of producing real GNP (Q_N). (In Chapter 14, we discuss classical theory with regard to the price level, P.)

The Inherently Stable–Inherently Unstable Category. Classical economists believed that the economy is inherently stable. The economy can smoothly and quickly equilibrate itself at full employment, or natural, real GNP.

The Effective–Ineffective Category. Classical economists believed in the principle of laissez-faire—that government should not interfere in the nation's economy. Such interference would be ineffective at solving economic problems; it would lead to more problems, not fewer.

KEYNESIAN THEORY: BACKGROUND
■

On the morning of October 10, 1932, John Maynard Keynes, age 49, walked into a lecture hall at Cambridge University in Cambridge, England. He began to speak: "Gentlemen, the change in the title of these lectures—from 'The Pure Theory of Money' to 'The Monetary Theory of Production' is significant." The impact of that lecture, and the 29 that followed over a period of four years, was felt far and wide. The discussions of economists, presidents, and prime ministers soon had to take into account the theories of John Maynard Keynes. The first shot of the Keynesian revolution had been fired.

Some economists argue that there would not have been a Keynesian revolution had there not been a Great Depression. (See the interview with Paul A. Samuelson in this chapter.) During these years, many economists and laypersons alike viewed the severe economic downturn as more than a temporary departure from classical theory equilibrium at natural real GNP. There was a general feeling that perhaps something more fundamental was wrong. Between 1929 and 1933, real GNP fell by approximately 30 percent; over the same period of time, the unemployment rate rose from 3.2 percent to 24.9 percent, real investment declined 75 percent, and real consumption dropped 20 percent. The macroeconomic policy of laissez-faire was being challenged. In such unusual and distressful economic circumstances, many persons wondered out loud why the government couldn't help. In this setting, Keynes wrote his *General Theory* (short for *The General Theory of Employment, Interest and Money*). We begin our discussion of Keynesian theory by pointing out a few of Keynes's criticisms of classical theory.

Keynes on Say's Law

Say's law maintained that there will always, or nearly always, be enough total demand or purchasing power in the economy to buy the full-employment, or natural, real GNP. Keynes disagreed, citing both empirical and theoretical reasons.

The Great Depression itself was enough of an empirical reason. Massive unemployment and a sharp decline in real GNP called Say's law into question.

On a theoretical level, Keynes argued that *it is possible to have saving (a leakage) greater than investment (an injection) such that total spending will be insufficient to buy the goods produced, resulting in a turndown in economic activity*. The classical view said interest rate flexibility would ensure a balance between saving and investment. Keynes emphasized that individuals save and invest for a host of reasons and that no single factor, such as the interest rate, links these activities. Furthermore, he believed that saving is more responsive to changes in income than to changes in the interest rate and that investment is more responsive to technological changes, business expectations, and innovations than to changes in the interest rate. In summary, whereas the classical economists believed that saving and investment depend on the interest rate, Keynes believed that both saving and investment depend on a number of factors that may be far more influential than the interest rate.

Consider the difference between Keynes and the classical economists on saving. As we noted earlier, the classical economists held that saving is directly related to the interest rate: As the interest rate goes up, saving rises; as the interest rate goes down, saving falls, *ceteris paribus.*

Keynes thought this might not always be true. If individuals are saving for a certain goal—say, a retirement fund of $100,000—then they might save less per period at an interest rate of 12 percent than at an interest rate of 5 percent, since a higher interest rate means that less saving is required per period to meet the goal within a set time. For example, if the interest rate is 5 percent, $50,000 saved earns $2,500 in interest income per year; if the interest rate is 10 percent, $25,000 saved earns $2,500.

As to investment, although Keynes believed that the interest rate is important in determining the level of investment, he did not think it is as important as other variables, such as the expected rate of profit on investment. Keynes argued that if business expectations are pessimistic, then it is unlikely there will be much investment, no matter how low the interest rate.

Empirical Evidence: Saving and Interest Rates

The classical economists stated that a *strong direct relationship* exists between saving and the interest rate (in other words, changes in the interest rate greatly affect saving). Keynes argued that a *weak direct relationship* exists between the two (changes in the interest rate mildly affect saving). Who is right?

In a study published in 1978, economist Michael Boskin calculated that a 10 percent increase in the real after-tax interest rate caused U.S. saving to increase between 2 and 6 percent. So the Boskin study supports the idea of a strong direct relationship between saving and the interest rate—score one for the classical economists.

However, a study published in 1983 by economists Irwin Freund and Joel Hasbrouck found that U.S. saving is not affected by changes in the real after-tax interest rate—score one for Keynes. Additionally, in a 1984 study, economists Vito Tanzi and Eytan Sheshinski found a time period in which U.S. saving actually fell as real after-tax interest rates were rising. Given the difference in the empirical results, the relationship between saving and interest rates (strong direct: classical; weak direct: Keynes; or negative: Tanzi and Sheshinski) is still up in the air. Why is it so hard for economists to establish the true relationship between saving and interest rates? We can only list some possibilities: (1) The relationship may be different at different times. (2) Measuring the real after-tax interest rate may be difficult (for example, measuring the real interest rate requires knowing something about the expectations of individuals with respect to future prices, and this is not easy to calculate). (3) Not all other things can be held constant as economists try to find the relationship between the two variables.

Keynes on Wage–Price Flexibility

Recall that the classical economists believed that not only a change in the interest rate but also changes in prices and wages will obtain natural real GNP. Keynes also disagreed with the classical economists on the issue of wage–price flexibility, citing two points.

On Prices.   Keynes noted that the internal structure of an economy is not always competitive enough to allow prices to fall. Recall from Chapter 3 how the forces of supply and demand operated when price was above equilibrium. In this case, a surplus was generated and price fell until the quantity supplied of the good equaled the quantity demanded. Keynes suggested that perhaps because of anti-competitive or monopolistic elements in the economy, price would not fall.

On Wages.   Keynes believed that there was a natural resistance from employees to employer's proposed wage cuts. Also, labor unions would resist wage cuts. According to Keynes, the wage rate may be inflexible in the downward direction.

The difference between classical economists and Keynes on the degree of flexibility in wage rates has theoretical consequences. We illustrate with the aid of Exhibit 9–2. Suppose we start at point 1 in (a). The economy here is in a recessionary gap, since the real GNP the economy is producing, Q_1, is less than natural real GNP, Q_N. This means the unemployment rate that exists is greater than the natural unemployment rate. According to the classical view of how the economy works, wage rates will soon fall. As this happens, the short-run aggregate supply (*SRAS*) curve shifts rightward, ultimately intersecting the aggregate demand curve at point 2. The economy is now in long-run equilibrium producing the natural real GNP.

EXHIBIT 9–2
Classical and Keynesian Views Contrasted

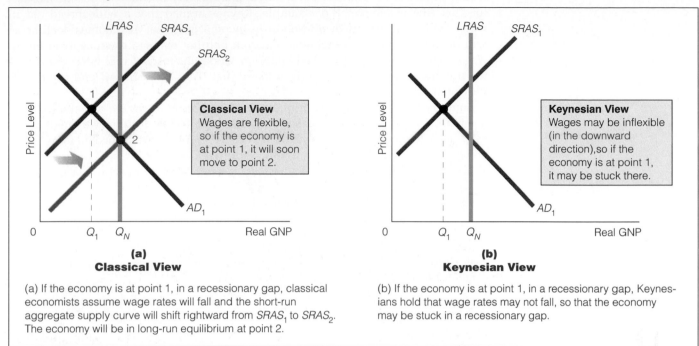

(a) If the economy is at point 1, in a recessionary gap, classical economists assume wage rates will fall and the short-run aggregate supply curve will shift rightward from $SRAS_1$ to $SRAS_2$. The economy will be in long-run equilibrium at point 2.

(b) If the economy is at point 1, in a recessionary gap, Keynesians hold that wage rates may not fall, so that the economy may be stuck in a recessionary gap.

Now let's look at how things turn out if wage rates do not fall. Suppose we start at point 1 in (b). Again, the economy is in a recessionary gap with the unemployment rate greater than the natural unemployment rate. According to the Keynesian view of how the economy works, wage rates may not fall. But if wage rates do not fall, then the *SRAS* curve will not shift to the right. And if the *SRAS* curve doesn't shift to the right, then the economy is stuck in a recessionary gap.

In summary, *the classical view that wages are flexible logically implies that the economy can eliminate a recessionary gap by itself. An economy doesn't get stuck in a recessionary gap. The Keynesian view that wages are inflexible (in the downward direction) implies that the economy may not be able to eliminate a recessionary gap by itself. An economy may get stuck in a recessionary gap.*

Keynes thus believed that the economy was inherently unstable—that is, it may not automatically cure itself of a recessionary gap: It may not easily and smoothly move toward full-employment, or natural, real GNP. In conclusion, equilibrium—or the balance of forces—in the economy may not be where the economy is producing natural real GNP, but in fact may be at some real GNP level below natural real GNP, for example, at Q_1 in Exhibit 9–2b.

This view is, of course, diametrically opposed to the classical view, which held that the economy is inherently stable and thus capable of moving itself to the position of producing natural real GNP.

On Prices and Wages. Keynes also made the point that even if prices and wages were flexible in the downward direction, this would not ensure a move to full-employment, or natural, real GNP. Here Keynes criticized the classical economists for confusing the consequences of a (single) price decline with a decline in the price level. Simply because a decline in the price of a single good or resource causes the quantity demanded of the good or resource to rise, it does not follow that a decrease in the prices of *all* goods and resources will bring about the same result. In short, what is true for a single market may not be true for all markets together (the economy).[2] For example, Keynes argued that a widespread cut in wages will result in a widespread cut in incomes and that as incomes decline, so will demand. Thus, he concluded, far from helping matters, a widespread cut in wages will make an already bad situation worse. Instead of real GNP rising and the unemployment rate falling, it is likely that real GNP will fall and the unemployment rate will rise.

Contrary to the classical position on unemployment—that we are always at or near full employment—Keynes believed that high levels of unemployment could exist for extended periods of time. Accordingly, it follows that the economy is not always close to or on its production possibilities frontier.

The revolutionary aspect of Keynesianism has been captured by L. Tarshis:

> I was also a bit surprised by his [Keynes's] concern over too low a level of output [real GNP]. I had been assured by all I had read that the economy would bob to the surface, like a cork held under water—and output would rise, of its own accord, to an acceptable level. But Keynes proposed something far more shocking: that the economy could reach an *equilibrium* position, with output far below capacity [far below natural real GNP or full-employment real GNP].[3]

A Modification of Keynesian Theory

Many economists criticized earlier versions of the Keynesian theory because, they argued, it didn't offer a rigorous explanation for inflexible wages. Some of the later versions made up for this deficiency by focusing on, among other things, long-term contracts and efficiency reasons for firms paying higher than market wages.

For example, some economists argue that long-term labor contracts are often advantageous to both employers and workers. The benefits firms may perceive from long-term contracts include fewer labor negotiations (labor negotiations can be costly) and the decreased likelihood of worker strikes (the firms have a breathing spell during the time of the contract). The benefits workers may perceive from long-term contracts include fewer strikes (which can be costly for them, too) and the added sense of security long-term contracts provide.

Long-term contracts come with costs as well as benefits for both firms and workers, but some economists believe that in many instances the benefits outweigh the costs and that firms and workers enter into the long-term contracts for mutually advantageous reasons. When they do, (nominal) wage rates are "locked in" for the period of the contract, and therefore cannot adjust downward to market-clearing levels given a fall in aggregate demand. The result is that the economy may get stuck at point 1 in Exhibit 9–2b for a long time and there may be high levels of unemployment lasting for many years. Keynesian economists believe that the theory explains the long-run levels of unemployment characteristic of some business cycles.

In a similar vein, economists who work with efficiency wage models also believe that there are (other) solid microeconomic reasons for inflexible wages. Economist George Akerlof argues that firms sometimes find it in their best interest to pay wage rates above market-clearing levels. According to the **efficiency wage models,**

Efficiency Wage Models
These models hold that it is sometimes in the best interest of firms to pay their employees higher than equilibrium wage rates.

[2]The view that what is true for a part of the whole is true for the whole is the fallacy of composition (see Chapter 1).

[3]L. Tarshis, "Keynesian Revolution," in *The New Palgrave: A Dictionary of Economics,* vol. 3 (London: The Macmillan Press, 1987), p. 48.

186

Interview: George Akerlof

George Akerlof has made major contributions to economic theory in the areas of asymmetric information, methodology, and labor market behavior. He is one of the major innovators of efficiency wage models. Akerlof is currently at the University of California, Berkeley.

Professor Akerlof, Keynesians have often argued that sticky wages, or wages that are inflexible in the downward direction, can prevent labor markets from clearing, thus causing the economy to get stuck at less than full-employment output. You, and others who have worked with efficiency wage models, have put forth reasons why it may be rational for firms to pay wages above market-clearing levels. What are a few of these reasons?

Firms sometimes pay wages above market-clearing levels because higher wages can lead to increased productivity. There are five basic reasons why this is the case. The most basic of these has to do with higher worker morale. Workers in firms with higher profits feel they deserve high wages, and firms with high profits pay higher wages than firms with low profits. If the firms do not pay these high wages, the workers invaria-

bly find a way of retaliating. Other reasons firms pay high wages are because they want to lower quit rates, stop unionization, give workers an incentive not to shirk, and attract a higher quality worker.

The efficiency wage model holds that in some labor markets, labor productivity is a function of the real wage paid by the firm. Specifically, as wages are cut, productivity falls, and as wages rise, productivity rises. Do you have a specific example where this is the case?

The most dramatic example of a rise in productivity following an increase in

wages came after Henry Ford's payment to his workers of the $5-a-day wage in 1914. Prior to his announcement, there was massive worker turnover at the Ford Motor Company. After the announcement, quits fell to an extremely low level.

One of the implicit messages of the efficiency wage model is that firms would rather stabilize wages than employment. That is, they'd rather lay off workers than cut wages. Wouldn't you think that layoffs might demoralize workers more than wage cuts, therefore prompting larger declines in productivity?

Certainly, both wage cuts and layoffs cause demoralization, but there is a big difference as to where the demoralized person ends up if he gets a wage cut than if he gets laid off. With wage cuts, the demoralized person stays at the firm. With layoffs, the demoralized person stays at home or looks for another job. As far as the firm goes, it is probably better to have the demoralized person at home than at the firm working. Also, when there are layoffs, the workers who stay with the firm are likely to be thankful they were not laid off, and in fact their morale may improve.

labor productivity depends on the wage rate the firm pays employees. Specifically, a cut in wages can cause labor productivity to decline, which, in turn, raises the firm's costs. By paying a wage higher than the market level, firms provide an incentive to workers to be productive and to minimize shirking, among other things. If shirking declines, so do the monitoring (management) costs of the firm.

The economist Robert Solow has argued that "the most interesting and important line of work in current macroeconomic theory is the attempt to reconstruct plausible microeconomic underpinnings for a recognizably Keynesian macroeconomics."[4] Many Keynesian economists believe the efficiency wage models can perform this task. They believe that although these models are fairly new, they have already provided a solid microeconomic explanation for inflexible wages, and

[4]Robert Solow, "Another Possible Source of Wage Stickiness," in *Efficiency Wage Models of the Labor Market*, edited by George Akerlof and Janet Yellen (Cambridge: Cambridge University Press, 1986), p. 41.

thus are capable of explaining the facts characteristic of continuing unemployment problems in some economies.

Keynes: The Classical Theory Is a Special Case

Keynes called his major work *The General Theory of Employment, Interest and Money.* Keynes did not believe that his theory was true only under special conditions. He did, however, view the classical theory as a theory that held only under special conditions: (1) when prices and wages are perfectly flexible (particularly in the downward direction); (2) perhaps in less severe economic downturns when it is possible to adjust back to full employment without massive and widespread wage cuts; and (3) in situations where investment and saving are somewhat responsive to changes in interest rates. Keynes stressed this point in the opening words of the *General Theory.*

> I shall argue that the postulates of the classical theory are applicable to a special case only and not to the general case, the situation which it assumes being a limiting point of the possible positions of equilibrium. Moreover, the characteristics of the special case assumed by the classical theory happen not to be those of the economic society in which we actually live, with the result that its teaching is misleading and disastrous if we attempt to apply it to the facts of experience.[5]

KEYNESIANISM:
THE COMPONENTS OF TOTAL EXPENDITURES

Keynesianism was a response to a real event and to a theory. The event was the Great Depression. The theory was classical theory, which some say did not predict and could not explain the high levels of unemployment that existed during the years of the Great Depression. So, for both empirical and theoretical reasons, the focus of Keynesian theory was unemployment. In terms of our P–Q category, unemployment relates to real GNP (Q).[6] That is, if the unemployment rate is too high, it could only mean that real GNP is too low (relative to natural real GNP).

We know from the AD–AS framework that aggregate demand and aggregate supply determine real GNP. For example, in Exhibit 9–3, AD_1 and $SRAS_1$ bring about real GNP. It follows that if real GNP is too low, it must mean one of three things.

1. Short-run aggregate supply is too low. Graphically, this means the $SRAS$ curve intersects the AD curve to the left of natural real GNP. In Exhibit 9–3, this is where $SRAS_2$ intersects AD_1 at point A.
2. Aggregate demand is too low. Graphically, this means the AD curve intersects the $SRAS$ curve to the left of natural real GNP. In Exhibit 9–3, this is where AD_2 intersects $SRAS_1$ at point B.
3. Both aggregate demand and short-run aggregate supply are too low. In Exhibit 9–3, this is where AD_2 intersects $SRAS_2$ at point C.

[5]John Maynard Keynes, *The General Theory of Employment, Interest and Money* (1936; reprint, London: Macmillan, 1970), p. 3.
[6]L. Tarshis, in *The New Palgrave: A Dictionary of Economics* (vol. 3, London: The Macmillan Press, 1987, p. 48) says that "after several years of plunging production, followed by a sluggish recovery, his [Keynes's] decision to examine the forces that determined output [real GNP] made sense, but after even more decades of regarding prices as the proper object of enquiry for economists the shift was not easy" (vol. 3, p. 48).

EXHIBIT 9–3
If Real GNP Is Too Low It Means . . .

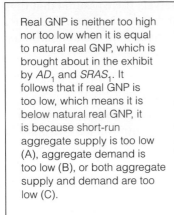

Real GNP is neither too high nor too low when it is equal to natural real GNP, which is brought about in the exhibit by AD_1 and $SRAS_1$. It follows that if real GNP is too low, which means it is below natural real GNP, it is because short-run aggregate supply is too low (A), aggregate demand is too low (B), or both aggregate supply and demand are too low (C).

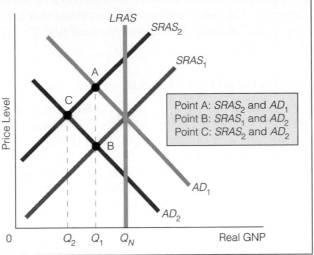

Point A: $SRAS_2$ and AD_1
Point B: $SRAS_1$ and AD_2
Point C: $SRAS_2$ and AD_2

Keynesian economics, usually emphasizes (2), aggregate demand being too low, so we need to understand something about the components of aggregate demand.

In Chapter 8, we stated that "at a given price level, anything that decreases any of the four components of total expenditures decreases aggregate demand and shifts the *AD* curve to the left." We deduce that if aggregate demand is too low, it must mean that, at a given price level, total expenditures are too low. The components of total expenditures are (1) household spending, or consumption (*C*), (2) business spending, or investment (*I*), (3) government spending, or government expenditures (*G*), and (4) foreign sector spending, or net exports ($X - M$). We focus our attention, therefore, on each of the four components of total expenditures.

First, we discuss a private economy, where there is a household, business, and foreign sector but no government sector. This will give us an understanding of the Keynesian view on how the private economy works. In the next chapter, we introduce government into the picture to get an idea of how many Keynesians view the government's impact on the private economy.

THE PRIVATE ECONOMY

■

Our purpose is to study the components of total expenditures in a private economy so that we understand what affects aggregate demand, and indirectly, real GNP and unemployment. In a private economy without government, there are three types of spending: consumption, investment, and net exports. The theoretical framework in which we study these three types of expenditures makes the following assumptions:

1. Wages and prices are fixed. Throughout most of the analysis (there are a few exceptions), all magnitudes (such as consumption, investment, and net exports) are real, or inflation-adjusted, magnitudes (such as real consumption, and so on). Remember this point, not only as you read, but as you view the exhibits, too.

2. The monetary side of the economy is excluded. For the most part, we do not discuss how changes in the money supply might affect the economy.

3. There is no government sector. When there is no government, there are no taxes or government transfer payments. Because of this, national income is *nearly* equal to disposable income. It makes no difference to our analysis if we assume that they are equal. Y is the symbol used for national income and Y_d is the symbol used for disposable income. Throughout our analysis, $Y = Y_d$, and both are denominated in real terms.

The Consumption Function

Keynes made three basic points about consumption and disposable income: (1) Consumption depends on disposable income. (2) Consumption and disposable income move in the same direction. (3) When disposable income changes, consumption changes by less.

These three points make a specific statement about the relationship between consumption and disposable income. The statement specifying this relationship is called the **consumption function.** We represent the consumption function as

$$C = C_0 + MPC(Y_d)$$

We know that C is consumption and that Y_d is disposable income. Let us discuss the MPC and C_0.

MPC. This stands for **marginal propensity to consume,** which is the ratio of the change in consumption to the change in income.

$$MPC = \Delta C / \Delta Y$$

The symbol Δ stands for "change in." We would read it this way: "The MPC is equal to the *change in* consumption divided by the *change in* income." To illustrate, suppose consumption rises from $800 to $900 as income rises from $1,000 to $1,200. If we divide the change in consumption, which is $100, by the change in income, which is $200, we see that the MPC equals .50.

C_0. This is **autonomous consumption.** Autonomous consumption does not change as income changes; it changes due to factors *other* than income.

Think of consumption as being made up of two parts: one part that is independent of income—called *autonomous consumption*—and a second part that is dependent on income—called **induced consumption.**

Look again at the consumption function. Suppose $C_0 = \$800$, $MPC = .80$ and $Y_d = \$1,500$. If we were to plug the numbers into the consumption function—$C = C_0 + MPC(Y_d)$—we would see that $C = \$2,000$ (since $\$2,000 = \$800 + .80 (\$1,500))$. With an eye on the consumption function, here are three ways in which C can be increased:

1. Raise autonomous consumption. Say autonomous consumption goes from $800 to $1,000. This would raise consumption, C, to $2,200 (since $2,200 = $1,000 + .80 ($1,500)).
2. Raise disposable income. Say disposable income goes from $1,500 to $1,800. This would raise C to $2,240 (since $2,400 = $800 + .80 ($1,800)). The $400 increase in consumption from $2,000 to $2,400 is due to an increase of $400 in *induced consumption.* Specifically, the increased consumption was *induced* by an increase in disposable income.
3. Raise the MPC. Suppose the MPC rises to .90. This would raise C to $2,150 (since $2,150 = $800 + .90 ($1,500)).

Consumption Function
The relationship between consumption and disposable income; in the consumption function used here, consumption is directly related to disposable income and is positive even at zero disposable income: $C = C_0 + MPC(Y_d)$.

Marginal Propensity to Consume (MPC)
The ratio of the change in consumption to the change in income: $MPC = \Delta C / \Delta Y$

Autonomous Consumption
That part of consumption that is independent of income.

Induced Consumption
That part of consumption that changes as income changes.

In Exhibit 9–4, we have calculated different levels of consumption spending for different levels of income. We have set C_0 equal to $200 billion and MPC equal to .80; thus, we have $C = \$200$ billion $+ .8(Y_d)$. Additionally, we have calculated different saving levels at different income levels. How did we calculate this? Since we know that $C = C_0 + MPC(Y_d)$, and we also know that households can only consume or save, it follows that saving is the difference between disposable income and consumption: $S = Y_d - (C_0 + MPC(Y_d))$.

The MPC and the MPS

In Exhibit 9–4, for every $1 change in income, there is an $.80 change in consumption. For example, at an income of $1,200 billion, consumption is $1,160 billion; but at an income of $1,400 billion, consumption is $1,320 billion. This is a difference of $160 billion, or $.80 additional consumption for every $1 of extra income. This means the $MPC = .80$.

The **marginal propensity to save** *(MPS)* is the ratio of the change in saving to the change in income.

$$MPS = \frac{\Delta S}{\Delta Y}$$

Marginal Propensity to Save (MPS)
The ratio of the change in saving to the change in income: $MPS = \Delta S/\Delta Y$.

Since we know that additions to income can only be used for consumption or saving, that is, $\Delta C + \Delta S = \Delta Y$, it follows that the marginal propensity to consume *(MPC)* plus the marginal propensity to save *(MPS)* must equal 1.

$$MPC + MPS = 1$$

In Exhibit 9–4, since we set the marginal propensity to consume at .80, it follows that the marginal propensity to save is .20. Notice that for every $1 change in income, saving changes by $.20; or, for every $200 change in income (column 2), there is a $40 change in saving (column 6).

The *APC* and *APS*

Return to Exhibit 9–4. If we were to calculate the marginal propensity to consume *(MPC)* at an income level of $1,400, we would find it equal to $160/$200, or .80

EXHIBIT 9–4
Consumption and Saving at Different Levels of Real Disposable Income (Real National Income) (in billions)

Since there is no government sector, real national income (Y) = real disposable income (Y_d). Our consumption function is $C = C_0 + MPC(Y_d)$, where C_0 has been set at $200 billion and $MPC = .80$. Since we know that saving is the difference between Y_d and C, then $S = Y_d - (C_0 + MPC(Y_d))$.

(1) Real Disposable Income (Real National Income), $Y_d = Y$	(2) Change in Real Disposable Income, ΔY_d	(3) Consumption, $C = C_0 + MPC(Y_d)$	(4) Change in Consumption, $\Delta C = MPC(\Delta Y_d)$	(5) Saving, $S = Y_d - (C_0 + MPC(Y_d))$	(6) Change in Saving, $\Delta S = \Delta Y_d - \Delta C$
$ 800	$ ___	$ 840	$ ___	-$40	$__
1,000	200	1,000	160	0	40
1,200	200	1,160	160	40	40
1,400	200	1,320	160	80	40
1,600	200	1,480	160	120	40
1,800	200	1,640	160	160	40

Average Propensity to Consume (APC)
Consumption divided by income: $APC = C/Y$.

Average Propensity to Save (APS)
Saving divided by income: $APS = S/Y$.

$(MPC = \Delta C/\Delta Y)$. Now suppose we were to calculate C/Y at the same income level. This would give us $\$1,320/\$1,400$, or .94. This fraction (C/Y) is called **average propensity to consume** *(APC)*. It is the proportion of income spent on consumption.

$$APC = \frac{C}{Y}$$

A similar concept, the **average propensity to save** *(APS)*, is the proportion of income saved.

$$APS = \frac{S}{Y}$$

Once again, since saving and consumption are the only ways households can dispose of income, it follows that

$$APC + APS = 1$$

In summary, it is important to differentiate between "marginal" and "average" magnitudes. Although they may sound alike, the *MPC* and *APC,* and the *MPS* and *APS,* are not one and the same. The average magnitudes, *APC* and *APS,* refer to the *fractions of income* that are consumed and saved, respectively. On an individual basis, if a person has an income of $\$1,000$ and her consumption is $\$600$ and her saving is $\$400$, then $APC = .60$ and $APS = .40$. The marginal magnitudes, *MPC* and *MPS,* refer to the *fractions of any change in income* that are consumed and saved, respectively. On an individual basis, if a person's income rises by $\$100$, and her consumption rises by $\$70$, and her saving rises by $\$30$, then $MPC = .70$ and $MPS = .30$.

Shifts in the Consumption Function

Exhibit 9–5 diagrams a consumption function. Notice that we did not start the consumption function at the origin. This is because given our consumption function, $C = C_0 + MPC(Y_d)$, consumption (C) is greater than zero even when dispos-

EXHIBIT 9–5
The Consumption Function, $C = C_0 + MPC(Y_d)$

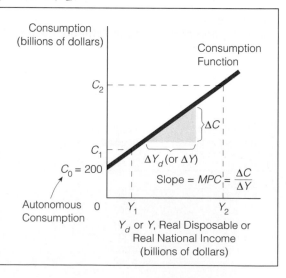

Even at a real national or real disposable income of 0 ($Y = Y_d = 0$), consumption is positive as long as $C_0 > 0$. A change in Y or Y_d will lead to a movement along the consumption function. A change in the following factors will lead to a shift in the consumption function: wealth, expectations about future prices and income, the price level, the interest rate, and taxes (assuming real national income, not real disposable income, is on the horizontal axis). Since we have assumed that prices are fixed, the consumption (C) on the vertical axis is "real cosumption."

able income is zero.[7] Previously, we specified that C_0 equals $200 billion and that the MPC is .80. Therefore, consumption (C) equals $200 billion when disposable income is zero [$C = \$200 + .8(0) = \$200$]. Also, in our exhibit, the slope of the consumption function represents the marginal propensity to consume.

At this point, we need to distinguish between a *shift* in the consumption function and a *movement* along the consumption function. The distinction between a shift in a curve and a movement along a curve was made in Chapter 3 when we discussed demand curves. We said there that a change in price *moved* us from one point on the demand curve to another point on the same curve, but that a change in preferences, a change in the price of substitutes, a change in the price of complements, and so on would *shift* the entire demand curve.

For the consumption function, a change in real national income will lead to a movement along the consumption function. This is easily seen by picking two points on the horizontal axis in Exhibit 9–5 and drawing a line upward (from each point) until it touches the consumption function. For example, at Y_1 consumption is C_1, and at Y_2 consumption is C_2. There is a different level of consumption spending at each income level.

A shift in the consumption function may be brought about by a host of factors. We refer to these factors as the nonincome determinants of consumption, which include wealth, expectations about future prices and income, the price level, the interest rate, and taxes. *The effects of the nonincome determinants of consumption are captured in the C_0 (autonomous consumption) term.* Exhibit 9–6 illustrates factors leading to a shift in the consumption function.

[7]For a consumption function that does begin at the origin, see the appendix to this chapter, where we discuss the permanent-income hypothesis.

EXHIBIT 9–6
Factors that Shift the Consumption Function

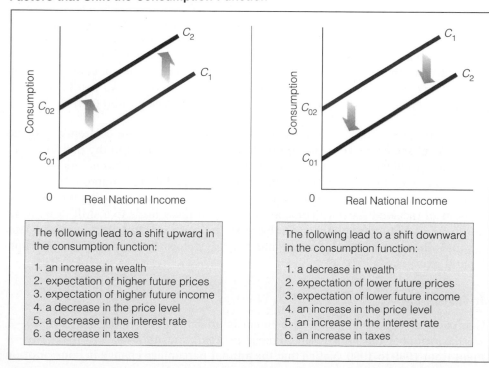

The following lead to a shift upward in the consumption function:

1. an increase in wealth
2. expectation of higher future prices
3. expectation of higher future income
4. a decrease in the price level
5. a decrease in the interest rate
6. a decrease in taxes

The following lead to a shift downward in the consumption function:

1. a decrease in wealth
2. expectation of lower future prices
3. expectation of lower future income
4. an increase in the price level
5. an increase in the interest rate
6. an increase in taxes

Wealth. Individuals consume, not only on the basis of their present income, but also on the basis of their wealth. Consider two individuals, each receiving an income of $30,000 a year. One has $75,000 in the bank, and the other has no assets at all. Which would you expect to spend more of her income on consumption goods this year? We would expect the person with the $75,000 in the bank to consume the greater amount. Greater wealth makes individuals feel financially more secure and thus more willing to spend. Increases in wealth shift the consumption function upward, and decreases in wealth shift the consumption function downward (see Exhibit 9–6).

Expectations about Future Prices and Income. If individuals expect higher future prices, they will tend to increase current consumption expenditures in order to buy goods at the lower current prices. If individuals expect lower future prices, they will do the opposite. An expectation of a higher future income will shift the consumption function upward; an expectation of a lower future income will shift the consumption function downward (see Exhibit 9–6).

The Price Level. (See the discussion of the real balance effect in Chapter 8.) As the price level rises, the purchasing power of money declines, and individuals are less wealthy. As a result, they consume less; thus, the consumption function shifts downward. As the price level falls, the purchasing power of money rises, and individuals are more wealthy. As a result, they consume more; thus, the consumption function shifts upward.

Note that the effect on the consumption function we are describing here works through changes in *wealth,* not *income.* We learned earlier that an increase in income moves us up along the consumption function, and a decrease in income moves us down along the consumption function.

In summary, a change in income moves us *along* the consumption function; a change in wealth *shifts* the consumption function (see Exhibit 9–6).

Interest Rate. Current empirical work shows that spending on consumer durables is sensitive to the interest rate. Since many of these items are financed by borrowing, an increase in the interest rate increases the monthly payments linked to their purchase and thereby reduces their consumption, shifting the consumption function downward. A decrease in the interest rate generally works in the opposite direction, shifting the consumption function upward (see Exhibit 9–6).

Taxes. We have been discussing the mechanics of a private economy with no government sector. Suppose for a minute we add government to the picture. With government comes taxation, and taxes can influence consumption. As taxes increase, we would expect less consumer spending for the same amount of received income; as taxes decrease, we would expect more consumer spending for the same amount of received income. Thus, an increase in taxes leads to a shift downward in the consumption function, and a decrease in taxes leads to a shift upward. (This assumes that real national income, and not real disposable income, is on the horizontal axis.)

Investment

Compared with consumption, investment is unstable and volatile. In Exhibit 9–7, we have plotted the percentage changes in (real) consumption and (real) investment from 1969 to 1990. Notice that the annual percentage change in consumption

EXHIBIT 9–7
Percentage Changes in Consumption and Investment, 1969–90.

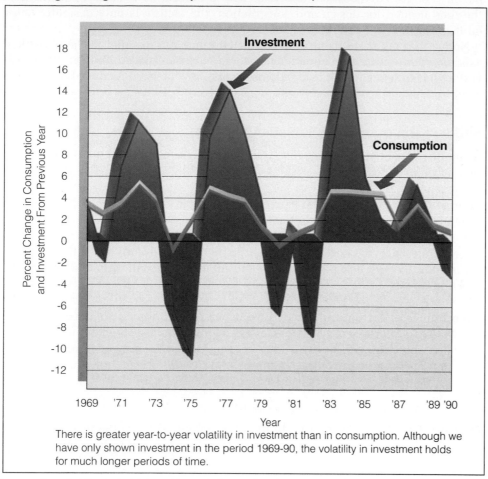

There is greater year-to-year volatility in investment than in consumption. Although we have only shown investment in the period 1969-90, the volatility in investment holds for much longer periods of time.

SOURCE: Council of Economic Advisers, *Economic Report of the President,* 1991 (Washington, D.C.: U.S. Government Printing Office, 1991).

is less volatile than the annual percentage change in investment. One reason that investment is more volatile than consumption is that expectations play a more important role in determining investment spending than consumption spending. We say more about this when we discuss the factors that can shift the investment function. First, however, we need to identify it.

The Investment Function

In our theory, investment is autonomous. Stated differently, investment does not depend on income. Our investment function specifies that

$$I = I_0$$

which says that (total) investment is autonomous investment; or (total) investment is equal to its autonomous component only (Exhibit 9–8).

The investment function we have specified ($I = I_0$) is consistent with Keynes's ideas about investment in the short run, mainly, that most current investment

EXHIBIT 9–8
The Investment Function

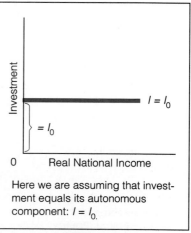

Here we are assuming that investment equals its autonomous component: $I = I_0$.

195

expenditures result from past investment expenditure decisions. For example, a business might have decided two years ago to build a new factory, but owing to the time needed for design and construction, the factory is only currently being built.

Notice that the investment function in Exhibit 9–8 is parallel to the horizontal axis on which (current) real national income has been placed, indicating that investment is independent of real national income: A change in income, from a lower level to a higher level or vice versa, does not lead to a change in investment.

Shifts in the Investment Function

A number of factors can shift the investment function (Exhibit 9–9). We explain each of them as follows.

Interest Rate.   Whether a firm borrows the funds to invest or uses its own funds, it incurs an opportunity cost in the form of interest lost. As the interest rate rises, the cost of a given investment project rises, and there is less investment; as the interest rate falls, the cost of a given investment project falls, and there is more investment, *ceteris paribus*. A rise in the interest rate will shift the investment function downward; a fall in the interest rate will shift it upward.

Expectations about Future Sales.   Businesses invest because they expect to sell the goods they produce. If businesses become optimistic about future sales, investment spending will grow; if they become pessimistic about future sales, investment spending will contract. Optimism of this kind leads to an upward shift in the investment function; pessimism leads to a downward shift in the investment function.

Business Taxes.   Again, let us add the government sector to the discussion. In a model that includes government, business taxes are relevant to investment spend-

EXHIBIT 9–9
Factors that Shift the Investment Function

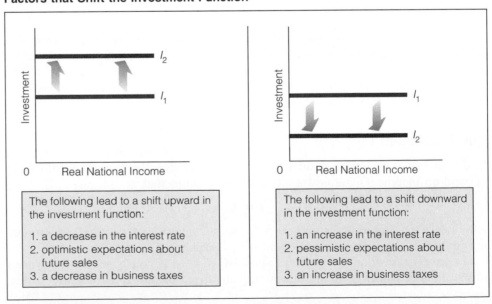

ing decisions. Businesses naturally consider expected after-tax profits when making their investment decisions. An increase in business taxes will lower expected profitability and decrease investment spending; a decrease in business taxes will raise expected profitability and increase investment spending. An increase in business taxes shifts the investment function downward; a decrease in business taxes shifts the investment function upward.

The Net Exports Function

To round out our discussion of the private economy, we discuss net exports. We know that net exports = exports − imports. In our simple model, there is no change in exports as (U.S.) real national income changes; in other words, exports are autonomous. Imports, though, rise as (U.S.) real national income rises. This is based on the idea that as Americans have more income, they buy more goods, some of which are foreign goods.

In Exhibit 9–10a, notice that the exports function is drawn parallel to the real national income axis, indicating no change in exports as real national income changes. In Exhibit 9–10b, the imports function is drawn sloping upward, indicating that as U.S. real national income rises, imports rise.

In Exhibit 9–10c, we have drawn the net export function. Since net exports = exports − imports, we have simply (a) taken exports at three different income

EXHIBIT 9–10
The Net Exports Function

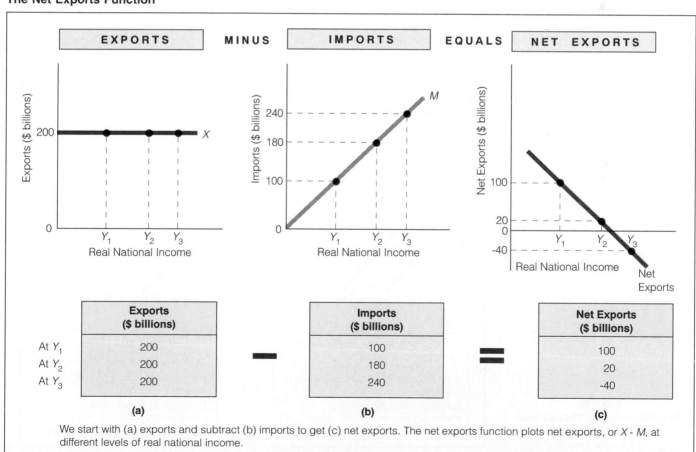

	Exports ($ billions)		Imports ($ billions)		Net Exports ($ billions)
At Y_1	200		100		100
At Y_2	200		180		20
At Y_3	200		240		-40
	(a)		(b)		(c)

We start with (a) exports and subtract (b) imports to get (c) net exports. The net exports function plots net exports, or X - M, at different levels of real national income.

197

levels, (b) subtracted imports at the same three income levels, and (c) plotted the respective net export dollar amounts at the three income levels. The downward-sloping curve that connects the three points is the net exports function.

Shifts in the Net Exports Function

A number of factors can shift the net exports function (Exhibit 9–11). We explain each of them as follows.

Foreign Real National Income.   As foreign real national income rises, foreigners buy more U.S. goods and services; thus, U.S. exports rise.[8] This shifts the export function upward (see Exhibit 9–10a). As a result, at every level of U.S. real national income (Y_1, Y_2, and Y_3 in Exhibit 9–10), net exports rises. The net export function shifts upward. Applying the same logic, if foreign real national income falls, the net export function shifts downward.

Price Levels in the U.S. and in Foreign Nations.   As the foreign price level rises relative to the U.S. price level, U.S. goods look more attractive to both foreigners and Americans. Consequently, exports rise and imports fall, and the net exports function shifts upward. As the foreign price level falls relative to the U.S. price level, foreign goods look more attractive to foreigners and Americans. Consequently, exports fall and imports rise, and the net exports function shifts downward.[9]

---

[8]As in Chapter 8, we assume that as the physical quantity of U.S. goods that foreigners buy rises, so does exports (X). Recall that exports refer to the total dollar spending on domestic goods, not to the physical goods themselves. In other words, exports is a dollar amount.

[9]Saying that the foreign price level rises (falls) relative to the U.S. price level is the same as saying that the U.S. price level falls (rises) relative to the foreign price level.

EXHIBIT 9–11
Factors that Shift the Net Exports Function

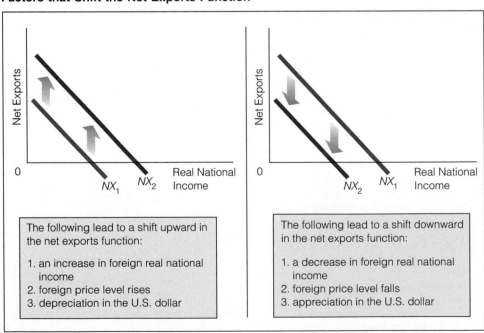

The following lead to a shift upward in the net exports function:

1. an increase in foreign real national income
2. foreign price level rises
3. depreciation in the U.S. dollar

The following lead to a shift downward in the net exports function:

1. a decrease in foreign real national income
2. foreign price level falls
3. appreciation in the U.S. dollar

The Depreciation and Appreciation of the U.S. Dollar. The **exchange rate** is the price of one currency in terms of another currency; for example, $1.50 = £1. A currency has **appreciated** in value if it takes more of a foreign currency to buy it. A currency has **depreciated** in value if it takes more of it to buy a foreign currency. For example, a movement in the exchange rate from $1.50 = £1 to $1.80 = £1 means that more dollars are necessary to buy one pound, so the pound has appreciated. And since more dollars are necessary to buy one pound, the dollar has depreciated.

A depreciation in a nation's currency makes foreign goods more expensive. Consider an English coat that is priced at £200 when the exchange rate is $1 = £1. To buy the English coat for £200, an American has to pay $200, or $1 for every £1. Now suppose the dollar depreciates to $2 = £1. The American has to pay $400 for the coat. Things are symmetrical here, so an appreciation in a nation's currency makes foreign goods cheaper. For example, if the exchange rate goes from $1 = £1 to $.80 = £1, the American no longer has to pay $200 for the English coat, but only $160 ($.80 per pound *times* £200 = $160).

The depreciation and appreciation in the U.S. dollar affect the net exports function. As the dollar depreciates, foreign goods become more expensive, Americans cut back on imported goods, and foreigners (whose currency has appreciated) increase their purchases of U.S. exported goods. If exports rise and imports fall, net exports increase, shifting the net exports function upward.

As the dollar appreciates, foreign goods become cheaper, Americans increase their purchases of imported goods, and foreigners (whose currency has depreciated) cut back on their purchases of U.S. exported goods. If exports fall and imports rise, net imports decrease, shifting the net exports function downward.

Changes in Consumption, Investment, and Net Exports and Changes in Aggregate Demand

In Chapter 8, we stated that *at a given price level,* anything that increases total expenditures increases aggregate demand and shifts the *AD* curve to the right; and *at a given price level,* anything that decreases total expenditures decreases aggregate demand and shifts the *AD* curve to the left.

Since we know that total expenditures in an economy is composed of (1) consumption, (2) investment, (3) government expenditures, and (4) net exports, we can reword our statement to read, *At a given price level,* anything that increases consumption, investment, government expenditures, or net exports increases aggregate demand and shifts the *AD* curve to the right, and *at a given price level* anything that decreases consumption, investment, government expenditures, or net exports decreases aggregate demand and shifts the *AD* curve to the left.

In this section, we have discussed those factors that can increase and decrease (1) consumption, (2) investment, and (3) net exports. It follows that we indirectly have been discussing those factors that can increase and decrease aggregate demand and consequently can shift the *AD* curve rightward and leftward, respectively.[10]

[10]In discussing consumption, we stated that an increase in the price level shifts the consumption function downward and a decrease in the price level shifts the consumption function upward. It is perhaps easy to conclude that since a change in the price level changes consumption, a change in the price level changes aggregate demand, too. This is incorrect, however. Remember, in our discussion of changes in aggregate demand, we are holding the price level constant ("At a *given* price level . . .") We repeat: A change in the price level does not change aggregate demand; it changes the quantity demanded of real GNP or real national income.

Exchange Rate
The price of one currency in terms of another currency; for example, $1.50 = £1.

Appreciation
An increase in the value of one currency relative to other currencies. A currency has appreciated if it takes more of a foreign currency to buy it.

Depreciation
A decrease in the value of one currency relative to other currencies. A currency has depreciated if it takes more of it to buy a foreign currency.

TOTAL EXPENDITURES (TE)
AND
TOTAL PRODUCTION (TP)

■

Here we focus on the three possible relationships between total expenditures (*TE*) and total production (*TP*). Our discussion is similar to that in Chapter 8 concerning the three possible relationships between real GNP (Q) and natural real GNP (Q_N). Whereas Q and Q_N are standard fare in the *AD–AS* framework, *TE* and *TP* are standard fare in the income–expenditure (*I–E*) framework, a framework of analysis that is Keynesian in its origins.

In this section, we allow prices and wages to change, but we exclude the monetary sector and government.

Three Possible States

We learned that the three possible states between real GNP (Q) and natural real GNP (Q_N) are (1) $Q = Q_N$; (2) $Q < Q_N$; and (3) $Q > Q_N$. These three states of the economy can also be discussed in terms of *total expenditures (TE)* and *total production (TP)*. Throughout our discussion, we assume that business firms collectively want to hold $300 billion worth of goods in inventory: no more, no less.

1. TE = TP. We start with firms holding their optimum inventory level, $300 billion worth of goods. Then firms produce $4,000 billion worth of goods, and members of the three sectors (household, business, and foreign) buy $4,000 billion worth of goods. In short, total expenditures (*TE*) equal total production (*TP*); the economy is in equilibrium.

2. TP > TE. We start with firms holding their optimum inventory level, $300 billion worth of goods. Then firms produce $4,000 billion worth of goods, and members of the three sectors buy $3,800 billion worth of goods and services. Since producers produce more than individuals buy, the difference adds to inventories. Inventory levels *unexpectedly* rise to $500 billion, which is $200 billion more than the $300 billion firms see as optimal.

This unexpected rise in inventories signals to firms that they have overproduced. Consequently, they cut back on the quantity of goods they produce, or cut prices, or both. The cutback in production causes real GNP to fall, bringing real GNP closer to the (lower) real GNP that members of the three sectors want to buy.

3. TE > TP. We start with firms holding their optimum inventory level, $300 billion worth of goods. Then firms produce $3,900 billion worth of goods, and members of the three sectors buy $4,100 billion worth of goods. But how can individuals buy more than firms produce? The answer is that firms make up the difference out of inventory. In our example, inventory levels fall from $300 billion to $100 billion, since individuals purchase $200 billion more of goods than firms produced (to be sold). In fact, this example points out the reason firms maintain inventories in the first place: to be ready to meet an unexpected increase in sales.

The unexpected fall in inventories signals to firms that they have underproduced. Consequently, they increase the quantity of goods they produce, or raise prices, or both. The rise in production causes real GNP to rise, in the process bringing real GNP closer to the (higher) real GNP that members of the three sectors want to buy.

The Graphical Representation of the Three States of the Economy

The three states of the economy can be represented by the *total expenditures (TE)* curve. We develop the curve by the following procedure.

1. In a private economy with no government, total expenditures consists of (a) consumption, (b) investment, and (c) net exports.

2. We know that there is an autonomous and induced component to consumption. Overall, consumption rises as real GNP rises (Exhibit 9–12a).[11]

3. Investment is assumed to be autonomous; it does not change as real GNP rises (Exhibit 9–12b).

4. Exports are assumed to be autonomous; exports do not change as real GNP rises (Exhibit 9–12c).

5. Imports are assumed to rise as real GNP rises (Exhibit 9–12d).

6. Total expenditures in a private economy without government equals $C + I + (X - M)$. In Exhibit 9–12, we have summed consumption, investment, and net export expenditures at two real GNP levels, Q_1 and Q_2. Plotting this in Exhibit 9–12e gives us two points, A and B. The curve that connects them is the total expenditures curve.

Now look at the income–expenditure diagram in Exhibit 9–13. On the horizontal axis you will find real GNP, and on the vertical axis you will find total production *(TP)*. Midway between the two is a 45-degree line. Any point on the 45-degree line is equidistant from the two axes; that is, any point on the line has the characteristic that real GNP equals total production.

Also, in the exhibit, you will see the *TE* curve superimposed. We add *TE* to the vertical axis as a result.

Let's now view three real GNP levels, Q_E, Q_1, and Q_2. Q_E represents equilibrium real GNP, since at this real GNP level, $TE = TP$. (*TE* is obtained by running a line up from Q_E to the *TE* curve, and *TP* is obtained by running a line up from Q_E to the 45-degree line. We see that *TE* and *TP* are $3,450 billion.)

At Q_1, $TP > TE$, $4,800 billion > $4,000 billion. Here the members of the three sectors purchase less than is being produced. What happens? As we learned earlier, this results in inventories higher than planned, which signals firms that they have overproduced, which causes firms to cut back on production, which decreases real GNP. The economy tends to move from Q_1 to Q_E.

At Q_2, $TE > TP$, $3,000 billion > $2,000 billion. Here the members of the three sectors purchase more than is being produced. What happens? As we learned earlier, this results in inventories lower than planned, which signals firms that they have underproduced, which causes firms to increase their production, which increases real GNP. The economy tends to move from Q_2 to Q_E.

THE MULTIPLIER

According to Keynesian theory, a change in any autonomous spending component can cause a multiple change in real GNP or real national income. There are three

---

[11]We have made a subtle change here. Instead of speaking about *real national income,* we use the term *real GNP.* This is acceptable since in Chapter 6 we learned that GNP = national income + indirect business taxes + capital consumption allowance + statistical discrepancy. To simplify things, economists occasionally let GNP = NI. Of course, in our discussion so far, there is no government and thus no indirect business taxes, and therefore the difference between GNP and national income is smaller than it would be if government were in the picture. However, even if government were in the picture, we could permit GNP to serve as a proxy for national income since we are interested in the *directional* and *magnitudinal* changes in GNP and national income, and they tend to move up and down together. Now, if GNP = NI, we can let real GNP = real national income.

EXHIBIT 9-12
The Derivation of the Total Expenditures (*TE*) Curve

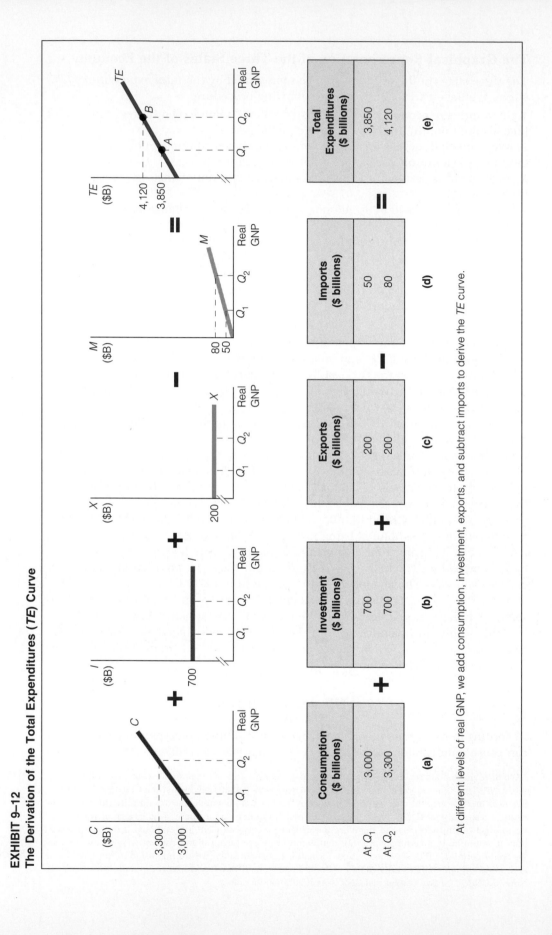

	Consumption ($ billions)		Investment ($ billions)		Exports ($ billions)		Imports ($ billions)		Total Expenditures ($ billions)
At Q_1	3,000	+	700	+	200	−	50	=	3,850
At Q_2	3,300		700		200		80		4,120
	(a)		(b)		(c)		(d)		(e)

At different levels of real GNP, we add consumption, investment, exports, and subtract imports to derive the *TE* curve.

EXHIBIT 9–13
The Income–Expenditure Diagram

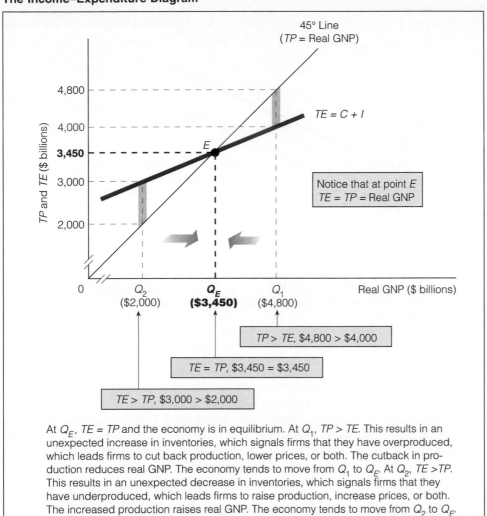

At Q_E, $TE = TP$ and the economy is in equilibrium. At Q_1, $TP > TE$. This results in an unexpected increase in inventories, which signals firms that they have overproduced, which leads firms to cut back production, lower prices, or both. The cutback in production reduces real GNP. The economy tends to move from Q_1 to Q_E. At Q_2, $TE > TP$. This results in an unexpected decrease in inventories, which signals firms that they have underproduced, which leads firms to raise production, increase prices, or both. The increased production raises real GNP. The economy tends to move from Q_2 to Q_E.

autonomous spending components we noted when we discussed total expenditures in a private economy without government: *autonomous consumption, autonomous investment,* and *autonomous exports.* We describe the multiplier process by introducing a change in autonomous investment.

Investment and the Multiplier

Suppose the relevant total expenditures curve is TE_1 and the economy is in equilibrium at E_1 (Exhibit 9–14). Suppose now that the interest rate falls, causing an increase in autonomous investment. An increase in investment will cause the total expenditures (TE) curve to shift upward from TE_1 to TE_2. (The vertical distance between the two TE curves is the amount by which autonomous investment has increased.) Now TE_2 is the relevant total expenditures curve and the economy is in equilibrium at E_2. It is important to notice that the change in real GNP from Q_1 to Q_2 is greater than the change in autonomous investment. We see that arrow 2, which indicates the change in real GNP, is longer than arrow 1, which indicates

EXHIBIT 9–14

A Change in Autonomous Investment Spending Relative to a Change in Real National Income

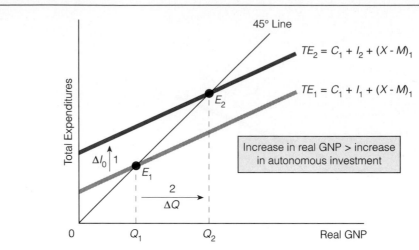

An increase in autonomous investment spending shifts the *TE* curve from TE_1 to TE_2 and brings about an increase in real GNP from Q_1 to Q_2. The increase in real GNP is greater than the increase in real autonomous investment spending—compare the length of arrow 2 with the length of arrow 1.

the change in autonomous investment. In other words, a change in autonomous investment of amount X brings about a change greater than X (say, $X+$) in real GNP; a change in autonomous investment changes real GNP by some multiple.

Multiplier (m)
The number that is multiplied by the change in autonomous spending to obtain the change in real GNP: $m = 1/(1 - MPC)$.

The multiple is called the **multiplier.** It is the number that is multiplied by the change in autonomous spending to obtain the change in real GNP. It is equal to

$$\text{Multiplier } (m) = \frac{1}{1 - MPC}$$

Let's work through an example (Exhibit 9–15).

1. We start with a $60 increase in autonomous investment spending (column 2).
2. This increase in autonomous investment spending generates income equal to itself: $60 spent on goods by one person is $60 received as income by some other person (column 3).
3. We assume that the $MPC = .80$. So if income increases by $60, then consumption changes by 80 percent of $60, or $48.
4. The $48 is spent, generating income equal to itself.
5. Again, if $MPC = .80$, then consumption changes by 80 percent of $48, or $38.40.
6. And so on.

The total change in real GNP or real national income is $300. Here is the formula we used:

$$\Delta \text{ Real GNP} = m \times \Delta \text{ Autonomous spending}$$

In our example, $MPC = .80$, so the multiplier equals 5 ($1/1 - MPC = 5$). The change in autonomous (investment) spending was $60; $60 times 5 equals $300.

EXHIBIT 9–15

Autonomous Investment and the Multiplier

A $60 change in autonomous investment ultimately changes real GNP or real national income by $300 ($MPC = .80$). The process begins with an increase in autonomous investment, which leads to a change in income, a change in consumption, another change in income, another change in consumption, and so on.

(1) EXPENDITURE ROUND	(2) CHANGE IN AUTONOMOUS INVESTMENT	(3) CHANGE IN REAL GNP OR REAL NATIONAL INCOME	(4) MPC	(5) CHANGE IN CONSUMPTION
Round 1	$60.00	$ 60.00	.80	$ 48.00
Round 2		48.00	.80	38.40
Round 3		38.40	.80	30.72
Round 4		30.72	.80	24.57
All other rounds		122.88	.80	98.88
TOTALS		$300.00		$240.00 (Approx.)

The Multiplier and Reality

We have discussed the multiplier in simple terms: A change in autonomous spending leads to an even larger change in real GNP.

We must note two points, however. First, the multiplier takes time to work itself out. In a textbook or on a blackboard, we go from an initial increase in autonomous investment spending to a multiple increase in real GNP in seconds. In the real world, it takes many months.

Second, for the multiplier to increase real GNP (the way we have described), idle resources must exist at each expenditure round.

Recall that one of the simplifying assumptions in our original theoretical framework (page 189) is that prices and wages are fixed or constant. It follows that if we experience an increase in real GNP (output is increasing) at each expenditure round, idle resources must be available to be brought into production. If this were not the case, then increased spending would simply result in higher prices and no increase in real GNP. Thus, there would be an increase in GNP ($P \times Q$), but not in real GNP (Q).

Question:

Does the multiplier analysis work in reverse? That is, if there had been a decrease in autonomous investment spending of $60, and the MPC equaled .80, would there have been a decrease in real GNP of $300?

Answer:

Yes.

KEYNESIAN THEORY IN THE *AD–AS* FRAMEWORK

■

In this section, we introduce the aggregate supply curve and discuss Keynesian theory within the *AD–AS* framework.

Three Other Aggregate Supply Curves

You are accustomed to seeing the (short-run) aggregate supply curve drawn as upward sloping. There are three other possible aggregate supply curves.

Horizontal *AS* Curve. Suppose we draw the aggregate supply curve as horizontal, as in Exhibit 9–16a. Here we are assuming that the price level will remain fixed no matter how aggregate demand changes. (You can see this by noting the light *AD* curves superimposed on the aggregate supply curve.) If the aggregate demand curve shifts rightward from AD_1 to AD_2, the price level remains at P_1. If the aggregate demand curve shifts leftward from AD_1 to AD_3, the price level remains at P_1. The only effect of a change in aggregate demand (when the aggregate supply curve is horizontal) is a change in real GNP.

Some economists posit that the economy's aggregate supply curve would be horizontal when there are many idle resources in the economy, perhaps during a deep recession or depression. In such a setting, an increase in aggregate demand may not put any upward pressure on prices.

Kinked *AS* Curve. Another aggregate supply curve has two distinct portions: It is horizontal up to the full-employment, or natural, real GNP level, and then it is vertical, as in Exhibit 9–16b. Changes in the horizontal section will affect real GNP only, as a shift from AD_1 to AD_2 illustrates. An increase in aggregate demand that shifts the aggregate demand curve out of the horizontal section into the vertical section increases the price level and real GNP, as the shift from AD_2 to AD_3 illustrates. Finally, any change in aggregate demand in the vertical section changes only the price level, as the shift from AD_3 to AD_4 illustrates.

EXHIBIT 9–16
Three Aggregate Supply Curves

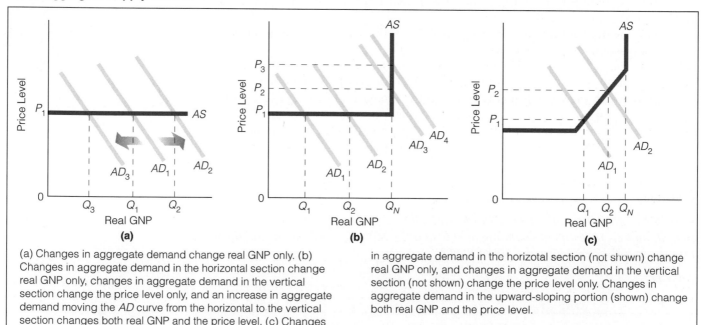

(a) Changes in aggregate demand change real GNP only. (b) Changes in aggregate demand in the horizontal section change real GNP only, changes in aggregate demand in the vertical section change the price level only, and an increase in aggregate demand moving the *AD* curve from the horizontal to the vertical section changes both real GNP and the price level. (c) Changes in aggregate demand in the horizotal section (not shown) change real GNP only, and changes in aggregate demand in the vertical section (not shown) change the price level only. Changes in aggregate demand in the upward-sloping portion (shown) change both real GNP and the price level.

What Caused the Great Depression?
A Keynesian Answer

Many people believe that the stock market crash caused the Great Depression. To most economists, however, the stock market crash was primarily an effect, not a cause. They would say that deeper, more fundamental, problems in the economy caused the stock market crash. But what were these problems? The Keynesian explanation for the Great Depression emphasizes investment spending. To grasp the entire story, we need to see what was going on in the years before the Great Depression.

Keynesians point to the sharp increase in investment demand in the early 1920s. They argue that this increased demand arose for a number of reasons.

First, World War I had left much of Europe in ruins; Europeans therefore turned to the United States for many goods. Increased European demand for American goods (U.S. exports) led to greater production in U.S. factories and to increased U.S. investment

spending (on factories and machinery) to meet the new higher demand.

Second, the end of the war unleashed American consumers' pent-up demand for goods. As a result, firms began to produce and invest more. Third, people after the war were optimistic about the future; they believed that the world was entering a period of peace and that the newest changes in technology would lead to a higher standard of living. Some economists argue that this heightened positive outlook encouraged business firms to invest beyond the level that reality indicated.

In the middle of the 1920s, the productive capacity of many industries caught up with the increased European and unleashed American demand for goods. In some industries, firms had excess productive capacity. As a result, investment demand began to fall. Then the multiplier, which brings about a greater fall in real GNP

than in investment, came into play. In turn, the decline in real GNP led to a fall in consumption, suggesting even less need for productive capacity and therefore less investment spending. In this process, the economy folded in on itself: A decline in investment led to a decline in real GNP, which led to a decline in consumption, which led to a decline in real GNP, and so on.

Not all economists agree with this explanation of the Great Depression, which explicitly maintains that the cause of the Depression was a reduction in investment spending coming off an investment boom. Some economists argue that investment was not the destabilizing element that caused the Great Depression, but rather that investment was itself destabilized by other factors. Was any factor particularly destabilizing? As we see in Chapter 14, one group of economists—called monetarists—argue that the money supply can be singled out.

Three-Stage *AS* Curve. Another scenario is for the aggregate supply curve to begin to slope upward between the point at which there are many idle resources and full-employment, or natural, real GNP. For example, the *AS* curve in Exhibit 9–16c has three sections: a horizontal section, indicating many idle resources; a vertical section at natural real GNP; and a section that slopes upward between the other two sections where resources are becoming shorter in supply but full employment has not yet been reached. Changes in aggregate demand in the horizontal section affect real GNP only;[12] changes in aggregate demand in the vertical section affect the price level only; and changes in the upward-sloping portion affect both the price level and real GNP, as the shift from AD_1 to AD_2 illustrates.

[12]In the case where the aggregate supply curve is horizontal, an increase in aggregate demand will increase real GNP only and have no effect on the price level. Some economists have referred to this as the *passive supply hypothesis,* which posits that no matter how much demand increases, supply (output) rises to meet it. With this in mind, consider a major difference between classical theory and Keynesian theory (with a horizontal *AS* curve): Whereas the classical notion was that *supply creates its own demand,* the Keynesian notion has been characterized as *demand creates its own supply.*

Here is a very Keynesian notion: the economy can be in equilibrium, and stuck in a recessionary gap, too.

■

Keynesian Theory in the *AD–AS* Framework: Equilibrium and a Recessionary Gap

In Exhibit 9–17a, equilibrium in the income–expenditure framework is at point E where the *TE* curve crosses the 45-degree line. This equilibrium point, E, corresponds to *one point* on the aggregate demand curve, namely point E', in (b). In (c), we add the short-run aggregate supply curve and see that the economy is in equilibrium at point E'. Notice that the equilibrium real GNP, Q_E, is lower than natural real GNP, Q_N: The economy is in a recessionary gap. We remind ourselves of the words of L. Tarshsis: "Keynes proposed something far more shocking: that the economy could reach *equilibrium* position, with output far below capacity [far below natural real GNP, or full-employment real GNP]." Here, then, is a very Keynesian notion: The economy can be in equilibrium and stuck in a recessionary gap, too.

According to many Keynesian economists, the economy is stuck in a recessionary gap because aggregate demand is too low. For example, if aggregate demand were represented in (d) by AD_2 instead of AD_1, then the economy would not be stuck in a recessionary gap. But, of course, saying that aggregate demand is too low is the same as saying that total expenditures in (a) are too low. In short, private spending—composed of household spending (consumption), business spending (investment), and foreign spending (net exports)—is too low to stabilize the economy at its natural real GNP level.

So what should be done? Many Keynesians would argue that the federal government should enter the economic picture to implement actions and policies that would stimulate the economy toward natural real GNP. In short, government ought to pursue those macroeconomic policies that increase aggregate demand. The key policy Keynesians propose is fiscal policy, which we discuss in the next chapter.

THINKING LIKE AN ECONOMIST

An economist's *view of the economy* and his *policy suggestions* are often linked. For example, classical economists, who view the economy as inherently stable, believe in a policy of laissez-faire: Government should keep hands off the economy. Keynesians, however, who view the economy as inherently unstable, suggest an economic role for government to play. In short, policy suggestions are sometimes a consequence of how one views the internal or inherent workings of an economy.

Major Tenets of Keynesian Theory

The P–Q Category.   Keynesian theory focuses on high unemployment and a too-low level of real GNP, Q. It is less concerned with the price level, P.

The Inherently Stable–Inherently Unstable Category.   Keynesian economists believe that the economy is inherently unstable. The economy cannot always smoothly and quickly equilibrate itself at full-employment, or natural, real GNP.

The Effective–Ineffective Category.   Keynesian economists believe that government has a role to play in managing the economy and that it can do so effectively. Keynesians do not advocate laissez-faire (see Chapter 10).

PART III
MACROECONOMIC THEORY AND
FISCAL POLICY

■

EXHIBIT 9–17

A Keynesian View of the Economy: In Equilibrium and Stuck in a Recessionary Gap, Too.

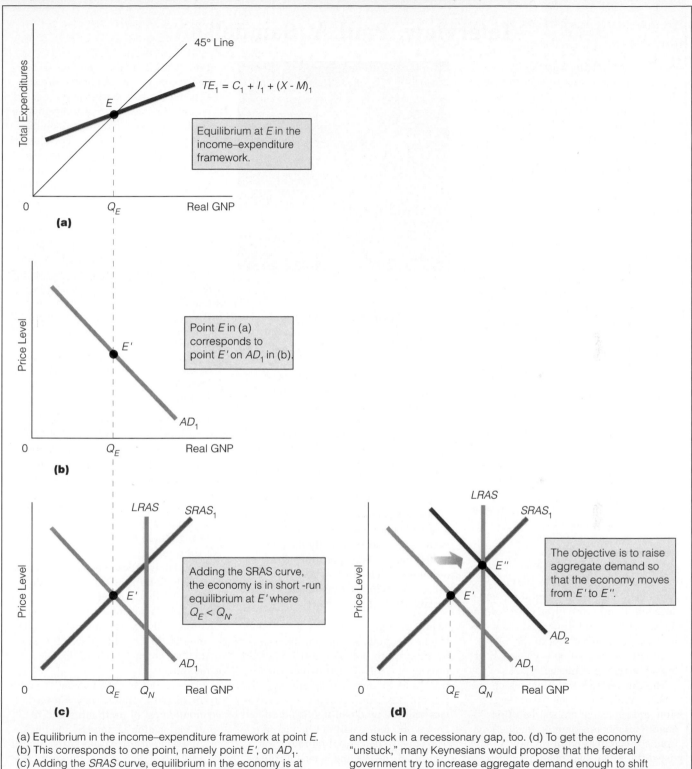

(a) Equilibrium in the income–expenditure framework at point *E*.
(b) This corresponds to one point, namely point *E'*, on AD_1.
(c) Adding the *SRAS* curve, equilibrium in the economy is at point *E'*, where real GNP is less than natural real GNP. This is a very Keynesian notion: The economy can be in equilibrium and stuck in a recessionary gap, too. (d) To get the economy "unstuck," many Keynesians would propose that the federal government try to increase aggregate demand enough to shift the *AD* curve from AD_1 to AD_2.

Interview: Paul A. Samuelson

Paul A. Samuelson was the first American economist to win the Nobel Prize in Economics (1970). He has made fundamental contributions to economic theory and greatly raised the level of scientific analysis in all branches of economics. When academic Keynesianism first came to the United States, it entered the door through Harvard University, where Samuelson was a graduate student and research fellow. Samuelson is currently at the Massachusetts Institute of Technology.

Professor Samuelson, you were a graduate student and junior fellow at Harvard University during the time the Keynesian revolution was occurring. You've said of this time that "Harvard was precisely the right place to be." Would you tell us something about the excitement you felt learning and doing research in economics during this period?

First, let me emphasize that I had my undergraduate training at the University of Chicago, and that was a great period there for neoclassical, pre-Keynesian economics. I did not want to leave Chicago, I would have stayed there forever, but the Social Science Research Council gave me an unusual fellowship, the only requirement being that I had to go elsewhere. So choosing between Columbia and Harvard, I went to Harvard. And I've always been grateful for that decision because the three great revolutions that were to follow, and were taking place in the last part of the 1930s, were largely ignored by my teachers at the University of Chicago.

The Keynesian revolution, which you refer to, grew out of the Great Depression and gave economists their first handle on macroeconomic fluctuations from a theoretical point of view. I resisted the Keynesian revolution because of my firm neoclassical training, and

I've never regretted that because it made me fully aware of the insecure microeconomic foundations of Keynesianism. But the big moment came when I realized that I'd rather have an imperfect theory that could grapple with the facts than an elegant one that really had no room in it for the phenomenon of mass unemployment in 1933.

The economist Axel Leijonhufvud has stated that the "central issue in macroeconomic theory is . . . the extent to which the economy may be regarded as a self-regulating system. In short, the issue is how well or badly its 'automatic' mechanisms perform." Professor Samuelson, how well or badly do you think the economy's "automatic" mechanisms perform?

There are efficient markets at the micro level—the modern theory of finance is a triumph when it comes to the relative pricing of General Motors preferred stock and common stock and put and call options. But it provides no guarantees that the whole of the Standard and Poor's 500 Index will not be pulled upward to 150 percent of reproduction cost of all the earning assets of American capitalism.

I don't think it is a superhuman task to make the mixed economy more stable, using the free market to do most of the day's business, but with the government in there as the ultimate stabilizer. [See Chapter 10.] Today we have just as much material for mass bankruptcies and debtor default and great banks failing (leading small banks to have runs on them) as we ever did in 1929. Still, I'm quite confident that nothing like what I lived through in the Midwest is going to happen. Under populist democracy, the rather simple things that can be done will be done to prevent the whole financial system from creating a self-fulfilling downward movement, not unlike the self-fulfilling mania for tulips in seventeenth-century Holland on the upside.

Generally, what are your thoughts on laissez-faire capitalism and a mixed economy?

My generation of economists were taught, from textbooks written about 1929, that laissez-faire capitalism was pretty much optimal. Not until John Maynard Keynes did we have a handle to diagnose and prescribe for the Great Depression that was erupting around us and that was departing from the market-clearing utopia of neoclassical equilibrium.

Fortunately modern economists have been able to build upon, and improve upon, orthodox economics. We came to grips with departures from perfect competition, and devised theories of welfare economics that could analyze income inequality characteristic of market economies.

Pure capitalism gave way everywhere to the mixed economy. In the mixed economy most of production and resource allocation is done by the market mechanisms of prices and costs, of profits and losses, and of self-interest. Why? Because experience has taught societies

Interview: Paul A. Samuelson

the hard way that alternative modes of economic organization cannot match *market efficiency.*

Efficiency divorced from human equity and welfare is without point. Democracies have converged toward the mixed economy in which the extremes of inequality and instability are moderated—under a process of law—by fiscal taxes and transfers, by regulations, and by macroeconomic stabilization poli-

cies. Since none of us can know in advance which of us will be most hurt and most blessed by the vicissitudes of dynamic markets, the Welfare State is our form of mutual insurance, and we choose it out of the same long-run self-interest and limited altruism that motivates market behavior.

Long study of the evidence of history and experience has impressed on me that economics does need *both a cool*

head and a warm heart. One is pointless without the other; the other degenerates merely into wishful thinking.

Sophie Tucker, a famous nightclub singer at the period between the Great Wars, used to say: "I've been rich. I've been poor. Believe me, rich is better." Autobiographically, I've lived under pure and under modified capitalism. Believe me, the mixed economy is better.

CHAPTER SUMMARY

Classical Theory

■ Classical theory holds that the economy is always close to or on its production possibilities frontier, which means the economy is always close to or at the point of producing natural real GNP; it is always close to or at full employment; and whatever real GNP that is produced is demanded.

■ All economists believe that Say's law (supply creates its own demand) holds in a barter economy. Here, there can be no general overproduction or underproduction of goods and services. Classical economists believed that Say's law also holds in a money economy. In their view, even if there is a leakage (saving) from the spending stream, economic forces are at work producing an equal and offsetting injection (investment).

■ In classical theory, interest rates, wages, and prices are flexible.

Keynes on Classical Economics

■ Keynes believed that the classical case (where the economy settled into equilibrium at full employment) was a special case. Keynes called his theory the "general theory."

■ Contrary to Say's law, Keynes believed that it is possible to have saving (a leakage) greater than investment (an injection), such that total spending will be insufficient to buy the goods produced. Keynes challenged the classical notion of interest rate flexibility, which "guaranteed" that increases in saving would be offset by equal increases in investment. He argued that saving and investment are dependent on other factors besides the interest rate and that the interest rate is actually one of the less important factors when it comes to changes in saving and investment.

■ Keynes's view that wages and prices are inflexible in the downward direction implies that the economy may get stuck in a recessionary gap.

■ Some economists have argued that there are microeconomic reasons why wages are inflexible in the downward direction. First, there are contracts that may lock wages in for a few years. These contracts may benefit both firms and employees. Second, efficiency wage theorists argue that firms sometimes find it in their best interest to pay wage rates above market-clearing levels since labor productivity depends on the wage the firm pays employees. Specifically, a cut in wages can cause labor productivity to decline, which, in turn, raises the firm's costs.

The Consumption, Investment, and Net Export Functions

■ Keynes made three points about consumption and disposable income: (1) Consumption depends on disposable income. (2) Consumption and disposable income move in the same direction. (3) As disposable income changes, consumption changes by less. These three ideas are incorporated into the consumption function, $C = C_0 + MPC(Y_d)$, where C_0 is autonomous consumption, MPC is the marginal propensity to consume, and Y_d is disposable income.

■ The way the consumption function is specified, consumption is greater than zero even when disposable income is zero.

■ A change in income will lead to a movement along the consumption function. A change in any one of the following factors will shift the consumption function: wealth, expectations about future prices and income, the price level, the interest rate, and taxation.

■ The investment function in the basic theory, $I = I_0$, is consistent with Keynes's idea that investment in the short run is independent of real national income, mainly, that most investment expenditures in the current period are a result of investment spending decisions made in past periods.

■ A change in any one of the following factors will shift the investment function: the interest rate, expectations about future sales, and business taxes.

■ A change in any one of the following factors will shift the net exports function: foreign real national income, price levels in the United States and in foreign nations, and the appreciation and depreciation of the U.S. dollar.

Total Expenditures and Total Production

■ If total expenditures (*TE*) equal total production (*TP*), the economy is in equilibrium. If *TP* > *TE*, the economy is in disequilibrium and inventories unexpectedly rise, signaling firms to cut back production, lower prices, or both. If *TE* > *TP*, the economy is in disequilibrium and inventories unexpectedly fall, signaling firms to increase production, raise prices, or both.

The Multiplier

■ A change in autonomous spending will bring about a multiple change in real national income or real GNP. This multiple change will be equal to $1/(1 - MPC)$ (the multiplier) times the change in autonomous spending. For example, if the multiplier = 5, and the change in autonomous investment = $400, then the change in real national income or real GNP = $2,000.

A Keynesian Theme

■ Keynes proposed that the economy could reach its equilibrium position with real GNP below natural real GNP; that is, the economy can be in equilibrium and be stuck in a recessionary gap, too.

Key Terms and Concepts

Say's Law

Involuntary
  Unemployment

Laissez-faire

Efficiency Wage Models

Consumption Function

Marginal Propensity to
  Consume

Autonomous
  Consumption

Induced Consumption

Marginal Propensity to
  Save

Average Propensity to
  Consume

Average Propensity to
  Save

Exchange Rate

Appreciation

Depreciation

Multiplier

QUESTIONS AND PROBLEMS

1. Given that classical economists believe in Say's law and interest rate and wage–price flexibility, what would the classical aggregate supply curve look like and why?

2. The economist Axel Leijonhufvud said, "The central issue in macroeconomic theory is . . . the extent to which the economy, or at least its market sectors, may properly be regarded as a self-regulating system. . . . How well or badly, do its automatic mechanisms perform?" Is there any debate between classical and Keynesian economists on this point? What does each group say?

3. Answer the following questions:

a. Suppose the MPC = .80 and that it is the same at all real income levels. Suppose autonomous consumption decreases by $500. How much does real national income change?

b. Suppose the MPS = .10 and that it is the same at all real income levels. Suppose autonomous investment increases by $100. How much does real national income change?

c. Suppose the MPC = .70 and that it is the same at all real income levels. Suppose autonomous consumption increases by $500 and autonomous investment decreases by $80. How much does real national income change?

4. In this chapter, a distinction was made between a shift in a curve or function and a movement along a curve or function. With respect to consumption, we saw that a change in real disposable income (or real national income) would lead to a movement along the consumption function, whereas a change in wealth, the price level, and so on would shift it. To add some jargon here, real disposable income is considered to be a "movement parameter" (in that a change in real disposable income will bring about a movement along a given consumption function), and wealth and so on are referred to as "shift parameters" (in that a change in wealth will bring about a shift in the consumption function). In terms of Exhibit 9–5, how does one distinguish between a movement and shift parameter?

5. Economists are often asked to make predictions. Suppose, for simplicity's sake, that the economy could be accurately summarized in the following two equations: $C = C_0 + MPC(Y_d)$ and $I = I_0$. Furthermore, assume that you know I = $1,000 and C_0 = $750, currently. Someone asks you to predict what equilibrium real national income will be one year from today. What problems might you encounter in making this prediction? Do you think it is easier for economists to explain or to predict? Why?

6. Explain the difference between the classical and Keynesian theory applied to the following: (a) leakages and injections; (b) full-employment, or natural, real GNP; (c) wage–price flexibility; (d) laissez-faire.

7. Suppose the aggregate supply curve has three portions to it: One is flat, or horizontal; one is upward sloping; and one is vertical. Explain why the effect on the price level is not always unambiguous, given a change (increase or decrease) in aggregate demand.

8. What happens if total expenditures is greater than total production? What happens if total production is greater than total expenditures?

9. Give two reasons why wage rates may be inflexible in the downward direction?

10. According to Akerlof, why might firms want to stabilize wages instead of employment?

11. What did Keynes mean when he said that classical theory is "applicable to a special case only"?

12. Explain the effect on the total expenditures (*TE*) curve of each of the following: (a) an increase in foreign national income, (b) depreciation of the U.S. dollar, (c) a fall in business taxes, (d) appreciation of the U.S. dollar, (e) an increase in wealth.

13. What is the classical view of the economy? What is the Keynesian view of the economy?

14. What is the relationship between a school's (for example, classical or Keynesian) view of the economy and its position on laissez-faire?

APPENDIX C

THE MULTIPLIER–ACCELERATOR THEORY OF THE BUSINESS CYCLE

Many Keynesians often point to changes in business investment, residential construction, and/or government spending as the cause of the business cycle. For example, a business cycle contraction might result from a decrease in business investment or government spending that lowers aggregate demand and imposes a net loss of sales on business firms. Since in Keynesian theory (nominal) wages are assumed inflexible in the downward direction, the major consequence of a fall in aggregate demand will come in the form of reduced output or real GNP instead of lower prices. A decline in output gets translated into a fall in income, and since consumption is a function of income, consumption will fall, which leads to an even lower level of aggregate demand. The original decrease in business investment or government spending snowballs into lower levels of consumption that generate a multiple (remember the multiplier?) decrease in output.

THE ACCELERATOR PRINCIPLE AND THE MULTIPLIER–ACCELERATOR PROCESS

The multiplier process just described postulates a cause–effect relationship running from decreases in business investment to multiple decreases in output. Many business cycle theorists have stated that often the cause–effect relationship runs the other way: from decreases in output to decreases in investment. The idea that investment depends on output, in particular the *growth* of output—given the condition of a constant relationship between an economy's capital stock and output—is captured in what economists call the **accelerator principle.** We illustrate how the accelerator principle works in Exhibit 9C–1, where all dollar figures are in millions.

Exhibit 9C–1 displays data for two industries: the furniture industry and the furniture machine industry. We assume that $2 of furniture machines are needed for every $1 of furniture produced. For example, if the furniture industry wants to

Accelerator Principle
The idea that investment depends on the growth rate of output. The accelerator principle assumes a constant relationship between an economy's capital stock and output.

215

EXHIBIT 9C–1

The Accelerator Principle

All numbers are in millions. The accelerator principle here shows that (1) if the growth rates of annual furniture sales decrease, net investment, gross investment, and furniture machine sales decrease in absolute terms; (2) the furniture industry moves from boom to bust even though annual furniture sales by the furniture industry do not decrease at all.

		FURNITURE INDUSTRY					FURNITURE MACHINE INDUSTRY
	(1)	(2)	(3)	(4)	(5)	(6)	(7)
	Annual Furniture Sales	Furniture Machines Needed	Furniture Machines On Hand	Net Investment in Furniture Machines = (2) − (3)	Furniture Machines That Require Replacement	Gross Investment In Furniture Machines = (4) + (5)	Sales Of Furniture Machines = (6)
Year 1	$10 ↑40%	$20	$20	$ 0	$2	$ 2	$ 2
Year 2	14 ↑42%	28	20	8	2	10	10
Year 3	20 ↑10%	40	28	12	2	14	14
Year 4	22 0%	44	40	4	2	6	6
Year 5	22 0%	44	44	0	2	2	2
Year 6	22	44	44	0	2	2	2

produce $10 million worth of furniture (see first entry in column 1), this requires $20 million worth of furniture machinery (see first entry in column 2). We also assume that each year the furniture industry needs to replace $2 million worth of machinery because of normal wear and tear (depreciation). Let us look at the situation for each of six years.

Year 1: Annual furniture sales are $10 million (column 1). This requires $20 million worth of furniture machinery (column 2). The industry currently has $20 million worth of machinery on hand (column 3). Column 4 notes the *net* investment the industry will need to make in furniture machinery this year. The dollar amount ($0) is found by subtracting the dollar worth of machines the industry has on hand from the dollar worth of machines the industry needs to satisfy its annual sales—that is, the dollar figure in column 2 minus the dollar figure in column 3. Column 5 notes the replacement investment in machinery the industry will need to make. Column 6 notes the industry's *gross* investment in machinery. This is equal to any net investment plus the replacement investment of $2 million—column 4 + column 5. Gross investment equals $2 million in year 1. Finally, in column 7, we note the dollar sales of furniture machines made by the furniture machine industry. This is equal to the gross investment of the furniture industry. In year 1, this is $2 million.

Year 2: Annual furniture sales increase 40 percent to $14 million. Since it takes $2 worth of furniture machines for every $1 worth of furniture produced, $28 million worth of furniture machines is required. Currently, the furniture industry has $20 million worth of furniture machines. This means it will need to make a net investment in furniture machines of $8 million. Adding its replacement investment this year ($2 million, column 5) to its net investment ($8 million, column 4), we obtain a total of $10 million gross investment (column 6). This is equal to furniture machines sales in year 2.

Year 3. In this year, furniture sales are $20 million, 42 percent higher than they were last year. This results in a gross investment of $14 million (column 6) and furniture machines sales of the same amount.

Year 4. In this year, furniture sales are $22 million, $2 million higher than in year 3, but the growth rate in sales (10 percent) is less than in the previous year (42 percent). What is the result? Gross investment in furniture machines falls from $14 million to $6 million. Furniture machine sales fall to $6 million.

Year 5. In this year, furniture sales are exactly what they were last year, $22 million. As a result, gross investment in furniture falls to $2 million, as do furniture machine sales.

Year 6: Once again, furniture sales are exactly what they were last year, $22 million. Gross investment and furniture machine sales are steady at $2 million. From this we can make the following conclusions:

1. If the *growth* rate of annual furniture sales increases, net investment, gross investment, and furniture machine sales increase in absolute terms.

2. If the *growth* rate of annual furniture sales decreases, net investment, gross investment, and furniture machine sales decrease in absolute terms. To put it differently, even if annual furniture sales increase or remain constant in absolute terms, as long as the *growth* rate in furniture sales decreases, net investment, gross investment, and furniture machine sales will also decrease.

3. The furniture machine industry moves from boom to bust (from sales of $2 million to $10 million to $14 million at the peak, down to $6 million and then to $2 million), even though annual furniture sales by the furniture industry do not decrease at all.

THE MULTIPLIER–ACCELERATOR EXPLANATION OF THE BUSINESS CYCLE

Combining the multiplier and the accelerator, we have an explanation of the business cycle. We describe the process by assuming that the economy is tending toward full employment, real GNP is rising, and business sales are rising at an *increasing* rate. Because of the accelerator, this results in increased investment. And because of the multiplier, the increased investment increases real GNP by a multiple of itself. In short, the accelerator and multiplier work together to expand the economy and move it faster toward full-employment output.

In time, however, the economy approaches full employment. At this point, the growth rate in business sales slows down. Because of the accelerator, investment falls. And because of the multiplier, there is a multiple decrease in real GNP. As real GNP falls, sales decrease further, leading to another round of cuts in investment. At some point, the economy will bottom out and the process is likely to repeat itself.

What we have here, then, is a story of boom and bust: a story of the business cycle. It is important to notice, too, that the multiplier–accelerator theory of the business cycle holds that the boom naturally leads into the bust, and the bust naturally leads into the boom. The theory implies that the private sector itself contains the seeds of the business cycle. As the believers in the multiplier–accelerator theory of the business cycle might say, the private economy is inherently unstable.

■ The accelerator principle holds that investment is dependent on output, or more specifically, the *growth rate of output.* In the accelerator analysis, there is a constant relationship between an economy's capital stock and output.

■ The multiplier-accelerator theory of the business cycle holds that if the economy is growing toward full employment, and sales are increasing at an increasing rate, then investment will increase, and via the multiplier, real GNP will increase by some multiple. Once the economy nears full employment, there is a slowdown in the growth rate of sales, investment falls, and via the multiplier, there is a multiple decrease in real GNP, which, in turn, leads to a further decrease in sales, investment, and real GNP. Once the economy bottoms out, the process reverses itself. A key implication of the multiplier-acceleratory theory of the business cycle is that the private economy is inherently unstable.

QUESTIONS AND PROBLEMS

1. Some economists criticize the multiplier-accelerator theory of the business cycle as being too mechanical and rigid. What do you think they mean by this? Is this a fair criticism? Would it be better to criticize the theory's predictions instead of its structure? Why?

2. Suppose the dollar amounts in column (1) of Exhibit 9C–1 are $12 million, $20 million, $24 million, $26 million, $26 million, and $26 million. Furthermore, suppose that $2 of furniture machines are needed for every $1 of furniture produced and that currently $20 million worth of furniture machines are on hand (first entry in column 3). Given this data, fill in the dollar amounts in columns (2)–(7).

APPENDIX

D

THE PERMANENT-INCOME HYPOTHESIS

Take another look at Exhibit 9–5 on page 192. You will notice that the consumption function does not go through the origin, but instead starts at a level of consumption spending of $200 billion. We specified an autonomous consumption component (C_0), which means that even if disposable income is 0 ($Y_d = 0$), consumption (C) will be greater than 0 because C_0 is positive; that is, $C = C_0 + MPC(Y_d)$.

Do real-world consumption functions take on the shape of the hypothetical consumption function in Exhibit 9–5? The answer is that some do and some do not. We explain by first discussing two types of statistical studies: cross-sectional studies and time-series studies.

In a cross-sectional study of the consumption function, the researcher does the following: (1) She divides the population into different income groups. (2) She then notes the consumption spending of the average family in the different income groups. Note that consumption spending is examined at one particular point in time. That is, in a cross-sectional study, the researcher picks one point in time, takes a cross section of families (which means that she categorizes or groups families according to some criterion), and records the consumption of the average family in each group.

When plotted, the data from cross-sectional studies of consumption take on the shape of the consumption function in Exhibit 9–5. That is, there is a direct relationship between consumption and disposable income; the consumption function does not start at the origin, but at some level of consumption spending above zero; and, following from the latter, the marginal propensity to consume is different from the average propensity to consume.

Finally, the data show that as disposable income increases, the average propensity to consume decreases; that is, high-income groups consume less and save more (in percentage terms) of their disposable incomes than do low-income groups. This finding is consistent with the way we have drawn our consumption function in Exhibit 9–5. Specifically, while the *MPC* is the slope of the consumption function, the *APC* is the slope of a ray extending from the origin to a point on the consumption function. You can visualize that the slope of this ray will become less as disposable income increases. (To see this, draw rays extending from the origin to different points on the consumption function.)

A Cross-Sectional and a Time-Series Consumption Function: Does the Permanent-Income Hypothesis Explain Why There Are Two?

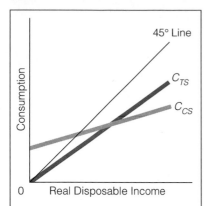

Plotting cross-sectional consumption data gives the consumption function C_{CS}. Plotting time-series consumption data gives the consumption function C_{TS}.

Thus, we can conclude that in cross-sectional consumption studies, the consumption function looks like the consumption function in Exhibit 9–5.

In time-series consumption studies, this is not the case. Here we find that the consumption function looks like the consumption function C_{TS} in Exhibit 9D–1.

Notice that this consumption function is different from the consumption function generated through cross-sectional studies (labeled C_{CS}). First, it extends outward from the origin; second, it always lies below the 45° line (this is not the case for C_{CS}); third, the *MPC* (measured by the slope of the consumption function) is equal to the *APC* (measured by the slope of the ray extending through the origin to a point on the consumption function).

In a time-series study of consumption, the researcher does the following: (1) He chooses his time period (for example, five years). (2) He decides how many periods within each year he will collect data on total consumption and total income (for example, in a quarterly time-series study, the researcher collects data on total consumption and total income in each of the four quarters of the year). The difference between a cross-sectional and time-series study is that in the former data are collected at one point in time, while in the latter, data are collected over time. Simply put, it is the difference between a snapshot, which gives us a picture of what is happening at an instant in time, and a movie, which gives us a picture of what is happening over time.

In summary, the empirical evidence suggests that there are two consumption functions: a cross-sectional consumption function and a time-series consumption function. Sometimes these are referred to as the short-run consumption function and the long-run consumption function, respectively. The two consumption functions are different. The short-run consumption function says the *APC* declines as disposable income increases, whereas the long-run consumption function says that it is constant over disposable income. Many economists believe that the existence of the two consumption functions and the inconsistency between them can be explained with the aid of the permanent-income hypothesis.

The permanent-income hypothesis, suggested by Nobel Prize–winner Milton Friedman, states that consumption is a function of permanent income, not current disposable income (as our consumption function in this chapter holds). A person's permanent income is her average, normal, or long-run income over some period of time. The time period over which she "calculates" her permanent income can be anywhere from a couple of years to many years. Suppose, for example, that Walters "calculates" her permanent income over a five-year time period. Walters expects the following disposable income for each year: year 1 = $50,000, year 2 = $55,000, year 3 = $120,000, year 4 = $60,000, year 5 = $20,000. Her average or permanent income is $61,000. The permanent-income hypothesis holds that consumption will be a function of this dollar figure, $61,000, in each of the five years, not the different dollar amounts in the different years.

A consumption function that specifies consumption as a function of current (disposable) income and one that specifies consumption as a function of permanent, or long-run, income often have quite different implications. For example, consider year 3 where Walters's current (disposable) income is $120,000, but her permanent income is $61,000—only $1,000 more than one-half of her current income. The permanent-income hypothesis holds that Walters's consumption in year 3 will be based on $61,000. The consumption function that specifies consumption as a function of current income holds that Walters's consumption in year 3 will be based on $120,000. The absolute difference in consumption spending between the two models is likely to be quite large.

In addition, the change in consumption spending between year 2 and year 3 will be different in the two hypotheses. The current-income hypothesis holds that there will be a rather large jump in consumption spending from year 2 to year 3 because there is a rather large jump in income during this period. The permanent-income hypothesis, however, holds that even though current income has taken a large jump between the two years, permanent income has not—and consumption spending is a function of the latter.

Now let us put this information together with our two consumption functions in Exhibit 9D–1. When a researcher is deriving a consumption function based on cross-sectional data, it is likely that (at that particular point in time) she will find many high-income persons are receiving current incomes that are above their permanent incomes and that their *APS*s are high (relative to others) and their *APC*s are low (relative to others) because they are spreading out their consumption over time: a little less consumption now, a little more consumption later. On the other hand, at the same point in time, many low-income persons are probably receiving current incomes that are below their permanent incomes, and therefore their *APS*s are low (relative to others) or negative, and their *APC*s are high (relative to others) because they, too, are spreading out their consumption over time: a little more consumption now, a little less consumption later. At low-income levels, then, we might expect to see dissaving: consumption expenditures greater than current income.[13] For both high-income and low-income groups, their *APC*s and *APS*s are likely to be different over time than they are at one particular point in time. And when we compare the *APC*s and *APS*s in the cross-sectional (short-run) studies with the *APC*s and *APS*s in the time-series (long-run) studies, this is what we find.

In short, the permanent-income hypothesis holds that we will (empirically) observe two consumption functions: one for the short run, or one based on cross-sectional data; and one for the long run, or one based on time-series data. The short-run consumption function is a picture of consumption spending while individuals are spreading out their consumption spending; the long-run consumption function is a picture of consumption spending after it has been spread out.

APPENDIX SUMMARY

■ In a cross-sectional study of consumption, the researcher divides the population into different income groups and notes the consumption spending of the average family in the different income groups. In a time-series study of consumption, the researcher chooses a time period and then decides how many periods within the time period she will collect data on consumption and income. The difference between a cross-sectional and time-series study is that in the former data are collected at one point in time, while in the latter, data are collected over time.
■ Milton Friedman hypothesized that consumption is a function of permanent income, not current income. A person's permanent income is her average, normal, or long-run income over some time period.

[13]Consider the case of a poor medical student who, because he believes his future income as a physician will be quite large, dissaves in the present.

■ The permanent income hypothesis holds that permanent changes in income have a major effect on consumption while transitory changes have a minor effect.
■ The permanent income hypothesis holds that we will (empirically) observe two consumption functions: one for the short run, or one based on cross-sectional data; and one for the long run, or one based on time series data. The short-run consumption function is a picture of consumption spending while individuals are spreading out their consumption spending; the long-run consumption function is a picture of consumption spending after it has been spread out.

QUESTIONS AND PROBLEMS

1. A person's average income is $37,000 a year for 10 years. In the eleventh year, his income unexpectedly jumps to $80,000, but there is little chance that this higher income level will continue into the future. According to the permanent income hypothesis, would we expect a large or small increase in consumption spending? Explain your answer.

2. Explain why the cross-sectional consumption function lies above the time-series consumption function at low levels of income but not at high levels of income.

3. Explain why poor medical students often dissave.

CHAPTER 10

FISCAL POLICY

WHAT THIS CHAPTER IS ABOUT

Can the federal government's spending and taxing powers be successfully used to stabilize the economy—that is, to eliminate both recessionary and inflationary gaps? This question underlies much of our discussion in this chapter. In other terms, it asks whether fiscal policy is effective or ineffective at meeting certain macroeconomic goals.

FISCAL POLICY

■

In this section, we define a budget deficit, a budget surplus, and a balanced budget, and describe the workings of fiscal policy.

The Federal Budget: Expenditures and Tax Receipts

The federal budget is composed of two, not necessarily equal, parts: expenditures (G) and tax receipts or revenues (T). If expenditures outstrip tax receipts, a **budget deficit** exists—which the federal government has had each year since 1970; if tax receipts outstrip expenditures, a **budget surplus** exists; and if expenditures equal tax receipts, a **balanced budget** exists.

What Is Fiscal Policy?

Fiscal policy refers to changes in government expenditures and taxation to achieve particular macroeconomic goals, such as low unemployment, stable prices, and economic growth. For example, fiscal policy might be used to move the economy out of a recessionary or inflationary gap. If it is used to increase either aggregate demand or aggregate supply, it is called **expansionary fiscal policy.** If it is used to decrease either aggregate demand or aggregate supply, it is called **contractionary fiscal policy.** A particular fiscal policy that is deliberately brought about through government action is referred to as **discretionary fiscal policy.** It follows that there can be either (1) discretionary expansionary fiscal policy or (2) discretionary contractionary fiscal policy.

In contrast, a policy measure that occurs automatically in response to economic events and is the result of past governmental decisions is referred to as **automatic fiscal policy** (or built-in fiscal policy). It follows that there can either be (1) automatic expansionary fiscal policy or (2) automatic contractionary fiscal policy.

As Exhibit 10–1 illustrates, discretionary expansionary fiscal policy includes deliberate actions by policy makers that increase government spending, decrease taxes, or both. Discretionary contractionary fiscal policy includes deliberate actions by government that decrease government spending, increase taxes, or both.

Notice that unemployment compensation and welfare payments are examples of both automatic expansionary and automatic contractionary fiscal policies. For example, if the economy turns down (real GNP declines), more people will become unemployed and eligible for unemployment benefits. We would also expect that some people would become eligible for welfare assistance. Unemployment compensation and welfare payments soften an economic downturn by preventing consumption spending (and therefore aggregate demand) from falling as much as it would if these two programs had not been in place. In short, during an economic downturn, unemployment compensation and welfare payments are automatic expansionary fiscal measures that reduce the intensity of the fall.

The two programs also moderate the intensity of an economic upturn. As individuals find jobs, many no longer receive welfare payments or unemployment compensation. Instead, increased deductions from payrolls for state and local programs and for union unemployment funds reduce the increase in disposable income going to employed workers.

Budget Deficit
Government expenditures outstrip tax receipts.

Budget Surplus
Tax receipts outstrip government expenditures.

Balanced Budget
Government expenditures equal tax receipts.

Fiscal Policy
Changes in government expenditures and taxation to achieve particular macroeconomic goals, such as low unemployment, stable prices, economic growth, and so on.

Expansionary Fiscal Policy
Fiscal policy designed to increase aggregate demand or aggregate supply.

Contractionary Fiscal Policy
Fiscal policy designed to decrease aggregate demand or aggregate supply.

Discretionary Fiscal Policy
Deliberate changes of government expenditures and taxes to achieve particular economic objectives.

Automatic Fiscal Policy
Changes in government expenditures or taxes that occur automatically without (additional) congressional action.

Question:

Does discretionary expansionary fiscal policy result in a budget deficit?

EXHIBIT 10–1
Four Types of Fiscal Policy

	Expansionary	Contractionary
Discretionary	Policymakers ↑G or ↓T or both **(1)**	Policymakers ↓G or ↑T or both **(2)**
Automatic	Unemployment Compensation Welfare Payments **(3)**	Unemployment Compensation Welfare Payments **(4)**

In this exhibit, G = government spending; T = taxes. The four types of fiscal policy include (1) discretionary expansionary, (2) discretionary contractionary, (3) automatic expansionary, and (4) automatic contractionary. Notice that unemployment compensation and welfare payments are examples of automatic expansionary fiscal policy and automatic contractionary fiscal policy.

Answer:

It can, but not necessarily. Whether it does depends on (1) the state of the budget before the expansionary fiscal policy is enacted and (2) the amount of expansionary fiscal stimulus. Suppose there is a budget surplus of $100 billion and government spending is increased by $20 billion. As a result, the surplus shrinks—but there is still a surplus. But if the budget was balanced before the increased spending, a deficit results. Finally, if the budget was in deficit before the increased spending, the expansionary fiscal action will increase the size of the deficit.

THE RISE OF DISCRETIONARY FISCAL POLICY

Discretionary fiscal policy did not always play as important a role as it did in the 1960s, and '70s. The story of the rise of discretionary fiscal policy—from the halls of academia to the hallways of Congress and the White House—is an interesting one, which we summarize briefly here.

The Old-Time Fiscal Religion

Before the Keynesian revolution in economics, laypersons and economists alike generally accepted the following standards:

1. The federal budget should be balanced. The Adam Smith notion that "what is prudence in the conduct of every private family, can scarce be folly in that of a great kingdom" was generally accepted. Since most persons believed that it was wrong for individuals to go into debt, particularly year after year, it was also widely accepted that a country should not pile up debt by running annual deficits. There was, however, one exception to the balanced budget rule. It was permissible for countries to run budget deficits during wartime. But after the war, a surplus was required to counteract the earlier deficits.

2. Increased federal spending should be tied to higher taxes so that individuals can clearly and correctly judge the true cost of government. The Swedish economist Knut Wicksell argued that individuals could only make an informed evaluation of various proposals for government expenditure if they were presented with a tax bill at the same time the proposal for additional spending was made. This was what we call the "menu approach to government spending." Next to each government program or activity would be its tax price. Citizen-taxpayers would review the menu, consider the prices (taxes) they would have to pay if they chose A over B, or B over C, and then make their choices—with their eyes wide open and with reality in full view.

3. Government spending and taxing powers should be directed to providing the citizenry with publicly demanded goods and services and should not be used to manipulate macroeconomic variables. People believed that it is beyond the proper role of government to manage the economy; the government's only proper role is to provide demanded goods and services that the economy cannot privately, through ordinary market forces, supply for itself. Related to this was the belief that the market economy is inherently stable. This is the classical notion that the economy naturally self-equilibrates at the full-employment, or natural, real GNP level.

Discretionary Fiscal Policy Moves to Center Stage

Beginning in the 1930s, many economists came to accept the Keynesian notion that the economy may be inherently unstable. The old-time fiscal religion was thrust aside by the new fiscal religion, which stated that expansionary fiscal policy should be implemented when aggregate demand is "too low," or when there is a recessionary gap—even if this meant budget deficits; and contractionary fiscal policy should be implemented when aggregate demand is "too high," or when there is an inflationary gap—even if this meant budget surpluses.

In the 1960s and '70s, the political implications of the new fiscal religion became explicit. To some economists, it seemed that expansionary fiscal policy—where government spending (G) was increased and/or taxes (T) reduced—was much easier to implement than contractionary fiscal policy—where government spending was decreased and/or taxes raised. Politicians, it was suggested, would readily increase G or lower T because these measures were popular with voters. But they would not so readily, if at all, call for decreases in G or increases in T because this usually met with voter resistance. Some economists began to ask if there was a political bias to the new fiscal religion. Would expansionary fiscal policy become the order of the day and contractionary fiscal policy be relegated to the dustbin? Would the political bias of the new fiscal religion result in a long string of annual budget deficits?

Question:

Do individuals who favor discretionary fiscal policy also favor big government?

Answer:

This is not necessarily the case. For example, consider two persons, Connors and Jordan. Connors favors "big government" and Jordan favors "small government." Is it possible for both of them also to favor discretionary fiscal policy? The answer is yes. Connors, who favors "big government," will advocate increases in government spending if he thinks the situation calls for expansionary fiscal policy. On the other hand, Jordan, who favors "small government," will advocate decreases in taxes.

Both measures—increased spending and decreased taxes—are expansionary fiscal measures. Similarly, if Connors thinks contractionary fiscal policy is required, he will advocate increases in taxes, while Jordan will advocate decreases in government spending. So one can be in favor of big government or small government and still advocate the use of discretionary fiscal policy.

DEMAND-SIDE FISCAL POLICY

Government spending and taxation can affect the demand or the supply side of the economy. We focus on the demand side in this section and discuss the supply side in the next section. First, we examine fiscal policy in the Keynesian theory; then we discuss the effectiveness of, and problems associated with, fiscal policy.

How Do Changes in *G* and *T* Affect Aggregate Demand?

Before discussing demand-side fiscal policy, we need to know the mechanics of how fiscal policy actually affects aggregate demand. Since fiscal policy deals with both increases and decreases in *G* and *T,* we need to know (1) how an increase in *G* affects aggregate demand; (2) how a decrease in *G* affects aggregate demand; (3) how an increase in *T* affects aggregate demand; and (4) how a decrease in *T* affects aggregate demand.

In Chapter 8, we said that *at a given price level,* anything that increases total expenditures—the components of which are consumption, investment, government expenditures, and net exports—increases aggregate demand and shifts the *AD* curve to the right; and *at a given price level,* anything that decreases total expenditures decreases aggregate demand and shifts the *AD* curve to the left. As we can see, an increase in government expenditures—which is a component of total expenditures—increases aggregate demand and shifts the *AD* curve to the right; a decrease in government expenditures decreases aggregate demand and shifts the *AD* curve to the left.[1]

A change in taxes can directly affect either or both consumption and investment, both of which are components of total expenditures. For example, a decrease in income taxes will increase disposable (after-tax) income, and households can, and perhaps will, consume more goods and services at a given price level—thus shifting the *AD* curve to the right. An increase in income taxes will decrease disposable (after-tax) income and lead to the opposite effect.

Fiscal Policy in Keynesian Theory

In Exhibit 10–2a, the economy is initially at point 1 and in a recessionary gap. Aggregate demand is too low to move the economy to equilibrium at the natural real GNP level. A familiar Keynesian prescription is to enact discretionary expansionary fiscal policy measures (an increase in government spending, a decrease in taxes, or both) to shift the aggregate demand curve rightward from AD_1 to AD_2 and move the economy to point 2 and to the natural real GNP level.

[1]We question this stated effect on aggregate demand of an increase or decrease in government expenditures later in the chapter when we discuss the issue of crowding out.

EXHIBIT 10–2
Fiscal Policy in Keynesian Theory: Ridding the Economy of Recessionary and Inflationary Gaps

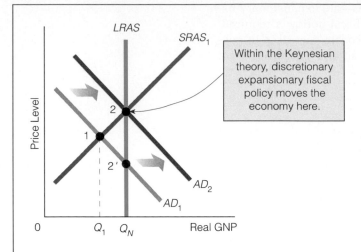

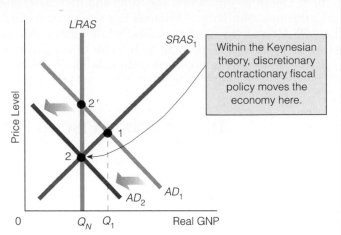

Within the Keynesian theory, discretionary expansionary fiscal policy moves the economy here.

Within the Keynesian theory, discretionary contractionary fiscal policy moves the economy here.

(a)
**Discretionary Expansionary Fiscal Policy
for a Recessionary Gap**

(b)
**Discretionary Contractionary Fiscal Policy
for an Inflationary Gap**

(a) Discretionary expansionary fiscal policy is used within Keynesian theory to eliminate a recessionary gap. Increased government spending, decreased taxes, or both lead to a rightward shift in the aggregate demand curve from AD_1 to AD_2, restoring the economy to the natural level of real GNP, Q_N. (b) Discretionary contractionary fiscal policy is used to eliminate an inflationary gap. Decreased government spending, increased taxes, or both lead to a leftward shift in the aggregate demand curve from AD_1 to AD_2, restoring the economy to the natural level of real GNP, Q_N.

Of course, at this point someone might ask, Why not simply wait for the short-run aggregate supply curve to shift rightward and intersect the aggregate demand curve at point 2'? The Keynesians have usually responded that (1) the economy is stuck at point 1 and won't move naturally to point 2'; or (2) it takes too long for the short-run aggregate supply curve to shift rightward, and in the interim we must deal with the high cost of unemployment and lower level of real GNP.

In Exhibit 10–2b, the economy is initially at point 1 and in an inflationary gap. In this situation, Keynesians are likely to propose a discretionary contractionary fiscal measure (a decrease in government spending, an increase in taxes, or both) to shift the aggregate demand curve leftward from AD_1 to AD_2 and move the economy to point 2.

The Calculations

According to Keynesian economists, a change in government spending will change real GNP by some multiple of itself. (This is the multiplier principle we discussed in Chapter 9.) Specifically, the change in real GNP is equal to the multiplier (m), which is $1/1 - MPC$, times the change in autonomous spending. In our example, the "change in autonomous spending" is equal to the "change in government spending."

$$(1) \quad \Delta Q = m \times \Delta G$$

For example, if the marginal propensity to consume is .80 (80 percent), then the multiplier is 5. So, if there is an increase in government spending of $4 billion, the increase in real GNP is five times this amount, or $20 billion.

Now instead of raising government spending by $4 billion, let's lower taxes by $4 billion. Assuming the same multiplier, will this raise real GNP by $20 billion? In other words, is a decrease in taxes of $4 billion equal in its expansionary fiscal effects to an increase in government spending of $4 billion?

The answer is no. Look at it this way. When government spending increases, 100 percent of every dollar of increased spending immediately goes to increase total expenditures. But when taxes are decreased, households experience an increase in disposable income. Some part of the tax cut is spent and some is saved. The amount that goes for saving depends on the marginal propensity to save. For example, if the marginal propensity to save is 20 percent, then 20 percent of each tax dollar reduction goes for saving, and the remainder (80 percent) goes for consumption, which in turn goes to increase aggregate demand.

What do we conclude? A dollar spent by government is a dollar spent; a dollar tax cut is a dollar partly saved and partly spent.

To calculate the change in real GNP given a change in taxes (T), we use the following formula:

$$(2) \quad \Delta Q = -MPC(m) \times \Delta T$$

In our example, a $4 billion cut in taxes increases real GNP by $16 billion. The arithmetic is simple: $-MPC(m) = -.80(5) = -4$, which we then multiply by the change in taxes ($-$$4 billion) to get $16 billion. We conclude that a $4 billion increase in government spending increases real GNP by more than a $4 billion tax cut does.

With this knowledge, now consider the net effect of an increase in government spending of $4 billion, which is an expansionary fiscal measure, and a simultaneous increase in taxes of $4 billion, which is an equal contractionary fiscal measure. Assuming we started from a position of a balanced budget, we are maintaining this state of affairs by raising taxes to the same degree we raise government expenditures.

What will be the change in real GNP? We obtain our answer by breaking down the problem into two parts. First we ask, What will be the increase in real GNP if government spending is increased by $4 billion? Then we ask, What will be the decrease in real GNP if taxes are increased by $4 billion? Finally, we note the difference, if any, between the two dollar amounts.

Assuming $MPC = .80$, the multiplier is 5, so that the increase in real GNP given an increase in government spending of $4 billion is $20 billion. (We have simply plugged the numbers into equation 1.) The change in real GNP given an increase of $4 billion in taxes is $-$$16 billion (equation 2). The difference between the two dollar amounts is a positive $4 billion.

We conclude: If government spending is increased $4 billion and taxes are increased $4 billion (to maintain the balance between expenditures and revenues), real GNP increases by $4 billion. In general terms: The change in real GNP is equal to the change in government spending when government spending and taxes change by the same dollar amount and in the same direction. This is what economists call the **balanced budget theorem.**

Question:

Simply, the balanced budget theorem seems to say that if government spending goes up by $X, and taxes go up by $X, real GNP will go up by $X. Is this correct?

Balanced Budget Theorem
A change in real GNP is equal to the change in government spending when government spending and taxes change by the same dollar amount and in the same direction.

229

Answer:

Yes. What the balanced budget theorem implies is that it is possible to increase government spending, maintain the budget in balance, and increase real GNP as well. For many persons, this is an ideal situation.

Crowding Out: Calling the Effectiveness of Fiscal Policy into Question

Many of the criticisms of the predicted effects of fiscal policy on aggregate demand and real GNP, as well as the multiplier analysis and the balanced budget theorem, come under the general heading of **crowding out.** This term refers to a decrease in private expenditures (consumption and so on) as a consequence of increased government spending or the financing needs of the deficit. The following are all possible examples of crowding out:

1. The government spends more on public libraries, and individuals buy fewer books at bookstores.[2]
2. The government spends more on public education, and individuals spend less on private education.
3. The government spends more on public transportation, and individuals spend less on private transportation.
4. The government spends more on social programs and defense without increasing taxes; the size of the deficit increases; the government is required to borrow more loanable funds to finance the larger deficit; real interest rates rise; as a result, investment decreases.

Believers in the existence of the crowding-out phenomenon argue that because of higher real interest rates (example 4) and the direct substitution of public services for consumer spending (examples 1–3), increases in government spending induce consumers and investors to spend less. Government spending crowds out private spending—either directly (examples 1–3) or indirectly (example 4).[3]

Furthermore, crowding out can be either complete or incomplete.[4] **Complete crowding out** occurs when the decrease in one or more components of private spending completely offsets the increase in government spending. For example, if government spending on public education increases by $100 million, and individual spending on private education drops $100 million as a result, we have complete crowding out.

Incomplete crowding out occurs when the decrease in one or more components of private spending only partially offsets the increase in government spending. For example, government spending on public libraries increases by $25 million, and individuals spend $5 million less on books at bookstores.

Whether we are dealing with complete or incomplete crowding out, the crowding-out effect suggests that discretionary expansionary fiscal policy will have an impact on aggregate demand and real GNP less than the Keynesian theory predicts.

Crowding Out
The decrease in private expenditures that occurs as a consequence of increased government spending or of the financing needs of the deficit.

Complete Crowding Out
The decrease in one or more components of private spending completely offsets the increase in government spending.

Incomplete Crowding Out
The decrease in one or more components of private spending only partially offsets the increase in government spending.

---

[2]We are not saying *if* government spends more on public libraries, individuals will *necessarily* buy fewer books at bookstores; rather, if they do, this would be an example of crowding out. The same holds for examples 2, 3, and 4.
[3]Some economists refer to the direct substitution of public services for private spending as *direct crowding out* and the decrease in investment caused by higher real interest rates as *indirect crowding out.*
[4]Alternatively, crowding out can be zero (no crowding out), complete (100 percent), or incomplete (somewhere between zero and complete).

In Exhibit 10–3, we illustrate the consequences of complete and incomplete crowding out. We also compare each with the case in Keynesian theory.

In 10–3, the economy is initially at point 1, Q_1. In Keynesian theory, expansionary fiscal policy increases the aggregate demand curve to AD_2 and moves the economy to point 2, Q_N. This implicitly assumes there is zero, or no, crowding out. With incomplete crowding out, the aggregate demand curve only increases (on net) to AD_2' because the initial stimulus in aggregate demand, due, say, to increased government spending, is partially offset by a fall in private expenditures. The economy moves to point 2', Q_2'. In the case of complete crowding out, the initial stimulus in aggregate demand, due to increased government spending, is completely offset by a fall in private expenditures such that the aggregate demand curve does not move (on net) at all. With complete crowding out, expansionary fiscal policy has no effect on the economy. The economy remains at point 1, Q_1.

Crowding out calls the effectiveness of fiscal policy into question.

Crowding Out, the Real Interest Rate, and Foreign Loanable Funds

Will there be less crowding out if, in response to higher real interest rates, loanable funds are attracted from abroad? Suppose the federal government either increases government spending or cuts taxes, and runs a larger budget deficit. The financing of the larger deficit increases the demand for loanable funds (demand for credit) and the real interest rate. Because of the higher real interest rate, investment declines. There is crowding out.

Now suppose we return to the point where real interest rates increased and ask ourselves if something might have been left out of the story. Many economists argue that the higher real interest rates will attract loanable funds from abroad. Foreigners, in search of the highest rates of return (actually, the highest after-tax real returns) will help finance the deficit by lending funds to the federal government through their purchases of U.S. Treasury securities. This action increases the supply of loanable funds (supply of credit) and keeps the real interest rate from rising, or rising as much.

How does the inflow of foreign funds affect crowding out? At first glance, it might appear to moderate it, since it dampens the increase in the real interest rate and thus the fall in investment. But a closer look is required. Before foreigners buy

EXHIBIT 10–3
Zero, Incomplete, and Complete Crowding Out

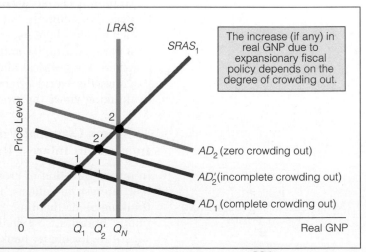

The effects of zero, incomplete, and complete crowding out in the *AD–AS* framework. Starting at point 1, expansionary fiscal policy shifts the aggregate demand curve to AD_2 and moves the economy to point 2 and Q_N. The Keynesian theory that predicts this outcome assumes zero, or no, crowding out; an increase in, say, government spending does not reduce private expenditures. With incomplete crowding out, an increase in government spending causes private expenditures to decrease by less than the increase in government expenditures. On net, the aggregate demand curve shifts to AD_2'. The economy moves to point 2' and Q_2'. With complete crowding out, an increase in government spending is completely offset by a decrease in private expenditures, and on net aggregate demand does not increase at all. The economy remains at point 1 and Q_1.

The increase (if any) in real GNP due to expansionary fiscal policy depends on the degree of crowding out.

231

Economic thinking views the world as essentially one country.

■

U.S. Treasury securities, they must exchange their domestic currency for U.S. dollars. This action increases the demand, and price, of U.S. dollars in the foreign exchange market. In short, the dollar will appreciate in value relative to other currencies: More of other currencies will be required to buy a dollar. In turn, this will make foreign goods cheaper for Americans, and American goods more expensive for foreigners. Economists predict that Americans will import more and export less. We conclude that some of the crowding out of private expenditures will come in the form of a decrease in net exports.

Question:

Does it follow that an increase in the size of the federal budget deficit can affect U.S. international trade?

Answer:

Trade Deficit
The situation where the value of exports is less than the value of imports.

Yes. To explain more fully, the United States is said to have a **trade deficit** if the value of its exports is less than the value of its imports. Let's suppose that the United States currently has a budget deficit of $100 billion and a trade deficit of $60 billion. The Congress increases government expenditures but does not raise taxes. As a result, the deficit becomes larger. Consequently, the U.S. Treasury demands more funds in the loanable funds market and the real interest rate rises. Then, as we said, the higher real interest rate causes foreign lenders to purchase interest-paying U.S. Treasury securities. In order to buy the securities, foreigners end up increasing their demand for U.S. dollars; thus, the dollar appreciates in value relative to foreign currencies. This makes foreign goods cheaper for Americans and American goods more expensive for foreigners. Americans import more and export less, thus widening the trade deficit beyond the original $60 billion. This is how a bigger budget deficit can lead to a bigger trade deficit.

Economic changes, like a stone thrown into a lake, often have a ripple effect. We have just seen how an increase in government spending can affect (1) the budget deficit, (2) interest rates, (3) the value of the dollar relative to other currencies, (4) the purchases of both foreigners and Americans, and (5) the U.S. trade deficit. These are quite a few ripples, and there are plenty more that we have not discussed. Economists have a mindset that takes the ripple effect into account: A change over here brings about a change way over there. Simply put, this means the laws of economics do not take notice of a nation's borders; economic effects do not ripple outward until they reach a national frontier and then stop, but may be worldwide in scope. This is where the political and economic way of thinking differ. Political thinking views the world as composed of hundreds of sovereign nations; economic thinking views the world as essentially one country.

The New Classical View of Fiscal Policy: Crowding Out with No Increase in Interest Rates

In our explanation of crowding out, we emphasized both direct substitution and real interest rate effects. In the first case, crowding out is a result of individuals thinking along this line: "Government has increased its expenditures on books in public libraries, so I shall decrease my private spending on books, which is a substitute for library books." In the second case, employers are thinking this way:

"The real interest rate has gone up (as a result of increased financing needs related to the deficit), so we shall reduce investment spending." Here, then, are two ways of understanding individuals' motives behind the crowding-out phenomenon.

According to the *new classical school of economics* there is yet another way of looking at what people may do. These economists believe that individuals, in response to expansionary fiscal policy measures, a larger deficit, and greater deficit-financing requirements, think the following: "A larger deficit implies more debt this year and higher future taxes. I'll simply save more in the present so I can pay the higher future taxes required to pay interest and to repay principal on the new debt."

Thus, the new classical macroeconomics theory offers a few predictions:

1. Current consumption will fall as a result of expansionary fiscal policy. An increase in government spending that increases the size of the deficit and the amount of debt financing will cause individuals to save more (consume less) to pay the higher future taxes.

2. Deficits do not bring higher real interest rates. The reason is simple: Deficits merely substitute future taxes for current taxes. Individuals save more to pay for their higher future taxes. The increased saving increases the supply of loanable funds and offsets the increased demand for loanable funds that is a consequence of the financing requirements of the deficit.

We illustrate these two new classical predictions in Exhibit 10–4. In (a), the economy is initially at point 1. If individuals do not anticipate higher future taxes as a result of expansionary fiscal policy, the aggregate demand curve will shift rightward from AD_1 to AD_2. However, new classical economists believe that individuals do anticipate higher future taxes, and therefore will reduce their consumption (and increase their saving) to pay the higher future taxes. In this case, the aggregate demand curve does not shift at all. What is the conclusion? Expansionary fiscal policy, given the condition of anticipated higher future taxes, leaves real GNP, unemployment, and the price level unchanged. Expansionary fiscal policy is not stimulative—it is not effective.

In (b), the loanable funds market is initially in equilibrium at point 1 and the real interest rate is i_1. As a result of the government implementing an expansionary fiscal policy measure, we have a deficit. The deficit requires financing, and so the demand for loanable funds shifts rightward from D_1 to D_2. At the same time, individuals perceive the deficit in terms of higher future taxes and increase their saving by enough to offset the higher future taxes. This action shifts the supply of loanable funds from S_1 to S_2. What is the conclusion? There is no change in the real interest rate.

The new classical position on expansionary fiscal policy might be summarized as follows: As long as expansionary fiscal policy is translated into higher future taxes (which new classical economists think is likely), there will be no change in real GNP, unemployment, the price level, or real interest rates. The analysis also holds for contractionary fiscal policy.

Question:

It doesn't seem that people will necessarily save enough to offset their higher future taxes completely, since many people won't live long enough to pay the higher future taxes. Won't some simply say, "I'd rather the government run a deficit today, and have lower taxes now, because when the higher future taxes roll around, I

EXHIBIT 10–4
The New Classical View of Expansionary Fiscal Policy

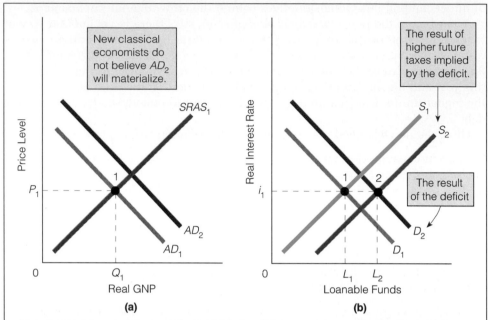

New classical economists argue that individuals will link expansionary fiscal policy to higher future taxes and decrease their current consumption and increase their saving as a result. (a) The decreased consumption prevents the aggregate demand curve from shifting rightward from AD_1 to AD_2. (b) The increased saving causes the supply of loanable funds to shift rightward from S_1 to S_2, thus offsetting the increased demand for loanable funds and maintaining the existing level of real interest rates. The new classical position on both (anticipated) expansionary and contractionary fiscal policy is that neither affects real GNP, unemployment, the price level, or real interest rates.

won't be here. Future taxpayers will have to pay for the increased government expenditures that I enjoyed."

If many of these assumed savers won't be paying the future taxes, there will be no reason to save more. Have the new classical economists thought of this?

Answer:

They have. One new classical economist, Robert Barro, points to the fact that individuals leave bequests to their children, implying that they care about their children's welfare and, indirectly, about the tax burden their children will one day face. He argues that today's taxpayers, reacting to an increased budget deficit, will increase their saving in order to leave more to their children, who will have to pay the higher future taxes.

On the topic of deficits and interest rates, there is some empirical evidence. In August 1981, the Congress passed a tax reduction bill that was to be phased in over the following three years. According to the new classical position, individuals would likely see this as resulting in a larger deficit, more debt financing, and higher future taxes. In reaction, they would increase their saving so that they, or their children, would be able to pay off the higher future taxes. Did they respond in kind? Most economists think not. The personal saving rate fell after 1981 from approximately 6.3 percent to an average of 4.8 percent in 1982–85.

Although this calls into question the new classical position on deficits, saving, and interest rates, there is some support for the position. For one thing, numerous empirical studies have found no statistically significant direct relationship between annual changes in the budget deficit and real interest rates. On the other hand, some economists have pointed out that although such a short-term relationship has not been found, the persistently high deficits of the early and mid-1980s were associated with high real interest rates. The question whether deficits cause higher real interest rates has not been definitely answered.

Lags and Discretionary Fiscal Policy

Suppose it were proved, beyond a shadow of a doubt, that discretionary fiscal policy is effective at changing real GNP. Would it hold that discretionary fiscal policy ought to be used to solve the problems of inflationary and recessionary gaps? Many economists would answer "not necessarily." The reason is because of lags. There are five types of lags.

1. The data lag. Policymakers are not aware of what is happening in the economy the day or week after it happens. For example, if the economy turns down in January, this may not be apparent for two to three months.

2. The wait-and-see lag. Once policymakers are aware of a downturn in economic activity, they are not likely to enact counteractive measures immediately. Instead, they probably will adopt a more cautious, wait-and-see attitude. They will want to be sure that the observed events are more than a very short-run phenomenon.

3. The legislative lag. Once policymakers decide that some type of fiscal policy measure is required, Congress or the president will have to propose the measure, build political support for it, and get it passed. This can take many months.

4. The transmission lag. Once a fiscal policy measure is enacted, it takes time to put the policy into effect. For example, a discretionary expansionary fiscal policy measure of increased spending for public works projects will require construction companies to submit bids for the work, prepare designs, negotiate contracts, and so on.

5. The effectiveness lag. Once a policy measure is actually implemented, it takes time for it to affect the economy. If government spending is increased on Monday, the aggregate demand curve does not shift rightward on Tuesday.

Taking these five lags together, some economists argue that discretionary fiscal policy is not likely to have the impact on the economy that policymakers will be hoping for. The problem is that, by the time the full impact of the policy is felt, the economic problem the policy was designed to solve may no longer exist, or may not exist to the degree it once did, or the problem may have changed altogether.

We illustrate this point in Exhibit 10–5. Suppose the economy is currently in a recessionary gap at point 1. The recession is under way before government officials recognize it. Once recognized, however, Congress and the president consider enacting expansionary fiscal policy in the hopes of shifting the AD curve from AD_1 to AD_2 and intersecting the $SRAS$ curve at point 1', at natural real GNP. But in the interim, unknown to everybody, the economy is "healing" itself: The $SRAS$ curve is shifting to the right. Government officials don't see this yet because it takes time to collect and analyze data on the economy.

Thinking that the economy is not healing itself, or not healing itself quickly enough, Congress begins the process of enacting expansionary fiscal policy. In

EXHIBIT 10–5
Fiscal Policy May Destabilize the Economy

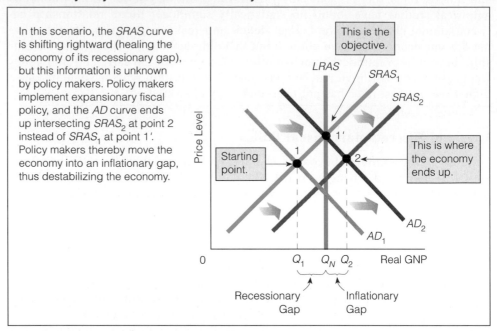

In this scenario, the *SRAS* curve is shifting rightward (healing the economy of its recessionary gap), but this information is unknown by policy makers. Policy makers implement expansionary fiscal policy, and the *AD* curve ends up intersecting *SRAS*$_2$ at point 2 instead of *SRAS*$_1$ at point 1'. Policy makers thereby move the economy into an inflationary gap, thus destabilizing the economy.

time, the *AD* curve shifts rightward. But by the time the increased demand is felt in the goods and services markets, the *AD* curve intersects the *SRAS* curve at point 2. In short, the government has moved the economy from point 1 to point 2, and not, as it had hoped, from point 1 to point 1'. The government has moved the economy into an inflationary gap. Instead of stabilizing and moderating the business cycle, it has intensified it.

Crowding Out, Lags, and the Effective–Ineffective Category

The issue of crowding out and lags may be placed in the effective–ineffective category (see Chapter 5). Specifically, those economists who believe crowding out is zero and that the lags are insignificant conclude that fiscal policy is *effective* at moving the economy out of a recessionary gap. Those economists who believe crowding out is complete and/or that the lags are significant conclude that fiscal policy is *ineffective* at moving the economy out of a recessionary gap. Keynesians usually view fiscal policy as effective, and new classical economists usually view it as ineffective.

SUPPLY-SIDE FISCAL POLICY
■

Fiscal policy effects may be felt on the supply side as well as the demand side of the economy. For example, a reduction in tax rates may alter an individual's incentive to work and produce, thus altering aggregate supply. We discuss the relevant issues in this section.

Marginal Tax Rates and Aggregate Supply

When fiscal policy measures affect tax rates, they may affect the aggregate supply curve as well as the aggregate demand curve. Consider a reduction in an individ-

Interview: Alice Rivlin

Alice M. Rivlin was the director of the Congressional Budget Office (CBO) from its inception in 1973 until 1983. As such, she is an economist with extensive knowledge of the budget process. In 1985 Dr. Rivlin became the first woman to be elected president of the American Economic Association. She is currently at the Brookings Institution.

Dr. Rivlin, what is the role of the CBO in the budget process, and what is a typical workday like for the director?

The CBO is the informational and analytical arm of the congressional budget process. It provides information, analysis, and projections to the Congress as it considers budget alternatives. In a sense it is a counterpart to the Office of Management and Budget (OMB), which provides the president with the information, analysis, and projections that go into his budget proposals. It is different than the OMB in the sense that the CBO works for the Congress and therefore has to be a nonpartisan agency. It doesn't make recommendations to the Congress in the way that the OMB might make recommendations to the president. It always gives options and alternatives to the Congress to consider.

The director of the CBO spends part of the time directing the agency itself, considering what projections to make about the economic situation and the budget itself, reviewing reports the agency is going to put out, and interacting with the staff over the actual product. Part of the time the director spends explaining these things to the Congress and to the world at large. My time was spent in meetings with staff, in testimony before the Congress (when the Congress was in session I sometimes testified several times a week), and talking to other parts of the federal government, state and local governments, university groups, and others interested in the budget process.

What did you like best about being the director of the Congressional Budget Office?

I enjoyed having the chance to create an organization that makes high quality economic analyses available to political decision-makers. Policy decisions are always hard, but I believe the chances of good policy are improved by having the best analyses available of the consequences of alternative choices. That's what we tried to do at CBO.

From your discussions with members of Congress, which factor—politics or fiscal policy considerations—more sharply influences the size and composition of the budget?

I don't think most politicians make a sharp distinction in their minds between "politics" and "right fiscal policy" most of the time. Nor do I find it easy to make the distinction myself. Most politicians try to do what they think is in the national interest and especially in the interest of their constituents. They are very concerned with being perceived as "fair." In practice, most of them become persuaded that policies that especially benefit their areas are indeed good for the country, or are, at least, "fair." If they have defense industries in their district, they

become genuinely convinced of the need for a strong defense and the importance to that defense of the particular weapons produced in their district. If they have a large farming constituency, they become dedicated to the idea that the national interest involves strong support for farmers.

The fact that politicians tend to see the national interest in terms of what is good for their constituents does not strike me as a major problem. That is how representative democracy is supposed to work. The fact that political campaigns are heavily financed by private money, however, is a serious problem. It enhances the power of people and industries with strong economic interest and plenty of cash, often to the detriment of the rest of the population.

What is the major long-run consequence of running annual budget deficits?

If the government is using a large fraction of the nation's savings to finance the budget deficit, less is available to finance productive investment. It is possible to compensate by borrowing the savings of other countries, but this leaves us indebted to them. In the long run, persistent federal deficits cut domestic investment and reduce the future standard of living.

Occasionally you are on television answering economic questions for members of the press. Are you impressed or disappointed in the press's knowledge of economics?

Many reporters are knowledgeable about economics—and some are not—but television coverage of economic matters seems to be extremely poor. The networks apparently assume that most people find economics boring and can only tolerate a 30 second sound byte, not a full explanation of what is happening. The networks also like to feature economists with extreme views

237

and tend to neglect the more sensible middle-of-the-road views of the bulk of the profession. In general, I believe the major newspapers do a much better job than the television networks of explaining economic issues.

What are the consequences of economic illiteracy on the individual's level? on society's level?

Individuals who fail to master the rudiments of economics increase the chances that they will make bad economic decisions themselves—about careers, purchases, investments, retirement plans, and so on. If a large part of

the public is illiterate about economic issues, it is much harder for the political system to make constructive decisions about economic policy. The federal deficit persists, for example, because most people do not understand why it is so important for the future of the country to get it down.

What got you interested in economics?

My interest in economics grew out of concern for improving public policy, both domestic and international. I was a teenager in the tremendously idealistic period after World War II when it seemed terribly important to get nations

working together to solve the world's problems peacefully. I was initially interested in foreign aid, economic development in poorer countries, and facilitating international trade generally.

My interest shifted later to the domestic economy, but never away from public policy issues. My interest in economics has always revolved around such issues as: how to make the tax system fairer; how to make the economy more productive; how to make the education and health systems work better, and so on.

Marginal Tax Rate
The change in a person's tax payment divided by a change in the person's taxable income: Δtax payment/Δtaxable income.

ual's marginal income tax rate. The **marginal tax rate** is equal to the change in a person's tax payment divided by a change in the person's taxable income: Δtax payment/Δtaxable income.

For example, if Smith's taxable income increases by $1, and her tax payment increases by $.40, her marginal tax rate is 40 percent; if her taxable income increases by $1, and her tax payment increases by $.28, then her marginal tax rate is 28 percent. All other things held constant, lower marginal tax rates increase the incentive to engage in productive activities (work) relative to leisure and tax-avoidance activities. As resources shift from the latter to the former, short-run aggregate supply increases. If the lower marginal tax rates are permanent, and not simply a one-shot affair, most economists predict that not only will the short-run aggregate supply curve shift rightward but the long-run aggregate supply curve will shift rightward, too. In Exhibit 10–6, we illustrate the predicted effect of a permanent marginal tax rate cut on aggregate supply.

Question:

Why would individuals want to work more and take less leisure if marginal tax rates were reduced? It seems that they would probably want to do the opposite. After all, with lower marginal tax rates, individuals will be left with higher disposable incomes and therefore will have less need to work.

Answer:

What we actually have here are two forces, pulling in opposite directions. Given a cut in marginal tax rates, two things will happen: (1) Individuals will have more disposable income. (2) The amount of money they can earn (and keep) by working increases. As a result of effect 2, individuals will choose to work more (would you want to work more or fewer hours if you could keep 90 cents out of every dollar earned as opposed to, say, 50 cents out of every dollar earned?). As a result of effect 1, individuals will choose to work less. Overall, what happens on net, whether an individual works more or less, depends on whether effect 1 or effect

EXHIBIT 10–6

The Predicted Effect of a Permanent Marginal Tax Rate Cut on Aggregate Supply Only

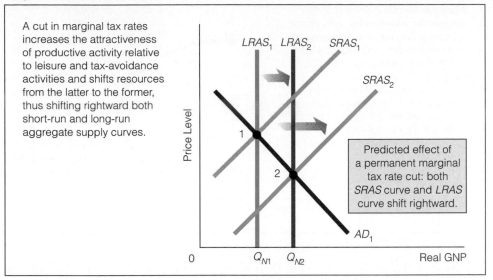

A cut in marginal tax rates increases the attractiveness of productive activity relative to leisure and tax-avoidance activities and shifts resources from the latter to the former, thus shifting rightward both short-run and long-run aggregate supply curves.

Predicted effect of a permanent marginal tax rate cut: both *SRAS* curve and *LRAS* curve shift rightward.

2 is stronger. If effect 2 is stronger than effect 1, the individual (on net) will work more; if effect 1 is stronger than effect 2, the individual will (on net) work less. In the analysis of marginal tax rates and aggregate supply, we implicitly assumed that in the aggregate, a marginal tax rate cut (on net) increases work activity.[5]

The Laffer Curve: Tax Rates and Tax Returns

If (marginal) income tax rates were reduced, would income tax revenues increase or decrease? Most people think the answer is obvious—lower tax rates mean lower tax revenues. The economist Arthur Laffer explained why this may not be the case.

As the story is told, Arthur Laffer, while dining with a journalist at a restaurant in Washington, D.C., drew the curve in Exhibit 10–7 on a napkin. The curve came to be known as the **Laffer curve.** Laffer's objective was to explain the different possible relationships between tax rates and tax revenues.

In the exhibit, tax revenues are on the horizontal axis and tax rates are on the vertical axis. Laffer made three major points using the curve:

1. There are two (marginal) tax rates at which zero tax revenues are collected—0 and 100 percent. Obviously, no tax revenues will be raised if the tax rate is zero, and if the tax rate is 100 percent, no one would work and earn income if the entire amount was to be taxed away.

2. An increase in tax rates could cause an increase in tax revenues. For example, an increase in tax rates from X percent to Y percent will increase tax revenues from T_X to T_Y.

3. A decrease in tax rates could cause an increase in tax revenues. For example, a decrease in tax rates from Z percent to Y percent will increase tax revenues from T_Z to T_Y. This was the point that brought public attention to the Laffer curve.

---

[5]Students of microeconomics will recognize "effect 1" as the *income effect* and "effect 2" as the *substitution effect.*

Laffer Curve
The curve, named after Arthur Laffer, that shows the relationship between tax rates and tax revenues. According to the Laffer curve, as tax rates rise from zero, tax revenues rise, reach a maximum at some point, and then fall with further increases in tax rates.

EXHIBIT 10–7
The Laffer Curve

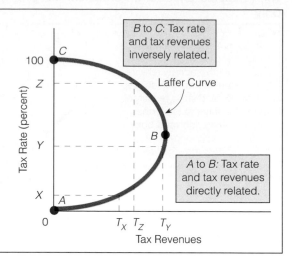

When the tax rate is either 0 or 100 percent, tax revenues are zero. Starting from a zero tax rate, increases in tax rates first increase (region A to B) and then decrease (region B to C) tax revenues. Starting from a 100 percent tax rate, decreases in tax rates first increase (region C to B) and then decrease (region B to A) tax revenues. This suggests there is some tax rate that maximizes tax revenues.

B to C: Tax rate and tax revenues inversely related.

Laffer Curve

A to B: Tax rate and tax revenues directly related.

Tax Base
When referring to income taxes, the total amount of taxable income. The (average) tax rate × tax base = tax revenues.

How is it that at different times both an increase in tax rates and a decrease in tax rates can increase tax revenues? This can happen because of the interrelationship of tax rates, the **tax base,** and tax revenues.

Tax revenues equal the tax base times the (average) tax rate.[6]

$$\text{Tax revenues} = \text{tax base} \times \text{(average) tax rate}$$

For example, a tax rate of 20 percent multiplied by a tax base of $100 billion generates $20 billion tax revenues.

Now, obviously, tax revenues are a function of two variables: the tax rate and the tax base. Whether tax revenues increase or decrease as the average tax rate is lowered depends on whether the tax base expands by a greater or lesser percentage than the percentage reduction in the tax rate. Exhibit 10–8 illustrates the point.

We start with a tax rate of 20 percent, a tax base of $100 billion, and tax revenues of $20 billion. We assume that as the tax rate is reduced, the tax base expands:

[6]First, the average tax rate is equal to an individual's tax payment divided by his or her taxable income (tax payment/taxable income). Second, a lower average tax rate requires a lower marginal tax rate. This follows from the average–marginal rule, which says that if the marginal magnitude is below the average magnitude, then the average is pulled down; and if the marginal is above the average, the average is pulled up. Simply put, if an individual pays less tax on an additional taxable dollar (which is evidence of a marginal tax rate reduction), then his or her average tax rate naturally falls.

EXHIBIT 10–8
Tax Rates, the Tax Base, and Tax Revenues
Tax revenues equal the tax base times the (average) tax rate. If the percentage reduction in the tax rate is greater than the percentage increase in the tax base, tax revenues decrease (Case 1); if the percentage reduction in the tax rate is less than the percentage increase in the tax base, tax revenues will increase (Case 2). All numbers are in billions of dollars unless otherwise noted.

	(1) TAX RATE	(2) TAX BASE	(3) TAX REVENUES (1) × (2)	SUMMARY	
Start with:	20%	$100	$20	—	
Case 1:	15	120	18	↓ Tax rate	↓ Tax revenues
Case 2:	15	150	22.5	↓ Tax rate	↑ Tax revenues

The rationale is that individuals work more, invest more, enter into more exchanges, and shelter less income from taxes at lower tax rates.

However, the real question is, How much does the tax base expand following the tax rate reduction? Suppose the tax rate in Exhibit 10–8 is reduced to 15 percent. In Case 1, this increases the tax base to $120 billion: A 25 percent decrease in the tax rate (from 20 to 15 percent) brings on a 20 percent increase in the tax base (from $100 billion to $120 billion). Tax revenues drop to $18 billion.

In Case 2, the tax base expands by 50 percent to $150 billion. Since the tax base increases by a greater percentage than the percentage decrease in the tax rate, tax revenues increase (to $22.5 billion).

Of course, either case is possible. In the Laffer curve, tax revenues increase if a tax rate reduction is made in the downward-sloping portion of the curve (between points C and B); tax revenues decrease following a tax rate reduction in the upward-sloping portion of the curve (between points A and B).

Question:

Suppose a country's income tax rate is 30 percent. Would it follow that a reduction in the tax rate to 25 percent would increase tax revenues?

Answer:

It would depend on whether the 30 percent tax rate was in the downward-sloping portion of the Laffer curve (between points C and B in Exhibit 10–7) or in the upward-sloping portion (between points A and B). If the former, then tax revenues would increase; if the latter, then tax revenues would decrease. This is largely an empirical issue. We say "largely" because most economists believe it is obvious that a tax rate reduction from an extreme 100 percent to some lower rate will increase tax revenues.

Contrast the way economist Laffer thinks about a tax cut with the way the layperson thinks about it. As we said earlier, the layperson probably believes that a reduction in tax rates brings a reduction in tax revenues. The layperson is focused on the "arithmetic" of the situation. Laffer, however, is focused on the economic incentives. He asks, What does a lower tax rate imply in terms of a person's incentive to engage in productive activity? How does a lower tax rate affect one's tradeoff between work and leisure?

The layperson likely sees only the "arithmetic" effect of a tax cut; the economist sees the incentive effect.

CHAPTER SUMMARY

Fiscal Policy: General Remarks

■ Fiscal policy refers to changes in government expenditures and taxation to achieve particular macroeconomic goals. Fiscal policy falls into one of four categories: discretionary expansionary, discretionary contractionary, automatic expansionary, and automatic contractionary.

■ The old-time fiscal religion emphasized balanced budgets except during wartime. The new fiscal religion advised the use of budget deficits and budget surpluses to help smooth out the business cycle.

■ Discretionary fiscal policy may be favored by those who favor big government, as well as by those who favor small government. An advocate of small government will favor reductions in taxes and in government spending as expansionary and contractionary fiscal policy measures, respectively. An advocate of big government will favor increases in government spending and in taxes as expansionary and contractionary fiscal policy measures, respectively.

Fiscal Policy in Keynesian Theory

■ In Keynesian theory, a change in government spending will change real GNP by more than an equal change in taxes. The relevant formulas are (1) $\Delta Q = m \times \Delta G$, where m = multiplier; and (2) $\Delta Q = -MPC(m) \times \Delta T$.

■ The balanced budget theorem holds that a change in real GNP is equal to the change in government spending when government spending and taxes change by the same dollar amount and in the same direction. For example, if government spending increases by \$5 billion, and taxes are raised \$5 billion, real GNP is predicted to increase by \$5 billion.

Crowding Out

■ Crowding out refers to the decrease in private expenditures that occurs as a consequence of increased government spending and/or the greater financing needs of the budget deficit. The crowding-out effect suggests that discretionary expansionary fiscal policy does not work to the degree that Keynesian theory predicts.

■ Complete (incomplete) crowding out occurs when the decrease in one or more components of spending completely (partially) offsets the increase in government spending.

■ New classical economists argue that crowding out occurs when individuals decrease consumption spending in order to increase saving to pay the higher future taxes brought on by debt financing of the deficit.

Supply-Side Fiscal Policy

■ When fiscal policy measures affect tax rates, they may affect the aggregate supply curve as well as the aggregate demand curve. It is generally accepted that a marginal tax rate reduction increases the attractiveness of work relative to leisure and tax-avoidance activities, and thus leads to an increase in aggregate supply.

■ Tax revenues equal the tax base multiplied by the (average) tax rate. Whether tax revenues decrease or increase as a result of a tax rate reduction depends on whether the percentage increase in the tax base is greater or lesser than the percentage reduction in the tax rate. If the percentage increase in the tax base is greater than the percentage reduction in the tax rate, then tax revenues will increase. If the percentage increase in the tax base is less than the percentage reduction in the tax rate, then tax revenues will decrease.

Key Terms and Concepts

Budget Deficit

Budget Surplus

Balanced Budget

Fiscal Policy

Expansionary Fiscal
Policy

Contractionary Fiscal
Policy

Discretionary Fiscal
Policy

Automatic Fiscal Policy

Balanced Budget
Theorem

Crowding Out

Complete Crowding Out

Incomplete Crowding
Out

Trade Deficit

Marginal Tax Rate

Tax Base

Laffer Curve

QUESTIONS AND PROBLEMS

1. Explain three ways crowding out may occur.

2. Why is crowding out an important issue in the debate over the use of discretionary fiscal policy?

3. Some economists argue for the use of discretionary fiscal policy to solve economic problems; some argue against its use. What are some of the arguments on both sides?

4. Assume $MPC = .80$ and that taxes are cut by $4 billion and government spending is increased by $7 billion. By what dollar amount will Keynesian economists predict real GNP will increase?

5. The debate over using government spending and taxing powers to stabilize the economy involves more than technical economic issues. Do you agree or disagree? Explain your answer.

6. The Laffer curve, which shows (among other things) that a tax rate reduction can increase tax revenues, became very popular and was widely cited a couple of years before, during, and for a few years after the presidential election of 1980. Why do you think this happened?

7. Is crowding out equally likely under all economic conditions? Explain your answer.

8. Tax cuts will likely affect aggregate demand and aggregate supply. Does it matter which is affected more? Explain in terms of the *AD–AS* framework.

9. Explain how a growing federal budget deficit may lead to a growing trade deficit.

10. What does complete crowding out imply about the value of the multiplier? Explain your answer.

11. Assume $MPC = .75$ and that taxes are raised by $5 billion and government spending is decreased by $12 billion. By what dollar amount will Keynesian economists predict real GNP will decrease?

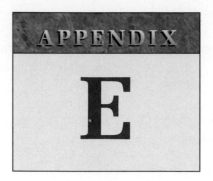

APPENDIX

E

FISCAL POLICY IN AN OPEN ECONOMY: INTERNATIONAL EFFECTS AND DOMESTIC FEEDBACKS

A budget deficit may have both (1) domestic effects and (2) international effects that feed back into the domestic economy. Consider each alone:

Domestic Effects

The domestic effects were outlined in this chapter in our discussion of Keynesian theory and expansionary fiscal policy. Here we saw that Keynesians (assuming zero crowding out) believed expansionary fiscal policy increased aggregate demand (see Exhibit 10–2a).

International Feedback Effects on the Domestic Economy

Here is an example. Start with a budget deficit. Suppose the Congress then adds an additional spending program and maintains everything else at status quo. As a result—one more spending program, no fewer spending programs, and no more taxes—the budget deficit grows. To finance the growing budget deficit, the U.S. Treasury borrows more funds in the credit or loanable funds market than it would have had to borrow if the latest spending program had not been passed. The increased demand for loanable funds raises the real interest rate. The higher U.S. interest rate attracts foreign capital. The demand for dollars in the foreign exchange market rises, and the dollar appreciates. Dollar appreciation has two effects: one relates to aggregate demand, the other to aggregate supply.

1. Aggregate Demand. As the dollar appreciates, foreign goods become cheaper; thus, Americans increase their purchases of imported goods and foreigners (whose currency has depreciated) cut back on their purchases of U.S. exported goods.[7] If exports fall and imports rise, net imports decrease and so do total expenditures. As we learned in Chapter 8, at a given price level, a decline in total expenditures causes the AD curve to shift leftward.

2. Aggregate Supply.   American producers not only buy resources or inputs from other Americans but they buy resources from foreigners, too. When the price of foreign resources falls, this leads to a rightward shift in the SRAS curve. Dollar appreciation causes foreign resource prices to drop (just as when the dollar appreciates, foreign goods become cheaper). So, dollar appreciation causes the SRAS curve to shift rightward.

Now, suppose the U.S. AD curve shifts leftward by more than the SRAS curve shifts rightward, which most economists believe happens as a result of dollar appreciation. The result is said to be a decline in real GNP.

Domestic Effects and International Feedback Effects Together

So we have this situation: (1) The rising budget deficit affects the domestic economy directly and pushes real GNP upward; but (2) increased deficit financing raises U.S. real interest rates and prompts increased foreign capital inflows, an increased demand for dollars, and dollar appreciation; and, under typical conditions, an appreciated dollar feeds back into the domestic economy and pushes real GNP downward. Obviously, what happens on net depends on how strong the international feedback effects are on the domestic economy. Are they strong enough to offset the initial expansionary push in real GNP?

Even if the international feedback effects on the domestic economy do not outweigh the initial expansionary push in real GNP, and real GNP rises on net, still

[7]This was discussed in Chapter 9.

EXHIBIT 10E–1
Expansionary Fiscal Policy in Open and Closed Economies

Expansionary fiscal policy raises real GNP more in a closed economy than in an open economy. For example, expansionary fiscal policy (in Keynesian theory) shifts the AD curve from AD_1 to AD_2. Because of the higher real interest rates, increased foreign capital inflows, and dollar appreciation, the AD curve shifts leftward from AD_2 to AD_3, and the SRAS curve shifts rightward from $SRAS_1$ to $SRAS_2$. In a closed economy, real GNP ends up at a lower level, Q_3.

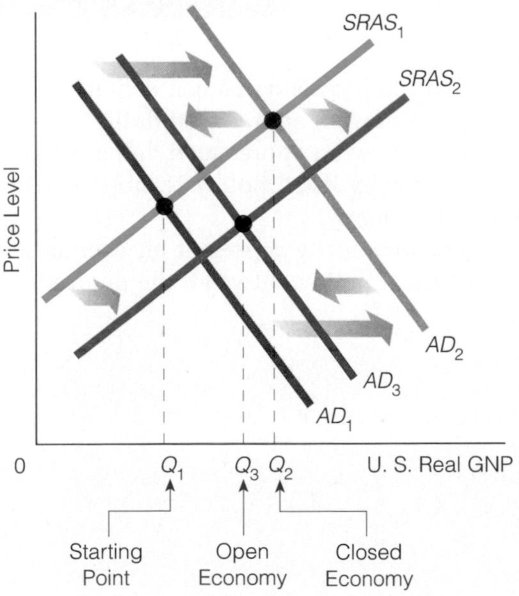

Closed Economy
An economy that does not trade goods and services with other nations.

Open Economy
An economy that trades goods and services with other nations.

we can conclude that expansionary fiscal policy raises real GNP more in a **closed economy** than in an **open economy.** This is because in a closed economy the international feedback effects that reduce real GNP (see point 2) are absent.

Exhibit 10E–1 illustrates our point. In the Keynesian theory, expansionary fiscal policy shifts the aggregate demand curve from AD_1 to AD_2. But because of the higher real interest rates, increased foreign capital inflows, and dollar appreciation, the AD curve shifts leftward from AD_2 to AD_3, and the $SRAS$ curve shifts rightward from $SRAS_1$ to $SRAS_2$. In a closed economy, real GNP rises from Q_1 to Q_2. In an open economy, where international feedback effects play a role, real GNP ends up at a lower level, Q_3.

The rising budget deficit affects the domestic economy directly and pushes real GNP upward; but increased deficit financing raises U.S. real interest rates and prompts increased foreign capital inflows, an increased demand for dollars, and dollar appreciation; and, under typical conditions, an appreciated dollar feeds back into the domestic economy and pushes real GNP downward. What happens on net depends on how strong the international feedback effects are on the domestic economy. If the international feedback effects outweigh the domestic effects, real GNP declines. If the domestic effects outweigh the international feedback effects, real GNP rises. Even if the domestic effects outweigh the international feedback effects, still real GNP will rise by a smaller amount in an open economy than in a closed economy.

1. Explain how a rising budget deficit can cause the dollar to appreciate.
2. Explain how an appreciated dollar affects the AD curve.
3. Explain how an appreciated dollar affects the $SRAS$ curve.
4. Explain why fiscal policy is more expansionary in a closed economy than in an open economy.
5. Diagrammatically represent an economy where the international feedback effects of fiscal policy outweigh the domestic effects of fiscal policy.

PART

IV

MONEY, MACROECONOMIC THEORY, AND MONETARY POLICY

MONEY AND BANKING

WHAT THIS CHAPTER IS ABOUT

In our study of macroeconomics so far, we have focused on three variables: the price level (*P*), real GNP (*Q*), and the unemployment rate. Many economists believe that in order to understand why these variables change, it is important to understand money. We begin our discussion of money in this chapter, and continue to examine the topic in Chapters 12–15.

Money is any good that is widely accepted for purposes of exchange.

∎

The story of money starts with a definition and a history lesson. In this section, we discuss what money is and isn't (the definition) and how money came to be (the history lesson).

Money: A Definition

To the layperson, the words *income, credit,* and *wealth* are synonyms for *money.* In each of the next three sentences, the word *money* is used incorrectly; the word in parentheses is the word an economist would use.

1. "How much money (income) did you earn last year?"
2. "Most of her money (wealth) is tied up in real estate."
3. "It sure is difficult to get much money (credit) in today's tight mortgage market."

In economics, the words *money, income, credit,* and *wealth* are not synonyms. The most general definition of **money** is any good that is widely accepted for purposes of exchange (payment for goods and services).

Three Functions of Money

Money has three major functions. It functions as a medium of exchange, unit of account, and store of value.

Money As a Medium of Exchange. If there were no money, goods would have to be exchanged by **barter.** Suppose you wanted a shirt. You would have to trade some good in your possession, say, a jackknife, for the shirt. This would require you to locate a person who has a shirt *and* wants to trade it for a knife. In a money economy, this is not necessary. You can simply (1) exchange money for a shirt or (2) exchange the knife for money and then the money for the shirt. The buyer of the knife and the seller of the shirt do not have to be the same person. Money is the medium through which exchange occurs; hence, it is a **medium of exchange.** As such, money reduces the **transaction costs** of making exchanges. Exchange is easier and less time consuming in a money economy than in a barter economy.

Money As a Unit of Account. A **unit of account** is a common measurement in which values are expressed. Consider a barter economy. The value of *every* good is expressed in terms of *all other* goods. For example, one horse might equal 100 bushels of wheat, or 200 bushels of apples, or 20 pairs of shoes, or 10 suits, or 55 loaves of bread, and so on. This is not the case in a money economy. Here a person doesn't have to know what an apple's price is in terms of oranges, pizzas, chickens, or potato chips, as would be the case in a barter economy. He or she only needs to know the price in terms of money. And since all goods are denominated in money, determining relative prices is easy and quick. For example, if 1 apple is $1 and 1 orange is 50 cents, then 1 apple = 2 oranges.

Money As a Store of Value. The **store of value** function refers to a good's ability to maintain its value over time. This is the least exclusive function of money, since other goods—such as paintings, houses, and stamps—can do this, too. There have been times when money has not maintained its value well—for example, during high inflationary periods. For the most part, though, money has served as a satisfactory store of value. This allows us to accept payment in money for our pro-

Money
Any good that is widely accepted for purposes of exchange.

Barter
Exchanging goods and services for other goods and services without the use of money.

Medium of Exchange
Anything that is generally acceptable in exchange for goods and services. A function of money.

Transaction Costs
The costs associated with the time and effort needed to search out, negotiate, and consummate an exchange.

Unit of Account
A common measurement in which relative values are expressed. A function of money.

Store of Value
The ability of an item to hold value over time. A function of money.

ductive efforts and to hold on to that money until we decide how we want to spend it.

From a Barter to a Money Economy: The Origins of Money

At one time, there was trade but no money. Instead, there was barter. An apple would trade for two eggs, a banana for a peach.

Today we live in a money economy. How did we move from a barter to a money economy? Did some king or queen issue the edict "Let there be money"? Not likely. Money evolved in a much more natural, market-oriented manner.

Making exchanges takes longer (on average) in a barter economy than in a money economy. Suppose Smith wants to trade apples for oranges. He locates Jones who has oranges. Smith offers to trade apples for oranges, but Jones tells Smith that she does not like apples, she would rather have peaches.

In this situation Smith must either (1) find someone who has oranges and wants to trade oranges for apples or (2) find someone who has peaches and wants to trade peaches for apples, after which he must return to Jones and trade peaches for oranges.

Suppose Smith continues to search and finds Brown, who has oranges and wants to trade oranges for (Smith's) apples. In economics terminology, Smith and Brown are said to have a **double coincidence of wants.** Two people have a double coincidence of wants if what the first person wants is what the second person has and what the second person wants is what the first person has. A double coincidence of wants is a necessary condition for trade to take place.

Now in a barter economy some goods are more readily accepted in exchange than other goods. This may originally have been the result of chance, but after traders notice the difference, their behavior tends to reinforce the effect. Suppose there are ten goods, A–J, and that good G is the most marketable of the ten. On average, good G is accepted 5 out of every 10 times it is offered in an exchange, while the remaining goods are accepted, on average, only 2 out of every 10 times. Given this difference, some individuals accept good G *simply because of its relatively greater marketability,* even if they have no plans to consume it. They accept good G because they know that it can be easily traded for most other goods at a later time (unlike the item originally in their possession).

The effect snowballs. The more people who come to accept good G for its relatively greater marketability, the greater its relative marketability becomes, which in turn causes more people to agree to accept it. This is how money evolved. Once the process of accepting good G evolves to the point where good G is *widely accepted for purposes of exchange,* good G is *money.* Historically, goods that have evolved into money include gold, silver, copper, cattle, rocks, and shells.

Double Coincidence of Wants
In a barter economy, a requirement that must be met before a trade can be made. It specifies that a trader must find another trader who is willing to trade what the first trader wants and at the same time wants what the first trader has.

Question:

Isn't money an invention of government? After all, didn't the kings and emperors of long ago stamp their likenesses on money?

Answer:

Kings and emperors might have stamped their likenesses on a certain form of money—coins—but neither kings nor emperors, nor any government, invented money. Money predates government. Money largely evolved out of the self-interested actions of individuals who were trying to reduce the time and effort it took to make exchanges in a barter economy.

What Gives Money Its Value?

In the days when the dollar was backed by gold, people would say that gold gave paper money its value. Very few ever asked, But what gives gold *its* value?

Today there is no gold backing for our money. Our money has value because of its *general acceptability.* For example, you accept the dollar bill in payment for your goods and services because you know others will accept the dollar bill in payment for their goods and services. It sounds odd, but think about it.

Suppose one day the grocery store clerk doesn't accept the paper dollars you have in your wallet as payment for the groceries you want to buy. Also, neither the plumber nor the gas station attendant accepts your paper dollars for fixing your kitchen drain or for gas. If this were to happen, would you be as likely to accept paper dollars in exchange for what you sell? We think not. You accept paper dollars because you know that other people will accept paper dollars later when you try to spend them. Money is valued by you, and by others, because it is widely accepted in exchange for other goods that are valuable.

DEFINING THE MONEY SUPPLY

Money is any good that is widely accepted for purposes of exchange. We now ask ourselves: Is a ten-dollar bill money? Is a dime money? Is a checking account or a savings account money? What is included in the term *money,* that is, in the money supply? We turn next to a discussion of two of the more frequently used definitions of the money supply, M1 and M2.

M1

M1
Includes currency held outside banks + demand deposits + other checkable deposits + traveler's checks.

Currency
Includes coins and paper money.

Federal Reserve Notes
Paper money issued by the Fed.

Demand Deposits
A deposit of funds that can be withdrawn without restrictions and is transferable by check.

Commercial Banks
Privately owned, profit-seeking institutions that offer a wide range of services (checking accounts, savings accounts, loans) to customers.

M1 is sometimes referred to as the narrow definition of the money supply. M1 consists of currency held outside banks, demand deposits, other checkable deposits, and traveler's checks.[1] **Currency** includes coins minted by the U.S. Treasury and paper money. About 99 percent of the paper money in circulation is **Federal Reserve Notes** issued by the Federal Reserve District Banks. (Look at the paper money you have in your possession. At the top it reads "Federal Reserve Note.")

Demand deposits are funds that we place or have in our *checking accounts.* They are deposits that can be withdrawn *on demand,* or made payable to a third party by writing a check. In essence, they are "checkbook money." **Commercial banks** are the sole issuers of demand deposits. Other checkable deposits besides demand deposits include NOW (negotiable order of withdrawal) accounts at banks, savings banks, and savings and loan associations, and CUSD (credit union share draft) accounts.[2] M1 also includes traveler's checks.

M1 = currency outside banks + demand deposits + other checkable deposits + traveler's checks

Of the four major components of M1, the other checkable deposits component is the largest. For example, in 1990, demand deposits equaled $277.5 billion, other

---

[1]"Currency held outside banks" may sound awkward, but think of it this way: Say there is a total of $200 billion worth of currency. Some of this currency is in bank vaults ("currency inside banks") and some of this currency is in the wallets of people ("currency outside banks"). In short, currency has to be in one of two places: inside or outside a bank. M1 only takes into account that currency which is outside banks. We explain the reason for this distinction later.
[2]NOW accounts are interest-earning accounts on which checks can be written; CUSD accounts are similar to NOW accounts but are held by credit union members.

checkable deposits equaled $293.8 billion, and currency held outside banks equaled $245.9 billion. Traveler's checks were $8.3 billion. M1, the sum of these figures, was $825.5 billion (Exhibit 11–1). Exhibit 11–2 gives M1 figures between 1980 and 1990.

Question:

Listening to the news, one may hear that the money supply has increased by, say, 4 percent on an annual basis. Is the news broadcast referring to the growth in M1 when it refers to the money supply?

Answer:

Most of the time it is. Sometimes the news commentator will even use the term *M1*. There are, however, other major money supply figures that are sometimes mentioned. The most common of these is M2. This alternative measure of the money supply is introduced next.

EXHIBIT 11–1
The Components of M1

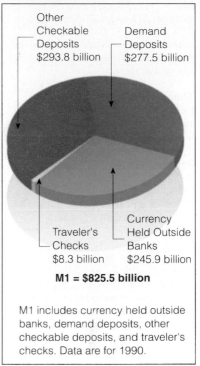

Other Checkable Deposits $293.8 billion

Demand Deposits $277.5 billion

Traveler's Checks $8.3 billion

Currency Held Outside Banks $245.9 billion

M1 = $825.5 billion

M1 includes currency held outside banks, demand deposits, other checkable deposits, and traveler's checks. Data are for 1990.

SOURCE: Board of Governors of the Federal Reserve System.

EXHIBIT 11–2
M1 and M2, 1980–90

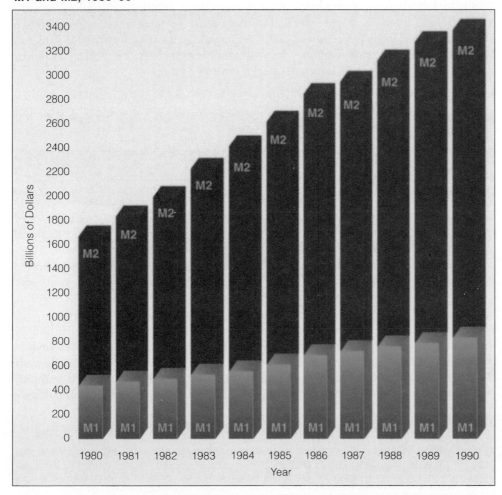

M2

M2
Includes M1 + small-denomination time deposits + savings deposits + money market accounts + overnight repurchase agreements + overnight Eurodollar deposits.

Time Deposits
Interest-earning deposits that have a stated maturity date and carry penalties for early withdrawal.

Savings Deposit
A type of time deposit. In principle (though not always in practice), the depositor can be required to give advance written notice prior to withdrawal.

Money Market Accounts
Accounts with banks (called money market deposit accounts, MMDA) or mutual fund companies (called money market mutual fund accounts, MMMF) that pay interest and offer limited check-writing privileges.

Liquid Asset
An asset that can easily and quickly be turned into cash. Some assets are more liquid than others; that is, assets differ as to the degree of liquidity.

Overnight Repurchase Agreements
An agreement by a financial institution to sell short-term securities to its customers, combined with an agreement to repurchase them at a higher price at a specified future date.

Overnight Eurodollar Deposits
Dollar-denominated deposits in banks outside the United States.

M2 is sometimes referred to as the (most common) broad definition of the money supply. M2 is made up of M1 plus small-denomination time deposits, savings deposits, money market accounts, overnight repurchase agreements, and overnight Eurodollar deposits held by U.S. residents. **Time deposits** are interest-earning deposits with a specified maturity date that are subject to penalties for early withdrawal. "Small-denomination" time deposits are deposits of less than $100,000. Small-denomination time deposits are ordinarily the largest component of M2.

A **savings deposit** is a type of time deposit because in principle, although not always in practice, the depositor can be required to give advance written notice prior to withdrawal. Other than such notice, a savings deposit has no stipulated date of maturity.

Money market accounts with banks (called money market deposit accounts, MMDA) or with mutual fund companies (called money market mutual fund accounts, MMMF) are accounts that pay interest and offer limited check-writing privileges (privileges may be limited by restricting the number of checks or setting a minimum check denomination that may be written). Money market mutual funds invest in short-term, highly **liquid assets.**

Overnight repurchase agreements consist of an agreement by a financial institution to sell short-term securities to its customers, combined with an agreement to repurchase them at a higher price at a future date. For customers, the difference between the purchase price (lower price) and resale price (higher price) is interest. **Overnight Eurodollar deposits** are deposits denominated in U.S. dollars at banks and other financial institutions outside the United States.

M2 = M1 + small-denomination time deposits + savings deposits + money market accounts + overnight repurchase agreements + overnight Eurodollar deposits

Refer to Exhibit 11–2 for M2 figures between 1980 and 1990.[3]

Question:

Earlier it was said that money is any good that is widely accepted for purposes of exchange. It is easy to see how currency, a check written on a local bank (demand deposit), and a traveler's check would fit this definition, since all are widely accepted for purposes of exchange. But a person cannot go into a store and buy what he wants with a savings deposit. Why, then, count it as part of the money supply?

Answer:

First, a savings deposit is *not* counted in the most basic, or narrow, definition of the money supply, M1. Instead it is counted in M2. Many economists believe it should be part of the money supply, broadly defined, because a savings deposit can be turned into currency without incurring appreciable costs. If you wanted, you could turn your savings account into currency in just a short time. These economists thus see a difference in *degree,* but not in *substance,* between a savings deposit and currency. They think it should be counted as part of the money supply,

[3]Besides M1 and M2, there are two other money supply definitions, M3 and L. M3 includes M2 plus larger time deposits ($100,000 or more), term repurchase agreements, and Eurodollar deposits (these are longer-term repurchase agreements and Eurodollar deposits than are included in M2), and institutional money market mutual funds. L consists of short-term Treasury securities, commercial paper, savings bonds, and bankers' acceptances. In 1989, figures for M3 and L were $4,044.3 billion and $4,881.2 billion, respectively.

if only in M2 and not in M1. By the way, some economists speak of M1 as money and some components of M2 and other broader measures of the money supply as *near monies*. The language of "money" and "near money" addresses the point raised in the question.

Where Do Credit Cards Fit In?

Credit cards are commonly referred to as money—plastic money. But they are not money. A credit card is an instrument or document that makes it easier for the holder to obtain a loan. When Tina Ridges hands the department store clerk her MasterCard or Visa, she is, in effect, spending someone else's money (that already existed). The department store submits the claim to the bank, the bank pays the department store, and then the bank bills the holder of its credit card. By using her credit card, Tina has spent someone else's money and she ultimately must repay her credit card debt with money. These transactions shift around the existing quantity of money between various individuals and firms but do not change the total.

HOW BANKING DEVELOPED

■

Just as money evolved, so did banking. This section discusses the origins of banking. The discussion will shed some light on, and aid in our understanding of, modern banking.

The Early Bankers

Our money today is easy to carry and transport. But it was not always this way. For example, when money was principally gold coins, carrying it about was neither easy nor safe. First, gold is heavy. Second, transporting thousands of gold coins is an activity that can easily draw the attention of thieves. Individuals wanted to store their gold in a safe place. The person most individuals turned to was the goldsmith because he was already equipped with safe storage facilities. Goldsmiths were the first bankers. They took in other people's gold and stored it for them. To acknowledge that they held deposited gold, goldsmiths issued receipts called *warehouse receipts* to their customers.

Once people's confidence in the receipts had been established, they used the receipts to make payments in place of the gold itself (gold was not only inconvenient for customers to carry, it was also inconvenient for merchants to accept). In short, the paper warehouse receipts circulated as money. For instance, if Franklin wanted to buy something from Mason that was priced at 10 gold pieces, he might give his warehouse receipt to Mason instead of going to the goldsmith, obtaining the gold, and then delivering it to Mason. Using the receipts was easier than dealing with gold itself, for both Franklin and Mason.

At this stage of banking, warehouse receipts were fully backed by gold; they simply represented gold in storage. Goldsmiths later began to recognize that on an average day few people came to redeem their receipts for gold. Many individuals were simply trading the receipts for goods and seldom requested the gold that the receipts represented. In short, the receipts had become money, widely accepted for purposes of exchange.

Sensing opportunity, some goldsmiths began to lend out some of their customers' gold, thinking they could earn interest on the loans without defaulting on their pledge to redeem the warehouse receipts when presented. In most cases, the borrowers of the gold preferred warehouse receipts to the actual gold, and so the goldsmiths ended up writing out warehouse receipts beyond gold on deposit. The consequence of this lending activity was an increase in the money supply—measured in terms of gold and the paper warehouse receipts issued by the goldsmith-bankers. This was the beginning of **fractional reserve banking.** Under a fractional reserve system, banks create money by holding on reserve only a fraction of the money deposited with them and lending the remainder. Our modern-day banking system operates under a fractional reserve banking arrangement.

The Federal Reserve System

In the next chapter, we discuss the structure of **the Fed** (the popular name for the **Federal Reserve System**) and the tools it uses to change the money supply. Here we need only note that the Federal Reserve System is the central bank, which essentially is a bank's bank and has as its chief function to control the nation's money supply.

THE MONEY CREATION PROCESS

This section describes the important money supply process, specifically, how the banking system, working under a fractional reserve requirement, creates money.

The Bank's Reserves and More

Many banks have an account with the Fed, in much the same way that an individual has a checking account with a commercial bank. Economists refer to this account with the Fed as either a "reserve account" or "bank deposits at the Fed." Banks also have currency or cash in their vaults—simply called "vault cash"—on the bank premises.[4] If we add (1) bank deposits at the Fed and (2) the bank's vault cash, we get (total bank) **reserves.**

Reserves = bank deposits at the Fed + vault cash

For example, suppose someone walks into a bank and deposits $100,000 in cash. This $100,000 is added to the bank's vault cash; thus, it becomes part of the bank's *reserves.* Furthermore, if the bank previously had $2.4 million in its account with the Fed and zero dollars in vault cash, the $100,000 in vault cash brings the bank's total reserves to $2.5 million.

The Fed mandates that member commercial banks must hold a certain fraction of their deposits in reserve form (that is, in the form of a bank deposit at the Fed or as vault cash). This fraction, say, 1/10 or 10 percent, is called the **required reserve ratio (r).** The actual dollar amount of deposits held in reserve form is called **required reserves.**

Required reserves = r × demand deposits

For example, assume that customers have deposited $10 million in a neighborhood bank. If the Fed mandates that a 10 percent reserve be maintained against total deposits, required reserves for the bank equal $1 million—.10 × $10 million = $1 million.

---

[4]Earlier we said that there is "currency outside banks" and "currency inside banks." Vault cash is "currency inside banks."

Fractional Reserve Banking
A banking arrangement that allows banks to hold reserves equal to only a fraction of their deposit liabilities.

The Federal Reserve System (the Fed)
The central bank of the United States.

Reserves
The sum of bank deposits at the Fed and vault cash.

Required-Reserve Ratio (r)
A percentage of each dollar deposited that must be held on reserve (at the Fed or in the bank's vault).

Required Reserves
The minimum amount of reserves a bank must hold against its deposits as mandated by the Fed.

The difference between a bank's (total) reserves and its required reserves is its **excess reserves.**

$$\text{Excess reserves} = \text{Reserves} - \text{Required reserves}$$

For example, if the bank's (total) reserves are $2.5 million, but its required reserves are $1 million, then it holds excess reserves of $1.5 million.

Banks make loans with excess reserves. If the bank uses the $1.5 million excess reserves to make loans, it earns interest income. If it does not make any loans, it does not earn interest income. Hence banks have an incentive to make loans.

Excess Reserves
Any reserves held beyond the required amount. The difference between total reserves and required reserves.

The Banking System Creates Demand Deposits: The Money Expansion Process

The banks in the banking system are prohibited from printing their own currency. Nevertheless, *the banking system can create money by creating demand deposits,* which, as we learned earlier, are part of the money supply.[5] Here is how this happens.

We start the process with Fred (his name rhymes with Fed), who has the ability to snap his fingers and create, out of thin air, $1,000. One day he snaps his fingers and does just this. He instantly deposits the newly created $1,000 into an account at Bank A. We can see this transaction in the following **T-account.** A T-account is a simplified balance sheet that records the *changes* in the bank's assets and liabilities.

T-Account
A simplified balance sheet that shows the changes in a bank's assets and liabilities.

BANK A

Assets		Liabilities	
Reserves	+$1,000	Demand deposits	+$1,000

Because the deposit initially is added to vault cash, the bank's reserves have increased by $1,000. The bank's demand deposit liabilities also have increased by $1,000.

Next, the banker divides the $1,000 reserves into two categories: required reserves and excess reserves. As previously stated, the amount of required reserves depends on the required-reserve ratio specified by the Fed. We'll set the required-reserve ratio at 10 percent. This means the bank is required to hold $100 in reserves against the deposit, and is holding an additional $900 in excess reserves. The previous T-account can be modified to show this:

BANK A

Assets		Liabilities	
Required reserves	+$100	Demand deposits	+$1,000
Excess reserves	+$900		

On the left-hand side of the T-account, we have a total of $1,000, and on the right-hand side we also have a total of $1,000. By dividing total reserves into "required" and "excess," we can see how many dollars the bank is holding over and above the Fed requirements. These excess reserves can be used to make new loans.

Suppose that Bank A makes a loan of $900 to Jenny Johnson. The left-hand side (assets side) of the bank's T-account looks like this:

[5]When we use the term *money supply,* we are referring to M1.

BANK A

Assets		Liabilities
Required reserves	+$100	
Excess reserves	+$900	See the next T-account.
Loans	+$900	

The dollars Jenny borrowed are placed in a (checking) account, shown in the bank's T-account by an increase in demand deposit liabilities of $900, as shown here:

BANK A

Assets	Liabilities	
See the previous T-account.	Demand deposits	+$1,000
	Demand deposits (Jenny Johnson)	+$ 900

Before we continue, notice that the money supply has increased. When Jenny Johnson borrowed $900 and the bank put that amount into her account, no one else in the economy had any less money and Jenny Johnson had more than before. Her new demand deposit is money. (Again, demand deposits are a part of M1.) Consequently, the money supply has increased.

Now suppose that Jenny spends the $900 on a new stereo. She writes a $900 check to the stereo retailer, who deposits the full amount of the check into Bank B. First, what happens to Bank A? It uses its excess reserves to honor Jenny Johnson's check when it is presented by Bank B, and simultaneously reduces her account balance by $900 to zero. Bank A's situation is shown here:

BANK A

Assets		Liabilities	
Required reserves	+$100	Demand deposits	+$1,000
Excess reserves	−$900	Demand deposits (Jenny Johnson)	−$900
Loans	+$900		

The situation for Bank B is different. Because of the stereo retailer's deposit, it now has $900 that it didn't have previously. This increases Bank B's reserves and demand deposit liabilities by $900:

BANK B

Assets		Liabilities	
Reserves	+$900	Demand deposits (stereo retailer)	+$900

Note that as a result of the stereo purchase there has been no change in the overall money supply. Dollars have moved from Jenny Johnson's checking account to the stereo seller's checking account.

The process continues in much the same way for Bank B as it did earlier for Bank A. Only a fraction (10 percent) of the retailer's $900 has to be kept on reserve (required reserves on $900 = $90), and the remainder constitutes excess reserves ($810), which can be lent to still another borrower. That loan will create $810 in new demand deposits and thus expand the money supply by that amount. The process continues with Banks C, D, E, and so on until the dollar figures become so small that things come to a halt. Exhibit 11–3 summarizes what happens as the $1,000 originally created by a snap of Fred's fingers works its way through the banking system.

Looking back over the entire process, this is what has happened.

- Fred created $1,000 worth of money out of thin air and instantly deposited it into an account at Bank A.
- The reserves of Bank A (a member of the banking system) increased. The reserves of no other bank decreased.
- The banking system, with Fred's new $1,000 in hand, created demand deposits (created money).

We started with $1,000 in *new* funds deposited in Bank A, and that was the basis of several thousand dollars worth of new bank loans and demand deposits. In this instance, the $1,000 initially injected into the economy ultimately caused bankers to create $9,000 in demand deposits. When this amount is added to Fred's $1,000, we can see that the money supply has expanded by $10,000. A formula that shows how we arrive at this result is

$$\text{Maximum } \Delta DD = 1/r \times \Delta R$$

where ΔDD = the change in demand deposits; r = the required-reserve ratio; and

EXHIBIT 11–3
The Banking System Creates Demand Deposits (Money)
In this exhibit, the required-reserve ratio is 10 percent, and the simple deposit multiplier is 10 ($1/r = 1/.10 = 10$). We have assumed that there is no cash leakage and that excess reserves are fully lent out; that is, banks hold zero excess reserves.

(1) BANK	(2) NEW DEPOSITS (new reserves)	(3) NEW REQUIRED RESERVES	(4) DEMAND DEPOSITS CREATED BY EXTENDING NEW LOANS (equal to new excess reserves)
A	$1,000.00	$100.00	$900.00
B	900.00	90.00	810.00
C	810.00	81.00	729.00
D	729.00	72.90	656.10
E	656.10	65.61	590.49
⋮	⋮	⋮	⋮
TOTALS (rounded)	$10,000	$1,000	$9,000

ΔR = the change in reserves resulting from the original injection of funds.[6] The arithmetic for this example is

$$Maximum \ \Delta DD = 1/.10 \times \$1,000$$
$$= 10 \times \$1,000$$
$$= \$10,000$$

Simple Deposit Multiplier
The reciprocal of the required-reserve ratio, 1/r.

In the formula, $1/r$ is known as the **simple deposit multiplier.** It is the reciprocal of the required-reserve ratio (r).

$$Simple \ deposit \ multiplier = 1/r$$

Why Maximum? Answer: No Cash Leakages and Zero Excess Reserves

Cash Leakage
Occurs when funds are held as currency instead of being deposited into a checking account.

There are a few things to notice about the money expansion process. First, we implicitly assumed that all monies were deposited into bank checking accounts. For example, when Jenny Johnson wrote a check to the stereo retailer, the retailer endorsed the check and deposited the *full amount* into Bank B. In reality, the retailer might have deposited less than the full amount and kept a few dollars in cash balances. This is referred to as a **cash leakage.** If there had been a cash leakage of $300, then Bank B would not have received $900, but only $600. This would change the second number in column 2 in Exhibit 11–3 to $600 and the second number in column 4 to $540. Therefore, the totals in column 2 of Exhibit 11–3 would be much smaller. Reducing the flow of dollars into banks by a cash leakage means that banks have fewer dollars to lend. Fewer loans mean banks put less into borrowers' accounts, so less money is created than in the earlier case (when cash leakages = 0).

Second, it was also implicitly assumed that every bank lent out *all* its excess reserves, leaving every bank with zero excess reserves. Following Fred's $1,000 deposit, for example, Bank A had excess reserves of $900, and it made a new loan for the full amount. Banks generally want to loan out all of their excess reserves to earn additional interest income, but there is no law, natural or legislated, that says every bank has to lend out every penny of excess reserves. If banks do not lend all their excess reserves, then demand deposits and the money supply will increase by less than in the original situation (where banks did lend all their excess reserves).

Who Created What?

There were two major players in the demand deposit expansion process we described: (1) Fred and (2) the banking system. *Together* they created or expanded the money supply by $10,000. Fred *directly* created $1,000 and thus made it possible for banks to create $9,000 in demand deposits as a by-product of extending new loans. In short, Fred created money *out of thin air,* and the banking system created money *out of money.*

An easy formula for finding the maximum change in demand deposits (money

[6]Since only demand deposits, and no other component of the money supply, change in this example, we can rewrite "Maximum $\Delta DD = 1/r \times \Delta R$" as "Maximum $\Delta M = 1/r \times \Delta R$" where ΔM = the change in the money supply. In this chapter, the only component of the money supply that we allow to change is demand deposits. For this reason, we can talk about changes in demand deposits and the money supply as if they are the same—which they are, given our specification.

supply) *brought about by the banking system,* or the maximum change in demand deposits *after* the initial deposit of Fred's $1,000, is

Maximum ΔDD (brought about by the banking system) = $1/r \times \Delta ER$

where ΔDD = the change in demand deposits; r = the required-reserve ratio; ΔER = the change in excess reserves of the first bank to receive the new injection of funds.[7]

The arithmetic here is

Maximum ΔDD (brought about by the banking system) = $1/.10 \times \$900 = 10 \times \$900 = \$9,000$

Question:

What would have happened if Fred had decided to keep the original $1,000 in his pocket rather than depositing it in Bank A?

Answer:

If Fred had kept the money rather than depositing it, the process (of money expansion) would not have gone as described in Exhibit 11–3. For the money expansion process to continue as described, dollars must be deposited in checking accounts, and banks must extend loans. This process began once Fred had placed the $1,000 into his checking account.

It Works In Reverse: The "Money Destruction" Process

In the preceding example, Fred created $1,000 out of thin air and instantly deposited it into a demand deposit account at Bank A. This simple act created a multiple increase in demand deposits and the money supply. The process also works in reverse. Suppose Fred withdraws the $1,000 and destroys it with a snap of his fingers. As a result, bank reserves decline. The multiple deposit contraction process is symmetrical to the multiple deposit expansion process. This is what happens.

Again, we set the required-reserve ratio at 10 percent. The situation for Bank A looks like this:

BANK A

Assets		Liabilities	
Reserves	− $1,000	Demand deposits	− $1,000

Losing $1,000 in reserves places Bank A in a reserve deficiency position. Specifically, it is $900 short. Remember, Bank A held $100 reserves against the initial $1,000 deposit, so it loses $900 in reserves that backed other deposits ($1,000 − $100 = $900). The bank must take immediate action to correct this reserve deficiency. What can it do? One of the things it can do is to reduce its outstanding loans. Funds from loan repayments can be applied to the reserve deficiency *rather than being used to extend new loans.* As borrowers repay $900 worth of loans,

[7]Once again, since only demand deposits, and no other component of the money supply, change in this example, we can rewrite "Maximum ΔDD (brought about by the banking system)" as "Maximum ΔM (brought about by the banking system)."

they draw down their checking balances by that amount, causing the money supply to decline by $900.

Let's assume that the $900 loan repayment to Bank A is written on a check issued by Bank B. Once the check has cleared, reserves and customer deposits at Bank B fall by $900. This situation is reflected in Bank B's T-account.

BANK B

Assets		Liabilities	
Reserves	− $900	Demand deposits	− $900

Bank B now faces a situation similar to Bank A's earlier situation. Losing $900 in reserves places Bank B in reserve deficiency. It is $810 short. Remember, Bank B held $90 against the $900 deposit, so it loses $810 that backed other deposits ($900 − $90 = $810). Bank B seeks to recoup $810 by reducing its outstanding loans by an equal amount.

If a customer is asked to pay off an $810 loan and does so by writing a check on his account at Bank C, that bank's reserves and deposits both decline by $810. As a result, Bank C is now in reserve deficiency; it is $729 short. Remember, Bank C held $81 against the $810 deposit, so it is short $729 that backed other deposits ($810 − $81 = $729).

As you can see, the figures are exactly the same ones given in Exhibit 11–3, with the exception that each change is negative rather than positive. When Fred withdrew and destroyed the $1,000 (that he had earlier created and deposited), the money supply ended up declining by $10,000.

In Exhibit 11–4, we show the money supply expansion and contraction process in brief.

We Change Our Example: No More Fred

Let's change our example somewhat. This time there is no Fred. No such person exists; no one can snap his fingers and create $1,000, or any other amount, out of thin air. This time we speak about Jack, a mere mortal who does not possess the unusual talents of Fred. Jack cannot create money out of thin air.

EXHIBIT 11–4
The Money Supply Expansion and Contraction Processes

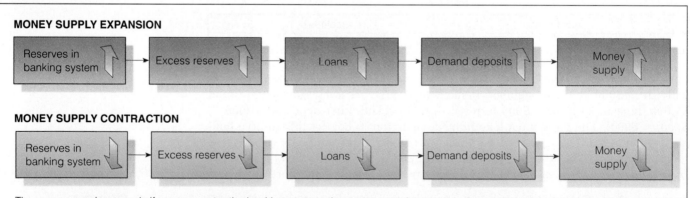

The money supply expands if reserves enter the banking system; the money supply contracts if reserves exit the banking system. In expansion, reserves rise, thus excess reserves rise, more loans are given out, and demand deposits rise. Since demand deposits are part of the money supply, the money supply rises. In contraction, reserves fall, thus excess reserves fall, fewer loans are given out, and demand deposits fall. Since demand deposits are part of the money supply, the money supply falls.

Suppose that Jack currently has $1,000 in cash in a shoebox in his bedroom. He decides that he doesn't want to keep this much cash around the house, so he takes it to Bank A and opens up a checking account. This act, as far as it has gone, does not change the money supply. Initially, the $1,000 in the shoebox was currency outside a bank, and thus part of the money supply. When Jack took the $1,000 from his shoebox and placed it in a bank, there was $1,000 *less* currency outside a bank and $1,000 *more* demand deposits. *So far,* this act has changed the *composition* of the money supply, not its *size*.

The $1,000 could not create a multiple of itself when it was in a shoebox in Jack's bedroom. However, once that $1,000 is placed in a checking account, the banking system has $1,000 more reserves than before, and thus has excess reserves that can be used to extend new loans. This means the money supply can expand in much the same way as we saw earlier. Recall that new demand deposits are created with each new loan. At maximum, the banking system can create $9,000 worth of new loans and demand deposits, just as in the Fred example. (We have assumed again that $r = .10$.) The primary difference between the two examples is where they began. Fred created $1,000 in new money, whereas banks created $9,000 by making new loans. Together they created $10,000. Jack deposited previously existing dollars—a transaction that does not directly affect the money supply—whereas banks used the new reserves to make $9,000 in new loans. In this case, the money supply increased by $9,000. Except for Fred's ability to create money, the two cases are identical.

Although we seldom notice, the money supply expands (as new loans are made) and contracts (as existing loans are paid off) every day. The "multiplier effect" is the result of a fractional reserve system of banking. Under fractional reserve banking, those who deposit cash in checking accounts maintain the same amount of money (both cash and demand deposits are money) and the bank where the cash is deposited has excess reserves that it can lend. Whatever funds the borrower receives is money also, so the money supply has increased. Further rounds of money expansion result when the loan is spent and funds are deposited in other banks.

Transferring Funds with a Push of a Button

Checks are useful instruments for transferring funds, but processing them generates a lot of paperwork that can be costly. It costs an estimated several billion dollars a year to process all the checks written in the United States (including losses due to bad checks). In recent years, check-processing costs have been going up relative to the costs of computer services, so many banks have begun to use the *electronic funds transfer system (EFTS)*—a system in which payments are made by electronic telecommunications.

Here's how the system works for a consumer. Suppose Jean goes into a store and decides to buy a pair of shoes priced at $50. Instead of paying cash or writing a check, Jean hands the shoe clerk her *debit card*. The debit card allows funds to be transferred out of Jean's bank account into the shoe store's account. The clerk runs the debit card through a desktop device much like the devices stores currently use to verify MasterCard and Visa purchases. The clerk enters the amount of Jean's purchase, and Jean enters her (secret) personal identification number (PIN). This permits Jean to access her checking account by remote terminal. She then commands a $50 fund transfer from her account to the store's account, probably at another bank. The operation takes a matter of seconds. As soon as the store has verified that the funds transfer has been completed, Jean leaves the store with her shoes.

The Savings and Loan Crisis

The story of the savings and loan crisis, which has made headlines in the past few years, can be told in two ways: in general terms of what happened and why and in terms of a specific person and institution. We'll tell it both ways. First, this is what happened and why.

A savings and loan, like a bank, accepts deposits from some people and lends the funds to others. For most of its history, the savings and loan industry, unlike the banking industry, has principally lent funds to home-buyers at a fixed interest rate. Also, for most of its history, it has lived under *Regulation Q,* which made it illegal for savings and loans to pay their depositers an interest rate higher than the stipulated interest rate ceiling mandated by government.

All went well for awhile. Then, in the 1970s, the inflation rate began to rise and savings and loans began to get squeezed. Money market mutual fund (MMMF) institutions, which were not under the jurisdiction of Regulation Q, began to proliferate and offer depositers higher rates of interest. Even though savings and loan depositers' deposits were insured by the federal government (up to $40,000 per account at the time), and MMMF deposits were not, still, for many people, the higher interest rates paid by the MMMFs made up for the difference (especially since MMMF money was largely "invested" in low-risk Treasury securities). Savings and loans began to lose deposits. Consequently, they had to borrow funds from other sources to avoid selling off their loans and other assets to repay depositers. Since these deposits cost savings and loans more interest than the interest they earned on mortgages and other assets, their profits were negative for the year. After a few years, the investments of savings and loan owners would be completely

dissipated and the savings and loan would be bankrupt.

Before that could happen, in 1982 Congress passed the Garn—St. Germain Act. Among the law's many provisions, savings and loans were given the right to invest in high risk ventures—quite unlike the home loans they were accustomed to making. To increase their earnings above interest expenses, many savings and loans became involved in speculative ventures about which their managers knew little. Faced with the prospect of failure, savings and loan owners were willing to bet their future on the possibility of large payoffs. Since depositors were insured—by this time up to $100,000 per account—they had little to lose from bad investments, and, as noted, savings and loan managers and owners had little chance of surviving without making radical changes in their way of doing business.

Against this background, many savings and loans began making loans to high risk oil exploration companies, commercial real estate, and other businesses. This was a kind of one-sided bet. Any profits they might earn would be theirs to keep; any loss would fall on taxpayers, who would have to repay depositors at failed savings and loans.

In any event, many of the high-risk, high-payoff ventures did not come through, and by the late 1980s, one-third of all the savings and loan institutions in the country were in financial trouble. The federal government had to offer a bailout that would end up costing American taxpayers between $200 to $400 billion.

Now consider the case of one individual and one savings and loan.[8] In

[8]Much of this story is from Martin Mayer's *The Greatest-Ever Bank Robbery: The Collapse of the Savings and Loan Industry* (New York: Charles Scribner's Sons, 1990).

June 1983, Ranbir Sahni, a former Air India pilot, acquired Tokay Savings and Loan Association, which was renamed American Diversified Savings Bank of Lodi, California. With capital requirements of only 3 percent of total assets, Sahni's American Diversified could own $100 million in assets. All Sahni had to do to get $100 million in assets was put up $3 million himself and then promise people that he would pay them a high interest rate if they would place their savings in his institution. At the time, American Diversified paid the highest return in the country, and the average account was $80,807, which was 10 times the average account in the average savings and loan. Between June 1983 and December 1985, American Diversified's assets increased from $11.7 million to $1.1 billion.

The money at American Diversified was "invested" in financial futures, options, stocks, shopping centers, condominiums, junk bonds, windmill farms, and a chicken farm (with which it was hoped chicken excrement could be processed into methane to power a new type of automobile).

In 1988, American Diversified was declared insolvent. Its losses totaled $800 million.

The Emerging Crisis in the Banking Industry

Between 1942 and 1980, 198 banks failed. In two years, 1989 and 1990, 362 banks failed. In the late-1980s and early-1990s, commercial banks began to fail in record numbers, causing some people to wonder if the banks would go the way of the savings and loans. What caused so many banks to fail at this time? Many economists argued that the problems in the banking industry were similar to the problems in the savings and loan industry: inflation in the 1970s led savers to leave the banks and move toward money market mutual funds and the like. Bank managers for the first time in a long time had to scramble to offer their depositers a higher return. They turned to higher-risk loans, first in agriculture and oil and gas, then to Third World nations, and finally to junk bonds and real estate. Many of those loans ended up turning bad.

A Last Word

Some say the savings and loan crisis was created by greedy S&L owners who didn't operate according to sound and conservative banking practices. In short, the banker was a gambler. Economists would disagree. Economists don't place as much emphasis on *individuals* as the cause of economic events as on *institutions* and *policies*. The economist would ask, Under what conditions, institutions, or policies is the banker likely to act like a gambler? For example, would the S&L owner be more careful with other peoples' money if he had to invest more of his own funds and could pass less of the risk on to taxpayers? Would depositers be more watchful of the S&Ls if there were less or no deposit insurance? Institutions and policies matter. Economists do not believe that S&L owners are careless, and depositers are asleep, under *all* institutions and policies—only under some. To economists, economic crises are not caused by "bad" people, but rather by "wrong" policies.

No cash was used, no checks were written, only a card was put through a machine and a few buttons were punched. Some people predict that this type of fund transfer will become so commonplace that soon the United States will become a cashless, checkless society.

We are not at that point yet. And some say we never will be as long as people are afraid that computer thieves can gain access to their accounts. As you read this, companies that provide EFT services are working to improve computer security so that potential debit card users will feel more comfortable with the new technology.

CHAPTER SUMMARY

What Money Is

■ Money is any good that is widely accepted for purposes of exchange.
■ Money serves as a medium of exchange, a unit of account, and a store of value.
■ Money evolved out of a barter economy as traders attempted to make exchange easier. A few goods that have been used as money include gold, silver, copper, cattle, rocks, and shells.
■ Money existed before formal governments existed.
■ Our money today has value because of its general acceptability.

The Money Supply

■ M1 includes currency held outside banks, demand deposits, other checkable deposits, and traveler's checks. M2 includes M1, small-denomination time deposits, savings deposits, money market accounts, overnight repurchase agreements, and overnight Eurodollar deposits. Credit cards are not money. When a credit card is used to make a purchase, a liability is incurred. This is not the case when money is used to make a purchase.

The Money Creation Process

■ Banks in the United States operate under a fractional reserve system in which they maintain only a fraction of their deposits in the form of reserves (that is, in the form of deposits at the Fed and vault cash). Excess reserves are typically used to extend loans to customers. When banks make these loans, they credit borrowers' checking accounts and thereby increase the money supply. When banks reduce the volume of loans outstanding, they reduce demand deposits and decrease the money supply.

■ A change in the *composition* of the money supply can change the *size* of the money supply. For example, suppose M1 = $400, where the breakdown is $150 in currency outside banks and $250 in demand deposits. Suppose now the $150 is placed into a demand deposit account. Initially, this changes the composition of the money supply but not its size. M1 is still $400 with $0 in currency outside banks and $400 in demand deposits. Later, when the banks have had time to create new loans (demand deposits) with the new reserves provided by the $150 deposit, the money supply expands.

Key Terms and Concepts

Money	Demand Deposits	Fractional Reserve Banking
Barter	Commercial Banks	
Medium of Exchange	M2	Federal Reserve System (the Fed)
Transaction Costs	Time Deposit	
Unit of Account	Savings Deposit	Reserves
Store of Value	Money Market Account	Required Reserve Ratio
Double Coincidence of Wants	Liquid Asset	Required Reserves
	Overnight Repurchase Agreement	Excess Reserves
M1		T-Account
Currency	Overnight Eurodollar Deposits	Simple Deposit Multiplier
Federal Reserve Notes		Cash Leakage

QUESTIONS AND PROBLEMS

1. Suppose, magically, 10,000 new dollars (never seen before) fall from the sky into the hands of Joanna Ferris. What are the minimum increase and the maximum increase in the money supply that may result? Assume the required-reserve ratio is 10 percent.

2. In question 1, suppose the $10,000 Joanna Ferris deposited into her demand deposit account had come from a friend, Ethel, instead of out of the sky. Additionally, Ethel gave Joanna the money by writing a check on her checking account.

Would the maximum increase in the money supply still be what you found it to be in question 1? Explain your answer.

3. Suppose that instead of Joanna getting $10,000 from the sky, or a check from a friend, she gets it from her mother who had it buried in a can in her back yard. In this case, would the maximum increase in the money supply be what you found it to be in question 1? Explain your answer.

4. What is the important point to be learned from the answers to questions 1, 2, and 3?

5. During the Civil War, both gold dollars and U.S. paper dollars (or greenbacks) existed. The North printed a tremendous number of greenbacks to finance the war with the South. There was no fixed exchange rate between the gold dollars and the greenbacks. Would you predict that the paper dollars would or would not drive the gold dollars out of circulation?

6. Does inflation, which is an increase in the price level, affect the three functions of money? If so, how?

7. Some economists have proposed that the Fed move to a 100 percent required-reserve ratio. This would make the simple deposit multiplier 1 ($1/r = 1/1.00 = 1$). Do you think banks would argue for or against the move? Explain your answer.

8. Money makes exchange easier. Would twice the money supply make exchange twice as easy? Would half the money supply make exchange one-half as easy?

9. Explain why gold backing is not necessary to give paper money value.

10. Describe the money supply contraction process.

CHAPTER 12

THE FEDERAL RESERVE SYSTEM

WHAT THIS CHAPTER IS ABOUT

We stated in the last chapter, but have not yet showed, that changes in the money supply are important to understanding changes in the price level (P), real GNP (Q), and the unemployment rate. If this is true, then the institution that actually changes the money supply is important, too. This institution is the Federal Reserve System, which we discuss in this chapter.

THE FEDERAL RESERVE SYSTEM

Economists of almost all persuasions agree that the money supply plays an important role in the economy. In the previous chapter, we defined the money supply and showed how the banking system could expand or contract it. An important part of the money expansion and contraction process is the total amount of bank reserves. We see in this chapter that the Fed is able to influence the money supply by controlling bank reserves. Before explaining how the Fed does that, we talk about the structure of the institution itself.

The Structure of the Federal Reserve System

The Federal Reserve System is the central bank of the United States. Other nations' central banks include the Bank of Sweden, the Bank of England, the Banque de France, the Bank of Japan, the Deutsche Bundesbank, and so on. The Federal Reserve System came into existence with the Federal Reserve Act of 1913 and began operations in November 1914. Its principal components are the Board of Governors, the 12 Federal Reserve District Banks, and the approximately 6,000 member commercial banks (Exhibit 12–1). A map showing the 12 Federal Reserve Districts appears in Exhibit 12–2.

EXHIBIT 12–1
The Federal Reserve System

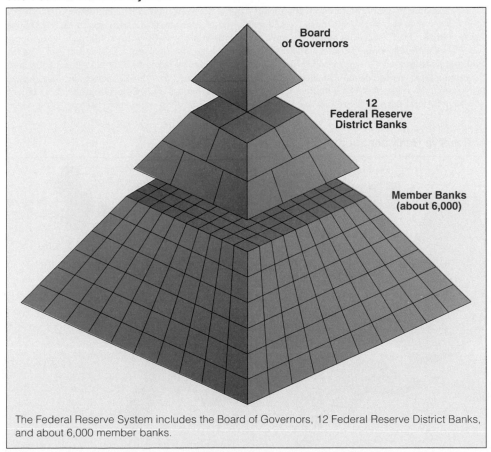

Board of Governors

12 Federal Reserve District Banks

Member Banks (about 6,000)

The Federal Reserve System includes the Board of Governors, 12 Federal Reserve District Banks, and about 6,000 member banks.

The most important responsibility of the Fed is to control the nation's money supply.

■

Board of Governors
The governing body of the Federal Reserve System.

Federal Open Market Committee (FOMC)
The 12-member policy-making group within the Fed. This committee has the authority to conduct open market operations.

Open Market Operations
The buying and selling of government securities by the Fed.

The **Board of Governors** controls and coordinates the activities of the Federal Reserve System. The Board is made up of seven members, each appointed to 14-year terms by the president with Senate approval. To reduce political influence on Fed policy, the terms of the governors are staggered—with one new appointment every other year—so a president cannot "pack" the Board. The president also designates one member as chairman of the Board for a four-year term.[1]

The major policy-making group within the Fed is the **Federal Open Market Committee (FOMC).** Authority to conduct **open market operations**—or the buying and selling of government securities—rests with the FOMC (more on open market operations later). The FOMC has 12 members, including the seven-member Board of Governors and five Federal Reserve District Bank presidents (four of the five positions are rotated among the Federal Reserve District Bank presidents). The president of the Federal Reserve Bank of New York holds a permanent seat on the FOMC, owing to the large amount of financial activity that takes place in New York City and the New York Fed's responsibility for executing open market operations.

The most important responsibility of the Fed is to control the nation's money supply. In meeting its responsibility, it is theoretically independent of politics, the Congress, and the president of the United States. It is not obligated to seek the advice of Congress or the president on monetary matters; it must only inform both of its plans. Many economists argue, however, that although the Fed is theoretically independent, there have been times when that independence has not been asserted. In general, it may be accurate to say that the Fed is independent of pol-

[1]The chairman plays an important role as a member of the Board of Governors. Economist Edward Kane tells a story that amusingly illustrates this: "During one of his last days as Chairman of the Federal Reserve Board, Paul Volcker is reputed to have treated the rest of the Governors to lunch. So as not to waste the Governors' valuable time, a waiter arrived quickly to take their orders. Ordering first, Volcker said that he would have the prime rib, which happened to be the restaurant's blue-plate special that day. Presuming that a trained economist such as Volcker would not want to order a la carte, the waiter asked, 'What about the vegetables?' Paul replied, '*They* can order for themselves.'" Edward J. Kane, "The Impact of a New Federal Reserve Chairman," *Contemporary Policy Issues,* vol. 6 (January 1988), p. 89.

EXHIBIT 12–2
Federal Reserve Districts and Federal Reserve Bank Locations

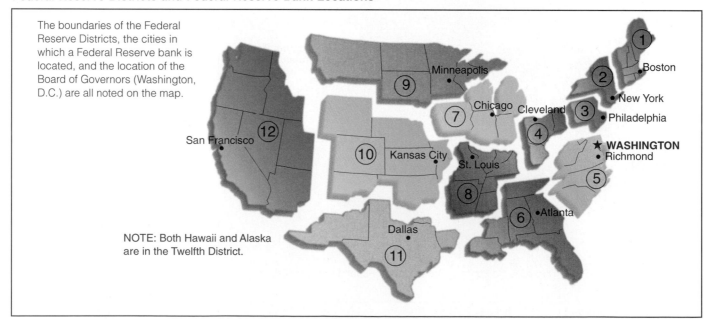

The boundaries of the Federal Reserve Districts, the cities in which a Federal Reserve bank is located, and the location of the Board of Governors (Washington, D.C.) are all noted on the map.

NOTE: Both Hawaii and Alaska are in the Twelfth District.

itics on a day-to-day basis, but probably subject to political influence (to what degree is a point of debate) over longer periods when general policy directions are set.

Functions of the Federal Reserve System

The Fed has eight major responsibilities or functions, the first of which we have noted.

1. Control the money supply. A full explanation of how the Fed does this comes later in this chapter.

2. Supply the economy with paper money (Federal Reserve Notes). The Federal Reserve banks have Federal Reserve Notes on hand to meet the demands of the banks and the public. Suppose it is the Christmas season and more people are going to their banks and withdrawing larger-than-usual amounts of $1, $5, $20, $50, and $100 notes. Commercial banks will need to replenish their vault cash, and so they will turn to their Federal Reserve banks. The Federal Reserve banks will meet this cash need by issuing more paper money (they act as passive suppliers of paper money). The actual printing of the paper money takes place at the Bureau of Engraving and Printing in Washington, D.C., but it is issued to commercial banks by the 12 Federal Reserve banks. On each Federal Reserve Note, an emblem on the left front side indicates which Federal Reserve District Bank issued the note. Check one and see. (In the trivia department, we note that today's Federal Reserve Notes are 6.14 × 2.61 inches and .0043 inches thick, which means a stack of 233 notes measure an inch high.)

3. Provide check-clearing services. When someone in New York writes a check to a person in Los Angeles, the Fed plays a role in moving money from the New Yorker's account to the Californian's account. It happens this way. Harriet Dodson writes a check on her New York bank and sends the check to George Adams in Los Angeles. George takes the check to his local bank, endorses it, and deposits it into his checking account. George's Los Angeles bank sends the check to the Federal Reserve Bank of San Francisco, which serves as the clearinghouse for checks in that particular district. The Federal Reserve Bank of San Francisco then sends the check to the Federal Reserve Bank of New York, which sends the check to Harriet's local New York bank, which sends the check back to Harriet with her monthly statement. There is a corresponding movement of funds in the opposite direction: Harriet's account is reduced, and dollars are forwarded by her bank to the New York Fed, to the San Francisco Fed, to George's Los Angeles bank, to George's account.

4. Hold depository institutions' reserves. As noted in our last chapter, banks are required to keep reserves against customer deposits either in the vault or in reserve accounts at the Fed. These accounts are maintained by the 12 Federal Reserve banks for member banks in their respective districts.

5. Supervise member banks. Without warning, the Fed can examine the books of member commercial banks to see the nature of the loans they have made, monitor compliance with bank regulations, check the accuracy of bank records, and so on. If the Fed finds that a bank has not been maintaining established banking standards, it can pressure it to do so.

6. Serve as the government's banker. The federal government collects and spends large sums of money. As a result, it needs a checking account for many of the same reasons an individual does. Its primary checking account is with the Fed. The Fed is the government's banker.

7. Serve as the lender of last resort. A traditional function of a central bank is to

Everything You Wanted to Know About Federal Reserve Notes but Were Too Busy Spending Them to Ask

Did you know the following facts about Federal Reserve Notes?

1. The average life of a typical $1 bill is 18 months. After 18 months, the typical note has been handled so often that it is worn out or badly torn.

2. Old money is sent to Federal Reserve District Banks to be exchanged for new.

3. Old used money is destroyed by machines that shred it to one-sixteenth of an inch.

4. If you have more than one-half of a Federal Reserve Note (say, one-third has been torn off), you can redeem it at a Federal Reserve bank. If you have less than one-half of a note, it will not be redeemed unless the treasurer of the United States is satisfied that the remainder of the note was totally destroyed.

5. Federal Reserve banks pay about 3 cents for each note produced by the Bureau of Engraving and Printing.

6. If you find a star at the end of the serial number on a Federal Reserve Note, this means the note is (a) a replacement for a note damaged in the printing process, (b) a replacement for a note found to be damaged on inspection at the Bureau of Engraving and Printing, or (c) the last note in a 100,000,000-note series.

7. On the back of the $1 note is the Great Seal of the United States. The Latin inscription, *E Pluribus Unum,* means "Out of Many, One." On the seal's reverse (located on the left side of the back of the note) are two inscriptions: *Annuit Coeptis,* meaning "He Has Favored Our Undertakings," and *Novus Ordo Seclorum,* meaning "A New Order of the Ages." Also on the reverse of the seal in Roman numerals, at the base of an unfinished pyramid, is the year the Declaration of Independence was signed, 1776.

---

serve as the lender of last resort for banks suffering cash management, or liquidity, problems.

8. Serve as a fiscal agent for the Treasury. The U.S. Treasury often issues (auctions) Treasury bills, notes, and bonds. These **U.S. Treasury securities** are sold to raise funds to pay the government's bills. The Federal Reserve District Banks receive the bids for these securities and process them in time for weekly auctions.

U.S. Treasury Securities
Bonds and bondlike securities issued by the U.S. Treasury when it borrows.

Question:

What is the difference between the Treasury and the Fed?

Answer:

The U.S. Treasury is a budgetary agency, the Fed a monetary agency. When the federal government spends funds, it is the Treasury's job to collect the taxes and borrow the funds needed to pay suppliers and others.[2] In short, the Treasury has an obligation to manage the financial affairs of the federal government. Except for coins, the Treasury does not issue money. It cannot create money "out of thin air" as the Fed can. The Fed is principally concerned with the availability of money and credit for the entire economy. It does not issue Treasury securities. It does not have an obligation to meet the financial needs of the federal government. Its responsibility is to provide a stable monetary framework for the economy.

---

[2]The Internal Revenue Service (IRS) is within the Treasury.

The Monetary Base and Money Multiplier

■

In this section, we discuss the monetary base and the money multiplier—what the monetary base is and the relationship between it and the money supply.

The Monetary Base

The **monetary base** (sometimes called *high-powered money* or *base money)* is composed of reserves plus currency held by the nonbanking public.

Monetary base (B) = reserves (R) + currency outside banks (C)

In abbreviated form, $B = R + C$. If we openly identify what reserves equal, we can rewrite the equation as

Monetary base =
bank deposits at the Fed + vault cash + currency outside banks

Every time the Fed buys or sells something, the monetary base changes.[3] For example, suppose the Fed hires an economic consultant and pays her with a $50,000 check written on its own account. Where did the $50,000 that the Fed pays the economic consultant come from? The answer, odd as it sounds, is "out of thin air."[4]

That's correct: *The Fed can create money out of thin air.* This simply means that the Fed has the legal authority to create money. The difference between you and the Fed is as follows: You have a checking account and the Fed has a checking account. There is a balance in each account. The Fed can take a pencil and increase the balance in its account at will—legally. If you do this, however, and then write a check for a dollar amount you don't have in your account, your check bounces. Fed checks don't bounce.

To return to our example, once the $50,000 check is in the hands of the economic consultant, it is part of the monetary base. Specifically, the $50,000 will end up in one of three places: as a deposit at the Fed, as vault cash, or as currency outside a bank. Decisions made by the economic consultant and her bank influence to a great degree which of these destinations is most likely.

First, suppose the consultant deposits the check into her checking account at her local bank. The bank in turn sends the check to the Fed for collection. The Fed then increases the bank's balance in its reserve account (at the Fed) by $50,000. In this case, the $50,000 adds to bank reserves.

Second, the bank could have asked the Fed for the $50,000 in cash and then put the cash in its own vault. This too would have added to reserves.

Third, instead of depositing the $50,000 into her checking account, the economic consultant could have simply asked her local bank to cash the check. The Fed's check then would have been turned into currency outside a bank.

Regardless of the route taken—as a bank's deposit at the Fed, as vault cash, or as currency outside a bank—the Fed's check has contributed $50,000 to the monetary base. (Remember, monetary base = reserves [which equal bank deposits at the Fed + vault cash] + currency outside banks.) And in each instance the money supply will also increase. As we learned in Chapter 11, if the $50,000 is added to bank reserves, the money supply will expand by a multiple of that amount. If the

Every time the Fed buys or sells something, the monetary base changes. As the monetary base changes, so does the money supply—often by a multiple of the change in the base.

■

Monetary Base
The sum of reserves and currency outside banks.

---

[3]What the Fed usually buys and sells are government securities. For now, though, it is buying the services of an economic consultant.

[4]Recall the Fred example in the last chapter. The Fed and Fred are a lot alike: Both can create money out of thin air.

$50,000 is converted to currency, the money supply will increase by an equal amount.

The process can work in reverse. The Fed can decrease the monetary base and the money supply by selling something. Suppose the Fed sells a $10,000 government security from its asset portfolio to a private investor. Hannah Ferris writes a check to the Fed on her local account in order to buy the security. (Alternatively, Hannah might have paid for the security with currency, although that is unlikely.) The Fed first collects the funds the check represents (which reduces either the bank's deposit at the Fed or its vault cash) which *removes the funds from the economy altogether*. Since either vault cash or deposits at the Fed fall, bank reserves decline and, following a contraction of loans and deposits, the money supply falls.

Question:

It is difficult to understand how the Fed "removes funds from the economy altogether." For example, if Natalie sells something to Teresa, money moves from Teresa to Natalie, and then Natalie spends the money. It doesn't leave the economy. Does something different happen when the Fed is doing the selling?

Answer:

Yes, it is different when the Fed is doing the selling. When the Fed makes a sale, it collects the money, and it is as if the money has disappeared. Dollars held by the Fed are not considered part of the money supply or bank reserves.

Follow-up Question:

The text states that if either vault cash or deposits at the Fed increase, the monetary base increases, and so does the money supply. Also, if either vault cash or deposits at the Fed decrease, the monetary base decreases, and so does the money supply. In short, the monetary base and money supply move up and down together. But does the money supply move up or down by the same amount as the monetary base? For example, if the monetary base goes up by $1 million, does the money supply go up by $1 million, too?

Answer:

No, it usually doesn't. The monetary base includes bank reserves, and since we operate under a *fractional* reserve banking system, another $1 million in reserves can be used by banks to create a *multiple* expansion in the total volume of demand deposits. The exception occurs when the monetary base grows as a result of the public acquiring more currency. If individuals or businesses prefer to hold the new base money as currency—permanently—then the money supply does rise dollar for dollar with the monetary base. However, this is unlikely in practice. In the general case, the money supply will increase by a multiple of the monetary base growth.

From the Simple Deposit Multiplier to the Money Multiplier

We saw in Chapter 11 that the simple deposit multiplier is equal to $1/r$ (where r is the required-reserve ratio). If we multiply the simple deposit multiplier by any incremental excess reserves injected into the banking system, we obtain the *max-*

imum possible change in demand deposits (money supply) that the banking system can generate. The simple deposit multiplier *does not* adjust for cash leakages or positive excess reserves. Since such things as cash leakages and positive excess reserves really do exist, the simple deposit multiplier *overstates* the *actual* change in the money supply that follows a change in reserves. A more complete multiplier, such as the **money multiplier,** does not. The money multiplier measures the *actual change* in the money supply for a dollar change in the monetary base. For example, if the money multiplier is 3.4, then a $1 million increase in the monetary base leads to a $3.4 million increase in the money supply. For a $1 rise in the monetary base, there is a $3.40 rise in the money supply. We compute the multiplier this way:

$$\text{Money multiplier} = \text{money supply/monetary base}$$

In December 1990, the M1 money supply was $825 billion, whereas the monetary base was $309 billion. Dividing the money supply by the monetary base suggests that the money multiplier was 2.67. Consequently, each $1 worth of monetary base resulted in $2.67 worth of money supply.

Rearranging terms in equation 1, we see that

$$\text{Money supply} = \text{money multiplier} \times \text{monetary base}$$

Now if we are told that the monetary base increases to $315 billion, we can multiply that figure by the money multiplier to find that M1 equals $841 billion (2.67 × $315 billion = $841 billion, rounded off).

Question:

If the Fed knows the money multiplier, and the Fed controls the monetary base, then can't the Fed control the money supply precisely? It seems as if it should be able to hit any money supply target it wants. For example, if it wants to increase the money supply by $10 million, and the money multiplier is 2.67, the monetary base should be increased by $3.74 billion, since 2.67 times 3.74 billion equals $10 million. All the Fed has to do is buy $3.74 billion worth of government securities to bring this about. Isn't this so?

Answer:

That is not exactly the case. The Fed is aware of past values for the money multiplier, but can't be certain what it will be next week or next month. Fluctuations in currency holdings by the public and in excess reserves held by banks affect the money multiplier's value, yet remain outside the Fed's control. Although such factors do not change by much, they are not constant and often prove difficult to predict in advance. For that reason, the degree of precision implied in the question is not possible. (Exhibit 12–3 shows money multipliers from 1970 to 1990.)

FED TOOLS FOR CONTROLLING THE MONEY SUPPLY

■

The three major tools the Fed has at its disposal to influence the money supply are (1) open market operations, (2) the required-reserve ratio, and (3) the discount rate.

EXHIBIT 12–3
The Money Multiplier, 1970–90
The money multiplier is defined as the ratio of M1 to the monetary base. Specifically, it is the M1 money multiplier.

YEAR	MONEY MULTIPLIER
1970	3.02
1971	3.01
1972	3.02
1973	2.95
1974	2.85
1975	2.80
1976	2.78
1977	2.77
1978	2.75
1979	2.71
1980	2.68
1981	2.71
1982	2.74
1983	2.76
1984	2.73
1985	2.83
1986	3.00
1987	2.90
1988	2.86
1989	2.88
1990	2.67

SOURCE: Board of Governors of the Federal Reserve System.

Open Market Operations

Recall that any time the Fed buys or sells anything, it affects the monetary base and thus the money supply. The main "thing" it buys and sells is U.S. government securities, which are bonds the government originally sold to investors when it needed to borrow funds.[5] When the Fed buys and sells such securities in the financial markets, it is said to be engaged in *open market operations*.

Open Market Purchases. Consider an open market purchase of government securities by the Fed. If the Fed buys $5 million worth of government securities from Bank ABC in Minneapolis, the securities leave the possession of the bank and go to the Fed. The Fed pays for the securities by increasing Bank ABC's reserves on deposit at the Fed by $5 million. As we learned in Chapter 11, this increases (total bank) reserves in the banking system by $5 million (remember that reserves = bank deposits at the Fed + vault cash). The transaction shows up in the Fed's T-account as follows:

THE FED

Assets	Liabilities
Government securities + $5 million	Reserves on deposit in Bank ABC's account + $5 million

As we can see, the Fed has assets of $5 million more in government securities, and it is holding (as liabilities) $5 million more for Bank ABC.

The situation for Bank ABC looks like this:

BANK ABC

Assets	Liabilities
Government securities − $5 million Reserves on deposit at the Fed + $5 million	No change

Bank ABC has $5 million less in securities and $5 million more in *reserves*.[6] We saw in Chapter 11 that as the reserves of one bank increase with no offsetting decline in reserves for other banks, the money supply expands through a process of increased loans and demand deposits. In summary, an open market purchase by the Fed increases the money supply.

This example illustrates an earlier point. When the Fed purchases government securities, it is creating money out of thin air by issuing currency or by issuing checks that banks and the general public accept. By reversing the process, the Fed can reduce the money supply.

Question:

If the Fed buys a government security from a bank, from whom did the bank get the security in the first place?

[5]Actually, what the Fed buys and sells when it conducts an open market operation are U.S. Treasury bills, notes, and bonds and government agency bonds. Government securities is a broad term that includes all of these financial instruments.

[6]Economists will sometimes say that an open market purchase changes the monetary base and at other times that an open market purchase changes reserves. These are equivalent statements. If currency outside banks is unchanged, a change in reserves equals a change in the monetary base.

Answer:

The bank probably gets the security from the U.S. Treasury. Suppose the federal government wants to spend $1 trillion and tax revenues are $850 billion. This means there is a budget deficit of $150 billion. This deficit has to be financed: The federal government has to find some way of raising the $150 billion. It is the U.S. Treasury's task to raise the $150 billion by offering (for sale) *Treasury securities*—which include Treasury bills, notes, and bonds. These Treasury securities are promises to pay the holder of them. For example, if Taylor buys a Treasury security (for, say, $9,500) and the face value of it is $10,000, then the U.S. Treasury is making a promise to Taylor that it will redeem the security at maturity for $10,000.

Suppose a bank has purchased some Treasury securities a few months ago. Later, the Fed comes along and offers to buy those Treasury securities from the bank. The bank agrees. This, then, is an open market purchase of government (Treasury) securities.

Open Market Sales.   Open market sales refer to Fed sales of government securities to banks and others. Suppose the Fed sells $5 million worth of government securities to Bank XYZ in Atlanta. The Fed surrenders securities to Bank XYZ and is paid with $5 million previously deposited in Bank XYZ's account at the Fed. Reserves in the banking system and the monetary base both decline by $5 million.

The transaction shows up in the Fed's T-account as follows:

THE FED

Assets	Liabilities
Government securities − $5 million	Reserves on deposit in Bank XYZ's account − $5 million

The situation for Bank XYZ looks like this:

BANK XYZ

Assets	Liabilities
Government securities + $5 million Reserves on deposit at the Fed − $5 million	No Change

Now that Bank XYZ's reserves have declined by $5 million, it is reserve deficient. As Bank XYZ (and other banks) adjust to the lower level of reserves, they reduce their total loans outstanding, which reduces the total volume of demand deposits and money in the economy. Exhibit 12–4 gives a summary of how open market operations affect the money supply.

The Required-Reserve Ratio

The Fed can also influence the money supply by changing the required-reserve ratio. Recall the Fred example from the previous chapter. When Fred snaps his fingers, $1,000 appears out of thin air. Fred deposits the $1,000 in Bank A, so if the required-reserve ratio (r) is 10 percent, then Bank A must hold $100 worth of reserves. That leaves $900 for Bank A to loan out, at which time an equal amount of new deposits is created. If we assume no cash leakage and if banks hold none of the newly deposited funds as excess reserves, then the banking system as a whole can create $9,000 in new demand deposits (money). Adding this to the

EXHIBIT 12–4
Open Market Operations
An open market purchase increases reserves (and the monetary base), which leads to an increase in the money supply. An open market sale decreases reserves (and the monetary base), which leads to a decrease in the money supply. (Note: We have assumed here that the Fed purchases government securities from, and sells government securities to, commercial banks.)

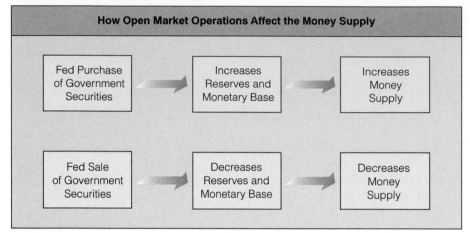

How Open Market Operations Affect the Money Supply

Fed Purchase of Government Securities → Increases Reserves and Monetary Base → Increases Money Supply

Fed Sale of Government Securities → Decreases Reserves and Monetary Base → Decreases Money Supply

$1,000 created by Fred, the money supply is $10,000 higher than originally. The relevant formula is

$$\text{Maximum } \Delta DD = 1/r \times \Delta R$$
$$= 1/.10 \times \$1,000$$
$$= 10 \times \$1,000$$
$$= \$10,000$$

But suppose Fed officials decide to increase the required-reserve ratio from 10 percent to 20 percent. Now when Fred deposits the original $1,000, Bank A is required to hold $200 on reserve and can only create $800 worth of new loans and demand deposits. The money supply will be less when r = 20 percent than it was when r was 10 percent. Here are the calculations:

$$\text{Maximum } \Delta DD = 1/.20 \times \$1,000$$
$$= 5 \times \$1,000$$
$$= \$5,000$$

If the Fed were to lower the required-reserve ratio to 5 percent, Bank A could make a $950 loan and create $950 worth of new demand deposits. Other banks could also create new demand deposits. The money supply would be larger as a result (relative to when r = 10 percent). When r = 5 percent,

$$\text{Maximum } \Delta DD = 1/.05 \times \$1,000$$
$$= 20 \times \$1,000$$
$$= \$20,000$$

So we conclude that an increase in the required-reserve ratio leads to a decrease in the money supply, and a decrease in the required-reserve ratio leads to an increase in the money supply. In other words, there is an inverse, or opposite, relationship between the required-reserve ratio and the money supply. As r goes up, the money supply goes down; as r goes down, the money supply goes up.

The Discount Rate

Banks not only provide loans to their customers but they also borrow funds when they need them. Consider Bank ABC. Currently, it has zero excess reserves: It is fully loaned up. Then one of two things happens:

- **Case 1:** Brenda Tappen walks into the bank and applies for a loan to buy new equipment for her horse ranch. The bank loan officer believes she is a good credit risk and that the bank could profit by granting her the loan. But the bank has no funds to lend.
- **Case 2:** Andrew Ferguson walks into the bank and closes down his checking account. As a result, the bank loses reserves and now is reserve deficient.

In Case 1, the bank *wants* funds so that it can make a loan to Brenda Tappen and increase its profits. In Case 2, the bank *needs* funds to meet its **reserve requirements.** In either case, there are two major places the bank can go to acquire a loan: to the **federal funds market,** which basically means the bank goes to another commercial bank for the loan, or to the Fed (to its Federal Reserve District Bank). At both places, the bank will pay an interest rate. The rate it pays for the loan in the federal funds market is called the **federal funds rate.** The rate it pays for the loan from the Fed is called the **discount rate.** Bank ABC will try to minimize its costs by borrowing where the interest rate is lower, *ceteris paribus.* Suppose the discount rate is much lower than the federal funds rate; thus Bank ABC goes to the Fed for funds. If we assume the Fed grants the bank a loan, the Fed's T-account looks like this:

THE FED

Assets		Liabilities	
Loan to Bank ABC	+$1 million	Reserves on deposit in Bank ABC's account	+$1 million

Bank ABC's T-account reflects the same transaction from its perspective.

BANK ABC

Assets		Liabilities	
Reserves on deposit at the Fed	+$1 million	Loan from the Fed	+$1 million

Notice that when Bank ABC borrows from the Fed, its reserves increase while the reserves of no other bank decrease. The result is increased reserves for the banking system as a whole, so the money supply increases. We can summarize by saying that when a bank borrows at the Fed's *discount window,* the money supply increases.

Question:

Do banks borrow from other banks when the discount rate is greater than the federal funds rate and borrow from the Fed when the discount rate is less than the federal funds rate?

Answer:

That is not always the case. Banks do not particularly care to borrow from the Fed for a number of reasons, which we discuss shortly. If the federal funds rate and

Reserve Requirement
The rule that specifies the amount of reserves a bank must hold to back up deposits.

Federal Funds Market
A market where banks lend reserves to one another, usually for short periods.

Federal Funds Rate
The interest rate in the federal funds market; the interest rate banks charge one another to borrow reserves.

Discount Rate
The interest rate the Fed charges depository institutions that borrow reserves from it.

the discount rate were equal (say, both were 7 percent), most banks would prefer to borrow funds from other banks than to borrow from the Fed. But, of course, as the discount rate falls relative to the federal funds rate (say, the discount rate falls to 5 percent, and the federal funds rate stays at 7 percent), this preference on the part of banks becomes more expensive to satisfy; and banks will be less likely to satisfy it. It comes down to this: As the discount rate falls relative to the federal funds rate, banks are more likely to borrow from the Fed. As the discount rate rises relative to the federal funds rate, banks are more likely to borrow from other banks. In effect, it is the spread (or difference) between the two rates that often matters. We discuss this next.

The Spread Between Discount Rate and Federal Funds Rate

The discount rate may be lower than the federal funds rate, and a bank may still go to the federal funds market for a loan. Here are the reasons why:

1. The bank may know that the Fed is hesitant to extend loans to banks that want to take advantage of profit-making opportunities such as the loan to Brenda Tappen (Case 1).
2. The bank doesn't want to have to deal with the Fed bureaucracy that regulates it, particularly if Fed officials interpret a request for a loan as mismanagement.
3. The bank realizes that acquiring a loan from the Fed is a privilege and not a right, and the bank doesn't want to wear this privilege too thin too quickly; it never knows when it may need the borrowing privilege the Fed has extended to it more than it currently needs it.

Banks basically look at the spread (the difference) between the federal funds rate and the discount rate in deciding where to borrow funds. If the discount rate is only slightly lower (1/4–1/2 percent lower) than the federal funds rate, most banks will pay the extra charge and borrow from other commercial banks. If the discount rate is significantly lower than the federal funds rate (2–3 percent lower), most banks will borrow from the Fed.

It follows that an increase in the discount rate relative to the federal funds rate reduces bank borrowings from the Fed. As banks borrow less from the Fed and *pay back* Fed loans previously taken out, reserves fall, and ultimately the money supply declines.

A decrease in the discount rate relative to the federal funds rate increases bank borrowings from the Fed. As banks borrow more from the Fed, reserves rise, and ultimately the money supply increases.

A summary of the effects of the different monetary tools of the Fed can be found in Exhibit 12–5.

Question:

Does the Fed use one monetary tool more than the others when it wants to change the money supply? If so, which one and why?

Answer:

The Fed today uses open market operations much more than the other two tools. It feels that open market operations have certain advantages over the other two tools. These advantages include the following:

EXHIBIT 12–5
Fed Monetary Tools and Their Effects on the Money Supply
The following Fed actions increase the money supply: purchasing government securities on the open market, lowering the required-reserve ratio, and lowering the discount rate relative to the federal funds rate. The following Fed actions decrease the money supply: selling government securities on the open market, raising the required-reserve ratio, and raising the discount rate relative to the federal funds rate.

FED MONETARY TOOL	MONEY SUPPLY
OPEN MARKET OPERATION	
Buys government securities	Increases
Sells government securities	Decreases
REQUIRED-RESERVE RATIO (r)	
Raises r	Decreases
Lowers r	Increases
DISCOUNT RATE	
Raises rate (relative to the federal funds rate)	Decreases
Lowers rate (relative to the federal funds rate)	Increases

1. Open market operations are flexible. The Fed can buy or sell small, medium, or large amounts of government securities and can control the size of the transaction.

2. Open market operations can easily be reversed. If yesterday the Fed purchased $50 million worth of government securities, but now realizes that $40 million would have been a more appropriate figure, it can sell $10 million worth of securities today to correct the situation.

3. Open market operations can be implemented quickly. If the Fed decides it wants to change the monetary base and therefore the money supply, it places an order with a government securities dealer, and the trade is executed immediately.

The Best Is Yet to Come

This chapter is as important for the questions it raises as for the questions it answers:

- Why would the Fed want to increase the money supply?
- Why would the Fed want to decrease the money supply?
- Can the Fed create too much money? What happens if it does?
- Can the Fed create too little money? What happens if it does?

These questions are answered in chapters to come. This chapter has only scratched the surface of what there is to know about money matters. The most interesting part of the story has yet to be told.

CHAPTER SUMMARY

The Federal Reserve System

- The Federal Reserve System is made up of a seven-member Board of Governors, 12 Federal Reserve District Banks, and about 6,000 member banks. The major policy-making group within the Fed is the Federal Open Market Committee. It is a 12-member group, made up of the seven members of the Board of Governors and five Federal Reserve District Bank presidents.

■ The major responsibilities of the Fed are to (1) control the money supply, (2) supply the economy with paper money (Federal Reserve Notes), (3) provide check-clearing services, (4) hold depository institutions' reserves, (5) supervise member banks, (6) serve as the government's banker, (7) serve as a lender of last resort, and (8) serve as a fiscal agent for the Treasury.

Monetary Base

■ The monetary base equals reserves plus currency outside banks.

■ Every time the Fed buys or sells anything, it automatically changes the monetary base.

Money Multiplier

■ The money multiplier measures the actual change in the money supply for a dollar change in the monetary base. It is the ratio of the money supply to the monetary base. Stated differently, the money supply is the product of the money multiplier times the monetary base (money supply = money multiplier × monetary base).

Controlling the Money Supply

■ The following Fed actions increase the money supply: lowering the required-reserve ratio, purchasing government securities on the open market, and lowering the discount rate relative to the federal funds rate. The following Fed actions decrease the money supply: raising the required-reserve ratio, selling government securities on the open market, and raising the discount rate relative to the federal funds rate.

Open Market Operations

■ An open market purchase by the Fed increases the money supply. An open market sale by the Fed decreases the money supply.

Changes in the Required-Reserve Ratio

■ An increase in the required reserve ratio leads to a decrease in the money supply. A decrease in the required-reserve ratio leads to an increase in the money supply.

Changes in the Discount Rate

■ An increase in the discount rate relative to the federal funds rate leads to a decrease in the money supply. A decrease in the discount rate relative to the federal funds rate leads to an increase in the money supply.

Key Terms and Concepts

Board of Governors

Federal Open Market
  Committee (FOMC)

Open Market
  Operations

Monetary Base

Money Multiplier

Reserve Requirement

Federal Funds Market

Federal Funds Rate

Discount Rate

QUESTIONS AND PROBLEMS

1. Is it possible for the monetary base to increase without an increase in reserves? If so, explain how.

2. Money supply = money multiplier × monetary base. This means that if the money supply is to rise, either the money multiplier or the monetary base must rise. Between 1980 and 1990, the M1 money supply doubled. After taking a look at the money multiplier during this period (see Exhibit 12–4), answer the following question: What was largely responsible for this increase?

3. Explain how an open market purchase increases the money supply.

4. Suppose the Fed raises the required-reserve ratio. This is normally thought to reduce the money supply. However, commercial banks find themselves with a reserve deficiency after the required-reserve ratio is increased and are likely to react by requesting a loan from the Fed. Does this action prevent the money supply from contracting as predicted by the theory?

5. Suppose Bank A borrows reserves from Bank B. Now that Bank A has more reserves than previously, will the money supply increase?

6. If the simple deposit multiplier turned out to be equal to the money multiplier (which isn't likely), what would this imply?

7. There are two towns in two different Federal Reserve Districts. One is a tourist town, the other is not. In which town would you expect to find more Federal Reserve Notes issued by Federal Reserve District Banks *other than* the one in the district in which the town is located? Explain why.

8. Suppose you read in the newspaper that all last week the Fed conducted open market purchases and that on Tuesday of last week it lowered the discount rate. What would you say the Fed was up to?

9. Suppose the Fed increases the monetary base by $350 million. Does it matter whether the $350 million is all in reserves, or all in currency, to how much the money supply will expand? Explain your answer.

10. Some people have referred to the Fed as a "legal counterfeiter." Explain why you think such terminology either is or is not a misrepresentation of the Fed's role.

11. Fill in the blank.

Money Supply ($ billions)	Monetary Base ($ billions)	Money Multiplier
715	A	4.2
B	209	3.1
802	241	C
692	D	2.5
E	321	2.6
796	255	F

INFLATION

WHAT THIS CHAPTER IS ABOUT

In *P–Q* terms, this chapter relates to the price level, or *P*. Specifically, it relates to a *rising price level,* which is what inflation is. In this chapter, we discuss both the causes and effects of inflation.

WHAT IS INFLATION, AND HOW DO WE MEASURE IT?

In everyday usage, the word **inflation** refers to *any* increase in the price level.[1] Economists, though, like to differentiate between *two types* of increases in the price level: a *one-shot* increase and a *continued* increase. This gives us two types of inflation, which we discuss in this section.

One-Shot Inflation

One-shot inflation is exactly what it sounds like: it is a one-shot, or one-time, increase in the price level. Suppose the CPI for years 1–5 is as follows:

Year	CPI
1	100
2	110
3	110
4	110
5	110

Notice that the price level is higher in year 2 than in year 1, but that after year 2 it does not change. In other words, it takes a "one-shot" jump in year 2 and then stabilizes. This is an example of *one-shot inflation.*

Continued Inflation

Now suppose the CPI for years 1–5 is as follows:

Year	CPI
1	100
2	110
3	120
4	130
5	140

Notice that the CPI goes from 100 to 110, then from 110 to 120, and so on. Each year the CPI is higher than in the year before. We have a *continued* increase in the price level. This is an example of **continued inflation.**

Measuring the Inflation Rate

The nightly news reporter usually speaks of a percentage change in the price level—that is, of an *inflation rate.* Calculating an inflation rate is a simple matter. We can use either of the two commonly used price indices, the consumer price index (CPI) or the GNP deflator. Suppose we choose the consumer price index. We learn that the CPI this year is 121 and that the CPI last year was 110. To find the annual inflation rate, we use this formula:

$$\text{Annual inflation rate} = \frac{\text{CPI this year} - \text{CPI last year}}{\text{CPI last year}} \times 100$$

In this case, the annual inflation rate is 10% [(121 − 110)/110 × 100 = 10%].

[1]Remember from Chapter 7 that the price level can be measured using the CPI or the GNP deflator.

Inflation
An increase in the price level.

One-Shot Inflation
A one-time increase in the price level. An increase in the price level that does not continue.

Continued Inflation
A continued increase in the price level.

One-shot inflation can
originate on the demand
side or on the supply
side of the economy.

■

Question:

*Suppose there is an increase in a particular price, say, the price of television sets,
but not in the price level. Is this inflation?*

Answer:

No, it isn't. The reason is that a rise in the price of one good may be offset by a
decline in the price of another good, leaving the price level unchanged. A rise in
a *single price* is not inflation. A rise in the *price level* is inflation.

THEORIES OF ONE-SHOT INFLATION
■

In Chapter 8, we learned that a shift rightward in the *AD* curve, or a shift leftward
in the *SRAS* curve, would raise the price level. We conclude that one-shot inflation
can originate on either the demand-side, or the supply-side, of the economy.

One-Shot Inflation: Demand-Side Induced

In Exhibit 13–1a, the economy is initially in long-run equilibrium at point 1. The
real GNP the economy is producing (Q_1) is the same as the natural real GNP (Q_N).
Suppose now the aggregate demand curve shifts rightward from AD_1 to AD_2. As
this happens, the economy moves to point 2, where the price level is P_2 and real
GNP is Q_2.

EXHIBIT 13–1
One-Shot Inflation: Demand-Side Induced

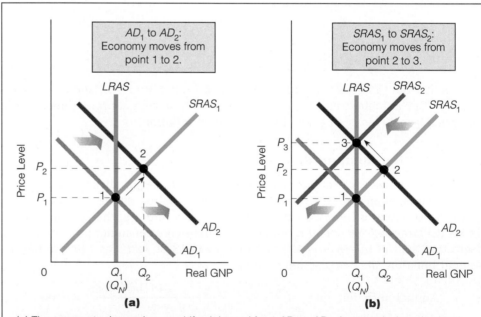

(a) The aggregate demand curve shifts rightward from AD_1 to AD_2. As a result, the price level
increases from P_1 to P_2; the economy moves from point 1 to point 2. (b) Since the real GNP
the economy produces (Q_2) is greater than the natural real GNP, the unemployment rate that
exists is less than the natural unemployment rate. Wage rates rise and the short-run aggregate
supply curve shifts leftward from $SRAS_1$ to $SRAS_2$. Long-run equilibrium is at point 3.

PART IV
MONEY, MACROECONOMIC THEORY
AND MONETARY POLICY

■

Starting in panel (b) at point 2, we notice that the real GNP the economy is producing (Q_2) is greater than natural real GNP. This means that the unemployment rate that exists in the economy is lower than the natural unemployment rate (see Chapter 8). Consequently, as old wage contracts expire, workers are paid higher wage rates because unemployment is relatively low. As wage rates rise, the SRAS curve shifts leftward from $SRAS_1$ to $SRAS_2$. The long-run equilibrium position is at point 3. The price level and real GNP at each of our three points are as follows:

Point	Price Level	Real GNP
1 (start)	P_1	$Q_1 = Q_N$
2	P_2	Q_2
3 (end)	P_3	$Q_1 = Q_N$

Notice that at point 3 the economy is at a *higher* price level, but at the *same* real GNP level, as at point 1.

Question:

In the example, the price level goes from P_1 *to* P_2 *to* P_3. *Is this a one-shot increase in the price level (one-shot inflation) or a continued increase in the price level (continued inflation)?*

Answer:

In the example, the price level rises (from P_1 to P_2 to P_3) and then stabilizes at P_3. Since the price level *stabilizes*, we cannot characterize it as *continually rising*, and so the change in the price level in our example is *not* representative of continued inflation. We have here one-shot inflation.

One-Shot Inflation: Supply-Side Induced

In Exhibit 13–2a, the economy is initially in long-run equilibrium at point 1. The real GNP the economy is producing (Q_1) is the same as the natural real GNP (Q_N). Suppose now the short-run aggregate supply curve shifts leftward from $SRAS_1$ to $SRAS_2$. As this happens, the economy moves to point 2 where the price level is P_2 and real GNP is Q_2.

Starting in panel (b) at point 2, we notice that the real GNP the economy is producing (Q_2) is less than natural real GNP. This means that the unemployment rate that exists in the economy is greater than the natural unemployment rate. Consequently, as old wage contracts expire, workers are paid lower wage rates because unemployment is relatively high. As wage rates fall, the short-run aggregate supply curve shifts rightward from $SRAS_2$ to $SRAS_1$. The long-run equilibrium position is at point 1 again. (If wage rates are somewhat inflexible, it may take a long while to move from point 2 to point 1.) The price level and real GNP at each of our three points are as follows:

Point	Price Level	Real GNP
1 (start)	P_1	$Q_1 = Q_N$
2	P_2	Q_2
1 (end)	P_1	$Q_1 = Q_N$

Notice that at point 3 the economy is at the *same* price level, and at the *same* real GNP level, as at point 1.

EXHIBIT 13–2
One-Shot Inflation: Supply-Side Induced

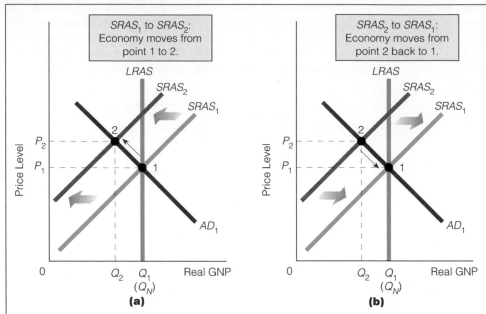

(a) The short-run aggregate supply curve shifts leftward from $SRAS_1$ to $SRAS_2$. As a result, the price level increases from P_1 to P_2; the economy moves from point 1 to point 2. (b) Since the real GNP the economy produces (Q_2) is less than the natural real GNP, the unemployment rate that exists is greater than the natural unemployment rate. Some economists argue that wage rates fall and the short-run aggregate supply curve shifts rightward from $SRAS_2$ (back) to $SRAS_1$. Long-run equilibrium is at point 1.

Confusing Demand-Induced and Supply-Induced One-Shot Inflation

Demand-induced and supply-induced one-shot inflation can be easily confused.[2] To illustrate, suppose the Federal Reserve System increases the money supply. Because there is more money in the economy, there can be greater total spending at any given price level. Consequently, the AD curve shifts rightward.

Next, prices begin to rise. Soon after, wage rates begin to rise. Many employers, perhaps unaware that the money supply has increased, certainly are aware that they are paying their employees higher wages. Thus, it is possible that they will think the higher price level is due to higher wage rates and not to the increased money supply that preceded the higher wage rates. In conclusion, what may look like a supply-induced rise in the price level is really a demand-induced rise in the price level.

Now let's explain this same story in terms of our diagrams in Exhibit 13–1. In (a), the AD curve shifts rightward because, as we said, the money supply increases. Employers, however, are unaware of what is happening in panel (a). What they see is panel (b). They end up paying higher wage rates to their employees and the $SRAS$ curve shifts leftward. Unaware that the AD curve shifted rightward in (a), but aware that the $SRAS$ curve shifted leftward in (b), they mistakenly conclude that the rise in the price level originated with a supply-side factor (higher wage rates) and not with a demand-side factor (an increase in the money supply).

[2]Sometimes the terms ''demand-side inflation'' and ''supply-side inflation'' are used.

PART IV
MONEY, MACROECONOMIC THEORY
AND MONETARY POLICY

288

It is a common phenomenon to believe that what we see with our eyes, or experience in our daily lives, *causes* the effects we notice. Witness, in our last example, employers' mistaken belief that the stimulus for the rise in the price level was a rise in wage rates (which they had first-hand experience of) and not an increase in the money supply (which they probably did not know had occurred). But the economist knows that the *cause* of something may be far removed from our personal orbit. This awareness is part of the way an economist thinks.

THEORY OF CONTINUED INFLATION

■

The CPI and GNP deflator figures for the United States for 1960–1990 are noted in Exhibit 13–3. Both price indices have *continually* increased, indicating *continued inflation* in the United States. For this reason, our discussion of continued inflation in this section is extremely relevant.

EXHIBIT 13–3
Consumer Price Index and GNP Deflator, 1960–90
Notice that both the CPI and the GNP deflator have continually increased during the period 1960–90. The U.S. inflation of the past three decades has been *continued inflation.*

YEAR	CONSUMER PRICE INDEX (1982–84 = 100)	GNP DEFLATOR (1982 = 100)
1960	29.6	30.9
1961	29.9	31.2
1962	30.2	31.9
1963	30.6	32.4
1964	31.0	32.9
1965	31.5	33.8
1966	32.4	35.0
1967	33.4	35.9
1968	34.8	37.7
1969	36.7	39.8
1970	38.8	42.0
1971	40.5	44.4
1972	41.8	46.5
1973	44.4	49.5
1974	49.3	54.0
1975	53.8	59.3
1976	56.9	63.1
1977	60.6	67.3
1978	65.2	72.2
1979	72.6	78.6
1980	82.4	85.7
1981	90.9	94.0
1982	96.5	100.0
1983	99.6	103.9
1984	103.9	107.7
1985	107.6	110.9
1986	109.6	113.8
1987	113.6	117.4
1988	118.3	121.3
1989	124.0	126.3
1990	130.7	131.5

SOURCE: Council of Economic Advisers, *Economic Report of the President, 1991* (Washington, D.C.: U.S. Government Printing Office, 1991).

From One-Shot Inflation to Continued Inflation

What can turn one-shot inflation into continued inflation? The answer is *continued increases in aggregate demand*. This process is illustrated in Exhibit 13–4.

Beginning at point 1 in Exhibit 13–4a, the aggregate demand curve shifts rightward from AD_1 to AD_2. The economy moves from point 1 to point 2. We know from our previous discussion that this is not the end of the story. At point 2, the unemployment rate that exists in the economy is less than the natural unemployment rate. As a result, wage rates rise and cause the short-run aggregate supply curve to shift leftward from $SRAS_1$ to $SRAS_2$. The economy moves from point 2 to point 3. At point 3, the economy is in long-run equilibrium.

Suppose that starting at point 3, the economy experiences another rightward shift in the aggregate demand curve (to AD_3). The process repeats itself, and the economy moves from point 3 to point 4 to point 5. Still another rightward shift in the aggregate demand curve moves the economy from point 5 to point 6 to point 7. We have stopped at point 7, but we could have continued. We notice that the result of this process is a continually rising price level—from P_1 to P_7 and beyond. We conclude that *continued increases in aggregate demand cause continued inflation.*

Suppose now we look at things from the supply-side of the economy. Beginning at point 1 in Exhibit 13–4b, the short-run aggregate supply curve shifts leftward

EXHIBIT 13–4
Changing One-Shot Inflation into Continued Inflation

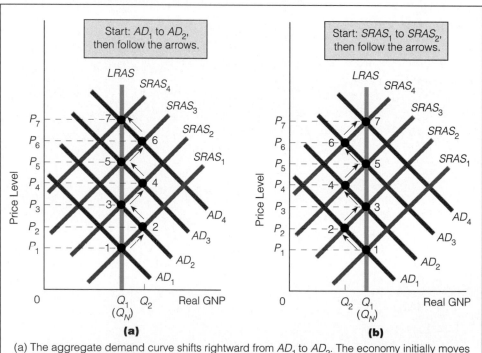

(a) The aggregate demand curve shifts rightward from AD_1 to AD_2. The economy initially moves from point 1 to point 2 and finally to point 3. Continued increases in the price level are brought about through continued increases in aggregate demand. (b) The short-run aggregate supply curve shifts leftward from $SRAS_1$ to $SRAS_2$. The economy initially moves from point 1 to point 2. The economy will return to point 1 unless there is an increase in aggregate demand. We see here, as in (a), that continued increases in the price level are brought about through continued increases in aggregate demand.

from $SRAS_1$ to $SRAS_2$. The economy moves from point 1 to point 2. At point 2, the unemployment rate that exists in the economy is greater than the natural unemployment rate. According to some economists, there is a natural tendency for wage rates to fall and the $SRAS$ curve to shift rightward, moving the economy back to point 1.

This natural tendency of the economy to return to point 1 will be offset, however, if the aggregate demand curve shifts rightward. Then, instead of moving from point 2 back to point 1, the economy moves from point 2 to point 3. At point 3, the economy is in long-run equilibrium, and a higher price level exists than existed at point 2.

Suppose the economy experiences another leftward shift in the aggregate supply curve ($SRAS_3$). The economy moves from point 3 to point 4, and would naturally return to point 3 unless aggregate demand shifted rightward. If the latter occurs, the economy moves to point 5. The same process moves the economy from point 5 to 6 to 7, where we have decided to stop. We notice that the result of this process results in a continually rising price level—from P_1 to P_7 and beyond. Again, we conclude that *continued increases in aggregate demand cause continued inflation.*

Question:

Can't continued declines in short-run aggregate supply (SRAS) also propel the price level continually higher? For example, suppose a labor union continually bargains for and receives higher wage rates for its members. Each time the union receives higher wage rates, the SRAS curve shifts leftward. And each time the SRAS curve shifts leftward, wouldn't the economy experience a higher price level?

Answer:

Theoretically, continued declines in $SRAS$ can lead to continued rises in the price level, *ceteris paribus.* It is possible, but not likely, that $SRAS$ continually declines. For it to do so, however, workers would have to continually increase their wage demands as unemployment rises above its natural level. This is not consistent with our supply-and-demand model outlined in Chapter 3, where we learned that a surplus leads to downward pressure on price (wages).

(See Economics in Our Times, "A Lot of Finger Pointing Goes on During a Rapid Inflation.")

What Causes Continued Increases in Aggregate Demand?

So far, we know that continued increases in aggregate demand cause continued inflation. But what causes continued increases in aggregate demand?

To answer this question, think back to Chapter 8. There we stated that *at a given price level, anything that increases total spending increases aggregate demand and shifts the AD curve to the right.* With this in mind, consider an increase in the money supply. If there is more money in the economy, there can be greater total spending at a given price level. Consequently, aggregate demand increases and the *AD* curve shifts rightward.

Economists are widely agreed that the *only factor* that can change continually in such a way as to bring about continued increases in aggregate demand is the *money supply.* Specifically, *continued increases in the money supply lead to continued increases in aggregate demand, which generate continued inflation.*

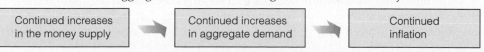

A Lot of Finger Pointing Goes on During a Rapid Inflation

During a rapid and continued rise in the price level, individuals usually point fingers at the persons or group they feel are responsible for the inflation. Labor unions are often the target of finger pointing. Some individuals will make the following argument (see if you can pick out the analytical error).

Labor unions bargain for and receive higher wage rates, and the higher wage rates get translated into higher prices. Because of the higher prices, labor unions again bargain for and receive higher wage rates (their members can't make ends meet on the old wages), and again higher wage rates get translated into higher prices, and on and on. Here we have a *wage–price spiral,* prompted by the labor unions.

Do unions cause continued inflation? The answer is no, at least not directly. To illustrate, when a labor union bargains for and receives higher wage rates, the short-run aggregate supply curve shifts leftward, as in Exhibit 13–5. A shift in the short-run aggregate supply curve from $SRAS_1$ to $SRAS_2$ raises the price level from P_1 to P_2 and lowers real GNP from Q_1 to Q_2. As real GNP falls, the unemployment rate rises. If labor unions respond to the higher price level by again bargaining for and receiving higher wages, the $SRAS$ curve will shift leftward again, with the same results—a higher price level, a lower real GNP, and a higher unemployment rate.

Are labor unions likely to push the $SRAS$ curve leftward *continually?* It is unlikely, since such a policy only leads to higher unemployment. Labor unions are not likely to go against their long-run employment objectives.

EXHIBIT 13–5
Do Unions Cause Continued Inflation?

Suppose a labor union bargains for and receives higher wage rates for its members, pushing the short-run aggregate supply curve leftward. The price level rises and real GNP falls. At the lower real GNP level, the unemployment rate is higher. Will the union continue such actions? It is unlikely it will. Continued (successful) attempts at pushing the $SRAS$ curve leftward will put increasingly more union members out of work.

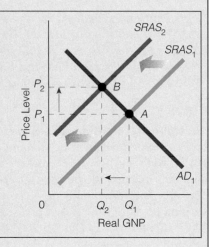

It is important to realize that the money supply can continually increase without reducing one of the four components of total spending—that is, consumption, investment, government expenditures, or net exports.

We note this because someone might ask, Can't government expenditures increase continually, too? First, there are both real and political limits beyond which government expenditures cannot go. The real upper limit is 100 percent of GNP. We do not know what the political upper limit is, but it is likely that it is less than 100 percent of GNP. In either case, once the limit is reached, government expenditures can no longer increase.

Second, some economists argue that government expenditures that are not financed with new money may crowd out one of the other components of total spending (see the discussion of crowding out in Chapter 10). Thus, increases in government expenditures are not guaranteed to raise total spending, because if government expenditures rise, consumption, say, may fall to the degree that government expenditures have increased. For example, for every additional dollar government spends on public education, households may spend one less dollar on private education.

The emphasis on the money supply as the only factor that can continue to increase and thus cause continued inflation has led most economists to agree with Nobel Laureate Milton Friedman that "inflation is always and everywhere a monetary phenomenon." (The "inflation" that Friedman is referring to is "continued inflation.")

Question:

Suppose the following scenario occurs: (1) The federal government runs continual budget deficits, that is, government expenditures are greater than tax revenues year after year. (2) The U.S. Treasury finances the budget deficit by selling Treasury securities to the public. (3) In response to step 2, the Fed conducts open market operations and purchases a large percentage of the Treasury securities. As long as steps 1 through 3 are repeated continually, would continued inflation result?

Answer:

This question is based on a condition, and the answer is "Yes, given the condition specified, and holding all other things constant." If there are *continued* deficits, and if the Fed *continues* to conduct open market purchases in response to Treasury financing of the deficits, continued increases in aggregate demand and continued inflation will occur. Notice, though, that the *money supply* is continuing to increase; thus, inflation has a monetary origin.

THE EFFECTS OF INFLATION
■

In this section, we discuss a few of the many effects of inflation. It is important to keep in mind that inflation may be *anticipated* or *unanticipated*. Unanticipated inflation catches people off guard. With anticipated inflation, people expect it and try to adjust for it. But simply because people anticipate inflation doesn't mean they necessarily anticipate the proper *rate* of inflation. They may either *correctly* anticipate inflation ("I said there would be a 5 percent inflation rate this year, and there is") or they may *incorrectly* anticipate inflation ("I said there would be a 5 percent inflation rate this year and it turned out to be 8 percent instead"). Here and throughout the remaining macroeconomic chapters, we develop the idea that the effects of inflation may be different depending on whether inflation is unanticipated, correctly anticipated, or incorrectly anticipated.

In this section, we discuss the effects mainly of unanticipated inflation. From time to time, you will see how things might be different if inflation is either correctly or incorrectly anticipated.

Who Does Inflation Hit and What Does It Do?

Savers, borrowers, and people who hold money are some of the people who feel the effects of inflation. How does inflation affect these people, and what are some of its other effects?

Inflation and People Who Hold Money.   With inflation, the purchasing power of money declines. For example, if the inflation rate is 10 percent this year, then it

Does Dog Racing Cause Continued Inflation?

Look at the data in Exhibit 13–6. There you will see 1980–88 data for the CPI, M1, consumption, government expenditures, and dog races. Dog races?

The theory of continued inflation states that continued increases in the money supply cause continued inflation. Is this confirmed by the small set of data presented in the exhibit? Yes, since a quick look at columns (2) and (3) shows that both the CPI and the money supply have continually increased during the period 1980–88.

But, of course, a look at column (2) and any column (4)–(6) shows the same thing. In column (4) consumption has continually increased; in col-

umn (5) government expenditures have continually increased; and in column (6) the number of dog races has continually increased.

Let's conduct a simple experiment. Suppose you lose the knowledge that you have gained in this chapter. Answer the following questions the way you would have answered them before you learned the cause of continued inflation.

1. If shown the data in columns (2) and (4) and then told that continued increases in consumption *cause* continued inflation, would you have believed us? ☐ Yes ☐ No

2. If shown the data in columns (2) and (5) and then told that continued increases in government expenditures *cause* continued inflation, would you have believed us? ☐ Yes ☐ No

3. If shown the data in columns (2) and (6) and then told that continued increases in dog races *cause* continued inflation, would you have believed us? ☐ Yes ☐ No

Most readers will answer "yes" to questions 1–2 and "no" to question 3. Perhaps you did, too. Why? The answer is probably that the data in columns 4–5 are economic data, and it seems plausible that continued changes in economic data could

EXHIBIT 13–6

Continued Increases in Several Factors

Here we show data for the CPI, money supply, consumption, investment, government expenditures, and (number of) dog races for the period 1980–88. Notice that there is a continued increase in all factors.

(1) Year	(2) Consumer Price Index (1982–84 = 100)	(3) M1 Money Supply ($ billions)	(4) Consumption ($ billions)	(5) Government Expenditures ($ billions)	(6) Dog Races
1980	82.4	408.9	1,732.6	530.3	5,855
1981	90.9	436.5	1,915.1	588.1	6,379
1982	96.5	474.5	2,050.7	641.7	6,499
1983	99.6	521.2	2,234.5	675.0	8,257
1984	103.9	552.1	2,430.5	735.9	8,661
1985	107.6	620.1	2,629.4	820.8	9,590
1986	109.6	724.7	2,797.4	872.2	10,654
1987	113.6	750.4	3,009.4	921.4	11,156
1988	118.6	787.5	3,238.2	962.5	12,904
	↑ Continued increases in CPI	↑ Continued increases in money supply	↑ Continued increases in consumption	↑ Continued increases in government expenditures	↑ Continued increases in number of dog races

SOURCES: Council of Economic Advisers, *Economic Report of the President*, 1991 (Washington, D.C.: U.S. Government Printing Office, 1991) and U.S. Bureau of the Census, *Statistical Abstract of the United States, 1990* (Washington, D.C.: U.S. Government Printing Office, 1990).

cause continued inflation. But the data in column 6 are not economic data and therefore the link between changes in it and continued inflation is less certain. Also, to most persons it seems unbelievable that the number of dog races has anything to do with continued inflation.

Consider this: You may have accepted the consumption or government expenditures theory of inflation over the "dog races" theory simply because either one of the first two theories *seems plausible* and the third does not. But, in truth, all three theories are incorrect.

In addition, what may seem like a *cause* of continued inflation may in fact be an *effect* of some other factor. For example, couldn't it be the case that continued increases in consumption is the *effect* of continued increases in the money supply?

The lesson is one that was stated in Chapter 1: Association is not causation. Simply because two events are associated it does not necessarily follow that one is the cause and the other is the effect. But in the flurry of economic facts and theories, this is a lesson that is easily forgotten.

---

takes $110 this year to buy what $100 bought the year before. Economists often refer to inflation as a "tax" on peoples' money holdings, because like a real tax it reduces their ability to buy as many goods and services.

Inflation and Savers. Suppose Michael and Melissa Pearson put $6,000 into a savings account that pays interest at a fixed annual rate of 5.25 percent. Furthermore, suppose the annual inflation rate turns out to be 10 percent. What has inflation done to the real (inflation-adjusted) return on Michael and Melissa's savings? It has caused it to be negative. Michael and Melissa will end up with $6,315 at the end of the year, but because of the 10 percent inflation rate they will need $6,600 to purchase what they could have purchased with $6,000 the year before. The real return on their savings is *minus* 4.75 percent ($+5.25\% - 10\% = -4.75\%$).

Today most savings accounts pay an interest rate that has been (upwardly) adjusted for an *expected inflation rate.* The rate they pay is the **nominal interest rate,** which is equal to the **real interest rate** plus the expected inflation rate.[3]

Nominal interest rate = real interest rate + expected inflation rate

Simply because most savings accounts offer an interest rate to savers that has been adjusted upward for the expected inflation rate, it doesn't necessarily follow that savers are guaranteed a positive real return on their savings. After all, the expected inflation rate may turn out to be much less than the actual inflation rate.

To illustrate, we need to distinguish between the **ex ante real interest rate** and the **ex post real interest rate.** *Ex ante* means "before" and *ex post* means "after." Here, *ex ante* refers to *before* the actual inflation rate has been realized, and *ex post* refers to *after* the actual inflation rate has been realized.

Ex ante real interest rate = nominal interest rate − expected inflation rate

Ex post real interest rate = nominal interest rate − actual inflation rate

Suppose the nominal interest rate is 8 percent and the expected inflation rate is 4 percent. It follows that the ex ante real interest rate is 4 percent. Now suppose

Nominal Interest Rate
The interest rate actually charged (or paid); the market interest rate. Nominal interest rate = real interest rate + expected inflation rate.

Real Interest Rate
In general, the inflation-adjusted interest rate. However, sometimes it is better to refer to either the *ex ante real interest rate* or the *ex post real interest rate* (see below).

Ex ante real interest rate
The nominal interest rate minus the expected inflation rate.

Ex post real interest rate
The nominal interest rate minus the actual inflation rate.

---

[3]A broader definition is nominal interest rate = real interest rate + expected rate of change in the price level, because we will not always be dealing with an expected inflation rate; we could be dealing with an expected deflation rate. (Deflation is a fall in the price level.) Saying "the expected rate of change in the price level" allows for either inflation or deflation.

the actual inflation rate turns out to be 9 percent. This means the ex post real interest rate is −1 percent.

Inflation and Lenders and Borrowers. Suppose Susan, a borrower, borrows $1,000 from Joann, a lender. Furthermore, suppose Susan agrees to pay Joann back in one year at a 7 percent rate of interest. If there is unanticipated inflation, Susan will be paying back the loan with dollars worth less in terms of their purchasing power than the dollars Joann lent her. We conclude that unanticipated inflation redistributes buying power from lenders to borrowers.

Inflation and Social Tension. Does inflation cause social tension? Some of the effects of inflation on savers, creditors, and homebuyers are likely to lead to a degree of social tension. It is not uncommon for affected individuals to blame certain persons or groups (sometimes mistakenly) for the inflation. Scapegoats abound. For example, corporations or labor unions are easy targets.

Inflation and Past Decisions. Inflation often turns past decisions into mistakes. Consider the contractor who last year contracted to build a shopping mall for $50 million. He agreed to this dollar figure based on his estimates of the prices of the resources he would need to build the mall. All of a sudden, inflation hits. Prices of labor, concrete, trucks, nails, tile, roofing, and so forth rise. Now the contractor may look back on his decision to build the mall for only $50 million as a mistake, a costly mistake for him.

Inflation and Uncertainty. Staying with our contractor, suppose he takes a loss on the shopping mall. Time passes, and he is offered the opportunity to bid on the construction of another mall. He notes a few important facts: (1) He took a loss on the last shopping mall because unanticipated inflation hit. (2) At present, there is a specific inflation rate, say, 4 percent, but the contractor doesn't know if the inflation rate next year will be 4 percent, less than 4 percent (if so, how much less?), or more than 4 percent (if so, how much more?). (3) The contractor realizes that he doesn't know what the future will bring on the inflation front, and because of this, his bid on the shopping mall, if accepted, may result in another financial disaster for him. Our point is simply that with inflation comes uncertainty, and this added uncertainty is likely to cause some individuals to decide not to enter into long-term contracts. It follows that many mutually advantageous exchanges will go unrealized.

Inflation and Hedging against Inflation. What do individuals in an inflation-prone economy do that individuals in a stable price economy do not do? They try to hedge against inflation. They try to figure out what investments offer the best protection against inflation. Would gold, real estate, or fine art be the best hedge? They travel to distant cities to hear "experts" talk on inflation. They subscribe to newsletters that claim to predict future inflation rates accurately. All this, obviously, requires an expenditure of resources—resources, we remind ourselves, that once expended in the effort to protect against inflation can no longer be used to build factories or produce shoes, houses, or cars. An effect of inflation is that it causes individuals to try to hedge against it, thereby diverting resources away from strictly productive activities.

Inflation and International Competitiveness

We live in a world economy where the U.S. inflation rate relative to other nations' inflation rates matters. To illustrate, suppose the U.S. CPI is 110 and the French CPI is 110, too. In relative terms, the U.S. and France are on equal footing. Now suppose the U.S. CPI rises to 120 and the French CPI rises to 112. The U.S. inflation rate is 9 percent and the French inflation rate is 1.8 percent. In relative terms, U.S. goods have become more expensive and French goods have become cheaper. Both Americans and the French end up buying more French goods and fewer American goods, *ceteris paribus.* The United States has become less competitive relative to France. In Exhibit 13–7 we note the inflation rate for selected nations during the period 1983–88.

Expectations, Nominal Interest Rates, and Inflation

In the preceding discussion, we mentioned that individuals form an expected inflation rate, which is included in the nominal interest rate (the nominal interest rate equals the real interest rate *plus* the expected inflation rate). Here we focus on the expected inflation rate and the nominal interest rate, specifically, on two major questions: (1) How is the expected inflation rate formed? (2) Since a change in the money supply can affect the two components of the nominal interest rate— that is, the real interest rate and the expected inflation rate—what is the directional pattern and time path traveled by the nominal interest rate in response to a change in the money supply?

The Expected Inflation Rate: How Is It Formed?

Two theories of expectations seek to explain how individuals form the expected inflation rate. One is **adaptive expectations;** the other is **rational expectations.** Adaptive expectations theory holds that individuals form the expected inflation rate based on past inflation rate experience and that they only gradually modify their expectations as the present and future unfold. For example, suppose the inflation rate has been 5 percent for the past seven years. Adaptive expectations theory would predict that the expected inflation rate in year 8 would be 5 percent. This would be the case *even if* the chairman of the Fed's Board of Governors said

Adaptive Expectations
Expectations that individuals form from past experience and modify slowly as the present and the future become the past (as time passes).

Rational Expectations
Expectations that individuals form based on past experience and also on their predictions about the effects of present and future policy actions and events.

EXHIBIT 13–7
Inflation Rates, Selected Nations and Selected Years

NATION	1983–84	1984–85	1985–86	1986–87	1987–88
United States	4.3	3.6	1.9	3.7	4.0
Argentina	626.7	672.1	90.1	98.2	(NA)
Brazil	197.0	226.9	145.2	229.7	682.3
Canada	4.3	4.0	4.2	4.4	4.0
France	7.4	5.8	2.5	3.3	2.7
Israel	373.8	304.6	48.1	19.9	16.2
Japan	2.3	2.0	.6	—	.7
Switzerland	2.9	3.4	.8	1.4	1.9
United Kingdom	5.1	6.1	3.4	4.2	4.9

SOURCE: U.S. Bureau of the Census, *Statistical Abstract of the United States,* 1990 (Washington, D.C.: U.S. Government Printing Office, 1990).

that the Fed expected to immediately and sharply increase the money supply growth rate. Since this piece of information does not relate to *past* inflation rate experience (but rather to *future* inflation), adaptive expectations theory assumes it is not taken into consideration.

Rational expectations theory holds that individuals form the expected inflation rate, not only on the basis of their past experience with inflation, but also on their predictions about the effects of present and future policy actions and events. In short, the expected inflation rate is formed by looking at the past, present, and future. Again, suppose the inflation rate has been 5 percent for the past seven years. All of a sudden, individuals hear the chairman of the Fed's Board of Governors talking about sharply "stimulating the economy." Rational expectationists would argue that the expected inflation rate might automatically jump upward, based on the current words of the chairman.

A major difference between adaptive and rational expectations is the speed at which the expected inflation rate changes. If the expected inflation rate is formed adaptively, then it is slower to change (since it is based only on the past, and individuals will wait until the present and the future become the past before they change their expectations) than if it is formed rationally (where it is based on the past, present, and future).

As we see in later chapters, whether the expected inflation rate is formed adaptively or rationally will have important consequences on the effects of monetary and fiscal policy. In this chapter, however, we are concerned about its effects on the nominal interest rate. The slower the expected rate of inflation changes, the slower the nominal interest rate adjusts to its long-run position, given a change in the money supply; the faster the expected rate of inflation changes, the faster the nominal interest rate adjusts to its long-run position, given a change in the money supply. We illustrate this in the next section.

Increases in the Money Supply and Changes in the Nominal Interest Rate

As we said earlier, the money supply can affect the two components of the nominal interest rate—the real interest rate and the expected inflation rate. Here we first review how the money supply affects the real interest rate and then how it affects the expected inflation rate.

How the Money Supply Affects the Real Interest Rate.   Suppose the Federal Reserve buys government securities from the public. As we learned in Chapter 12, this open market purchase increases the reserves of the banking system and ultimately leads to more bank lending. In short, it leads to an increase in the supply of loanable funds. An increase in the supply of loanable funds leads to a decrease in the price of loanable funds, or a decrease in the real interest rate. Because the real interest rate falls, so does the nominal interest rate, since the nominal rate is equal to the real rate plus the expected inflation rate. This decrease in the real and nominal interest rates due to an increase in the supply of loanable funds is referred to as the **liquidity effect.**

We also know from Chapter 11 that an increase in bank lending activity increases the money supply. The increase in the money supply leads to an increase in aggregate demand and to an increase in GNP. (In terms of our *AD–AS* diagram, an increase in the money supply shifts the *AD* curve rightward, which causes both the price level, *P,* and real GNP, *Q,* to rise in the short run. Since both *P* and *Q* rise, so does GNP, which is *P times Q*.) Most economists hold that an increase in

Liquidity Effect
The decrease in the real and nominal interest rates due to an increase in the supply of loanable funds.

GNP will bring about an increase in the demand for loanable funds (greater than the increase in supply). The notion here is that with rising GNP, many individuals who ordinarily would not have tried to borrow will demand credit. This increased demand for loanable funds puts upward pressure on the real interest rate and therefore the nominal interest rate, too. This increase in the real and nominal interest rates brought on by the increase in GNP is referred to as the **income effect.**

How the Money Supply Affects the Expected Inflation Rate.   Earlier, we established that continued increases in the money supply cause continued inflation. We also established that the expected inflation rate, using either adaptive or rational expectations, is a function of past inflation rates (although using rational expectations, it is a function of more than simply this).

It follows that there is an indirect link between the expected inflation rate and increases in the money supply. We would expect that the greater the increases in the money supply, the greater the inflation rate and the higher the expected inflation rate, *ceteris paribus.* From this we can conclude that the higher the expected inflation rate, the higher the nominal interest rate. The increase in the nominal interest rate due to a higher expected inflation rate is referred to as the **expectations effect.**[4]

In summary, the money supply affects the real interest rate and therefore the nominal interest rate via the liquidity and income effects. In addition, the money supply affects the expected inflation rate, and therefore the nominal interest rate, via the expectations effect. We conclude that the money supply affects the nominal interest rate via three effects: liquidity, income, and expectations. Exhibit 13–8 illustrates these three effects.

Income Effect
The increase in the real and nominal interest rates brought on by an increase in GNP.

Expectations Effect
The increase in the nominal interest rate due to a higher expected inflation rate.

Question:

A look at Exhibit 13–8 might lead one to conclude that given an increase in the money supply, the liquidity effect kicks in first, the income effect occurs next, and lastly the expectations effect occurs. Is this the ordering of occurrence: liquidity effect, income effect, and then expectations effect?

Answer:

No. Exhibit 13–8 does not illustrate the sequence of effects; it simply illustrates the effects. For one, we learn that given an increase in the money supply the liquidity effect pushes the nominal interest rate downward, and the income and expectations effects push it upward. The exhibit also illustrates that the income effect is approximately the same size as the liquidity effect and more or less offsets it. (To see this, notice in the exhibit that the income effect moves i_1 up by about the same amount that the liquidity effect moves i_2 down.) Thus, the net effect on the nominal interest rate is derived from the expectations effect.

Timing of the Adjustment

Exhibit 13–8 raises an important question, mainly, how much time passes between point 1 and point 4? Or, to put it differently, how long is the period between the increase in the money supply (point 1) and the full impact of the liquidity, income, and expectations effects (points 1–4) on the nominal interest rate? Early research,

---

[4]Sometimes the expectations effect is called the *Fisher effect* after economist Irving Fisher who described it in detail.

EXHIBIT 13–8
The Liquidity, Income, and Expectations Effects

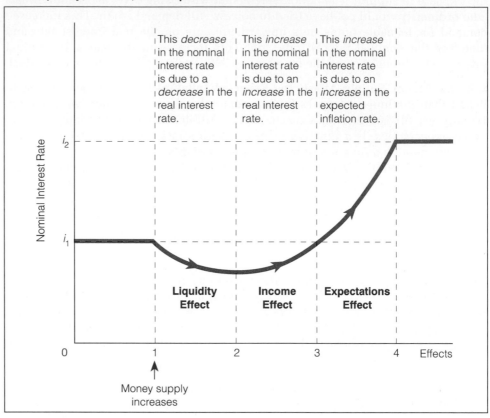

using data from 1945 through the 1960s, estimated that the liquidity effect lasted between 4 to 9 months, the income effect lasted about 6 months, and the time period between points 1 and 4 was several years. Some recent studies, however, based on more recent data, show that the liquidity effect is dominant for only about one month. From this we conclude that (1) the expectations effect is kicking in more quickly, and (2) the time period between points 1 and 4 has been reduced.

What accounts for this? Most economists explain it by saying that over time individuals appear to have formed their expectations of the future inflation rate based on present monetary growth and past inflation rates, instead of only past inflation rates. As a consequence, the expectations effect starts to occur earlier than in the past. This experience lends support to the rational expectations view of inflation expectations.

CHAPTER SUMMARY

The Definition of Measurement of Inflation

■ Inflation is an increase in the price level. One-shot inflation is a one-time increase in the price level. Continued inflation is a continued increase in the price level.

■ The consumer price index (CPI) and the GNP deflator are both used to measure inflation.

One-Shot Inflation

■ One-shot inflation can result from an increase in aggregate demand or a decrease in short-run aggregate supply.

■ Both an increase in aggregate demand and a decrease in short-run aggregate supply have short- and long-run effects on real GNP and the price level (see Exhibits 13–1 and 13–2). Starting from long-run equilibrium, the short-run effects of an increase in aggregate demand are that real GNP and the price level increase. The long-run effects of an increase in aggregate demand are that real GNP returns to its original level and the price level increases. Starting from long-run equilibrium, the short-run effects of a decrease in short-run aggregate supply are that real GNP decreases and the price level increases. The long-run effects of a decrease in short-run aggregate supply are that real GNP and the price level return to their original levels.

Continued Inflation

■ To change temporary inflation into continued inflation, it is necessary and sufficient to have a continued increase in aggregate demand.

■ Continued increases in the money supply cause continued increases in aggregate demand and continued inflation.

The Effects of Inflation

■ The effects of inflation are often different depending on whether inflation is unanticipated, correctly anticipated, or incorrectly anticipated. In this chapter, we discussed mainly the effects of unanticipated inflation.

■ Inflation is a "tax" on peoples' money holdings.

■ Inflation either lowers the real rate of return on savings or turns it negative.

■ Inflation redistributes purchasing power from lenders to borrowers.

■ Inflation can lead to social tension, particularly if individuals do not understand the cause of inflation.

■ Inflation may turn past decisions into mistakes.

■ Inflation causes increased uncertainty and may cause some individuals to choose not to enter into long-term contracts.

■ Inflation causes individuals to try to hedge against it; in the process they divert resources away from strictly productive activities.

■ An increase in the U.S. inflation rate relative to its trading partners' inflation rates leads to a decline in U.S. competitiveness in the international marketplace.

Expectations, Nominal Interest Rates, and Inflation

■ The nominal interest rate = real interest rate + expected inflation rate.

■ Both the adaptive expectations and rational expectations theories explain how individuals form the expected inflation rate. Adaptive expectations holds that individuals form the expected inflation rate based on past inflation rates. Rational expectations holds that individuals form the expected inflation rate based on past inflation rates and on their predictions of the effects of present and future policy actions and events.

■ A major difference between adaptive and rational expectations is the speed at which the expected inflation rate changes. If the expected inflation rate is formed adaptively, it changes more slowly (since it is based only on the past and individuals must wait until the present and the future become the past before they change their expectations) than if it is formed rationally (where it is based on the past, present, and future).

The Money Supply and Nominal Interest Rates

■ The money supply affects both the real interest rate and the expected inflation rate; hence it follows that the money supply also affects the nominal interest rate since the nominal interest rate = real interest rate + expected inflation rate.
■ The money supply affects the nominal interest rate via three effects: liquidity, income, and expectations. The decrease in the real and nominal interest rates due to an increase in the supply of loanable funds is referred to as the liquidity effect. The increase in the real and nominal interest rates brought on by an increase in GNP is referred to as the income effect. The increase in the nominal interest rate due to a higher expected inflation rate is referred to as the expectations effect.

Key Terms and Concepts

Inflation	Ex Ante Real Interest Rate	Rational Expectations
One-Shot Inflation		Liquidity Effect
Continued Inflation	Ex Post Real Interest Rate	Income Effect
Nominal Interest Rate		Expectations Effect
Real Interest Rate	Adaptive Expectations	

QUESTIONS AND PROBLEMS

1. "A loaf of bread, a computer, and automobile tires have gone up in price; therefore, we are experiencing inflation." Do you agree or disagree with this statement? Explain your answer.

2. What is the difference in the long run between a one-shot increase in aggregate demand and a one-shot decrease in short-run aggregate supply?

3. In recent years, economists have argued over what the truc value of the real interest rate is at any one time and over time. Given that the nominal interest rate = real interest rate + expected inflation rate, it follows that the real interest rate = nominal interest rate − expected inflation rate. Why do you think there is so much disagreement over the true value of the real interest rate?

4. Suppose there has been an increase in the price level in each of the last three years. Does this mean the money supply must have increased during this three-year period?

5. Here is the CPI for a few years. Calculate the inflation rate for 1981–89.

Year	CPI
1980	82.4
1981	90.9
1982	96.5
1983	99.6
1984	103.9
1985	107.6
1986	109.6
1987	113.6
1988	118.3
1989	124.0
1990	130.7

6. "One-shot inflation may be a demand-side (of the economy) or supply-side phenomenon, but continued inflation is likely to be a demand-side phenomenon." Do you agree or disagree with this statement? Explain your answer.

7. How might the Fed influence the international competitiveness of the United States?

8. "An increase in the money supply causes continued inflation." Explain why this statement is false.

9. Explain how demand-induced one-shot inflation may appear as supply-induced one-shot inflation.

10. What would we have to observe before we could conclude that continued inflation was a supply-side phenomenon?

CLASSICAL AND MONETARIST THEORY: EMPHASIS ON THE PRICE LEVEL AND GNP

WHAT THIS CHAPTER IS ABOUT

In Chapter 9, we learned that the main focus of Keynesian theory is on high unemployment and therefore on "real GNP that is below natural real GNP." In P–Q terms, Keynesians are interested in Q. In this chapter, we discuss classical economics and monetarism. Classical economics looks at the price level, or P, and monetarism emphasizes GNP, or P times Q. Both classical economists and monetarists regard the money supply as the major explanatory variable of changes in P and GNP.

CLASSICAL MONETARY THEORY

■

Classical monetary theory revolves around the equation of exchange and the simple quantity theory of money.

The Equation of Exchange

The equation of exchange is an identity that states that the money supply (M) multiplied by velocity (V) must be equal to the price level (P) times real GNP (Q).

$$MV = PQ$$

What is **velocity?** It is the average number of times a dollar is spent to buy final goods and services in a year. Think of an economy with only 10 one-dollar bills. In January, the first of the 10 one-dollar bills moves from Smith's hands to Jones's hands to buy good X. Then in June it goes from Jones's hands to Brown's hands to buy good Y. And in December it goes from Brown's hands to Peterson's hands to buy good Z. Over the course of the year, this dollar bill has changed hands 3 times.

The other dollar bills also change hands during the year. The second dollar bill changes hands 5 times, the third 6 times, the fourth 2 times, the fifth 7 times, the sixth 1 time, the seventh 2 times, the eighth 2 times, the ninth 3 times, and the tenth 4 times. Given this information, we calculate the number of times the average dollar changes hands in making a purchase. In this case the number is 3.5. This number (3.5) is velocity.

In a large economy such as ours, it is impossible to figure out how many times each dollar changes hands, and therefore it is impossible to calculate velocity the way we have done here. Instead a different way is used.

First, we calculate GNP; next, we calculate the average money supply; finally, we divide GNP by the average money supply to obtain velocity. For example, if $4,800 billion worth of transactions occur in a year, and the average money supply during the year is $800 billion, a dollar must have been used on average 6 times during the year to purchase goods and services. In symbols, we have

$$V \equiv \text{GNP}/M$$

(The sign $\equiv$ means "must be equal to"; this is an identity.) Since we know that GNP is equal to $P \times Q$, we can rewrite this as

$$V \equiv P \times Q/M$$

If we multiply both sides by M, we get

$$M \times V \equiv P \times Q$$

which is the **equation of exchange.** Exactly what the equation of exchange tells us can be interpreted in different ways. Here are a few of them:

1. The money supply multiplied by velocity must equal the price level times real GNP: $M \times V \equiv P \times Q$.
2. The money supply multiplied by velocity must equal GNP: $M \times V \equiv \text{GNP}$ (since $P \times Q \equiv \text{GNP}$). (Recall that when we use the letters "GNP" alone, we are referring to nominal GNP.)
3. Total spending (measured by MV) must equal the total sales revenues of business firms (measured by PQ): $MV \equiv PQ$.

In fact, the third way of explaining the equation of exchange is perhaps the most intuitively simple to understand. It simply says that the total expenditures (of

Velocity
The average number of times a dollar is spent to buy final goods and services in a year.

Equation of Exchange
An identity stating that the money supply times velocity must be equal to the price level times real GNP.

Simple Quantity Theory of Money
The theory that assumes that V and Q are constant and predicts that changes in M lead to strictly proportional changes in P.

buyers) must equal the total sales (of sellers). Consider a simple economy where there is only one buyer and one seller. If the buyer buys a book for $20, then the seller receives $20. Stated differently, the money supply in the example, or $20, times velocity, 1, is equal to the price of the book, $20, times the quantity of the book, 1.

From the Equation of Exchange to the Simple Quantity Theory of Money

Saying that the money supply times velocity must equal GNP is not a theory of the macroeconomy. For example, if M increases, it does not necessarily follow that GNP increases. Why? Because as M increases, V may decrease, and therefore MV may not increase at all. And if MV does not increase, neither will GNP.

To turn the equation of exchange into a theory, we need to make some assumptions about the variables in the equation. Many eighteenth-century classical economists, as well as the American economist Irving Fisher (1867–1947) and the English economist Alfred Marshall (1842–1924), assumed that changes in velocity are so small that for all practical purposes velocity can be assumed constant (especially over short periods of time) and that real GNP, or Q, is fixed in the short run. Hence, they turned the equation of exchange, which is simply true by definition, into a theory by assuming that both V and Q are fixed, or constant. With these two assumptions, we have the **simple quantity theory of money.** If V and Q are constant, we would predict that changes in M will bring about *strictly proportional* changes in P. This point is illustrated in Exhibit 14–1.

On the left side of the exhibit, the key assumptions of the simple quantity theory are noted: V and Q are constant. Also, $M \times V = P \times Q$ is noted. We use the equal sign ($=$) instead of the identity sign ($\equiv$) because we are speaking about the simple quantity theory and not the equation of exchange. (The $=$ sign here represents "is predicted to be equal"; that is, given our assumptions, $M \times V$, or MV, is predicted to be equal to $P \times Q$, or PQ.)

Starting with the first row, the money supply is $500, velocity is 4, real GNP (Q) is 1,000 units, and the price level, or price index, $2.[1] GNP therefore equals $2,000. In the second row, the money supply increases by 100 percent—from $500 to $1,000—and both V and Q are constant, at 4 and 1,000, respectively. The price level moves from $2 to $4. On the right-hand side of the exhibit, we see that a 100 percent increase in M predicts a 100 percent increase in P. Changes in P are predicted to be strictly proportional to changes in M.

[1]You are perhaps used to seeing real GNP written as a dollar figure and a price index as a number without a dollar sign in front of it. We have switched things for purposes of this example, as it is easier to think of Q as "so many units of goods" and P as the average price paid per unit of these goods.

EXHIBIT 14–1
Assumptions and Predictions of the Simple Quantity Theory of Money
The simple quantity theory of money assumes that both V and Q are constant. (A bar over each indicates this in the exhibit.) The prediction is that changes in M lead to strictly proportional changes in P. (Note: For purposes of this example, think of Q as "so many units of a good" and of P as the "average price paid per unit of these goods.")

ASSUMPTIONS OF SIMPLE QUANTITY THEORY								PREDICTIONS OF SIMPLE QUANTITY THEORY	
M	$\times$	$\overline{V}$	$=$	P	$\times$	$\overline{Q}$	$=$	GNP	% Change in M = % Change in P
$ 500		4		$2		1,000		$2,000	
1,000		4		4		1,000		4,000	+100% +100%
1,500		4		6		1,000		6,000	+ 50 + 50
1,200		4		4.80		1,000		4,800	− 20 − 20

Does the Fed Think in Terms of $MV = PQ$?

There is some evidence that the Fed looks at the economy in terms of $MV = PQ$. A few research economists at the Fed have proceeded this way:

First, they set M equal to the actual money supply (they use $M2$, so let's set $M2$ equal to $3,600 billion). Then they set V equal to the long-run average velocity of the money supply (they use $M2$ velocity, which is relatively stable with a mean value of 1.59). Next, they set Q in the equation equal to Q_N, or natural real GNP. The implicit assumption here is that the economy moves toward its natural real GNP level.

By checking whether the current unemployment rate is near the natural unemployment rate, economists know whether the current real GNP (Q) is or is not approximately equal

to natural real GNP (Q_N). For now, let's say the economy is currently operating at natural unemployment, so that the current real GNP and the natural real GNP are the same at $4,200 billion. Placing the numbers (dollars in billions) into our equation, we get:

$$M \times V = P \times Q$$

$$\$3,600 \times 1.59 = ? \times \$4,200$$

On the left side of the equation, we get $5,724 (which is $M \times V$). On the right side of the equation, we get $4,200P$ (which is P times Q). Solving for P, we get 1.36 ($5,724/$4,200 = P = 1.36$). Multiplying by 100, we get 136.

What does the number "136" tell us? It tells us simply that if (1) the economy is moving toward its natural real GNP level, (2) velocity is stable at 1.59, and (3) the money supply is

$3,600 billion, then the price level that will be established by the economy in the long run is 136.

Fed economists could then compare the predicted long-run price level (136) with the current price level—say, as measured by the GNP deflator. Suppose the current GNP deflator (124) is lower than the predicted long-run price level (136). Fed economists may conclude that current monetary policy (recall that the current money supply in our example is $3,600) will tend to raise the price level in the long run. In short, current monetary policy is inflationary. This gives Fed officials information about where the economy is headed if they simply hold fast. Of course, if price stability is currently a major goal, they may want to reverse course.

In the third row, M increases by 50 percent, and P is predicted to increase by 50 percent. In the fourth row, M decreases by 20 percent, and P is predicted to decrease by 20 percent.

In summary, the simple quantity theory assumes that both V and Q are constant in the short run, and therefore predicts that changes in M lead to strictly proportional changes in P.

Question:

A key question would seem to be: Are V and Q constant in the short run as the classical economists assumed? If they are not, then shouldn't the simple quantity theory of money, which assumes that they are, be disregarded?

Answer:

To a degree, the answer depends on how we define the short run. If we consider the short run as 24 hours, it is unlikely that either V or Q is going to change. If the time frame is a period of months, it is likely that V and Q would only register tiny changes, so small, in fact, that we might want to overlook them. Over a longer period, though, both V and Q can and do change. For example, the average annual change in velocity during the period 1987–1990 was approximately 3.0 percent, and the average annual change in real GNP during this period was approximately 2.8 percent.

Suppose we found that both velocity and real GNP were not constant, even for reasonably short periods of time. In short, suppose the assumptions of the theory

CHAPTER 14
CLASSICAL AND MONETARIST
THEORY: EMPHASIS ON THE PRICE
LEVEL AND GNP

■

are not 100 percent accurate. Is this a good enough reason to discard the theory? Many economists answer no. They argue that a theory should be evaluated in terms of the accuracy of its predictions instead of the degree of realism of its assumptions (see Chapter 1).

Follow-up Question:

Well, then, perhaps the question should be: Does the simple quantity theory of money predict well? Does it make predictions that are consistently substantiated by the facts?

Answer:

The simple quantity theory of money says that changes in the money supply bring about strictly proportional changes in prices. We do not always observe this strict proportionality. But what we do observe is that countries with higher money supply growth rates tend to have higher price level growth rates than those countries with lower money supply growth rates. And this definitely is a theme of the simple quantity theory of money. To illustrate briefly, during the period 1969–84, Argentina's annual money supply growth rate was 79.3 percent, and its annual growth rate in prices was 80.6 percent. During the period 1950–83, the annual growth rate in the U.S. money supply was 5.3 percent, and its annual growth rate in prices was 4.3 percent. As Exhibit 14–1 makes clear, the simple quantity theory of money predicts that larger percentage increases in the money supply will bring about greater percentage increases in the price level.

MONETARISM

Economists who call themselves *monetarists* have not been content to rely on the simple quantity theory of money. For one, they do not hold that velocity is constant; instead, they believe that velocity moves in a predictable way. They conclude that changes in the money supply and/or money demand change GNP.

The Demand for Money

Before pursuing monetarist theory, we need to discuss the demand for money (or money demand). Following are several statements that explain this phenomenon.

1. Money is a good and thus there is a demand for it. In Chapter 11, we defined money as a good—specifically, a good that is widely accepted for purposes of exchange. There is a demand for money, just as there is a demand for apples, telephones, socks, music keyboards, and other goods.

2. Individuals demand money in order to hold it, not to consume it. If a person demands an orange, most likely she buys it in order to consume it. The demand for money is not the same. People demand money, not to consume it, but to *hold* it. One of many reasons people hold money is to be ready to take advantage of opportunities that may arise in the future. In short, gains can be made from demanding, or holding, the most liquid asset of all—money.

3. Money is not the same as income, or anything else that might be incorrectly equated with money. Money is a *stock,* income is a *flow.* A stock is measured at one point in time; a flow is measured over time. For example, Alice may say that she has $25,000. This is a given amount of money at one instant in time. The

$25,000 is a stock; specifically, Alice's *money stock.* Alternatively, Alice may say that she earns $1,000 per month. In this case, we have a time period, one month. The $1,000 is Alice's income.

Suppose George, an employee at a furniture company, tells us that he is going to demand more money from his boss. Do you think George is demanding more *money* or more *income?* He said money, which is a stock, but it is likely that he means income. He probably doesn't want more money at one instant in time—a lump-sum payment right now—but rather a greater money flow *over time;* that is, a higher income every month.

When we talk about the demand for money, we are talking about the demand for a stock.

4. The quantity supplied of money must necessarily equal the quantity (or amount) of money that people actually hold. We shall let the symbol M^S stand for "quantity supplied of money" and the symbol M^{AH} stand for the "quantity of money actually held." So we are saying that $M^S = M^{AH}$.

Suppose M1 is $800 billion. It follows that the quantity of money that people actually hold must *also* be $800 billion. The reason is simple: Someone must be holding the money, the money must belong to someone.[2]

5. The quantity supplied of money (or the quantity of money people actually hold) does not necessarily equal the quantity demanded of money. We shall let the symbol M^d stand for "quantity demanded of money." So we are saying that M^S (and therefore M^{AH}, too) does not necessarily equal M^d.

To see this, suppose, once again, that M^S (and M^{AH}) is $800 billion. It does not necessarily follow that the quantity demanded of money (M^d) is also $800 billion. The quantity demanded of money may be more or less than $800 billion. For example, suppose that at the current level of GNP, the quantity demanded of money is $750 billion. This means that individuals are actually holding more money than they desire to hold given the present economic environment. As we shall soon see, this will bring about a particular behavioral response.

The Money Market Equilibrium Condition

In our discussion of supply and demand in Chapter 3, we noted that market equilibrium exists at the point at which the quantity supplied of a good equals the quantity demanded of the good ($Q_s = Q_d$). Money is a good, and therefore the same condition describes money market equilibrium. Money market equilibrium occurs when the quantity supplied of money equals the quantity demanded of money.

The money market equilibrium condition is

$$M^S = M^d$$

Since $M^S = M^{AH}$, the money market equilibrium condition can be rewritten as

$$M^S = M^{AH} = M^d$$

It follows that there is disequilibrium in the money market when M^S (or M^{AH}) is greater than, or less than, M^d.

---

[2]If you come across any money that does not belong to you, nor to anyone else, please write the author a letter telling him where it can be found. Many thanks.

The Demand for Money in the *MV–PQ* Framework

Again, consider the equation of exchange, $MV \equiv PQ$. The M in the exchange stands for the quantity supplied of money; thus $M = M^S$. Additionally, PQ is the same as GNP. We can rewrite the equation of exchange as

$$M^S \times V \equiv PQ$$

or

$$M^S \times V \equiv \text{GNP}$$

Now we add a piece of information we have recently acquired: When the money market is in equilibrium, $M^S = M^d$. Knowing that $M^S = M^d$ in equilibrium, we can substitute M^d in the equation of exchange for M^S. We get

$$M^d \times V = PQ$$

We then divide both sides of the modified equation of exchange by V. This gives us

$$M^d = 1/V \times PQ$$

If we let the fraction, $1/V$, equal k (that is, $k = 1/V$), we have

$$M^d = kPQ$$

This says that the quantity demanded of money equals k (a fraction, or the reciprocal of velocity, $1/V$) times PQ, or GNP.

With this simple equation in front of us, it is immediately clear that M^d increases if either k, P, or Q increases and that M^d decreases if either k, P, or Q decreases.

Of course, the net effect on M^d depends on the percentage change in one variable measured against the percentage change in another variable. For example, an *increase* in k accompanied by a proportionally greater *decrease* in P would *decrease* M^d. What are the economic reasons (as opposed to the arithmetical reasons) why M^d increases as P and Q increase?

First, consider P, the price level. As the price level increases, more money is needed to buy a specific bundle of goods—for example, a week's worth of groceries. Next, consider that as Q (real GNP) increases, the number and magnitude of transactions are usually assumed to increase, so individuals will hold larger money balances.[3]

In Exhibit 14–2, PQ, or GNP, is plotted against M^d. We see that as PQ increases, M^d increases; as PQ decreases, M^d decreases. Connecting different levels of PQ, or GNP, with different levels of M^d, we obtain a **money demand line.** Our money demand line represents the direct relationship between the quantity demanded of money and GNP. Changes in PQ, or GNP, will move us from one point on the money demand line to another point on the same line.

Money Demand Line
The graphical representation of the direct relationship between the quantity demanded of money and GNP.

k and *V*: What Variables Affect Them?

Given the equation $M^d = kPQ$, we know that a change in k will bring about a change in the quantity demanded of money: If k increases, so will M^d; if k decreases, so will M^d. But what factors will change k? We discuss three. Note, also, that any variable that changes k also changes velocity (V) since $k = 1/V$. Thus, the following variables can change both k and V.

PART IV
MONEY, MACROECONOMIC THEORY
AND MONETARY POLICY
■
310

[3]It follows that as the price level decreases, less money is needed to buy any specific bundle of goods. As real GNP decreases, the number and magnitude of transactions are usually assumed to decrease, so that individuals will hold smaller money balances.

Interest Rate. Holding money comes with certain benefits and costs. The cost of holding money is approximated by the interest rate (return) on close substitutes for money, such as bonds, stocks, and savings accounts. If the interest rate on these close substitutes increases (relative to the net return on holding money), individuals desire to hold a smaller fraction of their incomes in money balances, causing a decrease in k.

A similar point can be made of velocity. If the interest rate on the close substitutes for money increases, individuals desire to hold lower money balances and turn over more quickly those money balances they do hold. In short, velocity increases.

Alternatively, if the interest rate on close substitutes for money decreases (relative to the net return on holding money), individuals desire to hold a larger fraction of their incomes in money balances, causing an increase in k. This is the same as saying that velocity decreases.

We summarize: As the interest rate increases, k decreases, and V increases; as the interest rate decreases, k increases, and V decreases.[4]

Expected Rate of Inflation. When individuals expect an increase in the inflation rate, they desire to hold a smaller fraction of their incomes in money balances. The reason is that as the inflation rate rises, the purchasing power of money falls. (In Chapter 13, we said that inflation acts as a tax on peoples' money holdings.) We conclude, then, that an expected increase in the inflation rate will decrease k and increase V. On the other hand, when individuals expect a decrease in the inflation rate, they desire to hold a larger fraction of their incomes in money balances; therefore k increases and V decreases.

The Frequency with Which Employees Receive Paychecks. Economists argue that the more frequently an employee receives a paycheck, the less money (on average) that employee will hold—which implies that the smaller k is. For example, an employee who receives a paycheck twice a month will hold less money (on average) than if he or she receives a paycheck once a month, even if the annual salary is the same in both cases. To illustrate, consider two cases for an employee, Liz.

■ *Case 1:* Here Liz earns $24,000 a year and is paid on the first of each month ($2,000 a month). We assume that she always maintains a $1,000 minimum balance in her checking account. On the first day of the month, when Liz deposits her $2,000 monthly check into her checking account, the balance rises to $3,000. We shall assume that her checking account decreases a little each day as she makes purchases and that by the end of each month she has spent her entire monthly income. This means that on the last day of the month—the day before payday—her checking account balance is $1,000. Therefore, her average checking account balance—or her average money balance holding—is $2,000 (which is halfway between $3,000 and $1,000). If we divide her $24,000 annual income by her average money balance holding of $2,000, we obtain her personal velocity. This is 12.

■ *Case 2:* Now suppose Liz's workplace decides to pay its employees twice a month. Every two weeks, Liz receives a $1,000 paycheck instead of a $2,000 pay-

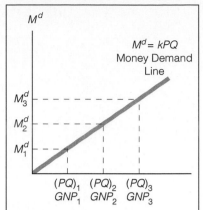

EXHIBIT 14–2
Plotting M^d against PQ, or GNP

As PQ, or GNP, increases, the quantity demanded of money, M^d, increases; as PQ, or GNP, decreases, the quantity demanded of money decreases. The money demand line represents this direct relationship.

[4]Economists tend to speak about "the" interest rate when, in fact, they are referring to one specific rate among several. We follow this practice in this text. As our present discussion has shown, there is an interest rate (return) on savings, an interest rate (return) on bonds, and an interest rate (return) on stocks. In reality, an individual compares the interest rate (return) on each of these close substitutes for money with the net return on money in order to decide how much money to hold. Speaking about "the" interest rate may incorrectly suggest that only one asset is being compared with money.

check every month. On the first of the month, Liz deposits $1,000 into her checking account and her checking balance rises to $2,000 (remember, she always has a $1,000 minimum balance). Again, we shall assume that Liz draws down the account until on the day before payday she has only the $1,000 minimum balance in her account. Her average money balance holding is now $1,500 (halfway between $1,000 and $2,000). Her personal velocity this time is 16 ($24,000/$1,500 = 16).

Comparing cases 1 and 2, we conclude that the more frequently Liz gets paid, the smaller the money balance that she holds. When she got paid *once* a month, her average money holding was *$2,000;* when she got paid *twice* a month, her average money holding was *$1,500.* This means that the more frequently Liz gets paid, the less money she needs to hold to cover a given number of transactions.

In more technical terms, we can say that the more frequently Liz gets paid, the larger V is and the smaller k is.

For a quick review of the factors that can affect k and V, see Exhibit 14–3.

As *k* Changes, the Money Demand Line Rotates

Anything that causes k or V to change causes the money demand line to rotate. To illustrate, as k decreases—meaning individuals desire to hold a smaller fraction of their income in money balances—the money demand line rotates downward from M_1^d to M_2^d (Exhibit 14–4). This is because as k decreases, M^d falls at a given level of GNP. In the exhibit, M^d falls from $200 billion to $100 billion at a GNP level of $1,000.

As k increases—meaning individuals desire to hold a larger fraction of their income in money balances—the money demand line rotates upward from M_1^d to M_3^d. This is because as k increases, M^d rises at a given level of GNP. In the exhibit, M^d rises from $200 billion to $333 billion at a GNP level of $1,000 billion.

An Increase in the Money Supply

We previously stated that the money market is in equilibrium when $M^s = M^{AH} = M^d$. It is important to remember this as we proceed.

First, consider Exhibit 14–5. At point 1, the money market equilibrium condition is satisfied: $M^s = M^{AH} = M^d$. Now suppose the Fed increases the money supply from M_1^s to M_2^s, or from $600 billion to $700 billion.

EXHIBIT 14–3
Changes in *k* and *V*
An increase in the interest rate, an expected increase in the inflation rate, and an increase in the frequency with which employees receive paychecks all decrease k and increase V. A decrease in the interest rate, an expected decrease in the inflation rate, and a decrease in the frequency with which employees receive paychecks all increase k and decrease V.

CONDITIONS	*k*	*V*
Increase in interest rate	Decreases	Increases
Decrease in interest rate	Increases	Decreases
Expected increase in the inflation rate	Decreases	Increases
Expected decrease in the inflation rate	Increases	Decreases
Increase in the frequency with which employees receive paychecks	Decreases	Increases
Decrease in the frequency with which employees receive paychecks	Increases	Decreases

EXHIBIT 14–4
As *k* Changes, the Money Demand Line Rotates

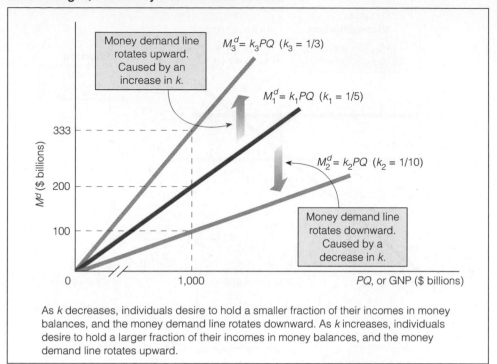

As *k* decreases, individuals desire to hold a smaller fraction of their incomes in money balances, and the money demand line rotates downward. As *k* increases, individuals desire to hold a larger fraction of their incomes in money balances, and the money demand line rotates upward.

Initially, GNP does not change: it remains at $4,000 billion. However, now M^s and M^{AH} are greater than M^d: $700 billion is greater than $600 billion. This can be seen at point 2.

When $M^s = M^{AH} > M^d$, we say that individuals are *holding too much money* (holding excess money balances) at the current level of GNP.

But can individuals really ever be holding too much money? The answer is yes: Individuals can hold too much money *relative* to other goods they desire—such as bonds, stocks, cars, houses, paintings, television sets, and so on. In fact, when individuals are holding too much money, they trade money for other goods; that is, they increase their spending. As a consequence, prices and/or output (*P* and/or *Q*) increase. This leads to an increase in *PQ*, or GNP.

But what happens as *PQ*, or GNP, rises? As we stated earlier, M^d rises since $M^d = kPQ$. The economy moves up the money demand line from point 1 in Exhibit 14–5 to point 3. At point 3, the money market is in equilibrium, since $M^s = M^{AH} = M^d$.

We conclude that an increase in the money supply increases GNP, *ceteris paribus*.

A Decrease in the Money Supply

Consider Exhibit 14–6. At point 1, the money market equilibrium condition is satisfied: $M^s = M^{AH} = M^d$. Now suppose the Fed decreases the money supply from M_1^s to M_2^s, or from $700 billion to 600 billion.

Initially, GNP does not change: it remains at $4,666 billion. However, now the M^s and M^{AH} are less than M^d: $600 billion is less than $700 billion. This can be seen at point 2.

EXHIBIT 14–5
An Increase in M^s

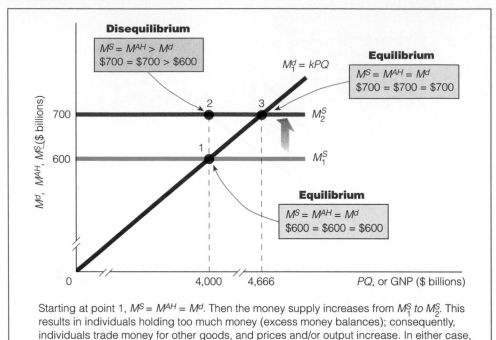

Starting at point 1, $M^S = M^{AH} = M^d$. Then the money supply increases from M_1^S to M_2^S. This results in individuals holding too much money (excess money balances); consequently, individuals trade money for other goods, and prices and/or output increase. In either case, GNP increases. As this occurs, the economy moves up the demand line. Equilibrium is at point 3, where once again $M^S = M^{AH} = M^d$.

When $M^s = M^{AH} < M^d$, we say that individuals are *holding too little money* (holding deficient money balances) at the current level of GNP. In fact, when individuals are holding too little money, they cut back on their spending in order to accumulate more money. As a consequence, prices and/or output (P and/or Q) decrease. This leads to a decrease in PQ, or GNP.

But what happens as PQ, or GNP, falls? As we stated earlier, M^d falls since $M^d = kPQ$. The economy moves down the money demand line from point 1 in Exhibit 14–6 to point 3. At point 3, the money market is in equilibrium, since $M^s = M^{AH} = M^d$. We conclude that a decrease in the money supply decreases GNP, *ceteris paribus*.

Three States of the Economy in Monetarism

In earlier chapters, we noted that the economy had to be in one of three states: recessionary gap ($Q < Q_N$), inflationary gap ($Q > Q_N$), or long-run equilibrium ($Q = Q_N$). Two of these states—recessionary and inflationary gaps—are disequilibrium states of the economy and one is not.

This threefold classification of the economy can also be used to categorize monetarism. Using our terms M^s, M^{AH}, and M^d, the economy is always in one of the following states:

1. $M^s = M^{AH} > M^d$
2. $M^s = M^{AH} < M^d$
3. $M^s = M^{AH} = M^d$

EXHIBIT 14–6
A Decrease in M^s

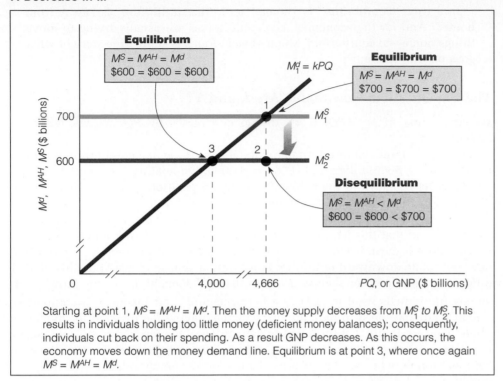

Starting at point 1, $M^S = M^{AH} = M^d$. Then the money supply decreases from M_1^S to M_2^S. This results in individuals holding too little money (deficient money balances); consequently, individuals cut back on their spending. As a result GNP decreases. As this occurs, the economy moves down the money demand line. Equilibrium is at point 3, where once again $M^S = M^{AH} = M^d$.

In short, individuals can hold (1) too much, (2) too little, or (3) the right amount of money. The first two are disequilibrium states and the third is not. In Exhibit 14–7 we show these three states and note what happens to spending and GNP in each case.

"Equilibrium" and "disequilibrium" are important categories for the economist: A market is either in equilibrium or disequilibrium; an economy is either in equilibrium or disequilibrium. When a market or an economy is in equilibrium, the economist knows that economic forces are in balance. When a market or an economy is in disequilibrium, the economist knows that there

EXHIBIT 14–7
The Monetarist Position

If $M^s = M^{AH} > M^d$, individuals are holding too much money, they increase their spending, and GNP rises. If $M^s = M^{AH} < M^d$, individuals are holding too little money, they then decrease their spending, and GNP falls. If $M^s = M^{AH} = M^d$, individuals are holding the right amount of money and do not change their spending.

CONDITION	INDIVIDUALS ARE HOLDING . . .	SPENDING . . .	GNP . . .
$M^s = M^{AH} > M^d$ (Disequilibrium)	Too Much Money	Increases	Rises
$M^s = M^{AH} < M^d$ (Disequilibrium)	Too Little Money	Decreases	Falls
$M^s = M^{AH} = M^d$ (Equilibrium)	The Right Amount of Money	Does Not Change	Does Not Change

are changes to be made. The economist then tries to figure out what those changes will be and why.

In a way, "equilibrium" is "home," and "disequilibrium" is "away from home." And for the economist, economic forces are usually trying to move things home—to equilibrium. Much of economics is simply the story of what goes on during the trip.

The Big Question: How Stable Are k and V?

We know that $M^d = kPQ$. If we divide both sides by PQ, we are left with $M^d/PQ = k$.

With this in mind, let us return to Exhibit 14–5. At the first equilibrium position, point 1, $M^d = \$600$ billion and $(PQ)_1 = \$4,000$. Calculating k at point 1, we get .15. Now let us move to the second equilibrium position, point 2, where $M^d = \$700$ billion and $(PQ)_2 = \$4,666$. Calculating k at point 2, we get .15. It is noticeable that k equals .15 at both equilibrium positions. In short, where we increased M^s, and found that this led to an increase in PQ, or GNP, k did not change.

What does it mean if k does not change? It means that the money demand line does not rotate downward or upward since only a change in k will do this. Stated differently, if k does not change, it means that the demand for money (how much money individuals want to hold as a percentage of their incomes) is completely stable. Again, we need to remind ourselves that saying the demand for money is stable does not imply that the quantity demanded of money is stable. The demand for money refers to either the money demand line or the percentage of income held as money, whereas the quantity demanded of money refers to the absolute number of dollars held. As we said, it is possible for individuals to maintain money balances at 15 percent (of their incomes) no matter what their incomes, while at the same time holding more money (in absolute terms) at a GNP of $4,666 billion than at $4,000 billion.

Most monetarists do not maintain that k and V are completely stable (that is, never changing), but do hold that both are highly stable. They allow for small changes in k and V; furthermore, they hold that these changes are predictable.

Whether k and V are highly stable and predictable is an empirical issue. Here we simply ask what the implications would be if the monetarist position on k and V is correct.

First, and most important, the monetarist position implies that changes in the money supply strongly affect GNP in a predictable manner (Exhibit 14–8).

Consider two extreme cases: case 1, where k and V are completely stable; and case 2, where k and V are largely unstable. Suppose the money supply increases from M_1^s to M_2^s. In case 1, k is completely stable, so the economy moves from point A to point B and GNP rises from GNP_1 to GNP_2.

In case 2, as the money supply increases, k increases, and because k increases, the money demand line rotates upward from M_1^d to M_2^d.[4] We have greatly accentuated this upward rotation in the money demand line, so much that our new equilibrium is at point C, giving us the same GNP level we had at point A before the money supply increased. Because of this large change in k, and consequent large change in the money demand line, the initial impact of an increased money supply on GNP is *completely offset*.

We conclude that the degree to which an increase in the money supply leads to

[5]We are implicitly assuming that as the money supply increases, the interest rate decreases. As we have learned, when the interest rate decreases, k increases, rotating the money demand line upward.

EXHIBIT 14–8
The Demand for Money and GNP

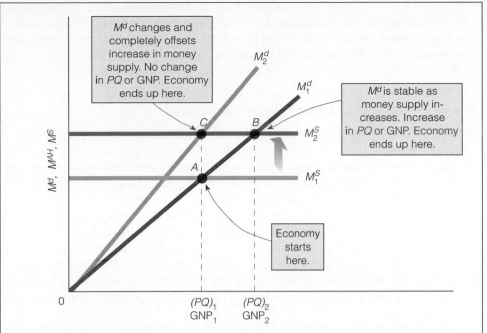

M^d changes and completely offsets increase in money supply. No change in PQ or GNP. Economy ends up here.

M^d is stable as money supply increases. Increase in PQ or GNP. Economy ends up here.

Economy starts here.

Two extreme cases are illustrated here. Starting at point A, the money supply increases from M_1^S to M_2^S. If the demand for money is stable—that is, k, or V, is stable—then the economy moves to point B. GNP increases from GNP$_1$ to GNP$_2$. If, however, k increases as the money supply increases, then the money demand line rotates upward. We have accentuated the rotation in the demand line so that we end up at point C. We conclude that the degree to which an increase in the money supply increases GNP depends on the degree to which k rises in response to an increase in the money supply.

an increase in GNP depends on the degree to which k rises in response to an increase in the money supply. The less k rises, the greater the increase in GNP given an increase in the money supply; the more k rises, the smaller the increase in GNP given an increase in the money supply.

In summary, the monetarist position specifies that the demand for money is highly stable. To put it differently, monetarists maintain that V and k are highly stable and predictable. This means that both change, but only slightly, and not in an erratic or random way. The monetarist conclusion–prediction is that changes in the money supply will strongly affect GNP.

Stating Monetarism *MV–PQ* Terms

We have presented monetarism in terms of the money demand equation, $M^d = kPQ$, and M^s. Since in equilibrium $M^s = M^d$, it is easy to replace M^d with M^s, and we see that in equilibrium $M^s = kPQ$. What does this tell us? It tells us that a change on the left-hand side of the equation—in M^s—will bring about a strictly proportional change on the right-hand side of the equation, in PQ, if k is constant. For example, suppose $M^s = \$600$ billion, $PQ = \$4,000$ billion, and $k = .15$. Now let M^s rise to $\$700$ billion, which is a 16.6 percent increase. If k is constant, then PQ rises to $\$4,666$ billion—or by a 16.6 percent increase. In more general terms,

CHAPTER 14
CLASSICAL AND MONETARIST
THEORY: EMPHASIS ON THE PRICE
LEVEL AND GNP

■

317

monetarism states that the smaller the change in k, the closer the percentage change in PQ will come to equaling the percentage change in M^s.

What we have just said about monetarism can be translated into MV–PQ terms. This is because the two equations, $M^d = kPQ$ and $M^s = kPQ$, are no more than a rewritten version of $MV = PQ$ since $k = 1/V$. Speaking in $MV = PQ$ terms, monetarism states that the smaller the change in V, the closer the percentage change in PQ will come to equaling the percentage change in the money supply.

Keynesian and Monetarist Theory Contrasted

In Chapter 9, we learned that Keynesians focus on the spending components of total expenditures—C, I, G, and net exports. Monetarists take a broader-brush approach by focusing on the money supply and money demand. This is indicated by their use of the equation of exchange, $MV = PQ$, and the money demand equation, $M^d = kPQ$.

In Keynesian theory, a change in any of the autonomous spending components of $C, I, G,$ or net exports affects GNP through the *multiplier*. Since Keynesians want to know *how much* GNP will change given a change in an autonomous spending component, they are naturally interested in the value of the multiplier. Much of the work in Keynesian theory has been on the value of the multiplier and whether it is stable. (What is it equal to today? Will it be the same next month or next year?)

In monetarist theory, a change in the money supply affects GNP through velocity. For example, if $V = 5$, a \$1 change in the money supply affects PQ, or GNP, by \$5, whereas if $V = 2$, a \$1 change in the money supply affects PQ, or GNP, by \$10. Since monetarists want to know how much PQ, or GNP, will change given a change in the money supply, they are naturally interested in the value of velocity. Much of the work in monetarism has been on the value of velocity and whether it is stable.

For Keynesians, a change in the money supply has to affect one of the three spending components of the private sector—consumption, investment, or net exports—before it affects GNP. In short, the link between changes in the money supply and changes in GNP is an indirect one. Monetarists believe there is a direct link between changes in the money supply and GNP. As we have discussed in this chapter, an increase in money supply causes individuals to find they are holding *too much money* at the given GNP level; consequently, they increase their spending, driving GNP up.

Association Is Not Causation: That Lesson Again

Monetarists hold that changes in the money supply bring about changes in GNP. Their theoretical explanation of this cause–effect relationship has been outlined in this chapter. Empirically, they have showed that, true enough, there is a strong association between changes in the money supply and changes in GNP. But association is not causation. It is possible that X and Y move up and down together, but knowing this doesn't indicate if (1) X is the cause and Y is the effect; or (2) Y is the cause and X is the effect; or (3) both X and Y are the effects of some, yet undetermined, cause.

What holds for X and Y might hold for the money supply and GNP. Monetarists state that money supply changes are the cause of GNP changes. But might it be the other way around? Keynesians sometimes argue that a decrease in autonomous

What Caused the Great Depression? A Monetarist Answer

In Chapter 9, we presented the Keynesian explanation of the Great Depression: A major drop in investment spending led to a multiple change in real GNP, which, in turn, prompted reductions in consumption and investment. In the background, the Keynesian theme—"the economy does not necessarily equilibrate at full-employment output"—could be heard.

The monetarist explanation of the Great Depression, mainly why the Great Depression was as long and severe as it was, focuses on the money supply and on government programs that worked against the natural full-employment tendencies of the economy.

For example, the monetarists point to the sharp drop in the money supply between 1929 and 1933 during which M1 fell by slightly more than one-fourth. Their theoretical framework indicates that such a drop is sure to depress GNP. (Think of what a decrease in the money supply does to the aggregate demand curve: The *AD* curve shifts leftward.)

Most monetarists argue that the economy could have recovered from its depressed state in a shorter period of time (the Depression lasted about ten years), even after the sharp drop in the money supply, if wages and prices had been allowed to fall to free-market levels. Instead, monetarists argue, government pursued policies that propped up prices and wages. (Think of what this does to the *SRAS* curve; it shifts leftward.) For example, monetarists point to President Franklin D. Roosevelt's National Recovery Act, which was designed to allow price-fixing agreements among firms. In addition, they point to the many farm programs that were established to boost crop prices and to new regulations in the communications industry that stifled price cutting. Finally, on the wage front, the monetarists maintain that major labor legislation passed at the time strengthened the hand of labor unions in bargaining for wage increases. Monetarists claim that together these policies and programs made the Depression more severe and longer lasting.

consumption and/or autonomous investment will lower GNP and lead to a drop in the money supply. The drop in the money supply is due to individuals borrowing less as a result of the decreased economic activity. In short, Keynesians have argued that the line of cause and effect may run from total spending to GNP to the money supply, while monetarists have argued that it runs from the money supply to GNP.

If we observe that changes in the money supply and GNP are positively associated, which line of causation—Keynesian or monetarist—should be given greater credence? The answer is neither or both. A Keynesian can rightfully argue that a strong positive association between money supply and GNP is as consistent with the "GNP–money supply" line of causation as it is with the monetarist "money supply–GNP" line of causation.

Monetarists build support for their explanation of the money supply–GNP link by pointing to monetary episodes where money supply changes have not been prompted by economic conditions. One of the best examples of such an episode occurred in 1936–37 when the Federal Reserve increased reserve requirements to improve its control of monetary policy. As a result, the money supply declined. Monetarists contend that this drop in the money supply was not the result of the Fed responding to economic conditions (the Great Depression was in full force), and therefore comes close to being a "controlled experiment," wherein one variable is changed independently of others. What were the consequences? Soon after the money supply fell, GNP fell. Monetarists point to this monetary episode, and to a few characteristically similar ones, as evidence that their explanation of the cause–effect relationship between money supply and GNP is correct. Not all economists have accepted the monetarist explanation, however.

A Change in GNP Without a Change in the Money Supply

Within the (general) monetarist framework, it is possible to get a change in GNP even if the money supply does not change. Suppose the economy is currently at point 1 in Exhibit 14–9. At point 1, the money market equilibrium condition is satisfied: $M^s = M^{AH} = M^d$. Now suppose k decreases (demand for money falls), causing the money demand line to rotate downward from M^d_1 to M^d_2, or from \$700 billion to \$600 billion at the original GNP level.

Initially, GNP does not change: It remains at \$4,200 billion. However, now M^s and M^{AH} are greater than M^d: \$700 billion is greater than \$600 billion. This can be seen at point 2.

When $M^s = M^{AH} > M^d$, we say that individuals are *holding too much money* at the current level of GNP. They increase their spending, and prices and/or output rise. This leads to an increase in PQ, or GNP.

But what happens as PQ, or GNP, rises? As we stated earlier, M^d rises since $M^d = kPQ$. The economy moves up M^d_1 from point 2 in Exhibit 14–9 to point 3. At point 3, the money market is in equilibrium, since $M^s = M^{AH} = M^d$. We conclude that a fall in k, or a decrease in the demand for money, will increase GNP, *ceteris paribus*. It follows that a rise in k, or an increase in the demand for money, will decrease GNP, *ceteris paribus*.

EXHIBIT 14–9
A Decrease in M^d

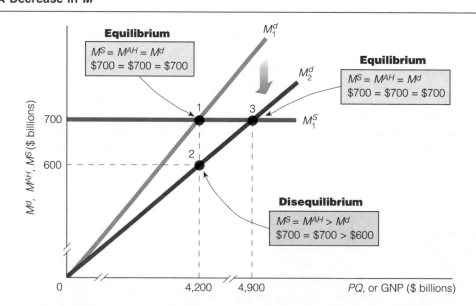

Starting at point 1, $M^S = M^{AH} = M^d$. Then money demand decreases from M^d_1 to M^d_2. This results in individuals holding too much money (excess money balances); consequently, individuals trade money for other goods, and prices and/or output increase. In either case, GNP increases. As this occurs, the economy moves up the money demand line. Equilibrium is at point 3, where once again $M^S = M^{AH} = M^d$.

Interview: Allan Meltzer

Allan Meltzer, a leading proponent of monetarism, has made significant contributions to the modern quantity theory of money. He is well known for his proposed monetary rule, which many monetarists believe, if implemented, would stabilize the price level. Meltzer is currently at Carnegie-Mellon University.

What in your mind are the main propositions of monetarism?

I think there are three main propositions. The first is the importance of the rate of money growth for short-run determination of output and for long-run inflation. The second is that steady, reliable monetary growth is a condition for stable long-term growth of economic activity, and stable, long-term growth in the money stock (in relation to real output growth) is the necessary condition for avoiding inflation. The third is the importance of rules vs. discretionary policy actions to reduce risk, uncertainty, and variability.

What do you predict will be a major economic problem the United States will have to face in the mid-1990s and how do you think it should solve that problem?

My ability to forecast the future is limited, but I expect the United States will have difficulty adjusting to a world in which several other countries are as wealthy and productive as the United States. U.S. policies—political and social as well as economic—will have to reflect this continuing change in relative wealth. We could accept our position and continue to accept our high standard of living. We may want to increase our efficiency or our growth rate. If so, we must improve the quality of our educational system and devote more resources to investment. We should remove the bias in favor of current consumption in our tax and government spending policies and give more choice of schools and curricula.

What do you think has been the most promising research development in economics in the past decade?

Two areas have developed—finance and political economy or public choice. Finance theory has developed a much improved understanding of how markets work. Political economy has replaced the assumption that the government acts to achieve the public's interest with an analysis of how collective decisions are made when individuals act in their own (enlightened) interest.

What got you interested in economics?

Economics is a social science. At its best it is concerned with ways (1) to improve well being by allowing individuals the freedom to achieve their personal aims or goals and (2) to harmonize their individual interests. I find working on such issues challenging, and progress is personally rewarding.

You are actively involved in economics research. What questions are you currently trying to answer?

For the past decade, I have been trying to learn more about why people willingly choose the tax, spending, and monetary policies that they do, how they decide on the amount of income redistribution and the form the redistribution takes. I took some time out, however, to read most of the collected papers of John Maynard Keynes and to write a book about them.

Would you give an example to illustrate how economists think about problems?

Two of the most important ideas in economics are the law of demand and the law of supply. These laws tell us that as price falls, quantity demanded increases and quantity supplied falls. These laws are very general. People respond to price and cost changes even if markets are not organized. Many people either do not believe these laws work, or they do not understand them. They favor policies that try to prevent adjustment to price changes or to prevent prices from changing.

Question:

Earlier, it was stated that monetarists believe the demand for money, or k *or* V, *is highly stable. This implies that monetarists would predict that changes in GNP are (for the most part) brought about by changes in the money supply instead of changes in the demand for money. Is this true?*

CHAPTER 14
CLASSICAL AND MONETARIST THEORY: EMPHASIS ON THE PRICE LEVEL AND GNP

■

321

Answer:

Yes, it is true.

Changes in Money Supply and Money Demand and Consequent Changes in Aggregate Demand

In Chapter 13, when we discussed inflation, we learned that an increase in the money supply would shift the *AD* curve rightward and a decrease in the money supply would shift the *AD* leftward.

Besides changes in the money supply, changes in money demand also change aggregate demand. To illustrate, suppose we start in equilibrium where $M^s = M^{AH} = M^d$. Now suppose money demand falls, giving us $M^s = M^{AH} > M^d$. In this setting, individuals are holding *too much money* and therefore increase their spending. As a result of increased spending, the *AD* curve shifts rightward (Exhibit 14–10).

Next, suppose that starting from equilibrium, money demand rises. Thus, we have $M^s = M^{AH} < M^d$. In this setting, individuals are holding *too little money* and therefore they decrease their spending. As a result of decreased spending, the *AD* curve shifts leftward.

Monetarism in the *AD–AS* Framework

Monetarist theory is easy to view in terms of the *AD–AS* framework. Let's start in long-run equilibrium in our *AD–AS* framework ($Q = Q_N$) and where $M^s = M^{AH} = M^d$ in our monetarist framework. Now suppose the Federal Reserve decreases the money supply. As we know, this brings about $M^s = M^{AH} < M^d$. In this setting,

EXHIBIT 14–10
Money Supply, Money Demand, and the *AD* Curve

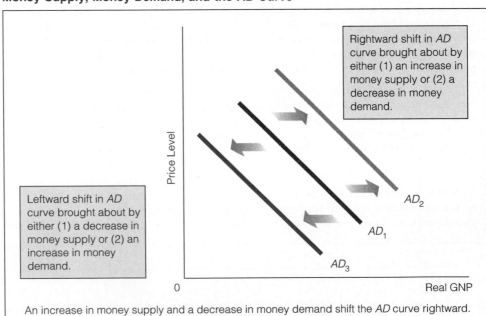

Rightward shift in *AD* curve brought about by either (1) an increase in money supply or (2) a decrease in money demand.

Leftward shift in *AD* curve brought about by either (1) a decrease in money supply or (2) an increase in money demand.

An increase in money supply and a decrease in money demand shift the *AD* curve rightward. A decrease in money supply and an increase in money demand shift the *AD* curve leftward.

people are holding too little money, and thus they decrease their spending. A decrease in spending shifts the aggregate demand (*AD*) curve leftward from AD_1 to AD_2 in Exhibit 14–11. Real GNP decreases from Q_1 to Q_2, and the economy is now in a recessionary gap at point 2. Whereas Keynesians might say that the economy would get stuck at point 2 (because of inflexible wages in the downward direction), monetarists argue that wages are flexible enough to rid the economy of a recessionary gap. For monetarists, wages will fall in a recessionary gap, the short-run aggregate supply (*SRAS*) curve will shift rightward from $SRAS_1$ to $SRAS_2$, and the economy will again be in long-run equilibrium. Since real GNP has moved back to its original level, monetarists say that monetary policy has no lasting (long-run) effect on the real side of the economy. They believe the main effect is on the price level (P). And because monetarists believe that the economy is inherently stable and that it equilibrates itself at natural real GNP, they, like classical economists, believe the government has only a minimal role to play in the economy.

Major Tenets of Monetarism

Using our three macroeconomic categories, here is what monetarism has to say.

The P–Q Category. Monetarism states that changes in money supply and money demand are the major determinants of changes in *P times Q*, or GNP.

The Inherently Stable–Inherently Unstable Category. Unlike Keynesians, monetarists believe that the economy is inherently stable and that it equilibrates at natural real GNP. The economy may find itself in either a recessionary or inflationary gap, but this is only a temporary state of affairs.

The Effective–Ineffective Category. Similar to the classical economists, monetarists believe that the government should not interfere in the nation's economy, that such interference often leads to more problems, not fewer. In the next chapter, we learn that monetarists advocate certain rules (in particular, a monetary rule) for

EXHIBIT 14–11
Monetarist Theory in the *AD–AS* Framework

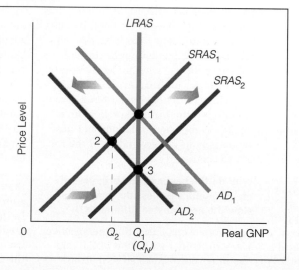

The economy is initially at point 1 in long-run equilibrium. Then the Federal Reserve decreases the money supply. As a result, people end up holding too little money and they cut back on their spending. A decrease in spending shifts the aggregate demand curve from AD_1 to AD_2. The economy is now in a recessionary gap at point 2. Monetarists believe that wages are flexible and that they will fall in a recessionary gap, shifting the short-run aggregate supply curve leftward from $SRAS_1$ to $SRAS_2$. In time, the economy is back again in long-run equilibrium.

Interview: Milton Friedman

Milton Friedman has made significant and lasting contributions in the areas of economic methodology, monetary theory, consumption theory, political economy and more. Friedman won the Nobel Prize in Economics in 1976. He is currently at the Hoover Institution.

What is the monetarist view of how the economy works?

There is no monetarist view of how the economy works. Monetarism is concerned with one aspect of the economy and one aspect only. That aspect is the effect of changes in monetary institutions and in the quantity of money on the price level in the long run and on fluctuations in output and prices in the short run. Communist China, laissez-faire Hong Kong, the quasi-socialist United States are economies that work very differently. However, all of them have monetary institutions and all of them have a medium of circulation called money. Hence, the general principles of monetary theory apply to all three economies.

What do you think is the main contribution of each of the following macroeconomic schools of thought: classical, Keynesian, monetarist, and new classical?

In a comment at an American Economic Association session some years back entitled "What Have We Learned about Money in the Past Twenty-five Years?" I said that it was easier to say what we had learned in the past 25 years than to say what we had learned in the past 200 years. Classical views about money are often oversimplified by limiting them to the long-period relationship between the nominal quantity of money and the price level. That was one aspect of classical teaching that has survived the test of experience, but the classical writers on money from David Hume to

Henry Thornton to Irving Fisher presented a much more sophisticated and subtle analysis which covered the short run as well as the long run. They provided us with our fundamental understanding of monetary phenomena. The Keynesian school changed the problems on which scholars put major emphasis but, in my opinion, contributed no substantive and lasting results about the relations between money and other magnitudes. The major impact was on the language that we use. The contribution of the monetarist school was essentially to revive, refurbish, restate, and test the analysis of the classical school. Its major contribution, as I see it, was its emphasis on testing the propositions of monetary theory, whether Keynesian or classical, by empirical evidence. The new classical school has fostered greater attention to the price theoretical foundations of monetary relations and has expanded our understanding of the role of expectations.

Why do the best and the brightest of the economics profession sometimes view the economy so differently?

For two reasons. First, time perspective. Many differences arise out of the relative importance attached to the short

period and over the long period. Second, differences in values, in particular the values attached to equality on the one hand and freedom on the other.

Would you give an example to illustrate how economists think about problems?

Consider the argument so often made that the U.S. cannot compete against foreign countries, say specifically Japan, because U.S. wages are higher than Japanese wages. The economist will reply, "Wages? The Japanese worker is paid in yen; the American worker is paid in dollars. How are you comparing the Japanese wage and the American wage? What determines the exchange rate between dollars and yen?" Suppose at the existing exchange rate, Japanese producers could price every product lower than United States producers could. The Japanese would sell, but what would the Japanese do with the dollars they received? By assumption, they don't want to buy American goods since they are all more expensive; they want to buy Japanese goods. But they can only buy Japanese goods with yen. To get yen, they must induce someone to sell them yen for dollars. The only way they can do that is by offering a higher dollar price for yen. But as the dollar price of yen goes up, Japanese goods become more expensive in the United States, U.S. goods become cheaper in Japan, and pretty soon there are some items, those for which in economists' jargon the U.S. has a comparative advantage, that the Japanese will start buying from the United States. The exchange rate will not settle down until the Japanese find a use for all the dollars they acquire by selling goods to the United States either by buying American goods, investing the dollars in the United States, or buying goods made in other countries that want to use the dollars to spend or invest in the U.S.

What got you interested in economics?

When I started college in 1928, I intended to be an actuary and I planned to major in mathematics. For reasons I no longer recall, I started taking some economics courses. The Great Depression hit about that time and economics clearly became a vital subject. When I graduated, I was offered a scholarship in applied mathematics at Brown and a scholarship in economics at Chicago. The choice was easy in 1932.

What do you think has been the most promising research development in economics in the past decade?

It takes more than a decade to recognize a promising development. In the past several decades I believe that the most promising research developments have been public choice and rational expectations.

What persons have had the greatest influence on your thinking and how would you summarize what you learned from each of them?

The persons who had the greatest influence on my thinking were Arthur R. Burns, Jacob Viner, Frank Knight, Wesley Mitchell, Friedrich Hayek. From Arthur Burns, I learned the importance of carefulness, thoroughness, and attention to detail in statistical and economic research. From Jacob Viner, I received my first exposure to the beauty of economic theory. Frank Knight made me realize the broader aspects of economics and the ramifications of economics in many other directions. Wesley Mitchell impressed on me the importance of clear, accurate, concise exposition of scientific findings. Friedrich Hayek made clear the dynamic role of the price system as a mode of transmitting information.

What do you consider your best piece of work and why?

I regard *The Theory of the Consumption Function* as my best piece of work. It presents an original hypothesis, deduces its implications, and tests those implications with a wide range of evidence. It comes closer than anything else I have done to corresponding to the ideal of positive economics that I stated in my essay on "The Methodology of Positive Economics." I trust that the rest of my work has many of the same characteristics, even though it may not exemplify them so comprehensively.

You have expressed a strong admiration for Adam Smith and Thomas Jefferson. Are there individuals in other disciplines—such as literature and philosophy—for whom you have a strong admiration, or who have had a strong influence on your life?

A. V. Dicey through his book, *Lectures on the Relation between Law and Public Opinion in the Nineteenth Century;* the authors of the Federalist Papers—Alexander Hamilton, James Madison, and John Jay; Karl Popper, the philosopher, both through his work on methodology and through his writings on an open society; and George Orwell through his extensive writings. I find it hard to single out any one or two persons in literature who had a special influence on me.

---

government to follow, which would seem to suggest that monetarists want government to act in some way in the economy. However, since these rules restrict government, they are best viewed as part of an overall laissez-faire approach. What many monetarists are proposing that government do is to limit or restrict itself so that it cannot play an active role in managing the economy.

We started with a simple diagram of money demand and supply (such as Exhibit 14–5). Looking at this diagram, it was easy to see that a change in either would change GNP. But this leads us to ask: Who or what can change the money supply? Who or what can change money demand?

We know that the Fed, the banks, and the public can change the money supply (Chapters 11, 12). The Fed can affect the money supply by changing bank reserves, the banks by changing the percentage of excess reserves they choose to lend out, and members of the public by changing the percentage of their funds they choose to deposit into a bank. Knowing this makes the analysis richer.

We have seen in this chapter that a change in k (or V) will change money demand. But what factors can change k? We have noted three: the interest

THINKING LIKE AN ECONOMIST

CHAPTER 14
CLASSICAL AND MONETARIST
THEORY: EMPHASIS ON THE PRICE
LEVEL AND GNP

rate, the expected rate of inflation, and the frequency with which employees receive paychecks.

Notice the process of analysis here. We started with the two main variables that can change GNP—money supply and money demand—and proceeded to examine them in depth. In doing so, we learned specifically what can change GNP. We learn more about the "economic puzzle" by taking the bigger pieces and breaking them down into smaller ones.

$MV \equiv PQ$

■ The equation of exchange is an identity: $M \times V \equiv P \times Q$. Exactly what the equation tells us can be interpreted in different ways. Here are a few: (1) The money supply multiplied by velocity must equal the price level times real GNP: $M \times V \equiv P \times Q$. (2) The money supply multiplied by velocity must equal GNP: $M \times V \equiv GNP$. (3) Total expenditures (measured by MV) must equal the total sales revenues of business firms (measured by PQ): $MV \equiv PQ$

■ The equation of exchange is not a theory of the macroeconomy. However, the equation of exchange can be turned into a theory if assumptions are made about some of the variables in the equation. For example, if we assume that both V and Q are constant, then we have the simple quantity theory of money, which predicts that changes in the money supply cause strictly proportional changes in the price level.

M^s, $M^{AH,}$ and M^d

■ The quantity supplied of money (M^s) necessarily equals the quantity of money that people actually hold (M^{AH}). The quantity demanded of money (M^d) may be equal to, greater than, or less than M^s and M^{AH}.
■ In equilibrium, $M^s = M^{AH} = M^d$.
■ When $M^s = M^{AH} > M^d$, individuals are holding too much money; consequently, spending increases and GNP rises.
■ When $M^s = M^{AH} < M^d$, individuals are holding too little money; consequently, spending decreases and GNP falls.

Money Demand

■ $M^d = kPQ$. This says that the quantity of money demanded is a function of k, P, and Q. Anything that causes k, P, and Q to rise (fall) will increase (decrease) the quantity demanded of money.
■ The following decrease k: (1) an increase in the interest rate; (2) an expected increase in the inflation rate; and (3) an increase in the frequency with which employees receive paychecks. The following increase k: (1) a decrease in the interest rate; (2) an expected decrease in the inflation rate; and (3) a decrease in the frequency with which employees receive paychecks.

Changes in the Money Supply, Money Demand, and Aggregate Demand

■ An increase in the money supply will lead to a rightward shift in the *AD* curve. A decrease in the money supply will lead to a leftward shift in the *AD* curve. A decrease in money demand will lead to a rightward shift in the *AD* curve. An increase in money demand will lead to a leftward shift in the *AD* curve.

Monetarism, *k*, and velocity

■ Monetarists believe that *k,* or *V,* is stable and predictable. They conclude that changes in GNP are largely brought about by changes in money supply.

How Monetarists View the Economy

■ Monetarists view the economy as stable and as equilibrating at natural real GNP.

Key Terms and Concepts

Velocity

Equation of Exchange

Simple Quantity Theory
of Money

Money Demand Line

QUESTIONS AND PROBLEMS

1. If the money supply increases by 10 percent, velocity increases by 1 percent, and real GNP (Q) decreases by 2 percent, what would monetarists predict that the percentage increase in the price level will be? Explain your answer.

2. What are different ways of saying that the demand for money is stable?

3. If credit cards become more widely used in the economy, what, if anything, will happen to velocity and why?

4. Using the *MV–PQ* framework of analysis, assume that *M, V,* and *Q* can all change and therefore can affect *P.* List the different configurations of *M, V,* and *Q* that are predicted to lead to a rise in *P.*

5. What is the difference between the equation of exchange and the simple quantity theory of money?

6. Calculate M^d at each of the following different levels of *k* and *PQ:* (a) $k = 1/4$; $PQ = \$350$ billion; (b) $k = 1/5$; $PQ = \$700$ billion; (c) $k = 1/10$; $PQ = \$1,000$ billion; (d) $k = 1/3$; $PQ = \$1,250$ billion; (e) $k = 1/8$; $PQ = \$2,000$ billion.

7. Suppose M^d is $300 billion at a GNP level of $900 billion in year 1 and $400 billion at a GNP level $1,000 billion in year 2. Is the demand for money the same in both years? Explain your answer.

8. If individuals collectively are holding too much money, how can they ever hold the optimum or right amount of money, since no one is ever going to burn money or throw it away?

9. In this chapter, we listed three factors that can change *k:* the interest rate, the expected rate of inflation, and the frequency with which employees receive paychecks. What other factors do you think might change *k*?

10. Suppose $M^{AH} = \$300$, $M^d = \$250$, and $PQ = \$1,200$ (all numbers in billions). From this, we know that $M^{AH}/PQ > M^d/PQ$. We also know that we are in monetary disequilibrium. If k in $M^d = kPQ$ is the same at the new monetary equilibrium point as it is at present, by how much must PQ increase?

11. What would be the directional change in GNP, given the following changes: (a) a decrease in the interest rate; (b) an increase in the expected rate of inflation; (c) an increase in money supply; (d) a decrease in money demand.

12. Suppose you are explaining to a friend who has had no training in economics that there are times when individuals find themselves holding too much money. Your friend says that that would never happen to her. She says that she has never held too much money, but rather that she has always held too little money. As she says this, she hands a ten-dollar bill to the cashier in the grocery store. What could you say that would help your friend understand that individuals can and do sometimes find that they are holding too much money?

13. In this chapter, we learned that PQ does not change unless either M or V changes (recall that $MV = PQ$). This implies that before a fiscal policy measure can affect GNP, or PQ, it must affect V. Do you think a change in government spending or taxes would affect V directly or indirectly through a change in some variable that directly affects V? If indirectly, what variable do you suggest?

15

MONETARY POLICY

WHAT THIS CHAPTER IS ABOUT

The goals of **monetary policy** are to stabilize the price level (P), achieve low unemployment (which is related to changes in real GNP, or Q), and promote economic growth (which is also related to Q), among other things. Economists generally agree that monetary policy affects the economy. However, they disagree over the degree to which, and under what conditions, it does this. This chapter focuses more on the disagreements than the agreements economists have over monetary policy.

Monetary Policy
Changes in the money supply, or in the rate of change of the money supply, to achieve particular macroeconomic goals.

Demand Curve for Money (Balances)
Represents the inverse relationship between the quantity demanded of money balances and the price of holding money balances.

THE MONEY MARKET

■

Like all markets, the money market has two sides: a demand side and a supply side.[1] We discuss both in this section.

The Demand Curve for Money

To illustrate a demand curve for a good, we place the price of the good on the vertical axis and the quantity of the good on the horizontal axis (see Chapter 3). To illustrate the **demand curve for money balances** (and money is a *good)*, we place the *price of holding money balances* on the vertical axis and the quantity of money on the horizontal axis. But before we do this, we must ask: What is the price of holding money balances?

The price of holding money balances—specifically, the opportunity cost of holding money—is the *interest rate.* In previous chapters, we learned that money is one of many forms in which individuals may hold their wealth and that by holding money they forfeit the opportunity to hold as much of their wealth in other forms. For example, the person who holds $1,000 in cash gives up the opportunity to purchase a $1,000 asset (for example, a bond) that yields interest. Thus, the interest rate is the opportunity cost of holding money. One pays the price of forfeited interest by holding money.

Exhibit 15–1a illustrates the demand curve for money (balances). As the interest rate increases, the opportunity cost of holding money increases, and individuals choose to hold less money. As the interest rate decreases, the opportunity cost of holding money decreases, and individuals choose to hold more money.

[1]In everyday langauge, the term *money market* is often used to refer to the market for short-term securities, where there is a demand for, and supply of, short-term securities. This is not the money market we are discussing. In our money market, there is a demand for, and supply of, money.

EXHIBIT 15–1
The Demand Curve For, and Supply Curve of, Money

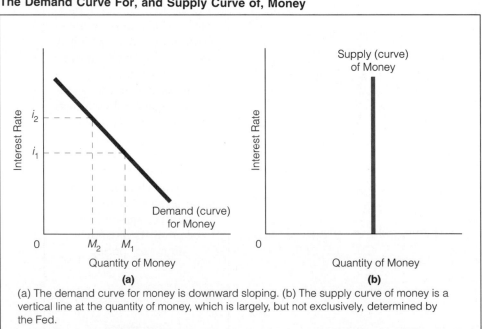

(a) The demand curve for money is downward sloping. (b) The supply curve of money is a vertical line at the quantity of money, which is largely, but not exclusively, determined by the Fed.

The Supply Curve of Money

In Exhibit 15–1b, we have drawn the supply curve of money as a vertical line at the quantity of money largely determined by the Fed. The money supply is not exclusively determined by the Fed because, as we learned in Chapters 11 and 12, both the banks and the public are important players in the money supply process. For example, if banks do not lend out their entire excess reserves, the money supply will not be as large as it will be if they do.

Equilibrium in the Money Market

Equilibrium in the money market exists when the quantity demanded of money equals the quantity supplied. In Exhibit 15–2, equilibrium exists at the interest rate i_1. At a higher interest rate, i_2, the quantity supplied of money is greater than the quantity demanded, and there is an excess supply of money. At a lower interest rate, i_3, the quantity demanded of money is greater than the quantity supplied of money, and there is an excess demand for money. Only at i_1 are the quantity demanded and the quantity supplied of money equal. Here there are no "shortages" or "surpluses" of money, no excess demands or excess supplies. Individuals are holding the amount of money they want to hold.

TRANSMISSION MECHANISMS
■

Consider two markets: the money market and the goods and services market. Economists have different ideas about the *degree of impact* that changes in the money market have on the goods and services market and whether that impact is *direct* or *indirect.* The routes or channels that ripple effects created in the money market travel to affect the goods and services market are known as the **transmission mechanism.** We discuss two major transmission mechanisms: the Keynesian and the monetarist.

Transmission Mechanism
The routes or channels that ripple effects created in the money market travel to affect the goods and services market (represented by the aggregate demand and aggregate supply curves in the *AD–AS* framework).

EXHIBIT 15–2
Equilibrium in the Money Market

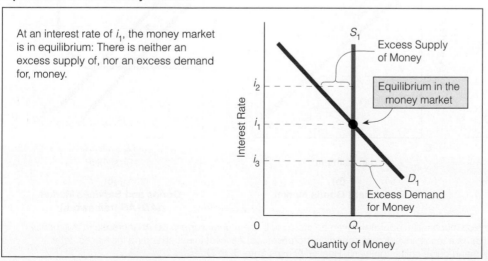

At an interest rate of i_1, the money market is in equilibrium: There is neither an excess supply of, nor an excess demand for, money.

The Keynesian Transmission Mechanism: Indirect

The Keynesian link between the money market and the goods and services market is an indirect one. With the aid of Exhibit 15–3, we describe the Keynesian transmission mechanism market by market.

The Money Market. Suppose the money market is in equilibrium at the interest rate i_1 in (a). Suddenly, the Fed increases the reserves of the banking system through an open market purchase. This results in an increase in the money supply. (See Exhibit 15–3a where the money supply shifts rightward from S_1 to S_2.) The process, we recall, is that increasing the reserves of the banking system in turn increases the excess reserves of the system and results in more loans being made. A greater supply of loans puts downward pressure on the price of a loan (the interest rate), as reflected in the movement from i_1 to i_2 in (a).

The Investment Goods Market. A fall in the interest rate stimulates investment spending. In the investment goods market in (b), investment spending rises from I_1 to I_2.

The Goods and Services Market (_AD–AS_ Framework). An increase in investment spending increases total expenditures, and anything that increases total expenditures at a given price level shifts the aggregate demand curve to the right, as shown in (c). If we assume the economy is in the horizontal section of the aggregate supply curve, which is relevant to the basic Keynesian theory, real GNP rises from Q_1 to Q_2 and there is no change in the price level. As a result of the increase in real GNP, the unemployment rate drops.

In summary, when the money supply increases, the Keynesian transmission mechanism works as follows: An increase in the money supply lowers the interest rate, which causes investment spending to rise and the AD curve to shift rightward. As a result, real GNP increases and the unemployment rate drops. The process works in reverse for a decrease in the money supply.

EXHIBIT 15–3
The Keynesian Transmission Mechanism

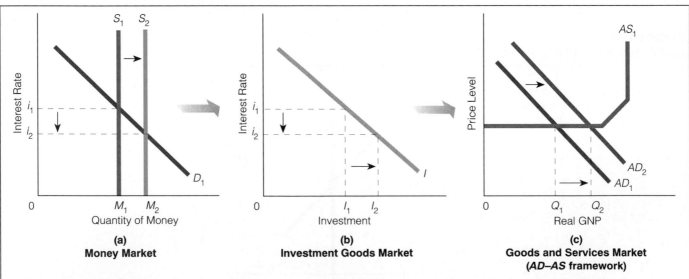

Here is the way the Keynesian transmission mechanism operates given an increase in the money supply. (a) An increase in the money supply brings on a lower interest rate. (b) As a result, investment spending increases. (c) As investment spending increases, total expenditures rise and the aggregate demand curve shifts rightward. Real GNP rises from Q_1 to Q_2.

The Keynesian Mechanism May Get Blocked

As we said earlier, the Keynesian transmission mechanism is indirect. Changes in the money market do not directly affect the goods and services market (and thus real GNP) since the investment goods market stands between the two markets. This means that it is possible (although not likely) that the link between the money market and the goods and services market could be broken in the investment goods market. We explain.

Interest-Insensitive Investment. In Chapter 9, we learned that, in contrast to the classical economists, Keynes believed that investment is not always responsive to interest rates. For example, when business firms are pessimistic about future economic activity, a decrease in interest rates will do little, if anything, to increase investment spending. When investment is completely insensitive to changes in interest rates, the investment demand curve is vertical, as in Exhibit 15–4a.

Consider what this means in terms of Exhibit 15–3. If the investment demand curve is vertical, a fall in interest rates will not increase investment spending, and if investment spending does not increase, neither will aggregate demand or real GNP. In addition, unemployment won't fall. Thus, the Keynesian transmission mechanism would be short-circuited in the investment goods market, and the link between the money market in (a) of Exhibit 15–3 and the goods and services market in (c) would be broken.

The Liquidity Trap. Keynesians have sometimes argued that the demand curve for money could become horizontal at some low interest rate. Before we discuss why this might be, we need to understand the consequences of it. First, notice that in Exhibit 15–4b, the demand curve for money becomes horizontal at i_1. This horizontal section of the demand curve for money is referred to as the **liquidity trap**.

Liquidity Trap
The horizontal portion of the demand curve for money.

EXHIBIT 15–4

Breaking the Link between the Money Market and the Goods and Services Market: Interest-Insensitive Investment and the Liquidity Trap

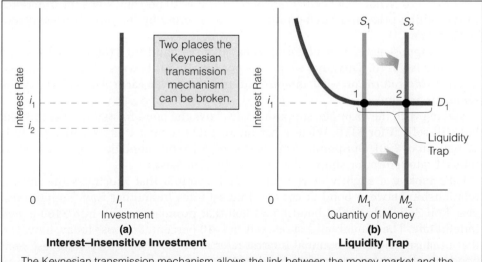

(a)
Interest–Insensitive Investment

(b)
Liquidity Trap

The Keynesian transmission mechanism allows the link between the money market and the goods and services market to be broken in two places. (a) If investment spending is totally interest insensitive, a change in the interest rate will not change investment spending; therefore, aggregate demand, real GNP, and unemployment will not change. (b) If the money market is in the liquidity trap, an increase in the money supply will not lower the interest rate. It follows that there will be no change in aggregate demand, real GNP, and unemployment.

What happens if the money supply is increased when the money market is in the liquidity trap, for example, from S_1 to S_2? The money market moves from point 1 to 2, and individuals are *willing to hold all the additional money supply* at the given interest rate.

What does this mean in terms of the Keynesian transmission mechanism illustrated in Exhibit 15–3? Obviously, if an increase in the money supply does not lower the interest rate, then there will be no change in investment spending, aggregate demand, or real GNP. The liquidity trap can break the link between the money market and the goods and services market.

The Keynesian transmission mechanism, being indirect, allows for both interest-insensitive investment demand and the liquidity trap; therefore, Keynesians conclude, there may be times when monetary policy will be unable to increase real GNP and decrease unemployment. Viewing the money supply as a string, some economists have argued that "you can't push on a string." In other words, you can't always force real GNP up by increasing (pushing upward) the money supply.

Question:

The liquidity trap, or the horizontal section of the demand curve for money, seems to come out of the clear blue sky. Why might the demand curve for money become horizontal at some low interest rate?

Answer:

To understand the explanation of the liquidity trap, one must first understand the relationship between bond prices and interest rates, which is the topic of the next section.

Bond Prices and Interest Rates

Consider Jessica Howard who buys good X for $100 today and sells it one year later for $110. What is her actual rate of return? It is 10 percent, since the difference in the selling price and buying price (or $10) divided by the buying price ($100) is 10 percent.

Now suppose good X is a bond: Jessica buys the bond for $100 and sells it one year later for $110. This time we phrase our question this way: What is her actual *interest rate return,* or what interest rate did the buyer earn? The answer is the same: 10 percent.

Staying with the example, suppose Jessica buys the bond for $90 instead of $100, but still sells it for $110. What is her interest rate return? It is 22 percent ($20 is 22 percent of $90). Our point is simple: As the price of a bond decreases, the actual interest rate return, or simply the interest rate, increases.

Let's look at a slightly more complicated example that illustrates the inverse relationship between bond prices and interest rates in another way. Suppose last year Rob Zelicki bought a bond for $1,000 that promises to pay him $100 a year indefinitely. The annual interest rate return is 10 percent. Suppose today, however, that because market or nominal interest rates are higher than they were last year, bond suppliers have to promise to pay $120 a year to any bondholder who buys a $1,000 bond today.

What will this do to the price Rob can get in the market for his $1,000 bond bought last year, assuming he wants to sell it? Will anyone pay Rob $1,000 for an (old) bond that pays $100 a year when a new $1,000 bond that pays $120 a year can be purchased? The answer is a definite no. This means that Rob will have to lower the price of his bond below $1,000. How far below $1,000 will he have to lower it? The price will have to be far enough below $1,000 so that the interest rate return on his old bond will be competitive with (equal to) the interest rate return on *new* bonds. Rob's bond will sell for $833. At a price of $833 for the old bond, a buyer of the bond will receive $100 a year and an interest rate of 12 percent, which is the same interest rate he or she would receive by buying a new bond for $1,000 and receiving $120 a year. Thus, $100 is the same percentage of $833 as $120 is of $1,000—12 percent. Looking back, we conclude that an increase in the market interest rate is inversely related to the price of old or existing bonds.

Keeping this in mind, consider the liquidity trap again. The reason an increase in the money supply does not result in an excess supply of money at a low interest rate is because individuals believe bond prices are so high (since low interest rates mean high bond prices) that an investment in bonds is likely to turn out to be a bad deal. Individuals would rather hold all the additional money supply than use it to buy bonds, which, they believe, are priced so high that they have no place to go but down. As an aside, we might mention that empirical evidence has not supported the existence of the liquidity trap.

Question:

If interest rates and bond prices move in opposite directions, shouldn't people buy bonds when they expect interest rates to fall and sell bonds when they expect interest rates to rise?

Answer:

That's correct. The objective is to buy low and sell high. Bond prices are at their lowest when interest rates are at their highest, so when interest rates appear to be at their highest, buy bonds. The flip side says that bond prices are at their highest when interest rates are at their lowest, so when interest rates appear to be at their lowest, sell bonds. By the way, all this is easier said than done. Predicting interest rates is a tough business, and economic forecasters often miss the mark. However, they still do better than noneconomists (which, depending on how one looks at these things, might not be saying much).

The Monetarist Transmission Mechanism: Direct

In monetarist theory, there is a direct link between the money market and the goods and services market. The monetarist transmission mechanism is short. Changes in the money market have a direct impact on aggregate demand, as illustrated in Exhibit 15–5. An increase in the money supply from S_1 to S_2 in (a) leaves individuals with an excess supply of money. They increase their spending on a wide variety of goods. Households buy more refrigerators, personal computers, television sets, clothes, and vacations. Businesses purchase additional machinery. The aggregate demand curve in (b) is directly affected. In the short run, real GNP rises from Q_1 to Q_2 and unemployment falls.

MONETARY POLICY AND THE PROBLEM OF INFLATIONARY AND RECESSIONARY GAPS

■

In Chapter 10, we discussed how discretionary expansionary and contractionary fiscal policies might be used to rid the economy of recessionary and inflationary gaps, respectively. Later, we questioned the effectiveness of discretionary fiscal

The Keynesian transmission mechanism is indirect from the money market to the goods and services market; the monetarist transmission mechanism is direct.

■

EXHIBIT 15–5
The Monetarist Transmission Mechanism

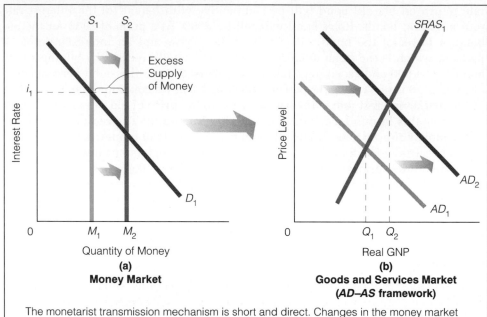

The monetarist transmission mechanism is short and direct. Changes in the money market directly affect aggregate demand in the goods and services market. For example, an increase in the money supply leaves individuals with an excess supply of money that they spend on a wide variety of goods.

policy. In this section, we discuss how monetary policy might be used to eliminate both recessionary and inflationary gaps.

In Exhibit 15–6, the economy is in a recessionary gap at point 1; aggregate demand is too low to bring the economy into equilibrium at its natural level of real GNP. Economist A argues that in time the short-run aggregate supply curve will shift rightward and pass through point 2′, so it is best to leave things alone. Economist B states that it takes too long for the economy to get to point 2′ on its own, and in the interim the economy suffers the high cost of unemployment and a lower level of output. Economist C maintains that the economy is *stuck* in the recessionary gap. Economists B and C propose expansionary monetary policy to move the economy along to its natural real GNP level. An appropriate increase in the money supply will shift the aggregate demand curve rightward to AD_2, and the economy will be in long-run equilibrium at point 2. The recessionary gap is eliminated through the use of expansionary monetary policy.[2]

In (b), the economy is experiencing an inflationary gap at point 1. Economist A argues that in time the economy will move to point 2′, so it is best to leave things alone. Economist B argues that it would be better to decrease the money supply so that aggregate demand shifts leftward to AD_2, and the economy moves to point 2. Economist C agrees with B and says that the price level is lower at point 2 than at 2′, although real GNP is the same at both points.

[2]In a static framework, expansionary monetary policy refers to an increase in the money supply, and contractionary monetary policy refers to a decrease in the money supply. In a dynamic framework, expansionary monetary policy refers to an increase in the *growth rate* of the money supply, while contractionary monetary policy refers to a decrease in the *growth rate* of the money supply. In the real world, where things are constantly changing, the growth rate of the money supply is more indicative of the direction of monetary policy.

EXHIBIT 15-6
Monetary Policy: Ridding the Economy of Recessionary and Inflationary Gaps

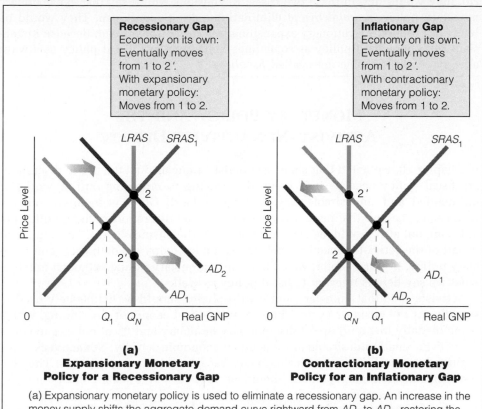

Recessionary Gap
Economy on its own:
Eventually moves
from 1 to 2'.
With expansionary
monetary policy:
Moves from 1 to 2.

Inflationary Gap
Economy on its own:
Eventually moves
from 1 to 2'.
With contractionary
monetary policy:
Moves from 1 to 2.

(a)
Expansionary Monetary
Policy for a Recessionary Gap

(b)
Contractionary Monetary
Policy for an Inflationary Gap

(a) Expansionary monetary policy is used to eliminate a recessionary gap. An increase in the money supply shifts the aggregate demand curve rightward from AD_1 to AD_2, restoring the economy to the natural level of GNP, Q_N. (b) Contractionary monetary policy is used to eliminate an inflationary gap. A decrease in the money supply shifts the aggregate demand curve leftward from AD_1 to AD_2, restoring the economy to Q_N.

Most Keynesians believe that the natural forces of the market economy work much more quickly and assuredly at eliminating an inflationary gap than a recessionary gap. In terms of Exhibit 15–6, they argue that it is much more likely that the short-run aggregate supply curve in (b) will shift leftward and pass through point 2', eliminating the inflationary gap, than that the short-run aggregate supply curve in (a) will shift rightward and pass through point 2', eliminating the recessionary gap. The reason is that wages and prices rise more quickly than they fall. (Recall that many Keynesians believe wages are inflexible *in the downward direction*.) Consequently, Keynesians are more likely to advocate expansionary monetary policy to eliminate a stubborn recessionary gap than contractionary monetary policy to eliminate a not-so-stubborn inflationary gap. As a result, it has been argued that Keynesian monetary policy has an inflationary bias to it. Keynesians often retort that this is not necessarily bad if, indeed, wages and prices are less flexible downward than upward.

Question:

Would Keynesians advocate expansionary monetary policy to eliminate a recessionary gap if they believed that the money market was in the liquidity trap or that investment spending was interest insensitive?

Answer:

No, they would not. In these two cases, Keynesians would say that expansionary monetary policy is *ineffective* at eliminating a recessionary gap. They would be likely to propose discretionary expansionary fiscal policy instead. Because Keynesians view monetary policy as sometimes ineffective and fiscal policy as always effective, they are sometimes called *fiscalists*.

MONETARY POLICY AND THE ACTIVIST–NONACTIVIST DEBATE

In Chapter 10, we noted that some economists argue against the use of discretionary fiscal policy because it is ineffective (owing to crowding out) or works in unintended and undesirable ways (owing to lags). Other economists, notably Keynesians, believe that neither is the case and that discretionary fiscal policy not only can, but also should, be used to smooth out the business cycle. This argument is part of the activist–nonactivist debate, which encompasses both fiscal and monetary policy. In this chapter, we address only monetary policy, although much of what we say here is relevant to fiscal policy as well.

Activists state that monetary and fiscal policies should be deliberately used to smooth out the business cycle. They are in favor of economic **fine tuning,** which is the (usually frequent) use of discretionary monetary and fiscal policies to counteract even small undesirable movements in economic activity. **Nonactivists** argue against the use of deliberate discretionary fiscal and monetary policies. They believe that discretionary policies should be replaced by a stable and permanent monetary and fiscal framework and that rules should be established in place of activist discretionary policies. For example, nonactivists advocate a balanced budget rule on the fiscal side and a **monetary rule**—a monetary policy based on a predetermined steady growth rate in the money supply—on the monetary side. The activist ranks are mostly made up of Keynesians; the nonactivist ranks are mostly made up of monetarists and new classical economists.[3]

The Case for Activist Monetary Policy

The case for activist monetary policy rests on three major claims:

1. The economy does not always equilibrate quickly enough at the natural real GNP or full-employment output. Consider the economy at point 1 in Exhibit 15–6a. If left to its own workings, some economists maintain, the economy will eventually move to point 2′. Activists often argue that it takes too long for the economy to move from point 1 to 2′ and that too much lost output and too high an unemployment rate must be tolerated in the interim. They believe that an activist monetary policy speeds things along so that higher output and a lower unemployment rate can be achieved more quickly.

2. Activist monetary policy works; it is effective at smoothing out the business cycle. Activists are quick to point to the undesirable consequences of the constant (nonactivist) monetary policy of the mid-1970s. In 1973, 1974, and 1975, the

[3]Because an economist is a Keynesian, it does not follow that he or she *always* advocates activist monetary and fiscal policies. Nor does it follow that a monetarist or new classical economist *always* advocates nonactivist monetary and fiscal policies. We are speaking of the general policy inclinations of Keynesians, monetarists, and new classical economists.

Activists
Persons who argue that monetary and fiscal policies should be deliberately used to smooth out the business cycle.

Fine-tuning
The (usually frequent) use of discretionary monetary and fiscal policies to counteract even small undesirable movements in economic activity.

Nonactivists
Persons who argue against the deliberate use of discretionary fiscal and monetary policies. They believe in a permanent, stable, rule-oriented monetary and fiscal framework.

Monetary Rule
Describes monetary policy that is based on a predetermined steady growth rate in the money supply.

money supply growth rates were 5.5 percent, 4.3 percent, and 4.8 percent, respectively. These percentages represent a near constant growth rate in the money supply. The economy, however, went through a recession during this time (real GNP fell between 1973 and 1974 and between 1974 and 1975). Activists argue that an activist and flexible monetary policy would have reduced the high cost the economy had to pay in terms of lost output and higher unemployment.

3. Activist monetary policy is flexible; nonactivist monetary policy, which is rule oriented, is not. Flexibility is a desirable quality in monetary policy; inflexibility is not. The implicit judgment of activists is that the more closely monetary policy can be designed to meet the *particulars* of a given economic environment, the better. For example, at certain times the economy requires a sharp increase in the money supply; at other times, a sharp decrease; at still other times, only a slight increase or decrease. They argue that activist monetary policy can change as the monetary needs of the economy change; nonactivist, rule-oriented, "the-same-for-all-seasons" monetary policy cannot.

The Case for Nonactivist Monetary Policy

The case for nonactivist monetary policy rests on three major claims:

1. There is sufficient flexibility in wages and prices in modern economies to allow the economy to equilibrate at reasonable speed at the natural level of real GNP. For example, nonactivists point to the sharp drop in union wages in 1982 in response to high unemployment. In addition, they argue that government policies largely determine how flexible wages and prices turn out to be. For example, when government decides to cushion people's unemployment (such as through unemployment compensation), wages will not fall as quickly as when government does nothing. Nonactivists believe that a laissez-faire, hands-off approach by government would promote speedy wage and price adjustments and therefore a quick return to natural real GNP.

2. Activist monetary policies may not work. Economists who believe individuals form their expectations rationally (rational expectations) argue that there are really two types of monetary policy—monetary policy that is anticipated by the public and monetary policy that is unanticipated. Anticipated monetary policy *may not* be effective at changing real GNP or the unemployment rate. This is a subject we discuss in detail in the next chapter, but here is a brief explanation.

Suppose the public correctly anticipates that the Fed will soon increase the money supply by 10 percent. Consequently, the public reasons that aggregate demand will increase and prices will rise. (Recall that an increase in the money supply shifts the *AD* curve rightward; Exhibit 15–7.) Workers are particularly concerned about the expected higher price level because they know higher prices decrease the buying power of their wages. In an attempt to maintain their *real wages,* workers bargain for and receive higher money wage rates—which shifts the *SRAS* curve to the left. Now if the *SRAS* curve shifts leftward (owing to higher wage rates) *to the same degree* as the *AD* curve shifts rightward (owing to the increased money supply), then there is no change in real GNP. Real GNP stays constant at Q_1. We conclude that an *anticipated* increase in the money supply will be ineffective at raising real GNP.

3. Activist monetary policies are likely to be destabilizing rather than stabilizing; they are likely to make matters worse rather than better. Nonactivists point to lags as the main reason that activist monetary policies are likely to be destabilizing. For example, economist Robert Gordon has estimated that the total lag in monetary

EXHIBIT 15–7
Expansionary Monetary Policy and No Change in Real GNP

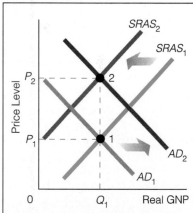

If expansionary monetary policy is anticipated (thus a higher price level is anticipated), workers may bargain for and receive higher wage rates. It is possible that the *SRAS* curve will shift leftward to the degree that expansionary monetary policy shifts the *AD* curve rightward. Result: no change in real GNP.

339

Monetary policy may sometimes destabilize the economy.

policy (consisting of the data, recognition, legislative, transmission, and effectiveness lags discussed in Chapter 10) is 13.3 months.[4] To nonactivists, such a long lag makes it almost impossible to conduct effective activist monetary policy. They maintain that by the time the Fed's monetary stimulus arrives on the scene, the economy may not need any stimulus, and thus it will likely destabilize the economy.[5] The stimulus in this instance makes things worse rather than better.

We illustrate this last point in Exhibit 15–8. Suppose the economy is currently in a recessionary gap at point 1. The recession is underway before Fed officials recognize it. Once recognized, however, Fed officials consider expanding the money supply in the hopes of shifting the AD curve from AD_1 to AD_2 and intersecting the $SRAS$ curve at point 1', at natural real GNP. In the interim, however, unknown to everybody, the economy is healing itself: The $SRAS$ curve is shifting to the right. Fed officials don't see this yet because it takes time to collect and analyze data on the economy.

Thinking that the economy is not healing itself, or not healing itself quickly enough, Fed officials go ahead and implement expansionary monetary policy. The AD curve shifts rightward. By the time the increased money supply is felt in the goods and services markets, the AD curve intersects the $SRAS$ curve at point 2. In short, the Fed has moved the economy from point 1 to point 2, and not as it had hoped, from point 1 to point 1'. The Fed has moved the economy into an inflationary gap. Instead of stabilizing and moderating the business cycle, it has intensified it.

[4]Robert Gordon, *Macroeconomics,* 4th ed. (Boston: Little, Brown & Co., 1987), p. 423.
[5]Some nonactivists have recently argued that the 1990–91 U.S. recession was as moderate as it was because neither activist fiscal nor monetary policy was enacted.

EXHIBIT 15–8
Monetary Policy May Destabilize the Economy

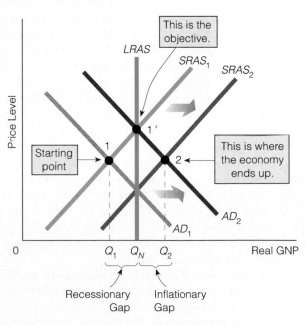

In this scenario, the *SRAS* curve is shifting rightward (healing the economy of its recessionary gap), but this information is unknown by Fed officials. Fed officials implement expansionary monetary policy and the *AD* curve ends up intersecting *SRAS₂* at point 2 instead of *SRAS₁* at point 1'. Fed officials end up moving the economy into an inflationary gap and thus destabilizing the economy.

Ask an economist a question and you are likely to get a conditional answer. For example, if you ask an economist whether monetary policy stabilizes or destabilizes the economy, she may answer that it can do either—depending on conditions. For instance, starting in a recessionary gap, *if* expansionary monetary policy shifts the *AD* curve rightward by just the right amount to intersect the *SRAS* curve and the *LRAS* curve at natural real GNP, *then* monetary policy stabilizes the economy. But *if* it shifts the *AD* curve rightward by more than this amount, it may move the economy into an inflationary gap, and *then* monetary policy destabilizes the economy. If–then thinking is common in economics, as are if–then statements.

THINKING LIKE AN ECONOMIST

NONACTIVIST MONETARY PROPOSALS

Activists are largely content to have monetary policy implemented by a discretionary Fed. Nonactivists are of the opposite mind. Here we outline two nonactivist monetary proposals: a monetary rule and a gold standard.

A Monetary Rule

As we noted earlier, a *monetary rule* describes monetary policy that is based on a predetermined steady growth rate in the money supply. The most direct and obvious, but not the only, objective of a monetary rule is to stabilize the price level. Some economists would like the monetary rule (monetary policy) to read as follows: *The annual money supply growth rate will be constant at the average annual growth rate of real GNP.* For example, if the average annual real GNP growth rate is approximately 3.3 percent, the money supply will be put on automatic pilot and will be permitted to grow at an annual rate of 3.3 percent. This will be the case no matter what the state of the economy. Some economists predict that such a policy will bring about a stable price level over time.

The prediction is based on the equation of exchange ($MV = PQ$). If the average annual growth rate in real GNP (Q) is 3.3 percent, and the money supply (M) grows at 3.3 percent, the price level should remain stable over time. (If Q is below 3.3 percent and M remains constant at 3.3 percent, P must increase so that PQ will still be equal to MV.) Monetary rule advocates argue that there will be some years when the growth rate in real GNP is below its average rate, bringing on an increase in the price level, and some years when the growth rate in real GNP is above its average rate, bringing on a fall in the price level, but over time the price level will be stable.

Critics point out that this monetary rule makes two assumptions: (1) Velocity is constant (there have been periods when it has not been constant). (2) The money supply is defined correctly. Critics argue that it is not clear yet which definition of the money supply (M1, M2, or some broader monetary measurement) is the proper one and therefore which money supply growth rate ought to be fixed.

Largely in response to the charge that velocity is not always constant, some monetary rule advocates would prefer that the monetary rule (monetary policy) read this way: *The annual growth rate in the money supply will be equal to the average annual growth rate in real GNP minus the growth rate in velocity.* With this monetary rule, the growth rate of the money supply is *not fixed*. It can vary from year to year, yet it is predetermined in that it is dependent on the growth rate in real GNP and on velocity.[6] To illustrate the workings of the rule, consider the following extended version of the equation of exchange.

$$\%\Delta M + \%\Delta V = \%\Delta P + \%\Delta Q$$

Suppose the percentage change in Q is $+3$ percent and the percentage change in V is $+1$ percent. The monetary rule here would specify that the growth rate in the money supply would be 2 percent ($3\% - 1\% = 2\%$). This would keep the price level stable; there would be a zero percent change in P:

$$\%\Delta M + \%\Delta V = \%\Delta P + \%\Delta Q$$
$$2\% + 1\% = 0\% + 3\%$$

Finally, some monetary rule proponents claim that even if a monetary rule does not adjust for changes in velocity, there is little cause for concern. Velocity instability is largely the result of unpredictable and volatile monetary policy. Once monetary policy is predictable and fixed, changes in velocity will be small and will occur within a narrow range.

Question:

If a monetary rule would bring about price level stability, why don't governments implement a monetary rule?

Answer:

First, not everyone is convinced that a monetary rule would bring about price level stability, owing to the problems of velocity and the correct definition of the money supply. Second, some people are strongly convinced that discretionary monetary policy is still much more effective at smoothing out the business cycle than non-activist monetary policy.

A Gold Standard

Gold Standard
The monetary arrangement whereby a nation backs its paper money totally or partially with gold.

If a nation backs its paper money totally or partially with gold, the nation is said to be on a **gold standard.** Most proponents of a gold standard maintain that it would stabilize the price level over time and restrain the money-creating activities of politicians, bureaucrats, and activist policy makers. Under a gold standard, the money supply would be tied to the stock of gold. As we can see, proponents of a monetary rule and proponents of a gold standard share the same objectives: to stabilize the price level over time and to reduce the amount of political and economic tinkering that can be applied to the money supply process.

The mechanics of a gold standard are as follows:

1. **The government pegs the price of gold at some dollar amount.** Most proponents of the gold standard claim that the dollar amount should be the market price of gold. Let's pick a price of $400. This, then, becomes the official price of gold. Initially, the free market price and the official price of gold are one and the same.
2. **The government promises to buy and sell gold at the official price.** Thus, if Schultz wants to buy gold from (or sell gold to) the government, the government will sell (or buy) gold at the price of $400. It is this government action that maintains the official price of gold equal to the market price and, according to the gold standard proponents, keeps the price level constant.

[6]This rule is based on the monetary rule put forth by Allan Meltzer, a long-standing monetarist. We omit some of the more technical points that are relevant to the Meltzer rule.

We explain the second point with the aid of Exhibit 15–9. In (a), the demand and supply curves represent the demand for and supply of gold in the private market, where gold is used as a commodity (jewelry, etc.). Because of inflation, the market price for gold rises to, say, $425, which is above the official price of $400, the price at which the government has agreed to buy and sell gold. This price discrepancy presents a profit opportunity to individuals. It is now possible for individuals to *buy* gold from the government at the $400 official price and *sell* gold in the market at the $425 market price, realizing a $25 profit (not taking into account exchange and transportation costs).

This transaction has an impact on the money supply, the market price of gold, and ultimately the price level. As individuals buy gold from the government, they exchange their cash or demand deposits (which are part of the money supply) for gold. The money supply in privately held hands is reduced, thus reducing aggregate demand and inflationary forces that originally pushed up gold prices. In the private gold market the policy increases the supply of gold; the supply curve shifts rightward from S_1 to S_2 until it intersects the demand curve at point 2, and thus the market price of gold falls until it hits the official price.

Proponents of the gold standard argue that by keeping the market price of gold constant over time—by selling gold to the market when the market price of gold is above the official price, as we have illustrated—the price level will be kept constant over time, too.

Consider the gold standard at work when the economy is in a recessionary gap and the price level is declining. In (b) the forces of supply and demand equilibrate at a $380 market price for gold. The official gold price, $400, is above the market

EXHIBIT 15–9
The Market for Gold and the Workings of a Gold Standard

(a)
Market Price > Official Price

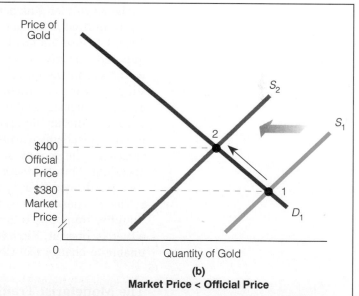

(b)
Market Price < Official Price

(a) The market price for gold is greater than the official price. This will cause individuals to buy gold from the government and sell it in the private market for $425. This action will result in an increase in the supply of gold in the private market (from S_1 to S_2), a fall in the price of gold to the official level, a contraction in the money supply, and a lower price level.

(b) The market price for gold is below the official price. This will cause individuals to buy gold in the private market for $380 and sell it to the government for $400. This action will result in a decrease in the supply of gold in the private market (from S_1 to S_2), a rise in the price of gold to the official level, an expansion in the money supply, and a higher price level.

price, $380, so individuals have a monetary incentive to *buy* gold in the market at the lower price and *sell* it to the government at the higher price. Dollars received from government increase the privately held money supply. This increases aggregate demand and offsets deflationary tendencies in the economy. In the private gold market, the policy reduces the supply of gold and the supply curve shifts leftward from S_1 to S_2 until it intersects the demand curve at point 2. The market price of gold increases. The impact on the money supply, market price of gold, and price level has been to increase all three. A "too low" price level, represented by a market price for gold lower than the official price, has been pushed upward. The objective is to maintain the price level that is consistent with a $400 market price for gold. Neither price levels below nor above are acceptable.

Critics charge that a gold standard is no guarantee against inflation. For example, if a cheap source of gold is discovered, the supply of gold on the market will increase, driving the market price down below the official price, which in turn will place upward pressure on the money supply and price level. This is what happened soon after the California gold rush of 1849.

Critics also charge that a reduction in national output and an increase in unemployment will result if prices do not fall in the same proportion when the gold-backed money supply is reduced. For example, if money wages do not fall as quickly as the prices of other goods and services, *real wages* will rise, reducing the quantity demanded of labor services and output production.

CHAPTER SUMMARY

The Keynesian Transmission Mechanism

■ The Keynesian link between the money market and the goods and services market is indirect. Changes in the money market must affect the investment goods market before the goods and services market is affected. Assuming no liquidity trap and that investment is not interest insensitive, the transmission mechanism works as follows for an increase in the money supply: An increase in the money supply lowers the interest rate and increases investment spending. This increases aggregate demand and thus shifts the *AD* curve rightward. Consequently, real GNP rises and the unemployment rate falls. Under the same assumptions, the transmission mechanism works as follows for a decrease in the money supply: A decrease in the money supply raises the interest rate and decreases investment spending. This decreases aggregate demand and thus shifts the *AD* curve leftward. As a result, real GNP falls and the unemployment rate rises.

■ The Keynesian transmission mechanism may be short-circuited either by the liquidity trap or by interest-insensitive investment. Both are Keynesian notions. If either is present, Keynesians predict that expansionary monetary policy will be unable to change real GNP or unemployment.

The Monetarist Transmission Mechanism

■ The monetarist link between the money market and the goods and services market is direct. Changes in the money supply affect aggregate demand, period. An increase in the money supply causes individuals to increase their spending on a wide variety of goods.

Bond Prices and Interest Rates

■ Interest rates and the price of old or existing bonds are inversely related.

The Activist–Nonactivist Debate

■ Activists argue that monetary and fiscal policies should be deliberately used to smooth out the business cycle; they are in favor of economic fine-tuning. Nonactivists argue against the use of deliberate and discretionary fiscal and monetary policies; they propose a stable and permanent monetary and fiscal framework guided by rules.

■ The case for activist monetary policy rests on three major claims: (1) The economy does not always equilibrate quickly enough at the natural level of real GNP. (2) Activist monetary policy works. (3) Activist monetary policy is flexible, and flexibility is a desirable quality in monetary policy.

■ The case for nonactivist monetary policy rests on three major claims: (1) There is sufficient flexibility in wages and prices in modern economies to allow the economy to equilibrate in reasonable speed at the natural level of real GNP. (2) Activist monetary policies may not work. (3) Activist monetary policies are likely to make matters worse rather than better.

Nonactivist Monetary Proposals

■ A monetary rule describes monetary policy that is based on a predetermined steady growth rate in the money supply. In this chapter, we discussed two similar monetary rules. One proposes that the annual money supply growth rate remain constant at the average annual growth rate of real GNP. The second proposes that the annual money supply growth rate equal the average annual growth rate in real GNP minus the growth rate in velocity.

■ Critics of monetary rules state that flexible monetary policy, as in activist-discretionary monetary policy, is more effective at smoothing out the business cycle. Also, they argue that (1) velocity changes, and therefore a fixed money supply growth rule that doesn't take velocity changes into account will be destabilizing; (2) it is unclear what monetary aggregate the rule ought to apply to. Proponents of a monetary rule retort that (1) a monetary rule that takes velocity changes into account can be devised; (2) velocity would be more stable once a monetary rule was implemented, since the velocity instability that exists is due to unpredictable and volatile monetary policy.

■ A nation operates on a gold standard if it backs its paper money totally or partially with gold. The gold standard operates in the following way: If the market price of gold falls below the official price, individuals buy gold in the market and sell it to the government. In the process, the money supply expands; the predicted effect is a rise in the price level. If the market price of gold is above the official price, individuals buy gold from the government and sell it in the market. In the process, the money supply contracts; the predicted effect is a fall in the price level.

Key Terms and Concepts

Monetary Policy	Activists	Monetary Rule
Transmission Mechanism	Fine Tuning	Gold Standard
Liquidity Trap	Nonactivists	

1. Consider the following: Two researchers, A and B, are trying to determine whether eating fatty foods leads to heart attacks. Researchers A and B proceed differently. Researcher A builds a model where fatty foods *may* first affect *X* in one's body, and if *X* is affected, then *Y* may be affected, and if *Y* is affected, then *Z* may be affected. Finally, if *Z* is affected, the heart is affected, and the individual has an increased probability of suffering a heart attack. Researcher B doesn't proceed in this step-by-step fashion. She conducts an experiment to see if people who eat many fatty foods have a higher, lower, or equal incidence of heart attacks as people who eat few fatty foods. Which researcher's methods have more in common with the research methodology implicit in the Keynesian transmission mechanism? Which researcher's methods have more in common with the research methodology implicit in the monetarist transmission mechanism? Explain your answer.

2. If bond prices fall, will individuals want to hold more or less money? Explain your answer.

3. It has been suggested that nonactivists are not concerned with the level of real GNP and unemployment, since most (if not all) nonactivist monetary proposals set as their immediate objective the stabilization of the price level. Discuss.

4. Suppose the combination of more accurate data and better forecasting techniques made it easy for the Fed to predict a recession 10 to 16 months in advance. Would this strengthen the case for activism or nonactivism? Explain your answer.

5. Suppose it were proved that there is no liquidity trap and that investment is not interest insensitive. Would this be enough to disprove the Keynesian claim that expansionary monetary policy is not always effective at changing real GNP? Why or why not?

6. Both activists and nonactivists make good points for their respective positions. Do you think there is anything an activist could say to a nonactivist to convince him or her to accept the activist position, and vice versa? If so, what is it? If not, why not?

7. In the discussion of supply and demand in Chapter 3, we noted that if two goods are substitutes, the price of one and the demand for the other are directly related. For example, if Pepsi-Cola and Coca-Cola are substitutes, an increase in the price of Pepsi-Cola will increase the demand for Coca-Cola. Suppose that bonds and stocks are substitutes. We know that interest rates and bond prices are inversely related. What do you predict is the relationship between stock prices and interest rates? Explain your answer.

8. Argue the case for and against a gold standard.

9. Conduct the following exercise. Pick any week of the year. Quickly read through all the issues of the *Wall Street Journal* for that week, and write down the number of articles in which the word *Fed* is used, along with a brief summary of each article. Usually, the article will have to do with monetary policy. Many articles will also relate opinions as to what the Fed has done, is doing, and will do. The chief economist at a major firm may say that he thinks the Fed is positioning itself to ease up on money supply growth in the upcoming months. An economic forecaster at a major bank may say she thinks the newest member of the Board of Governors will be persuasive in arguing for a slight tightening of the money supply because of his reputation as a fierce opponent of inflation.

What is the point of this exercise? First, the large number of articles in which the Fed is mentioned will show you how important the Fed and monetary policy are to the economics, political, banking, and business communities. Second, the quotations from people (supposedly) in the know will show you how much guessing and difference of opinion surrounds Fed monetary policy. Third, the factors cited as influencing Fed actions will give you a rough idea of how individuals think the Fed determines monetary policy.

After you conduct this exercise, sit down and reflect on the following questions:

a. Is the Fed implementing an activist monetary policy?

b. How does the Fed go about deciding whether it should increase or decrease the rate of growth of the money supply?

c. Would there be as many articles in the *Wall Street Journal* on monetary policy if there were a monetary rule or gold standard? If not, why not?

d. Would I be better off or worse off if I could accurately predict monetary policy? What monetary institutions are necessary for the accurate prediction of monetary policy?

e. Is the secrecy and guessing that surrounds Fed monetary policy a small price to pay for what the Fed has done to stabilize the economy, or is it a high price to pay for what the Fed has done to destabilize the economy?

If answers to these questions are not easily forthcoming, do not be concerned. As long as you can either ask or recognize questions relevant to monetary policy, and possess some knowledge of what the answers may be, you are ready to join the interesting and continuing debate on monetary policy. That is an important accomplishment.

APPENDIX F

MONETARY POLICY IN AN OPEN ECONOMY

Monetary policy, like fiscal policy, can be discussed in a closed economy (where there is no international trade) and in an open economy (where there is international trade). In this chapter, we have discussed the effect of monetary policy in a closed economy. In this appendix, we enlarge the picture and look at both expansionary and contractionary monetary policy in an open economy.

Expansionary Monetary Policy

We have learned that expansionary monetary policy causes the AD curve to shift rightward according to Keynesian theory (without a liquidity trap and without interest-insensitive investment) and according to monetarist theory. In Exhibit 15F-1a, the AD curve shifts rightward from AD_1 to AD_2. It also affects the exchange value of the dollar and net exports. Here's how.

The Exchange Value of the Dollar. One consequence of expansionary monetary policy is an initial decline in interest rates. If U.S. interest rates decline relative to foreign nations' interest rates, then this will lead to an outflow of capital from the United States (in search of higher interest rate returns). Americans will supply more dollars in the foreign exchange market and demand more foreign currencies. As the supply of dollars increases, and the demand for foreign currencies increases, the U.S. dollar depreciates and foreign currencies appreciate. This affects both the AD and $SRAS$ curves.

AD Curve (Affected by Net Exports). As the dollar depreciates and foreign currencies appreciate, U.S. goods become cheaper for foreigners, and foreign goods become more expensive for Americans. In turn, U.S. exports rise, U.S. imports fall, and U.S. net exports rise. An increase in net exports shifts the AD curve rightward. In Exhibit 15F-1a, the AD curve shifts from AD_2 to AD_3.

EXHIBIT 15F-1
Expansionary and Contractionary Monetary Policy in Open and Closed Economies

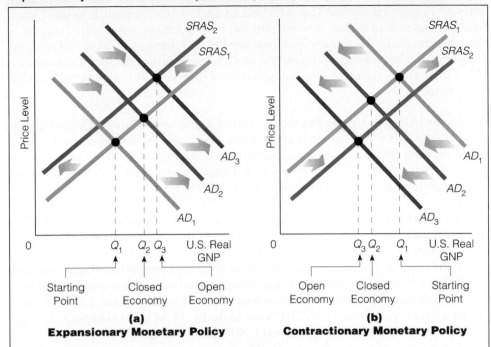

(a)
Expansionary Monetary Policy

(b)
Contractionary Monetary Policy

The consequences of expansionary monetary policy for both open and closed economies.
(a) The Fed increases the money supply and the AD curve shifts from AD_1 to AD_2. Real GNP rises from Q_1 to Q_2. The increased money supply leads to lower interest rates in the short run, promoting U.S. capital outflow and a depreciated dollar, which raises U.S. exports, lowers U.S. imports, and raises U.S. net exports. Higher net exports shift the AD curve rightward from AD_2 to AD_3. The depreciated dollar shifts the $SRAS$ curve leftward from $SRAS_1$ to $SRAS_2$. In the end, real GNP rises from Q_2 to Q_3. (Here we have drawn the AD curve shifting rightward by more than the $SRAS$ curve shifts leftward, which is typical given the initial event.) Expansionary monetary policy raises real GNP more in an open economy than in a closed economy.
(b) Contractionary monetary policy lowers real GNP more in an open economy than in a closed economy.

$SRAS$ Curve (Affected by Dollar Depreciation). As the dollar depreciates, foreign inputs become more expensive for Americans. As a result, the $SRAS$ curve shifts leftward from $SRAS_1$ to $SRAS_2$ in Exhibit 15F-1a.

A quick look at Exhibit 15F-1a, after both domestic and international feedback effects have been noted, shows us that monetary policy is more expansionary in an open economy than in a closed economy. In a closed economy, expansionary monetary policy increases real GNP from Q_1 to Q_2. In an open economy, expansionary monetary policy increases real GNP from Q_1 to Q_3.

This is in contrast to fiscal policy in an open economy, which we examined in Appendix E in Chapter 10. There we found that expansionary fiscal policy was less expansionary in an open economy than in a closed economy.

Contractionary Monetary Policy

As we have learned, contractionary monetary policy causes the AD curve to shift leftward. In Exhibit 15F-1b, the AD curve shifts rightward from AD_1 to AD_2. It also affects the exchange value of the dollar and net exports. Here's how.

The Exchange Value of the Dollar.   One consequence of contractionary monetary policy is an initial rise in interest rates. If U.S. interest rates rise relative to foreign nations' interest rates, then this will lead to an inflow of capital into the United States (in search of higher interest rate returns). Foreigners will supply more of their currencies in the foreign exchange market and demand more dollars. As the supply of foreign currencies increases, and the demand for dollars increases, the U.S. dollar appreciates and foreign currencies depreciate. This affects both the *AD* and *SRAS* curves.

AD Curve (Affected by Net Exports).   As the dollar appreciates and foreign currencies depreciate, U.S. goods become more expensive for foreigners and foreign goods become cheaper for Americans. In turn, U.S. exports fall, U.S. imports rise, and U.S. net exports fall. A decrease in net exports shifts the *AD* curve leftward. In Exhibit 15F-1a, the *AD* curve shifts from AD_2 to AD_3.

SRAS Curve (Affected by Dollar Appreciation).   As the dollar appreciates, foreign inputs become cheaper for Americans. As a result, the *SRAS* curve shifts rightward from $SRAS_1$ to $SRAS_2$ in Exhibit 15F-1b.

A quick look at Exhibit 15F-1b, after both domestic and international feedback effects have been noted, shows us that monetary policy is more contractionary in an open economy than in a closed economy. In a closed economy, contractionary monetary policy decreases real GNP from Q_1 to Q_2. In an open economy, contractionary monetary policy decreases real GNP from Q_1 to Q_3.

APPENDIX SUMMARY

■ Expansionary monetary policy affects the exchange rate of the dollar, which in turn affects net exports. The process works this way: (1) Expansionary monetary policy initially causes interest rates to decline; (2) If U.S. interest rates decline relative to foreign nations' interest rates, then there is an outflow of capital from the United States; (3) Americans supply more dollars and demand more foreign currencies; (4) As the supply of dollars increases, the dollar depreciates and foreign currencies appreciate; (5) Dollar depreciation makes U.S. goods cheaper for foreigners and foreign goods more expensive for Americans; (6) U.S. exports rise, U.S. imports fall, and U.S. net exports rise.

■ Contractionary monetary policy affects the exchange rate of the dollar, which in turn affects net exports. The process works this way: (1) Contractionary monetary policy initially causes interest rates to rise; (2) If U.S. interest rates rise relative to foreign nations' interest rates, then there is an inflow of capital into the United States; (3) Foreigners demand more dollars and supply more of their currencies; (4) As the demand for dollars increases, the dollar appreciates and foreign currencies depreciate; (5) Dollar appreciation makes U.S. goods more expensive for foreigners and foreign goods cheaper for Americans; (6) U.S. exports fall, U.S. imports rise, and U.S. net exports fall.

■ Monetary policy is more expansionary in an open economy than in a closed economy.

■ Monetary policy is more contractionary in an open economy than in a closed economy.

1. Explain why monetary policy is more expansionary in an open economy than in a closed economy.

2. Explain why monetary policy is more contractionary in an open economy than in a closed economy.

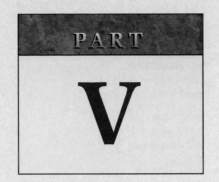

PART

V

EXPECTATIONS, MACROECONOMIC THEORY, AND POLICY ISSUES

V

JOB SEARCH THEORY, PHILLIPS CURVE ANALYSIS, AND NEW CLASSICAL THEORY: ENTER EXPECTATIONS

WHAT THIS CHAPTER IS ABOUT

In this chapter we discuss three related topics: job search theory, Phillips curve analysis, and new classical theory. Job search theory addresses unemployment and inflation expectations; Phillips curve analysis addresses inflation, unemployment, and inflation expectations; new classical theory addresses inflation, unemployment, inflation expectations, and economic policy.

THE ECONOMIC THEORY OF JOB SEARCH

■

How long does an unemployed person search for a job? The quick, and sometimes wrong, answer is until he or she finds a job. Consider Shirley Babbins, who voluntarily left her job as a secretary at a medical office three months ago. Since quitting her job, she has been offered work as a secretary in three other medical offices, as a secretary in two law offices, and as a part-time news reporter on a local radio station. She has turned down all six job offers and continues to search. In our example and in real life, a person doesn't necessarily search for a job only for as long as it takes to find a job. In this section, we discuss the economic theory of job search and relate it to the unemployment rate.

The Rational Search for Jobs

The economic theory of job search maintains that individuals are rational in their job searches: They consider both the costs and the benefits of searching for a job, and they search until the additional costs and additional benefits are equal. In practice, this translates into job searchers comparing *wages offered* with *reservation wages.*

The Wage Offer Curve. Most job searchers do not accept the first job they are offered because they cannot be sure that a better job is not waiting around the corner. In economic terms, job searchers do not possess complete information about job opportunities.

Consider 1,000 individuals searching for jobs. To simplify the analysis, let's assume that each individual compares the jobs he or she is offered only in terms of wages offered. If we were to plot the wage offers of each of the 1,000 individuals, we would no doubt find that some individuals received their highest wage offer with their first job offer, some received their highest wage offer with their tenth job offer, and many fell between the two extremes. On average, we would expect wage offers to increase (up to a point) as the job search period is extended. The wage offer curve in Exhibit 16–1a illustrates this pattern.

EXHIBIT 16-1
The Wage Offer and Reservation Wage Curves

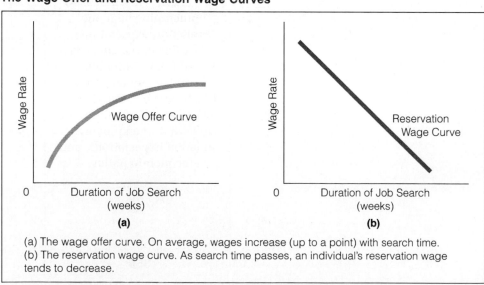

(a) The wage offer curve. On average, wages increase (up to a point) with search time.
(b) The reservation wage curve. As search time passes, an individual's reservation wage tends to decrease.

The Reservation Wage Curve. Individuals searching for jobs realize that the search is costly to them. Most of the cost consists of the wages they could have been earning had they accepted the last offer and not extended the search. For this reason, each job searcher has some notion of a wage offer that is good enough to accept without extending the search. The lowest wage a person will accept at any time in the job search process is called that person's **reservation wage.**

As search time passes, an individual's reservation wage tends to decrease for several reasons. First, individuals searching for jobs usually start out optimistic and often overestimate their market worth to employers. As time passes, they gain information about themselves and the labor market, and thus become more realistic. Second, long periods of unemployment draw down savings accounts and put pressure on the job searchers to return to work. Third, unemployment benefits do not extend indefinitely. The relationship between the reservation wage and time is illustrated by the *reservation wage curve* in Exhibit 16–1b.

The Optimal Search Time. When does a job searcher stop searching? The answer is when he or she receives a wage offer that equals his or her reservation wage. To put it differently, if the wage offer (W) is less than the reservation wage (R), the individual continues to search. The job searcher stops searching when $W = R$. Exhibit 16–2 represents the process. The optimal search time is X weeks, which is the length of time it takes until W equals R. Before X weeks have passed, $R > W$, and the job searcher continues to search because he has not received a wage offer high enough to stop him from searching further. In short, he evaluates his wage offers as being too low. As time passes, however, wage offers rise (on average), and the reservation wage falls. Eventually, the two are equal. At this point, the job search ends.

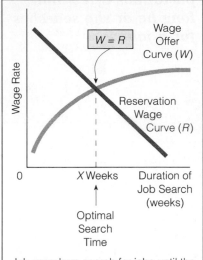

When economists explain and predict behavior, they are usually *comparing* things. For example, in job search theory, *wages offered* are compared with *reservation wages* to explain and predict how long a person searches for a job. In the theory of supply and demand, the quantity demanded of a good is compared with the quantity supplied of a good to see if the market is in equilibrium. In the theory of opportunity cost, what one *is* doing is compared with what one *could be* doing to determine cost. Last, when discussing wages, economists assume that people are more interested in their real wages—their money wages compared with the price level—than in their money wages alone.

Comparing things illustrates that to know where we are, or how we are doing, it is important to have a reference point. Jones doesn't know whether a wage offer of $2,000 a month is good or not until she knows her opportunity costs. Smith doesn't know whether his salary increase makes him better off or not until he measures the percentage increase in his salary against the percentage increase in the price level. So, when economists compare things, they are acting on the knowledge that a reference point is often necessary to tell us how we stand.

Optimal Search Time and the Unemployment Rate

An increase in optimal search time is followed by an increase in the unemployment rate, *ceteris paribus*. Here is a simple numerical example to illustrate the point.

CHAPTER 16
JOB SEARCH THEORY, PHILLIPS
CURVE ANALYSIS, AND NEW
CLASSICAL THEORY: ENTER
EXPECTATIONS

357

Suppose the civilian labor force is composed of 100 individuals and there are 10 unemployed persons. It follows that the unemployment rate is 10 percent. Now consider two cases. In Case 1, the optimal search time is one week, and each week 10 persons become unemployed. In Case 2, the optimal search time is two weeks, and each week 10 persons become unemployed. As we can see, the only difference between Case 1 and Case 2 is that the optimal search time is longer in Case 2. Does an increase in the optimal search time increase the unemployment rate?

To help us answer this question, we turn to Exhibit 16–3. Consider Case 1. In week 1, there are 10 persons unemployed, so the unemployment rate is 10 percent. In week 2, 10 persons accept job offers (recall that the optimal search time is one week), and 10 persons become unemployed. We subtract 10 persons from, and add 10 persons to, the number of unemployed at the end of week 1. This gives us a total of 10 persons unemployed in week 2 and an unemployment rate of 10 percent. In week 3, 10 persons accept job offers, and 10 persons become unemployed. We subtract 10 persons from, and add 10 persons to, the number of unemployed persons at the end of week 3. This gives us a total of 10 persons unemployed in week 3 and an unemployment rate of 10 percent.

We turn now to Case 2, where the optimal search time is two weeks. Beginning in week 1, there are 10 persons unemployed, so the unemployment rate is 10 percent. In week 2, 10 persons are added to the ranks of the unemployed, but none of the previously unemployed accepts a job offer (recall that the optimal search time is two weeks). It follows that there are 20 persons unemployed in week 2 and that the unemployment rate is 20 percent. In week 3, 10 persons accept job offers (the two weeks optimal search time has passed), and 10 persons become unemployed. We therefore subtract 10 persons from, and add 10 persons to, the number of unemployed at the end of week 2. The total number of persons unemployed in week 3 is 20, and the unemployment rate is 20 percent. Our conclusion is that *as the optimal search time increases, the unemployment rate increases.*

Inflation Expectations and Optimal Search Time

A worker's inflation expectations affect how long he or she searches for a job. Consider Helen Rodriguez's job search. She has some idea of what she can buy

EXHIBIT 16-3
Optimal Search Time and the Unemployment Rate
Starting with a civilian labor force of 100 persons and 10 unemployed persons, we consider two cases: Case 1, where the optimal search time is one week, and each week 10 persons become unemployed; and Case 2, where the optimal search time is two weeks, and each week 10 persons become unemployed. As optimal search time increases, so does the unemployment rate—from 10 percent in Case 1 to 20 percent in Case 2.

CASE 1: OPTIMAL SEARCH TIME = 1 WEEK			
	Week 1	**Week 2**	**Week 3**
Unemployed persons	10	$10 - 10 + 10 = 10$	$10 - 10 + 10 = 10$
Unemployment rate	$\frac{10}{100} = 10\%$	$\frac{10}{100} = 10\%$	$\frac{10}{100} = 10\%$

CASE 2: OPTIMAL SEARCH TIME = 2 WEEKS			
	Week 1	**Week 2**	**Week 3**
Unemployed persons	10	$10 + 10 = 20$	$20 - 10 + 10 = 20$
Unemployment rate	$\frac{10}{100} = 10\%$	$\frac{20}{100} = 20\%$	$\frac{20}{100} = 20\%$

with the pay she is being offered. For example, if she is offered a salary of $40,000 per year, she has an idea of what $40,000 will buy over the period of time she receives it. Suppose, though, that her idea of what the $40,000 will buy is based on an expected inflation rate of 15 percent. The actual inflation rate, however, turns out to be 5 percent. Does her "too high" expected inflation rate, relative to the actual inflation rate, influence the time she spends searching for a job? Most likely it does. She believes that any salary offered to her has less purchasing power than it actually has, and therefore she is likely to search longer for a job (stay voluntarily unemployed longer) than she would if her expected inflation rate were accurate (equal to the actual inflation rate).

Unemployment Benefits and the Unemployment Rate

Can higher unemployment benefits raise the unemployment rate? Yes, if there is a relationship between unemployment benefits and optimal search time. But for this relationship to exist, a change in unemployment benefits must shift either the wage offer curve or the reservation wage curve. Does it?

Suppose the government announces that the amount of unemployment benefits paid per week will increase and that benefits will be available for more weeks. Instead of the average unemployment benefit being, say, $100 per week for 20 weeks, it will be $150 per week for 30 weeks. As a result, we predict that individuals' reservation wages will increase. One reason for this is that the job search pressure on savings isn't as great. As reservation wages increase, the reservation wage curve shifts rightward from R_1 to R_2 (Exhibit 16–4). As a result, the optimal search time increases from X_1 weeks to X_2 weeks, and the unemployment rate increases from U_1 to U_2.

The existence of unemployment benefits may explain why many jobs go unfilled, even in the midst of a high-unemployment period. For example, in 1982, when

EXHIBIT 16-4
Unemployment Benefits and the Unemployment Rate

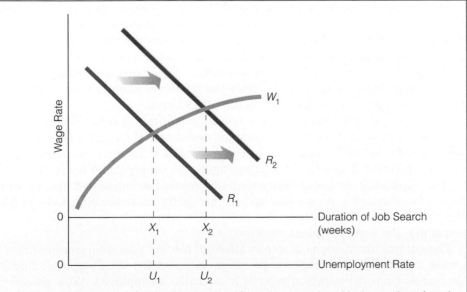

An increase in the amount of unemployment benefits paid per week and in the number of weeks benefits are available shifts the reservation wage curve (R) to the right; this increases the number of weeks a person searches for a job and, thus, the unemployment rate.

CHAPTER 16
JOB SEARCH THEORY, PHILLIPS
CURVE ANALYSIS, AND NEW
CLASSICAL THEORY: ENTER
EXPECTATIONS

■

359

the unemployment rate was at a relatively high 9.7 percent, there were slightly more than 6 million job openings. If unemployment benefits are high enough so that the monetary difference between being employed and being unemployed is small, we would expect that more persons will stay unemployed than if the difference between being employed and being unemployed is large.

This is not an argument against unemployment benefits or increases in unemployment benefits. We are simply pointing out that because unemployment benefits exist, the unemployment rate is higher than it would be otherwise. For other reasons, a society may prefer higher unemployment benefits and higher unemployment rates to lower unemployment benefits and lower unemployment rates. For example, some economists argue that there are benefits from individuals spending more time searching for a better job match.

When an economist argues that higher unemployment benefits raise the unemployment rate, the layperson may conclude that the economist is against a system of unemployment benefits. But this misrepresents what the economist is saying. Economists who do positive economics ("what is" as opposed to "what should be") are not necessarily for or against a particular system or policy. Their world is the world of cause and effect. The economist who argues that higher unemployment benefits will increase the unemployment rate is not necessarily against raising unemployment benefits. He is simply showing us that there are no free lunches: There is a cost to higher unemployment benefits. Science advances when researchers tell us the truth as they see it—regardless of whether they like the particular truth or not.

The *LRAS* Curve Is Not Carved in Stone

Up to this point, we have said little about a shift in the *LRAS* curve. When we talked about a supply-side shift, it has been a shift in the short-run aggregate supply (*SRAS*) curve. What about the *LRAS* curve? Can it shift?

The answer is yes. The logic is easy to follow: Since the *LRAS* curve is set at the natural real GNP level (Q_N)—which corresponds to the natural unemployment rate (U_N)—anything that either increases or decreases the natural unemployment rate will automatically shift the *LRAS* curve leftward or rightward, respectively. More specifically, anything that changes either of the two components of the natural unemployment rate—that is, either the frictional unemployment rate or the structural unemployment rate—shifts the *LRAS* curve.

Here is an example. Suppose the economy in Exhibit 16–5 is at the natural real GNP level of Q_{N1} and the natural unemployment rate of U_{N1}, or 6 percent (where the frictional unemployment rate is 2 percent and the structural unemployment rate is 4 percent). The relevant long-run aggregate supply curve is $LRAS_1$.

Now suppose government permanently increases the length and amount of unemployment benefits. As we saw earlier, this shifts the reservation wage curve to the right (see Exhibit 16–4). As this happens, the optimal search time rises; consequently, the unemployment rate rises.

The natural unemployment rate is affected, too. As unemployment benefits increase and extend over more weeks, the pressure on the unemployed to find jobs decreases. Consider a person who is frictionally unemployed. With greater unemployment benefits, she doesn't have to find another job as quickly, and so she stretches out the job search. All other things held constant, this increases the frictional unemployment rate. But if the frictional unemployment rate rises, so does

EXHIBIT 16-5
A Shift in the *LRAS* Curve

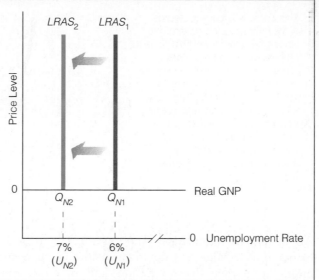

Anything that changes the natural unemployment rate causes a shift in the *LRAS* curve. For example, a permanent increase in unemployment benefits causes the frictional unemployment rate to rise. As a result, the natural unemployment rate increases (say, from 6% to 7%) and the *LRAS* curve shifts leftward from $LRAS_1$ to $LRAS_2$.

the natural unemployment rate. In our example, if the frictional unemployment rate goes up from 2 to 3 percent, and the structural unemployment rate is constant at 4 percent, then the natural unemployment rises to 7 percent.

In Exhibit 16–5, the economy moves leftward along the unemployment rate axis from U_{N1} (6 percent) to U_{N2} (7 percent) and leftward along the real GNP axis from Q_{N1} to Q_{N2}.

Given these changes, is $LRAS_1$ still the relevant long-run aggregate supply curve? The answer is no. The relevant long-run supply curve is now $LRAS_2$. In other words, since the natural unemployment rate has increased, the *LRAS* curve has shifted to the left. If the natural unemployment rate had decreased, the *LRAS* curve would have shifted to the right.

In summary, anything that raises the natural unemployment rate shifts the *LRAS* curve to the left; anything that lowers the natural unemployment rate shifts the *LRAS* curve to the right.

PHILLIPS CURVE ANALYSIS

In this section, we begin our discussion of the Phillips curve by focusing on the work of three economists, A. W. Phillips, Paul Samuelson, and Robert Solow.

1958: The Phillips Curve

In 1958, A. W. Phillips of the London School of Economics published a paper entitled "The Relation between Unemployment and the Rate of Change of Money Wages in the United Kingdom, 1861–1957," in the economics journal *Economica*. As the title suggests, Phillips collected data on the rate of change in money wages, sometimes referred to as *wage inflation,* and unemployment rates in the United Kingdom over a period of time. He then plotted the rate of change in money wages against the unemployment rate for each year. Finally, he fit a curve to the data points (Exhibit 16–6).

EXHIBIT 16-6
The Original Phillips Curve

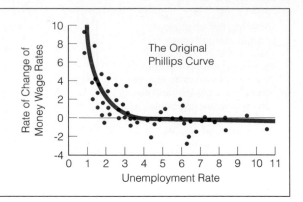

This curve was constructed by A. W. Phillips, using data for the United Kingdom from 1861 to 1913. (The relationship here is also representative of the experience of the United Kingdom through 1957). The original Phillips curve suggests an inverse relationship between wage inflation and unemployment; it represents a wage inflation–unemployment trade-off. (Note: Each dot represents a single year.)

Phillips Curve
A curve that originally showed the relationship between wage inflation and unemployment. Now it more often shows the relationship between price inflation and unemployment.

An Inverse Relationship. The curve came to be known as the **Phillips curve.** Notice that the curve is downward sloping, suggesting that the rate of change of money wage rates (wage inflation) and unemployment rates are inversely related. This inverse relationship suggests a trade-off between wage inflation and unemployment. Higher wage inflation means lower unemployment; lower wage inflation means higher unemployment. Policy makers concluded from the Phillips curve that it was impossible to lower both wage inflation *and* unemployment; one could do one or the other. So, the combination of low wage inflation *and* low unemployment was not likely. This was the bad news. The good news was that rising unemployment and rising wage inflation did not go together either. Thus, the combination of high unemployment *and* high wage inflation was also not likely.

The Theoretical Explanation for the Phillips Curve. What is the reason for the inverse relationship between wage inflation and unemployment? Early explanations centered on the state of the labor market given changes in aggregate demand. When aggregate demand is increasing, businesses expand production and hire more employees. As the unemployment rate falls, the labor market becomes tighter, and it becomes increasingly difficult to hire workers at old wages. Businesses end up offering higher wages to obtain additional workers. Unemployment and money wage rates move in opposite directions.

1960: Samuelson and Solow: The Phillips Curve Is Americanized

In 1960, two American economists, Paul Samuelson and Robert Solow, published an article in the *American Economic Review* in which they fit a Phillips curve to the U.S. economy from 1935 to 1959. Besides using American data instead of British data, they measured price inflation rates (instead of wage inflation rates) against unemployment rates. They found an inverse relationship between (price) inflation and unemployment (see Exhibit 16–7).[1]

From viewing the Phillips curve (such as the one in 16–7), economists concluded that **stagflation,** or high inflation together with high unemployment, was

Stagflation
The simultaneous occurrence of high rates of inflation and unemployment.

PART V
EXPECTATIONS, MACROECONOMIC
THEORY AND POLICY ISSUES

[1]Today, when economists speak of the Phillips curve, they are usually referring to the relationship between price inflation rates and unemployment rates, instead of wage inflation rates and unemployment rates.

extremely unlikely. The economy could register high unemployment and low inflation *or* low unemployment and high inflation.

Also, economists noticed that the Phillips curve presented policy makers with a *menu of choices.* For example, policy makers could choose to move the economy to any of the points on the Phillips curve in Exhibit 16–7. If they decided that a point like *A,* with high unemployment and low inflation, was preferable to a point like *D,* with low unemployment and high inflation, then so be it. It was simply a matter of reaching the right level of aggregate demand. To Keynesian economists, who were gaining a reputation for advocating *fine-tuning* the economy, that is, using small-scale measures to counterbalance undesirable economic trends, this conclusion seemed to be consistent with their theories and policy proposals.

Question:

If the Phillips curve presents policy makers with a menu of choices (such as 5 percent inflation and 3 percent unemployment or 2 percent inflation and 4.5 percent unemployment, and so on), this implicitly assumes that the menu of choices does not change over time. The same combinations of inflation and unemployment rates exist year after year. Is it really this way in the real world?

Answer:

As we soon explain, the real world is not like this.

EXHIBIT 16-7
The Phillips Curve and a Menu of Choices

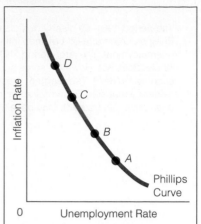

Samelson and Solow's early work using American data showed that the Phillips curve was downward sloping. Economists reasoned that stagflation was extremely unlikely and that the Phillips curve presented policy makers with a menu of choices—point *A, B, C,* or *D.*

THE CONTROVERSY BEGINS

Next we discuss the work of Milton Friedman and the hypothesis that there are two, not one, Phillips curves.

The 1970s and 1980s: Things Aren't Always As We Thought

In the 1970s and early 1980s, economists began to question many of the conclusions about the Phillips curve. Their questions were largely prompted by events in the period after 1969. Consider Exhibit 16–8, which shows U.S. inflation and unemployment rates for the years 1961–90. The 1961–69 period, which is shaded, depicts the original Phillips curve trade-off between inflation and unemployment. The remaining period, 1970–90, as a whole does not, although some subperiods, such as 1976–79, do.

Focusing on the period 1970–90, we note two things: (1) Stagflation—high unemployment and high inflation—is possible. For example, 1975, 1981, and 1982 are definitely years of stagflation. Furthermore, the existence of stagflation implies that a trade-off between inflation and unemployment may not always exist. (2) Cycles of unemployment and inflation rates appear to have gravitated around a 6 percent unemployment rate—identified by the vertical line in Exhibit 16–8. This suggests that the unemployment rate tends to move toward some natural level in the long run.

Flashback to 1967: Friedman and the Natural Rate Hypothesis

Milton Friedman, in his presidential address to the American Economic Association in 1967 (published in the *American Economic Review),* attacked the idea of a permanent downward-sloping Phillips curve. Friedman's key point was that

CHAPTER 16
JOB SEARCH THEORY, PHILLIPS
CURVE ANALYSIS, AND NEW
CLASSICAL THEORY: ENTER
EXPECTATIONS

363

The period 1961–69 clearly depicts the original Phillips curve trade-off between inflation and unemployment. The later period, 1970–90, as a whole, does not. However, some subperiods do, such as 1976–79. The diagram presents empirical evidence that stagflation may exist; an inflation–unemployment trade-off may not always hold.

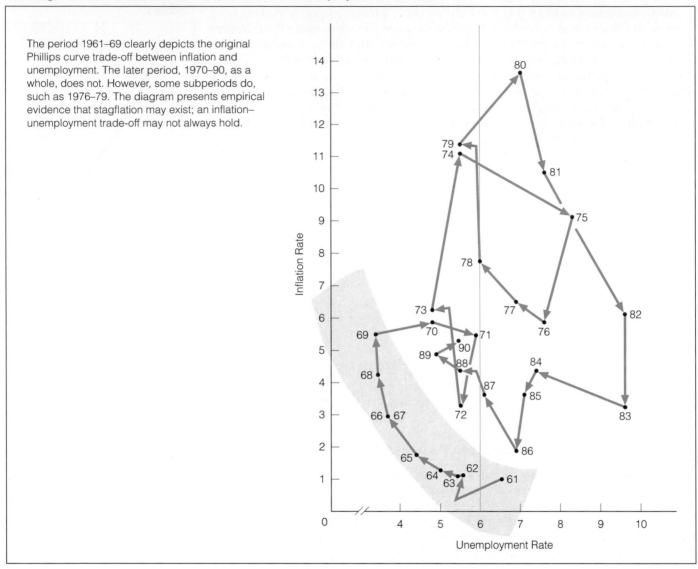

there are two, not one, Phillips curves: a short-run Phillips curve and a long-run Phillips curve. Friedman said, "There is always a temporary trade-off between inflation and unemployment; there is no permanent trade-off." In other words, there is a trade-off in the short run, but not in the long run. Friedman's discussion not only introduced two types of Phillips curves—short run and long run—to the analysis but also opened the macroeconomics door wide, once and for all, to expectations theory, that is, to the idea that peoples' expectations about economic events affect economic outcomes.

It is easy to illustrate both the short-run and long-run Phillips curves with the aid of Exhibit 16–9. We start with the economy in long-run equilibrium, operating at Q_1, which is equal to Q_N. This is shown in Window 1. In the main diagram, the economy is at point 1 at the natural rate of unemployment. Further, and most

EXHIBIT 16-9
Short-Run and Long-Run Phillips Curve

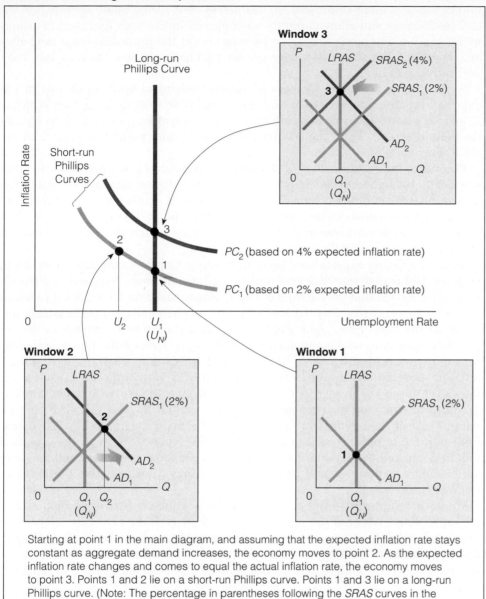

Window 3

Window 2

Window 1

Starting at point 1 in the main diagram, and assuming that the expected inflation rate stays constant as aggregate demand increases, the economy moves to point 2. As the expected inflation rate changes and comes to equal the actual inflation rate, the economy moves to point 3. Points 1 and 2 lie on a short-run Phillips curve. Points 1 and 3 lie on a long-run Phillips curve. (Note: The percentage in parentheses following the *SRAS* curves in the windows refers to the expected inflation rate.)

important, we assume that the expected inflation rate and the actual inflation rate are the same, at 2 percent.

Now suppose government *unexpectedly* increases aggregate demand from AD_1 to AD_2, as shown in Window 2. As a result, the actual inflation rate increases (say, to 4 percent), but in the short run (immediately after the increase in aggregate demand), individual decision makers do not know this. Consequently, the expected inflation rate remains at 2 percent. In short, we have aggregate demand increasing at the same time that people's expected inflation rate remains constant. Because of this combination of events, certain things happen.

CHAPTER 16
JOB SEARCH THEORY, PHILLIPS
CURVE ANALYSIS, AND NEW
CLASSICAL THEORY: ENTER
EXPECTATIONS

■

365

First, the higher aggregate demand causes temporary shortages and higher prices. Businesses respond to higher prices and higher profits by increasing output. Higher output requires more employees, so businesses start hiring more workers. Job vacancies increase and many currently unemployed individuals find work. Furthermore, many of the newly employed persons accept the prevailing wage rate; after all, they think the wages will have greater purchasing power than, in fact, they will turn out to have.

So far, the results of an increase in aggregate demand with no change in the expected inflation rate are (1) an increase in real GNP from Q_1 to Q_2 (see Window 2) and (2) a corresponding decrease in the unemployment rate from U_1 to U_2 (see the main diagram). Thus, the economy has moved from point 1 to point 2 in the main diagram.

This raises the question: Is point 2 a stable equilibrium? Friedman answered that it was not. He argued that as long as the *expected* inflation rate is not equal to the *actual* inflation rate, the economy is not in long-run equilibrium. For Friedman, as for most economists today, the movement from point 1 to point 2 on PC_1 is a short-run movement. Economists refer to PC_1, along which short-run movements occur, as a *short-run Phillips curve.*

In time, inflation expectations begin to change. As prices continue their climb, wage earners realize that their real (inflation-adjusted) wages have fallen. In hindsight, they realize that they accepted money wages based on an expected inflation rate (of 2 percent) that was too low. They revise their inflation expectations upward. At the same time, some wage earners quit their jobs because they do not choose to continue working at such low real wages. Eventually, the combination of some workers quitting their jobs and most (if not all) workers revising their inflation expectations upward causes wage rates to move upward. Higher wage rates shift the short-run aggregate supply curve from $SRAS_1$ to $SRAS_2$ (see Window 3), ultimately moving the economy back to the natural level of real GNP and the natural rate of unemployment (at point 3 in the main diagram). The movement from point 2 to point 3 was prompted by a discrepancy between the expected inflation rate and the actual inflation rate. The curve that connects point 1, where the economy started out, and point 3, where it ended up, is called the *long-run Phillips curve.*

Thus, the short-run Phillips curve exhibits a trade-off between inflation and unemployment, whereas the long-run Phillips curve does not. This is the idea implicit in what has come to be called the **natural rate hypothesis.** According to this hypothesis, in the long run, the economy returns to its natural rate of unemployment; lower unemployment cannot permanently be bought by higher inflation.

Natural Rate Hypothesis
The idea that in the long run, unemployment is at its natural rate. Within the Phillips curve framework, the natural rate hypothesis specifies that there is a long-run Phillips curve, which is vertical at the natural rate of unemployment.

RATIONAL EXPECTATIONS AND NEW CLASSICAL THEORY

■

Rational expectations has played a major role in the developing discussion of the Phillips curve controversy. The work of economists Robert Lucas, Robert Barro, Thomas Sargent, and Neil Wallace is relevant here. We turn to a discussion of rational expectations next.

1973: Rational Expectations and the New Classical Ratex Theory

In the early 1970s, a few economists, including Robert Lucas of the University of Chicago, began to question if there was even a short-run trade-off between inflation and unemployment. Essentially, what Lucas did was combine the natural rate hypothesis with rational expectations (sometimes simply referred to as **"ratex"**).[2]

Lucas and other *new classical economists,* as they came to be called, pointed out that the traditional natural rate hypothesis was based on adaptive expectations. As stated in Chapter 13, adaptive expectations theory holds that individuals form their inflation expectations based on past inflation rate experience. Stated differently, if people form the expected inflation rate *adaptively,* they are always looking over their shoulders to see what *has happened* (in the *past*)—as opposed to what *is* happening (in the *present)*, or what they think *will* happen (in the *future*).

The new classical economists thought individuals formed their inflation expectations rationally; that is, taking into account not only what *has happened* but also what *is happening* and what *will happen*—in short, on all available and relevant information. But, of course, to say that individuals base their inflation expectations on, among other things, the effects of what will happen—for example, future policy actions—implies that individuals *anticipate* policy actions. Before we examine the details of the natural rate hypothesis with the rational expectations twist, let us discuss whether people do anticipate policy.

Do People Anticipate Policy?

Suppose you picked a person at random on the street and asked him or her this question: What do you think the Fed will do in the next few months? Do you think you would be more likely to receive (1) an intelligent answer or (2) the response, "What's the Fed"? Most readers of this text will probably choose answer (2). There is a general feeling that the person on the street knows little about economics or economic institutions. The answer to our question—Do people anticipate policy?—seems to be no.

But suppose you were to ask the same question of a person picked at random on Wall Street. This time you would likely receive an informed answer. In this case, the answer to our larger question—Do people anticipate policy?—is likely to be yes.

We suggest that not all persons need to anticipate policy; as long as some do, the consequences may be the same *as if* all persons do. For example, Juanita Estevez is anticipating policy if she decides to buy 100 shares of SKA, because her best friend, Tammy Higgins, heard from her boyfriend, Kenny Urich, that his broker, Roberta Gunter, had told him that SKA's stock was going to go up. Juanita is anticipating policy because it is likely that Roberta Gunter obtained her information from a researcher in the brokerage firm who makes it his business to "watch the Fed" and to anticipate its next move. (In fact, many New York investment firms pay their professional "Fed watchers" a quarter of a million dollars per year or more. There is a life in economics beyond taking tests.)

Of course, anticipating policy is not done just for the purpose of buying and selling stocks. Labor unions hire professional forecasters to predict future inflation rates, which is important information to have during contract wage negotiations. Banks hire professional forecasters to predict inflation rates, which they incorporate into the interest rate they charge. Export businesses hire professional forecasters to predict the future exchange value of the dollar. The average investor may

As long as some people anticipate policy, the consequences may be the same as if all persons do.

■

Ratex
Short for rational expectations.

[2]Rational expectations came on the economic scene in 1961 with the publication of the article "Rational Expectations and the Theory of Price Movements" by John Muth in the journal *Econometrica.* For about ten years, the article received little attention from the economics profession. Then, in the early 1970s, with the work of Robert Lucas, Thomas Sargent, Neil Wallace, Robert Barro, and other economists, the article began to be noticed.

CHAPTER 16
JOB SEARCH THEORY, PHILLIPS
CURVE ANALYSIS, AND NEW
CLASSICAL THEORY: ENTER
EXPECTATIONS

■

367

subscribe to a business or investment newsletter in order to predict interest rates, the price of gold, or next year's inflation rate more accurately. The person thinking of refinancing his mortgage watches "Wall Street Week" on television to hear what this week's guest has to say about the Congress's most recent move and how it will affect interest rates in the next three months.

New Classical Theory: The Effects of Unanticipated and Anticipated Policy

There are two major assumptions of new classical theory: (1) Expectations are formed rationally. (2) Wages and prices are flexible. With these in mind, we discuss new classical theory in two settings: one where policy is unanticipated and the other where policy is anticipated.

Unanticipated Policy. Consider Exhibit 16–10a. The economy starts off at point 1, where $Q_1 = Q_N$. *Unexpectedly,* the Fed begins to buy government securities, and the money supply and aggregate demand increase. The aggregate demand curve shifts rightward from AD_1 to AD_2. Since the policy action was unanticipated, individuals are caught off guard, so the anticipated price level (P_1), on which the short-run aggregate supply curve is based, is not likely to change immediately.[4] In

[4]This is similar to saying, as we did in the discussion of the Friedman natural rate hypothesis, that individuals' expected inflation rate is less than the actual inflation rate.

EXHIBIT 16-10
Rational Expectations in an *AD–AS* Framework

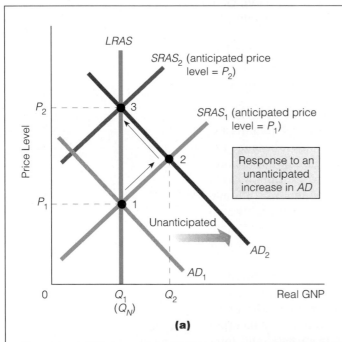

(a)

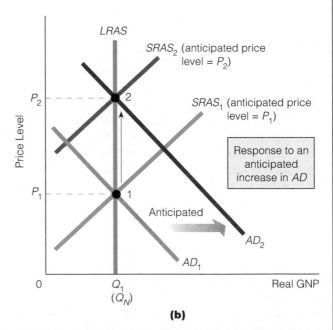

(b)

The economy is in long-run equilibrium at point 1 in both (a) and (b). In (a), there is an unanticipated increase in aggregate demand. In the short run, the economy moves to point 2. In the long run, it moves to point 3. In (b), there is an anticipated increase in aggregate demand. Because the increase is anticipated, the short-run aggre-

gate supply curve shifts from $SRAS_1$ to $SRAS_2$ at the same time the aggregate demand curve shifts from AD_1 to AD_2. The economy moves directly to point 2, which is comparable to point 3 in (a).

the short run, the economy moves from point 1 to point 2, from Q_1 to Q_2. (In Phillips-curve terms, the economy has moved up the short-run Phillips curve to a higher inflation rate and lower unemployment rate.) In the long run, workers correctly anticipate the higher price level and increase their wage demands accordingly. The short-run aggregate supply curve shifts leftward from $SRAS_1$ to $SRAS_2$ and the economy moves to point 3.

Anticipated Policy. Now consider the difference if policy is anticipated, in particular if it is *correctly* anticipated. When individuals anticipate that the Fed will buy government securities and that the money supply, aggregate demand, and prices will increase, they will adjust their present actions accordingly. For example, workers will bargain for higher wages so that their real wages will not fall when the price level rises. As a result, the short-run aggregate supply curve will shift leftward from $SRAS_1$ to $SRAS_2$ at the same time that the aggregate demand curve shifts rightward from AD_1 to AD_2 (see Exhibit 16–10b). The economy moves directly from point 1 to point 2. Real GNP does not change; throughout the adjustment period, it remains at its natural level. It follows that the unemployment rate does not change either. Simply put, there is no short-run trade-off between inflation and unemployment. The short-run Phillips curve and the long-run Phillips curve are one and the same; and the curve is vertical.

Question:

What is a simple, everyday (preferably noneconomic) example that illustrates the operation and effects of rational expectations in a setting where "policy" is unanticipated and one where it is anticipated?

Answer:

Suppose Jim's psychology class starts at 9 A.M. and it is "natural" for him to arrive one minute before class starts. In other words, his "natural waiting time" is one minute.

The first day of class, Jim arrives at 8:59, his instructor arrives at 8:59:30, and she starts class promptly at 9 A.M.

The second day of class, Jim arrives at 8:59, his instructor arrives at 9:01:30, and she starts class at 9:02. On this day, Jim has waited three minutes, which is above his natural waiting time of one minute.

The third, fourth, and fifth days of class are the same as the second. So, for the second through fifth days of class, Jim is operating at above his natural waiting time.

Finally, Jim adjusts. Instead of arriving at 8:59, he arrives at class at 9:01. This day the instructor again arrives at 9:01:30 and begins class at 9:02. Jim is back at his natural waiting time of one minute.

In this case, Jim did not initially anticipate that his instructor would be late: A change in the instructor's policy from the first day of class (when she arrived at 8:59:30) to the second through fifth days of class (when she arrived at 9:01:30) was unanticipated. As a result, Jim was moved away from his natural waiting of time for a few days. Finally, he adjusted back to it.

Now suppose that a change in the instructor's policy is anticipated. For example, the instructor announces on the first day of class that she will begin class two minutes late from now on. Knowing this, Jim no longer plans to arrive to class at

CHAPTER 16
JOB SEARCH THEORY, PHILLIPS
CURVE ANALYSIS, AND NEW
CLASSICAL THEORY: ENTER
EXPECTATIONS

■

369

8:59, but instead at 9:01; thus, he maintains his natural waiting time at one minute; never does he rise above or fall below it.

Policy Ineffectiveness Proposition (PIP)

Using rational expectations, we showed (see Exhibit 16–10) that if the rise in aggregate demand is *unanticipated,* there is a short-run increase in real GNP, but if the rise in aggregate demand is *correctly anticipated,* there is no change in real GNP.

We have studied two types of macroeconomic policies—fiscal and monetary—both of which theoretically can increase aggregate demand. For example, assuming there is no crowding out or incomplete crowding out, expansionary fiscal policy shifts the *AD* curve rightward. Expansionary monetary policy does the same. In both cases, expansionary policy is *effective* at increasing real GNP and lowering the unemployment rate in the short run. But what new classical economists call into question is just this. They argue that (1) if the expansionary policy change is *correctly anticipated,* (2) individuals form their expectations rationally, and (3) wages and prices are flexible, neither expansionary fiscal policy nor expansionary monetary policy will be able to increase real GNP and lower the unemployment rate in the short run. This is called the **policy ineffectiveness proposition (PIP).**

Think what this means. If, under certain conditions, expansionary monetary and fiscal policy are not effective at increasing real GNP and lowering the unemployment rate, the case for government fine-tuning the economy is called into question.

Policy Ineffectiveness Proposition (PIP)

If (1) a policy change is correctly *anticipated,* (2) individuals form their expectations rationally, and (3) wages and prices are flexible, then neither fiscal policy nor monetary policy is effective at meeting macroeconomic goals.

Question:

Are new classical economists saying that monetary and fiscal policies are never effective?

Answer:

No, they are saying that monetary and fiscal policies are not effective under a certain condition: When policy is correctly anticipated, people form their expectations rationally, and wages and prices are flexible.

Follow-up Question:

I know a number of people who do not anticipate policy and who do not seem to form their expectations by looking to the past, present, and future. Isn't this evidence that new classical theory is assuming things that are wrong and therefore is of little value?

Answer:

Remember, we do not judge a theory by its assumptions, but instead by the accuracy of its predictions. Certainly, all of us can find people who do not anticipate policy and who do not form their expectations rationally. But the point is whether these people are great enough in numbers to upset the prediction of the theory. It may be that enough people form their expectations rationally, and enough people anticipate policy, so that it is *as if* everyone does. New classical theory does not purport to describe reality perfectly. All theories—whether classical, Keynesian, monetarist, or new classical—are abstractions from reality.

Rational Expectations and Incorrectly Anticipated Policy

Suppose that wages and prices are flexible and people form their expectations rationally and anticipate policy—but this time they anticipate policy incorrectly. What happens?

To illustrate, consider Exhibit 16–11. The economy is in long-run equilibrium at point 1 where $Q_1 = Q_N$. The public believes the Fed will increase aggregate demand by increasing the money supply, but it incorrectly anticipates the *degree* to which aggregate demand will be increased. The public, thinking aggregate demand will increase from AD_1 to AD_2, immediately revises its anticipated price level to P_2 (the long-run equilibrium position of the AD_2 curve and the *LRAS* curve), and as a result the short-run aggregate supply curve shifts leftward from $SRAS_1$ to $SRAS_2$.

A problem arises, however, when the aggregate demand curve only shifts rightward from AD_1 to AD'_2. In short, the actual increase in aggregate demand is less than anticipated. As a result, the economy moves to point 2′; to a lower real GNP and a higher unemployment rate. From this we conclude that a policy designed to increase real GNP and lower unemployment can do just the opposite if the policy is less expansionary *than anticipated*.

EXHIBIT 16-11
The Short-Run Response to an Aggregate Demand-Increasing Policy That Is Less Expansionary Than Anticipated (in the New Classical Ratex Theory)

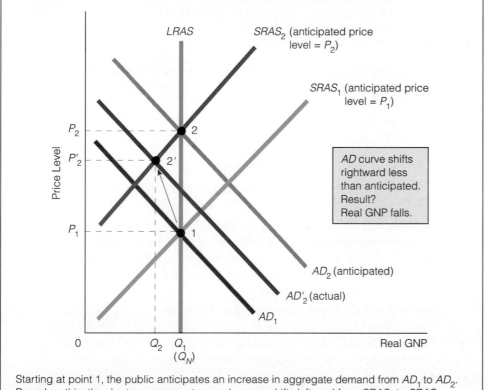

Starting at point 1, the public anticipates an increase in aggregate demand from AD_1 to AD_2. Based on this, the short-run aggregate supply curve shifts leftward from $SRAS_1$ to $SRAS_2$. It turns out, however, that the aggregate demand curve only shifts rightward to AD'_2 (less than anticipated). As a result, the economy moves to point 2′, to a lower real GNP and a higher unemployment rate.

CHAPTER 16
JOB SEARCH THEORY, PHILLIPS
CURVE ANALYSIS, AND NEW
CLASSICAL THEORY: ENTER
EXPECTATIONS

371

One Implication of Rational Expectations: If You Say You're Going to Do It, You Had Better Do It, Because If You Don't, Next Time No One Will Believe You, and That Could Cause Problems

Suppose the public sees the following scenario played out three times in three years. The federal government runs a deficit. It finances the deficit by borrowing from the public (issuing Treasury bills, notes, and bonds). The Fed conducts open market operations and buys many of the government securities. Aggregate demand increases and the price level rises. At the same time all this is going on, every elected representative says he or she will do what needs to be done to bring inflation under control. The chairman of the Fed says the Fed will soon move against inflation.

Three times elected representatives and the Fed chairman say they will move against inflation; three times they don't. This can create a situation like the one illustrated in Exhibit

16–11. Indeed, some economists believe such events go a long way toward explaining the 1981–82 recession. They maintain that the following scenario occurred: (1) President Reagan proposed, and the Congress approved, tax cuts in 1981. (2) Notwithstanding what some economists (namely, some supply-siders) were saying at the time—that the tax cuts would stimulate so much economic activity that tax revenues would increase—the public believed that tax cuts would decrease tax revenues and increase the size of the budget deficit. (3) People translated larger deficits into more government borrowing. (4) They anticipated greater money supply growth connected with larger deficits (they had experienced this before). (5) Greater

money supply growth would mean an increase in aggregate demand and the price level. (6) The Fed said it wouldn't finance the deficits (buy government bonds), but it had said this before and acted contrarily, so few people believed it this time. (7) The Fed actually did not increase the money supply as much as individuals thought it would. (8) This meant that monetary policy was not as expansionary as individuals had anticipated. (9) As a result, the economy moved to a point like 2′ in Exhibit 16–11. Real GNP fell and unemployment increased; a recession ensued. Some economists contend that the 1981–82 scenario would have been different if in the past the Fed had done what it said it was going to do.

Major Tenets of New Classical Theory

In terms of our three macroeconomic organizational categories, here is what new classical theory has to say.

The P–Q Category. In new classical theory, there is a strong tendency for the economy to always return to its natural real GNP level (Q_N). Also, when policy is (correctly) anticipated, expectations are formed rationally, and wages and prices are flexible, policy changes affect only the price level (P) and not real GNP (Q), too. For example, see Exhibit 16–10b.

The Inherently Stable–Inherently Unstable Category. Unlike Keynesians, new classical economists believe that the economy is inherently stable and that it equilibrates at natural real GNP. The economy may find itself in either a recessionary or inflationary gap, but this is only a temporary state of affairs.

The Effective–Ineffective Category. New classical economists believe that under certain conditions—namely, policy is (correctly) anticipated and people form their expectations rationally, and wages and prices are flexible—neither fiscal nor monetary policy is effective. Like classical economists and monetarists, new classical economists largely advocate laissez-faire.

Interview: Thomas Sargent

As a graduate student at Harvard, Thomas Sargent developed a discomfort with macroeconomic models that assumed individual agents respond passively to economic policy. Today, he is considered one of the pioneers of rational expectations theory. Sargent is currently at Stanford University's Hoover Institution.

Professor Sargent, what is the basic property of the rational expectations model?

The rational expectations model basically has the property that all the agents in the model are doing the best that they can do whatever their situation is. They may be in very complicated situations, where they face a lot of uncertainty and have very imperfect information, but they are basically doing the best that they can do.

Some of the critics of rational expectations theory argue against its policy implications, a major one being that short-run government stabilization policies are ineffective. Are there others, however, who criticize the essence of the theory itself, that is, the idea that expectations are formed rationally? If so, what is their major criticism and how do you respond to it?

The first thing is that the so-called "policy ineffectiveness proposition" occurred only within a very special class of models that a lot of us don't think are very interesting. The main interest in rational expectations is to figure out how various policies are effective and to take into account dynamic effects that involve some element of imperfect foresight on the part of individuals. The really tough problems, and the scientifically challenging ones, are those that get us to study exactly how government policy matters and how you can optimally plan intervention in contexts in which it does matter.

Basically, the policy ineffectiveness proposition got started like this: Robert Lucas, Neil Wallace, and I worked with some models that embodied the transmission mechanism that was in the Keynesian models of the late-1960s. That mechanism had the property that the main effects (and in some models, all the effects) of monetary and fiscal policy were intermediated through policy surprises. For example, if you take a model in which all effects of policy are intermediated through surprises, and then take away the ability of the government to manipulate surprises—which is what you automatically do when you impose rational expectations—you get policy ineffectiveness. But that was a very special class of models, and much more interesting are the models where government policy has effects because it introduces distortions of various kinds—both good ones and bad ones: models in which there are externalities, models in which taxes distort effort, models in which monetary policy distorts effort, and this is the general case. When you do that, you get the result that policy matters.

As to the second part of the question, if you look at economic theory in general, rational expectations is now the dominant equilibrium concept. Nobody uses anything else. It is used in game theory. It was somewhat controversial in the 1970s, but I don't see it as controversial now.

It has been said that in the world of rational expectations, decision makers are like chess players: They anticipate the next move. Or is it better to say that they anticipate the next two moves? In fact, is it reasonable to ask how many moves ahead rational expectations theorists assume individuals anticipate? Or does this question miss the mark as to what rational expectations is about?

No, it doesn't miss the mark at all. It is exactly right. In a rational expectations equilibrium, you're in effect assuming that agents (to the best of their abilities) go an infinite number of moves ahead.

In the *Journal of Economic Literature* in March 1982, Maddock and Carter wrote a dialogue between two imaginary graduate students discussing rational expectations. One graduate student, Bernie, says that rational expectations "suggests that people anticipate the *effects* of policy." The other graduate student, Ernie, asks, "How on earth are people supposed to anticipate the effects of policy? I just can't see it. Have they all got econometric models under the sink?" How would you answer Ernie's question?

Well, they certainly don't have econometric models under the sink. I guess the way you can think of it is that people are trying to forecast what the policies are. If you're a person who is going to get affected by the corporate tax rate, or some kind of windfall profits tax, or a change in monetary regulation, it is in your interest to follow what is going on. And if you talk to people who are greatly affected by tax law, not only do they try to forecast it, they try to influence it, and they probably have a lot more information than you could get from an econometric model. For example, they know which congressman is voting for what.

Some people say that rational expectations is revolutionary. Is it?

It is revolutionary in two ways. One is in terms of a whole host of technical issues, in terms of the way people construct and estimate macroeconomic models. There are essentially huge changes in econometric practices and huge changes in the way you set up models. It's a revolution in the sense that it requires tooling up with a different set of tools. One of the ways to think about it is to realize that Keynes talked about expectations, but he didn't have any tools to work with it. And the Keynesian models up to the late-1960s were always fudged. Theorists basically fit distributed lags and left them uninterpreted. The way rational expectations got started is that persons within that tradition were trying to figure out what those distributed lags meant.

The second way in which rational expectations is revolutionary is in the sense that the disparity between micro and macro tends to vanish when you do rational expectations. You start to build models the exact same way.

EXHIBIT 16-12
The Short-Run Response to Aggregate Demand-Increasing Policy (in the New Keynesian Ratex Theory)

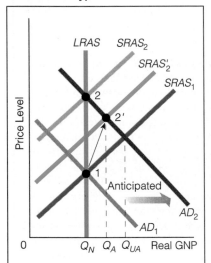

Starting at point 1, an increase in aggregate demand is anticipated. As a result, the short-run aggregate supply curve shifts leftward, but not all the way to $SRAS_2$ (as would be the case in the new classical ratex model). Instead it shifts only to $SRAS'_2$ because of some wage and price rigidities; the economy moves to point 2' (in the short run), and real GNP increases from Q_N to Q_A. If the policy had been unanticipated, real GNP would have increased from Q_N to Q_{UA}.

THE NONCLASSICAL OR NEW KEYNESIAN RATEX THEORY

We have seen that new classical theory assumes complete flexibility of wages and prices, since in the theory, an increase in the anticipated price level results in an immediate and equal rise in wages and prices, and the aggregate supply curve immediately shifts to the long-run equilibrium position.

In response to the assumption of flexible wages and prices, a few economists began to develop what has come to be known as the "nonclassical ratex theory," or the "New Keynesian ratex theory." This theory assumes that rational expectations is a reasonable characterization of how expectations are formed, but drops the assumption of complete wage and price flexibility. Economists who work with this theory argue that long-term labor contracts often prevent wages and prices from fully adjusting to changes in the anticipated price level. (Prices and wages are somewhat sticky, rigid, or inflexible.)

Consider the possible situation at the end of the first year of a three-year wage contract. Workers may realize that the anticipated price level is higher than they expected when they negotiated the contract, but will be unable to do much about it because their wages are locked in for the next two years. Price stickiness might also arise because firms often engage in fixed-price contracts with their suppliers. As we learned in Chapter 9, Keynesian economists today put forth microeconomic-based reasons why long-term labor contracts and above-market wages (efficiency wage theory) are sometimes in the best interest of both employers and employees.

To see what the theory predicts, look at Exhibit 16–12. The economy is initially in long-run equilibrium at point 1. The public anticipates an increase in aggregate demand from AD_1 to AD_2. As a result, the anticipated price level changes; because of some wage and price rigidities, however, the short-run aggregate supply curve does not shift all the way from $SRAS_1$ to $SRAS_2$, and the economy does not move from point 1 to point 2 (as in new classical theory). The short-run aggregate supply curve shifts instead to $SRAS'_2$ because some rigidities prevent complete wage and price adjustments. In the short run, the economy moves from point 1 to point 2', from Q_N to Q_A. It is interesting to note that had the policy been unanticipated, real GNP would have increased from Q_N to Q_{UA} in the short run.

Interview: Robert Solow

Robert Solow is the 1987 winner of the Nobel Prize in Economics. His major contributions have been in the field of economic growth theory. Solow is currently at the Massachusetts Institute of Technology.

In 1960, you and Paul Samuelson published a paper on the U.S. Phillips curve. What did you want your fellow economists to learn from this paper?

First, we wanted to suggest how hard it is to make inferences about causality from observed data on wage inflation and changes in unemployment. We knew that one shouldn't easily leap from a statistical relationship between the two variables to a causal relationship. We also wanted to get across that there was a price to pay in terms of inflation if there was an attempt to stimulate or expand the economy through the use of expansionary policy.

The question I often ask myself, and that other people ask me, is did we think there was a permanent trade-off between inflation and unemployment. Whereas the article contains the qualifications that work against a permanent trade-off, there is no doubt in my mind that we were very likely too optimistic about the stability of even the short-run trade-off. So, although in a court of law, so to speak, a jury would say "Yes, you said all the things you needed to say so you cannot be convicted of error," still we perhaps left a more optimistic impression of things than now seems to be justified.

What caused you to revise your degree of optimism—events or someone else's theoretical work?

It was a bit of both. In my case, it had to do more with events than the later work of Phelps and Friedman—to this day, I am not a believer in a meaningfully stable natural rate of unemployment. I think both the theory and the econometric evidence that underlie the

standard notions are flimsy. This doesn't mean that the picture we presented in 1960 is the right one. I would do it quite differently now. But I think what turned me into somewhat of a pessimist is the experience of the 1970s.

What do you think of the work of the rational expectation theorists?

I think that the notion of rational expectations is worth studying. There are places in economic and social life that are its natural habitat—like securities markets. One certainly wouldn't want to approach a study of stock or bond pricing with a mechanical theory of expectations. On the other hand, it does not seem to me that the labor market is a natural place for rational expectations to be functioning.

It is also important to keep in mind the distinction between the strong and weak versions of rational expectations. By the strong version, I mean either that expectations held by market participants are consistent with the true model of the economy, or that they are consistent with any detailed model of the economy. By the weak version, I mean that obvious hints from events will be picked up by participants. It seems to me that the weak version is much more closely related with reality than the strong version.

Why do you think rational expectationists persist in holding on to the extreme version of rational expectations in places like the labor market?

I think it is primarily because the strong version of rational expectations makes it possible to write down neat, complete theories, and weak versions are sloppy and indeterminate and less easy to deal with. And I also think that the rational expectations school prefers to sacrifice consistency with common observation in order to have a neat theory.

Is the world, to your way of thinking, a lot sloppier than these theories would suggest?

Yes, and I think any rational expectationist would agree that the world is sloppier than theories of this kind would suggest. But I would go further and say the world is sloppy enough that it would lead to outcomes that are quite different from those that a strict rational expectationist would find plausible.

Isn't this a major distinction between Keynesians and monetarists and between Keynesian and new classical economists? Keynesians always did seem to feel intuitively that the world is a lot messier than the others thought.

Well, yes, I think your description is right, and it may be for historical reasons. If you look at Keynes's own writings or his letters of the time, he placed a lot of importance on the fact that investment is a shot in the dark. The state of what he called long-term expectations was hardly probabilistic at all. It was affected by a whole host of things. So there was that historical connection.

Have you considered that economists of different schools might have different psychological inclinations? Some people I meet seem to see the world as pretty much black and white, whereas others see it as so many different shades of gray. I wonder if there is

something from one's childhood that inclines a person to believe that things are shaded or black and white when it comes to the economy.

In thinking about the people one knows—economists and others—the dichotomy you mention is visible. We all know people who can't stand ambiguity, and then there are others that don't mind it at all. And I think you could describe this as part of someone's psychological makeup. But I don't know any reason to suppose that its origins are in childhood. This could be something you learn in the course of your life.

Do you think economists' psychological makeup matters to the macroeconomics debate?

It matters in the sense that the schools people join have something to do with this. But I don't think it matters to the outcome of the debate. I am enough of an optimist to believe that no matter what my psychological reasons for believing something, if it doesn't stand up to logical analysis and fact, then I am going to lose.

What do you think has been the most promising Keynesian research development in the past decade?

I think the most promising theoretical research in macroeconomics is the line that leads to models of the economy that have more than one equilibrium. There are now several examples of this.

The usual background is that if you model the economy as having imperfect competition, then that gets you to the fact that business firms have to form expectations about what demand curves they will face in the future. And in order to do that, they normally have to form some expectations about aggregate demand in the economy. This leads to both high-level and low-level equilibria. In high-level equilibria, business firms think aggregate demand will be pretty good, and so they invest a lot and produce a lot and, consequently, aggregate demand *is* pretty good. On the other hand, if they were all pessimists, they would lay off workers and cut back investment, and they might bring on a type of low-level equilibria. It is that type of theorizing that strikes me as most promising. I hardly know whether to call it Keynesian or not, because he shared it with many others, but it is the most promising line of research for those who believe the economy is not quickly and immediately self-equilibrating.

What do you predict will be a major economic problem the United States will have to face in the mid-1990s, and how should it solve that problem?

I will guess that a main problem will be a continued slow erosion relative (not absolute) to other industrial countries—Germany, Japan, and so on. I don't think we will find this easy to deal with in terms of our own attitudes or in

terms of economic policy. What we ought to do to solve this problem is provide incentives for research and development, for a better workplace, and to save and invest.

What got you interested in economics?

I grew up in the 1930s and it was very hard not to be interested in economics. If you were a high school student in the 1930s, you were conscious of the fact that our economy was in deep trouble and no one knew what to do about it.

How would you describe how economists think?

I won't try to give you a deep answer to that question, but I believe there are two major ways of thinking economists use to approach problems. Let me describe it this way. The first thought many economists have about any question is to ask themselves how it fits into the notion of supply and demand. The first thought other economists have is to ask themselves how it fits into the notion of optimization. They observe something peculiar and ask themselves under what circumstances would it turn out to be the absolutely rational thing to do.

I am a supply-and-demand economist. When I come across something, I ask myself what is being transferred here and where does the supply come from and where does the demand come from.

CHAPTER SUMMARY

The Job Search Process

■ The economic theory of job search maintains that individuals are rational in their job search; they consider both the costs and benefits of searching for a job, and they search until the additional costs and additional benefits of the job search are equal. In practice, this means they search until they receive a wage offer that is equal to their reservation wage.

- The optimal search time is the time it takes until the wage offer (W) equals the reservation wage (R). If the optimal search time increases, the unemployment rate increases; if the optimal search time decreases, the unemployment rate decreases.

The Phillips Curve

- A. W. Phillips plotted a curve to a set of data points that exhibited an inverse relationship between wage inflation and unemployment. This curve came to be known as the Phillips curve. From the Phillips curve relationship, economists concluded that neither the combination of low inflation and low unemployment *nor* the combination of high inflation and high unemployment (stagflation) was likely.
- Economists Samuelson and Solow fit a Phillips curve to the U.S. economy. Instead of measuring wage inflation against unemployment rates (as Phillips did), they measured price inflation against unemployment rates. They found an inverse relationship between inflation and unemployment rates.
- Based on the findings of Phillips and Samuelson and Solow, economists concluded the following: (1) Stagflation, or high inflation and high unemployment, is extremely unlikely. (2) The Phillips curve presents policy makers with a menu of choices between different combinations of inflation and unemployment rates.

The Natural Rate Hypothesis

- Milton Friedman pointed out that there are two types of Phillips curves: a short-run Phillips curve and a long-run Phillips curve. The short-run Phillips curve exhibits the inflation–unemployment trade-off; the long-run Phillips curve does not. Consideration of both short-run and long-run Phillips curves opened macroeconomics to expectations theory.
- The natural rate hypothesis holds that *in the short run,* a decrease (increase) in inflation is linked to an increase (decrease) in unemployment, but that *in the long run,* the economy returns to its natural rate of unemployment. In other words, there is a trade-off between inflation and unemployment in the short run, but not in the long run.
- Originally, the natural rate hypothesis was expressed in terms of adaptive expectations. Individuals formed their inflation expectations by considering past inflation rates. Later, the natural rate hypothesis came to be expressed in terms of rational expectations, too. Rational expectations theory holds that individuals form their expected inflation rate by considering present and past inflation rates, as well as all other available and relevant information—in particular, the effects of present and future policy actions.

New Classical Theory

- Implicit in the new classical theory are two assumptions: (1) Individuals form their expectations rationally. (2) Wages and prices are completely flexible.
- In new classical theory, policy has different effects (1) when it is unanticipated and (2) when it is anticipated. For example, if the public anticipates an increase in aggregate demand, the short-run aggregate supply curve will likely shift leftward at the same time the aggregate demand curve shifts rightward. If the public does not anticipate an increase in aggregate demand (but one occurs), then the short-run aggregate supply curve will not shift leftward at the same time the aggregate

CHAPTER 16
JOB SEARCH THEORY, PHILLIPS
CURVE ANALYSIS, AND NEW
CLASSICAL THEORY: ENTER
EXPECTATIONS

■

377

demand curve shifts rightward; it will shift leftward sometime later. If policy is anticipated, expectations are formed rationally, and wages and prices are completely flexible, then an increase or decrease in aggregate demand will change only the price level but not real GNP or the unemployment rate. The new classical theory casts doubt on the belief that the short-run Phillips curve is always downward sloping. Under certain conditions, it may be vertical (as is the long-run Phillips curve).

■ If policies are anticipated, but not credible, and rational expectations is a reasonable characterization of how individuals form their expectations, then certain policies may have unintended effects. For example, if the public believes that aggregate demand will increase by more than it (actually) increases (because policy makers have not done in the past what they said they would do), then anticipated inflation will be higher than it would have been, the short-run aggregate supply curve will shift leftward by more than it would have, and the (short-run) outcome of a policy that increases aggregate demand will be lower real GNP and higher unemployment (see Exhibit 16–11).

Nonclassical or New Keynesian Ratex Theory

■ Implicit in the nonclassical or New Keynesian ratex theory are two assumptions: (1) Individuals form their expectations rationally. (2) Wages and prices are not completely flexible (in the short run).

■ If policy is anticipated, the economic effects predicted by the new classical theory and nonclassical or New Keynesian theory are not the same (in the short run). Since the nonclassical or New Keynesian ratex theory assumes that wages and prices are not completely flexible in the short run, it follows that given an anticipated change in aggregate demand, the short-run aggregate supply curve cannot immediately shift to its long-run equilibrium position. The nonclassical or New Keynesian ratex theory predicts that there is a short-run trade-off between inflation and unemployment (in the Phillips curve framework) (see Exhibit 16–12).

Key Terms and Concepts

Reservation Wage	Natural Rate Hypothesis	Policy Ineffectiveness
Phillips Curve	Ratex	Proposition (PIP)

QUESTIONS AND PROBLEMS

1. Optimal search time will change if the wage offer curve shifts, the reservation wage curve shifts, or both curves shift. Name three factors that can change each curve. In each case, specify the directional change in the curve and the effect on optimal search time. Give reasons for the factors you choose and the directional changes you specify.

2. What is a major difference between adaptive and rational expectations? Give an example.

3. It has been said that the policy ineffectiveness proposition (connected with new classical theory) does not eliminate policy makers' ability to reduce unemployment through aggregate demand-increasing policies, since they can always increase aggregate demand by more than the public expects. What might be the weak point in this argument?

4. Why does the new classical theory have the word "classical" associated with it? Also, why has it been said that the classical theory failed where the new classical theory succeeds, as the former could not explain the business cycle ("the ups and downs of the economy"), but the latter can?

5. Suppose there were a permanent downward-sloping Phillips curve that offered a menu of choices of different combinations of inflation and unemployment rates to policy makers. How do you think society would go about deciding which point on the Phillips curve it wanted to occupy?

6. Suppose a short-run trade-off between inflation and unemployment currently exists. How would you expect this trade-off to be affected by a change in technology that permits the wider dispersion of economic policy news? Explain your answer.

7. Nonclassical or New Keynesian ratex theory holds that because of such things as long-term labor contracts, wages are not completely flexible. New classical economists often respond that experience teaches labor leaders to develop and bargain for contracts that allow for wage adjustments. Do you think the new classical economists have a good point? Why?

8. What evidence can you point to that suggests individuals form their expectations adaptively? What evidence can you point to that suggests individuals form their expectations rationally?

9. Explain both the short-run and long-run movements of the natural rate hypothesis if expectations are formed adaptively.

10. Explain both the short-run and long-run movements of the natural rate hypothesis if expectations are formed rationally and policy is unanticipated.

11. "Even if some people do not form their expectations rationally, this does not necessarily mean that new classical theory is of no value." Discuss.

12. Illustrate graphically what would happen if (1) individuals form their expectations rationally, (2) prices and wages are flexible, and (3) individuals underestimate the decrease in aggregate demand.

CHAPTER 16
JOB SEARCH THEORY, PHILLIPS
CURVE ANALYSIS, AND NEW
CLASSICAL THEORY: ENTER
EXPECTATIONS

■

379

BUSINESS CYCLES: THEORIES OF ECONOMIC EXPANSION AND CONTRACTION

WHAT THIS CHAPTER IS ABOUT

This chapter is about the business cycle—recurrent swings (up and down) in real GNP, or *Q*. Essentially, we bring together much of the material that we have discussed in previous chapters, such as Keynesian, monetarist, and new classical theories; different views of the economy; expectations theory; and more.

PRELIMINARIES

■

In this section, we define some terms and introduce several issues that will shape our discussion of **business cycles.** These can be summarized in four points:

1. There are four stages of the business cycle: expansion, peak, contraction, and trough. These four stages are often summarized by the words "boom and bust." In fact, the business cycle is sometimes called the *boom-and-bust cycle.* The contractionary, or bust, part of the business cycle is formally known as **recession.**

2. To many persons, the word *cycle* connotes both a certain period of time and inevitability. For example, a person might think that business cycles are always five years long and that they naturally occur every ten years. Neither idea is correct. First, business cycles can be long and they can be short. Business cycles have ranged in length from 1 to 12 years. Second, not all economists believe that business cycles are inevitable. Although some (perhaps many) economists argue that business cycles are extremely likely to occur, they are reluctant to state that business cycles will necessarily occur. For these reasons, many economists prefer to speak, more neutrally, of business *fluctuations* rather than business *cycles.*

3. Two important issues are relevant to a discussion of business cycles. One concerns the *cause* of the business cycle. Obviously, if there is a period of boom and bust, we are prompted to ask what caused it. The other concerns the economy's *adjustment path.* For example, if real GNP drops below the natural level, we are interested in knowing (a) whether it will adjust in the direction of the natural level and (b) how long the adjustment period will last.

4. What a person views as the cause of the business cycle, and what information he holds relevant to the economy's adjustment path, will influence the types of policies he proposes as a means of smoothing out the business cycle. For example, if a person believes the business cycle is a consequence of political factors, he will most likely propose particular political reforms to solve the problem. If someone thinks that the business cycle is caused by the inherent instabilities of the private sector, he is likely to propose that government stabilization policies be implemented.

Business Cycle
Recurrent swings (up and down) in real GNP.

Recession
A decline in real GNP that lasts for two consecutive quarters (six months) or more.

BUSINESS CYCLE ORIGINS: DEMAND SIDE OR SUPPLY SIDE

■

Within the *AD–AS* framework of analysis, picture the economy at its long-run equilibrium position. This is where the three curves—*AD, SRAS,* and *LRAS*—intersect at the natural real GNP level. Within this framework, think of (1) what has to change to bring about a contraction in real GNP, and (2) what has to change to bring about an expansion in real GNP.

A Contraction in Real GNP (the Bust of the Business Cycle). A contraction in real GNP can be brought about by a change on the demand side of the economy or by a change on the supply side of the economy. On the demand side, a contraction in real GNP can be brought about by a decline in aggregate demand (Exhibit 17–1a). On the supply side, a contraction in real GNP can be brought about by a reduction in short-run aggregate supply (c) or a reduction in long-run aggregate supply (e).

An Expansion in Real GNP (the Boom of the Business Cycle). An expansion in real GNP can be brought about by a change on the demand side of the economy

EXHIBIT 17–1
Business Contractions and Expansions

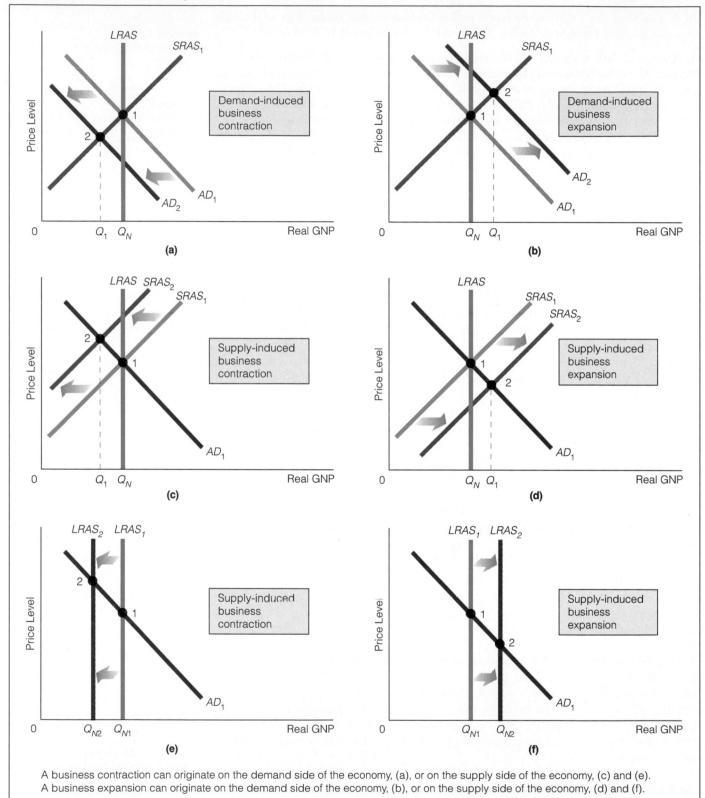

A business contraction can originate on the demand side of the economy, (a), or on the supply side of the economy, (c) and (e).
A business expansion can originate on the demand side of the economy, (b), or on the supply side of the economy, (d) and (f).

or by a change on the supply side of the economy. On the demand side, an expansion in real GNP can be brought about by an increase in aggregate demand (Exhibit 17–1b). On the supply side, an expansion in real GNP can be brought about by an increase in short-run aggregate supply (d) or an increase in long-run aggregate supply (f).

Keep Exhibit 17–1 in mind as we discuss the different business cycle theories in this chapter. Obviously, every business cycle contraction has to fit into panels (a), (c), or (e) in Exhibit 17–1, and every business cycle expansion has to fit into panels (b), (d), or (f). An entire business cycle—incorporating both the contraction and the expansion—must fit into any *two* panels in Exhibit 17–1, one chosen from the left side of the exhibit (the contraction) and the other chosen from the right side of the exhibit (the expansion). For example, a given business cycle may be explained using (a) to describe the contraction and (b) to describe the expansion. If so, this business cycle would have been totally demand induced—since both the contraction and the expansion originate on the demand side of the economy.

THREE DEMAND-INDUCED BUSINESS CYCLE THEORIES

Here we discuss three demand-induced business cycle theories: (1) the Friedman natural rate theory, (2) the new classical theory under the conditions of unanticipated and incorrectly anticipated policy, and (3) the Keynesian theory (old and new). We summarize these three theories, which have been discussed more fully in earlier chapters.

The Friedman Natural Rate Theory

In the Friedman natural rate theory, the business cycle occurs because there is a difference between individuals' expected inflation rate and the actual inflation rate. To put it differently, the business cycle is a consequence of imperfect information. Obviously, if there were perfect information, there would be no difference in the expected and actual inflation rates; people would know exactly what to expect.

A business cycle expansion in the Friedman natural rate theory is illustrated in Exhibit 17–2. Starting at point 1, the aggregate demand curve shifts rightward from AD_1 to AD_2. At first, the expected inflation rate does not increase even though the actual inflation rate is increasing. Why? Because in this theory, expectations are formed adaptively. In practical terms, workers are accepting jobs at lower real wages than they think they are accepting. The economy moves from point 1 to point 2, from Q_1 to Q_2—largely because workers are being "fooled" into accepting the lower real wages (this has prompted some economists to refer to the theory as the Friedman "fooling" theory). Later, workers learn that the inflation rate has increased, and they revise their expected inflation rate upward. The (short-run) aggregate supply curve shifts leftward and the economy moves to point 3.

Question:

If an increase in aggregate demand can cause the business cycle expansion, can a decrease in aggregate demand cause the business cycle contraction? If so, then what causes these increases and decreases in aggregate demand, and therefore the business cycle, in the Friedman natural rate theory?

EXHIBIT 17–2
A Business Cycle Expansion in the Friedman Natural Rate Theory

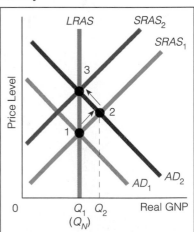

In the Friedman natural rate theory, the business cycle occurs because there is a difference between individuals' expected inflation rate and the actual inflation rate. Starting at point 1, the aggregate demand curve shifts rightward from AD_1 to AD_2. At first, the expected inflation rate does not rise to the new (higher) inflation rate. As a result, the economy moves from point 1 to point 2, from Q_1 to Q_2. Later, the expected inflation rate is revised upward and the economy moves to point 3.

Answer:

First, it is correct that an increase in aggregate demand can cause the business cycle expansion and that a decrease in aggregate demand can cause the business cycle contraction. As to what can cause these changes in aggregate demand in the Friedman natural rate theory, the answer involves the *causes* of the business cycle, which we discuss in an upcoming section. But since Friedman is a monetarist, an educated guess would be that changes in the money supply change aggregate demand.

The New Classical Theory (under the Conditions of Unanticipated Policy and Incorrectly Anticipated Policy)

When policy is unanticipated, the new classical theory generates the same results, and offers the same explanations, as the Friedman natural rate theory. In the short run, there is a change in real GNP, but in the long run, the economy returns to its natural real GNP level when the actual expected inflation rate is the same as the expected inflation rate.

In the case of incorrectly anticipated policy, the new classical theory generates a business cycle in the following way. Starting at point 1 in Exhibit 17–3, the

EXHIBIT 17–3
A Business Cycle Contraction in the New Classical Theory

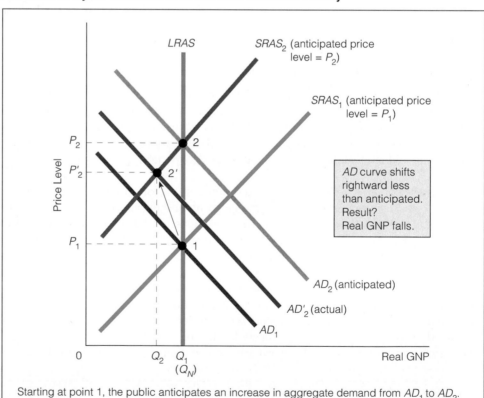

Starting at point 1, the public anticipates an increase in aggregate demand from AD_1 to AD_2. Based on this, the short-run aggregate supply curve shifts leftward from $SRAS_1$ to $SRAS_2$. It turns out, however, that the aggregate demand curve only shifts rightward to AD_2' (less than anticipated). As a result, the economy moves to point 2′, to a lower real GNP and a higher unemployment rate.

public anticipates an increase in aggregate demand from AD_1 to AD_2. Based on this, the short-run aggregate supply curve shifts leftward from $SRAS_1$ to $SRAS_2$, which is consistent with the expected long-run equilibrium price level of P_2. Later, it turns out that the aggregate demand curve only shifts rightward from AD_1 to AD_2', which is less than the public anticipated (the public anticipated incorrectly). As a result, the economy moves to point $2'$, to a lower real GNP level.

The Keynesian Theory: Old and New

In Exhibit 17–4, the economy is initially at point 1. The aggregate demand curve shifts leftward from AD_1 to AD_2. As a result, the economy moves from Q_1 to Q_2, from point 1 to point 2. At point 2, the Keynesian theory holds, the economy may get *stuck*. This is based on the key assumption of inflexible wage rates in the downward direction. Earlier (old) versions of Keynesian theory were criticized for arbitrarily assuming that wage rates were inflexible downward or not thoroughly explaining why wage rates were inflexible. Some of the later (new) versions of Keynesian theory made up for this deficiency by focusing on, among other things, long-term contracts and efficiency reasons for firms paying higher than market wages.

The argument (see Chapter 9) is as follows. Long-term labor contracts are often advantageous to both employers and workers. The benefits firms may perceive from long-term contracts include fewer labor negotiations and the decreased likelihood of worker strikes. The benefits workers may perceive from long-term contracts include fewer strikes and an added sense of security.

So, in many instances, the benefits of long-term contracts outweigh the costs, and firms and workers enter into long-term contracts for mutually advantageous

EXHIBIT 17–4
A Business Cycle Contraction in the Keynesian Theory

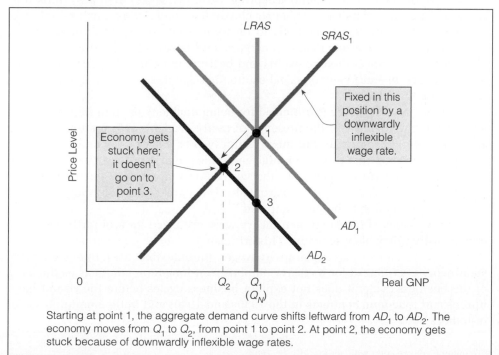

Starting at point 1, the aggregate demand curve shifts leftward from AD_1 to AD_2. The economy moves from Q_1 to Q_2, from point 1 to point 2. At point 2, the economy gets stuck because of downwardly inflexible wage rates.

reasons. When they do, (nominal) wage rates are locked in for the period of the contract, and therefore cannot adjust downward to market-clearing levels with a fall in aggregate demand. The result is that the economy may get stuck at point 2 in Exhibit 17–4 for a long time, and there may be high levels of unemployment lasting for many years. The theory, according to Keynesians, explains the long-run levels of unemployment characteristic of some business cycles.

Similarly, economists who work with efficiency wage models also believe that there are (other) solid microeconomic reasons for inflexible wages. Economist George Akerlof argues that firms sometimes find it in their best interest to pay wage rates above market-clearing levels. According to the *efficiency wage models,* labor productivity depends on the wage rate the firm pays employees. A cut in wages can cause labor productivity to decline, which, in turn, raises the firm's costs. By paying a wage higher than the market level, firms provide an incentive to workers to be productive and to minimize **shirking,** among other things. If shirking declines, so do the monitoring (management) costs of the firm.

Many Keynesian economists today believe that although the long-term contract and efficiency wage theories are fairly new, they have already provided a solid microeconomic explanation for inflexible wages and thus the characteristics of continuing unemployment problems in some economies.

Efficiency Wage Models
These models hold that it is sometimes in the best interest of firms to pay their employees higher than equilibrium wage rates.

Shirking
Behavior descriptive of a person who is putting forth less than the agreed-to effort when doing a job.

Question:

Assuming that every theory has its critics, how have economists criticized the Friedman natural rate theory, the new classical theory (under the conditions of unanticipated and incorrectly anticipated policy), and the Keynesian theory?

Answer:

The Friedman natural rate theory is criticized on the ground that it assumes workers will continually be fooled into accepting lower real wages than they think they are accepting. New classical economists charge that the Friedman natural rate theory does not allow for expectations to be formed rationally. They argue that if workers often see aggregate demand increase, and later notice the price level rise, they will soon connect the two events and begin to anticipate the latter when the former occurs. In short, new classical economists say it is not rational for workers to continue to be fooled.

The new classical theory is criticized for being unable to explain *long-term* high levels of unemployment in the presence of easily available information on prices and a key variable such as the money supply. For example, economist George Akerlof has argued that to say the high unemployment rate Great Britain experienced during the 10-year period in the late 1970s and early 1980s "is due to an unanticipated shock is simply unreasonable. Ten years is much too long a period of time for something to be unanticipated."[1]

Earlier versions of the Keynesian theory were criticized for arbitrarily assuming downwardly inflexible wage rates. This criticism cannot be made of later versions, since these versions try to explain why wages are inflexible. Still, the new Keynesian theory is criticized for its heavy emphasis on long-term contracts as the basis of the business cycle; it does not explain business cycles before the rise of labor unions and long-term contracts in the 1930s and 1940s and in the nonunion sector of today's economy.

[1]Telephone conversation with author, July 12, 1988.

Wages, Prices, and Business Cycles

In the Friedman natural rate theory and in the new classical theory, wages and prices are implicitly assumed to be flexible—the economy does not get stuck in a recessionary gap, and it always returns to the natural real GNP level. In the Keynesian theory, wages and prices are assumed to be inflexible.

Why not settle at least part of the debate among the three demand-induced theories of the business cycle by finding out whether wages and prices are flexible or not? There is a problem. To illustrate, clearly, some wages and prices are not instantly flexible: They do not rise immediately after an increase in demand, and they do not fall immediately after a decrease in demand. First, a decrease in aggregate demand is not instantly noticed by firms in the economy. Second, there may be some solid economic reasons why firms would want to keep prices constant over some period of time.

Consider a restaurant owner who has just finished printing new menus and posting new prices. If demand rises the week after the new menu is on the tables, it is unlikely the restaurant owner will immediately throw the new menus out and put newer ones in their place. There is a certain cost to having new menus printed. Also, the restaurant owner might reason that her customers will get angry at seeing new, higher prices posted in just one week's time. So, there is little doubt that some prices are somewhat inflexible in the real world. (The prices of financial securities are not; they can change by the minute.)

The real questions economists want answers to are (1) how many prices are inflexible, (2) how long are they inflexible, and (3) even if there are inflexible prices in the economy, is there any loss in predictive power from assuming that the economy works *as if* all prices are flexible.

Once again, we see theory at odds with reality. For example, new classical theory, which assumes flexible wages and prices, is at odds with a world in which some wages and prices are inflexible. But the real question we have to continue to ask is, Does it matter? Does the real world perform *as if* the simplified and abstract theory accurately describes its workings?

Our discussion here should not be read as an endorsement of any one business cycle theory. We simply want to bring out a key consideration in the theories—that is, the degree of flexibility in wages and prices, which in turn reflects on the inherent stability properties of an economy—and to once again remind us that a theory, however abstract, may still capture the essence of the way an economy works.

Forecasting Business Cycles

Think of yourself when you have the flu. There are usually three periods in the illness: (1) when you are coming down with the flu; (2) when you have the flu; and (3) when you are getting over the flu (but do not yet feel your old self). In each period, there is an indicator of what is happening.

In the first period, when you are coming down with the flu, you feel a little sluggish and tired. We might call this a *leading indicator* of the flu, in that it precedes the flu; it lets you know what's coming. In the period when you have the flu, you feel achy and you might have a slight fever. We shall call this a *coincident indicator* of the flu, in that it coincides with having the flu. Finally, in the period when you are getting over the flu, your temperature returns to normal and you are slightly more alert but you don't have all your energy back. We shall call this a *lagging indicator* of the flu. Thus, we have established a few indicators of your health and sickness.

Similarly, economists have devised a few indicators of the health and sickness of the economy. These indicators—called *leading, coincident,* and *lagging* indicators—are purported to do what their names suggest: *lead* economic upturns or downturns, *coincide* with economic upturns or downturns, and *lag* economic upturns or downturns. We would expect a leading indicator to rise before a boom and fall before a bust; we would expect a coincident indicator to reach its high (low) point coincident with a boom (bust); and finally, we would expect a lagging indicator to reach its high (low) point sometime after a boom (bust). The leading economic indicators are of particular interest to economists and business managers, since individuals often want to know what's coming.

An often-cited statistic is the *index of leading economic indicators*—composed of such factors as new orders for consumer goods, contracts for orders and new plant and equipment, and so on. No matter what it does—go up, go down, or stay the same—it is announced in the news media much the same way as the Dow Jones Industrial Average (DJIA) of stock prices. A decrease in the index portends a rocky economic road ahead; an increase, smoother sailing and generally good times.

How reliable is the index when it comes to predicting economic upturns and downturns? It is fairly reliable, but far from perfect. Many times it has dropped a few months before an economic downturn (pretty good), a few times it has dropped a whole year before an economic downturn (not so good), and a few times it has dropped and no economic downturn has materialized (bad). Despite the mixed bag of results, the index is still widely used.

Question:

Would it be correct to conclude from economists' less-than-perfect record of predicting and forecasting major economic movements that economics is not a science?

Answer:

We need to make two points. First, it would be incorrect to conclude from economists' prediction record that economics is not a science. Is physics, chemistry, or biology any less a science because the record of physicists, chemists, or biologists is not perfect when it comes to prediction?

Second, prediction and forecasting is not the be-all and end-all of a science. Sometimes, what we learn by scientifically approaching economic problems or issues is that we cannot predict perfectly.

In other words, there is a difference between approaching the study of the world in a scientific manner and being able to predict perfectly. *Sometimes, no matter how scientific one is, perfect prediction still remains beyond one's reach.*

CAUSES OF THE BUSINESS CYCLE

In the three theories discussed previously, a business cycle contraction or expansion is caused by a shift leftward or rightward, respectively, in the aggregate demand curve. But this leaves unanswered the question, What causes the aggregate demand curve to shift? In this section, we present a few of the answers economists have given to this question.

Money Supply Changes: Accelerators and Brakes

Many of the economists who endorse the Friedman natural rate theory are monetarists. We might guess from this that they would focus on the money supply when explaining the business cycle.

Monetarist empirical work on business cycles illustrates that, typically, money supply growth drops before economic contractions and rises before economic expansions. For most monetarists, severe contractions are caused by a large drop in either the absolute money supply or money supply growth rates. In everyday language, they say the Fed "slammed the monetary brakes on too hard."

On the other hand, major economic upturns or booms are caused by a large rise in the absolute money supply or money supply growth rates. In everyday terms, monetarists say the Fed "put the monetary accelerator to the floor." It is the movement from "hard on the monetary accelerator" to "hard on the monetary brakes" that most monetarists see as the direct cause of business cycles.

Question:

What is the monetarist solution to the business cycle?

Answer:

Monetarists are nonactivists when it comes to discretionary monetary policy (see Chapter 15). They advocate a monetary rule. In short, they argue that the money supply should grow by a fixed annual rate that is consistent with the average annual growth rate in real GNP and (in some versions of the monetary rule) adjusted for changes in velocity.

Business Investment, Residential Construction, and Government Spending

Many Keynesians often point to changes in business investment, residential construction, or government spending as the cause of the business cycle. For example, a business cycle contraction might result from a decrease in business investment or government spending that lowers aggregate demand and imposes a net loss of sales on business firms. The major consequence of a fall in aggregate demand will come in the form of reduced output and increased unemployment. A decline in output is translated into a fall in income, and since consumption is a function of income, consumption will fall, which leads to an even lower level of aggregate demand. The original decrease in business investment or government spending snowballs into lower levels of consumption that generate a multiple (remember the multiplier from Chapter 9) decrease in total output.

The Political Business Cycle

Some economists theorize that the underlying motivation of the business cycle is political. The theory of the "political business cycle" has different hypotheses, each of which focuses on different political factors.

One hypothesis is that the political business cycle is largely prompted at the congressional level, where elected representatives are motivated to enact economic expansionary fiscal measures, such as tax cuts or spending hikes, shortly before they go up for reelection. Another is that the Fed is a political–monetary institution that responds to political pressures exerted on it, as well as to bureaucratic and self-preserving proclivities internal to itself, and this goes a long way to explain the ups and downs of the economy. A third hypothesis is that the business cycle is largely prompted by presidential action. To illustrate, we sketch a possible scenario in terms of the Phillips curve framework developed in the last chapter.

The Phillips Curve as Political Toy.   Some economists have argued that if there is a short-run trade-off between inflation and unemployment, it can be exploited for political gain. Of course, saying that a short-run inflation–unemployment trade-off *can be* exploited for political gain does not mean it *will be* exploited. We say more about this later. For now, consider Exhibit 17–5.

Suppose Edward Sumner is elected president of the United States in the year 2000. A few months after the election, the economy is at point 1 experiencing a (relatively) high inflation rate. No one blames President Sumner for the high inflation rate since he only recently took office. However, the president wants to get the inflation rate down because he is already thinking about his reelection. He proposes higher taxes and a cut in government spending (contractionary fiscal policy). His economic advisers tell him this will reduce aggregate demand and lower the inflation rate. The great majority of his proposals are accepted by the Congress since he is still in the "honeymoon" period (almost all presidents enjoy a "honeymoon" at the beginning of their terms when Congress passes their programs without much opposition). In addition, President Sumner starts putting both

EXHIBIT 17–5
Can Politicians Use the Inflation–Unemployment Trade-Off to Get Votes?

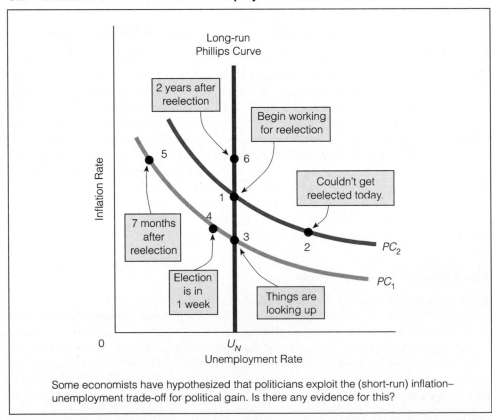

Some economists have hypothesized that politicians exploit the (short-run) inflation–unemployment trade-off for political gain. Is there any evidence for this?

public and private pressure on the Fed to reduce the money supply. To a large degree, the Fed complies.

As a result of these policies to reduce aggregate demand, the economy moves to point 2. The inflation rate falls, but at the (short-run) price of a huge increase in the unemployment rate. Newspaper editors all over the country begin saying that President Sumner's economic policies put people out of work. The public opinion polls show that President Sumner couldn't win reelection today if his life depended on it. For the most part, the president stays in the White House and says very little. He isn't too worried because the election is still a long time off, and his economic advisers assure him that things will soon be getting better. Sure enough, the economy begins to move toward its natural rate of unemployment as people revise their inflation expectations downward; that is, eventually, the economy moves to point 3. Inflation has been lowered considerably (relative to what it was at point 1), and in recent months the unemployment rate has fallen. President Sumner's standing rises in the polls. The same newspaper editors who were criticizing the president a few months ago are now praising him. The president and his advisers remind themselves that the public has a short memory.

Time passes, and it looks as if President Sumner will have to run against an extremely popular candidate from the other political party. The president decides to use the economy to help his reelection efforts. Starting at point 3, he proposes a cut in taxes (politically popular) and an increase in government spending (politically popular with groups receiving government benefits); he also urges the Fed to increase the money supply. The Congress doesn't cut taxes, but it does increase government spending, and the Fed does increase the money supply. As election day approaches, the economy moves toward point 4. One week before the election, unemployment is lower than it was at point 3, the inflation rate is slightly higher (but still not so much higher as to cause too much concern), and the economy appears to be strong and growing. President Sumner's campaign stresses that he has brought down both inflation and unemployment from the levels they were at when he took office (compare points 1 and 4). He moves up in the polls. On election day, President Sumner carries 42 of the 50 states and receives 61 percent of the popular vote.

The expansionary economic policies are still bubbling through the economy after the reelection; after seven months, the economy is at point 5. Two years after the reelection, the economy is at point 6—with a higher inflation rate and the same unemployment rate as when President Sumner first moved into the White House.

Is there a *political business cycle?* Might the ups and downs in the economy be largely the consequence of politicians trying to arrange the inflation and unemployment rates in a politically popular configuration before election day?[2] There are a number of points to consider. First, even if a president, or other elected representatives, wanted to exploit the short-run Phillips curve trade-off, there is no guarantee that it could be done. The economy can be pushed and shoved in different directions, but it doesn't always move exactly where elected representatives want it to move. In our story of President Sumner, the economy might have been at point 5 (with high inflation) instead of at point 4 (with low inflation) one week before the election if the *lags* in the economy had been shorter. What would that have done to the president's reelection prospects?

[2]On January 14, 1990, President Bush appointed two new members of the Board of Governors of the Federal Reserve System. Both members were said to be in favor of lower interest rates (brought about through expansionary monetary policy). Some speculated that Bush appointed these two members because of their views on lowering interest rates: With an impending economic recession and Bush facing reelection at the end of 1991, an expansionary monetary policy was the political medicine that Bush needed to increase the probability of a successful presidential campaign.

■

According to some, a business cycle contraction can be brought about by a major supply-side change that reduces the capacity of the economy to produce.

∎

Second, there is no guarantee that the Congress and the Fed will do what the president wants them to do.

Third, although we have seen instances of presidents pushing for expansionary economic policies shortly before an election (a notable example is Richard Nixon in 1971–72),[3] there are also instances where presidents have not—even when high levels of unemployment existed and, one would think, their political careers were on the line.

Finally, new classical economists argue that under certain conditions there is no short-run trade-off between inflation and unemployment to exploit. Politicians can't exploit a trade-off between inflation and unemployment that largely doesn't exist.

Question:

Many people believe that government is trying its best to smooth out the business cycle and to achieve stable prices and low unemployment. This is, after all, what our elected representatives say they are trying to do. However, the economists who believe in the political business cycle theory imply that elected representatives are not trying to do what they say they are trying to do. The implication is that the economy is largely a toy to be pulled this way and that for political purposes. This is a serious charge. Is the economics profession agreed that this is happening?

Answer:

No, the economics profession is not agreed on this, although there are economists who believe the business cycle is largely politically induced. The research in this area continues.

We can say that whereas the political business cycle theory, like any other business cycle theory, may not explain all business cycles, it may explain some. For example, some presidents may be more likely than others to try to use the economy for political ends and thus prompt a politically induced business cycle.

A SUPPLY-INDUCED BUSINESS CYCLE THEORY

∎

Business cycles may originate on the supply side as well as the demand side of the economy. One particular supply-induced business cycle theory that has generated research and controversy in recent years is the **real business cycle theory.**

The Real Business Cycle

Real Business Cycle Theory
The theory that business cycle contractions are generally brought about by aggregate supply changes that reduce the economy's capacity to produce.

Real business cycle theorists argue that a business cycle contraction can be brought about by a major supply-side change that reduces the capacity of the economy to produce. The illustration of one variant of the real business cycle in Exhibit 17–6 helps explain the argument that business cycles that *appear* to originate in aggregate demand changes may, in fact, be prompted by aggregate supply changes.

We start with an adverse supply shock that reduces the capacity of the economy to produce. (We give an example in the next section.) This is represented by a shift inward in the production possibilities frontier of the economy, or a leftward

---

[3]Richard Nixon was quite aware that the state of the economy can affect a candidate's bid for the presidency. In his memoirs, Nixon blamed his loss to John Kennedy in 1960 on the fact that President Eisenhower didn't push to reduce unemployment at the end of his term (when Nixon was his vice president).

EXHIBIT 17–6
Real Business Cycle Theory

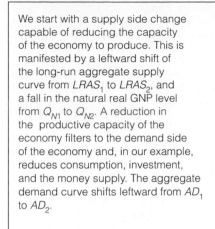

We start with a supply side change capable of reducing the capacity of the economy to produce. This is manifested by a leftward shift of the long-run aggregate supply curve from $LRAS_1$ to $LRAS_2$, and a fall in the natural real GNP level from Q_{N1} to Q_{N2}. A reduction in the productive capacity of the economy filters to the demand side of the economy and, in our example, reduces consumption, investment, and the money supply. The aggregate demand curve shifts leftward from AD_1 to AD_2.

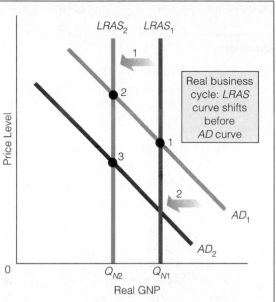

shift in the long-run aggregate supply curve from $LRAS_1$ to $LRAS_2$, which moves the economy from point 1 to 2. As we showed in Chapter 16, a leftward shift in the long-run aggregate supply curve means that the natural real GNP level has fallen.

As a result of the leftward shift in the $LRAS$ curve, real GNP declines, which in this example is coincident with firms reducing their demand for labor and scaling back employment. Due to the lower demand for labor (which puts downward pressure on money wages) and the higher price level, real wages fall.

As real wages fall, workers choose to work less, and unemployed persons choose to extend the length of their job search. Due to less work and lower real wages, workers have less income. Lower incomes soon lead workers to reduce consumption.

Because consumption has fallen, or because businesses have become pessimistic (prompted by the decline in the productive potential of the economy), or both, businesses have less reason to invest. As a result, firms borrow less from banks, the volume of outstanding loans falls, and therefore the money supply falls. A decrease in the money supply causes the aggregate demand curve to shift leftward, from AD_1 to AD_2 in Exhibit 17–6, and the economy moves to point 3.

Real business cycle theorists sometimes point out how easy it is to confuse a demand-induced business cycle with a supply-induced business cycle. In our example, both the aggregate supply *and* the aggregate demand side of the economy change, although the aggregate supply side changes first. However, if the change in aggregate supply is overlooked, and only the changes in aggregate demand are observed (or, specifically, a change in one of the variables that can change aggregate demand, such as the money supply), then the business cycle will appear to be demand induced. In terms of Exhibit 17–6, the leftward shift in the $LRAS$ curve would be overlooked, but the leftward shift in the AD curve would be observed, giving the impression that the contraction is demand induced.

If real business cycle theorists are correct, the cause–effect analysis of the business cycle would be turned upside down. To take but one example, monetary changes may be a *result* of the business cycle, not its *cause*.

Question:

Why can't it be argued that the fall in the money supply caused the business cycle contraction illustrated in Exhibit 17–6? After all, didn't the fall in the money supply cause the aggregate demand curve to shift leftward?

Answer:

For the fall in the money supply to have caused the business cycle, it must have caused real GNP to decline. In Exhibit 17–6, this is not the case. In the exhibit, the business cycle contraction—evidenced by the fall in real GNP from Q_{N1} to Q_{N2}—is the result of a shift leftward in the long-run aggregate supply curve from $LRAS_1$ to $LRAS_2$. In short, because of this change in the $LRAS$ curve, the economy moved from point 1 to 2. Afterward, the aggregate demand curve shifted leftward from AD_1 to AD_2, but this shift did not decrease real GNP (it had already decreased). Instead, the shift in the AD curve only lowered the price level. This is why real business cycle theorists say that the money supply change is a *result* of the business cycle. In their view, the money supply responds to the real (supply-side) forces at work in the economy.

The Middle East, the *LRAS* Curve, College Graduates, and You

On August 2, 1990, Saddam Hussein's Iraqi forces moved into Kuwait and, some say, threatened the free flow of oil to the western world. Some western authorities argued that if Hussein, a despot, got hold of Kuwait's oil, he would then turn his attention to Saudi Arabia's oil fields. If Hussein were successful in his move against Saudi Arabia, he would control a sizable percentage of the world's oil and be able to raise the price of it by reducing its supply on the world market. Perhaps for this reason, among others, the United Nations ordered Hussein to withdraw his troops from Kuwait. President Bush did the same. January 15, 1990, at midnight, was set as the deadline date. The message to Hussein was, Get out of Kuwait or else!

Let's put the politics and national defense issues aside for a minute, and consider the economics of the situation. If western authorities were right about Hussein's intent, what effect would this have on the U.S. economy if Hussein's intent were realized? Business cycle theory gives us the answer.

Reducing the world's supply of oil is an adverse supply shock. With less oil, an important resource in the production process, the productive capability of the U.S. economy would decline (perhaps because the high price of oil would make it too costly to use certain types of machinery). The *LRAS* curve in the United States would shift leftward, as in Exhibit 17–6. Consequently, real GNP would fall and the unemployment rate would rise—the U.S. economy would have contracted.

What might this mean to current college graduates? With an economic recession underway, their chances of locating suitable employment would be diminished. In short, a despot, thousands of miles away, could affect their standard of living. The lesson? Political intrigue, military adventures, and ambitious designs for territorial and economic expansion on the opposite side of the globe can flow through economic channels—to you.

Interview: Charles Plosser

Charles Plosser is one of the major developers, and proponents, of real business cycle theory. Plosser is currently at the University of Rochester.

What is the essence of the real business cycle theory?

Modern real business cycle theory is comprised of two key elements. First, the models are equilibrium models. Second, and perhaps more distinctive, is that the models stress the importance of real rather than nominal shocks to the economic system as the primary source of impulses to the business cycle.

Would you give a few examples of how a real business cycle could get started? Is there evidence that real business cycles exist?

A real business cycle can be initiated in any number of ways. The formal models sometimes talk in terms of productivity or technological shocks which could include natural disasters. More generally, we can think of any sort of real disturbance or collection of disturbances that set off a business cycle. Some of these may be natural or unavoidable, others may be the result of specific policies. For example, the Arab oil embargo and associated rapid rise in oil prices in the mid-70s is an excellent example. More recently, the Gulf War and the resulting fall in consumer confidence combined with a brief spurt in oil prices could also be called an impulse to a real business cycle. Policy shocks can also be important. For example, a large temporary increase in income taxes and the elimination of the

investment tax credit in 1968 could be important real impulses to the mild recession of 1969–70.

What are the policy implications of real business cycle theory?

A key feature of most real business cycle models is that they are equilibrium models and do not stress the role of market failures or externalities in generating or propagating the business cycle. As a result, the role for stabilization policy is nil. Nevertheless, changes in policy (e.g. tax and regulatory policy) can be a source of real disturbances and therefore contribute to the variability of the economy.

What do you predict will be a major economic problem the United States will have to face in the mid-1990s and how should it solve that problem?

That's a tough question and I'm not sure I have a comparative advantage in answering it. Nevertheless, I will speculate that world trade will continue to be

a major economic issue through the 1990s. In some ways, this is surprising because most economists agree that free trade is superior to managed trade or protectionist policies. Yet, most public discussions perpetuate the idea that trade is a zero sum game. Economists must continue to explain why this is a false premise that runs counter to the very essence of what makes market economies so successful.

What do you think has been the most promising research development in economics in the past decade?

In the area of macroeconomics, I think that research on real business cycles has been a very important development. It has stimulated useful discussion both pro and con and challenged the conventional wisdom. As a result, it has changed the terms of debate and dramatically influenced the way economists think about economic fluctuations.

What got you interested in economics?

I was an engineer as an undergraduate with little knowledge of economics. I went to the University of Chicago Graduate School of Business to get an MBA and there became fascinated with economics. I was impressed with the seriousness with which economics was viewed as a way of organizing one's thoughts about the world to address interesting questions and problems. After working for a couple of years, I returned to the university to get my Ph.D.

Supply-and-demand theorizing is a major part of the way economists think— both on the micro- and macroeconomic level. Economists are quick to take events like the Iraqi invasion of Kuwait and see if and how they fit into a supply and demand framework.

THINKING LIKE AN ECONOMIST

The Friedman Natural Rate Theory, the New Classical Theory under Specific Conditions, and the Keynesian Theory

■ In the Friedman natural rate theory, the business cycle is a consequence of the difference between individuals' expected inflation rate and the actual inflation rate. To put it differently, the business cycle is a consequence of imperfect information. Sometimes, the Friedman natural rate theory is called the "fooling" theory, because it views the business cycle expansion (contraction) as the result of workers being fooled into thinking their real wages are higher (lower) than, in fact, they are.

■ The new classical theory explains the business cycle under conditions of unanticipated policy (in the same way the Friedman natural rate theory does) and incorrectly anticipated policy.

■ In the Keynesian theory, a decrease in aggregate demand can bring on a business cycle contraction. In both the earlier (old) and later (new) versions of the theory, wage rates are assumed to be downwardly inflexible. Critics charge that this assumption was arbitrarily made in the earlier version. In later versions, inflexible wage rates are said to be a consequence of voluntary long-term contracts and efficiency considerations.

Causes of the Business Cycle

■ Many causes of the business cycle have been suggested. Changes in aggregate demand can generate the business cycle, but this raises another question: What causes aggregate demand to change? Many monetarists hold that sharp changes in the money supply lead to sharp changes in aggregate demand and to the business cycle. Keynesians tend to stress changes in factors such as business investment, residential construction, and government spending. Some economists hold that the business cycle is largely the consequence of political factors, usually those directed at reelection. Real business cycle theorists generally emphasize aggregate supply changes as the cause of business cycles.

Real Business Cycle Theory

■ Real business cycles originate on the supply side of the economy. A real business contraction might follow this pattern: (1) An adverse supply shock reduces the economy's ability to produce. (2) The *LRAS* curve shifts leftward. (3) As a result, real GNP declines and the price level rises. (4) The number of persons employed falls, as do real wages, owing to a decrease in the demand for labor, which lowers money wages, and a higher price level. (5) Incomes decline. (6) Consumption and investment decline. (7) The volume of outstanding loans declines. (8) The money supply falls. (9) The *AD* curve shifts leftward.

Key Terms and Concepts

Business Cycle	Efficiency Wage Model	Real Business Cycle Theory
Recession		

1. Each of the following pertains to a theory or cause of the business cycle discussed in this chapter. Identify the cause or theory: (a) slamming on the monetary brakes too hard; (b) a change in real GNP when policy is incorrectly anticipated; (c) votes; (d) changes in natural real GNP; (e) investment spending sharply declines; (f) adverse supply shock; (g) individuals' expected inflation rate does not equal the actual inflation rate.

2. Which theory of the business cycle might justifiably be called a disequilibrium theory? Why?

3. How might the explanations of the business cycle of a monetarist and a real business cycle theorist differ?

4. How does the issue of wages and prices figure into business cycle theories?

5. Explain why wage rates may be inflexible.

6. Is the political business cycle theory a demand-induced or supply-induced theory? Explain your answer.

7. What is the difference in both the short run and the long run between the Friedman natural rate theory and the new classical theory under the condition of unanticipated policy?

8. Since some wages and prices in the economy are inflexible, the Keynesian theory, which assumes inflexible wages and prices, must be correct. Discuss.

9. When might adaptive expectations and rational expectations yield the same results?

10. Since it seems unreasonable to assume that workers are consistently fooled, the Friedman natural rate theory must be incorrect. Discuss.

18

BUDGET DEFICITS
AND THE NATIONAL DEBT

WHAT THIS CHAPTER IS ABOUT

Both the federal budget deficit and the national debt have received much public attention in the past decade, and it is likely this will continue in the immediate years to come. We discuss both the deficit and the debt in this chapter.

DEFICITS AND DEBT

■

A **budget deficit** occurs when government expenditures outstrip tax receipts during any single year; the **national debt,** which is sometimes called the federal or public debt, is the total sum of what the federal government owes its creditors. The debt at a given time is the sum of all past budget deficits minus repayments. The debt is a **stock** variable, the deficit is a **flow** variable. Think of the debt as the water in a bathtub, and the deficit as the water that flows out of the faucet into the tub. The more water that flows out of the faucet (the larger the deficits), the more water in the tub (the larger the debt). Exhibit 18–1 shows the deficit, deficit/GNP ratio, the debt, and debt/GNP ratio for the period 1980–90.

Who Bears the Burden of the Debt?

Who bears the burden of the debt? Or, to put it differently, who bears the burden of public spending financed by borrowing from the public? There are two main schools of thought here. One argues that the current generation bears the burden of the debt. The other argues that the future generation bears the burden of the debt.

One Answer: The Current Generation Bears the Burden of the Debt

According to this view, public borrowing only imposes a burden on the current generation. To illustrate, suppose government increases its spending on national defense, and finances the spending by borrowing the funds. Because more resources are devoted to building planes, ships, and tanks, fewer resources are available to produce television sets, radios, and cars. Some economists argue that the current generation must give up private goods (television sets and the like) to pay for the increased national defense.

But what happens when the bonds issued in the current year come due, say, 30 years later? Don't future taxpayers have to pay them off? The economist Abba Lerner answered yes, but added that as long as the debt is domestically held (only

Budget Deficit
Occurs when government expenditures outstrip tax receipts.

National Debt
The total sum of what the federal government owes its creditors.

Stock
A variable that is measured at one point in time.

Flow
A variable that is measured over a period of time. Flow variables are measured in terms of units per time period.

EXHIBIT 18-1
Deficits and Debt
Here we show the deficit, deficit/GNP ratio, the debt, and debt/GNP ratio for the period 1980–90.

Year	Budget Deficit ($ billions)	Deficit as a Percentage of GNP	National Debt ($ billions)	Debt as a Percentage of GNP
1980	61.3	2.24	709.3	25.96
1981	63.8	2.09	784.8	25.68
1982	145.9	4.60	919.2	29.03
1983	176.0	5.16	1,131.0	33.20
1984	169.6	4.49	1,300.0	34.46
1985	196.9	4.90	1,499.4	37.34
1986	206.9	4.88	1,736.2	41.02
1987	158.2	3.50	1,888.1	41.81
1988	141.7	2.90	2,050.3	42.06
1989	134.3	2.58	2,190.3	42.11
1990	161.3	2.96	2,410.4	44.12

SOURCE: Council of Economic Advisers, *Economic Report of the President, 1991* (Washington, D.C.: U.S. Government Printing Office, 1991).

Americans hold the debt), American taxpayers will be making payments to American bondholders. And if we lump both taxpayers and bondholders together, and realize that together they make up the future generation, then we can say that the future generation doesn't pay the debt. There is simply a *transfer* of funds from one part of the future generation, taxpayers, to another part of the future generation, bondholders. This is the *we owe it to ourselves* argument. According to this view, the future generation, as a whole, sacrifices nothing for the increased government expenditures in an earlier period.[1]

Question:

Is the entire national debt held by Americans?

Answer:

No, it isn't. In the past 10 years, foreigners have held approximately 15–20 percent of the national debt.

Follow-up Question:

If the entire debt is not held exclusively by Americans, then won't future taxpaying Americans have to pay off some of the debt to foreigners? If so, what would be the response of the economists who believe that only the current generation bears the burden of the debt?

Answer:

They'd say that to the degree that the national debt is held by foreigners, the future American generation (specifically, future American taxpayers) does not completely escape the burden of the debt.

Another Answer: The Future Generation Bears the Burden of the Debt

Economist James Buchanan has argued that although resources are drawn from the private sector when debt-financed public expenditures are made, the people who give up these resources do not pay for, or bear the burden of, the public expenditures secured. To illustrate, suppose again that the government issues debt to pay for more national defense. Some people buy the government bonds—these are current bondholders. As a result of this voluntary exchange, resources shift from the private to the public sector. Society ends up with more planes, ships, and tanks and fewer television sets and the like. So far, the debt situation is the same as described earlier.

Have the bondholders paid for the weapons systems? Buchanan would say no. What the bondholders have done, he argues, is entered into a voluntary trade; they have voluntarily decided to consume a little less today (by buying bonds they have less income to devote to consumption) and to consume a little more when their

[1]In our discussion, we assumed that the current generation gives up consumer goods (television sets and the like) and not capital goods. If it gives up capital goods, some economists within this general school of thought would argue that the capital stock passed on to future generations is smaller because of the debt-financed public expenditures, and therefore the future generation bears the burden of the debt in the form of a reduced capital stock.

bonds are paid off (since they will receive the principal plus interest, they can consume more over their lifetimes than if they had not purchased the bonds). What bondholders have paid for by sacrificing current private consumption is more future private consumption; they have not paid for more weapons systems. Buchanan argues that the persons who pay for the weapons systems are the future taxpayers, who must retire the debt when it comes due.

In summary, Buchanan's argument works like this: The government in year 1 says, "Who among you want to buy our government bonds?" Some people voluntarily raise their hands. What they are buying and "paying for" is the opportunity to increase their private consumption in the future over and above what it would have been had they not purchased the bonds. When the future comes, say, year 30, and the bonds need to be paid off, the government doesn't say, "Who among you want to pay your taxes so that the debt can be paid off?" Instead, it simply takes the funds from taxpayers—persons who back in year 1 were *future taxpayers*. These taxpayers are not paying for the opportunity of greater future private consumption, as were the bondholders in year 1; they are paying for debt-financed expenditures in year 1.

How does Buchanan deal with the fact that in year 30 there are both taxpayers *and* bondholders, both of whom made up the future generation from the perspective of year 1? Once again, since the taxpayers in year 30 pay the bondholders in year 30, and what the taxpayers lose, the bondholders gain, wouldn't it follow that *on net* the burden of the debt for this generation is zero?

As we learned earlier, some economists would answer yes. But Buchanan states that the argument is misleading. The bondholders in year 30 don't really gain anything; all they do is trade one asset (bonds) for another asset (money) of equal value. This generation of bondholders gains no more from this transaction than if it had exchanged a $20 bill for four $5 bills. The taxpayers in year 30 do, however, lose something—taxes. In conclusion, bondholders do not gain anything, and taxpayers lose something, so *on net* the next generation loses.

Real Deficits and Debt

Some economists believe that much of the talk about deficits and debt is misdirected. Economist Robert Eisner argues that deficits and debt should be viewed in real terms, not nominal terms. If this is done, the picture does *look* different (whether it *is* different, however, is what economists debate).

Eisner says that to obtain the real deficit, the national debt should be adjusted each year for inflation and subtracted from the actual or nominal deficit. Suppose, in 1994, the national debt is $3,000 billion. During the year, the federal government runs a $200 billion deficit. The $200 billion adds to the national debt, so that at the end of the year the debt has increased to $3,200 billion (the increase in the national debt from one year to the next equals the deficit over the year).

Now suppose the price level rises by 5 percent during 1994. This means the real value of the original $3,000 billion debt declines by 5 percent. In short, the nominal national debt rises from $3,000 to $3,200 billion during the year, but inflation reduces the real value of the debt by $150 billion ($3,000 billion $\times$ .05 = $150 billion). In effect, this $150 billion is as much a receipt for government as if it were a tax. If we take this "inflation tax" into account, the conventionally measured deficit is reduced to $50 billion ($200 billion − $150 billion = $50 billion). Currently, government accounting procedures do not adjust the debt for inflation.

Question:

To reduce the deficit, it seems necessary either to cut government expenditures or to raise tax receipts. In the preceding example, neither was done. How, then, did the deficit go from $200 billion to $50 billion?

Answer:

When the real value of the debt is reduced, the result is the same *as if* inflation had raised tax receipts. Consider a simple example. Suppose the federal government spends $200 billion and has tax receipts of $80 billion. In this case, the deficit is $120 billion. We'll assume that the national debt was zero before the deficit is run, so that the debt equals $120 billion after the deficit is run. Thus, in our simple model, the national debt = the deficit.

Now let the price level increase by 10 percent. If we adjust the national debt for the rise in prices, the real value of the debt falls by 10 percent—or $12 billion. But if the *real value* of the debt falls by $12 billion because of the rise in prices, the result is the same *as if* government had raised $12 billion more in taxes. One can think of it this way: A person borrows $100 and promises to pay back the $100 in a year, but during the year the price level rises 10 percent. She ends up paying back the loan with dollars that have 10 percent less purchasing power than the dollars she borrowed. For the lender, it is *as if* he received 10 percent fewer dollars than he thought he would receive at the time the loan was made. Increases in the price level redistribute buying power from creditors to debtors. With regard to the national debt, the federal government is a debtor.

How Is Some Legislation Like a Bond?

When the government issues debt in the form of a bond, it promises to make a monetary payment to the bondholder in the future. The federal government also has other ways of promising to make a monetary payment in the future: It can make a promise through legislation. The best example of this is Social Security. Under Social Security legislation, the federal government promises benefits to future retirees that must be paid out of future tax revenues. Some economists believe that Social Security promises and the like should be viewed as the *implicit national debt.* Arthur Andersen & Co., an accounting firm, in 1986 estimated that if the implicit obligations of the federal government (implicit national debt) were added to the explicit obligations of the federal debt (explicit national debt), the national debt would be approximately three times as large as the official estimate.

The Deficit: International Considerations

Is there a link between the budget deficit ($G > T$) and the trade deficit ($M > X$)? In the appendix to Chapter 6, we demonstrated such a link. The substance of the argument is as follows: (1) If the deficit grows larger, the Treasury has to borrow more credit. This increases the demand for credit, and drives the interest rate up. (2) A higher U.S. interest rate will bring about an increase in foreign capital inflows (to receive the relatively higher rate of return). (3) This will result in a greater demand for the U.S. dollar and thus the appreciation of the dollar. (4) The appreciation of the dollar makes U.S. goods more expensive and foreign goods cheaper.

(5) As a result, we would expect people to buy more foreign goods and fewer U.S. goods—thus U.S. exports decline and imports rise. (6) A fall in exports and a rise in imports simply increases the size of the trade deficit. In theory, then, the budget deficit can affect the trade deficit.

An Example: When it Comes to Economics, Do National Borders Really Mean Much Any More?   Suppose there are two persons, Jones and Smith, both of whom live in the same small town in the Midwest. Jones is a farmer and Smith owns a small business in which he makes unique clocks, many of which he sells in Europe.

One day Jones and other farmers from across the country go to Washington to lobby for more generous federal benefits. They tell their elected representatives that times are hard and that the American farmer needs help—immediately. Soon afterward, the Congress increases federal spending on agricultural programs. We will assume that no other program in the budget is cut, taxes are not raised, and there is a budget deficit at the time the farm spending program is put into effect. As a result, the budget deficit widens.

The process we described earlier begins: (1) To finance the additional spending, the Treasury increases the demand for credit. (2) Interest rates rise. (3) There is an increased inflow of foreign capital. (4) There is greater demand for the U.S. dollar. (5) The dollar appreciates in value. (6) U.S. exports fall and imports rise. One of the persons initially hurt by the higher (international) value of the dollar is Smith, our clockmaker.

One day, farmer Jones is in Smith's store looking for a clock to buy for his wife on their 30th anniversary. Smith is showing him around. The two start talking about this and that. Smith mentions to Jones that his business has been slow recently because his customers in Europe are not buying as many of his clocks as they used to buy. Jones asks Smith what he thinks is the problem. Smith tells him that the rise in the value of the dollar has hurt him greatly. Jones sympathizes with him and says that the rise in the value of the dollar has even started to hurt his wheat sales to foreigners. "Do you have any idea how the dollar got to be so much higher?" Jones asks Smith. Smith says, "No idea at all." Then he adds, "I don't know who to blame for this." Jones says, "I don't either." Then Jones apologizes to Smith for having to buy one of the cheaper clocks in the store. "Because," he says, "things just aren't looking too good right now." Smith just sighs. He knows.

Our example is fictional, but not unrealistic. It shows that it is possible for our actions as Americans to help us in the short run, but hurt us in the long-run. Jones, who lobbies for and receives additional federal benefits today, undertakes an action the long-run effects of which harm him and other farmers who sell their produce abroad. Also, sometimes the actions of one American (Jones) can adversely affect another American (Smith). It is likely that Jones and Smith, talking together in Smith's clock shop, had very little idea of where their problems originated. Jones probably didn't think that a small part of his current problems originated with himself. He might have blamed anyone from his elected representatives, to major corporations, to the oil-producing nations, to the president of the United States for the fact that an appreciated dollar is making it harder for him to sell his produce abroad. Similarly, it is unlikely that Smith, standing in his shop talking to Jones, would have accused him, a neighbor, as part of the source of his current economic woes. After all, what does an American farmer have to do with the international value of the U.S. dollar?

Economic actions have ripple effects—often far dispersed from the source.

We sometimes see news reports on television of the rise and fall of the U.S. dollar on international exchange markets, often accompanied by film of men and women sitting packed together in a room in London, Zurich, New York, or Tokyo, each in front of a green-screened computer monitor with a telephone in both hands. The atmosphere is hectic, if not frantic. The sounds are of currency prices: so many German marks or French francs for the U.S. dollar. To the average viewer, there is no connection between such sights and sounds and the activities of a Midwestern farmer, perhaps plowing the fields, many thousands of miles away. To the economist, however, the connection is immediately apparent. The price of the dollar affects the farmer's sales abroad, for example. He knows that economic actions have ripple effects—often far dispersed from the source.

THE BALANCED BUDGET AMENDMENT

Deficits do not occur in a political vacuum. Neither do proposals to reduce deficits. In this section, we discuss a few deficit-reduction proposals. One proposal, in particular, has been widely discussed throughout the 1980s. It is the balanced budget amendment The balanced budget amendment seeks to solve the deficit problem at the constitutional level. Other proposals include the presidential-line veto, a national consumption tax, a value-added tax, and privatization.

The Balanced Budget Amendment

The balanced budget amendment contains the following provisions:

1. Congress must legislate annual budgets "in which total outlays are no greater than total receipts."
2. Total receipts may not rise "by a rate greater than the rate of increase in national income."
3. "The Congress and the President shall . . . ensure that actual outlays do not exceed the outlays set forth in the budget statement."
4. These provisions may be overridden in time of war or other emergencies.

Critics of the balanced budget amendment have raised a number of points:

1. To adopt a budget statement "in which total outlays are no greater than total receipts," the Congress must rely on economic forecasts of how the economy will perform. Different forecasters come up with different forecasts, raising the question, Whose forecasts should the Congress accept? In addition, if the chosen forecast turns out to be wrong, then the Congress will have failed to abide by the amendment and thus will be in violation of the law.
2. What happens if the Congress doesn't abide by the amendment? Will all members of Congress be put in jail?
3. Congress can evade the amendment by moving expenditures "off-budget."[2]
4. Abiding by the discipline of a balanced budget may cause the government to enact the wrong kind of fiscal policy. For example, suppose the economy experiences a recession, real GNP declines, and tax revenues fall. If the budget were previously in balance, either an expenditure cut or a tax increase would be nec-

[2]Currently, the federal government does not include all its expenditures in its official budget; some expenditures are moved "off-budget."

Proposals to Deal with the Deficit

The balanced budget amendment is not the only proposal that has been put forth to deal with large budget deficits. Some of the other proposals include the presidential line-item veto, a consumption tax, a value-added tax, and privatizing certain government functions.

The Presidential Line-Item Veto

The president submits a budget to the Congress in January or February of each year. Between then and October 1, the first day of the fiscal year, different subcommittees and full appropriations committees in both houses of Congress meet and put together appropriations bills to be voted on by the full Congress. Once passed by Congress, these appropriations bills are sent to the president for approval or veto. In recent years, the Congress has been sending the president *fewer* but *larger* appropriations bills. Large bills contain some things the president wants and some things the president does not want. But under existing law, the president can either sign the entire bill or veto the entire bill. The president cannot go through the large appropriations bill and veto certain lines of expenditure. Critics have pointed out that Congress can throw "pork-barrel" spending projects into a large appropriations bill, knowing full well that the president isn't likely to veto a bill that contains a number of vital appropriations. Currently, many spending projects that couldn't pass on their own—if examined one by one—are tossed into a large appropriations bill that the president must accept fully or not at all.

The presidential line-item veto would allow the president to go through a large appropriations bill and draw a line through (veto) specific appropriations. No longer would it be a matter of all or nothing. Proponents of the line-item veto say this will permit the president to hold the line on federal spending, and thus have an impact on the deficit in the right direction—down. Opponents sometimes argue that it will shift spending authority from the Congress to the president, contrary to the design of the Constitution. Others note that the line-item veto is a good idea when you agree with the president's choice of items to veto, but a bad idea when you do not. A conservative president is likely to veto different appropriations than a liberal president. Some line-item-veto advocates retort that no matter what type of president occupies the White House, a line-item veto will still restrain runaway federal spending (even though people won't always agree with the particular items vetoed). Restraining federal spending, they maintain, is of greater importance than the composition of federal spending.

National Consumption Tax

When considering proposals for a new tax, one must ask, Is this tax to be added to the current tax system, or is it a substitute for a current tax?

A national consumption tax is similar to a state sales tax, but it would be applied to all Americans. Is the proposed consumption tax an additional tax or is it to be a substitute for the income tax? Those who want the consumption tax as an additional tax often argue that it will add to total tax revenues and thereby lower the deficit. Those who want it as a substitute for the income tax rarely discuss the deficit at all; instead, they maintain that the consumption tax is preferable to the income tax; that is, consumption is a better base to tax than income.

The actual operation of a consump-

tion tax would be simple. Suppose Liz Warner's income is $20,000 this year and that she saves 10 percent of this amount, or $2,000. The $18,000 difference between saving and income, or consumption, is taxed, say, at 5 percent. One of the arguments in favor of a consumption tax, which is unrelated to the deficit, is that it would encourage more saving, thus permitting more investment.

Value-Added Tax

Like the consumption tax, the value-added tax (VAT) is proposed by some as a supplementary revenue source and by others as a substitute for a current tax or taxes. Those who propose it as an additional tax often say that it is needed to reduce the deficit.

A value-added tax is essentially a multistage sales tax that is collected from firms (not from individuals like an income or consumption tax) at each stage in the production and distribution process. The base of a VAT is the *value added* to a good at each stage of its production. The value added is equal to the price a firm receives for a good minus its purchases of material inputs from other firms. Consider three firms: Firm A, a manufacturer; Firm B, a wholesaler; and Firm C, a retailer. Suppose Firm A hires workers and manufacturers a good that it sells to Firm B for $700. In this case, the value added by Firm A is $700, since Firm A sells a good to Firm B for $700, and it does not purchase any materials from other firms ($700 − $0 = $700). Firm B distributes the good to a retailing firm, Firm C, for $900. What is the value added by Firm B? The answer is $200, because Firm B had purchased the good from Firm A for $700 ($900 − $700 = $200). Finally, Firm C sells the good to a consumer for $1,000. What is the value added by Firm C? The answer is $100 because Firm C had purchased the good for $900 from Firm B ($1,000 − $900 = $100).

A VAT would tax the value added by each firm. The value added by Firm A ($700) would be taxed, as would the value added by Firm B ($200), and the value added by Firm C ($100). Notice that the total value added $700 + $200 + $100 = $1,000 is equal to the sales price of the good. In short, the tax base of a value-added tax is the same as a retail sales tax.

If firms are allowed to deduct purchases of capital goods, then the tax base essentially becomes total consumption in the economy. This makes the VAT and the consumption tax sound similar, and in this regard they are. They are different, though, in that the consumption tax is assessed against individuals (it is a direct tax), and the VAT is assessed against firms. Even though individuals are the only ones that can ultimately pay taxes, critics of a VAT argue that its taxes are "hidden" from individuals. If a hidden tax is easier to raise than a visible tax, as some economists believe, then a value-added tax is more likely to lead to an overall greater tax burden in the long run than a consumption or income tax.

Privatization

Some economists maintain that the federal government currently performs some functions that could be done better and less expensively by the private sector and that such functions should be turned over to the private sector, or *privatized*. This would lower the deficit in three ways. First, through reduced spending. Second, through increased revenues due to the sale of government assets. And in some cases, third, by eliminating government promises to provide future benefits. So far, such proposals have not been widely discussed or accepted. Privatization proposals have included Social Security (by expanding Individual Retirement Accounts as a private alternative to Social Security), the postal service, the wastewater grant program, and public housing, among other things.

essary to maintain the balance. However, both of these actions would worsen the recession in the Keynesian model.

The proponents of the balanced budget amendment also make several points:

1. Budget institutions should convey to the public the costs of government expenditures as clearly and directly as possible. Taxes are a clearer, more direct, more understandable way to do this than deficit financing is.
2. Continued deficits have harmful effects on the economy (maybe just as much or more than the "wrong" fiscal policy). Some economists have hypothesized that deficits lead to higher interest rates, crowding out (less private investment), lower long-run real GNP, and inflation.
3. The burden of the debt is paid for by future generations, and running up deficits and placing such a burden on future generations is wrong.

CHAPTER SUMMARY

Ownership and Burden of the Debt

■ Americans have to pay off the national debt, and it is mostly Americans to whom the debt will be paid off. The percentage of the debt owned by foreigners has been between 15 and 20 percent in the past decade.
■ There is a continuing debate in economics on who bears the burden of the national debt. Economists who hold that the burden of the debt falls on the current

generation argue that resources are used up only in the periods when spending programs take place. Thus, if government debt finances an expenditure on, say, weapons, the resources that go into producing the weapons must be given up by some persons during that current period, not later.

■ Economists who hold that the burden of the debt falls on future generations state that when government debt finances an expenditure, it issues debt that is purchased by bondholders. These bondholders voluntarily trade one asset (money) for another (bonds). What they purchase is greater future consumption, not the government expenditure. The people who pay for the government expenditure are those who pay higher taxes to retire the previously issued debt.

Real Deficits and Debt

■ Economist Robert Eisner maintains that deficits and debt ought to be discussed in real, not nominal, terms. The national debt should be adjusted each year for inflation and subtracted from the actual deficit to obtain the real deficit. For example, suppose the national debt rises from $1,000 billion to $1,100 billion in one year, but at the same time the price level rises by 10 percent. The nominal deficit for the year is $100 billion, but the real deficit is zero because the value of the national debt falls by $100 billion ($1,000 billion $\times$ .10 = $100 billion). If we subtract $100 billion from the nominal deficit, we have zero.

The Implicit National Debt

■ Some economists state that the national debt should take into account not only the explicit national debt but also the implicit national debt. (The official measurement of the national debt only includes the explicit debt.) They argue that legislation can be like a bond. A bond is a promise to make a monetary payment in the future, and some legislation (for example, Social Security) is similar, if not for all practical purposes the same.

Proposals to Reduce the Deficit

■ One major proposal to reduce budget deficits is the balanced budget amendment.
■ Critics of the balanced budget amendment make several points: (1) Balancing the budget depends on accurate forecasts of expenditures and revenues. Which forecasts should the Congress use? If the chosen forecast turns out to be wrong, then the Congress has failed to abide by the amendment and is in violation of the law. (2) What happens if the Congress does not abide by the amendment? Will all members of Congress be put in jail? (3) Congress can evade the amendment by moving expenditures "off-budget." (4) A balanced budget amendment makes it difficult to enact stabilizing fiscal policy.
■ Proponents of the balanced budget amendment also make several points: (1) Budget institutions should convey to the public the costs of government expenditures as clearly and directly as possible. The balanced budget amendment is such a budget institution. (2) Continued deficits have harmful effects on the economy (maybe just as much or even more than the "wrong" fiscal policy). (3) It is wrong to debt finance current government expenditures and have future generations pay for them.
■ Besides the balanced budget amendment, other measures such as the presidential line-item veto, a consumption tax, a value-added tax, and privatization have been proposed to deal with large deficits.

Key Terms and Concepts

Budget Deficit   Stock   Flow
National Debt

QUESTIONS AND PROBLEMS

1. The national debt in year 1 is $1,500 billion, the national debt in year 2 is $1,575 billion. The price level in year 2 is 20 percent higher than it was in year 1. What is the nominal deficit and the real deficit?

2. Suppose the U.S. economy is in recession and the deficit is $146 billion. Using the Keynesian model, what are the predicted effects on the economy if the balanced budget amendment is in force?

3. "The national debt is a fraction of the GNP. The Jensens private debt is equal to their family income. It follows that the national debt is less of a problem than the Jensens private debt. Since you rarely hear anyone getting upset about the Jensens private debt, there is even less reason to get upset about the national debt. All this discussion about the seriousness of the national debt is simply empty talk." Discuss.

4. Economists are quick to point out that economics and politics are often at war with each other over deficits and debt. What do you think this means?

5. "A liberal president would not use the presidential line-item veto to restrain government spending, but a conservative president would." Discuss.

6. Are you in favor of the balanced budget amendment? Why? To what degree does your answer depend on your view of the stabilizing effects of fiscal policy?

7. In the 48 years between 1944 and 1991, the United States has witnessed a budget deficit in 36 years and a budget surplus in 12 years. Some people have concluded that recent U.S. fiscal history shows a bias toward running budget deficits. Offer some explanations for this deficit bias.

MICROECONOMICS

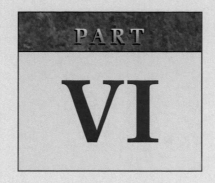

PART

VI

MICROECONOMIC FUNDAMENTALS

CHAPTER 19

AN INTRODUCTION TO MICROECONOMICS

WHAT THIS CHAPTER IS ABOUT

The objective of this chapter is to introduce and describe the major players in microeconomics and to develop a microeconomics mindset: a means by which we can focus on key factors as we study microeconomics.

413

THE MICROECONOMIC PLAYERS

■

In the marketplace, people buy and sell goods, services, and factors of production. Microeconomics examines the decisions to buy and sell, or alternatively, the decisions to refrain from buying and selling. Economists place those who participate in the market economy into one of four groups: consumers, firms, factor owners,[1] and government. An individual may fall into two or more of these categories at different times even during a single day, since the categories describe economic functions rather than a person's role in life.

Consumers, firms, and factor owners share a few things in making economic decisions. They all have *objectives,* or goals, which they hope to promote in market transactions. They all face *constraints* on their actions, which make it necessary for them to sacrifice some things in order to obtain other things. Finally, they all make *choices* in ways they feel will promote their own interests.

Consumers

Consumers buy goods and services produced by firms. This advances their *objective* of maximizing their utility, or satisfaction. Yet very few people can buy all the goods they might like to consume. Consumers purchases are *constrained* by their limited incomes and by the positive prices for each good. Each purchase subtracts from the consumer's available income, and eventually nothing remains. Given limited purchasing ability, the consumer will attempt to gain as much utility as possible from each dollar spent. In practice, this is done by *choosing* to use **marginal analysis** in making consumption decisions—by comparing the additional (marginal) benefits and additional (marginal) costs of each purchase. We examine how marginal analysis works in the next chapter.

Firms

Firms *hire* productive factors or resources, combine them in a certain way to *produce* a final good, then *sell* that good to consumers. In short, firms play two roles in the economy: They are the buyers of factors and the sellers of goods.

Firms as Buyers.   When they hire workers and other productive factors, the *objective* of firm managers is to maximize **profits.** Among other things, this implies that they will hire a mix of factors that will minimize their costs of producing the desired amount of output. Their hiring decisions are *constrained* by the positive price of factors and by the need to cover opportunity costs. Firm managers achieve their objectives by *choosing* to hire only those factors that contribute more at the margin to the firm's output and sales receipts than the additional cost of employing them. The marginal analysis employed by firms as buyers is the subject of a later chapter.

Firms as Sellers.   When they decide how many units of a good to produce or what price to charge for it, the *objective* of firm managers is to maximize profits. If they are successful in purchasing resources and managing the production process, the *constraints* on sellers are those imposed by consumers, who search for

Marginal Analysis
Weighing additional benefits of a change against the additional costs of a change with respect to current conditions.

Profit
The difference between total revenue and total cost.

[1]Factor owners own the factors of production, or resources, which include land, labor, capital, and entrepreneurship.

lower prices and higher quality, and competitors, who attempt to undercut prices charged by other sellers or produce a more desirable product.[2] The manager of a firm will maximize profits by *choosing* to produce and sell those units of output that contribute more at the margin to the firm's sales revenues than they add to its costs. We examine the marginal analysis of the profit maximizing firm in a later chapter.

Factor Owners

Factor owners (or resource owners) sell the factors or resources to firms that firms use to produce goods and services. Just as the sellers of goods and services have as their *objective* to maximize profits, so do the sellers of factors. Since factors are not infinite, factor owners are *constrained* by the prices paid for their services in the marketplace and by the finite amount of factors they have to sell. For example, you, as the owner of your labor, can sell only as much labor as you have in a 24-hour day (where approximately 8 hours are needed for sleep). Factor owners achieve their objective by *choosing* to sell those units (of the factor) for which the additional (marginal) benefit, in terms of price offered for the resource, is greater than or equal to the additional (marginal) cost. For example, how much of your labor you choose to sell will depend on the value you place on what you could be doing if you didn't work (your opportunity costs) in relation to the price per hour you are offered for one hour's worth of your labor.

Government

Government buys goods and services just as consumers do, but we are not interested in this particular role of government here. Instead, in our study of microeconomics, we are interested in government as the entity that performs the following functions: (1) assigns and adjudicates property rights, (2) taxes, (3) subsidizes, and (4) regulates consumers, firms, and resource owners.

MICROECONOMICS IS ABOUT OBJECTIVES, CONSTRAINTS, AND CHOICES

■

We have seen that consumers, firms, and factor owners all have objectives and all face constraints. In a world of constraints, it is impossible to reach one's objective without making choices. Finally, it is important *how* the choice is made. For example, a firm may be faced with the choice of buying more labor or buying more capital. Does it "choose" by flipping a coin, or in some other way? Economists answer that it chooses in some other way and they go on to define that particular way. This is where marginal decision making comes into the picture—the process of choosing by weighing additional benefits against additional costs.

In our study of microeconomics, you will observe the trilogy of objective–constraint–choice coming up again and again. The way choices are made—by comparing additional benefits and additional costs—will also be a permanent piece of the microeconomics landscape.

[2]In later chapters, we discuss the particular constraints that firms in different market structures face.

MICROECONOMICS IS ABOUT MARKETS

■

Different Market Types

Microeconomics is about the interactions between consumers and firms, and between firms and factor owners, in market settings. As stated in Chapter 3, there are two sides to every market: a buying side (demand) and a selling side (supply). We now differentiate between two types of markets: **product markets** and **factor (or resource) markets.** In product markets, we deal with consumers and firms: Consumers are demanders of products and firms are suppliers of products. In factor markets, we deal with firms as the buyers of factors and factor owners as the suppliers of resources.

Within the broad outline of product markets, there are two general types—*price-taker* and *price-searcher* product markets. The same classification exists for factor markets, too.

Product Markets
Markets where goods and services are bought and sold.

Factor (or Resource) Markets
Markets where the factors of production or resources are bought and sold.

Different Market Settings

A key to understanding markets is the degree of competition in them. One of the factors that influences the degree of competition is the number of buyers and sellers. For example, in one product market (say, the market for wheat), there may be *many buyers* and *many sellers,* and in another product market (say, the market for cars), there may be *many buyers* and *few sellers.*

Similarly, in one product market, there may exist easy entry, so that a firm that wanted to enter the market and produce and sell its product could do so without difficulty. And in another product market, there may exist high barriers to entry, so that a firm that wanted to enter and produce and sell its product either could do so only with much difficulty or simply couldn't do so because of prohibitively high entry costs.

Different conditions on different sides of the market may result in consumers and firms having unequal market power. In one product market the suppliers may have much more control over the price a good sells for than in another market.

MICROECONOMICS IS ABOUT THE WORKINGS OF MARKETS WITH AND WITHOUT GOVERNMENT INTERVENTION

■

Microeconomics is about the workings of markets with and without government intervention of some sort. In our study of consumers, firms, and factor owners in different market settings, we look at what happens when government is *not involved* in affecting the behavior of any or all of the three microeconomics players and when government *is involved* in affecting the behavior of the players.

When government is involved, we examine both the *purpose* and the *effects* of its involvement. The effects, in particular, can be related to the objectives, constraints, and choices of consumers, firms, and factor owners. To illustrate, suppose the government decides to tax firms. We would want to know how the tax affects the objectives, constraints, and choices of the firm, and then how the (perhaps) changed behavior on one side of the market (supply side) affects overall market outcomes.

A MICROECONOMICS MINDSET

■

The Players and Their Environment

Let's summarize the points we have made so far and try to develop a *mindset* for our study of the subject matter that is before us:

1. Microeconomics is about consumers, firms, and factor owners.
2. Consumers, firms, and factor owners each have objectives.
3. They try to achieve their objectives in the face of certain constraints.
4. Because they try to achieve objectives in a world of constraints, they are forced to make choices.
5. They make their choices in a certain way: by weighing additional benefits against additional costs.
6. Consumers and firms, and firms and factor owners, interact in market settings. In any market, there is always something being bought and something being sold.
7. There exist different types of market settings.
8. Government can affect the behavior of consumers, firms, and factor owners, and thus affect overall market outcomes.

So, our microeconomic mindset is centered around three ideas: (1) Consumers, firms, and factor owners deal with objectives, constraints, and choices. (2) Consumers and firms, and firms and factor owners, interact in market settings—where not all market settings are alike. (3) Government can affect consumers, firms, and factor owners and thus affect overall market outcomes.

Translating Pictures into Economics

The average person sees hundreds of real pictures, or scenes, each day. One of these pictures is illustrated in Exhibit 19–1. Here we have a "Pizza Palace" next to a "Taco Hut." Also in the picture are three people on their way into the Pizza Palace, a cook inside tossing a pizza, a "Help Wanted" sign outside the door, and a sign outside advertising the Pizza Palace lunch special. In all, just a picture, one you've seen many times before.

One thing you will notice, as you make your way through the study of microeconomics, is that over time you will be able to take ordinary, everyday pictures and see the economics behind them. Let us illustrate.

The layperson sees three persons walking into the Pizza Palace. The economist sees consumers, or buyers, who represent the demand side of the market.

The layperson sees the Pizza Palace advertised special on the sign. The economist sees a firm informing potential customers that it is willing to supply pizzas at a certain price (a point on a supply curve, perhaps).

The layperson sees a cook inside tossing a pizza. The economist sees the process of production; she acknowledges that the cook was hired in a factor market.

The layperson sees a Taco Hut next door to the Pizza Palace. The economist sees tacos and burritos as substitutes for pizzas and the Taco Hut as competition for the Pizza Palace.

The layperson sees a "Help Wanted" sign. The economist sees information relating to a factor market.

The layperson sees the Pizza Palace and the customers about to do business. The economist sees an exchange in a product market.

EXHIBIT 19–1
Can You See the Economics in the Picture?
Once you learn economics, it is easy to see it in everyday places.

Item in the "Picture":	The Economist "Sees":
Persons walking into the Pizza Palace	Consumers or buyers; the demand side of the market.
Pizza Palace advertised special	A firm informing potential customers it is willing to supply pizzas at a certain price.
Cook tossing a pizza	Production in the works; a person hired in a factor market.
Taco Hut	Tacos and burritos are substitutes for pizza; Taco Hut is Pizza Palace's competitor.
Help Wanted sign	Information relating to a factor market.
Pizza Palace and customers about to do business	An exchange in a product market.

CHAPTER SUMMARY

Microeconomic Players

■ In microeconomics, there are four principal players: consumers, firms, factor owners, and government.

What Microeconomics Is About

■ Microeconomics is about objectives, constraints, and choices that face consumers, firms, and factor owners.

■ Microeconomics is about markets where consumers and firms, and firms and factor owners, interact.
■ Microeconomics is about the workings of markets with and without government intervention.

Key Terms and Concepts

Marginal Analysis

Profit

Product Markets

Factor (or Resource) Markets

QUESTIONS AND PROBLEMS

1. What is the objective of each of the following: consumers, firms, and factor owners?

2. In what markets do consumers and firms interact? firms and factor owners?

3. What is (are) the constraint(s) for each of the following: consumers, firms, and factor owners?

4. What are the ways in which government can affect consumers, firms, and factor owners.

5. How might market settings differ?

CHAPTER 20

THE LOGIC
OF CONSUMER CHOICE

WHAT THIS CHAPTER IS ABOUT

In this chapter, we focus our attention on consumers. We discuss their objective—to maximize utility—and the process by which they attempt to realize their objective—by employing marginal analysis.

UTILITY THEORY

■

Water is cheap and diamonds are expensive. But water is necessary to life and diamonds are not. Isn't it odd—paradoxical?—that what is necessary to life is cheap and what is not necessary to life is expensive? This is the question that the economist Adam Smith wondered about. He observed that often things that have the greatest value in use, or are the most useful, have a relatively low price, and things that have little or no value in use have a high price. Smith's observation came to be known as the **diamond–water paradox,** or the paradox of value. The paradox challenged economists, and they sought a solution to it. In this section, we begin to develop parts of the solution they found.

Utility, Total and Marginal

To say that a good gives you **utility** is to say that it has the power to satisfy wants, or that it gives you satisfaction. For example, suppose you buy your first unit of good *X.* You obtain a certain amount of utility, say, 10 **utils** from it. (Utils are an artificial construction with which to "measure" utility; we realize you have never seen a util; no one has.)

You buy a second unit of good *X.* Once again, you get a certain amount of utility from this second unit, say, 8 utils. You purchase a third unit and receive 7 utils. If we sum the amounts of utility you obtain from each of the three units, we would have the **total utility** you receive from purchasing good *X*—which is 25 utils. Total utility is the total satisfaction one receives from consuming a particular quantity of a good (in this example, three units of good *X).*

Total utility is different from **marginal utility.** Marginal utility is the additional utility gained from consuming an additional unit of good *X.* Marginal utility is the *change* in total utility divided by the *change* in the quantity consumed of a good: $MU = \Delta TU/\Delta Q$ (where the change in the quantity consumed of a good is usually equal to one unit).

To illustrate, suppose you receive 50 utils of total utility from consuming one apple and 80 utils of total utility from consuming two apples. What is the marginal utility of the second apple, or, in other words, what is the additional utility of consuming an additional apple? It is 30 utils.

Law of Diminishing Marginal Utility

Do you think the marginal utility of the second unit is greater than, less than, or equal to the marginal utility of the first unit? Before answering, consider the difference in marginal utility between the third unit and the second unit, or between the fifth unit and the fourth unit (had we extended the number of units consumed). In general, we are asking whether the marginal utility of the unit that comes next is greater than, less than, or equal to the marginal utility of the unit that comes before.

Economists have generally answered "less than." The **law of diminishing marginal utility** states that for a given time period, the marginal utility gained by consuming equal successive units of a good will decline as the amount consumed increases. In terms of our artificial units, utils, this means that the number of utils gained by the consumption of the first unit of the good is greater than the number of utils gained by the second (which is greater than the number gained by the

Diamond–Water Paradox
The observation that those things that have the greatest value in use sometimes have little value in exchange and those things that have little value in use sometimes have the greatest value in exchange.

Utility
A measure of the satisfaction, happiness, or benefit that results from the consumption of a good.

Util
An artificial construct used to measure utility.

Total Utility
The total satisfaction a person receives from consuming a particular quantity of a good.

Marginal Utility
The additional utility a person receives from consuming an additional unit of a particular good.

Law of Diminishing Marginal Utility
The marginal utility gained by consuming equal successive units of a good will decline as the amount consumed increases.

third, which is greater than the number gained by the fourth, and so on). We illustrate the law of diminishing marginal utility in Exhibit 20–1.

In (a), we see both the total utility of consuming a certain number of units of a good and the marginal utility of consuming additional units; in (b), total utility; and in (c), marginal utility. Notice in (b) and (c) that total utility can increase as marginal utility decreases. This will be important in helping unravel the diamond–water paradox.

The law of diminishing marginal utility is based on the idea that if a good has a variety of uses, but only one unit of the good is available, the consumer will use the first unit to satisfy his or her most urgent want. If two units are available, the consumer will use the second unit to satisfy a less urgent want.

To illustrate, suppose that good X can be used to satisfy wants A through E, with A being the most urgent want and E being the least urgent want, and B being

EXHIBIT 20–1
Total Utility, Marginal Utility, and the Law of Diminishing Marginal Utility

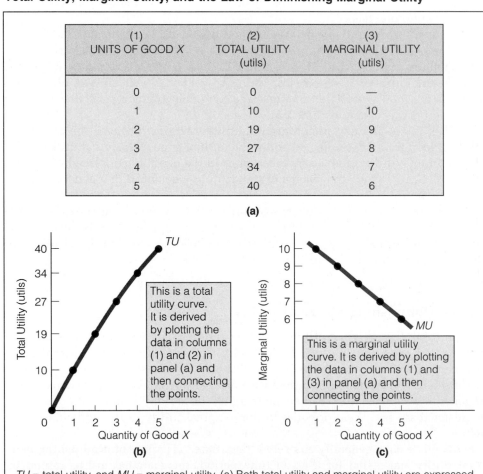

(1) UNITS OF GOOD X	(2) TOTAL UTILITY (utils)	(3) MARGINAL UTILITY (utils)
0	0	—
1	10	10
2	19	9
3	27	8
4	34	7
5	40	6

(a)

This is a total utility curve. It is derived by plotting the data in columns (1) and (2) in panel (a) and then connecting the points.

(b)

This is a marginal utility curve. It is derived by plotting the data in columns (1) and (3) in panel (a) and then connecting the points.

(c)

TU = total utility, and MU = marginal utility. (a) Both total utility and marginal utility are expressed in utils. Marginal utility is the change in total utility divided by the change in the quantity consumed of the good, $MU = \Delta TU/\Delta Q$. (b) Total utility. (c) Marginal utility. Together, (b) and (c) demonstrate that total utility can increase (b) as marginal utility decreases (c).

more urgent than *C*, *C* being more urgent than *D*, and *D* being more urgent than *E*. We can chart the wants as follows:

		Wants		
A	*B*	*C*	*D*	*E*

Most Urgent ← ... → **Least Urgent**

Suppose the first unit of good *X* can satisfy any one—but only one—of the wants *A* through *E*. Which want will an individual choose to satisfy? The answer is "the most urgent want—A." The individual chooses to satisfy *A* instead of *B, C, D,* or *E* because people will ordinarily satisfy their most urgent want before all others. If you were dying of thirst in a desert (having gone without water for three days), and came across a quart of water, would you drink it or use it to wash your hands? You would drink it, of course. You would satisfy your most urgent want first. Washing your hands in the water would give you less utility than drinking the water.

Utility and the Hundredth Game of Chess

As we defined the law of diminishing marginal utility—the marginal utility gained by consuming equal successive units of a good will decline as the amount consumed increases—it follows that marginal utility begins to decline with the second unit of a good consumed. Occasionally, this doesn't appear to be the case. For example, someone will mention that his first chess game did not give him as much utility as his hundredth game, because when he played his first chess game, he did not know how to play chess very well, but when he played his hundredth, he did. The same can be said of other games such as golf and tennis. In short, sometimes you derive more utility from something as you get better at it. Does this invalidate the law of diminishing marginal utility? Some economists think not. They argue that a person's first game of chess may not be the same good as his hundredth game. Although to an onlooker the first and the hundredth games may appear to be much alike (they use the same board and so forth), from the viewpoint of the chess player, there may be a large difference between the first game of chess and the hundredth. In fact, the difference may be so large that we are dealing with two different goods.

This general problem has led some economists to refer to the less emphatic *principle* of diminishing marginal utility, rather than to the *law* of diminishing marginal utility. Other economists have simply noted that there are exceptions to the law of diminishing marginal utility. Still others have said that it is important to define the law (or principle) of diminishing marginal utility as follows: *The marginal utility associated with consuming equal successive units of a good will eventually decline as the amount consumed increases.* The key word here is *eventually.* These economists state that a person may enjoy, say, the first piece of pizza immensely, and the second even more, but eventually there comes a point when one piece of pizza (say, the fourth) brings less utility than the previous piece (the third). This last version of the law of diminishing marginal utility is consistent with the law expressed by William Stanley Jevons, one of the founders of marginal utility theory. Jevons said that "the degree of utility varies with the quantity of commodity, and ultimately decreases as that quantity increases."

The Millionaire and the Pauper: What the Law Says and Doesn't Say

Does a poor man get more or less utility from one more dollar than a millionaire? Most people would say that a poor man gets more utility from one more dollar than a millionaire because the poor man has so many fewer dollars than the millionaire. "What's an extra dollar to a millionaire?" they ask. They then answer, "Nothing. A millionaire has so many dollars, one more doesn't mean a thing."

Some people think the law of diminishing marginal utility substantiates the claim that a millionaire gets less utility from one more dollar than a poor man. Unfortunately, though, this is a misreading of the law. In terms of our example, the law says that for the millionaire an additional dollar is worth less than the dollar that preceded it; and for the poor man, an additional dollar is worth less than the dollar that preceded it. Let's say the millionaire has $2 million, and the poor man has $1,000. We now give each of them one more dollar. The law of diminishing marginal utility says that the additional dollar is worth less to the millionaire than his two-millionth dollar; and the additional dollar is worth less to the poor man than his one-thousandth dollar. That is all the law says. We do not and cannot know whether the additional dollar is worth more or less to the millionaire than it is to the poor man. In summary, the law tells us something about the millionaire and about the poor man (both persons value the last dollar more than the next-to-last dollar), but it does not tell us anything about the millionaire's utility compared with the poor man's.

To compare the utility the millionaire gets from the additional dollar with the utility the poor man gets from it is to fall into the trap of making an **interpersonal utility comparison.** Utility obtained by one person cannot be scientifically or objectively compared with the utility obtained from the same thing by another person because utility is subjective. Who knows for certain how much satisfaction (utility) the millionaire gets from the additional dollar compared with the poor man? The poor man may care little for money; he may shun it, consider it the root of all evil, and prefer to consume the things in life that do not require money. On the other hand, the millionaire may be interested only in amassing more money. We should not be so careless as to "guess" at the utility one person obtains from consuming a certain item, compare it to our "guess" of the utility another person obtains from consuming the same item, and then call these "guesses" scientific facts.

Interpersonal Utility Comparison
Comparing the utility one person receives from a good, service, or activity with the utility another person receives from the same good, service, or activity.

The Solution to the Diamond–Water Paradox

Goods have both total utility and marginal utility. Take water, for example. Water is extremely useful; we cannot live without it. We would expect its total utility (its total usefulness) to be high. But we would also expect its marginal utility to be low. Why? We would expect this because water is in relatively plentiful supply, and as the law of diminishing marginal utility states, the utility of successive units of a good diminishes as consumption of the good increases. In short, water is immensely useful, but there is so much of it that individuals place relatively little value on another unit of it.

In contrast, diamonds are not as useful as water. We would expect the total utility of diamonds to be lower than the total utility of water. However, we would also expect the marginal utility of diamonds to be high. Why? Because there are relatively few diamonds in the world, the consumption of diamonds (in contrast to the consumption of water) takes place at relatively high marginal utility. Diamonds, which are rare, get used only for their few valuable uses. Water, being

Do You Know Why You Sometimes Get Bored?

For the past eight years, O'Brien has spent his annual two-week vacation in Hawaii. The first two or three times in Hawaii, he had a good time and was excited. The last two or three times, he has been bored. He has decided that on his next vacation he will go somewhere else.

Excitement is usually connected with high utility; boredom with low utility. The road from excitement (high utility) to boredom (low utility) is by way of repetition: doing the same thing repeatedly.

"Doing the same thing repeatedly" is similar to consistently consuming

additional units of a good—to which the law of diminishing marginal utility applies. Question: Does the law of diminishing marginal utility explain why we get bored? We think it does. Here are some examples.

Driving a long distance in a car. Usually, the first few miles of a long-distance trip are the most exciting. As day passes on, and the miles roll by, boredom sets in. Are yawns the sign of boredom? Are yawns the sign of the law of diminishing marginal utility at work?

First week on the new job. Usually, the first week on a new job is the most exciting. As the weeks pass, and you know more about the job and your coworkers, boredom often sets in.

Seeing a movie. Few people have the desire to see a movie more than once. They know they will probably be bored seeing the movie the second time. Not wanting to see a movie more than once implicitly recognizes the validity of the law of diminishing marginal utility.

plentiful, gets used for its many valuable uses and for its not-so-valuable uses (such as spraying the car with the hose for two more minutes even though you are 99 percent sure that the soap is fully rinsed off).

In conclusion, the total utility of water is high because water is extremely useful; the total utility of diamonds is low in comparison because diamonds are not as useful as water. The marginal utility of water is low because water is so plentiful that people end up consuming it at low marginal utility; the marginal utility of diamonds is high because diamonds are so scarce that people end up consuming them at high marginal utility.

Do prices reflect total or marginal utility? We know that they reflect marginal utility; after all, diamonds are more expensive than water.

Question:

Aren't there times when water would be more expensive than diamonds?

Answer:

Yes, there are. If the supply of water is unusually limited for some reason, say, a drought, the price of water is likely to be higher than the price of diamonds. In some arid parts of the world, water is in unusually short supply, and people have been known to trade their diamonds and precious metals as well as fight for some of it.

Is Gambling Worth It?

Is gambling in a fair game worth it? The answer for those persons who derive no pleasure from gambling itself, but only gamble to win, is no.

First, let's define a fair game. A fair game is one in which the value of the expected gain equals the wager made. For example, if you bet $1 to have a 10 percent chance to win $10, the game is fair: $1 (the wager) is equal to the probability of winning (10 percent) times the win ($10).

But now consider the diminishing marginal utility of *money:* The last dollar brings less utility than the next-to-last dollar, and so on. This means that the money potentially lost from a wager has a higher per-unit utility than an equal amount of money potentially gained. Specifically, losing a dollar bet in a fair game causes you to lose more utility than winning a dollar causes you to gain utility. We conclude that under the conditions stated—a fair game and no pleasure derived from gambling itself—gambling is a losing proposition.

CONSUMER EQUILIBRIUM AND DEMAND
■

Here we identify the condition necessary for consumer equilibrium and then discuss the relationship between it and the law of demand. The analysis that follows is based on the assumption that individuals seek to maximize utility.

Equating Marginal Utilities per Dollar

Suppose there are only two goods in the world, apples and oranges. At present, a consumer is spending his entire income consuming 10 apples and 10 oranges a week. We assume that the marginal utility and price of each are as follows:[1]

$$MU_{\text{oranges}} = 30 \text{ utils}$$

$$MU_{\text{apples}} = 20 \text{ utils}$$

$$P_{\text{oranges}} = \$1$$

$$P_{\text{apples}} = \$1$$

The marginal (last) dollar spent on apples returns 20 utils per dollar, and the marginal (last) dollar spent on oranges returns 30 utils per dollar. The ratio of MU_O/P_O (O = oranges) is greater than the ratio of MU_A/P_A (A = apples): $MU_O/P_O > MU_A/P_A$.

A consumer who found himself in this situation one week would redirect his purchases of apples and oranges the next week. He would think: If I buy an orange, I receive more utility (30 utils) than if I buy an apple (20 utils). It's better to buy one more orange with a dollar and one less apple. I gain 30 utils from buying the orange, which is 10 utils more than if I buy the apple.

But what happens as the consumer buys one more orange and one less apple? The marginal utility of oranges falls (recall what the law of diminishing marginal utility says happens as a person consumes additional units of a good), and the marginal utility of apples rises (the consumer is consuming fewer apples). Because the consumer has bought one more orange and one less apple, he now has 11

[1]You may wonder where these marginal utility figures come from. These are points on hypothetical marginal utility curves, such as the one in Exhibit 20–1. What is important here is the fact that one number is greater than the other. We could easily have picked other numbers, such as 300 and 200, and so on.

oranges and 9 apples. At this combination of goods, the new situation looks like this:

$$MU_{\text{oranges}} = 25 \text{ utils}$$

$$MU_{\text{apples}} = 25 \text{ utils}$$

$$P_{\text{oranges}} = \$1$$

$$P_{\text{apples}} = \$1$$

Here the ratio MU_O/P_O equals MU_A/P_A. The consumer is getting exactly the same amount of utility (25 utils) per dollar from the two goods. There is no way the consumer can redirect his purchases (buy more of one good and less of another good) and be made better off. Thus, the consumer is in equilibrium. In short, a consumer is in equilibrium when he or she derives the same marginal utility per dollar for all goods. The condition for **consumer equilibrium** is[2]

$$MU_A/P_A = MU_B/P_B = MU_C/P_C = \ldots = MU_Z/P_Z$$

where the letters A–Z represent all the goods a person buys.

Consumer Equilibrium
Occurs when the consumer has spent all income and the marginal utilities per dollar spent on each good purchased are equal: $MU_A/P_A = MU_B/P_B = MU_C/P_C = \ldots = MU_Z/P_Z$, where the letters A–Z represent all the goods a person buys.

Question:

If a person is in consumer equilibrium, does it follow that she has maximized her total utility?

Answer:

Yes, it does. By spending her dollars on goods that give her the greatest marginal utility and in the process bringing about the consumer equilibrium condition, she is adding as much to her total utility as she can possibly add.

Consumers have an objective—to maximize (total) utility; they are constrained by income and prices; and they do make choices in a particular way—by equating the marginal utility–price ratio (MU/P) for all goods purchased—that is, by equating marginal utilities per dollar. The key word here is *marginal*. Economists rely on the idea of marginal magnitudes because they are the magnitudes that count when economic actors seek to meet their objectives. Thinking in terms of marginal magnitudes is part of the economic way of thinking.

Consumer Equilibrium and the Law of Demand

Suppose the consumer purchases 11 oranges and 9 apples and $MU_O/P_O = MU_A/P_A$. Then the price of oranges falls from \$1 each to \$.50. The situation is as follows:

$$MU_{\text{oranges}} = 25 \text{ utils}$$

$$MU_{\text{apples}} = 25 \text{ utils}$$

$$P_{\text{oranges}} = \$.50$$

$$P_{\text{apples}} = \$1.00$$

[2]We are assuming here that the consumer exhausts his or her income and that saving is treated as a good.

We now have $MU_O/P_O > MU_A/P_A$. The fall in the price of oranges has thrown the consumer out of equilibrium into disequilibrium. He will attempt to restore equilibrium by buying more oranges because he derives more utility per dollar from buying oranges than apples. Here we have the inverse relationship between (own) price and quantity demanded expressed in the law of demand.

We can see another example in Exhibit 20–2. There are two goods, *A* and *B*. Currently, the price of both goods is \$1 each. At this price the consumer buys 1 unit of good *A* and 6 units of good *B*. As we see from the exhibit, the marginal utility of the first unit of good *A* is 12 utils, and the marginal utility of the sixth unit of good *B* is also 12 utils. The consumer is in equilibrium where

$$MU_A/P_A = MU_B/P_B$$
$$12 \text{ utils}/\$1.00 = 12 \text{ utils}/\$1.00$$

Now suppose the price of good A falls to \$.50. This changes the situation to the following:

$$MU_A/P_A > MU_B/P_B$$
$$12 \text{ utils}/\$.50 > 12 \text{ utils}/\$1.00$$

In this situation, the consumer is gaining more utility per dollar by purchasing good *A* than good *B*. She decides to buy more of good *A* and less of good *B*. We see that she buys 5 more units of good *A*, to make a total of 6, and 2 fewer units of good *B*, to make a total of 4. As she buys more units of good *A*, the marginal

EXHIBIT 20–2
Consumer Equilibrium and a Fall in Price

Good *A* (Original Purchase: 1 unit → New Purchase: 6 units)

Units of Good *A*	1	2	3	4	5	6	7
Marginal Utility (utils)	12	11.5	11	10	9	8	7

Good *B* (Original Purchase: 6 units → New Purchase: 4 units)

Units of Good *B*	1	2	3	4	5	6	7
Marginal Utility (utils)	22	20	18	16	14	12	10

Original Purchase

Good *A*		Good *B*
$\frac{12 \text{ utils}}{\$1.00}$	=	$\frac{12 \text{ utils}}{\$1.00}$

New Purchase

Good *A*		Good *B*
$\frac{8 \text{ utils}}{\$.50}$	=	$\frac{16 \text{ utils}}{\$1.00}$

Initially, the price of both good *A* and good *B* is \$1. The consumer is in equilibrium buying 1 unit of good *A* and 6 units of good *B*. Then the price of good A falls to \$.50. No longer is the consumer in equilibrium. To restore herself to equilibrium, she buys more of good *A* and less of good *B*. As she does this, the marginal utility of good *A* decreases and the marginal utility of good *B* increases. At the new set of prices, \$.50 for *A* and \$1 for *B*, the consumer is back in equilibrium when she purchases 6 units of good *A* and 4 units of good *B*.

utility of good A decreases (law of diminishing marginal utility). The marginal utility of the sixth unit of good A is 8 utils. As the consumer cuts back on her purchases of good B, we notice that the marginal utility of good B increases. The marginal utility of the fourth unit of good B is 16 utils. At the new set of prices, \$.50 for good A and \$1.00 for good B, the consumer is in equilibrium when she buys 6 units of good A and 4 units of good B. We have the following condition:

$$MU_A/P_A \;=\; MU_B/P_B$$

$$8 \text{ utils}/\$.50 \;=\; 16 \text{ utils}/\$1.00$$

The consumer receives equal marginal utility per dollar from purchasing goods A and B.

Are Rats Rational?

How rational do you have to be to have a downward-sloping demand curve? Empirical research seems to say "as rational as a white rat." Several researchers at Texas A&M University undertook to study the "buying" behavior of two white rats. The rats were put in laboratory cages with two levers: one they could push to obtain root beer, the other they could push to obtain nonalcoholic collins mix. Each day, each of the rats was given a "fixed income" of 300 pushes. (After 300 pushes the lever could not be pushed down until the next day.) The prices of root beer and collins mix were both 20 pushes per milliliter of beverage. Given this income and the price of root beer and collins mix, one rat settled in to consuming 11 milliliters of root beer and 4 milliliters of collins mix. The other rat settled in to consuming almost all root beer.

Then the prices of the two beverages were changed. The price of collins mix was halved while the price of root beer was doubled. Using economic theory, we would predict that with these new prices, the consumption of collins mix would increase and the consumption of root beer would decrease. This is exactly what happened. Both rats began to consume more collins mix and less root beer. In short, both rats had downward-sloping demand curves for collins mix and root beer.

Should the Government Provide the Necessities of Life for Free?

Sometimes you will hear people say, "Food and water are necessities of life. No one can live without them. It is wrong to charge for these goods. The government should provide them free to everyone."

Or you might hear, "Medical care is a necessity to those who are sick. Without it, people will either experience an extremely low quality of life (you can't experience a high quality of life when you are feeling bad) or die. Making people pay for medical care is wrong. The government should provide it free to the people who need it."

Or someone might say, "A college education has become a necessity of life in this day and age. Without a college degree, you can't get a good job and earn a decent salary. You are stuck in a big hole with no way to get out. The government should provide a college education free to anyone who wants it."

Each of these statements labels something as a necessity of life (food and water, medical care, college education) and then makes the policy proposal that government should provide the necessity for free.

Suppose government did give food and water, medical care, and college education to everyone for free—in other words, at zero price (although not at zero taxes). At zero price, people would want to consume these goods up to the point of zero marginal utility for each good. They would do so because if the marginal utility of the good (expressed in dollars) is greater than its price, one could derive more utility from purchasing the good than one would lose in parting with the dollar price of the good. In other words, if the price of a good is $5, an individual will continue purchasing it as long as the marginal utility she derives from its purchase is greater than $5. If the price is $0, she will continue to consume the good as long as the marginal utility she derives from it is greater than 0.

Since resources must be used to produce every unit of a good consumed, the government is using scarce resources to provide a good that has low marginal utility. Thus, if some resources were withdrawn from producing these goods, total utility would fall very little. The resources could then be redirected to producing goods with a higher marginal utility, thereby raising total utility.

The people who argue that certain goods should be provided free implicitly assume that the not-so-valuable uses of food and water, medical care, and college education are valuable enough to warrant a system of taxes to pay for the complete provision of these goods at zero price. It is questionable, however, if the least valuable uses of food and water, medical care, and college education are worth the sacrifices of other goods that would necessarily be forfeited if more of these goods were produced.

Think about these questions: Currently, water is relatively cheap, and people use it to satisfy its more valuable uses and its not-so-valuable uses, too. But suppose water were cheaper than it is? Suppose it were zero price? Would it be used to satisfy its more valuable uses, not-so-valuable uses, and its absolutely least valuable use? If food had a zero price, would it follow that it too would be used to satisfy its more valuable uses, not-so-valuable uses, and its absolutely least valuable use (food fights perhaps)? Would the same be true of medical care? If medical care were free, would some people visit their doctor simply for a social outing? If college education were free, would some people go to college just to "hang out"?

Income and Substitution Effects

Consider what happens when the absolute price of one good falls and the absolute prices of all other goods remain constant. Suppose the absolute price of computers falls, and the absolute prices of all other goods remain constant. Two things occur: First, the relative price of computers falls.[3] Second, a consumer's **real income,** or purchasing power, rises.

Real Income
Income adjusted for price changes. A person has more (less) real income as the price of a good falls (rises), *ceteris paribus.*

A person's real income, or purchasing power, rises if with a given absolute (or dollar) income he or she can purchase more goods and services. To illustrate, suppose Barbara's income is $100 per week, and there are only two goods in the world, *A* and *B,* whose prices are $50 and $25, respectively. With her $100 income, Barbara purchases 1 unit of good *A* and 2 units of good *B* per week, for a total of 3 units of the two goods.

Suppose that the price of good *A* falls to $25, *ceteris paribus.* Now Barbara can purchase a greater combination of the two goods. She purchases 2 units of good *A* and 2 units of good *B,* for a total of 4 units of the two goods. Given this, we say

[3]In Chapter 3, we explained the process by which a fall in absolute price brings about a decrease in relative price, *ceteris paribus.*

that Barbara's real income has risen as a result of the fall in the price of good *A*. With her $100 income, Barbara is able to purchase more goods.

To recap, a fall in the absolute price of a good leads to (1) a fall in the relative price of the good and (2) a rise in real income.

We learned in Chapter 3 that a fall in the relative price of a good will, and a rise in real income can, lead to greater purchases of the good.[4] That portion of the change in the quantity demanded of a good that is attributable to a change in its relative price is referred to as the **substitution effect.** That portion of the change in the quantity demanded of a good that is attributable to a change in real income, brought about by the change in absolute price, is referred to as the **income effect.**

Suppose the price of normal good *A* falls from $10 to $8, *ceteris paribus*. As a result, the quantity demanded of good *A* rises from 100 units to 143 units. A portion of the 43-unit increase in the quantity demanded is due to the relative price of good *A* falling; and a portion of the 43-unit increase in quantity demanded is due to real income rising. Suppose quantity demanded rises from 100 to 129 units because the relative price of good *A* falls. This would be the extent of the substitution effect: People purchase 29 more units of good *A* because it has become relatively cheaper to purchase. The difference between 143 units and 129 units, or 14 units, constitutes the extent of the income effect: People purchase 14 more units of good *A* because their real incomes have risen.

Marginal Utility, Price, and Income

What has to change before buying behavior changes?

Part of the answer is supplied by the condition for consumer equilibrium—which is that the marginal utility—price ratio (MU/P) for all goods and services has to be the same. If either MU changes or P changes, we know that the consumer will be moved into disequilibrium, and his or her buying behavior will change. For example, starting in consumer equilibrium in a two-good world, where $MU_{good\ 1}/P_{good\ 1} = MU_{good\ 2}/P_{good\ 2}$, a rise in the marginal utility of good 1 will increase the consumption of good 1.

A change in income can also change buying behavior. Suppose that starting from a position of consumer equilibrium, a person receives an increase in her (money) income. As a result, she decides to buy more of good 1, which is a normal good. As a result, the marginal utility of good 1 declines and the MU–P ratio of good 1 falls relative to the MU–P ratio of good 2. To reestablish consumer equilibrium, the consumer purchases more of good 2. Here we see that it is possible for an increase in income to increase the consumption of more than just one good.

Now let's use these three concepts—marginal utility, price, and income—in a real-world situation. In 1991, the California housing market had slowed considerably. Houses that once sold in two weeks were taking many months to sell. The situation went from frantic buying and selling to very little buying and selling. Some real estate companies closed a few of their branch offices; some real estate agents left the business. Sellers, potential buyers, and the remaining real estate agents wondered, When would buying behavior (in the California real estate market) pick up?

An economist would reword this question and ask, What needs to change before buying behavior picks up? The answer is, one of three things—marginal utility of the good, the price of the good, or peoples' incomes.

Substitution Effect
That portion of the change in the quantity demanded of a good that is attributable to a change in its relative price.

Income Effect
That portion of the change in the quantity demanded of a good that is attributable to a change in real income (brought about by a change in absolute price).

[4]Specifically, a rise in real income *will* lead to greater purchases of a good if the good is a normal good. It will not, if the good is an inferior good. See the discussion of normal and inferior goods in Chapter 3.

At this time in California, many sellers were actively trying to influence buyers' marginal utility of the houses for sale. For example, if a house was located near a good school, the seller would be sure to bring this point up to parents with children. This was a different state of affairs from the boom days of California real estate when sellers did little more than simply post a price and wait for buyers to knock at their doors.

Our three economic concepts can also be used to make a prediction. Assuming that the buyers' marginal utility of the houses for sale does not change, and income does not change, we predict that before buying will pick up, prices will have to fall.

Is this useful information? It certainly would be to a potential buyer of California real estate. In short, asking the right question—What has to change before buying behavior changes?—and then answering the question, can lead to an accurate prediction and to a boon to one's wallet.

Consumers' Surplus

Consumers' Surplus
The difference between the price buyers pay for a good and the maximum or highest price they would have paid for the good. It is a dollar measure of the benefit gained by being able to purchase a unit of a good for less than one is willing to pay for it.

Consumers' surplus is the difference between the price buyers pay for a good and the maximum, or highest, price they would have paid for the good. It is a dollar measure of the benefit gained by being able to purchase a unit of a good for less than one is willing to pay for it. For example, if Joanne would have paid $10 to see the movie at the Cinemax, but only paid $4, her consumer surplus if $6.

Consumers' surplus is represented as the shaded triangle in Exhibit 20–3a. This triangle is the area under the demand curve and above the equilibrium price out to the equilibrium quantity. Keeping in mind that consumers' surplus is highest price minus price paid, notice in the window of the exhibit that consumers would

EXHIBIT 20–3
Consumers' Surplus

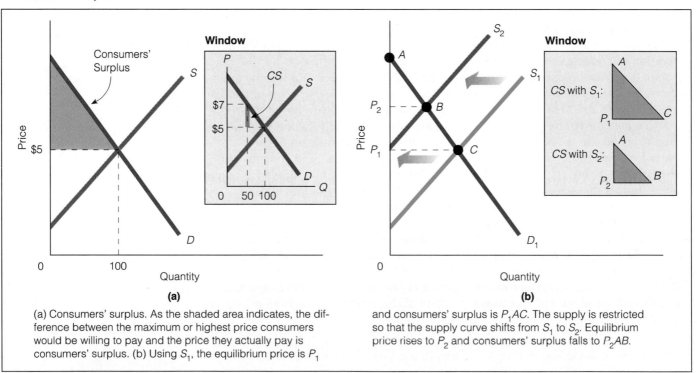

(a) Consumers' surplus. As the shaded area indicates, the difference between the maximum or highest price consumers would be willing to pay and the price they actually pay is consumers' surplus. (b) Using S_1, the equilibrium price is P_1 and consumers' surplus is P_1AC. The supply is restricted so that the supply curve shifts from S_1 to S_2. Equilibrium price rises to P_2 and consumers' surplus falls to P_2AB.

have been willing to pay $7 for the 50th unit, but instead paid $5. Thus, the consumers' surplus on the 50th unit of the good is $2. If we add the consumers' surplus on each unit of the good between and including the first and the 100th (100 units being the equilibrium quantity), we obtain the shaded (consumers' surplus) triangle.

Using Consumers' Surplus

Here is an example to illustrate the use of consumers' surplus. In Exhibit 20–3b, suppose D_1 and S_1 are the effective demand and supply curves, respectively, and P_1 is the equilibrium price. The consumers' surplus under this condition is represented by the area P_1AC.

Now suppose government regulations or a private monopoly restrict the supply of the good.[5] This causes the supply curve to shift leftward from S_1 to S_2 and for equilibrium price to rise from P_1 to P_2. As a result, the area of consumers' surplus shrinks from P_1AC to P_2AB.

We conclude that government regulations or monopolists which reduce supply lower consumers' welfare as measured by the economic concept of consumers' surplus.

CHAPTER SUMMARY

The Law of Diminishing Marginal Utility

■ The law of diminishing marginal utility holds that as the amount of a good consumed increases, the marginal utility of the good decreases.
■ The law of diminishing marginal utility should not be used to make interpersonal utility comparisons. For example, the law does not say that a millionaire receives less (or more) utility from an additional dollar than a poor man. Instead, it says that the last dollar has less value for both the millionaire and the poor man than the next-to-last dollar.

The Diamond–Water Paradox

■ The diamond–water paradox states that what has great value in use sometimes has little value in exchange and what has little value in use sometimes has great value in exchange. A knowledge of the difference between total utility and marginal utility is necessary to unravel the diamond–water paradox.
■ A good can have high total utility and low marginal utility. Take water, for example. Its total utility is high; but because water is so plentiful, its marginal utility is low. In short, water is immensely useful, but it is so plentiful that individuals place relatively low value on another unit of it. In contrast, diamonds are not as useful as water, but because there are few diamonds in the world, the marginal utility of diamonds is high. In sum, a good can be extremely useful and have a low price if the good is in plentiful supply (high value in use, low value in exchange). On the other hand, a good can be of little use and have a high price if the good is in short supply (low value in use, high value in exchange).

[5]In Chapter 3, we discussed how government restrictions (such as a quota) would reduce supply.

Consumer Equilibrium

■ Individuals seek to equate marginal utilities per dollar. For example, if a person receives more utility per dollar spent on good *A* than *B*, she will reorder her purchases and buy more *A* and less *B*. There is a tendency to move away from this condition, $MU_A/P_A > MU_B/P_B$, to this condition, $MU_A/P_A = MU_B/P_B$. The latter condition represents consumer equilibrium (in a two-good world).

Marginal Utility Analysis and the Law of Demand

■ Marginal utility analysis can be used to illustrate the law of demand. The law of demand states that price and quantity demanded are inversely related, *ceteris paribus*. Starting from consumer equilibrium in a world in which there are only two goods, *A* and *B*, a fall in the price of *A* will cause MU_A/P_A to be greater than MU_B/P_B. As a result, the consumer will purchase more of good *A* to restore herself to equilibrium.

Key Terms and Concepts

Diamond-Water Paradox	Total Utility	Interpersonal Utility Comparison
Utility	Marginal Utility	
Utils	Law of Diminishing Marginal Utility	Consumers' Surplus

QUESTIONS AND PROBLEMS

1. If we take $1 away from a rich person and give it to a poor person, the rich person loses less utility than the poor person gains. Comment.

2. Is it possible to get so much of a good that it turns into a bad? If so, give an example.

3. If a person consumes fewer units of a good, will marginal utility of the good increase as total utility decreases? Why?

4. If the marginal utility of good *A* is 4 utils and its price is $2, and the marginal utility of good *B* is 6 utils and its price is $1, is the individual consumer maximizing (total) utility if she spends a total of $3 buying one unit of each good? If not, how can more utility be obtained?

5. Individuals who buy second homes usually spend less for them than they do for their first homes. Why is this the case?

6. Think of five everyday examples where you or someone else makes an interpersonal utility comparison.

7. Is there a logical link between the law of demand and the assumption that individuals seek to maximize utility? (Hint: Think of how the condition for consumer equilibrium can be used to express the inverse relationship between price and quantity demanded.)

8. List five sets of two goods (each set is composed of two goods; for example, diamonds and water is one set) where the good with the greater value in use has lower value in exchange than the good with the lower value in use.

9. Do you think people with high IQs are in consumer equilibrium (equate marginal utilities per dollar) more often than people with low IQs? Why?

APPENDIX

G

BUDGET CONSTRAINT AND INDIFFERENCE CURVE ANALYSIS

In this chapter we used marginal utility theory to discuss consumer choice. Sometimes budget constraint and indifference curve analysis is used instead, especially in upper-division economics courses. We examine this important topic in this appendix.

THE BUDGET CONSTRAINT

Societies have production possibilities frontiers (see Chapter 2), and individuals have **budget constraints.** The budget constraint is built on two prices and the individual's income. To illustrate, consider O'Brien who has a monthly income of $1,200. In a world of two goods, X and Y, O'Brien can spend his total income on X, he can spend his total income on Y, or he can spend part of his income on X and part on Y. Suppose the price of X is $100 and the price of Y is $80. Given this, if O'Brien spends his total income on X, he can purchase a maximum of 12 units; if he spends his total income on Y, he can purchase a maximum of 15 units. Locating these two points on a two-dimensional diagram and then drawing a line between them, as we have done in Exhibit 20G–1, gives us O'Brien's budget constraint. Any point on the budget constraint, as well as any point below it, represents a possible combination (bundle) of the two goods available to O'Brien.

The slope of the budget constraint has special significance. The absolute value of the slope represents the relative prices of the two goods, X and Y. This slope, or P_X/P_Y, is equal to 1.25, indicating that the relative price of 1 unit of X is 1.25 units of Y.

What Will Change the Budget Constraint?

As we stated, the budget constraint is built on two prices and the individual's income. This means that if any of the three variables changes (either of the prices or the individual's income), the budget constraint changes. Not all changes are alike, however. First, consider a fall in the price of good X from $100 to $60. With

Budget Constraint
All the combinations or bundles of two goods a person can purchase given a certain money income and prices for the two goods.

EXHIBIT 20G–1
The Budget Constraint

An individual's budget constraint gives us a picture of the different combinations (bundles) of two goods available to the individual (this assumes a two-good world; for a many-good world, we could put one good on one axis and "all other goods" on the other). The budget constraint is derived by finding the maximum amount of each good an individual can consume (given his or her income and the prices of the two goods) and connecting these two points.

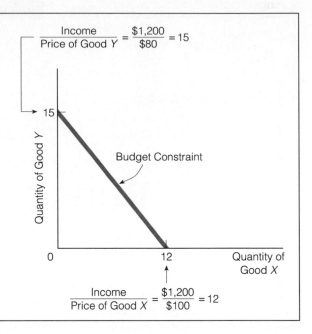

$$\frac{\text{Income}}{\text{Price of Good } Y} = \frac{\$1,200}{\$80} = 15$$

$$\frac{\text{Income}}{\text{Price of Good } X} = \frac{\$1,200}{\$100} = 12$$

this change the maximum number of units of good X purchasable with an income of $1,200 rises from 12 to 20. The budget constraint revolves away from the origin in a counterclockwise direction, as shown in (Exhibit 20G–2a). Notice that the number of O'Brien's possible combinations of the two goods increases; there are more bundles of the two goods available after the price decrease than before.

Consider what happens to the budget constraint if the price of good X rises. If it goes from $100 to $150, the maximum number of units of good X falls from 12 to 8. The budget constraint revolves toward the origin in a clockwise direction. As a consequence, the number of bundles available to O'Brien decreases. We conclude that a change in the price of either good changes the slope of the budget constraint, with the result that relative prices and the number of bundles available to the individual also change.

We turn now to a change in income. If O'Brien's income rises to $1,600, the maximum number of units of X rises to 16 and the maximum number of units of Y rises to 20. The budget constraint shifts rightward (away from the origin) and is parallel to the old budget constraint. As a consequence, the number of bundles available to O'Brien increases (Exhibit 20G–2b). If O'Brien's income falls from $1,200 to $800, the extreme end points on the budget constraint become 8 and 10 for X and Y, respectively. The budget constraint shifts leftward (toward the origin) and is parallel to the old budget constraint. As a consequence, the number of bundles available to O'Brien falls (Exhibit 20G–2b).

INDIFFERENCE CURVES

■

An individual can, of course, choose any bundle of the two goods on or below the budget constraint. We assume that she spends her total income and therefore chooses a point on the budget constraint. This raises two important questions:

EXHIBIT 20G–2
Changes in the Budget Constraint

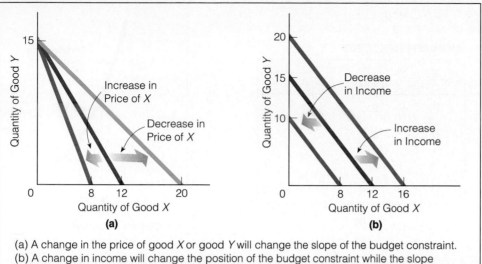

(a) A change in the price of good *X* or good *Y* will change the slope of the budget constraint.
(b) A change in income will change the position of the budget constraint while the slope remains constant. Whenever a budget constraint changes, the number of combinations (bundles) of the two goods available to the individual changes, too.

(1) Which bundle of the many bundles of the two goods does the individual choose? (2) How does the individual's chosen combination of goods change given a change in prices or income? Both questions can be answered by combining the budget constraint with the graphical expression of the individual's preferences— that is, indifference curves.

Constructing an Indifference Curve

Is it possible to be indifferent between two bundles of goods? Yes, it is. Suppose bundle *A* consists of 2 pairs of shoes and 6 shirts and bundle *B* consists of 3 pairs of shoes and 4 shirts. A person who is indifferent between these two bundles is implicitly saying that it doesn't matter which bundle he ends up with; one is as good as the other. He is likely to say this, though, only if he receives equal total utility from the two bundles: If this were not the case, he would prefer one bundle to the other.

If we were to tabulate all the different bundles from which the individual receives equal utility, we would have an **indifference set.** If we then plotted the data in the indifference set, we would have an **indifference curve.** Consider the indifference set illustrated in Exhibit 20G–3a. There are four bundles of goods, *A–D*; each bundle gives the same total utility as every other bundle. These equal-utility bundles are plotted in Exhibit 20G–3b. Connecting these bundles in a two-dimensional space gives us an indifference curve.

Characteristics of Indifference Curves

Indifference curves for goods have certain characteristics that are consistent with reasonable assumptions about consumer behavior. We present a list of them here.

■ **Indifference curves are downward sloping** (from left to right). The assumption that consumers always prefer more of a good to less requires that indifference

Indifference Set
Group of bundles of two goods that give an individual equal total utility.

Indifference Curve
Represents an indifference set. A curve that shows all the bundles of two goods that give an individual equal total utility.

EXHIBIT 20G–3
An Indifference Set and an Indifference Curve

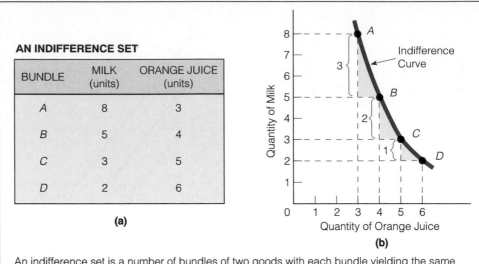

An indifference set is a number of bundles of two goods with each bundle yielding the same total utility. An indifference curve represents an indifference set. In this exhibit, data from an indifference set (a) are used to derive an indifference curve (b).

curves slope downward left to right. Consider the alternatives to downward sloping: vertical, horizontal, and upward sloping (left to right). A horizontal or vertical curve would combine bundles of goods some of which had more of one good and no less of another good than other bundles (Exhibit 20G–4a–b). (If bundle *B* contained more of one good and no less of another good than bundle *A,* would an individual be *indifferent* between the two bundles? No, he or she wouldn't. Individuals prefer more to less.) An upward-sloping curve would combine bundles of goods some of which had more of *both* goods than other bundles (Exhibit 20G–4c). A simpler way of putting it is to say that indifference curves are downward sloping because a person has to get more of one good in order to maintain his or her level of satisfaction (utility) when giving up some of another good.

■ **Indifference curves are convex to the origin.** This implies that the slope of the indifference curve becomes flatter as we move down and to the right along the indifference curve. For example, at 8 units of milk (point *A* in Exhibit 20G–3b), the individual is willing to give up 3 units of milk to get an additional unit of orange juice (and thus move to point *B*). At point *B,* where she has 5 units of milk, she is only willing to give up 2 units of milk to get an additional unit of orange juice (and thus move to point *C*). Finally, at point *C,* with 3 units of milk, she is now only willing to give up 1 unit of milk to get an additional unit of orange juice. We conclude that the more of one good that an individual has, the more units he or she will give up to get an additional unit of another good; the less of one good that an individual has, the fewer units he or she will give up to get an additional unit of another good. Is this reasonable? The answer is yes. Our observation is a reflection of diminishing marginal utility at work. As the quantity of a good consumed increases, the marginal utility of that good decreases; therefore we reason that the more of one good an individual has, the more units he or she can (and will) sacrifice to get an additional unit of another good and still maintain total utility. Stated differently, if the law of diminishing marginal utility did not exist,

EXHIBIT 20G–4
Indifferences Curves for Goods Do Not Look Like This

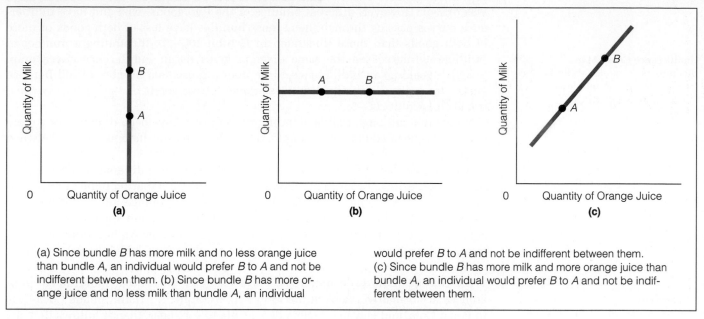

(a) Since bundle *B* has more milk and no less orange juice than bundle *A*, an individual would prefer *B* to *A* and not be indifferent between them. (b) Since bundle *B* has more orange juice and no less milk than bundle *A*, an individual

would prefer *B* to *A* and not be indifferent between them.
(c) Since bundle *B* has more milk and more orange juice than bundle *A*, an individual would prefer *B* to *A* and not be indifferent between them.

then it would not make sense to say that indifference curves of goods are convex to the origin.

An important peripheral point about marginal utilities is that *the absolute value of the slope of the indifference curve*—which is called the **marginal rate of substitution**—*represents the ratio of the marginal utility of the good on the horizontal axis to the marginal utility of the good on the vertical axis:*

$$\frac{MU_{\text{good on horizontal axis}}}{MU_{\text{good on vertical axis}}}$$

Let's look carefully at the words in italics. First, we said that the absolute value of the slope of the indifference curve is the marginal rate of substitution. The marginal rate of substitution (*MRS*) is the amount of one good an individual is willing to give up to obtain an additional unit of another good and maintain equal total utility. For example, in Exhibit 20G–3b we see that moving from point *A* to *B*, the individual is willing to give up 3 units of milk to get an additional unit of orange juice, with total utility remaining constant (between points *A* and *B*). The marginal rate of substitution is therefore 3 units of milk for 1 unit of orange juice in the area between points *A* and *B*. And as we said, the absolute value of the slope of the indifference curve, the marginal rate of substitution, is equal to the ratio of the *MU* of the good on the horizontal axis to the *MU* of the good on the vertical axis. How can this be? Well, if it is true that an individual giving up 3 units of milk and receiving 1 unit of orange juice maintains his total utility, it follows that (in the area under consideration) the marginal utility of orange juice is approximately three times the marginal utility of milk. In general terms

Absolute value of the slope of the indifference curve

$$= \text{marginal rate of substitution} = \frac{MU_{\text{good on horizontal axis}}}{MU_{\text{good on vertical axis}}}$$

Marginal Rate of Substitution
The amount of one good an individual is willing to give up to obtain an additional unit of another good and maintain equal total utility.

■ **Indifference curves that are farther from the origin are preferable because they represent larger bundles of goods.** In Exhibit 20G–3b only one indifference curve was drawn. However, different bundles of the two goods exist and have indifference curves passing through them; these bundles have less of both goods or more of both goods than those illustrated in Exhibit 20G–3b. Illustrating a number of indifference curves on the same diagram gives us an **indifference curve map.** Strictly speaking, an indifference curve map represents a number of indifference curves for a given individual with reference to two goods. A "mapping" is illustrated in Exhibit 20G–5.

Notice that although only five indifference curves have been drawn, many more could have been added. For example, there are many indifference curves between I_1 and I_2.

Also notice that the farther away from the origin an indifference curve is, the higher total utility it represents. You can see this by comparing point A on I_1 and point B on I_2. At point B there is the same amount of orange juice as at point A, but more milk. Point B is therefore preferable to point A, and since B is on I_2 and A is on I_1, I_2 is preferable to I_1. The reason for this is simple: An individual receives more utility at any point on I_2 (because more goods are available) than at any point on I_1.

■ **Indifference curves do not cross.** The reason for this is that individuals' preferences are **transitive.** Look at the following example. If Kristin prefers Coca-Cola to Pepsi-Cola, and she also prefers Pepsi-Cola to root beer, then it follows that she prefers Coca-Cola to root beer. If she preferred root beer to Coca-Cola, she would be contradicting her earlier preferences. To say that an individual has transitive preferences means that he or she maintains a logical order of preferences during a given time period. Consider what indifference curves that crossed (intersected) would represent. In Exhibit 20G–6, indifference curves I_1 and I_2 intersect at point A. Notice that point A lies on *both* I_1 and I_2. Comparing A and B, we hold that the individual must be indifferent between them because they lie on the same indif-

Indifference Curve Map
Represents a number of indifference curves for a given individual with reference to two goods.

Transitivity
The principle whereby if A is preferred to B, and B is preferred to C, then A is preferred to C.

EXHIBIT 20G–5
An Indifference Map

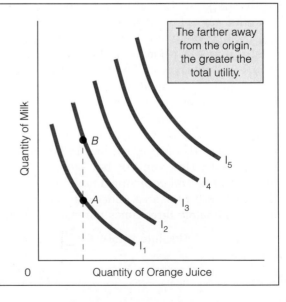

A few of the many possible indifference curves have been drawn. Any point in the two-dimensional space is on an indifference curve. Indifference curves farther away from the origin represent greater total utility than those closer to the origin.

The farther away from the origin, the greater the total utility.

ference curve. The same holds for *A* and *C*. But if the individual is indifferent between *A* and *B,* and between *A* and *C,* it follows that she must be indifferent between *B* and *C.* But a quick glance at the exhibit tells us that *C* has more of both goods than *B,* and thus the individual will not be indifferent between *B* and *C;* she will prefer *C* to *B.* We cannot have transitive preferences and make sense of crossing indifference curves. We can, however, have transitive preferences and make sense of noncrossing indifference curves. We go with the latter.

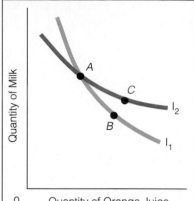

Point *A* lies on both indifference curves I_1 and I_2. This means that the individual is indifferent between *A* an *B* and between *A* an *C,* which results in her (supposedly) being indifferent between *B* and *C.* But individuals prefer "more to less" (when it comes to goods) and, thus, would prefer *C* to *B.* We cannot have transitive preferences and make sense of crossing indifference curves.

THE INDIFFERENCE MAP AND THE BUDGET CONSTRAINT COME TOGETHER

At this point we bring the indifference map and the budget constraint together to illustrate consumer equilibrium. We have the following facts: (1) The individual has a budget constraint. (2) The absolute value of the slope of the budget constraint is the relative prices of the two goods under consideration, say, P_X/P_Y. (3) The individual has an indifference map. (4) The absolute value of the slope of the indifference curve at any point is the marginal rate of substitution, which is equal to the marginal utility of one good divided by the marginal utility of another good; for example, MU_X/MU_Y. With this information, what is the necessary condition for consumer equilibrium? Obviously the individual will try to reach a point on the highest indifference curve she can reach. This point will be where the slope of the budget constraint is equal to the slope of an indifference curve (or where the budget constraint is tangent to an indifference curve). At this point consumer equilibrium is established and the following condition holds:

Slope of budget constraint = slope of indifference curve

or

$$\frac{P_X}{P_Y} = \frac{MU_X}{MU_Y}$$

This condition is met in Exhibit 20G–7 at point *E.* Note that it looks similar to the

EXHIBIT 20G–7
Consumer Equilibrium

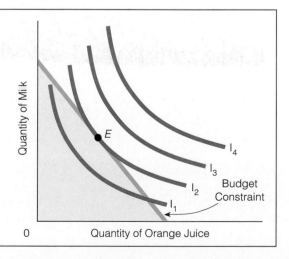

Consumer equilibrium exists at the point where the slope of the budget constraint is equal to the slope of an indifference curve, or where the budget constraint is tangent to an indifference curve. In the exhibit, this point is *E.* Here $P_X/P_Y = MU_X/MU_Y$; or rearranging, $MU_X/P_X = MU_Y/P_Y$.

condition for consumer equilibrium that we found early in Chapter 20. By rearranging the terms in the condition, we get[1]

$$\frac{MU_X}{P_X} = \frac{MU_Y}{P_Y}$$

We now see that the condition for consumer equilibrium is the same whether we use a marginal utility approach or a budget constraint–indifference curve approach.

From Indifference Curves to a Demand Curve

We can now derive a demand curve within a budget constraint–indifference curve framework. In Exhibit 20G–8a there are two budget constraints, one reflecting a $10 price for good X and the other reflecting a $5 price for good X. Notice that as

[1]Start with $P_X/P_Y = MU_X/MU_Y$ and cross multiply. This gives us $P_X MU_Y = P_Y MU_X$. Next divide both sides by P_X. This gives us $MU_Y = P_Y MU_X/P_X$. Finally, divide both sides by P_Y. This gives us $MU_Y/P_Y = MU_X/P_X$.

EXHIBIT 20G–8
From Indifference Curves to a Demand Curve

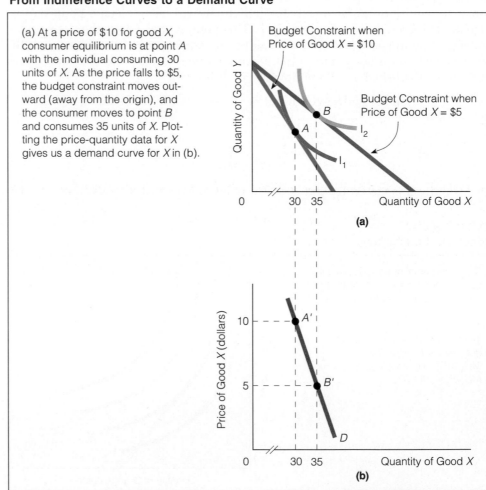

(a) At a price of $10 for good X, consumer equilibrium is at point A with the individual consuming 30 units of X. As the price falls to $5, the budget constraint moves outward (away from the origin), and the consumer moves to point B and consumes 35 units of X. Plotting the price-quantity data for X gives us a demand curve for X in (b).

the price of X falls, the consumer moves from point A to B. At B, 35 units of X are consumed; at A, 30 units of X were consumed. We conclude that a lower price for X results in greater consumption of X. By plotting our relevant price and quantity data, we derive a demand curve for good X in (b).

APPENDIX SUMMARY

■ A budget constraint represents all combinations or bundles of two goods a person can purchase given a certain money income and prices for the two goods.
■ An indifference curve shows all the combinations or bundles of two goods that give an individual equal total utility.
■ Indifference curves are downward sloping, convex to the origin, and do not cross. The further from the origin an indifference curve is, the greater total utility it represents for the individual.
■ Consumer equilibrium comes where the slope of the budget constraint equals the slope of the indifference curve.

QUESTIONS AND PROBLEMS

1. Diagram the following budget constraints:

    a. income = $4,000; P_X = $50; P_Y = $100
    b. income = $3,000; P_X = $25; P_Y = $200
    c. income = $2,000; P_X = $40; P_Y = $150

2. Explain why indifference curves are (a) downward sloping, (b) convex to the origin, and (c) do not cross.
3. Explain why consumer equilibrium is equivalent using marginal utility and indifference curve analysis.
4. Derive a demand curve using indifference curve analysis.

ELASTICITY

WHAT THIS CHAPTER IS ABOUT

This chapter is divided into two parts. Part 1 defines price elasticity of demand, explains how it is calculated, and describes the relationship between it and total revenue (total expenditure). This information is important to understanding the firm and market structures, which are discussed in upcoming chapters. Part 2 discusses the determinants of price elasticity of demand, along with cross elasticity of demand, income elasticity of demand, and price elasticity of supply.

ELASTICITY: PART 1

■

The law of demand states that price and quantity demanded are inversely related, *ceteris paribus.* What we don't know is by *what percentage* quantity demanded changes as price changes. Suppose price rises by 10 percent. As a result, quantity demanded falls. But by *what percentage* does it fall? We can answer this question by applying the notion of *price elasticity of demand.* The general concept of *elasticity* provides a technique for estimating the response of one variable to changes in some other variable. It has numerous applications in economics.

Price elasticity of demand is a measure of the responsiveness of quantity demanded to changes in price.

■

Price Elasticity of Demand

Price elasticity of demand is a measure of the responsiveness of quantity demanded to changes in price. Who might be interested in price elasticity of demand? The answer is just about anyone who sells anything. The person who sells running shoes wants some idea of how much quantity demanded will fall if she raises shoe prices 5 percent. The car salesman wants to know how much quantity demanded will rise if he lowers car prices 10 percent. The university administration wants to know how much enrollment will drop if it raises tuition by 7 percent.

    Economists measure price elasticity of demand quite simply: They divide the percentage change in the quantity demanded of a good by the percentage change in its price. For example, if the quantity demanded of good *X* falls by 20 percent as a result of a 10 percent rise in the price of good *X*, price elasticity of demand is 2 (20 percent/10 percent = 2). In short:

$$E_d = \frac{\text{percentage change in quantity demanded}}{\text{percentage change in price}} = \frac{\%\Delta Q_d}{\%\Delta P}$$

where E_d stands for "coefficient of price elasticity of demand," or simply "elasticity coefficient," and Δ stands for "change in."

Price Elasticity of Demand
A measure of the responsiveness of quantity demanded to changes in price.

Question:

Suppose the elasticity coefficient is 2. What does this mean?

Answer:

It means that if prices were raised from the prevailing rate, the percentage change in quantity demanded would be 2 times the percentage change in price. For example, if price were raised 1 percent, quantity demanded would fall 2 percent. Consider an example closer to home. Suppose the university raises tuition by 10 percent and the enrollment falls off by 20 percent. Here the elasticity coefficient is 2. This number is a shorthand way of saying that a 10 percent rise in tuition brought about a 20 percent (2 times the percentage change in price) fall in enrollment.

Follow-up Question:

If the elasticity coefficient is 2, which means quantity demanded falls by 2 times the percentage rise in price, shouldn't there be a minus sign (−) in front of the number 2?

EXHIBIT 21–2
Price Elasticity of Demand

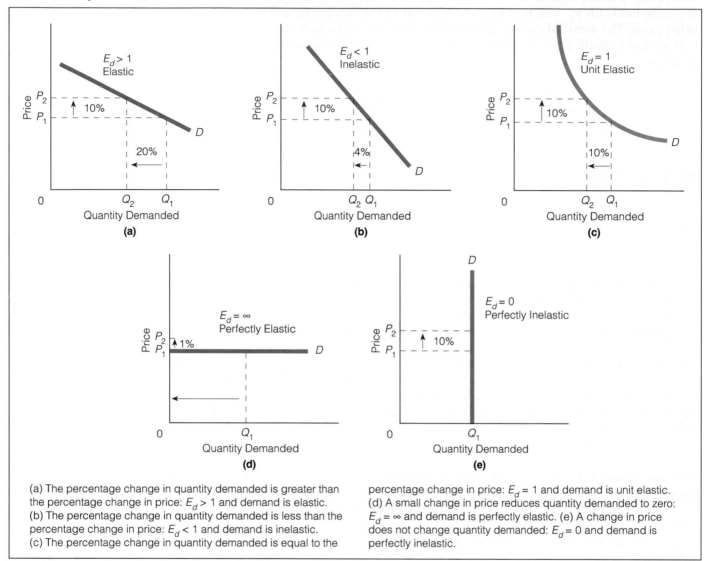

(a) The percentage change in quantity demanded is greater than the percentage change in price: $E_d > 1$ and demand is elastic.
(b) The percentage change in quantity demanded is less than the percentage change in price: $E_d < 1$ and demand is inelastic.
(c) The percentage change in quantity demanded is equal to the percentage change in price: $E_d = 1$ and demand is unit elastic.
(d) A small change in price reduces quantity demanded to zero: $E_d = \infty$ and demand is perfectly elastic. (e) A change in price does not change quantity demanded: $E_d = 0$ and demand is perfectly inelastic.

Unit Elastic Demand
The percentage change in quantity demanded is equal to the percentage change in price. Quantity demanded changes proportionately to price changes.

Unit Elastic Demand ($E_d = 1$). If the numerator (percentage change in quantity demanded) equals the denominator (percentage change in price), the elasticity coefficient is one (1). This means quantity demanded changes proportionately to price changes. For example, a 10 percent increase in price brings about a 10 percent decrease in quantity demanded ($E_d = 1$). Demand exhibits unitary elasticity or is **unit elastic.**

Perfectly Elastic Demand
A small percentage change in price brings about an extremely large percentage change in quantity demanded (from buying all to buying nothing).

Perfectly Elastic Demand ($E_d = \infty$). If quantity demanded is extremely responsive to changes in price, demand is **perfectly elastic.** For example, buyers are willing to buy all units of a seller's good at $5 per unit, but nothing at $5.10. A small percentage change in price brings about an extremely large percentage change in quantity demanded (from buying all to buying nothing). The percentage is so large, in fact, that economists say it is "infinitely large."

Perfectly Inelastic Demand ($E_d = 0$). If quantity demanded is completely unresponsive to changes in price, demand is **perfectly inelastic.** For example, buyers are willing to buy 100 units of good X at $10 each, and if price rises to $11, they are still willing to buy 100 units. A change in price brings about no change in quantity demanded.

Perfectly Inelastic Demand
Quantity demanded does not change as price changes.

Question:

Suppose the price of "Dogs Love It" dog food rises 10 percent, and Jeremy doesn't buy any less of it per week for his dog, Napsie. Does it follow that Jeremy's demand for "Dogs Love It" dog food is perfectly inelastic?

Answer:

Yes, it is perfectly inelastic, between the initial price and the 10 percent higher price. We qualify this because if price rises another 10 percent, Jeremy may cut back on his weekly purchases of "Dogs Love It" dog food and buy some other kind of dog food instead. In the next section, we show how price elasticity of demand changes as we move up some demand curves from lower to higher prices.

Question:

Aren't all demand curves downward sloping because they express the inverse relationship between price and quantity demanded, ceteris paribus? In (d) and (e) in Exhibit 21–2, neither of the demand curves is downward sloping. Why?

Answer:

In the real world, there are no perfectly elastic or perfectly inelastic demand curves *at all prices.* Thus, we ought to view the perfectly elastic and perfectly inelastic demand curves in Exhibit 21–2 as representations of the extreme limits between which all real-world demand curves fall.

We should add, however, that a few real-world demand curves *approximate* the perfectly elastic and inelastic demand curves in (d) and (e). In other words, they come very close. For example, the demand for a particular farmer's wheat approximates the perfectly elastic demand curve in (d). We discuss this in detail in Chapter 24.

Price Elasticity of Demand and Total Revenue (Total Expenditure)

Total revenue equals the price of a good times the quantity of the good sold.[1] For example, if the hamburger stand down the street sells 100 hamburgers today at $1.50 each, its total revenue is $150.

Suppose the hamburger vendor were to raise the price of hamburgers to $2 each. What do you predict will happen to total revenue? Most people say it will increase; there is a widespread belief that higher prices bring higher total revenue. But total revenue may decrease, or it may remain constant. Suppose price rises to $2, but because of the higher price, the quantity of hamburgers sold falls to 50. Total

Total Revenue
Price times quantity sold.

---

[1] In the discussions here, "total revenue" and "total expenditure" are equivalent terms. Total revenue equals price times the quantity sold. Total expenditure equals price times the quantity purchased. If something is sold, it must be purchased, making total revenue equal to total expenditure. The term "total revenue" is used when looking at things from the point of view of sellers in a market. The term "total expenditure" is used when looking at things from the point of view of the buyers in a market. Buyers make expenditures, sellers receive revenues.

revenue is now $100 (whereas it was $150). Whether total revenue rises, falls, or remains constant after a price change depends on whether the *percentage change in quantity demanded* is less than, greater than, or equal to the *percentage change in price*. We are back to price elasticity of demand.

If demand is elastic, the percentage change in quantity demanded is greater than the percentage change in price. Given a price rise of, say, 5 percent, quantity demanded falls *by more than* 5 percent—say, 8 percent. What happens to total revenue? If quantity demanded falls, or sales fall off, by a greater percentage than price rises, total revenue decreases. In short, *if demand is elastic, a price rise decreases total revenue.*

But suppose demand is elastic and price falls? What happens to total revenue? In this case, quantity demanded rises (price and quantity demanded are inversely related) by a greater percentage than price falls, causing total revenue to increase. In short, *if demand is elastic, a price fall increases total revenue.*

If demand is inelastic, the percentage change in quantity demanded is less than the percentage change in price. If price rises, quantity demanded falls, but by a smaller percentage than price rises. As a result, total revenue increases. *If demand is inelastic, a price rise increases total revenue.* If, however, price falls, quantity demanded rises by a smaller percentage than price falls. Total revenue decreases. *If demand is inelastic, a price fall decreases total revenue.*

If demand is unit elastic, the percentage change in quantity demanded equals the percentage change in price. If price rises, quantity demanded falls by the same percentage as price rises. Total revenue does not change. If price falls, quantity demanded rises by the same percentage as price falls. Once again, total revenue does not change. *If demand is unit elastic, a rise or fall in price leaves total revenue unchanged.* For a quick review of the material in this section, see Exhibit 21–3.

When Is a Half-Packed Auditorium Better Than a Packed One?

Suppose you are the manager of a famous rock group, which will soon go on a tour of 30 U.S. cities. In each of the 30 cities, the group will play in an auditorium. The auditorium in St. Louis, Missouri, seats, say, 20,000 people. Is it better to sell all 20,000 tickets for the rock group's performance or to sell less than 20,000 tickets, perhaps 10,000 tickets?

Most people will say it is better to sell 20,000 tickets than 10,000 tickets. But is it necessarily better? To sell 20,000 tickets, the price per ticket will have to be lower than the price per ticket to sell 10,000 tickets. Suppose that to sell all 20,000 tickets, the ticket price must be $10. In that case, the total revenue will be $200,000. Suppose, however, that at $25 per ticket, 10,000 tickets (and no more) can be sold. In that case, the total revenue will be $250,000. In other words, a $10 ticket price fills the auditorium to capacity and generates $200,000 total revenue. A $25 ticket price only fills half the auditorium but generates $250,000 total revenue.

Question:

Doesn't the analysis implicitly assume that only one ticket price, either $25 or $10, can be charged? If more than one price can be charged, then the 10,000 good seats in the auditorium might be sold for $25 each, and the remaining 10,000 not-so-good seats might be sold for $10 each. The total revenue would be $350,000 ($25 × 10,000 + $10 × 10,000 = $350,000). In short, if only one price can be charged,

EXHIBIT 21–3
Elasticities, Price Changes, and Total Revenue

If demand is elastic, a price rise leads to a decrease in total revenue and a price fall leads to an increase in total revenue. If demand is inelastic, a price rise leads to an increase in total revenue and a price fall leads to a decrease in total revenue. If demand is unit elastic, a rise or fall in price does not change total revenue.

PRICE ELASTICITY OF DEMAND	PRICE	TOTAL REVENUE
Elastic	↑ ↓	↓ ↑
Inelastic	↑ ↓	↑ ↓
Unit Elastic	↑ ↓	No Change / No Change

If Cars Get More Miles Per Gallon, Will There Be More or Less Car Pollution?

The concept of elasticity relates to a change in one thing (such as price) relative to a change in something else (such as quantity demanded). With this in mind, consider this question: If fuel economy standards are raised, will there be more or less car pollution?

The answer that most people will give is "less car pollution." They reason this way: (1) If fuel economy standards are raised, the average miles per gallon for a car will rise—say, from 27 mpg to 40 mpg. (2) With more miles per gallon, people will have to buy fewer gallons to get from one point to another, say, from home to university. (3) Consequently, people will buy and burn less gas. (4) This results in less car pollution since burning gas causes carbon dioxide (pollution).

This sounds like a reasonable argument and it could very well be true. But it is not necessarily true. Things could unfold this way. (1) Because fuel economy standards are raised from an average of 27 mpg to 40 mpg, the cost per mile of travel declines. For example, if the price of one gallon of gas is $1.20 and a car gets 27 mpg, the cost per mile is $.044 per mile, but if the price is $1.20 and the car gets 40 mpg, the cost per mile is

$.03 per mile of travel. (2) At a lower cost per mile of travel, people will decide to travel more—after all, we assume the demand curve for travel is downward sloping.

What is the result? Will a rise in fuel economy standards increase, decrease, or leave constant the gallon consumption per month of gasoline? Obviously, it depends on how much gas consumption declines because of a higher mpg relative to how much gas consumption rises because of a lower cost per mile of travel. If the decline in gas consumption because of a higher mpg is greater than the rise in gas consumption because of a lower cost per mile, then on net gas consumption declines and car pollution falls. If the decline in gas consumption because of a higher mpg is less than the rise in gas consumption because of a lower cost per mile, then on net gas consumption rises and car pollution rises. Finally, if the decline in gas consumption because of a higher mpg is equal to the rise in gas consumption because of a lower cost per mile, then on net gas consumption remains the same as does car pollution.

Our answer, we see, depends on how much gas consumption falls because of one thing (higher mpg) *rela-*

tive to how much gas consumption rises because of something else (lower cost per mile). This is similar to our discussion of total revenue, where the net change in total revenue depended on how much total revenue decreased owing to a drop in price and how much total revenue increased owing to a rise in quantity demanded.

Thinking Like an Economist

Following the logic of economics sometimes leads us to counter-intuitive conclusions—that is, conclusions against one's intuition. For example, intuition tells most people that if cars get more miles per gallon, there will be less car pollution. But as we have explained, this may not be the case. It could be that higher fuel efficiency standards (deemed "good") will result in more car pollution (deemed "bad"). The fact that something good could lead to something bad is, for most people, counter-intuitive. Economists don't think counterintuitively, but in "doing economics," they sometimes reach counterintuitive conclusions. So, economic analysis has the ability to surprise us, since any counterintuitive conclusion is, by definition, something unexpected.

a half-packed auditorium may, under certain conditions, generate more revenue than a packed auditorium. But if two prices can be charged, isn't a packed auditorium preferable to a half-packed auditorium?

Answer:

True, the assumption is that only one price can be charged; that is, all seats must be priced at either $10 or $25, not some seats at $10 and some seats at $25. Furthermore, charging a higher price for good seats and a lower price for not-so-good seats actually happens at rock concerts, plays, basketball games, and so forth. The example has demonstrated why.

Elasticity: Part 2

■

In this section, we discuss the elasticity ranges of a straight-line downward-sloping demand curve and the determinants of price elasticity of demand, along with cross price elasticity of demand, income elasticity of demand, and price elasticity of supply.

Price Elasticity of Demand Along a Demand Curve

The price elasticity of demand for a straight-line downward-sloping demand curve varies from highly elastic to highly inelastic. We illustrate this important point with the aid of Exhibit 21–4.

Notice that as we move down the demand curve from higher to lower prices, from $8 to $7 to $6, and so on, the price elasticity of demand (as measured by the elasticity coefficient in column 4) decreases, from 2.14 to 1.44 to 1.00, and so on. As we move up the demand curve from lower to higher prices, price elasticity of demand increases. There are three elasticity ranges on the demand curve: an inelastic range, an elastic range, and a unit elastic range.

We can easily understand this result by recalling that price elasticity of demand is a ratio of the percentage change in quantity demanded to the percentage change in price. At the upper end of the demand curve, where quantities demanded are lower and prices are higher, a 1-unit change in quantity demanded is a relatively large percentage change in quantity demanded, and a $1 price change is a relatively small percentage change in price.

At the lower end of the demand curve, where quantities demanded are higher and prices are lower, the situation is reversed. A 1-unit change in quantity demanded is a relatively small percentage change in quantity demanded, and a $1 price change is a relatively large percentage change in price.

EXHIBIT 21–4
Price Elasticity of Demand along a Demand Curve

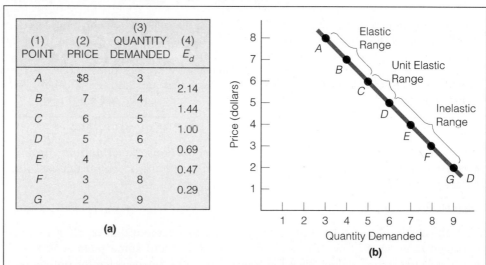

(1) POINT	(2) PRICE	(3) QUANTITY DEMANDED	(4) E_d
A	$8	3	
			2.14
B	7	4	
			1.44
C	6	5	
			1.00
D	5	6	
			0.69
E	4	7	
			0.47
F	3	8	
			0.29
G	2	9	

(a)

(b)

On the straight-line, downward-sloping demand curve, price elasticity of demand is greater at higher prices than lower prices. The demand curve has three elasticity ranges. By calculating total revenue at each price, it is obvious that total revenue is maximized where demand is unit elastic.

Determinants of Price Elasticity of Demand

There are three major determinants of price elasticity of demand: (1) the number of substitutes, (2) the percentage of one's budget spent on the good, and (3) time. Since all three factors interact, we discuss each holding all other things constant.

Number of Substitutes.   Suppose good *A* has 2 substitutes and good *B* has 15 substitutes. We shall assume that each of the 2 substitutes for good *A* is as good (or close) a substitute for that good as each of the 15 substitutes is for good *B*.

Let the price of each good rise by 10 percent. The quantity demanded of each good decreases. Would we expect the "percentage change in quantity demanded of good *A*" to be greater or less than the "percentage change in quantity demanded of good *B*"? In short, will quantity demanded be more responsive to the 10 percent price rise in the good that has 2 substitutes (good *A)* or the good that has 15 substitutes (good *B*)? The answer is the good with 15 substitutes, good *B*. This occurs because the more chance of substituting one good for another (there is more chance of substituting a good for *B* than for *A*), the less of a good will be purchased if its price rises. For example, when the price of good *A* rises 10 percent, people can turn to 2 substitutes; quantity demanded of good *A* falls, but not by as much as if there had been 15 substitutes, as there were for good *B*.

The relationship between the availability of substitutes and price elasticity is clear: *The more substitutes for a good, the higher the price elasticity of demand; the fewer substitutes for a good, the lower the price elasticity of demand.*

For example, the price elasticity of demand for Chevrolets is higher than the price elasticity of demand for all cars. This is because there are more substitutes for Chevrolets than for cars. Everything that is a substitute for a car (bus, train, walking, bicycle, and so on) is also a substitute for a specific type of car, Chevrolet; but some things that are a substitute for a Chevrolet (Ford, Toyota, Chrysler, Mercedes-Benz, and so on) are not substitutes for a car. Instead, they are simply *types* of cars. Thus, we can state the rule: The more broadly defined the good, the fewer the substitutes; the more narrowly defined the good, the greater the substitutes. There are more substitutes for this economics textbook than there are for all economics textbooks. There are more substitutes for Coca-Cola than there are for all soft drinks.

Percentage of One's Budget Spent on the Good.   Claire Rossi has a monthly budget of $3,000. Of this monthly budget, she spends $30 per month on pens and $400 per month on dinners at restaurants. In percentage terms, she spends 1 percent of her monthly budget on pens and 13 percent of her monthly budget on dinners at restaurants. Suppose both the price of pens and the price of dinners at restaurants double. Would Claire be more responsive to the change in the price of pens or dinners at restaurants? The answer is the price of dinners at restaurants. The reason is that a doubling in price of a good on which a person spends 1 percent of her budget is not felt as strongly as a doubling in price of a good on which she spends 13 percent. Claire is more likely to shrug off the doubling in the price of pens than the doubling in the price of dinners at restaurants. Buyers are (and thus quantity demanded is) more responsive to price the larger the percentage of their budget that goes for the purchase of the good. In short, *the greater the percentage of one's budget that goes to purchase a good, the higher the price elasticity of demand; the smaller the percentage of one's budget that goes to purchase a good, the lower the price elasticity of demand.*

Time. As time passes, buyers have greater opportunities to be responsive to a price change. If the price of electricity went up today, and you knew about it, you probably would not change your consumption of electricity today as much as you would three months from today. As time passes, you have more chances to change your consumption by finding substitutes (natural gas), changing your life style (buying more blankets and turning down the thermostat at night), and so on. We conclude that *the more time that passes (since the price change), the higher the price elasticity of demand for the good; the less time that passes, the lower the price elasticity of demand for the good.*[2] In other words, price elasticity of demand for a good is higher in the long run than in the short run.

Take the case of gasoline consumption patterns in the period 1973–75. Gasoline prices increased a dramatic 71 percent during this period. The consumption of gasoline didn't fall immediately and sharply. Motorists didn't immediately stop driving big gas-guzzling cars. As time passed, however, many car owners traded in their big cars for compact cars. Car buyers became more concerned with the miles per gallon a car received. People began to form car pools. The short-run price elasticity of demand for gasoline was estimated at 0.2; the long-run price elasticity of demand for gasoline was estimated at 0.7, 3½ times larger.

OTHER ELASTICITY CONCEPTS
■

In this section, we discuss three other elasticities: cross elasticity of demand, income elasticity of demand, and price elasticity of supply.

Cross Elasticity of Demand

Cross Elasticity of Demand
Measures the responsiveness in quantity demanded of one good to changes in the price of another good.

Cross elasticity of demand measures the responsiveness in the quantity demanded of one good to changes in the price of another good. It is defined as *the percentage change in the quantity demanded of one good divided by the percentage change in the price of another good.*

$$E_c = \frac{\text{percentage change in quantity demanded of one good}}{\text{percentage change in price of another good}}$$

where E_c stands for coefficient of cross elasticity of demand, or elasticity coefficient.[3]

This concept is often used to determine whether two goods are substitutes or complements and the degree to which one good is a substitute or complement to another. Consider two goods: Skippy peanut butter and Jif peanut butter. Suppose that there is a 10 percent increase in the price of Jif peanut butter and that the

[2]If we say, "The more time that passes (since the price change), the higher the price elasticity of demand," wouldn't it follow that price elasticity of demand gets steadily larger? For example, might it be that on Tuesday the price of good X rises, and five days later, $E_d = 0.70$, 10 days later it is 0.76, 20 days later it is 0.90, and so on toward infinity? This is not exactly the case. Obviously, there comes a time when quantity demanded is no longer adjusting to a change in price (just as there comes a time when there are no longer any ripples in the lake from the passing motorboat). Our conditional statement ("the more time that passes . . .") implies this condition.

[3]A question naturally arises: How can E_d and E_c both be the elasticity of coefficient? It is a matter of convenience. When speaking about price elasticity of demand, the coefficient of price elasticity of demand is referred to as the "elasticity coefficient." When speaking about cross elasticity of demand, the coefficient of cross elasticity of demand is referred to as the "elasticity coefficient." This practice holds for other elasticities as well.

quantity demanded of Skippy peanut butter increases by 45 percent. The cross elasticity of demand for Skippy with respect to the price of Jif is written

$$E_c = \frac{\text{percentage change in quantity demanded of Skippy}}{\text{percentage change in price of Jif}}$$

This is a positive 4.5. When the elasticity coefficient is positive, we know that the percentage change in the quantity demanded of one good (numerator) moves in the same direction as the percentage change in the price of another good (denominator). This is representative of goods that are substitutes. In short, as the price of Jif rises, the demand curve for Skippy shifts rightward, causing the quantity demanded of Skippy to increase at each and every price.[4] We conclude that if $E_c > 0$, the two goods are substitutes.

If the elasticity coefficient is negative, $E_c < 0$, the two goods are complements. A negative number occurs when the percentage change in the quantity demanded of one good (numerator) and the percentage change in the price of another good (denominator) move in opposite directions. Consider an example. Suppose the price of cars increases by 5 percent and the quantity demanded of car tires decreases by 10 percent. To calculate the cross price elasticity of demand, we have -10 percent/5 percent $= -2$. Cars and car tires are complements.

The concept of cross elasticity of demand can be very useful. Suppose a company sells cheese. A natural question might be, What goods are substitutes for cheese? The answer would shed some light on who the competitors of the company are. We could find out which goods are substitutes for cheese by calculating the cross elasticity of demand between cheese and other goods. A positive cross elasticity of demand would indicate that the two goods were substitutes; and the higher the cross elasticity of demand, the greater the degree of substitution.

Income Elasticity of Demand

Income elasticity of demand measures the responsiveness of quantity demanded to changes in income. It is defined as *the percentage change in quantity demanded of a good divided by the percentage change in income.*

Income Elasticity of Demand
Measures the responsiveness of quantity demanded to changes in income.

$$E_y = \frac{\text{percentage change in quantity demanded}}{\text{percentage change in income}}$$

where $E_y =$ coefficient of income elasticity of demand, or elasticity coefficient.

*Income elasticity of demand is positive, $E_y > 0$, for a normal good. A **normal good** is one whose demand, and thus quantity demanded, increases, given an increase in income; thus, the variables in the numerator and denominator in the income elasticity of demand formula move in the same direction. Income elasticity of demand for an **inferior good** is negative, $E_y < 0$. In calculating the income elasticity of demand of a good, we use the same midpoint approach that we used for calculating price elasticity of demand.

Normal Good
A good the demand for which rises (falls) as income rises (falls).

Inferior Good
A good the demand for which falls (rises) as income rises (falls).

$$E_y = \frac{\dfrac{\Delta Q_d}{(Q_{d1} + Q_{d2})/2}}{\dfrac{\Delta Y}{(Y_1 + Y_2)/2}}$$

[4]In Chapter 3, we explained that if two goods are substitutes, a rise in the price of one good causes the demand for the other good to increase.

where Y_1 represents the first income, Y_2 the second income, and Q_{d1} and Q_{d2} the respective quantities demanded.

Suppose income increases from \$500 to \$600 per month and that as a result quantity demanded of good X increases from 20 units to 30 units per month. We have

$$E_y = \frac{\dfrac{10}{(20 \ + \ 30)/2}}{\dfrac{100}{(500 \ + \ 600)/2}} = \frac{\dfrac{10}{25}}{\dfrac{100}{550}} = 2.2$$

Since E_y is a positive number, good X is a normal good. Also, since $E_y > 1$, demand for good X is said to be **income elastic.** This means the percentage change in quantity demanded of the good is greater than the percentage change in income. If $E_y < 1$, the demand for the good is said to be **income inelastic.** If $E_y = 1$, then it is **income unit elastic.**

Income Elastic
The percentage change in quantity demanded of a good is greater than the percentage change in income.

Income Inelastic
The percentage change in quantity demanded of a good is less than the percentage change in income.

Income Unit Elastic
The percentage change in quantity demanded of a good is equal to the percentage change in income.

Question:

Are there any real-world applications for income elasticity of demand?

Answer:

Yes, there are. Suppose Lisa Neiman is considering buying stocks in the stock market. We'll assume her objective is to earn as much profit as possible. Furthermore, suppose she believes that individuals' incomes will be increasing over the next few months and years. Would it be better for her to buy stocks in companies that produce inferior goods (income increases, demand for the good decreases) or in companies that produce normal goods (income increases, demand for the good increases)? Clearly, the answer is "in companies that produce normal goods."

Having established this, would it be better for her to go with companies that produce normal goods that are highly income elastic, unit income elastic, or income inelastic? It would be better for her to go with companies that produce normal goods that are highly income elastic, where quantity demanded is highly responsive to increases in income.

We add a proviso: Simply because a good was highly income elastic last year, or for the past few years, it does not necessarily follow that it will be so this year or in the next few years. The future does not always mirror the past. This means that income elasticity of demand, if used as a predictive tool, should be used with caution.

Question:

Can a good be both normal and income inelastic?

Answer:

Yes, it can. A normal good means $E_y > 0$. An income inelastic good means $E_y < 1$. Suppose that for good X, $E_y = 0.8$. This is a positive number (hence, X is a normal good) that is less than one (hence, X is income inelastic). Food, tobacco, and health-related drugs have been calculated to have elasticity coefficients greater than 0 but less than 1.

Price Elasticity of Supply

Price elasticity of supply measures the responsiveness of quantity supplied to changes in price. It is defined as the percentage change in quantity supplied of a good divided by the percentage change in the price of the good.

$$E_s = \frac{\text{percentage change in quantity supplied}}{\text{percentage change in price}}$$

where E_s stands for coefficient of price elasticity of supply, or elasticity coefficient. We use the midpoint approach to calculate price elasticity of supply.

In addition, we may classify supply as elastic, inelastic, unit elastic, perfectly elastic, or perfectly inelastic (Exhibit 21–5). Elastic supply ($E_s > 1$) refers to a percentage change in quantity supplied that is greater than the percentage change

Price Elasticity of Supply
Measures the responsiveness of quantity supplied to changes in price.

EXHIBIT 21–5
Price Elasticity of Supply

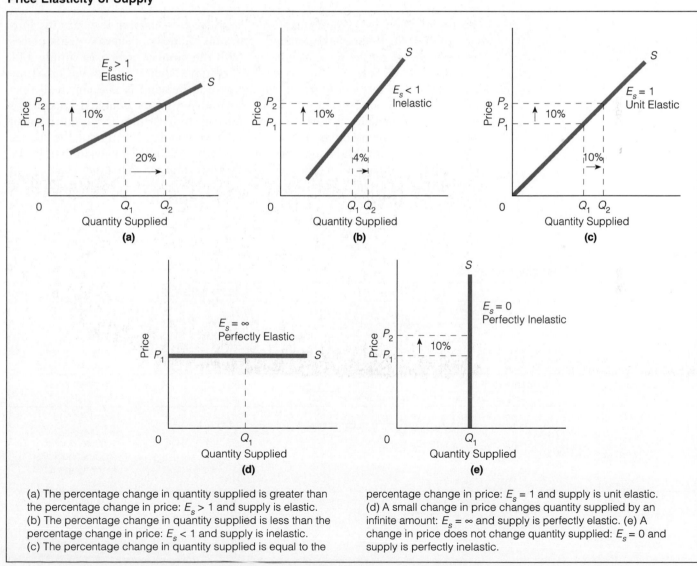

(a) The percentage change in quantity supplied is greater than the percentage change in price: $E_s > 1$ and supply is elastic.
(b) The percentage change in quantity supplied is less than the percentage change in price: $E_s < 1$ and supply is inelastic.
(c) The percentage change in quantity supplied is equal to the percentage change in price: $E_s = 1$ and supply is unit elastic.
(d) A small change in price changes quantity supplied by an infinite amount: $E_s = \infty$ and supply is perfectly elastic. (e) A change in price does not change quantity supplied: $E_s = 0$ and supply is perfectly inelastic.

in price. Inelastic supply ($E_s < 1$) refers to a percentage change in quantity supplied that is less than the percentage change in price. Unit elastic supply ($E_s = 1$) refers to a percentage change in quantity supplied that is equal to the percentage change in price. Perfectly elastic supply ($E_s = \infty$) represents the case where a small change in price changes quantity supplied by an infinitely large amount (and thus the supply curve, or a portion of the overall supply curve, is horizontal). Perfectly inelastic supply ($E_s = 0$) represents the case where a change in price brings no change in quantity supplied (and thus the supply curve, or a portion of the overall supply curve, is vertical).

Price Elasticity of Supply and Time

The longer the period of adjustment to a change in price, the higher the price elasticity of supply. (We are speaking of goods whose quantity supplied *can* increase with time. This covers most goods. It does now, however, cover original Picasso paintings.) There is an obvious reason for this: Additional production takes time.

For example, suppose the demand increases for new housing in your city. Further, suppose this increase in demand comes all at once on Tuesday. This places upward pressure on the price of housing. Will the number of houses supplied be much different on Saturday than it was on Tuesday? No, it won't. It will take time for suppliers to figure out whether the increase in demand is permanent (if they consider it a temporary state of affairs, not much will be done). If contractors decide it is permanent, it takes time to move resources from the production of other things into the production of additional new housing. Simply put, the change in quantity supplied of housing is likely to be different in the long run than in the short run given a change in price. This translates into a higher price elasticity of supply in the long run than in the short run. See Exhibit 21–6 for a quick review of elasticity concepts.

EXHIBIT 21–6
Summary of the Four Elasticity Concepts

TYPE	DEFINITION	POSSIBILITIES	
Price elasticity of demand	$\dfrac{\text{percentage change in quantity demanded}}{\text{percentage change in price}}$	$E_d > 1$	Elastic
		$E_d < 1$	Inelastic
		$E_d = 1$	Unit elastic
		$E_d = \infty$	Perfectly elastic
		$E_d = 0$	Perfectly inelastic
Cross elasticity of demand	$\dfrac{\text{percentage change in quantity demanded of one good}}{\text{percentage change in price of another good}}$	$E_c < 0$	Complements
		$E_c > 0$	Substitutes
Income elasticity of demand	$\dfrac{\text{percentage change in quantity demanded}}{\text{percentage change in income}}$	$E_y > 0$	Normal good
		$E_y < 0$	Inferior good
		$E_y > 1$	Income elastic
		$E_y < 1$	Income inelastic
		$E_y = 1$	Income unit elastic
Price elasticity of supply	$\dfrac{\text{percentage change in quantity supplied}}{\text{percentage change in price}}$	$E_s > 1$	Elastic
		$E_s < 1$	Inelastic
		$E_s = 1$	Unit elastic
		$E_s = \infty$	Perfectly elastic
		$E_s = 0$	Perfectly inelastic

Why Pays the Tax: Elasticity Matters

Many people think that if government *places* a tax on firm X, firm X actually *pays* the tax. As we shall see, there is a difference between the placement and the payment of a tax, and furthermore placement does not guarantee payment.

Suppose the government places a tax on VCR tape producers: They are taxed $1 for every tape they sell. VCR tape producers are enjoined: Sell a tape, send $1 to government. This action changes equilibrium in the VCR tape market. To illustrate, in Exhibit 21–7, *before* the tax is imposed, the equilibrium price and quantity of tapes are $8 and Q_1, respectively. The tax per tape shifts the supply curve up and leftward from S_1 to S_2. The vertical distance between the two supply curves represents the $1 per tape tax.

(Why does the vertical distance between the two curves represent the $1 per tape tax? This is because what matters to the producers is how much they get to keep for each tape sold, not how much the consumers pay. For example, if they get to keep $8 per tape for Q_1 tapes before the tax is imposed, then they must get to keep $8 per tape for Q_1 tapes after the tax is imposed. But if the tax is $1, the only way they can get to keep $8 per tape for Q_1 tapes is to charge $9 per tape. They receive $9 per tape from the consumer, turn over $1 to government, and keep $8 for themselves. In other words, each quantity on the new supply curve, S_2, corresponds to a $1 higher price than on the old supply curve, S_1. It does not follow, though, that the new equilibrium price will be $1 higher than the old equilibrium price.)

The new equilibrium comes at a price of $8.50 and quantity Q_2. Consumers pay $8.50 per tape (after the tax is imposed) as opposed to $8.00 (before the tax was

EXHIBIT 21–7
Who Pays the Tax?

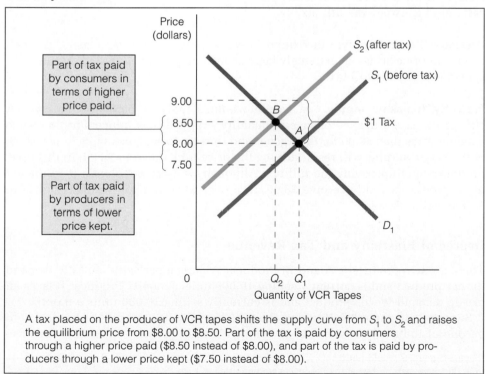

A tax placed on the producer of VCR tapes shifts the supply curve from S_1 to S_2 and raises the equilibrium price from $8.00 to $8.50. Part of the tax is paid by consumers through a higher price paid ($8.50 instead of $8.00), and part of the tax is paid by producers through a lower price kept ($7.50 instead of $8.00).

imposed). The difference between the new price and the old price is the amount of the $1 tax that consumers pay per tape. In this example, consumers pay 50 cents, or one-half of the tax, of the $1 tax per tape.

The producers *receive* $8.50 per tape from consumers (after the tax is imposed) as opposed to $8.00 per tape (before the tax was imposed), but do not get to *keep* the $8.50 per tape. One dollar has to be turned over to the government, leaving the producers with $7.50. Before the tax was imposed, however, the producers received and kept $8.00 per tape.[5] As we noted, it is the price that the producers get to keep that is relevant to them. The difference between $8.00 and $7.50 is the amount of the tax per tape that the producers pay. In this example, the producers pay 50 cents of the $1 tax per tape. In short, the producers pay one-half of the tax. We conclude that the full tax was placed on the producers, but they paid only one-half of the tax, whereas none of the tax was placed on consumers but they paid one-half of the tax, too. What is the lesson? Government can place a tax on whomever it wants, but the determination of who ends up paying the tax depends on the laws of economics.

We can derive another lesson from this example. The percentage or share of the tax actually paid by consumers and producers depends on price elasticity of demand and supply. For example, you noticed that in this example both the consumers and the producers paid one-half of the tax. It did not have to be this way, however, as the following four cases illustrate.

Perfectly Inelastic Demand. In Exhibit 21–8a, demand is perfectly inelastic. A change in price brings no change in quantity demanded. In this case, consumers pay the full $1 tax per tape even though the tax is placed entirely on producers.

Perfectly Elastic Demand. In Exhibit 21–8b, demand is perfectly elastic. A small change in price brings an extremely large change in quantity demanded. In this case, producers pay the full tax.

Perfectly Elastic Supply. In Exhibit 21–8c, supply is perfectly elastic. A small change in price brings an extremely large change in quantity supplied. In this case, consumers pay the full tax.

Perfectly Inelastic Supply. In Exhibit 21–8d, supply is perfectly inelastic. A change in price brings no change in quantity supplied. If producers try to charge a higher price than $8.00 for their good (and thus try to get consumers to pay some of the tax), a surplus will result driving the price back down to $8.00. In this case, producers end up paying the full tax. Although we have not shown it in the exhibit, producers would receive $8.00, turn over $1 to the government, and keep $7 for each unit sold.

Degree of Elasticity and Tax Revenue

There are two producers: A and B. Producer A faces a perfectly inelastic demand for her product and is currently selling 10,000 units a month. Producer B faces an elastic demand for his product and is currently selling 10,000 units a month.

Suppose government is thinking about placing a $1 tax per unit of product sold on one of the two producers. If government's objective is to maximize tax reve-

[5]Some economists would put it this way: The tax drives a *wedge* between what the producers receive from the consumers and what the producers are permitted to keep.

EXHIBIT 21–8
Different Elasticities and Who Pays the Tax

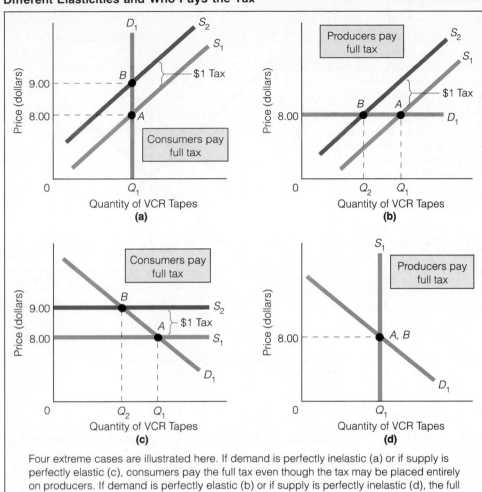

Four extreme cases are illustrated here. If demand is perfectly inelastic (a) or if supply is perfectly elastic (c), consumers pay the full tax even though the tax may be placed entirely on producers. If demand is perfectly elastic (b) or if supply is perfectly inelastic (d), the full tax is paid by the producers.

nues, which producer will it place the tax on and why? The answer is producer A, the producer with the inelastic demand curve. We explain with the aid of Exhibit 21–9.

The demand curve facing producer A is D_1; the demand curve facing producer B is D_2. S_1 represents the supply curve for both firms. Currently, both firms are at equilibrium at point A selling 10,000 units.

Government then places a $1 tax per unit sold on producer A. The supply curve shifts to S_2 and equilibrium is now at point C. However, since demand is perfectly inelastic, producer A is still selling 10,000 units. Tax revenue equals the tax ($1) times 10,000 units, or $10,000.

If government had placed the $1 tax per unit sold on producer B, tax revenues would have only been $8,000. This is because the tax shifted the supply curve to S_2 and moved equilibrium to point B, at which only 8,000 units were sold.

The lesson is: Given the $1 tax per unit sold, tax revenues are maximized by placing the tax on the producer that faces the more inelastic (less elastic) demand curve.

EXHIBIT 21–9
Maximizing Tax Revenues

Two producers, A and B, are each currently selling 10,000 units of the good they produce. Producer A faces the demand curve D_1, and producer B faces D_2. If the objective is to maximize tax revenues with a $1 tax per unit of product sold, and only one producer can be taxed, taxing producer A will maximize tax revenues and taxing producer B will not. To illustrate, we note that after the tax has been placed, the supply curve shifts from S_1 to S_2. Producer A is in equilibrium at point C, selling 10,000 units, and producer B is in equilibrium at point B, selling 8,000 units. Since tax revenues equal the tax per unit times the quantity of output sold, taxing producer A raises $10,000 in tax revenues whereas taxing producer B raises $8,000.

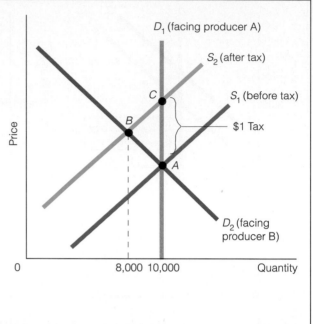

In Perspective

In a previous chapter, we said that the microeconomics mindset is centered around three ideas: (1) Consumers, firms, and factor owners deal with objectives, constraints, and choices. (2) Consumers and firms, and firms and factor owners, interact in market settings. (3) Government can affect consumers, firms, and factor owners and thus affect overall market outcomes.

In this chapter, we have seen the microeconomics mindset at work. First, consider the concept of price elasticity of demand with respect to the firm's objective, which is to maximize profit. One way to maximize profit is to ensure that the difference between total revenue (what comes in) and total cost (what goes out) is as large as possible. Price elasticity of demand affects total revenue—for example, if demand is inelastic, a price rise will increase total revenue—and therefore it indirectly affects maximizing profit.

Second, consider that government can influence consumers and firms and thus affect overall market outcomes. We learned that if government imposes a per-unit tax on a firm, this causes the supply side of the market to initially react (the supply curve shifts leftward); consequently, equilibrium price rises and equilibrium quantity falls. When the demand curve is downward sloping, both consumers and producers end up paying part of the tax: Consumers pay in the form of higher prices paid and producers pay in the form of a lower price kept.

Part 1
Price Elasticity of Demand

- Price elasticity of demand is a measure of the responsiveness of quantity demanded to changes in price: E_d = percentage change in quantity demanded/percentage change in price.
- If the percentage change in quantity demanded is greater than the percentage change in price, demand is elastic. If the percentage change in quantity demanded is less than the percentage change in price, demand is inelastic. If the percentage change in quantity demanded is equal to the percentage change in price, demand is unit elastic. If a small change in price brings on an infinitely large change in quantity demanded, demand is perfectly elastic. If a change in price brings on no change in quantity demanded, demand is perfectly inelastic.
- The coefficient of price elasticity of demand (E_d) is negative, signifying the inverse relationship between price and quantity demanded. For convenience, however, the absolute value of the elasticity coefficient is used.

Total Revenue and Price Elasticity of Demand

- Total revenue equals price times quantity sold. Total expenditure equals price times quantity purchased. Total revenue equals total expenditure.
- If demand is elastic, price and total revenue are inversely related: As price rises (falls), total revenue falls (rises).
- If demand is inelastic, price and total revenue are directly related: As price rises (falls), total revenue rises (falls).
- If demand is unit elastic, total revenue is independent of price: As price rises (falls), total revenue remains constant.

Part 2
Determinants of Price Elasticity of Demand

- The more substitutes for a good, the higher the price elasticity of demand; the fewer substitutes for a good, the lower the price elasticity of demand.
- The greater the percentage of one's budget that goes to purchase a good, the higher the price elasticity of demand; the smaller the percentage of one's budget that goes to purchase a good, the lower the price elasticity of demand.
- The more time that passes (since a price change), the higher the price elasticity of demand; the less time that passes, the lower the price elasticity of demand.

Cross Elasticity of Demand

- Cross elasticity of demand measures the responsiveness in the quantity demanded of one good to changes in the price of another good: E_c = percentage change in quantity demanded of one good/percentage change in the price of another good.
- If $E_c > 0$, two goods are substitutes. If $E_c < 0$, two goods are complements.

Income Elasticity of Demand

■ Income elasticity of demand measures the responsiveness of quantity demanded to changes in income: E_y = percentage change in quantity demanded/percentage change in income.

■ If $E_y > 0$, the good is a normal good; if $E_y < 0$, the good is an inferior good.

■ If $E_y > 1$, demand is income elastic; if $E_y < 1$, demand is income inelastic; and if $E_y = 1$, demand is income unit elastic.

Price Elasticity of Supply

■ Price elasticity of supply measures the responsiveness of quantity supplied to changes in price: E_s = percentage change in quantity supplied/percentage change in price.

■ If the percentage change in quantity supplied is greater than the percentage change in price, supply is elastic. If the percentage change in quantity supplied is less than the percentage change in price, supply is inelastic. If the percentage change in quantity supplied is equal to the percentage change in price, supply is unit elastic.

■ Price elasticity of supply is higher in the long run than in the short run.

Key Terms and Concepts

Price Elasticity of Demand	Perfectly Inelastic Demand	Inferior Good
Elastic Demand	Total Revenue	Income Elastic
Inelastic Demand	Cross Elasticity of Demand	Income Inelastic
Unit Elastic Demand	Income Elasticity of Demand	Income Unit Elastic
Perfectly Elastic Demand	Normal Good	Price Elasticity of Supply

QUESTIONS AND PROBLEMS

1. Explain how a seller can determine whether the demand for his or her good is inelastic, elastic, or unit elastic between two prices.

2. Suppose the current price of gasoline at the pump is $1 per gallon and that one million gallons are sold per month. A politician proposes to add a 10-cent tax to the price of a gallon of gasoline. She says the tax will generate $100,000 tax revenues per month (one million gallons × 10 cents = $100,000). What assumption is she making?

3. A college in the South raises its annual tuition from $2,000 to $2,500, and its student enrollment falls from 4,877 to 4,705. Compute the price elasticity of demand. Is demand elastic or inelastic?

4. Suppose a straight-line, downward-sloping demand curve shifts rightward. Is the price elasticity of demand higher, lower, or the same between any two prices on the new (higher) demand curve than on the old (lower) demand curve?

5. Suppose Oklahoma City is hit by a tornado that destroys 25 percent of the housing in the area. Would you expect the total expenditure on housing after the tornado to be higher than, less than, or equal to what it was before the tornado?

6. Which of the following goods has the higher price elasticity of demand: (a) airline travel in the short run or airline travel in the long run; (b) television sets or Sony television sets; (c) cars or Toyotas; (d) telephones or AT&T telephones; (e) popcorn or Orville Redenbacker popcorn?

7. How might you determine whether toothpaste and mouthwash manufacturers are in competition with each other?

8. Assume the demand for cocaine is perfectly inelastic. Further, assume that the users of cocaine get the funds to pay for the cocaine by stealing. If the supply of cocaine decreases, what happens to the price of cocaine? What happens to the amount of crime committed by cocaine users?

9. Suppose you learned that the price elasticity of demand for wheat is 0.7 between the current price for wheat and a price $2 higher per bushel. Do you think farmers collectively would try to reduce the supply of wheat and drive the price up $2 higher per bushel? Why? Assuming that they would try to reduce supply, what problems might they have in actually doing so?

10. It has been said that if government wishes to tax certain goods, it should tax goods that have inelastic rather than elastic demand. What is the rationale for this?

11. In 1947, the U.S. Justice Department brought a suit against the DuPont Company (which at the time sold 75 percent of all the cellophane in the United States) for monopolizing the production and sale of cellophane. In court, the DuPont Company tried to show that cellophane was only one of several goods in the market in which it was sold. It argued that its market was not the cellophane market but the "flexible packaging materials" market, which included (besides cellophane) waxed paper, aluminum foil, and so forth. DuPont pointed out that it had only 20 percent of all sales in this more broadly defined market. Using this information, discuss how the concept of cross elasticity of demand would help establish whether Dupont should have been viewed as a firm in the cellophane market or as a firm in the "flexible packaging materials" market.

THE FIRM

WHAT THIS CHAPTER IS ABOUT

Firms are one of the three principal players in our study of microeconomics, the other two being consumers and factor owners. In this chapter, we begin our discussion of firms—a discussion that will occupy much of our attention in the chapters to come, too.

WHY FIRMS EXIST

∎

A **business firm** is an entity that employs resources, or factors of production, to produce goods and services to be sold to consumers, other firms, or the government. In this section, we start with a very basic question, Why do firms exist?[1]

The Market and the Firm: Invisible Hand versus Visible Hand

The market we examined in Chapter 3 guides and coordinates individuals' actions. Moreover, the market does this in an impersonal manner. No one orders buyers to reduce quantity demanded when price increases; they just do it. No one orders sellers to increase quantity supplied when price increases; they just do it. No one orders more resources to be moved into the production of personal computers when the demand and price for personal computers increase. The market *guides* individuals, from the production of one good into the production of another good, for example; and it *coordinates* individuals' actions, so that suppliers and demanders find mutual satisfaction at equilibrium, for example. As the economist Adam Smith observed, individuals in a market setting are "led by an invisible hand to promote an end which was no part of their intention."

Contrast the invisible hand of the market with the visible hand of a manager in a firm. Who tells the employee on the assembly line to make more computer chips? The manager does. Who tells the employee to design a new engine, to paint the lamps green, to put steak and lobster on the menu? The manager does. Thus, both the *invisible hand* of the market and the *visible hand* of the manager of a firm guide and coordinate individuals' actions. There is, in other words, **market** and **managerial coordination.**

If the market is capable of guiding and coordinating individuals' actions, why did firms (and managers) arise in the first place? In other words, why do firms exist? Two economists have suggested a possible answer.

The Alchian and Demsetz Answer.   Economists Armen Alchian and Harold Demsetz suggest that firms are formed when benefits can be obtained from individuals working as a team.[2] Sometimes the sum of what individuals can produce as a team is greater than the sum of what they can produce alone: sum of team production > sum of individual production. Consider 11 individuals, all making shoe boxes. Each working alone produces 10 shoe boxes per day, for a total daily output of 110. If they work as a team, however, the same 11 individuals can produce 140 shoe boxes; the added output (30 shoe boxes) may be reason enough for them to work together as a team.

> Before answers, come questions. The most important question is sometimes simply "Why?" The economist asks, Why do firms exist? This may seem as obvious as asking, "Why is there a sun?" or "Why does the sun set in the west?" But as we have seen, asking seemingly obvious questions, as well as

Sometimes the sum of what individuals can produce as a team is greater than the sum of what they can produce alone.

∎

Business Firm
An entity that employs factors of production (resources) and produces goods and services to be sold to consumers, other firms, or the government.

Managerial Coordination
The process in which managers direct employees to perform certain tasks.

Market Coordination
The process in which individuals perform tasks, such as producing certain quantities of goods, based on changes in the market forces such as supply, demand, and price.

THINKING LIKE
AN ECONOMIST

---

[1]The word *firm* usually refers to profit-seeking business enterprises, which is how we use it here. Occasionally, we speak of "business firms" or of "businesses" as a reminder that these terms can be used interchangeably with "firm." Of course, there are other types of firms besides business firms. We discuss a few at the end of the chapter.
[2]Armen Alchian and Harold Demsetz, "Production, Information Costs, and Economic Organization," *American Economic Review* 62 (December 1972):777–95.

less obvious ones, and then attempting to answer them, can expand our knowledge of the world. Why is the price of a car $15,000? Why do consumers buy more when price falls? Economists and other scientists are a lot like kids: They are forever asking why.

Shirking in a Team

Team production also brings disadvantages. One problem of team production is **shirking,** which refers to workers putting forth less than the agreed-to effort. The amount of shirking increases in teams because the costs of shirking to individual team members are lower than when they work alone.

Consider five individuals, Tom, Sue, Mark, Genia, and John, who form a team to produce lightbulbs because they realize that the sum of their team production will be more than the sum of their individual production. They agree to team-produce lightbulbs, sell the lightbulbs, and split the proceeds five equal ways. On an average day, they produce 140 lightbulbs and sell each one for $2. Total revenue per day is $280, with each of the five team members receiving $56. Then Mark begins to shirk. Owing to his shirking, production falls to 135 lightbulbs per day, and total revenue falls to $270 per day; each person now receives $54. Notice that Mark did all the shirking and that total revenue fell by $10, but that Mark's reduction in pay was only $2, one-fifth of this amount.

In situations (such as team production) where one person receives all the benefits from shirking and pays only a part of the costs, we predict there will be more shirking than in the situation where the person who shirks bears the full cost of his or her shirking.

Question:

Suppose a firm is made up exclusively of extremely conscientious and hard-working people. Would shirking still be a problem?

Answer:

Even though individuals may have different inclinations to shirk (given the chance, some people will shirk more than others), this does not mean that their behavior is *independent* of a change in the cost of shirking. As long as shirking is considered a *good* (Isn't it a form of leisure?) from which individuals obtain utility, lowering the cost of shirking will cause individuals to "consume" more shirking, *ceteris paribus.*

The Monitor (Manager): Taking Care of Shirking

The **monitor** (or manager) plays an important role in the firm. He is the person who reduces the amount of shirking by firing shirkers and rewarding the productive members of the firm. In doing this, the monitor can preserve the benefits that often come with team production (increased output) and reduce, if not eliminate, the costs associated with team production (increased shirking). But this raises another question: *Who or what monitors the monitor?* In other words, how can the monitor be kept from shirking?

One possibility is to give the monitor an incentive not to shirk by making him a **residual claimant** of the firm. A residual claimant receives the excess of revenues over costs (profits) as his income. If the monitor shirks, then profits are likely to be lower (or even zero or negative), and therefore the monitor will receive less income.

Can Above-Market Wages Cause People To Shirk Less?

Recently, some economists have argued that firms may find it in their best interest to pay wage rates above market levels. At first sight, this seems nonsensical. Why would an employer pay $10 per hour per worker to hire 200 workers when she can pay the market wage rate of, say, $9 per hour? Such an action would seemingly raise her costs and lower her profits.

But some economists maintain that there is more to the story. Above-market wage rates, they say, make it less likely for employees to shirk or more likely to monitor themselves. The reason is that when workers are paid above-market wage rates, they have a greater incentive to hold on to their job; after all, if they lose the job that pays above-market wages, they will likely have to settle for a new job that pays less. The strong desire to hold on to their above-market-wage job causes them to be more conscientious in their work and to shirk less. And if shirking is reduced, so are the monitoring (management) costs of the firm. In short, for the firm that pays above-market wage rates, its labor costs may be higher, but its monitoring costs will be lower. Overall, economists who advance the above-market-wage theory, which is more commonly referred to as the *efficiency wage theory,* predict that firms would only be willing to pay above-market wage rates if their monitoring costs went down by more than their labor costs went up.

Marginal analysis, which is an integral part of our microeconomics mindset, involves weighing "additional benefits" against "additional costs" when making a decision. This type of thinking is employed in efficiency wage theory. Suppose a firm is considering paying its employees wage rates $1 above the current market level. The action comes with potential benefits and costs. The firm's owners must ask themselves two questions: (1) How much are the additional benefits that arise from lower monitoring costs? (2) How much are the additional costs that arise from higher labor costs? Then the firm's owners must compare the two dollar amounts and take the appropriate action. If monitoring costs fall by more than labor costs rise, efficiency wage economists predict that the firm's owners will pay above-market wages; if not, they won't.

Markets: Outside and Inside the Firm

What do we see when we put the firm under the microeconomic microscope? Basically, we see a market of sorts at work. Economics, as we know, is largely about trades or exchanges; it is about market transactions. In supply-and-demand analysis, the exchanges are between buyers of goods and services and sellers of goods and services. In the theory of the firm, the exchanges take place at two levels: (1) at the level of individuals coming together to form a team and (2) at the level of workers "choosing" a monitor.

Looking at the theory of the firm in the context of exchange, individuals initially come together realizing that the sum of what they can produce as a team is greater than the sum of what they can produce as individuals. In essence, each individual "trades" working alone for working in a team as long as he receives exactly the same from others. Later, once the team has been formed, the team members learn that shirking reduces the amount of the added output they came together to capture in the first place. Now the team members enter into another trade or market transaction: They trade some say-so over their daily behavior—specifically, they trade a low-cost shirking environment for a high-cost shirking environment—in order to receive a larger absolute amount of the potential benefits that drew them together. It is in this trade that the monitor appears: Some individuals "buy" the monitoring services that other individuals "sell."

As you continue in your study of microeconomics, look for the "markets" that appear at different levels of analysis.

The Objective of the Firm

What is the objective of the firm? Most economists say that the firm's goal, or objective, is to maximize profits. Not all economists agree, however. William Baumol, for example, claims that firms seek to maximize sales. A. A. Berle and Gardner Means maintain that **separation of ownership from control (or management)** in business firms (especially large firms) has allowed managers to pursue their own goals, such as increasing the size of the firm or increasing the number of employees working for them, at the expense of the profit-maximization goal of the stockholders (owners) of the firm. Richard Cyert, James March, and Herbert Simon argue that rather than trying to maximize profits, the firm seeks only to achieve some satisfactory target profit level (referred to by Simon as **satisficing behavior**) and then pursues other goals.

Although these so-called sales and managerial theories of the firm explain some relevant aspects of the business firm, many economists believe they do not offer a significant alternative to profit maximization as the goal of business firms. It may be true that business firms do not attempt only to maximize profits, and goals other than profit do sometimes motivate the behavior of firms. Nonetheless, one must ask whether the theories built on the profit-maximization assumption satisfactorily describe, explain, and predict the firm's behavior. As we see in later chapters, they apparently do this quite well.

Separation of Ownership from Control (or Management)
Refers to the division of interests between owners and managers that may occur in large business firms.

Satisficing Behavior
Behavior directed to meeting some satisfactory (not maximum) profit target.

Question:

Firm A decides to maximize profits over a three-year time span, while firm B decides to maximize profits over a shorter time period, say, one year. To the observer, who does not know the time span each firm has picked, firm B may appear to be attempting to maximize profits while firm A does not. In short, long-run profit maximization (three years in this example) may involve short-run behavior that appears contrary to profit maximization. And, of course, it may be contrary to profit maximization in the short run but not in the long run. Isn't this a problem with the profit-maximization hypothesis?

Answer:

That depends on how the word *problem* is used. Certainly, this example does not call the profit-maximization hypothesis into question. In other words, nothing in this example suggests that firms do not attempt to maximize profits. Instead, the example correctly points out that (1) not all firms necessarily maximize profits over the same time period and (2) failure to understand this can result in the idea that a firm does not maximize profits when, in fact, it does.

TYPES OF BUSINESS FIRMS

Business firms differ in many ways. They differ in what they produce, the number of people they employ, their revenues, their costs, where they are located, the type of advertising campaigns they run, their relationship with the government, the amount of taxes they pay, and in hundreds of other details. Many of the differences among business firms are minor, but some are not. One major difference is the firm's legal categorization. Business firms commonly fall into one of three legal categories: proprietorships, partnerships, and corporations.

Proprietorships

A **proprietorship** is a form of business that is owned by one individual who makes all the business decisions, receives the entire profits, and is legally responsible for the debts of the firm.

Being legally responsible for the debts of the business means that the sole proprietor has **unlimited liability;** that is, a sole proprietor is responsible for settling all debts of the firm even if this means selling his or her personal property (car, house, and so on) to do so.

As Exhibit 22–1 shows, proprietorships are the most numerous form of business firm in the United States; in 1986, 70.7 percent of all firms were proprietorships. They accounted for only 6.0 percent of total business revenues, however. Using this latter criterion, the much less numerous corporations are the dominant form of business firm.

Advantages of Proprietorships.   There are certain advantages to proprietorships. The first advantage is that *proprietorships are easy to form and to dissolve.* To start a proprietorship, one need only meet broadly defined health and zoning regulations and register the name of the business. To dissolve the proprietorship, one need only stop doing business. The second advantage is that *all decision-making power resides with the sole proprietor.* He or she need not consult anyone as to what product will be produced, how many units will be produced, or who will do what and when. The third advantage is that *the profit of the proprietorship is taxed only once.* The profit of the proprietorship is the income of the sole proprietor, and as such only personal income taxes apply to it.

Disadvantages of Proprietorships.   There are three major disadvantages of proprietorships. The first disadvantage is that *the sole proprietor faces unlimited liability.* As we noted, this means that the owner is responsible for all debts of the proprietorship and that his or her personal property can be used to settle these debts. In short, the liability of the firm can extend beyond the confines of the business to the proprietor's home, car, boat, and savings account. The second disadvantage is that *proprietorships have limited ability to raise funds for business expansion.* This partly explains why proprietorships are usually small business firms. Proprietorships do not find borrowing funds easy, because lenders are not eager to lend funds to business firms whose success depends on only one person. The third disadvantage is that *proprietorships usually end with the death of the proprietor.* From the point of view of the business community and the firm's employees, this is a disadvantage. Employees usually like to work for firms that offer a degree of permanency and the possibility of upward career mobility.

Proprietorship
A form of business that is owned by one individual who makes all the business decisions, receives the entire profits, and is legally responsible for the debts of the firm.

Unlimited Liability
A legal term that signifies that the personal assets of the owner(s) of a firm may be used to pay off the debts of the firm.

Partnerships

A **partnership** is a form of business that is owned by two or more co-owners, called partners, who share any profits the business earns and who are legally responsible for any debts incurred by the firm. A partnership may be viewed as a proprietorship with more than one owner. Partners in a partnership may contribute different amounts of financial capital to the formation of the firm; they may agree to have different responsibilities within the firm; and they may agree to different "cuts" of the profit pie.

Advantages of Partnerships. Since partnerships are much like proprietorships, they share many of the same advantages and disadvantages. First, *a partnership is easy to organize*. Second, *a partnership is usually an effective form of business organization in situations where team production involves skills that are difficult to monitor*. For example, physicians and attorneys often form partnerships. Names like the Smithies and Yankelovich law firm or the Matson, Bradbury, and Chan medical clinic are not uncommon. Monitoring the job performance of such professionals would be difficult. We could not know whether our fictional Dr. Matson was doing a good job or not when he talked gruffly to Mrs. Brown about her "moving aches and pains." Was he trying to short circuit her hypochondria, or was he simply being rude? Since Dr. Matson is a partner in the partnership, he is a residual claimant, and thus has an incentive to monitor his own work performance effectively.

Third, *in a partnership, the benefits of specialization can be realized*. If, for example, one partner in an advertising agency is better at public relations and another is better at art work, then they can work at the tasks for which they are best suited.

Fourth, *the profit of the partnership is the income of the partners, and only personal income taxes apply to it*.

Disadvantages of Partnerships. First, *the partners in a partnership have unlimited liability*. In a way, this is even more of a disadvantage than it is in a proprietorship. In a proprietorship, the proprietor incurs only his or her own debts and is solely responsible for them. In a partnership, one partner might incur the debts, but all partners are responsible for them. For example, if partner Matson incurs a debt by buying an expensive piece of medical equipment without the permission of partners Bradbury and Chan, that is too bad for partners Bradbury and Chan. They are still legally responsible for the debts incurred by Matson.

Second, *decision making in a partnership can be complicated or frustrating*. Suppose, in our fictional law firm, that Smithies wants to move the partnership in one direction, to specialize in corporate law, say, and Yankelovich wants to move it in another direction, to specialize in family law. Who makes the decision in this tug-of-war? Possibly no one will make the decision and things will stay as they are, which may not be a good thing for the growth of the partnership.

Third, *voluntary withdrawal by a partner from the firm, or the death of a member of a firm, can cause the partnership to dissolve or to be restructured*. This presents partnerships with a continuity problem, similar to the one proprietorships experience.

Question:

Isn't there such a thing as a limited partnership that avoids some of the problems of unlimited liability?

Answer:

Yes; in a **limited partnership** there are usually general partners and limited partners. General partners continue to have unlimited liability, but limited partners do not. The limited partner's liability is restricted to the amount he or she has invested in the firm. Usually, limited partners do not participate in the management of the firm, nor do they enter into contractual agreements on behalf of the firm.

Corporations

A **corporation** is a legal entity that can conduct business in its own name in the same way an individual does; ownership of the corporation resides with stockholders who have limited liability in the debts of the corporation. As Exhibit 22–1 shows, in 1986 corporations made up only 19.6 percent of all U.S. firms but accounted for 89.8 percent of total business revenues. Corporations with which most of us are familiar include Exxon, Ford Motor Company, General Motors, AT&T, IBM, Procter & Gamble, and NBC, to name only a few.

Advantages of Corporations. First, *the owners of the corporation (the stockholders) are not personally liable for the debts of the corporation;* they have **limited liability.** Limited liability assures the owners (stockholders) that if the corporation should incur debts that it cannot pay, creditors do not have recourse to the owners' personal property for payment. This means that an owner of a corporation cannot lose more than his or her investment. For example, if a person buys 100 shares of stock in corporation XYZ at $50 a share for a total purchase price of $5,000, he cannot lose more than $5,000.

Second, *corporations continue to exist even if one or more owners of the corporation sell their shares or die.* This is because the corporation is a legal entity in and of itself.

Third, since the corporation's life is independent of the life of any one of the owners of the corporation, and because there is limited liability, *corporations are usually able to raise large sums of financial capital for investment purposes.* Limited liability is a plus from the point of view of the potential investor in a corporation. She knows that she can only lose her investment and nothing more. In addition, because corporations can sell bonds and issue stock, they have means of raising financial capital that do not exist for proprietorships or partnerships. We discuss bonds and stocks in more detail later in the chapter.

EXHIBIT 22–1
Forms of Business Organizations
Two criteria commonly used for classifying business firms include percentage of U.S. firms and percentage of total business revenues. Nearly three out of every four firms is a proprietorship, but they generate only 6.0 percent of total business revenues. Corporations, though relatively few in number, generate 89.8 percent of total business revenues. All data are for 1986.

TYPE OF FIRM	PERCENTAGE OF U.S. FIRMS	PERCENTAGE OF TOTAL BUSINESS REVENUES
Proprietorship	70.7%	6.0%
Partnership	9.7	4.1
Corporation	19.6	89.8

SOURCE: U.S. Bureau of the Census, *Statistical Abstract of the United States, 1990* (Washington, D.C.: U.S. Government Printing Office, 1990).

Disadvantages of Corporations. The major disadvantage of corporations is that the *profits of the corporation are taxed twice.* For example, suppose corporation XYZ earns a $3 million profit this year. This amount is subject to the corporate income tax. If the corporate tax is 25 percent, then $750,000 is paid in taxes and $2.25 million remains for **dividends** and other uses. Next, suppose half of this $2.25 million is distributed as dividends to stockholders. This is income for the stockholders and is taxed at personal income tax rates. In short, the $3 million profit was subject to both the corporate income tax and the personal income tax. Contrast this situation with the profit earned by a proprietorship. If a proprietorship had earned the $3 million in profit, it would only have been subject to one tax: the personal income tax.

A second disadvantage of corporations is that they are *often subject to problems associated with the separation of ownership from control,* where the owners of the corporation are different persons from the managers who control it on a day-to-day basis and owners and managers do not always agree on what the corporation's objectives should be.

The objective of the owners might be to increase profits and raise the value of the stock they hold. The manager might want to increase the size of the corporation or hire additional personnel or contribute to the local community—all of which may work against profitability.

This possible difference in objectives between managers and owners is the subject of controversy in the economics profession. Many economists discount this problem. According to their argument, stockholders do not need to know what the managers of their corporation are doing on a daily basis; to find out how the managers are doing, stockholders can simply watch the value of their stock. If it goes down, they can reason that present management is not doing a good job and can organize to remove them; in short, they can monitor the managers by reading the stock market pages of their local newspaper. Also, the stockholders can make the managers "one of them" by issuing stock to the managers. The idea here is to ensure the correspondence of objectives of managers and stockholders. Finally, entrepreneurially oriented managers are usually waiting in the wings, willing and able to make the case to stockholders that the present management is doing a bad job and needs to be replaced (by them). Their presence restrains present management from satisfying its objectives at the expense of the objective(s) of stockholders.

Exhibit 22–2 summarizes the advantages and disadvantages of corporations and compares them with proprietorships and partnerships.

Japanese Proprietorships and American Corporations

Proprietorships in Japan receive approximately 50 percent of the retail sales in Japan, whereas proprietorships in the United States receive only about 6 percent of retail sales in the United States. In this country, retails sales are largely dominated by corporations, which receive approximately 90 percent of retails sales.

The difference between the type of firm that receives the majority of retails sales in the two countries has consequences for international trade. For the Japanese to enter the U.S. retail market in a major way, they need to do business with one of the major U.S. retail corporations—such as K-Mart. But for Americans to enter the Japanese retail market in a major way, they would need to strike a deal with hundreds of Japanese proprietorships. All other things held constant, it is much easier to strike a deal with one major U.S. retail corporation than with hundreds of Japanese proprietorships.

EXHIBIT 22–2

Advantages and Disadvantages of Different Types of Business Firms

TYPE OF BUSINESS FIRM	EXAMPLES	ADVANTAGES	DISADVANTAGES
Proprietorship	1. Local barbershop 2. Many restaurants 3. Family farm 4. Carpet cleaning service	1. Easy to form and to dissolve. 2. All decision-making power resides with the sole proprietor. 3. Profit is taxed only once.	1. Proprietor faces unlimited liability. 2. Limited ability to raise funds for business expansion. 3. Usually ends with death of proprietor.
Partnership	1. Some medical offices 2. Some law offices 3. Some advertising agencies	1. Easy to organize. 2. Deals effectively with team production that involves skills difficult to monitor. 3. Benefits of specialization can be realized. 4. Profit is taxed only once.	1. Partners face unlimited liability (one partner can incur a debt and all partners are legally responsible for payment of the debt). 2. Decision making can be complex and frustrating. 3. Withdrawal or death of a partner can end partnership or cause its restructuring.
Corporation	1. IBM 2. AT&T 3. General Motors	1. Owners (stockholders) have limited liability. 2. Corporation continues if owners sell their shares of stock or die. 3. Usually able to raise large sums of financial capital.	1. Profit is taxed twice. 2. Problems may arise owing to separation of ownership from control (some suggest "separation of ownership from control" is more illusory than real).

Some economists have argued that the difference in the types of firms that control the majority of retails sales in the two countries puts the United States at a disadvantage relative to Japan when it comes to retail exports. This is a nontariff and nonquota barrier to trade, they say, which has a negative effect on the U.S. balance of trade.

THE BALANCE SHEET OF A FIRM

■

All business firms—proprietorships, partnerships, and corporations alike—have a balance sheet. A **balance sheet** presents a picture of the financial status of a firm; it is an accounting of the assets and liabilities (and hence the net worth) of a firm. Exhibit 22–3 illustrates a balance sheet for a fictional corporation, American Computers, Inc.

Balance Sheet
An accounting of the assets, liabilities, and net worth of a business firm.

EXHIBIT 22–3

A Balance Sheet for American Computers, Inc.

The left-hand side of the balance sheet lists the corporation's assets; the right-hand side of the balance sheet lists liabilities and net worth (equity or capital stock). The net worth of a business firm is equal to assets minus liabilities. This means liabilities plus net worth equal assets, and the right-hand side of the balance sheet exactly "balances" the left-hand side.

ASSETS ($ MILLIONS)		LIABILITIES ($ MILLIONS)	
Cash	$ 5	Accounts payable	$ 10
Accounts receivables	15	Short-term debt	15
Inventory	25	Long-term debt	30
Equipment	40	Total liabilities	$ 55
Land and building	60	Net worth	90
Total assets	$145	Total liabilities and net worth	$145

Assets
Anything of value to which the firm has a legal claim.

Liabilities
A debt of the business firm.

Net Worth (Equity or Capital Stock)
Value of the business firm to its owners; it is determined by subtracting liabilities from assets.

On the left-hand side of the balance sheet, **assets** are listed. An asset is anything of value to which the firm has a legal claim. On the right-hand side of the balance sheet, **liabilities** are listed. A liability is a debt of the firm. Also listed on the right-hand side of the balance sheet is **net worth.** Net worth, also known as **equity,** or **capital stock** (when dealing with a corporation), is the value of the business firm to its owners; it is determined by subtracting liabilities from assets. According to American Computers' balance sheet, if the company sold off its assets and paid off its liabilities, it would have $90 million left over. This amount, or the net worth of the firm, represents the owners' claims on the assets of the firm. If liabilities should exceed assets, then the firm would have a negative net worth. Since a firm's net worth is equal to its assets minus its liabilities, it follows that liabilities plus net worth equal a firm's assets. In other words, the left-hand side of the balance sheet exactly "balances" the right-hand side.

$$\text{Net worth} = \text{assets} - \text{liabilities}$$

so it follows that

$$\text{Assets} = \text{liabilities} + \text{net worth}$$

FINANCING CORPORATE ACTIVITY

We mentioned earlier that corporations have options for raising financial capital that do not exist for proprietorships and partnerships. All firms can raise financial capital by borrowing from banks and other lending institutions. Corporations, however, have two other avenues: They can *sell bonds* (sometimes referred to as *issuing debt),* and they can *issue (or sell) additional shares of stock.*

Stocks and Bonds

Bond
An IOU statement that promises to pay a certain sum of money (the principal) at maturity and also to pay periodic fixed sums until that date.

Face Value (Par Value)
Dollar amount specified on the bond.

A **bond** is a promise to pay for the use of someone else's money. Specifically, it is an IOU statement that promises to pay a certain sum of money (the principal) at maturity and also to pay periodic fixed sums until that date. All bonds specify the following: (1) the maturity date, which is some date in the future, say, 1999; (2) a dollar figure, which is called the **face value (par value)** of the bond, say, $1,000;

476

(3) a **coupon rate** (of interest), which is stated in percentage terms. We pick 10 percent as our coupon rate.

When someone buys the bond we have just described from a corporation, the following process takes place: (1) The person who buys the bond pays some dollar amount for the bond (not necessarily the face value). Since this person will be receiving periodic payments, and will receive a fixed sum of money at the maturity date, we say that the person has lent money to the corporation, or that the corporation has borrowed money from the person who bought the bond. (2) The person who buys the bond receives annual payments from the corporation equal to the coupon rate times the face value of the bond. For our bond this amounts to $100 (10% × $1,000 = $100). These $100 payments will continue each year through 1999, the maturity date. (3) When the maturity date arrives, the person who bought the bond receives the face value of the bond—$1,000.

Instead of selling bonds, a corporation may issue **stock** to raise financial capital. A share of stock is a claim on the assets of the corporation that gives the purchaser a share of the ownership of the corporation. Whereas the buyer of a corporate bond is lending funds to the corporation, the buyer of a share of stock is acquiring an ownership right in the corporation.

Coupon Rate
The percentage of the face value of the bond that is paid out regularly (usually quarterly or annually) to the holder of the bond.

(Shares of) Stock
A claim on the assets of a corporation that gives the purchaser a share of the ownership of the corporation.

Question:

In recent years, we have heard a lot about **junk bonds.** *What are they?*

Answer:

Junk bonds are considered risky bonds that offer high coupon rates. In fact, the coupon rate is higher than for most bonds because the risk is higher ("there are no free lunches"). What makes junk bonds risky is that the people who buy them are the least likely to be paid what is owed to them by the issuer of the junk bonds, if the issuer gets into financial trouble.

Junk Bonds
Risky bonds that offer high coupon rates.

Follow-up Question:

Why would anyone buy junk bonds if they are so risky?

Answer:

For some people, the higher risk that comes with junk bonds is offset by the higher expected return.

Nonprofit Firms

There are firms other than business firms. It is important to know about them and to understand how and why they differ from business firms. In this short section, we discuss *nonprofit* firms, both private and public.

Nonprofit firms are firms in which there are no residual claimants; any revenues over costs must be plowed back into the operation of the firm so that "what comes in" equals "what goes out." Churches, charitable organizations, colleges, and mutual insurance companies are a few examples of nonprofit firms. All these organizations are without residual claimants. For example, in a college, the college president does not pocket any of the funds over and above the costs of running the college. Any funds that come into the college—through tuition fees, state appropriations, or monetary gifts—must be used for the operation of the college.

Nonprofit Firms
Firms in which there are no residual claimants; any revenues over costs must be plowed back into the operation of the firm so that "what comes in" equals "what goes out."

The Monkey and the Economist

Here are two facts about stocks: (1) Stocks are bought and sold (traded) with the future in mind. Rollins might buy 100 shares of IBM because he thinks the price of IBM stock will rise. (2) People act quickly on information about the future performance of a corporation whose stock is traded. If Carpenter, who owns stock in United Artists, hears that the company is headed for bad times, she won't wait long to act on this information. Taking the two facts together, we conclude that *stock prices quickly reflect individuals' most recently acquired information about the future performance of the corporations that issued the stock.*

Consider two stocks: IBM stock and Ford Motor stock. Suppose both companies' stock is selling for the same price—$100 a share. One day, individuals learn that IBM has made a major breakthrough in the market for computers and that it is headed for better times. On the same day, individuals learn that one of Ford's models is about to be recalled, and the company is headed for rough times. What will happen to the prices of IBM and Ford stock? We would expect the price of IBM stock to be bid up and the price of Ford stock to fall. At the end of the day, IBM stock will be selling for $100+ and Ford Motor stock will be selling for $100−.

Many economists predict that the price of Ford Motor stock will fall sufficiently (and the price of IBM stock will rise sufficiently) so that after the price adjustments have taken place, Ford stock is no worse and no better a buy for the price than IBM stock. Furthermore, since individuals act quickly on information relating to future corporate performance, the new equilibrium between the stocks' prices is likely to be achieved rapidly.

What all this suggests is that there are no *uniquely* good or bad buys in the stock market. In equilibrium, IBM stock will be as *good or as bad a buy* as Ford stock, even though the expected future performances of the two corporations may not be the same. In theory, the prices of the two stocks will instantaneously adjust for the differences in the expected future performances of the two corporations.

Enter the monkey and the economist. Is one more capable than the other of choosing stocks within broad classes? In other words, is a monkey who "chooses" stocks by throwing darts at the stock market page of the *Wall Street Journal* any better or worse than an economist who sits at his desk pouring over stock market facts and figures? Unless the economist has *inside information,* or can *better evaluate given information* (than other analysts), he can do no better than the dart-throwing monkey at choosing stocks. As shocking as this sounds, it is simply a consequence of the extreme speed with which the stock market processes information relating to the future performance of companies whose stocks are traded.

As Paul Samuelson, a Nobel Prize–winner in economics, has noted, "Even the best investors seem to find it hard to do better than the comprehensive common-stock averages, or better on the average than random selection among stocks of comparable variability."[3] If you replace the words

[3]Paul Samuelson, "Proof That Properly Discounted Present Values of Assets Vibrate Randomly," *Bell Journal of Economics and Management Science* 4 (Autumn 1973):369–74.

"random selection" with "monkey selection," you have the story we have told here.

A Postscript

In 1967, the editors of *Forbes* magazine taped the stock market page of a newspaper to the wall and threw darts at it 28 times. In each of the 28 "hit" companies, they invested a hypothetical $1,000.

By 1984, the original $28,000 had grown to $132,000, not counting dividends. This was a 370 percent gain, or ten times better than the performance of the Dow Jones industrial average. Few highly trained professional stock analysts did as well.

Unfortunately for them, the editors of *Forbes* did not invest real money in the venture. Obviously, they didn't trust the power of the dart.

Question:

Some people have been sent to jail for using inside information. What is inside information? Is it hard to get? And what's wrong with using it?

Answer:

Inside information is information that is not yet public; it is known only to a small group of people, called *insiders*. The following example explains how someone might get inside information.

Diana Jenkins works as an accountant for a major pharmaceutical company. She has a friend, David Thompson, who works as a researcher for the company. One day David tells Diana that he and others in the research department are working on a drug that represents a major advance in cancer treatment. Months pass, and then one day David tells Diana (in whispers) that the research team has perfected the drug and it will soon be sold on the market.

This is a piece of inside information. "No one knows about this except a handful of people in the executive offices and the research team," says David to Diana, "so please be sure to keep it quiet."

Inside information is hard to get because companies often do not want to release it. For example, the company that David works for might not want the information to get out too soon because it is afraid that its competitors might

speed up production of a cancer-curing drug they are working on. By releasing the inside information, David is probably breaking a contract with his employer to keep this information secret.

It has been argued that since no residual claimants exist in a nonprofit firm, no one within the firm has an incentive (or, at least, as strong an incentive as in a profit-maximizing business firm with residual claimants) to monitor shirking. We predict, then, that there will be more shirking in a nonprofit firm than in a profit-seeking business firm. For example, we would expect more shirking at the Division of Motor Vehicles (DMV) than at the local computer store.

Also, since any funds in excess of costs cannot be taken out of the firm, it is argued that top administrators in nonprofit firms will attempt to use these "surplus" funds to make their lives more comfortable *within* the firm. The administrators might have large, luxurious offices and private dining rooms, pay out higher salaries than necessary in order to acquire quality personnel, or take frequent pleasurable "business" trips.

Nonprofit firms are either private or public. A charitable organization such as the United Way is a private nonprofit firm. A police force that receives state-appropriated funds is a public nonprofit firm. One major difference between the two is who pays the costs of the firm.

In a private nonprofit firm, private citizens pay the costs. For example, the salaries of the persons who work for the local church are paid by private citizens mostly through voluntary contributions. In a public nonprofit firm, *taxpayers* pay the costs. The salaries of the police in your town are paid by taxpayers.

At times the difference is not so clear-cut. Sometimes a nonprofit firm will receive some funds from private citizens, who purchase the goods or services the nonprofit firm sells, and some funds from taxpayers. State universities receive funds both from private citizens (students), as consumers of education, and also from taxpayers. Is the state university a private nonprofit firm or a public nonprofit firm? The answer is that it is a public nonprofit firm because it is operated by persons who must answer to members of the public sector: the state governor and the regents, who are elected or publicly appointed.

Public Nonprofit Firms and Taxes. A private nonprofit firm (such as a charitable organization) that doesn't satisfy the persons who contribute the funds—its customers, so to speak—is more likely to go out of business than a public nonprofit firm that doesn't satisfy its customers. The reason is that the latter receives taxpayer funds whereas the former does not. If the customers of the private nonprofit firm do not wish to continue buying what the firm is selling or wish to stop contributing, they do just that. They show their change in preferences, or their dissatisfaction with the firm, by stopping the flow of dollars.

The customers-as-taxpayers of the public nonprofit firm are not in the same situation. They may not like the way the public nonprofit firm is treating them, or

Inside Information
Information that is not yet public; it is known only to a small group of people called insiders.

they may think the firm is doing an extremely poor job at delivering services, but unless they can convince their elected representatives to stop allocating tax funds for the public nonprofit firm, the flow of tax dollars is likely to continue.

CHAPTER SUMMARY

The Firm

■ Alchian and Demsetz argue that firms are formed when there are benefits from individuals working as a team; specifically, when the sum of what individuals can produce as a team is greater than the sum of what individuals can produce alone: sum of team production > sum of individual production.

■ There are both advantages and disadvantages to team production. The chief advantage (in many cases) is the positive difference between the output produced by the team and the sum of the output produced by individuals working alone. The chief disadvantage is the increased shirking in teams. The role of the monitor in the firm is to preserve the increased output and reduce or eliminate the increased shirking. The monitor has a monetary incentive not to shirk his monitoring duties because he is a residual claimant.

Different Types of Business Firms

■ A proprietorship is a form of business that is owned by one individual who makes all the business decisions, receives the entire profits, and is legally responsible for the debts of the firm. The sole proprietor has unlimited liability. The advantages of a proprietorship include the following: (1) It is easy to form and to dissolve. (2) All decision-making power resides with the sole proprietor. (3) The profits of the proprietorship are taxed only once. The disadvantages include the following: (1) The sole proprietor faces unlimited liability. (2) It has limited ability to raise funds for business expansion. (3) It usually ends with the death of the proprietor.

■ A partnership is a form of business that is owned by two or more co-owners (partners) who share any profits the business earns and who are legally responsible for any debts incurred by the firm. The advantages of a partnership include the following: (1) It is easy to organize. (2) It is an effective form of business organization in situations where team production involves skills that are difficult to monitor. (3) The benefits of specialization can be realized. (4) The profits of the partnership are taxed only once. The disadvantages include the following: (1) The partners have unlimited liability. (2) Decision making can be complicated and frustrating. (3) The voluntary withdrawal of a partner from the firm or the death of a partner can cause the partnership to be dissolved or restructured.

■ A corporation is a legal entity that can conduct business in its own name. Corporations account for the vast majority of total business revenues (approximately 90 percent). The advantages of a corporation include the following: (1) The owners (stockholders) of the corporation are not personally liable for the debts of the corporation; there is limited (not unlimited) liability. (2) The corporation continues to exist even when an owner sells his or her shares of stock or dies. (3) Corporations are usually able to raise large sums of financial capital for investment purposes. The disadvantages include the following: (1) The profits of the corporation are taxed twice. (2) There are problems associated with separation of ownership from control (although some economists maintain that no serious problems exist here that cannot be solved).

The Balance Sheet of a Firm

■ A balance sheet is a picture of the financial status of a firm. Principally, a balance sheet lists a firm's assets, liabilities, and net worth. An asset is anything of value to which the firm has a legal claim. A liability is a debt of the firm. Net worth is the difference between assets and liabilities.

Financing Corporate Activity

■ Corporations can either issue bonds or additional shares of stock to raise funds. A bond is an IOU statement that promises to pay back a certain fixed sum of money at a specific point in time and to pay a fixed sum of money periodically. A share of stock is a claim on the assets of the corporation that gives the purchaser a share of the ownership of the corporation. A bondholder of corporation X, for example, does not have an ownership right in corporation X, but a stockholder of the corporation does.

Nonprofit Firms

■ Nonprofit firms are firms in which there are no residual claimants. There are both private and public nonprofit firms. One major difference between the two types is who pays the costs of the firms. In private nonprofit firms, private citizens as (voluntary) contributors or consumers do; in public nonprofit firms, taxpayers do. Since there are no residual claimants in nonprofit firms, we would expect the incentive to monitor shirking to be less, leading to more shirking than in business firms. In addition, since none of the "surplus" funds can be taken out of the firm, we would expect to see top administrators in nonprofit firms using the funds in personal ways to enhance their comfort, pleasure, and status. Some economists believe that empirical evidence fails to reject this theory.

Key Terms and Concepts

Business Firm	Unlimited Liability	Liabilities
Market Coordination	Partnership	Net Worth (Equity or Capital Stock)
Managerial Coordination	Limited Partnership	
	Corporation	Bond
Shirking	Limited Liability	Face Value (Par Value)
Monitor	Dividends	Coupon Rate
Residual Claimant	Balance Sheet	(Shares of) Stock
Efficiency Wage Theory	Assets	Junk Bonds
Proprietorship		Inside Information

1. Explain the difference between managerial coordination and market coordination.

2. Is the managerial coordination that goes on inside a business firm independent of market forces? Explain your answer.

3. Explain why even conscientious workers will shirk more when the cost of shirking falls.

4. What does the phrase "separation of ownership from control" refer to?

5. Discuss the different types of liability (limited versus unlimited) that proprietorships, partnerships, and corporations face.

6. The chapter implied that business firms might operate differently from nonprofit firms. What might make this so?

7. Profit sharing is more often found in partnerships, where the number of owners is small, than in corporations where the number of owners tends to be relatively large. Could there be an economic reason for this? If so, what could it be?

8. Your economics class can be viewed as a team. You come together with other individuals to learn economics. There is a hierarchical scheme in the classroom. Your instructor is the monitor, and he or she tells you what to read and when the tests will be given, and then grades your performance. Consider what would happen if, instead of this system, you were not graded. Would you shirk more or less? Explain your answer. In which setting would you expect to learn more economics? Why? Can you relate any of your answers to the performance of an employee in a firm? If so, explain how.

9. What differences, if any, do you think there might be between the behavior of the president of your college or university, as chief administrator of a nonprofit firm, and the behavior of the president of a corporation as chief administrator of a business firm?

PRODUCTION AND COSTS

WHAT THIS CHAPTER IS ABOUT

Just as there are two sides to a market, a buying side (demand) and selling side (supply), there are two sides to a firm: a cost side and a revenue side. This chapter looks principally at the cost side.

ALL ABOUT COSTS

■

Cost connotes sacrifice; and sacrifices can be made, and alternatives can be forfeited, without money changing hands.

■

Explicit Cost
A cost that is incurred when an actual (monetary) payment is made.

Implicit Cost
A cost that represents the value of resources used in production for which no actual (monetary) payment is made.

We discussed the concept of opportunity costs in Chapters 1 and 2. This chapter presents other types of costs—12 different cost concepts, to be specific. In this section, we focus on three: explicit cost, implicit cost, and sunk cost.

Explicit Cost and Implicit Cost

Opportunity cost is a measure of what is given up when one action is taken instead of another. "What is given up" may either be explicit or implicit; hence, opportunity costs may be either **explicit costs** or **implicit costs.**

Let's look at a pizzeria in town. The owner of the pizzeria buys napkins, cheese, and soft drinks from her suppliers. The dollar payments she makes for these supplies are referred to as explicit costs (or accounting costs). An explicit cost is a cost that is incurred when an actual (monetary) payment is made.

An implicit cost is a cost that represents the value of resources used in production for which no actual (monetary) payment is made; it is a cost incurred as a result of a firm using resources that it owns or that the owners of the firm contribute to it.

Suppose that if the owner of the pizzeria had chosen not to own and work at the restaurant, she would have worked for an insurance company and earned $50,000 per year. In other words, by choosing to own and work at the pizzeria (and not to work for the insurance company), she *forfeits* a $50,000 salary. The $50,000 is an implicit cost.

With implicit costs, no money changes hands. But, of course, money need not change hands before a cost can be incurred. Cost connotes sacrifice; and sacrifices can be made, and alternatives can be forfeited, without money changing hands.

Question:

Are opportunity costs different in any way from explicit costs and implicit costs?

Answer:

No, they are not. There are two *subsets* of opportunity cost: the explicit-cost subset and the implicit-cost subset. Perhaps it would be clearer to say "explicit opportunity cost" and "implicit opportunity cost." But, as noted in Chapter 1, economists often leave out the word "opportunity" when speaking of costs.

Economic Profit and Accounting Profit

Economic Profit
The difference between total revenue and total (opportunity) cost, including both its explicit and implicit components.

Economic profit is the difference between total revenue and total opportunity cost, including both its explicit and implicit components.

$$\text{Economic profit} = \text{total revenue} - \text{total opportunity cost}$$

or

$$\text{Economic profit} = \text{total revenue} - (\text{explicit} + \text{implicit costs})$$

Accounting Profit
The difference between total revenue and explicit costs.

Accounting profit is the difference between total revenue and explicit costs.[1]

---

[1]Don't jump to the conclusion that accounting profit is what accountants calculate and economic profit is what economists calculate. What we have here are simply two different profit concepts. It is possible for anyone (an accountant, an economist, a computer analyst, a nurse, and so forth) to calculate either type of profit.

484

$$\text{Accounting profit} = \text{total revenue} - \text{explicit costs}$$

An example will help differentiate between economic profit and accounting profit. McDowell, an attorney working for the law firm of Zale and Zenzer, earns an annual salary of $60,000. One day he quits his job and opens up a copying shop across from the university. For the first year of operation, his explicit costs are $50,000. His total revenue is $130,000. What is his accounting profit? The answer is $80,000. We get this figure by subtracting $50,000 explicit costs from $130,000 total revenue. McDowell's economic profit is $20,000. We get this figure by subtracting both explicit costs ($50,000) and implicit costs ($60,000) from total revenue.

In calculating economic profit, we take into account the salary McDowell could be earning working for Zale and Zenzer (but is not earning because he chose to work for himself) and subtract it from total revenue. In calculating accounting profit, we do not take into account the salary McDowell could be earning working for Zale and Zenzer.

Question:

When most people use the word profit, *which profit do they mean? Which concept of profit is it better to use?*

Answer:

When most noneconomists use the word *profit,* they usually mean accounting profit. It is economic profit, however, that directs economic activity, as the following example illustrates.

Suppose one month after graduating from college, Marta gets a good-paying job working for a long distance telephone company. Three years later, she thinks about leaving the company to start her own. Will what Marta has to give up to start her company, including her well-paying job, job security, pension benefits, and so on be important in her decision of whether to strike out on her own? We think she'll say yes, it is important. This, then, tells us that not only do explicit costs matter but that implicit costs matter, too.

We conclude that if we seek to understand and predict economic behavior, it is better to think in terms of economic profit than accounting profit.

Zero Economic Profit Is Not as Bad as It Sounds

Economic profit is usually lower (never higher) than accounting profit, because economic profit is the difference between total revenue and total opportunity costs, including both explicit and implicit costs, whereas accounting profit is the difference between total revenue and only explicit costs. Thus, it is possible for a firm to earn both a positive accounting profit *and* a zero economic profit. In economics, a firm that makes zero economic profit is said to be earning a **normal profit:** zero economic profit = normal profit.

Should an owner of a firm be worried if he has made zero economic profit for, say, the year just ending? The answer is no. A zero economic profit—as bad as it may sound—means the owner has generated total revenues sufficient to cover total opportunity costs; that is, both explicit *and* implicit costs. If, for example, the owner's implicit cost is a (forfeited) $100,000 salary working for someone else, then earning a zero economic profit means he has done as well as he could have in his next best (alternative) line of employment.

Normal Profit
Zero economic profit. A firm that earns normal profit is earning revenues equal to its total opportunity costs. This is the level of profit necessary to keep resources employed in that particular firm.

When we realize that zero economic profit (or normal profit) means "doing as well as could have been done," we understand that it isn't bad to make zero economic profit. Zero accounting profit is something altogether different; it implies that some part of total opportunity costs has not been covered by total revenue.

Sunk Cost

Sunk cost is a cost incurred in the past that cannot be changed by current decisions and therefore cannot be recovered. For example, suppose a firm must purchase a $10,000 government license before it can legally produce and sell lamp poles. Furthermore, suppose the government will not buy back the license, nor allow it to be resold. The $10,000 the firm spends to purchase the license is a sunk cost. It is a cost that, once it has been incurred (the $10,000 was spent), cannot be changed by a current decision (we cannot go back into the past and undo what was done), and cannot be recovered (the government will not buy back the license, nor allow it to be resold).

Question:

Suppose Alicia purchases a pair of shoes, wears them for a few days, and then realizes that they are uncomfortable. Furthermore, suppose she can't return the shoes for a refund. Are the shoes considered a sunk cost? Would an economist recommend that Alicia continue wearing the shoes?

Answer:

The purchase of the shoes represents a cost (1) incurred in the past that (2) cannot be changed by a current decision and (3) cannot be recovered; therefore, it is a sunk cost. An economist would recommend that Alicia not base her current decision to wear or not wear the shoes on what has happened and cannot be changed. If a person lets what she has done, and can't undo, influence her present decision, she runs the risk of compounding mistakes.

To illustrate, if Alicia decides to wear the uncomfortable shoes because she thinks it is a waste of money not to, then she may end up with an even bigger loss: certainly less comfort and possibly a trip to the podiatrist later. The relevant question she must ask herself is, What *will* I give up by wearing the uncomfortable shoes? and not, What *did* I give up by buying the shoes? The message here is that only the future can be affected by a present decision, never the past. Bygones are bygones, sunk costs are sunk costs.

"I Have to Get a Job as an Accountant, I've Invested Four Years in Accounting"

Sunk cost is most often discussed in terms of the production of a good. We illustrate here how it might also be relevant to you or a friend in college.

Consider a senior in college who is about to graduate. She has spent a little over four years in college and has majored in accounting. In her last semester, she finally admits to herself what she began to suspect in her junior year: She dislikes accounting work. She is, however, currently interviewing with accounting firms for a job as an accountant upon graduation. A friend asks her why, if she dislikes accounting so intensely, she wants to be an accountant. She says that she has spent more than four years and a lot of money learning to be an accountant and that she must now become one to recapture some of the cost incurred.

But we ask, Is it possible to recapture some of the cost incurred? Aren't the costs she has incurred to learn accounting—the dollars spent on tuition and books, the time spent studying accounting—sunk? Yes, they are. There is no way to undo the past. Whether our senior works as an accountant or not, the costs incurred in becoming an accountant cannot be recovered. Saying this does not imply that the senior should or should not work as an accountant, only that the decision to work as one is best made by ignoring the past. The relevant cost-related questions for the senior to ask herself are, "What *will I give up* if I choose to work as an accountant?" Or, "What *will I give up* if I go back to school and learn something else?" It is not, "What *have I given up* to learn accounting?"

Microeconomics emphasizes that all economic actors deal with objectives, constraints, and choices. Briefly, let us focus on *constraints*. All economic actors would prefer to have fewer constraints than more and constraints that offer more latitude rather than less. For example, a firm would probably prefer to be constrained in having to buy its resources from five resource suppliers rather than only one. A consumer would rather have a budget constraint of $4,000 a month instead of $2,000 a month.

Think of two persons, A and B. Person A considers sunk cost when she makes a decision, and person B ignores it when she makes a decision. Does one person face fewer constraints, *ceteris paribus?* The answer is that the person who ignores sunk cost when making a decision, person B, faces fewer constraints. What person A does, in fact, is act as if a constraint is there—the constraint of sunk cost, the constraint of having to rectify a past decision—when it really exists simply because person A thinks it does.

In this sense, the "constraint" of sunk cost is very different from the constraint of, say, scarcity. Whether a person believes scarcity exists or not, it exists. People are constrained by scarcity, as they are by the force of gravity, whether they know it or not. But people are not constrained by sunk cost if they choose not to be constrained by it. If you choose to let bygones be bygones, if you realize that sunk cost is a cost that has been incurred and cannot be changed, then you will not be constrained by it when making a current decision.

Economists look at things this way: There are already enough constraints in the world. You are not made better off by behaving as if there is one more than there actually is.

PRODUCTION AND COSTS IN THE SHORT RUN

Production involves costs and takes time to complete. In other words, there is a link between production, costs, and time. In this section, we discuss production and costs in the short run. In the next, we discuss production and costs in the long run.

Fixed and Variable Inputs; Fixed and Variable Costs

The production of a good requires factors of production, or inputs; essentially there are two types: **fixed inputs** and **variable inputs.** A fixed input is an input whose

Fixed Input
An input whose quantity cannot be changed as output changes in the short run.

Variable Input
An input whose quantity can be changed as output changes in the short run.

487

What Does Sunk Cost Have to Do with Zen?

Economics can be found in more places than we may think. Economics can even be found in books about Zen. Compare the words of the economist speaking about sunk cost with the words of the Zen Master speaking about life:

The economist says that sunk cost is a part of life, nothing can change this, and it is better to face this fact than to ignore it.

The Zen Master says, "There *is* one thing in life that you can always rely on: life being as it is."*

The economist realizes that it is sometimes hard to ignore sunk cost because we don't want to admit that we have made a mistake.

The Zen Master says, "We have to pay attention to this very moment,

*All the quotes relating to Zen are from Charlotte Joko Beck, *Everyday Zen*, edited by Steve Smith (New York: Harper & Row, 1989).

the totality of what is happening right now. And the reason we don't want to pay attention is because it's not always pleasant. It doesn't suit us."

The economist urges us to face the fact that sunk costs cannot be recaptured, that bygones are bygones, and that if we act accordingly we will not compound mistakes.

The Zen Master takes this principle to the *n*th degree and says, "Trust in things being as they are is the secret of life."

The economist says that when we try in vain to recapture sunk costs (to bring back the past) we lose out on the present and perhaps the future. A person cannot be looking over his shoulder and in front of him, too.

The Zen Master puts this in context and says, "Sometimes a man or a woman dreams of an ideal partner; they dream and they dream. But when we live life in dreams and

hopes, then what life *can* offer, that man or woman sitting right next to us—ordinary, unglamorous—the wonder of that life escapes us because we are hoping for something special, for some ideal."

In sum, the economist, when discussing sunk costs, urges us to see the world as it is, to realize that bygones are bygones, that trying to undo something that cannot be undone can only lead us to lose the present and perhaps the future, too. To a large degree, this is the message of Zen—which emphasizes reality (good or bad), the now (as opposed to the past or the future), and living in accordance with the way life is (as opposed to the way we might want it to be).

If economics can be found in a book about Zen, think of how many other places it may be found, too.

quantity cannot be changed as output changes in the short run. A variable input is an input whose quantity can be changed as output changes in the short run. The following example illustrates a fixed input.

The McMahon and McGee Typewriter Company has rented a factory for which it has a six-month lease: McMahon and McGee have contracted to pay the $2,300 monthly rent for six months—no matter what. This means whether McMahon and McGee produce 1 typewriter or 7,000 typewriters, the $2,300 rent on the factory must still be paid. The factory is an input in the production process of typewriters; specifically, it is a fixed input.

Fixed Costs
Costs that do not vary with output.

Costs are associated with a fixed input. These are **fixed costs.** A fixed cost is a cost that does not change as output changes. The $2,300 rent for the factory is a fixed cost; it does not change with the number of typewriters McMahon and McGee produce. Whether they produce 0, 1, or 7,000, the rent is still the same. Such things as payments for fire insurance, payments for liability insurance, and the rental payments for a factory and machinery are usually considered fixed costs. They are independent of the level of output produced.

Examples of variable inputs for the McMahon and McGee Typewriter Company include typewriter ribbons, typewriter rollers, and plastic keys for the typewriter keyboards. These inputs can and (most likely) will change as the production of typewriters changes. As more typewriters are produced, more of these inputs will be purchased by McMahon and McGee; as fewer typewriters are produced, fewer of these inputs will be purchased. Labor might also be a variable input for McMahon and McGee. As they produce more typewriters, they might hire more employees; as they produce fewer typewriters, they might lay off some employees. Costs are associated with variable inputs. These costs are **variable costs.** A variable cost is a cost that changes as output changes.

If we add fixed costs to variable costs, we have **total cost.** Total cost is the sum of fixed and variable costs.

Periods of Production: Short Run and Long Run

We now turn to the two periods in which production takes place: the **short run** and the **long run.** The short run is a period in which some inputs are fixed. This implies that any changes in output can only be brought about by a change in the quantity of variable inputs. The long run is a period in which all inputs can be varied (no inputs are fixed). Exhibit 23–1 reviews periods of production, inputs, and costs connected with the production process.

Computing and Graphing Total, Average, and Marginal Cost Curves

In Exhibit 23–2, we have computed and graphed the following: total fixed cost (*TFC*), total variable cost (*TVC*), total cost (*TC*), **average fixed cost** (*AFC*), **average variable cost** (*AVC*), **average total cost** (*ATC*) or **unit cost,** and marginal cost. Here is a step-by-step explanation.

First, we entered some hypothetical data in column 2, which represents total fixed cost (*TFC*), and in column 4, which represents total variable cost (*TVC*).

Second, we summed the *TFC* and *TVC* dollar amounts to compute total cost (*TC*), shown in column 6 (on the following page).

Third, we took each total cost magnitude—*TFC*, *TVC*, and *TC*—and turned it into an average cost magnitude. This is done by dividing *TFC*, *TVC*, and *TC* each by the quantity of output. Simply put, we computed average fixed cost (*AFC*) by

Variable Costs
Costs that vary with output.

Total Cost
The sum of fixed and variable costs.

Short Run
A period of time in which some inputs are fixed.

Long Run
A period of time in which all inputs can be varied (no inputs are fixed).

Average Fixed Cost
Total fixed cost divided by quantity of output: $AFC = TFC/Q$.

Average Variable Cost
Total variable cost divided by quantity of output: $AVC = TVC/Q$.

Average Total Cost (Unit Cost)
Total cost divided by quantity of output: $ATC = TC/Q$.

EXHIBIT 23–1
Periods of Production, Inputs, and Costs
In the short run, there are both fixed and variable inputs and fixed and variable costs. In the long run, all inputs are variable and, therefore, the only costs are variable costs.

PERIOD OF PRODUCTION	INPUTS USED	COSTS ASSOCIATED WITH INPUTS	DEFINITION OF COSTS
Short run	Fixed	Fixed Costs	Costs that do not change as output changes. If there are 2 fixed inputs, *A* and *B*, then fixed costs equal $P_AQ_A + P_BQ_B$ where P_A = price of input A, P_B = price of input B, Q_A = quantity of input A, Q_B = quantity of input B.
	Variable	Variable costs	Costs that change as output changes. If there are three variable inputs, *X, Y,* and *Z,* then variable costs equal $P_XQ_X + P_YQ_Y + P_ZQ_Z$ where P_X = price of input X, Q_X = quantity of input X, and so on.
Long run	Variable	Variable Costs	Costs that change as output changes.

EXHIBIT 23–2
Total, Average, and Marginal Costs

TFC equals $100 (column 2) and *TVC* is as noted in column 4. From the data, we calculate *AFC, AVC, TC, ATC,* and *MC. TFC, AFC, TVC, AVC, TC, ATC,* and *MC* are shown in diagrams at the bottom of the corresponding columns. (Note: Scale is not the same for all diagrams.)

(1) QUANTITY OF OUTPUT, *Q* (units)	(2) TOTAL FIXED COST (*TFC*)	(3) AVERAGE FIXED COST (*AFC*) $AFC = TFC/Q$ = (2)/(1)	(4) TOTAL VARIABLE COST (*TVC*)	(5) AVERAGE VARIABLE COST (*AVC*) $AVC = TVC/Q$ = (4)/(1)
0	$100	—	$ 0	—
1	100	$100.00	50	$50.00
2	100	50.00	80	40.00
3	100	33.33	100	33.33
4	100	25.00	110	27.50
5	100	20.00	130	26.00
6	100	16.67	160	26.67
7	100	14.28	200	28.57
8	100	12.50	250	31.25
9	100	11.11	310	34.44
10	100	10.00	380	38.00

dividing each *TFC* dollar amount by the quantity of output. For example, if *TFC* is $100 and the quantity of output is 2 units, then *AFC* is $50. In short $AFC = TFC/Q$, $AVC = TVC/Q$, and $ATC = TC/Q$. In column 3, you will find the *AFC* figures; in column 5, the *AVC* figures; and in column 7, the *ATC* figures.

Next, in column 8, we computed **marginal cost** (*MC*). Marginal cost, an extremely important cost concept in economics, is *the change in total cost that results from a change in output.* Alternatively, we could say that marginal cost is the change in *total variable cost* that results from a change in output. Since $TC = TFC + TVC$, and *TFC* does not change as output changes, it follows that any change in *TVC* will equal the change in *TC*.

To illustrate, consider both the change in *TVC* and in *TC* in Exhibit 23–2 when the firm moves from producing one unit to two units. The change in *TVC* is $30 (from $50 to $80), and the change in *TC* is also $30 (from $150 to $180). Calculating marginal cost, we get $30—whether we use the formula $MC = \Delta TVC/\Delta Q$ or $MC = \Delta TC/\Delta Q$.

Each of the cost concepts we have calculated is diagrammed under the appropriate column.

Marginal Cost
The change in total cost or total variable cost that results from a change in output: $MC = \Delta TC/\Delta Q = \Delta TVC/\Delta Q$.

EXHIBIT 23–2
continued

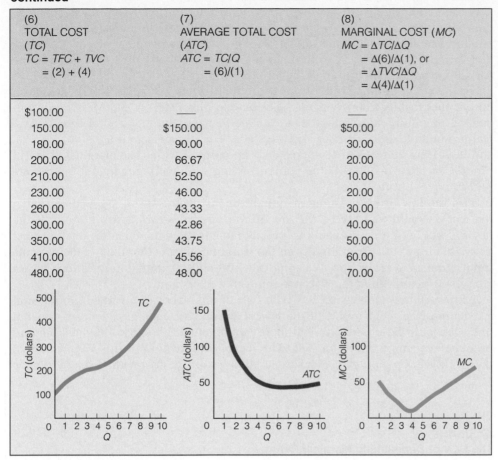

(6) TOTAL COST (TC) $TC = TFC + TVC$ $= (2) + (4)$	(7) AVERAGE TOTAL COST (ATC) $ATC = TC/Q$ $= (6)/(1)$	(8) MARGINAL COST (MC) $MC = \Delta TC/\Delta Q$ $= \Delta(6)/\Delta(1)$, or $= \Delta TVC/\Delta Q$ $= \Delta(4)/\Delta(1)$
$100.00	—	—
150.00	$150.00	$50.00
180.00	90.00	30.00
200.00	66.67	20.00
210.00	52.50	10.00
230.00	46.00	20.00
260.00	43.33	30.00
300.00	42.86	40.00
350.00	43.75	50.00
410.00	45.56	60.00
480.00	48.00	70.00

The Law of Diminishing Marginal Returns

A quick look at the marginal cost curve in Exhibit 23–2 shows that it has a downward-sloping and an upward-sloping portion. The reason the marginal cost curve looks the way it does is due to the (short-run) **law of diminishing marginal returns.**

In the nineteenth century, the English economist David Ricardo noted that agricultural land was essentially fixed in supply. He believed that as more and more variable inputs, such as labor and capital, were added to a fixed input, such as land, the variable inputs would yield smaller and smaller additions to output. Ricardo's theory came to be known as the law of diminishing marginal returns.

Specifically, the law states that *as ever larger amounts of a variable input are combined with fixed inputs, eventually the marginal physical product of the variable input will decline.*

Consider the production of a good that requires two inputs. One input is labor, the other is capital. The capital input is fixed; the labor input is variable. (Note that we must be dealing in the *short run,* because the short run is the period of time in which some inputs are fixed.) We add more and more units of the variable

Law of Diminishing Marginal Returns
As ever-larger amounts of a variable input are combined with fixed inputs, eventually the marginal physical product of the variable input will decline.

input, labor, to the fixed input, capital. As we do this, output increases. This is illustrated in columns 1–3 in Exhibit 23–3.

We are interested next in *how much additional output is produced for each additional unit of variable input employed;* that is, we are interested in the **marginal physical product** of the variable input, labor. The marginal physical product of a variable input is equal to the change in output that results from changing the variable input by one unit, holding all other inputs fixed.

For example, the marginal physical product of labor is equal to the change in output that results from changing labor by one unit ($MPP = \Delta Q/\Delta L$). This is calculated in column 4 of Exhibit 23–3. Notice that in column 4, the marginal physical product of labor first rises and then falls. The numbers go from 18 to 19 to 20, and then from 20 to 19 to 18 and so on. The point at which the marginal physical product of labor declines is the point at which diminishing marginal returns are said to have "set in."

Does the law of diminishing marginal returns make sense? Ask yourself what the world would look like *if the law of diminishing returns did not hold.* If the law *did not* hold, then it would be possible to continue to add additional units of a variable input to a fixed input, and the marginal physical product of the variable input would never decline. We could increase output indefinitely as long as we continued to add units of a variable input to a fixed input.

A firm produces television sets with two inputs, labor (the variable input) and a machine (the fixed input). If the law of diminishing marginal returns did not hold, it would be possible to add more laborers continually to the machine and produce ever more television sets. The logical implication of this would be that the world's supply of television sets could be produced by one firm operating one

Marginal Physical Product
The change in output that results from changing the variable input by one unit, holding all other inputs fixed.

EXHIBIT 23–3
The Law of Diminishing Marginal Returns

In the short run, as additional units of a variable input are added to a fixed input, the marginal physical product of the variable input increases at first. Eventually the marginal physical product of the variable input decreases. The point at which marginal physical product decreases is the point at which diminishing marginal returns have set in.

(1) VARIABLE INPUT, LABOR (Workers)	(2) FIXED INPUT, CAPITAL (units)	(3) QUANTITY OF OUTPUT, Q (units)	(4) MARGINAL PHYSICAL PRODUCT OF VARIABLE INPUT (units) $\Delta(3)/\Delta(1)$
0	1	0	
			18
1	1	18	
			19
2	1	37	
			20
3	1	57	
			19
4	1	76	
			18
5	1	94	
			17
6	1	111	
			16
7	1	127	
			10
8	1	137	
			–4
9	1	133	
			–8
10	1	125	

machine in one location. In agriculture, it would be possible to grow the world's supply of corn in a flowerpot.

We do not see the world's supply of television sets being produced by one firm using one machine in one location. Nor do we see the world's corn supply being grown in a flowerpot. Why? The law of diminishing marginal returns says that as more units of the variable input are hired, *each one has fewer units of the fixed input to work with;* consequently, output eventually rises at a *decreasing rate.*

Average Productivity

Suppose that one worker can produce 10 units of output a day, and two workers can produce 18 units of output a day. Marginal physical product is 8 units. *Average physical product,* which is output divided by the number of laborers ($AP = Q/L$), is equal to 9 units.

Usually, in the newspaper and in government documents, when the term *labor productivity* is used, it refers to the average (physical) productivity of labor on an hourly basis. By computing the average productivity of labor for different countries, and by noting the annual percentage changes, we can get some idea of how countries compare.

Government statisticians have chosen 1977 as a benchmark year (a year against which we measure other years). They have also set a productivity index, which is a measure of productivity, for 1977 equal to 100. Then, by computing a productivity index for other years and noting whether each index is above, below, or equal to 100, they know whether productivity is rising, falling, or remaining constant, respectively. Finally, by computing the percentage change in productivity indices from one year to the next, they know the rate at which productivity is changing.

Suppose the productivity index for the United States is 120 in year 1 and 125 in year 2. Since the productivity index is higher in year 2 than in year 1, we know that labor productivity increased over the year; that is, output produced increased per hour of labor expended.

Next, if we compute the percentage increase, we see it is 4.17 percent. This percentage is obtained by dividing the absolute change in the productivity index (which is 5) by the productivity index in year 1 (which is 120). Exhibit 23–4 compares productivity data for four countries over a specified time period.

The Law of Diminishing Marginal Returns and Marginal Cost

Marginal cost is a reflection of the marginal physical product of the variable input. We can see this arithmetically in Exhibit 23–5. Column 5 lists the total fixed cost associated with the fixed input. Column 6 lists the total variable cost associated with the variable input. We obtained the dollar figures in this column by first assuming that each worker costs $20 per day and then multiplying this cost times the number of workers. Adding total fixed cost and total variable cost, we get total cost in column 7. Finally, we calculate marginal cost in column 8.

Notice that marginal cost first falls and then rises. Furthermore, notice the important relationship between marginal cost and the marginal physical product of labor: *As the marginal physical product of labor increases, marginal cost decreases; and as the marginal physical product of labor decreases, marginal cost increases.* This relationship can be seen by looking at the marginal physical pro-

EXHIBIT 23–4
Productivity Changes in Four Nations*

We have noted the productivity index for four nations in four different years (top part of exhibit) and calculated the average annual percentage change in productivity for three time periods for four nations (bottom part of exhibit). Japan has witnessed the greatest growth rate in productivity in the time periods specified.

Year	United States	Japan	Canada	United Kingdom
1970	80.8	64.8	75.6	80.3
1980	101.4	122.7	98.2	101.9
1985	123.6	161.1	117.3	134.1
1988	136.2	190.0	124.3	154.9
Average Annual Percentage Change in Productivity				
1970–80	2.3	6.6	2.6	2.4
1980–85	4.0	5.6	3.6	5.6
1985–88	3.3	5.7	1.9	4.9

*1977 = 100.

SOURCE: Bureau of the Census, *Statistical Abstract of the United States 1990* (Washington, D.C.: U.S. Government Printing Office, 1990).

EXHIBIT 23–5
Marginal Physical Product and Marginal Cost

(a) The marginal physical product of labor curve. The curve is derived by plotting the data from columns 1 and 4 in the exhibit. (b) The marginal cost curve. The curve is derived by plotting the data from columns 3 and 8 in the exhibit. Notice that as the *MPP* curve rises, the *MC* curve falls; and as the *MPP* curve falls, the *MC* curve rises.

(1) VARIABLE INPUT, LABOR (Workers)	(2) FIXED INPUT, CAPITAL (units)	(3) QUANTITY OF OUTPUT, Q (units)	(4) MARGINAL PHYSICAL PRODUCT OF VARIABLE INPUT (units) Δ(3)/Δ(1)	(5) TOTAL FIXED COST (dollars)	(6) TOTAL VARIABLE COST (dollars)	(7) TOTAL COST (dollars) (5) + (6)	(8) MARGINAL COST (dollars) Δ(7)/Δ(3) or Δ(6)/Δ(3)
0	1	0		$40	$ 0	$40	
			18				$1.11
1	1	18		40	20	60	
			19				$1.05
2	1	37		40	40	80	
			20				$1.00
3	1	57		40	60	100	
			19				$1.05
4	1	76		40	80	120	
			18				$1.11
5	1	94		40	100	140	
			17				$1.17
6	1	111		40	120	160	
			16				$1.25
7	1	127		40	140	180	

(a) Marginal Physical Product (MPP) Curve

(b) Marginal Cost (MC) Curve

494

duct (*MPP*) curve under column 4 in conjunction with the marginal cost (*MC*) curve under column 8.

We see that as the marginal physical product curve rises, the marginal cost curve falls; and as the marginal physical product curve falls, the marginal cost curve rises. This is common sense: As marginal physical product rises, or to put it differently, as the productivity of the variable input rises, we would expect costs to decline. And as the productivity of the variable input declines, we would expect costs to rise.

In general, what the marginal cost curve looks like depends on what the marginal physical product curve looks like (which, we remind ourselves, must have a declining portion to it because of the law of diminishing marginal returns). If the marginal physical product curve first rises then falls, it follows that the marginal cost curve first falls then rises.

An easy way to see that *MPP* and *MC* move in opposite directions is to define marginal cost as equal to the additional cost of hiring an additional unit of the variable input divided by its marginal physical product. In Exhibit 23–5, using the variable input labor, this turns out to be $MC = W/MPP$, where MC = marginal cost, W = wage, and MPP = marginal physical product. The following table, which reproduces columns 4 and 8 from Exhibit 23–5 and notes the wage, shows what we mean.

MPP	Variable Cost (W)	MC = W/MPP
18 units	$20	$20/18 = $1.11
19	20	20/19 = 1.05
20	20	20/20 = 1.00
19	20	20/19 = 1.05
18	20	20/18 = 1.11
17	20	20/17 = 1.17
16	20	20/16 = 1.25

As you can see by comparing the marginal cost figures in the last column in the table with the marginal cost figures in column 8 in Exhibit 23–5, whether we define *MC* as equal to $\Delta TC/\Delta Q$ ($= \Delta TVC/\Delta Q$) or as equal to *W/MPP*, we get the same results. The latter way of defining marginal cost, however, explicitly shows that as *MPP* rises, *MC* falls, and as *MPP* falls, *MC* rises.

$$\downarrow MC = \frac{W}{MPP\uparrow}$$

$$\uparrow MC = \frac{W}{MPP\downarrow}$$

The Average-Marginal Rule

What do the average total and average variable cost curves look like in relation to the marginal cost curve? To explain, we need to discuss the **average-marginal rule**, which is best defined with an example.

Suppose there are 20 persons in a room and each person weighs 170 pounds. Your task is to calculate the average weight. This is accomplished by summing the individual weights and dividing by 20. Obviously, this average weight will be 170 pounds. Now let an additional person enter the room. We shall refer to this *additional* person as the *marginal* person and the *additional* weight he brings to the room as the *marginal* weight.

Average-Marginal Rule
When the marginal magnitude is above the average magnitude, the average magnitude rises; when the marginal magnitude is below the average magnitude, the average magnitude falls.

495

Let the weight of the marginal person be 275 pounds. If we were to calculate a new average weight based on 21 persons instead of 20, it would be 175 pounds. The new average weight is greater than the old average weight. It was pulled up by the weight of the last person. In short, *when the marginal magnitude is above the average magnitude, the average magnitude rises.* This is one part of the average-marginal rule.

Suppose, however, that the weight of the marginal person had been less than the average weight of 170 pounds, for example, 65 pounds. Then the new average would have been 165 pounds. It was pulled down by the weight of the last person. Thus, *when the marginal magnitude is below the average magnitude, the average magnitude falls.* This is the other part of the average-marginal rule.

Now suppose we apply the average-marginal rule to find out what the average total and average variable cost curves look like in relation to the marginal cost curve. The following analysis holds for both the average total cost curve and the average variable cost curve, although we speak only in terms of the latter.

We reason that if marginal cost is below (less than) average variable cost, average variable cost is falling; and if marginal cost is above (greater than) average variable cost, average variable cost is rising. This reasoning implies that the relationship between the average variable cost curve and the marginal cost curve must look like that in Exhibit 23–6a. In Region 1 of (a), marginal cost is below average variable cost and, consistent with the average-marginal rule, average variable cost is falling. In Region 2 of (a), marginal cost is above average variable cost, and average variable cost is rising. In sum, the relationship between the average variable cost curve and the marginal cost curve in Exhibit 23–6a is consistent with the average-marginal rule.

EXHIBIT 23–6
Average and Marginal Cost Curves

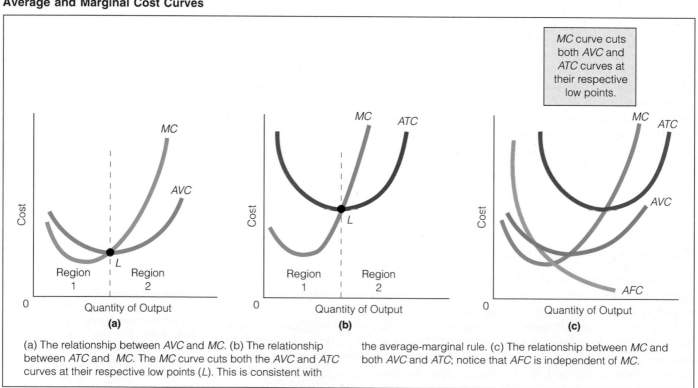

(a) The relationship between *AVC* and *MC*. (b) The relationship between *ATC* and *MC*. The *MC* curve cuts both the *AVC* and *ATC* curves at their respective low points (*L*). This is consistent with the average-marginal rule. (c) The relationship between *MC* and both *AVC* and *ATC*; notice that *AFC* is independent of *MC*.

In addition, since average variable cost is being pulled down when marginal cost is below it and pulled up when marginal cost is above it, it follows that the marginal cost curve *must* intersect the average variable cost curve at the latter's lowest point. This lowest point is labeled "*L*" in Exhibit 23–6a.

In Exhibit 23–6c, there are three average cost curves and a marginal cost curve. We now know that (1) the marginal cost curve has the shape it has because of the marginal physical product curve and the law of diminishing marginal returns; and (2) when the marginal cost curve is below the average variable and average total cost curves, the two curves are falling; when the marginal cost curve is above the average variable and average total cost curves, the two curves are rising.

But what about the average fixed cost curve? Is there any relationship between it and the marginal cost curve? The answer is no. We indirectly see why by recalling that average fixed cost is simply total fixed cost (which is constant over output) divided by output ($AFC = TFC/Q$). As output (Q) increases and total fixed cost (TFC) remains constant, it follows that average fixed cost (TFC/Q) must decrease continuously (see Exhibit 23–6c).

PRODUCTION AND COSTS IN THE LONG RUN

In this section, we discuss production and long-run costs. As we noted previously, in the long run there are no fixed inputs and no fixed costs. Consequently, the firm has greater flexibility in the long run than in the short run.

Long-Run Average Total Cost Curve

In the long run, variable costs *are* total costs. The reason is simple: In the short run, there are fixed costs and variable costs; therefore, total cost is the sum of the two. But in the long run, there are no fixed costs, so variable costs are total costs.

Here we focus on (1) what the long-run average total cost (*LRATC*) curve is and (2) what it looks like.

Consider the manager of a firm that produces bedroom furniture. When all inputs are variable, the manager must decide what situation he wants to be in in the (upcoming) short-run period. For example, when it comes to plant size, he must decide whether the plant will be small, medium-sized, or large. Once this decision is made, he is locked in to a specific plant size; he is locked in for the short run.

Suppose the manager must choose from among three different plant sizes. Associated with each size is a short-run average total cost (*SRATC*) curve. (Since here we discuss both short-run and long-run average total cost curves, we distinguish between the two with prefixes: *SR* for short run and *LR* for long run. In the previous section, it was not necessary to add *SR*, since short-run costs were the only costs we were discussing.) The three short-run average total cost curves, representing the different plant sizes, are illustrated in Exhibit 23–7a.

Suppose the manager of the firm wants to produce output level Q_1. Which plant size will he choose? Obviously, he will choose the plant size represented by $SRATC_1$, since this gives him a lower unit cost of producing Q_1 than the plant size represented by $SRATC_2$. The latter plant size comes with a higher unit cost of producing Q_1 ($6 as opposed to $5).

Suppose, though, the manager chooses to produce Q_2. Which plant size will he choose now? He will choose the plant size represented by $SRATC_3$, because the

EXHIBIT 23–7
Long-Run Average Total Cost Curve (*LRATC*)

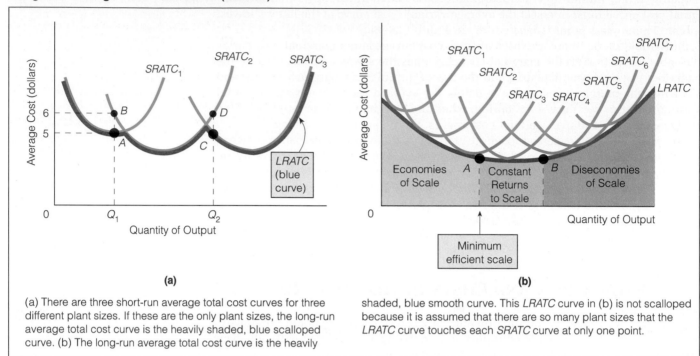

(a)

(b)

(a) There are three short-run average total cost curves for three different plant sizes. If these are the only plant sizes, the long-run average total cost curve is the heavily shaded, blue scalloped curve. (b) The long-run average total cost curve is the heavily

shaded, blue smooth curve. This *LRATC* curve in (b) is not scalloped because it is assumed that there are so many plant sizes that the *LRATC* curve touches each *SRATC* curve at only one point.

**Long-Run Average Total Cost
(*LRATC*) Curve**
A curve that shows the lowest (unit) cost at which the firm can produce any given level of output.

unit cost of producing Q_2 is lower with the plant size represented by $SRATC_3$ than it is with that represented by $SRATC_2$.

If we were to ask the same question for every (possible) output level, we would derive the **long-run average total cost (*LRATC*) curve.** The *LRATC* curve shows the lowest unit cost at which the firm can produce any given level of output. In Exhibit 23–7a, it is those portions of the three *SRATC* curves that are tangential to the blue curve. The *LRATC* curve is the scalloped blue curve.

In Exhibit 23–7b, we have a host of *SRATC* curves and a *LRATC* curve. In this case, you will notice that the *LRATC* curve is not scalloped, as in (a), but instead is smooth. The reason is that in (b) we assume there are many plant sizes in addition to the three represented in (a). In other words, although they have not been drawn, in (b) there exist short-run average total cost curves representing different plant sizes between $SRATC_1$ and $SRATC_2$ and between $SRATC_2$ and $SRATC_3$ and so on. In this case, the *LRATC* would be smooth and would only touch each *SRATC* curve at one point.

Economies of Scale, Diseconomies of Scale, and Constant Returns to Scale

Economies of Scale
Exist when inputs are increased by some percentage and output increases by a greater percentage, causing unit costs to fall.

Suppose two inputs, labor and capital, are used together to produce a particular good. If inputs are increased by some percentage (say, 100 percent), and output increases by a greater percentage (more than 100 percent), unit costs falls, and **economies of scale** are said to exist.

If inputs are increased by some percentage and output increases by an equal percentage, unit costs remain constant, and **constant returns to scale** are said to exist.

If inputs are increased by some percentage and output increases by a smaller percentage, unit costs rise, and **diseconomies of scale** are said to exist.

Here is an arithmetical example that illustrates economies of scale. Good X is made with two inputs, Y and Z, and it takes $20Y$ and $10Z$ to produce 5 units of X. The cost of each unit of input Y and Z is $1. Thus, a total cost of $30 is required to produce 5 units of X; the unit cost (average total cost) of good X is $6 ($ATC = TC/Q$).

Now consider a doubling of inputs Y and Z to $40Y$ and $20Z$, and a more than doubling in output, say, to 15 units. This means a total cost of $60 is required to produce 15 units of X, and the unit cost (average total cost) of good X is $4.

If, in the production of a good, economies of scale give way to constant returns to scale or diseconomies of scale, as in Exhibit 23–7b, the point at which this occurs is referred to as the **minimum efficient scale.** The minimum efficient scale is the lowest output level at which average total costs are minimized. Point A represents the minimum efficient scale in Exhibit 23–7b.

Constant Returns to Scale
Exist when inputs are increased by some percentage and output increases by an equal percentage, causing unit costs to remain constant.

Diseconomies of Scale
Exist when inputs are increased by some percentage and output increases by a smaller percentage, causing unit costs to rise.

Minimum Efficient Scale
The lowest output level at which average total costs are minimized.

Question:

Is there any special significance to the minimum efficient scale of output?

Answer:

Yes, there is. If we look at the long-run average total cost curve in Exhibit 23–7b, we see that between points A and B there are constant returns to scale; the average total cost is the same over the various output levels between the two points. This means that larger firms (firms producing greater output levels) within this range do not have a cost advantage over smaller firms that operate at the minimum efficient scale.

Question:

Are economies of scale, diseconomies of scale, and constant returns to scale relevant to the short run, the long run, or both?

Answer:

They are only relevant to the long run. Implicit in the definition of the terms, and explicit in the arithmetical example of economies of scale, all inputs necessary to the production of a good are changeable. Since no input is fixed, economies of scale, diseconomies of scale, and constant returns to scale must be relevant only to the long run.

In addition, the three conditions can be easily seen in the $LRATC$ curve. If economies of scale are present, the $LRATC$ curve is falling; if constant returns to scale are present, the curve is flat, and if diseconomies of scale are present, the curve is rising (see Exhibit 23–7b).

We must not confuse *diminishing (marginal) returns* with *diseconomies of scale.* Diminishing returns are the result of using, say, a given plant size more intensively. Diseconomies of scale result from changes in the size of the plant.

Why Economies of Scale

Up to a certain point, long-run unit costs of production fall as a firm grows. There are two main reasons for this: (1) In growing firms there are greater opportunities for employees to specialize. Individual workers can become highly proficient at more narrowly defined tasks, often producing more output at lower unit costs. (2) Growing firms (especially large, growing firms) can take advantage of highly efficient mass production techniques and equipment that ordinarily require large setup costs and thus are only economical if they can be spread over a large number of units. For example, assembly line techniques are usually "cheap" when millions of units of a good are produced, and are "expensive" when only a few thousand units are produced.

Why Diseconomies of Scale?

Diseconomies of scale usually arise at the point at which a firm's size produces coordination, communication, and monitoring problems. In very large firms, managers often find it difficult to coordinate work activities, communicate their directives to the right persons in satisfactory time, and monitor personnel effectively. The business operation simply gets "too big." There is, of course, a monetary incentive not to pass the point of operation where diseconomies of scale exist. Firms will usually find ways to avoid diseconomies of scale. They will reorganize, divide operations, hire new managers, and so on.

Minimum Efficient Scale and Number of Firms in an Industry

Some industries are composed of a smaller number of firms than other industries. Or, we can say there is a different degree of concentration in different industries.

Exhibit 23–8 lists the *minimum efficient scale (MES)* for six industries as a percentage of U.S. consumption or total sales for that industry. Notice that firms in some industries continue to experience economies of scale up to output levels that are a higher percentage of industry sales than firms in other industries. For example, cigarette firms reach the minimum efficient scale of plant, and thus exhaust economies of scale, at an output level of 6.6 percent of total industry sales. On the other hand, petroleum refining firms experience economies of scale only up to an output level of 1.9 percent of total industry sales. Consequently, we would expect to find fewer firms in the cigarette industry than in the petroleum refining industry. By dividing the *MES* as a percentage of U.S. consumption into 100, we can estimate the number of efficient firms it takes to satisfy U.S. consumption for a particular product. For cigarettes, it takes 15 firms (100/6.6 = 15). For petroleum refining, it takes 52 firms.

EXHIBIT 23–8
Minimum Efficient Scale (*MES*) for Six Industries

INDUSTRY	*MES* AS A PERCENTAGE OF U.S. CONSUMPTION
Refrigerators	14.1%
Cigarettes	6.6
Beer brewing	3.4
Petroleum refining	1.9
Paints	1.4
Shoes	0.2

SOURCE: F. M. Scherer, Alan Bechenstein, Erich Kaufer, and R. D. Murphy, *The Economics of Multiplant Operation* (Cambridge, Mass.: Harvard University Press, 1975), p. 80.

SHIFTS IN COST CURVES

In discussing the shape of short-run and long-run cost curves, we assumed that certain factors remained constant. We discuss a few of these factors here and illustrate how changes in them can shift cost curves.

Taxes

Consider a tax on each unit of a good produced. Suppose Company X has to pay $3 for each unit of X it produces. What effects will this have on the firm's cost curves? First, will the tax affect the firm's fixed costs? No, it won't. The reason is that the tax is paid only when output is produced, and fixed costs are present even if output is zero. (Note that if the tax had been a lump-sum tax, requiring the company to pay a lump sum no matter how many units of goods it produced, this would have affected fixed costs.) We conclude that the tax does not affect fixed costs and therefore cannot affect average fixed cost.

  Will the tax affect variable cost? Yes, it will. As a consequence of the tax, the firm has to pay out more for each unit of the good it produces. Variable costs rise along with total cost. This means that average variable cost and average total cost rise, and the representative cost curves shift upward. Finally, since marginal cost is the change in total cost (or variable cost) divided by the change in output, marginal cost rises and the marginal cost curve shifts upward.

Input Prices

A rise or fall in input prices brings about a corresponding change in the firm's average total, variable, and marginal cost curves. For example, if the price of steel rises, the variable costs of building skyscrapers rise, and so must average variable cost, average total cost, and marginal cost. The cost curves shift upward. If the price of steel falls, we get the opposite effects.

Technology

Technological changes often bring either (1) the capability of using fewer inputs to produce a good (for example, the introduction of the personal computer reduced the hours necessary to type and edit a manuscript) or (2) lower input prices (technological improvements in the area of transistors have led to price reductions in the transistor components of calculators). In either case, technological changes of this variety lower variable costs, and consequently, lower average variable cost, average total cost, and marginal cost.

CHAPTER SUMMARY

Explicit and Implicit Cost

■ An explicit cost is incurred when an actual (monetary) payment is made. An implicit cost represents the value of resources used in production for which no actual (monetary) payment is made.

Economic and Accounting Profit

■ Economic profit is the difference between total revenue and total opportunity cost, including both its explicit and implicit components. Accounting profit is the difference between total revenue and explicit costs. Economic profit is usually lower (never higher) than accounting profit. Economic profit (not accounting profit) motivates economic behavior.

Sunk Cost

■ Sunk cost is a cost incurred in the past that cannot be changed by current decisions and therefore cannot be recovered. A person or firm that wants to minimize losses will hold sunk costs to be irrelevant to present decisions. For example, Janet buys good X for $10 on Monday with the idea of reselling it at a higher price in the near future. A week passes and the price of good X falls to $6. Some people argue that Janet should not sell good X because she will incur a loss. According to their argument, Janet should look over her shoulder, note the higher price she paid for the good, and let this fact influence her present decision. But bygones are bygones. Janet needs to ask herself: Do I expect the price of good X to go up or down? If the answer is down, then it is better to sell today at $6 than to sell tomorrow at an even lower price. If the answer is up, then Janet may want to sell later.

Production and Costs in the Short Run

■ The short run is a period in which some inputs are fixed. The long run is a period in which all inputs can be varied. The costs associated with fixed and variable inputs are referred to as fixed costs and variable costs, respectively.
■ Marginal cost is the change in total cost (or total variable cost) that results from a change in output.
■ The law of diminishing marginal returns states that as ever larger amounts of a variable input are combined with fixed inputs, eventually the marginal physical product of the variable input will decline. As this happens, marginal cost rises.
■ The average-marginal rule states that if the marginal magnitude is above (below) the average magnitude, the average magnitude rises (falls).
■ The marginal cost curve intersects the average variable cost curve at its lowest point. The marginal cost curve intersects the average total cost curve at its lowest point. There is no relationship between marginal cost and average fixed cost.

Production and Costs in the Long Run

■ In the long run, there are no fixed costs, so variable costs equal total costs.
■ The long-run average total cost curve is the envelope of the short-run average total cost curves. It shows the lowest unit cost at which the firm can produce any given level of output.
■ If inputs are increased by some percentage and output increases by a greater percentage, unit costs fall, and economies of scale exist. If inputs are increased by some percentage and output increases by an equal percentage, unit costs remain constant, and constant returns to scale exist. If inputs are increased by some percentage and output increases by a smaller percentage, units cost rise, and diseconomies of scale exist.

■ The minimum efficient scale is the lowest output level at which average total costs are minimized.

Shifts in Cost Curves

■ A firm's cost curves will change owing to a change in taxes, input prices, or technology.

Key Terms and Concepts

Explicit Cost	Variable Costs	Law of Diminishing Marginal Returns
Implicit Cost	Total Cost	
Economic Profit	Short Run	Marginal Physical Product
Accounting Profit	Long Run	Average-Marginal Rule
Normal Profit	Average Fixed Cost	Long-Run Average Total Cost Curve
Sunk Cost	Average Variable Cost	
Fixed Inputs	Average Total Cost (Unit Cost)	Economies of Scale
Variable Inputs		Constant Returns to Scale
Fixed Costs	Marginal Cost	Diseconomies of Scale
		Minimum Efficient Scale

QUESTIONS AND PROBLEMS

1. Illustrate the average-marginal rule in a noncost setting.

2. "People who earn big salaries are less likely to go into business for themselves than people who earn small salaries, because their implicit costs are higher." Do you agree or disagree? Explain your answer.

3. A quick glance at Exhibit 23–6c shows that the average variable cost curve and the average total cost curve get closer to each other as output increases. What explains this?

4. When would total costs equal fixed costs?

5. Is studying for an economics exam subject to the law of diminishing marginal returns? If so, what is the fixed input? What is the variable input?

6. Some individuals decry the decline of the small family farm and its replacement with the huge corporate megafarm. Discuss the possibility that this is a consequence of economies of scale.

7. We know that there is a link between productivity and costs. For example, recall the link between the marginal physical product of the variable input and marginal cost. With this in mind, what link might there be between productivity and prices?

8. Some people's everyday behavior suggests that they do not hold sunk costs irrelevant to present decisions. Give some examples.

9. Explain why a firm might want to produce its good even after diminishing marginal returns have set in and marginal cost is on the rise.

10. Fill in the blanks.

(1) Quantity of Output, Q (units)	(2) Total Fixed Cost (TFC)	(3) Average Fixed Cost (AFC) AFC = TFC/Q = (2)/(1)	(4) Total Variable Cost (TVC)	(5) Average Variable Cost (AVC) AVC = TVC/Q = (4)/(1)	(6) Total Cost (TC) TC = TFC + TVC = (2) + (4)	(7) Average Total Cost (ATC) ATC = TC/Q = (6)/(1)	(8) Marginal Cost (MC) MC = ΔTC/ΔQ = Δ(6)/Δ(1) or = ΔTVC/ΔQ = Δ(4)/Δ(1)
0	$200	_____	0		_____		
1	200	_____	30	_____	_____	_____	_____
2	200	_____	50	_____	_____	_____	_____
3	200	_____	60	_____	_____	_____	_____
4	200	_____	65	_____	_____	_____	_____
5	200	_____	75	_____	_____	_____	_____
6	200	_____	95	_____	_____	_____	_____
7	200	_____	125	_____	_____	_____	_____
8	200	_____	165	_____	_____	_____	_____
9	200	_____	215	_____	_____	_____	_____
10	200	_____	275	_____	_____	_____	_____

MICROECONOMIC THEORIES (PRODUCT MARKETS)

CHAPTER

24

PERFECT COMPETITION

WHAT THIS CHAPTER IS ABOUT

The farmer in Iowa and the Ford Motor Company find themselves in different *market structures.* The term **market structure** refers to the particular environment of a firm, the characteristics of which influence the firm's pricing and output decisions. In this and the following two chapters, we discuss four theories of market structures: perfect competition (Chapter 24), monopoly (Chapter 25), and monopolistic competition and oligopoly (Chapter 26).

507

THE THEORY OF PERFECT COMPETITION

■

A perfectly competitive firm is a price taker.

■

The theory of **perfect competition** is built on four assumptions.

1. There are many sellers and many buyers, none of which is large in relation to total sales or purchases. This assumption speaks to both demand (number of buyers) and supply (number of sellers). Since there are many buyers and sellers, it is reasonably assumed that each buyer and each seller acts independently of other buyers and sellers, respectively, and each is *so small a part of the market that he or she has no influence on price.*

2. Each firm produces and sells a homogeneous product. This means each firm sells a product that is indistinguishable from all other firms' products in a given industry (for example, the buyer of wheat cannot distinguish between Farmer Stone's and Farmer Gray's wheat). As a consequence, buyers are indifferent to whom they buy the product from.

3. Buyers and sellers have all relevant information about prices, product quality, sources of supply, and so forth. Buyers and sellers know who is selling what, at what prices, at what quality, and on what terms. In short, they know everything that relates to buying, producing, and selling the product.

4. Firms have easy entry and exit. New firms can enter the market easily, and existing firms can exit the market easily. There are no barriers to entry or exit.

Examples of perfect competition include some agricultural markets and a small subset of the retail trade. The stock market, where there are hundreds of thousands of buyers and sellers of stock, is also sometimes cited as an example of perfect competition.

Market Structure
The particular environment a firm finds itself in, the characteristics of which influence the firm's pricing and output decisions.

Perfect competition
A theory of market structure based on four assumptions: there are many sellers and buyers, sellers sell a homogeneous good, buyers and sellers have all relevant information, and there is easy entry into and exit from the market.

A Perfectly Competitive Firm Is a Price Taker

A perfectly competitive firm is a **price taker.** A price taker is a seller that does not have the ability to control the price of the product it sells; it *takes* the price determined in the market. For example, if Farmer Stone is a price taker, it follows that he can increase or decrease his output without significantly affecting the price of the product he sells.

Why is a perfectly competitive firm a price taker? A firm is restrained from being anything but a price taker if it finds itself one among many firms where its supply is small relative to the total market supply (assumption 1 in the theory of perfect competition), and it sells a homogeneous product (assumption 2) in an environment where buyers and sellers have all relevant information (assumption 3).

Price Taker
A seller that does not have the ability to control the price of the product it sells; it takes the price determined in the market.

Question:

If the assumptions of the theory guarantee that the perfectly competitive firm is a price taker, then aren't economists choosing the assumptions necessary to give them what they want?

Answer:

No, they aren't. Economists do not start out wanting the perfectly competitive firm to be a price taker, and then choose the assumptions that will make this so. Instead, economists start out with certain assumptions, and then logically conclude that the firm for which these assumptions hold, or that behaves *as if* these assumptions hold, is a price taker; that is, it has no control over price. Afterward, economists test the theory by observing whether it accurately predicts and explains the real-world behavior of some firms.

The Demand Curve for a Perfectly Competitive Firm Is Horizontal

In the perfectly competitive setting, there are many sellers and many buyers. Together, all buyers make up the market demand curve; together, all sellers make up the market supply curve. An equilibrium price is established at the intersection of the market demand and market supply curves (Exhibit 24–1a). Once the equilibrium price has been established, we see that a single perfectly competitive firm faces a horizontal (flat, perfectly elastic) demand curve at the equilibrium price. In short, the firm "takes" the equilibrium price as given—hence, the firm is a price taker—and sells all quantities of output at this price.[1] (As an aside, we learned in Chapter 21 that the more substitutes for a good, the higher the price elasticity of demand. In the perfectly competitive market setting, there are many substitutes for the firm's product—so many, in fact, that the firm's demand curve is perfectly elastic.)

If the perfectly competitive firm were to charge a price higher than the market-established equilibrium price, it wouldn't sell any of its product. This is because the firm sells a homogeneous product, its supply is small relative to the total market supply, and all buyers are informed about where they can obtain the product at the lower price.

Also, if the firm is attempting to maximize profits, it would not offer to sell its good at a lower price than the equilibrium price. Why should it? It can sell all it wants at the market-established equilibrium price. Therefore, this is the only relevant price for the perfectly competitive firm.

Question:

In an earlier chapter, it was noted that demand curves are downward sloping. Now it appears that the demand curve for a perfectly competitive firm is not downward sloping, but horizontal. How can this be?

Answer:

The *market demand curve* in Exhibit 24–1a is downward sloping, positing an inverse relationship between price and quantity demanded, *ceteris paribus*. The demand curve faced by a *single* perfectly competitive firm does not contradict this relationship; it simply represents the pricing situation in which the single perfectly competitive firm finds itself. It says that a single perfectly competitive firm's supply is such a small percentage of the total market supply that the firm cannot perceptibly influence price by changing its quantity of output. To put it differently, the firm's supply is so small compared with the total market supply that the inverse relationship between price and quantity demanded, although present, cannot be observed on the firm's level, although it is observable on the market level.

[1]The horizontal demand curve does not mean that the firm can sell an *infinite* amount at the equilibrium price; rather, it means that price will be virtually unaffected by the variations in output that the firm may find it practicable to make.

EXHIBIT 24–1
Market Demand Curve and Firm Demand Curve in Perfect Competition

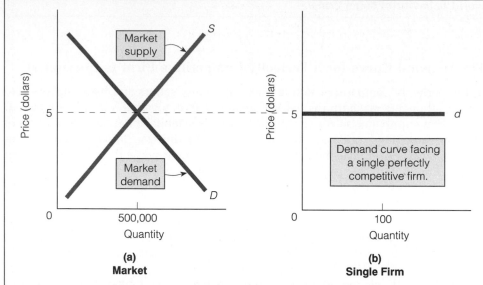

(a)
Market

(b)
Single Firm

(a) The market, composed of all buyers and sellers, establishes the equilibrium price. (b) A single perfectly competitive firm then faces the horizontal (flat, perfectly elastic) demand curve. We conclude that the firm is a price taker; it "takes" the eqilibrium price established by the market and sells any and all quantities of output at this price. (The large *D* represents the market demand curve; the small *d* represents the single firm's demand curve.)

The Marginal Revenue Curve of the Perfectly Competitive Firm Is the Same as Its Demand Curve

Consider a simple numerical example. If the equilibrium price is $5, as in Exhibit 24–1, and the perfectly competitive firm sells 100 units of its good, its total revenue is $500 ($5 × 100 = $500). Now suppose the firm sells an additional unit, bringing the total number of units sold up to 101. Its total revenue is now $505 ($5 × 101 = $505).

The firm's **marginal revenue**—the change in total revenue that results from selling one additional unit of output ($MR = \Delta TR/\Delta Q$)—is $5. Notice that marginal revenue ($5) at any output level is always equal to the equilibrium price ($5). We conclude that for a perfectly competitive firm, price is equal to marginal revenue ($P = MR$). It follows that if price is equal to marginal revenue, the marginal revenue curve for the perfectly competitive firm is the same as its demand curve.

A demand curve plots price against quantity, whereas a marginal revenue curve plots marginal revenue against quantity. If price equals marginal revenue, then the demand curve and marginal revenue curve are the same (Exhibit 24–2).

The Importance of "As If" in Economic Theories

The theory of perfect competition describes how firms act in a market structure where (1) there are many buyers and sellers, none of which is large in relation to total sales or purchases; (2) sellers sell a homogeneous product; (3) buyers and sellers have all relevant information; and (4) there is easy entry and exit exist. These assumptions are closely met in some real-world markets.

Marginal Revenue
The change in total revenue that results from selling one additional unit of output.

(1) PRICE	(2) QUANTITY	(3) TOTAL REVENUE = (1) x (2)	(4) MARGINAL REVENUE = $\Delta TR/\Delta Q$ = Δ(3)/Δ(2)
$5	1	$5	$5
5	2	10	5
5	3	15	5
5	4	20	5

Plotting columns 1 and 2 gives us the demand curve; plotting columns 2 and 4 gives us the marginal revenue curve.

(a)

(b)

(a) By computing marginal revenue, we find that it is equal to price. (b) By plotting columns 1 and 2, we obtain the firm's demand curve; by plotting columns 2 and 4, we obtain the firm's marginal revenue curve. The two curves are the same.

These assumptions are also *approximated* in some other markets. In such markets, the number of sellers may not be large enough so that every firm is a price taker, but still the amount of control the firm has over price may be negligible. The amount of control may be so negligible, in fact, that the firm acts *as if* it were a perfectly competitive firm.

Similarly, buyers may not have all relevant information concerning price and quality, but they may still have a great deal of information, and the information they do not have may not matter. The products that the firms in the industry sell may not be homogeneous, but the differences may be inconsequential. In short, a market that does not meet the assumptions of perfect competition may nonetheless approximate those assumptions to such a degree that it behaves *as if* it were a perfectly competitive market. If so, it follows that the theory of perfect competition can be used to predict the market's behavior.

PERFECT COMPETITION IN THE SHORT RUN

We have seen that the perfectly competitive firm is a price taker, that (for it) price is equal to marginal revenue, and therefore the perfectly competitive firm's demand curve is the same as its marginal revenue curve. We turn now to a discussion of how much output the firm will produce in the short run.

The Profit-Maximization Rule: *MR = MC*

Consider the situation in Exhibit 24–3. The perfectly competitive firm's demand curve and marginal revenue curve (one and the same) are drawn at the equilibrium price of $5. The firm's marginal cost curve is also shown. On the basis of these curves, what quantity of output will the firm produce?

The firm will continue to produce units of output as long as marginal revenue is greater than marginal cost; that is, as long as more is coming in than is going out on the marginal unit. It will not produce units of output for which marginal

EXHIBIT 24–3
The Quantity of Output the Perfectly Competitive Firm Will Produce

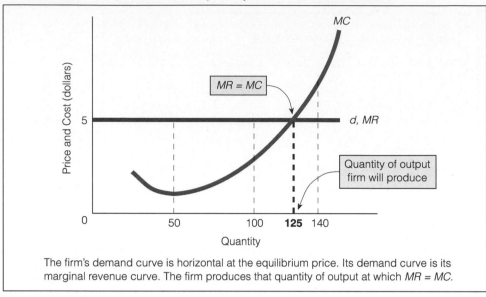

The firm's demand curve is horizontal at the equilibrium price. Its demand curve is its marginal revenue curve. The firm produces that quantity of output at which $MR = MC$.

Profit-maximization Rule
Profit is maximized by producing the quantity of output at which $MR = MC$.

revenue is less than marginal cost. We conclude that the firm will stop producing when marginal revenue and marginal cost are equal. The **profit-maximization rule** for the firm says, *Produce the quantity of output at which MR = MC.*[2] In Exhibit 24–3, this is at 125 units of output. For the perfectly competitive firm, the profit-maximization rule can be rewritten as $P = MC$ (since for the perfectly competitive firm $P = MR$). In perfect competition, $P = MR = MC$ when profit is maximized.

***

Question:

Why doesn't the firm in Exhibit 24–3 stop producing at 50 units of output? This is where the largest difference between marginal revenue and marginal cost occurs. Why does the firm continue to produce until marginal revenue equals marginal cost?

Answer:

Suppose the firm did stop producing with the 50th unit of output. Then it wouldn't have produced the 51st, which, as Exhibit 24–3 illustrates, comes with a greater marginal revenue than marginal cost. Nor would it have produced the 52nd unit, for which marginal revenue is also greater than marginal cost. In short, the firm would have not produced some units of output for which a marginal (additional) profit could have been made; thus, it would not have been maximizing profit. What matters is whether *MR* is greater than *MC, not how much greater MR is than MC.*

***

To Produce or Not to Produce: That Is the Question?

The following cases illustrate three applications of the profit-maximization (loss-minimization) rule by a perfectly competitive firm.

[2]The profit-maximization rule is the same as the loss-minimization rule, since it is impossible to maximize profits without minimizing losses. The profit-maximization rule also holds for all firms, whether they are perfectly competitive or not.

Case 1: Price Is above Average Total Cost. Exhibit 24–4a illustrates the perfectly competitive firm's demand and marginal revenue curves. If the firm follows the profit-maximization rule, and produces the quantity of output at which marginal revenue equals marginal cost, it will produce 100 units of output. This will be the profit-maximizing quantity of output. Notice that at this quantity of output, price is above average total cost. Using the information in the exhibit, we can make the following calculations:

Case 1	
Equilibrium price	= $15
Quantity of output produced	= 100 units
Total revenue ($P \times Q = \$15 \times 100$)	= $1,500
Total cost ($ATC \times Q = \$11 \times 100$)	= $1,100
Total Variable cost ($AVC \times Q = \$7 \times 100$)	= $700
Total Fixed Cost ($TC - TVC = \$1,100 - \$700$)	= $400
Profits ($TR - TC = \$1,500 - \$1,100$)	= $400

We conclude that if price is above average total cost for the perfectly competitive firm, the firm maximizes profits by producing the quantity of output at which $MR = MC$.

EXHIBIT 24–4
Profit Maximization and Loss Minimization for the Perfectly Competitive Firm: Three Cases

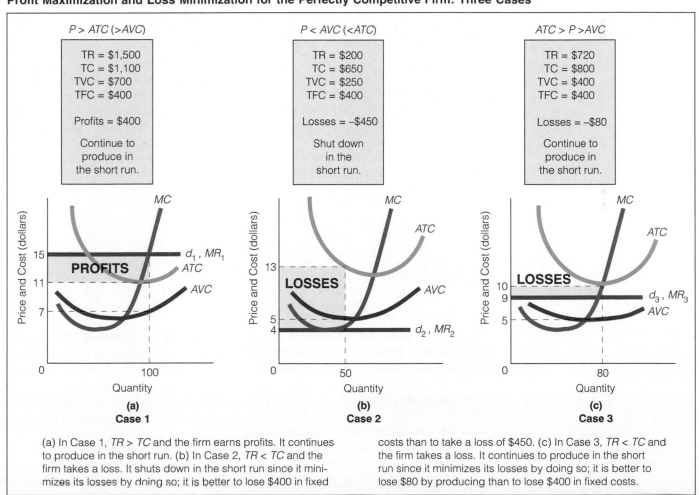

(a) In Case 1, $TR > TC$ and the firm earns profits. It continues to produce in the short run. (b) In Case 2, $TR < TC$ and the firm takes a loss. It shuts down in the short run since it minimizes its losses by doing so; it is better to lose $400 in fixed costs than to take a loss of $450. (c) In Case 3, $TR < TC$ and the firm takes a loss. It continues to produce in the short run since it minimizes its losses by doing so; it is better to lose $80 by producing than to lose $400 in fixed costs.

Case 2: Price Is below Average Variable Cost. Exhibit 24–4b illustrates the case in which price is below average variable cost. The equilibrium price at which the perfectly competitive firm sells its good is $4. At this price, total revenue is less than both total cost and total variable cost, as the following calculations indicate. To minimize its loss the firm should shut down.

Case 2		
Equilibrium price	=	$4
Quantity of output indicated by profit-maximization rule	=	50 units
Total revenue ($P \times Q = \$4 \times 50$)	=	$200
Total cost ($ATC \times Q = \$13 \times 50$)	=	$650
Total variable cost ($AVC \times Q = \$5 \times 50$)	=	$250
Total fixed cost ($TC - TVC = \$650 - \$250$)	=	$400
Losses ($TR - TC = \$200 - \$650$)	=	$-\$450$

As one can see from the computation, if the firm produces in the short run, it will take a loss of $450. If it shuts down, its loss will be less. It will lose its fixed costs, which amount to the difference between total cost and variable cost (since $TFC + TVC = TC$, then $TC - TVC = TFC$). This is $400 ($650 − $250). So, between the two options of producing in the short run or shutting down, the firm minimizes its losses by choosing to shut down; it will lose $400 by shutting down, whereas it will lose $450 by producing in the short run.

We conclude that if price is below average variable cost, the perfectly competitive firm minimizes losses by choosing to shut down; that is, by not producing.

Case 3: Price Is below Average Total Cost but above Average Variable Cost. Exhibit 24–4c illustrates the case in which price is below average total cost but above average variable cost. Here the equilibrium price at which the perfectly competitive firm sells its good is $9. If the firm follows the profit-maximization rule, it will produce 80 units of output. At this price and quantity of output, total revenue will be less than total cost (hence there will be a loss), but total revenue will be greater than total variable cost.

Case 3		
Equilibrium price	=	$9
Quantity of output produced	=	80 units
Total revenue ($P \times Q = \$9 \times 80$)	=	$720
Total cost ($ATC \times Q = \$10 \times 80$)	=	$800
Total variable cost ($AVC \times Q = \$5 \times 80$)	=	$400
Total fixed cost (TC $TVC - \$800 - \$400$)	=	$400
Losses ($TR - TC = \$720 - \$800$)	=	$-\$80$

If the firm decides to produce in the short run, it will take a loss of $80. Should it shut down instead? If it does, it will lose its fixed costs, which, in this case, will be $400 ($TC - TVC = \$800 - \$400 = \$400$). It is better to continue to produce in the short run than to shut down: Losses are minimized by producing.

We conclude that if price is below average total cost but above average variable cost, the perfectly competitive firm minimizes its losses by continuing to produce in the short run instead of shutting down.

We also conclude that a firm produces in the short run as long as price is *above* average variable cost (Cases 1 and 3). Or, a firm shuts down in the short run if price is *less than* average variable cost (Case 2).

We can summarize the same information in terms of total revenue and total variable costs. A firm produces in the short run as long as total revenue is greater than total variable costs (Cases 1 and 3). A firm shuts down in the short run if total revenue is less than total variable costs (Case 2).

The Perfectly Competitive Firm's Short-Run Supply Curve

Since the firm produces (supplies output) in the short run if price is above average variable cost, and it shuts down if price is below average variable cost (does not supply output), it follows that the **short-run supply curve** of the firm is that portion of its marginal cost curve that lies above the average variable cost curve. In other words, only a price above average variable cost will induce the firm to supply output. The short-run supply curve of the firm is illustrated in Exhibit 24–5.

Job Security and Fixed Costs in the Short Run

Consider two firms, X and Y, each with the same total costs but with different variable and fixed costs, as illustrated in Exhibit 24–6. For firm X, fixed costs are 33 percent of total costs; and for firm Y, fixed costs are 17 percent of total costs. This difference will affect the shut-down decision for the two firms. Firm Y will shut down if total revenue falls to the level of total variable cost ($500). But for firm X, total revenue has to fall to a lower level of total variable cost ($400) before it will shut down. In short, when total revenue is between $500 and $400, firm X will still operate, but firm Y will shut down. Note that this result holds for firms that have the same total cost.

We can conclude that the greater the fixed cost–total cost ratio (*TFC/TC*), the more likely the firm will operate in the short run; the smaller the fixed cost–total cost ratio, the less likely the firm will operate in the short run, *ceteris paribus*.

Now consider the input labor. Suppose that labor's objective is to attain as much job security as possible. Given this objective, which firm would employees prefer to work for? The answer is firm X. The reason is that total revenue can fall farther for firm X than for firm Y without it shutting down.

Employees who value job security have not ignored the fact that the firms with higher fixed cost–total cost ratios are less likely to shut down in the short run. For example, in the past two decades in particular, labor representatives have often argued for greater fringe benefits as an alternative to taking all gains in higher hourly wages. These fringe benefits often take the form of health, life, and accident insurance, contributions to pension funds, and the like. These fringe benefits are often negotiated so that the firm has to pay them for a period of time (six months to a year is common) after *it has shut down*. This means that part of the employees' payment and fringe benefit package is a fixed cost to the firm. Since this compensation is a fixed cost (as opposed to wages, which are a variable cost to the firm), it follows that fixed costs will be higher for a given level of total costs, and the firm's fixed cost–total cost ratio will also be higher. Consequently, the firm is less likely to shut down in the short run, and job security increases.

A simple numerical example illustrates the point. For a given time period, a firm has total costs of $10,000, total variable costs (which are exclusively labor costs) of $7,000, and fixed costs of $3,000 per week. Employees then propose to their employer that their total wages be reduced to $6,000, but that they now receive health insurance benefits worth $1,000 (they received $0 before) that will continue for a period of six months after the firm has shut down. The total costs of the firm

EXHIBIT 24–5
The Perfectly Competitive Firm's Short-Run Supply Curve

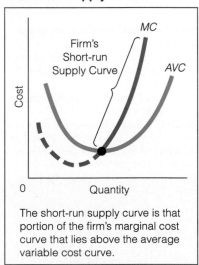

The short-run supply curve is that portion of the firm's marginal cost curve that lies above the average variable cost curve.

515

EXHIBIT 24–6

EXHIBIT 24–6
Fixed (and Variable) Costs as a Percentage of Total Cost and the Shut-Down Decision

Both firms have the same total cost; however, firm X has a higher total fixed cost–total cost ratio than firm Y. It follows that firm X is less likely to shut down in the short run. Firm X will shut down when total revenue falls to $400. Firm Y will shut down when total revenue falls to $500. It follows that firm Y would shut down before firm X would (since total revenue could fall to $500 and not fall to $400, but the reverse isn't true.)

FIRM X
TC = $600
TVC = $400
TFC = $200
$\dfrac{TVC}{TC} = \dfrac{\$400}{\$600} = .67$
$\dfrac{TFC}{TC} = \dfrac{\$200}{\$600} = .33$

FIRM Y
TC = $600
TVC = $500
TFC = $100
$\dfrac{TVC}{TC} = \dfrac{\$500}{\$600} = .83$
$\dfrac{TFC}{TC} = \dfrac{\$100}{\$600} = .17$

Short-Run Industry (Market) Supply Curve
The horizontal summation of all existing firms' short-run supply curves.

Long-Run Competitive Equilibrium
The condition where $P = MC = SRATC = LRATC$. There are zero economic profits, firms are producing the quantity of output at which price is equal to marginal cost, and no firm has an incentive to change its plant size.

will not change if this proposal is accepted, but fixed costs as a percentage of total costs will rise from 30 percent to 40 percent. If the firm does not accept the employees' proposal, it will shut down if total revenue falls to $7,000. If it does accept the employees' proposal, it will shut down if total revenue falls to $6,000. The firm's acceptance of the employees' proposal increases employee job security—at least in the short run.

From Firm to Market (Industry) Supply to Short-Run Competitive Equilibrium

Once we know that the firm's short-run supply curve is that part of its marginal cost curve that is above its average variable cost curve, it is a simple matter to derive the **short-run market (industry) supply curve**.[3] We horizontally sum the short-run supply curves for all firms in the market or industry.

Consider, for simplicity, an industry made up of two firms, A and B. At a price of $4, firm A supplies 100 units of good X and firm B supplies 150 units. One point on the market supply curve thus corresponds to $4 on the price axis and 250 units (100 units + 150 units) on the quantity axis.[4] By following this procedure for all prices, we would have the short-run market supply curve.

The market demand curve, as we saw in Chapter 3, is obtained using the same approach; this time, however, we sum the quantity demanded by each demander at every price. The interplay of market demand and short-run market supply finally establishes equilibrium price and quantity; thus, this interplay characterizes the process and outcome of short-run competitive equilibrium. The derivation of the short-run market supply curve, the market demand curve, and short-run competitive equilibrium is illustrated in Exhibit 24–7.

PERFECT COMPETITION IN THE LONG RUN

■

The number of firms in a perfectly competitive market may not be the same in the short run as in the long run. For example, if the typical firm is making economic profits in the short run, new firms will be attracted to the industry, and the number of firms will expand. If the typical firm is sustaining losses, some existing firms will exit the industry, and the number of firms will contract. We explain the process in greater detail in later sections. First, we outline the conditions of long-run competitive equilibrium.

The Conditions of Long-Run Competitive Equilibrium

The following conditions characterize **long-run competitive equilibrium:**

1. Economic profit is zero: Price is equal to short-run average total cost ($P = SRATC$). (SR = short run and LR = long run.) The logic of this condition can be understood by asking what would happen if price were above or below short-run average total cost. If it were above, positive economic profits would attract firms to the industry in order to obtain the profits. If price were below, losses would result and some firms would want to exit the industry. We could not have long-run competitive equilibrium if firms have an incentive to enter or exit the industry

[3]In discussing market structures, the words *industry* and *market* are often used interchangeably when a single-product industry is under consideration, which is the case here.
[4]We add one qualification: Each firm's supply curve is drawn on the assumption that the prices of its variable inputs are constant.

EXHIBIT 24–7
The Process of Short-Run Competitive Equilibrium

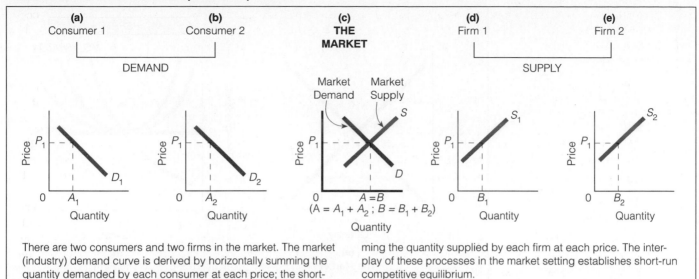

There are two consumers and two firms in the market. The market (industry) demand curve is derived by horizontally summing the quantity demanded by each consumer at each price; the short-run industry (market) supply curve is derived by horizontally sum- ming the quantity supplied by each firm at each price. The interplay of these processes in the market setting establishes short-run competitive equilibrium.

in response to positive economic profits or losses, respectively. For long-run equilibrium to exist, there can be no incentive for firms to enter or exit the industry. This condition is brought about by zero economic profit (normal profit), which is a consequence of the equilibrium price being equal to short-run average total cost.

2. Firms are producing the quantity of output at which price is equal to marginal cost ($P = MC$). As previously noted, perfectly competitive firms naturally move toward the output level at which marginal revenue (or price, since $MR = P$ for a perfectly competitive firm) equals marginal cost.

3. No firm has an incentive to change its plant size to produce its current output; that is, $SRATC = LRATC$ at the quantity of output at which $P = MC$. To understand this condition, suppose $SRATC > LRATC$ at the quantity of output established in condition 2. The firm then has an incentive to change plant size in the long run, because it wants to produce its product with the plant size that will give it the lowest average total cost (unit cost). It will have met this condition, and thus have no further incentive to change plant size, when it is producing the quantity of output at which price equals marginal cost and $SRATC$ equals $LRATC$.

The three conditions necessary for long-run competitive equilibrium can be stated: *Long-run competitive equilibrium exists when $P = MC = SRATC = LRATC$* (Exhibit 24–8).

Question:

It appears that long-run competitive equilibrium exists when there is no incentive for firms to make any changes. Is this correct?

Answer:

Yes, it is. Specifically, long-run competitive equilibrium exists when all of the following occur:

EXHIBIT 24–8
Long-Run Competitive Equilibrium

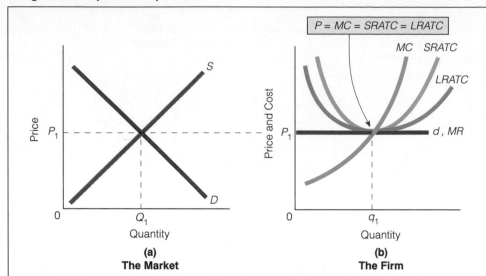

(a) Equilibrium in the market. (b) Equilibrium for the firm. In (b), $P = MC$ (the firm has no incentive to move away from the quantity of output at which this occurs, q_1); $P = SRATC$ (there is no incentive for firms to enter or exit the industry); and $SRATC = LRATC$ (there is no incentive for the firm to change its plant size). Note that the MC curve in the exhibit is the short-run marginal cost ($SRMC$) curve. Although not illustrated, the long-run marginal cost ($LRMC$) curve would also pass through the point where the demand, $LRATC$, and $SRATC$ curves are tangent. In short, long-run competitive equilibrium may be specified as $P = SRMC = LRMC = SRATC = LRATC$.

1. There is no incentive for firms to enter or exit the industry. This means there are no economic profits or losses. There is, instead, zero economic profit (or normal profit), which can only come about if $P = SRATC$.

2. There is no incentive for firms to produce more or less output. This requires firms to produce the quantity of output at which P (MR) $= MC$, since any other output level does not maximize profits or minimize losses.

3. There is no incentive for firms to change plant size. Firms naturally want to produce at the lowest average total cost (unit cost) possible. If, for example, $SRATC >$ $LRATC$ at the output level at which $MR = MC$, the firm has an incentive to change its plant size in the long run in order to produce the same output level at lower units costs.

Industry Adjustment to an Increase in Demand

Suppose we start at long-run competitive equilibrium, where, as noted, $P = MC$ $= SRATC = LRATC$. Then market demand rises for the product produced by the firms in the industry. What happens? Equilibrium price rises; as a consequence, the demand curve faced by an individual firm (which is its marginal revenue curve) shifts upward; next, existing firms in the industry increase quantity of output since marginal revenue now intersects marginal cost at a higher quantity of output. In the long run, new firms begin to enter the industry since price is currently above average total cost and there are positive economic profits. As new firms enter the industry, the market (industry) supply curve shifts rightward. As a consequence, equilibrium price falls. It falls until long-run competitive equilibrium is reestablished; that is, until there is, once again, zero economic profit.

If you look at the process again, from the initial increase in the market demand to the reestablishment of long-run competitive equilibrium, you will notice that price first increased in the short run (owing to the increase in demand), and then decreased in the long run (owing to the increase in supply). Also, profits first increased (owing to the increase in demand and consequent increase in price) and then decreased (owing to the increase in supply and consequent decrease in price); they went from zero to some positive amount and then back to zero.

We emphasize the up-and-down movements in both price and profits in response to an increase in demand. Too often people only see the primary upward movements in both price and profits and ignore or forget the secondary downward movements. The secondary effects in price and profits are as important as the primary effects.

The process of adjustment we have described brings up an important question. If price first rises owing to an increase in market demand, and later falls owing to an increase in market supply, will the new equilibrium price be greater than, less than, or equal to the original equilibrium price? For example, if equilibrium price is $10 before the increase in market demand, will the new equilibrium price (after market and firm adjustments have taken place) be greater than, less than, or equal to $10? The answer depends on whether increasing cost, decreasing cost, or constant cost, respectively, describes the industry in which the increase in demand has taken place. We discuss the three cases.

Constant-Cost Industry.   A **constant-cost industry** is an industry in which average total costs (unit costs) do not change as output increases or decreases, as firms enter or exit the market or industry. If market demand increases for a good produced by firms in a constant-cost industry, price will initially rise and finally fall to its *original level.* This is illustrated in Exhibit 24–9a.

We start from a position of long-run competitive equilibrium where there are zero economic profits. This is at point 1, which is one point on the long-run supply curve (*LRS*). We now experience an increase in demand. Price rises from P_1 to P_2; at P_2 there are positive profits, which cause the firms currently in the industry to expand output. We move up the supply curve, S_1, from point 1 to point 2. Next, new firms, drawn by the profits, enter the industry, causing the supply curve to shift rightward.

For a constant-cost industry, output is increased without a change in the price of inputs. Because of this, the firms' cost curves do not shift. But, of course, if costs do not rise to reduce the profits in the industry, this means price must fall. (Profits can be reduced in two ways: through a rise in costs or a fall in price.) We know, then, that price must fall to its original level (P_1) before profits are zero. This implies that the supply curve shifts rightward by the same amount that the demand curve shifts rightward. In the exhibit, this is a shift from S_1 to S_2. Connecting the two long-run equilibrium points (1 and 3), where economic profits are zero, gives us the **long-run (industry) supply curve.** A constant-cost industry is characterized by a horizontal long-run supply curve.

Increasing-Cost Industry.   An **increasing-cost industry** is an industry in which average total costs (unit costs) increase as output increases and decreases as output decreases, as firms enter and exit the industry, respectively. If market demand

Constant-Cost Industry
An industry in which average total costs do not change as (industry) output increases or decreases, as firms enter or exit the industry, respectively.

Long-Run Industry Supply Curve
Graphic representation of the quantities of output that the industry is prepared to supply at different prices after the entry and exit of firms is completed.

Increasing-Cost Industry
An industry in which average total costs increase as output increases and decrease as output decreases, as firms enter and exit the industry, respectively.

519

EXHIBIT 24–9
Long-Run Industry Supply Curves

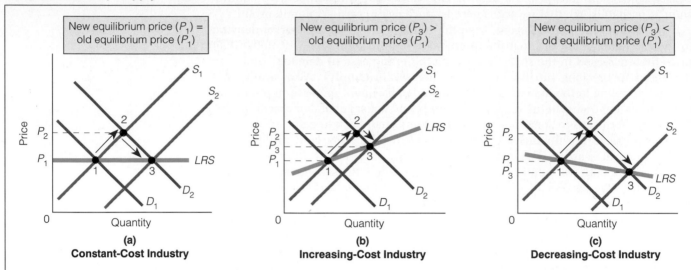

New equilibrium price (P_1) =
old equilibrium price (P_1)

(a)
Constant-Cost Industry

New equilibrium price (P_3) >
old equilibrium price (P_1)

(b)
Increasing-Cost Industry

New equilibrium price (P_3) <
old equilibrium price (P_1)

(c)
Decreasing-Cost Industry

LRS = long-run industry supply. Each part illustrates the same scenario, but with different results depending on whether the industry has (a) constant costs, (b) increasing costs, or (c) decreasing costs. In each part, we start at long-run competitive equilibrium (point 1). Demand increases, price rises from P_1 to P_2, and there are positive economic profits. Consequently, existing firms expand output, and new firms are attracted to the industry.

In (a), input costs remain constant as output increases, so the firms' cost curves do not shift. Profits fall to zero through a decline in price. This implies that in a constant-cost industry, the supply

curve shifts rightward by the same amount as the demand curve shifts rightward.

In (b), input costs increase as output increases. Profits are squeezed by a combination of rising costs and falling prices. The new equilibrium price (P_3) for an increasing-cost industry is higher than the old equilibrium price (P_1).

In (c), input costs decrease as output increases. The new equilibrium price (P_3) for a decreasing-cost industry is lower than the old equilibrium price (P_1).

Decreasing-Cost Industry
An industry in which average total costs decrease as output increases and increase as output decreases, as firms enter and exit the industry, respectively.

increases for a good produced by firms in an increasing-cost industry, price will initially rise and finally fall to a level *above its original level.*

Consider the situation in Exhibit 24–9b. We start, as before, in long-run competitive equilibrium. Demand increases and price rises from P_1 to P_2. This brings about positive economic profits, which cause firms in the industry to expand output and new firms to enter the industry. So far this is the same process we described for a constant-cost industry. The difference, however, is that in an increasing-cost industry, as firms purchase more inputs to produce more output, some input prices rise and cost curves shift. In short, as industry output expands, profits are caught in a two-way squeeze: Price is coming down, and costs are rising. (If costs are rising as price is falling, then it is not necessary for price to fall to its original level before zero economic profits rule once again. Price will not have to fall as far to restore long-run competitive equilibrium in an increasing-cost industry as in a constant-cost industry.) We would expect, then, that given an increase in demand in an increasing-cost industry, the new equilibrium price will be higher than the old equilibrium price. This means the supply curve shifts rightward by less than the demand curve shifts rightward. An increasing-cost industry is characterized by an upward-sloping long-run supply curve.

Decreasing-Cost Industry. A **decreasing-cost industry** is an industry in which average total costs (unit costs) decrease as output increases and increase as output decreases, as firms enter and exit the industry, respectively. If market demand increases for a good produced by firms in a decreasing-cost industry, price will initially rise and finally fall to a level *below its original level.* In Exhibit 24–9c, price initially moves from P_1 to P_2 and then to P_3. In such an industry, average total costs decrease as new firms enter the industry, so price must fall below its original level in order to eliminate profits. A decreasing-cost industry is characterized by a downward-sloping long-run supply curve.

Entry into the Industry and Price Declines

In 1969, the first hand-held calculator was introduced in the United States; it sold for $395. In 1975, Sony sold the first videocassette recorder (VCR) for a price of $1,400. In 1977, Apple Computer Corporation sold the first personal computer—it had only 4K random access memory (RAM)—for just under $1,300. In 1992, the prices of all three goods were much lower in both nominal and real (inflation-adjusted) terms and the quality was generally considered much higher than in the years when the goods were first introduced. Hand-held calculators of higher quality than the one introduced in 1969 were selling for approximately $10. Videocassette recorders of higher quality than those in 1975 were selling for approximately $325. Personal home computers of higher quality than those in 1977 were selling for approximately $500.

What brought about this sharp decrease in price and increase in quality? The entry of new firms into the calculator, VCR, and personal computer industries was partly responsible. Positive economic profits, realized by the first companies in the different industries, attracted new firms, the supply of the goods increased, and prices fell.[5] In 1970, one year after the first hand-held calculator was introduced, Texas Instruments, Inc., entered the industry. It was quickly followed by Canon, Hewlett-Packard, National Semi-Conductor, and Sears, to name only a few well-known companies. In the VCR industry, Sony was soon followed by RCA, General Electric, Zenith, and many others. In the personal computer industry, Apple was quickly followed by Tandy (Radio Shack), Xerox, IBM, Nippon Electric, Casio, Digital Equipment, and a host of others.

These examples illustrate how easy entry into the market can affect price and profits. They also suggest the potential benefits that exist for incumbent firms that can successfully limit entry into the industry. (Consider the profits Sony would have realized if it could have legally prohibited other firms from entering the videocassette recorder industry.)

Industry Adjustment to a Decrease in Demand

Demand can decrease as well as increase. The analysis we outlined for an increase in demand can be reversed to explain industry adjustment to a decrease in demand. Starting at long-run competitive equilibrium, market demand decreases; as a consequence, in the short run the equilibrium price falls, effectively shifting the firm's demand curve (marginal revenue curve) downward; following this, some firms in the industry will decrease production since marginal revenue intersects marginal cost at a lower level of output, and some firms will shut down.

In the long run, some firms will leave the industry because price is below average total cost and they are taking continual losses. As firms leave the industry, the

[5]Changes in technology also occurred around the same time.

market supply curve shifts leftward. As a consequence, the equilibrium price rises. It will rise until long-run competitive equilibrium is reestablished; that is, until there are, once again, zero economic profits (instead of negative economic profits). Whether the new equilibrium price is greater than, less than, or equal to the original equilibrium price depends on whether decreasing cost, increasing cost, or constant cost, respectively, describes the industry in which demand decreased.

Question:

What motivates long-run adjustment?

Answer:

Profit seeking by firms is behind long-run adjustment. For example, suppose that in the short run, the typical firm is earning profits. In the long run, new firms will enter the industry, causing the number of firms to expand, supply to increase, and prices to fall.

Differences in Costs, Differences in Profits: Now You See It, Now You Don't

Two farmers, Hancock and Cordero, produce wheat. Farmer Cordero grows his wheat on fertile land; Farmer Hancock grows his wheat on poor soil. Both farmers sell their wheat for the same price, but because of the difference in the quality of their land, Cordero has lower average total costs than Hancock. This is represented in Exhibit 24–10.

EXHIBIT 24–10
Differences in Costs, Differences in Profits: Now You See It, Now It's Gone

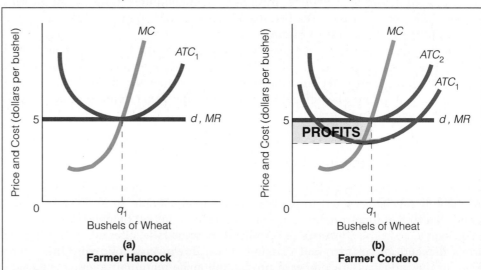

At ATC_1 for both farmers, Cordero earns profits and Hancock does not. The reason Cordero is earning profits is because the land he farms is of higher quality (more productive) than Hancock's land. Eventually, this fact is taken into account, either by Cordero paying higher rent for the land or by incurring higher implicit opportunity costs for it. This moves Cordero's ATC curve upward to the same level as Hancock's, and Cordero earns zero economic profits. The profits have gone as payment (implicit or explicit) for the higher quality, more productive land.

If we compare initial situations for the two farmers (see each farmer's ATC_1), we notice that Cordero is earning profits and Hancock is not. Cordero is earning profits because he pays lower average total costs than Hancock as a consequence of his farming higher quality land than Hancock. But is this situation likely to continue? Is Cordero likely to continue earning profits? The answer is no. Individuals will bid up the price of the fertile land that Cordero farms vis-à-vis the poor quality land that Hancock farms. In other words, if Cordero is renting his farmland, the rent he pays will increase to reflect the superior quality of the land. The rent will increase by an amount equal to the profits per time period; that is, an amount equal to the shaded portion in (b). If Cordero owns the land, the superior quality of the land will have a higher implicit (opportunity) cost attached to it (Cordero can rent it out for more than Hancock can rent out his land, assuming Hancock owns his land), and this fact will be reflected in the average total cost curve.

In Exhibit 24–10b, ATC_2 reflects either the higher rent Cordero must pay for the superior land or the full implicit opportunity cost he incurs by farming land he owns. In either case, once the average total cost curve reflects *all costs,* Cordero will be in the same situation as Hancock; he, too, will be earning zero economic profits.

Where has the profit gone? It has gone for payment to the higher quality, more productive resource responsible for the lower average total costs in the first place. Consequently, average total costs are no longer relatively lower for the person or firm that employs the higher quality, more productive resource or input.

Profit and Discrimination

How does a firm's discriminatory behavior affect its profits in the context of the model of perfect competition? Let's start at the position of long-run competitive equilibrium where firms are earning zero economic profits. Consider the owner of a firm who chooses not to hire an excellent worker (a worker who is above average, let's say) simply because of that worker's race, religion, or sex.

If the owner of the firm discriminates in any way, what happens to his profits? First, if he chooses not to employ high-quality employees because of their race, religion, or sex, then the firm owner's costs will rise above the costs of his competitors who hire the best employees—irrespective of race, religion, or sex. Since he is initially earning zero profit, where $TR = TC$, this act of discrimination will raise TC and push him over into taking economic losses.

Also, owners may decide to replace managers of firms earning subnormal profits; thus profit maximization by shareholders works to reduce discrimination.

Our conclusion is that if a firm finds itself in a perfectly competitive market structure, there are penalties it will pay if it chooses to discriminate. Discrimination costs.

TOPICS FOR ANALYSIS WITHIN THE THEORY OF PERFECT COMPETITION

In this section, we briefly analyze three topics within the theory of perfect competition: higher costs and higher prices, advertising, and setting prices.

Do Higher Costs Mean Higher Prices?

Suppose there are 600 firms in an industry. Each firm sells the identical product at the same price. Suppose that one of these firms experiences a rise in its marginal costs of production. Someone immediately comments, "Higher costs for the firm today, higher prices for the consumer tomorrow." Her assumption is that firms that experience a rise in costs simply pass on these higher costs to consumers in the form of higher prices.

Will this occur in a perfectly competitive market structure? Remember that each firm in the industry is a price taker; furthermore, only one firm has experienced a rise in marginal cost. Since this firm supplies only a tiny percentage of the total market supply, it is unlikely that there will be anything other than a negligible change in the market supply curve. And if the market supply curve does not change, neither will equilibrium price. In short, a rise in costs incurred by one of many firms does not mean consumers will pay higher prices. The situation would have been different, of course, if many of the firms in the industry had experienced a rise in costs. In this case, the market supply curve would have been affected, along with price.

Will the Perfectly Competitive Firm Advertise?

Do individual farmers advertise? Have you ever seen an advertisement, say, for Farmer Johnson's milk? We think not. First, since Farmer Johnson sells a homogeneous product, advertising his milk is the same as advertising every dairy farmer's milk. Second, since Farmer Johnson finds himself in a perfectly competitive market, he can sell all the milk he wants at the going price. So, why should he advertise? From his viewpoint, advertising has costs and no benefits.

Will a perfectly competitive *industry* advertise? For example, if Farmer Johnson won't advertise his milk, will the milk industry advertise milk? It may. The industry as a whole may advertise milk in the hope of shifting the market demand curve for milk to the right. This is actually what the milk industry hopes to do with its commercial message: "Milk, it does a body good."

Supplier-set Price versus Market-determined Price: Collusion or Competition

Suppose the only thing you know about a particular industry is that all firms within it sell their products at the same price. To explain this, some people argue that the firms are colluding—that is, the firms come together, pick a price, and stick to it.

This, of course, is one way all firms can arrive at the same price for their products. But it is not the only way. Another way has been described in this chapter. It could be that all firms are price takers; that is, the firms find themselves in a perfectly competitive market structure. There is no collusion here.

Two or more explanations may seem equally reasonable. For example, observing that all firms within an industry sell their product for the same price, both the explanation that the firms collude on price and the explanation that the firms are price takers seem equally reasonable. But for the economist, a reasonable explanation is not sufficient; what she wants is the correct explanation. The economist is skeptical of any explanation that simply sounds reasonable. She has to have evidence that fails to reject the explanation.

Suppose your history professor comes to class each day cleanly shaved and attired in dress slacks, a shirt and tie, and a sports jacket. One day he ambles in unshaved, in cut-off jeans and a T-shirt. You notice the difference and try to explain it. Perhaps his alarm clock didn't go off this morning; he got up with only 20 minutes to spare, grabbed the first set of clothes in sight, and ran off to class as fast as he could. Your explanation sounds reasonable.

Your classmate, though, suggests a different explanation. She suggests your history professor is going through a midlife crisis, and dressing this new way is one of the forms it is taking. Your classmate's explanation sounds reasonable, too.

How would you determine which one of you, if either, has come up with the correct explanation? The question an economist would ask is, "If my explanation is correct, what would I expect to see?" Here the economist attempts to test the explanation by gathering real-world evidence.

If the evidence fails to reject the alarm-clock explanation, we would expect to see the history professor come to the next class cleanly shaved and attired in dress slacks, a shirt and tie, and a sports jacket. If the evidence fails to reject the midlife crisis explanation, we would expect to see the history professor come to the next class unshaved and in cut-off jeans and a T-shirt, or wearing something equally different from his customary attire.

So, what separates the layperson from the economist is that the layperson stops trying to figure out something once he or she has heard a reasonable explanation. For the economist, a reasonable explanation is not enough.

> *A perfectly competitive firm exhibits resource allocative efficiency: it produces the quantity of output at which $P = MC$.*

RESOURCE ALLOCATIVE EFFICIENCY AND PRODUCTIVE EFFICIENCY

Perfect competition is often put forth as a benchmark against which other market structures are judged. Two of the reasons for this are *resource allocative efficiency* and *productive efficiency*.

Resource Allocative Efficiency

A firm that produces the quantity of output at which $P = MC$ is said to exhibit **resource allocative efficiency.** A perfectly competitive firm is such a firm. It produces the quantity of output at which $MR = MC$, and since for it $P = MR$, it follows that $P = MC$.

Resources are allocated efficiently when the (exchange) value of the resources to demanders equals the opportunity cost of the resources. Put differently, resource allocative efficiency is said to exist when the marginal benefit to demanders of the resources in the goods they purchase is equal to the marginal cost to suppliers of the resources they use in producing the goods. Resource allocative efficiency is established when firms produce the quantity of output at which price, or the market representation of the exchange value or marginal benefit of the resources to demanders, is equal to marginal cost. Continuing to produce a good until its price equals its marginal cost ensures that all units of the good are produced that are of greater value to demanders than the alternative goods that might have been produced.

An important point to notice is that for a perfectly competitive firm, profit maximization and resource allocative efficiency are not at odds. (Might they be for other market structures? See the next two chapters.) The firm seeks to maximize profit by producing the quantity of output at which $MR = MC$, and since for the

Resource Allocative Efficiency
The situation that exists when firms produce the quantity of output for which price equals marginal cost.

Interview: George Stigler

George Stigler won the Nobel Prize in Economics in 1982. His major contributions in economics have been in the areas of industrial structures, the functioning of markets, and the effects of public regulatory activities. Stigler is currently at the University of Chicago.

Professor Stigler, What is it that sometimes makes theories built on unrealistic assumptions predict better than theories built on realistic assumptions?

The main explanation for the power of an abstract theory is that it has not specified a lot of factual content. If I specify factual content, if I get descriptive in my assumptions, there is a great danger that while I can tell a very good story, it doesn't tell me anything about the world. A striking example is the theory of monopolistic competition of the Chamberlin variety, which now is no longer used. It paid attention to things such as the fact that every seller differs from every other seller in location, or the charm of his personality, or the fact that his brand of toothpaste is advertised differently from another brand, and so forth. All those things are realistic, but they are part of a theory that doesn't tell us anything that is seriously interesting, different, or more insightful than the abstract theory of perfect competition.

You once said that abstraction and generality are virtually synonyms. Is this your point here—that an abstract theory is a general theory, that it has the potential to tell us more about the world?

Yes, you can subject it to a wider range of challenging applications. For example, consider the standard assumption of competition: that the rate of return tends to equality in all the areas in which returns are allowed to flow. We can use that in a million applications.

Some economists have suggested that there is more agreement in microeconomics than in macroeconomics because economists ask harder questions in macroeconomics than in microeconomics. Do you agree?

I think many of the people in macroeconomics are extremely bright people, and they certainly have a good command of the techniques of economics. Given this, I have to conclude that they are singularly less successful in predicting and understanding the phenomena they work with because they are working with a harder set of phenomena than the microeconomist deals with. Macroeconomics has not reached anything like the stability or universality of acceptance that microeconomics has achieved. If I compare the Ph.Ds from different universities, they all use the same microeconomics, but they still vary a good deal in their macroeconomics. So probably I'm a lazy man: I'd rather work on subjects that we economists are awfully good at rather than those subjects that, however important, we're not as good at.

If you could snap your fingers and have the answer to any economic question, what question would you like to have answered?

There are some things anyone would like to solve. For example, if we could finally nail down the true theory of oligopoly, of the behavior of small groups or of coalitions, that would be an enormous contribution both to industrial organization in the private sector and to the theory of interest groups and their influence on political phenomena. It would be a stunning advance if we could show the logic of collusion and competition among groups.

Economics is interesting, don't you think, because there are so many challenging puzzles to solve?

If a field ever got to the dreadful state that there were no more interesting questions left, it would be terrible. I always say that just as in science we owe it to our successors to leave them a lot of unsolved problems—a duty, by the way, we completely fulfill—it is also true in social affairs.

You joined the faculty of the University of Chicago in 1958. You had been recommended by the Department of Economics for a position there 12 years earlier, but the university's acting president rejected the appointment because he was unimpressed by the results of his interview of you. Could you tell us a little more of this story?

On that occasion when I was interviewed, I was on a kick on how important empirical studies are to a scientist. Most likely the acting president of the university thought I was overdoing it. By the way, he, too, was a man of limited skill on that day. I thought at the time what an outrage it was. But a few weeks later, they took that same job and offered it to Milton Friedman. I said to myself, What a wonderful contribution I have made to the university.

firm $P = MR$, it automatically accomplishes resource allocative efficiency ($P = MC$) when it maximizes profit ($MR = MC$).

Productive Efficiency

A firm that produces its output at the lowest possible per unit cost (lowest *ATC*) is said to exhibit **productive efficiency.** The perfectly competitive firm does this in long-run equilibrium, as a glance back at Exhibit 24–8 shows. This is a desirable situation from society's standpoint, since it means that perfectly competitive firms are economizing on society's scarce resources and therefore not wasting them. To illustrate, suppose the lowest unit cost at which good X can be produced is $3—this is the minimum *ATC*. If a firm produces 1,000 units of good X, its total cost is $3,000. Now suppose the firm had produced good X, not at its lowest unit cost of $3, but at a slightly higher unit cost of $3.50. Total cost would now equal $3,500. This would mean that $500 worth of resources were employed producing good X that could have been used to produce other goods had the firm exhibited productive efficiency. The society could have been "richer" in goods and services, but now is not.

In Perspective

In Chapter 19 we stated that microeconomics is about objectives, constraints, and choices. In this chapter we learned that perfectly competitive firms have as their *objective* to maximize profit or, in its absence, to minimize losses. Second, they are *constrained* by the demand curve they face—they cannot charge a higher price than that established by the market. Finally, within this setting, they maximize profits (or minimize losses) by *choosing* to produce where $MR = MC$.

CHAPTER SUMMARY

The Theory of Perfect Competition

■ The theory of perfect competition is built on four assumptions: (1) There are many sellers and many buyers, none of which is large in relation to total sales or purchases. (2) Each firm produces and sells a homogeneous product. (3) Buyers and sellers have all relevant information with respect to prices, product quality, sources of supply, and so on. (4) There is easy entry into and exit from the industry.
■ The theory of perfect competition predicts the following: (1) Economic profits will be squeezed out of the industry in the long run by the entry of new firms—that is, zero economic profit exists in the long run. (2) In equilibrium, firms produce the quantity of output at which price equals marginal cost. (3) In the short run, firms will stay in business as long as price covers average variable costs. (4) In the long run, firms will stay in business as long as price covers average total costs. (5) In the short run, an increase in demand will lead to a rise in price; whether the price in the long run will be higher than, lower than, or equal to its original level depends on whether the firm finds itself in an increasing-, decreasing-, or constant-cost industry.

The Perfectly Competitive Firm

■ A perfectly competitive firm is a price taker. It sells its product only at the market-established equilibrium price.

■ The perfectly competitive firm faces a horizontal (flat, perfectly elastic) demand curve. Its demand curve and marginal revenue curve are one and the same.

■ The perfectly competitive firm (as well as all other firms) maximizes profits (or minimizes losses) by producing the quantity of output at which $MR = MC$.

■ For the perfectly competitive firm, price equals marginal revenue.

Production in the Short Run

■ If $P > ATC$, the firm earns economic profits and will continue to operate in the short run.

■ If $P < AVC < ATC$, the firm takes losses. It will shut down since the alternative (continuing to produce) increases the losses.

■ If $ATC > P > AVC$, the firm takes losses. Nevertheless, it will continue to operate in the short run since the alternative (shutting down) increases the losses.

■ Since the firm only produces in the short run when price is greater than average variable cost, the portion of its marginal cost curve that lies above the average variable cost curve is the firm's short-run supply curve.

Conditions of Long-Run Competitive Equilibrium

■ Long-run competitive equilibrium exists when (1) there is no incentive for firms to enter or exit the industry; (2) there is no incentive for firms to produce more or less output; (3) there is no incentive for firms to change plant size. We formalize these conditions as follows: (1) Economic profits are zero (this is the same as saying there is no incentive for firms to enter or exit the industry). (2) Firms are producing the quantity of output at which price is equal to marginal cost (this is the same as saying there is no incentive for firms to produce more or less output; after all, when $P = MC$, it follows that $MR = MC$ for the perfectly competitive firm, and thus the firm is maximizing profits). (3) $SRATC = LRATC$ at the quantity of output at which $P = MC$ (this is the same as saying firms do not have an incentive to change plant size).

Industry Adjustment to a Change in Demand

■ In a constant-cost industry, an increase in demand will result in a new equilibrium price equal to the original equilibrium price (before demand increased); in an increasing-cost industry, an increase in demand will result in a new equilibrium price that is higher than the original equilibrium price; in a decreasing-cost industry, an increase in demand will result in a new equilibrium price that is lower than the original equilibrium price.

■ The long-run supply curve for a constant-cost industry is horizontal (flat, perfectly elastic); the long-run supply curve for an increasing-cost industry is upward sloping; the long-run supply curve for a decreasing-cost industry is downward sloping.

Perfect Competition, Resource Allocative Efficiency, and Productive Efficiency

■ A perfectly competitive firm is resource allocative efficient because it produces the quantity of output at which $P = MC$; that is, the exchange value of resources to demanders equals the opportunity cost of the resources.

■ A perfectly competitive firm exhibits productive efficiency because it produces its output in the long run at the lowest possible per unit cost (lowest ATC).

Key Terms and Concepts

Market Structure

Perfect Competition

Price Taker

Marginal Revenue

Profit-Maximization
Rule

Short-Run (Firm)
Supply Curve

Short-Run Market
(Industry) Supply
Curve

Long-Run Competitive
Equilibrium

Constant-Cost Industry

Long-Run (Industry)
Supply Curve

Increasing-Cost Industry

Decreasing-Cost
Industry

Resource Allocative
Efficiency

Productive Efficiency

QUESTIONS AND PROBLEMS

1. True or false. The firm's entire marginal cost curve is its short-run supply curve. Explain your answer.

2. True or false. In a perfectly competitive market, firms always operate at the lowest per-unit cost. Explain your answer.

3. "Firm A, one firm in a competitive industry, faces higher costs of production. As a result, consumers end up paying higher prices." Discuss.

4. Suppose each firm in a perfectly competitive market structure is in long-run equilibrium. Then demand for the firms' product increases. Initially, price and economic profits rise. Soon afterward, the government decides to tax away most (but not all) of the economic profits, arguing that the firms in the industry did not earn them—the profits were simply the result of an increase in demand. What effect, if any, would the tax have on market adjustment?

5. Explain why one firm sometimes appears to be earning higher profits than another, but in reality is not.

6. Profit maximization for a perfectly competitive firm does not conflict with resource allocative efficiency. Do you agree? Explain your answer.

7. The perfectly competitive firm does not increase its quantity of output without limit even though it can sell all it wants at the going price. Why not?

8. Suppose you read in a business magazine that computer firms are reaping high profits. With the theory of perfect competition in mind, what would you expect to happen over time to the following: computer prices, the profits of computer firms, the number of computers on the market, the number of computer firms?

9. In your own words, explain resource allocative efficiency.

10. The term *price taker* can apply to buyers as well as sellers. A price-taking buyer is one who cannot influence price by changing the amount she buys. What goods do you buy for which you are a price taker? What goods do you buy for which you are not a price taker?

11. Why study perfect competition if it does not exist in the real world?

12. Explain why a perfectly competitive firm will not produce in the short run if price is lower than average variable cost, but it will produce if price is below average total cost (but above average variable cost).

13. In long-run competitive equilibrium, $P = MC = SRATC = LRATC$. Since we know that $P = MR$, we can rewrite the condition as $P = MR = MC = SRATC = LRATC$. Now let's look at the condition as being made of four parts: (a) $P = MR$, (b) $MR = MC$, (c) $P = SRATC$, and (d) $SRATC = LRATC$. If we were to explain *why* $MR = MC$ (b), we would say because the perfectly competitive firm attempts to maximize profits and this is how it does it. What is the *why* for (a), (c), and (d)?

14. Why is perfect competition used as a benchmark to judge other market structures?

15. Suppose the government imposes a production tax on one perfectly competitive firm in the industry. For each unit the firm produces, it must pay $1 to the government. Will consumers in this market end up paying higher prices because of the tax? Why?

16. Given the following information, state whether the firm should shut down or continue to operate in the short run.

a. $Q = 100$; $P = \$10$; $AFC = \$3$; $AVC = \$4$.

b. $Q = 70$; $P = \$5$; $AFC = \$2$; $AVC = \$7$.

c. $Q = 150$; $P = \$7$; $AFC = \$5$; $AVC = \$6$.

MONOPOLY

WHAT THIS CHAPTER IS ABOUT

This chapter presents the theory of monopoly. Monopoly theory, like the theory of perfect competition, may not perfectly describe any real-world market, but it may explain and predict the behavior of some real-world markets. Also, keep in mind that a monopoly market structure is 180-degrees away from a perfectly competitive market structure. Monopoly and perfect competition are at opposite ends of the market structure spectrum. It will be useful to compare the two market structures as we proceed in our discussion.

THE THEORY OF MONOPOLY

■

Monopoly
A theory of market structure based on three assumptions: There is one seller, it sells a product for which no close substitutes exist, and there are extremely high barriers to entry.

The theory of **monopoly** is built on three assumptions:

1. There is one seller. This means that the firm *is* the industry. Contrast this situation with perfect competition, where many firms make up the industry.
2. The single seller sells a product for which there are no close substitutes. Because there are no close substitutes for its product, the single seller, the *monopolist* or *monopoly firm,* faces little, if any, competition.
3. There are extremely high barriers to entry. In the theory of perfect competition, we assumed it was easy for a firm to enter the industry. In the theory of monopoly, we assume it is very hard (if not impossible) for a firm to enter the industry; there are extremely high barriers that keep new firms out. We discuss the nature of these barriers shortly.

Examples of monopoly include many public utilities (local public utilities such as electricity, water, gas, and local telephone service) and the postal service (in the delivery of first-class mail).

Question:

One of the assumptions in the theory of monopoly is that the single seller sells a product for which there are no close substitutes. Isn't deciding what constitutes a close substitute for a product a subjective matter?

Answer:

Yes, it is. For example, someone might argue that writing a letter is a close substitute for making a telephone call, and someone else might maintain that it is not. Recall, however, that we are not trying to determine whether close substitutes exist or not, we are simply *assuming* that there are no close substitutes. This is part of our theory, which we hope will explain and predict the behavior of firms in some real-world markets. If, for example, the theory accurately predicts behavior in market X, even though some people may argue that market X does not *perfectly* meet the assumption that there are no close substitutes, some economists would say, "No matter, the market behaves *as if* the assumption is met."

We add that even if the critics are right and a range of substitutes exists, it is impossible to know beforehand how close a substitute must be before the theory (that assumes no close substitutes) is not useful. In other words, even if there is a "slightly close" substitute for a seller's product, "slightly close" may not be close enough to matter.

Barriers to Entry

If a firm is a single seller of a product, why don't other firms enter the market and produce the same product? Legal barriers, economies of scale, or one firm's exclusive ownership of a scarce resource may make it difficult or impossible for new firms to enter the market.

Public Franchise
A right granted to a firm by government that permits the firm to provide a particular good or service and excludes all others from doing the same.

Legal Barriers. These include public franchises, patents, and government licenses. A **public francise** is a right granted to a firm by government that permits the firm to provide a particular good or service and excludes all others from doing the same (thus eliminating potential competition by law). For example, the U.S. Postal Service has been granted the exclusive franchise to deliver first-class mail. Many public utilities operate under state and local franchises, as do food and gas suppliers along many state turnpikes.

In the United States, *patents* are granted to inventors of a product or process for a period of 17 years. During this time, the patent holder is shielded from competitors; no one else can legally produce and sell the patented product or process. The rationale behind patents is that they are necessary to encourage innovation in an economy. It is argued that few persons will waste their time and money trying to invent a new product if their competitors can immediately copy the product and sell it.

Entry into some industries and occupations requires a government-granted *license.* For example, radio and television stations cannot operate without a license from the Federal Communications Commission (FCC). In most states, a person needs to be licensed to join the ranks of physicians, dentists, architects, nurses, embalmers, barbers, veterinarians, and lawyers, among others.

Economies of Scale. In some industries, low average total costs are only obtained through large-scale production. This means that if new entrants are to be competitive in the industry, they must enter it on a large scale. But this is risky and costly and acts as a barrier to entry. If economies of scale are so pronounced in an industry that only one firm can survive in the industry, this firm is called a **natural monopoly.** Often-cited examples of natural monopoly include public utilities that provide gas, water, electricity, and local telephone service. In a later chapter, we will discuss government regulation of a natural monopoly.

Natural Monopoly
The condition where economies of scale are so pronounced in an industry that only one firm can survive.

Exclusive Ownership of a Necessary Resource. Existing firms may be protected from the entry of new firms by the exclusive or near-exclusive ownership of a resource needed to enter the industry. The classic example here is the Aluminum Company of America (Alcoa), which for a time controlled almost all sources of bauxite in the United States; Alcoa was the sole producer of aluminum in the country from the late nineteenth century until the 1940s. Many people today view the DeBeers Company of South Africa as a monopoly because it controls a large percentage of diamond production and sales. Strictly speaking, though, DeBeers is more of a *marketing cartel* than a monopolist, although, as we see in the next chapter, a successful cartel acts much like a monopolist.

Barriers to Entry and the Legal Prohibition of Competition: Government Monopoly and Market Monopoly

As we have seen, sometimes high barriers to entry exist because competition is legally prohibited; sometimes they exist independently. Where high barriers take the form of public franchises, patents, or government licenses, competition is legally prohibited. In contrast, where high barriers take the form of economies of scale or exclusive ownership of a resource, competition is not legally prohibited. In these cases, nothing *legally* prohibits rival firms from entering the market and competing, even though they may choose not to do so. The high barrier to entry does not have a sign attached to it that reads "No competition allowed."

Some economists use the term *government monopoly* to refer to monopolies that are legally protected from competition and *market monopoly* to refer to monopolies that are not legally protected from competition. But these terms do not imply that one type is better or worse than the other.

Price Searcher
A seller that has the ability to control to some degree the price of the product it sells.

MONOPOLY PRICING AND OUTPUT DECISIONS

■

A monopolist is a **price searcher;** that is, it is a seller that has the ability to control to some degree the price of the product it sells. In contrast to a price taker, a price searcher can raise its price and still sell its product—although not as many units as it could sell at the lower price. The pricing and output decisions of the price-searching monopolist are discussed in the next sections.

The Monopolist's Demand and Marginal Revenue

In the theory of monopoly, the monopoly firm is the industry, the industry is the monopoly firm—they are one and the same. It follows that the monopoly firm faces the market demand curve, which is downward sloping. A downward-sloping demand curve posits an inverse relationship between price and quantity demanded: More is sold at lower prices than at higher prices, *ceteris paribus.* Unlike the perfectly competitive firm, the monopolist can raise its price and still sell its product (though not as much).

Suppose the monopolist wants to sell an additional unit of its product. What must it do? Since it faces a downward-sloping demand curve, it must necessarily lower price. For example, if the monopoly seller is selling two units of X at $10 each, and it wishes to sell three units, it must lower price, say, to $9.75. It sells all three units at $9.75.[1] To sell an *additional* unit, it must lower price on all *previous units.*

The monopoly seller both gains and loses by lowering price, as Exhibit 25–1 shows. It gains $9.75, the price of the additional unit sold because price was low-

[1]We are discussing here how a *single-price monopolist* behaves. This is a monopolist that sells all units of its product for the same price. Later we discuss a *price-discriminating monopolist.*

EXHIBIT 25–1
The Dual Effects of a Price Reduction on Total Revenue

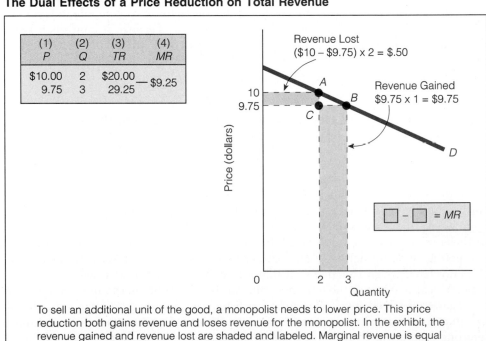

(1) P	(2) Q	(3) TR	(4) MR
$10.00	2	$20.00	$9.25
9.75	3	29.25	

To sell an additional unit of the good, a monopolist needs to lower price. This price reduction both gains revenue and loses revenue for the monopolist. In the exhibit, the revenue gained and revenue lost are shaded and labeled. Marginal revenue is equal to the larger shaded area minus the smaller.

ered. It loses 50 cents—25 cents on the first unit it used to sell at $10, plus 25 cents on the second unit it used to sell at $10. Gains are greater than losses here; the monopolist's net gain from selling the additional unit of output is $9.25 ($9.75 − .50 = $9.25). This is its marginal revenue: the change in total revenue that results from selling one additional unit of output. (Check this out. Total revenue is $20 when two units are sold at $10 each. Total revenue is $29.25 when three units are sold at $9.75 each. The change in total revenue that results from selling one additional unit of output is $9.25.)

Notice that the price of the good ($9.75) is greater than the marginal revenue ($9.25), $P > MR$. This is the case for a monopoly seller, or any price searcher. (Recall that for the firm in perfect competition, $P = MR$.)

Step by step, the effects of a price reduction can be summarized as follows:

1. To sell an additional unit of a good (per time period), the monopolist must lower price. In our example, the monopolist must lower price from $10 to $9.75.
2. The monopolist gains and loses by doing this.
3. What is gained equals the price of the product times one (one additional unit). Let's call this the *revenue gained.* In our example, this is $9.75 × 1 = $9.75. We see that price equals revenue gained ($P =$ revenue gained).
4. What is lost equals the difference between the new lower price ($9.75) and the old higher price ($10) times the units of output sold *before* price was lowered. In our example, this is 25 cents × 2 = 50 cents. Let's call this the *revenue lost.*
5. Marginal revenue can be defined as revenue gained minus revenue lost.
6. Since $P =$ revenue gained
   and $MR =$ revenue gained − revenue lost
   and revenue lost is > 0
   therefore $P > MR$.

Question:

Earlier, it was said that to sell an additional unit, the monopolist must lower price on all previous units. This is confusing. How does the monopolist lower price on units it has already sold?

Answer:

We shouldn't think of *previous* and *additional* as referring to an actual sequence of events. The firm doesn't sell 100 units of a good and then decide to sell one more unit. The firm is in an either–or situation. *Either* the firm sells 100 units over some period of time, *or* it sells 101 units over the same period of time. If it wants to sell 101 units, the price per unit has to be lower than if it wants to sell 100 units.

The Monopolist's Demand and Marginal Revenue Curves Are Not the Same

In perfect competition, the firm's demand curve is the same as its marginal revenue curve. In monopoly, the firm's demand curve is not the same as its marginal revenue curve. The monopolist's demand curve lies above its marginal revenue curve.

The demand curve plots price and quantity (P and Q); the marginal revenue curve plots marginal revenue and quantity (MR and Q). Because for a monopolist price is *greater than* marginal revenue, its demand curve necessarily lies *above* its marginal revenue curve. (Note that price and marginal revenue are the same for the first unit of output, so the demand curve and the marginal revenue curve will share one point in common.) The correct relationship between a monopolist's demand and marginal revenue curves is illustrated in Exhibit 25–2.

A Digression: The Revenue-maximizing Price Is Usually Not the Profit-maximizing Price

We assume that all firms, whether price searchers or price takers, seek to maximize profits. Many of us easily fall into the trap of thinking that the price that maximizes revenues is necessarily the price that maximizes profits. Only under one condition is this the case: when the firm has no variable costs.

Profit is the difference between total revenue and total cost: profit = $TR - TC$. If the firm has no variable costs, then total cost equals total fixed cost (remember that fixed cost is constant as output changes). Thus, profit can be rewritten as the difference between total revenue and total fixed cost: profit = $TR - TFC$, since $TC = TFC$. It follows that maximizing total revenue is the same as maximizing profit, since every time total revenue increases, the difference between it and total cost (total fixed cost)—that is, profit—increases, too.

We conclude that maximizing revenues is the same as maximizing profits only when the firm has no variable costs. It is unlikely, though, that the firm will be without variable costs. In the numerous cases in which variable costs exist, the price that maximizes revenues is not the same as the price that maximizes profits.

An Application: Revenue-Maximizing Price versus Profit-Maximizing Price

Let us begin with a single fact: The island dogs are calling to each other.

It is night. My grandfather listens to them and does not like the sound. In that melody of hounds all the elegiac loneliness of my part of the world is contained. The island dogs are afraid. It is October 4, 1944, ten o'clock in the evening. The tide is rising and will not be full until 1:49 the next morning.

—From *The Prince of Tides* by Pat Conroy

Pat Conroy, the novelist, sells millions of copies of his novels (which include *The Great Santini, The Lords of Discipline, The Prince of Tides,* and others). As far as he's concerned, all those books are priced too high. Conroy, like any author, wants his books to be priced lower than the publisher wants them to be priced. This is because the author earns more income if they are priced lower.

Consider the facts. There are two main entities involved in producing a Pat Conroy novel: Conroy, who writes the book, and the publishing company, which prints, markets, and distributes the book. Pat Conroy incurs no costs in publishing or selling the book; the publishing company does. This means that once Conroy finishes writing the book and turns it over to the publishing company, he incurs no further costs. His marginal costs of publishing and selling the book are zero (he has no variable costs).

But this is not the situation for the publishing company. Its marginal costs are positive. The publishing company incurs an additional cost for each copy of the book that is published and sold. This difference in cost positions between the author and the publisher affects the price at which each wishes to sell the book.

Let's look at Exhibit 25–3, which shows a demand curve and marginal revenue curve for the book. Note that there are two marginal cost curves. The one for the

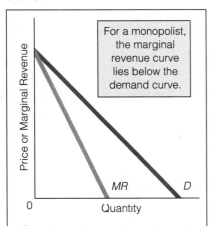

EXHIBIT 25–2
Demand and Marginal Revenue Curves

For a monopolist, the marginal revenue curve lies below the demand curve.

The demand curve plots price and quantity. The marginal revenue curve plots marginal revenue and quantity. Since for a monopolist $P > MR$, the marginal revenue curve must lie below the demand curve. (Note that when a demand curve is a straight line, the marginal revenue curve bisects the horizontal axis halfway between the origin and the point where the demand curve intersects the horizontal axis.)

EXHIBIT 25–3
The Publisher and the Author Opt for Different Prices

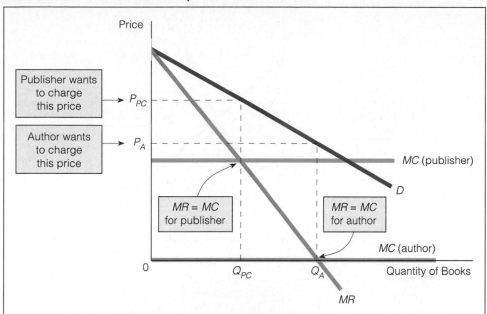

The author faces zero costs of publishing and selling the book; the publishing company faces positive (and we assume) constant marginal costs. Both the author and the publishing company want to equate *MR* and *MC*. The difference, though, is that they do not have the same marginal cost. The author wants Q_A books produced and sold at a price of P_A; the publishing company wants Q_{PC} books produced and sold at a price of P_{PC}.

publishing company is positive and (we have assumed) constant. The other marginal cost curve is for the author and is zero at all levels of output. In all, the exhibit shows one demand curve, one marginal revenue curve, and two marginal cost curves. (Since most authors receive a fixed percentage of total receipts from the sale of the book, the publisher's demand and marginal revenue curves are relevant to the author.) The author wants to sell the quantity of books at which marginal revenue equals his marginal cost. This is at Q_A. The highest price per book at which this quantity of books can be sold is P_A. This is the author's best price. Since the author is paid a fixed percentage of total sales revenues, he wants to maximize revenues. This occurs where $MR = 0$.

Assuming that the publishing company wants to maximize profits, it will want to sell the quantity of books at which marginal revenue equals its marginal cost. This is at Q_{PC}. The highest price per book at which this quantity of books can be sold is P_{PC}. Notice that P_{PC} is higher than P_A—the best price for the publisher is higher than the best price for the author.

Monopoly Price and Output for a Profit-maximizing Monopolist

The monopolist that seeks to maximize profits produces the quantity of output at which $MR = MC$ (as did the profit-maximizing perfectly competitive firm) and *charges the highest price per unit at which this quantity of output can be sold.* In Exhibit 25–4, the highest price at which Q_1, the quantity at which $MR = MC$, can

EXHIBIT 25–4
The Monopolist's Profit-maximizing Price and Quantity of Output

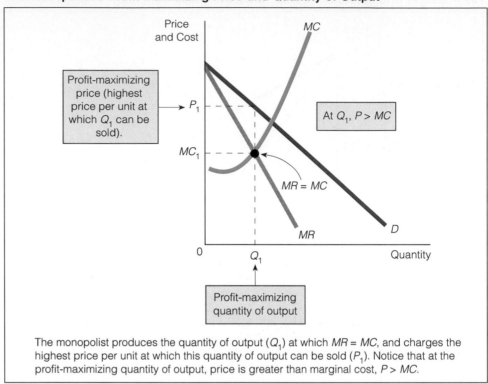

The monopolist produces the quantity of output (Q_1) at which $MR = MC$, and charges the highest price per unit at which this quantity of output can be sold (P_1). Notice that at the profit-maximizing quantity of output, price is greater than marginal cost, $P > MC$.

be sold is P_1. Notice that at Q_1 the *monopolist charges a price that is greater than marginal cost, $P > MC$.*

Whether profits are earned depends on whether P_1 is greater or less than average total cost at Q_1. In short, the profit-maximizing price may be the loss-minimizing price. Both monopoly profits and monopoly losses are illustrated in Exhibit 25–5.

Question:

Isn't it unrealistic to suggest that the monopolist can take a loss? After all, if the monopolist is the only seller in the industry, how can it take a loss?

Answer:

Just because a firm is the only seller of a particular product does not guarantee it will earn profits. Remember, a monopolist cannot charge *any* price it wants for its goods; it charges the highest price that the demand curve allows it to charge. In some instances, the highest price may be lower than its average total costs (unit costs). If so, there is a loss.

Differences between Perfect Competition and Monopoly

There are some important differences between perfect competition and monopoly. Here are two.

EXHIBIT 25–5
Monopoly Profits and Losses

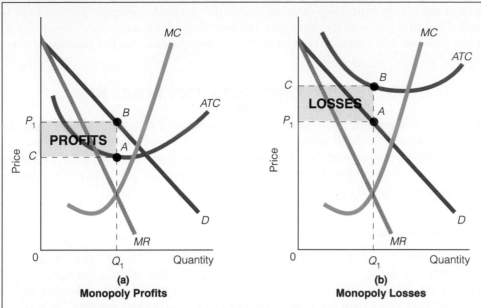

A monopoly seller is not guaranteed any profits. In (a), price is above average total cost at Q_1, the quantity of output at which $MR = MC$, and therefore TR (the area $0P_1BQ_1$) is greater than TC (the area $0CAQ_1$) and profits equal the area CP_1BA. In (b), price is below average total cost at Q_1, and TR (the area $0P_1AQ_1$) is less than TC ($0CBQ_1$) and losses equal P_1CBA.

1. **For the perfectly competitive firm, $P = MR$; for the monopolist, $P > MR$.** The perfectly competitive firm's demand curve is its marginal revenue curve; the monopolist's demand curve lies above its marginal revenue curve.

2. **The perfectly competitive firm charges a price equal to marginal cost; the monopolist charges a price greater than marginal cost.** See Exhibit 25–4 for the monopoly case and Exhibit 24–3 in the last chapter for the perfect competition case.

$$\text{Perfect competition: } P = MR \text{ and } P = MC$$
$$\text{Monopoly: } P > MR \text{ and } P > MC$$

In Perspective

Our trilogy of objective–constraint–choice is useful here. Like the perfectly competitive firm, the monopoly firm has as its objective to maximize profit. Again like the perfectly competitive firm, the monopoly firm is constrained by the height of the demand curve. Neither the perfectly competitive firm nor the monopoly firm can charge a higher price than is warranted by the demand curve it faces. Finally, the monopolist, like the perfectly competitive firm, chooses to maximize profits by equating marginal revenue with marginal cost.

One major difference between the perfectly competitive firm and the monopoly firm is the number of constraints each faces. As we said in an earlier chapter, the fewer the constraints, the better.[2] Whereas the perfectly competitive firm faces the

[2]In this case, we are talking about the seller. Fewer constraints for the seller may be better for it, but fewer constraints for the seller may not necessarily be better for, say, the consumer.

constraint of competition from sellers who sell an identical product, the monopolist does not. To see just how constrained the perfectly competitive firm is relative to the monopoly firm, keep in mind that if the perfectly competitive firm tries to sell its product for a price other than the market price, it will sell nothing and its total revenue will be zero. This, of course, is not the case for the monopoly firm.

MONOPOLY PROFITS IN THE LONG RUN

In perfect competition, economic profits were reduced to zero in the long run by the entry of new firms. In monopoly, profits cannot be reduced to zero by the entry of new firms because extremely high barriers to entry prevent this. However, other forces may reduce profits. These include the capitalization of profits and monopoly rent-seeking activity.

The Capitalization of Profits

Suppose the owners of a profit-earning monopoly firm decide to sell it. What price will they ask for it? No doubt they will ask a price that reflects the value of the profits. As a result, the buyers of the monopoly firm will be faced with higher average total costs than were faced by the former owners of the firm. It is likely that the average total costs will be higher by an amount sufficient to return only zero economic profits to the new owners. This is illustrated in Exhibit 25–6.

The former owners of the monopoly firm had an ATC curve that was low enough to provide them with profits equal to the area CP_1BA. When they sold the monopoly firm, they asked for a price that reflected the value of the monopoly profits. The new owners have a higher ATC curve as a result; this ATC curve is likely to be high enough to provide only zero economic profits to the new owners. In short, through the capitalization of future profits into the firm's market value, the new owners of a monopoly firm will receive only zero economic profits.

Question:

If the new owners are paying a price that reflects the value of profits, and therefore end up receiving zero economic profits, why would they buy the monopoly firm?

Answer:

Perhaps they think they can operate the monopoly firm more efficiently and at lower cost than the previous owners; that is, they believe they can lower their ATC curve over time and make profits in the future. Or perhaps they believe the demand for the product the monopoly firm produces will rise. Of course, simply making their opportunity cost (which is what they do when they earn zero profits) may be enough to induce them to buy the monopoly firm.

The Politics of Monopoly: Monopoly Rent Seeking

Economic or Monopoly Rent
A payment in excess of opportunity cost.

If profits are earned by a monopoly, these monopoly profits are sometimes referred to as **economic rent** or **monopoly rent.** Economic or monopoly rent is a payment in excess of opportunity cost.

How is it that monopoly profits are monopoly rents? The answer is simple. The opportunity costs of the monopolist are reflected in its ATC curve. If price is above

EXHIBIT 25–6
The Capitalization of Profits

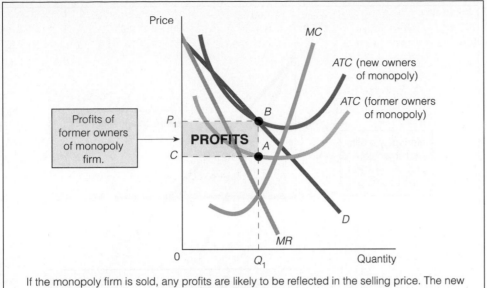

If the monopoly firm is sold, any profits are likely to be reflected in the selling price. The new owners' *ATC* curve is likely to be sufficiently higher than the former owners' *ATC* curve such that the new owners will receive zero economic profits.

average total costs, profits are earned, and if these profits cannot be competed down by the entry of new competitors, then they are rent.

Market participants normally compete for monopoly profits or rent. Activity directed to the accomplishment of this goal is referred to as **rent seeking**.[3]

Consider the following example of rent seeking. Assume the government plans to award some firm a monopoly right to produce good *X*. Suppose firms desiring to produce *X* believe this right is worth $40 million. How will these firms compete for this right? Each firm will spend money (use resources) to convince government officials that it should be awarded the right: It will hire lobbyists, donate money to political campaigns, wine and dine politicians, and so forth. How much will each firm be expected to spend on rent seeking? If firm A is 40 percent sure it can win the right, we predict it will spend $16 million ($40 million × .40 = $16 million). Such an expenditure will dissipate some of the monopoly rents the firm is seeking. In a later section, we explain why this rent-seeking activity is socially wasteful even though it is rational economic activity for the individual firm.

Rent Seeking
Actions of individuals and groups who spend resources to influence public policy in the hope of redistributing (transferring) income to themselves from others.

THE CASE AGAINST MONOPOLY

■

Monopoly is often said to be inefficient in comparison with perfect competition. Here we examine some of the shortcomings that are associated with monopoly.

The Welfare Cost Triangle

Exhibit 25–7 shows demand, marginal revenue, marginal cost, and average total cost curves. We have made the simplifying assumption that the product is pro-

[3]The term *rent seeking* was introduced into economics in the context we are discussing here by economist Anne Krueger in her article "The Political Economy of the Rent-Seeking Society," *American Economic Review* 64 (June 1974):291–303.

EXHIBIT 25-7
Welfare Cost and Rent Seeking as Social Costs of Monopoly

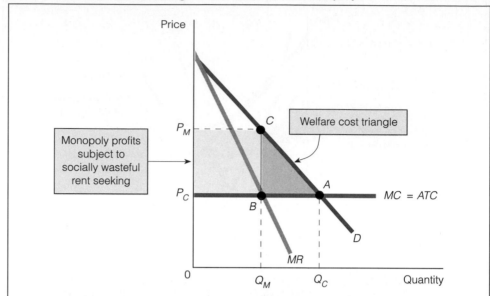

The monopolist produces Q_M and the perfectly competitive firm produces the higher output level Q_C. The welfare cost of monopoly is the triangle (*BCA*) between these two levels of output. Rent-seeking activity is directed to obtaining the monopoly profits, represented by the area $P_C P_M CB$. Rent seeking is a socially wasteful activity because resources are expended to affect a transfer and not to produce goods and services.

duced under constant-cost conditions; as a consequence, marginal cost equals long-run average total cost.[4]

If the product is produced under perfect competition, output Q_C would be produced and sold at a price of P_C. At the competitive equilibrium output level, $P = MC$. If the product is produced under monopoly, output Q_M would be produced and sold at a price of P_M. At the monopoly equilibrium, $P > MC$.

Notice that greater output is produced under perfect competition than under monopoly. The net value of the difference in these two output levels is said to be the **welfare cost of monopoly.** In Exhibit 25-7, we can see that the value to buyers of increasing output from Q_M to Q_C is equal to the maximum amount they would pay for this increase in output. This amount is designated by the area $Q_M CAQ_C$. The costs that would have to be incurred to produce this additional output are designated by the area $Q_M BAQ_C$. The difference between the two is the triangle *BCA*. This is the amount buyers value the additional output over and above the opportunity costs of producing the additional output. It is the welfare loss attached to not producing the competitive quantity of output. The triangle *BCA* is referred to as the **welfare cost triangle.** We conclude that monopoly produces a quantity of output that is "too small" in comparison to the quantity of output produced in perfect competition; thus, this difference in output results in a welfare loss to society.

Welfare Cost of Monopoly
The net value (value to buyers over and above costs to suppliers) of the difference between the monopoly quantity of output (where $P > MC$) and the competitive quantity of output (where $P = MC$).

Welfare Cost Triangle
A diagram of the welfare cost to society associated with monopoly.

[4]A simplifying assumption makes the analysis simpler without significantly affecting the results.

Arnold Harberger was the first economist who tried to determine the actual size of the welfare cost of monopoly in the manufacturing sector of the U.S. economy.[5] He estimated the welfare cost to be a small percentage of the economy's total output. Additional empirical work by other economists puts the figure at approximately 1 percent of total output.

In rent seeking, resources are used to obtain a transfer, not to produce more goods.

■

Rent Seeking Is Socially Wasteful

The economist Gordon Tullock maintains that the welfare cost is not the only cost of monopoly to society.[6] We have identified the monopoly profits as $P_C P_M CB$ in Exhibit 25–7, and noted that they may reasonably be viewed as a transfer from consumers to the monopolist. Tullock asks two questions: First, will individuals compete for this transfer? Second, what are the consequences of people competing for transfers?

The answer to the first question is yes. There is no reason to believe that individuals will turn their backs on monopoly rents; they can be expected to compete for them. As a consequence, individuals will expend resources to bring about a simple transfer from others to themselves. Such rent-seeking behavior is socially wasteful, because resources that could be used to produce goods and services are used instead to transfer income from one group of persons to another.

Suppose group A is currently receiving monopoly rents of $20 million. Groups B, C, and D compete to take the monopoly position away from group A, and with it the monopoly rents. Groups B, C, and D hire lawyers, accountants, lobbyists, secretaries, and research staffs to accomplish their goal. Resources are expended. In the end, group B unseats group A and takes over the monopoly position and the monopoly rents (if any are left after the resource expenditure necessary to obtain the monopoly position). From society's perspective, it does not matter whether group A or group B receives the monopoly rents. What does matter is that the resources used in rent seeking were used in nonproductive instead of productive ways. *Resources were used to obtain a transfer, not to produce more goods.* Moreover, if the desire for the monopoly profits is intense, it is possible that resources valued at the total amount of the transfer—the monopoly rent of $20 million in our example—will be wasted in seeking the transfer. Or this is area $P_C P_M CB$ in Exhibit 25–7. When added to the welfare cost triangle, this increases the cost of monopoly to society.

Question:

Is the motivation for rent seeking the same or different from the motivation for profit seeking?

Answer:

It is the same, since monopoly profit is monopoly rent. There is a difference, however, between profit seeking under perfect competition and monopoly profit (rent) seeking under monopoly. In the former, where there is easy entry into the industry, profit seeking leads to the entry of new firms into the industry, an increase in industry output, and a decrease in price. In monopoly, where high barriers to entry

[5] Arnold Harberger, "Monopoly and Resource Allocation," *American Economic Review* 44 (May 1954): 77–87.

[6] Gordon Tullock, "The Welfare Cost of Tariffs, Monopolies, and Theft," *Western Economic Journal* 5 (June 1967):244–32.

Interview: Gordon Tullock

Gordon Tullock is considered one of the founders of public choice theory, along with James Buchanan (see Chapter 34). Tullock is also the major developer of the theory of rent seeking. He is currently at the University of Arizona.

Professor Tullock, what is rent seeking? What are some current examples of it?

Rent seeking is the use of special resources to get some kind of special privilege. Most of the current examples involve lobbying or something similar in order to get government protection but it is quite possible to find examples in the private market.

A major point in your 1967 article on rent seeking was that the welfare cost of monopoly was greater than economists thought. The article has sparked an outpouring of research efforts in rent-seeking theory. How did you come to write this article?

The story is somewhat amusing. You may remember the first X-efficiency article by Harvey Leibenstein. In some ways, this article shocked me; in other ways, the argument put forth in it seemed plausible. My most serious criticism of it, though, was that I didn't think allocative efficiency meant *only* the absence of tariffs and monopoly. Nevertheless, the empirical data, which Leibenstein mentioned and I had read elsewhere, did indicate that neither tarrifs nor monopoly led to very much inefficiency.

I wrote a response to this article and sent it off to the *American Economic Review*. I got a negative referee report from someone I thought had not understood it at all, along with an apologetic letter from John Gurley, the managing editor, who agreed that the referee hadn't understood the article, but nevertheless said he wasn't going to publish

it. Soon afterward, I received a letter from Alice Vandermeulen who was working for the new *Western Economic Journal*. She asked me if I had anything to submit to the journal. I looked over my rent-seeking article, made some minor changes, and sent it to her. At this point, the article was entitled "The Welfare Effects of Tariffs and Monopolies." She decided to add the word *theft* to the title, so it became "The Welfare Effects of Tariffs, Monopolies, and Theft."

I incorporated this paper into my standard lecture which I gave traveling around to various places. At the time, I was convinced that my arguments were right and that the whole matter of rent seeking should be given more attention by economists. But I didn't realize the outpouring of further research that would occur.

In fact, the word *outpouring* is somewhat symbolic here. If a number of logs are drifting downstream and get jammed, old-fashioned lumberjacks would look for a single log, called the "key log," which when pulled out would cause things to break loose. In my opinion, we have something of the same thing here. A very large amount of

research that should have been done in the last 30 to 40 years had not been done because this particular "rent-seeking" key log still remained in place. When it was pulled out, an immense volume of research burst forth.

You have said that rent seeking is a socially wasteful activity. How might things be changed so that there is less rent seeking in the world and thus less waste?

This is a difficult question. It is easy to think of ways to remedy particular situations, but the general issue is very difficult. In fact, most governments throughout history have been dominated by rent-seeking activity. For some time in the nineteenth century, most of northwestern Europe was not—but this is an exceptional period. I think we ought to look for explanations of why that period was the way it was, instead of explanations of why we have returned to the normal, yet less desirable, state of affairs.

Anyway, all I can recommend is that economists talk about the social wastefulness of rent seeking and try to convince people that it is undesirable. Some economists have said that economic education does pay off. It seems to me that nineteenth-century northwestern Europe is an example of a place and a time where it did, and with some pressure it may do so again. In any case, David Ricardo and his friends were successful, and I see no reason why we can't be, too.

Turning to a more general topic, would you give us an example to illustrate how economists think about problems.

An obvious example is the minimum wage. The average uneconomically educated person thinks that the purpose of the minimum wage is to give certain poor people higher wages. The economist thinks that it will lead to certain poor people being driven into unemployment because their product is not good enough to justify paying them that wage.

What got you interested in economics?

That's a little hard to say. I took a compulsory course in economics in law school at the University of Chicago, and apparently I had a natural affinity for the subject because I almost immediately began treating economics as a major hobby. Now I am paid very well to pursue my hobby.

What do you like about economics?

I'm not sure. To repeat what I said before, I appear to have a natural affinity and do economics casually when I walk or drive. What it is that attracts me

about it I don't know. On the other hand, I also can't tell you why I like chocolate.

What do you think has been the most promising research development in economics in the past decade?

The most promising research development in economics in the past decade has been the development of experimental economics. At the same time, there has been much progress in a number of other areas—law and economics, for another example, and, of course, public choice.

What do you consider your best piece of work and why?

In many ways the best piece of work I ever did was a book that was never published. It was a study of the eco-

nomics of ants, termites, and other social insects entitled Coordination without Command: The Economics of the Social Insects. It involved the application of economic thought in an area that was far, far from its normal field. Yet economics worked out well. I think of it as an economic tour de force and regret that it was not published. Incidentally, there's a social reason why it's unfortunate that it was not published. It never occurred to me that we should model human behavior after that of the animal societies or that animal societies taught us very much about human society. If this book had been published before Wilson's *Sociobiology,* the great uproar about his use of sociobiology to offer policy advice on human beings might never have occurred.

---

exist, monopoly profit (rent) seeking does not lead to additional output and lower price. Often it simply leads to a transfer of profits or rents and a socially wasteful expenditure of resources.

X-Inefficiency

Economist Harvey Leibenstein maintains that the monopolist is not under pressure to produce its product at the lowest possible cost.[7] It is possible for the monopolist to produce its product above the lowest possible unit cost and still survive. Certainly, the monopolist benefits if it can and does lower its costs, but the point is that it doesn't have to in order to survive (with the proviso that average total costs cannot rise so high as to be higher than price). Leibenstein refers to monopolists operating at higher than lowest possible costs, and to the organizational slack that is directly tied to this, as **X-inefficiency.**

It is hard to obtain accurate estimates of X-inefficiency, but whatever its magnitude, there are forces working to mitigate it. For example, if a market monopoly is being run inefficiently, persons realizing this may attempt to buy the monopoly, and if successful, lower costs to make higher profits.

X-Inefficiency
The increase in costs and organizational slack in a monopoly resulting from the lack of competitive pressure to push costs down to their lowest possible level.

PRICE DISCRIMINATION

■

Sometimes monopoly sellers and other price searchers are able to practice price discrimination. Price discrimination has a certain unlooked-for consequence: the

[7]Harvey Leibenstein, "Allocative Efficiency vs. X-Efficiency," *American Economic Review* 56 (June 1966): 392–415.

production of a quantity of output by the monopolist that is equal to the quantity of output that would be produced under perfectly competitive conditions.

What Is Price Discrimination?

We have so far assumed that the monopoly seller sells all units of its product for the same price (it is a single-price monopolist). Under certain conditions, though, it could practice **price discrimination.** This occurs when the seller charges different prices for the product it sells, and the price differences do not reflect cost differences.

There are three types of price discrimination: perfect price discrimination, second-degree price discrimination, and third-degree price discrimination.

Suppose a monopolist produces and sells 1,000 units of good X. If it sells each unit separately and charges the highest price each consumer would be willing to pay for the product rather than go without it, the monopolist is said to practice **perfect price discrimination.** This is sometimes called *discrimination among units.*

If it charges a uniform price per unit for one specific quantity, a lower price for an additional quantity, and so on, the monopolist practices **second-degree price discrimination.** This is sometimes called *discrimination among quantities.* For example, the monopolist might sell the first 10 units for $10 each, the next 20 units at $9 each, and so on.

If it charges a different price in different markets, or charges a different price to different segments of the buying population, the monopolist practices **third-degree price discrimination.** This is sometimes called *discrimination among buyers.* For example, if your local pharmacy charges senior citizens lower prices for medicine than it charges nonsenior citizens, it practices third-degree price discrimination.

Why Would the Monopolist Want to Price Discriminate?

Suppose these are the maximum prices at which the following units of a product can be sold: first unit, $10; second unit, $9; third unit, $8; fourth unit, $7. If the monopolist wants to sell four units, and it charges the same price for each unit (it is a single-price monopolist), its total revenue is $28 ($7 $\times$ 4).

Now suppose the monopolist *can* and *does* practice perfect price discrimination. It charges $10 for the first unit, $9 for the second unit, $8 for the third unit, and $7 for the fourth unit. Its total revenue is $34 ($10 + $9 + $8 + $7). A comparison of total revenue when the monopolist does and does not price discriminate tells us why the monopolist would want to price discriminate. A perfectly price-discriminating monopolist receives the maximum price for each unit of the good it sells; a single-price monopolist does not.

If the monopolist *perfectly price discriminates,* then for it, price equals marginal revenue, $P = MR$. To illustrate, when the monopolist sells its second unit for $9 (having sold the first unit for $10), its total revenue is $19—or its marginal revenue is $9, which is equal to price.

Conditions of Price Discrimination

It is obvious why the monopolist would want to price discriminate. But what conditions must exist before it can? To price discriminate, the following conditions must hold.

1. The seller must exercise some control over price; it must be a price searcher.

Price Discrimination
Occurs when the seller charges different prices for the product it sells, and the price differences do not reflect cost differences.

Perfect Price Discrimination
Occurs when the seller charges the highest price each consumer would be willing to pay for the product rather than go without it.

Second-Degree Price Discrimination
Occurs when the seller charges a uniform price per unit for one specific quantity, a lower price for an additional quantity, and so on.

Third-Degree Price Discrimination
Occurs when the seller charges different prices in different markets, or charges a different price to different segments of the buying population.

2. The seller must be able to distinguish among customers who would be willing to pay different prices.

3. It must be impossible or too costly for one buyer to resell the good to other buyers. The possibility of **arbitrage,** or "buying low and selling high," must not exist.

If the seller is not a price searcher, it has no control over price and therefore cannot sell a good at different prices to different buyers. Also, unless the seller can distinguish among buyers who would pay different prices, it cannot price discriminate. After all, how would it know to whom to charge the higher (lower) prices? Finally, if a buyer can resell the good, there can be no price discrimination because buyers who buy the good at a lower price will simply turn around and sell the good to other buyers for a price lower than the seller's higher price. In time, no one will pay the higher price.

Many movie theaters charge lower prices to matinee moviegoers than to evening moviegoers. It is possible to price discriminate this way because matinee moviegoers cannot resell their seats to evening moviegoers.

Moving to $P = MC$ through Price Discrimination

The perfectly competitive firm exhibits resource allocative efficiency; it produces the quantity of output at which $P = MC$.

What about the single-price monopolist? It produces the quantity of output at which $P > MC$. A quick glance back at Exhibit 25–4 confirms this. At Q_1, price is P_1, which is higher than marginal cost (MC_1). The single-price monopolist produces an inefficient level of output. But what about the monopolist that can and does practice perfect price discrimination? Does it, too, produce an inefficient level of output?

The answer is no. A perfectly price-discriminating monopolist does not lower price on all previous units in order to sell an additional unit of its product. For it, $P = MR$ (as was the case for the perfectly competitive firm). Naturally, when the perfectly price-discriminating monopolist produces the quantity of output at which $MR = MC$, it automatically produces the quantity where $P = MC$. In short, the perfectly price-discriminating monopolist and the perfectly competitive firm both exhibit resource allocative efficiency.

Some important points are reviewed in Exhibit 25–8. In (a), we see that the perfectly competitive firm produces where $P = MC$. In (b), the single-price monopolist produces where $P > MC$. In (c), the perfectly price-discriminating monopolist produces where $P = MC$. Notice one important difference between the perfectly competitive firm and the perfectly price-discriminating monopolist. Although both produce where $P = MC$, the perfectly competitive firm charges the same price for each unit of the good it sells, and the perfectly price-discriminating monopolist charges a different price for each unit of the good it sells.

Question:

Suppose a firm charges one person $40 for its product and charges another person only $33. Isn't the first person paying a higher price so that the second person can pay a lower price?

Answer:

No, this is not the case. Suppose there are two persons, O'Neill and Stevens. The maximum price O'Neill will pay for good X is $40; the maximum price Stevens

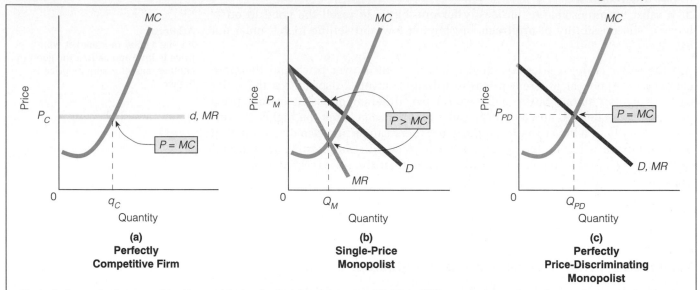

(a)
Perfectly Competitive Firm

(b)
Single-Price Monopolist

(c)
Perfectly Price-Discriminating Monopolist

For both the perfectly competitive firm and the perfectly price-discriminating monopolist, $P = MR$ and the demand curve is the marginal revenue curve. Both produce where $P = MC$. The single-price monopolist, however, produces where $P > MC$, since for it $P > MR$ and its demand curve lies above its marginal revenue curve. One difference between the perfectly competitive firm and the perfectly price-discriminating monopolist is that the former charges the same price for each unit of the good it sells, and the latter charges a different price for each unit of the good it sells.

will pay for good X is \$33. If a monopolist can and does perfectly price discriminate, it charges O'Neill \$40 and Stevens \$33.

Is O'Neill somehow paying the higher price so that Stevens can pay the lower price? It is easy to see that O'Neill is not by asking if the monopolist would have charged O'Neill a price under \$40 if Stevens's maximum price had been \$39 instead of \$33. Probably it wouldn't—why should it when it could have received O'Neill's maximum price of \$40?

Our point is that the perfectly price-discriminating monopolist tries to get the highest price from each customer, irrespective of what other customers pay. In short, the price O'Neill is charged is independent of the price Stevens is charged.

It Looks Like a Deal, It Sounds Like a Deal, but Is It a Deal?

Sellers sometimes advertise one unit of their good for \$X, but two units of the same good for less than \$2X. For example, a department store might advertise one pair of men's trousers at \$40, but two pairs for \$70 (which is \$10 less than \$40 twice). At first sight, this might appear to be quite a deal. Whether it is or not is a personal judgment. What it is for certain, however, is an act of price discrimination.

Look at the situation in terms of an individual's demand curve for trousers. In Exhibit 25–9, Brennen's demand curve tells us he will buy only one pair of trousers if the price is \$40 a pair, but that he will buy two pairs if the price is \$30 a pair.

Suppose the department store wishes to sell Brennen two pairs of trousers. How might it go about this? It could price trousers at \$30 a pair, and Brennen would buy two pairs. Under this pricing scheme, the department store receives $60 total revenue. Or it could price the first pair at $40, and the second pair at $30—for a total of $70 for two. Will Brennen be willing to pay $40 for the first pair of trousers and $30 for the second pair? From his demand curve, we see that he will. Under this pricing scheme, the department store receives $70 total revenue.

Here's another point to think about. Trousers can be resold. It is possible for Brennen to buy hundreds of pairs of trousers—at $70 for each two pairs—and then resell them for, say, $39 a pair; thus, he is undercutting the department store by a dollar (assuming there are numerous buyers who have the same demand curve, or close to the same demand curve, that Brennen has for trousers). In short, there is room for arbitrage here. However, taking advantage of buying low and selling high may be too costly for Brennen. For him, it may not be worth buying hundreds of pairs of trousers, setting up a shop, advertising trousers for sale, and putting up with customer hassles. We conclude that price discrimination can occur, even if arbitrage is possible—as long as arbitrage is too costly for anyone to engage in.

This raises another question: Is Brennen likely to engage in arbitrage if a home-building company offers to sell one house at $95,000 and two houses (of the same quality) at $180,000—$10,000 less than twice the price of one house? Probably he will. In this case, Brennen will likely decide that the cost he must incur to resell one or both of the houses is worth $10,000.

You Can Have the Comics, Just Give Me the Coupons Section

Third-degree price discrimination, or discrimination among buyers, is sometimes employed through the use of cents-off coupons. (Remember that third-degree price discrimination exists if a seller sells the same product at different prices to different segments of the population.)

As you know, one of the conditions of price discrimination is that the seller has to be able to distinguish among customers who would be willing to pay different prices.

Ask yourself if people who value their time highly are more willing to pay a higher price for a product than people who do not? Some sellers think so. They argue that people who place a high value on their time want to economize on the *shopping time* connected with the purchase of the product. If sellers want to price discriminate between these two types of customers—charging more to customers who value time more and charging less to customers who value time less—they must determine the category into which each of their customers falls.

How would you go about this if you were a seller? What many real-world sellers do is place cents-off coupons in newspapers and magazines. They hypothesize that people who value their time relatively low will spend it clipping and sorting coupons. The people who place a relatively high value on their time will not.

In effect, things work much like this in, say, a grocery store:

1. The posted price for all products is the same for all customers.
2. Both Linda and Josh put product X in their shopping carts.
3. When Linda gets up to the counter, the clerk asks, "Do you have any coupons today?" Linda says no. She is therefore charged the posted price for all products, including X.
4. When Josh gets up to the counter, the clerk asks, "Do you have any coupons today?" Josh says yes and pulls out a coupon for product X. Josh pays a lower price for product X than Linda pays.

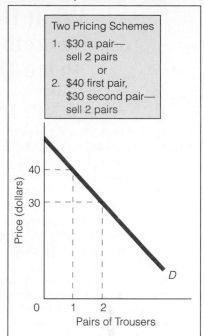

Two Pricing Schemes
1. $30 a pair—
   sell 2 pairs
   or
2. $40 first pair,
   $30 second pair—
   sell 2 pairs

Given the demand curve in the exhibit, two different pricing schemes present themselves. First, $30 can be charged for each pair of trousers, at which price two pairs of trousers will be sold and total revenue will be $60. Second, $40 can be charged for the first pair of trousers, $30 for the second, and two pairs of trousers will be sold bringing in total revenue of $70.

What Do High Grades, Low Income, and Basketball Star Quality Have To Do with Price Discrimination at Your College or University?

Scholarships are often given out by universities. Usually, these scholarships are given to students with (1) low incomes, (2) excellent grades, or (3) some athletic ability (to top-notch basketball or football players for example). Many economists have argued that the university is price discriminating when it gives out these scholarships.

First, the low-income student might not come to the university unless he or she receives a lower tuition price (than what other students pay). The scholarship, in effect, reduces the tuition the low-income student has to pay.

Second, the high-academic achiever and the high-athletic achiever have numerous universities competing for them. Consequently, a university will have to offer them a lower tuition price in order to secure them as stu-

dents. The academic scholarship accomplishes this for the high-academic achiever just as the athletic scholarship does so for the high-athletic achiever. In other words, both the high-academic and high-athletic achiever have a high elasticity of demand for education at a given university, since they have so many substitutes (other universities) from which to choose.* A university acknowledges this fact when it practices price discrimination through scholarships.

Finally, let us consider if the university meets the conditions of a price discriminator. First, it is a price searcher, since not all universities are alike, nor do they sell a homogeneous

good as they do in the case of perfect competition (price taker).

Second, the university can distinguish between students (customers) who would be willing to pay different prices. For example, the student with few universities seeking him would probably be willing to pay more than the student with many options.

Third, the service being purchased cannot be resold to someone else. For example, it would be difficult to resell an economics lecture. You could of course tell someone what was covered in the lecture, perhaps for a small payment or perhaps for a promise to do the same for you at a later time, but it would be similar to telling someone about a movie instead of the person seeing the movie herself. It is often difficult or impossible to resell something that is consumed on the premises.

*In Chapter 21, we noted that the more substitutes there are for a good, the greater the price elasticity of demand.

In conclusion, one of the uses of the cents-off coupon is to make it possible for the seller to charge a higher price to one group of customers than to another group. (We say *one* of the uses, because cents-off coupons are also used to induce customers to try a product and so forth.)

In Perspective

We know that firms prefer to face fewer and more flexible constraints than more and less flexible constraints. With this in mind, consider the issues of rent seeking and price discrimination.

Rent Seeking. If a firm could choose to be either a perfectly competitive firm or a monopoly firm, it would prefer to be a monopoly firm, *ceteris paribus.* This is because a monopoly firm faces fewer constraints: A perfectly competitive firm faces the constraint of competition from sellers of a homogeneous product; a monopoly firm does not.

So, monopoly rent-seeking behavior can be viewed as directed toward a particular objective: to "buy" a monopoly position where fewer constraints are faced. In short, if the monopoly position is more valuable to a seller than the perfectly competitive position—since in perfect competition there is competition from sellers of homogeneous goods and in monopoly there is not—then we would expect that firms would spend resources to "buy" the fewer-constraint monopoly position. In the objective–constraint–choice framework, rent seeking is an activity directed at buying fewer constraints.

Price Discrimination.   The single-price monopolist is constrained in its behavior: It must charge the same price to all its customers. We would expect the single-price monopolist to try to find ways around this particular constraint, since it would rather charge each customer the highest price he or she would be willing to pay. We know, though, that before a firm can price discriminate it must (1) exercise some control over price, and (2) be able to distinguish among customers who would be willing to pay different prices. In addition, (3) it must be impossible or too costly for one buyer to resell the good to other buyers. We predict that we would see some firms in the real world working toward the establishment of one or more of these conditions.[8] The use of cents-off coupons, discussed earlier, can be seen in this light; it is an attempt by sellers to distinguish among customers who would be willing to pay different prices.

Consider also a common practice among car salespersons. It is customary when buying a new or used car to do some haggling and not simply pay the sticker price. However, the salesperson wants to sell the car for a price as close to the sticker price as possible. In his attempt to meet this objective, he will often ask the customer what kind of work he or she does. If the customer answers truthfully, the salesperson then has some idea of the customer's income. For example, if the customer says that she is a physician, the salesperson will know that the person is a high-income earner and will be able, if not necessarily willing, to pay a higher price for the car than a blue-collar worker. In short, the salesperson's attempt to secure this kind of information is part of his attempt to distinguish among customers who *may be* willing to pay different prices for the car.

CHAPTER SUMMARY

The Theory of Monopoly

■ The theory of monopoly is built on three assumptions: (1) There is one seller. (2) The single seller sells a product for which there are no close substitutes. (3) There are extremely high barriers to entry into the industry.
■ High barriers to entry may take the form of legal barriers (public franchise, patent, government license), economies of scale, and exclusive ownership of a scarce resource.

[8]A firm need not work toward the establishment of all three conditions if one or more is already met. For example, a firm may already be a price searcher and thus exert some control over its price, and it may sell a product that is difficult for customers to resell. Since it already satisfies two out of three conditions needed to price discriminate, we would expect to see it trying to distinguish among customers who would be willing to pay different prices.

Monopoly Pricing and Output

■ The profit-maximizing monopolist produces the quantity of output at which $MR = MC$ and charges the highest price per unit at which this quantity of output can be sold.

■ For the single-price monopolist, $P > MR$; therefore, its demand curve lies above its marginal revenue curve.

■ The single-price monopolist sells its output at a price higher than its marginal cost, $P > MC$.

Monopoly Profits in the Long Run

■ Monopoly profits are not competed away by the entry of new firms into the industry (as profits are in perfect competition). In monopoly, there are barriers to entering the industry. However, profits may be (1) capitalized into the price of the monopoly firm if it is being sold or (2) competed for indirectly through rent-seeking actions.

Rent Seeking

■ Economic or monopoly rent is a payment in excess of opportunity cost. Monopoly profits are rents. Activity directed at competing for and obtaining rent is referred to as rent seeking. From society's perspective, rent seeking is a socially wasteful activity. People use resources to affect a transfer of the rent from others to themselves instead of producing goods and services.

Price Discrimination

■ Price discrimination occurs when a seller charges different prices for its product, and the price differences are not due to cost differences.

■ Before a seller can price discriminate, certain conditions must hold: (1) The seller must be a price searcher. (2) The seller must be able to distinguish among customers who would be willing to pay different prices. (3) It must be impossible or too costly for a buyer to resell the good to others.

■ A seller that practices perfect price discrimination (charges the maximum price for each unit of product sold) sells the quantity of output at which $P = MC$. It exhibits resource allocative efficiency.

■ The single-price monopolist is said to produce too little output, since it produces less than would be produced under perfect competition. This is not the case for a perfectly price-discriminating monopolist.

Key Terms and Concepts

Monopoly	Welfare Cost of Monopoly	Perfect Price Discrimination
Public Franchise	Welfare Cost Triangle	Second-Degree Price Discrimination
Natural Monopoly	X-Inefficiency	
Price Searcher	Price Discrimination	Third-Degree Price Discrimination
Economic or Monopoly Rent		Arbitrage

1. The perfectly competitive firm exhibits resource allocative efficiency ($P = MC$), and the single-price monopolist does not. What is the reason for this difference?

2. Since the monopolist is a single seller of a product with no close substitutes, is it able to obtain any price for its good that it wants?

3. When a single-price monopolist maximizes profits, price is greater than marginal cost. This means that consumers would be willing to pay more for additional units of output than they cost to produce. Given this, why doesn't the monopolist produce more?

4. Is there a welfare cost triangle if the firm produces the quantity of output at which price equals marginal cost?

5. It has been noted that rent seeking is individually rational, but socially wasteful. Explain.

6. Occasionally, students accuse their instructors, rightly or wrongly, of practicing grade discrimination. What these students mean is that the instructor "charges" some students a higher price for a given grade than other students (by requiring some students to do more or better). Grade discrimination involves no money, price discrimination does. Discuss the similarities and differences between the two types of discrimination. Which do you prefer less or perhaps dislike more? Why?

7. Make a list of real-world price discrimination practices. Do they meet the conditions posited for price discrimination?

8. For many years in California, car washes would advertise "Ladies Day." This was one day out of the week when a woman could have her car washed for a price lower than a man could have his car washed. It was argued that this was a form of sexual discrimination. The argument was accepted, and a California court ruled that there could no longer be a "Ladies Day." Do you think this was a case of sexual discrimination or price discrimination? Explain your answer.

9. Make a list of both market monopolies and government monopolies. Which list is longer? Why do you think this is so?

10. Fast-food stores often charge higher prices for their products in high-crime areas than in low-crime areas. Is this an act of price discrimination? Why?

11. Coupons are usually more common on small-ticket items than on big-ticket items. Explain why.

12. Fill in the blanks.

Price ($)	Quantity Demanded	Total Revenue ($)	Marginal Revenue ($)	Total Cost ($)	Marginal Cost ($)	Profit or Loss
18	0	_____		10		
15	2	_____	_____	14	_____	_____
11	5	_____	_____	19	_____	_____
9	7	_____	_____	25	_____	_____
7	10	_____	_____	31	_____	_____
0	25	_____	_____	38	_____	_____

MONOPOLISTIC COMPETITION AND OLIGOPOLY

WHAT THIS CHAPTER IS ABOUT

In this chapter, we discuss monopolistic competition and oligopoly. Monopolistic competition is a market structure that is said to combine elements of both perfect competition and monopoly. Oligopoly is a market structure that is dominated by a small number of firms, for which several theories have been developed.

THE THEORY OF MONOPOLISTIC COMPETITION

The theory of **monopolistic competition** is built on three assumptions:

1. There are many sellers and buyers. This assumption held for perfect competition, too. For this reason, you might think the monopolistic competitor is a price taker, but this is not the case. It is a price searcher, basically because of the following assumption.

2. Each firm (in the industry) produces and sells a slightly differentiated product. Differences among the products may be due to brand names, packaging, location, credit terms connected with the sale of the product, friendliness of the salespeople, and so forth. Product differentiation may be real or imagined. For example, aspirin may be aspirin, but if some people view a name-brand aspirin (such as Bayer) as better than a generic brand, product differentiation exists.

3. There is easy entry and exit. Monopolistic competition resembles perfect competition in this respect. There are no barriers to entry and exit, legal or otherwise.

Examples of monopolistic competition include retail clothing, restaurants, textbook publishing, and service stations.

Monopolistic Competition
A theory of market structure based on three assumptions: many sellers and buyers, firms producing and selling slightly differentiated products, and easy entry and exit.

Question:

Is the breakfast cereal industry an example of monopolistic competition? After all, there are many different cereals on the market: Crispix, Cracklin' Oat Bran, Apple Cinnamon Squares, Frosted Mini-Wheats, Cheerios, Cocoa Krispies, Rice Krispies, Raisin Bran, Corn Flakes, Frosted Flakes, Nutri-Grain, Product 19, Apple Raisin Crisp, to name only a few.

Answer:

With the exception of Cheerios, all the cereals mentioned are produced by *one* firm, Kellogg. Cheerios is made by General Mills. Just because there are many different cereals, it does not necessarily follow that many firms make these cereals. In fact, there are relatively few firms in the cereal industry; thus, the cereal industry is an example of oligopoly (few sellers). We discuss this market structure later.

You Already Know More about Monopolistic Competition than You Think: Answer These Questions and See

You have already studied two theories of market structures, perfect competition and monopoly. Using your knowledge of these theories and the assumptions of the theory of monopolistic competition, what do you think the theory of monopolistic competition predicts?

First, do you think the monopolistic competitor (or monopolistic competitive firm) faces a horizontal or downward-sloping demand curve? The answer is downward sloping. The assumption of product differentiation tells us this. Because of product differentiation, each monopolistic competitor has some control over the price of the product it sells. Because its product is slightly different from other firms', it can raise price and still sell some of its product. In short, it is a *price searcher.*

Second, is the demand curve facing the monopolistic competitive firm more elastic or less elastic than the demand curve facing the monopoly seller? It is more elastic. Why? As the discussion of elasticity in Chapter 21 explained, the more substitutes a good has, the greater the price elasticity of demand for the good. In monopolistic competition, there are substitutes; in monopoly, there are none. Therefore, we predict that the demand curve facing a monopolistic competitor will be more elastic than the demand curve facing a monopoly seller.

Third, will $P = MR$ (as in perfect competition), or will $P > MR$ (as in monopoly)? The answer is $P > MR$. The reason is that the monopolistic competitor faces a *downward-sloping* demand curve. This means it has to lower price to sell an additional unit of the good. It follows that in monopolistic competition, the demand curve facing the firm lies above its marginal revenue curve.

Fourth, does the monopolistic competitor exhibit resource allocative efficiency? The answer is no. Since it maximizes profits by producing the quantity of output at which $MR = MC$ (all firms, no matter what the market structure, do this), and $P > MR$, it follows that $P > MC$ at the quantity of output at which the monopolistic competitive firm produces. Like the monopolist, the monopolistic competitor produces the quantity of output at which $MR = MC$ and charges the highest possible price per unit for the output (Exhibit 26–1a).

Fifth, will there be economic profits in the long run? Most likely, there won't be. The assumption of easy entry and exit precludes this. If firms in the industry are earning profits, new firms will enter the industry and compete them away (Exhibit 26–1b).

Question:

To the question of whether there will be profits in the long run, the answer was "Most likely, there won't be." Why was the answer qualified by "most likely"? Why not simply "no"?

Answer:

The answer was qualified by "most likely" because monopolistic competition differs from perfect competition, where short-run profits attract new firms that produce the *identical* product produced by existing firms in the industry. In monopolistic competition, new firms usually produce a *close substitute* for the product produced by existing firms. Is this enough of a difference to upset the zero economic profit condition in the long run? In some instances, it may be. An existing firm may differentiate its product sufficiently in the minds of the buying public that although new firms enter the industry and compete with it, it still continues to earn profits. Firms that try to differentiate their products from those of other sellers in ways other than in price are said to be engaged in *nonprice competition*. This may take the form of advertising or trying to establish a brand name that is well respected, among other things. For example, soft drink companies' advertising often tries to stress the uniqueness of their product. Dr. Pepper has been advertised as "the unusual one," 7-Up as "the uncola." IBM has a well-respected name in personal computers, Bayer in aspirin, Hilton in hotels. Such well-respected names sometimes differentiate products enough in the minds of the buying public so that short-run profits are not easily, or completely, competed away by the entry of new firms into the industry.

Excess Capacity Theorem
States that a monopolistic competitor in equilibrium produces an output smaller than the one that would minimize its costs of production.

Excess Capacity: What Is It, and Is It "Good" or "Bad"?

The theory of monopolistic competition makes one major prediction, which is generally referred to as the **excess capacity theorem.** It states that in equilibrium,

EXHIBIT 26–1

The Monopolistic Competitor in the Short Run and in the Long Run

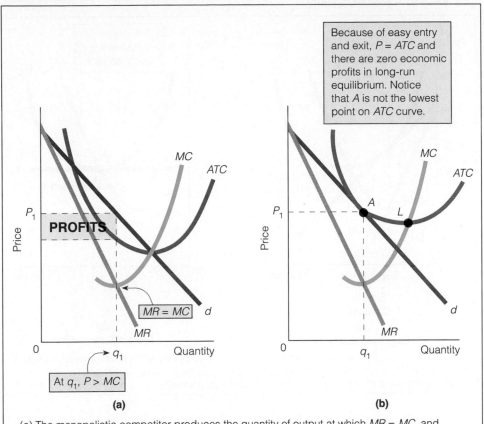

Because of easy entry and exit, $P = ATC$ and there are zero economic profits in long-run equilibrium. Notice that A is not the lowest point on ATC curve.

(a)

(b)

(a) The monopolistic competitor produces the quantity of output at which $MR = MC$, and charges the highest price per unit consistent with this output. Notice that at q_1, $P > MC$. This seller is receiving short-run profits. It is not likely that these profits will continue, however, because there is easy entry in the theory of monopolistic competition. (b) Because of easy entry, any short-run profits will most likely be competed away in the long run by new firms entering the industry. Because of easy exit, any short-run losses will disappear in the long run owing to some firms exiting the industry. In long-run equilibrium, price equals short-run average total cost, and there will be zero economic profits.

a monopolistic competitor will produce an output smaller than the one that would minimize its costs of production.

To illustrate, look at point A in Exhibit 26–2a. At this point, the monopolistic competitor is in long-run equilibrium since profits are zero ($P = ATC$). Now notice that point A is *not* the lowest point on the average total cost curve. The lowest point on the average total cost curve is point L. We conclude that in long-run equilibrium, when the monopolistic competitor earns zero economic profits, it is not producing the quantity of output at which average total costs (unit costs) are minimized for the given scale of plant.

In Exhibit 26–2, we also can contrast the perfectly competitive firm and the monopolistic competitor in long-run equilibrium. In (b), the perfectly competitive firm is earning zero economic profits and price (P_{C1}) equals average total cost (ATC). Furthermore, the point at which price equals average total cost (point L) is the lowest point on the average total cost curve. In long-run equilibrium, the per-

EXHIBIT 26–2

A Comparison of Perfect Competition and Monopolistic Competition: The Issue of Excess Capacity

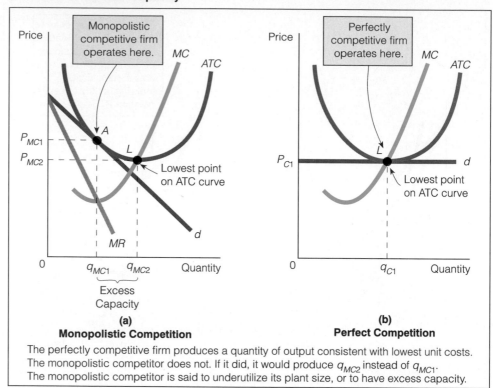

(a)
Monopolistic Competition

(b)
Perfect Competition

The perfectly competitive firm produces a quantity of output consistent with lowest unit costs. The monopolistic competitor does not. If it did, it would produce q_{MC2} instead of q_{MC1}. The monopolistic competitor is said to underutilize its plant size, or to have excess capacity.

fectly competitive firm produces the quantity of output at which unit costs are minimized.

Now look back at (a). Here the monopolistic competitor is earning zero economic profits and price (P_{MC1}) equals average total cost. As previously noted, the monopolistic competitor does not produce the quantity of output at which unit costs are minimized. If it did, it would produce quantity of output q_{MC2}. Because of this, it has been argued that the monopolistic competitor produces "too little" output (q_{MC1} instead of q_{MC2}) and charges "too high" a price (P_{MC1} instead of P_{MC2}). With respect to the former, "too little" output translates into the monopolistic competitor *underutilizing* its present plant size. It is said to have *excess capacity*. In (a), the excess capacity is equal to the difference between q_{MC2} and q_{MC1}.

It is sometimes argued that the monopolistic competitor operates at excess capacity because it faces a downward-sloping demand curve. To see this, once again turn to Exhibit 26–2a. Notice that the only way the firm would not operate at excess capacity is if its demand curve were tangent to point L—the lowest point on the *ATC* curve. But for this to occur, the demand curve must be horizontal, which would require *homogeneous products*. There is no possible way for a downward-sloping demand curve to be tangent to point L. In short, the monopolistic competitor operates at excess capacity as a consequence of its downward-sloping demand curve, and its downward-sloping demand curve is a consequence of differentiated products. We leave you with a question many economists ask, but do not always answer the same way: If excess capacity is the price we pay for differentiated products (more choice), is it too high a price?

Oligopoly: Assumptions and Real-World Behavior

There is no one theory of **oligopoly** as there is for perfect competition, monopoly, and monopolistic competition. The different theories of oligopoly do make some common assumptions, however:

1. **There are few sellers and many buyers.** It is usually assumed that the few firms of an oligopoly are mutually interdependent; each one is aware that its actions will influence the other firms and that the actions of other firms affect it. The interdependence among firms is a key characteristic of oligopoly.

2. **Firms produce and sell either homogeneous or differentiated products.** Steel is a homogeneous product produced in an oligopolistic market; cars are a differentiated product produced in an oligopolistic market. The oligopolist is a price searcher. Like all other types of firms, it produces the quantity of output at which $MR = MC$.

3. **There are significant barriers to entry.** Economies of scale are perhaps the most significant barrier to entry in oligopoly theory, but patent rights, exclusive control over an essential resource, and legal barriers also act as barriers to entry here.

Oligopoly in the Real World

Which industries today are dominated by a small number of firms? Economists have developed the **concentration ratio** to help answer this question. This is the percentage of industry sales (or assets, output, labor force, or some other factor) accounted for by *x*-number of firms in the industry. The "*x*-number" in the definition is usually four or eight, but it can be any number (although it is usually small). A high ratio implies that few sellers make up the industry; a low concentration ratio implies that more than a few sellers make up the industry.

Suppose we calculate a four-firm concentration ratio for industry Z. Total industry sales for a given year are $5 million, and the four largest firms in the industry account for $4.5 million in sales. The four-firm concentration ratio would be .90 or 90 percent ($4.5 million is .90 of $5 million). Industries with high four- and eight-firm concentration ratios in recent years include cigarettes, cars, tires and inner tubes, cereal breakfast foods, telephone and telegraph, farm machinery, and soap and other detergents, to name a few.

Note, however, that although concentration ratios are often used to determine the extent (or degree) of oligopoly, they are not perfect guides to industry concentration. Most important, they do not take into account foreign competition and competition from substitute domestic goods. For example, the U.S. automobile industry is highly concentrated, but it still faces stiff competition from abroad. A more relevant concentration ratio for this particular industry might be computed on a worldwide basis.

Price and Output Under Oligopoly: Three Theories

Oligopoly is a more difficult market structure to analyze than perfect competition, monopoly, and monopolistic competition, largely owing to the interdependence among firms in oligopoly. When such interdependence exists, the significant variable becomes the reaction of one firm to the actions of one or more of the other

Oligopoly
A theory of market structure based on three assumptions: few sellers and many buyers, firms producing either homogeneous or differentiated products, and significant barriers to entry.

Concentration Ratio
The percentage of industry sales (or assets, output, labor force, or some other factor) accounted for by *x*-number of firms in the industry.

firms. Because many possible assumptions can be made about a firm's reactions, a number of different oligopoly theories exist. Here we discuss three: the kinked demand curve theory, the price leadership theory, and the cartel theory.

The Kinked Demand Curve Theory

Kinked Demand Curve Theory
A theory of oligopoly that assumes that if a single firm in the industry cuts price, other firms will do likewise, but if it raises price, other firms will not follow suit. The theory predicts price stickiness or rigidity.

The behavioral assumption in the **kinked demand curve theory** is that if a single firm lowers price, other firms will do likewise, but if a single firm raises price, other firms will not follow suit. Suppose there are five firms in an industry, A, B, C, D, and E. If firm A raises its price, the other firms maintain their prices. If firm A cuts its price, the other firms match the price cut.

The kinked demand curve theory, developed in the 1930s by Paul Sweezy, is portrayed in Exhibit 26–3. The current price being charged by the firm is $25. If the firm raises its price to $27, other firms will not match it, and therefore the firm's sales will drop off (from 20 to 10). In short, the demand curve for the firm above $25 is highly elastic. However, if the firm should lower its price to, say, $23, other firms will match the price cut, and therefore the firm's sales will not increase by much (only from 20 to 22). Demand is much less elastic below $25 than above it. We conclude that there is a *kink* in the firm's demand curve at the current price (the letter *K* in Exhibit 26–3). The kink signifies that other firms respond radically differently to a single firm's price hikes than to its price cuts.

EXHIBIT 26–3
Kinked Demand Curve Theory

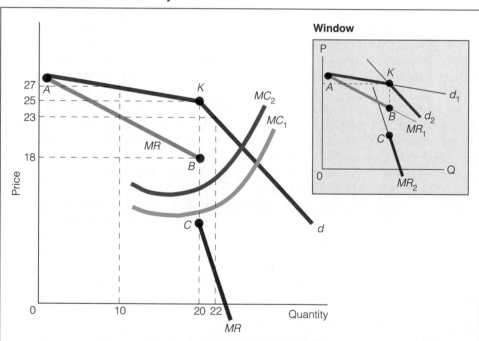

The key behavioral assumption of the theory is that rival firms will not match a price hike but will match a price cut. The theory predicts that changes in marginal costs in area *B* to *C* will not bring changes in price or output. In the window in the exhibit, we see two demand curves and two marginal revenue curves. The firm believes it faces d_2, the more inelastic demand curve, if it cuts price; the firm believes it faces d_1, the more elastic demand curve, when it raises price. The relevant portions of each demand curve are indicated by heavy lines. We show only the relevant parts of the demand curves in the main diagram in the exhibit.

Actually, there are two demand curves and two marginal revenue curves, as we have shown in the window in Exhibit 26–3. Only the thicker portions of the curves in the window are relevant, however, and thus appear in the main diagram. To illustrate, starting at a price of $25, the firm believes price cuts will be matched but price hikes will not. This says that when considering a price cut, the firm believes it faces the more inelastic of the two demand curves, d_2 instead of d_1, and the corresponding marginal revenue curve, MR_2 instead of MR_1. But when considering a price hike, the firm believes it faces the more elastic of the two demand curves, d_1 instead of d_2, and the corresponding marginal revenue curve, MR_1 instead of MR_2. It follows that the demand curve and the marginal revenue curve the firm faces are part of d_2 and part of MR_2, and part of d_1 and part of MR_1, respectively, dependent on whether it is considering a price cut or hike.

Question:

Why do firms match price cuts but not price hikes?

Answer:

It has been argued that firms match price cuts because failure to do so will result in their losing a large share of the market. They do not match price hikes because they hope to gain in market share.

Price Rigidity and Oligopoly.   Notice the marginal revenue curve for the oligopolist in the main diagram of Exhibit 26–3. Directly below the kink, it drops off sharply. In fact, we may see the marginal revenue curve as three segments: a line from point *A* to point *B*, which corresponds to the upper part of the demand curve; a gap between points *B* and *C*, which comes directly below the kink in the demand curve; and a line from point *C* onward, which corresponds to the lower part of the demand curve from point *K* onward.

The gap between points *B* and *C* represents the sharp change in marginal revenue that comes about once price is lowered below the kink on the demand curve. The gap helps explain why prices might be less flexible (more rigid) in oligopoly than in other market structures. We recall that the oligopolistic firm produces the output at which marginal revenue equals marginal cost. For the firm in Exhibit 26–3, though, marginal cost can change between points *B* and *C*, and the firm will continue to produce the same quantity of output and charge the same price. For example, an increase in marginal cost from MC_1 to MC_2 will not lead to a change in production levels or price.

To put it differently, prices are "sticky" if oligopolistic firms face kinked demand curves. Costs can change within certain limits, and such firms will not change their prices because they expect that none of their competitors will follow their price hikes, but that all will match their price cuts.

Criticisms of the Kinked Demand Curve Theory.   The kinked demand curve (and resulting *MR* curve) posits that prices in oligopoly will be less flexible (or more rigid) than in other market structures. The theory has been criticized on both theoretical and empirical grounds. On a theoretical level, looking at Exhibit 26–3, the theory fails to explain how the original price of $25 came about. In other words, why does the *kink* come at $25? It is a theory that is better at explaining things once the kink (the current price) has been identified than in explaining the placement of the kink.

On empirical grounds, the theory has been challenged as a *general theory of oligopoly*. For example, economist George Stigler found no evidence that the oligopolists he examined were more reluctant to match price increases than price cuts, which calls into question the behavioral assumption behind the kinked demand curve.

The Price Leadership Theory

Price Leadership Theory
In this theory of oligopoly, the dominant firm in the industry determines price, and all other firms take their price as given.

The key behavioral assumption in the **price leadership theory** is that one firm in the industry—called the dominant firm—determines price, and all other firms take this price as given. Suppose there are ten firms in an industry, A–J, and that firm A is the dominant firm; assume also that it is much larger than its rival firms (although the dominant firm need not be the largest firm in the industry, it could be the low-cost firm). The dominant firm sets the price that maximizes its profits, and all other firms take this price as given. All other firms, then, are seen as price takers; thus, they will equate price with their respective marginal costs.

This explanation suggests that the dominant firm acts without regard to the other firms in the industry but simply forces other firms to adapt. This is not quite correct. The dominant firm sets the price based on information it has on the other firms in the industry. We see this in Exhibit 26–4.

In (a), the market demand curve and the horizontal sum of the marginal cost curves of the fringe firms (all firms other than the dominant firm) are shown. Since

EXHIBIT 26–4
Price Leadership Theory

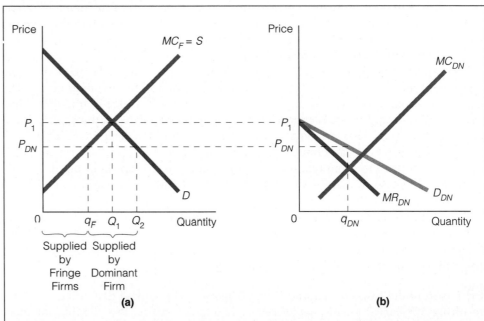

Here we have a dominant firm and a number of fringe firms. (a) The horizontal sum of the marginal cost curves of the fringe firms gives us the supply curve. At P_1, the fringe firms supply the entire market. (b) The dominant firm derives its demand curve by computing the difference between market demand, D, and MC_F at each price below P_1. It then produces q_{DN} and charges P_{DN}. P_{DN} becomes the price that the fringe firms take. They equate price and marginal cost and produce q_F in (a). The remainder of the output—the difference between Q_2 and q_F—is produced by the dominant firm.

these fringe firms are price takers, the marginal cost curve in (a) is the supply curve. The dominant firm observes that at a price of P_1, the fringe firms alone can supply the entire market. They will supply Q_1. In short, P_1 and Q_1 is the situation in the industry or market *that excludes the dominant firm.*

Now add the dominant firm. It derives its demand curve, D_{DN}, by noting how much is left over for it to supply at each given price. For example, at a price of P_1, we noted that the fringe firms would supply the entire market and nothing would be left for the dominant firm to supply. So a price of P_1 and an output of zero is one point on the dominant firm's demand curve, which we see in (b). (Sometimes the dominant firm's demand curve is referred to as the "residual demand curve," for obvious reasons.) The dominant firm continues to locate other points on its demand curve by noting the difference between the market demand curve (D) and MC_F at each price.

Once the dominant firm calculates its residual demand curve, it produces the quantity of output at which its marginal revenue equals its marginal cost. This level is q_{DN} in Exhibit 26–4b. It charges the highest price for this quantity of output, which is P_{DN}. This is the price that the dominant firm sets and the fringe firms take. Since they act as price takers here, they equate P_{DN} with marginal cost and produce q_F, as shown in (a). The remainder of the total output produced by the industry—the difference between Q_2 and q_F—is produced by the dominant firm. This means that the distance from the origin to q_{DN} in (b) is equal to the difference between Q_2 and q_F in (a).

At one time or another, the following firms have been price leaders in their industries: R. J. Reynolds (cigarettes), General Motors (autos), Kellogg (breakfast cereals), and Goodyear Tires and Rubber (tires).

The Cartel Theory

The key behavioral assumption of the **cartel theory** is that oligopolists in an industry act as if there were only one firm in the industry. In short, they form a **cartel** in order to capture the benefits that would exist for a monopolist. A *cartel* is an organization of firms that reduces output and increases price in an effort to increase joint profits.

First, let's illustrate the benefits that may arise from forming and maintaining a cartel. In Exhibit 26–5, we show an *industry* in long-run competitive equilibrium. The price is P_1 and the quantity of output is Q_1. The industry is producing the output at which price equals marginal cost and there are zero economic profits. Now suppose the firms that make up the industry form a cartel and reduce output to Q_C. The new price becomes P_C (cartel price), and there are profits equal to CP_CAB, which can be shared among the members of the cartel. With no cartel, there were no profits; with a cartel, profits are earned. Thus, an incentive exists to form a cartel and behave cooperatively rather than competitively. But even with such an incentive, this does not mean that one can be formed, or if formed, that it will be successfully maintained. Several problems await firms that wish to form and maintain a cartel, in addition to the fact that legislation prohibits certain types of cartels in the United States. There are costs as well as benefits in organizing and forming a cartel.

The Problem of Forming the Cartel. Even if it were legal, getting the sellers of an industry together to form a cartel can be costly, especially when the number of sellers is large. Each potential cartel member might resist incurring the costs of forming the cartel because it stands to benefit more if someone else does it. In

Cartel Theory
In this theory of oligopoly, oligopolistic firms act as if there were only one firm in the industry.

Cartel
An organization of firms that reduces output and increases price in an effort to increase joint profits.

As paradoxical as it first appears, once the cartel agreement is made, there is an incentive . . . to cheat on the agreement.

■

other words, each potential member has an incentive to become a free rider: to stand by and take a free ride on the actions of others.

The Problem of Formulating Cartel Policy.   Suppose the first problem is solved, and potential cartel members form a cartel. Now comes the problem of formulating policy. For example, firm A might propose that each cartel member reduce output by 10 percent, while firm B advocates that all bigger cartel members reduce output by 15 percent and all smaller members reduce output by 6 percent. There may be as many policy proposals as there are cartel members. Reaching agreement may be difficult. Such disagreements are harder to resolve the greater the differences between cartel members in costs, size, and so forth.

The Problem of Entry into the Industry.   Even if the cartel members manage to agree on a policy that generates high profits, those high profits will provide an incentive for firms outside the industry to join the industry. If current cartel members cannot keep new suppliers from entering, the cartel is likely to break up.

The Problem of Cheating.   As paradoxical as it first appears, once the cartel agreement is made, there is an incentive for cartel members to cheat on the agreement. Consider Exhibit 26–6, which shows a representative firm of the cartel. We compare three situations for this firm: first, the situation before the cartel is formed; second, the situation after the cartel is formed when all members adhere to the cartel price; third, the situation if the firm cheats on the cartel agreement, but the other cartel members do not.

  Before the cartel is formed, the firm is in long-run competitive equilibrium; it produces q_1 and charges price P_1. It earns zero economic profits. Next, it reduces its output to q_C as directed by the cartel (the cartel has set a quota for each member), and it charges the cartel price of P_C. It earns profits equal to CP_CAB. Now note what happens if the firm cheats on the cartel agreement and produces q_{CC} instead of the stipulated q_C. As long as other firms do not cheat, this firm views

EXHIBIT 26–5
The Benefits of a Cartel (to Cartel Members)

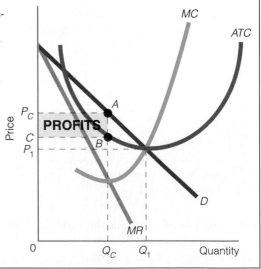

We assume the industry is in long-run competitive equilibrium, producing Q_1 and charging P_1. There are no profits. A reduction in output to Q_C through the formation of a cartel raises price to P_C and brings profits of CP_CAB. (Note: In Chapter 24, we worked with a horizontal demand curve that faced the firm. Here we work with a downward-sloping demand curve that faces the industry. Don't be misled by this difference. No matter what type of demand curve we use, long-run competitive equilibrium comes where $P = MC = SRATC = LRATC$.)

EXHIBIT 26–6
The Benefits of Cheating on the Cartel Agreement

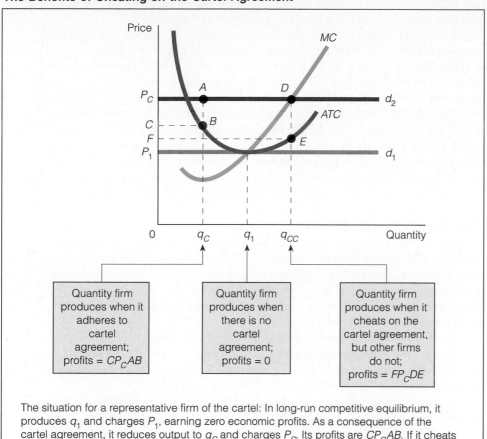

Quantity firm produces when it adheres to cartel agreement; profits = CP_CAB

Quantity firm produces when there is no cartel agreement; profits = 0

Quantity firm produces when it cheats on the cartel agreement, but other firms do not; profits = FP_CDE

The situation for a representative firm of the cartel: In long-run competitive equilibrium, it produces q_1 and charges P_1, earning zero economic profits. As a consequence of the cartel agreement, it reduces output to q_C and charges P_C. Its profits are CP_CAB. If it cheats on the cartel agreement and others do not, the firm will increase output to q_{CC} and reap profits of FP_CDE. Note, however, that if this firm can cheat on the cartel agreement, so can others. Given the monetary benefits that exist from cheating, it is unlikely that the cartel will be around long.

its demand curve as horizontal at the cartel price (P_C). The reason is simple: It is one of a number of firms so it cannot affect price by changing output. Therefore, it can produce and sell additional units of output without lowering price. We conclude that if the firm decides to cheat on the cartel agreement, and other firms do not, then the cheater firm can increase its profits from the smaller amount CP_CAB to the larger amount FP_CDE. Of course, if all firms cheat, we are back where we started—with no cartel agreement and at price P_1.

This illustrates a major theme of cartels: Firms have an incentive to form a cartel, but once it is formed, they have an incentive to cheat. As a result, some economists have concluded that even if cartels can be formed successfully, it is unlikely that they will be effective for long.

An Enforcer of the Cartel Agreement

We often hear that the government is in the business of breaking up cartels. This has happened. However, the role government has played and continues to play in cartels is mixed. On occasion, government has actually helped to create and maintain a cartel instead of breaking it up. There are even cases where the cartel in question wouldn't exist without the government's assistance.

For example, in agriculture, the acreage allotment program (in which the government restricts the number of acres a farmer can plant of a given crop) is aimed at reducing the supply of a crop; this is an objective of farmers who expect a reduction in supply to bring about higher prices, higher revenues, and higher profits. Could the farmers collectively reduce the supply of their crop without government assistance? Would a cartel agreement specifying a lower level of output work? It's not likely. The problems of forming and maintaining a noncheating cartel would probably be too great to overcome. However, a government program that restricts production gets around these problems. A government program that restricts production and a cartel that restricts production have the same outcome.

Along the same lines, consider the Civil Aeronautics Board (CAB) in the days of airline regulation. The CAB was created to protect the airlines from "cutthroat competition." It had the power to set air fares, allocate air routes, and prevent the entry of new carriers into the airline industry. In the days before deregulation, the federal government's General Accounting Office estimated that airline fares would have been, on average, as much as 52 percent lower if the CAB had not been regulating them. Clearly, the CAB was doing for the airlines—preventing price competition among airlines, allocating routes, and preventing competition—what an airline cartel would have done.

As to the Interstate Commerce Commission (ICC), Judge Richard Posner has observed that "the railroads supported the enactment of the first Interstate Commerce Act, which was designed to prevent railroads from price discrimination, because discrimination was undermining the railroad's cartels."[1]

Government is not always the glue that holds a cartel together, but there are numerous examples where it is.

How Is a New Year's Resolution Like a Cartel Agreement?

In a cartel, one firm makes an agreement with another firm or other firms. In a New Year's resolution, you essentially make an agreement with yourself. So in both cases—the cartel and the resolution—there is an agreement.

There is also the possibility of cheating on the agreement in both cases. Suppose your New Year's resolution is to exercise more, take better notes in class, and read one "good" book a month. You might set such objectives for yourself because you know you will be better in the long run if you do these things. But then the short run interjects itself into the picture. You have to decide between exercising today and plopping yourself down in your favorite chair and watching some television. You have to decide between starting on *Moby Dick* and catching up on the latest entertainment news in *People* magazine. The part of you that wants to hold to the resolution is at odds with the part of you that wants to watch television or read *People* magazine. Often the television-watching, *People* magazine-reading part wins out. It is just too easy to break a New Year's resolution—as you perhaps already know.

Similarly, it is easy to break a cartel agreement. For the firm that has entered into the agreement, the lull of higher profits is often too strong to resist. In addition,

[1]Richard A. Posner, "Theories of Regulation," *Bell Journal of Economics and Management Science* 5 (Autumn 1984):337.

the firm is concerned that if it doesn't break the agreement (and cheat), some other firm might, and then it would have lost out completely.

In short, both resolutions and cartel agreements take a lot of will power to hold together. And will power, it seems, is in particularly short supply.

What, then, can take the place of will power? What do both a resolution and a cartel agreement need in order to sustain long life? The answer is an enforcer. Both need an enforcer to enact some penalty on the party that breaks the resolution or cartel agreement. Government sometimes plays this role for firms. Family members and friends will occasionally play this role for individuals by reminding or reprimanding them if they fail to live up to their resolutions. (Usually, though, this is a poor enforcement mechanism.)

We conclude the following: First, an agreement is at the heart of both a New Year's resolution and a cartel. Second, both the resolution and the cartel are subject to cheating behavior. Third, often the resolution and the cartel need an outside enforcer if they are to sustain long life.

In economics, there are moving targets. Consider the target of higher profits for the firms in an oligopolistic industry. Once the firms have formed a cartel to capture the higher profits, the target of higher profits moves—to where a cartel member must cheat on the cartel to "hit" it. But if all cartel members take aim at the new position of the target, the target moves back to its original position—to where cartel members must agree to stop cheating.

The layperson may think that an economic objective, or economic target, is stationary. All that an economic actor has to take is careful aim in order to hit it. But the economist knows that sometimes the target moves and that careful aim is not always enough.

GAME THEORY AND OLIGOPOLY

Game theory is a mathematical technique used to analyze the behavior of decision makers who try to reach an *optimal position* through game playing or the use of *strategic behavior,* are fully aware of the *interactive nature of the process* at hand, and *anticipate the moves* of other decision makers. Game theory is often used to study situations fundamentally like that of two persons playing chess. Chess has all the necessary ingredients. First, it has decision makers who are trying to reach an optimal position (I want to place my opponent in checkmate). Second, each player plans a strategy to meet his or her objective (I will move my pawn here and my castle there, so that my opponent will be forced to move his knight). Third, chess players are aware of the interactive nature of a chess game (what she does influences what I do), and they anticipate each others' moves (I think he will move here, so if I move there now, I will be in a better position).

Prisoner's Dilemma

A well-known game in game theory, called *prisoner's dilemma,* illustrates a case where individually rational behavior leads to a jointly inefficient outcome. It has been described this way: "You do what is best for you, I'll do what is best for me, and somehow we end up in a situation that is not best for either of us." Here are the mechanics of the prisoner's dilemma game.

Game Theory
A mathematical technique used to analyze the behavior of decision makers who try to reach an optimal position for themselves through game playing or the use of strategic behavior, are fully aware of the interactive nature of the process at hand, and anticipate the moves of other decision makers.

The Facts.   Two men, Bob and Nathan, are arrested and charged with jointly committing a crime. They are put in separate cells so that they cannot communicate with each other. The district attorney goes to each man separately and says the following:

- If you confess to the crime and agree to turn state's evidence, and your accomplice does not confess, I will let you off with a $500 fine.
- If your accomplice confesses to the crime and agrees to turn state's evidence, and you do not confess, I will fine you $5,000.
- If both you and your accomplice remain silent and refuse to confess to the crime, I will charge you with a lesser crime (which I can prove you committed), and both you and your accomplice will end up paying a fine of $2,000.
- If both you and your accomplice confess, I will fine each of you $3,000.

The Options and Consequences.   Each man has two choices: confess or not confess. We show these choices on the grid in Exhibit 26–7. According to the possibilities laid out by the district attorney, if both men do not confess, each pays a fine of $2,000. This is shown in Box 1 in the exhibit.

If Nathan confesses and Bob does not, then Nathan gets off with the light fine of $500, and Bob pays the stiff penalty of $5,000. This is shown in Box 2.

If Nathan does not confess and Bob confesses, then Nathan ends up with the stiff penalty of $5,000, and Bob pays the light fine of $500. This is shown in Box 3.

Finally, if both men confess, each pays $3,000. This is shown in Box 4.

What Nathan Thinks.   Nathan considers his choices and possible outcomes. He reasons to himself, I have two options, confess or not confess, and Bob has the same two options. Let me ask myself two questions:

- First, *if Bob chooses not to confess, what is the best thing for me to do?* The answer is confess, since if I do not confess, I will end up in Box 1 paying $2,000,

EXHIBIT 26–7
Prisoner's Dilemma

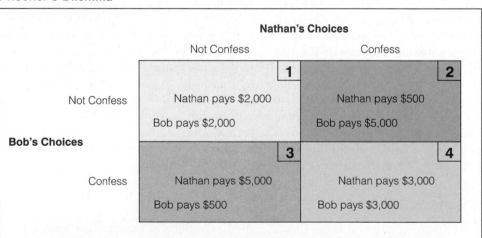

Nathan and Bob each have two choices: confess or not confess. No matter what Bob does, it is always better for Nathan to confess. No matter what Nathan does, it is always better for Bob to confess. Both Nathan and Bob confess and end up in Box 4 where each pays a $3,000 fine. Both men would have been better off had they not confessed. That way they would have ended up in Box 1 paying a $2,000 fine.

but if I confess I will end up in Box 2 paying only $500. No doubt about it, if Bob chooses not to confess, I ought to confess.

■ Second, *if Bob chooses to confess, what is the best thing for me to do?* The answer is confess, since if I do not confess, I will end up in Box 3 paying $5,000, but if I confess I will pay $3,000. No doubt about it, if Bob chooses to confess, I ought to confess.

Nathan's Conclusion.   Nathan concludes that no matter what Bob chooses to do, not confess or confess, he is always better off if he confesses. Nathan decides to confess to the crime.

The Situation Is the Same for Bob.   Bob goes through the same mental process that Nathan does. Asking himself the same two questions Nathan asked himself, Bob gets the same answers and makes the same conclusion. Bob decides to confess to the crime.

The Outcome.   The DA goes to each man and asks what he has decided. Nathan says, "I confess." Bob says, "I confess." The outcome is shown in Box 4 with each man paying a fine of $3,000.

Look Where They Could Be.   Is there an outcome, represented by one of the four boxes, that is better for *both* Nathan *and* Bob than the outcome where each pays $3,000? Yes, there is; it is Box 1. In Box 1, both Nathan and Bob pay $2,000. To get to Box 1, all the two men had to do was keep silent and not confess.

Changing the Game.   What would happen if the DA gave Nathan and Bob another chance? Suppose she tells them that she will not accept their confessions. Instead, she wants them to *talk it over together* for ten minutes, after which time she will come back, place each man in a separate room, and ask for his decision. The second time she will accept each man's decision, no matter what.

Will this change the outcome? Most people will say yes, arguing that Nathan and Bob will now see that their better choice is to remain silent, so that each ends up with a $2,000 fine instead of a $3,000 fine. Let's assume this happens, that Nathan and Bob enter into a gentlemen's agreement to remain silent.

Nathan's Thoughts on the Way to His Room.   The DA returns and takes Nathan to a separate room. On the way, Nathan thinks to himself, I'm not sure I can trust Bob. Suppose he goes back on our agreement and confesses. If I hold to the agreement and he doesn't, he'll end up with a $500 fine and I'll end up paying $5,000. Of course, if I break the agreement and confess and he holds to the agreement, then I'll reduce my fine down to $500. Maybe the best thing for me to do is break the agreement and confess, hoping that he doesn't and I'll only pay $500. If I'm not so lucky, at least I'll protect myself from paying $5,000.

Once in the room, the DA asks Nathan what his decision is. He says, "I confess."

The Situation Is the Same for Bob.   Bob sees the situation the same way Nathan does and chooses to confess again.

The Outcome Again.   Both men end up confessing a second time. Each pays $3,000, realizing that if they had been silent and kept to their agreement, their fine would only be $2,000 each.

Prisoner's Dilemma and Oligopolists

Oligopolists may be a lot like our prisoners, Nathan and Bob. Sometimes they, too, find themselves in a prisoner's dilemma. Suppose we approximate the prisoners' situation using two firms, A and B, that sell the same product and are in stiff competition. Currently, the competition between them is so stiff that each earns only $10,000 profits. Soon the two firms decide to enter into a *cartel agreement* in which each agrees to raise prices and, once raised, not to undercut the other. If they hold to the agreement, each firm will earn profits of $50,000. But if one firm holds to the cartel agreement, and the other does not, the one that does not hold to the agreement will earn profits of $100,000, and the one that does will earn $5,000 profits. Of course, if neither holds to the agreement, then both will be back where they started—earning $10,000 profits. We have outlined the choices for the two firms and the possible outcomes in Exhibit 26–8.

Each firm is likely to behave the way our two prisoners behaved. Each firm will see the chance to earn $100,000 by breaking the agreement (instead of $50,000 by holding to it); it will also realize that if it does not break the agreement and the other firm does, it will be in a worse situation than when it was in stiff competition with the other firm. Most economists predict that the two firms will end up in Box 4 in Exhibit 26–8, earning the profits they did before they entered into the agreement. In sum, they will *cheat* on the cartel agreement and again be in competition—the very situation they wanted to escape.

Constraints and Oligopolists

We are accustomed to thinking that the fewer constraints an economic actor has, the better. But the prisoner's dilemma raises an interesting issue, namely, that the oligopolists who seek to form and benefit from a cartel agreement would be better off (receive higher profits) if they were *constrained* from cheating on the agreement. Here, then, is an example where adding a constraint makes it easier to meet an

EXHIBIT 26–8
Cartels and Prisoner's Dilemma

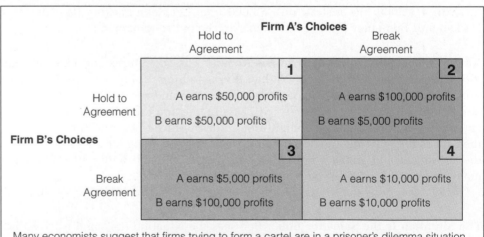

Many economists suggest that firms trying to form a cartel are in a prisoner's dilemma situation. Both firms A and B earn higher profits holding to a (cartel) agreement than not, but each will earn even higher profits if it breaks the agreement while the other firm holds to it. If cartel formation is a prisoner's dilemma situation, we predict that cartels will be short-lived.

objective. We conclude that constraints come in two varieties: those that make it more difficult to meet an objective and those that make it less difficult. Economists predict that economic actors will try to *remove* those constraints that make it *harder* to meet an objective (for instance, a single-price monopolist tries to find a way to distinguish among customers who will pay different prices, so that it will no longer be constrained in having to sell its product to each customer for the same price) and to *add* those constraints that make it *easier* to meet an objective (firms sometimes lobby government to constrain them from cheating on a cartel agreement).

THE THEORY OF CONTESTABLE MARKETS: CHALLENGING ORTHODOXY

■

Our discussion of market structures, from perfect competition to oligopoly, has focused on the number of sellers in each market structure. In perfect competition there were many sellers; in monopoly there was only one; in monopolistic competition there were many; in oligopoly there were few. The message was that the number of sellers in a market influences the behavior of the sellers within the market. For example, the monopoly seller is more likely to restrict output and charge higher prices than the perfect competitor.

Recently, economists have shifted emphasis from the number of sellers in a market toward the issue of entry into and exit from an industry. This new focus is a result of the work of economists like William Baumol and others who have put forth the idea of contestable markets.[2]

A **contestable market** is one in which the following conditions are met: (1) There is easy entry into the market and costless exit from the market. (2) New firms entering the market can produce the product at the same cost as current firms. (3) Firms exiting the market can easily dispose of their fixed assets by selling them elsewhere (less depreciation; thus, fixed costs are not sunk but recoverable).

To illustrate, suppose there are currently eight firms in an industry, all of which are earning profits. Firms outside the industry notice this and decide to enter the industry (nothing prevents entry). They acquire the necessary equipment and produce the product at the same cost as current producers. Time passes, and the firms that entered the industry decide to exit it. They can either switch their machinery into another line of production or sell their equipment for what they paid for it, less depreciation.

Perhaps the most important element of a contestable market is "hit-and-run" entry and exit. New entrants can enter—hit—produce the product and compete away the profits of current firms; then they exit costlessly—run.

The theory of contestable markets has been criticized because of its assumptions—in particular, the assumption that there is extremely free entry into, and costless exit from, the industry. However, although this theory, like most theories, is a caricature of the real world, this does not of itself destroy its usefulness.

Currently, the theory of contestable markets is being tested. It is still relatively young (as market structure theories go), and it is difficult to tell what its overall

Contestable Market
A market in which entry is easy and exit is costless, new firms can produce the product at the same cost as current firms, and exiting firms can easily dispose of their fixed assets by selling them.

[2]William J. Baumol, "Contestable Markets: An Uprising in the Theory of Industry Structure," *American Economic Review* 72 (March 1982):1–15. For a critique of the contestable markets theory, see William G. Shepherd, "Contestability' vs. Competition," *American Economic Review* 74 (September 1984): 572–87.

worth will turn out to be. It has, at minimum, rattled orthodox market structure theory. Here are a few of its conclusions:

1. Even if an industry is composed of a small number of firms, or simply one firm, this is not evidence that the firms perform in a noncompetitive way. They might be extremely competitive if the market they are in is contestable.
2. Profits can be zero in an industry even if the number of sellers in the industry is small.
3. If a market is contestable, inefficient producers cannot survive. Cost inefficiencies invite lower-cost producers into the market, driving price down to minimum *ATC* and forcing inefficient firms to change their ways or exit the industry.
4. If as conclusion 3 suggests, a contestable market encourages firms to produce at their lowest possible average total cost and charge $P = ATC$, it follows that they will also sell at a price equal to marginal cost. (Recall that the marginal cost curve intersects the average total cost curve at its minimum point.)

The theory of contestable markets has also led to a shift in policy perspectives. To some (but certainly not all) economists, the theory suggests that efforts directed at lowering entry and exit costs might do more to encourage firms to act as perfect competitors (such as selling at $P = MC$) than direct interference in the behavioral patterns of firms.

THE FOUR MARKET STRUCTURES REVIEWED

With the discussion of oligopoly, our examination of the four different market structures—perfect competition, monopoly, monopolistic competition, and oligopoly—comes to an end. Exhibit 26–9 reviews some of the characteristics and consequences of the different market structures.

The first four columns of the exhibit simply summarize the characteristics of the different market structures. In the last column, we have noted the long-run market tendency between price and average total cost in the different market structures. This indicates whether long-run profits are possible. Note that for three of the four market structures (monopoly, monopolistic competition, and oligopoly), super-

EXHIBIT 26–9
Characteristics and Consequences of Market Structures

Market Structure	Number of Sellers	Type of Product	Barriers to Entry	Long-run Market Tendency of Price and *ATC*
Perfect competition	Many	Homogeneous	No	$P = ATC$ (zero economic profits)
Monopoly	One	Unique	Yes	$P > ATC$ (positive economic profits)[a,c]
Monopolistic competition	Many	Slightly differentiated	No	$P = ATC$ (zero economic profits)[b]
Oligopoly	Few	Homogeneous or differentiated	Yes	$P > ATC$ (positive economic profits)[a,c]

[a]It is possible for positive profits to turn to zero profits through the capitalization of profits or rent-seeking activities.
[b]It is possible for the firm to make positive profits in the long run if it can differentiate its product sufficiently in the minds of the buying public.
[c]It is possible for positive profits to turn to zero profits if the market is contestable.

Interview: William Baumol

William Baumol is one of the key persons associated with the development of the contestable markets theory. Besides contestable markets, Baumol is well known for his work on the *sales maximization theory,* which says that firms maximize sales subject to a minimum-profit constraint, instead of attempting to maximize profits. Baumol is currently at New York University and Princeton University.

Professor Baumol, what insights into the market does the contestable markets theory provide?

One of its key insights is the suggestion that freedom of entry can act as a supplement to, or as a substitute for, actual competition.

One of the things contestable markets theory teaches us is that the number of firms in an industry may not affect a firm's behavior as much as whether the industry is contestable. Would you go so far as to say that contestability is the major criterion by which we ought to measure markets?

Really, you are asking here whether freedom of entry, or contestability, is more important than actual competition. And to this I would say no. The way I have presented it (including cases where I have testified) is to say that there are two sets of sufficient conditions for effective competitiveness of a market, and the presence of either or both is a sufficient guarantee for the purpose.

To your knowledge, what industries either are, or behave as if they are, contestable?

The answer is it's a matter of degree. For example, we had originally thought that airlines would be highly contestable, and there is still some evidence that they are characterized by a consid-

erable degree of contestability, but we now believe that airlines are not nearly as contestable as we had thought earlier.

Two examples of industries that we do believe are highly contestable are barges and trucks. Let me explain why. Both trucks and barges deal primarily with industrial rather than consumer products. That means that much of their business is carried out by contract. And contract makes the difference here. For example, if the market is exploited by a monopolist, then a prospective entrant can say to the customers of the monopolist, "Look, if I come in without a contract, the monopolist will undercut me and drive me out, and you'll be back in your old position. But if you sign a contract with me for five years, cutting their profits down by 90 percent, we will both benefit." This sort of thing makes that market contestable. In contrast, airlines deal with thousands and thousands of passengers so that contracts are unworkable and do not occur and therefore the incumbents can, if they choose, punish an entrant by cutting prices that drive him out.

Can you provide us with some specific examples of how contestable markets

theory has been used by courts and government agencies?

Its most effective use by government agencies has been of two sorts. One is, in effect, acting in accord with, or in the spirit of, the merger guidelines. That is, saying in effect that before we will say a particular industry involves monopoly or market power, we must consider the combination of ease of entry and the number of incumbents, rather than the number of incumbents alone. And there have been a number of cases of that sort.

The second is that regulatory agencies have used it in formulating rules for regulation. That is to say, what they have rightly been persuaded to do is to act as substitutes for contestability in markets that were not contestable. The agencies, therefore, have required the regulated firms to tailor their behavior to that which would prevail if the market had been contestable. Now what this means is that they have removed those regulations that are unnecessary to achieve those results, and strengthened the regulations that were needed for the purpose.

My final comment is that the concept of market contestability has also been misused by lawyers who were tempted to claim that the entire world is contestable, a position that neither I nor my coauthors hold.

Is it somewhat surprising to you that the courts and government agencies have so readily adopted contestable markets theory?

I was surprised, and I was flattered. As I said before, my impression is that when the courts and the regulatory agencies have used it, it has been used sensibly. But when it was used for partisan purposes, it was in a number of cases abused. And it was embarrassing

ECONOMICS IN OUR TIMES

for me and my coauthors because we ended up being characterized as believing what we do not believe—that is, that everything is all for the best, without government interference. It is my belief that you have to examine things case by case, you have to get the evidence to find out whether a particular market is or is not contestable. The only point we're making that is different from what was known before, but is crucial as I now hope to convince you,

is that the perfectly competitive model, which had been used as a guide by regulators and the courts before, simply does not apply to most of the cases that are at issue, because most of those cases are cases with economies of scale (which makes for large firms). If the firms weren't large in the first place, nobody would worry about them, and it is not only by accident that the perfectly competitive model, with its multiplicity of tiny firms, must assume the existence

of constant returns to scale. What our analysis says is that similar rules, which are equally demanding, and which are equally suitable for protecting consumers, can be applied for the first time to cases with large firms and with economies of scale. But I want to emphasize that we don't want to be any less tough when there is monopoly than does anyone else.

script letters beside the possible profits refer you to notes that describe alternative market tendencies given different conditions. For example, the market tendency in oligopoly is for $P > ATC$ and for profits to exist in the long run. The reason is that there are significant barriers to entry in oligopoly, and short-run profits cannot be competed away through the entry of new firms into the industry. As we have just learned, however, the market tendency of price and average total cost may be different if the particular oligopolistic market is contestable.

CHAPTER SUMMARY

Monopolistic Competition

■ The theory of monopolistic competition makes the following assumptions: (1) There are many sellers and buyers. (2) Each firm in the industry produces and sells a slightly differentiated product. (3) There is easy entry and exit.

■ The monopolistic competitor is a price searcher.

■ For the monopolistic competitor, $P > MR$, and its marginal revenue curve lies below its demand curve.

■ The monopolistic competitor produces the quantity of output at which $MR = MC$. It charges the highest price per unit for this output.

■ Unlike the perfectly competitive firm, the monopolistic competitor does not exhibit resource allocative efficiency.

■ The monopolistically competitive firm does not earn profits in the long run (because of easy entry into the industry) unless it can successfully differentiate its product (for example, by brand name) in the minds of the buying public.

Excess Capacity Theorem

■ The excess capacity theorem states that a monopolistic competitor will, in equilibrium, produce an output smaller than the one at which average total costs (unit costs) are minimized.

Oligopoly Assumptions

■ There are many different oligopoly theories. All are built on the assumptions that (1) there are few sellers and many buyers, (2) firms produce and sell either homogeneous or differentiated products, and (3) there are significant barriers to entry.

■ One of the key characteristics of oligopolistic firms is their mutual interdependence.

Oligopoly Theories

■ The kinked demand curve theory assumes that if a single firm lowers price, other firms will do likewise, but if a single firm raises price, other firms will not follow suit.

■ The price leadership theory assumes that the dominant firm in the industry determines price and all other firms take this price as given.

■ The cartel theory assumes that firms in an oligopolistic industry act in a manner consistent with there being only one firm in the industry.

■ The kinked demand curve theory predicts that an oligopolistic firm will experience price stickiness or rigidity. This is because there is a gap in its marginal revenue curve, along which the firm's marginal cost can rise or fall; hence, the firm can still produce the same quantity of output and charge the same price. The evidence in some empirical tests rejects the theory. For example, Stigler found no evidence that the oligopolists he examined were more reluctant to match price increases than price decreases.

■ Four problems are associated with cartels: (1) the problem of forming the cartel, (2) the problem of formulating policy, (3) the problem of entry into the industry, and (4) the problem of cheating.

■ Firms that enter into a cartel agreement are in a prisoner's dilemma situation where individually rational behavior leads to a jointly inefficient outcome.

The Theory of Contestable Markets

■ A contestable market is one in which the following conditions are met: (1) There is easy entry into the market and costless exit from it. (2) New firms entering the market can produce the product at the same costs as current firms. (3) Firms exiting the market can easily dispose of their fixed assets by selling them elsewhere (less depreciation). The theory of contestable markets lays more emphasis on the issue of entry into and exit from an industry and less emphasis (than orthodox market structure theories) on the number of sellers in an industry.

Key Terms and Concepts

Monopolistic
   Competition

Excess Capacity
   Theorem

Oligopoly

Concentration Ratio

Kinked Demand Curve
   Theory

Price Leadership
   Theory

Cartel Theory

Cartel

Game Theory

Contestable Market

1. What, if anything, do all firms in all four market structures have in common?

2. Why does the marginal revenue curve have the unusual look that it does in the kinked demand curve model?

3. Would you expect cartel formation to be more likely in industries that comprise a few firms or many firms? Explain your answer.

4. Does the theory of contestable markets shed any light on oligopoly pricing theories?

 5. There are 60 types or varieties of product X on the market. Is product X made in a monopolistically competitive market?

6. Why does interdependence of firms play a major role in oligopoly, but not in perfect competition or monopolistic competition?

7. Airline companies sometimes fly airplanes that are one-quarter full between cities. Some people point to this as evidence of economic waste. What do you think? Would it be better to have fewer airline companies and more full planes?

8. Concentration ratios have often been used to note the tightness of an oligopoly market. A high concentration ratio indicates a tight oligopoly market, and a low concentration ratio indicates a loose oligopoly. Would you expect firms in tight markets to reap higher profits, on average, than firms in loose markets? Would it matter if the markets were contestable?

9. Market theories are said to have the happy consequence of getting individuals to think in more focused and analytical ways. Has this happened to you? Give examples to illustrate.

10. Give an example of a prisoner's dilemma situation other than the two mentioned in this chapter.

11. How are oligopoly and monopolistic competition alike? How are they different?

12. In Exhibit 26–3, what is the highest dollar amount marginal cost can rise to without changing price? Explain.

MICROECONOMIC THEORIES
(FACTOR MARKETS)

FACTOR MARKETS: WITH EMPHASIS ON THE LABOR MARKET

WHAT THIS CHAPTER IS ABOUT

In the chapters on perfect competition, monopoly, monopolistic competition, and oligopoly, the firm was a *seller* of products. In this chapter, the firm is a *buyer* of factors (resources or inputs). We approach this subject by first examining some principles that are relevant to factor markets in general. Then we turn to a specific factor market, the labor market.

FACTOR MARKETS

■

A firm may be a buyer in one market and a seller in another. For example, IBM sells computers; it is a seller in the computer market. But IBM also buys paper, plastic, paint, and labor; it is a buyer in numerous factor markets.

As was explained in previous chapters, a seller may be a price taker or a price searcher. In short, the firm faces either a horizontal or a downward-sloping demand curve. Here we refer to a seller that is a price taker in a product market as a **product price taker.** A seller that is a price searcher in a product market is a **product price searcher.**

The price taker–price searcher model, which was used to describe the firm in its role as a seller of products, is also relevant to the firm in its role as a buyer of factors. For example, a firm is a price taker in a factor market—or **factor price taker**—if it can buy all of a factor it wants at the equilibrium price. In this situation, it faces a horizontal (flat, perfectly elastic) supply curve of factors. For example, the department store at the local mall is a price taker in hiring salesclerks. This means the store can hire salesclerks one right after another, all for the same wage rate, and not drive up the wage rate.

A firm that is a price searcher in a factor market—a **factor price searcher**—faces an upward-sloping supply curve of factors. If it buys an additional factor unit, it drives up factor price. For example, if the department store is a price searcher in hiring salesclerks, then as it hires additional clerks, it must pay a higher wage rate, not only to the extra person hired, but to all those hired previously, too.

A firm may fall into four possible categories, which are illustrated in Exhibit 27–1:

1. A product price taker and a factor price taker (box I).
2. A product price searcher and a factor price taker (box II).
3. A product price taker and a factor price searcher (box III).
4. A product price searcher and a factor price searcher (box IV).

The exhibit shows the relevant demand and supply curves for each case.

We now turn to a discussion of two of the four categories: (1) the firm as product price taker and factor price taker (*PT–PT)* and (2) the firm as product price searcher and factor price taker (*PS–PT).*

The Firm as Product Price Taker and Factor Price Taker, *PT–PT*

Why do firms purchase factors? The answer is obvious—to produce products to sell. This goes for all firms, no matter what type. General Motors buys steel in order to build cars to sell to car buyers. Farmers buy tractors and fertilizer in order to produce grain to sell.

The demand for factors is a **derived demand.** It is derived from, and directly related to, the demand for the product that the resources go to produce. If the demand for the product rises, the demand for the factors used to produce the product rises; if the demand for the product falls, the demand for the factors used to produce the product falls. For example, if the demand for a university education falls, so does the demand for university professors. If the demand for computers rises, so does the demand for skilled computer workers.

When the demand for a seller's product rises, the seller needs to have some idea of how much more of a factor it should buy. The concepts of marginal revenue product and marginal resource cost are relevant here.

Product Price Taker
A firm that faces a horizontal demand curve for the product it sells. It can sell as many units of its good as it wants without affecting price. The perfectly competitive firm is a product price taker.

Product Price Searcher
A firm that faces a downward-sloping demand curve for the product it sells. It sells fewer units at higher prices than lower prices. The monopoly, monopolistic competitive, and oligopoly firms are product price searchers.

Factor Price Taker
A firm that can buy all of a factor it wants at the equilibrium price. It faces a horizontal (flat, perfectly elastic) supply curve of factors.

Factor Price Searcher
A firm that drives up factor price if it buys an additional factor unit. It faces an upward-sloping supply curve of factors.

Derived Demand
Demand that is the result of some other demand. For example, factor demand is the result of the demand for the products that the factors go to produce.

EXHIBIT 27–1
The Firm, Two Markets, Four Categories

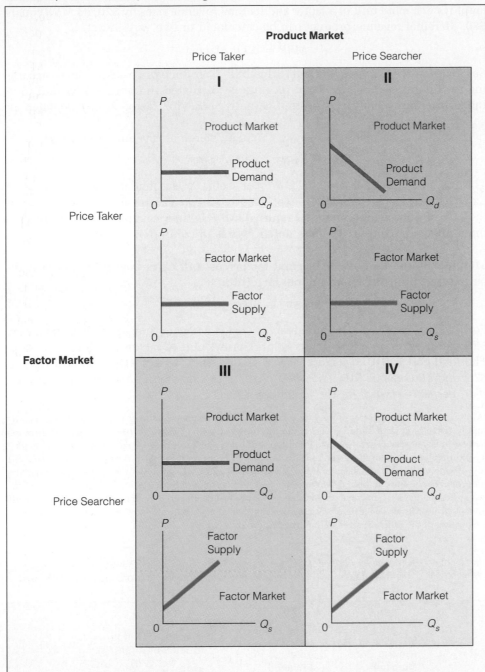

P = price. In the product and factor markets, *P* stands for "product price" and "factor price," respectively. A firm may be either a price taker or a price searcher in product markets; and it may be either a price taker or a price searcher in factor markets. Thus, a firm may fall into one of four possible categories. The demand and supply curves for a firm in each category are depicted in the four boxes.

Marginal Revenue Product (*MRP*)
The additional revenue generated by employing an additional factor unit.

Marginal Revenue Product. Marginal revenue product (*MRP*) is the additional revenue generated by employing an additional factor unit. For example, if a firm employs one more unit of a factor and its total revenue rises by $20, its *MRP* equals $20. Marginal revenue product can be calculated in two ways. First,

$$MRP = \Delta TR/\Delta\text{factor}$$

See Exhibit 27–2, where the data illustrate a product price taker since, according to column 4, $P = MR$. Total revenue is calculated in column 5 by multiplying price times quantity of output. Finally, *MRP* for factor X is calculated in column 6.

The other, more common, way to calculate marginal revenue product is

$$MRP = MR \times MPP$$

The marginal physical product (*MPP*) of factor X is calculated in column 3 of Exhibit 27–2, using the method explained in Chapter 23 (recall the discussion of the law of diminishing marginal returns). *MRP* is then calculated by multiplying the numbers in column 3 by the dollar figures in column 4.

Marginal Factor Cost
The additional cost incurred by employing an additional factor unit.

Marginal Resource Cost. Marginal factor cost (*MFC*) is the additional cost incurred by employing an additional factor unit:

$$MFC = \Delta TC/\Delta\text{factor}$$

For a factor price taker, marginal factor cost is constant and equal to factor price, $MFC = P$. Suppose a firm wants to purchase 1 unit of factor Y at a price of $10. The total cost is $10. If it purchases a second unit, it pays $10, total cost rises to $20, and *MFC* equals $10. *The MFC curve, or the factor supply curve, is horizontal (flat, perfectly elastic) for the factor price taker.*[1]

[1]Although the *MFC*, or factor supply, curve for the single factor price taker is horizontal, the *market* supply curve is upward sloping. This is similar to the situation for the perfectly competitive firm described in Chapter 24. There we noted that the firm's demand curve was horizontal but that the market (or industry) demand curve was downward sloping. In factor markets, we are simply talking about the supply side of the market instead of the demand side. The firm's supply curve is flat because it can hire additional factor units without driving up the price of the factor; it buys a relatively small portion of the factor. For the industry, however, higher factor prices must be offered to entice factors (such as workers) from other industries. The difference in the two supply curves—the firm's and the industry's—is basically a reflection of the different sizes of the firm and the industry.

EXHIBIT 27–2
Marginal Revenue Product Schedule
Using the data provided in the exhibit, *MRP* is calculated in two ways: $MRP = \Delta TR/\Delta\text{factor}$, and $MRP = MR \times MPP$. Marginal revenue product is the additional revenue generated by employing one more factor unit. We have assumed that the firm is a product price taker and that all factors other than X are fixed.

(1) Units of Factor X	(2) Quantity of Output	(3) Marginal Physical Products of X (MPP_x) $MPP_x = \dfrac{\Delta(2)}{\Delta(1)}$	(4) Product Price, Marginal Revenue ($P = MR$)	(5) Total Revenue $TR = P \times Q$ $= (4) \times (2)$	(6) Marginal Revenue Product of X (MRP_x) $MRP_x = \dfrac{\Delta TR}{\Delta X} = \dfrac{\Delta(5)}{\Delta(1)}$ $= MR \times MPP_x = (4) \times (3)$
0	10*	0	$5	$ 50	$ 0
1	19	9	5	95	45
2	27	8	5	135	40
3	34	7	5	170	35
4	40	6	5	200	30
5	45	5	5	225	25

*Seeing that the quantity of output is 10 at 0 units of factor X indicates that other factors (not shown in the exhibit) must also be used to produce the good.

The *MRP* = *MRC* Rule: Maximizing Profits. Employing marginal analysis, the firm continues to purchase units of a given factor as long as $MRP > MFC$. It stops where $MRP = MFC$. By doing this, the firm maximizes profits; it buys factors as long as their purchase adds more to revenues than to costs. In Exhibit 27–3, *MRP* equals *MFC* at a factor quantity of Q_1.

In Perspective

In the product market, the firm produces that quantity of output at which marginal revenue equals marginal cost, $MR = MC$. In the factor market, the firm buys the factor quantity at which marginal revenue product equals marginal factor cost, $MRP = MFC$. The economic principle of *equating additional benefits with additional costs* holds in both markets.

Question:

In Exhibit 27–3, why is the MFC *curve horizontal at* P_1?

Answer:

The *MFC* curve is horizontal at P_1 because we have assumed that the firm is a factor price taker; it can buy all of a factor it wants at the equilibrium price without driving up the price of the factor.

The *MRP* Curve Is the Firm's Factor Demand Curve. The factor demand curve tells us how many factor units the firm will buy at different prices (for example, 500 units at $2 per unit, 600 units at $1.50 per unit, and so forth). As Exhibit 27–4 illustrates, the firm's *MRP* curve is its factor demand curve, because the *MRP* curve shows exactly how much of a factor the firm buys at different prices (which is what any demand curve shows).

Suppose the price of the factor in Exhibit 27–4 is P_1. Since the firm is a factor price taker and thus can buy as many factor units at this price as it wants, P_1 equals MFC_1. At P_1, the firm chooses Q_1 factor units. If price rises to P_2, the firm chooses Q_2. At a lower factor price, the firm buys more factor units; at a higher factor price, the firm buys fewer factor units. The *MRP* curve maps out the quantity of a factor the firm is willing and able to buy at different factor prices.

Question:

Why is the MRP *curve downward sloping?*

Answer:

The *MRP* curve is downward sloping because (after some point) the more of a factor that is used, the lower its *MRP* will be (because of the law of diminishing marginal returns). In short, since $MRP = MR \times MPP$, and *MPP* declines at some point, so must *MRP*.[2]

Value Marginal Product. Value marginal product (**VMP**) is equal to the price of the product times the marginal physical product of the factor:

$$VMP = P \times MPP$$

[2]If the firm is a product price searcher, there is an additional reason: namely, that higher levels of sales mean a lower *MR*, along with a declining *MPP*.

EXHIBIT 27–3
Equating *MRP* and *MFC*

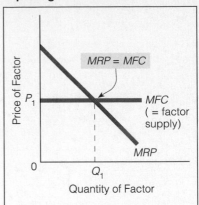

The firm continues to purchase a factor as long as its *MRP* exceeds its *MFC*. In the exhibit, the firm purchases Q_1.

EXHIBIT 27–4
The *MRP* Curve Is the Firm's Factor Demand Curve

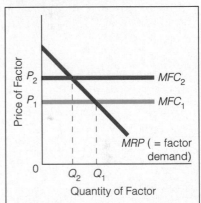

The *MRP* curve shows the various quantities of the factor the firm is willing to buy at different prices, which is what a demand curve shows. For example, at P_1 the firm buys Q_1; at P_2 it buys Q_2.

Value Marginal Product (*VMP*)
The price of the good multiplied by the marginal physical product of the factor: $VMP = P \times MPP$. For a product price taker, $P = MR$, and thus $MRP = VMP$. For a product price searcher, $P > MR$, and $VMP > MRP$.

For example, if price is $10 and marginal physical product is 9 units, then *VMP* is $90. The *VMP* is a measure of the value that each factor unit adds to the firm's product. Think of it as the marginal physical product measured in dollars.

Question:

Is VMP = MRP *for a price taker in a product market?*

Answer:

Yes, it is. Since for a product price taker $P = MR$, and we know that $VMP = P \times MPP$ and $MRP = MR \times MPP$, it follows that $VMP = MRP$. Exhibit 27–2 shows this. In the last column, one way of calculating *MRP* is by multiplying *MR* times *MPP*, or multiplying the dollar amounts in column 4 times the unit amounts in column 3. If we were to calculate *VMP*, we would multiply *P* times *MPP*, which again would be column 4 times column 3.

A Summary.   The following conditions hold for a firm that is a price taker in both the product and factor markets:

1. The firm buys and employs the factor quantity at which $MRP = MFC$.
2. MFC = factor price. This is because the firm is a factor price taker.
3. The *MRP* curve is the firm's factor demand curve.
4. $VMP = MRP$. This is because the firm is a product price taker. It follows that this firm's *VMP* curve will be identical to its *MRP* curve (Exhibit 27–5a).
5. At the profit-maximizing factor quantity, $VMP = MRP = MFC$ = factor price.

The Firm as Product Price Searcher and Factor Price Taker, *PS–PT*

For the product price searcher, $P > MR$; therefore *VMP* $(P \times MPP)$ does not equal *MRP* $(MR \times MPP)$. Instead, $VMP > MRP$. Therefore, the following conditions hold:

1. The firm buys and employs the factor quantity at which $MRP = MFC$.
2. MFC = factor price. This is because the firm is a factor price taker.
3. The *MRP* curve is the firm's factor demand curve.
4. $VMP > MRP$. This is because the firm is a product price searcher. It follows from this that if we were to derive the firm's *VMP* and *MRP* curves, the *MRP* curve would lie *below* the *VMP* curve (Exhibit 27–5b).
5. At the profit-maximizing factor quantity, $VMP > MRP = MFC$ = factor price.

The Least-Cost Rule: Applicable When There Is More Than One Factor

Suppose a firm requires two factors, labor and capital, to produce its product. How does it combine these two factors to minimize costs? Does it combine 20 units of labor with 5 units of capital, or perhaps 15 units of labor with 8 units of capital?

Simply put, the firm purchases the two factors until the ratio of *MPP* to price for one factor equals the ratio of *MPP* to price for the other factor. In other words,

$$\frac{MPP_L}{P_L} = \frac{MPP_K}{P_K}$$

(L = Labor and K = Capital)

EXHIBIT 27-5

MRP and VMP Curves for a Product Price Taker and Product Price Searcher

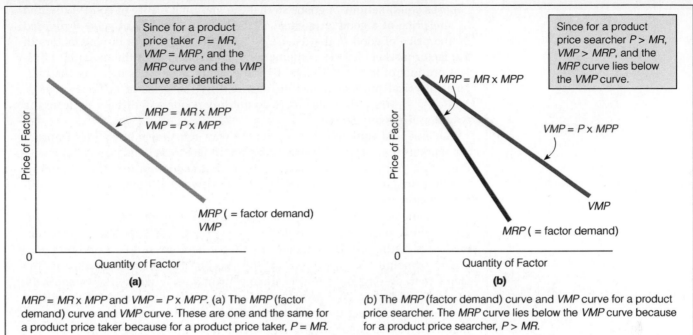

Since for a product price taker $P = MR$, $VMP = MRP$, and the MRP curve and the VMP curve are identical.

$MRP = MR \times MPP$
$VMP = P \times MPP$

MRP (= factor demand)
VMP

Price of Factor

Quantity of Factor

(a)

Since for a product price searcher $P > MR$, $VMP > MRP$, and the MRP curve lies below the VMP curve.

$MRP = MR \times MPP$

$VMP = P \times MPP$

VMP

MRP (= factor demand)

Price of Factor

Quantity of Factor

(b)

$MRP = MR \times MPP$ and $VMP = P \times MPP$. (a) The MRP (factor demand) curve and VMP curve. These are one and the same for a product price taker because for a product price taker, $P = MR$.

(b) The MRP (factor demand) curve and VMP curve for a product price searcher. The MRP curve lies below the VMP curve because for a product price searcher, $P > MR$.

This is the **least-cost rule.** To understand the logic behind it, suppose that (1) the price of labor is $5, (2) the price of capital is $10, (3) an extra unit of labor results in an increase in output of 25 units, and (4) an extra unit of capital results in an increase in output of 25 units. Finally, the firm currently spends an extra $5 on labor and an extra $10 on capital.

Notice that MPP_L/P_L is greater than MPP_K/P_K: $25/\$5 > 25/\$10$. Thus, in our example, a dollar spent on labor is more effective at raising output than a dollar spent on capital. In fact, it is *twice* as effective.

The firm is not minimizing costs. As is, it spends an additional $15 ($5 on labor and $10 on capital) and produces 50 additional units of output. Instead, it could spend $10 on labor only, spending $0 on capital, and produce the 50 additional units of output, saving $5. To minimize costs, the firm will rearrange its purchases of factors until the least-cost rule is met.

Least-Cost Rule
Specifies the combination of factors that minimizes costs. This requires that the following condition be met: $MPP_1/P_1 = MPP_2/P_2 = \ldots = MPP_n/P_n$, where the numbers stand for the different factors.

Question:

If $MPP_L/P_L > MPP_K/P_K$, *how does the firm equalize the two ratios?*

Answer:

It buys more labor and less capital. As this happens, the *MPP* of labor falls, and the *MPP* of capital rises, bringing the two ratios closer in line. The firm continues to buy more of the factor whose *MPP*-to-price ratio is larger. It stops when the two ratios are equal. This type of equilibrating process was described in Chapter 20 in the discussion of marginal utility and consumer choice.

Compare the firm's least-cost rule with the way buyers allocate their consumption dollars (see Chapter 20). A buyer of goods in the product market chooses combinations of goods so that the marginal utility of good A divided by the price of a good A is equal to the marginal utility of good B divided by the price of good B; that is, $MU_A/P_A = MU_B/P_B$. A firm buying factors in the factor market chooses combinations of factors so that the marginal physical product of factor X divided by the price of factor X is equal to the marginal physical product of factor Y divided by the price of factor Y, that is, $MPP_X/P_X = MPP_Y/P_Y$. Consumers do not buy goods any differently from the way that firms buy factors.

The essential equivalence between the way consumers buy goods in product markets and the way firms buy factors in factor markets points out something that you may have already sensed: that economic principles are few, but they sometimes seem numerous because we find them in so many different settings.

The same economic principle lies behind equating the MU/P ratio for different goods in the product market and equating the MPP/P ratio for different resources in the resource market.[3] In short, there are not two different economic principles at work—one in the product market and another in the factor market—but only one economic principle at work in two markets, product and factor. That principle simply says that economic actors will, in their attempt to meet their objectives, arrange their purchases in such a way that they receive equal additional benefits per dollar of expenditure.

Seeing how a *few* economic principles operate in *many* different settings is part of the economic way of thinking.

THE LABOR MARKET

Labor is a factor of special interest because at one time or another, most people find themselves in the labor market. In this section, we first discuss the demand for labor, next the supply of labor, and finally the two together. We focus our discussion on the firm that is a price taker in both the product and factor markets[4] (see box I in Exhibit 27–1).

Shifts in the Firm's *MRP*, or Factor Demand, Curve

As we said earlier, the firm's *MRP* curve is its factor demand curve, and marginal revenue product equals marginal revenue times marginal physical product:

$$MRP = MR \times MPP \tag{1}$$

Since for a product price taker, $P = MR$, we can rewrite (1) as

$$MRP = P \times MPP \tag{2}$$

Now consider the demand for a specific factor input, labor. As the price of the product that labor produces changes, the factor demand curve for labor shifts. In Exhibit 27–6, we start with a product price of $10 and curve MRP_1. At the wage rate of W_1, the firm hires Q_1 workers.

[3]The "P" in MU/P stands for product price; the "P" in MPP/P stands for factor price.
[4]It is important to keep in mind that the labor market we are discussing here is a labor market in which neither buyers nor sellers have any control over wage rates. Because of this, supply and demand are our analytical tools. In the next chapter, we modify this analysis.

EXHIBIT 27-6
Shifts in the Firm's *MRP*, or Factor Demand, Curve

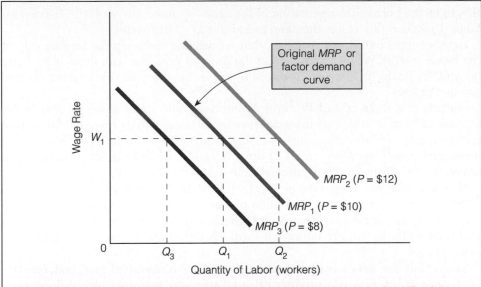

It is always the case that $MRP = MR \times MPP$. For a product price taker, since $P = MR$, it follows that $MRP = P \times MPP$. If P changes, MRP will change. For example, if product price rises, MRP rises, and the firm's MRP curve (factor demand curve) shifts rightward. If product price falls, MRP falls, and the firm's MRP curve (factor demand curve) shifts leftward. If MPP rises (reflected in a shift in the MPP curve), MRP rises, and the firm's MRP curve shifts rightward. If MPP falls, MRP falls, and the firm's MRP curve shifts leftward.

Suppose product price rises to $12. As we can see from equation (2), *MRP* rises. At each wage rate, the firm wants to hire more workers. For example, at W_1, it wants to hire Q_2 workers instead of Q_1. In short, a rise in product price shifts the firm's *MRP*, or factor demand, curve rightward.

If product price falls from $10 to $8, *MRP* falls. At each wage rate, the firm wants to hire fewer workers. For example, at W_1 it wants to hire Q_3 instead of Q_1 workers. In short, a fall in product price shifts the firm's *MRP*, or factor demand, curve leftward.

It is also the case that changes in the *MPP* of the factor—reflected in a shift in the *MPP* curve—also change the firm's *MRP* curve. As we can see from equation (2), an increase in, say, the *MPP* of labor will increase *MRP* and shift the *MRP*, or factor demand, curve rightward. A decrease in *MPP* will decrease *MRP* and shift the *MRP*, or factor demand, curve leftward.[5]

Question:

Considering the factor labor, if there is either a change in the price of the product labor produces or a change in the MPP *of labor (reflected in a shift in the* MPP *curve), the (factor) demand curve for labor shifts. Is this correct?*

Answer:

Yes, that is correct.

---

[5]Notice here that we are talking about a change in *MPP* that is reflected in a shift in the *MPP* curve; we are not talking about a movement along a given *MPP* curve.

Market Demand for Labor

We now discuss the market demand curve for labor. Normally, we would expect this to be the horizontal summation of the firms' demand curves (MRP curves) for labor. However, this is not the case, as Exhibit 27–7 illustrates.

Here we have two firms, A and B, that we assume make up the buying side of the factor market. We also assume that the product price for both firms is P_1: Parts (a) and (b) in the exhibit show the MRP curve for the two firms based on this product price.

Starting at a wage rate of W_1, firm A purchases 100 units of labor. This is the amount of labor at which its marginal revenue product equals marginal factor cost (or the wage). At this same wage rate, firm B purchases 150 units of labor. If we horizontally sum the MRP curves of firms A and B, we get the MRP curve in (c), where the two firms together purchase 250 units of labor at W_1.

Now increase the wage rate to W_2. In (c), firms A and B move up the given MRP_{A+B} curve and purchase 180 units of labor. This may seem to be the end of the process, but, of course, it is not. A higher wage rate increases each firm's costs and thus shifts its supply curve leftward. This leads to an increase in product price to P_2.

Recall that the firm's marginal revenue product is equal to marginal revenue (and price, if the firm is a product price taker) times marginal physical product, $MRP = MR$ or $(P) \times MPP$. If price rises, so does MRP; thus, each firm faces a *new* MRP curve at the wage rate W_2. Parts (a) and (b) in Exhibit 27–7 illustrate these new MRP curves for firms A and B, and (c) shows the horizontal summation of the new MRP curves. The firms together now purchase 210 units of labor at W_2.

Once all adjustments have been made, connecting the units of labor purchased by both firms at W_1 and W_2 gives us the *market demand curve* in (c).

EXHIBIT 27–7
The Derivation of the Market Demand Curve for Labor

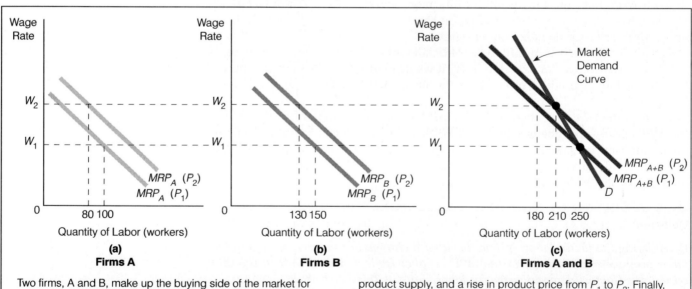

Two firms, A and B, make up the buying side of the market for labor. At a wage rate of W_1, firm A purchases 100 units of labor, and firm B purchases 150 units. Together, they purchase 250 units, as illustrated in (c). The wage rate rises to W_2, and the amount of labor purchased by both firms initially falls to 180 units. Higher wage rates translate into higher costs, a fall in product supply, and a rise in product price from P_1 to P_2. Finally, an increased price raises MRP. We obtain new MRP curves for each firm. The horizontal summation of the new MRP curves shows they purchase 210 units of labor. Connecting the units of labor purchased by both firms at W_1 and W_2 gives us the market demand curve.

The Elasticity of Demand for Labor

The **elasticity of demand for labor** is the percentage change in the quantity demanded of labor divided by the percentage change in the price of labor (the wage rate).

$$E_{\mathrm{L}} = \frac{\text{percentage change in quantity demanded of labor}}{\text{percentage change in wage rate}}$$

where E_{L} = coefficient of elasticity of demand for labor, or simply elasticity coefficient. For example, if the wage rate were to change by 20 percent and the quantity demanded of a particular type of labor changed by 40 percent, the elasticity of demand for this type of labor would be 2 (40 percent/20 percent); the demand between the old wage rate and the new wage rate would be elastic. There are three main determinants of elasticity of demand for labor.

Elasticity of Demand for the Product That Labor Produces.   If the demand for the product that labor produces is highly elastic, a small percentage increase in price (say, owing to a wage increase that shifts leftward the supply curve for the product) will decrease quantity demanded of the product by a relatively large percentage. In turn, this will greatly reduce the quantity of labor needed to produce the product, implying the demand for labor is highly elastic, too.

  The relationship between the elasticity of demand for the product and the elasticity of demand for labor is as follows: *The higher the elasticity of demand for the product, the higher the elasticity of demand for the labor that produces the product; the lower the elasticity of demand for the product, the lower the elasticity of demand for the labor that produces the product.*

Ratio of Labor Costs to Total Costs.   Labor costs are a part of total costs. Consider two situations: one where labor costs are 90 percent of total costs and one where labor costs are only 5 percent of total costs. Now suppose there is a $2 per hour increase in wages. Total costs are affected more where labor costs are 90 percent of total costs (the $2 per hour wage increase is being applied to 90 percent of all costs) than where labor costs are only 5 percent. Price rises by more in the case where labor costs are a larger percentage of total costs. And, of course, the more price rises, the more quantity demanded of the product falls. It follows that labor, being a derived demand, is affected more. In short, the decline in the quantity demanded of labor is greater for a $2-per-hour wage increase when labor costs are 90 percent of total costs than when labor costs are 5 percent of total costs. The relationship between the labor cost–total cost ratio and the elasticity of demand for labor is as follows: *The higher the labor cost–total cost ratio, the higher the elasticity of demand for labor (the greater the cutback in labor for any given wage increase); the lower the labor cost–total cost ratio, the lower the elasticity of demand for labor (the less the cutback in labor for any given wage increase).*

Number of Substitute Factors.   The more substitutes there are for labor, the more sensitive buyers of labor will be to a change in the price of labor. This is a principle that was established in Chapter 21 when we discussed price elasticity of demand. The more chances of substituting other factors for labor, the more likely firms that purchase labor will cut back on their use of labor if the price of labor rises. *The more substitutes for labor, the higher the elasticity of demand for labor; the fewer substitutes for labor, the lower the elasticity of demand for labor.*

Elasticity of Demand for Labor
Percentage change in the quantity demanded of labor divided by the percentage change in the wage rate.

EXHIBIT 27–8
The Market Supply of Labor

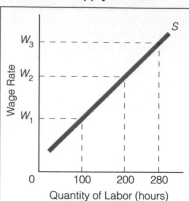

A direct relationship exists between the wage rate and the quantity of labor supplied. As the wage rate rises, more individuals will have their opportunity costs met and will be willing to supply their labor on the market. In short, as the wage rate rises, more individuals are willing to work.

The Market Supply of Labor

As the wage rate rises, the quantity supplied of labor rises, *ceteris paribus*. The upward-sloping labor supply curve in Exhibit 27–8 illustrates this. At a wage rate of W_1, individuals are willing to supply 100 labor hours; at the higher wage rate of W_2, individuals are willing to supply 200 labor hours (this is because some individuals who were not willing to work at a wage rate of W_1 are willing to work at a wage rate of W_2, and also because some individuals who were working at W_1 will be willing to supply more hours at W_2); at the even higher wage rate of W_3, individuals are willing to supply 280 labor hours.

For any given individual, the wage he receives must cover his opportunity costs—the wage he could receive in his next best line of employment. If an employer does not pay this amount to an employee, the employee will not work for the employer. For example, if Miller can work for Cusack for $1,000 a month, and Richards offers Miller $500 a month, then Richards is not meeting Miller's opportunity costs and therefore will not be successful in employing him.

Question:

A person who could be working for a major corporation earning $150,000 a year instead works at a small private college where she earns $54,000 a year. Obviously, her employer isn't paying her "next best alternative wage." Isn't it the case that the employer is not meeting the person's opportunity costs?

Answer:

No, it isn't. In speaking about the supply of labor, we assume that "all other things are held constant." This takes into account the nonmoney or nonpecuniary benefits individuals receive in their work. The person who chooses to work at the $54,000 job instead of the $150,000 job is probably receiving some nonmoney benefits at the private college that compensate her for the reduced income she is earning.

For example, she might be working at a more leisurely pace than she would in the big corporation, or maybe what she is doing is more enjoyable, or the hours are shorter. If we add nonmoney benefits to the overall pay package a person receives in his or her work, we conclude that an employer must provide an employee a wage-plus-nonmoney-benefits package at least equal to the employee's next best wage-plus-nonmoney-benefits package before the person will work for that employer.

Changes in the Supply of Labor

Changes in the wage rate change the quantity supplied of labor. But what changes the entire labor supply curve? Two factors of major importance are wage rates in other labor markets and the nonmoney or nonpecuniary aspects of a job.

Wage Rates in Other Labor Markets.   Deborah currently works as a technician in a television manufacturing plant. She has skills suitable for a number of jobs. One day she learns that the computer manufacturing plant on the other side of town is offering 33 percent more pay per hour. Since she is also trained to work as a computer operator, Deborah decides to leave her current job and apply for work at the computer manufacturing plant. In short, the wage rate offered in other labor markets can bring about a change in the supply of labor in a particular labor market.

Nonmoney or Nonpecuniary Aspects of a Job.   Other things held constant, people prefer to avoid dirty, heavy, dangerous work in cold climates. An increase in the overall "unpleasantness" of a job (for example, an increased probability of contracting lung cancer working in an asbestos factory) will cause a decrease in the supply of labor to that firm or industry. An increase in the overall "pleasantness" of a job (employees are now entitled to a longer lunch break and use of the company gym) will cause an increase in the supply of labor to that firm or industry.

Putting Supply and Demand Together

Exhibit 27–9 illustrates a particular labor market. The equilibrium wage rate and quantity of labor are established by the forces of supply and demand. At a wage rate of W_2, there is a surplus of labor. Some people who want to work at this wage rate will not be able to find jobs. A subset of this group will begin to offer their services for a lower wage rate. The wage rate will move down until it reaches W_1. At the wage rate W_3, there is a shortage of labor. Some demanders of labor will begin to bid up the wage rate until it reaches W_1. At the equilibrium wage rate, W_1, the quantity supplied of labor equals the quantity demanded of labor.

Why Wage Rates Differ

Why do wage rates differ? To answer this, we must ask what conditions would be necessary for everyone to receive the same pay.

Assume the following conditions hold: (1) The demand for every type of labor is the same. (Throughout our analysis, any wage differentials caused by demand are short-run differentials.) (2) There are no special nonpecuniary aspects to any job. (3) All labor is ultimately homogeneous and can costlessly be trained for different types of employment. (4) All labor is mobile at zero cost.

EXHIBIT 27–9
Equilibrium in a Particular Labor Market

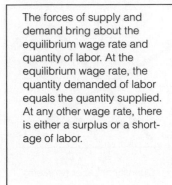

The forces of supply and demand bring about the equilibrium wage rate and quantity of labor. At the equilibrium wage rate, the quantity demanded of labor equals the quantity supplied. At any other wage rate, there is either a surplus or a shortage of labor.

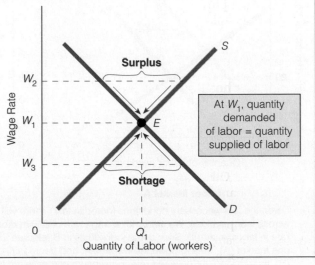

Given these conditions, there would be no difference in wages rates in the long run. Consider Exhibit 27–10, where two labor markets, A and B, are shown. Initially, the supply conditions are different, with a greater supply of workers in labor market B (represented by S_B) than in labor market A (represented by S_A). Because of the different supply conditions, more workers are working in labor market B (Q_B) than in labor market A (Q_A), and the equilibrium wage rate in labor market B ($10) is lower than the equilibrium wage rate in labor market A ($30).

The differences in the wage rates between the two labor markets will not last. We have previously assumed that labor can move costlessly from one labor market to another (so why not move from the lower-paying job to the higher-paying job?), that there are no special nonpecuniary aspects to any job (there is no nonpecuniary reason for not moving), that labor is ultimately homogeneous (workers who work in labor market B can work in labor market A), and that if workers need training to make a move from one labor market to another, they are not only capable of being trained but also can acquire the training costlessly. As a result, some workers in labor market B will relocate to labor market A, decreasing the supply of workers to S_B' in labor market B and increasing the supply of workers to S_A' in labor market A. The relocation of workers ends when the equilibrium wage rate in both markets is the same—$20.

We conclude that wage rates will not differ if our four conditions hold. But, in reality, they do not hold. Therefore, we can direct our attention to why wage rates differ. Obviously, they differ because demand conditions are not the same in all labor markets (important to explain short-run wage differentials *only*), nor are supply conditions; there are nonpecuniary aspects to different jobs, labor is not homogeneous, labor cannot be retrained without cost, and labor is not costlessly mobile.

EXHIBIT 27–10
Wage Rate Equilization across Labor Markets

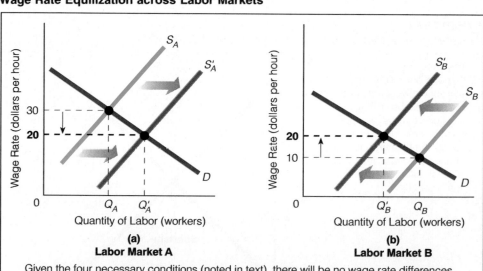

(a)
Labor Market A

(b)
Labor Market B

Given the four necessary conditions (noted in text), there will be no wage rate differences across labor markets. We start with a wage rate of $30 in labor market A and a $10 wage rate in labor market B. Soon some individuals in B relocate to A, increasing the supply in one market (A), driving down the wage rate, and decreasing the supply in the other market (B), thus driving up the wage rate. Equilibrium comes when the same wage rate is paid in both labor markets. This outcome critically depends on the necessary conditions holding.

Why Demand and Supply Curves Differ in Different Labor Markets

Saying that wage rates differ because demand and supply conditions in different labor markets differ raises the question of why this is the case.

First, consider demand. We know that the firm's *MRP* curve is its factor demand curve, so we need to look at what affects the components of *MRP*, namely, *MR* and *MPP*. Product supply and demand conditions determine price and therefore indirectly affect marginal revenue (since $MR = \Delta TR/\Delta Q$ and $TR = P \times Q$) and factor demand. In short, since the supply and demand conditions in *product markets* are different, it follows that the demand for labor in different *labor markets* will be different, too.

The second factor, the marginal physical product of labor, is affected by individual workers' *own abilities and skills* (both innate and learned), the *degree of effort* they put forth on the job, and the *other factors of production* they work with. With respect to the latter, American workers are more productive than workers in many other countries because they work with many more capital goods and much more technical know-how. If all individuals had the same innate and learned skills and abilities, applied the same degree of effort on the job, and worked with the same amount and quality of other factors of production, wages would differ less than they currently do.

What about supply? Why are the supply conditions in different labor markets different? First, as we noted earlier, jobs have *different nonpecuniary qualities.* Working as a coal miner in West Virginia is not as attractive a job as working as a gardener at a lush resort in Hawaii. We would expect this fact to be reflected in the supply of coal miners and gardeners.

Second, supply is also a reflection of *the number of persons who can actually do a job.* Williamson may want to be a nuclear physicist, but may not have the ability in science and mathematics to be one. Johnson may want to be a basketball player, but may not have the ability to be one.

Third, even if individuals have the ability to work at a certain job, they may perceive *the training costs as too high* (relative to the perceived benefits) to train for it. Miller may have the ability to be a brain surgeon, but views the years of schooling required to become one too high a price to pay.

Fourth, sometimes supply in different labor markets reflects a difference in the *cost of moving* across markets. Wage rates might be higher in Alaska than in Alabama for comparable labor because the workers in Alabama find the cost of relocating to Alaska too high relative to the benefits of receiving a higher wage.

Question:

Do the same factors that affect the demand for and supply of labor also affect the wage rate labor is paid?

Answer:

Yes, they do. Since the wage rate is determined by supply and demand forces, the factors that affect these forces indirectly affect wage rates. Exhibit 27–11 summarizes these factors.

Why Did You Choose the Major That You Chose?

It is interesting to note that our lives are influenced by what happens in labor markets. Consider a college student choosing a major. The decision comes down

EXHIBIT 27–11
The Wage Rate

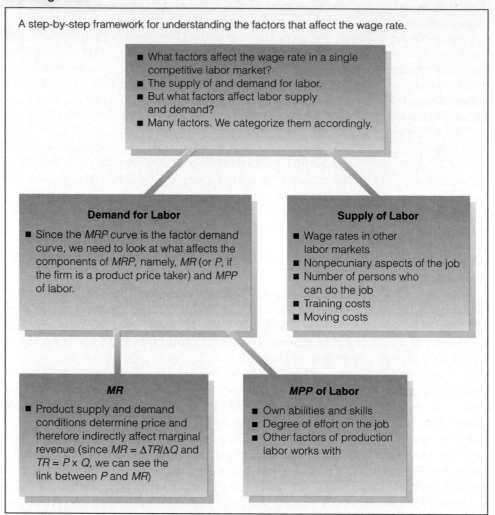

A step-by-step framework for understanding the factors that affect the wage rate.

- What factors affect the wage rate in a single competitive labor market?
- The supply of and demand for labor.
- But what factors affect labor supply and demand?
- Many factors. We categorize them accordingly.

Demand for Labor
- Since the *MRP* curve is the factor demand curve, we need to look at what affects the components of *MRP*, namely, *MR* (or *P*, if the firm is a product price taker) and *MPP* of labor.

Supply of Labor
- Wage rates in other labor markets
- Nonpecuniary aspects of the job
- Number of persons who can do the job
- Training costs
- Moving costs

MR
- Product supply and demand conditions determine price and therefore indirectly affect marginal revenue (since $MR = \Delta TR/\Delta Q$ and $TR = P \times Q$, we can see the link between P and MR)

MPP of Labor
- Own abilities and skills
- Degree of effort on the job
- Other factors of production labor works with

to a choice between accounting and English. The student believes that English is more fun and interesting, but that accounting, on average, will earn her enough additional income to compensate for the lack of fun in accounting. Specifically, at $40,000 annual salary for accounting and at $30,000 annual salary for English, the student is indifferent between accounting and English. But at $41,000 for accounting and $30,000 for English, accounting moves ahead.

Of course, what accounting "pays" is determined by the demand for and supply of accountants. Once we realize this, we understand that other people influenced our person's decision to go into accounting. To illustrate, suppose the Congress passes more intricate tax laws that require more accountants to figure them out. This increases the demand for accountants which, in turn, ends up raising the wage rate for accountants. And an increase in the wage rate that accountants receive increases the probability that more people—perhaps you—will major in accounting and not in English, philosophy, or history.

As you can see, economics—of which markets play a major part—helps explain why part of your life is the way it is.

If the Tax Is Divided Equally, Why Do I Pay It All?

When Congress established the Social Security system, it instituted Social Security taxes and split the tax between the employer and employees. By doing this, it intended to split the cost of the system. In 1991, the tax was $15.30 per $100 on annual maximum taxable earnings of $53,400. Half of the $15.30 per $100, or $7.65, was *placed* on the employer, and the other half was *placed* on the employee.

Economists know that sometimes taxes *placed* on one group of persons are actually *paid* for by another group. To a large extent, this is the case with the Social Security tax. Although half of the tax is placed on the employer, and half is placed on the employee, the employee ends up *paying* almost all of the tax.

Exhibit 27–12 approximates this conclusion. We say "approximates," because most economists believe that the supply curve for labor *in the aggregate* is extremely inelastic. For simplicity, we have drawn the supply curve as perfectly inelastic, or vertical. In short, our supply curve approximates the actual supply curve. In a situation where no Social Security tax is placed on the employer, D_1 is the relevant demand curve for labor. The equilibrium wage rate is $9, meaning that employers are willing to pay a maximum of $9 per hour (per worker) for Q_1 workers. (Remember that a demand curve gives us the *maximum amount* per unit a buyer is willing to pay for alternative quantities. In the case of the labor market, this is the *maximum wage* rate per worker for alternative quantities of labor.)

Now consider placing the entire Social Security tax on the employer in-

stead of half on the employer and half on the employee. Suppose employers calculate the Social Security tax on an hourly basis and find that they have to "pay" $1 per hour for every employee they hire. If $9 was the equilibrium wage rate *before the tax,* then employers are not willing to pay any more for the same number of workers *after the tax.* Employers are only willing to pay labor $9 per hour

minus the hourly computed tax. In short, from the employer's perspective, the demand curve for labor falls by $1 for each alternative quantity of labor. Employers are now willing to pay only a maximum of $8 per hour per workers for Q_1 workers. Given a vertical supply curve, $8 per hour is the new equilibrium wage rate.

Reviewing the situation, we see that if (what turns out to be) a $1 per

EXHIBIT 27–12
Who Pays the Social Security Tax?

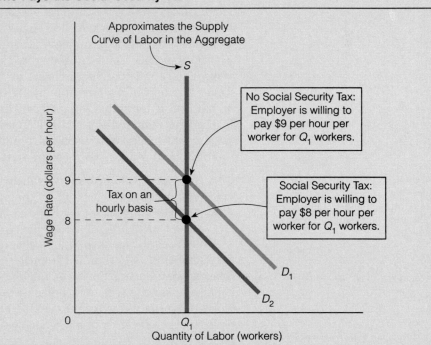

With no Social Security tax, the equilibrium wage rate is $9 per hour; employers are willing to pay a maximum of $9 per hour (per worker) for Q_1 workers. With the Social Security tax fully placed on employers, and computed on an hourly basis, employers are willing to pay $9 per hour minus the hourly computed tax for Q_1 workers. Since we have assumed the hourly tax is $1 per employee and the supply curve for labor is perfectly inelastic in the aggregate, the new equilibrium wage rate is $8. Under the conditions stated, the employee ends up paying the full Social Security tax in the form of lower wages.

hour Social Security tax is placed on employers, they will only be willing to pay up to a maximum of $8, instead of $9, per worker for Q_1 workers. Workers who received $9 before the tax will now receive $8 per hour after the tax.

Who really pays the employer's portion of the Social Security tax? The employees pay it in the form of lower hourly wages.

Question:

If the employer portion of the Social Security tax is actually paid by the employee indirectly in terms of lower wages, and the employee also has to pay his or her portion of the tax directly, what did a person earning, say, $40,000 in 1991 pay in total Social Security Taxes?

Answer:
The contribution rate for both employer and employee was 7.65 percent in 1991. Since the employee pays approximately the full Social Security tax, we can simply say that the contribution for the employee was 15.30 percent (7.65 × 2 = 15.30). The employee would have paid $6,120 ($40,000 × .1530 = $6,120).

Marginal Productivity Theory

Here are some things we know:

1. If a firm is a factor price taker, marginal factor cost is constant and equal to factor price, $MFC = P$. Suppose we have a factor price taker that hires labor. For the firm, $MFC = W$, where W is the wage rate.
2. Firms hire the factor quantity at which $MRP = MFC$.
3. Taking points 1 and 2 together, we know that a factor price taker pays labor a wage equal to its marginal revenue product, $W = MRP$. That is, since $MFC = W$ (point 1), and $MRP = MFC$ (point 2), it follows that $W = MRP$.
4. If a firm is a product price taker, $MRP = VMP$.
5. If a firm is both a product price taker *and* a factor price taker, it pays labor a wage equal to its value marginal product, $W = VMP$. That is, since $W = MRP$ (point 3), and $MRP = VMP$ (point 4), it follows that $W = VMP$.

Marginal Productivity Theory
States that firms in competitive or perfect product and factor markets pay factors their marginal revenue products.

This is the **marginal productivity theory,** which states that if a firm sells its product and purchases its factors in competitive or perfect markets (that is, it is a product price taker and a factor price taker; see box I in Exhibit 27–1), it pays its factors their *MRP* or *VMP* (since the two are equal for a product price taker).

In other words, the theory holds that under the competitive conditions specified, if a factor unit is withdrawn from the productive process, and the amount of all other factors remains the same, the *decrease in the value of the product produced* equals the factor payment received by the factor unit. To illustrate, suppose Wilson works for price taker firm X producing good X. One day he quits his job (but nothing else relevant to the firm changes). As a result, the total revenue of the firm falls by $100. If Wilson was paid $100, then he received his *MRP*. He was paid a wage equal to his contribution to the productive process.[6]

Question:

Aren't some workers paid less than their MRPs (less than their contributions to the productive process)? If so, isn't this evidence sufficient to reject the marginal productivity theory?

[6]Recall that there are two ways to calculate *MRP*: $MRP = \Delta TR/\Delta factor$, and $MRP = MR \times MPP$. In this example, we used the first method. When Wilson quits his job, the change in the denominator is 1 factor unit. If, as a result, *TR* falls by $100, then the change in the numerator is $100.

Answer:

The theory specifies that the firm sells its product and purchases its factors in competitive, or perfect, markets. Not all firms fit into this category; thus, certainly some workers are not paid their *MRP*s. (We discuss marginal productivity theory and market imperfections in the next chapter.)

Follow-up Question:

Are workers who work for firms that "sell their products and purchase their factors in competitive markets" paid their MRP*s?*

Answer:

The proponents of marginal productivity theory argue that employees in this setting are paid wages that over time closely approximate their *MRP*s. In other words, not all employees are paid their exact *MRP*s, but most employees in this setting are paid *close to* their *MRP*s. The critics of the theory point out that it is very difficult for firms to measure the value of their employees' marginal products accurately. The proponents argue that the firms have a monetary incentive to make a reasonable estimate. They add that firms interview and screen potential employees, as well as regularly evaluate current employees, to acquire information on workers' *MRP*s.

LABOR MARKETS AND INFORMATION

We now look at job hiring, employment practices, and employment discrimination and how information, or the lack of it, affects these processes.

Employee Screening: Or What Is Your GPA?

Employers typically do not know exactly how productive a potential employee will be on the job. What the employer wants, but lacks, is complete information about the potential employee's future job performance.

This raises two questions. First, why would an employer want complete information about a potential employee's future job performance? Second, what does the employer do because he or she lacks complete information?

The answer to the first question is obvious. Employers have a strong monetary incentive to hire good, stable, quick-learning, responsible, hard-working, punctual employees. One study found that corporate spending on training employees reached $40 billion annually. Obviously, corporations would like to see the highest return possible for their training expenditures. This requires that they hire employees who will make the training pay off. This is where **screening** comes in.

Screening is the process used by employers to increase the probability of choosing "good" employees based on certain criteria. For example, an employer might ask a young college graduate searching for a job what his GPA was in college. This is a screening mechanism. The employer might know from past experience that people with high GPAs turn out to be better employees, on average, than persons with low GPAs.

Promoting from Within

Sometimes employers promote from within the company because they have more information on company employees than on potential employees.

One's GPA is sometimes a screening device in the labor market.

■

Screening
The process used by employers to increase the probability of choosing "good" employees based on certain criteria.

Suppose the executive vice president in charge of sales is retiring from Trideck, Inc. The president of the company could hire an outsider to replace the vice president, but often she will select an insider about whom she has some knowledge. What may look like discrimination to outsiders—"That company discriminates against persons not working for it"—may simply be a reflection of the difference in costs to the employer of acquiring relevant information on employees inside and outside the company.

Is It Discrimination or Is It an Information Problem?

Suppose the world is made up of people with characteristic X and people with characteristic Y. We call them X people and Y people, respectively. Over time, we observe that most employers are X people and that they tend to hire and promote proportionally more X than Y people. Are the Y people being discriminated against?

It could be. Nothing that we have said so far would rule this out. But, then, it may be that X people rarely hire or promote Y people because over time X employers have learned that Y people on average do not perform as well as X people.

So, in this example, we simply state that X people are not discriminating against Y people, but instead that Y people are not being hired and promoted as often as X people because, for whatever reason, Y people on average are not as productive as X people.

Suppose in this environment an extremely productive Y person comes along and applies for a job with an X employer. The problem is that the X employer does not know—she lacks complete information—about the full abilities of the Y person; furthermore, it is costly to acquire complete information. She bases her decision to reject the Y person's job application based on what she knows about Y people, which is that on average they are not as productive as X people. She doesn't do this because she has something against Y people, but because it is simply *too costly* for her to acquire complete information on every potential employee—X or Y.

We do not mean to imply that everything that looks like discrimination is really a problem of the high cost of information. Nonetheless, sometimes what looks like discrimination ("he doesn't like me, I'm a Y person") is a consequence of living in a world where acquiring complete information is "too costly."

CHAPTER SUMMARY

Price Takers, Price Searchers

■ The price taker–price searcher model can be used to describe firms as buyers in factor markets, just as it is used to describe firms as sellers in product markets.
■ A factor price taker can buy all of a factor it wants at the equilibrium price. It faces a horizontal (flat, perfectly elastic) supply curve of factors.
■ A factor price searcher drives up factor price if it buys an additional factor unit. It faces an upward-sloping supply curve of factors.
■ Two types of firms discussed in this chapter are (1) the product price taker and factor price taker and (2) the product price searcher and factor price taker.

Derived Demand

■ The demand for a factor is derived—hence, it is called a derived demand. Specifically, it is derived from, and directly related to, the demand for the product that the factor goes to produce; for example, the demand for auto workers is derived from the demand for autos.

MRP, MFC, VMP

■ Marginal revenue product (*MRP*) is the additional revenue generated by employing an additional factor unit. Marginal factor cost (*MFC*) is the additional cost incurred by employing an additional factor unit. The profit-maximizing firm buys that factor quantity at which $MRP = MFC$.

■ The *MRP* curve is the firm's factor demand curve; it shows how much of a factor the firm buys at different prices.

■ Whereas $MRP = MR \times MPP$, $VMP = P \times MPP$. For a product price taker, $P = MR$, so $MRP = VMP$. For a product price searcher, $P > MR$, so $VMP > MRP$. The *VMP* is a measure of the value that each factor unit adds to the firm's product.

■ For the firm that is a price taker in both product and factor markets, $VMP = MRP = MFC = $ *factor price* at the profit-maximizing factor quantity.

■ For the firm that is a price searcher in the product market and a price taker in the factor market, $VMP > MRP = MFC = $ *factor price* at the profit-maximizing factor quantity.

The Least-Cost Rule

■ The firm minimizes costs by buying factors in the combination at which the *MPP*–price ratio for each is the same. For example, if there are two factors, labor and capital, the least-cost rule reads

$$MPP_L/P_L = MPP_K/P_K$$

Labor and Wages

■ A change in the price of the product labor produces, or a change in the marginal physical product of labor (reflected in a shift in the *MPP* curve), will shift the demand curve for labor.

■ The higher (lower) the elasticity of demand for the product labor produces, the higher (lower) the elasticity of demand for labor. The higher (lower) the labor cost–total cost ratio, the higher (lower) the elasticity of demand for labor. The more (fewer) substitutes for labor, the higher (lower) the elasticity of demand for labor.

■ As the wage rate rises, the quantity supplied of labor rises, *ceteris paribus*.

■ At the equilibrium wage rate, the quantity supplied of labor equals the quantity demanded of labor.

Marginal Productivity Theory

■ Marginal productivity theory states that firms in competitive or perfect product and factor markets pay factors their marginal revenue products.

Key Terms and Concepts

Product Price Taker	Derived Demand	Least-Cost Rule
Product Price Searcher	Marginal Revenue	Elasticity of Demand for
Factor Price Taker	Product	Labor
Factor Price Searcher	Marginal Factor Cost	Marginal Productivity
	Value Marginal Product	Theory
		Screening

QUESTIONS AND PROBLEMS

1. The supply curve is horizontal for a single price taker in a factor market; however, the industry supply curve is upward sloping. Explain how this can be.

2. What forces and factors determine the wage rate for a particular type of labor?

3. What is the relationship between labor productivity and wage rates?

4. What might be one effect of government legislating wage rates?

5. Using the theory developed in this chapter, explain the following: (a) why a worker in Ethiopia is likely to earn much less than a worker in Japan; (b) why the army expects recruitment to be up during economic recessions; (c) why basketball stars earn relatively large incomes; (d) why jobs that carry a health risk offer higher pay than jobs that do not, *ceteris paribus*.

6. Discuss the factors that might prevent the equalization of wage rates for identical or comparable jobs across labor markets.

7. Prepare a list of questions that an interviewer is likely to ask an interviewee in a job interview. Try to identify which of the questions are part of the interviewer's screening process.

8. Explain why the market demand curve for labor is not simply the horizontal summation of the firms' demand curves for labor.

9. Discuss the firm's objective, its constraints, and how it makes its choices in its role as buyer of resources.

10. Explain the relationship between each of the following: (a) elasticity of demand for a product and the elasticity of demand for labor that produces the product; (b) labor cost–total cost ratio and the elasticity of demand for labor; (c) the number of substitutes for labor and the elasticity of demand for labor.

11. Fill in the blanks.

(1) Units of Factor X	(2) Quantity of Output	(3) Marginal Physical Product of X (MPP_X) $MPP_X = \dfrac{\Delta(2)}{\Delta(1)}$	(4) Product Price, Marginal Revenue ($P = MR$)	(5) Total Revenue $TR = P \times Q$ $= (4) \times (2)$	(6) Marginal Revenue Product of $X(MRP_X)$ $MRP_X = \dfrac{\Delta TR}{\Delta X} = \dfrac{\Delta(5)}{\Delta(1)}$ $= MR \times MPP_X = (4) \times (3)$
0	15	0	$8	____	____
1	24	____	8	____	____
2	32	____	8	____	____
3	39	____	8	____	____
4	45	____	8	____	____
5	50	____	8	____	____

CHAPTER

28

WAGES, UNIONS, AND LABOR

WHAT THIS CHAPTER IS ABOUT

In this chapter, we discuss labor unions. We start with a few facts and figures, followed by a brief history of the labor union movement. Next, we examine the objectives and practices of labor unions. Finally, we look at the effects of labor unions on wage rates and prices.

THE FACTS AND FIGURES OF LABOR UNIONS

■

Here we discuss the different types of labor unions, and give some statistics that place unions within the overall labor force.

Types of Unions

Economists often speak of three different types of labor unions: craft (trade) unions, industrial unions, and public employee unions. A **craft or trade union** is a union whose membership is made up of individuals who practice the same craft or trade. Examples include the plumbers', electricians', and musicians' unions.

An **industrial union** is a union whose membership is made up of workers who work in the same firm or industry but do not all practice the same craft or trade. Examples include the autoworkers' and the steelworkers' unions. For an industrial union to be successful, it must unionize all firms in an industry. If not, union firms will face competition from (possibly lower-cost) nonunion firms, which may lead to a decrease in the number of union firms and workers.

A **public employee union** is a union whose membership is made up of workers who work for the local, state, or federal government. Examples include teachers', police, and firefighters' unions. Over the past two decades, this has been one of the fastest-growing subsets of the union movement.

Besides these three types of unions, some economists hold that employee associations such as the American Medical Association (AMA), the American Association of University Professors (AAUP), and the American Bar Association (ABA) are a type of union. An **employee association** is an organization whose members belong to a particular profession. At first sight, it may seem odd to place professional employee associations into the union category. Some economists argue, however, that employee associations often have the same objectives and implement the same practices to meet those objectives as craft, industrial, and public employee unions; consequently, these associations should be considered unions.

A Few Facts and Figures

Union membership as a percentage of the labor force (total number of union members divided by total work force) was 5.6 percent in 1910, rising to about 12 percent in 1920. By 1930, it was down to around 7.4 percent, and in 1934 it fell to approximately 5 percent. From the late 1930s until the middle-1950s, union membership as a percentage of the labor force grew. It reached its peak of 25 percent in the mid-1950s. In recent years, it has declined. In 1991, it was approximately 17 percent.

HISTORY OF THE LABOR MOVEMENT

■

In this section, we focus on some of the people, events, legislation, and judicial decisions that comprise the history of the labor movement, which began to emerge in the United States after the Civil War.

The Knights of Labor

In 1869, a group of Philadelphia tailors, led by Uriah S. Stephens, organized the Knights of Labor. Seventeen years later, in 1886, its membership totaled approxi-

---

Craft (Trade) Union
A union whose membership is made up of individuals who practice the same craft or trade.

Industrial Union
A union whose membership is made up of individuals who work in the same firm or industry but do not all practice the same craft or trade.

Public Employee Union
A union whose membership is made up of individuals who work for the local, state, or federal government.

Employee Association
An organization whose members belong to a particular profession.

mately 800,000. The Knights of Labor welcomed anyone who worked for a living—farmers, skilled craft workers, unskilled workers—with a few exceptions, such as liquor dealers. The Knights of Labor sought certain political objectives as well as economic ones. Among other things, it called for the establishment of workers' cooperatives, higher wages, an eight-hour working day, and the replacement of capitalism with socialism.

On May 4, 1886, approximately 100,000 members of the Knights of Labor demonstrated in front of the McCormick Harvester Works in Haymarket Square in Chicago. A group of anarchists tossed a bomb into the crowd of people, and a riot erupted in which several people were killed. Public sentiment soon turned against the Knights of Labor, although no wrongdoing on their part was proved, and the union began to lose membership until 1917 when it collapsed.

The American Federation of Labor

The American Federation of Labor (AFL) was formed in 1886 under the leadership of Samuel Gompers, who ran the organization until his death in 1924. Gompers believed that the AFL should consist mainly of skilled craft workers; he thought that the gains skilled craft workers could obtain through the union would be diminished if unskilled and semiskilled workers were admitted. Membership in the AFL was approximately 2 million in 1904, rising to 5 million in 1920, and then falling to around 3 million in 1930.

Unlike the Knights of Labor, the AFL concentrated on basic economic issues. It sought to work within the capitalist system, instead of advocating an overthrow of private property and the advancement of socialist principles. Its activities were almost solely directed to lobbying for better pay and improved working conditions for its members.

The Courts in the Early Days

In the early days of the labor union movement, the courts treated unions as illegal conspiracies. Union leaders were regularly prosecuted and sued for damages. In 1842, in an important case decided by the Supreme Court of Massachusetts, the court ruled that unions were not illegal per se, but that certain union practices were. In the early 1900s, the Sherman Antitrust Act (which declares, among other things, that "every person who shall monopolize, or attempt to monopolize, or combine or conspire with any other person or persons, to monopolize any part of the trade or commerce along the several States, or with foreign nations, shall be deemed guilty of a misdemeanor") was applied to labor unions, although many persons believed this was not the intent of Congress. During this period, injunctions were used against labor unions to prevent strikes, pickets, and boycotts. (Injunctions are court orders that were originally designed to prevent damage to property when it was thought that the court processes would be too slow.) Owing to the use of injunctions by employers during this period, labor unions found it very difficult to carry out a strike.

The Norris–LaGuardia and Wagner Acts

The legal climate in which labor unions operated changed dramatically in 1932 with the passage of the Norris–LaGuardia Act by the U.S. Congress. The main thrust of the act was to restrain the use of injunctions. It declared that workers should be "free from the interference, restraint, or coercion of employers" in choosing their union representatives.

In 1935, the Congress passed the Wagner Act, which required employers to bargain in good faith with workers; it also made it illegal for employers to interfere with their employees' rights to organize or join a union. In addition, the act set up the National Labor Relations Board (NLRB) to investigate unfair labor practices. Union membership grew by leaps and bounds as a result of the Norris–LaGuardia and Wagner acts.

The Congress of Industrial Organizations (CIO)

Because of the better legal climate for labor unions, a push to unionize the major production industries such as steel, automobiles, and rubber began. This, however, caused some discontent within the AFL. The craft unionists in the AFL did not believe that long-lasting unions could be formed in industries; they wanted new members to be part of the craft unions. In 1938, John L. Lewis of the United Mine Workers, who led the opposition to the craft unionists, and other like-minded union leaders broke with the AFL and formed the Congress of Industrial Organizations (CIO). The CIO successfully unionized the steel, rubber, textile, meat-packing, and automobile industries.

For a time, both the AFL and the CIO increased their membership. Then after World War II, membership in the CIO began to decline. Some thought that the bickering between the AFL and CIO was the cause. In 1955, the craft-union AFL and the industrial-union CIO merged under the leadership of George Meany. The merger did not prevent the decline in membership, nor did it stop the discord between the AFL and the CIO.

The Taft–Hartley Act

The congressional sentiment that made the Wagner Act possible in 1935 began to shift after World War II. A few particularly damaging strikes in 1946 set the stage for the Taft–Hartley Act in 1947. This act gave states the right to pass **right-to-work laws.** These laws prohibit unions from requiring employers to establish union membership as a condition of employment. The Taft–Hartley Act also outlawed certain union practices, such as strikes and boycotts aimed at forcing self-employed persons to join unions, and gave the president of the United States the right to issue an injunction in cases where a strike could seriously disrupt the economy.

The evaluation of Taft–Hartley depends on the observer. Many labor union leaders and members see it as a strongly anti-union piece of legislation. Many other persons believe that it neutralizes some of the undesirable consequences of union action.

Right-to-Work Laws
Laws that make it illegal to require union membership for purposes of employment.

The Landrum–Griffin Act

The Landrum-Griffin Act was passed in 1959 with the expressed intent of policing the internal affairs of labor unions. It calls for regular union elections and secret ballots and requires union leaders to report on the union's finances. It also prohibits ex-convicts and communists from holding union office.

OBJECTIVES OF LABOR UNIONS

■

Labor unions usually seek one of three objectives: to employ all their members, to maximize the total wage bill, or to maximize income for a limited number of union members.

Employment for All Members

One possible objective of a labor union is employment for all its members. To illustrate, suppose the demand curve in Exhibit 28–1 represents the demand for labor in a given union. Also suppose that the total membership of the union is Q_1. If the objective of the union is to have its total membership employed, then the wage rate that must exist in the market is W_1; at W_1 firms want to hire the total union membership.

Maximizing the Total Wage Bill

The total wage bill received by the membership of a union is equal to the wage rate times the number of labor hours worked. One possible objective of a labor union is to maximize this dollar amount; that is, to maximize the number of dollars coming *from* the employer *to* union members. In Exhibit 28–1, the wage rate that maximizes the total wage bill is W_2. This is where the quantity of labor is Q_2, and the elasticity of demand for labor is equal to 1. We recall from Chapter 21 that total revenue (or total expenditure) is maximized when price elasticity of demand is equal to 1, or demand has unit elasticity. It follows that the total wage bill is maximized at that point where the demand for labor is unit elastic. Note, however,

EXHIBIT 28–1
Labor Union Objectives

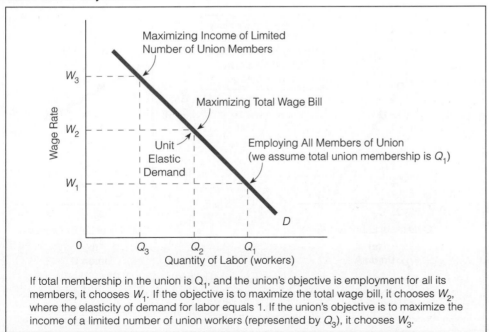

If total membership in the union is Q_1, and the union's objective is employment for all its members, it chooses W_1. If the objective is to maximize the total wage bill, it chooses W_2, where the elasticity of demand for labor equals 1. If the union's objective is to maximize the income of a limited number of union workers (represented by Q_3), it chooses W_3.

that fewer union members are working at W_2 than at W_1, telling us that there is a trade-off between higher wages and the employment of union members.

Maximizing Income for a Limited Number of Union Members

Some economists have suggested that a labor union might want neither total employment of its membership nor maximization of the total wage bill; instead it might prefer to maximize income for a limited number of union members, perhaps those with the most clout or seniority in the union. Suppose this group is represented by Q_3 in Exhibit 28–1. The highest wage at which this group can be employed is W_3; thus, the union might seek this wage rate instead of any lower wage.

Question:

Exhibit 28–1 suggests that the union must make a wage–employment trade-off. It can get higher wage rates, but some of the union members will lose their jobs in the process. Is this correct?

Answer:

Yes, a higher wage rate means fewer union members employed, *ceteris paribus*. The union is likely to be aware that this wage–employment trade-off exists. Notice also that this wage–employment trade-off depends on the elasticity of demand for labor.

Consider the demand for labor in two unions, A and B, in Exhibit 28–2. If both unions bargain for a wage increase from W_1 to W_2, the quantity of labor falls off

EXHIBIT 28–2
The Wage–Employment Trade-Off: Two Cases

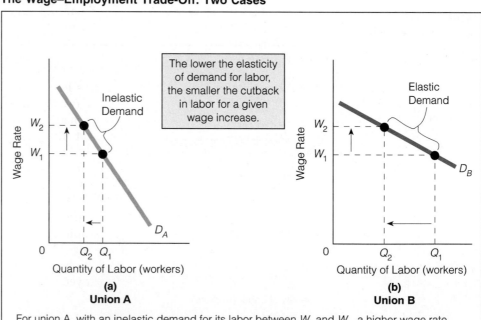

For union A, with an inelastic demand for its labor between W_1 and W_2, a higher wage rate brings about a smaller cutback in workers than for union B, with an elastic demand for its labor between W_1 and W_2. We predict that union B will be less likely to push for higher wages than union A because its wage–employment trade-off is more pronounced.

much more in union B, where demand for labor is elastic between the two wage rates, than in union A, where the demand for labor is inelastic between the two wage rates. We would expect that union B will be less likely to push for higher wages than union A, *ceteris paribus*. The reason is that the wage–employment trade-off is more pronounced for union B than union A. It is simply costlier (in terms of union members' jobs) for union B to push for higher wages than it is for union A.

The lower the elasticity of demand for labor, the smaller the cutback in labor for any given wage increase.

■

PRACTICES OF LABOR UNIONS

■

Labor unions try to meet their objectives by influencing one or more of the following factors: the elasticity of demand for labor, the demand for labor, and the supply of labor.

Elasticity of Demand for Union Labor

We saw in Exhibit 28–2 that the lower the elasticity of demand for labor, the smaller the cutback in labor for any given wage increase. Obviously, the smaller the cutback in labor for a given wage increase, the better it is from the viewpoint of the labor union. Between losing 200 jobs because of a wage rate increase of $2 and losing 50 jobs, the labor union prefers to lose the smaller number of jobs. This raises the question of how the labor union might go about lowering the elasticity of demand for its labor.

Availability of Substitute Products. Consider the autoworkers' union, whose members produce American automobiles. We know from Chapter 27 that the lower the elasticity of demand for American automobiles, the lower the elasticity of demand for the labor that produces automobiles. We would expect, then, that unions would attempt to reduce the availability of substitutes for the products they produce, such as through import restrictions. The autoworkers' union, for example, has in recent years proposed restrictions on Japanese car imports.

Availability of Substitute Factors. The fewer the substitute factors for union labor, the lower the elasticity of demand for union labor. There are two general substitutes for union labor: nonunion labor and certain types of machines—for example, a musical synthesizer (that can sound like many different instruments) is a substitute for a group of musicians playing different instruments. Labor unions often have attempted to reduce the availability of substitute factors for themselves, both of the nonunion labor variety and the nonhuman variety. Thus, labor unions commonly oppose the relaxation of immigration laws, they usually favor the repatriation of illegal aliens, they generally are in favor of a high minimum wage (which increases the relative price of nonunion labor vis-à-vis union labor), and they usually oppose machines that can be substituted for their labor. Also, in the area of construction, unions usually specify which jobs can be done by, say, electricians only (thus prohibiting substitute factors from being employed on certain jobs).

The Demand for Union Labor

Another objective of labor unions is to increase the demand for union labor. All other things held constant, this leads to higher wage rates and more union labor employed. How can labor unions increase the demand for their labor? Consider the following possibilities.

Increasing Product Demand. Unions occasionally urge the buying public to buy the products they produce. Unions advertise, urging people to "look for the union label" or to look for the label that reads "Made in the U.S.A." As we mentioned earlier, they sometimes also support legislation that either keeps out imports altogether or makes them more expensive.

Increasing Substitute Factor Prices. If union action leads to a rise in the relative price of factors that are substitutes for union labor, the demand for union labor rises. (Recall from Chapter 3 that if X and Y are substitutes, and the price of X rises, so does the demand for Y.) For this reason, unions have often lobbied for an increase in the minimum wage—the wage received mostly by unskilled labor, which is a substitute for skilled union labor. The first minimum wage legislation was passed at a time when many companies were moving from the unionized North to the nonunionized South. The minimum wage made the nonunionized, relatively unskilled labor in the South more expensive and is said to have slowed the movement of companies to the South.

Increasing Marginal Physical Product. If unions can increase the productivity of their members, the demand for their labor will rise. With this in mind, unions prefer to add skilled labor to their ranks, and they sometimes undertake training programs for new entrants.

The Supply of Union Labor

A third objective of labor unions is to decrease the supply of labor. A decreased supply translates into higher wage rates. How might the labor union decrease the supply of labor from what it might be if the labor union did not exist? One possibility is to control the supply of labor in a market.

Craft unions in particular have been moderately successful in getting employers to hire only union labor. In the past, they were successful at turning some businesses into closed shops. A **closed shop** is an organization in which an employee must belong to the union before he or she can work. Once unions can determine, or at least control in some way, the supply of labor in a given market, they can decrease it from what it would ordinarily have been. They can do this by restricting membership, by requiring long apprenticeships, or by rigid certification requirements. The closed shop was prohibited by the Taft–Hartley Act.

The union shop, however, is legal in many states today. A **union shop** is an organization that does not require individuals to be union members in order to be hired, but does require them to join the union within a certain period of time after becoming employed. Today, unions typically argue for union shops and against the prohibition of closed shops. They also typically argue against state right-to-work laws (which some, but not all, states have), which make it illegal to require union membership for purposes of employment. (The Taft–Hartley Act allowed states to pass right-to-work laws and thus to override federal legislation that legalized union shops.) In short, the union shop is illegal in right-to-work states.

Affecting Wages Directly: Collective Bargaining

Besides increasing wage rates indirectly through changes in the demand for and supply of their labor, unions can directly affect wage rates through collective bar-

Closed Shop
An organization in which an employee must belong to the union before he or she can be hired.

Union Shop
An organization in which a worker is not required to be a member of the union to be hired, but must become a member within a certain period of time after being employed.

gaining. **Collective bargaining** is the process whereby wage rates are determined by the union bargaining with management on behalf of all its members. In collective bargaining, union members act together as a single unit in order to increase their bargaining power with management. On the other side of the market, the employers of labor may also band together and act as one unit. Their objective is the same as the union's: to increase their bargaining power.

From the viewpoint of the labor union, collective bargaining is unlikely to be successful unless the union can strike. A **strike** occurs when unionized employees refuse to work at a certain wage or under certain conditions. Exhibit 28–3 illustrates the effects of successful union collective bargaining.

Suppose the initial wage rate that exists in the labor market is the competitive wage rate of W_1. This is the wage rate that would exist if each employee were to bargain separately with management.

Management and the union (which represents *all* labor in this market) now sit down at a collective bargaining session. The union specifies that it wants a wage rate of W_2 and says that *none of its members will work at a lower wage rate.* This means the union holds that the new supply curve is $S'S$—or the heavy supply curve. In effect, the union is telling management that it cannot hire anyone for a lower wage rate than W_2 and if it wants to hire more people than want to work at this wage rate—represented by Q_3—it will have to increase the wage rate.

Whether the union can bring this higher wage rate (W_2) about depends on whether it can prevent labor from working at less than this wage. That is, if management does not initially agree to W_2, the union will have to call a strike and show management that it cannot hire any labor for a wage rate lower than W_2. It

Collective Bargaining
The process whereby wage rates and other issues are determined by a union bargaining with management on behalf of all union members.

Strike
The situation where union employees refuse to work at a certain wage or under certain conditions.

EXHIBIT 28–3
Successful Collective Bargaining by the Union

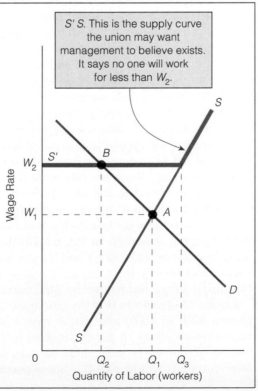

We start at a wage rate of W_1. The union's objective is to increase the wage rate to W_2. This means the union holds that the new supply curve of labor is $S'S$ —the heavy supply curve. To convince management that the new supply curve looks as the union says it does, the union will either have to threaten a strike or call one. We assume that the union is successful at raising the wage rate to W_2. As a consequence, fewer individuals will work in this labor market than would have worked at W_1.

$S'S$. This is the supply curve the union may want management to believe exists. It says no one will work for less than W_2.

has to convince management that the new supply curve looks the way the union says it looks. We assume here that the strike threat, or actual strike, is successful for the union and management agrees to the higher wage rate of W_2. As a result, fewer workers work in this labor market than worked at W_1. The new equilibrium is at point B instead of point A.

Strikes

It is clear that the purpose of a strike is to convince management that the supply curve is what the union says it is. Often, this depends on the ability of striking union employees to prevent nonstriking and nonunion employees from working for management at a lower wage rate than the union is seeking through collective bargaining. For example, if management can easily hire individuals at a wage rate lower than W_2 in Exhibit 28–3, it will not be convinced that the heavy supply curve is the relevant supply curve.

EFFECTS OF LABOR UNIONS

■

What are the effects of labor unions on wage rates? Are the effects the same in all labor markets? We address these two questions in the next sections.

The Case of Monopsony

Monopsony
A single buyer in a factor market.

A single buyer in a factor market is known as a **monopsony.** Some economists refer to a monopsony as a "buyer's monopoly." Monopoly, we recall, refers to a single seller of a product; a monopsony is a single buyer of a factor.

Suppose there is a firm in a small town with no other firms for miles around that is the only buyer of labor. This firm would be considered a monopsony. Because it is a monopsony, it cannot buy additional units of a factor without increasing the price it pays for the factor (in much the same way that a monopolist in the product market cannot sell an additional unit of its good without lowering price). The reason is that the supply of labor it faces is the industry supply of labor.

For the monopsonist, marginal factor cost increases as it buys additional units of a factor, and the supply curve of the factor and the monopsonist's marginal factor cost curve are different. We see that marginal factor cost increases as additional units of the factor are purchased in Exhibit 28–4. In (a), notice that as workers are added, the wage rate rises. For example, for the monopsonist to have two workers working, the wage rate must rise from $6.00 per hour to $6.05. To have three workers working, the monopsonist must offer to pay $6.10. Comparing column 2 with column 4, we notice that the marginal factor cost for a monopsonist is greater than the wage rate (in the same way that for a monopolist, price is greater than marginal revenue). In (b), we illustrate the supply curve the monopsonist faces by plotting columns 1 and 2, and we illustrate the MFC curve the monopsonist faces by plotting columns 1 and 4. Since $MFC >$ wage rate, it follows that the supply curve lies below the MFC curve.

Exhibit 28–4b shows that the monopsonist chooses to purchase Q_1 units of labor (where $MRP = MFC$) and that it pays a wage rate of W_1 to labor (W_1 being the wage rate necessary to get Q_1 workers to offer their services). If the monopsonist were to pay workers what their services were worth to it (as represented by the MRP curve), it would pay W_2. Some persons contend that labor unions and col-

PART VIII
MICROECONOMIC THEORIES
(FACTOR MARKETS)

■

610

EXHIBIT 28–4
The Labor Union and the Monopsonist

(1) Workers	(2) Wage Rate	(3) Total Labor Cost (1) × (2)	(4) Marginal Factor Cost $\frac{\Delta(3)}{\Delta(1)}$
0	—	—	—
1	$6.00	$6.00	$6.00
2	6.05	12.10	6.10
3	6.10	18.30	6.20
4	6.15	24.60	6.30
5	6.20	31.00	6.40

(a)

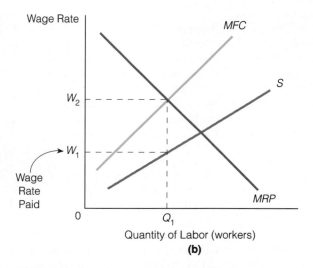

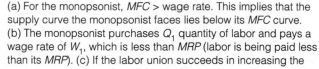

(b)

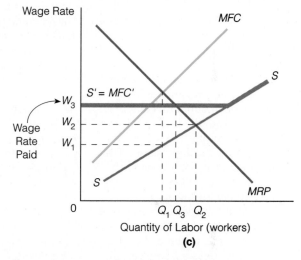

(c)

(a) For the monopsonist, *MFC* > wage rate. This implies that the supply curve the monopsonist faces lies below its *MFC* curve. (b) The monopsonist purchases Q_1 quantity of labor and pays a wage rate of W_1, which is less than *MRP* (labor is being paid less than its *MRP*). (c) If the labor union succeeds in increasing the wage rate from W_1 to W_3 through collective bargaining, then the firm will also hire more labor (Q_3 instead of Q_1). We conclude that in the case of monopsony, higher wage rates (over a range) do not imply fewer persons working.

lective bargaining are necessary in situations such as this, where labor is being paid less than its marginal revenue product. Furthermore, they argue that successful collective bargaining on the part of the labor union in this setting will not be subject to the wage–employment trade-off it encounters in other settings. This is illustrated in (c).

Successful collective bargaining by the labor union moves the wage rate from W_1 to W_3 in (c). The labor union is essentially saying to the monopsonist that it cannot hire any labor below W_3. This changes the monopsonist's marginal factor cost curve from *MFC* to *MFC'*, which corresponds to the new supply curve the

College Sports and the NCAA

Sometimes firms that sell a similar good try to band together in a cartel and act as a monopoly. Can this behavior occur when firms buy a factor? Do firms that buy a specific factor sometimes try to band together in a cartel to act as a monopsony? No doubt you know such a "firm." Many universities and colleges have banded together to buy the services of college-bound athletes. In other words, they have entered into a cartel agreement to reduce the monetary competition among themselves for college-bound athletes. The National Collegiate Athletic Association (NCAA) is the cartel or monopsony enforcer. How does all this work?

The NCAA sets certain rules and regulations that its member universities and colleges must abide by or else face punishment and fines. For example, universities and colleges are prohibited from offering salaries to athletes to play on their teams. They are prohibited from "making work" for them at the university or paying them relatively high wage rates for a job that usually pays much less—for example, paying athletes $20 an hour to reshelve books in the university library. Universities and colleges are also prohibited from offering inducements such as cars, clothes, and trips to attract athletes.

The stated objectives of such NCAA regulations are to maintain the amateur standing of college athletes, to prevent the rich schools from getting all the good players, and to enhance the competitiveness of college sports. Some economists suggest that some schools may have other objectives. They note that college athletics can be a revenue-raising activity for schools, and that these institutions would rather pay college athletes less than their marginal revenue products (the way a monopsony does) to play ball.

Currently, universities and colleges openly compete for athletes by offering scholarships, free room and board, and school jobs. They also compete in terms of their academic reputations and the reputations of their sports programs (obviously, some find it easier to do this than others). Although it is prohibited, some universities and colleges compete for athletes in ways not sanctioned by the NCAA; that is, they compete "under the table." This is evidence, some economists maintain, that they are cheating on the cartel agreement. Such cheating usually benefits the college athletes who receive a "payment" for their athletic abilities that is closer to their marginal revenue products. For example, it has occasionally been noted that some college athletes, many of whom come from families of modest means, drive flashy and expensive cars in

college. Where do they get these cars? Often they come from community friends of the university or boosters of its sports program. Such payments to college athletes may be prohibited by the NCAA, but as we saw earlier, members of cartels (of the monopoly or monopsony variety) usually find ways of evading the rules.

Question:

Are all economists agreed that the NCAA is a cartel?

Answer:
No, they aren't. Some economists argue that paying college athletes would diminish the reputation of college athletics, which would decrease the public demand for college sports programs. They conclude that the NCAA imposes its rules and regulations—one of which is that college athletes should not be paid to play sports—in order to keep college sports nonprofessional and in relatively high demand, and not to suppress players' wages.

Within this perspective, under-the-table payments to college athletes are not evidence of cheating on the cartel, but simply disregard for NCAA rules and regulations—in much the same way that driving over the speed limit is disregard for the traffic laws.

monopsonist faces, $S'S$. The monopsonist once again purchases that quantity of labor at which $MRP = MFC$, but this time equality comes at Q_3 workers at a wage rate of W_3. We conclude that over a range, there is no wage–employment trade-off for the labor union when it faces a monopsonist. It is possible to raise the wage rate *and* the number of workers working, too.

Question:

Chapter 4 explained that the minimum wage, which is an example of a price floor, reduces the number of persons working in the labor market in which it is effective.

In the monopsony setting, however, this does not seem to be the case. In fact, if W_3 in Exhibit 28–4c is considered a minimum wage—in that the monopsonist cannot hire anyone for a lower wage—then it seems to increase rather than decrease employment. Is this right?

Answer:

Yes, that is right. Consider two peripheral points, though. First, W_3 is a higher wage rate than the wage rate that would maximize total employment. The wage rate that maximizes total employment comes where supply and demand intersect. In Exhibit 28–4c, this comes where the *MRP* curve, or the factor demand curve, intersects the supply curve (*SS*) of labor. Here Q_2 workers would be employed at a wage rate of W_2.

Second, notice that even in a monopsony setting, it is not possible to raise wage rates continually and increase employment, too. For example, in (c), if the wage rate were raised above W_3, fewer individuals would be working.

Follow-up Question:

Are there many instances of monopsony in the real world?

Answer:

The evidence seems to show that there are few instances of (pure) monopsony in the real world (some economists argue that many firms have some degree of monopsony power—that is, their *MFC* curves are not perfectly elastic). Historically, the "company town" fit the description of monopsony. Today, it is quite easy for labor to move from city to city and from firm to firm, so that most workers have opportunities to work for a number of firms, not just one.

An economist rarely answers questions without specifying the *condition* under which the answer is true. For example, if asked, "Does the minimum wage increase or decrease the number of persons working in the unskilled labor market?" the economist would answer, "In the case of monopsony, the minimum wage can increase the number of persons working; in the case of perfect competition, a minimum wage decreases the number of persons working." Sometimes the layperson misunderstands this type of response, thinking the economist is giving an ambiguous answer or hedging his bets. But the economist is simply trying to be as precise as possible.

THINKING LIKE AN ECONOMIST

Unions' Effects on Wages

Most studies show that some unions have increased their members' wages substantially, whereas other unions have not increased their members' wages at all. Work by H. Gregg Lewis concludes that over the period 1920–79, the *average* wage of union members was 10 to 15 percent higher than that of comparable nonunion labor.[1] (It is important to keep in mind, though, that the *union–nonunion wage differential* can differ quite a bit in different years and between industries.) Ad-

[1]See H. Gregg Lewis, *Unionism and Relative Wages in the United States* (Chicago: University of Chicago Press, 1963); *Union Relative Wage Effects: A Survey* (Chicago: University of Chicago Press, 1986); and "Union Relative Wage Effects: A Survey of Macro Estimates," *Journal of Labor Economics* (1983).

ditional studies by Weiss, Freeman, and Medoff and by Stafford also show that unions raise union workers' wages relative to those of nonunion workers.[2]

We illustrate the theoretical underpinning of the observation that higher union wages lead to lower nonunion wages, or to a union–nonunion wage gap, in Exhibit 28–5. Two sectors of the labor market are shown: (a) the unionized sector and (b) the nonunionized sector. We assume that labor is homogeneous and that the wage rate is W_1 in both sectors.

The labor union either collectively bargains its way to a *higher* wage rate of W_2 or manages to reduce supply so that W_2 comes about (we have drawn the case for a decrease in supply). As a consequence, fewer individuals are employed in the unionized sector. If we hold that the persons who now are not working in the unionized sector can work in the nonunionized sector, it follows that the supply of labor in the nonunionized sector increases from S_{NU} to S'_{NU} and that the wage rate in the nonunionized sector *falls* to W_2. We conclude that there are theoretical and empirical reasons for believing that labor unions increase the wages of union employees and decrease the wages of nonunion employees.

Do the higher wages that union employees receive through unionization outweigh the lower wages that nonunion employees receive in terms of the percentage of the national income that goes to labor? It appears not. The percentage of the national income that goes to labor (union plus nonunion labor) has been fairly constant over time. In fact, it was approximately the same when unions were weak and union membership was relatively low as when unions were strong and union membership was relatively high.

[2]L. Weiss, "Concentration and Labor Earnings," *American Economic Review* (March 1966); Richard Freeman and James Medoff, "The Two Faces of Unionism," *The Public Interest* (Fall 1979); *What Do Unions Do?* (New York: Basic Books, 1984); and Frank Stafford, "Concentration and Labor Earnings: A Comment," *American Economic Review* 58 (March 1968).

EXHIBIT 28–5
The Effect of Labor Unions on Union and Nonunion Wages

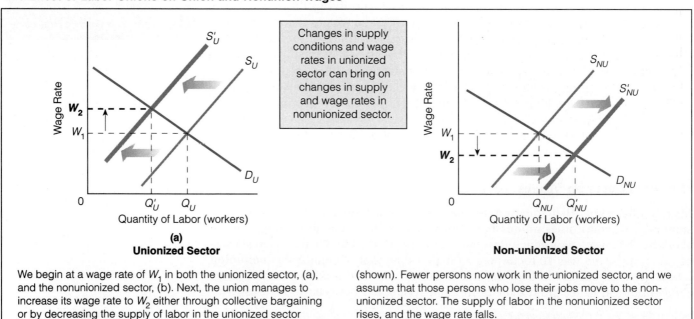

Changes in supply conditions and wage rates in unionized sector can bring on changes in supply and wage rates in nonunionized sector.

(a)
Unionized Sector

(b)
Non-unionized Sector

We begin at a wage rate of W_1 in both the unionized sector, (a), and the nonunionized sector, (b). Next, the union manages to increase its wage rate to W_2 either through collective bargaining or by decreasing the supply of labor in the unionized sector

(shown). Fewer persons now work in the unionized sector, and we assume that those persons who lose their jobs move to the nonunionized sector. The supply of labor in the nonunionized sector rises, and the wage rate falls.

Question:

The layperson's view of labor unions is that they are able to do better for their members at the expense of the owners of the firms, not at the expense of other workers. The foregoing comments suggest this may not be true. Why don't the higher wages that go to union employees come out of profits?

Answer:

It is important to differentiate between the short run and the long run here. In the theory of perfect competition, when there were short-run profits, new firms entered the industry, the industry supply curve shifted rightward, prices fell, and profits were competed away. In the long run, there was zero economic profit.

In addition, when there were short-run losses, firms exited the industry, the industry supply curve shifted leftward, price increased, and losses finally disappeared. In the long run, there was zero economic profit.

Within this market structure, consider a labor union that manages to obtain higher wages for its members. It is possible that in the short run these higher wages will diminish profits—the way any cost increase would diminish profits, *ceteris paribus*—but in the long run there will be adjustments as firms exit the industry, supply curves shift, and prices change. In the long run, zero economic profit will exist. We conclude that it is possible in the short run for "higher wages to come out of profits," but in the long run this isn't likely to be the case.

The economist is trained to make the important distinction between primary and secondary effects, or between what happens in the short run and what happens in the long run. For example, we have just seen that higher wages may initially come at the expense of profits, but as time passes, this may not continue to be the case.

THINKING LIKE AN ECONOMIST

Unions' Effects on Prices

We have seen that union wages are relatively higher and nonunion wages are relatively lower than would have been the case in the absence of the labor union. The higher union wages mean higher costs for the firms that employ union labor, and higher costs affect supply curves, which in turn affect product prices. We conclude that the higher union wages will bring about higher prices for the products that the labor union produces. Conversely, lower nonunion wages mean lower costs for the firms that employ nonunion labor and thus lower prices for the products produced by nonunion labor.

Unions' Effects on Productivity and Efficiency: Two Views

There are two major views of the effects labor unions have on productivity and efficiency.

The Traditional (or Orthodox) View. The traditional view holds that labor unions have a negative impact on productivity and efficiency. Its proponents make the following arguments: (1) Labor unions often have unnecessary staffing requirements and insist that only certain persons be allowed to do certain jobs (see the section "Availability of Substitute Factors" earlier in this chapter). Because of this, the economy operates below its potential—that is, inefficiently. (2) Strikes disrupt production and prevent the economy from realizing its productive potential. (3) Labor unions drive an artificial wedge between the wages of comparable labor in the union and nonunion sectors of the labor market.

This last point warrants elaboration. Once again turn to Exhibit 28–5. Remember that we are dealing with homogeneous labor and that we start out with the same wage rate in both sectors of the labor market. Union efforts increase the wage rate in the union sector and decrease the wage rate in the nonunion sector.

At this point, the marginal revenue product of persons who work in the union sector is higher than the marginal revenue product of individuals who work in the nonunion sector (we are farther up the factor demand curve, or *MRP* curve, in the union than nonunion sector). If labor were to move from the nonunionized sector into the unionized sector, it would be moving from where it is worth less to where it is worth more. But this cannot happen owing to the supply-restraining efforts of the union. Economists call this a misallocation of labor; not all labor is employed where it is most valuable.

A New View: The Labor Union as a Collective Voice. There is evidence that in some industries union firms have a higher rate of productivity than nonunion firms. Economists explain this by the labor union's role as a collective voice mechanism for its members. Without a labor union, workers who are disgruntled with their jobs, feel taken advantage of by their employers, or feel unsafe in their work would leave their jobs and seek work elsewhere. This "job exiting" comes at a cost; it raises the turnover rate, results in lengthy job searches during which individuals are not producing goods and services, and raises training costs. Such costs can be reduced, it is argued, when a labor union acts as a collective voice for its members. Instead of individual employees having to discuss ticklish employment matters with their employer, the labor union does it for them. Overall, the labor union makes the employees feel more confident, less intimidated, and more secure in their work; such positive feelings usually mean happier, more productive employees. Some proponents of this view also hold that the employees are less likely to quit their jobs. In fact, there is evidence that unionism does indeed reduce job quits.

Critics have contended, though, that the reduced job quits are less a function of the labor union as a collective voice mechanism than of the labor union as an institution capable of increasing its members' wages. It has also been noted that the productivity-increasing aspects of the labor union, which are linked to its role as a collective voice mechanism, are independent of the productivity-decreasing aspects of the labor union in its role as "monopolizer of labor."

CHAPTER SUMMARY

Types of Unions

■ There are three different types of labor unions: craft (or trade) unions, industrial unions, and public employee unions. Some economists hold that employee associations are also a type of union.

Objectives of a Union

■ Objectives of a union include (1) employment for all its members, (2) maximizing the total wage bill, and (3) maximizing the income for a limited number of union members. A labor union faces a wage–employment trade-off; higher wage rates mean less labor union employment. There is an exception, however. When a labor union faces a monopsonist, it is possible for the union to raise both wage rates and employment of its members (over a range). Exhibit 28–4c illustrates this.

Practices of a Labor Union

■ To soften the wage–employment trade-off, a labor union seeks to lower the elasticity of demand for its labor. Ways of doing this include (1) reducing the availability of substitute products and (2) reducing the availability of substitute factors for labor.

■ Union wage rates can be increased by increasing the demand for union labor, reducing the supply of union labor, or collective bargaining. To increase demand for its labor, a union might try to (1) increase the demand for the good it produces, (2) increase substitute factor prices, or (3) increase its marginal physical product. To decrease the supply of its labor, a union might argue for closed and union shops and against right-to-work laws.

■ In a way, successful collective bargaining on the part of a labor union changes the supply curve of labor that the employer faces. The labor union is successful if, through its collective bargaining efforts, it can prevent the employer from hiring labor at a wage rate below a union-determined level. In this case, the supply curve of labor becomes horizontal at this wage rate. See Exhibit 28–3.

Monopsony

■ For a monopsonist, marginal factor cost rises as it buys additional units of a factor, and the supply curve lies below the marginal factor cost curve. The monopsonist buys the factor quantity at which $MRP = MFC$. Since the price of the factor is less than the monopsonist's marginal factor cost, the monopsonist ends up paying the factor less than its marginal revenue product.

Effects of Unions

■ There is evidence that labor unions generally have the effect of increasing their members' wage rates (over what they would be without the union) and lowering the wage rates of nonunion labor.

■ The traditional view of labor unions holds that they negatively affect productivity and efficiency. They do this by (1) arguing for and often obtaining unnecessary staffing requirements, (2) calling strikes that disrupt production, and (3) driving an artificial wedge between the wages of comparable labor in the union and nonunion sectors. The "new" view of labor unions holds that labor unions act as a collective voice mechanism for individual union employees and cause them to feel more confident in their jobs and less intimidated by their employers. This leads to more productive employees, who are less likely to quit, and so forth.

Key Terms and Concepts

Craft (Trade) Union   Right-to-Work Laws   Collective Bargaining

Industrial Union   Closed Shop   Strike

Public Employee Union   Union Shop   Monopsony

Employee Association

QUESTIONS AND PROBLEMS

1. What view is a labor union like to hold on each of the following issues: (a) easing of the immigration laws; (b) a quota on imported products; (c) free trade; (d) a decrease in the minimum wage?

2. Most actions or practices of labor unions are attempts to affect one of three factors. What are these three factors?

3. Explain why the monopsonist pays labor a wage rate less than labor's marginal revenue product.

4. It has been suggested that organizing labor unions is easier in some industries than others. What industry characteristics make unionization easy?

5. What is the effect of labor unions on nonunion wage rates?

6. Some persons argue that a monopsony firm exploits its workers if it pays them less than their marginal revenue products. Others disagree. They say that as long as the firm pays the workers their opportunity costs (which must be the case or the workers would not stay with the firm), the workers are not being exploited. This suggests that there are two definitions of exploitation: (a) paying workers below their marginal revenue products (even if wages equal the workers' opportunity costs) and (b) paying workers below their opportunity costs. Keeping in mind that this may be a subjective judgment, which definition of exploitation do you think is more descriptive of the process and why?

7. A discussion of labor unions will usually evoke strong feelings. Some persons argue vigorously against labor unions, others argue with equal vigor for labor unions. Some persons see labor unions as the reason why the workers in this country enjoy as high a standard of living as they do; others see labor unions as the reason the country is not as well off economically as it might be. Speculate on why the topic of labor unions generates such strong feelings and emotions and often such little analysis.

8. What forces may lead to the breakup of an employer (monopsony) cartel?

9. Fill in the blanks.

(1) Workers	(2) Wage Rate	(3) Total Labor Cost	(4) Marginal Factor Cost
0			
1	——	$12.00	$12.00
2	$12.10	24.20	——
3	12.20	——	——
4	——	——	12.60

INTEREST, RENT, AND PROFIT

WHAT THIS CHAPTER IS ABOUT

We first noted in Chapter 2 that there are four categories of resources: land, labor, capital, and entrepreneurship. In Chapter 27, we discussed labor; specifically, how wage rates are determined. In this chapter, we examine the payments to capital, land, and entrepreneurship. This knowledge is critical to understanding how markets operate and economies function.

INTEREST

■

The word *interest* is used in two ways in economics. Sometimes it refers to the price for **loanable funds.** For example, Lars borrows $100 from Rebecca and a year later pays her back $110. The interest is $10.

Interest can also refer to the return earned by capital as an input in the production process. A person who buys a machine (a capital good) for $1,000 and earns $100 a year by using the productive services of the machine is said to earn $100 interest, or a 10 percent interest rate, on the capital.

The reason economists often refer to both the price for loanable funds and the return on capital goods as interest is that there is tendency for the two to become equal. We show this later.

Loanable Funds
Funds that someone borrows and another person lends, for which the borrower pays an interest rate to the lender.

Question:

Is there a difference between interest and the interest rate?

Answer:

Yes, there is. Interest refers to an absolute dollar amount; the interest rate is a ratio of the annual interest to the principal amount. Suppose someone lends Maria $100 and she pays back $120 in a year. She pays $20 in interest. The ratio of the interest to the principal ($20/$100) gives us the interest as an (annual) percentage of the loan, or the interest rate; it is 20 percent.

Loanable Funds: Demand and Supply

The equilibrium interest rate, or the price for loanable funds, is determined by the demand for, and supply of, loanable funds. The demand for loanable funds is composed of the demand for consumption loans, the demand for investment loans, and government's demand for loanable funds. With respect to the latter, the U.S. Treasury may need to finance budget deficits by borrowing (demanding) loanable funds in the loanable funds market. In this chapter, we focus on the demand for consumption loans and the demand for investment loans.

The supply of loanable funds comes about through people's saving and newly created money. In this chapter, we discuss only people's saving.

In sum, the demand for loanable funds (in our discussion) is composed of (1) the demand for consumption loans and (2) the demand for investment loans. The supply of loanable funds is composed of people's saving.

The Supply of Loanable Funds. Savers are people who consume less than their current income. Without savers, there would be no supply of loanable funds. Savers receive an interest rate for the use of their funds, and the amount of funds saved and loaned is directly related to the interest rate.[1] Specifically, the supply curve of loanable funds is upward sloping: The higher the interest rate, the greater the quantity supplied of loanable funds; the lower the interest rate, the less the quantity supplied of loanable funds.

PART VIII
MICROECONOMIC THEORIES
(FACTOR MARKETS)

■

620

---

[1]Because a higher interest rate may have both a substitution effect and an income effect, many economists argue that a higher interest rate can lead to either more saving or less saving, depending on which effect is stronger. We will ignore these complications at this level of analysis and hold that the supply curve of loanable funds (from savers) is upward sloping.

The Demand for Loanable Funds: Consumption Loans. Loanable funds are demanded by consumers because they have a **positive rate of time preference;** that is, consumers prefer earlier availability of goods to later availability. For example, most people would prefer to have a car today than a car five years from today.

There is nothing irrational about a positive rate of time preference—most, if not all, people have it. People differ, though, as to the degree of their preference for earlier, compared with later, availability. Some people have a high rate of time preference, signifying that they greatly prefer present to future consumption (I've got to have that new car today). Other people have a low rate, signifying that they prefer present to future consumption only slightly. (Ask yourself this: Would people with a high or a low rate of time preference be more likely to save, that is, postpone consumption? The answer is people with a low rate of time preference.)

Because consumers have a positive rate of time preference, there is a demand for consumption loans. Consumers borrow today in order to buy today; they will pay back the borrowed amount plus interest tomorrow. The interest payment is the price consumers-borrowers pay to obtain the earlier availability of goods.

The Demand for Loanable Funds: Investment Loans. Investors (or firms) demand loanable funds so they can invest in capital goods and finance **roundabout methods of production.** A firm using a roundabout method of production first directs its efforts to producing capital goods and then uses those goods to produce consumer goods.

Consider both a direct and a roundabout method of catching fish. In the direct method, a person uses his hands to catch fish. In the roundabout method, the person weaves a net (which is a capital good) and then uses the net to catch fish. Let's suppose that by using the direct method, Charlie can hand-catch 4 fish per day. Using the roundabout method, he can net-catch 20 fish per day.

Furthermore, let's suppose it takes Charlie 10 days to weave a net. This means if Charlie does not weave a net and instead hand-catches fish, he can catch 1,460 fish per year (4 fish per day times 365 days). If, however, Charlie spends 10 days weaving a net (during which time he catches no fish), he can catch 3,550 the first year (10 fish per day times 355 days). We conclude that the capital-intensive roundabout method of production is highly productive.

The highly productive nature of roundabout methods of production prompts investors to borrow funds to invest in them. For example, our hand-catching fisherman might reason as follows: "I'm more productive if I weave a fishing net, but to do so, I'll need to take 10 days off from hand-catching fish and devote all my energies to weaving a net. What will I eat during the 10 days? Perhaps I can borrow some fish from my neighbor. Suppose I borrow 40 fish for the next 10 days. Since I must make it worthwhile for my neighbor to enter into this arrangement, I will promise to pay her back 50 fish at the end of the year; thus, my neighbor will lend me 40 fish today in exchange for 50 fish at the end of the year. I realize I'm paying an interest rate of 25 percent (since the interest payment of 10 fish is 25 percent of the number of fish borrowed, 40), but still it will be worth it." It is the highly productive nature of the capital-intensive roundabout method of production that makes it worthwhile.

The reasoning in our fish example is repeated whenever a firm makes a capital investment. Making computers on an assembly line is a roundabout method of production compared with making them one by one by hand. Making copies on a copying machine is a roundabout method of production compared with copying by hand. In both cases, firms are willing to borrow now, use the borrowed funds

Positive Rate of Time Preference
Preference for earlier availability of goods over later availability of goods. A person's rate of time preference equals the percentage increase in future consumption that the person needs to obtain before he or she will sacrifice some amount of present consumption.

Roundabout Method of Production
The production of capital goods that enhance productive capabilities and ultimately bring about increased consumption.

EXHIBIT 29–1
Loanable Funds Market

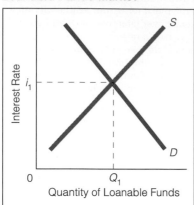

The demand curve shows the different quantities of loanable funds demanded at different interest rates. The supply curve shows the different quantities of loanable funds supplied at different interest rates. Through the forces of supply and demand, the equilibrium interest rate and the quantity of loanable funds are established as i_1 and Q_1.

to invest in roundabout methods of production, and pay back the loan with interest later. If roundabout methods of production were not productive, firms would not be willing to do this.

Adding the demand for consumption loans to the demand for investment loans gives us the total demand for loanable funds. The demand curve for loanable funds is downward sloping. As interest rates rise, consumers' cost of earlier availability of goods rises, and they curtail their borrowing. Also, as interest rates rise, some investment projects that would be profitable at a lower interest rate will no longer be profitable. We conclude that the interest rate and quantity demanded of loanable funds are inversely related.

Exhibit 29–1 illustrates both the demand for, and supply of, loanable funds. The equilibrium interest rate is the interest at which the quantity demanded of loanable funds equals the quantity supplied of loanable funds.

Question:

When would a project be profitable at lower interest rates but not at higher interest rates?

Answer:

Suppose a firm estimates that if it buys a particular capital good, the return next year will be 10 percent. The price of the loanable funds needed to buy the capital good is 8 percent. Given this, the firm will go ahead and borrow the funds and buy the capital good. If, however, the price of the loanable funds rises to 10.5 percent, the firm will not buy the capital good.

Price for Loanable Funds and Return on Capital Goods Tend to Equality

As we said earlier, both the price for loanable funds and the return on capital are referred to as *interest* because they tend to equality. To illustrate, suppose again that the return on capital is 10 percent and the price for loanable funds is 8 percent. In this setting, firms will borrow in the loanable funds market and invest in capital goods. As they do this, the quantity of capital increases, and its return falls (capital is subject to diminishing marginal returns). In short, the return on capital and the price for loanable funds begin to approach each other.

Suppose, instead, that things are reversed and the price for loanable funds is 10 percent and the return on capital is 8 percent. In this situation, no one will borrow loanable funds at 10 percent to invest at 8 percent. Over time, the capital stock will decrease (capital depreciates over time, it doesn't last forever), its marginal physical product will rise, and the return on capital and the price for loanable funds will eventually equal each other.

PART VIII
MICROECONOMIC THEORIES
(FACTOR MARKETS)

■

622

In economics, it is not uncommon for factors to converge. For example, in our discussion of supply-and-demand analysis, we learned that the quantity demanded, and the quantity supplied, of a good tend to equality (through the equilibrating process). In our discussion of consumer theory, we learned that the marginal utility–price ratios for different goods tend to equality. And we have just seen that the price of loanable funds and the return on capital tend to equality. But *why* do many things tend to equality in economics? It is because equality is often representative of *equilibrium*. When quantity demanded equals quantity supplied, a market is said to be in equilibrium. When the marginal utility–price ratio for all goods is the same, the consumer is said to be in equilibrium. Inequality, therefore, often signifies disequilibrium. When the price of loanable funds is greater than the return on capital, there is disequilibrium. The next logical question is, "So what happens now?"

The economist, knowing that equality often signifies equilibrium, looks for inequalities and then asks, "So what happens now?"

Why Interest Rates Differ

The supply-and-demand analysis in Exhibit 29–1 may suggest that there is only one interest rate in the economy. In reality, there are many. For example, a major business is not likely to pay the same interest rate for an investment loan to purchase new machinery as the person next door pays for a consumption loan to buy a stereo set. Some of the factors that affect interest rates are discussed in the following paragraphs. In each case, the *ceteris paribus* condition holds.

Risk. Any time a lender makes a loan, there is a possibility that the borrower will not repay it. Some borrowers are better credit risks than others. A major corporation with a long and established history is probably a better credit risk than a person who has been unemployed three times in the last seven years. The more risk associated with a loan, the higher the interest rate; the less risk associated with a loan, the lower the interest rate.

Term of the Loan. In general, the longer the term of the loan, the higher the interest rate; the shorter the term of the loan, the lower the interest rate. Borrowers are usually more willing to pay higher interest rates for long-term loans because this gives them greater flexibility. Lenders require higher interest rates to part with funds for extended periods.

Cost of Making the Loan. A loan for $1,000 and a loan for $100,000 may require the same amount of record keeping, making the larger loan cheaper (per dollar) to process than the smaller loan. Also, some loans require frequent payments (such as payments for a car loan), whereas others do not. This difference is likely to be reflected in higher administrative costs for those with more frequent payments. We conclude that loans that cost more to process and administer will come with higher interest rates than loans that cost less.

Nominal and Real Interest Rates

The **nominal interest rate** is the interest rate determined by the forces of supply and demand in the loanable funds market; it is the interest rate in current dollars, unadjusted for *expected inflation*. The nominal interest rate will change if the demand for, or supply of, loanable funds changes. One of the factors that can change both is individuals' expectations of inflation. Inflation occurs when the money prices of goods, on average, increase over time. To see exactly how this can affect the nominal interest rate, look at Exhibit 29–2.

We start out with an interest rate of 8 percent and an actual and expected inflation rate of zero (actual inflation rate = expected inflation rate = 0 percent). Later,

Nominal Interest Rate
The interest rate determined by the forces of supply and demand in the loanable funds market; the interest rate in current dollars, unadjusted for expected inflation.

EXHIBIT 29–2
Expected Inflation and Interest Rates

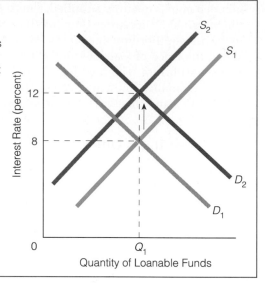

We start at an 8 percent interest rate and an actual and expected inflation rate of 0 percent. Later, both borrowers and lenders expect an inflation rate of 4 percent. Borrowers are willing to pay a higher interest rate because they will be paying off their loans with cheaper dollars. Lenders require a higher interest rate because they will be paid back in cheaper dollars. The demand and supply curves shift such that at Q_1 borrowers are willing to pay and lenders require a 4 percent higher interest rate. The nominal interest rate is now 12 percent. The real interest rate is 8 percent (real interest rate = nominal interest rate − expected inflation rate).

both the demanders and suppliers of loanable funds expect a 4 percent inflation rate. What will this 4 percent expected inflation rate do to the demand for, and supply of, loanable funds? Borrowers (demanders of loanable funds) will be willing to pay 4 percent more interest for their loans because they expect to be paying back the loans with dollars that have 4 percent less buying power than the dollars they are being lent. (Another way of looking at this is to say that if they want to buy goods, the prices of the goods they want will have risen by 4 percent. To beat the price increase, they will be willing to pay up to 4 percent more to borrow and purchase the goods now.) In effect, the demand for loanable funds curve shifts rightward, so that at Q_1 borrowers are willing to pay a 4 percent higher interest rate.

On the other side of the loanable funds market, the lenders (suppliers of loanable funds) require a 4 percent higher interest rate (that is, 12 percent) to compensate them for the 4 percent less valuable dollars in which the loan will be repaid. In effect, the supply of loanable funds curve shifts leftward, so that at Q_1 lenders will receive an interest rate of 12 percent.

We see that an expected inflation rate of 4 percent increases the demand for loanable funds and decreases the supply of loanable funds, so that the interest rate is 4 percent higher than it was when there was a zero inflation rate. In this example, 12 percent is the nominal interest rate; that is, the interest rate in current dollars, the interest rate including the expected inflation rate.

If we were to adjust for the expected inflation rate, we would have the **real interest rate.** The real interest rate is the nominal interest rate *adjusted* for the expected inflation rate; that is, it is the nominal interest rate minus the expected inflation rate. In our example, the real interest rate is 8 percent (real interest rate = nominal interest rate − expected inflation rate).

It is the real interest rate, not the nominal interest rate, that matters to borrowers and lenders. Consider a lender who grants a $1,000 loan to a borrower at a 20 percent nominal interest rate at a time when the expected inflation rate (and later

Real Interest Rate
The nominal interest rate adjusted for expected inflation; that is, the nominal interest rate minus the expected inflation rate.

the *actual* inflation rate) is 15 percent. The amount repaid to the lender is $1,200, but $1,200 with a 15 percent inflation rate does not have the buying power that $1,200 with a zero inflation rate has. Therefore, since the 15 percent inflation rate wipes out much of the gain, the lender is not getting a real return of 20 percent on the loan, but rather only 5 percent. Thus, the rate lenders receive and borrowers pay (and therefore the rate they care about) is the real interest rate.

Question:

When a person calls a bank to find out what interest rate he or she would pay for a loan, which interest rate is being quoted, the nominal or the real?

Answer:

The bank will quote the nominal interest rate. Remember, the nominal interest rate is the interest rate that is determined by the current forces of supply and demand; it is the interest rate expressed in current dollars, unadjusted for expected inflation.

Follow-up Question:

Are the nominal interest rate and the real interest rate ever the same?

Answer:

They are the same when the expected inflation rate is zero. Since the real interest rate = nominal interest rate − expected inflation rate (alternatively, this can be written as nominal interest rate = real interest rate + expected inflation rate), if the expected inflation rate is zero, real interest rate = nominal interest rate.

Present Value: What Is Something Tomorrow Worth Today?

We know that because of people's positive rate of time preference, $100 today is worth more than $100 a year from now. (Don't you prefer $100 today to $100 in a year?) Thus, since $100 today is worth more than $100 in a year, $100 a year from now must be *worth less* than $100 today. But if $100 a year from now is worth less than $100 today, *how much is it worth today?*

This question introduces the concept of **present value.** Present value refers to the current worth of some future dollar amount (of receipts or income). In our example, present value refers to what $100 next year is worth today.

Present value (*PV*) is computed by using a rather simple formula:

$$PV = A_n/(1 + i)n$$

where A_n is the actual amount of income or receipts in a particular year in the future, i is the interest rate (in decimals), and n refers to the particular year in the future. Computing the present value of $100 one year in the future, at a 10 percent interest rate, we get $90.91:

$$PV = \$100/(1 + .10)^1$$
$$= \$90.91$$

This means that the right to receive $100 a year from now is worth $90.91 today. Another way to look at this is to realize that if a person today put $90.91 in a savings account paying a 10 percent interest rate, it would equal $100 in a year.

Present Value
The current worth of some future dollar amount of income or receipts.

How Much Is That Medical Degree Worth?

Present values are important for many things besides the investment decisions of business firms. Lawyers, for example, often call on economists to calculate the present value of someone's future income. Accident cases involving personal injuries and divorce suits are examples of cases in which a lawyer might need to know the present value of a future income.

Consider a couple, Carol and Jack, who got married in 1974. Shortly after, Jack entered medical school, while Carol went to work to help pay Jack's medical school expenses.

In 1991, Jack and Carol realize that their marriage is in trouble. They seek professional help, but things don't work out. They both agree to a divorce and say they'll split the assets: the house, the cars, the furniture, the silverware, the paintings, the Persian carpets. There is one hitch, however. Carol claims that Jack's medical degree is an asset, and that she has invested in it because she helped pay his way through medical school. Jack's lawyer objects to this reasoning, and the case ultimately goes before a judge.

Before the case goes to trial, Carol's lawyer has to determine how much the medical degree is worth. After all, if Carol is to get part of the value of the medical degree, it is important to know what that value is. The lawyer consults an economist and asks him to find the present value of the degree. He estimates that as a medical doctor Jack will earn $100,000 a year. He also estimates that Jack will be practicing medicine for the next 25 years. Using an interest rate of 4 percent, the economist calculates the present value of $100,000 a year for 25 years. Of course, the economist's estimates will be subject to close scrutiny by Jack's lawyer ("How do you know my client will be practicing for 25 years or that he will be making $100,000 a year?"), but our concern here is the role present value plays in the process, not the legal issues.

In any case, the economist calculates the present value of $100,000 a year for 25 years at 4 percent interest to be approximately $1.57 million. Now the court must decide if the medical degree is an asset whose proceeds should be divided between Carol and Jack and if so, what portion of the proceeds should go to Carol and over what period of time.

Now suppose we wanted to know what a particular future income stream was worth today. That is, instead of finding out what a particular future dollar amount is worth today, our objective is to find out what a number of future dollar amounts in the future are worth today. Consider a firm that buys a machine that will earn $100 for the next three years. What is this future income stream—$100 per year for three years—worth today? What is its present value? At a 10 percent interest rate, this income stream has a present value of $248.74:

$$PV = A_1/(1 + .10)^1 + A_2/(1 + .10)^2 + A_3/(1 + .10)^3$$
$$= \$100/1.10 + \$100/1.21 + \$100/1.331$$
$$= \$90.91 + \$82.64 + \$75.13 = \$248.68$$

Investment Decisions and Present Value

Business firms often compute present values when deciding whether to buy a capital good. Again, consider the firm's machine that will earn $100 for the next three years. Suppose we assume that after the three-year period the machine must be scrapped and that it will have no scrap value. The firm will consider the present value of the future income generated by the machine ($248.68) against the cost of the machine. Suppose the cost of the machine is $250. Since the cost of the machine is greater than the present value of the income stream the machine will generate, the firm decides not to buy the machine.

Would the business firm buy the machine if the interest rate had been 4 percent instead of 10 percent? Recalculating the present value of $100 for three years at 4 percent interest, we get $278. Comparing this amount with the cost of the machine ($250), we see that the firm is likely to buy the machine. We conclude that as interest rates decrease, present values increase, and firms will buy more capital goods; as interest rates increase, present values decrease, and firms will buy fewer capital goods, all other things held constant.

RENT

■

Mention the word *rent,* and people naturally think of someone living in an apartment who makes monthly payments to a landlord. This is not the type of rent we are discussing here. To an economist, rent means **economic rent.** Economic rent is a payment in excess of opportunity costs. There is also a subset of economic rent called **pure economic rent.** This is a payment in excess of opportunity costs when opportunity costs are zero. Historically, the term *pure economic rent* was first used to describe the payment to the factor land, which is perfectly inelastic in supply.

Exhibit 29–3 gives an example. As we can see, the total supply of land is fixed at Q_1 acres; there can be no more, and no less, than this amount of land. We know that the payment for land will be determined by the forces of supply and demand; this turns out to be R_1.

It is important to notice that R_1 is more than sufficient to bring Q_1 acres into supply. In fact, we know by looking at the fixed supply of land (the supply curve is perfectly inelastic), that Q_1 acres would have been forthcoming at a payment of zero dollars. In short, this land has *zero opportunity costs.* Therefore, the full payment, all of R_1, is referred to as pure economic rent.

Question:

In other words, pure economic rent only exists if the supply curve of the factor is perfectly inelastic. Is this correct?

Answer:

Yes, it is.

Follow-up Question:

Can economic factors besides land receive pure economic rent?

Answer:

Yes, they can, as long as the supply curve of these factors is perfectly inelastic.

David Ricardo, the Price of Grain, and Land Rents in New York and Tokyo

In nineteenth-century England, people were concerned about the rising price of grains, which were a staple in many English diets. Some argued that grain prices were rising because land rents were rising rapidly. Fingers began to be pointed at the landowners, as people maintained that the high rents the landowners received

Economic Rent
Payment in excess of opportunity costs.

Pure Economic Rent
A category of economic rent where the payment is to a factor that is in fixed supply, implying that it has zero opportunity costs.

EXHIBIT 29–3
Pure Economic Rent and the Total Supply of Land

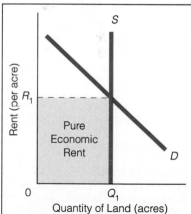

The total supply of land is fixed at Q_1. The payment for the services of this land is determined by the forces of supply and demand. Since the payment is for a factor in fixed supply, it is referred to as pure economic rent.

627

for their land made it more and more costly for farmers to raise grains; these higher costs, in turn, were passed on to the consumers in the form of higher prices. According to this argument, the solution was to lower rents, which would lead to lower costs for farmers and eventually to lower prices for consumers.

The English economist David Ricardo thought this reasoning was faulty. He contended that grain prices weren't high because rents were high (as most individuals thought), but rather that rents were high because grain prices were high.

His argument, put in current economic terminology, went like this: Land is a factor of production; therefore, the demand for it is derived. Also, land is in fixed supply; therefore, the only thing that will change the payment made to land is a change in the demand for land (the supply curve isn't going to shift, and thus the only thing that can change price is a shift in the demand curve). Landowners have no control over the demand for land. Demand comes from other persons who want to use it. In nineteenth-century England, the demand came from farmers who were raising grains and other foodstuffs. Therefore, landowners could not have pushed up land rents because they had no control over the demand for their land. It follows that if rents were high, this must have been because the demand for land was high, and the demand for land was high because grain prices were high.

Today, the same confusion between high rents and high prices still exists. For example, many people complain that prices in stores and restaurants in New York City and Tokyo are high. When they notice that land rents are also high, they reason that prices are high because land rents are high. But, as Ricardo pointed out, the reverse is true; land rents are high because prices are high. If the demand for living, visiting, and shopping in New York City and Tokyo were not as high as it is, prices for goods would not be as high; in turn, the demand for land would not be as high, and therefore the payments to land would not be as high. Economists put it this way: Land rents are price determined, not price determining.

The Supply Curve of Land Can Be Upward Sloping

Exhibit 29–3 depicts the supply of land as fixed. This is the case when the *total* supply of land is in question. For example, there are only so many acres of land in this country, and that amount is not likely to change.

Most subparcels of land, however, have competing uses. Consider 25 acres of land on the periphery of a major city. It can be used for farmland, a shopping mall, or a road. Once we note that a particular parcel of land (as opposed to all land, or the total supply of land) has competing uses, it follows that that parcel of land has opportunity costs. Land that is used for farming could have been used to house a shopping mall. To reflect the opportunity cost of that land, we draw its supply curve as upward sloping. This implies that if individuals want more land for a specific purpose—say, for a shopping mall—they must bid high enough to attract existing land away from other uses (farming, for example). This is illustrated in Exhibit 29–4, where the equilibrium payment to land is R_1. The shaded area indicates the economic rent.

Economic Rent and Other Factors of Production

As we mentioned earlier, the concept "economic rent" applies to economic factors besides land; for example, labor. Suppose Hanson works for company X and is paid $40,000 a year. Furthermore, suppose that in his next best alternative job he would be earning $37,000. Is Hanson receiving economic rent working for com-

EXHIBIT 29–4
Economic Rent and the Supply of Land (Competing Uses)

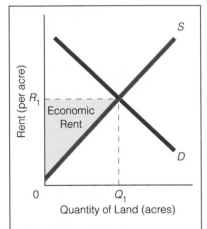

A particular parcel of land, as opposed to the total supply of land, has competing uses, or positive opportunity costs. For example, to obtain more land to build a shopping center, the developers must bid high enough to attract existing land away from competing uses. The supply curve is upward sloping. At a payment of R_1, economic rent is identified as the payment in excess of (positive) opportunity costs.

pany X? Yes, he is receiving a payment in excess of his opportunity costs; thus, he is receiving economic rent.

Or consider the local McDonald's that hires teenagers. It pays all its beginning employees the same wage. But not every beginning employee has *the same* opportunity costs as every other employee. Suppose two teenagers, Tracy and Paul, sign on to work at McDonald's for $5.00 an hour. Tracy's next best alternative wage is $5.00 an hour working for her mother's business, and Paul's next best alternative wage is $4.25 an hour. Tracy receives no economic rent in her McDonald's job, but Paul receives 75 cents an hour economic rent in the same job.

What usually happens over time is that teenagers and other beginning employees find that their opportunity costs rise (owing to continued schooling and job experience) and that the McDonald's wage no longer covers their opportunity costs. When this happens, they quit their jobs.

The Perspective from Which the Factor Is Viewed Matters

Economic rent will differ depending on the perspective from which the factor is viewed. Let's look at a baseball star who earns $1 million a year playing baseball. Suppose that if he weren't playing baseball, he would be a coach at a high school; therefore, the difference between what he is currently paid ($1 million a year) and what he would earn as a coach (say, $30,000 a year) is economic rent. This amounts to $970,000. This way of identifying economic rent requires that we ask what is the alternative to our baseball star playing baseball.

We could, however, identify economic rent in a different way. We could ask what is the alternative to our baseball star playing baseball *for his present team.* The answer is probably that he can play baseball for another team. For example, if he weren't playing for the Boston Red Sox, he might be playing for the Pittsburgh Pirates and earning $950,000 a year. His economic rent in this instance is only $50,000.

Our baseball player's economic rent as a player for the Boston Red Sox is $50,000 a year (his next best alternative is playing for the Pittsburgh Pirates earning $950,000 a year). But his economic rent as a baseball player is $970,000 (his next best alternative is being a high school coach earning $30,000 a year).

Competing for Artificial and Real Rents

Individuals and firms will compete for *artificial rents* and *real rents*. An artificial rent is an economic rent that is artificially contrived by government; it would not exist without government. Suppose government decides to award a monopoly right to one firm to produce good X. In so doing, it legally prohibits all other firms from producing good X. If the firm with the monopoly right receives a price for good X in excess of its opportunity costs, it receives a "rent" or "monopoly profit" because of government's supply-restraining efforts. Firms that compete for the monopoly right to produce good X and receive the "rent" expend resources in a socially wasteful manner.[2] They use resources to lobby politicians in the hope of effecting a transfer—resources that (from society's perspective) are better used to produce goods and services.

[2]This may sound familiar. The process described here where individuals expend resources lobbying government for a special privilege was described as rent-seeking in Chapter 25 on monopoly. See the interview with Gordon Tullock in that chapter.

Uncertainty and risk are not the same. Risk comes with a probability, uncertainty does not.

■

Competing for real rents is something different, however. Where the rent is real, where it has not been artificially created, and where there are no barriers to competing for it, resources are used in a way that is socially productive. For example, suppose firm Z currently receives economic rent in the production of good Z. Government does not prohibit other firms from competing with firm Z, so some do. In the process, these other firms produce good Z, thus increasing the supply of the good and lowering its price. The lower price reduces the rent firm Z receives in its production of good Z. In the end, firm Z has less rent, while society has more of good Z and pays a lower price for it.

PROFIT
■

The "profits" that appear in newspaper headlines are *accounting profits,* not economic profits. Economic profit, as we learned in Chapter 23, is the difference between total revenue and total cost, where both explicit and implicit costs are included in total cost.

Economists emphasize economic profit over accounting profit because economic profit determines entry into and exit from an industry. For the most part, this is how economic profit figured into our discussion of market structures in Chapters 24–26.

In this section, we go beyond the entry-and-exit role of profit. First, we discuss the *source* of profits, to find out why economic profit exists. Second, we examine why the full value of the product produced by firms is not divided up among the factors land, labor, and capital. As with many other issues in economics, economists do not agree on the answers to these questions.

Theories of Profit

Several different theories address the question of where profit comes from, or the source of profit. One theory holds that profit would not exist in a world of certainty; hence, uncertainty is the source of profit. Another theory holds that profit is the return for alertness to (broadly defined) arbitrage opportunities. A third theory holds that profit is the return to the entrepreneur as innovator.

Profit and Uncertainty. Uncertainty exists when a potential occurrence is so unpredictable that a probability cannot be estimated. (For example, what is the probability that the United States will enter a world war in 1997? Who knows?) Risk, which many people mistake for uncertainty, exists when the probability of a given event can be estimated (for example, there is a 50–50 chance that a toss of a coin will come up heads). It follows that risks may be insured against, uncertainties cannot.

Anything that can be insured against can be treated as just another cost of doing business. Insurance coverage is an input in the production process. Only events that are uncertain can generate results where a firm's revenues diverge from costs (including insurance costs). The investor-decision maker who is adept at making business decisions under conditions of uncertainty earns a profit. For example, based on experience and some insights, an entrepreneur may believe that 75 percent of college students next year will buy personal computers. This assessment, followed up by the act of investing in a chain of retail computer stores near college campuses, will ultimately prove to be right or wrong. The essential point is that the entrepreneur's judgment is not something that can be insured against. If correct, the entrepreneur will earn a profit; if incorrect, a loss.

Profit and Arbitrage Opportunities.   The way to make profit, the advice goes, is to "buy low and sell high." Usually, what is being bought (low) and sold (high) is the same item. For example, someone might buy an ounce of gold in New York for $400 and sell the same ounce of gold in London for $410. We might say that the person is *alert* to where she can buy low and sell high, thereby earning profits. She is alert to an arbitrage opportunity.

Sometimes buying low and selling high does not refer to the same item. Sometimes it refers to buying factors in one set of markets at the lowest possible prices, combining the factors into a finished product, and then selling the product for the highest possible price. An example of this would be buying oranges and sugar (in the oranges and sugar markets), combining the two, and selling orange juice (in the orange juice market). If doing this results in profit, we would then say that the person who undertook the act was *alert* to a (broadly defined) arbitrage opportunity; he saw that oranges and sugar together, in the form of orange juice, would fetch more than the sum of oranges and sugar separately.

Profit and Innovation.   In this theory, profit is the return to the entrepreneur as innovator: the person who *creates* new profit opportunities by devising a new product, production process, or marketing strategy. Viewed in this way, profit is the return to "innovative genius." People such as Thomas Edison, Henry Ford, and Richard Sears and Alvah Roebuck are said to have had it.

Unlike land, labor, and capital, entrepreneurship cannot be measured. There are no units of entrepreneurship.

■

Question:

If profit is the "return" to entrepreneurship, what exactly is entrepreneurship, and how does it differ from the other factors of production?

Answer:

In Chapter 2, we said that entrepreneurship "refers to the particular talent that some people have for organizing the resources of land, labor, and capital into the production of goods, and for seeking new business opportunities and developing new ways of doing things." More narrowly, an entrepreneur bears uncertainty, is alert to arbitrage opportunities, and exhibits innovative behavior. Most entrepreneurs probably exhibit different degrees of each. For example, Thomas Edison may have been more the innovator-entrepreneur than the arbitrageur-entrepreneur.

Unlike the other factors of production (land, labor, capital), entrepreneurship cannot be measured. There are no entrepreneurial *units,* as there are labor, capital, and land units. Furthermore, an entrepreneur receives profit as a residual after the other factors of production have been paid.

Monopoly Profits

Monopolies can earn positive economic profits owing to the high barriers to entry. In contrast to the temporary profits that exist where barriers to entry are low or nonexistent, monopoly profits can exist for a long time. Remember, however, that monopoly profits may be competed for, may become capitalized, and may disappear altogether if the monopoly market is contestable. (For a review, see Chapter 25.)

Profit and Loss as Signals

Too often we simply see profit and loss in terms of the benefit or hurt they bring to particular persons. We need to go beyond this and see both profit and loss as *signals* (see Chapters 24–26).

When one firm earns a profit, entrepreneurs in other industries view this as a signal that the profit-earning firm is producing and selling a good that buyers value more than the factors that go to make the good. The profit causes entrepreneurs to move resources into the production of the particular good to which the profit is linked. In short, resources follow profit.

On the other hand, if a firm is taking a loss, this is a signal to the entrepreneur that the firm is producing and selling a good that buyers value less than the factors that go to make the good. The loss causes resources to move out of the production of the particular good to which the loss is linked. Resources turn away from losses.

THINKING LIKE AN ECONOMIST

Throughout history, interest, land rent, and profits have often been attacked. At various times, philosophers and religious leaders have maintained that it is morally wrong for one person to make a loan to another person and charge interest. Interest is both improper and unjust. The early communists also held this view.

As for land rents, Henry George (1839–1897), who wrote the influential book *Progress and Poverty,* believed that all land rents were pure economic rents and should be heavily taxed. Landowners benefited simply because they had the good fortune to own land. In George's view, landowners did nothing productive. He maintained that the early owners of land in the American West reaped higher land rents, not because they made their land more productive, but because individuals from the East began to move West, driving up the price of land. In arguing for a heavy tax on land rents, George said there would be no supply response in land owing to the tax because land was in fixed supply.

Profits have also frequently come under attack. High profits are somehow thought to be evidence of corruption or manipulation. Those who earn profits are sometimes considered no better than thieves.

The economist thinks of interest, land rent, and profits differently from many laypersons. The economist understands that all are returns to resources or factors of production. Most people find it easy to understand that labor is a factor of production and that wages are the return to this factor. But understanding that land, capital, and entrepreneurship are also genuine factors of production with returns that flow to them seems to be more difficult.

Another point that is overlooked is that interest exists largely because individuals naturally have a positive rate of time preference. Those who dislike interest are in fact criticizing individuals because of the way they naturally happen to be. If they could somehow make individuals not weigh present consumption over future consumption, interest would diminish.

A similar point can be made about profit. Some say profit is the consequence of living in a world of uncertainty. If those who do not like profit could make this world of ours less uncertain, or bring certainty to it, then profit would disappear.

Question:

Do interest, rent, and profits together make up a larger or smaller percentage of national income than wages alone do?

Answer:

The percentage is quite a bit smaller. In most years, wages' share of national income is about 75 percent, leaving 25 percent for interest, rent, and profit together.

CHAPTER SUMMARY

Interest

■ *Interest* refers to (1) the price paid by borrowers for loanable funds and (2) the return on capital in the production process. There is a tendency for these two to become equal.

■ The equilibrium interest rate (in terms of the price for a loanable fund) is determined by the demand for, and supply of, loanable funds. The supply of loanable funds comes from savers, people who consume less than their current incomes. The demand for loanable funds comes from the demand for consumption and investment loans.

■ Consumers demand loanable funds because they have a positive rate of time preference; they prefer earlier availability of goods to later availability. Investors (or firms) demand loanable funds so that they can invest in productive roundabout methods of production.

■ The nominal interest rate is the interest rate determined by the forces of supply and demand in the loanable funds market. It is the interest rate in current dollars, unadjusted for expected inflation. The real interest rate is the nominal interest rate adjusted for expected inflation. Specifically, real interest rate = nominal interest rate − expected inflation rate (which means nominal interest rate = real interest rate + expected inflation rate).

Rent

■ Economic rent is a payment in excess of opportunity costs. A subset of this is pure economic rent, which is a payment in excess of opportunity costs when opportunity costs are zero. Historically, the term *pure economic rent* was used to describe the payment to the factor land, since land (in total) was assumed to be fixed in supply (perfectly inelastic supply curve). Today, the terms *economic rent* and *pure economic rent* are also often used when speaking about economic factors other than land.

■ David Ricardo argued that grain prices weren't high because land rents were high but that rents were high because grain prices were high. Land rents are price determined, not price determining.

■ How much economic rent a factor receives depends on the perspective from which the factor is viewed. For example, a university librarian earning $50,000 a year receives $2,000 economic rent if his next best alternative income at another university is $48,000. Or the economic rent may be $10,000 if his next best alternative in a nonuniversity position pays $40,000.

Profit

■ Several different theories of profit address the question of the source of profit. One theory holds that profit would not exist in a world of certainty; hence, uncertainty is the source of profit. Another theory holds that profit is the return for alertness to arbitrage opportunities. A third theory holds that profit is the return to the entrepreneur as innovator.

■ Taking the three profit theories together, we can say that profit is the return to entrepreneurship, where entrepreneurship entails bearing uncertainty, being alert to arbitrage opportunities, and exhibiting innovativeness.

Key Terms and Concepts

Loanable Funds	Nominal Interest Rate	Economic Rent
Positive Rate of Time Preference	Real Interest Rate	Pure Economic Rent
Roundabout Method of Production	Present Value	

QUESTIONS AND PROBLEMS

1. What type of people are most willing to pay high interest rates?

2. Some persons have argued that in a moneyless (or barter) economy, interest would not exist. Is this true?

3. In what ways are a baseball star who can do nothing but play baseball and a parcel of land similar?

4. What is the overall economic function of profits?

5. "The more economic rent a person receives in his job, the less likely he is to leave the job, and the more content he will be on the job." Do you agree or disagree? Explain your answer.

6. It has been said that a society with a high savings rate is a society with a high standard of living. What is the link (if any) between saving and a relatively high standard of living?

7. Make an attempt to calculate the present value of your future income.

8. What do you think each of the following events would do to individuals' rate of time preference, and thus to interest rates? (a) a technological advance that raises longevity; (b) an increased threat of war; (c) growing older.

9. "As the interest rate falls, firms are more inclined to buy capital goods." Do you agree or disagree? Explain your answer.

10. Compute the following:

a. The present value of $25,000 each year for 4 years at a 7 percent interest rate.

b. The present value of $152,000 each year for 5 years at a 6 percent interest rate.

c. The present value of $60,000 each year for 10 years at a 6.5 percent interest rate.

PART

IX

MICROECONOMIC PROBLEMS AND PUBLIC POLICY

30

AGRICULTURE: PROBLEMS AND POLICIES

WHAT THIS CHAPTER IS ABOUT

This chapter discusses the problems in agriculture, the policies enacted to deal with them, and the effects of those policies. Three groups of people are involved in the story we tell here: farmers, consumers, and taxpayers. And, of course, there is government, which, as you will see, through its policies, affects all three.

AGRICULTURE: THE ISSUES

■

From the perspective of some farmers, there are three issues of major concern: high productivity in the agricultural sector, income inelasticity for specific foods (income elasticity less than 1), and price inelasticity for specific foods (price elasticity of demand less than 1). Related to these three issues is the issue of price instability in the agricultural sector.

Agriculture and High Productivity

At the beginning of this century, one farmer produced enough food to feed 8 people. Today, one farmer produces enough food to feed 35 people. Obviously, farmers have become more productive over the years. In fact, the productivity of the agricultural sector has increased faster than productivity in the economy as a whole. A recent *Economic Report of the President* states: "Over much of the 20th century, agriculture has been one of the most innovative and productive sectors in the U.S. economy. . . . Farmers in the United States represent less than 3 percent of the civilian labor force, but they produce enough food to feed the entire domestic population, while maintaining the capacity to export large quantities to the rest of the world."[1]

Increased productivity in the agricultural sector has pushed the supply curve of farm products rightward. From the perspective of the consumer, this is good. Increased supply means more food at lower prices. But from the perspective of farmers, lower prices do not necessarily mean higher revenues. For example, if the demand curve for a particular food is inelastic, a lower price brings lower, not higher, revenues.

In Exhibit 30–1 we have illustrated a rightward shift in the supply curve for a particular food, due to an increase in productivity. As a result, equilibrium price falls and equilibrium quantity rises. Since the demand curve between the two equilibrium points, E_1 and E_2, is inelastic, total revenue is less at E_2 than at E_1. In summary, increased productivity results in lower prices for consumers and lower revenues for farmers.

Question:

Why don't farmers simply agree among themselves to be less productive, since greater productivity seems to work to their disadvantage?

Answer:

That is easy to say but hard to do. Ideally, each farmer wants to be as productive as possible, while wanting his fellow farmers to be as unproductive as possible. We can see why by considering the following hypothetical example.

Suppose on Tuesday all farmers agree to restrict output in one of two ways: indirectly, by being less productive, or directly, by taking certain acreage out of production.[2] On Wednesday, Farmer Jenkins thinks to himself, If everyone abides by the agreement to restrict output, the supply curve will shift leftward and a

---

[1]Council of Economic Advisers, *Economic Report of the President,* 1987 (Washington, D.C.: U.S. Government Printing Office, 1987), pp. 147–48.

[2]The transaction costs of getting all farmers together are probably so high that all farmers wouldn't meet to make an agreement like the one described here. We omit this real-world complexity to make our main point: Even if all farmers could get together to agree to be less productive, the agreement probably wouldn't last. The farmers would be in a prisoner's dilemma situation (see Chapter 26).

EXHIBIT 30–1
High Productivity Doesn't Always Benefit Farmers as a Group

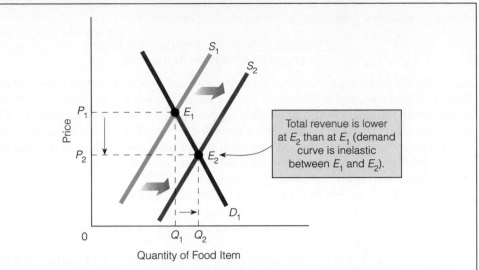

Owing to increased agricultural productivity, the supply curve shifts rightward from S_1 to S_2. As a result, equilibrium price falls and equilibrium quantity rises. The demand curve between E_1 and E_2 is inelastic, so total revenue is lower at E_2 than at E_1. In summary, increased productivity results in lower prices for consumers and lower revenues for farmers.

higher price will result. It certainly would be nice if once that higher price arrives on the scene, I have a lot to sell. So it seems that the best thing for me to do is forget the agreement and, in fact, increase output (or at least do nothing to decrease it), and in the interim hope that all other farmers do not think and behave the way I do.

The problem here is that Jenkins is not the only farmer who can or will think this way. Other farmers will behave similarly. In the end, any farmers' agreement to restrict output is not likely to hold, because each farmer will reason that he will be better off if he increases output while others do not.

Economists think in terms of *incentives.* In the foregoing example, the farmers initially had an incentive to form an agreement to reduce the supply of the product they sold on the market. Once the agreement was made, that particular incentive no longer existed. It was replaced by another. The economist asks, Given the agreement, is there any incentive an individual farmer has currently that he or she didn't have before the agreement was made? The answer is yes. The individual farmer has the incentive to break the agreement (and hope that other farmers do not).

By asking if any incentives exist to change current behavior, the economist alerts himself to possible changes in behavior and thus is better able to predict what will happen. If, after having asked whether farmers have an incentive to form an agreement to reduce supply, the economist had not gone on to ask whether farmers have an incentive to break the agreement soon after it is made, then the economist would likely have made the erroneous prediction that an agreement would be made and adhered to instead of that an agreement would be made and broken.

CHAPTER 30
AGRICULTURE: PROBLEMS AND
POLICIES

■

Agriculture and Income Inelasticity

In Chapter 21, we defined **income elasticity of demand** as the responsiveness of a change in quantity demanded to changes in income:

$$E_y = \frac{\text{percentage change in quantity demanded}}{\text{percentage change in income}}$$

If $E_y < 1$, the percentage change in quantity demanded is less than the percentage change in income—and the demand for the good in question is income inelastic. In the United States, studies show that as real income has been increasing, the per-capita demand for food has been increasing by much less. Many studies put U.S. income elasticity for food at less than 0.2, which means that as income increases 10 percent, food purchases increase by less than 2 percent.

If we put the income inelasticity of demand for food together with high agricultural productivity, we see that whereas demand for food has been increasing (owing largely to population growth), the supply of food has been increasing even more (Exhibit 30–2). Of course, supply increases that outstrip demand increases lead to falling prices.

In fact, if we look at the **parity price ratio,** which is a ratio of an index of prices that farmers receive to an index of prices that farmers pay, it is evident that in much of this century prices of agricultural products have fallen *relative* to other prices (Exhibit 30–3). The ratio uses the years 1910–14, which was a period of unusual peacetime prosperity for farmers, as a base period. If the ratio falls below the base-period ratio of 100, this means that prices of agricultural products have fallen relative to other prices; if the ratio rises above the base-period ratio of 100, this means that prices of agricultural products have risen relative to other prices. As we can see from Exhibit 30–3, for most of the period measured, prices of agricultural products have fallen relative to the prices of other goods.

EXHIBIT 30–2
High Productivity and Income Inelasticity Together

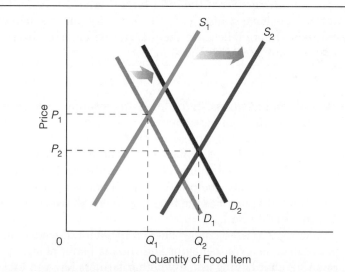

Both the demand for, and supply of, food have been increasing (here we show the demand for, and supply of, a particular food) for most of this century. High productivity in the agriculture sector, relative to income inelasticity for food, has meant that supply has increased by more than demand. As a result, prices have fallen.

EXHIBIT 30–3
Parity Price Ratio

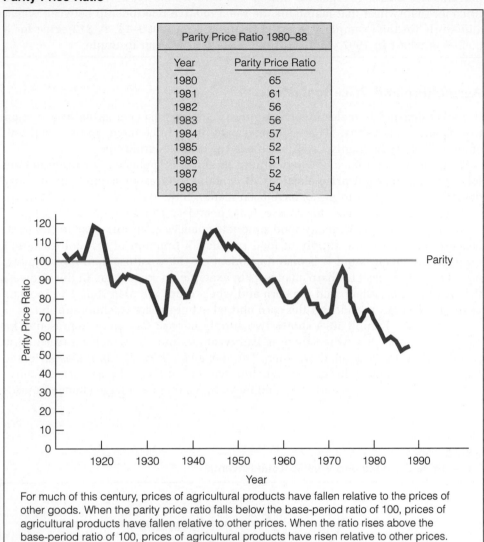

Parity Price Ratio 1980–88	
Year	Parity Price Ratio
1980	65
1981	61
1982	56
1983	56
1984	57
1985	52
1986	51
1987	52
1988	54

For much of this century, prices of agricultural products have fallen relative to the prices of other goods. When the parity price ratio falls below the base-period ratio of 100, prices of agricultural products have fallen relative to other prices. When the ratio rises above the base-period ratio of 100, prices of agricultural products have risen relative to other prices.

Source: Department of Agriculture; U.S. Bureau of the Census, *Statistical Abstract of the United States, 1991* (Washington, D.C.: U.S. Government Printing Office, 1991).

Question:

What do farmers want when they ask for parity? Do they want the same prices for their products today that existed in the period 1910–14?

Answer:

They want the same *relative* prices today that existed in the period 1910–14. Suppose that in 1910–14, a bushel of wheat sold for $1 and a shirt could be purchased for $1. This meant that the price of wheat in terms of a shirt (or the *relative price* of a bushel of wheat) was one shirt: 1 bushel of wheat = 1 shirt. Now suppose that in 1992 one bushel of wheat sells for $6 and a shirt can be purchased for $12.

The relative price of a bushel of wheat has fallen to 1/2 shirt. Parity would be 50 percent. When farmers argue for full, or 100 percent, parity, they are arguing for a price for their wheat that maintains the same relative relationship between wheat and shirts (in the example) as existed in the period 1910–14. A $12 price for a bushel of wheat in 1992 would maintain full parity in our example.

Agriculture and Price Inelasticity

If market demand is inelastic, and supply is subject to severe shifts from season to season, it follows that (1) price changes are likely to be large, and (2) total revenue is likely to be highly volatile. This is the case in agriculture.

First, the demand for many agricultural products is inelastic. For example, the following estimates of **price elasticity of demand** (the responsiveness of quantity demanded to changes in price) have been made: cattle, 0.68; chickens, 0.74; corn, 0.54; eggs, 0.23; milk used for cheese, 0.54; potatoes, 0.11; and soybeans, 0.61.

Price elasticity of demand
Measures the responsiveness of quantity demanded to changes in price.

Second, the supply of many food products changes from one year to the next, because not only is the supply of food products a function of technological and productivity changes but it is also dependent on the weather—and as we know, the weather is subject to sharp changes. For example, in some years in the Midwest the weather is excellent, and the corn and wheat crops are plentiful. And in some years the weather is bad, and the corn and wheat crops are in short supply.

To illustrate, Exhibit 30–4 shows two supply curves: S_B, which represents the supply of a food item when there is bad weather, and S_G, which represents the supply when there is good weather. The demand curve, D_1, is inelastic in the region relevant to our discussion. Whether we start at S_B (bad weather) and move to S_G (good weather), or start at S_G and move to S_B, there is a large change in price

EXHIBIT 30–4
Large Price Changes and Volatile Total Revenue

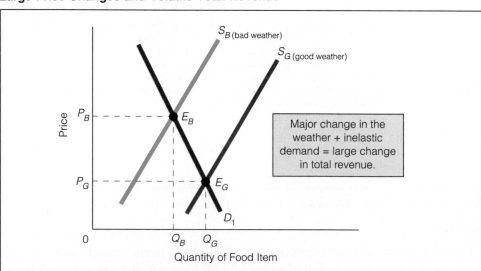

If demand is inelastic and supply is subject to severe changes from season to season, price changes will be large and total revenue (farmers' gross income) will be volatile. Suppose the supply curve shifts from S_B to S_G. As a result, price falls from P_B to P_G, and total revenue falls from $P_B \times Q_B$ to $P_G \times Q_G$.

due to the relatively high inelasticity of demand for the food item. We would expect, then, that large changes in supply, brought about by changes in weather conditions, would in turn bring about relatively large fluctuations in the price of agricultural products.

If there are large changes in price when demand is inelastic, it follows that there will be large changes in total revenue or farmers' gross income. Suppose demand is perfectly inelastic and quantity demanded is thus completely insensitive to changes in price. If price is $10 and quantity demanded is 100, total revenue is $1,000. If price drops by 50 percent to $5, total revenue falls by 50 percent to $500, too, since quantity demanded does not change at all. Thus, large changes in price bring about large changes in total revenue (farmers' gross income) when demand is inelastic.

The instability in price and total revenue (gross income) increases the uncertainties of farming. Typically, farmers argue that they have no idea what prices they will get for their products or what they will earn from one season to the next. Farmers see this as a major problem.

Why Bad Weather Is Sometimes Good

An individual farmer prefers good weather to bad weather, but farmers as a group may prefer bad weather to good weather. What's the explanation for this seeming inconsistency?

One of the things an individual farmer is interested in is her total revenue, or price times quantity ($P \times Q$). The P is determined by the market, and Q is largely determined by the individual farmer and the weather. The individual farmer prefers good weather to bad weather because the better the weather (up to some limit), the greater her Q, or output, and therefore the greater total revenue is. Farmers as a group prefer bad weather to good weather (up to some limit) because bad weather shifts the supply curve for their product leftward and raises P, and if demand is inelastic, total revenue rises.

Ideally, an individual farmer would want good weather for herself and bad weather for all other farmers. In other words, an individual farmer might vote for good weather for herself so that her Q will be high, but vote for bad weather for all other farmers so that total supply will be less and P will be high.

The Changing Farm Picture

Because of the problems directly and indirectly related to high productivity, income inelasticity, and price inelasticity, the farm picture today is different from what it was in years past. There are fewer farms in this country today than there were earlier in this century. The number of farms in 1990 was barely 37 percent of the number in 1900. The number of people living on farms has also steadily decreased. The farm population, which is defined as the civilian population living on farms in rural areas (regardless of occupation), has gone from approximately 25 million in the late 1940s to a little over 5 million today. Farm employment, which is defined as persons working on farms, has also declined, from approximately 10 million in the late 1940s to approximately 2.1 million today.

AGRICULTURE: POLICIES

Farmers could solve many of their problems if they could control the supply of their products. As we explained in the previous section, problems arise because

An individual farmer prefers good weather to bad weather, but farmers as a group may prefer bad weather to good weather.

(1) supply has grown faster than demand (the high productivity problem combined with the income inelasticity problem), which brings about falling relative prices for agricultural products, and (2) supply can and does severely change from season to season, which, together with the price inelasticity problem, brings about sharply fluctuating farm prices and total revenues, or farm incomes.

But farmers have not been able to control supply by themselves. And so they have turned to government for help. In this section, we discuss a few of the major government-implemented policies designed to help farmers. We also discuss the effects of these agricultural policies on consumers and taxpayers.

Price Supports

Price Support
A government-mandated minimum price for agricultural products; an example of a price floor.

An agricultural **price support** is an example of a price floor. It is a government-guaranteed minimum price. Some of the agricultural products that either have or have had price supports include wheat, cotton, feed grains, dairy products, peanuts, and tobacco. Suppose the price support for wheat is set at $6 per bushel, which is above the equilibrium price (Exhibit 30–5). At this price, quantity supplied is greater than quantity demanded, and there is a surplus of wheat. In addition, the amount of wheat bought by *private citizens* is less (Q_2) at the price support (price floor) than at the equilibrium price (Q_1). (We specify *private citizens* here because some of the wheat crop is purchased by government.) We would expect wheat buyers to dislike the price support program since they end up paying higher than equilibrium price for the wheat they buy.

What happens to the surplus? Farmers want to get rid of the surplus and could do so by lowering price. But, of course, there is no need to lower price. The price is supported *by government,* which buys the surplus at the support price.[3] The government's surplus wheat purchase needs to be stored, resulting in sometimes huge storage costs. For example, in the 1950s and early 1960s, storage costs for wheat escalated, reaching over $1 million per day at one period. For the taxpayers who ultimately had to pay the bill, this was not a happy state of affairs.

Thus, the effects of agricultural price supports are (1) a surplus, (2) fewer exchanges (less wheat bought by private citizens), (3) higher prices paid by consumers of wheat, and (4) government purchase and storage of the surplus wheat (for which taxpayers pay).

Restricting Supply

Prices of agricultural products can be increased directly by price supports or indirectly by restricting supply. Suppose the government and farmers want to raise the price of wheat from $4 to $6 per bushel. As we have just seen, one way is to set a price support for wheat at $6. Another way is to restrict the supply of wheat by a sufficient amount so that price will automatically rise to $6 per bushel. The objective is to shift the supply curve leftward from S_1 to S_2, as shown in Exhibit 30–6. Historically, government has used three methods to accomplish this

[3]In practice, the government does not just hand over dollars to the farmer for his surplus. The price support program works like this: Suppose a farmer harvests 10,000 bushels of wheat and the price support is $6 per bushel. If the harvest cannot be sold at $6 per bushel, the farmer can apply for a loan of $60,000 ($10,000 bushels × $6 per bushel) from a government agency called the Commodity Credit Corporation (CCC). If the price for wheat rises above the price support, the farmer can later sell the wheat and repay the loan. If the farmer cannot sell any of the wheat, he can "repay" the loan by turning the wheat over to the CCC. If the farmer sells part of the wheat, say, 4,000 bushels, he can turn over 6,000 bushels to the CCC along with $24,000 (4,000 bushels × $6 per bushel) and keep the remainder ($36,000) of the loan. In this roundabout way, the government pays the price support for the farmer's surplus wheat.

EXHIBIT 30–5
Effects of an Agricultural Price Support

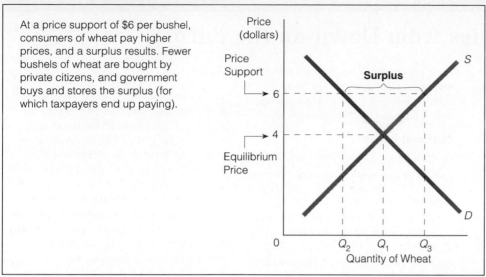

At a price support of $6 per bushel, consumers of wheat pay higher prices, and a surplus results. Fewer bushels of wheat are bought by private citizens, and government buys and stores the surplus (for which taxpayers end up paying).

objective: (1) assigning acreage allotments, (2) assigning market quotas, and (3) paying farmers not to produce as much of their crops. These three ways are called the acreage allotment program, the marketing quota system, and the soil bank program, respectively.

EXHIBIT 30–6
The Objective of Supply-Restricting Agricultural Policies

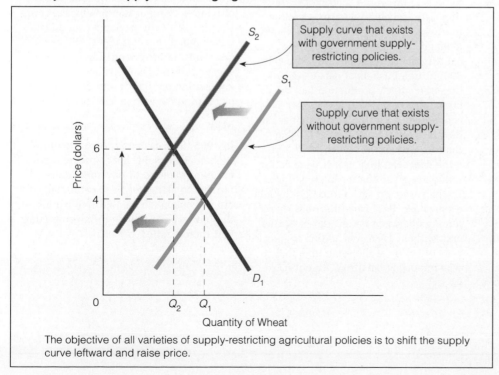

Supply curve that exists with government supply-restricting policies.

Supply curve that exists without government supply-restricting policies.

The objective of all varieties of supply-restricting agricultural policies is to shift the supply curve leftward and raise price.

Stories from Down on the Farm

Here are a few stories that describe the effects of U.S. agricultural policy.

Grain Instead of Cash

In 1983, the federal government established a supply-restricting program called *Payment-in-Kind,* or PIK. Under PIK, farmers agreed to set aside certain acres of farmland, not in exchange for cash, but for grain that the government had purchased and stored as a result of previous price support programs. The farmers could store the grain or sell it. The PIK program was supposed to (1) reduce supply, (2) stabilize prices and raise farm income, and (3) reduce or eliminate government stockpiles and reduce storage costs. Under PIK, it was possible for a farmer to take an entire farm out of production. The Department of Agriculture announced that farmers had taken 231 million acres out of production as a result of the program. As things turned out, more farmers signed up for the program than had been expected (some say because the grain payments to farmers were too generous), and as a result, the government depleted its entire stockpile of grain. In fact, the government did not have sufficient stockpiles to meet its commitments and had to buy grain on the market to do so. The PIK program was phased out after its first year.

Critics of PIK state that at the time the PIK program was in full force, a drought reduced the corn crop below normal levels; as a result, the combination of PIK and the bad weather reduced supply by more than government officials had wanted. Also, the supply of crops not affected by the drought did not fall by as much as expected. This was because farmers set aside their least-productive farmland and farmed their productive acreage more intensively. In short, supply fell by more than expected for some crops and by less than expected for other crops.

Oats and Barley

In the spring of 1988, the Quaker Oats Company ran some 60-second radio commercials in which it promised midwestern farmers "high bids for top-quality grain." One ad said, "We want to help you supply us." Another ad invited farm youths to enter an oats-growing contest. It said, "Quaker Oats is looking for you."

The Quaker Oats company was advertising for oats because the U.S. oats production was off. Oats production had declined because, as one South Dakota farmer said, "Why should I raise oats when I can get more money for barley?" (*Wall Street Journal,* June 10, 1988).

Producing less oats when the demand for oats is down is understandable, but producing less oats when the demand for oats is up would seem to be irrational. In the mid-1980s, oats production was down at the same time that the demand for oatmeal and oats-based cereal was rising. In 1985, approximately 500 million bushels of oats were produced; by 1987, production had declined to 374 million bushels. Many economists point to the fact that subsidies for barley were 96 cents higher than for oats as the reason for the decline. Farmers, they argue, were acting rationally given the incentive structure that government agricultural policy had established. Because of the subsidy differences between barley and oats, General Mills in 1988 was adding to its surplus of barley at the same time that it was importing oats from Argentina.

Sugar

At the urging of U.S. sugar producers, Congress has restricted the supply of sugar to U.S. consumers through the use of sugar quotas (limits on sugar imports). As a result, in recent years the price of sugar in the United States has been double the world price for sugar. For example, in 1990 the average world price for sugar was 12 cents per pound wholesale, while the average U.S. price for sugar was 23 cents per pound wholesale. According to a 1988 study by the Commerce Department, higher priced sugar ended up adding $3 billion a year to American consumers' grocery bills.

This may not be the end of the story, however. Because foreigners cannot sell as much sugar in the United States as they would like, their incomes are affected adversely. One study, cited in the *Economic Report of the President,* 1987, estimated that industrialized countries' sugar policies reduced the real income of people living in the developing countries by $2.1 billion. Some economists have argued that in some Caribbean and Central American countries, one-time sugar producers have turned to planting and selling marijuana and other illegal drugs to make up the lost income.

Milk

In 1985, then-Secretary of Agriculture Richard Lyng said that the federal government planned to pay some dairy farmers to slaughter their cattle and go out of business. The objective behind the plan was to reduce milk production and increase milk prices.

Acreage Allotment Program.   The acreage allotment program restricts output by limiting the number of farm acres that can be used to produce a particular crop. The allowable (total) acreage is distributed among farmers in a predetermined manner. In some cases, acreage allotment is based on a farmer's history of production.

To illustrate how the program works, suppose Farmer Thompson has a 10,000-acre farm on which he plants wheat. When the acreage allotment program is put into effect, he is limited to planting only 7,500 acres. The idea here is that if all wheat farmers reduce the number of acres they plant in wheat, the quantity of wheat brought to market will fall. As this happens, price rises, *ceteris paribus.*

One consequence of this program is that farmers begin to take their least-productive land out of production and to farm their remaining (allowable) acreage more intensively. Because of this effect, government is not always able to restrict the output of a crop to the degree it seeks.

Economists often remark that the acreage allotment program makes it more costly to produce crops. If farmers have an incentive to farm their alloted land more intensively, they tend to substitute more expensive resources such as fertilizer for less expensive resources such as land. (If farmers are combining resources such as fertilizer, land, and labor in the cheapest way possible before the program, any disturbance, such as restricting the use of land, causes a shift from a less costly to a more costly means of production.)

Marketing Quota System.   Under a marketing quota system, government does not restrict land usage, but instead sets a limit on the quantity of a product that a farmer is allowed to bring to market. In 1981, a large crop of oranges was harvested in California. As part of the marketing quota system, "excess" oranges were destroyed by dumping them in cow pastures.

Soil Bank Program.   In 1956, the Eisenhower administration initiated the soil bank program. Under this program, farmers were paid to take part of their land out of cultivation. (The difference between the acreage allotment program and the soil bank program is that under the former, farmers do not receive a direct payment.) Under the soil bank program, as under the acreage allotment program, farmers tend to take their least-productive land out of production and to farm their remaining acreage more intensively.

Target Prices

Another way in which government tries to aid farmers is by setting a guaranteed price called a **target price.** This is different from a price support in that consumers do not necessarily pay the target price. Also, with a target price, there is no surplus for the government to purchase and store. We show how it works with the aid of Exhibit 30–7.

Suppose government sets a target price for wheat at $6 per bushel. At this price, farmers choose to produce Q_1 bushels of wheat. However, consumers will not buy Q_1 bushels of wheat at $6 per bushel. The maximum price consumers will pay per bushel for Q_1 is $2. Under the target price system, this is exactly what consumers pay. Since the government has guaranteed a target price of $6 per bushel to farmers, it makes a *deficiency payment* of $4 per bushel to farmers (deficiency payment per bushel = target price per bushel − market price per bushel). The total deficiency payment that government makes to farmers equals $4 times Q_1 [($6 − $2) × Q_1]. With the target price system, consumers end up getting a lot of cheap wheat

Target Price
A guaranteed price; if the market price is below the target price, the farmer receives a deficiency payment equal to the difference between the market price and the target price.

EXHIBIT 30–7
The Target Price System

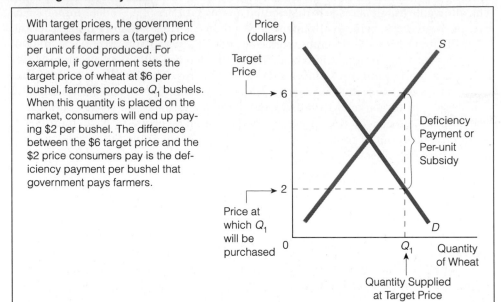

With target prices, the government guarantees farmers a (target) price per unit of food produced. For example, if government sets the target price of wheat at $6 per bushel, farmers produce Q_1 bushels. When this quantity is placed on the market, consumers will end up paying $2 per bushel. The difference between the $6 target price and the $2 price consumers pay is the deficiency payment per bushel that government pays farmers.

for which the government (taxpayers) pay. A problem with the target price program is that deficiency payments go to rich and poor farmers alike. For example, in fiscal 1986, farmers received a total of $26 billion in deficiency payments. It has been estimated that 15 percent of these payments went to farmers who had a net worth in excess of $1 million.

Consider a poor farmer who rents 200 acres on which to farm. A government program of, say, price supports is supposedly designed to help him. But does it? The layperson would say yes, since with a price support program in place the farmer sells his product for a higher dollar price than he would if there were no price support program. But since our farmer *rents* the land on which he farms, we would expect that the rent he pays the landowner will rise to reflect the higher expected profits from farming. In other words, the value of the price support subsidies will be *capitalized* into the value of the land that the farmer rents from the landowner. After all, the price support program has made farming more profitable, and therefore the land on which farming can be done is more valuable, too.

CHAPTER SUMMARY

Agriculture and High Productivity

■ Productivity in the agricultural sector has increased faster than productivity in the economy as a whole. This has not always been a blessing for farmers, because when productivity increases, the supply curve for their products shifts rightward and price falls. Decreases in price often lead to decreased revenues since the demand for many farm products is inelastic.

Agriculture and Income Inelasticity

■ The demand for many farm products is income inelastic, which means that quantity demanded changes by a smaller percentage than income changes. When combined with the high productivity problem, this means that the supply of farm products is likely to increase by more than the demand for them. Once again, this puts downward pressure on price.

Agriculture and Price Inelasticity

■ In addition to high productivity and income inelasticity, which tend to put downward pressure on farm prices, the demand for many agricultural goods is inelastic, which means falling price leads to falling total revenue (or gross farm income). Also, because demand is inelastic, shifts in supply—which are common-place in agriculture owing to changes in weather conditions—bring about (some-times) large changes in price and total revenue. Such unexpected (sometimes) large changes in price and total revenue increase the uncertainties of farming.

Parity Price Ratio

■ The parity price ratio is a ratio of an index of prices that farmers receive to an index of prices that farmers pay. The ratio uses the years 1910–14, which was a period of unusual peacetime prosperity for farmers, as a base period. For much of this century, the parity price ratio has been below 100, which means that prices of agricultural products have fallen relative to other prices.

Agricultural Policies

■ Three major agricultural policies are price supports, which attempt to set the prices of agricultural products directly; supply-restricting policies, which attempt to decrease supply and bring about a higher price for agricultural products indi-rectly; and target prices, which neither try to set prices directly nor decrease sup-ply, but instead pay farmers a deficiency payment if the market price for their goods does not equal the target price.

■ A price support is a government-guaranteed minimum price; it is an example of a price floor. If the price support is set above the equilibrium price (which is customary), then a surplus results. Historically, government has purchased the surplus and stored it.

■ The acreage allotment program, the market quota system, and the soil bank pro-gram are examples of supply-restricting agricultural policies. In the acreage allot-ment program, farmers are only permitted to produce crops on a percentage of their total acreage. In the market quota system, government sets the amount of a product that a farmer is allowed to bring to market. In the soil bank program, farmers are paid to take part of their land out of production.

■ In the target price program, government sets a target price for an agricultural product and then pays farmers the difference between the target price and the market price.

Key Terms and Concepts

Parity Price Ratio	Price Support	Target Price

1. What is the connection between inelastic demand and price instability?

2. Why don't all supply-restricting agricultural policies work as intended?

3. Some people argue that unless small family farms are assisted through price supports, target prices, or supply-restricting policies, they will soon disappear, and large (corporate) farms will control food production in this country. Agriculture will cease to be a perfectly competitive market and will become an oligopolistic market. Today, 5 percent of all farms have annual sales over $200,000 and are considered large farms. If the agriculture industry comes to be dominated by these large farms, is it likely that agriculture will become an oligopolistic market?

4. How might government reduce the amount of farm payments in the federal budget and still assist farmers?

5. Critics of present-day agricultural policies maintain that government does for farmers what they can't do for themselves: restrict supply and push prices up. Do you agree or disagree? Why?

6. Some people contend that the majority of Americans realize that they subsidize farmers through various government programs, but they don't mind doing this because they know they are preserving a desirable way of life. This argument assumes that the United States wouldn't be the same—would be in some way diminished—without family farms and that it is worth paying taxes to preserve them. What do you think of this argument? How would you go about determining how much truth there is in it?

7. Do you think the number of farmers in the United States will increase, decrease, or stay roughly the same during the next 20-years? Why?

THE DISTRIBUTION OF INCOME AND POVERTY

WHAT THIS CHAPTER IS ABOUT

Why are some persons rich and others poor? What does it mean to be poor? How is income inequality measured?

In this chapter, we seek answers to these and many other questions. We discuss the facts surrounding the distribution of income, the ways economists measure the degree of income inequality, the reasons why income inequality exists, and the problem of, and proposed solutions to, poverty.

SOME FACTS ABOUT INCOME DISTRIBUTION

In discussing public policy issues, we sometimes speak of a fact when we should speak of facts. A single fact is usually not as informative as facts are, in much the same way that a single snapshot in time does not tell as much of a story as a moving picture—a succession of snapshots through time. This section presents a few facts about the distribution of income.

Who Are the Rich and How Rich Are They?

By many interpretations, the *lowest fifth* (lowest 20 percent) of family income groups is considered poor, the top fifth is considered rich, and the three-fifths in between are considered middle income. Given this breakdown, what income do you think a family of four had to receive in 1987 to be considered rich—that is, to be in the top fifth of all income earners? The answer is $52,911. Many people regard that figure as low. They usually think the ranks of the rich are filled exclusively with millionaires and multimillionaires. Of course, millionaires and multimillionaires are rich, but then so is the family that earned $52,911 in 1987.

If we define as rich only those families that make up the *top 5 percent* of income earners, we find that a family in 1987 was rich if it had an income of $86,310 or more. In 1987, the lowest 20 percent (the poor) earned 4.6 percent of the total money income, and the highest 20 percent (the rich) earned 43.7 percent, or almost ten times as much as the poor. The highest 5 percent received 16.9 percent of the total money income, meaning that in 1987 they received approximately four times as much as the bottom 20 percent received (Exhibit 31–1).

The Income Distribution over a Period of Time

Has income distribution in the United States become less equal, more equal, or stayed about the same over time?[1] Exhibit 31–2 shows the income shares of family income groups in 1929 and 1987. In 1929, the highest- (top) fifth income group accounted for 54.4 percent of all income; in 1987, the percentage had fallen to 43.7. In 1929, the top 5 percent received 30 percent of all income; in 1987, the percentage had fallen to 16.9 percent (not shown in exhibit). At the other end of the income spectrum, in 1929, the lowest fifth received 3.9 percent of all income; in 1987, the percentage had risen to 4.6. The middle groups—the three-fifths of income recipients between the lowest fifth and the highest fifth—accounted for 41.7 percent of all income in 1929 and 51.8 percent in 1987. Thus, the facts show that the income distribution in this country became more equal between 1929 and 1987.

The Income Distribution Adjusted for Taxes and In-Kind Transfer Payments

Ex Ante Distribution (of Income)
The before-tax-and-transfer-payment distribution of income.

Government can change the distribution of income. One of the ways it does this is through the use of taxes and transfer payments. Economists speak of **ex ante**

[1]Semantically speaking, "less nearly equal" and "more nearly equal" are preferable to "less equal" and "more equal." However, we will adopt the more familiar usage. Note also that whenever we say "more equal" or "less equal," we could just as easily have said "less unequal" and "more unequal," respectively. To avoid confusion, though, we will speak of more or less equality for the most part (and not more or less inequality).

EXHIBIT 31–1
Distribution of Family Income and Income Shares, 1987

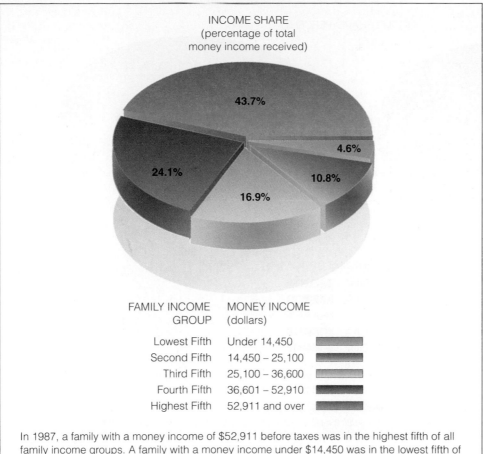

INCOME SHARE
(percentage of total
money income received)

43.7%

4.6%

24.1%

10.8%

16.9%

FAMILY INCOME GROUP	MONEY INCOME (dollars)	
Lowest Fifth	Under 14,450	
Second Fifth	14,450 – 25,100	
Third Fifth	25,100 – 36,600	
Fourth Fifth	36,601 – 52,910	
Highest Fifth	52,911 and over	

In 1987, a family with a money income of $52,911 before taxes was in the highest fifth of all family income groups. A family with a money income under $14,450 was in the lowest fifth of all family income income groups. A family with a money income of $86,310 was in the top 5 percent of all family income groups (not shown in exhibit).

* Income shares do not sum to 100 percent owing to rounding.
Source: U.S. Bureau of the Census, *Statistical Abstract of the United States, 1990* (Washington, D.C.: U.S. Government Printing Office, 1990).

and **ex post distributions** of income. The ex ante distribution of income is the before-tax-and-transfer-payment distribution of income. The ex post distribution of income is the after-tax-and-transfer-payment distribution of income. Transfer payments include welfare payments such as Aid to Families with Dependent Children (AFDC), food stamps, housing, education, and health care. **Transfer payments** are payments to persons that are not made in return for goods and services currently supplied.

The income distributions in Exhibit 31–2 do not take into account taxes, nor do they take into account **in-kind transfer payments,** that is, transfer payments, such as food stamps, medical assistance, and subsidized housing, that are paid in a specific good or service rather than cash. However, the distributions do take into account cash (monetary) transfer payments, such as direct monetary welfare assistance.

Ex Post Distribution (of Income)
The after-tax-and-transfer-payment distribution of income.

Transfer Payments
Payments to persons that are not made in return for goods and services currently supplied.

In-Kind Transfer Payments
Transfer payments, such as food stamps, medical assistance, and subsidized housing, that are made in a specific good or service.

653

EXHIBIT 31–2
Income Distribution, 1929 and 1987

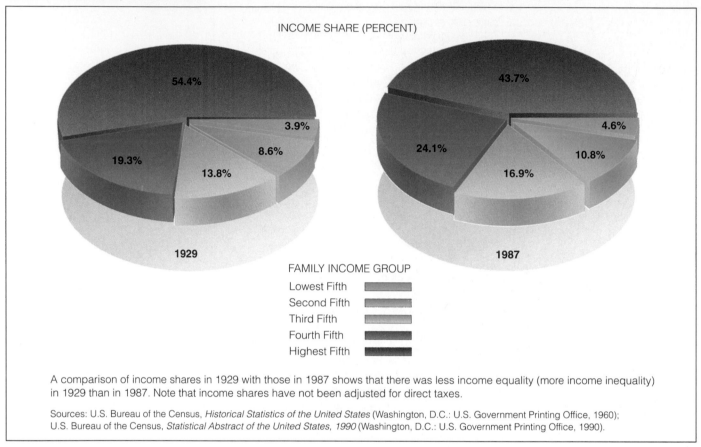

INCOME SHARE (PERCENT)

1929
54.4%
3.9%
8.6%
13.8%
19.3%

1987
43.7%
4.6%
10.8%
16.9%
24.1%

FAMILY INCOME GROUP
Lowest Fifth
Second Fifth
Third Fifth
Fourth Fifth
Highest Fifth

A comparison of income shares in 1929 with those in 1987 shows that there was less income equality (more income inequality) in 1929 than in 1987. Note that income shares have not been adjusted for direct taxes.

Sources: U.S. Bureau of the Census, *Historical Statistics of the United States* (Washington, D.C.: U.S. Government Printing Office, 1960); U.S. Bureau of the Census, *Statistical Abstract of the United States, 1990* (Washington, D.C.: U.S. Government Printing Office, 1990).

Economists Edgar Browning and William Johnson undertook to identify the ex post distribution of income in 1976 by adjusting for taxes (specifically, income and payroll taxes) and all transfers, both cash and in-kind transfer payments. Exhibit 31–3, which is based on their findings, shows that the adjusted income shares present a more equal income distribution than the unadjusted income shares do. For example, the unadjusted income share of the lowest-fifth income group in 1976 was 2.6 percent, but its adjusted income share was 6.2 percent. On the other end, the unadjusted income share for the highest-fifth income group in 1976 was 50.1 percent, but its adjusted income share was 42.0 percent.

The Effect of Age on the Income Distribution

We need to distinguish between people who are poor for long periods of time (sometimes their entire lives) and people who are poor temporarily. Consider Sherri Holmer, who attends college and works part-time as a waitress at a nearby restaurant. Currently, her income is so low that she falls into the lowest fifth of income earners. But it isn't likely that this will always be the case. After college, her income will probably rise. If she is like most people, her income will rise during her twenties, thirties, and forties. In her late forties or early fifties, her income will take a slight downturn and then level off.

EXHIBIT 31-3
Income Distribution Adjusted for Taxes and Transfers
Adjusted income shares (adjusted for taxes and transfers, both cash and in-kind) portray greater
income equality than unadjusted income shares.

Family Income Group	Income Share (Unadjusted)	Income Share (Adjusted for In-Kind and Cash Transfers and Income and Payroll Taxes)*
Lowest fifth	2.6%	6.2%
Second fifth	8.4	12.0
Third fifth	15.5	16.9
Fourth fifth	23.4	23.0
Highest fifth	50.1	42.0

*Income shares do not sum to 100 percent owing to rounding.
SOURCES: Edgar K. Browning and William R. Johnson, *The Distribution of the Tax Burden* (Washington, D.C.,
American Enterprise Institute, 1979); Edgar K. Browning and Jacqueline M. Browning, *Public Finance and the
Price System,* 3d ed. (New York: Macmillan, 1987), p. 243.

It is possible, in fact highly likely, that a person in her *late* twenties, thirties, or
forties will have a higher income than another person in her *early* twenties or
sixties, even though their total lifetime incomes will be identical. That is, if we
view each person *over time,* income equality is greater than if we view each person
at a particular point in time (say, when one is 58 years old and the other is 68).

Let's look at the case of John and Stephanie in different years. Starting in 1988,
in Exhibit 31-4, John is 18 years old and earning $10,000 per year and Stephanie
is 28 years old and earning $30,000. The income distribution between John and
Stephanie is unequal in 1988.

Ten years later, the income distribution is still unequal, with Stephanie earning
$45,000 and John earning $35,000. In fact, the income distribution is unequal in
every year shown in the exhibit. However, if we look at the total income earned
by each person in the five years specified, we see that each person earned $236,000,
giving us a perfectly equal income distribution over time.

A Simple Equation

Before we discuss the possible sources or causes of income inequality, we should
mention the factors that determine a person's income. Here we have combined

EXHIBIT 31-4
Income Distribution at One Point in Time and Over Time

Year	John's Age	John's Income	Stephanie's Age	Stephanie's Income
1988	18 years	$ 10,000	28 years	$ 30,000
1998	28	35,000	38	45,000
2008	38	52,000	48	60,000
2018	48	64,000	58	75,000
2028	58	75,000	68	26,000
Total		$236,000		$236,000

In each year, the income distribution between John and Stephanie is unequal, with either
Stephanie earning more than John (1988, 1998, 2008, and 2018) or John earning more than
Stephanie (2028). However, the total income earned by each person in the five years specified is
$236,000, giving a perfectly equal income distribution over time.

four of them—labor income, asset income, transfer payments, and taxes—in a simple equation:

Individual income = labor income + asset income + transfer payments − taxes

Labor income is equal to the wage rate an individual receives times the number of hours he or she works. Asset income consists of such things as the return to saving, the return to capital investment, and the return to land. Transfer payments and taxes we have already discussed. This equation gives us a quick way of focusing on the direct and indirect factors that affect an individual's income and the degree of income inequality. We next examine the conventional ways that income inequality is measured.

Question:

The income equation includes transfer payments, which may come in the form of cash or in-kind payments. According to the equation, if a person receives an in-kind transfer—such as free food—his income increases. But this doesn't make sense. How can a free good increase a person's income? After all, food isn't money.

Answer:

We are interested in how much a person can consume. An individual who earns $10,000 per year and doesn't have to pay apartment rent is better off (in having more goods and services) than a person who earns $10,000 per year and does have to pay apartment rent. The first person is better off than his absolute level of money income would lead us to believe. By including in-kind transfers, among other things, in individual income, we are trying to take into account this quality of being "better off." Although most government income figures do not take into account in-kind transfers, most economists would argue that simple money income is not as accurate a measure of one's command over goods and services as is a measurement of income that adjusts for in-kind transfers.

To many people, poor is poor. This is not the case for the economist. The economist wants to know *why* the person is poor. Is he poor because he is young and just starting out in life? Would he be poor if we were to consider the in-kind benefits he receives? The economist's attitude may sound cold and calculating; after all, some people argue, when someone is poor you don't ask questions, you simply try to help him out. But the economist knows that not everyone is in the same situation for the same reason, and the reason may make the difference as to whether you proceed with help, and if you do proceed, just *how* you do. Both the disabled elderly person and the young, smart college student may earn the same low income, but you may feel it more important to help the disabled elderly person than the college student.

MEASURING INCOME INEQUALITY
■

There are two commonly used measurements of income inequality. One is the Lorenz curve; the other is the Gini coefficient.

The Lorenz Curve

The **Lorenz curve** represents the distribution of income; it expresses the relationship between *cumulative percentage of families* and *cumulative percentage of income.* Exhibit 31–5 shows a hypothetical Lorenz curve.

The data in (a) are used to plot the Lorenz curve in (b). According to (a), the lowest-fifth income group has an income share of 10 percent, the second fifth has an income share of 15 percent, and so on. The Lorenz curve in (b) is derived by plotting five points. Point *A* represents the *cumulative* income share of the lowest-fifth income group (10 percent of income goes to the lowest-fifth income group). Point *B* represents the *cumulative* income share of the lowest-fifth income group *plus* the second fifth (25 percent of income goes to two-fifths, or 40 percent, of the income recipients). Point *C* represents the *cumulative* income share of the lowest fifth income group *plus* the second fifth *plus* the third fifth (45 percent of income goes to three-fifths, or 60 percent, of the income recipients). The same procedure is used for points *D* and *E.* Connecting these points gives us the Lorenz curve that represents the data in (a); the Lorenz curve is another way of depicting the income distribution in (a). Exhibit 31–6 illustrates the Lorenz curve for the United States based on the (money) income shares in Exhibit 31–1.

What would the Lorenz curve look like if there were *perfect income equality* among the different income groups? In this case, every income group would receive exactly the same percentage of total income, and the Lorenz curve would be the line of perfect income equality illustrated in Exhibit 31–5b. This is a 45° line, along which at any point cumulative percent of income (on the vertical axis) equals

Lorenz Curve
A graph of the income distribution. It expresses the relationship between cumulative percentage of families and cumulative percentage of income.

EXHIBIT 31–5
A Hypothetical Lorenz Curve

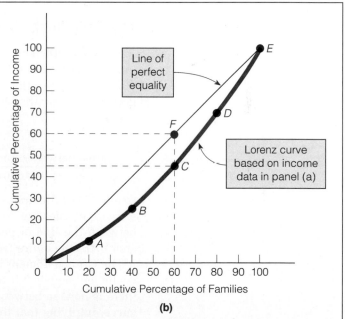

Family Income Group	Income Share (percent)	Cumulative Income Share (percent)
Lowest fifth	10%	10%
Second fifth	15	25
Third fifth	20	45
Fourth fifth	25	70
Highest fifth	30	100

(a)

(b)

The data in (a) was used to derive the Lorenz curve in (b). The Lorenz curve shows the cumulative percentage of income earned by the cumulative percentage of families. If all family income groups received the same percentage of total income, the Lorenz curve would be the line of perfect income equality. The bowed Lorenz curve shows an unequal distribution of income. The more bowed the Lorenz curve is, the more unequal the distribution of income.

EXHIBIT 31–6
Lorenz Curve for the United States, 1987

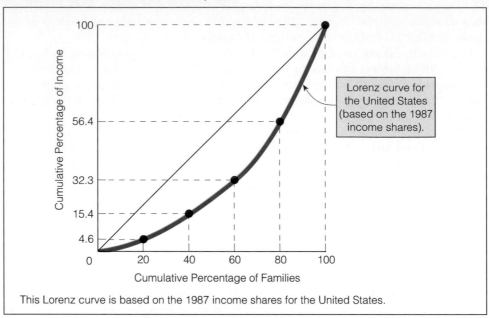

This Lorenz curve is based on the 1987 income shares for the United States.

cumulative percent of families (on the horizontal axis). We can see this by examining the characteristics of any point on the line of perfect income equality. For example, at point *F,* 60 percent of the families receive 60 percent of the total income.

The Gini Coefficient

Gini Coefficient
A measurement of the degree of inequality in the income distribution.

The **Gini coefficient,** which is a measurement of the degree of inequality in the income distribution, is used in conjunction with the Lorenz curve. It is equal to the area between the line of perfect income equality (or 45° line) and the actual Lorenz curve divided by the entire triangular area under the line of perfect income equality.

$$\text{Gini coefficient}$$
$$= \frac{\text{area between line of perfect income equality and actual Lorenz curve}}{\text{entire triangular area under the line of perfect income equality}}$$

Exhibit 31–7 illustrates both the line of perfect income equality and an actual Lorenz curve. The Gini coefficient is computed by dividing the shaded area (the area between the line of perfect income equality and the actual Lorenz curve) by the area 0*AB* (the entire triangular area under the line of perfect income equality).

The Gini coefficient is a number between 0 and 1. On the one extreme, the Gini coefficient equals 0 if the numerator in the equation is 0. A numerator of 0 means there is no area between the line of perfect income equality and the actual Lorenz curve, implying that they are one and the same. It follows that a Gini coefficient of 0 means perfect income equality.

At the other extreme, the Gini coefficient equals 1 if the numerator in the equation is equal to the denominator. If this is the case, the actual Lorenz curve is as far away from the line of perfect income equality as is possible. It follows that a

EXHIBIT 31–7
The Gini Coefficient

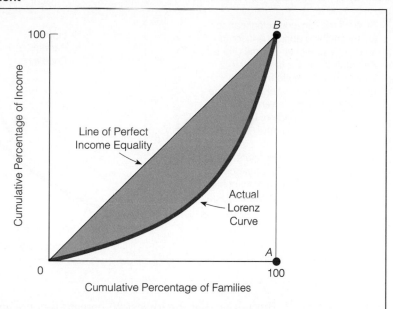

The Gini coefficient is a measurement of the degree of income inequality. It is equal to the area between the line of perfect income equality and the actual Lorenz curve divided by the entire triangular area under the line of perfect income equality. In the diagram, this is equal to the shaded portion divided by the triangular area 0AB. A Gini coefficient of 0 means perfect income equality; a Gini coefficient of 1 means complete income inequality. The larger the Gini coefficient, the greater the income inequality; the smaller the Gini coefficient, the less the income inequality.

Gini coefficient of 1 means complete income inequality. (What would the actual Lorenz curve look like if there were complete income inequality? It would represent a situation where one person had all of total income and no one else had any income. In Exhibit 31–7, a Lorenz curve representing complete income inequality would lie along the horizontal axis from 0 to A and then move from A to B.)

If a Gini coefficient of 0 represents perfect income equality and a Gini coefficient of 1 represents complete income inequality, then it follows that the larger the Gini coefficient, the greater the degree of income inequality; the smaller the Gini coefficient, the less the degree of income inequality.

A Limitation of the Gini Coefficient

Although we can learn the degree of inequality in the income distribution from the Gini coefficient, we should be careful not to misread what it is saying. For example, suppose the Gini coefficient is .33 in country 1 and .25 in country 2. We know that the income distribution is more equal in country 2 than in country 1. But would we know in which country the lowest income group receives the larger percentage of income? The natural inclination is to answer in the country with the more equal income distribution—country 2. However, this may not be true.

To see this, consider Exhibit 31–8, where two Lorenz curves are drawn. Overall, Lorenz curve 2 is closer to the line of perfect income equality than Lorenz curve 1; thus, the Gini coefficient for Lorenz curve 2 is smaller than the Gini coefficient

EXHIBIT 31–8
Limitation of the Gini Coefficient

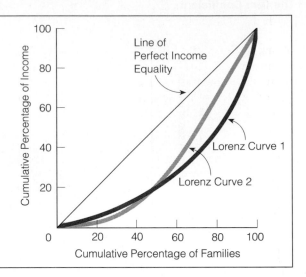

By itself the Gini coefficient cannot tell us anything about the income share of a particular income group. Although there is a tendency to believe that the bottom income group receives a larger percentage of total income the lower the Gini coefficient, this need not be the case. In the diagram, the Gini coefficient for Lorenz curve 2 is lower than the Gini coefficient for Lorenz curve 1. But as we can see, the bottom 20 percent income group obtains a smaller percentage of total income in the lower Gini coefficient case.

for Lorenz curve 1. But notice that the lowest 20 percent income group has a lower percentage of total income with Lorenz curve 2 than with curve 1.

Our point is that the Gini coefficient lacks the ability to tell us what is happening in different income groups. We should not jump to the conclusion that because in country 2 the Gini coefficient is lower than in country 1, the lowest income group has a greater percentage of total income in country 2 than in country 1.

WHY INCOME INEQUALITY EXISTS

Why does income inequality exist? How might income inequality be lessened? Both questions can be answered by focusing on the equation *individual income = labor income + asset income + transfer payments − taxes.* Generally, income inequality exists because people do not receive the same labor income, asset income, and transfer payments or pay the same taxes. If the objective is to reduce income inequality, one means of doing so is to increase transfer payments going to, and decrease taxes paid by, those persons with low labor and asset incomes; and decrease transfer payments going to, and increase taxes paid by, those with high labor and asset incomes. We discuss how this may be achieved in the section on poverty; here we concentrate on why income inequality exists.

Factors Contributing to Income Inequality

Six factors that contribute to income inequality are innate abilities and attributes, work and leisure, education and other training, risk taking, luck, and wage discrimination.

Innate Abilities and Attributes. Individuals are not all born with the same innate abilities and attributes. People vary in the degree of intelligence, good looks, and creativity they possess. Some individuals have more marketable innate abilities and attributes than others; for example, the man or woman born with exceptionally good looks, the "natural" athlete, the person who is musically gifted or mathematically adept. Such people are more likely to earn higher incomes than those with lesser abilities or attributes.

Work and Leisure. There is a trade-off between work and leisure: More work means less leisure, less work means more leisure. Some individuals will choose to work more hours (or take on a second job) and thus have less leisure. This choice will be reflected in their labor income. They will earn a larger income than those persons who choose not to work more, *ceteris paribus.*

Education and Other Training. Economists usually refer to schooling and other types of training as an "investment in human capital." Recall from the discussion of physical capital goods in Chapter 29 that in order to buy a capital good, or invest in one, a person has to forgo present consumption. A person does so in the hope that the capital good will increase his or her future consumption.

Schooling can be looked on as capital. First, one must forgo present consumption to obtain it. Second, by providing individuals with certain skills and knowledge, schooling can increase their future consumption over what it would be without the schooling. Schooling, then, is **human capital.** In general, human capital refers to education, the development of skills, and anything else that is particular to the individual and increases his or her productivity.

Contrast a person who has obtained an education with a person who has not. The educated person is likely to have certain skills, abilities, and knowledge that the uneducated person lacks. Consequently, he or she is likely to be worth more to an employer. Most college students know this. It is part of the reason they are college students.

Risk Taking. Individuals do not all have the same attitude toward risk. Some individuals are more willing to take on risk than others. Some of the individuals who are willing to take on risk will do well and rise to the top of the income distribution, and some will fall to the bottom. Those individuals who exhibit a preference for playing it safe aren't as likely to reach the top of the income distribution or hit the bottom.

Luck. When individuals can't explain why something has happened to them, they often say it was the result of good or bad luck. At times, the good or back luck explanation makes sense; at other times, it is more a rationalization than an explanation.

Good and bad luck may influence incomes. For example, the college student who studies biology only to find out in her senior year that the bottom has fallen out of the biology market has experienced bad luck. The farmer who hits oil while digging a well has experienced good luck. An automobile worker who is unemployed owing to a recession he had no part in causing is experiencing bad luck. A person who trains for a profession in which there is an unexpected increase in demand experiences good luck.

Although luck can and does influence incomes, it is not likely to have (on average) a large or long-run effect on incomes. The person who experiences good luck today, and whose income reflects this fact, isn't likely to experience luck-boosting income increases time after time. In the long run, such factors as innate ability and attributes, education, and personal decisions (how much work, how much leisure?) are more likely to have a larger, more sustained effect on income than good and bad luck.

Human Capital
Education, development of skills, and anything else that is particular to the individual and increases his or her productivity.

Even in a world with no discrimination, differences in income would still exist. (But would they be as great?)

■

Wage Discrimination
The situation that exists when individuals of equal ability and productivity (as measured by their contribution to output) are paid different wage rates.

Wage Discrimination. **Wage discrimination** exists when individuals of equal ability and productivity, as measured by their marginal revenue products, are paid different wage rates. It is a fact that the median income of blacks in the postwar period as a whole has been approximately 60 percent that of whites, and that since the late 1950s, women working full-time have earned approximately 60 percent of the male median income. Are these differences between white and black incomes, and between male and female incomes, due wholly to discrimination? Most empirical studies show that approximately half the differences are due to differences in education, productivity, and job training (although one may ask if discrimination has anything to do with the education, productivity, and job training differences). The remainder of the wage differential is due to other factors, one of which is hypothesized to be discrimination.

Most persons agree that discrimination exists, although they differ on the degree to which they think it affects incomes. Also, we should note that discrimination is not always directed at employees by employers. For example, consumers may practice discrimination—some white consumers may wish to deal only with white physicians and lawyers; some Asians may wish to deal only with Asian physicians and lawyers. Wage discrimination and a proposed means of dealing with it are discussed further in the Economics in Our Times about comparable worth.

Income Differences: Some are Voluntary, Some are Not

Even in a world with no discrimination, differences in income would still exist. Other factors, which we have noted, account for this. Some individuals would have more marketable skills than others, some individuals would decide to work harder and longer hours than others, some individuals would take on more risk than others, some individuals would undertake more schooling and training than others. Thus, some degree of income inequality is due to the fact that individuals are innately different and that they make different choices. Of course, this also implies that some degree of income inequality is due to factors unrelated to innate ability or choices; it might be due to discrimination or luck.

An interesting debate continues to be waged on the topic of discrimination-based income inequality. The opposing sides weight different factors differently. Some persons argue that wage discrimination would be lessened if markets were allowed to be more competitive, more open, more free. They believe that in an open and competitive market, with few barriers to entry and no government protection of privileged groups, discrimination would have a high price. Firms that didn't want to hire the best and the brightest—no matter what race, religion, or sex a person was—would suffer. They would ultimately pay for their act of discrimination. Individuals holding this view usually propose that government deregulate, reduce legal barriers to entry, and in general not hamper the workings of the free market mechanism.

Others contend that even if the government were to follow this script, much wage discrimination would still exist. They think government should play an active legislative role in reducing both wage discrimination and other types of discrimination that they believe ultimately result in wage discrimination. The latter include discrimination in education and discrimination in on-the-job training. Proponents of an active role for government usually believe that such policy programs as affirmative action, equal pay for equal work, and comparable worth (equal pay for comparable work) are beneficial in reducing both the amount of wage discrimination in the economy and the degree of income inequality.

Comparable Worth: What Is a Truck Driver Really Worth?

Accepting the view that discrimination does negatively affect the incomes of certain groups, the Congress, in 1963, passed the Equal Pay Act, which mandated equal pay for equal work. The next year, Title VII of the Civil Rights Act of 1964 prohibited employers from discriminating against women. These rules were relatively straightforward, but during the 1970s, a new concept, *comparable worth,* began to be discussed. The idea behind comparable worth is that equal pay should be paid for comparable work. The difficulty comes when we try to define *comparable.* Equal work is one thing, comparable work quite another. Most people believe that a woman who drives a truck loaded with oranges from Florida to Illinois does the same work as a man who drives a truck loaded with oranges from Florida to Illinois. But what is comparable work? Is working as a secretary in a major corporation comparable to working as an electrician? Is working as a registered nurse in a hospital comparable to working as a truck driver?

In one comparable worth case, a state employees' union brought a suit against the state of Washington, charging that the state had discriminated by paying lower wages to women in female-dominated jobs than it had paid men in "comparable" male-dominated jobs. Although the union ultimately lost the case, the state agreed to institute a comparable worth policy over a ten-year period.

To implement the program, the state had to determine which state jobs were comparable. Independent consultants were hired to conduct a study, and it was agreed that jobs would be evaluated on a point system according to four criteria: knowledge and skills, mental demands, accountability, and working conditions. The higher the number of points a job received, the higher the pay would be for the person occupying the job. Jobs receiving equal points were considered comparable; workers in comparable jobs would receive equal pay.

In the Washington study, a registered nurse received more points than a computer-systems analyst. A clerical supervisor received more points than a beginning secretary. Truck drivers received fewer points than retail clerks. The study found that clerk-typists were comparable to warehouse workers.

Skeptics wonder how the consultants evaluating different jobs could make sensible evaluations based on a factor such as "mental demands." How, they ask, does one evaluate the mental demands of a warehouse worker compared with a secretary? More important, though, critics charge that if expert-determined wage rates replace supply-and-demand-determined wage rates, undesirable consequences will emerge—even for those persons who initially think they will benefit from the implementation of the comparable worth doctrine.

For example, suppose the expert-determined wage for a secretary is $12 per hour while the supply-and-demand-determined wage is $7 per hour. What will happen if the supply-and-demand-determined wages are overturned by the legislatures or the courts and replaced by expert-determined wages?

First, employers of secretaries would hire fewer secretaries at $12 per hour than at $7 per hour (the demand curve for secretaries is downward sloping, no law can change that). Second, we would expect that more individuals will want to become secretaries at a wage rate of $12 per hour than at $7 per hour. Moreover, these persons are likely to be more qualified (higher skilled) than the persons working as secretaries at $7 per hour. Can you explain why? The persons who would not work as secretaries at $7 per hour largely did not because their opportunity costs were higher than $7 per hour. With a longer line of potential secretaries, and fewer secretarial positions, employers are likely to ration the available jobs to the most highly qualified persons. For the most part, the most highly qualified persons will be the persons who would not work as secretaries at $7 per hour, but will work as secretaries at $12 per hour. In the end, persons working as secretaries before comparable worth might not be working as secretaries after comparable worth.

NORMATIVE STANDARDS OF INCOME DISTRIBUTION

For hundreds of years, economists, political philosophers, and political scientists, among others, have debated what constitutes a proper, just, or fair distribution of income and have proposed different normative standards. Here we discuss three of the more well-known normative standards of income distribution. These include the marginal productivity normative standard, the absolute (complete) income equality normative standard, and the Rawlsian normative standard.

The Marginal Productivity Normative Standard

The marginal productivity theory of factor prices (discussed in Chapter 27) states that in a competitive setting, people tend to be paid their marginal revenue products.[2] The marginal productivity normative standard of income distribution holds that people *should be* paid their marginal revenue products.

We illustrate this idea in Exhibit 31–9a. The first "income pie" in (a) represents the actual income shares of eight individuals, A–H, who work in a competitive setting and are paid their respective *MRP*s. As we can see, the income distribution is unequal, since the eight persons do not contribute equally to the productive process. Some individuals are more productive than others.

The second income pie in (a), which is the same as the first, is the income distribution that the proponents of the marginal productivity normative standard believe should exist. In short, individuals should be paid their marginal revenue products.

Proponents of this position argue that it is just for individuals to receive their contribution (high, low, or somewhere in-between) to the productive process, no more and no less. Also, paying people according to their productivity gives them an incentive to become more productive. For example, individuals have an incentive to learn more and to become better trained if they know that they will be paid more as a consequence. According to this argument, without such incentives work effort would decrease, laziness would increase, and in time the entire society would feel the harmful effects. Critics respond that some persons are innately more productive than others and that rewarding them for innate qualities is unfair.

Question:

This discussion assumed a competitive setting where people were paid their MRP*s. Suppose a person is in a monopsony setting (discussed in Chapter 28) and is not being paid his or her* MRP. *Would the proponents of the marginal productivity normative standard argue that he or she should be?*

Answer:

Yes, they would. People who propose *normative standards* think the marginal productivity standard *should be* applied no matter what the current situation *is*. In other words, it is possible to be a proponent of the marginal productivity normative standard whether or not you believe people are currently being paid their marginal revenue products.

The Absolute Income Equality Normative Standard

Exhibit 31–9b illustrates the viewpoint of those persons who advocate the absolute income equality normative standard. The first income pie represents the income

[2]You may recall that in a competitive setting value marginal product (VMP) equals marginal revenue product (MRP). Thus we can say that the marginal productivity theory holds that in a competitive setting people tend to be paid their VMPs or MRPs.

EXHIBIT 31–9
Different Normative Standards of Income Distribution

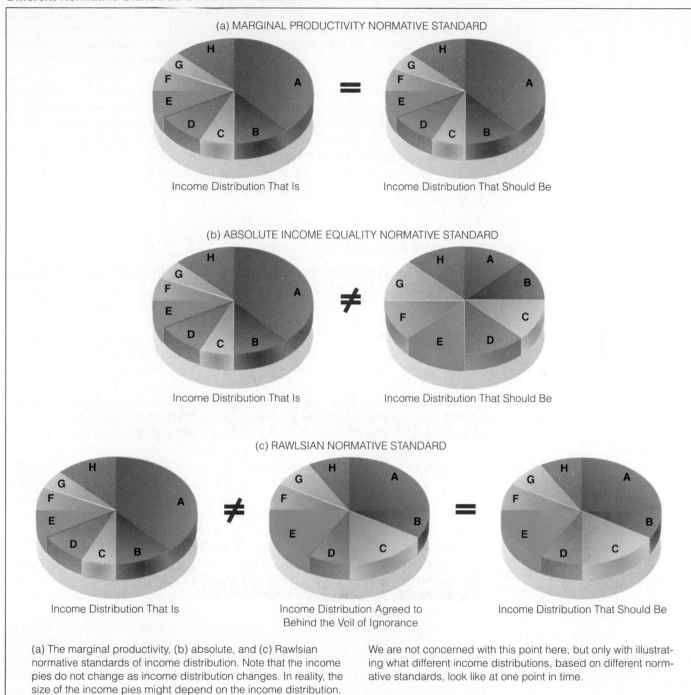

(a) MARGINAL PRODUCTIVITY NORMATIVE STANDARD

Income Distribution That Is   Income Distribution That Should Be

(b) ABSOLUTE INCOME EQUALITY NORMATIVE STANDARD

Income Distribution That Is   Income Distribution That Should Be

(c) RAWLSIAN NORMATIVE STANDARD

Income Distribution That Is   Income Distribution Agreed to   Income Distribution That Should Be
                                     Behind the Veil of Ignorance

(a) The marginal productivity, (b) absolute, and (c) Rawlsian normative standards of income distribution. Note that the income pies do not change as income distribution changes. In reality, the size of the income pies might depend on the income distribution.

We are not concerned with this point here, but only with illustrating what different income distributions, based on different normative standards, look like at one point in time.

distribution that exists—in which there is income inequality. The second income pie represents the income distribution that the persons who argue for absolute income equality believe should exist. Notice that each individual receives an equal percentage of the income pie. No one has any more or any less than anyone else.

Some hold that an equal distribution of income will lead to the maximization of total utility (in society). The argument goes this way: (1) Individuals are alike when it comes to how much satisfaction they receive from an added increase in income. (2) Receiving additional income is subject to the law of diminishing marginal utility; that is, each additional dollar is worth less to the recipient than the dollar that preceded it. (3) From points 1 and 2 it follows that redistributing income from the rich to the poor will raise total utility. The rich will not lose as much utility from the redistribution as the poor will gain. Overall, total utility (of society) will rise through the redistribution of income from the rich to the poor. Total utility will be maximized when all persons receive the same income.

Opponents of this position hold that it is impossible to know if all individuals receive equal utility from an added dollar of income, and that a rich person may receive far more utility from an added dollar of income than a poor person receives. If so, then redistributing income until it is equalized would not maximize total utility.

The Rawlsian Normative Standard

In *A Theory of Justice,* philosopher John Rawls states that individuals will argue for a different income distribution if they know what their position is in the current income distribution than if they don't know their position in the current income distribution.[3] We give an example to illustrate.

Patricia Jevons is thought to be a rich person; since her income is $300,000 per year, she is in the top 5 percent of income earners. Furthermore, the income distribution in which she occupies this position is largely unequal. There are few rich people and many poor people. Given that Patricia *knows* her position in the income distribution and considers it a comfortable position to occupy, she is less likely to argue for a more equal income distribution (and the high taxes that will be needed to bring it about) than if she were placed behind John Rawls's fictional **veil of ignorance.**

Veil of Ignorance
The imaginary veil or curtain behind which a person does not know his or her position in the income distribution.

The veil of ignorance is the imaginary veil or curtain behind which a person does not know her position in the income distribution; that is, a person does not know whether she will be rich or poor once the veil is removed. Rawls argues that behind the veil the "average" person would be more likely to vote for a more equal income distribution than she would vote for without the veil.

The full power of Rawls's veil of ignorance idea, and its impact on the income distribution, can be seen in the following scenario. On Monday, everyone knows his position in the income distribution. Some people are arguing for more income equality, but a sizable group do not want this. They are satisfied with the status-quo income distribution.

On Tuesday, everyone is somehow magically transported behind Rawls's veil of ignorance. Behind it, no one knows his position on the other side of the veil. No one knows whether he is rich or poor, innately talented or not, lucky or unlucky. As a group, the persons behind the veil must decide on the income distribution they wish to see once the veil is removed. Rawls believes that individuals are largely risk avoiders and will not want to take the chance that once the veil is removed, they will end up poor. They will opt for an income distribution that will assure them that if they do end up (relatively) poor, their standard of living is not too low.

[3]John Rawls, *A Theory of Justice* (Cambridge: Harvard University Press, 1971).

The Rawlsian normative standard is illustrated in Exhibit 31–9c, which shows three income pies. The first represents the income distribution that currently exists. The second represents the income distribution that individuals behind the veil of ignorance would accept. The third and last income pie, which is the same as the second, represents the income distribution that Rawls holds should exist— since it was agreed to in an environment where individuals were, in a sense, equal: No one knew how he or she would fare once the veil was removed.

Critics of the Rawlsian position state that individuals behind the veil of ignorance might not reach a consensus on the income distribution that should exist, and that they might not be risk avoiders to the degree Rawls assumes they will be.

Furthermore, the individuals behind the veil of ignorance will consider the trade-off between less income inequality and more output. As we hinted earlier, in a world where there is likely to be an unequal income distribution because of unequal individual productivities (sharply different marginal revenue products), reducing income inequality requires higher taxes and a lower reward for productive effort. In the end, this will lead to less productive effort being expended and less output for consumption. In short, the *size* of the income pie might change given different income distributions. Some of Rawls's critics maintain that individuals are likely to consider this information to a greater degree than Rawls assumes they will.

We can define poverty in absolute terms or in relative terms.

■

Question:

To expand on the last point: The way the income pies are drawn, the size of the pie does not change no matter what the income distribution is. Isn't this unlikely? For example, isn't it possible that the income pie over time will be larger with an unequal income distribution than with an absolutely equal income distribution? After all, individuals may not work as hard if they know that government is determined to make all incomes the same.

Answer:

That is correct. The income pies are drawn to illustrate what different income distributions, based on different normative standards, look like at one point in time, not over time. Over time the size of the pies might indeed change.

POVERTY
■

This section presents some facts about poverty and examines its causes and some proposed solutions.

What Is Poverty?

There are principally two views of poverty. One view holds that poverty should be defined in absolute terms; the other holds that poverty should be defined in relative terms.

A definition of poverty in absolute terms might be the following: Poverty exists if a family of four receives an income below $10,000 per year. A definition of poverty in relative terms might be the following: Poverty exists if a family of four receives an income that places it in the lowest 10 percent of family income recipients.

Viewing poverty in relative terms means that poverty will always exist—unless, of course, there is absolute income equality. Given any unequal income distribution, some persons will always occupy the bottom rung of the income ladder; thus, there will always be poverty. This holds no matter how high the absolute standard of living of the members of the society. For example, in a community of ten persons, where nine earn $1 million per year, and one earns $400,000 per year, the person earning $400,000 per year is in the bottom 10 percent of the income distribution and therefore is considered to be living in poverty if poverty is defined in relative terms.

The U.S. government defines poverty in absolute terms. The absolute poverty measurement was developed in 1964 by the Social Security Administration, based on the findings of the Department of Agriculture. Called the **poverty income threshold** or **poverty line,** it refers to the income below which people are considered to be living in poverty. Individuals or families with incomes below the poverty income threshold, or poverty line, are considered poor.

In 1988, the poverty income threshold was $12,092 for a family of four. It was $6,024 for an individual between 15 and 64 years of age and $5,674 for an individual 65 years of age or older. The poverty threshold is updated yearly to reflect changes in the consumer price index. In 1989, there were 6.8 million families living below the poverty line, or 10.3 percent of all families.

Poverty Income Threshold (Poverty Line)
Income level below which people are considered to be living in poverty.

Limitations of the Official Poverty Income Statistics

We need to be aware of certain limitations and shortcomings of the official poverty income statistics. First, the poverty figures are based solely on money incomes. Many money-poor persons receive in-kind benefits. For example, a family of four with a money income of $11,000 in 1988 was defined as poor, although it might have received in-kind benefits worth, say, $4,000. If the poverty figures are adjusted for in-kind benefits, the percentage of persons living in poverty drops. In 1986, on the basis of money income only, 13.6 percent of the population was said to be living in poverty, but when in-kind benefits were taken into account, the percentage dropped to 11.6.

In addition, poverty figures are not adjusted for unreported or illegal income, leading to an overestimate of poverty. Furthermore, poverty figures are not adjusted for regional differences in the cost of living, leading to both over- and underestimates of poverty.

Finally, government counters are unable to find some poor persons—such as some illegal aliens and some of the homeless—which leads to an underestimate of poverty.

Who Are the Poor?

Although the poor are made up of persons of all religions, colors, sexes, ages, and ethnic backgrounds, some groups are represented much more prominently in the poverty figures than others. For example, a greater percentage of blacks and Hispanics are poor than whites. In 1988, 31.6 percent of blacks, 26.8 percent of Hispanics, and 10.1 percent of whites lived below the poverty line. A greater percentage of families headed by females are poor than families headed by males, and families with seven or more persons are much more likely to be poor than families with fewer than seven persons. In addition, a greater percentage of young persons are poor than others, and the uneducated and poorly educated are more likely to be poor than the educated. Overall, a disproportionate percentage of the poor are black or Hispanic and live in large families headed by a female who is young and has little education.

If we look at poverty in terms of absolute numbers, instead of percentages, then most poor persons are white, largely because there are more whites in the total population than other groups. In 1988, 20.8 million whites, 9.4 million blacks, and 5.4 million Hispanics lived below the poverty line.

The Causes of Poverty: How Many, What Weight, Which One?

Why are some people poor? To a large degree, the causes and sources of poverty are the same as the causes and sources of inequality in the income distribution, which we discussed earlier.

It is difficult to assign a single cause to poverty. Some persons speak as if there is one. They argue that people are poor because they do not want to work. Others argue that people are poor because they are discriminated against in the workplace. Although most economists today believe poverty has more than one cause, they differ as to the weights they assign to the causes. And sometimes they (along with others) differ as to the cause of poverty in a particular case. We explain this latter point through a short fictional story.

Christine Berkley is 25 years old; she has only a seventh-grade education; she has three small children and no husband. Her days are spent watching television, taking care of her children, and generally staying around her apartment. Christine and her children live in poverty. Their total income comes from government cash and in-kind assistance.

Viewing this situation, one person comments that Christine is poor because of her own choosing. She chose not to get an education, to get pregnant outside of marriage, and to stay at home instead of work. This person says that the life Christine is living now—in poverty—is the consequence of decisions that she made years ago.

Another person sees the situation differently. He says that Christine was unlucky to be born in a family where the father was an alcoholic and neither parent stressed the importance of getting an education. He says that when Christine was young and attending school, she couldn't do her homework because conditions in her home were so disruptive—father yelling at mother, television turned up loud, and the like. Also, Christine has been discriminated against in the workplace, although with her lack of education, any job she could get would probably pay so little that she would not be able to afford day care for her children. He concludes that Christine is living in poverty because of bad luck and discrimination.

In broad terms, one person sees voluntary choice as the cause of Christine's poverty, the other sees factors outside her control as the cause. This is not the place to wage a full discussion about which person is closer to the truth or to try to answer the age-old question, Is one's life the result of fate or choice? Our purpose is simply to show that even though individuals may agree that poverty has more than one cause, it does not follow that they can agree about the specific cause in a specific case.

Proposed and Existing Ways of Reducing or Eliminating Poverty

In this section, we discuss three ways of reducing or eliminating poverty: the current welfare system, the negative income tax, and the market-oriented program.

Possible Justifications for Government Welfare Assistance

What is the justification for government involvement in welfare assistance, in redistributing income and goods from the rich to the poor? Some individuals would answer that there is no justification for government providing welfare assistance. This function is outside the proper role of government; playing Robin Hood is not the proper task of government. Persons who make this argument say they are not against helping the poor (for instance, they are usually in favor of private charitable organizations), but they are against government using its powers to take from some to give to others.

Persons who believe in government welfare assistance usually present the *public good–free rider* justification or the *social-insurance* justification.

Proponents of the public good–free rider position make the following arguments: (1) Most individuals in society would feel better if there were little or no poverty; it is distressing to view the sights of poverty—slums, hungry and poorly clothed people,

the homeless. Therefore, there is a demand for reducing or eliminating poverty. (2) The reduction or elimination of poverty is a *public good,* a good that if consumed by one person can be consumed by other persons to the same degree, and the consumption of which cannot be denied to anyone.* That is, once poverty is reduced or eliminated, everyone will benefit from no longer viewing the ugly and upsetting sights of poverty, and no one can be excluded from such benefits. (3) If no one can be excluded from experiencing the benefits of poverty reduction, then individuals will not have any incentive to pay for what they can get for free; thus, they will become *free riders.* The economist Milton Friedman sums up the force of the argument this way:

I am distressed by the sight of poverty: I am benefited by its alleviation; but I am benefited equally whether I or someone else pays for its alleviation; the benefits

of other people's charity therefore partly accrue to me. To put it differently, we might all of us be willing to contribute to the relief of poverty, *provided* everyone else did. We might not be willing to contribute the same amount without such assurance.**

Accepting the public good–free rider argument means that government is justified in taxing all persons to pay for welfare assistance for some.

The social-insurance justification is a different type of justification for government welfare assistance. It holds that individuals currently not receiving welfare think they might one day need welfare assistance and thus are willing to take out a form of insurance for themselves by supporting welfare programs (with their tax dollars and votes) today.

** Milton Friedman, *Capitalism and Freedom* (Chicago: University of Chicago Press, 1952), p. 191.

* We discuss public goods in Chapter 33.

The Current Welfare System.   The current welfare system largely aids the poor in two ways: by providing cash benefits and in-kind benefits. The major cash payment program is Aid to Families with Dependent Children (AFDC). In 1988, this program paid out $16.8 billion with an average monthly payment per family of $379.

The major in-kind forms of assistance to the poor include food stamps, public housing, and Medicaid. In 1988, the food stamp program paid out approximately $11.1 billion to 18.6 million recipients.

Some critics of the current welfare system comment that too little money is being spent to get people out of poverty. Others state either that too much money is being spent or that much that is being spent isn't reaching the right people (for example, in the past there have been reports of college students from rich families receiving food stamps).

Also, critics charge, the current welfare system has the unintended consequence of distorting the incentive individuals have to lessen their need. Consider the case of the fictional Barbara Sullivan. Barbara receives $496 per month in AFDC payments and $204 per month in food stamps. Barbara is currently not working, but she is seriously considering trying to find work soon. There is a problem, though: If she works and earns an income, her AFDC payments and food stamps will be cut. On the one hand, she earns income if she works; but on the other hand, she loses money (AFDC) and in-kind benefits (food stamps) if she works. The real question is how much she benefits by working relative to how much she loses. In many instances, the net benefit from working is small. In such instances, some individuals choose not to work; thus, we can reasonably say that welfare assistance acts as a disincentive to work.

In October 1988, the Congress passed by a wide margin legislation that requires welfare recipients who have children over the age of three to participate in work, training, or education programs approved of, or established by, the states. The measure also requires that states extend welfare benefits to two-parent families in which both parents are unemployed, as long as one parent works a minimum of 16 hours a week in a community-service job. This provision becomes effective October 1, 1993.

The Negative Income Tax. The negative income tax was designed to lessen the disincentive effects of the current welfare system. In popular jargon, the negative income tax is the policy that would solve the problem of poverty with a check. We explain how it would work with the aid of Exhibit 31–10.

The income and negative income tax figures in Exhibit 31–10 are hypothetical. The process of finding a family's negative income tax payment is quite easy. For example, if a family earns zero income (column 1), it would receive a negative income tax payment, or cash grant, of $5,000 (column 2). This would make its total income (column 3) $5,000. It follows that no family would be permitted to fall below an income of $5,000; this income would then be the **guaranteed income level.** Exactly what dollar figure would constitute the guaranteed income level would be decided through the political process.

Suppose now that the family that previously earned $0 earns $1,000. How will it be affected? Its negative income tax payment will fall—from $5,000 to $4,500—but not by the amount its earned income increased. For a $1,000 increase in earned

Guaranteed Income Level
Income level below which people are not allowed to fall.

EXHIBIT 31–10
Hypothetical Negative Income Tax
The negative income tax here has an implicit marginal tax rate of 50 percent and a guaranteed income of $5,000. A family that earns $0 receives a negative income tax payment of $5,000. If this same family earns $1,000, the negative income tax payment falls to $4,500.

(1) Earned Income	(2) Negative Income Tax Payment (Cash Grant)	(3) Total Income = Earned Income + Negative Income Tax Payment
$ 0	$5,000	$ 5,000
1,000	4,500	5,500
2,000	4,000	6,000
3,000	3,500	6,500
4,000	3,000	7,000
5,000	2,500	7,500
6,000	2,000	8,000
7,000	1,500	8,500
8,000	1,000	9,000
9,000	500	9,500
10,000	0	10,000

income, its negative income tax payment decreases by $500. This means the family's **implicit marginal tax rate** is 50 percent. The implicit marginal tax rate is the rate at which the negative income tax payment, or any cash grant or subsidy, is reduced as earned income increases.

For the family in our example, the implicit marginal tax rate is 50 percent for every $1,000 increase in earned income up to $10,000. The essence of the negative income tax is that a family can make itself substantially better off—as measured by its total income (column 3)—by working and earning income. This contrasts with many present welfare assistance programs that, at certain levels of assistance and in certain circumstances, impose a 100 percent implicit marginal tax rate on the welfare recipient. The message of such a (high-tax) welfare system is clear: Earn an additional dollar of income, lose a dollar of welfare assistance. With such a high implicit marginal tax rate, the disincentive to work and earn income is strong, as is the incentive to remain on welfare.

Question:

Wouldn't the negative income tax provide people with a sharp disincentive to work if the guaranteed income level were set too high? If the guaranteed income level were set at, say, $17,000, many people currently earning that income might decide to quit their jobs and collect negative income tax payments. Isn't this likely to be the case?

Answer:

Certainly, if the guaranteed income level is set too high, individuals currently not receiving welfare assistance would have an incentive to put themselves into a position where they would receive it. In this case, the negative income tax program might lead to more instead of fewer individuals receiving welfare assistance. The dollar amount of the guaranteed income is critical to the program having the desired effect.

The Market-Oriented Program. In both the current welfare system and the negative income tax scheme, government is actively involved in trying to reduce or eliminate poverty. Both use the approach of assisting poor persons directly by giving them cash or goods and services. The market-oriented program for reducing poverty does not take the direct assistance approach but rather advocates breaking down the existing legal barriers to employment, thereby indirectly assisting poor persons.

For example, advocates of this approach hold that the minimum wage actually hurts poor, unskilled persons by pricing them out of the labor market. They argue that a poor person with low skills is trapped into a life of idleness if he or she cannot get a job, and that the person isn't likely to get a job if the minimum wage mandates that an employer must pay the person more than he or she is worth.

Consider another example. In many major cities of the country a person must obtain an expensive medallion (license) before opening a taxi business. Advocates of the market-oriented approach to reducing poverty maintain that such licensing procedures keep some people in poverty. Their removal would promote a more open and entry-free market. They say that the poor will benefit immensely if job opportunities that are currently closed are opened up to them. If government were to become more involved in opening up the market, instead of working alongside those who wish to close it, poverty would quickly decrease, and the need for welfare-type programs would diminish.

Interview: John Kenneth Galbraith

To the public at large, one of the best-known economists is John Kenneth Galbraith. Two of his many books, *The Affluent Society* and *The New Industrial State,* have had a major impact on the way many people think about economics and the economy. Galbraith is a vocal critic of the free market system. He *argues against* giant corporations, which he believes manipulate the American economy, and he *argues for* more responsible government that will adequately address, among other things, the legitimate concerns of the poor. Galbraith is currently at Harvard University.

Market economists argue that the problems of poverty and income inequality are best solved by restraining government and freeing up the market. What is wrong with this approach? How are these problems best solved?

Market economists reach this conclusion out of convenience and not out of logic. It is what a great many conservative politicians want to hear.

You have had much to say about the poor and about income inequality. What do you consider an intolerable level of poverty and income inequality? What public actions would you propose on this front?

Certainly, I don't want to see anybody falling below the prescribed poverty level, but beyond that I would like to see greater equality of income distribution. And as to the instruments, there is none that is new. The government has to repair the substantial defaults of capitalism by an adequate minimum wage, a strong housing program (there is no industrialized country where capitalism builds good houses for the poor), and a strong health program for those who do not have access to medical care.

Do you think most Americans have the same priorities you do but that these priorities are not being transmitted properly through the political process, or do they have different priorities?

I don't think it is necessarily the role of an economist to be with the majority. The role of the economist is to state what he or she believes is right and should be done. I confess to the feeling that those of us who are asking for a more equitable society, and a more responsible and effective role for government, may well be in the minority.

What do you predict will be a major economic problem the United States will have to face in the mid-1990s, and how should it solve that problem?

I'll say the major economic problem is going to be our competitive position in the world plus the likelihood of some substantial recession in consequence of all the problems that were allowed to accumulate during the Reagan years.

What are some of the problems you are referring to?

Real estate speculation, weakness of the banks, and I think I would put my ma-

jor emphasis on the increasingly bad distribution of income and the growing problems of our central cities.

What persons have most influenced your thinking, and would you summarize what you have learned from each of them?

In economics, I was first greatly influenced by Alfred Marshall. He was important for me in getting under my belt the basic structure of neoclassical economics. And then came along John Maynard Keynes who helped me to see its shortcomings.

What got you interested in economics?

I was a student in agriculture in the 1930s in Canada. It occurred to me very strongly that there was no point in producing better livestock or better crops if you couldn't sell them. The issue wasn't the quality of the product, or the efficiency with which it was produced, but the larger economic problem in selling it, that is, getting a decent price for it. So I shifted from the study of animal husbandry to economics—agricultural economics. Then I went on to study agricultural economics further at [the University of California] Berkeley.

Which do you consider your best book?

I've always thought that my best book was *The New Industrial State,* and that position has been quite widely shared.

Interview: Walter Williams

Walter Williams is a well-respected economist who uses the tools of economics to discuss such controversial and important issues as poverty, discrimination, and economic issues related to different ethnic groups. Williams is currently at George Mason University.

What is the best way to address the problems of poverty and racial discrimination in this country?

I think the best way is through the free market. If you look around the world and you look for a general level of affluence, you see that affluence occurs in those societies where a greater proportion of the resources are allocated through the free market system. You can talk about Hong Kong, Korea, Taiwan, and Singapore and some other places. I think in terms of solving the problems of poverty in this country, we need to move toward the free market as opposed to government intervention. Most often government intervention exacerbates the problems of poverty—such as the minimum wage laws restricting jobs, or rent controls reducing the number of rental units, or welfare payments increasing dependency.

Is the free market the best way to proceed when it comes to racial discrimination?

Yes it is. For example, if you look at some of our legislation on the books, such as the Davis Bacon Act of 1931, it requires the payment of above-market wages on federally-funded or assisted construction projects. You'll read through the legislative history and find that white workers and white contractors called for the Davis Bacon Act explicitly to create monopoly privileges for white workers and price blacks out of the market.

In general, when there is a free market, people can offer compensating differences. For example, if you happen to be less preferred for a position for whatever reason—perhaps you are a minority, or a woman, or speak a foreign language—you can bid down your price and therefore become employed.

Why do you think the critics of the free market do not see how it can over time help lessen the problems of poverty and racial discrimination?

I think it has a lot to do with their vision of how the world operates. For example, if it is your vision that an employer needs so many workers in order to get a job done—in other words, as an economist would say the demand for labor is zero [perfectly inelastic demand curve for labor]—well, then, having a minimum wage means that workers will have a higher pay and the same number will be employed, and the higher wages will come out of profits. However, if it is your vision that employers can find substitutes, and that they will substitute one input for the other input whose price has risen—that is, there is non-zero elasticity of demand for labor [demand curves for labor slope downward]—then you can be for the low-skilled and come out against the minimum wage. In this vision, you see that

a minimum wage simply prices some people out of the market and prevents them from getting on-the-job training that is needed to increase their future wage.

In terms of race, if it is your vision that if a person can do something he will in fact do it, then you might come out for affirmative action. That is, if you assume that if an employer can discriminate that he will discriminate, regardless of what it costs, then you will have very little faith in the free market. But for the person who realizes there is an elasticity of demand for discrimination as well, that at some prices people just won't take discrimination, then things are different.

Do you think government has helped minorities in this country in the last two decades?

There is a yes and no answer to that. In terms of ensuring constitutional protections that have been long denied, I think the government indeed has helped—that is, today black Americans have the same guarantees as anybody else in the United States.

But for other government actions which have been taken in the name of helping minorities, such as affirmative action, it is questionable that they have helped. For example, there is a study that looks at black progress from 1940–80 and it says that much greater progress was made between 1940 and 1960, before affirmative action, than between 1960 and 1980, after affirmative action. Blacks received a lot of benefits from getting rid of just the crude forms of discrimination that existed as opposed to affirmative action or quota programs.

I think many government programs have harmed blacks in making achievements less credible. For example, whatever inspiration Harvard or the University of Virginia has in requiring so many articles in the law journals to be written by women or by minorities reduces the credibility of a black student or a female student having written for the law journal.

What got you interested in economics?

I was a major in sociology in 1963 and I concluded that it was not very rigorous. Over the summer I was reading a book by W.E.B. Dubois, *Black Reconstruction*, and somewhere in the book it said something along the lines that blacks could not melt into the mainstream of American society until they understood economics, and that was something that got me interested in economics. And then beyond that, I had some excellent professors at California State University where I got my B.A. degree and UCLA where I did my graduate work that stimulated a lot of interest.

Would you talk about the economic way of thinking?

One of the major things about the economic way of thinking is that economic theory suggests that one always weigh benefits against costs. Regardless of a benefit anyone will tell you about, we know that there are costs. We might not know the specific costs, but we know that the second law of thermodynamics and other laws of conservation suggest that there are no free lunches, there is no-something-for-nothing machine. And I think when you talk about costs and benefits you recognize that there are tradeoffs, and you get more of good X only by substituting good Y. I think that is the major contribution economists can give to thinking about analytical or political problems. It is in recognizing the importance of opportunity costs.

What is the best way to teach key economic concepts?

I think you have to do it through example. I know Armen Alchian, who was a tenacious mentor of mine at UCLA, said that the true test of your knowledge of your subject is whether you can teach someone who doesn't know anything about it and might even possibly be hostile to it. One way is to simply use examples.

For instance, one of the ways I teach students the difference between marginal cost and historical (sunk) cost is to say, suppose someone wants his teenage son to be in by 11 P.M. and he can offer two forms of punishment. One is that if the son comes in late at night he gets his car taken away from him for a week; the second is to tell him that for each minute he is out past 11 P.M. he has to forfeit one day of driving his car. Then I ask my students if the young man is out past 11 P.M. under which regime will he rush home. They say the second: when the marginal cost is not zero. Students can relate to that type of application.

How do you get students to think about economics?

You ask students questions that they have to puzzle over. I remember Jack Hirshliefer, a professor of mine at UCLA, asked me on my Ph.D. oral exam if whales had utility curves. I said of course they do. Then he asked me if I could construct an empirical test to confirm or reject the hypothesis. With Hirshliefer and Alchian, they weren't actually looking for a specific answer to their questions, but they wanted to know how an economist would go about trying to find the answer.

I take much of the same approach with my students. For example, I sometimes ask them questions that come out of the Bible. For example, I ask them why there is a prohibition in Deuteronomy about plowing a field with both an ox and an ass. Or why is there a prohibition that a man shall not wear that which pertaineth to a woman and a woman shall not wear that which pertaineth to a man. Or I might ask them what is the economic meaning of the commandment that thou shalt honor thy mother and father. And I don't know the answer for certain, but we talk about it, and perhaps [in the case of honoring thy mother and father] it is a social security clause of some sort.

CHAPTER SUMMARY

The Distribution of Income

■ The distribution of income is determined first in factor markets. The government can change the distribution of income through taxes and transfer payments. The evidence available shows that the ex post distribution of income is more equal than the ex ante distribution of income.

■ Individual income = labor income + asset income + transfer payments − taxes. Government affects the latter factors, transfer payments and taxes.

CHAPTER 31
THE DISTRIBUTION OF INCOME AND
POVERTY
■
675

■ The Lorenz curve represents the income distribution. The Gini coefficient is a measurement of the degree of inequality in the distribution of income. A Gini coefficient of 0 means perfect income equality; a Gini coefficient of 1 means complete income inequality.

■ Income inequality exists because individuals differ in their innate abilities and attributes, their choices of work and leisure, their education and other training, their attitudes about risk taking, the luck they experience, and the amount of wage discrimination directed against them. Some income inequality is the result of voluntary choices, some is not.

■ There are three major normative standards of income distribution: the marginal productivity normative standard, which holds that the income distribution should be based on workers being paid their marginal revenue products; the absolute income equality normative standard, which holds that there should be absolute or complete income equality; and the Rawlsian normative standard, which holds that the income distribution decided on behind the veil of ignorance (where individuals are equal) should exist in the real world.

Poverty

■ The income poverty threshold, or poverty line, is the income level below which a family or person is considered poor and living in poverty.

■ It is important to be aware of the limitations of poverty income statistics. The statistics are usually not adjusted for (1) in-kind benefits, (2) unreported and illegal income, and (3) regional differences in the cost of living; and (4) the statistics do not count the poor who exist but are out of sight, such as illegal aliens and some of the homeless.

■ Different ways of dealing with the problem of poverty have been proposed; some have been implemented. The current welfare system aids people through cash and in-kind payments. The negative income tax establishes a guaranteed level of income below which no one is allowed to fall; as a family earns income, its negative income tax payment is reduced by less than its earned income rises (up until a certain income level). An important consideration in this program is the level at which the guaranteed income is set. The market-oriented approach to reducing or eliminating poverty stresses breaking down the barriers to poor persons earning income.

Key Terms and Concepts

Ex Ante Distribution (of Income)

Ex Post Distribution (of Income)

Transfer Payments

In-Kind Transfer Payments

Lorenz Curve

Gini Coefficient

Human Capital

Wage Discrimination

Veil of Ignorance

Guaranteed Income Level

Implicit Marginal Tax Rate

1. "The Gini coefficient for country A is .35, and the Gini coefficient for country B is .22. From this it follows that the bottom 10 percent of income recipients in country B have a greater percentage of the total income than the bottom 10 percent of the income recipients in country A." Do you agree or disagree? Why?

2. Would you expect greater income inequality in country A, where there is great disparity in age, or in country B, where there is little disparity in age? Explain your answer.

3. What is a major criticism of the absolute income equality normative standard?

4. Would the work-disincentive effect of the negative income tax be less with a 10 percent implicit marginal tax rate than with a 50 percent implicit marginal tax rate, *ceteris paribus?*

5. A good welfare system is said to be one that takes care of the deserving without encouraging people to become undeserving. In other words, it helps the people who deserve to be helped, but doesn't distort incentives to the degree that the undeserving put themselves into situations where they can cash in on people's generosity. Discuss the current welfare system, the negative income tax, and the market-oriented program with this thought in mind.

6. In what ways does the Rawlsian technique of hypothesizing individuals behind a veil of ignorance help or not help us decide whether we should have a 55 mph speed limit or a higher one, a larger or smaller welfare system, and higher or lower taxes placed on the rich?

7. Welfare recipients would rather receive their benefits in cash than in-kind, but much of the welfare system provides benefits in-kind. Is there any reason for not giving recipients their welfare benefits the way they want to receive them? Would it be better to move to a welfare system that only provides benefits in cash?

8. Critics of the market-oriented program of reducing poverty often remark that it does too little and that it does not really address the root causes of poverty, such as discrimination. Do you agree or disagree? Why?

CHAPTER

32

ANTITRUST, BUSINESS REGULATION, AND DEREGULATION

WHAT THIS CHAPTER IS ABOUT

The television reporter sits across from the economist and asks him to explain what the recent economic news means. The economist responds. He talks about an economic theory (cleverly disguised) and cites a few facts and figures. The reporter asks: So, what do we do? The reporter wants to know what *policy* we (the American public, the government, the regulators, whoever) should implement.

This chapter is largely about economic policy, specifically, economic policy that relates to business—antitrust law and business regulation and deregulation.

678

ANTITRUST

■

We learned earlier that a monopoly produces a smaller output than is produced by a perfectly competitive firm with the same revenue and cost considerations, charges a higher price, and causes a welfare loss to society (see Chapter 25). Some economists argue that based on these facts, government should place certain restrictions on monopolies. Also, government should restrict the activities of cartels, since the objective of a cartel is to behave as if it were a monopoly.

Others hold that monopolies do not have as much market power as some people think—witness the competition some monopolies face from broadly defined substitutes and imports. As for cartels, they usually contain the seeds of their own destruction—therefore, it is only a matter of time (usually short) before they naturally crumble.

We are not concerned here with the debate about *whether* to restrict monopoly power. Instead, we examine the ways government has dealt with, and continues to deal with, monopoly power. Two of the ways government has done this are through the antitrust laws and through regulation. We examine antitrust law in this section, regulation in the next.

Antitrust law is legislation passed for the stated purpose of controlling monopoly power and preserving and promoting competition. First, let's look at how a few of the major antitrust acts have been used and the effects they have had.

> *Two of the ways government has dealt with monopoly power are through the antitrust laws and through regulation.*
>
> ■

Antitrust Law
Legislation passed for the stated purpose of controlling monopoly power and preserving and promoting competition.

Antitrust Acts

The seven major acts that constitute U.S. antitrust policy are the Sherman Act (1890), the Clayton Act (1914), the Federal Trade Commission Act (1914), the Robinson–Patman Act (1936), the Wheeler–Lea Act (1938), the Celler–Kefauver Antimerger Act (1950), and the Hart–Scott–Rodino Antitrust Procedural Improvements Act (1980).

The Sherman Act (1890). The Sherman Act was passed during a period when mergers of companies were common. At that time, the organization that companies formed by combining together was called a **trust;** this in turn gave us the word *antitrust.*

The Sherman Act contains two major provisions:

1. "Every contract, combination in the form of trust or otherwise, or conspiracy, in restraint of trade or commerce among the several states, or with foreign nations, is hereby declared to be illegal."
2. "Every person who shall monopolize, or attempt to monopolize, or combine or conspire with any other person or persons to monopolize any part of the trade or commerce . . . shall be guilty of a misdemeanor."

Some people have argued that the provisions of the Sherman Act are vague. For example, the act never explains which specific acts constitute "restraint of trade," although it declares such acts illegal.

The Clayton Act (1914). The Clayton Act made the following business practices illegal when their effects "may be to substantially lessen competition or tend to create a monopoly":

1. Price discrimination—charging different customers different prices for the same product where the price differences are not related to cost differences.

Trust
A combination of firms that come together to act as a monopolist.

2. Exclusive dealing—selling to a retailer on the condition that the seller not carry any rival products.

3. Tying contracts—arrangements whereby the sale of one product is dependent on the purchase of some other product(s).

4. The acquisition of competing companies' stock if the acquisition reduces competition. (Some say a major loophole of the act is that it did not ban the acquisition of competing companies' physical assets, and therefore did not prevent anticompetitive mergers as it was designed to do.)

5. Interlocking directorates—an arrangement whereby the directors of one company sit on the board of directors of another company in the same industry. These were made illegal, irrespective of their effects (that is, interlocking directorates are illegal at all times, not just when their effects "may be to substantially lessen competition. . .")

The Federal Trade Commission Act (1914). The Federal Trade Commission Act contained the broadest and most general language of any antitrust act. It declared illegal "unfair methods of competition in commerce." In essence, this amounts to declaring illegal those acts that are judged to be "too aggressive" in competition. The problem is how to decide what is fair and what is unfair, what is aggressive but not too aggressive. This act also set up the Federal Trade Commission (FTC) to deal with "unfair methods of competition."

The Robinson–Patman Act (1936). The Robinson–Patman Act was passed in an attempt to decrease the failure rate of small businesses by protecting them from the competition of large and growing chain stores. The large chain stores were receiving price discounts from their suppliers and, in turn, were passing the discounts on to their customers. As a result, small businesses had a difficult time competing, and many of them failed. The Robinson–Patman Act prohibited suppliers from offering special discounts to large chain stores unless they also offered the discounts to everyone else. Many economists believe that, rather than preserving and strengthening competition, the Robinson–Patman Act limited it. The act seemed to be more concerned about a certain group of competitors than about the process of competition and the buying public as a whole.

The Wheeler–Lea Act (1938). The Wheeler–Lea Act empowered the Federal Trade Commission to deal with false and deceptive acts or practices. Major moves in this area have been against advertising that the FTC has deemed false and deceptive.

The Celler–Kefauver Antimerger Act (1950). The Celler–Kefauver Act was designed to close the merger loophole that remained in the Clayton Act (see point 4 of the Clayton Act). It banned anticompetitive mergers that occurred as a result of one company acquiring the physical assets of another company.

The Hart–Scott–Rodino Antitrust Procedural Improvements Act (1980). This act required that pending mergers be reported in advance to the Federal Trade Commission and the Justice Department.

Unsettled Points in Antitrust Policy

It is not always clear where lines should be drawn in implementing antitrust policy. Which firms should be allowed to enter into a merger, which firms should be prohibited? What constitutes restraint of trade? Which firms should be termed "monopolists" and broken into smaller firms, and which firms should be left alone?

As we might guess, not everyone answers these questions the same way. In short, some points of antitrust policy are still unsettled. A few of the more important unsettled points are noted here.

Definition of the Market. Should a market be defined broadly or narrowly? The way it is defined will help determine whether a particular firm is considered a monopoly or not. For example, in an important antitrust suit in 1945, a court ruled that Alcoa (Aluminum Company of America) was a monopoly because it had 90 percent of the virgin aluminum ingot market. If the market Alcoa operated within had been broadened to include stainless steel, copper, tin, nickel, and zinc (some of the goods it had to compete with), it is unlikely that Alcoa would have been ruled a monopoly.

Later court rulings have tended to define markets broadly rather than narrowly. For instance, in the DuPont case in 1956, the market relevant to DuPont was ruled to be the flexible wrapping materials market rather than the narrower cellophane market.

In a well-publicized antitrust suit, the Justice Department filed antitrust charges against IBM, saying that it had monopolized the "general-purpose computer and peripheral-equipment" industry. After 13 years and 66 million pages of documents, the government decided to drop the suit. It did so largely on the basis of a broad interpretation of IBM's market. Although IBM did dominate the mainframe computer industry, there was little evidence that it dominated the minicomputer, word processor, or computer-services markets.

Concentration Ratios. Concentration ratios have often been used to gauge the amount of competition in an industry, but as we pointed out in Chapter 26, there are problems with such use. First, concentration ratios do not address the issue of foreign competition. For example, the four-firm concentration ratio might be very high, but still the four firms that make up the concentration ratio may face stiff competition from abroad. Furthermore, it is possible for a four-firm concentration ratio to remain stable over time even though there is competition among the four major firms in the industry.

In 1982, the Justice Department replaced the four- and eight-firm concentration ratios with the Herfindahl index, although it too is subject to some of the same criticisms as the concentration ratios. The **Herfindahl index** measures the degree of concentration in an industry. It is equal to the sum of the squares of the market shares of each firm in the industry:

$$\text{Herfindahl index} = (S_1)^2 + (S_2)^2 + \ldots + (S_n)^2$$

Herfindahl Index
Measures the degree of concentration in an industry. It is equal to the sum of the squares of the market shares of each firm in the industry.

where S_1 through S_n are the market shares of firms 1 through n. For example, if there are 10 firms in an industry, and each firm has a 10 percent market share, the Herfindahl index is 1,000 ($1,000 = 10^2 + 10^2 + 10^2 + 10^2 + 10^2 + 10^2 + 10^2 + 10^2 + 10^2 + 10^2$).

Exhibit 32–1 compares the Herfindahl index and the four-firm concentration ratio. Looking at the top four firms, A–D, we notice that together they have a 48 percent market share, which generally is thought to describe a concentrated industry. A merger between any of the top four firms and any other firm (say, between firm B and firm G) would give the new merger firm a greater market share than any existing firm and usually would incur frowns from the Justice Depart-

EXHIBIT 32–1

A Comparison of the Four-Firm Concentration Ratio and the Herfindahl Index
Using the old method (in this case, the four-firm concentration ratio), the top four firms in the industry have a 48 percent market share. A proposed merger between any of the top four firms and any other firm would likely be frowned on by the Justice Department. However, the Herfindahl index of 932 is representative of an unconcentrated industry, and any merger that didn't increase the index by more than 200 would most likely be allowed.

FIRMS	OLD METHOD (MARKET SHARE)	HERFINDAHL INDEX (MARKET SHARE SQUARED)
A	15%	225
B	12	144
C	11	121
D	10	100
E	8	64
F	7	49
G	7	49
H	6	36
I	6	36
J	6	36
K	6	36
L	6	36
Total	100%	932

Four-Firm concentration ratio = .48 or 48 percent

Herfindahl Index = 932

ment. The Herfindahl index for the industry is 932, however, and the Justice Department considers any number less than 1,000 to be representative of an unconcentrated industry. Furthermore, a merger between two firms that does not raise the Herfindahl index by more than 200 points (assuming the index is below 1,000 before the merger) will not bring on an antitrust action. For example, a merger between firm B (with a 12 percent market share) and firm G (with a 7 percent market share) will raise the Herfindahl index by 168 and is therefore likely to be permitted. (We obtain the number 168 by first finding the market share of the merged firm—which is 12 percent + 7 percent, or 19 percent—then squaring this, giving us 361, and finally finding the *difference* between 361 and the sum of the market share squared of both firms before the merger (which is 144 + 49, or 193; that is, 361 − 193 = 168).

The advantage of the Herfindahl index over the four- and eight-firm concentration ratios is that it provides information about the dispersion of firm size in an industry. For example, the Herfindahl index will be different between setting A, where, 3 firms together have a 50 percent market share and there are only 4 other firms in the industry, and setting B, where 3 firms together have a 50 percent market share and there are 150 other firms in the industry.

The Herfindahl index and the four- and eight-firm concentration ratios have been criticized for implicitly arguing *from firm size to market power*. Both assume that firms that have large market shares have market power that they are likely to be abusing. But, of course, size could be a function of efficiency, serving the buying public well.

Antitrust Decisions: Some Hits, Some Misses

The stated purpose of the antitrust laws may be worthwhile. Most people agree that promoting and strengthening competition is a good idea. Often, however, a difference arises between the stated purpose or objective of a policy and its effects. Some economists have argued that the antitrust laws have not, in all instances, accomplished their stated objective. (We have already hinted at this in our short discussion of the Robinson–Patman Act.) Here are a few cases that illustrate some of the ways the courts and government policy makers have approached antitrust issues.

Case 1: In 1966, the U.S. Supreme Court ruled on the legality of a merger between Von's Grocery Co. and Shopping Bag Food Stores, both of Los Angeles. Together the two grocery chains had a little over 7 percent of the grocery market in the Los Angeles area. However, the Supreme Court ruled that a merger between the two companies violated the Clayton Act. It based its ruling largely on the fact that between 1950 and the early

1960s, the number of small grocery stores in Los Angeles had declined sharply. The court took this as an indication of increased concentration in the industry.

Economists are quick to point out that the number of firms in an industry might be falling owing to technological changes, and when this happens, the average size of an existing firm rises. Justice Potter Stewart, in a dissenting opinion to the 1966 decision, argued that the Court had erroneously assumed that the "degree of competition is invariably proportional to the number of competitors."

Case 2: In 1967, the Salt Lake City-based Utah Pie Co. charged that three of its competitors in Los Angeles, Continental Baking Company, Carnation Company, and Pet Milk Company, were practicing price discrimination. Utah Pie charged that these companies were selling pies in Salt Lake City for lower prices than they were selling pies near their plants of operation. The Supreme Court ruled in favor of Utah Pie.

Some economists note, though, that Utah Pie charged lower prices for its pies than did its competitors, and that it continued to increase its sales volume and make a profit during the time its competitors were supposedly exhibiting anticompetitive behavior. They suggest that Utah Pie was using the antitrust laws to hinder its competitors.

Case 3: In 1978, Continental Airlines set out to acquire National Airlines. The Justice Department opposed the merger of the two companies on the grounds that the merged company would dominate the New Orleans air-traffic market. The Civil Aeronautics Board (CAB) did not oppose the merger because it said the market under consideration was contestable. As we noted in Chapter 26, firms in a contestable market that operate inefficiently or consistently earn positive economic profits will be joined by competing firms. It was implicitly argued that statistical measures, such as concentration ratios, mean less than whether the market is contestable.

REGULATION

This section examines the stated objectives of regulatory agencies and effects of regulation on natural and other monopolies.

The Case of Natural Monopoly

If economies of scale are so pronounced or large in an industry that only one firm can survive, that firm is called a **natural monopoly** (see Chapter 25). Firms that supply local electricity, gas, water, and telephone service are usually considered natural monopolies.

Consider the natural monopoly setting represented in Exhibit 32–2. Suppose there is one firm in the market and that it produces Q_1 units of output at an average total cost of ATC_1 (Q_1 is the output at which $MR = MC$, although to simplify the diagram the MR curve is not shown). At Q_1, we have an inefficient allocation of

Natural Monopoly
The condition where economies of scale are so pronounced in an industry that only one firm can survive; an industry in which it is not economical to have more than one firm providing a good.

683

EXHIBIT 32–2
The Natural Monopoly Situation

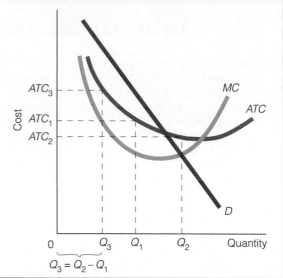

Here the only existing firm produces Q_1 at an average total cost of ATC_1. The resource-allocative efficient output level is Q_2. There are two ways to obtain this output level: (1) The only existing firm can increase its production to Q_2, or (2) a new firm can enter the market and produce Q_3, which is the difference between Q_2 and Q_1. The first way minimizes total cost, the second way does not. This, then, is a natural monopoly situation: One firm can supply the entire output demanded at a lower cost than two or more firms could.

resources. Why? As we learned in Chapter 24, resource-allocative efficiency exists when the marginal benefit to demanders of the resources used in the goods they buy equals the marginal cost to suppliers of the resources they use in the production of the goods they sell. In Exhibit 32–2, resource-allocative efficiency exists at Q_2, corresponding to the point where the demand curve intersects the MC curve.

There are two ways to reach the higher, efficient quantity of output, Q_2: (1) The firm currently producing Q_1 could increase its output to Q_2. (2) Another firm could enter the market and produce Q_3—the difference between Q_2 and Q_1.

Different costs are associated with each way. For example, if a new firm enters the market and produces Q_3, it incurs an average total cost of ATC_3. Thus, both firms *together* produce Q_2, but one firm incurs average total costs of ATC_3, and the other firm incurs average total costs of ATC_1.

If, instead, the firm currently in the market increases its production to Q_2, it incurs average total costs of ATC_2. As long as the objective is to increase output to the resource-allocative efficient level, it is cheaper (lower total costs) to do this by getting the firm currently in the market to increase its output to Q_2 than to have two firms together produce Q_2.

Natural monopoly exists where one firm can supply the entire output demanded at lower cost than two or more firms can. (From this, some economists argue that a natural monopoly is best defined as an industry in which it is not economical to have more than one firm produce a good.)

Will the natural monopolist change the monopoly price? Some economists say yes. See Exhibit 32–3, where the natural monopoly firm produces Q_1, at which marginal revenue equals marginal cost, and charges price P_1, which is the highest price per unit consistent with the output it produces.

Because it charges the monopoly price, some persons argue that the natural monopoly firm should be regulated. What form should the regulation take? We address this question next.

EXHIBIT 32–3
The Profit-Maximizing Natural Monopoly

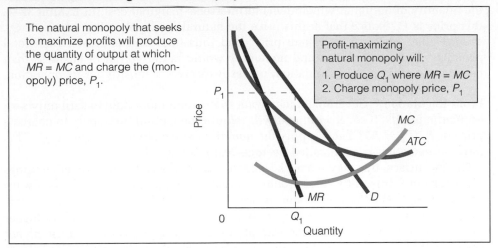

The natural monopoly that seeks to maximize profits will produce the quantity of output at which $MR = MC$ and charge the (monopoly) price, P_1.

Profit-maximizing natural monopoly will:

1. Produce Q_1 where $MR = MC$
2. Charge monopoly price, P_1

Question:

In many towns, because the local gas company is considered to be a natural monopoly, local government officials argue that no other firm can successfully compete with it (it can produce gas at a lower ATC than all other firms, therefore outcompeting them). Furthermore, the government officials prohibit other firms from even trying to compete with the gas company.

But why does government need to prohibit other firms from competing with the local gas company? If the gas company really is a natural monopolist, it can outcompete all newcomers. Why does it need government protection from the competitors it can outcompete anyway?

Answer:

One answer is that government isn't so much protecting the natural monopolist (the gas company) from competition as it is protecting the public from *inefficient entry* into the natural monopoly setting. According to this argument, if new firms are permitted to enter a natural monopoly setting to compete against the natural monopolist, they will be outcompeted, leave the industry, and the resources they used to enter the industry will have been wasted. The situation is analogous to preventing a 135-pound weakling from getting into the boxing ring with a 250-pound professional boxer. If you know the 135-pound weakling is going to lose anyway, it may be better (some say) to prevent him from wasting his time, and "society's" scarce resources, trying to do something he can't possibly do.

Other economists do not accept this argument. They point out that we don't protect the public from "inefficient entry" in other market structures, and therefore we should not do so here. In addition, they sometimes note, it is difficult to know for certain whether a particular firm's entry into an industry will turn out to waste resources or not.

Ways of Regulating the Natural Monopoly

The natural monopoly may be regulated through price, profit, or output regulation.

> *If profit is regulated to the extent that zero economic profits are guaranteed, then there will be little incentive to hold costs down.*

■

Price Regulation. *Marginal-cost pricing* is one form of price regulation. The objective is to set a price for the natural monopoly firm that equals marginal cost at the quantity of output at which demand intersects marginal cost. In Exhibit 32–4, this price is P_1. Notice that at this price the natural monopoly takes a loss. At Q_1, average total cost is greater than price, and thus total cost is greater than total revenue.[1] Obviously, the natural monopoly would rather go out of business than be subject to this type of regulation, unless it receives a subsidy for its operation.

Profit Regulation. Government may want the natural monopoly to earn only zero economic profits. If so, government will require the natural monopoly to charge a price of P_2 ($P_2 = ATC$) and supply the quantity demanded at that price (Q_2). This form of regulation is often called *average-cost pricing.*

On the surface, this may seem like a good way to proceed, but in practice things often turn out differently. The problem is that if the natural monopoly is always held to zero economic profits—and is not allowed to fall below or rise above this level—then it has an incentive to let costs rise. Higher costs—in the form of higher salaries or more luxurious offices—simply mean higher prices to cover the higher costs. In this case, it is unlikely that average cost pricing is an efficient way to proceed.

In recent years, the Federal Communications Commission (FCC) has experimented by relaxing some of their profit targets on American Telephone and Telegraph (AT&T). On some services, AT&T is permitted to increase profit by reducing production costs. Since this new procedure has been adopted, AT&T has initiated several cost-cutting practices.

---

[1]Remember that $TC = ATC \times Q$ and $TR = P \times Q$. Since here $ATC > P$, it follows that $TC > TR$.

EXHIBIT 32–4
Ways of Regulating a Natural Monopoly

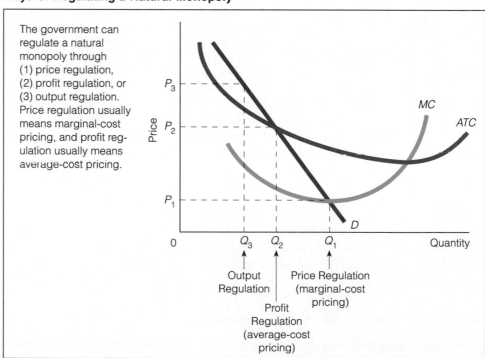

The government can regulate a natural monopoly through (1) price regulation, (2) profit regulation, or (3) output regulation. Price regulation usually means marginal-cost pricing, and profit regulation usually means average-cost pricing.

Output Regulation.   The government could mandate a quantity of output it wants the natural monopoly to produce. Suppose this is Q_3 in Exhibit 32–4. Here, there are positive economic profits, since price is above average total cost at Q_3. It is possible that the natural monopoly would want higher profits. At a fixed quantity of output, this can be obtained by lowering costs. In this setting, the natural monopolist might lower costs by reducing the quality of the good or service it sells, knowing that it faces no direct competition and that it is protected (by government) from competitors.

Problems with Regulating a Natural Monopoly

Regulation does not always turn out the way it was intended to turn out. The major problems with regulating a natural monopoly have to do with *incentives* and *information.*

As we have noted, government regulation of a natural monopoly—whether it takes the form of price, profit, or output regulation—can distort the incentives of those who operate the natural monopoly. To repeat, if profit is regulated to the extent that zero economic profits are guaranteed, then there will be little incentive to hold costs down. Furthermore, the owners of the natural monopoly also have an incentive to try to influence the government officials or other persons who are regulating the natural monopoly (more on this later).

In addition, each of the three types of regulation we have discussed requires information. For example, if the government wishes to set price equal to marginal cost or average cost for the natural monopoly, it must know the cost conditions of the firm. Three problems arise here: (1) The cost information is not easy to come by, even for the natural monopoly itself. (2) The cost information can be rigged (to a degree) by the natural monopoly, and therefore the regulators will not get a true picture of the firm. (3) The regulators have little incentive to obtain accurate information, since they are likely to keep their jobs and prestige even if they work with less-than-accurate information. (This raises another question: Who will ensure that the regulators do a good job?)

Last, there is the issue of **regulatory lag,** which is indirectly related to information. Regulatory lag refers to the period between the time when a natural monopoly's costs change and the time when the regulatory agency adjusts prices for the natural monopoly. For example, suppose the gas rates your local gas company charges customers are regulated. The gas company's costs rise, and it seeks a rate hike through the local regulatory body. This is not likely to happen quickly. The gas company will probably have to submit an application for a rate hike, document its case, have a date set for a hearing, argue its case at the hearing, and then wait for the regulatory agency to decide on the merits of the application. The time between the beginning of the process and the end may be many months; during that time the regulated firm is operating in ways and under conditions that both the firm and the regulatory body might not have desired.

Regulatory Lag
The period between the time when a natural monopoly's costs change and the time when the regulatory agency adjusts prices for the natural monopoly.

The public is perhaps naturally inclined to think that a solution (such as regulation) to a problem (such as monopoly) is better than no solution at all—that *something* is better than *nothing*. The economist has learned, though, that a "solution" can do one of three things: (1) solve a problem, (2) not solve a problem but do no damage, (3) make the problem worse. Thinking in terms of the entire range of *possibilities* is natural for an economist, who, after all, understands that solutions come with both costs and benefits.

THINKING LIKE
AN ECONOMIST

Regulating Industries That Are Not Natural Monopolies

Some firms are regulated even though they are not natural monopolies. For instance, in the past, government has regulated both the airline and trucking industries. In the trucking industry, the Interstate Commerce Commission (ICC) fixed routes, set minimum freight rates, and erected barriers to entry. In the airline industry, the Civil Aeronautics Board (CAB) did much the same. Some economists view the regulation of competitive industries as unnecessary; when it exists, they see it as evidence that the firms that are being regulated are controlling the regulation to reduce their competition. We discuss this in greater detail next.

The Capture Hypothesis

The **capture hypothesis** holds that no matter what the motive for the initial regulation and the establishment of the regulatory agency, eventually the agency will be "captured" (controlled) by the special interests of the industry that is being regulated. The following are a few of the interrelated points that have been put forth to support this hypothesis:

1. In many cases, persons who have been in the industry will be asked to regulate the industry, since they know the most about it. Such regulators are likely to feel a bond with those persons remaining in the industry, see their side of the story more often than not, and thus are inclined to cater to them.
2. At regulatory hearings, members of the industry will be there in greater force than taxpayers and consumers. For the industry, the regulatory hearing can affect it substantially and directly; for individual taxpayers and consumers, the effect (spread over millions of people) is usually small and indirect. Thus, regulators are much more likely to hear and respond to the side of the story presented by the groups being regulated.
3. Members of the regulated industry will make a point of getting to know the members of the regulatory agency. They will talk frequently about business matters, perhaps they will socialize. The bond between the two groups will grow stronger over time. This may have an impact on regulatory measures.
4. Once they either retire or quit their jobs, regulators often go to work for the industries they once regulated.

The capture hypothesis is markedly different from what has come to be called the **public interest theory of regulation.** This theory holds that regulators are seeking to do, and will do through regulation, what is in the best interest of the public or society at large. Here, then, are two interesting, different, and at first sight, believable hypotheses or theories of regulation. Economists have directed much effort to testing the two theories. There is no clear consensus yet, but in the area of business regulation, the adherents of the capture hypothesis have been increasing.

DEREGULATION

■

In recent years, government has moved to deregulate some industries. Two notable examples include airlines and telecommunications.

The Deregulation of Airlines

The Civil Aeronautics Act, which was passed in 1938, gave the Civil Aeronautics Authority (CAA) the authority to regulate air fares, the number of carriers on interstate routes, and the pattern of routes. The CAA's successor, the Civil Aeronautics Board (CAB), regulated fares in such a way that major air carriers could meet their average costs. An effect of this was that fares were raised so that high-cost, inefficient air carriers could survive. In addition, the CAB did not allow price competition between air carriers. As a result, air carriers usually competed in a nonprice dimension: by offering more scheduled flights, better meals, more popular in-flight movies, and so forth.

In 1978, things began to change. Under CAB chairman Alfred Kahn, an economist, the airline industry was deregulated. With deregulation, airlines can compete on fares, initiate service along a new route, or discontinue a route. Empirical research after deregulation showed that passenger miles increased and fares decreased. For example, in 1978, fares fell 20 percent, and between 1979 and 1984, fares fell approximately 14 percent.

A Question for George Stigler

Nobel Prize–winner George Stigler (see interview in Chapter 24) is closely associated with the capture hypothesis—that special interest groups tend to "capture" the regulatory system and use it to promote their own narrowly defined self-interest. In practice this usually means that the regulated firms get the regulations they want. But this raises an interesting question about deregulation, which we asked Professor Stigler:

Does it follow that where deregulation exists, the broadly based public interest has somehow come to outweigh the special interests?

I wish that were true, and people talk about the deregulation movement and some are occasionally so kind as to say that we economists at the University of Chicago were important in it. I don't really believe that is what happened. I believe that situations arise where the old regulatory schemes no longer work. For example, consider the cartel that fixed commission rates on the New York Stock Exchange. This held for 180 years or so. But it finally gave way because important new developments like the growth of large traders who were no longer using the New York Stock Exchange, and were working in a third market, brought enormous pressure for change. Then the SEC went along and agreed to the deregulation of fixed commission rates. I assume that the same theory that explains why interest groups get regulation explains why sometimes they want to get rid of it.

Deregulation and Technological Changes

Sometimes deregulation is the result of technological changes. Consider deregulation in the telecommunications sector. We quote from the *Economic Report of the President, 1991:*

> The early history of the telecommunications sector was characterized by extensive competition. In the period following the expiration of Alexander Graham Bell's original patents in 1893 and 1894, many new firms entered the telephone business, eroding the monopoly held by AT&T, which had evolved from Bell's original company. By 1907, 49 percent of installed telephones were controlled by non-Bell companies, and most Bell operating subsidiaries faced direct competition.
>
> AT&T then adopted an explicit strategy of reducing competition through mergers and acquisitions and willingly accepting regulation, both to exclude competitors legally and also to blunt public criticism of monopoly. By 1932, Bell's market share had returned to 79 percent, and direct competition had been virtually eliminated. With the passage of the

Why, If You Fly, Do You Always Have to Go Through Dallas or Chicago?

The shortest distance between two points is a straight line. Some say that the airline industry doesn't care much about straight lines (or, obviously, about short distances). It cares about *hubs* and *spokes*.

Suppose you want to go from Phoenix to New York City. The shortest route to take is the direct route: Phoenix *directly* to New York. Very likely, however, you won't be able to get a direct flight. Often (but not always) you will be routed through Dallas or Chicago. In other words, you will get on the plane in Phoenix, get off the plane in Dallas, get on another plane in Dallas, fly to New York, and finally get off the plane in New York. This is the hub-and-spoke delivery system illustrated in Exhibit 32–5 (it looks like a bicycle wheel). The hub represents the center of an airline network; the spokes, representing origin and destination cities, are always linked up through the hub.

The hub-and-spoke system has been used more often since airline deregulation. In several instances, airline departures from major hubs (such as Dallas and Chicago) have doubled. Most economists believe the increased use of the hub-and-spoke system, which makes average travel time longer, is the result of increased price competition brought on by deregulation. Airlines after deregulation were under greater pressure to compete on price; thus, it became more important to cut costs. One way to cut costs is to use bigger planes, since bigger planes cost less to operate per seat mile. Also, the bigger planes have to be filled. To accomplish both objectives—flying bigger planes that

are more fully occupied—it became necessary to gather passengers at one spot—the hub—and from there fly more of them to the same destination. For example, instead of flying people in Phoenix and people in Albuquerque directly but separately to New York, both groups of people are flown first to Dallas, and then the combined group is flown to New York.

There may be benefits that offset the costs of inconvenience and longer

travel time. Some people think it is better to pay lower airline ticket prices and reach one's destination a little later than to pay higher prices and get there sooner. They also maintain that increased use of the hub-and-spoke system has given passengers more options to travel on different airlines (once in Dallas, numerous airlines can fly you to New York) at more convenient times (numerous flights leave Dallas every hour).

EXHIBIT 32–5
The Hub-and-Spoke System

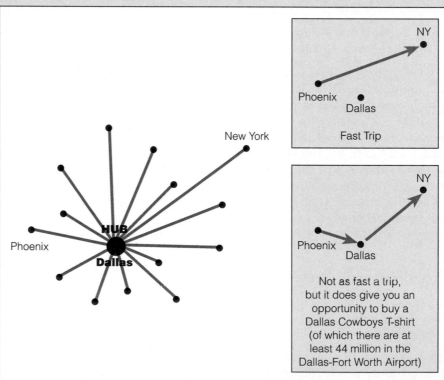

Since airline deregulation, the hub-and-spoke delivery system has been used increasingly. There are both benefits and costs to this system. A cost is longer average travel time. A benefit is a lower ticket price.

Interview: Murray Weidenbaum

Murray Weidenbaum was chairman of the Council of Economic Advisers under President Reagan from February 27, 1981, until August 25, 1982. Professor Weidenbaum is well known and respected for his work in the area of government regulation. He is currently at Washington University in St. Louis, where he is the director of the Center for the Study of American Business.

Would you give us a few of what you consider to be the "right" reasons for regulation and a few of the "wrong" reasons?

One of the right reasons for regulation is to deal with situations where large externalities are present. The best example I can think of is air and water pollution, where cleaning up a dirty river, or reducing the pollutants in the air, may generate far more benefits than costs to the society. More specifically, the situation is one where sometimes the polluter faces greater private costs than benefits from doing so, and so he does not clean up the pollution. But society as a whole receives greater benefits than costs from having the pollution cleaned up. This is the standard case for government intervention. There are debates, of course, as to what is the best way for the government to intervene, but that is a different matter.

Let me give another example. Consider the case where the consumer does not have adequate information about a product and thus does not know of the hidden hazards of the product. The important thing here is to provide the consumer with additional information. In technical areas, the simplest thing may be for the Consumer Product Safety Commission to set standards that companies must meet. In other cases, it may be more effective to give the consumer more information as to the nature of the

hazard. The same thing applies to the workplace.

As to the wrong reasons for regulation, examples include regulations that interfere with competition. Interstate trucking is an excellent example. Import restrictions are another. They reduce the choice to the consumer and raise price.

Most people suspect that regulation comes with a price tag, but they are uncertain how high or low that price is. Could you shed some light on this subject?

Let me first say that I view the costs of complying with regulation as a "hidden tax." And the very fact that it is hidden presents the basic problem for policy. Too often policy makers in promoting regulation crow about the visible benefits and do not have to worry about the costs because they are hidden in the form of higher prices paid for by the consumer.

So people see the benefits of regulation, but they don't realize the costs they are paying?

Precisely. Which of course brings up the need for cost–benefit analysis of

proposed regulations. But of course we must be aware that there is a natural tendency on the part of regulators, and the proponents of regulation, to overestimate the benefits and underestimate the costs, and conversely those persons (potentially) subject to the regulation tend to overestimate the costs and underestimate the benefits. A certain sense of detachment needs to be present in evaluating any specific set of numbers.

Please assess the past five years for us with the following words in mind—regulation and deregulation.

The past five years have produced a mixed bag in the area of government regulation. We have seen a slowdown, if not an end, to the rapid trend toward deregulation that began in mid-1970s and continued on to the mid-1980s. We have also seen a rapid upturn in new and expanded regulation. On net, there is more regulation facing the private sector today than five years ago. One way to look at it is the way we do here at the Center for the Study of American Business [at Washington University in St. Louis]. We tally up the budgets for the federal regulatory agencies and their work forces. In the first half of the 1980s, there was a noticeable decline in the head count and in total budgets for these agencies. In the last five years of the decade, the trend had reversed.

What is the cause for the rapid upturn in new and expanded regulation?

The concern for the environment.

Will it continue?

Yes, it will continue, but no one knows for exactly how long. Although, I should say that we have seen some of the limits to it. In November [1990], in every state where there was a Big Green initiative, it failed to carry.

What is the public turning against here, since it seems that the public does want some regulation in this area?

Oh, yes, it does, but in a sense the environmental activists have overstepped themselves. The idea of providing 40 pages of fine print containing all types of onerous requirements and then telling people you have to vote yes or no on this . . . well there is no way people want to read all that and they resent it.

What do you consider a reasonable economic approach to the problems of the environment?

First, I think we ought to remind ourselves that we are all interested in clean air, clean water, and so on. After all, even economists breathe the same air as real people, so by raising questions about ways to deal with the environment economists are not suggesting that environmental or ecological goals are not worthwhile. The economist, however, is quick to realize that there are different costs of trying to meet these goals in different ways. I think public policy makers must continue to search out the most efficient solutions, or cost-effective approaches.

Do you think the public would be more likely to understand what economists are doing in this area if they had a better idea of how economists think—of the fact that economists consider both the costs and the benefits of cleaning up the environment?

Yes, I think so. The sad thing is that the public rarely gets exposure to this type of thinking. For example, most of the public opinion polls dealing with the environment are worded in extreme ways, such as "Do you think we ought to clean up the environment despite the costs?" If you ask people the question that way, most of them will say yes. On the other hand, if you ask "Should we weigh the costs against the benefits and try to find the most efficient way of cleaning up the environment?" people will also say yes. In any event, the environmental movement has recently shifted its attention to the federal government. Noticeably, the same year in which many of the Big Green initiatives were turned down, a major expansion in the Clean Air Act was agreed to by Congress. It seems much easier to get items through the Congress than through the voters.

This is a pattern other groups have followed. What should Congress do to prevent groups from coming to them instead of taking the case to the public?

Unfortunately, the Congress is very susceptible to organized pressure groups—whatever you think of those pressure groups (whether they serve the public interest or not). I do think, however, that we are seeing the outer limits of Congress responding to pressure groups, mostly because of the Savings and Loan scandal.

Are you suggesting that the S&L scandal will have some carryover into other areas?

I think it will. The Congress may eventually learn that it has to say no instead of trying to please every constituent group.

What do you think has been the most promising development in the area of the economics of regulation in the past decade?

The most promising has been developing new ways of introducing economic incentives into the regulatory process: tradeable permits, for example. This is something that awhile back would have been laughed at. The concept has been embraced by environmentalists as well as economists because both groups see it as a way of achieving environmental improvements at minimum cost.

What got you interested in economics?

A specific professor got me interested in economics. He was very prescient: He correctly noted that while lawyers dominated the policy-making process up until then (the 1940s), in the future economics would be an important tool for developing public policy. And he was right.

What is it you like about economics or trying to solve economic problems?

In dealing with economic problems you wrestle with the kinds of issues that affect the welfare of people in a very fundamental way.

Communications Act of 1934, the regulated monopoly structure of the telephone system was completed. In 1970, AT&T controlled 95 percent of local and long-distance telephone revenues, and its Western Electric manufacturing subsidiary provided almost all of Bell's equipment needs.

Changing technology eventually made this monopoly regime unsustainable. As early as the 1950s, other companies sought permission to sell types of telephone equipment that AT&T did not produce. The development of economic microwave transmission technology made competition for long-distance telephone service feasible, and the FCC permitted a competitor to enter this market in a limited way in 1969. The completely regulated monopoly structure of the telecommunications industry might have made sense in 1930, but by the 1970s it clearly was incompatible with the new state of technology. Competition, not regulated monopoly, emerged as the appropriate policy for the equipment and long-distance components of the telephone industry.

The history of the cable television segment of the industry offers the same lesson. In the 1960s, cable TV provided television to remote areas that could not receive standard broadcast signals. Cable TV operators clearly had a monopoly over an important segment of the entertainment market in these areas, and the widespread practice by state and local governments of regulating cable TV rates developed in this era. Later, cable evolved in many areas into an alternative to "over-the-air" TV, and it also faced increasing competition in the broader entertainment market from direct satellite broadcasts and widely available videocassette rentals. Regulation of cable TV rates persisted, however, until the 1984 Cable Act deregulated them except in areas with limited broadcast competition. Again, policy had to change to recognize the change in the underlying industry conditions.

Thus, in telephone equipment, cable TV, and long-distance telephone service, a regulatory regime appropriate to a technology at one stage gave way, slowly and reluctantly, to a new policy appropriate to new technological realities . . ."[2]

CHAPTER SUMMARY

Dealing with Monopoly Power

■ A monopoly produces less than a perfectly competitive firm produces (assuming the same revenue and cost conditions), charges a higher price, and generally causes a welfare loss to society. This is the monopoly power problem, and solving it is usually put forth as a reason for antitrust laws and/or government regulatory actions. Some economists note, though, that government antitrust and regulatory actions do not always have the intended effect. Also, sometimes they are implemented where there is no monopoly power problem to solve.

Antitrust Laws

■ Two major criticisms have been directed at the antitrust acts. First, some argue that the language in the antitrust acts is vague; for example, even though the words "restraint of trade" are used in the Sherman Act, the act does not clearly explain what actions constitute a restraint of trade. Second, it has been argued that some antitrust acts appear to hinder, rather than promote, competition; for example, the Robinson–Patman Act.

■ There are a few unsettled points in antitrust policy. One centers around the proper definition of a market. Should a market be defined narrowly or broadly? How this question is answered will have an impact on which firms are considered monopolies. In addition, the use of concentration ratios for identifying monopolies or deciding whether to allow two firms to enter into a merger has been called into question. Recently, concentration ratios have been largely replaced (for purposes of implementing antitrust policy) with the Herfindahl index. This index is subject to some of the same criticisms as the concentration ratios.

[2]Council of Economic Advisers, *Economic Report of the President, 1991* (Washington, D.C.: U.S. Government Printing Office, 1991), p. 143–44.

Regulation

- Even if we assume that the intent of regulation is to serve the public interest, it does not follow that this will be accomplished. To work as desired, regulation must be based on complete information (the regulatory body must know the cost conditions of the regulated firm, for example), and it must not distort incentives (to keep costs down, for example). Many economists are quick to point out that neither condition is likely to be fully met. In itself, this does not mean that regulation should not be implemented, but only that regulation may not have the effects one expected.

- Government uses three basic types of regulation to regulate natural monopolies: price, profit, or output regulation. Price regulation usually means marginal-cost price regulation: setting $P = MC$. Profit regulation usually means zero economic profits. Output regulation specifies a particular quantity of output that the natural monopoly must produce.

- The capture hypothesis holds that no matter what the motive for the initial regulation and the establishment of the regulatory agency, eventually the agency will be "captured" (controlled) by the special interests of the industry that is being regulated. In contrast, the public interest theory holds that regulators are seeking to do, and will do through regulation, what is in the best interest of the public or society at large.

Key Terms and Concepts

Antitrust Law	Herfindahl Index	Capture Hypothesis
Trust	Natural Monopoly	Public Interest Theory of Regulation

QUESTIONS AND PROBLEMS

1. Explain why defining a market narrowly or broadly can make a difference in how antitrust policy is implemented.

2. What is the implication of saying that regulation is likely to affect incentives?

3. What is the major difference between the capture hypothesis (or capture theory of regulation) and the public interest theory of regulation?

4. A study of both unregulated and regulated electric utilities by George Stigler and Claire Friedland found no difference in the rates charged by them. One could draw the conclusion that regulation is ineffective when it comes to utility rates. What ideas or hypotheses presented in this chapter might have predicted this?

5. The courts have ruled that it is a *reasonable restraint of trade* (and therefore permissible) for the owner of a business to sell his business and sign a contract with the new owner saying he will not compete with her within a vicinity of, say, 100 miles, for a period of, say, 5 years. If this is a reasonable restraint of trade, can you give an example of what you would consider an unreasonable restraint of trade? Explain how you decide what is a reasonable restraint of trade and what isn't.

6. In your opinion, what is the best way to deal with the monopoly power problem? Do you advocate antitrust laws or regulation, or something else we didn't discuss? Give reasons for your answer.

7. It is usually asserted that public utilities such as electric companies and gas companies are natural monopolies. But an assertion is not proof. How would you go about trying to prove (disprove) that electric companies and the like are (are not) natural monopolies? (Hint: You might consider comparing the average total cost of a public utility that serves many customers with the average total cost of a public utility that serves relatively few customers.)

8. Discuss the advantages and disadvantages of business deregulation.

9. Calculate the Herfindahl index and the four-firm concentration ratio.

Firms	Market Share
A	17%
B	15
C	14
D	14
E	12
F	10
G	9
H	9

MARKET FAILURE: EXTERNALITIES, THE ENVIRONMENT, AND PUBLIC GOODS

WHAT THIS CHAPTER IS ABOUT

Market failure is a situation in which the market does not provide the ideal or optimal amount of a particular good. We saw an example of this in our discussion of monopoly; monopoly produces too little output. In this chapter, we discuss two other cases where some economists believe the market fails. The first deals with externalities, the second with public goods.

EXTERNALITIES

■

Sometimes, when goods are produced and consumed, side effects (spillover or third-party effects) occur that are felt by people who are not directly involved in the market exchanges. In general, these side effects are called **externalities** because the costs or benefits are *external* to the person(s) who caused them. In this section, we discuss two types of externalities, negative and positive.

Negative Externalities

Suppose Derrick lives in a house near an airport. Occasionally, airplanes fly over his home, creating noise and causing him some discomfort. The airplane pilot, who works for the airline company, undertakes an action (flying) in which a cost external to him is felt by some other person. In short, the flying generates an externality, and because it imposes a cost on a third party (sometimes called an "external cost"), it is referred to as a negative externality. A **negative externality** exists when a person's or group's actions cause a cost (adverse side effect) to be felt by others. A consequence of a negative externality is that *social costs* do not equal *private costs,* and the *socially optimal level of production* is not naturally obtained.

This is illustrated in Exhibit 33–1, where we see a downward-sloping demand curve for the good. The supply curve, S_1, represents the *private costs* of the producers of the good (we speak of a *marginal private cost (MPC)* curve instead of simply a marginal cost curve). Equilibrium in this market setting is at E_1; Q_1 is the output—specifically, the *market output.*

Now assume that negative externalities arise as a result of the production of the good. If the external costs, linked with the negative externalities, are to be taken into account, we add them (as best we can) to the marginal private costs and end up with a *marginal social cost (MSC)* curve, represented in Exhibit 33–1 by S_2. If *all* costs are taken into account (both external costs and private costs), equilibrium comes at E_2 at the quantity Q_2. This is sometimes referred to as the **socially optimal output.**

Notice that the market output (Q_1) is greater than the socially optimal output (Q_2) when negative externalities exist. The market is said to "fail" (hence, market failure) because it *overproduces* the good that is connected with the negative externality. The triangle noted in Exhibit 33–1 is the visible manifestation of the market failure: It is the net social cost of producing the market output (Q_1) instead of the socially optimal output (Q_2), or of moving from the socially optimal output to the market output.

Question:

How exactly does the triangle in Exhibit 33–1 represent the net social cost of moving from the socially optimal output to the market output?

Answer:

We explain this concept with the aid of Exhibit 33–2, where Q_2 is the socially optimal output and Q_1 is the market output. If "society" moves from Q_2 to Q_1, who specifically benefits and how do we represent these benefits? Buyers benefit (they are a part of society) since they will be able to buy more output at prices they are willing to pay; thus, the area under the *demand curve* between Q_2 and

A consequence of a negative externality is that social costs do not equal private costs.

■

Market Failure
A situation in which the market does not provide the ideal or optimal amount of a particular good.

Externality
A side effect of an action that affects the well-being of third parties.

Negative Externality
Exists when a person's or group's actions cause a cost (adverse side effect) to be felt by others.

Socially Optimal Output
The output level at which all benefits (external as well as private) and all costs (external as well as private) have been taken into account and adjusted for.

EXHIBIT 33–1
The Negative Externality Case

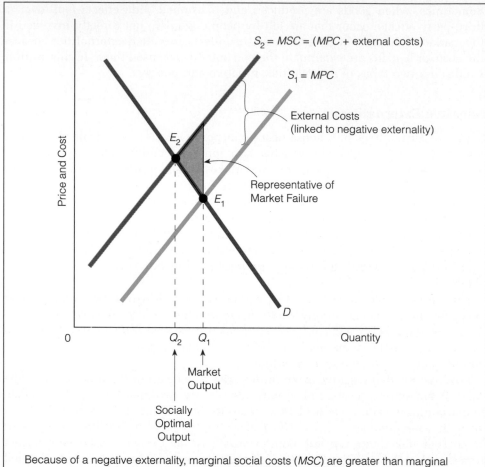

Because of a negative externality, marginal social costs (*MSC*) are greater than marginal private costs (*MPC*), and the market output is greater than the socially optimal output. The market is said to fail in that it overproduces the good.

Q_1 represents the benefits of moving from Q_2 to Q_1 (see the shaded area in Window 1 in Exhibit 33–2).

Next we ask, If society moves from Q_2 to Q_1, how can we illustrate the costs that are incurred? Sellers and third parties incur costs (sellers incur private costs, and third parties incur external costs), so the area under S_2 (not S_1, because S_1 only takes into account part of society—sellers—and ignores third parties) between Q_2 and Q_1 represents the full costs of moving from Q_2 to Q_1 (see the shaded area in Window 2).

Since the shaded area in Window 2 is larger than the shaded area in Window 1, the costs to sellers *and* third parties of moving from Q_2 to Q_1 outweigh the benefits to buyers of moving from Q_2 to Q_1. The difference between the shaded areas is the triangle; thus, costs outweigh benefits by the triangle. In short, the triangle in this example represents the net social cost of moving from Q_2 to Q_1, or producing Q_1 instead of Q_2.

EXHIBIT 33–2
The Triangle

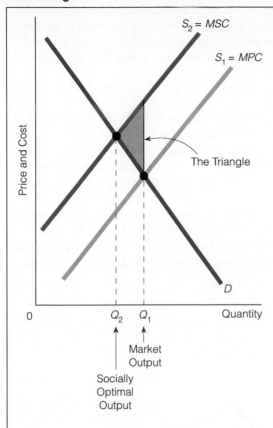

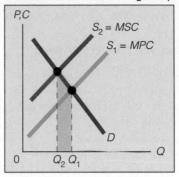

Window 1
Benefits of moving from Q_2 to Q_1

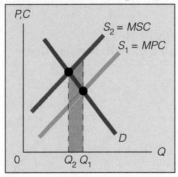

Window 2
Costs of moving from Q_2 to Q_1

Q_2 is the socially optimal output, Q_1 is the market output. If society moves from Q_2 to Q_1, buyers benefit by an amount represented by the shaded area in Window 1, but sellers and third parties together incur greater costs, represented by the shaded area in Window 2. The triangle (the difference between the two shaded areas) represents the net social costs to society of moving from Q_2 to Q_1 or producing Q_1 instead of Q_2.

Economists tend to think in terms of zero sum games, positive sum games, and negative sum games. A zero sum game exists if the gains to a winner are equally offset by the losses to a loser. For example, the game of blackjack is a zero sum game: What the winner wins (say, $40) is equally offset by what the loser loses ($40), so that the gains plus the losses equal zero. A positive sum game exists when the gains to the winner are greater than the losses to the loser, or when there are only gains and no losses. A negative sum game exists when the losses to the loser are greater than the gains to the winner, or when there are only losses and no gains.

Life can be looked at, economically, as a series of zero-, and positive-, and negative-sum games. For example, when discussing exchange, most economists will say that it is an example of a positive sum game: Both the seller and the buyer benefit from an exchange, else they would not have entered into it.

THINKING LIKE
AN ECONOMIST

CHAPTER 33
MARKET FAILURE: EXTERNALITIES,
THE ENVIRONMENT, AND PUBLIC
GOODS

■

A consequence of a positive externality is that social benefits do not equal private benefits.

■

Consider the position society is in when the market output is being produced and there exists a negative externality. As we showed in Exhibit 33–2, there is a net social cost when society produces the market output instead of the socially optimal output. This exists because the *costs* to sellers and third parties are greater at the market output than the *benefits* derived by buyers—losses are greater than gains, and we have a negative sum game.

Positive Externalities

Suppose Erica Evans is a beekeeper who lives near an apple orchard. Erica's bees occasionally fly over to the orchard and pollinate the blossoms, in the process making the orchard more productive. Thus, Erica undertakes an action—keeping bees—in which a benefit external to the action is felt by some person—namely, the orchard owner. Erica's beekeeping generates an externality, and because it results in a benefit to a third party (sometimes called an "external benefit"), it is referred to as a positive externality. A **positive externality** exists when a person's or group's actions cause a benefit (beneficial side effect) to be felt by others. A consequence of a positive externality is that social benefits do not equal private benefits, and the socially optimal level of production is not naturally obtained.

Positive Externality
Exists when a person's or group's actions cause a benefit (beneficial side effect) to be felt by others.

EXHIBIT 33–3
The Positive Externality Case

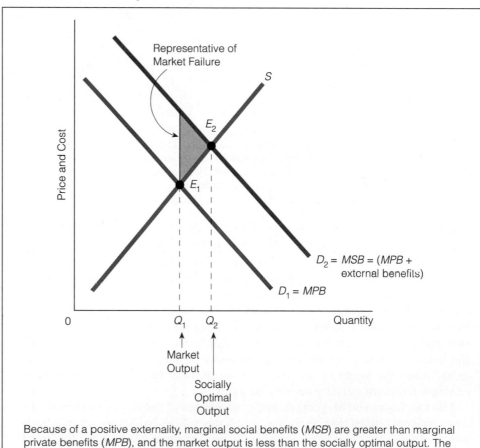

Because of a positive externality, marginal social benefits (*MSB*) are greater than marginal private benefits (*MPB*), and the market output is less than the socially optimal output. The market is said to fail in that it underproduces the good.

We illustrate this in Exhibit 33–3. The demand curve, D_1, represents the *private benefits* of the demanders of the good; we call D_1 a *marginal private benefit (MPB)* curve. Equilibrium in this market setting is at E_1; Q_1 is the market output.

Now assume that positive externalities are generated as a result of the production of the good. If the external benefits, linked with the positive externalities, are to be taken into account, we would add them (as best we could) to the marginal private benefits and end up with a *marginal social benefit (MSB)* curve, represented by D_2. If all benefits are taken into account (private and external benefits), output is Q_2. This is the socially optimal output.

Notice that the market output is less than the socially optimal output. The market is said to fail because it *underproduces* the good that is connected with the positive externality. The triangle in Exhibit 33–3 shows the market failure: It is the net social benefit of moving from the market output to the socially optimal output.

Question:

If Q_2 is the socially optimal output, does this mean that it is better to be at Q_2 than at Q_1?

Answer:

That is not necessarily the case. Economists usually answer this question by adding conditions. If the cost of moving from the market output to the socially optimal output—that is, if the cost of adjusting for the negative or positive externality—is less than the benefits, the answer is yes; if not, the answer is no.

All we have shown so far is that where negative and positive externalities exist, benefits can be gained (in the case of positive externalities) or costs can be lessened (in the case of negative externalities) by moving from the market output to the socially optimal output. However, there are costs associated with this adjustment.

INTERNALIZING EXTERNALITIES
■

An externality is **internalized** if the persons or group that generated the externality incorporate into their own private or *internal* cost–benefit calculations the external benefits (in the case of a positive externality) or the external costs (in the case of a negative externality) that third parties bear. Simply put, internalizing externalities is the same as adjusting for externalities. An externality has been internalized or adjusted for *completely* if, as a result, the socially optimal output emerges. A few of the numerous ways to adjust for, or internalize, externalities are presented in this section.

Persuasion

Many negative externalities in particular arise partly because persons or groups do not consider other individuals when they decide to undertake an action. Consider the person who plays his stereo loudly at three o'clock in the morning. Perhaps if he would consider the external cost his action imposes on his neighbors, he would either not play the stereo at all or would play it at low volume. The

Internalizing Externalities
An externality is *internalized* if the person(s) or group that generated the externality incorporate into their own private or *internal* cost–benefit calculations the external benefits (in the case of a positive externality) or the external costs (in the case of a negative externality) that third parties bear.

option of trying to persuade those who impose external costs on us to adjust their behavior to take these costs into account is one way to make the imposer adjust for—or internalize—externalities. In today's world, such slogans as "Don't Drink and Drive" and "Don't Litter" are attempts to persuade individuals to take into account the fact that their actions affect others. The religious commandment "Do unto others as you would have them do unto you" makes the same point.

Assigning Property Rights

Consider the idea that air pollution and ocean pollution—both of which are examples of negative externalities—are the result of the air and oceans being unowned. No one owns the air, no one owns the oceans, and because no one does, many individuals feel free to emit wastes into them. If private property, or ownership, rights in air and oceans could be established, the negative externalities would likely become much less. If someone owns the resources, then actions that damage the resources come with a price; namely, the resource owner can sue for damages.

For example, in the early West when grazing lands were unowned (common property) and open, many cattle ranchers allowed their herds to overgraze. The reasons for this were simple. No one owned the land, no one could stop the overgrazing to preserve the value of the land, and if one rancher decided not to allow his herd to graze, this simply meant that there was more grazing land for other ranchers. As a consequence of overgrazing, a future generation inherited barren, wasted land. From the point of view of future generations, the cattle ranchers who allowed their herds to overgraze were generating negative externalities.

What would have happened if the western lands had been privately owned? In this case, there would not have been any overgrazing, because the monetary interests of the owner of the land would not have permitted it. The landowner would have charged the rancher a fee for grazing his cattle, and more grazing would have entailed additional fees. There would have been less grazing of cattle at a positive fee than at a zero fee (the case when the lands were open and unowned). The externalities would have been internalized.

Question:

In the example of grazing lands, assigning private property rights, or establishing ownership rights, to unowned land lessened the externality problem. Establishing ownership rights in land is possible, but can this be done with the air and oceans?

The person who plays his stereo loudly at three o'clock in the morning would generate less of a negative externality (or none at all) if Amy Cohan, who lives next door to the stereo player, owned the air over her property and charged him for sending those music sounds through her air. This would put a price on his behavior, and thus the externalities would be internalized. But is it possible to assign property rights in air?

Answer:

It is very difficult and costly to establish ownership rights in air. Consequently, assigning property rights is not likely to be the method chosen to deal with externalities that arise as a consequence of unowned air. There are other ways of dealing with the problem, however.

Voluntary Agreements

Externalities can sometimes be internalized through individual voluntary agreements. Consider two persons, Pete and Sean, living on a tiny deserted island. Pete and Sean have agreed between themselves that Pete owns the northern part of the island and that Sean owns the southern part. Pete occasionally cooks early in the morning, and the breeze carries the cooking smells over to Sean's part of the island where he is sleeping. Often the cooking smells awaken Sean, who has a keen sense of smell. Pete and Sean have a negative externality problem. Pete wants to be free to cook in the morning, and Sean would like to continue to sleep.

Suppose that Sean values his sleep in the morning by a maximum of 6 oranges—he would give up 6 oranges to be able to sleep without Pete cooking. On the other hand, Pete values cooking in the morning by 3 oranges—he would give up a maximum of 3 oranges to be able to cook in the morning. Since Sean values his sleep by more than Pete values cooking in the morning, they have an opportunity to strike a deal. Sean can offer Pete some number of oranges greater than 3, but less than 6, to refrain from cooking in the morning. The deal will make both Pete and Sean better off. In this example, the negative externality problem is successfully addressed through the individuals voluntarily entering into an agreement. The condition for this outcome is that the **transaction costs,** or costs associated with making and reaching the agreement, must be low relative to the expected benefits of the agreement.

These last two ways of internalizing externalities—property rights assignments and voluntary agreements—can be combined, as in the following example.[1]

A rancher's cattle occasionally stray onto the adjacent farm and damage (eat) some of the farmer's crops. If the court assigns liability to the cattle rancher and orders him to prevent his cattle from straying, then a property rights assignment solves the externality problem. As a result, the rancher might put up a strong fence to prevent his cattle from damaging his neighbor's crops.

But there may be another solution. It is possible that the court's property rights assignment will be undone by the farmer and the cattle rancher if they find it in their mutual interest to do so. Suppose the rancher is willing to pay $100 a month to the farmer for permission to allow his cattle to stray onto the farmer's land, but the farmer is willing to give permission for only $70 a month. Assuming trivial or zero transaction costs, the farmer and the rancher will undo the court's property rights assignment. For a payment of $70 or more a month, the farmer will allow the rancher's cattle to stray onto his land.

But what would the resource allocative outcome have been if the court, instead of assigning liability to the cattle rancher, had given him the property right to allow his cattle to stray? With this (opposite) property rights assignment, the cattle would have been allowed to stray (which was exactly the outcome of the previous property rights assignment once the cattle rancher and farmer voluntarily agreed to undo it). We conclude that *in the case of trivial or zero transaction costs, the property rights assignment does not matter to the resource allocative outcome*. In a nutshell, this is the **Coase theorem.** The theorem can be expressed in other ways, two of which we mention here: (1) In the case of trivial or zero transaction costs, a property rights assignment will be undone (exchanged) if it benefits the relevant parties to undo it. (2) In the case of trivial or zero transaction costs, the resource allocative outcome will be the same no matter who is assigned the property right.

Transaction Costs
The costs associated with the time and effort needed to search out, negotiate, and consummate an exchange.

Coase Theorem
In the case of trivial or zero transaction costs, the property rights assignment does not matter to the resource allocative outcome.

[1]See Ronald Coase, "The Problem of Social Cost," *Journal of Law and Economics 3* (October 1960):1–44.

The Coase theorem is significant for two reasons: (1) It shows that under certain conditions the market can internalize externalities. (2) It provides a benchmark for analyzing externality problems—that is, it shows what would happen if transactions costs were trivial or zero.

Taxes and Subsidies

Taxes and subsidies are sometimes used as corrective devices for a market failure. A tax adjusts for a negative externality, a subsidy for a positive externality. First, consider the negative externality case in Exhibit 33–1.

The objective of the corrective tax is to move the supply curve from S_1 to S_2 (recall from earlier chapters that a tax can shift a supply curve) and therefore move from the market-determined output, Q_1 to the socially optimal output, Q_2.

In the case of a positive externality, illustrated in Exhibit 33–3, the objective is to subsidize the demand side of the market so that the demand curve moves from D_1 to D_2 and output moves from Q_1 to the socially optimal output, Q_2.

We need to keep in mind that there are costs and consequences to taxes and subsidies. For example, suppose government misjudges the external costs illustrated in Exhibit 33–4 and imposes a tax on the supplier of the good that moves the supply curve, not from S_1 to S_2, but instead from S_1 to S_3. As a result, the

EXHIBIT 33–4
A Corrective Tax Gone Wrong

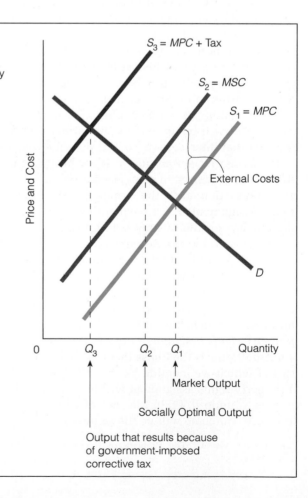

It is possible for government to miscalculate external costs and impose a tax that moves the supply curve from S_1 to S_3 instead of from S_1 to S_2. As a result, the output level will be farther away from the socially optimal output than before the "corrective" tax was applied. Q_3 is farther away from Q_2 than Q_1 is from Q_2.

$S_3 = MPC + $ Tax

$S_2 = MSC$

$S_1 = MPC$

External Costs

Price and Cost

D

0   Q_3 Q_2 Q_1 Quantity

Market Output

Socially Optimal Output

Output that results because of government-imposed corrective tax output level will be farther away from the socially optimal output than it was before the "corrective" tax was supplied.

Beyond Internalizing: Setting Regulations

One way to deal with externalities, in particular with negative externalities, is for government to apply regulations directly to the activity that generates the externalities. For example, factories producing goods also produce smoke that rises up through the smokestacks. The smoke is often seen as a negative externality. Government may decide that the factory must install pollution-reducing equipment, or that it can only put so much smoke into the air per day, or that it must move to an area that is less populated.

The critics of this approach often note that regulations, once instituted, are difficult to remove even if conditions warrant removal. Also, regulations are often applied across the board when circumstances dictate otherwise. For example, factories in relatively pollution-free cities might be required to install the same pollution control equipment as factories in smoggy, pollution-ridden cities.

Finally, there is the cost of regulation. If government is going to regulate, there must be regulators (whose salaries must be paid), offices (to house the regulators), word processors (to produce the regulations), typists (to do the typing), and more. As we previously noted, there may be benefits to dealing with externalities successfully, but the costs need to be taken into account as well.

Question:

Is there any one best way of dealing with externalities? It is not clear whether it is better to use persuasion or to use, say, taxes and subsidies.

Answer:

Almost all economists would agree that some methods of dealing with externalities are more effective in some situations than in others. For example, if the smoke from Vincent's neighbor's barbecue comes into his yard and bothers him, it is unlikely that any economist would think the negative externality situation at hand would warrant direct governmental involvement in the form of regulation or taxes. In this case, persuasion may be the best way to proceed. In the case of a factory emitting smoke into the air, however, persuasion might not be effective. Nor might voluntary agreements, since the transaction costs of entering into an agreement would very likely be high (getting together all or most persons affected by the factory's smoke is difficult, for example). In this case, the inclination to propose taxes or regulations would be strong.

Pigou vs. Coase

The first editor of the *Journal of Law and Economics* was Aaron Director. In 1959, Director published an article by Ronald Coase entitled "The Federal Communications Commission." In the article, Coase took issue with economist A. C. Pigou, a trailblazer in the area of externalities and market failure, who had argued that government should use taxes and subsidies to adjust for negative and positive externalities, respectively. Coase argued that in the case of negative externalities, it is not clear that the state should tax the person imposing the negative externality. First, Coase stressed the *reciprocal* nature of externalities, pointing out that it takes two to make a negative externality (it is not always clear who is harming whom).

Interview: Harold Demsetz

Harold Demsetz is well-known for his work in the area of property rights theory. His article, "Toward a Theory of Property Rights," is considered a classic in the field. Demsetz is currently at the University of California, Los Angeles.

Professor Demsetz, you have argued that property rights change to internalize externalities. Would you give us a few examples to illustrate this principle at work?

In my paper "Toward a Theory of Property Rights," I focused on the privatizing of lands by Indians in the eastern United States on the Canada–U.S. border. Anthropologists had discovered a correlation through time and across geography between the fur trade, whose source was in Europe, and the privatization of land among these Indians. I explain this correlation, and its absence among Indians in the Southwest, by considering the externality associated with treating animals as a free good. All hunters had access to fur-bearing animals that inhabited the forests of this region, and no hunter had a rational incentive to refrain from hunting in order to preserve or increase the stock of animals in these forests. This is because an animal left unhunted was an animal that other hunters had free access to hunt. Hence, refraining from hunting would neither enrich a hunter nor guarantee an increase in the stock of animals. There existed no incentive for hunters in the present to take account of the cost that might be borne by future generations as a result of depleting the stock of animals.

Before the coming of the fur trade, treating these animals as if access to them were costless probably did not do much damage to the stock of animals. The scale of hunting could not have been great when its only purpose was

to meet the purely personal needs of these Indians. The coming of the fur trade changed this by increasing the value of these furs and the scale of hunting. The stock of animals must have been put into jeopardy. What the Indians did to solve this problem was privatize land. This land had been treated as communal property, freely accessible to all. By privatizing the land, the Indians in effect privatized access to the animals because it is in the nature of forest animals to stay within fairly narrow territorial areas. Now, an Indian who refrained from hunting preserved the stock of animals on his land, so that the value of doing so accrued to him. An incentive to husband these animals was created by this act of privatization. The coming of the fur trade, by changing the benefits from husbanding the animals, made it profitable for the Indians to resolve the externality problem through this act of privatization.

In the southwestern United States, things were different. Here the animals were grazing animals, not forest animals. Someone with a right to land doesn't automatically get a right to the animals, too, because they graze over wide tracts of land and thus are very likely to go off to someone else's land.

In this case, it is very costly to husband animals because the Indians would need to fence in a very large tract of land. In cost–benefit terms, the situation did not argue for the privatizing of lands in the Southwest. In fact, the Indians did not privatize land in the Southwest, and buffalo herds were not able to withstand the scale of hunting that came about once Indians came into possession of rifles and horses.

Another example relates to the exploration of minerals under the earth. When it came to exploring for minerals, the general rule of law that governed the activity was called "rule of capture." What that meant was that anyone who wanted to could go down into his land and take the minerals out. With mineral resources, this doesn't cause any serious externality. A person takes iron ore or gold from his mine and no one else is affected. But when oil was discovered, what we had was a resource that flowed under pressure. And in this case, sinking a well and pumping crude oil reduced the pressure in the oil field and made it more costly to retrieve all the oil in the field.

With the rule of capture, there is a great incentive for people to take crude oil out as fast as they can because if they don't someone else will (since the pool of oil is large enough to extend across tracts of private lands owned by different persons). The response to this was the unitization of the oil field, which means that no longer can an owner of an oil well take as much oil out of the ground as he wants. Instead, he can take only the amount that is determined jointly by all owners of the land holding the oil pool.

A third example concerns air space. With the coming of air transport, something that once was a free good—air space—became a scarce good, especially air space near the ground. As a result, we got a change in property rights such that owners of land or homes near airports are entitled to quiet at certain times of the day.

You can go through a whole litany of cases in which you can see the relevance of externalities in the development of property rights. But I would put the proposition more generally than just in terms of externalities. We can look at property rights arrangements in cost–benefit terms. In some cases, demands and supplies change, and therefore the costs and benefits of privatizing change so that new rights replace old rights.

Within the property rights literature, two articles are widely cited. There is your article, "Toward a Theory of Property Rights," and Ronald Coase's "The Problem of Social Cost." What are the key insights of these two articles?

The articles appear to deal with the same subject but they really don't. The Coase article is not strictly about property rights. Coase takes the property rights system as completely defined and existing, then he gets into a debate with the Pigovians about externalities, showing that when transaction costs are zero, externalities don't exist. If transaction costs are positive, the usual prescription for dealing with them in the Pigovian framework is not necessarily the correct prescription.

In my paper, I am not really dealing with the externality problem in the same way, or even arguing with the Pigovians. What I'm trying to do is to explain why certain kinds of bundles of rights arise, and externalities (being a cost) are one clue as to why they arise. But as I stated earlier, a more general view is to look at costs and benefits of devising new property rights without special reference to the external costs associated with externalities.

In recent years, the media have reported on, and many people have viewed on television, the cruel clubbing to death of baby seals off Prince Edward Island in the Gulf of St. Lawrence. You have explained how this event is related to a particular property rights assignment. Will you repeat the main points of your argument for us?

There has been a legitimate public outcry about the hunt. The outcry has been about the inhuman behavior of the hunters, which is very paradoxical since the hunters are human. One shouldn't look to inhuman behavior to explain human behavior. One has to look elsewhere, and not very far.

The legal arrangement is such that annually some branch of the Canadian government decides how many seals are allowed to be taken, say, 50,000. Then the government allows a certain period of time—say, one or two weeks—for anybody to come in and take the seals until the total of 50,000 is taken. That means the hunters treat the seals as a free good up to 50,000. At 50,000, seals become an infinitely scarce good if the hunters abide by the law. That kind of legal arrangement is guaranteed to get very human people to hunt very quickly in order to get a large share of the seals before other people do and before the hunt ends. There is a great premium placed on fast hunting, and in hiring people who are agile, and on hiring people whose stomach doesn't turn when they hunt in this fashion.

You could of course avoid this behavior by prohibiting the hunt. But if you wanted to allow the hunt, you can get behavior that people would call more humane very easily. All you would have to do is sell people the right to take a number of seals. The hunters would then pay for the license to take a certain number of seals, with the total licenses being sold equal to the total number of seals the Canadian government wants to allow to be taken. And then the hunter could very patiently, and with greater humanity, take the seals that he is entitled to by virtue of now having a property right in those seals. The only way he could get the property right in the seals in the previous arrangement was by killing them, and by killing them quickly he got more. Under the arrangement I am proposing, the property right is created by the purchase, and the hunter is entitled to the seal, and he can take his time and handle the problem in a way that is more congenial to those people that have been complaining about the nature of the hunt.

Second, Coase proposed a market solution to externality problems that was not implicit in Pigou's work.

Aaron Director and others believed that Coase was wrong and that Pigou was right. Coase, who was teaching at the University of Virginia at the time, was invited to discuss his thesis with Director and a handful of well-known economists. The group included Martin Bailey, Milton Friedman, Arnold Harberger, Reuben Kessel, Gregg Lewis, John McGee, Lloyd Mints, George Stigler, and, of course, Director.

**CHAPTER 33
MARKET FAILURE: EXTERNALITIES, THE ENVIRONMENT, AND PUBLIC GOODS**

■

The group met at Aaron Director's house one night. Before Coase began to outline his thesis, the group took a vote and found that everyone (with the exception of Coase) sided with Pigou. Then the sparks began to fly. Friedman, it is reported, "opened fire" on Coase. Coase answered the intellectual attacks of his colleagues. At the end of the debate, another vote was taken. Everyone sided with Coase against Pigou. It is reported that as the members of the group left Director's home that night, they said to one another that they had witnessed history in the making. The Coase theorem had taken hold in economics.

THE ENVIRONMENT

The environment became a major economic, political, and social issue in the 1980s. For example, when the Group of Seven (United States, Japan, West Germany, Britain, France, Canada, and Italy) held its fifteenth annual economic summit in Paris in July 1989, environmental issues were a major focus for the first time. Problems of the environment are manifold and cover things such as acid rain, the greenhouse effect, deforestation, including the destruction of the rain forests, solid waste (garbage) disposal, water pollution, air pollution, and much more. In this section, we principally discuss air pollution.

There are three principal points that economists make about pollution. First, it is a negative externality. Second, and perhaps counterintuitively, no pollution is sometimes worse than some pollution. Third, the market can be used to deal with the problem of pollution.

Is No Pollution Worse Than Some Pollution?

When might some pollution be preferred to no pollution? The answer is, when all other things are not held constant. In short, most of the time.

Certainly, if all other things are held constant, less pollution is preferred to more pollution, and therefore no pollution is preferred to some pollution. But the world would be different with no pollution—and not only in terms of having cleaner air, rivers, and oceans. Pollution is a byproduct of the production of many goods and services. For example, it is unlikely that steel could be produced without some pollution as a byproduct. Given the current state of pollution technology, less steel pollution means less steel and fewer products made from steel.

Pollution is also a byproduct of many of the goods we use daily, including our cars. We could certainly end car pollution tomorrow, but this would mean that we would have to give up driving cars. Are there any benefits to driving cars? If there are, then perhaps we wouldn't choose zero car pollution. In short, zero pollution is not preferable to some positive amount of pollution once we take into consideration that we'll have fewer goods and services if we have less pollution.

The same conclusion can be reached through Coasian-type analysis. Suppose there are two groups: polluters and nonpolluters. For certain units of pollution, the value to polluters of polluting might be greater than the value of a less-polluted environment to nonpolluters. In the presence of trivial or zero transaction costs, a deal will be struck. The outcome will be characterized by some positive amount of pollution.

Two Methods to Reduce Pollution

One of the biggest movements of the 1990s is likely to be *market environmentalism:* the use of market forces to clean up the environment. This was the idea behind the Clean Air Act amendments, which President Bush signed in November 1990. The amendments lowered the maximum allowable sulfur dioxide emissions (the major factor in acid rain) for 111 utilities, but gave them the right to trade permits for sulfur dioxide emissions. In other words, the amendments to the Clean Air Act make it possible for the utilities to buy and sell the right to pollute.

"To buy and sell the right to pollute" may sound odd to ears accustomed to thinking about dealing with pollution through government regulations or standards. Let's consider these two methods of reducing pollution. Method 1 is by the government setting pollution standards. Method 2 is by government selling the right to pollute. Which is the least costly?

Method 1: Government Sets Pollution Standards. In Exhibit 33–5(a), we show the cost of eliminating the first through eighth units of pollution for three firms, X, Y, Z, located in the same area. For example, the cost of eliminating the first unit of pollution is $50, $70, and $800 for firms X, Y, and Z, respectively.

Currently, each firm is spewing 8 units of pollution for a total pollution level of 24 units. Now suppose the government wants to reduce the pollution level by half. If it tries to accomplish this objective by setting standards, it will order each of

EXHIBIT 33–5
Two Methods of Reducing 12 Units of Pollution

	Firm X	Firm Y	Firm Z
Cost of Eliminating:			
1st unit of pollution	$ 50	$ 70	$ 800
2nd unit of pollution	75	130	1,000
3rd unit of pollution	100	200	2,000
4th unit of pollution	150	300	3,000
5th unit of pollution	200	400	4,000
6th unit of pollution	300	500	5,000
7th unit of pollution	400	600	6,000
8th unit of pollution	500	700	7,000

(a)
Data

Cost to Firm X of Eliminating 4 Units	= $50 + 75 + 100 + 150 = $375
Cost to Firm Y of Eliminating 4 Units	= $70 + 130 + 200 + 300 = $700
Cost to Firm Z of Eliminating 4 Units	= $800 + 1,000 + 2,000 + 3,000 = $6,800
Total Units of Pollution Eliminated	= 4 + 4 + 4 = 12
Total Cost of Eliminating 12 Units of Pollution	= $375 + 700 + 6,800 = $7,875

Cost to Firm X of Eliminating 7 Units	= $50 + 75 + 100 + 150 + 200 + 300 + 400 = $1,275
Cost to Firm Y of Eliminating 5 Units	= $70 + 130 + 200 + 300 + 400 = $1,100
Cost to Firm Z of Eliminating 0 Units	= $0
Total Units of Pollution Eliminated	= 7 + 5 + 0 = 12
Total Cost of Eliminating 12 Units of Pollution	= $1,275 + 1,100 + 0 = $2,375

(b)
Setting Standards

(c)
Selling the Right to Pollute

(a) The cost of eliminating units 1–8 of pollution for each of three firms. (b) The cost for each firm of eliminating 4 units of pollution, and the total cost of eliminating 12 units of pollution ($7,875). (c) The cost for each firm of eliminating its chosen level of pollution under a system of pollution permits, and the total cost of eliminating 12 units of pollution ($2,375).

the three firms to cut its pollution level by four units. In (b), we see that the cost to firm X of reducing its pollution by four units is $375; the cost to firm Y is $700; and the cost to firm Z is $6,800. The total cost of eliminating 12 units of pollution is the sum of these figures, $7,875.

Method 2: Government Sells the Right to Pollute.   Again suppose the government wants the firms to eliminate 12 units of pollution. This time, however, the government decides to sell firms pollution permits for a price of $401 a permit.[2] For each permit a firm buys, it can emit one pollution unit into the atmosphere.

How many permits will firm X purchase? Since it can eliminate each pollution unit 1–7 for less than $401 per unit, but it cannot eliminate the eighth unit for less than $401, it will buy only one permit. In (c), we see that its cost of eliminating seven units of pollution turns out to be $1,275.

Similarly, firm Y can eliminate each pollution unit 1–5 for less than $401 per unit, but it cannot eliminate units 6–8 for less than $401 per unit. Firm Y buys 3 permits and its cost of eliminating five units of pollution is $1,100.

Firm Z cannot eliminate any of its pollution for less than $401 per unit, so it buys 8 tickets and eliminates zero units of pollution for a cost of $0.

Since firm X eliminates 7 units of pollution, and firm Y eliminates 5 units of pollution, a total of 12 units of pollution are eliminated for a total cost of $2,375.

Comparing Method 1 with Method 2, we notice that it is less costly to eliminate 12 units of pollution if the government sells the right to pollute than if it sets standards. This is why many economists propose *selling the right to pollute* over *setting standards.*

Question:

What about the price of the pollution permits that the firms had to buy? This wasn't added in as a cost of eliminating pollution. For example, it was stated that the cost of eliminating 7 units of pollution for firm X was $1,275. But shouldn't it have been $1,275 plus $401—which was the cost to the firm of buying one pollution permit. This would bring the total up to $1,676.

Answer:

The $401 price for the pollution permit is not a cost to society of eliminating pollution. It is the price paid to legally emit one unit of pollution into the air. Stated differently, it is a transfer of funds *from* firm X *to* government—that is all.

Look at it this way. We are interested in reducing a given level of pollution. We know that we cannot do this without expending some resources, but we want the resource cost to be as low as possible. Between the two methods outlined—standards and selling pollution permits—the latter accomplishes the goal at lower resource cost: $2,375 instead of $7,875.

The total price paid by the three firms for the 12 pollution permits purchased— 1 by firm X, 3 by firm Y, and 8 by firm Z—is $4,812 ($401 a permit × 12 permits = $4,812). Certainly, this is a real cost of business for the three firms, but it is not a cost that is directed toward eliminating pollution, nor is it a cost to society of

[2]We have simplified the analysis here by stating that the government sells pollution permits to firms. Actually, what happens is that the government issues (allocates) pollution permits to firms, after which the firms reallocate the permits (among themselves) by buying and selling them to each other. Our simplified analysis gives us the essence of the issue at hand without unnecessary complications.

Interview: Allen V. Kneese

Allen V. Kneese is best known for his research in the area of environmental economics. With environmental issues becoming increasingly more important in recent years, Kneese's work has come to the forefront of public policy discussions. Kneese is currently at Resources for the Future, a research organization.

How would you describe the economic approach to environmental issues?

I would like to answer this question rather fully. This background will permit me to answer subsequent questions much more compactly.

What happened in the late nineteen sixties and early seventies, when the environmental movement emerged, to make people, including economists, rather suddenly so acutely aware of environmental pollution? Three things which have come upon us slowly, but more or less simultaneously, are chiefly responsible, I think.

First, recent decades have seen immense increases in industrial production and energy conversion. Associated with this are massive flows of materials and energy from concentrated states in nature to degraded and diluted states in the environment. This has begun to alter the physical, chemical, and biological quality of the atmosphere and hydrosphere on a truly massive scale. Furthermore, scientists and technicians now have the means to detect even very small changes in these natural systems so that we are much more aware of what is happening than in the past.

Second, "exotic" materials are being introduced into the environment. The near-alchemy of modern physics and chemistry has recently subjected the world's biological systems to strange, unnatural inputs to which they cannot adapt (or at least not quickly); or adaption may occur in some species but not in others and thus the balance of species will be upset.

Third, ordinary folk in developed countries have come to expect standards of cleanliness, safety, and wholesomeness in their surroundings that were the exclusive province of the well-born or rich in earlier times.

What is to be done in the face of these profound new forces in the world? And why did our existing market institutions not cope with them at all well?

As a first step toward gaining insight into why this growing divergence between private ends and social ends came about, it is useful to invoke one of the most basic physical principles—that of mass balance. When minerals, fuels, gases, and organic materials are extracted and harvested from nature and used by producers and consumers, it is immediately apparent that their mass is not altered in these processes, except in trivial amounts. Material residuals are generated in production and consumption activities, and their mass must be about equal to that initially extracted from nature.

The services which material objects can yield are used, and market exchange works to allocate these services to those who desire them most, but their physical substance remains intact. The important implications this has for

the allocation of resources in a market system is that while most extractive harvesting, processing, and distributional activities can be conducted relatively efficiently through the medium of exchange of private ownership rights, the inevitable residual mass returned to the environment goes heavily into what the economists call common property resources. Common property resources are those valuable natural assets which cannot, or can only imperfectly, be reduced to private ownership. Examples are the air mantle, watercourse, complex ecological systems, large landscapes, and the electromagnetic spectrum. The nature of all these resources violates an important structural assumption for an efficient market to exist— that all valuable assets can be individually owned and managed.

It is obvious what will happen when open and unpriced access to such resources is permitted. From careful study of particular common property or common pool problems like oil and ocean fisheries, it is well known that unhindered access to such resources leads to overuse, misuse, and quality degradation. Market forces, while marvelously efficient in allocating owned resources, work to damage or destroy common property resources.

The law of conservation of mass was no doubt always held. But at lower levels of population size and economic activity, the return of "used" materials to the environment has only local effects, most of which can be dealt with by means of ordinances and other local government measures to improve sanitation in the immediate vicinity of cities. Thus sewers can be installed, and the streets can be cleared of trash and offal.

But, as economic development proceeds, more and more material tends to be returned to the environment pari passu with the increased production of material objects. Indeed, some forces press in the direction of increasing the proportion of residual waste to final usable output—resort to progressively lower-quality ores or the use of shales for the production of oil is a case in point. Larger "problem sheds" are affected and greater numbers of people more remotely located in both space and time suffer adverse impacts. Common property assets, which cannot enter into market exchange, are progressively degraded because the industries, governments, and individuals use them as dumps at no cost to themselves even though important assets arising from other uses are degraded or destroyed.

In summary, a profound asymmetry has developed in the effectiveness and efficiency of the system of economic incentives inherent in market systems. On the one hand, it works well in stimulating the exploitation of basic resources, and processing and distributing them, but it fails almost completely in the efficient disposal of residuals to common property resources.

What are some of the proposed solutions to environmental problems and how do you rate each one?

The policy debate about what to do in the face of the problems just discussed has focused on two broad approaches. One, mostly advocated by economists, would make heavy use of economic incentive approaches such as effluent or emissions taxes, or tradeable permits to discharge residuals. Lawyers and politicians, who are often one and the same, have usually favored what has come to be called the "command and control" approach, that is, the government should require specific discharge controls for each major source of residuals discharge. The issues are too intricate to go into here but most economists believe that economic incentives will be more "cost-effective" in achieving environmental goals than will command and control techniques and a large body of research tends to support that position. I believe we should place more emphasis on economic incentives in the

future development of environmental policy.

You have been quoted as saying that you are frustrated over the "difficulty of getting more than a few members of Congress to understand that environmental pollution is an economic problem as well as an environmental problem." Would you discuss what you mean when you say "environmental pollution is an economic problem," and speculate on why few members of Congress understand what you mean?

The answer to the question is, I think, explained in my answers to your earlier questions. But I believe that the quote is, by now, quite old and at least partly obsolete. It is true that lawyers, whose instinct is to issue orders, and environmentalists who tended to see environmental pollution as strictly a moral issue, have dominated environmental policy making in the past. But things have been changing. There are now a number of trained environmental economists in the Environmental Protection Agency and they are assuming a significant role in the continuing policy debate. In addition, more lawyers dealing with environmental issues have training in economics and even environmental organizations now have economists on their staffs. A recent manifestation of this change is the Clean Air Act of 1990 which relies heavily on an economic incentive approach for the control of acid rain.

Is ethics tied in with environmental issues?

Of course it is. Any statement of a "normative" nature about the environment is based on some system of ethical beliefs even though it is usually not made very explicit. But recognizing this does not mean that we should not care about economic costs or efficiency. They are necessary items of information in balancing off conflicting values. In a democratic society this conflict resolution properly takes place in the political arena.

What got you interested in economics?

A major factor was an inspiring professor I had as an undergraduate. Also economic theory, especially in its application to resources and environmental problems, provides a conceptual structure that can be used to integrate data and methods from many other disciplines e.g. ecology, engineering, physics. I have always had a strong interest in interdisciplinary research.

You are actively involved in environmental economics research. What questions are you currently trying to answer?

I am trying to understand the appropriate role of environmental economics in connection with such large new issues as nuclear waste disposal and climate change. On a less grand scale I am working with a team helping a federal agency to do a cost-effectiveness analysis of alternatives for restoring the salmon runs in the Columbia River Basin. Also I am working on a project on environment and development in China and another on environmental problems in Eastern Europe. Finally, I am continuing my long standing research on the role of economic incentives in environmental policy.

What do you predict will be the future of the environment in the United States?

If we pursue efficient policies I think the future quality of our air and water should continue to improve. We certainly have the means to make it so. Where the environmental problems seem to be almost, if not altogether, hopeless is in the formerly socialist economies of Eastern Europe and in the Soviet Union, despite the claim sustained over many years that socialist economies do not have pollution. In fact it is much worse there for reasons we do not have time to go into.

A major uncertainty in our situation surrounds what may, or may not, have to be done, to manage global climate change.

eliminating pollution. It is simply a *transfer* of funds: collectively the three firms have $4,812 less and the government has $4,812 more.

The distinction is between a *resource cost,* which signifies an expenditure of resources, and a *transfer,* which does not.

PUBLIC GOODS

Many economists maintain that the market fails to produce public goods. A **public good** is a good that, once produced and provided to one person, gives benefits to more than one person. The two characteristics of a public good are nonrivalry in consumption and nonexcludability.

Nonrivalry in Consumption

A good is **nonrivalrous in consumption** if its consumption by one person does not reduce its consumption by others. Consider national defense. Once produced, national defense protects all persons—not just some—in a designated geographical area (which may be as large as the entire United States). It is impossible to protect one person in Newark, New Jersey, from incoming missiles and not protect another person in New York City as well. And just as important, protecting the person in Newark does not reduce the degree of protection for the person in New York. National defense is nonrivalrous in consumption.

A good is **rivalrous in consumption** if its consumption by one person reduces its consumption by others. Let's look at an apple. If one person takes a bite out of an apple, there is that much less of the apple for someone else to consume. Many goods are rivalrous in consumption, such as cars, shoes, dresses, shirts, medical services, typewriters, pizzas, and hammocks. All such goods are known as private goods.

Nonexcludability

A good is **nonexcludable** if it is impossible, or prohibitively costly, to exclude someone from obtaining the benefits of the good once it has been produced. Again, once national defense is produced, it is impossible (or "prohibitively costly" if your penchant is to see nothing as impossible) to exclude someone from consuming its services. The same holds for flood control or large-scale pest control. Once the dam has been built, once the pest spray has been sprayed, it is impossible to exclude persons from benefiting from it.

A good is **excludable** if it is possible, or not prohibitively costly, to exclude someone from obtaining the benefits of the good once it has been produced. For example, a movie in a movie theater is excludable, in that persons who do not pay to see the movie can be excluded from seeing it. Other goods that fit into this category include typewriters, radios, rock concerts, swimming pools, tennis courts, and hotel rooms.

Nonrivalry Does Not Necessarily Imply Nonexcludability

There is a tendency to believe that any good that is nonrivalrous in consumption is also nonexcludable. This is erroneous. It is possible to have a good that is both nonrivalrous in consumption and excludable. Once again, consider a movie in a movie theater. The movie can be seen equally (or very nearly equally) by everyone in the theater. If Gloria views the movie, this does not prevent Franco from viewing it, too.

It is possible, though, to exclude someone from viewing the movie. If a person does not pay the admittance fee to see the movie, he will not be permitted into the movie theater—he will be excluded. A movie, then, is an example of a good that is both nonrivalrous in consumption and excludable.

The Free Rider

Free Rider
Anyone who receives the benefits of a good without paying for it.

When a good is nonexcludable, it is possible for individuals to obtain the benefits of the good without paying for it. Persons who do so are referred to as **free riders.** It is because of the so-called free rider problem that most economists hold that the market will fail to produce public goods, or fail to produce them at a desired level.

Consider someone contemplating the production of public good *X*. The good is nonrivalrous in consumption and nonexcludable; therefore, once it has been produced and provided to one person, there is no incentive for others to pay for it (even if they demand it) since they can receive its benefits without paying. No one is likely to supply a good for which no one has to pay in order to consume. The market, it is argued, will not produce public goods. The door then is opened to government involvement in the production of public goods. It is often stated that if the market will not produce public goods, although they are demanded, then the government must.

The free rider argument is the basis for accepting government (the public or taxpayers) provision of public goods. We need remind ourselves, though, that there is a difference between a *public good* and a *government-provided good*. A public good has already been defined: It is a good that is nonrivalrous in consumption and nonexcludable. A government-provided good is self-defined. In some instances, a government-provided good is a public good, such as when government furnishes national defense. But it need not be. Government furnishes mail delivery and education, two goods that are also provided privately, and are excludable and thus not subject to free riding.

Question:

It seems that the market only fails to produce a demanded good when the good is nonexcludable, because the free rider problem only arises if the good is nonexcludable. The rivalry vs. nonrivalry issue is not relevant to the issue of market failure; that is, a good can be rivalrous in consumption or nonrivalrous in consumption and still be produced by the market. Isn't this correct?

Answer:

That is correct. As we noted earlier, a movie may be nonrivalrous in consumption, but be excludable, too. And we know that the market has no problem producing movies and movie theaters. The free rider problem only occurs with goods that are nonexcludable. Also relevant to the question is the case of "the lighthouse in economics."[3] For a long time, a lighthouse was thought to have the two characteristics of a public good: (1) It is nonrivalrous in consumption—any ship can use the light from the lighthouse, and one ship's use of the light does not detract from another's. (2) It is also nonexcludable—it is difficult to exclude any nonpaying

[3]See Ronald Coase, "The Lighthouse in Economics," *Journal of Law and Economics 19* (October 1976).

ships from using the light. The lighthouse seemed to be a perfect good for government provision.

There is only one problem. Economist Ronald Coase found that in the eighteenth and early nineteenth centuries, many lighthouses were privately owned, which meant that the market had not failed to provide lighthouses. Economists were left to conclude either that the market could provide public goods or that the lighthouse wasn't a public good as had been thought. Closer examination showed the lighthouse was nonrivalrous in consumption, but the costs of excluding others from using it were fairly low. Lighthouse owners knew that usually only one ship was near the lighthouse at a time and that they could turn off the lights if a ship did not exhibit the flag of a paying vessel.

SOME EXTERNALITY AND PUBLIC GOODS ISSUES

Externality and public goods theory has a number of real-world applications. Here we present a few interesting issues that relate to externalities and public goods.

Acid Rain

Acid rain is a rain or mist that carries a mixture of sulfur-dioxide gases and nitrous-oxide emissions. When it falls to the earth, it is thought to destroy forests and pollute lakes and rivers, killing fish. Scientists are not agreed on the causes of acid rain. Some blame the emissions from industrial plants. Others say it is principally due to car exhausts.

In addition, scientists and nonscientists disagree about where acid rain first arises. The Canadians say it originates largely in the United States. Individuals who live in the East say it originates in the Midwest. Midwesterners say it originates in the East. Obviously, we have a problem here—specifically, a negative externality problem. But how do we solve it? Should we use persuasion? What about assigning property rights in the air? If we did this, we would still have a problem because even if a group of people owned the air, how would they know exactly who was polluting it? Will voluntary agreements work? One problem with voluntary agreements is that no one knows for sure who is creating the acid rain and to what degree. We could tax the activities that we think are generating the negative externality, but this does not place us on very solid ground. What about direct regulation? We still do not know whom to regulate and to what degree. Besides, there are costs to regulation. The problem of acid rain—a negative externality problem—is a sticky one that is not likely to be dealt with in a way that is satisfactory to everyone.

Question:

What is the significance of this acid rain example?

Answer:

First, it shows that acid rain is a negative externality problem, which may help some people to view it in a new way. Second, it illustrates that some negative externalities are more difficult to deal with than others. Acid rain is particularly difficult to deal with because, among other things, not everyone is agreed as to its cause or its birthplace.

Traffic Congestion

In most cases, roads are provided by government. The often-cited justification for this is that roads are public goods; they are nonrivalrous in consumption (for the most part, one person's driving on the road does not prevent another person from driving on the road) and nonexcludable (it might be prohibitively costly to exclude someone from driving on the road; the road owner would have to install gates everywhere).

The payment scheme worked out for the production of roads is quite simple. Taxes are raised and spent to construct roads; then once the roads are constructed, no one has to make a direct monetary payment to drive on most roads (turnpikes are the notable exception). We conclude that once a person has paid his or her taxes, there is a zero (money) price to driving on roads. And economists are quick to point out that the quantity demanded of a good is greater at a zero price than at some positive price.

The zero price of driving on roads often leads to traffic congestion (see Chapter 4). In many big cities around the world, traffic is bumper to bumper on major roadways during the rush hour period early in the morning and in the evening. Can anything be done about rush hour traffic, or must individuals simply grin and bear it?

Some economists have argued that roads are not, and never have been, public goods. First, although they are nonrivalrous in consumption at some times, such as when there are few cars on the roads, at other times, such as rush hour, they are rivalrous in consumption. Second, they are not nonexcludable (which means they are excludable). The existence of tolls and the like proves this. Does this mean government should sell the roads to private investors and permit private roads and private pricing schemes?

In Hong Kong, the government has started to experiment with a market approach to rationing road space. Cars are fitted with an electronic number plate, which is read by electronic devices buried under the roads at frequently congested intersections. The license number is relayed to a central computer that adds a fee to the car owner's monthly bill. A car owner can lower his monthly bill by deciding not to drive on certain roads. It is also possible for the price of driving on certain roads to increase at certain times of the day. For example, when the demand for the road space is high, the price will be higher than when the demand for the road space is low. By selling road space on a market basis, critics of government-provided roads charge, the continuing problems of shortages and surpluses of road space will be solved.

Smoking Sections in Restaurants

Recall the days before there were smoking and nonsmoking sections in most restaurants. Shelly Blevins, a nonsmoker, is seated at a table next to Diane Mueller, a chain smoker. Shelly is quietly eating her meal when cigarette smoke wafts its way over to her nose. She gives Diane a dirty look, but the latter doesn't notice because she is busy lighting up another cigarette. We have a negative externality situation that raises the question: Who has the right to do what? Does Shelly have the right to sit quietly in the restaurant and eat her meal in a smokeless environment? Does Diane have the right to sit quietly in the restaurant and enjoy herself by smoking a few cigarettes?

Can this externality problem be resolved through persuasion or voluntary agreement? Shelly could lean over to Diane and ask her to refrain from smoking. That might work. Or Shelly and Diane might try to enter into a voluntary agreement. If eating in a smokeless environment is worth more to Shelly than smoking cigarettes is to Diane, then Shelly could pay Diane not to smoke. But time spent in a restaurant is usually short and it is likely that most people will not work out voluntary agreements relevant to smoking and not smoking, nor will most persons try to persuade others to change their habits. Thus, the negative externality problem in the restaurant will probably not be solved through persuasion or voluntary agreements.

Local ordinances in many municipalities now require restaurant owners to separate the two groups of customers. Most restaurants now have smoking and nonsmoking sections. The negative externality problems has been solved, one would assume, in the least costly manner.

Is Charitable Giving Subject to Free Riding?

Some persons contend that charitable giving is a public good and subject to free riding. Consider the case of Bill McDonald, who is the type of person who receives utility when individuals less fortunate than he are being helped. When a homeless person is given a home, he feels good inside. When he learns that a rich entrepreneur in Dallas has decided to pay the college tuition of 20 poor, college-age students, it makes his day. Notice that charitable giving appears to be a public good. It is nonrivalrous in consumption and nonexcludable. If the rich entrepreneur in Dallas pays the tuition of 20 poor, college-age students, Bill McDonald receives utility from such a gesture as easily as the rich entrepreneur; and it is impossible to exclude him from receiving the utility once the rich entrepreneur's charitable giving has been reported.

We explained earlier that a public good is subject to free riding. Is Bill McDonald a free rider? Will he take a free ride on the charitable giving of others? Using the following line of reasoning, many persons argue that he will: (1) The average person's charitable contribution is a tiny percentage of total charitable contributions ($75 out of many millions). (2) Consequently, the average person realizes that even if he or she does not make a charitable contribution, charitable giving by others will not be much different (total charitable contributions will be less by only $75— a mere drop in the bucket). (3) A person has an incentive to become a free rider once the person realizes that his or her contribution will not affect total charitable contributions by more than the tiniest amount and that he or she can benefit from the charitable giving of others. What is the moral of the story? When a person feels that his contribution is insignificant to the total contribution, or that the benefits he receives from a good will not be appreciably different in the absence of his paying for it, then he has a strong incentive to become a free rider.

Free Riders and the Size of the Group: Can Committees Get Too Big?

As we have just seen, a person has a strong incentive to become a free rider if his contribution is insignificant to the total contribution, or the benefits he receives from a good will not be appreciably different in the absence of his paying for it. Now we ask, Is there anything that, if changed, would affect both the way a person views his contribution vis-à-vis the total contribution and the benefits received from a good in the absence of paying for it? The answer is *the size of the group*. All other things held constant, the larger the group size, the smaller or less significant the individual's contribution relative to the total contribution, and the less likely the benefits received from a good will be appreciably different in the absence of paying for it.

For example, if the group size is one million, then one person's contribution is a smaller percentage of the total contribution than if the group size is ten. We conclude that as the group size decreases, the incentive to become a free rider becomes less; as the group size increases, the incentive to become a free rider becomes greater. We would expect to find fewer free riders in small groups than in large groups.

Think about the size of a committee. A large committee of 20–30 persons is likely to contain more free riders than a committee of 4–6 persons. In a large committee, each individual's contribution is a smaller percentage of the total contribution of the group, and therefore doing little or nothing does not appreciably affect the results as much as it would in a small committee. One person taking a free ride in a large committee is not as likely to be noticed or felt as one person taking a free ride in a small committee. We would expect more free riding in large committees than in small committees. It follows that small committees are likely to accomplish more than large committees.

Economics 22,300 Miles High, or You Can See for Miles and Miles

Economics has moved beyond the classroom, the city, the state, and the nation. It has moved into outer space. The reason is simple; space has become scarce (and as you will recall from Chapter 1, the bedrock upon which economics rests is scarcity). Space is scarce today because of the increased use of satellites. These satellites are used to transmit live news reports or telephone calls from the other side of the world, to monitor weather conditions (for example, hurricanes), and to monitor the military operations of other countries. The best place to put these satellites for transmission purposes is 22,300 miles above the earth in an area called the geostationary orbital arc. The arcs of the orbital paths that are of greatest interest to the United States lie between 60 degrees and 135 degrees west longitude, because a satellite placed in this area can serve the entire continental United States. Unfortunately for the United States, this orbital arc is also of great interest to Canada, Mexico, and Latin America.

Owing to space congestion, these countries and their business firms cannot put as many satellites as they want into this area of space. To minimize the chance of collisions, as well as signal interference, satellites must be positioned a certain distance from one another. For example, each satellite must be placed approximately 2–3 degrees away from any other satellite using the same transmission frequency. This means there are only so many space slots for satellites to occupy. INTELSAT, the international telecommunications satellite organization, has projected that slots in some orbital arcs will be filled by the early 1990s.

Why Space Congestion Exists.   Space congestion exists in outer space because no one owns space. In 1967, the United Nations Committee on the Peaceful Uses of Outer Space drafted the Outer Space Treaty, which said that all nations have equal rights to the resources of space. In other words, space is communal property—all nations "own" it. But as we know, communal property rarely provides the incentives necessary for efficient use. Many economists predict that the present system of rationing space slots according to first-come-first-served (zero price) is bound to produce negative externalities in the future.

Suppose a particular space area already is congested. If one more satellite is launched into the area, it will increase the risks of signal interference and collision for all the other satellites in the area and will be viewed as a negative externality by the owners of the other satellites.

This situation is similar to the cattle rancher–farmer example we discussed earlier. What are each party's rights in the congested area? If space is owned by everyone, doesn't the nation that wants to put a satellite into space have the right to do so? But on the other hand, don't the nations and companies that already have satellites in space have the right to use "their" space property in a way that minimizes the risks to their satellites?

Assigning Property Rights to Space. One of the ways to solve the externality problem is to *assign property rights* in space slots. Let's say space slot 1 is assigned to company X (we will skirt the issue for now of who or what assigns the property right to whom). Since company X's computations show that space slot 1 can safely accommodate three satellites of a certain size and transmission frequency, it figures that it can maximize profits by limiting its satellite occupants to three. Therefore, it leases space in its space slot for $Y per time period. Any intruder satellites in its space will be dealt with harshly—after all, they will be on private property without permission.

If space is private property, space slots are likely to be put to their highest-valued use (in much the same way that an acre of land in the center of the city will be purchased by the person(s) who will put the land to its highest-valued use). The situation in space is analogous to the situation in a city with high rent districts, say, New York City. Just as prime lots in New York fetch high prices, prime slots in space would fetch high prices. The persons who buy the high-priced lots in New York make it worth their while by building tall skyscrapers and renting office space to thousands of tenants. The persons who buy high-priced slots in space would make it worth their while by building large satellites that carry many transponders, the devices that bounce back communication signals. Then the company that owns the satellite can rent out the transponders to clients. Since space is scarce, it may be better to have a few large satellites in space with many transponders than many small satellites with a few transponders. Clearly, allocating property rights in space will force people to economize on this scarce resource.

To Whom Do the Space Slots Go? Property rights in space can be allocated in numerous ways, none of which seems to generate unanimous approval. Some economists have proposed that space slots be auctioned off, but this has been criticized on the ground that poor countries will be at a disadvantage in the building. Some have proposed that each nation should receive a quota of slots. Then nations that currently lack the technology to put a satellite in space could rent out their slots or sell them. Others have proposed that a lottery be held with the winners chosen at random. As these proposals suggest, deciding the distribution of space slots raises the issue of equity. In many ways, equity is the stumbling block to assigning property rights in space, since it is doubtful that the nations of the world will agree on what is equitable.

We don't know when property rights will be assigned in space, nor do we know how these property rights will be assigned. We do predict, however, that sooner or later space will be subject to property rights assignments. The impending externality problems are the reason why.

Externalities

■ An externality is a side effect of an action that affects the well-being of third parties. There are two types of externalities: negative and positive. A negative externality exists when an individual's or group's actions cause a cost (adverse side effect) to be felt by others. A positive externality exists when an individual's or group's actions cause a benefit (beneficial side effect) to be felt by others.

■ When either negative or positive externalities exist, the market output is different from the socially optimal output. In the case of a negative externality, the market is said to overproduce the good connected with the negative externality (the socially optimal output is less than the market output). In the case of a positive externality, the market is said to underproduce the good connected with the positive externality (the socially optimal output is greater than the market output). See Exhibits 33–1 and 33–3.

■ Negative and positive externalities can be internalized or adjusted for in a number of different ways, including persuasion, the assignment of property rights, voluntary agreements, and taxes and subsidies. Also, regulations may be used to adjust for externalities directly.

The Coase Theorem

■ The Coase theorem holds that in the case of trivial or zero transaction costs, the property rights assignment does not matter to the resource allocative outcome. To put it differently, a property rights assignment will be undone if it benefits the relevant parties to undo it. The Coase theorem is significant for two reasons: (1) It shows that under certain conditions the market can internalize externalities. (2) It provides a benchmark for analyzing externality problems—that is, it shows what would happen if transaction costs were trivial or zero.

The Environment

■ No pollution is not likely to be a better situation than some pollution. The reason is that pollution comes with certain things people derive utility from, such as cars to drive.

■ There is more than one way to tackle problems of the environment. For example, both setting standards and selling pollution permits can be used to deal with pollution. The economist is interested in finding the cheapest way to solve environmental problems. Often, this tends to be through some measure of market environmentalism, such as selling pollution permits.

Public Goods

■ A public good is a good characterized by nonrivalry in consumption and nonexcludability. The market is said to fail in the provision of public goods as a consequence of the nature of a public good; a supplier of the good would not be able to extract payment for the good since its benefits can be received without making payment. In short, the market fails because of the free rider problem associated with public goods.

■ There is a difference between a public good and a government-provided good. A public good is a good that is nonrivalrous in consumption and nonexcludable. A government-provided good is any good provided by government. Sometimes a public good and a government-provided good are the same, such as national defense. Sometimes they are not.

Key Terms and Concepts

Externality	Transaction Costs	Rivalrous in Consumption
Negative Externality	Coase Theorem	Nonexcludability
Socially Optimal Output	Public Good	Excludability
Positive Externality	Nonrivalrous in Consumption	Free Rider
Internalizing Externalities		

QUESTIONS AND PROBLEMS

1. Give an example that illustrates the difference between private costs and social costs.

2. Consider two types of divorce laws. Law A allows either the husband or the wife to obtain a divorce without the other person's consent. Law B permits a divorce only if both parties agree to the divorce. Will there be more divorces under law A or law B, or will there be the same number of divorces under both laws? Why?

3. People have a demand for sweaters, and the market provides sweaters. There is evidence that people also have a demand for national defense, yet the market does not provide national defense. What is the reason the market does not provide national defense? Is it because government is providing national defense and therefore there is no need for the market to do so, or because the market won't provide national defense?

4. Education is often said to generate positive externalities. How might it do this?

5. Give an example of each of the following: (a) a good rivalrous in consumption and excludable; (b) a good nonrivalrous in consumption and excludable; (c) a good rivalrous in consumption and nonexcludable; (d) a good nonrivalrous in consumption and nonexcludable.

6. Some individuals argue that with increased population growth, negative externalities will become more common and there will be more instances of market failure and more need for government to solve externality problems. Other individuals believe that as time passes, technological advances will be used to solve negative externality problems. They conclude that over time there will be fewer instances of market failure and less need for government to deal with externality problems. What do you believe will happen? Give reasons to support your position.

7. Name at least five government-provided goods that are not public goods.

8. One view of life is that life is one big externality. Just about everything that someone does affects someone else either positively or negatively. To permit government to deal with externality problems is to permit government to tamper with everything in life. There is no clear dividing line between externalities government should and should not become involved in. Do you support this position? Why?

9. Economists sometimes shock noneconomists by stating that they do not favor the complete elimination of pollution. Explain the rationale for this position.

PUBLIC CHOICE: ECONOMIC THEORY APPLIED TO POLITICS

WHAT THIS CHAPTER IS ABOUT

The last chapter was about *market failure.* To a large degree, this chapter is about *government failure.* Government failure is said to exist when government enacts policies that produce inefficient or inequitable results as a consequence of the rational behavior of the participants in the political process—politicians, voters, special-interest groups, and bureaucrats.

Our subject is **public choice:** the branch of economics that deals with the application of economic principles and tools to public-sector decision making.

PUBLIC CHOICE THEORY

Public Choice
The branch of economics that deals with the application of economic principles and tools to public-sector decision making.

Public choice theorists reject the notion that people are like Dr. Jekyll and Mr. Hyde: exhibiting greed and selfishness in their transactions in the private (market) sector and altruism and public spirit in their actions in the public sector. The same people who are employers, employees, and consumers in the market sector are the politicians, bureaucrats, special-interest group members, and voters in the public sector. According to public choice theorists, differences between the behavior of people in the market sector and people in the public sector are due not to different motives (or the way people are) but to the different institutional arrangements in the two sectors.

Consider a simple example. Erin Bloom currently works for a private, profit-seeking firm that makes radio components. Erin is cost conscious, does her work on time, and generally works hard. She knows that she must exhibit this particular work behavior if she wants to be promoted.

Time passes. Erin leaves her job at the radio components company and takes a job with the Department of Health and Human Services (HHS) in Washington, D.C. Is Erin a different person (with different motives) working for HHS than she was working for the radio components company? Public choice theorists would say no.

But simply because Erin is the same person in and out of government, it does not necessarily follow that she will exhibit the same work behavior. The reason is that the costs and benefits of certain actions may be substantially different at HHS than at the radio components company.

For example, perhaps the cost of being late for work is less in Erin's new job at HHS than at her old job. In her job at the radio components company, she had to work overtime if she came in late; in her new job, her boss doesn't say anything when she comes in late. We predict that Erin is more likely to be late in her new job than she was in her old one. She is simply responding to costs and benefits as they exist in her new work environment.

Question:

Some people talk as if government is made up exclusively of good and giving people, who have nothing but the public good in mind. Other people talk as if government is made up exclusively of bad and grabbing people, who have nothing but their own welfare at stake. Are public choice theorists saying that both are caricatures of the real people who work in government?

Answer:

Yes, they are. As one of the first public choice theorists, James Buchanan, has said: "If men should cease and desist from their talk about and their search for evil men [and his sentiments include "purely good men," too] and commence to look instead at the institutions manned by ordinary people, wide avenues for genuine social reform might appear."[1]

THE POLITICAL MARKET

Economists who do positive economics want to understand the world they live in. This means not only understanding such things as the production and pricing of

[1]James Buchanan, *The Limits of Liberty, between Anarchy and Leviathan* (Chicago: University of Chicago Press, 1975), p. 149. An interview with Buchanan appears near the end of this chapter.

goods, unemployment, inflation, and the firm but also understanding political outcomes and political behavior. This section is an introduction to the political market.

Moving Toward the Middle: The Median Voter Model

I never lied to you, I always been cool
I want to be elected.
I got to get the votes, I talk about schools
I want to be elected.
Elected
Elected
I want to be elected . . .

—From the song *Elected,* by Alice Cooper

During political elections, voters often complain that the candidates for office are "too much alike." Some find this frustrating; they say they would prefer to have more choice.

As Exhibit 34–1 illustrates, two candidates running for the same office often sound alike because of the competition for votes: (a), (b), and (c) show a distribution of voters. The political spectrum goes from the "Far Left" to the "Far Right," and it should be noted that (relatively) few voters hold positions in either of these two extreme wings.

In addition, we assume that voters will vote for the candidate who comes closest to matching their own ideological or political views. The person whose views are in the Far Left of the political spectrum will vote for the candidate closest to the Far Left, and so on.

Our election process begins with two candidates, a Democrat and a Republican, occupying the positions D_1 and R_1 in (a), respectively. If the election were held today, the Republican would receive more votes than his Democratic opponent.

EXHIBIT 34–1
The Move toward the Middle

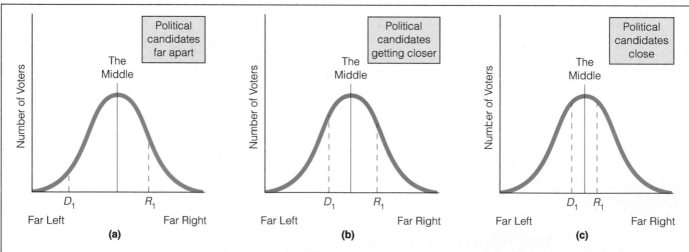

Here we see the tendency for political candidates to move toward the middle of the political spectrum. Starting with (a), the Republican receives more votes than the Democrat and would win the election if it were held today. To offset this (b), the Democrat moves inward toward the middle of the political spectrum. The Republican tries to offset the Democrat's movement inward by moving inward himself. As a result, both candidates move closer to each other over time toward the political middle (c).

724

The Republican would receive all the votes of the voters who position themselves to the right of R_1, the Democrat would receive all the votes of the voters who position themselves to the left of D_1, and the voters between R_1 and D_1 would be split down the middle between the two candidates. The Republican would receive more votes than the Democrat.

If, however, the election were not held today, the Democrat would likely notice (through polls and the like) that her opponent was doing better than she, and to offset this she would move toward the center, or middle, of the political spectrum to pick up some votes; (b) illustrates this move by the Democrat. Relative to her position in (a), the Democrat is closer to the middle of the political spectrum, and as a result she picks up votes. Voters to the left of D_2 vote for the Democrat, voters to the right of R_2 vote for the Republican, and the voters between the two positions split their votes equally between the two candidates. If the election were held now, the Democrat would win the election.

In (c) each candidate, in an attempt to get more votes than his or her opponent, moves toward the middle of the political spectrum. At election time, the likely position of the two candidates is *side by side at the political center or middle.* Notice that in (c) both candidates have become middle-of-the-roaders in their attempt to pick up votes. This tendency to move to a position at the center of the distribution—captured in the **median voter model**—is what causes many voters to complain that there is not much difference between the candidates for political office.

What Does the Theory Predict?

The theory we have just presented explains why politicians running for the same office often sound alike. But what does the theory predict? Here are a few of its predictions:

1. Candidates will label their opponents as either "too far right" or "too far left." The candidates know that the one closer to the middle of the political spectrum (in a two-person race) will win more votes and thus the election. As we noted earlier, to accomplish this feat, they will move toward the political middle. At the same time, they will say that their opponent is a member of the political fringe (that is, a person far from the center). A Democrat may argue that his Republican opponent is "too conservative"; a Republican that his Democratic opponent is "too liberal."

2. Candidates will call themselves "middle-of-the-roaders," not right- or left-wingers. In their move toward the political middle, candidates will try to portray themselves as moderates. In their speeches, they will make the point that they represent the majority of voters, that they are practical, not ideological, persons. They will not be likely to refer to themselves as "ultra-liberal" or "ultra-conservative," or as right- or left-wingers, because to do so would send the wrong message to the voters.

3. Candidates will take polls, and if they are not doing well in the polls and their opponent is, they will modify their positions to become more like their opponent. Polls tell candidates who the likely winner of the election will be. A candidate who finds out that she would lose the election (she is down in the polls) is not likely to sit back and do nothing. The candidate will change her positions. Often this means becoming more like the winner of the poll; that is, becoming more like her opponent in the political race (see Exhibit 34–1).

Two candidates running for the same office often sound alike because of the competition for votes.

Median Voter Model
Suggests that politicians in a two-person political race will move towards matching the preferences of the median voter (that is, that person's preferences which are at the center, or in the middle, of the political spectrum).

4. Candidates will speak in general, instead of specific, terms. Voters agree more on *ends* than on the *means* to accomplishing those ends. For example, voters of the left, right, and middle believe that a strong economy is better than a weak economy. They do not all agree on the best way to obtain a strong economy. The person on the right might advocate less government intervention as a way to strengthen the economy, while the person on the left might advocate more government intervention. Most political candidates soon learn that addressing the issues specifically requires them to discuss "means" and that doing so increases the probability they will have an extreme-wing label attached to them.

For example, the candidate who advocates less government intervention in the economy is more likely to be labeled a right-winger than a candidate who simply calls for a stronger national economy without discussing the specific means he would use to bring this about. In the candidate's desire to be perceived as a middle-of-the-roader, he is much more likely to talk about ends, on which voters agree, than about means, on which voters disagree.

THINKING LIKE AN ECONOMIST

The economist thinks about theories, and then tests them. She is not content if a theory—such as the one that says, in a two-person political race candidates will gravitate toward the center of the political distribution—sounds right. The economist asks herself, "If the theory is right, what should I expect to see in the real world? If the theory is wrong, what should I expect to see in the real world?" Such questions direct the economist to look to effects to see whether the theory has explanatory and predictive power. If we actually see the four predictions of the median voter theory occurring in the real world—candidates labeling themselves one way, speaking in general terms, and so on—then we can conclude that the evidence fails to reject the theory. But suppose we see that candidates en masse do not speak in general terms and so on; what then? Then we would know to reject the theory.

VOTERS AND RATIONAL IGNORANCE

The preceding section explained something about the behavior of politicians, especially near or at election time. We turn now to a discussion of voters.

The Costs and Benefits of Voting

Political commentators often remark that the voter turnout for a particular election was low. They might say, "Only 54 percent of the registered voters actually voted." Are voter turnouts low because Americans are apathetic or because they do not care who wins an election? Are they uninterested in political issues? Public choice economists often explain low voter turnouts in terms of the costs and benefits of voting.

Consider Mark Quincy who is thinking about voting in a presidential election. Mark may receive many benefits from voting. He may feel more involved in public affairs, or think that he has met his civic responsibility; he may see himself as more patriotic; he may believe he has a greater right to criticize government if he takes an active part in it. In short, he may benefit from seeing himself as a doer instead of a talker. Ultimately, however, he will weigh these positive benefits against the costs of voting, which include driving to the polls, standing in line,

Simple Majority Voting and Inefficiency: The Case of the Statue in the Public Square

The simple majority decision rule is often used to decide public questions. Most people think this is the fair and democratic way to do things. However, there are instances where a simple majority vote leads to a project being undertaken whose costs are greater than its benefits.

Consider a ten-person community. The names of the individuals in the community are listed in column 1 of Exhibit 34–2. The community is considering whether to purchase a statue (a replica of the Statue of Liberty) to put in the center of the public square. The cost of the statue is $1,000, and the community has previously agreed that if the statue is purchased, the ten individuals will share the cost equally—that is, each will pay $100 in taxes (see column 3).

Column 2 notes the dollar value of the benefits each individual will receive from the statue. For example, Applebaum places a dollar value of $150 on the statue, Browning places a dollar value of $140 on the statue, and so on. Column 4 notes the net benefit (+) or net cost (−) of the statue to each individual. There is a net benefit for an individual if the dollar value he or she places on the statue is greater than the tax (cost) he or she must incur. There is a net cost if the reverse holds true. Finally, column 5 indicates how each of the ten individuals would vote. If an individual believes there is a net benefit to the statue, he or she will vote for it. If

an individual believes there is a net cost to the statue, he or she will vote against it. Six individuals vote for the statue, and four individuals vote against it. The majority rules, and the statue is purchased and placed in the center of the public square.

Notice, though, that the total dollar value of benefits to the community ($812) is less than the total tax cost to the community ($1,000). Using the simple majority decision rule has resulted in a situation where a statue has been purchased although the benefits of the statue to the community are *less* than the costs of the statue to the community.

This outcome should not be shocking once it is understood that the simple majority decision rule does not take into account the intensity of individuals' preferences. No matter how strongly a person feels about the issue, he or she simply registers one vote. For example, even though Emerson places a net benefit of $1 on the statue, and Isley places a net cost of $90 on the statue, each individual has only one vote. There is no way for Isley to register that he does not want the statue more than Emerson wants it.

EXHIBIT 34–2
Simple Majority Voting and Inefficiency
The simple majority decision rule sometimes generates inefficient results. Here the statue is purchased even though the total dollar value of the benefits of the statue is less than the total dollar costs.

(1) Individuals	(2) Dollar Value of Benefits to Individual	(3) Tax Levied on Individual	(4) Net Benefit (+) or Net Cost (−)	(5) Vote for or Against
Applebaum	$150	$ 100	+ $50	For
Browning	140	100	+ 40	For
Carson	130	100	+ 30	For
Davidson	110	100	+ 10	For
Emerson	101	100	+ 1	For
Finley	101	100	+ 1	For
Gunter	50	100	− 50	Against
Harris	10	100	− 90	Against
Isley	10	100	− 90	Against
Janowitz	10	100	− 90	Against
Total	$812	$1,000		

and so on. If, in the end, Mark perceives the benefits of voting as greater than the costs, he will vote.

Suppose Mark believes that he only benefits from voting if his vote will have an impact on the election outcome. In other words, if his vote will make the difference between candidate X winning and candidate Y winning, then Mark sees voting as worthwhile; if not, he sees voting as a waste of time. In that case, it is not likely

Rational Ignorance
The state of not acquiring information because the costs of acquiring the information are greater than the benefits.

that Mark will vote. For example, in a presidential election, where millions of votes are cast, the probability that one voter's vote will affect the election outcome is very small. The truth of the matter is (probably) that with or without Mark's vote, the election outcome will be the same.

The point that public choice economists make is that if many individual voters will only vote if they perceive their vote as making a difference, then it is not likely they will vote because it is not likely that their vote will make a difference. The low turnouts that appear to be a result of voter apathy may instead be a result of cost–benefit calculations.

Rational Ignorance

"Democracy would be better served if only the voters took more of an interest in, and became better informed about, politics and government. They don't know much about the issues." How often have you heard this?

The problem is not that voters are too stupid to learn about the issues. Many persons who know little about politics and government are quite capable of learning about both, *but they choose not to learn.*

But why would many voter-citizens choose to be uninformed about politics and government? The answer is perhaps predictable: because the benefits of becoming informed are often outweighed by the costs of becoming informed. In short, many persons believe that becoming informed is simply not worth the effort; hence, on an individual basis, it makes sense to be uninformed about politics and government, to be in a state of **rational ignorance.**

Look at the case of Shonia Tyler. Shonia has many things she could be doing with her time: She could be reading a good novel, watching a television program, going out with friends. Shonia could also be becoming better informed about the candidates and the issues in the upcoming U.S. Senate race.

There are costs associated with becoming informed, however. If Shonia stays home and reads up on the issues, she can't go out with her friends. If she stays up late to watch a news program, she might be too tired to work efficiently the next day. These costs have to be weighed against the benefits of becoming better informed about the candidates and the issues. For Shonia, as for many people, the benefits aren't likely to be greater than the costs. Many persons see little personal benefit to becoming more knowledgeable about political candidates and issues. As with voting, this may be linked to the small impact any single individual can have in a large-numbers setting.

Question:

Earlier it was said that politicians move toward the middle of the political spectrum to increase the probability that they will win the election. Now it turns out that the voter in the middle of the political spectrum, or any other voter for that matter, isn't likely to be knowledgeable about the issues. Doesn't this imply that politicians are trying to match the political preferences of a group of largely uninformed voters?

Answer:

Yes, it does. Some persons believe this is one of the deficiencies of representative democracy.

SPECIAL-INTEREST GROUPS

■

Special-interest groups are subsets of the general population that hold (usually) intense preferences for or against a particular government service, activity, or policy. Often special-interest groups gain from public policies that may not be in accord with the interests of the general public. In recent decades, they have played a major role in government.

Informational Content and Lobbying Efforts

Basically, the general voter will be uninformed on the issues. The same does not hold for members of a special-interest group. For example, it is likely that teachers will know a lot about government education policies, farmers about government farm policies, and union members about government union policies. On "their" issue, the members of a particular special-interest group will know much more about the issue at hand than will the general voter. The reason for this is simple: The more directly and intensely issues affect them, the greater the incentive of individuals to become informed on the issues.

When we bring together the uninformed general voters and the informed members of a special-interest group, what we often observe is that the special-interest group is able to sway politicians in its direction—even if it means that the general public will be made worse off by such actions (which, of course, is not always the case).

Suppose special-interest group A, composed of 5,000 individuals, favors a policy that will result in the redistribution of $50 million from the general taxpayers to the group. The dollar benefit for each member of the special-interest group is $10,000. Given this substantial dollar amount, it is likely that the members of the special-interest group (1) will have sponsored or proposed the legislation, and (2) will lobby the politicians who will decide the issue.

But will the politicians also hear from the general voter (general taxpayer)? First, the general voter-taxpayer will be less informed on the legislation than the members of the special-interest group, and even if he or she were informed, it would be necessary for each person to calculate the benefits and the costs of lobbying against the proposed legislation. If the legislation passes, the average taxpayer will pay out approximately 50 cents. The benefits of lobbying against the legislation are probably not greater than 50 cents. Therefore, we would reasonably conclude that even if the general taxpayer were informed on the legislation at hand, he or she would not be likely to argue against it. It just wouldn't be worth the time and effort. We predict that special-interest bills have a good chance of being passed in our legislatures.

Question:

Is special-interest legislation necessarily bad legislation? Can't legislation proposed and lobbied for by a special-interest group benefit not only the special-interest (directly) but also the public interest (perhaps indirectly)?

Answer:

Special-interest legislation is not necessarily bad legislation, and certainly it is possible that such legislation can benefit the public interest. What we are saying is simply this: The costs and benefits of being informed on particular issues and of lobbying for and against issues are different for the member of the special-interest group and the member of the general public, and this can make a difference in the type of legislation that will be proposed, passed, and implemented.

Congressional Districts as Special-Interest Groups

Most people do not ordinarily think of congressional districts as special-interest groups. (Special-interest groups are commonly thought to include the ranks of public school teachers, steel manufacturers, automobile manufacturers, farmers, environmentalists, bankers, truck drivers, doctors, and so on). With some issues, however, a particular congressional district may be a special-interest group.

Suppose an air force base is located in one of the congressional districts of Texas. Along comes a Pentagon study that says the air force base is not needed; it advises the Congress of the United States to close it down. The Pentagon study demonstrates that the cost to the taxpayers of keeping the base open is greater than the benefits to the country of maintaining the base.

But closing the air force base would hurt the pocketbooks of the people in the congressional district that houses the base. Their congressional representative knows as much; she also knows that if she can't keep the base open, she isn't as likely to be reelected to office.

Therefore, she speaks to other members of Congress about the proposed closing. In a way, she is a lobbyist for her congressional district. Will the majority of the members of Congress be willing to go along with the Texas representative? If they do, they know that their constituents will be paying more in taxes than the Pentagon has said is necessary to assure the national security of the country. But if they don't, when they need a vote on one of their own special-interest (sometimes the word *pork barrel* is used) projects, the representative from Texas may not be forthcoming. In short, members of Congress sometimes trade votes: my vote on your air force base for your vote on subsidies to dairy farmers in my district.[2] This type of vote trading—the exchange of votes to gain support for legislation—is commonly referred to as **logrolling**.

Logrolling
The exchange of votes to gain support for legislation.

Public-Interest Talk, Special-Interest Legislation

Special-interest legislation usually isn't called by that name by the special-interest group lobbying for it. Instead, it is said to be legislation "in the best interest of the general public." A number of examples, both past and present, come to mind.

In the early nineteenth century, the British Parliament passed the Factory Acts, which put restrictions on women and children working. Those who lobbied for the restrictions said they did so for humanitarian reasons; for example, to protect young children and women from difficult and hazardous work in the cotton mills. There is evidence, however, that male workers in the factories were the main lobbyists for the Factory Acts and that a reduced supply of women and children directly benefited them by raising wages. The male factory workers appealed to individuals' higher sensibilities instead of letting it be known that they would benefit at the expense of others.

[2]Congressman Leon Panetta of California, speaking of the ways of Congress, said: "There is an unwritten rule around here. If I go to a member for help, at some point down the road they'll remember." *Wall Street Journal,* May 13, 1988, p. 18R.

A Simple Quiz You Are Likely to Fail (but That's Not Bad)

Rational ignorance is usually easier to see in others than in ourselves. We understand that most people are not well informed on politics and government, but we often fail to put ourselves into the same category, even when we deserve to be there. We can take a giant leap forward in understanding rational ignorance and special-interest legislation if we see ourselves more clearly. With this in mind, try to answer the following ten questions about politics or government.

1. What is the name of your most recently elected U.S. senator, and what party does he or she belong to?

2. How has your congressional representative voted in any of the last 20 votes in Congress?

3. What is the approximate dollar amount of federal government spending? What is the approximate dollar amount of federal government tax revenues?

4. Which political party controls the House of Representatives?

5. What is the name of your representative in the state legislature?

6. Name just one special-interest group and note how much it received in federal monies (within a broad range) in the last federal budget.

7. Explain what was at issue in the most recent local political controversy that did not have to do with someone's personality or personal life.

8. Approximately how many persons sit in your state's legislature?

9. What political positions (if any) did the governor of your state hold before becoming governor?

10. In what month and year will the next congressional elections in your state be held?

If you know the answers to only a few of the questions, then consider yourself rationally ignorant about politics and government. This is what we would expect.

Now ask yourself if you don't know the answers to the questions because they are too hard (and almost impossible) to answer or because you have not been interested in answering such questions.

Finally, ask yourself if you will now take the time to find the answers to the questions you couldn't answer. If you do not know the answer to question 6, are you going to take the time to find the answer? We think not. If we're right, then you should now understand—on a personal level—what rational ignorance is all about.

Today, those interests calling for, say, economic protection from foreign competitors or greater federal subsidies rarely explain that they favor this measure because it will make them better off while someone else foots the bill. Instead, they usually voice the public-interest argument. Economic protectionism isn't necessary to protect industry X, it is necessary to protect American jobs and the domestic economy. The special-interest message often is "Help yourself by helping us."

Sometimes this message holds true, and sometimes it does not. But it is likely to be as forcefully voiced in the latter case as in the former.

GOVERNMENT BUREAUCRACY

A discussion of politics and government is not complete without mention of the government bureau and bureaucrat. A **government bureaucrat** is an unelected person who works in a government bureau and is assigned a special task that relates to a law or program passed by the legislature.

Government Bureaucrat
An unelected person who works in a government bureau and is assigned a special task that relates to a law or program passed by the legislature.

731

Government Bureaus: Some Facts and Their Consequences

Consider a few facts about government bureaus:

1. A government bureau receives its funding from the legislature. Often its funding in future years depends on how much it spends carrying out its specified duties in the current year.

2. A government bureau does not maximize profits.

3. There are no transferable ownership rights in a government bureau. There are no stockholders in a government bureau.

4. Many government bureaus provide services for which there is no competition. For example, if a person wants a driver's license, there is usually only one place to go, the Department of Motor Vehicles.

5. If the legislation that established the government bureau in the first place is repealed, there is little need for the government bureau.

These five facts about government bureaus have several consequences. Many economists see these as follows:

1. Government bureaus are not likely to end the current year with surplus funds. If they do, then funding for the following year is likely to be less than it was for the current year. The motto is "spend the money, or lose it."

2. Since a government bureau does not attempt to maximize profits the way a private firm would, it does not watch its costs as carefully. Combining points 1 and 2, we conclude that government bureau costs are likely to remain constant or rise, but are not likely to fall.

3. No one has a monetary incentive to watch over the government bureau because no one "owns" the government bureau, and no one can sell an "ownership right" in the bureau. Stockholders in private firms have a monetary incentive to ensure that the managers of the firms do an efficient job. Since there is no analog to stockholders in a government bureau, there is no one to ensure that the bureau managers operate the bureau efficiently.

4. Government bureaus and bureaucrats are not as likely to try to please the "customer" as private firms because (in most cases) they have no competition and are not threatened by any in the future. If the lines are long in the Department of Motor Vehicles, this is just too bad. Customers have no place else to go to get what they need.

5. Government bureaucrats are likely to lobby for the continued existence and expansion of the programs they administer. To behave differently would go against their own best interests. To argue for the repeal of a program, for example, is to argue for the abolition of their jobs.

Question:

This description makes it sound as if government bureaucrats are petty, selfish people. Aren't many government bureaucrats nice, considerate people who work hard at their jobs?

Answer:

The point is *not* that government bureaucrats are bad people set on taking advantage of the general public, but that ordinary people will behave in certain predictable ways in a government bureau that is funded by the legislature, does not maximize profits, has no analog to private-sector stockholders, has little (if any)

Interview: James Buchanan

James Buchanan won the Nobel Prize in Economics in 1986 for his work in public choice theory. Most economists today view Buchanan and his long-time colleague, Gordon Tullock, as the founders of public choice. Buchanan is currently director of the Center for Study of Public Choice and University Professor at George Mason University in Fairfax, Virginia.

What is public choice theory?

Public choice theory is a body of analysis that explains how political or collective decisions are made. As with all scientific explanation, the analysis is limited in its objective. Public choice theory makes no claim to all-inclusive and comprehensive explanation. The tools and methods of economics are used in application to political decision making.

Please tell us something about the early history of the public choice movement.

For the most part, public choice theory was developed initially by economists, many of whom had worked with questions of public finance. Any analysis of taxing and spending decisions prompts questions concerning how decisions to tax and to spend public monies are made. Hence, economists such as Duncan Black were led to ask how political decisions get made. Black's work on how committees work was an early contribution. Knut Wicksell, even earlier, had recognized that members of legislatures represented differing interests and that the rules of voting were influential in determining political outcomes. Even earlier, many Italian public finance scholars argued for the necessity of developing a model of political decision making.

Black's work on committees and elections, Arrow's work on social choice,

Downs's work on democracy—these were the early contributions in the 1950s. Buchanan and Tullock's work on constitutions in the early 1960s tended to integrate the earlier work, and Buchanan and Tullock were, themselves, the entrepreneurs in establishing the Public Choice Society and in organizing the journal *Public Choice*.

Part of the public choice message is that politicians edge their way to the middle of the political spectrum, voters exhibit rational ignorance, and special-interest groups lobby hard to receive benefits paid for by others. If the message is true, is there any hope for the future? If so, in whom or what does it lie?

Looking forward, it is easy to be pessimistic, since the rent seeking [actions of individuals and groups who spend resources to influence public policy in the hope of transferring income from others to themselves] seems more pervasive than ever. But blatant rent seeking is subject to more and more criticism, and if we look backward for two decades and measure the change in the dialogue about politics, then we can be a bit optimistic.

Twenty-five years ago, when a college student took an economics course, he or she learned nothing about public choice theory because it was still in its infancy. Today, almost every economics principles text devotes a chapter to public choice. How is the college student better off because of this?

The college student who is exposed to any basic public choice theory takes away a more skeptical view of what government and politics can do and will do in response to social and economic problems. The student learns to take on a more realistic and less romantic view of politics and politicians.

You are actively involved in economics research. What questions are you currently trying to answer?

I am now primarily interested in the impact of ethical rules or norms on economic interdependence, and notably on the economic content of the work and saving ethic.

What got you interested in economics?

My own interest was serendipitous. I got a fellowship in economics in 1940, and this determined my career path.

What persons have had the greatest influence on your thinking, and how would you summarize what you learned from each of them?

Frank Knight—a critical spirit, a willingness to challenge anything and everything, no matter by whom asserted. Knut Wicksell—the constitutional emphasis. Rules and institutions matter.

competition, and whose existence depends on the continuance of certain legislation.

A View of Government

The view of government presented in this chapter is perhaps much different from the view presented by your elementary school social studies teacher. He may have described government as made up of people who were kind, charitable, altruistic, generous, and, above all, dedicated to serving the public good. No doubt some will say that the view of government in this chapter is cynical and exaggerated. It may very well be. But remember it is based on a *theory,* and most theories are not descriptively accurate. The real question is whether the theory of public-sector decision making presented here meets the test that any theory must meet: explaining and predicting real-world events. Numerous economists and political scientists have concluded that it does.

Politicians and the Middle

■ In a two-person race, candidates for the same office will gravitate toward the middle of the political spectrum to pick up votes. If a candidate does not do this, and his opponent does, the opponent will win the election. Candidates do a number of things around election time that indicate they understand where they are headed—toward the middle. For example, candidates attempt to label their opponents as either "too far right" or "too far left." Candidates usually pick labels for themselves that represent the middle of the political spectrum, they speak in general terms, and they take polls and adjust their positions accordingly.

Voting and Rational Ignorance

■ There are both costs and benefits to voting. Many potential voters will not vote because the costs of voting—in terms of time spent going to the polls and so on— outweigh the benefits of voting, measured as the probability of their single vote affecting the election outcome.
■ There is a difference between being unable to learn certain information and choosing not to learn certain information. Most voters choose not to be informed on political and governmental matters because the costs of becoming informed outweigh the benefits of becoming informed. They choose to be rationally ignorant.

Special-Interest Groups

■ Special-interest groups are usually well informed on their issue. Individuals have a greater incentive to become informed on issues the more directly and intensely the issue affects them.
■ Legislation that concentrates the benefits on a few and disperses the costs over many is likely to pass since the beneficiaries will have an incentive to lobby for it, whereas those who pay the bill will not lobby against it because each of them pays such a small part of the bill.

Bureaucrats

■ Public choice economists do not believe that government bureaucrats are bad people set on taking advantage of the general public. They believe that they are ordinary people (just like our friends and neighbors) who behave in predictable ways in a government bureau that is funded by the legislature, does not maximize profits, has no analog to private-sector stockholders, has little (if any) competition, and whose existence depends on the continuance of certain legislation.

Key Terms and Concepts

Public Choice	Special-Interest Groups	Government Bureaucrat
Rational Ignorance	Logrolling	

QUESTIONS AND PROBLEMS

1. Some observers maintain that not all politicians move toward the middle of the political spectrum to obtain votes. They often cite Barry Goldwater in the 1964 presidential election and George McGovern in the 1972 presidential election as examples. Are these exceptions to the theory developed in this chapter?

2. Would voters have a greater incentive to vote in an election in which there were only a few registered voters or many registered voters? Why?

3. Many individuals learn more about the car they are thinking of buying than about the candidates running for the presidency of the United States. Explain why.

4. If the model of politics and government presented in this chapter is true, what are some of the things we would expect to see?

5. It has often been remarked that Democratic candidates are more liberal in the Democratic primaries and Republican candidates are more conservative in the Republican primaries than either is in the general election, respectively. Explain why.

6. What are some ways of reducing the cost of voting to voters?

7. What are some ways of making government bureaucrats and bureaus more cost conscious?

8. Some individuals see national defense spending as benefiting the special interests—in particular, the defense industry. Others see it as directly benefiting not only the defense industry but the general public as well. Does this same difference in view exist for issues other than national defense? Name a few.

9. Evaluate each of the following proposals for reform in terms of the model presented in this chapter: (a) linking all spending programs to a visible tax hike; (b) a balanced budget amendment that stipulates that the Congress cannot spend more than total tax revenues; (c) a budgetary referenda process whereby the voters actually vote on the distribution of federal dollars to the different categories of spending (X percentage to agriculture, Y percentage to national defense, and so on), instead of the elected representatives deciding.

THE WORLD ECONOMY

PART

X

INTERNATIONAL ECONOMICS: THEORY AND POLICY

CHAPTER 35

INTERNATIONAL TRADE

WHAT THIS CHAPTER IS ABOUT

Economics is about trade, and trade crosses boundaries. People do not trade exclusively with people who live in their city, state, or nation. They trade with people in other countries, too (a person in Denver, Colorado, may step into a department store and purchase a Sony television set made in Japan). This chapter examines international trade and the prohibitions that are sometimes placed on it.

The reasons why we have international trade are the same as why we have any trade: individuals trade to make themselves better off.

In this section, we discuss some of the facts and figures of international trade, especially as they relate to the United States. We also introduce the important *law of comparative advantage.*

What Does the United States Export and Import?

In 1990, major U.S. exports included automobiles, computers, aircraft, corn, wheat, soybeans, scientific instruments, coal, and plastic materials. Its major imports included petroleum, automobiles, clothing, iron and steel, office machines, footwear, fish, coffee, and diamonds. Exhibit 35–1 shows the percentage breakdowns for broad categories of U.S. exports and imports for 1990.

Why Do People in Different Countries Trade with One Another?

The reasons why we have international trade are the same as why we have any trade, at any level. Individuals trade to make themselves better off. Pat and Zach, both of whom live in St. Paul, Minnesota, trade because they both value something the other has more than they value some of their own possessions. On an international scale, Elaine in the United States trades with Cho in China because Cho has something that Elaine wants.

Obviously, different countries have different terrain, climate, resources, skills, and so on. It follows that some countries will be able to produce some goods that other countries cannot produce or can produce only at extremely high costs.

EXHIBIT 35–1
U.S. Exports and Imports, 1990
SOURCE: Council of Economic Advisers, *Economic Report of the President, 1991* (Washington, D.C.: U.S. Government Printing Office, 1991).

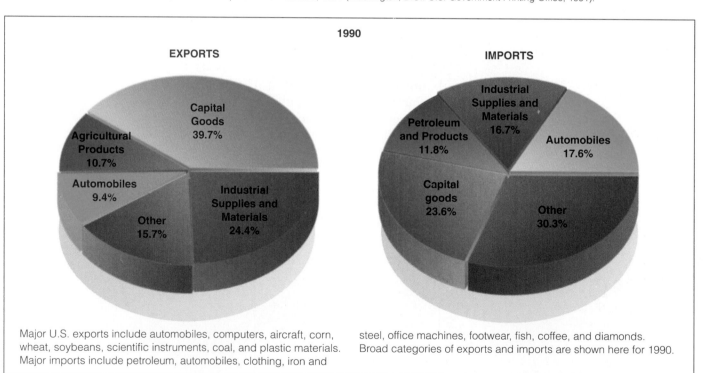

Major U.S. exports include automobiles, computers, aircraft, corn, wheat, soybeans, scientific instruments, coal, and plastic materials. Major imports include petroleum, automobiles, clothing, iron and steel, office machines, footwear, fish, coffee, and diamonds. Broad categories of exports and imports are shown here for 1990.

For example, Hong Kong has no oil, Saudia Arabia has a large supply. Bananas do not grow easily in the United States, but they flourish in Honduras. Americans could grow bananas, if they used hothouses, but it is cheaper for Americans to buy bananas from Hondurans than to produce bananas themselves.

How Do Countries Know What to Trade?

To explain how countries know what to trade, we need to discuss the concepts of *absolute advantage* and *comparative advantage.* Here is a simple model.

Absolute Advantage. Assume a two country–two good world. The countries are the United States and Japan, and the goods are food and clothing. Both countries can produce the two goods in the four different combinations listed in Exhibit 35–2. For example, with a given amount of resources, the United States can produce 90 units of food and 0 units of clothing, or 60 units of food and 10 units of clothing, and so on. With the same amount of resources used in the United States, Japan can produce 60 units of food and 0 units of clothing, and so on. Plotting the different combinations of the two goods each country can produce gives us the production possibilities frontiers in Exhibit 35–2.[1]

Notice that using the same amount of resources, the United States can produce more of one good (food) than Japan can, but Japan can produce more of another good (clothing) than the United States can. For example, using the same quantity of resources, the United States can produce 90 units of food whereas Japan can produce only 60 units, but Japan can produce 60 units of clothing whereas the United States can produce only 30 units. Economists would say that the United States has an **absolute advantage** in the production of food and Japan has an absolute advantage in the production of clothing.

A country has an absolute advantage in the production of a good if, using the same amount of resources as another country, it can produce more of a particular good. To put it differently, a country has an absolute advantage in the production of a good if, with fewer resources, it can produce the same amount of a good as another country.

Suppose now that the United States is producing and consuming the two goods in the combination represented by point *B* on its production possibilities frontier, and Japan is producing and consuming the two goods in the combination represented by point *C'* on its production possibilities frontier. The United States is producing and consuming 60 units of food and 10 units of clothing, and Japan is producing and consuming 20 units of food and 40 units of clothing. We refer to this as the *no specialization–no trade (NS–NT)* case (column 1 in Exhibit 35–3).

Now suppose the two countries decide to specialize and trade. We call this the *specialization–trade (S–T)* case. The United States specializes in the production of food, producing 90 units, and Japan specializes in the production of clothing, producing 60 units. In short, the United States moves to point *A* on its production possibilities frontier, and Japan moves to point *D'* on its production possibilities frontier (column 2 in Exhibit 35–3).

After they have specialized in production, the two countries must settle on the terms of trade; that is, how much food will trade for how much clothing. The United States faces the following situation: For every 30 units of food it does not

Absolute Advantage
The situation where a country can produce more of a good than another country can produce with the same quantity of resources.

[1]Notice that these are straight-line production possibilities frontiers, not curved ones. A straight-line production possibilities frontier indicates that resources can be transferred from the production of one good into another at *constant* opportunity cost. For a review, see Chapter 2.

EXHIBIT 35–2
Production Possibilities in Two Countries

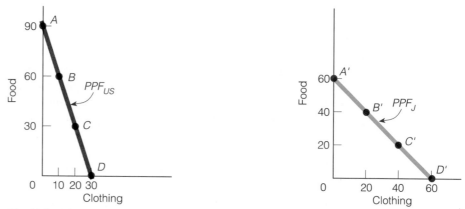

UNITED STATES			JAPAN		
Points on Production Possibilities Frontier	Food	Clothing	Points on Production Possibilities Frontier	Food	Clothing
A	90	0	A'	60	0
B	60	10	B'	40	20
C	30	20	C'	20	40
D	0	30	D'	0	60

The United States has an absolute advantage in the production of food; Japan has an absolute advantage in the production of clothing. Initially, the United States produces at point B on its production possibilities frontier, and Japan produces at point C' on its production possibilities frontier. If the United States specializes in food production, and Japan in clothing production, and the United States trades 20 units of food to Japan for 10 units of clothing, both countries will be made better off.

produce, it can produce 10 units of clothing (see Exhibit 35–2). Thus, 3 units of food come at an opportunity cost of 1 unit of clothing ($3F = 1C$), or 1 unit of food comes at a cost of 1/3 unit of clothing ($1F = 1/3C$). Meanwhile, Japan faces the following situation: For every 20 units of food it does not produce, it can produce 20 units of clothing. Thus, 1 unit of food comes at an opportunity cost of 1 unit of clothing ($1F = 1C$). Recapping, for the United States $3F = 1C$, and for Japan $1F = 1C$.

With these cost ratios, it would seem likely that both countries could agree on terms of trade that specify $2F$ for $1C$. The United States would prefer to give up 2 units of food instead of 3 units for 1 unit of clothing, whereas Japan would prefer to give up 1 unit of clothing and get 2 units of food instead of only 1. Suppose the two countries agree to the terms of trade of $2F = 1C$ and trade, in absolute amounts, 20 units of food for 10 units of clothing (column 3 in Exhibit 35–3).

Now the United States produces 90 units of food and trades (exports) 20 units to Japan, for which it receives in exchange (imports) 10 units of clothing. Thus, the United States consumes 10 units of clothing (received in trade from Japan)

EXHIBIT 35-3

Comparing the No Specialization–To Trade Case with the Specialization–Trade Case

	NO SPECIALIZATION– NO TRADE CASE (NS–NT)		SPECIALIZATION–TRADE CASE (S–T)				
Country	(1) Production and Consumption in the NS–NT Case		(2) Production in the S–T Case	(3) Exports (−) Imports (+) Terms of Trade are 2F = 1C	(4) Consumption in the S–T Case (2) + (3)	(5) Gains from Specialization and Trade (4) − (1)
UNITED STATES						
Food	60	Point B in	90	Point A in	− 20	70	10
Clothing	10	Exhibit 35–2	0	Exhibit 35–2	+ 10	10	0
JAPAN						
Food	20	Point C' in	0	Point D' in	+ 20	20	0
Clothing	40	Exhibit 35–2	60	Exhibit 35–2	− 10	50	10

Column 1: Both the United States and Japan operate independently of each other. The United States produces and consumes 60 units of food and 10 units of clothing. Japan produces and consumes 20 units of food and 40 units of clothing.

Column 2: The United States specializes in the production of food; Japan specializes in the production of clothing.

Column 3: The United States and Japan agree to the terms of trade of 2 units of food for 1 unit of clothing. They actually trade 20 units of food for 10 units of clothing.

Column 4: Overall, the United States consumes 70 units of food and 10 units of clothing. Japan consumes 20 units of food and 50 units of clothing.

Column 5: Consumption levels are higher for both the United States and Japan in the S–T case than in the NS–NT case.

plus 70 units of food it has left over (recall that it produced 90 units and only traded away 20 units). (Column 4 in Exhibit 35–3 shows the situation for the United States.)

Now Japan produces 60 units of clothing and trades (exports) 10 units to the United States, and receives in exchange (imports) 20 units of food. Thus, Japan consumes 20 units of food (received in trade from the United States) plus 50 units of clothing it has left over (it only traded away 10 of the 60 units of clothing it produced). (Column 4 in Exhibit 35–3 shows the situation for Japan.)

Comparing the consumption levels of both countries in the no specialization–no trade case with the specialization–trade case, we find that both countries consume more in the specialization–trade case. The United States consumes 10 more units of food and no less clothing; Japan consumes 10 more units of clothing and no less food. Both countries have made themselves better off through specialization and trade.

Question:

In the example, both countries had an absolute advantage in the production of one good. Isn't this why they both benefited from specialization and trade? Would both have benefited if one country, say, the United States, had had an absolute advantage in the production of both goods?

Answer:

Yes, they would. Even if the United States had had an absolute advantage in the production of both goods, it could still have gained through specialization and trade. The classical economist David Ricardo pointed this out in the early nineteenth century. The discussion of *comparative advantage* in the next section explains this point further.

CHAPTER 35
INTERNATIONAL TRADE

■

745

Comparative Advantage. Notice in Exhibit 35–4 that the United States is better than Japan at producing both food and clothing; it has an absolute advantage in the production of both goods. Now look at Exhibit 35–5, which shows that even under such conditions, both countries can gain from specialization and trade. Suppose, first, the two countries are not specializing or trading. The United States is producing and consuming the combination of the two goods represented by point *B* on its production possibilities frontier, and Japan is producing and consuming the combination of the two goods represented by point *B'* on its production possibilities frontier (column 1).

Now suppose the two countries decide to specialize and trade. Since the United States is better than Japan in the production of both goods, which good does the United States specialize in? Similarly, which good does Japan specialize in since it is not as efficient as the United States in the production of either good? The general answer to both questions is the same: *Countries specialize in the production of the good in which they have a* **comparative advantage.** A country has a comparative advantage in the production of a good when it can produce the good at lower opportunity cost than another country.

Comparative Advantage
The situation where a country can produce a good at lower opportunity cost than another country.

EXHIBIT 35–4
Production Possibilities in Two Countries

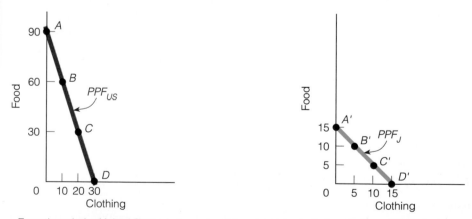

UNITED STATES			JAPAN		
Points on Production Possibilities Frontier	Food	Clothing	Points on Production Possibilities Frontier	Food	Clothing
A	90	0	A'	15	0
B	60	10	B'	10	5
C	30	20	C'	5	10
D	0	30	D'	0	15

Even though the United States has an absolute advantage in the production of both goods, both countries can be made better off by specializing in and trading the good in which each has a comparative advantage. Gains from specialization and trade depend on comparative advantage, not absolute advantage.

EXHIBIT 35–5
Even If One Country Has an Absolute Advantage in Both Goods, Both Countries Can Gain from Specialization and Trade

	NO SPECIALIZATION–NO TRADE CASE (NS–NT)		SPECIALIZATION–TRADE CASE (S–T)			
Country		(1) Production and Consumption in the NS–NT Case	(2) Production in the S–T Case	(3) Exports (−) Imports (+) Terms of Trade are 2F = 1C	(4) Consumption in the S–T Case (2) + (3)	(5) Gains from Specialization and Trade (4) − (1)
UNITED STATES						
Food	60 }	Point B in	90 }	Point A in	−20	70	10
Clothing	10 }	Exhibit 35–4	0 }	Exhibit 35–4	+10	10	0
JAPAN						
Food	10 }	Point B' in	0 }	Point D' in	+20	20	10
Clothing	5 }	Exhibit 35–4	15 }	Exhibit 35–4	−10	5	0

Column 1: Both the United States and Japan operate independently of each other. The United States produces and consumes 60 units of food and 10 units of clothing. Japan produces and consumes 10 units of food and 5 units of clothing.
Column 2: The United States specializes in the production of food; Japan specializes in the production of clothing.
Column 3: The United States and Japan agree to the terms of trade of 2 units of food for 1 unit of clothing. They actually trade 20 units of food for 10 units of clothing.
Column 4: Overall, the United States consumes 70 units of food and 10 units of clothing. Japan consumes 20 units of food and 5 units of clothing.
Column 5: Consumption levels are higher for both the United States and Japan in the S–T case than in the NS–NT case.

For example, in the United States, the opportunity cost of producing 1 unit of clothing is 3 units of food (since for every 10 units of clothing it produces, it forfeits 30 units of food), whereas the opportunity cost of producing 1 unit of food is 1/3 unit of clothing. In Japan, the opportunity cost of producing 1 unit of clothing is 1 unit of food (since for every 5 units of clothing it produces, it forfeits 5 units of food). To recap, in the United States the situation is $1C = 3F$ and $1F = 1/3C$; in Japan the situation is $1C = 1F$ or, turning it around, $1F = 1C$.

We see that the United States can produce food at a lower opportunity cost ($1/3C$ as opposed to $1C$ in Japan), whereas Japan can produce clothing at a lower opportunity cost ($1F$ as opposed to $3F$ in the United States). Thus, the United States has a comparative advantage in food, and Japan has a comparative advantage in clothing.

Suppose the two countries specialize in the production of the good in which they have a comparative advantage (column 2), agree to the terms of trade $2F = 1C$, and trade in absolute amounts 20 units of food for 10 units of clothing (column 3).

Now the United States produces 90 units of food and trades 20 units to Japan, receiving 10 units of clothing in exchange. It consumes 70 units of food and 10 units of clothing (column 4, U.S. entry).

Now Japan produces 15 units of clothing and trades 10 to the United States, receiving 20 units of food in exchange. It consumes 5 units of clothing and 20 units of food (column 4, Japan entry).

Comparing the consumption levels in both countries in the two cases, the United States and Japan each consume 10 more units of food and no less clothing in the specialization–trade case than in the no specialization–no trade case (column 5).

We conclude that even when a country has an *absolute advantage* in the production of both goods (or when a country has an absolute disadvantage in the production of both goods), it stands to gain by specializing in producing and trading the good in which it has a *comparative advantage.*

Question:

Specialization and trade appear to allow a country's inhabitants to consume at a level beyond its production possibilities frontier. Is this correct?

Answer:

Yes, that is correct. To see this, turn back to Exhibit 35–4 and look at the *PPF* for the United States. In the *NS–NT* case, the United States consumes 60 units of food and 10 units of clothing—that is, the United States consumes at point *B* on its *PPF*. In the *S–T* case, however, it consumes 70 units of food and 10 units of clothing. A point that represents this combination of the two goods is outside the country's *PPF*.

How Do Countries Know When They Have a Comparative Advantage?

Government officials of a country do not sit down with piles of cost data before them and determine what their country should specialize in producing and then trade. Countries do not plot production possibilities frontiers on graph paper or calculate opportunity costs. Instead, it is individuals' desire to make a dollar, a franc, or a pound that determines the pattern of international trade; it is the desire to earn a profit that determines what a country specializes in and trades.

Take the case of Geoffrey, an enterprising Englishman who visits the United States. Geoffrey observes that beef is relatively cheap in the United States (compared with the price in England) and tea is relatively expensive. Noticing the price differences for beef and tea between his country and the United States, he decides to buy some tea in England, bring it to the United States, and sell it for the relatively higher U.S. price. With his profits on the tea transaction, he buys beef in the United States, ships it to England, and sells it for the relatively higher English price. It is obvious that what Geoffrey is doing is buying low and selling high; he is buying in the country where the good is cheap and selling it in the country where the good is expensive.

What are the consequences of Geoffrey's activities? First, he is earning a profit. The larger the price differences in the two goods between the two countries, and the more he reshuffles goods between countries, the more profit Geoffrey earns.

Second, Geoffrey's activities are moving each country toward its comparative advantage. The United States ends up exporting beef to England, and England ends up exporting tea to the United States. Just as the pure theory predicts, individuals in the two countries specialize in and trade the good in which they have a comparative advantage. The outcome is brought about spontaneously through the actions of individuals trying to make themselves better off; they are simply trying to gain through trade.

TRADE RESTRICTIONS

■

International trade theory shows that countries gain from free international trade; that is, from specializing in the production of the goods in which they have a comparative advantage and trading these goods for other goods. In the real world, however, there are numerous types of trade restrictions, which raises the question: If countries gain from international trade, why are there trade restrictions? We answer this and related questions in this section.

Why Are There Trade Restrictions in the Real World?

In the previous section, we learned that specialization and international trade benefit individuals in different countries. This occurs *on net.* Every person may not gain. Suppose Pam Dickson lives and works in the United States making clock radios. She produces and sells 12,000 clock radios per year for a price of $40 each. As the situation stands, there is no international trade. Individuals in other countries who make clock radios do not sell their clock radios in the United States.

Then one day things change. The U.S. market is opened up to clock radios from Japan. It appears that the Japanese manufacturers have a comparative advantage in the production of clock radios. They sell their clock radios in the United States for $25 each. Pam realizes that she cannot compete with this price. Her sales fall off to such a degree that she goes out of business. For Pam, personally, the introduction of international trade, *in this one instance,* has harmed her.

This raises the issue of the distributional effects of trade. Using the tools of supply and demand, we concentrate on two groups: U.S. consumers and U.S. producers. But first let's consider consumers' and producers' surplus.

Consumers' and Producers' Surplus

Consumers' surplus is the difference between the price buyers pay for a good and the maximum or highest price they would have paid for the good. It is a dollar measure of the benefit gained by being able to purchase a unit of a good for less than one is willing to pay for it. For example, if Yakov would have paid $10 to see the movie at the Cinemax, but only paid $4, his consumer surplus is $6.

Producers' surplus is the difference between the price sellers receive for a good and the minimum or lowest price for which they would have sold the good. It is a dollar measure of the benefit gained by being able to sell a unit of output for more than one is willing to sell it. For example, if Joan sold her knit sweaters for $14 each, but would have sold them for as low (but no lower) than $4 each, her producer surplus is $10 per sweater. Consumers' surplus is the consumers' net gain from trade, and producers' surplus is the producers' net gain from trade.

Both consumers' and producers' surplus are represented in Exhibit 35-6. In (a), consumers' surplus is the shaded triangle. This triangle is the area under the demand curve and above the equilibrium price out to the equilibrium quantity. Recall that the definition of consumers' surplus is highest price minus price paid. For example, notice in the window in (a) that consumers would have been willing to pay $7 for the 50th unit, but instead paid $5. Thus, the consumers' surplus on the 50th unit of the good is $2. If we add the consumers' surplus on each unit of the good between and including the first and the 100th (100 units being the equilibrium quantity), we obtain the shaded (consumers' surplus) triangle.

In (b), producers' surplus is represented by the shaded triangle. This triangle is the area above the supply curve and under the equilibrium price out to the equilibrium quantity. Keep in mind the definition of producers' surplus—price paid minus lowest price. For example, notice in the window in (b) that suppliers would have sold the 50th unit for as low as $3 but actually sold it for $5. Thus, the producers' surplus on the 50th unit of the good is $2. If we add the producers' surplus on each unit of the good between and including the first and the 100th, we obtain the shaded (producers' surplus) triangle.

Consumers' Surplus
The difference between the price buyers pay for a good and the maximum or highest price they would have paid for the good. It is a dollar measure of the benefit gained by being able to purchase a unit of a good for less than one is willing to pay for it.

Producers' Surplus
The difference between the price sellers receive for a good and the minimum or lowest price for which they would have sold the good. It is a dollar measure of the benefit gained by being able to sell a unit of output for more than one is willing to sell it.

EXHIBIT 35–6
Consumers' and Producers' Surplus

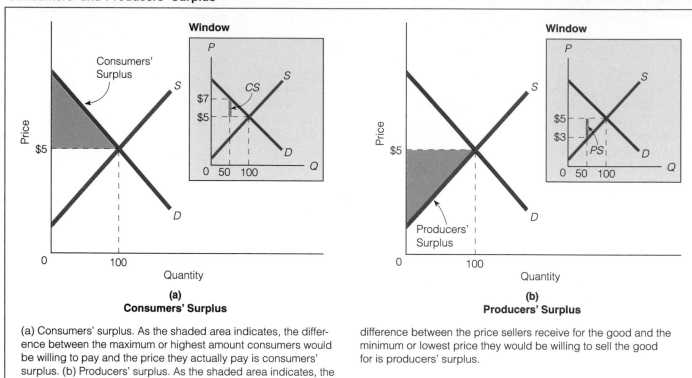

(a)
Consumers' Surplus

(b)
Producers' Surplus

(a) Consumers' surplus. As the shaded area indicates, the difference between the maximum or highest amount consumers would be willing to pay and the price they actually pay is consumers' surplus. (b) Producers' surplus. As the shaded area indicates, the difference between the price sellers receive for the good and the minimum or lowest price they would be willing to sell the good for is producers' surplus.

Exports Permitted and Prohibited

We now consider two cases: one where the U.S. government permits U.S. producers to export goods and one where it does not. Exhibit 35–7a illustrates the world market for wheat. The equilibrium world market price is P_W. At this price, U.S. consumers buy Q_1 amount of wheat in (b), and U.S. producers produce Q_2 amount of wheat. The difference between the two quantities $(Q_2 - Q_1)$ is the amount of wheat U.S. producers export to the rest of the world.

Now suppose exports are prohibited; U.S. producers are no longer allowed to export wheat to the rest of the world. Price is now determined by domestic demand and supply. In the short term, this results in a surplus of wheat in the United States and drives price down. As a result, the price that is relevant to American wheat buyers is P_N in (b). In equilibrium, U.S. consumers buy Q_3 amount of wheat, U.S. producers produce and sell Q_3 amount of wheat, and no U.S. wheat is exported. Now compare the situation for U.S. consumers and producers when exports are permitted and when they are prohibited.

The Effects on U.S. Consumers. If exports are *permitted,* consumers' surplus is represented by the area P_WAB. This is the area under the demand curve and above the world equilibrium price P_W (which is the relevant equilibrium price if exports are permitted).

If exports are *prohibited,* U.S. consumers receive consumers' surplus equal to the area P_NAD. This is the area under the demand curve and above the equilibrium price P_N (which is the relevant equilibrium price if exports are prohibited).

EXHIBIT 35-7
Exports Permitted and Prohibited: The Effects on U.S. Consumers and Producers

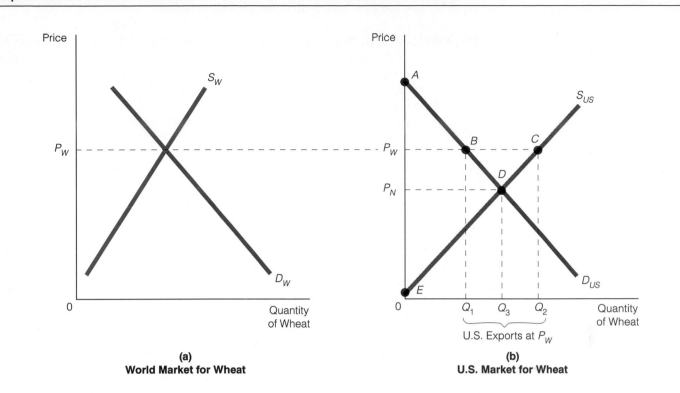

(a)
World Market for Wheat

(b)
U.S. Market for Wheat

U.S. CONSUMERS				U.S. PRODUCERS			
	Consumers' Surplus		Net Gain from Prohibiting Exports		Producers' Surplus		Net Gain from Permitting Exports
EXPORTS PERMITTED	P_WAB		P_WBDP_N	EXPORTS PERMITTED	P_WCE		P_WCDP_N
		Since $P_NAD > P_WAB$, U.S. consumers are better off if exports are prohibited.				Since $P_WCE > P_NDE$, U.S. producers are better off if exports are permitted.	
EXPORTS PROHIBITED	P_NAD			EXPORTS PROHIBITED	P_NDE		

P_WCDP_N is greater than P_WBDP_N by the area BCD. This area represents the net gain of a policy of permitting exports over a policy of prohibiting exports. In short, there are net gains to free trade.

(c)

If exports are permitted, consumers' surplus is P_WAB and producers' surplus is P_WCE. If exports are prohibited, consumers' surplus is P_NAD and producers' surplus is P_NDE. The net gain to consumers of a policy that prohibits exports over a policy that permits exports is P_WBDP_N. The net gain to producers of a policy that permits exports over a policy that prohibits exports is P_WCDP_N. Since $P_WCDP_N > P_WBDP_N$, there is a net gain to free trade represented by the area BCD.

Consumers' surplus is greater when exports are prohibited than when they are permitted: $P_N AD > P_W AB$. U.S. consumers are helped by a policy that prohibits exports; they are hurt by a policy that permits exports.

The Effects on U.S. Producers. If exports are permitted, producers' surplus is $P_W CE$. This is the area above the supply curve and under the world equilibrium price P_W (which is the relevant equilibrium price if exports are permitted).

If exports are prohibited, U.S. producers receive producers' surplus equal to $P_N DE$. This is the area above the supply curve and under the equilibrium price P_N (which is the relevant equilibrium price if exports are prohibited). Producers' surplus is greater if exports are permitted than if they are prohibited: $P_W CE > P_N DE$. U.S. producers are helped by a policy that permits exports; they are hurt by a policy that prohibits exports.

How much better off, on net, are U.S. consumers if exports are prohibited than if they are permitted? The answer is represented by the area $P_W BDP_N$ in (b). Since consumers' surplus is larger when exports are prohibited ($P_N AD$) than when exports are permitted ($P_W AB$), the net gain to consumers of having exports prohibited is the difference between the two consumers' surplus areas, which is $P_W BDP_N$.

How much better off, on net, are U.S. producers if exports are permitted than if they are prohibited? Since producers' surplus is larger when exports are permitted ($P_W CE$) than when they are prohibited ($P_N DE$), the net gain to producers of having exports permitted is the difference between the two producers' surplus areas, which is $P_W CDP_N$. Looking at this area in (b), you will notice that it *includes* the net benefit to consumers of having exports prohibited—that is, area $P_W BDP_N$. This means that the net gain to producers of having exports permitted is greater than the net gain to consumers of having exports prohibited. The former is greater than the latter by the area BCD. *The area BCD represents the net gain of a policy of permitting exports over a policy of prohibiting exports.* In other words, there are net gains to free trade. Exhibit 35–7c summarizes this analysis.

Imports Permitted and Prohibited: The Effects on U.S. Consumers and Producers

The analysis of permitting and prohibiting imports follows the same steps as in the previous section. We begin, as we did before, at the world equilibrium price of P_W (Exhibit 35–8a). At this price for cars, U.S. consumers wish to buy Q_2 cars in (b); Q_1 of these cars will be bought from the U.S. producers of cars, and the difference between Q_2 and Q_1 ($Q_2 - Q_1$) will be bought from the foreign producers of cars. In short, U.S. consumers import $Q_2 - Q_1$ cars. In this case, where imports are permitted, consumers' surplus is represented by the area $P_W AC$, and U.S. producers receive producers' surplus equal to the area $P_W DE$.

Now suppose government passes legislation prohibiting foreign car imports. As a result, price rises to P_N. At this equilibrium price, U.S. consumers buy Q_3 cars and American producers sell Q_3 cars. U.S. consumers receive consumers' surplus equal to the area $P_N AB$, and U.S. producers receive producers' surplus equal to the area $P_N BE$.

Comparing the two situations, we notice that U.S. consumers receive higher consumers' surplus when imports are permitted ($P_W AC > P_N AB$), and U.S. producers receive higher producers' surplus when imports are prohibited ($P_N BE > P_W DE$).

The net gain to U.S. consumers of a policy that permits imports over one that

EXHIBIT 35–8
Imports Permitted and Prohibited: The Effects on U.S. Consumers and Producers

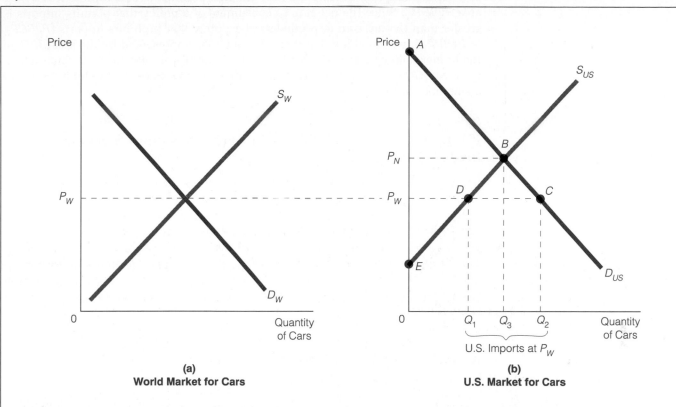

(a)
World Market for Cars

(b)
U.S. Market for Cars

	U.S. CONSUMERS			U.S. PRODUCERS	
	Consumers' Surplus	Net Gain from Permitting Imports		Producers' Surplus	Net Gain from Prohibiting Imports
IMPORTS PERMITTED	P_WAC	P_NBCP_W	IMPORTS PERMITTED	P_WDE	P_NBDP_W
	Since $P_WAC > P_NAB$, U.S. consumers are better off when imports are permitted			Since $P_NBE > P_WDE$, U.S. producers are better off when imports are prohibited.	
IMPORTS PROHIBITED	P_NAB		IMPORTS PROHIBITED	P_NBE	

P_NBCP_W is greater than P_NBDP_W by the area *BCD*. This area represents the net gain of a
policy of permitting imports over a policy of prohibiting imports. In short, there are net gains to free trade.

(c)

If imports are permitted, consumers' surplus is P_WAC and producers' surplus is P_WDE. If imports are prohibited, consumers' surplus is P_NAB and producers' surplus is P_NBE. The net gain to consumers of a policy that permits imports over a policy that prohibits imports is P_NBCP_W. The net gain to producers of a policy that prohibits imports over a policy that permits imports is P_NBDP_W. Since $P_NBCP_W > P_NBDP_W$, there is a net gain to free trade represented by the area *BCD*.

753

prohibits them is represented by the area P_NBCP_W. The net gain to U.S. producers of a policy that prohibits imports over one that permits them is represented by the area P_NBDP_W. Since the net gain to consumers of a policy that permits imports is greater than the net gain to producers of a policy that prohibits imports ($P_NBCP_W > P_NBDP_W$), we conclude that there is a net gain, represented by the area BCD, to the former policy (permits imports) over the latter (prohibits imports). Once again, the area BCD may be viewed as the net gain from free trade. See Exhibit 35–8c for a summary of the analysis.

If Free Trade Results in Net Gain, Why Do Nations Sometimes Restrict Trade?

Based on the preceding analysis, the case for free trade (no prohibitions on exports or imports) appears to be a strong one. The case for free trade has not gone unchallenged, however. Some persons maintain that at certain times, free trade should be restricted or suspended. In almost all cases, they argue that it is in the best interest of the public or country as a whole to do so. In short, they advance a public-interest argument. Other persons contend that the public-interest argument is only superficial; down deep, they say, it is a special-interest argument clothed in pretty words. As you might guess, the debate between the two groups is often heated.

Arguments for Trade Restrictions

Here are some arguments that have been advanced for trade restrictions.

The National-Defense Argument.   It is often stated that certain industries—such as aircraft, petroleum, chemicals, and weapons—are necessary to the national defense. Suppose the United States has a comparative advantage in the production of wheat and the Soviet Union has a comparative advantage in the production of weapons. Should the United States specialize in the production of wheat, and then trade wheat to the Soviet Union in exchange for weapons? Many Americans would answer no. It is too dangerous, they maintain, to leave weapons productions to another country—whether that country is the Soviet Union, or England, or Canada.

The national-defense argument may have some validity. But even valid arguments may be abused. Industries that are not really necessary to the national defense may maintain otherwise. In the past, the national-defense argument has been used by some firms in the following industries: pens, pottery, peanuts, papers, candles, thumbtacks, tuna fishing, and pencils.

The Infant-Industry Argument.   Alexander Hamilton, the first U.S. secretary of the treasury, argued that "infant" or new industries often need to be protected from older, established foreign competitors until they are mature enough to compete on an equal basis. Today, some persons voice the same argument. The infant-industry argument is clearly an argument for temporary protection. Critics charge, however, that once an industry is protected from foreign competition, removing the protection is almost impossible; the once infant industry will continue to maintain that it isn't old enough to go it alone. Critics of the infant-industry argument say that political realities make it unlikely that a benefit once bestowed will be removed.

Finally, the infant-industry argument, like the national-defense argument, may be abused. It may well be that all new industries, whether they could currently compete successfully with foreign producers or not, would argue for protection on infant-industry grounds.

The Antidumping Argument. Dumping is the sale of goods abroad at a price below their cost and below the price charged in the domestic market. If a French firm sells wine in the United States for a price below the cost of producing the wine and below the price charged in France, it is said to be *dumping* wine in the United States. Critics of dumping maintain that it is an unfair trade practice that puts domestic producers of substitute goods at a disadvantage. In addition, they charge that dumpers seek only to penetrate a market, drive out domestic competitors, and then raise prices. However, some economists point to the infeasibility of this strategy. Once the dumpers have driven out their competition and raised prices, their competition is likely to return. The dumpers, in turn, would have obtained only a string of losses (owing to their selling below cost) for their efforts. Second, opponents of the antidumping argument point out that domestic consumers benefit from dumping. They end up paying lower prices.

Dumping
The sale of goods abroad at a price below their cost and below the price charged in the domestic markets.

The Foreign-Export-Subsidies Argument.   Some governments subsidize the firms that export goods. If a country offers a below-market (interest rate) loan to a company, it is often argued that the government subsidizes the production of the good the firm produces. If, in turn, that firm exports the good to a foreign country, domestic producers of substitute goods call foul. They complain that the foreign firm has been given an unfair advantage that they should be protected against.[2] Others say that one should not turn one's back on a gift (in the form of lower prices). If foreign governments want to subsidize their exports, and thus give a gift to foreign consumers at the expense of their own taxpayers, then the recipients should not complain. Of course, the recipients are usually not the ones who are complaining. Usually, the ones complaining are the domestic producers who can't sell their goods at as high a price because of the gift domestic consumers are receiving from foreign governments.

The Low-Foreign-Wages Argument.   It is sometimes argued that American producers can't compete with foreign producers because American producers pay high wages to their workers, and foreign producers pay low wages to their workers. The American producers insist that free trade must be restricted or they will be ruined. What the argument overlooks is the reason American wages are high and foreign wages are low in the first place. In a word, the reason is productivity. High productivity and high wages are usually linked, as are low productivity and low wages. If an American worker, who receives $20 per hour, can produce (on average) 100 units of X per hour, working with numerous capital goods, the cost per unit may be lower than in the case of a foreign worker, who receives $2 per hour, but produces (on average) 5 units of X per hour, working by hand. In short, a country's high-wage disadvantage may be offset by its productivity advantage; a country's low-wage advantage may be offset by its productivity disadvantage. High wages do not necessarily mean high costs once productivity (and the costs of non-labor resources) are factored in.

[2]Words are important in this debate. For example, domestic producers who claim that foreign governments have subsidized foreign firms say that they are not asking for economic *protectionism*, but only for *retaliation*, or *reciprocity*, or simply *tit-for-tat*—words that have less negative connotation than the words their opponents use.

The Saving-Domestic-Jobs Argument. Sometimes the argument against completely free trade is made in terms of saving domestic jobs. Actually, we have already discussed this argument in its different guises. For example, the low-foreign-wages argument is one form of it. That argument continues along this line: If domestic producers cannot compete with foreign producers because foreign producers pay low wages and domestic producers pay high wages, domestic producers will go out of business and domestic jobs will be lost. The foreign-export-subsidies argument is another. Its proponents generally state that if foreign-government subsidies give a competitive edge to foreign producers, not only will domestic producers fail but as a result of their failure, domestic jobs will also be lost. The low-foreign-wages and foreign-export-subsidies arguments are also applied to the saving-domestic-jobs argument (so we will not repeat them here). In addition, critics of the saving-domestic-jobs argument (in all its guises) often argue that if a domestic producer is being outcompeted by foreign producers, and domestic jobs in a particular industry are being lost as a result, the world market is signaling that those labor resources could be put to better use in an industry in which the country holds a comparative advantage.

How Is Trade Restricted?

There are numerous ways to restrict free trade. Tariffs and quotas are two of the more commonly used methods.

Tariff
A tax on imports.

Tariffs. A **tariff** is a tax on imports. The primary effect of a tariff is to raise the price of the imported good to the domestic consumer. Exhibit 35–9 illustrates the effects of a tariff.

EXHIBIT 35–9
The Effects of a Tariff

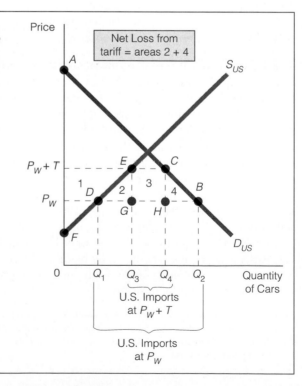

A tariff raises the price of cars from P_W to $P_W + T$, decreases consumers' surplus by areas $1 + 2 + 3 + 4$, increases producers' surplus by area 1, and generates tariff revenues collected by government equal to area 3. Since consumers lose more than producers and government gain, a net loss results from a tariff.

The world price for cars is P_W. At this price, U.S. consumers are buying Q_2 cars: Q_1 from U.S. producers and the difference between Q_2 and Q_1 ($Q_2 - Q_1$) from foreign producers. In other words, U.S. imports at P_W are $Q_2 - Q_1$. In this situation, consumers' surplus is $P_W AB$ and producers' surplus is $P_W DF$.

Now suppose a tariff is imposed. The new price for imported cars in the U.S. car market rises to $P_W + T$ (the world price plus the tariff). At this price, U.S. consumers buy Q_4 number of cars: Q_3 from U.S. producers of cars and $Q_4 - Q_3$ from foreign producers. U.S. imports are $Q_4 - Q_3$, which is a smaller number of imports than at the pretariff price. An effect of tariffs, then, is to reduce imports. At the price $P_W + T$, consumers' surplus is $(P_W + T)AC$, and producers' surplus is $(P_W + T)EF$.

Because of the tariff, consumers' surplus is reduced by an amount equal to the areas 1 + 2 + 3 + 4, and producers' surplus is increased by an amount equal to area 1. The government collects tariff revenues equal to area 3. This area is obtained by multiplying the number of imports ($Q_4 - Q_3$) times the tariff itself, which is the difference between $P_W + T$ and P_W ($P_W + T - P_W = T$).

In conclusion, the effects of the tariff are a decrease in consumers' surplus, an increase in producers' surplus, and tariff revenues for government. Since the loss to consumers (areas 1 + 2 + 3 + 4) is greater than the gain to producers (area 1) plus the gain to government (area 3), it follows that a net loss results from a tariff. This is the other side of the coin that reads "There is a net gain to free trade."

Quotas. A **quota** is a legal limit on the amount of a good that may be imported. For example, the government may decide to allow no more than 100,000 foreign cars to be imported, or 10 million barrels of OPEC oil, or 30,000 Japanese television sets. A quota, reduces the supply of a good and raises the price of imported goods to domestic consumers (Exhibit 35–10).

Quota
A legal limit on the amount of a good that may be imported.

EXHIBIT 35–10
The Effects Of a Quota

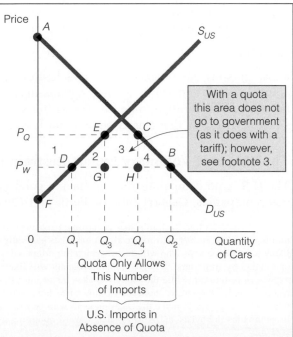

A quota that sets the legal limit of imports at $Q_4 - Q_3$ causes the price of cars to increase from P_W to P_Q. As a result, consumers' surplus decreases by the areas 1 + 2 + 3 + 4, producers' surplus increases by area 1, and importers receive higher total revenues on imports $Q_4 - Q_3$, or area 3. Since consumers lose more than producers and importers gain, a net loss results from a quota.

With a quota this area does not go to government (as it does with a tariff); however, see footnote 3.

Quota Only Allows This Number of Imports

U.S. Imports in Absence of Quota

Once again, consider the situation in the U.S. car market. At a price of P_W U.S. consumers buy Q_1 cars from U.S. car producers and import $Q_2 - Q_1$ from foreign car producers. Consumers' surplus is $P_W AB$ (as it was in the tariff example) and producers' surplus is $P_W DF$. Suppose now that the U.S. government sets a quota equal to $Q_4 - Q_3$. Since this is the number of foreign cars U.S. consumers imported when the tariff was imposed (see Exhibit 35–9), the new price of cars rises to P_Q in Exhibit 35–10 (which is equal to $P_W + T$ in Exhibit 35–9). At P_Q, consumers' surplus is $P_Q AC$ and producers' surplus is $P_Q EF$. The decrease in consumers' surplus due to the quota is equal to the areas $1 + 2 + 3 + 4$; the increase in producers' surplus is equal to area 1.

But what about area 3? Is this area transferred to government, as was the case when a tariff was imposed? No, it isn't. This area represents the additional revenue earned by the importers (and sellers) of $Q_4 - Q_3$. Without the quota, those importers and sellers of $Q_4 - Q_3$ sold their imported cars for P_W. Their total revenue was therefore $P_W \times (Q_4 - Q_3)$, or the area $Q_3 GHQ_4$. Because of the quota, the price rises to P_Q and their total revenue is $P_Q \times (Q_4 - Q_3)$, or the area $Q_3 ECQ_4$. The difference between total revenues on $Q_4 - Q_3$ imports without a quota and with a quota is the area 3.

In conclusion, the effects of a quota are a decrease in consumers' surplus (areas $1 + 2 + 3 + 4$), an increase in producers' surplus (area 1), and an increase in total revenue for the importers who sell the allowed number of imported units (area 3). Since consumers lose more than domestic producers and importers gain, a net loss results from a quota.[3]

Question:

It appears that the following statements are true:

1. Tariffs and quotas generate a net loss (consumers lose more than producers, importers, and governments gain).
2. Tariffs and quotas exist in the real world.
3. Neither tariffs nor quotas would or could exist without government sanction.

Given these facts, would it be reasonable to conclude that governments, at least on the issue of international trade, do not try to promote the general welfare?

Answer:

Many persons have come to this conclusion. However, others argue that things aren't as black and white as the diagrams may make them appear. They say that the reasons for limiting trade (see the earlier section) have to be considered alongside the diagrams that clearly show a net loss from limiting free trade.

The Effects of Voluntary Export Restraints

The U.S. auto companies did not have a good year in 1980. The Big Three U.S. auto companies, General Motors, Ford, and Chrysler, sold over 1 million fewer

---

[3]It is perhaps incorrect to imply that government receives *nothing* from a quota. Although it receives nothing directly, it may gain indirectly. Economists generally argue that since government officials are likely to be the persons who will decide which importers will get to satisfy the quota, they will naturally be lobbied by importers; thus government officials will likely receive *something,* if only dinner at an expensive restaurant, while the lobbyist makes his or her pitch. In short, in the course of the lobbying, resources will be spent by lobbyists as they curry favor with those government officials or politicians who have the power to make the decision as to who gets to sell the limited number of imported goods. In economics, lobbyists' activities, geared toward obtaining a special privilege, are referred to as *rent seeking.*

cars in 1980 than in 1979. The Big Three blamed Japanese car imports for their problems and lobbied for protectionism. They said they needed a little time to catch their breath, retool for smaller cars, change their production processes, and cut costs. In a way, they were voicing the infant-industry argument. Given the age of the industries, some have preferred to call it the senile-industry argument.

In 1981, some members of Congress argued strongly for severe protectionist measures to be slapped on Japanese car imports. To prevent this, the Reagan administration proposed, and the Japanese agreed to, a **"voluntary" export restraint (VER)**. A voluntary export restraint is an agreement between two countries in which the exporting country voluntarily agrees to limit its exports to the importing country. (The effects of a voluntary export restraint can be analyzed the same way as a quota.) In this case, the export restraint was not really voluntary in the way the word is usually understood. The Japanese accepted the VER because, some say, they feared much worse measures if they didn't.

What happened as a result of the VER? In a *Wall Street Journal* article, Robert Crandall of the Brookings Institution reported that the effects of VER were:

1. In 1983, Japanese car imports were selling for about $1,500 more than they would have without the restraints.
2. In 1984, Japanese car imports were selling for about $2,500 more than they would have without the restraints.
3. In the period 1984–85, U.S. consumers paid about $10 billion more for Japanese cars than they would have in the absence of the restraints.
4. The restraints on imports allowed U.S. car companies to raise their prices by about $1,000 per car.
5. American consumers paid about $16.6 billion more for U.S-produced cars in 1984–85 because of the restraints.[4]

At What Price Jobs?

Suppose the U.S. government imposes a tariff on imported good X. As a result, the domestic producers of good X sell their goods for higher prices, receive higher producers' surplus, and are generally better off. Some of the domestic workers who produce good X are better off, too. Perhaps without the tariff on imports of good X, some of them would have lost their jobs.

Such scenarios raise two important questions: How many domestic jobs in the firms that produce good X are saved because of the tariff? How much do consumers have to pay in higher prices to save these jobs? Economists are interested in answering such questions. Here are a few answers for different industries at different times.

In 1977, tariffs and quotas were imposed on imports of foreign footwear. An estimated 21,000 domestic jobs were protected in the domestic footwear industry as a result. The average worker in the industry earned $8,340 (in 1980 dollars). Domestic consumers paid $77,714 for *each* $8,340 domestic footwear job protected.

As we stated earlier, in 1981, voluntary export restraints were placed on Japanese car imports. The U.S. International Trade Commission estimated that 44,000 domestic jobs were protected—at a cost of $193,000 per job.

In 1988, the consumer cost of voluntary export restraints on machine tools was $48 million, while the gain to U.S. machine tool manufacturers was $11 million. The consumer cost per job saved turned out to be $120,000.

[4]Robert W. Crandall, "Detroit Rode Quotas to Prosperity," *Wall Street Journal*, January 29, 1986, p. 30.

"Voluntary" Export Restraint (VER)
An agreement between two countries in which the exporting country "voluntarily" agrees to limit its exports to the importing country.

Free-Trade Agreements

Several recent agreements have given worldwide impetus to free trade. We describe them here.

The United States of Europe.   At the end of 1992, the 12 nations that make up the European Community (EC) will essentially form a United States of Europe for trading purposes. In 1993, the seven nation European Free Trade Association will join the EC unification efforts to form the world's largest trading bloc, embracing 380 million consumers and accounting for 43 percent of world trade. A few of the European nations' objectives are to (1) abolish all tariffs and quotas on products traded by the nations, (2) establish a common system of tariffs for products imported into the nations, and (3) establish the free movement of capital and labor among the nations.

Economists are certain that the abolition of trade barriers among European nations will economically benefit those nations, although they note that if the United States of Europe raises trade barriers against the rest of the world, many of the benefits of the economic union will be dissipated.

The U.S.–Canadian Free-Trade Agreement.   Canada is the largest trading partner of the United States. In 1988, President Reagan and Canadian Prime Minister Mulroney signed the U.S.–Canadian Free-Trade Agreement. According to the agreement, tariffs and quotas between the two countries will be eliminated over a 10-year period. It has been estimated that the free-trade agreement will bring gains of between $1 billion and $3 billion a year to each nation.

The U.S.–Mexico Free-Trade Area.   Mexico is the third largest trading partner of the United States (Japan is the second). In 1990, President Bush and the president of Mexico endorsed the goal of a free-trade agreement between the two countries. In 1991, President Bush began negotiating with Mexico to achieve this free-trade agreement. This free-trade agreement, like the one that the United States has with Canada, will, if accepted by Congress, eventually eliminate completely the tariffs between the two nations, as well as other trade barriers.

International trade is a place where economics and politics often do battle. The simple tools of supply and demand and consumers' and producers' surplus tell us that there are net gains from free trade; limiting exports or imports serves only to make living standards, on the whole, lower than they would be if free trade were permitted.

But, on the other hand, are the harsh realities of life. Domestic producers may advocate quotas and tariffs to make themselves better off, but give little thought to the negative effects felt by foreign producers or domestic consumers. And domestic consumers may advocate policies that prohibit exports to make themselves better off, but give little thought to the negative effects felt by foreign consumers or domestic producers.

Perhaps the battle over international trade comes down to this: Policies are largely advocated, argued, and lobbied for based more on their *distributional effects* than on their aggregate or overall effects. On an aggregate level, free trade produces a net gain for society, whereas restricted trade produces a net loss. But economists understand that just because free trade *in the aggregate* produces a net gain, it does not necessarily follow that every single person benefits more from free trade than restricted trade. This chapter has presented numerous examples where a subset of the population gains more, in a par-

Interview: Lester Thurow

Lester Thurow is one of the more articulate, well-respected, and sometimes controversial economists on the public scene today. In recent years, he has appeared on numerous news programs to discuss such topics as international trade, industrial policy, productivity, and the trade deficit. He is currently at the Massachusetts Institute of Technology.

Professor Thurow, in your essay on declining industries in *The New Palgrave: A Dictionary of Economics*, you say, "Almost all countries protect their declining industries to some extent." They do this despite the fact that economists can show that protectionism comes with net costs to society. Why is there so much protectionism in the world?

I think the simple reason is that if you look at the pluses and the minuses from free international trade, the pluses may be bigger than the minuses but the pluses are spread over a very large number of people who all get a small addition to their incomes, and the minuses are spread over a relatively small number of people who take a huge cut in their incomes. For example, if we give $1 to all Americans, and take away $1,000 from each of 100 Americans, then the 100 Americans who are losing are going to put up a tremendous economic fight, and the millions of Americans who are winning are not, because what they are winning is a small amount of money ($1). And this would be the case even if the total winnings are greater than the total losses.

Which is one of the most protectionist nations in the world? Which is one of the least protectionist?

Hong Kong is clearly the least protectionist. Among industrial countries, Korea is one of the most protectionist.

Most Americans appear to believe that Japan is much more protectionist than the United States. Do you think this is true?

The two countries have about equal amounts of protection. At the end of the 1980s, about 25 percent of the products entering the United States were in some way restricted. Japan is no worse. The difference is that Japan has strategic protection while American's protection is "loser driven." Japan protects the strategic industries of the future such as amorphous metals. America protects those old dying industries that have political clout.

What do you predict will be a major economic problem in the United States in the mid-1990s, and how should it solve that problem?

In 1990, the weekly wages of what the Department of Labor calls nonsupervisory workers were 17 percent below where they were in 1973 after correcting for inflation. Low rates of productivity growth and what economists know as "factor price equalization" (in a world economy, unskilled American workers can be paid no more than unskilled workers in competing countries

such as Korea) will continue these trends in the 1990s. In the 1970s and 1980s, increasing female work effort meant that the average family could experience slowly rising real standards of living despite the fact that the wages of both husband and wife were falling. But the work potential of women has been almost fully utilized, and in the 1990s, falling wages will lead to falling family incomes as well.

You have had more opportunities than most economists to deal with the press, since in recent years you have been interviewed on a number of news programs. How would you rate the understanding of economics of most of the journalists who have interviewed you?

Somewhere between average and good. The real problem with the press, and especially the electronic press like television, is that they try to compress things into (at the most) 75 seconds, and there are many economic subjects that just cannot intelligently be discussed in that short time. So the problem is not ignorance, it is time.

Do you find this frustrating?

Well, you don't get frustrated when they interview you, because what they do is come to your office and take 45 minutes of tape and then they edit it down to 75 seconds. It is not so much the interview that is frustrating, it is what actually shows up on the air.

What got you interested in economics?

The belief, some would see it as naive belief, that economics was a profession where it would be possible to help make the world better.

ticular instance, from restricted trade than from free trade. In short, economists realize that real-world policies are often determined more by the answer to the question, How does it affect *me?* than by How does it affect *us?*

CHAPTER SUMMARY

Specialization and Trade

■ A country has an absolute advantage in the production of a good if, using the same amount of resources as another country, it can produce more of a particular good. A country has a comparative advantage in the production of a good it produces at lower opportunity cost than another country.

■ Individuals in countries that specialize and trade have a higher standard of living than would be the case if they did not specialize and trade.

■ Government officials do not sit down with cost data and determine what their country should specialize in and trade. Instead, the desire to earn a dollar, franc, or pound guides individuals' actions and produces the unintended consequence that countries specialize in and trade the good(s) in which they have a comparative advantage. However, trade restrictions can change this outcome.

International Trade: Distributional Effects

■ Consumers' surplus is greater if exports are prohibited than if they are permitted.

■ Producers' surplus is greater if exports are permitted than if they are prohibited.

■ Consumers' surplus is greater if imports are permitted than if they are prohibited.

■ Producers' surplus is greater if imports are prohibited than if they are permitted.

■ Producers lose more than consumers gain from a policy that prohibits exports. Thus, prohibiting exports results in a net loss.

■ Consumers lose more than producers gain from a policy that prohibits imports. Thus, prohibiting imports results in a net loss.

■ Producers gain more than consumers lose from a policy that permits exports. Thus, permitting exports results in a net gain.

■ Consumers gain more than producers lose from a policy that permits imports. Thus, permitting imports results in a net gain.

Arguments for Trade Restrictions

■ The national-defense argument states that certain goods—such as aircraft, petroleum, chemicals, and weapons—are necessary to the national defense and should be produced domestically whether the country has a comparative advantage in their production or not.

■ The infant-industry argument states that "infant" or new industries should be protected from free (foreign) trade so that they may have time to develop and compete on an equal basis with older, more established foreign industries.

■ The antidumping argument states that domestic producers should not have to compete (on an unequal basis) with foreign producers that sell products below cost and below the prices they charge in their domestic markets.

■ The foreign-export-subsidies argument states that domestic producers should not have to compete (on an unequal basis) with foreign producers that have been subsidized by their governments.

■ The low-foreign-wages argument states that domestic producers cannot compete with foreign producers that pay low wages to their employees when domestic producers pay high wages to their employees. In order that high-paying domestic firms may survive, limits on free trade are proposed.

■ The saving-domestic-jobs argument states that through low foreign wages or government subsidies (or dumping, and so forth), foreign producers will be able to outcompete domestic producers, and therefore domestic jobs will be lost. In order that domestic firms may survive, and domestic jobs not be lost, limits on free trade are proposed.

■ The arguments for trade restrictions are not accepted as valid by all persons. Critics often maintain that the arguments can be and are abused and, in most cases, are motivated by self-interest.

Tariffs and Quotas

■ A tariff is a tax on imports. A quota is a legal limit on the amount of a good that may be imported.

■ Both tariffs and quotas raise the price of imports.

■ Tariffs lead to a decrease in consumers' surplus, an increase in producers' surplus, and tariff revenues for the government. Consumers lose more through tariffs than producers and government (together) gain.

■ Quotas lead to a decrease in consumers' surplus, an increase in producers' surplus, and additional revenues for the importers that sell the quota. Consumers lose more through quotas than producers and importers (together) gain.

Key Terms and Concepts

Absolute Advantage	Producers' Surplus	Quota
Comparative Advantage	Dumping	"Voluntary" Export Restraint
Consumers' Surplus	Tariff	

QUESTIONS AND PROBLEMS

1. A production possibilities frontier is usually drawn for a country. One could, however, be drawn for the world. Picture the world's production possibilities frontier. Is the world positioned at a point on the curve or below the frontier? Give a reason for your answer.

2. Using the data in the table, answer the questions that follow: (a) In which good does Canada have a comparative advantage? (b) In which good does Italy have a comparative advantage? (c) What might be a set of favorable terms of trade for the two countries? (d) Prove that both countries would be better off in the specialization–trade case than in the no specialization–no trade case.

Points on Production Possibilities Frontier	CANADA		ITALY	
	Good X	Good Y	Good X	Good Y
A	150	0	90	0
B	100	25	60	60
C	50	50	30	120
D	0	75	0	180

3. "Whatever can be done by a tariff can be done by a quota." Discuss.

4. Consider two groups of domestic producers: those that compete with imports and those that export goods. Suppose the domestic producers that compete with imports convince the legislature to impose a high tariff on imports, so high, in fact, that almost all imports are eliminated. Does this policy in any way adversely affect domestic producers that export goods? How?

5. Suppose the U.S. government wants to curtail imports, would it be likely to favor a tariff or a quota to accomplish its objective? Why?

6. Suppose the land mass known to you as the United States of America had been composed, since the nation's founding, of separate countries instead of separate states. Would you expect the standard of living of the people who inhabit this land mass to be higher, lower, or equal to what it is today? Why?

7. Even though Jeremy is a better gardener and novelist than Bill is, he (Jeremy) still hires Bill as his gardener. Why?

8. Suppose that tomorrow a constitutional convention were called and you were chosen as one of the delegates from your state. You and the other delegates must decide whether it will be constitutional or unconstitutional for the federal government to impose tariffs and quotas or restrict international trade in any way. What would be your position?

9. Some economists have argued that since domestic consumers gain more from free trade than domestic producers gain from (import) tariffs and quotas, consumers should buy out domestic producers and rid themselves of costly tariffs and quotas. For example, if consumers save $400 million from free trade (through paying lower prices) and producers gain $100 million from tariffs and quotas, consumers can pay producers something more than $100 million but less than $400 million and get producers to favor free trade, too. Assuming this scheme were feasible, what do you think of it?

36

INTERNATIONAL FINANCE

WHAT THIS CHAPTER IS ABOUT

Chapter 35 presented the *real* side of international transactions—primarily, the goods being produced in one country and traded in others. Money did not figure prominently in the picture.

Chapter 36 presents the *monetary* side of international transactions. Here money does figure prominently in the picture. All types of monies are involved: U.S. dollars, Japanese yen, English pounds, French francs, Indian rupees, and more.

The two main topics of international finance are the balance of payments and exchange rates. We discuss both in this chapter.

THE BALANCE OF PAYMENTS

Countries keep track of their domestic level of production by calculating their gross national product; similarly, they keep track of the flow of their international trade (receipts and expenditures) by calculating their balance of payments. The **balance of payments** is a periodic statement (usually annual) of the money value of all transactions between residents of one country and residents of all other countries. The balance of payments provides information about a nation's imports and exports, domestic residents' earnings on assets located abroad, foreign earnings on domestic assets, gifts to and from foreign countries (including foreign aid), and official transactions by governments and central banks.

Balance of payments accounts record both debits and credits. A debit is indicated by a minus (−) sign, and a credit is indicated by a plus (+) sign. *Any transaction that supplies the nation's currency in the foreign exchange market is recorded as a* **debit.**

For example, if Americans buy Japanese television sets, they must first buy Japanese yen by selling (supplying) U.S. dollars. This import transaction is listed as a debit in the U.S. balance of payments.

Similarly, *any transaction that supplies a foreign currency in the foreign exchange market is recorded as a* **credit.** If the Japanese buy American computers, they must first buy U.S. dollars by selling (supplying) Japanese yen. This export transaction is listed as a credit in the U.S. balance of payments.

The international transactions that occur, and are summarized in the balance of payments, can be grouped into three categories, or three accounts: the current account, the capital account, and the official reserve account—and a statistical discrepancy. We have illustrated a U.S. balance of payments account for year Z in Exhibit 36–1. The data in the exhibit are hypothetical (to make our calculations simpler), but not unrealistic.

Question:

When Americans buy Japanese goods, they supply dollars and demand yen. When the Japanese buy American goods, they supply yen and demand dollars. Thus the first transaction is recorded as a debit (since it supplies the nation's currency) and the second as a credit (since it supplies a foreign currency) in the U.S. balance of payments. Is this correct?

Answer:

Yes, that is correct.

The Current Account

The **current account** includes all payments related to the purchase and sale of goods and services. There are three major components of the current account: exports of goods and services, imports of goods and services, and net unilateral transfers abroad.

Exports of Goods and Services. Americans export goods (say, cars), they export services (such as insurance, banking, transportation, and tourism), and they receive investment income on assets they own abroad. All three activities increase the

Sidebar definitions

Balance of Payments
A periodic statement (usually annual) of the money value of all transactions between residents of one country and residents of all other countries.

Debit
In the balance of payments, any transaction that either supplies the nation's currency or creates a demand for foreign currency in the foreign exchange market.

Credit
In the balance of payments, any transaction that either supplies a foreign currency or creates a demand for the nation's currency in the foreign exchange market.

Current Account
Includes all payments related to the purchase and sale of goods and services. Components of the account include exports, imports, and net unilateral transfers abroad.

EXHIBIT 36-1
U.S. Balance of Payments, Year Z

The data in this exhibit are hypothetical, but not unrealistic. All numbers are in billions of dollars. The plus and minus signs in the exhibit should be viewed as operational signs.

CURRENT ACCOUNT
1. EXPORTS OF GOODS AND SERVICES   +340
    a. Merchandise exports (including military sales)   +220
    b. Services   +30
    c. Income from U.S. assets abroad   +90
2. IMPORTS OF GOODS AND SERVICES   −390
    a. Merchandise imports (including military purchases)   −300
    b. Services   −40
    c. Income from foreign assets in U.S.   −50

Merchandise Trade Balance
Difference between value of merchandise exports (item 1a)
and value of merchandise imports (item 2a): +220 − 300 = −80

3. NET UNILATERAL TRANSFERS ABROAD   −11

Current Account Balance
Items 1, 2, 3: +340 − 390 − 11 = ⟶ **−61**

CAPITAL ACCOUNT
4. OUTFLOW OF U.S. CAPITAL   −16
5. INFLOW OF FOREIGN CAPITAL   +60

Capital Account Balance
Items 4 and 5: −16 + 60 = ⟶ **+44**

OFFICIAL RESERVE ACCOUNT
6. INCREASE (−) IN U.S. OFFICIAL RESERVE ASSETS   −4
7. INCREASE (+) IN FOREIGN OFFICIAL ASSETS IN U.S.   +3

Official Reserve Balance
Items 6 and 7: −4 + 3 = ⟶ **−1**

STATISTICAL DISCREPANCY   +18

TOTAL $0 $0
                       (always zero)

Balance of Payments =

Summary statistic of all ⟨⟩ items (items 1 - 7 and the statistical discrpancy)

+$340 − 390 − 11 − 16 + 60 − 4 + 3 + 18 = $0

or

Summary statistic of all ▪ items (current account balance, capital account balance, official reserve balance, and the statistical discrepancy)

−$61 + 44 − 1 + 18 = $0

Note: The pluses (+) and the minuses (−) in the exhibit serve two purposes. First, they distinguish between credits and debits. A plus is always placed before a credit, and a minus is always placed before a debit. Second, in terms of our calculations, we view the pluses and minuses as operational signs. In other words, if a number has a plus in front of it, we simply add it to our total. If a number has a minus in front of it, we simply subtract it from our total.

demand for U.S. dollars at the same time as they increase the supply of foreign currencies; thus, they are recorded as credits (+). For example, if a foreigner buys a U.S. computer, payment must ultimately be made in U.S. dollars. Thus, she is required to supply her nation's currency when she demands U.S. dollars. (We use *foreigner* in this chapter to refer to a resident of a foreign country.)

Imports of Goods and Services.   Americans import goods and services, and foreigners receive income on assets they own in the United States. These activities increase the demand for foreign currencies at the same time as they increase the supply of U.S. dollars to the **foreign exchange market;** thus, they are recorded as debits (−). For example, if an American buys a Japanese car, payment must ultimately be made in Japanese yen. Thus, he is required to supply U.S. dollars when he demands Japanese yen. Exhibit 36–1 shows that exports of goods and services totaled +$340 billion in year Z, and imports of goods and services totaled −$390 billion.[1]

If we look at the difference between the value of merchandise exports (1a in Exhibit 36–1) and the value of merchandise imports (2a in the exhibit), ignoring for now export and import services as well as income from U.S. assets abroad and income from foreign assets in the United States, we have the merchandise trade balance (or balance of trade). Specifically, the **merchandise trade balance** is the difference between the value of merchandise exports and the value of merchandise imports. In year Z, this was −$80 billion. If the value of a country's merchandise exports is less than the value of its merchandise imports, it is said to have a **merchandise trade deficit.** If the value of a country's merchandise exports is greater than the value of its merchandise imports, it is said to have a **merchandise trade surplus.** Exhibit 36–2 shows the U.S. merchandise trade balance from 1960 through 1989.

Foreign Exchange Market
The market in which currencies of different countries are exchanged.

Merchandise Trade Balance
The difference between the value of merchandise exports and the value of merchandise imports.

Merchandise Trade Deficit
The situation where the value of merchandise exports is less than the value of merchandise imports.

Merchandise Trade Surplus
The situation where the value of merchandise exports is greater than the value of merchandise imports.

Question:

In Exhibit 36–1, merchandise exports are +$220 billion (item 1a) and merchandise imports are −$300 billion (item 2a). Can't the merchandise trade balance be calculated simply by subtracting the merchandise imports from merchandise exports?

Answer:

Yes, it can be calculated by subtracting merchandise imports from merchandise exports. But we must be careful not to make the mistake of *subtracting a minus $300 billion from a positive $220 billion.* In other words, we don't say, Merchandise trade balance = $220 billion − (−$300 billion). This equals $520 billion. Instead, we simply subtract the *value of the merchandise imports,* which is $300 billion, from the value of the merchandise exports, which is $220 billion. In other words, Balance of trade = $220 billion − $300 billion. This equals −$80 billion.

In terms of calculations, the positive and minus signs in Exhibit 36–1 are operational signs. When a minus sign (−) appears in front of a number, we simply subtract that number from the total. When a positive sign (+) appears in front of a number, we add that number to the total.

---

[1]We realize that in everyday language, people do not say, "Exports were a *positive* $X billion, and imports were a *negative* $Y." Placing a plus sign (+) in front of exports and a minus sign (−) in front of imports simply reinforces the essential point that exports are credits and imports are debits. This is useful later when we calculate certain account balances.

Net Unilateral Transfers Abroad. *Unilateral transfers* are one-way money payments. They can go from Americans or the U.S. government to foreigners or to foreign governments. If an American sends money to a relative in a foreign country, or the U.S. government gives money to a foreign country as a gift or grant, or an American decides to retire in a foreign country and receives a Social Security check there, all these transactions are referred to as unilateral transfers.

Unilateral transfers can also go from foreigners or foreign governments to Americans or to the U.S. government. If a foreign citizen sends money to a relative living in the United States, this is a unilateral transfer.

If an American makes a unilateral transfer abroad, this gives rise to a demand for foreign currency and a supply of U.S. dollars; thus, it is entered as a debit item

EXHIBIT 36–2
U.S. Merchandise Trade Balance, 1960–89

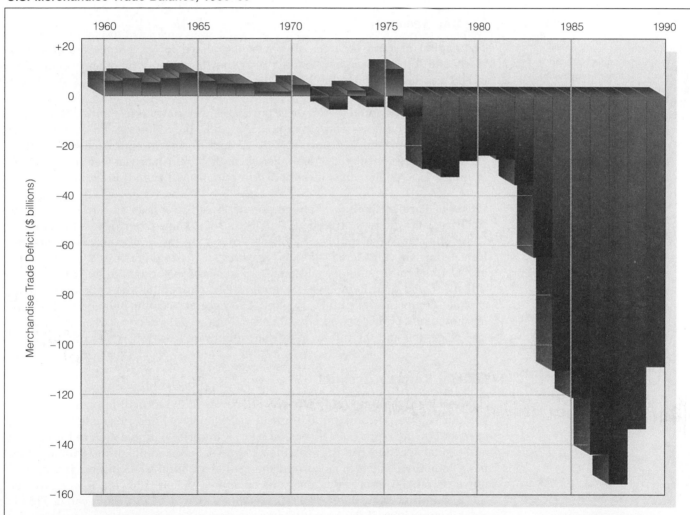

In the 1960s, there were numerous years with a merchandise trade surplus. In the 1970s and 1980s, there were numerous years with a merchandise trade deficit. The minus sign (–) in front of deficit figures signifies that merchandise exports were less than merchandise imports.

Source: Council of Economic Advisers, *Economic Report of the President, 1991* (Washington, D.C.: U.S. Government Printing Office, 1991), U.S. Commerce Department.

in the U.S. balance of payments accounts. If a foreigner makes a unilateral transfer to an American, this gives rise to a supply of foreign currency (and demand for U.S. dollars) and thus is entered as a credit item in the U.S. balance of payments accounts. For year Z, we have assumed that unilateral transfers made by Americans to foreign citizens were greater than unilateral transfers made by foreign citizens to Americans; thus, we get a negative *net* dollar amount, −$11 billion in this case. This is referred to as *net unilateral transfers abroad.*

Items 1, 2, and 3 in Exhibit 36–1—exports of goods and services, imports of goods and services, and net unilateral transfers abroad—are known as the current account. The **current account balance** is the summary statistic for these three items. In year Z, it is −$61 billion. The news media sometimes call the current account balance the *balance of payments.* To an economist, this is incorrect. As we shall soon see, the balance of payments includes several more items.

Capital Account

The **capital account** includes all payments related to the purchase and sale of assets and to borrowing and lending activities. Its major components are outflow of U.S. capital and inflow of foreign capital.

Outflow of U.S. Capital.   American purchases of foreign assets and U.S. loans to foreigners are outflows of U.S. capital. As such, they give rise to a demand for foreign currency and a supply of U.S. dollars on the foreign exchange market. Hence, they are considered a debit. For example, if an American wants to buy land in Brazil, U.S. dollars must be supplied to purchase (demand) Brazilian cruzados.

Inflow of Foreign Capital.   Foreign purchases of U.S. assets and foreign loans to Americans are inflows of foreign capital. As such, they give rise to a demand for U.S. dollars and to a supply of foreign currency on the foreign exchange market. Hence, they are considered a credit. For example, if a German buys a U.S. Treasury bill, German marks must be supplied to purchase (demand) U.S. dollars.

Items 4 and 5 in Exhibit 36–1—outflow of U.S. capital and inflow of foreign capital—comprise the capital account. The **capital account balance** is the summary statistic for these two items. It is equal to the difference between the outflow of U.S. capital and the inflow of foreign capital. In year Z, it is $44 billion.

Official Reserve Account

A government possesses official reserve balances in the form of foreign currencies, gold, its reserve position in the International Monetary Fund (discussed later), and *special drawing rights* (also discussed later). Countries with a deficit in the current and capital accounts can draw on their reserves. For example, if the United States has a combined deficit in its current and capital accounts of $5 billion, it can draw down its official reserves to meet this combined deficit. Viewing item 6, we see that the United States increased its reserve assets by $4 billion in year Z. This is a debit item since, if the United States acquires official reserves (say, through the purchase of a foreign currency), it has increased the demand for the foreign currency and supplied dollars. Thus, an increase in official reserves is like an outflow of capital in the capital account and appears as a payment with a negative sign. It follows that an increase in foreign official assets in the United States is a credit item. (Note: In recent years governments have not actively managed their reserve accounts.)

Current Account Balance
The summary statistic for exports of goods and services, imports of goods and services, and net unilateral transfers.

Capital Account
Includes all payments related to the purchase and sale of assets and to borrowing and lending activities. Components include outflow of U.S. capital and inflow of foreign capital.

Capital Account Balance
The summary statistic for the outflow of U.S. capital and the inflow of foreign capital. It is equal to the difference between the outflow of U.S. capital and the inflow of foreign capital.

Statistical Discrepancy

If someone buys a U.S. dollar with, say, Swiss francs, someone must sell a U.S. dollar. Thus, *dollars purchased = dollars sold.* In all the transactions discussed earlier—exporting goods, importing goods, sending money to relatives in foreign countries, buying land in foreign countries—dollars were bought and sold. The total number of dollars sold must always equal the total number of dollars purchased. However, balance of payments accountants do not have complete information; they can only record credits and debits that they observe. This means there may be more debits or credits than those observed in a given year. Suppose, in year Z, *all* debits are observed and recorded, but *not all* credits are observed and recorded—perhaps because of smuggling activities, secret bank accounts, people living in more than one country, and so on. To adjust for this, balance of payments accountants make use of the *statistical discrepancy,* which is that part of the balance of payments that adjusts for missing information. In Exhibit 36–1, the statistical discrepancy is +$18 billion. This means that $18 billion worth of credits (+) went unobserved in year Z. There may have been some hidden exports and unrecorded capital inflows that year.

What the Balance of Payments Equals

The balance of payments is the summary statistic for the following: exports of goods and services (item 1), imports of goods and services (item 2), net unilateral transfers abroad (item 3), the outflow of U.S. capital (item 4), the inflow of foreign capital (item 5), the increase in U.S. official reserve assets (item 6), the increase in foreign official assets in the United States (item 7), and the statistical discrepancy. Calculating the balance of payments, we have (in billions of dollars) $+340 - 390 - 11 - 16 + 60 - 4 + 3 + 18 = 0$.

Alternatively, the balance of payments is the summary statistic for the following: the current account balance, capital account balance, official reserve balance, and statistical discrepancy. Calculating the balance of payments we have (in billions of dollars) $-61 + 44 - 1 + 18 = 0$. The balance of payments for the United States in year Z equals *zero.* The fact is, the balance of payments *always* equals zero.

Question:

Why does the balance of payments always equal zero?

Answer:

The reason the balance of payments always equals zero is that the three accounts that comprise the balance of payments, when taken together, plus the statistical discrepancy, include all of the *sources* and all of the *uses* of dollars in international transactions. And since every dollar used must have a source, adding the sources (+) to the uses (−) necessarily gives us zero.

FLEXIBLE EXCHANGE RATES

■

If a U.S. buyer wants to purchase a good from a U.S. seller, the buyer simply turns over to the seller the required number of U.S. dollars. If, however, a U.S. buyer wants to purchase a good from a seller in France, it is a slightly different matter.

Exchange rate
The price of one currency in terms of another currency; for example, 1 dollar = 2 marks.

Flexible Exchange Rate System
The system whereby exchange rates are determined by the forces of supply and demand for a currency.

First, the U.S. buyer must exchange her U.S. dollars for French francs, and then with the French francs she buys the good from the French seller. The market in which currencies of different countries are exchanged, as we mentioned earlier, is the foreign exchange market.

In the foreign exchange market, currencies are bought and sold for a price; **exchange rate** exists. For instance, it might take $1.50 to buy a British pound, 17 cents to buy a French franc, 58 cents to buy a German mark, or seven-tenths of 1 cent to buy a Japanese yen. In this section, we discuss how exchange rates are determined in the foreign exchange market when the forces of supply and demand are allowed to rule. Economists refer to this as a **flexible exchange rate system.** In the next section, we discuss how exchange rates are determined under a fixed exchange rate system.

The Demand and Supply of Currencies

To simplify our analysis, we assume that there are only two countries in the world, the United States and Great Britain. This, then, means there are only two currencies in the world, the dollar ($) and the pound (£). In this two-country–two-currency world, what constitutes the demand for dollars or the supply of dollars on the foreign exchange market? What constitutes the demand for pounds or the supply of pounds?

Odd as it may appear at first sight, the demand for dollars and the supply of pounds are linked, as are the demand for pounds and the supply of dollars. Suppose an American wants to buy a British Rolls Royce. Before he can purchase the Rolls Royce, the American must buy British pounds—hence, British pounds are demanded. But the American buys British pounds with dollars; that is, he supplies dollars to the foreign exchange market in order to demand British pounds. We conclude that the American demand for British goods leads to a demand for British pounds and to a supply of U.S. dollars on the foreign exchange market.

The story is similar if a British buyer wants to buy an American Cadillac. Before she can purchase the Cadillac, the British buyer must buy dollars—hence, U.S. dollars are demanded. The British buyer buys the dollars with pounds. We conclude that the British demand for American goods leads to a demand for U.S. dollars and to a supply of British pounds on the foreign exchange market. This process is illustrated in Exhibit 36–3.

In (a), we see the market for British pounds. (Exhibit 36–3b shows the market for U.S. dollars, which mirrors what is happening in the market for British pounds.) On the horizontal axis is the "quantity of pounds," and on the vertical axis, the exchange rate—the dollar price per pound. Notice that the demand curve for British pounds is downward sloping, indicating that as the dollar price per pound increases, Americans buy fewer pounds, and as the dollar price per pound decreases, Americans buy more pounds. For example, if it takes $1.90 to buy one pound, Americans will buy fewer pounds than they would if it takes $1.50 to buy one pound. Simply put, the higher the dollar price per pound, the more expensive British goods are for Americans and the fewer British goods Americans will buy; thus, a smaller quantity demanded of pounds.

The supply of pounds is upward sloping. It is easy to understand why if we recall that the supply of British pounds is linked to the British demand for American goods and U.S. dollars. Consider a $1.90 price for a pound compared with a price of $1.50 a pound. At $1.50 = £1, a British buyer gives up one pound for which he receives $1.50 in return. But at $1.90 = £1, a British buyer gives up one pound and receives $1.90 in return. At which exchange rate are American goods *cheaper* for the British? The answer is at the exchange rate of $1.90 = £1.

Here is an illustration. Think of an American computer with a price tag of $1,000. At an exchange rate of $1.90 = £1, the British will have to pay approximately £526 to buy the American computer ($1,000/$1.90 = £526). But at an exchange rate of $1.50 = £1, the British will have to pay approximately £667 pounds ($1,000/$1.50 = £667). To the British, the American computer is cheaper at the exchange rate of $1.90 per pound than at $1.50 per pound. It follows, then, that the higher the dollar price per pound, the greater the quantity demanded of dollars by the British (because American goods will be cheaper), and therefore the greater the quantity supplied of pounds to the foreign exchange market. The upward-sloping supply curve for pounds illustrates this.[2]

The British demand for American goods leads to a demand for U.S. dollars and to a supply of British pounds on the foreign exchange market.

We learned that the demand for dollars is linked to the supply of pounds and that the demand for pounds is linked to the supply of dollars. Economists often think in terms of one activity being linked to another because economics, after all, is about exchange. In an exchange, one gives (supply) and gets (demand): John "supplies" $25 in order to demand the new book from the shopkeeper; the shopkeeper supplies the new book in order that he may "demand" the $25. In such a transaction, we usually diagrammatically represent the demand for, and supply of, the new book—but we could also dia-

THINKING LIKE AN ECONOMIST

[2]Actually, the supply curve here is upward sloping because we have assumed that the British demand for American goods is price elastic. This assumption will hold for most of this chapter. We bring price elasticity of demand into the discussion explicitly when we discuss the J-curve later in the chapter.

EXHIBIT 36–3

Translating U.S. Demand for Pounds into U.S. Supply of Dollars and British Demand for Dollars into British Supply of Pounds

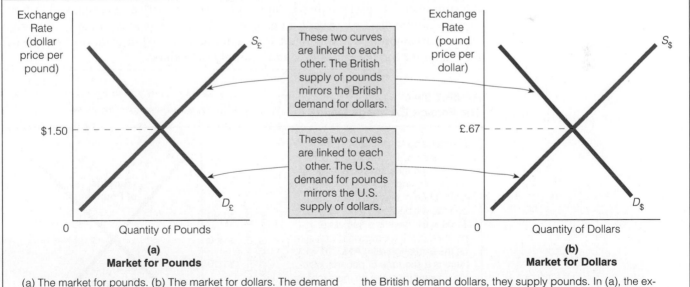

(a) The market for pounds. (b) The market for dollars. The demand for pounds in (a) is linked to the supply of dollars in (b): When Americans demand pounds, they supply dollars. The supply of pounds in (a) is linked to the demand for dollars in (b): When the British demand dollars, they supply pounds. In (a), the exchange rate is $1.50 = £1, which is equal to £.67 = $1 in (b). Exchange rates are the reciprocals of each other.

grammatically represent the demand for, and supply of, money. Of course, in international exchange, where monies are bought and sold *before* goods are bought and sold, this is exactly what we do.

The Equilibrium Exchange Rate

In a completely flexible exchange rate system, where the forces of supply and demand are allowed to rule, the equilibrium exchange rate (dollar price per pound) will be $1.50 = £1 in Exhibit 36–4. At this dollar price per pound, the quantity demanded of pounds equals the quantity supplied of pounds. There are no shortages or surpluses of pounds. At any other exchange rate, however, either an excess demand for pounds or an excess supply of pounds exists.

Let's look at the exchange rate of $1.90 = £1. At this exchange rate, a surplus of pounds exists. As a result, downward pressure will be placed on the dollar price of a pound (just as downward pressure would be placed on the dollar price of an apple if there were a surplus of apples). If, however, the exchange rate were $1.10 = £1, there would be a shortage of pounds, and upward pressure would be placed on the dollar price of a pound.

It is also important to note that exchange rates are reciprocals of each other. To take a simple example, if 1 pound = 2 dollars, then 1 dollar = ½ pound.

Question:

Are the demand and supply curves in Exhibit 36–4 related in any way to the U.S. balance of payments in Exhibit 36–1?

Answer:

Yes, they are. For example, U.S. exports represent a demand for U.S. dollars by foreigners (and therefore constitute the supply of foreign currencies), while U.S. imports represent the U.S. demand for foreign currencies (and therefore constitute the supply of U.S. dollars). In fact, any dollar amount with a plus sign (+) in front of it in Exhibit 36–1 represents a demand for U.S. dollars and a supply of foreign currencies, and any dollar amount with a minus sign (−) in front of it represents a demand for foreign currencies and a supply of dollars.

EXHIBIT 36–4
The Foreign Exchange Market

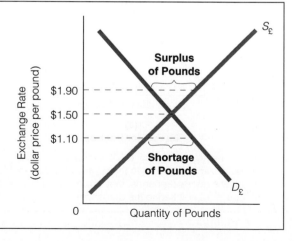

The demand for pounds is downward sloping: The higher the dollar price for pounds, the fewer pounds will be demanded; the lower the dollar price of pounds, the more pounds will be demanded. At $1.90 = £1, there is a surplus of pounds, placing downward pressure on the exchange rate. At $1.10 = £1, there is a shortage of pounds, placing upward pressure on the exchange rate. At the equilibrium exchange rate, $1.50 = £1, the quantity demanded of pounds equals the quantity supplied of pounds.

Changes in the Equilibrium Exchange Rate

In Chapter 3, we learned that a change in the demand for a good, or the supply of a good, or both would change the equilibrium price of the good. The same holds true for the price of currencies. A change in the demand for pounds, or the supply of pounds, or both will change the equilibrium dollar price per pound. If the dollar price per pound rises—say, from $1.50 = £1 to $1.80 = £1—the pound is said to have **appreciated** and the dollar to have **depreciated.**

A currency has appreciated in value if it takes more of a foreign currency to buy it. A currency has depreciated in value if it takes more of it to buy a foreign currency. For example, a movement in the exchange rate from $1.50 = £1 to $1.80 = £1 means that more dollars are necessary to buy one pound, so the pound has appreciated (the other side of the coin is that fewer pounds are necessary to buy one dollar). And since more dollars are necessary to buy one pound, the dollar has depreciated.

If the equilibrium exchange rate can change owing to a change in the demand for, and supply of, a currency, then it is important to understand what factors can change the demand for, and supply of, a currency. Three are presented here.

A Difference in Income Growth Rates. An increase in a nation's income will usually cause the nation's residents to buy more of both domestic and foreign goods. The increased demand for imports will result in an increased demand for foreign exchange.

Suppose U.S. residents experience an increase in income, but British residents do not. As a result, the demand curve for pounds shifts rightward, as illustrated in Exhibit 36–5. This causes the equilibrium exchange rate to rise from $1.50 = £1 to $1.80 = £1. *Ceteris paribus,* if one nation's income grows, and another's lags behind, the currency of the higher-growth-rate country *depreciates,* and the currency of the lower-growth-rate country *appreciates.* To many persons this is paradoxical; nevertheless, it is true.

Differences in Relative Inflation Rates. Suppose the U.S. price level rises 25 percent at a time when Great Britain experiences stable prices. An increase in the U.S. price level will make British goods relatively less expensive for Americans

Appreciation
An increase in the value of one currency relative to other currencies.

Depreciation
A decrease in the value of one currency relative to other currencies.

EXHIBIT 36–5
The Growth Rate of Income and the Exchange Rate

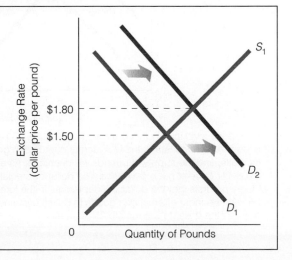

If U.S. residents experience a growth in income, but British residents do not, U.S. demand for British goods will increase, and with it, the demand for pounds. As a result, the dollar exchange rate will change; the dollar price of pounds will rise. The dollar depreciates, the pound appreciates.

and American goods relatively more expensive for the British. As a result, the American demand for British goods will increase, and the British demand for American goods will decrease.

How will this affect the demand for, and supply of, British pounds in Exhibit 36–6? The demand for British pounds will increase (British goods are relatively cheaper than they were before the U.S. price level rose), and the supply of British pounds will decrease (since American goods are relatively more expensive, the British buy fewer American goods; thus, they demand fewer U.S. dollars and supply fewer British pounds).

Purchasing Power Parity (PPP) Theory
States that exchange rates between any two currencies will adjust to reflect changes in the relative price levels of the two countries.

As Exhibit 36–6 shows, the result of an increase in the demand for British pounds and a decrease in the supply of British pounds is an appreciation in the pound and a depreciation in the dollar. It now takes more dollars and cents to buy one pound than it did before the U.S. price level increased 25 percent.

An important question is, How much will the U.S. dollar depreciate as a result of the rise in the U.S. price level vis-à-vis the British price level? (Recall that there is no change in the British price level.) The **purchasing power parity (PPP) theory** predicts that the U.S. dollar will depreciate by 25 percent.[3] This requires the dollar price of a pound to rise to $1.88 (since $1.88 − $1.50 = 38 cents, and 38 cents is approximately 25 percent of $1.50). A 25 percent depreciation in the dollar restores the original relative prices of American goods to British customers.

Consider a U.S. car with a price tag of $10,000. If the exchange rate is $1.50 = £1, a British buyer of the car will pay approximately £6,667. If the car price in-

[3]The PPP theory is sometimes referred to as the "inflation theory of exchange rates."

EXHIBIT 36–6
Inflation, Exchange Rates, and Purchasing Power Parity (PPP)

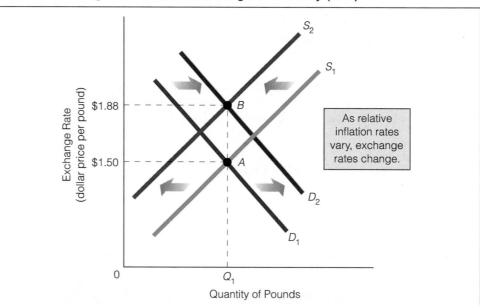

If the price level in the United States increases by 25 percent while the price level in Great Britain remains constant, the U.S. demand for British goods (and therefore pounds) will increase, and the supply of pounds will decrease. As a result, the exchange rate will change; the dollar price of pounds will rise. The dollar depreciates, and the pound appreciates. PPP theory predicts that the dollar will depreciate in the foreign exchange market until the original price (in pounds) of American goods to British customers is restored. In this example, this requires the dollar to depreciate 25 percent.

creases by 25 percent to $12,500, and the dollar depreciates 25 percent (to $1.88 = £1), the British buyer of the car will still only have to pay approximately £6,667 pounds.

In short, the purchasing power parity theory predicts that changes in the relative price levels of two countries will affect the exchange rate in such a way that one unit of a nation's currency will continue to buy the same amount of foreign goods as it did before the change in the relative price levels. In our example, because the higher U.S. inflation rate causes a change in the equilibrium exchange rate and leads to a depreciated dollar, one pound continues to have the same purchasing power it previously did.

On some occasions, the PPP theory of exchange rates has predicted accurately, whereas on others it has not. For the period 1973–86, it accurately predicted the exchange rate between the U.S. dollar and the Canadian dollar. It did not accurately predict the exchange rate between the U.S. dollar and the Japanese yen for the period 1973–79. In the period 1972–86, the theory accurately predicted the *trend* of the exchange rate between the U.S. dollar and British pound, but still the *actual exchange rate* between the two currencies diverged widely at times from the predicted exchange rate.

Many economists suggest that the theory does not always predict accurately because the demand for, and supply of, a currency are affected by more than the difference in inflation rates between countries. We have already noted that different income growth rates affect the demand for a currency and therefore the exchange rate. Shortly, we shall discuss other factors that affect the exchange rate. In the *long run,* however, and in particular when there is a *large difference* in inflation rates across countries, the PPP theory does predict exchange rates accurately.

Changes in Real Interest Rates.   As was evident from the U.S. balance of payments, illustrated in Exhibit 36–1, more than goods flow between countries. There is financial capital, too, the flow of which is dependent on different countries' **real interest rates**—interest rates adjusted for inflation. Suppose we start at a position where the real interest rate is 3 percent in both the United States and in Great Britain. Then the real interest rate in the United States increases to 4.5 percent. What will happen? The British will increase the demand for dollars, and therefore supply more pounds to purchase financial assets in the United States that pay a higher real interest rate than financial assets in Great Britain. As the supply of pounds increases on the foreign exchange market, the exchange rate (dollar price per pound) will change; fewer dollars will be needed to buy pounds. In short, the dollar will appreciate and the pound will depreciate.

Real Interest Rate
The inflation-adjusted interest rate.

Combined Current and Capital Account Balances with Flexible Exchange Rates

In the following discussion, the current and capital accounts are lumped together into one account: the combined current and capital account.

Once again, consider the exchange rate of $1.90 = £1 in Exhibit 36–4. As we noted, at this exchange rate there is a surplus of pounds; more pounds are supplied than are demanded. But what does this mean in terms of the flow of goods, services, and funds between the two countries? Simply put, since the British are supplying more pounds than Americans are demanding, it implies that the British are demanding more dollars (since the demand for dollars is a reflection of the supply of pounds) than Americans are demanding pounds.

How does this affect the U.S. combined current and capital account and Great Britain's combined current and capital account? In the United States, the effect is that the sum total of the numbers that have a plus (+) in front of them in this combined account is greater than the sum total of the numbers that have a minus (−) in front of them.[4] In Great Britain, the effect is that the sum total of numbers that have a minus (−) in front of them in this combined account is greater than the sum total of the numbers that have a plus (+) in front of them.[5] This is a roundabout way of saying that at the exchange rate $1.90 = £1, there is a surplus in the U.S. combined current and capital account (pluses outweigh minuses) and a deficit in the British combined capital and current account (minuses outweigh pluses).

This is a temporary state of affairs, though, because the combined current and capital account deficit in Great Britain and the corresponding surplus in the United States are both the result of the above-equilibrium exchange rate, which is temporary. As soon as the exchange rate reaches its equilibrium level, the quantity demanded and supplied of pounds will be equal, as well as the quantity demanded and supplied of dollars (if the pound market is in equilibrium, so is the dollar market). In short, both the U.S. and British combined current and capital account will be balanced.[6]

FIXED EXCHANGE RATES

■

The major alternative to the flexible exchange rate system is the **fixed exchange rate system.** This system works the way it sounds: Exchange rates are fixed or pegged, they are not allowed to fluctuate freely in response to the forces of supply and demand. The workings of the fixed exchange rate system are described in the next sections.

Fixed Exchange Rates and the Central Bank (the Fed)

Once again, we deal with a two-country–two-currency world. Suppose this time the United States and Great Britain agree to fix or peg their currencies; that is, instead of letting the dollar depreciate or appreciate relative to the pound, the two countries agree to set the price of one pound at $1.90. They agree to the exchange rate $1.90 = £1. Generally, we call this the fixed exchange rate or the *official price*

Fixed Exchange Rate System
The system where a nation's currency is set at a fixed rate relative to all other currencies, and central banks intervene in the foreign exchange market to maintain the fixed rate.

---

[4]Recall that a plus (+) indicates a credit for the United States; it represents the demand for U.S. dollars. A minus (−), on the other hand, represents a debit for the United States; it represents the supply of dollars to the foreign exchange market, or the demand for a foreign currency. Since we have already said that the demand for dollars is greater than the demand for pounds, it follows that in the U.S. combined current and capital account, the sum total of the numbers that have a plus before them must be greater than the sum total of numbers that have a minus before them.

[5]In the British balance of payments a plus (+) represents a credit or the demand for pounds. A minus (−) represents a debit or the demand for foreign currency, which is the same as the supply of pounds. Once again, since we have already noted that the demand for dollars is greater than the demand for pounds, it follows that in the British combined capital and current account, the sum total of the numbers that have a minus in front of them is greater than the sum total of the numbers that have a plus in front of them.

[6]This assumes there is no government intervention in the foreign exchange market.

of a pound.[7] Since we deal with more than one official price in our discussion, we refer to $1.90 = £1 as *official price 1* (Exhibit 36–7).

If the dollar price of pounds is above its equilibrium level (which is the case at official price 1), the pound is said to be **overvalued.** It follows that if the pound is overvalued, the dollar is **undervalued.** Similarly, if the dollar price of pounds is below its equilibrium level (which is the case at official price 2 in Exhibit 36–7), the pound is undervalued. It follows that if the pound is undervalued, the dollar must be overvalued.

Notice that at the fixed exchange rate, or official price 1, a surplus of pounds exists. As we previously pointed out, this means the quantity supplied of pounds is greater than the quantity demanded of pounds. Great Britain's combined current and capital account is in deficit.

But what about the U.S. combined current and capital account? Is it in deficit or surplus? Since the quantity supplied of pounds is greater than the quantity

Overvaluation
A currency is overvalued if its price in terms of other currencies is above the equilibrium price.

Undervaluation
A currency is undervalued if its price in terms of other currencies is below the equilibrium price.

[7]If the price of one pound is $1.90, it follows that the price of one dollar is approximately 52 pence. Thus, setting the official price of a pound in terms of dollars and cents automatically sets the official price of a dollar in terms of pounds and pence.

EXHIBIT 36–7
A Fixed Exchange Rate System

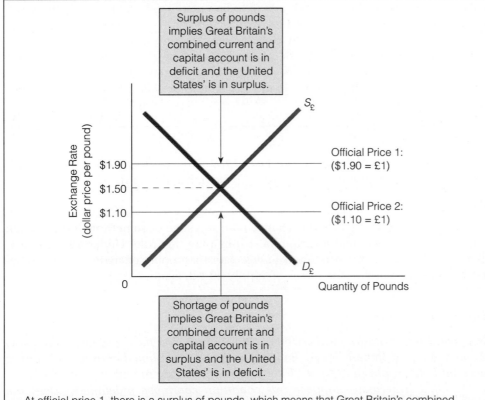

At official price 1, there is a surplus of pounds, which means that Great Britain's combined current and capital account is in deficit and the U.S. combined current and capital account is in surplus. To maintain the official price, the U.S. central bank, the Fed, could buy pounds. At official price 2, there is a shortage of pounds, which means Great Britain's combined current and capital account is in surplus and the U.S. combined current and capital account is in deficit. To maintain the official price, the Fed could sell pounds.

demanded of pounds, it follows that the quantity demanded of dollars is greater than the quantity supplied of dollars. (For a review of the link between the pound market and the dollar market, see Exhibit 36–3.)

If the United States and Great Britain were operating under a flexible exchange rate system, the exchange rate would soon fall to $1.50 = £1, and the disequilibrium condition in each nation's combined current and capital account would disappear. But the two nations are operating under a fixed exchange rate system. So what happens now?

To maintain the fixed exchange rate, the U.S. central bank, the Federal Reserve System (the Fed), could buy the surplus of pounds. This would show up in the official reserve account of the U.S. balance of payments as an increase in U.S. official reserve assets (see item 6 in Exhibit 36–1).

Alternatively, instead of the Fed buying pounds (to mop up the excess supply of pounds), the Bank of England could sell dollars (to eliminate the shortage of dollars, which is the other side of the coin of a surplus of pounds). Finally, there could be some combination of the two actions.

Suppose now that the exchange rate had been fixed at $1.10 = £1. This is *official price 2* in Exhibit 36–7. At this exchange rate, there is a shortage of pounds; the quantity demanded of pounds is greater than the quantity supplied. This implies a surplus in Great Britain's combined current and capital account and a consequent deficit in the U.S. combined current and capital account.

What happens? If the exchange rate is to be maintained, the Fed must now sell pounds to eliminate the shortage of pounds (alternatively, the Bank of England could buy dollars, or there could be some combination of the two actions). The United States will have to draw down the holdings of pounds that it might have acquired when the dollar price per pound was above the equilibrium level. Once again, this action will be recorded in the official reserve account of the U.S. balance of payments.

Question:

Why does the central bank, or the Fed, play a much larger role under a fixed exchange rate system than under a flexible exchange rate system?

Answer:

To support or maintain a fixed exchange rate, someone or something has to do the supporting or the maintaining. Central banks play this role. Under a flexible exchange rate system, there is no exchange rate to support or maintain; exchange rates simply respond to the forces of supply and demand.

Follow-up Question:

Suppose Great Britain and the United States agree to a fixed exchange rate, say, $1.90 = £1, and that at this exchange rate the U.S. combined current and capital account is in surplus and Great Britain's combined current and capital account is in deficit. Furthermore, suppose this condition continues indefinitely. Does the United States continue buying pounds indefinitely?

Answer:

A persistent deficit or surplus in a nation's combined current and capital account is usually dealt with in a way other than the nation continuing indefinitely to buy or sell the other nation's currency. We discuss this in the next section.

Options under a Fixed Exchange Rate System

A nation that persistently has a deficit or a surplus in its combined current and capital account has several options under a fixed exchange rate system. These include devaluation and revaluation, protectionist trade policies, and changes in macroeconomic policies.

Devaluation and revaluation.   Suppose the United States and Great Britain have agreed to fix or peg the exchange rate at $1.90 = £1, which results in a *persistent* surplus in the U.S. combined current and capital account and a *persistent* deficit in Great Britain's combined current and capital account. At some point, the U.S. authorities tire of supporting the exchange rate by buying pounds, and/or the British authorities tire of supporting the exchange rate by selling dollars. The countries agree to reset the official price of the pound and the dollar. Suppose they reset it at its equilibrium level of $1.50 = £1. Afterward, economists say there has been a devaluation of the pound and a revaluation of the dollar. A **devaluation** occurs when the official price of a currency is lowered. A **revaluation** occurs when the official price of a currency is raised. If the official price of a pound is moved from $1.90 = £1 (or $1 = 52 pence) to $1.50 = £1 ($1 = 67 pence), it now takes fewer dollars and cents to buy a pound—so the pound has been devalued. It also takes more pence to buy a dollar—so the dollar has been revalued. The devaluation of the pound and revaluation of the dollar have the effect of eliminating the persistent disequilibrium situations in the two nation's combined current and capital accounts—at least for now.

The situation could arise where one nation would want to reset the official price of the currencies and another nation would not. Suppose the United States is experiencing a surplus in its merchandise trade balance (exports of goods > imports of goods) at the official price of $1.90 = £1 and doesn't want to give this up. It may be that U.S. export businesses are lobbying U.S. authorities not to revalue the dollar. In short, U.S. export interests feel they are benefiting from the undervalued dollar (and overvalued pound) and want to keep things this way.

Protectionist trade policy (quotas and tariffs).   A nation that has a merchandise trade deficit can erect quotas and tariffs to stem the tide of imports into the country. We saw in our last chapter how both tariffs and quotas meet this objective. Economists are quick to point out that merchandise trade problems are sometimes used as an excuse to promote trade restrictions—many of which simply benefit special interests.

Changes in monetary policy.   Sometimes monetary policy can be used by a nation to support the exchange rate or the official price of its currency. Suppose the United States is continually running a merchandise trade deficit; year after year, imports are outstripping exports. To remedy this, the United States might enact a tight monetary policy to retard inflation and drive up interest rates (at least in the short run). The tight monetary policy will reduce the U.S. rate of inflation and thereby lower U.S. prices relative to prices in other nations. This will make U.S. goods relatively cheaper than they were before (assuming other nations didn't also enact a tight monetary policy) and promote U.S. exports and discourage foreign imports, as well as generate a flow of investment funds into the United States in search of higher real interest rates.

Some economists argue against fixed exchange rates because they think it unwise for a nation to adopt a particular monetary policy simply to maintain an interna-

Devaluation
An official governmental act that changes the exchange rate by lowering the official price of a currency.

Revaluation
An official governmental act that changes the exchange rate by raising the official price of a currency.

tional exchange rate. Instead, they believe domestic monetary policies should be used to meet domestic economic goals—such as price stability, low unemployment, low and stable interest rates, and so forth. This naturally leads us into a discussion of the case for and against fixed exchange rates for promoting international trade.

Promoting International Trade

Which are better, fixed or flexible exchange rates? Following is the case for each.

The Case for Fixed Exchange Rates. Proponents of a fixed exchange rate system often argue that fixed exchange rates promote international trade, whereas flexible exchange rates stifle it. A major advantage of fixed exchange rates is certainty: Individuals in different countries know from day to day what their nation's currency will trade for. With flexible exchange rates, individuals will not be as likely to enter into international trade because of the added risk of not knowing from one day to the next how many dollars or francs or pounds they will have to give up to get, say, 100 yen. Certainty is a necessary ingredient in international trade; flexible exchange rates promote uncertainty, which hampers international trade. Economist Charles Kindleberger, a proponent of fixed exchange rates, believes that having fixed exchange rates is analogous to having one currency in the entire United States instead of having one currency for each of 50 states: One currency in the United States promotes trade and 50 different currencies would hamper it. In Kindleberger's view:

> The main case against flexible exchange rates is that they break up the world market. . . . Imagine trying to conduct interstate trade in the USA if there were fifty different state monies, none of which was dominant. This is akin to barter, the inefficiency of which is explained time and again by textbooks.[8]

The Case for Flexible Exchange Rates. Advocates of flexible exchange rates, as we have noted, maintain that it is better for a nation to adopt the policies it wants to meet domestic economic goals than to sacrifice domestic economic goals to maintain an exchange rate. They also state that there is too great a chance that the fixed exchange rate will diverge greatly from the equilibrium exchange rate, creating persistent balance of trade problems. This leads deficit nations to impose trade restrictions (tariffs and quotas) that hinder international trade.

The Value of the Dollar and American Real Estate

When the dollar depreciates relative to the Japanese yen, dollar-denominated assets become cheaper for the Japanese to buy. During the last 20 years or so, the Japanese have begun to buy American hotels, businesses, land, apartment buildings, and so on. Some Americans have complained that the Japanese are buying out Americans and taking over the United States. A debate over the seriousness of the issue ensued.

Some people said the following:

1. Foreign investment in the United States unfairly drives up real estate prices for the American buyer. The idea here is that when the Japanese bid for real estate along with Americans, the price of real estate rises. Americans end up paying more

[8]Charles Kindleberger, *International Money* (London: Allen and Unwin, 1981), p. 174.

The Future Sometimes Looks Brighter with Futures: Or How to Lock in the Price of the Yen without Really Trying

Meet (the fictional) Bill Whatley, the owner of a Toyota dealership in San Diego. It is currently May, and Bill is thinking about buying a shipment of Toyotas in August. He knows that he must buy the Toyotas from Japan with yen, but he has a problem. At the present time, in May, the dollar price of yen is $.005. Bill wonders what will happen if the dollar price of yen rises in August when he plans to make his purchase. Suppose the dollar price of yen rises to $.006. If this happens, then instead of paying $15,000 for a Toyota priced at 3 million yen, he would have to pay $18,000.* This $3,000 difference may be enough to wipe out any profit on the sale of Toyotas.

*If a yen equals $.005, then a Toyota with a price tag of 3 million yen actually costs $15,000 ($.005 × 3,000,000 = $15,000). If a yen equals $.006, then a Toyota with a price tag of 3 million yen actually costs $18,000 (.006 × 3,000,000 = $18,000).

What is Bill to do? He could purchase a *futures contract* today for the needed quantity of yen in August. A futures contract is a contract in which the seller agrees to provide a particular good (in our example, a particular currency) to the buyer on a specified future date at an agreed-on price. In short, Bill can buy yen today at a specified dollar price and take delivery of the yen at a later date (in August).

But suppose the dollar price of yen falls to $.004 in August? If this happens, Bill would only have to pay $12,000 (instead of $15,000) for a Toyota priced at 3 million yen. Although this is true, Bill, like other car dealers, might not be interested in assuming the risk associated with changes in exchange rates. He may prefer to lock in a sure thing.

Who would sell yen to Bill? The answer is someone who is willing to assume the risk of changes in the value of currencies that Bill obviously is not—for example, Julie Jackson. Ju-

lie thinks to herself, "I think the dollar price of yen will go down between now and August. Therefore, I will enter into a contract with Bill stating that I will hand over to him 3 million yen in August for $15,000—the exchange rate specified in the contract being 1 yen = $.005. If I am right, and the *actual* exchange rate at the time is 1 yen = $.004, then I can purchase the 3 million yen for $12,000, and turn around and fulfill my contract with Bill by turning the yen over to him for $15,000. I walk away with $3,000 profit."

Many economists argue that futures contracts offer people a way of dealing with the risk associated with a flexible exchange rate system. If a person doesn't know what next month's exchange rate will be, and doesn't want to take the risk of waiting to see, then he or she can enter into a futures contract and effectively shift the risk to someone who voluntarily assumes it.

to buy real estate than if the demand was less. This is true enough; but the argument ignores the benefits to the sellers (perhaps American?) of American real estate. They benefit from the increased demand for real estate—whether it comes from other Americans, the Japanese, or someone else.

2. Foreign investment will result in foreign control of American businesses. The argument here is that if the Japanese, or other foreigners, buy American businesses, there will be a fundamental change in the nature of these businesses and ultimately Americans will be hurt. Looking at the opposite side of the coin, one may question whether foreigners will run American businesses differently from the way Americans run American businesses. Presumably, the Japanese buy American businesses to earn profits, which is the same reason Americans buy American businesses. The desire to earn profits limits one's behavior in a certain way, so that there will be little difference (if any) between a business in the United States owned by a foreigner and the same business owned by an American.

What Does the International Value of the Dollar Have to Do with Life on the Farm?

Peter Sutton, 36, is a farmer. His father is a farmer, as were his grandfather and great-grandfather. Peter hopes that his son, Ryan, will one day grow up to be a farmer.

In 1978, Peter bought a wheat farm in Kansas. At the time, farmland was selling at a premium, so Peter had to agree to meet stiff mortgage payments. Still, times were prosperous, and Peter could make the payments. He and his wife were working hard, but it was good, honest work, and they both enjoyed it.

In the meantime, the nation's elected representatives in Washington were discussing tax and spending cuts. In the end, however, not many of the spending cuts were passed, but the tax cuts were. The editor of the newspaper in the town near Peter's farm wrote a few editorials on expansionary fiscal policy. (She was proud that she had minored in economics in college.)

In late 1980s, Peter began to notice news stories about the increasingly

strong dollar (that is, appreciating dollar). He didn't think much about it at first. But then in 1982, the dollar appreciated more, and in 1983, it appreciated even more, and so on into 1984 and 1985. In 1983, Peter's profits began to decline. The appreciated dollar made it more difficult for him to sell his wheat abroad. Also, as the German mark went from 2 to 3 marks per dollar, a bushel of wheat that sold for 12 marks in Germany earned only $4 instead of $6 for the American farmer who produced the wheat. Peter began to feel the pinch. Less income was coming in, but he still had his mortgage payments to meet. He fell six months behind and the bank threatened to foreclose on his farm.

Peter tried to work harder; he sold one of his cars and even sold some of his furniture, but each month he fell farther behind in his mortgage payments. Finally, in mid-1984, Peter lost his farm.

Many of Peter's farmer neighbors were in the same predicament. Some

of them argued that the Congress should impose protectionist measures in order to decrease imports. The major television networks broadcast special features on the economic problems of farmers and their discontent with the government's policies.

Last week, Peter was visiting his brother in Oregon. His nephew, Jack, was home from college where he is a freshman. Jack, who is studious, was telling his Uncle Peter about what he had recently learned in his economics course. He also complained mildly that economics is too theoretical and doesn't relate to the real world. Unaware of his uncle's experiences, Jack mentioned the exchange rate value of the dollar as an example of economics that didn't really affect ordinary people.

Uncle Peter had a few things to say on the subject.

The Gold Standard

Once nations have decided to adopt the gold standard, they automatically fix their exchange rates. Suppose the United States defines a dollar as equal to $\frac{1}{20}$ of an ounce of gold and Great Britain defines a pound as equal to $\frac{1}{5}$ of an ounce of gold. This means that one ounce of gold could be bought with either $20 or £5. What, then, is the exchange rate between dollars and pounds? It is 4 dollars = 1 pound, or 1 dollar = $\frac{1}{4}$ pound. This is the *fixed* exchange rate between dollars and pounds.

To have an international gold standard, countries must do the following: (1) Define their currencies in terms of gold (for example, $1 = $\frac{1}{20}$ oz. of gold, £1 = $\frac{1}{5}$ oz. of gold, and so on). (2) Stand ready and willing to convert gold into paper money and paper money into gold at the rate specified (for example, the United States would buy and sell gold at $20 an ounce). (3) Link their money supplies to their holdings of gold. With this in mind, consider how a gold standard would work.

Let's again look at the two countries Great Britain and the United States, and assume that the exchange rate 1 dollar = $\frac{1}{4}$ pound is the equilibrium exchange rate. Then, a change occurs: Inflation raises British prices by 100 percent. A British tea set that was priced at £20 before the inflation is now priced as £40. At the fixed exchange rate, Americans find that they now have to give up $160 to buy the tea set, whereas before the British inflation they only had to give up $80. Consequently, Americans buy fewer tea sets; Americans import less.

At the same time, however, the British import more. The reason is that American prices are now relatively lower than before the British inflation. Suppose an American pair of shoes was $80 before the inflation. In relative terms, the cost was 1 British tea set, since the tea set cost £20 before the inflation and 1 dollar = ¼ pound. After the inflation, the American shoes are still $80 but the tea set is £40. This means the relative cost of American shoes has gone down to ½ British tea set (since 1 dollar = ¼ pound). To the British, the inflation in their country has made American goods relatively cheaper. The British end up buying more American goods; they import more.

We see, then, that the British inflation has decreased American imports and increased American exports; at the same time, it has decreased British exports and increased British imports. The U.S. merchandise trade balance moves into surplus; the British trade balance moves into deficit.

The British have to pay for the difference between their imports and exports with gold. Gold is therefore shipped to the United States. An increase in the supply of gold in the United States expands the U.S. money supply. A decrease in the supply of gold in Great Britain contracts the British money supply. Prices are affected in both countries. In the United States, prices begin to rise; in Great Britain, prices begin to fall. As U.S. prices go up and British prices go down, the earlier situation begins to reverse itself. American goods look more expensive to the British, and they begin to buy less, whereas British goods look cheaper to Americans, and they begin to buy more. Consequently, American imports begin to rise and exports begin to fall; British imports begin to fall and exports begin to rise. The gold standard, through changing domestic money supplies and price levels, begins to correct the initial trade balance disequilibrium.

The change in the money supply that the gold standard sometimes requires has prompted some economists to voice the same argument against the gold standard that is often heard against the fixed exchange rate system; that is, it subjects domestic monetary policy to international instead of domestic considerations. In fact, many economists cite this as part of the reason many nations abandoned the gold standard in the 1930s. At a time when unemployment was unusually high, many nations with trade deficits felt that matters would only get worse if they contracted their money supplies to live by the edicts of the gold standard. We explore this question in greater detail in the next section.

WHERE WE'VE BEEN, WHERE WE ARE

Historians are quick to point out that we can only understand where we are if we first understand where we've been. With this in mind, we discuss a few key past and present events in U.S. international finance.

The Crack-up of the Gold Standard

From the 1870s to the 1930s, many nations tied their currencies to gold. The United States, for example, stood ready to exchange an ounce of gold for $20.67. For most of this period—roughly from the 1870s to the end of World War I—the gold standard worked well. Critics say that the gold standard worked well because there were few problems for it to solve. For example, during this time, no major trading country found itself with persistent balance of payments problems.

Then, after World War I, things began to change. Some countries (most notably the United States) began to break the rules of the gold standard by not contracting their money supplies to the extent called for by the outflow of gold. Under these circumstances, the gold standard could not restore balance of trade equilibrium.

In the 1920s, Great Britain and France tried to restore the gold standard. They did so, however, by setting the "wrong" exchange rates: The pound was overvalued and the franc was undervalued. This action led to trade surpluses in France and high unemployment and trade deficits in Great Britain. To maintain the gold standard, both countries would have had to change their money supplies significantly. The countries began to feel that it was not worth subjecting their domestic economies to such sharp changes in order to abide by the discipline of the gold standard.

As we noted earlier, the Great Depression was perhaps the straw that broke the back of the gold standard. In the face of widespread high unemployment, nations with trade deficits began to feel that abiding by the rules of the gold standard and contracting their money supplies to restore balance of trade equilibrium was too high a price to pay. So they went off the gold standard.

The Bretton Woods System

In 1944, once it appeared that the Allies were certain to win World War II, major negotiators from the Allied countries met in Bretton Woods, New Hampshire, to map out a new international monetary system. This system came to be known as the *Bretton Woods system.* It was based on fixed exchange rates and an international central bank called the **International Monetary Fund (IMF).**[9] Under the Bretton Woods system, nations were expected to maintain fixed exchange rates (within a narrow range) by buying and selling their own currency for other currencies.[10] A nation experiencing a trade deficit could borrow international reserves from the IMF. It was expected that the nation that had borrowed reserves would, over time, generate a trade surplus with which it could pay off its loan. The IMF reserves were created by imposing a quota on each member nation—a fee based on the nation's trade and national income. Each member nation contributed 25 percent of its quota in gold or U.S. dollars and 75 percent in its own currency.

In the late 1960s, the IMF created a new international money to add to its international reserves fund. This was the **special drawing right (SDR).** In essence, SDRs are simply bookkeeping entries. However, once a country has an SDR account, it can use SDRs to settle a trade imbalance.

In the 1960s and early 1970s, the Bretton Woods system became strained at the seams. One of the major shortcomings of the system was that it encouraged speculative attacks on a currency. Suppose Great Britain is persistently running a trade

International Monetary Fund (IMF)
An international organization created by the Bretton Woods system to oversee the international monetary system. Although the Bretton Woods system no longer exists, the IMF does. It does not control the world's money supply, but it does hold currency reserves for member nations and makes loans to central banks.

Special Drawing Right
An international money, created by the IMF, in the form of bookkeeping entries; like gold and currencies, they can be used by nations to settle international accounts.

[9]The IMF is sometimes confused with the World Bank (or International Bank for Reconstruction and Development), although it is something different altogether. The World Bank, which was also part of the Bretton Woods agreement, was set up to provide long-term loans to assist developing nations in building roads, dams, and other capital projects that it was felt would contribute to their economic development.
[10]Actually, the Bretton Woods system was not an absolutely rigid fixed exchange rate system. Because it was not, it is sometimes referred to as the *adjustable peg system.* Exchange rates were set, and then a narrow band around each exchange rates was specified within which the exchange rate could move without central bank intervention. In addition, the IMF allowed for periodic realignment in exchange rates.

deficit and Germany is persistently running a trade surplus. Under these circumstances, speculators know that sooner or later Great Britain will have to devalue its currency, although government officials in Great Britain will probably deny this. Speculators will likely respond by selling the weak British pound (before it is devalued and they are left holding a bag full of less valuable pounds) and buying the strong currency—in our example, the German mark. Obviously, this speculative action will increase the supply of pounds on the foreign exchange market and cause the difference between the official price of pounds and the equilibrium price of pounds to increase. Thus, if the pound were overvalued before the speculative action, it is now even more overvalued; a bad situation has become worse.

This is, in fact, what happened to Great Britain in 1967. At the official price for a pound, the quantity supplied of pounds was greater than the quantity demanded of pounds. In short, the pound was overvalued, and Great Britain was faced with a combined current and capital account deficit. To maintain the official price (exchange rate), the Bank of England had to buy the excess supply of pounds. In doing this, though, it lost international reserves. By November 17, 1967, speculators began to suspect that despite IMF loans to Great Britain, the British pound would soon have to be devalued. They reasoned that Great Britain didn't have the reserves necessary to continue to maintain the official price of the pound. Speculators began to view a devaluation of the pound as (almost) certain and began to sell off pounds. This made the problem worse for the Bank of England because now, with more pounds on the foreign exchange market, it was forced to buy up more pounds to maintain the official price of the pound. On one day alone, the Bank of England had to buy $1 billion worth of pounds to keep the exchange rate from falling. Finally, the Bank of England realized that it could not continue to defend the pound successfully at its present official price, and soon after devalued the pound by 14 percent. This meant that the speculators who had sold $1 billion worth of pounds to the Bank of England collectively earned $140 million. How did they manage this? The dollars they had bought by selling pounds to the Bank of England had appreciated in value 14 percent. If they sold $1 billion worth of pounds, then they realized $140 million in profits (since 14 percent of $1 billion = $140 million). The Bank of England had found that defending its currency against speculative attack was expensive. Critics of the Bretton Woods system began to point out that any fixed exchange rate system has this failing; it can prompt speculative attacks on currencies.

In 1971, speculators began to speculate on the dollar. Before we can understand this action fully, we need to point out that the U.S. dollar was convertible into gold (for foreign governments and central banks only) at $35 an ounce. In the 1960s, the United States had witnessed an accelerating inflation that caused U.S. exports to become more expensive and U.S. imports to become less expensive. This difference in inflation rates between the United States and many other countries began to put pressure on exchange rates; more and more, it appeared that the dollar was overvalued at its official price. In short, there was a surplus of dollars. But this simply meant that some other currencies were undervalued and that there was an excess demand for them. According to the rules laid down under the Bretton Woods system, the countries whose currencies were in short supply had to buy up dollars and thus sell more of their currency to maintain exchange rates. For example, the German central bank, the Bundesbank, bought $2 billion of U.S. dollars between January and March 1971 to fulfill its obligation to keep the exchange rate fixed at 27 cents = 1 mark.

Now this meant that by buying dollars, the Bundesbank, and some other central banks, were increasing their holdings of dollars. But increasingly, central banks became reluctant to hold dollars. U.S. monetary authorities became worried because they knew that if central banks did demand gold (for dollars), the U.S. gold stock would be severely diminished if the United States maintained a $35 price for gold. Add to this the voiced anguish of many American exporters of goods who complained that they were being severely hurt by the overvalued dollar, and you knew something would soon have to happen.

It did. On Sunday evening, August 15, 1971, President Nixon addressed the nation and announced that the United States would no longer honor its IMF obligation to sell gold at $35 an ounce. Soon after, the U.S. dollar began to fluctuate in the foreign exchange market. The overvalued dollar soon depreciated against other major currencies. By 1973, the Bretton Woods system was dead.

The Current International Monetary System

Managed Float
A managed flexible exchange rate system, under which nations now and then intervene to adjust their official reserve holdings to moderate major swings in exchange rates; this is today's international monetary system.

Today's international monetary system is best described as a *managed flexible exchange rate system,* sometimes referred to more casually as a **managed float.** In a way, this is a rough compromise between the fixed and flexible exchange rate systems. The current system operates under flexible exchange rates, but not completely. Nations now and then intervene to adjust their official reserve holdings to moderate major swings in exchange rates. For example, the United States intervened in foreign exchange markets in 1978 to moderate the depreciation of the dollar. Recent intervention has involved coordinated efforts on the part of major industrial nations. In September 1985, the finance ministers of five industrial nations—France, Germany, Japan, Great Britain, and the United States—met at the Plaza Hotel in New York City and agreed to intervene in foreign exchange markets to achieve desired changes in exchange rates. At the time the meeting took place, the Group of Five (or G-5, as the countries came to be known) believed the dollar was overvalued and therefore agreed to achieve a depreciation of the dollar. In 1987, the Group of Five was joined by Canada and Italy and became known as the Group of Seven (G-7). At this time, the G-7 bought large quantities of dollars in the foreign exchange market in order to achieve appreciation of the dollar. The G-7 still periodically intervenes in foreign exchange markets to accomplish particular goals.

Proponents of the managed float system stress the following advantages:

1. It allows nations to pursue independent monetary policies. Under a (strictly) fixed exchange rate system, fixed either by agreement or by gold, a nation with a merchandise trade deficit might have to enact a tight monetary policy in order to retard inflation and promote its exports (see the discussion of the fixed exchange rate system). This would not be the case with the managed float. Its proponents argue that it is better to adjust one price—the exchange rate—than to adjust the price level to solve trade imbalances.

2. It solves trade problems without trade restrictions. As we stated earlier, with a fixed exchange rate system, nations sometimes impose tariffs and quotas to solve trade imbalances. For example, a deficit nation might impose import quotas so that exports and imports of goods will be more in line. With the current system, trade imbalances are usually solved through changes in exchange rates.

3. It is flexible and therefore can easily adjust to shocks. In 1973–74, the OPEC nations dramatically raised the price of oil, which resulted in many oil-importing nations running trade deficits. A fixed exchange rate system would have had a hard time accommodating such a major change in oil prices. The current system had little trouble, however. Exchange rates took much of the shock (there were large changes in exchange rates) and thus allowed most nations' economies to weather the storm with a minimum of difficulty.

Opponents of the current international monetary system stress the following disadvantages:

1. It promotes exchange rate volatility and uncertainty and results in less international trade than would be the case under fixed exchange rates. Under a flexible exchange rate system, exchange rates are volatile and therefore make it risky for importers and exporters to conduct business; as a result, international trade is less than it would be under a fixed exchange rate system. Opponents of the current system often point to the sharp depreciation of the U.S. dollar in 1986. Proponents often report that a futures market in currencies exists that allows importers and exporters to shift the risk of fluctuations in exchange rates to others.

For example, if an American company wants to buy a certain quantity of a good from a Japanese company three months from today, it can contract today for the desired quantity of yen it will need, at a specified price; it will not have to worry about a change in the dollar price of yen over the next three months. There is, of course, a cost to this, but it is usually modest.

2. It promotes inflation. As we have seen, the monetary policies of different nations are not independent of one another under a fixed exchange rate system. For example, a nation with a merchandise trade deficit is somewhat restrained from inflating because this will worsen the deficit problem—it will make its goods more expensive relative to foreign goods and promote the purchase of imports. In its attempt to maintain the exchange rate, a nation with a merchandise trade deficit would have to enact a tight monetary policy.

Under the current system, a nation with a merchandise trade deficit does not have to concern itself with maintaining exchange rates or trying to solve its deficit problem through changes in its money supply. Opponents of the current system argue that this frees nations to inflate. They predict more inflation will result than under a fixed exchange rate system.

3. Changes in exchange rates alter trade balances in the desired direction only after a long time; in the short run, a depreciation in a currency can make the situation worse instead of better. It is often argued that soon after a depreciation in a trade-deficit nation's currency, the trade deficit will increase (not decrease, as was hoped). The reason is that import demand is inelastic in the short run: Imports are not very responsive to a change in price. Suppose Great Britain is running a trade deficit with the United States at the present exchange rate of $1.50 = £1. At this exchange rate, the pound is overvalued, and Great Britain (we assume) buys 2,000 television sets each with a price tag of $500 from the United States. Great Britain therefore spends £666,666 on imports of American television sets. Now suppose the overvalued pound begins to depreciate, say, to $1.25 = £1. Furthermore, in the short run, British customers only buy 100 fewer American television sets; that is, they import 1,900 television sets. At a price of $500 each, and at an exchange rate of $1.25 = £1, the British now spend £760,000 on imports of American television sets.

In the short run, then, a depreciation in the pound has widened the trade deficit because the percentage by which imports falls (5 percent) was less than the percentage by which the price of imports (in terms of pounds) increased (16.7 percent).[11] As time passes, imports will fall off more (it takes time for British buyers

---

[11]In other words, the demand for imports in the short run is highly price inelastic. As time passes, the price elasticity of demand for imports increases, and the trade deficit problem begins to be solved.

EXHIBIT 36–8
The J-Curve

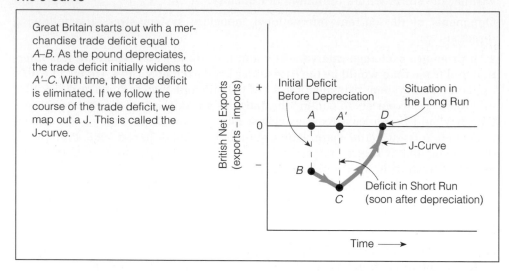

Great Britain starts out with a merchandise trade deficit equal to A–B. As the pound depreciates, the trade deficit initially widens to A'–C. With time, the trade deficit is eliminated. If we follow the course of the trade deficit, we map out a J. This is called the J-curve.

J-Curve
The curve that shows a short-run worsening in the trade deficit after a currency depreciation, followed later by an improvement.

to shift from higher-priced American goods to lower-priced British goods), and the deficit will shrink. If we graph this phenomenon—namely, that a depreciation in a nation's currency widens the trade deficit in the short run and shrinks it in the long run—we obtain a **J-curve** (Exhibit 36–8).

In the exhibit, we have plotted time on the horizontal axis and British net exports on the vertical axis. Net exports = exports − imports; therefore, negative net exports imply a trade deficit (imports > exports). As we can see, before the depreciation of the pound, Great Britain is experiencing a trade deficit equal to $A - B$. Next, the pound is depreciated and the trade deficit widens to $A' - C$. The movement from B to C is the first part of the J-curve. Next, as time passes, the trade deficit begins to shrink. The British are, with time, moving from American imports to domestic goods. At point D, British net exports are zero (exports = imports). The movement from C to D is the second part of the J-curve. The J-curve is represented by the movement from B to C and from C to D.

Question:

Does the J-curve phenomenon mean that a system of flexible exchange rates is undesirable?

Answer:

Some economists would say that if there is a J-curve phenomenon, changes in exchange rates are a rather crude way of solving a trade imbalance because in the short run they make things worse.

Balance of Payments

■ The balance of payments provides information about a nation's imports and exports, domestic residents' earnings on assets located abroad, foreign earnings on domestic assets, gifts to and from foreign countries, and official transactions by governments and central banks.

■ In a nation's balance of payments, any transaction that supplies the nation's currency in the foreign exchange market is recorded as a debit ($-$). Any transaction that supplies a foreign currency is recorded as a credit ($+$).

■ The three main accounts of the balance of payments are the current account, capital account, and official reserve account.

■ The current account includes all payments related to the purchase and sale of goods and services. The three major components of the account are exports of goods and services, imports of goods and services, and unilateral transfers.

■ The capital account includes all payments related to the purchase and sale of assets and to borrowing and lending activities. The major components are outflow of U.S. capital and inflow of foreign capital.

■ The official reserve account includes transactions by the central banks of various countries.

■ The merchandise trade balance is the difference between the value of merchandise exports and the value of merchandise imports. If exports are greater than imports, a nation has a trade surplus; if imports are greater than exports, a nation has a trade deficit. The balance of payments equals current account balance + capital account balance + official reserve balance + statistical discrepancy.

The Foreign Exchange Market and Flexible and Fixed Exchange Rates

■ The market in which currencies of different countries are exchanged is called the foreign exchange market. In this market, currencies are bought and sold for a price; an exchange rate exists.

■ If Americans demand British goods, they also demand British pounds and supply U.S. dollars. If the British demand American goods, they also demand U.S. dollars and supply British pounds. When the residents of a nation demand a foreign currency, they must supply their own currency.

■ Under flexible exchange rates, the foreign exchange market will equilibrate at the exchange rate where the quantity demanded of a currency equals the quantity supplied of a currency; for example, the quantity demanded of dollars equals the quantity supplied of dollars.

■ If the price of a nation's currency increases against a foreign currency, the nation's economy is said to have appreciated. For example, if the dollar price of a pound rises from $1.50 = £1 to $1.80 = £1, the pound has appreciated. If the price of a nation's currency decreases against a foreign currency, the nation's currency is said to have depreciated. For example, if the pound price of a dollar falls from 66 pence = $1 to 55 pence = $1, the dollar has depreciated.

■ Under a flexible exchange rate system, the equilibrium exchange rate is affected by a difference in income growth rates between countries, a difference in inflation rates between countries, and a change in (real) interest rates between countries.

- Under a fixed exchange rate system, countries agree to fix the price of their currencies. The central banks of the countries must then buy and sell currencies to maintain the agreed-on exchange rate. If a persistent deficit or surplus in a nation's combined current and capital account exists at a fixed exchange rate, the nation has a few options to deal with the problem: devalue or revalue its currency, enact protectionist trade policies (in the case of a deficit), or change its monetary policy.

The Gold Standard

- To have an international gold standard, nations must do the following: (1) Define their currencies in terms of gold. (2) Stand ready and willing to convert gold into paper money and paper money into gold at a specified rate. (3) Link their money supplies to their holdings of gold. The change in the money supply that the gold standard sometimes requires has prompted some economists to voice the same argument against the gold standard that is often heard against the fixed exchange rate system: It subjects domestic monetary policy to international instead of domestic considerations.

The Current International Monetary System

- Today's international monetary system is described as a managed flexible exchange rate system, or managed float. For the most part, the exchange rate system is flexible, although nations do periodically intervene in the foreign exchange market to adjust exchange rates. Since it is a managed float system, it is difficult to tell if nations will emphasize the "float" part or the "managed" part in years to come.
- Proponents of the managed flexible exchange rate system believe it offers several advantages: (1) It allows nations to pursue independent macroeconomic policies. (2) It solves trade problems without trade restrictions. (3) It is flexible and therefore can easily adjust to shocks. Opponents of the managed flexible exchange rate system believe it has several disadvantages: (1) It promotes exchange rate volatility and uncertainty, and thus results in less international trade than would be the case under fixed exchange rates. (2) It promotes inflation. (3) It corrects trade deficits only a long time after a depreciation in the currency; in the interim, it can make matters worse. This is the J-curve phenomenon.

Key Terms and Concepts

Balance of Payments	Current Account Balance	Fixed Exchange Rate System
Debit	Capital Account	Overvaluation
Credit	Capital Account Balance	Undervaluation
Current Account	Exchange Rate	Devaluation
Foreign Exchange Market	Flexible Exchange Rate System	Revaluation
Merchandise Trade Balance	Appreciation	International Monetary Fund (IMF)
Merchandise Trade Deficit	Depreciation	Special Drawing Right
Merchandise Trade Surplus	Purchasing Power Parity Theory	Managed Float
	Real Interest Rate	J-curve

1. The following foreign exchange information appeared in a newspaper:

	U.S. $ Equivalent		Currency per U.S. $	
	FRI.	THRS.	FRI.	THRS.
France (franc)	.1577	.1578	6.3410	6.3400
Japan (yen)	.007503	.007493	133.27	133.45
German (mark)	.5370	.5364	1.8563	1.8583

(a) Between Thursday and Friday, did the dollar appreciate or depreciate against the French franc? (b) Between Thursday and Friday, did the dollar appreciate or depreciate against the Japanese yen? (c) Between Thursday and Friday, did the dollar appreciate or depreciate against the German mark?

2. Suppose the United States and Greece are on a flexible exchange rate system. Explain whether each of the following events will lead to an appreciation or depreciation in the U.S. dollar and Greek drachma: (a) U.S. real interest rates rise above Greek real interest rates. (b) The Greek inflation rate rises relative to the U.S. inflation rate. (c) Greece puts a quota on imports of American radios. (d) Americans learn on the nightly news that terrorists at the Athens airport boarded a plane that they subsequently skyjacked with American citizens aboard. As a result, American tourism to Athens (Greece) drops off substantially.

3. Give an example that illustrates how a change in the exchange rate changes the relative price of domestic goods in terms of foreign goods.

4. Suppose the media report that the United States has a deficit in its current account. What does this imply about the U.S. capital account balance and official reserve account balance?

5. Suppose that Great Britain has a merchandise trade deficit and France has a merchandise trade surplus. Since the two countries are on a flexible exchange rate system, the franc appreciates and the pound depreciates. It is noticed, however, that soon after the depreciation of the pound, Great Britain's trade deficit grows instead of shrinks. Why might this be?

6. What are the strong and weak points of the flexible exchange rate system? What are the strong and weak points of the fixed exchange rate system?

7. Individuals do not keep a written account of their balance of trade with other individuals. For example, John doesn't keep an account of how much he sells to Alice and how much he buys from Alice. In addition, neither cities nor any of the 50 states calculate their balance of trade with all other cities and states. However, nations do calculate their merchandise trade balance with other nations. If nations do it, should individuals, cities, and states do it? Why?

8. Since every nation's balance of payments equals zero, does it follow that each nation is on an equal footing in international trade and finance with every other nation? Explain your answer.

9. Suppose your objective is to predict whether the British pound and the U.S. dollar will appreciate or depreciate on the foreign exchange market in the next two months. What information would you need to help you make your prediction? Specifically, how would this information help you predict the direction of the foreign exchange value of the pound and dollar? Next, explain how a person who could accurately predict exchange rates could become extremely rich in a short time.

PART

XI

ECONOMIC GROWTH, DEVELOPMENT, AND ALTERNATIVE ECONOMIC SYSTEMS

ECONOMIC GROWTH AND DEVELOPMENT

WHAT THIS CHAPTER IS ABOUT

What would your life be like if you had been born in Ethiopia, India, or Tanzania instead of the United States? Most likely you wouldn't be driving a car because you wouldn't own one. You wouldn't have new clothes, a compact disc player, or a personal computer. You wouldn't go out to restaurants and movies regularly. You wouldn't be enrolled in a college or university studying economics!

You largely have what you have—things that Ethiopians, Indians, and Tanzanians do not have because you were born to parents who live in a country that has experienced relatively more economic growth and development than most countries of the world. In this chapter, we examine the role economic growth and development play in a nation's life.

ECONOMIC GROWTH

■

Real Economic Growth
An increase from one period to the next in real GNP.

Per-Capita Real Economic Growth
An increase from one period to the next in per-capita real GNP, which is real GNP divided by population.

The term *economic growth* refers to either real economic growth or to per-capita real economic growth. **Real economic growth** is an increase from one period to the next in *real GNP*. **Per-capita real economic growth** is an increase from one period to the next in *per-capita real GNP,* which is real GNP divided by population.

Most economists think the per-capita measurement is more useful, since it, unlike absolute economic growth, tells us how much better or worse off the average person is in one period compared with another, assuming a given income distribution. For example, India has a higher real GNP than Norway. But it also has 171 times the population. It turns out that per-capita real GNP in Norway is approximately 50 times as high as per-capita real GNP in India.

Per-capita real economic growth is a relatively new phenomenon. In the preindustrial world, real economic growth often encouraged the population to increase beyond the increase in real GNP, and consequently people's standard of living fell. It was only in sixteenth-century England and the Netherlands that per-capita real economic growth first appeared on a sustainable basis. This means that before this time, a son's standard of living was much like his father's, his grandfather's, and so on back a few more generations. To get an idea of the changes that have occurred, just think of how much higher your standard of living is than that of persons who lived in the United States only 50 years ago.

Question:

Suppose the real GNP of country X is $1 billion and the population is 1,000,000 persons. The per-capita real GNP is $1,000. In country Y, the real GNP is $1 million and the population is 2,000 persons. The per-capita real GNP is $500. Does it necessarily follow that the average person in country X is better off than the average person in country Y (at least in material goods)?

Answer:

No, it does not. It could be that in country X one person has the entire real GNP, and in country Y the real GNP is spread evenly over the entire population. In short, per-capita real GNP does not tell us anything about the income distribution. This is not an argument against using the measure of per-capita real GNP, only against its misuse. As an example of its proper use, if for a given country and a given income distribution, the per-capita real GNP is higher in 1991 than in 1990, then it is accurate to say that the average person is better off in terms of material goods.

Growth in a Production Possibilities Frontier Framework

Growth can be seen in a production possibilities frontier (PPF) framework, as Exhibit 37–1 illustrates. On the horizontal axis, we have placed agricultural goods, and on the vertical axis, manufactured goods. There are two production possibilities frontiers: PPF_{1991} and PPF_{1996}. The distance between the two frontiers represents the increased productive capabilities that can, but may not, be realized by the economy. If the economy actually realizes these increased capabilities (and moves from a point on PPF_{1991} to a point on PPF_{1996}), then growth has occurred between 1991 and 1996. If it does not, then growth has not been realized. The

EXHIBIT 37–1
Economic Growth

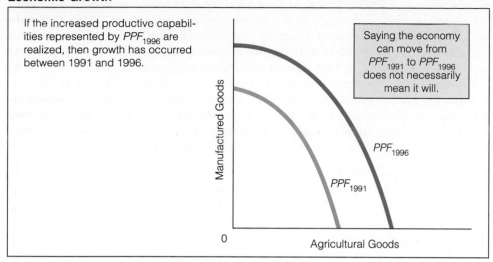

If the increased productive capabilities represented by PPF_{1996} are realized, then growth has occurred between 1991 and 1996.

Saying the economy can move from PPF_{1991} to PPF_{1996} does not necessarily mean it will.

Manufactured Goods

PPF_{1996}

PPF_{1991}

0   Agricultural Goods

latter case would be analogous to discovering a new field of oil or inventing a new technology and doing nothing about it. Potential growth exists, but actual growth is not realized.

Question:

Suppose country A experiences a 3 percent growth rate in real GNP each year for five years, and country B experiences a 6 percent growth rate in real GNP each year for five years. Does it follow that the residents of country B are better off in terms of material goods than the residents of country A?

Answer:

No, it doesn't. Think about this in terms of the *PPF* and per-capita real economic growth. First, the *PPF* for country B might be much closer to the origin than the *PPF* for country A. If this is the case, then fewer goods are produced in country B, even though it has the higher growth rate. Second, we need to know something about the populations of the two countries. It might be that the per-capita real GNP growth rate of country A is greater than the per-capita real GNP growth rate of country B, even though country B has witnessed greater real economic growth.

The United States and Japan: Shifting *PPFs*

Positive economic growth shows up as an outward shift in a country's production possibilities frontier. Let's look at the United States and Japan. Each country has been experiencing economic growth, which means each country's *PPF* has been shifting outward. Exhibit 37–2 shows how much each country's *PPF* has shifted outward for different periods and years. In the exhibit, a positive growth rate represents an outward shift in the country's production possibilities frontier. For most periods and years cited in the exhibit, the growth rate in Japan was greater than the growth rate in the United States.

What Factors Affect Growth?

Why do some countries experience economic growth while others do not? Why do some countries experience fast economic growth and others, slow economic growth? Is there a necessary factor for economic growth? For example, does a country need factor X before it can grow? Is there a sufficient factor for growth? If a country has factor Z, is that enough (sufficient) to guarantee growth?

Unfortunately, economists do not have answers to all these questions. No one theory of economic growth is universally accepted. But economists are agreed on a few factors that are linked to economic growth, although they differ as to how heavily each of the factors should be weighted. The factors are natural resources, capital formation, technological advances, and property rights structure.

Natural Resources.   People often think that countries that have a plentiful supply of natural resources experience economic growth, whereas countries that are short on natural resources do not. In fact, some countries with an abundant supply of natural resources have experienced rapid growth (like the United States), and some have experienced no growth or only slow growth (like Bolivia and Ghana). Also, some countries that are short on natural resources, like Hong Kong, grow very fast. It appears that natural resources are neither a sufficient nor a necessary factor for growth: Nations rich in natural resources are not guaranteed economic growth, whereas nations poor in natural resources may grow. Having said all this, it is still more likely for a nation rich in natural resources to experience growth, *ceteris paribus.* For example, if Hong Kong had been blessed with much fertile soil instead of only a little, and many raw materials instead of almost none, it might have experienced more economic growth than it has.

Capital Formation.   Capital formation includes two types of capital: physical and human. Physical capital, such as a tractor or a machine, and human capital, such as knowledge and skills, increase the ability of an individual to produce (that is, there is a predictable relationship between capital formation and labor productivity). For example, modern American farmers produce much more than their grandfathers largely because they have certain physical capital goods, such as tractors, that their grandfathers didn't have, and they know much more about the science of farming. In short, they possess more physical *and* human capital than their grandfathers.

Both physical and human capital formation do not come without cost. Tractors, computers, and factory machines do not fall from the sky. Education and knowl-

EXHIBIT 37–2

U.S. and Japanese Growth Rates in Real GNP, 1961–90

A positive growth rate represents an outward shift in a country's production possibilities frontier (*PPF*). As the exhibit shows, for most periods and specific years, Japan's *PPF* has been shifting outward by a greater percentage than the United States' *PPF*. Figures for 1990 are preliminary estimates.

	Growth Rates in Real GNP, 1961–90 (Percentage Change)										
COUNTRY	AVERAGE ANNUAL 1961–65	AVERAGE ANNUAL 1966–70	AVERAGE ANNUAL 1971–75	AVERAGE ANNUAL 1976–83	1984	1985	1986	1987	1988	1989	1990
Japan	12.4%	11.0%	4.3%	4.4%	5.1%	4.9%	2.5%	4.6%	5.7%	4.9%	6.1%
United States	4.6	3.0	2.2	2.5	6.8	3.4	2.7	3.4	4.5	2.5	0.9

SOURCE: Council of Economic Advisers, *Economic Report of the President, 1991* (Washington, D.C.: U.S. Government Printing Office, 1991).

edge are not obtained by snapping one's fingers. Sacrifices have to be made. To produce capital goods, which are not directly consumable, present consumption must be sacrificed. Robinson Crusoe, alone on an island fishing with a spear, must give up some of his present consumption of fish to weave a net (a physical capital good) with which he hopes to catch more fish.

If Crusoe gives up some of his present consumption, if he chooses not to consume now, he is in fact saving. There is a link between *non*consumption, or saving, and capital formation. As the savings rate increases, capital formation increases, and so does economic growth. Take the case of the United States and Japan. In the period 1961–90, Japan's per-capita real GNP growth rate was double that of the United States. Modern research indicates that Japan's higher per-capita real GNP growth rate is due to its higher savings rate, which is almost 75 percent higher than the U.S. savings rate.

Exhibit 37–3 makes this point. Suppose that in 1990, the production possibilities frontier was the same for both the United States and Japan. The United States decided to locate at point *A*, producing relatively more consumption goods and fewer investment goods than Japan, which decided to locate at point *B*. Because the two countries decided to produce a different investment-goods-to-consumption-goods ratio in 1990, they have different *PPF*s in 1998. Because Japan had a higher savings rate than the United States, which brought about greater investment in Japan than in the United States, it experienced greater growth than the United States.

Technological Advances. Technological advances make it possible to obtain more output from the same amount of resources. Compare the amount of work that can be done by a business that uses computers with the amount accomplished by a business that does not. The world has witnessed major technological advances in the past 100 to 200 years. Consider what your life would have been like if you

EXHIBIT 37–3
The Effect of Consumption/Investment Choices on Economic Growth

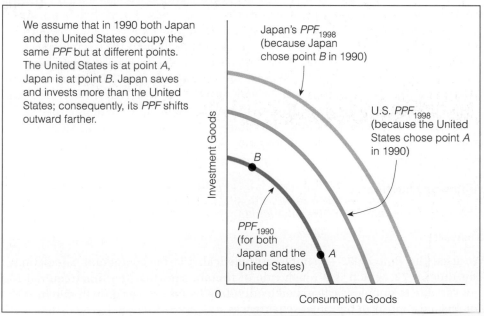

We assume that in 1990 both Japan and the United States occupy the same *PPF* but at different points. The United States is at point *A*, Japan is at point *B*. Japan saves and invests more than the United States; consequently, its *PPF* shifts outward farther.

Japan's *PPF*₁₉₉₈ (because Japan chose point *B* in 1990)

U.S. *PPF*₁₉₉₈ (because the United States chose point *A* in 1990)

Investment Goods

B

*PPF*₁₉₉₀ (for both Japan and the United States)

A

0   Consumption Goods

had lived 200 years ago, around 1790. Most of the major technological achievements we take for granted today—the car, computer, telephone, electricity, mass production techniques—did not exist. It is sometimes said, and it is probably true, that a person living in the late 1700s had a living standard that was closer to the living standard of people living in the year 1 A.D. than of people living today.

Property Rights Structure.   Some economists have argued that per-capita real economic growth first appeared in those areas where a system of institutions and property rights had evolved that encouraged individuals to direct their human capital and energy to effective economic projects. Here *property rights* refers to the range of laws, rules, and regulations that define rights over the use and transfer of resources.

Consider two property rights structures: one in which people are allowed to keep the full fruits of their labor and one in which people are allowed to keep only one-half of the fruits of their labor. Many economists would predict that the first property rights structure would stimulate more economic activity than the second, *ceteris paribus*. Individuals will invest more, take more risks, and work harder when the property rights structure allows them to keep more of the fruits of their investing, risk taking, and labor.

Question:

Do economic growth rates matter that much in the long run? For example, suppose one country has a growth rate of 4 percent per year for 20 years and another country has a growth rate of 3 percent per year for 20 years. Will the total growth be different in the two countries over a period of 20 years?

Answer:

There will be a sizable difference. For example, in 1990, in the United States, a 1 percent higher annual growth rate represented approximately $54 billion worth of output. As far as growth over the long run is concerned, the example of compound interest illustrates what happens. If you put $100 into a savings account at a 10 percent annual interest rate, in a year you will have $110. And then if you keep the $110 in the savings account at the same annual interest rate, the following year you have $121. It takes only about 7 years to double your $100 savings. And, of course, the higher the interest rate is, the quicker your savings doubles. For instance, at an interest rate of 12 percent, your money doubles in approximately 6 years. It works the same way with growth rates. At a 4 percent growth rate (per year), it will take 18 years to double in size. At a 3 percent growth rate (per year), it takes 24 years to double—or 6 years longer. Thus, a 1 percent increase in the growth rate can mean a lot in the long run.

Follow-up Question:

How was the number of years calculated?

Answer:

We used the *Rule of 72*—a simple arithmetical rule for compound calculations. The Rule of 72, which is a rough rule of thumb, says that the time required for any variable to double is calculated by dividing its percentage growth rate into 72. For instance, an economy that experiences a 5 percent annual growth rate will take approximately 14.4 years (72/5 = 14.4) to double in size. The United States had an average annual growth rate in real GNP of 2.8 percent during the period 1986–90. If this annual growth rate were to continue, it would take 25.7 years (72/2.8 = 25.7) for the U.S. economy to double in size. During the same period, the Japanese average annual growth rate in real GNP was 4.7 percent. If this annual growth rate were to continue, it would take 15.3 years (72/4.7 = 15.3) for the Japanese economy to double in size.

When discussing economic growth, economists think in terms of tangibles and intangibles. The tangibles include natural resources, capital formation, and technological advancements. The intangibles include the property rights structure, which directly affects the incentives individuals have to apply the tangibles to the production of goods and services. No amount of resources, capital, and technology can do it alone. People must be motivated to put them all together; in addition, the degree of motivation matters to the result. In a world in which it is easy to think that only those things that occupy physical space matter, the economist is there to remind us that we often need to look further.

Productivity Slowdown

In the early 1970s, the United States began to experience a decline in real economic growth. This was noticed and recorded by many economists, in particular, by Edward Denison of the Brookings Institution. Denison calculated that the real national income growth rate was approximately twice as high for the United States in the period 1948–73 as it was in the period 1973–82.[1] This slowdown in economic growth appeared to be largely the result of a slowdown in labor productivity, as measured by output per hour of labor. But this, then, prompted individuals to ask what caused the slowdown in labor productivity. We note a few of the more frequently cited reasons here.

Decline in Capital per Hour Worked.   We have discussed how labor, combined with capital goods, is more productive than labor alone. Recall that the farmer with a tractor is more productive than the farmer working alone. If we put capital goods on one hand and labor hours worked on the other, we can then look at one in terms of the other and speak of *capital per hour worked*. In the 1970s, the ratio of capital to labor hours worked began to decline. There were two reasons for this: (1) Growth of the capital stock slowed down. (2) Growth in labor hours worked speeded up. Thus, both components of the ratio were affected. The growth in labor hours worked increased because a large number of women moved from home activity into the labor force during the seventies.

Why, however, did the growth of the capital stock decline? One economist, Martin Feldstein, argued that inflation and a tax system that did not adjust for inflation gains (but treated them instead as real gains) combined to overtax savings. As a result, saving, which is necessary for capital formation, was discouraged.

Decline in the Quality of the Labor Force.   The early 1970s saw an increase in the number of women and young people who entered the labor force. As men-

[1] Edward Demison, *Trends in American Economic Growth, 1929–1982* (Washington, D.C.: Brookings Institution, 1985).

Do Special-Interest Groups Zap Productivity?

Economist Mancur Olson has proposed a theory that he and some others believe explains the productivity slowdown of the 1970s, among other things. Olson argues that when countries experience a long period of political stability, special-interest groups (or distributional coalitions, which often want to redistribute income from others to themselves) have an opportunity to grow and achieve political power. For example, labor union special-interest groups will use their increasing economic and political power to set wages and prevent employers from hiring nonunion labor, introducing labor-saving technology, and the like. Business-oriented special-interest groups will lobby government for preferential treatment in the form of subsidies, tariffs, and quotas.

Olson argues that the United States, having experienced a long period of political stability, currently has powerful special-interest groups that can often accomplish their goals. In comparison, Japan and Germany, having lost World War II, had their societies turned upside down, and in the process once-powerful special-interest groups were dismantled; as yet these groups have not had the time to reestablish themselves and become as strong as their American counterparts. Olson implies that this gives the economic edge to Japan:

If the argument so far is correct, it follows that countries whose distributional coalitions have been emasculated or abolished by totalitarian government or foreign occupation should grow relatively quickly after a free and stable legal order is established. This can explain the postwar "economic miracles" in the nations that were defeated in World War II, particularly those in Japan and West Germany.*

In the Olson theory, powerful special-interest groups reduce the economy's flexibility and slow down its ability to adapt to changing circumstances and technologies (they suffer, in Olson's words, from *institutional sclerosis*). For example, if demand in the economy falls, business- and labor-oriented special-interest groups will react slowly; thus, wages and prices are likely to stay fixed for some time, and unemployment will rise. Overall, the economy will not react smoothly and quickly to a new reality. National output and labor productivity will suffer.

*Mancur Olson, *The Rise and Decline of Nations: Economic Growth, Stagflation, and Social Rigidities* (New Haven, Conn.: Yale University Press, 1982), p. 75.

tioned earlier, many of the women entering the labor force had come from home activity. The young people were largely the "baby boomers" who were coming of age and getting their first jobs. Some economists contend that because these two groups initially lacked work experience, they pulled down the average quality of labor during this time and prompted the slowdown in labor productivity. Denison's studies, however, suggest that this played only a minor part in the slowdown of labor productivity.

Major Oil Price Increases. It is occasionally argued that the substantial oil price increases of the 1970s caused the relative price of labor compared with energy to decrease, prompting businesses to hire more labor and thus acquire less capital than they might ordinarily have acquired. Related to this, the sharp oil price increases caused much of the economy's capital stock to become obsolete. For example, many generators and gas-guzzling trucks had to be retired because high oil prices made them too costly to operate. Some say this reduction in the capital stock reduced labor productivity substantially. Others, like economist Michael Darby, believe that the energy crises and high oil prices played no role in the slowdown in labor productivity. In fact, Darby's work shows that there was no productivity slowdown. He notes that economists who use *output per hour of labor* as a measure of productivity fail to adjust for quality changes in labor and thus necessarily bias their results. In his work, Darby adjusted for quality changes in labor and concluded that hourly labor productivity has grown at a stable rate throughout the twentieth century.

Regulation. The 1970s witnessed an increase in the number of government safety, environmental, and health regulations that affected businesses. Some maintain that since businesses were required to invest in equipment to meet these regulations, they could not invest as heavily in standard plant and equipment and this led to the slowdown in economic growth.

A Combination of Factors. Economist Lester Thurow has argued that no single factor was decisive for the productivity slowdown, but that many factors together—inflation, regulation, oil price increases—all played a part. Thurow has compared the many-factor explanation of the productivity slowdown to "death by a thousand cuts."

Two Worries over Future Economic Growth

It would not be unreasonable for someone who has read this far to conclude that growth is good and no growth is bad. If you have this impression, it is because we have not yet painted the full picture. Not everyone believes growth is better than no growth, or that faster growth is better than slower growth.

Two worries commonly crop up in discussions of economic growth. One concerns the *costs* of growth. Some individuals argue that more economic growth comes with more pollution, more factories (and thus fewer open spaces), more crowded cities, more emphasis on material goods and getting ahead, more rushing around, more psychological problems, more people using drugs, more suicides, and so on. They argue for less growth instead of more.

Others maintain there is no evidence that economic growth (or faster as opposed to slower economic growth) causes all or most of these problems. They argue that growth brings many positive things: more wealth, less poverty, a society that is better able to support art projects and museums, less worry in people's lives (not having enough is a huge worry), and so forth. As for pollution and the like, such "undesirables" would be diminished if the courts were to establish and strictly enforce property rights—for example, in the rivers and the air (which are often the first to become polluted).

As you can no doubt see, the debate between those who favor more growth and those who favor less is not a simple one. Economists have become engaged in it, as have psychologists, biologists, sociologists, and many others. The debate promises to continue for a long time.

Another debate surrounds the issue of economic growth and the future availability of resources. Some people believe that continued economic and population growth threatens the very survival of the human race, since such growth will simply hasten the time when the world runs out of resources; inevitably, a time will come when there will be no more natural resources, no more clean air, no more pure water, no more land for people to live on comfortably. They urge social policies that will slow down growth and preserve what we have.

Critics of this position often charge that such "doomsday forecasts," as they have come to be called, are based on unrealistic assumptions, oversights, and flimsy evidence. For example, economist Julian Simon points out that, contrary to the doomsday forecasts, the quantity of arable land has increased in recent years owing to swamp drainage and land improvement, that there is not an inverse relationship between population growth and per-capita income growth, that the incidence of famine is decreasing, that we are not running out of natural resources, and that if and when scarcity of natural resources becomes a problem, rising relative prices of the resources will cause individuals to conserve them and stimulate economic activity to find substitutes.

Question:

It is easy to say that as oil reserves decline, for example, that the relative price of oil will rise, causing individuals to buy less oil and to search for a substitute for oil. But how can anyone be sure a good substitute will be found? Aren't the critics of the doomsday forecasts doing what they charge the doomsdayers with doing: simply making a claim instead of proving it?

Answer:

Probably some of them do this, and we need to watch out for it. But, then, the fact that someone can't come up with a substitute for X doesn't mean that a substitute won't one day be found. For example, it would have been hard for anyone living in eighteenth-century America to know that the car would one day be a substitute for the horse.

ECONOMIC DEVELOPMENT

In this section, we discuss the less-developed countries (LDCs), sometimes referred to as developing nations or third-world countries. Mainly, we are concerned with the question, Why are some nations poor?

The Problems of the Less-Developed Countries (LDCs): Why Some Nations Are Poor

Less-Developed Country (LDC)
A country with a low per-capita GNP.

A **less-developed country (LDC)** is a country with a low per-capita GNP. About three-quarters of the world's people live in LDCs.[2] Not all LDCs are alike; they differ in economic and political systems, culture, and ethnicity, to mention a few important factors.

To get some idea what a "low" per-capita GNP figure is, consider a few nations with "high" per-capita GNP figures. In 1987, Switzerland had a per-capita GNP of $27,300, the United States per-capita GNP was approximately $18,570, and Japan had a per-capita GNP of $19,410. Countries with low per-capita GNP figures include (to name only a few) Afghanistan, Bangladesh, Cambodia, China, Chad, Ethiopia, India, Nigeria, Pakistan, Somalia, Tanzania, Uganda, and Zambia. For example, in 1987, the per-capita GNP of India was $307, in China it was $438, and in Uganda it was $236. The developed nations, as a group, accounted for approximately 80 percent of the world's GNP in 1987; the LDCs for 20 percent. Per-capita GNP in the developed nations is, on average, approximately 12 times that in the LDCs.

Why has economic growth and development largely bypassed the people of the LDCs? Why are some nations so poor? Here are a few of the obstacles that some economists believe stifle economic development in the LDCs.

[2]When China and India have multiplied their per-capita incomes by about five times—to about where Greece is today—then three-quarters of the world's population will live in "rich" countries. Many experts think this will happen in less than 100 years.

Rapid Population Growth. It is commonly noticed that the population growth rate is higher in LDCs than in developed nations. The population growth rate in developed nations has been around one-half of 1 percent to 1 percent, whereas it has been around 2 to 3 percent for LDCs. The population growth rate is equal to the birthrate minus the deathrate. If in country X the birthrate is 3 percent in a given year, and the deathrate is 2 percent, the population growth rate is 1 percent.[3]

What has caused the relatively fast population growth rate in the LDCs? First, the birthrate tends to be higher than in developed nations. In countries where pensions, Social Security, and the like do not exist, and where the economy revolves around agriculture, children are often seen as essential labor and as security for parents in their old age. In this setting, people tend to have more children.

Second, in the past few decades in the LDCs, the deathrate has fallen, largely owing to medical advances. The combination of higher birthrates and declining deathrates explains why the population grows more rapidly in LDCs than in developed nations.

But is this faster population growth rate an obstacle to economic development? In Exhibit 37–4, many of the countries with the fastest-growing populations are relatively poorer on a per-capita basis than those countries with the slowest-growing populations. But this is still not proof that rapid population growth causes poverty. Many of the developed nations today witnessed faster population growth rates when they were developing than the LDCs do today.

Also, when we check population density (instead of population growth), there are a number of examples where high-density populations are much richer than low-density populations. Japan is more densely populated than India and has a higher per-capita income. The same is true for Taiwan vis-à-vis China.

Nonetheless, some still argue that rapid population growth, though not necessarily a deterrent to economic development, can stifle it. This is because in countries with fast-growing populations, the dependency ratio rises. The **dependency ratio** is the number of children under a certain age plus the number of the elderly (age 65 and over) divided by the total population. For example, if the number of

Dependency Ratio
The number of children under a certain age plus the number of the elderly (aged 65 and over) divided by the total population.

[3]In many cases, the birth- and deathrates are not given in percentage terms but in births or deaths per thousand. For example, the birthrate of country X is cited as "30 per thousand."

EXHIBIT 37–4
Some Countries with Fast and Slow Growing Populations
For the most part, countries with fast growing populations tend to be poorer than countries with slow-growing populations. There are exceptions, though. (Population figures are estimates.)

Some Countries with Fast-Growing Populations			Some Countries with Slow-Growing Populations		
	POPULATION IN 1989 (MILLIONS)	AVERAGE ANNUAL GROWTH RATE 1980–90 (PERCENT)		POPULATION IN 1989 (MILLIONS)	AVERAGE ANNUAL GROWTH RATE 1980–90 (PERCENT)
Qatar	0.5	7.7%	United States	248.0	0.9%
Saudi Arabia	16.1	5.0	Switzerland	6.6	0.4
Kuwait	2.0	4.2	Greece	10.0	0.4
Kenya	24.3	4.2	France	55.9	0.4
Bahrain	0.5	3.9	Czechoslovakia	15.6	0.3
Ivory Coast	11.6	3.6	Norway	4.2	0.3
Syria	12.0	3.6	Italy	57.5	0.2
Rwanda	7.3	3.6	Bulgaria	8.9	0.2
Iraq	18.0	3.5	United Kingdom	57.0	0.1
Ghana	14.8	3.5	Luxembourg	0.3	0.1
Equatorial Guinea	0.3	3.2	Hungary	10.5	−0.2

SOURCE: U.S. Bureau of the Census *Statistical Abstract of the United States, 1990* (Washington, D.C.: U.S. Government Printing Office, 1990).

children and elderly equals 500 and the total population is 1,500, the dependency ratio is 33 percent. The high dependency ratio in LDCs like India, Bangladesh, and Egypt puts added burdens on the productive working-age population.

Low Savings Rate. Economic growth and development requires investment, among other things. Capital formation increases labor productivity and economic growth. To accumulate capital, though, it is necessary to save; that is, to lower one's current consumption so that resources may be released for investment. It is generally argued that since living standards in the LDCs are barely above the subsistence level, and incomes must largely go for the necessities of life, there is little (if any) left over for saving. In short, LDCs are poor because they can't save and invest, but they can't save and invest because they are poor. Here we have what is usually referred to as the **vicious circle of poverty.**

Critics charge that low (or subsistence) incomes cannot possibly be a permanent barrier to development since high (or above-subsistence) incomes were not always a feature of today's developed nations.

Vicious Circle of Poverty
The idea that countries are poor because they do not save (and invest) and that they cannot save (and invest) because they are poor.

Cultural Differences. Do some of the LDCs have cultures that retard economic growth and development? Some people think so. For example, some cultures are reluctant to deviate from the status quo. People may think that things ought to stay the way they always have been; they view change as dangerous and risky. In these countries, it is not uncommon for a person's economic and social status to depend on who his parents were rather than on who he is or what he does; mobility is limited. In some cultures, the people are fatalistic—as measured by Western standards. They believe that a person's good or bad fortune in life is more dependent on fate than on how hard one works, or how much he or she learns, or how hard he or she strives to succeed.

Political Instability and Government Expropriation of Private Property. Individuals in both developed nations and LDCs sometimes do not invest in businesses in the LDCs because they are afraid either that the current leaders of an LDC will be toppled and thrown out of office or that the government might expropriate private property. Both political instability and the risk of government expropriation of private property substantially increase an investor's risk and therefore reduce total investment in a country. Probably the worst thing many governments of LDCs can do is to hint that they might nationalize industries. This usually scares off both domestic and foreign investors.

High Tax Rates. Some economists, like Alvin Rabushka, argue that high marginal tax rates (the *change* in a person's tax payment divided by the *change* in the person's taxable income) affect economic development. Rabushka undertook a study of the 1960–82 tax structures of 54 LDCs and categorized each LDC as a high-, low-, or medium-tax-rate nation. LDCs with top marginal tax rates of 50 percent or lower were classified as low-tax nations, whereas LDCs with top marginal tax rates of 50 percent or more that applied to incomes less than $10,000 were categorized as high-tax nations. Rabushka found that the nation with the lowest marginal tax rate, Hong Kong, had the highest growth rate in per-capita income during the period under study; low-tax nations overall had an average growth rate in per-capita income of 3.7 percent, whereas the high-tax nations had an average growth rate in per-capita income of 0.7 percent.

Interview: Irma Adelman

Irma Adelman is one of the world's leading economists in the area of economic development. She has been a consultant to the United Nations, the World Bank, and numerous other national and international organizations. Adelman currently is at the University of California at Berkeley.

Why are some countries wealthy and others poor?

Historically, what mattered was whether a country had sufficient institutional development to benefit from the Industrial Revolution. Those countries that did not have the institutional conditions—either because of colonialism (e.g. India) or because of backwardness (e.g. Russia)—were unable to benefit from the revolution in technology. It was not a question of natural resources; in fact, most developing countries are, on the average, resource-rich rather than resource-poor. Even now, differences in economic performance among developing countries are much more a matter of institutional development policy choices.

Are there specific institutions that encourage development?

Yes; institutions that allow for factor mobility and political institutions that allow for a choice of policies that would be beneficial to the development of a modern industrial base.

Do you think the nations of Eastern Europe, the Soviet Union, and the People's Republic of China currently have the institutional development to make a major leap forward in economic growth and development?

No; this is what they are struggling with now. And by the way, I would distinguish between Eastern Europe and the U.S.S.R. In Eastern Europe, the human resources are still competitive with one another and eager to take the initiative, whereas in the Soviet Union, that is no longer true.

What do you predict will be the most pressing economic problem of less-developed countries in the mid-1990s?

I think it will be trade problems—specifically, trade barriers that exist in the developed world. And the other problem is ethnic-religious cleavages.

Is the latter problem insurmountable?

No one has developed a good method for handling ethnic–religious cleavages throughout history. And that is not a matter of development levels because we have some developed countries that are plagued with those problems.

Do you think the United States has a responsibility to less-developed countries?

Yes, it does. Its responsibility is to assist with a sensible development process and to use its influence to provide an international environment so that development is possible.

How do you think it is meeting this responsibility now?

On the aid front, very poorly; on the trade front, not too badly. The total amount of foreign assistance is small, and 80 percent of the foreign assistance is disbursed on political–strategic grounds. So there is very little that remains to be disbursed on economic and need criteria. Unfortunately, I don't see this changing. If anything, it is going to get worse.

Why worse?

The aftermath of the Gulf War.

You once said that "in countries in which you start out from a very unequal allocation of assets and opportunities, the market may work against reducing poverty." Why do you think things turn out this way given the condition you have specified?

One major reason is political. The wealthy capture the political apparatus and make sure that the government enacts policies that favor their interests. When the distribution of assets, including human assets, is not very uneven, industrialization eventually produces a middle class. And the middle class is capable of reorienting political policies in such a way that things are less unequal.

How would you describe the economic way of thinking?

Well, I am at odds with the general way of thinking in economics. Economists pretend that the way to approach problems is through hypothesis testing. But I believe that there are too many plausible hypotheses out there and we know too little to be able to formulate the hypotheses sharply enough so that hypothesis testing will, in general, be a fruitful approach.

What is an alternative to doing things the current way?

In statistics the approach goes by the name of exploratory data analysis. The approach applies fairly powerful statistical techniques to real-world data in such a way as to reduce the complexity of the data. Then one uses the results to help formulate hypotheses.

What got you interested in economics?

I hesitate to say because it sounds arrogant. My reason was that I wanted to benefit humanity. And my perception at the time was that economic problems were the most important problems that humanity has to face. That is what got me into economics and into economic development.

Why do you say it sounds arrogant?

Because it is arrogant to think that one person can make a real difference.

You said that "my perception at the time was that economic problems were the most important problems that humanity has to face." Has your perception changed?

Yes, a little bit. In the sense that I now recognize politicians can do a lot to change the situation—either for the better or the worse. But politics isn't my comparative advantage.

Question:

This approach to explaining why some nations are poor seems to be a "throw everything into the pot" approach—the poverty that some nations experience could be because of a low saving rate, and could be because of high population growth, and could be because of this and that. Aren't there some explanations that apply to all LDCs?

Answer:

This is one of the frustrations of research that we warned about earlier. Unfortunately, economists are not agreed on "the" reason why some nations are poor. It is not hard, however, to find *an* economist who will tell you what he or she thinks "the" reason is. Some economists might tell you that some nations are poor because they do not put free market practices into effect. Other economists will tell you that a very unequal wealth distribution retards economic development. With time and more and better research, we may be able to throw out a few of the things that are currently in the pot.

Fungibility

Fungibility
A term that is Latin in origin, meaning "such that any unit is substitutable for another." Fungibility means substitutable.

Fungibility is a key concept in economics. It comes from a Latin term that means "such that any unit is substitutable for another." In short, it simply means *substitutable*. For example, points in a basketball game are fungible. Team A plays team B in basketball and beats it by two points; the last two points are scored in the last second of the game by player Robinson, who is carried off the basketball court on the shoulders of his teammates. The headline in the newspaper the next day reads "Robinson Wins Game."

But what about player Petrie's two points in the first minute of the game? Had Petrie not gotten those two points, Robinson's two points would not have "won" the game. Why not then say that Petrie's two points were as important as Robinson's two points?

Well, that doesn't seem quite as exciting. But, nevertheless, it is true. Petrie's and Robinson's points are fungible: They are substitutable.

Money is fungible, too. Suppose Jack's parents hand over $200 to him and tell him to buy his textbooks with the money. Will the $200 actually be used to buy textbooks? Possibly, it will; Jack may take the $200 and buy his books. But possibly it won't. The $200 Jack's parents gave him can be used to buy clothes, and the $200 he earned last week can now be used to pay for his books. In the latter case, what did Jack's money really pay for—the books or the clothes? Since money is fungible, there is no sensible way to answer this question.

Now consider foreign aid. One government gives another government $100 million and makes the recipient government promise to use the money for project X. Is the money really used for project X? The answer is, not necessarily. Money, remember, is fungible. The $100 million might be used for project X, but then the recipient government has money it might have used for project X that it can now use on any project it wants.

Let's say country Z has $400 million to spend, and it would like to complete the following projects:

1. Build factories for $200 million.
2. Build roads and schools for $100 million.
3. Upgrade agriculture for $100 million.
4. Build a lavish palace for the leader of the country for $100 million.

Currently, the country can only complete projects 1–3.

Now the United States, say, gives $100 million to country Z and specifies that the money must be used to build roads and schools. So country Z does as the United States says. But now it has $100 million that can be used to build a lavish palace for the leader of the country. Did the U.S. money go for schools and roads or for a palace? Once again, money is fungible.

Question:

Is this an argument against the United States giving money to poor nations?

Answer:

No, it isn't. The point is simply that money given may not always be used for the purpose that the donor nation would prefer. However, the United States, or any other country for that matter, may decide that giving the money is preferable to not giving it, even though some of the money may be spent for purposes the donor has not intended.

The World Debt Crisis

Throughout the 1980s, there was much talk about a world debt crisis. Some of the LDCs—Mexico, Argentina, Brazil, the Philippines, Chile, and Nigeria, for example—had huge outstanding loans they were scheduled to repay to (mostly) Western banks, many of them in the United States. At the time, some people thought that the LDCs would default on the loans and that one major U.S. bank after another would fail.

How did this situation develop? Is the crisis over? What will happen? Most economists believe that the debt crisis had its origin in the quadrupling of oil prices by OPEC in 1973. After the price increase, the oil-rich nations began to run huge current account surpluses. The OPEC nations, in turn, deposited much of their oil money in U.S. banks. At the same time, many of the LDC oil-importing nations began to run deficits in their current accounts. The U.S. banks began to *recycle* the oil money to the LDCs. Some of this money went for worthwhile investment projects, some did not. For example, in some countries the borrowed funds were used for consumption rather than for investment.

In the late 1970s, some of the oil-exporting LDCs, such as Mexico, began to borrow huge sums from U.S. banks. Why did the U.S. banks extend them credit? Since oil prices were still rising, it looked as if Mexico and others would have no trouble paying off the loans. (If you are poor today, but your bank believes you will be rich tomorrow, then it will most likely be happy to extend you credit.) Then in 1981, the price of oil began to fall.

In August 1982, Mexico told Citibank of New York that it could not pay its loans on time. Other countries in a similar position began to follow suit. The list included both oil-importing LDCs, which had gotten into debt because of the rising price of oil in the 1970s, and oil-exporting LDCs, which had gotten into debt because of the falling price of oil in the early-to-mid 1980s. Lending banks were largely forced into *restructuring* and *rescheduling* the debt—extending the payback period, reducing interest payments, and so on. In this environment, LCDs have few funds to invest in new capital projects required for economic growth.

What the outcome will be largely depends on the state of the world economy (Will it grow enough so that debtor nations can export goods and earn the currency needed to meet their loan payments? Will it stagnate?) and the domestic economic policies that the LDCs with debt problems implement (Will they cut back on extravagant spending?). Some economists argue that the huge interest payments that some LDCs have to pay on their loans will prevent them from becoming developed nations for some time.

CHAPTER SUMMARY

Economic Growth

■ The term *economic growth* refers to either *real economic growth* or to *per-capita real economic growth*. Real economic growth is an increase from one period to the next in *real GNP.* Per-capita real economic growth is an increase from one period to the next in *per-capita real GNP,* which is real GNP divided by population.

■ Economists often argue that economic growth is dependent on a society's natural resources, rate of capital formation (physical and human), technological advances, and property rights structure. More natural resources, more and better capital goods and human capital, more and better technological advances, and a property rights structure that largely allows individuals to keep the fruits of their labor are thought to promote per-capita economic growth. This does not mean, however, that a nation with, say, many natural resources will necessarily experience faster per-capita economic growth than a nation with a few natural resources. There could be offsetting factors.

■ When calculating how long it will take a nation's economy to double in size, economists use the Rule of 72: To calculate the time required for any variable to double, divide its percentage growth rate into 72.

Productivity Slowdown

■ The decline in U.S. economic growth in the 1970s was largely caused by a slowdown in labor productivity which, it has been argued, was caused by one or more of the following: a decline in capital per hour worked, a decline in the quality of the labor force, major oil price increases, and regulation.

The Problems of the LDCs

■ Most economists cite one or more of the following problems as the reason(s) the LDCs are poor: rapid population growth rate (high dependency ratio), low savings rate, a culture that does not lend itself to economic growth, political instability and the threat of government expropriation of private property, and high tax rates.

Key Terms and Concepts

Real Economic Growth	Less-Developed Country	Vicious Circle of
Per-Capita Real	(LDC)	Poverty
Economic Growth	Dependency Ratio	Fungibility

QUESTIONS AND PROBLEMS

1. Suppose the population growth rate of country X is 3 percent and the population growth rate of country Y is 0.5 percent. How long will it take before the population of each country has doubled?

2. How do you explain that some countries with plentiful natural resources are developed whereas others are less developed (LDCs)? How do you explain that some countries with few natural resources are developed whereas some countries with plentiful natural resources are less developed?

3. What is one of the major failings of "doomsday" forecasts?

4. Would you expect the birthrate in LDCs to go up or down as a result of per-capita economic growth and economic development?

5. If, before you had read this chapter, someone had asked you why the LDCs were poor and what they should do to promote economic development, what would you have said? What would you say now? Is there much difference between the two views? To what do you attribute the difference?

6. Absolute economic growth is about increasing the size of the economic pie. Per-capita economic growth is about increasing the size of the economic pie faster than the population is growing, so not only is there more but also there is more per person. Explain how different property rights structures might help or hinder both absolute and per-capita economic growth.

7. Some people argue that the LDCs will not grow and develop without foreign aid from developed countries. Other people say that foreign aid actually limits growth and development (they see it as a handout that distorts the incentive to produce) and propose in its place a reliance on foreign trade. In the real world, there is some of both. Do you think, however, that an increase in the aid-to-trade ratio (amount of foreign aid received divided by the amount of foreign trade) would decrease, increase, or leave unchanged the economic development of an LDC? What about a decrease? Explain your answers.

CHAPTER 38

ALTERNATIVE ECONOMIC SYSTEMS: THEORY, PRACTICE, AND EVOLUTIONARY ASPECTS

WHAT THIS CHAPTER IS ABOUT

The bulk of this book has described the workings of the economic system that is best known as *mixed capitalism*. It is the economic system that, to different degrees, exists in the United States, Canada, Australia, and Japan, to name only a few countries. In this chapter, we discuss a few of the alternatives to mixed capitalism. The list includes *pure capitalism, command-economy socialism,* and *decentralized socialism.*

We also discuss the economies of the Soviet Union, China, and Japan.

Economic Systems and Shared Economic Realities

First, we define mixed capitalism and its alternatives and discuss the economic realities facing all economic systems. Then, we examine some of the similarities and differences of the various systems.

Mixed Capitalism and Its Alternatives

Mixed capitalism is an economic system characterized by largely private ownership of the factors of production, market allocation of resources, and decentralized decision making; most economic activities take place in the private sector, but government plays a substantial economic and regulatory role.

Pure capitalism is an economic system characterized by purely private ownership of the factors of production, market allocation of resources, and decentralized decision making; most economic activities take place in the private sector, and government plays a small role or no role at all in the economy.

Command-economy socialism is an economic system characterized by government ownership of the nonlabor factors of production, government allocation of resources, and centralized decision making; most economic activities take place in the public sector, and government plays a very large role in the economy.

Decentralized socialism is an economic system characterized by government ownership of the nonlabor factors of production, largely market allocation of resources, and decentralized decision making; most economic activities take place in the public sector, and government plays a major overseer role in the economy.

See Exhibit 38–1 for a review of the principal properties of the four economic systems outlined here.

Question:

Suppose seven countries are identified as mixed capitalist. Does it follow that the seven are mixed capitalist to the same degree?

Answer:

No, that is not exactly the case. An analogy is class grades. Suppose Jerry gets an 89 on a test and Trenton gets an 81. Both of them receive a B for a grade and thus

Mixed Capitalism
An economic system characterized by largely private ownership of the factors of production, market allocation of resources, and decentralized decision making; most economic activities take place in the private sector in this system, but government plays a substantial economic and regulatory role.

Pure Capitalism
An economic system characterized by private ownership of the factors of production, market allocation of resources, and decentralized decision making; most economic activities take place in the private sector, and government plays a small role or no role at all in the economy.

Command-Economy Socialism
An economic system characterized by government ownership of the nonlabor factors of production, government allocation of resources, and centralized decision making; most economic activities take place in the public sector, and government plays a very large role in the economy.

Decentralized Socialism
An economic system characterized by government ownership of the nonlabor factors of production, largely market allocation of resources, and decentralized decision making; most economic activities take place in the public sector, and government plays a major overseer role in the economy.

EXHIBIT 38–1
Four Economic Systems
The principal properties of four economic systems are summarized.

ECONOMIC SYSTEM	OWNERSHIP OF FACTORS OF PRODUCTION	ALLOCATION OF RESOURCES	DECISION MAKING	WHERE DO MOST ECONOMIC ACTIVITIES TAKE PLACE?	ROLE GOVERNMENT PLAYS IN THE ECONOMY
Mixed Capitalism	Largely private	Market allocation	Decentralized	Private sector	Plays a substantial economic and regulatory role
Pure Capitalism	Purely private	Market allocation	Decentralized	Private sector	Small or no role
Command-Economy Socialism	Government ownership of nonlabor factors of production	Government allocation	Centralized	Public sector	Very large role
Decentralized Socialism	Government ownership of nonlabor factors of production	Largely market allocation	Decentralized	Public sector	Major role

both are B students. We can't really say which student is more of a B student, but we can say that Jerry, who is a B student, is a little closer to being an A student than Trenton, who is also a B student. Similarly, we might say that country X, with a mixed capitalist economic system, is closer to pure capitalism than country Y, or that country Y, with a mixed capitalist economic system, is closer to decentralized socialism than country X.

Shared Economic Realities

All economies share some features. We outline them here.

Scarcity. In Chapters 1 and 2, we introduced the concept of scarcity, which is the condition where wants outstrip the resources available to satisfy them. We already know that mixed capitalist economies must face up to the reality of scarcity. But what about pure capitalist, command-economy socialist, and decentralized socialist economies? Do they have to deal with scarcity? They certainly do. All economic systems must deal with scarcity. The people in the United States, the Soviet Union, the People's Republic of China, Japan, Venezuela, Saudi Arabia, and every other country in the world must grapple with it. What distinguishes economic systems is not that some economic systems have to deal with scarcity and others do not, but rather how different economic systems deal with scarcity.

Opportunity Cost, or No Free Lunch. We learned in earlier chapters that opportunity cost is a consequence of scarcity. It follows, therefore, that since all economic systems must deal with scarcity, all economic systems are faced with opportunity cost. In short, in all societies there is no such thing as a free lunch. This is the case in the United States, the Soviet Union, India, Chile, the People's Republic of China, and every other country.

Rationing Devices. Since all economic systems are faced with scarcity, all economic systems must ration goods. In the United States, for example, this is largely done through (dollar) price. Cars, houses, television sets, computers, toothbrushes, clocks, books, and much more are rationed by price. If, in some societies, money price is seen as a less than desirable rationing device, then some other rationing device must be put in its place. It may be first-come-first-served, political power, or something else, but in a world of scarcity, societies must always decide on a rationing device or devices.

The Law of Demand. Does the law of demand only hold for mixed capitalist economies and not for command-economy or decentralized socialist economies? It certainly does not. The law of demand holds for all economic systems. If the dollar price of television sets rises, Americans will buy fewer television sets, *ceteris paribus.* And if the ruble price of television sets rises, Russians will buy fewer television sets, *ceteris paribus.*

Rational Self-Interested Behavior. Rational self-interested behavior means to act in such a way as to maximize the difference between the benefits and costs as perceived by the individual. It is generally assumed that individuals all over the world, no matter what their economic system, exhibit this type of behavior.

What Goods will be Produced? How will the Goods be Produced? For Whom will the Goods be Produced? All economic systems must decide what goods will be produced, how the goods will be produced, and for whom the goods will be produced.

For example, will the economy produce more books or more fax machines? Implicit here is the question who decides what the economy produces. Will it be the marketplace, composed of millions of buyers and sellers, or a central government committee?

Once this question is answered, the economic system must decide how the goods will be produced. For example, will food staples be produced on private farms, or on large state-operated collective farms?

Finally, for whom are these goods produced? Are they produced for the people who pay the prices for them? Are they produced for whomever the government decides needs or should have them? Socialists often argue that capitalism produces houses for people who can pay the money prices for the houses and that socialism produces houses for people who need houses. Critics charge that socialism produces low-quality houses for people the government officials believe need houses and that need usually is linked to political party loyalty.

In our discussion of the shared economic realities of different societies, we noted that economists assume that individuals all over the world, no matter what their economic system, exhibit rational self-interested behavior. This does not mean, though, that individuals in different societies necessarily exhibit the same behavior because the costs and benefits of particular actions in different societies will be different. For example, in society A the costs of expressing one's opinion (say, about government political and economic policies) may be higher than the benefits and therefore an individual chooses not to express his opinions; whereas in society B the costs of expressing one's opinion are lower than the benefits and one does express his opinion. Is the individual in society A exhibiting rational self-interested behavior and the individual in society B not? Or are they both exhibiting rational self-interested behavior, while simply responding to a different configuration of costs and benefits? The economist will say it is the latter.

PURE CAPITALISM

Pure capitalism sometimes goes by the names *laissez-faire capitalism, anarcho-capitalism,* or *libertarianism.* Adherents to the pure capitalism position are usually referred to as *libertarians.* Libertarians either see a very limited role or no role at all for government. The former principally see government's role as protecting property rights and enforcing contracts. Some libertarians add the provision of national defense to this list. The latter argue that any government at all is too much government. They maintain that the free market is capable of providing roads, courts, police protection, and so forth. In this section we discuss the libertarians' case for pure capitalism.

Arguing the Pure Capitalism Case

For most libertarians, many public problems are caused by too much government. As a solution to these problems, libertarians usually recommend less government and greater reliance on the forces of the free market. Here are a few things libertarians say.

1. **Professional licensing.** Professional licensing reduces the supply of a service and increases its price. For example, because medical licensing makes it more difficult for individuals to become physicians and for nurses to compete directly with physicians, licensing increases the price of medical care. In a pure capitalist economy, professional licensing would not exist; that it largely does exist today is because government, by licensing certain trades, serves as the cartel enforcer of a special-interest group.

2. **Minimum wage law.** Minimum wage laws are a restraint on free trade. Setting a minimum wage guarantees that individuals whose present skills are worth less than the minimum wage will go unemployed. Individuals have the (natural) right to work for whatever wage they voluntarily agree to, and government, by passing a minimum wage law, prevents individuals from exercising this right in some instances. The minimum wage would not exist under pure capitalism.

3. **The U.S. Postal Service.** Private companies can and should be allowed to deliver first-class mail. Under pure capitalism, a number of competing mail services would deliver first-class mail, and such competition would drive prices down and quality up.

4. **Restraints on price.** All restraints on price, either price floors or price ceilings, reduce voluntary exchange to a level below that which would exist in a pure capitalist economy. Libertarians are against interest rate ceilings, minimum wages (as noted earlier), agricultural price supports, and rent controls.

5. **Discretionary fiscal and monetary policies.** Government intervention in the economy, via fiscal policy (taxing and spending policies) and monetary policy, often has negative effects—such as high interest rates, inflation, recession, and high unemployment. The free market is inherently stable and capable of equilibrating at full-employment output.

6. **The Federal Reserve.** The Federal Reserve System, the central bank of the United States, should be eliminated. It is an "engine of inflation," far too political, and the cause of unnecessary and harmful ups and downs in the economy. In monetary policy, libertarians usually favor an automatic monetary mechanism as opposed to a discretionary one. This translates into a monetary rule or a gold standard.

7. **Antitrust policy.** Government antitrust policy too often stifles market competition and is used to attack firms for no other reason than that they are big. Pure capitalism, which maximizes competitive forces, is the best antitrust policy. Firms are much more afraid of successful competitors than they are of government antitrust policy. In a related argument, libertarians maintain that antitrust policy is sometimes used by firms to limit their competition. For example, firm X, in competition with firm Y, may argue before the antitrust authorities against the merger between firm Y and firm Z. Too often, the authorities will accept the argument and a merger that possibly might increase productivity, reduce costs, and ultimately increase quality and lower price will not be permitted.

8. **Quotas and tariffs.** Quotas and tariffs increase prices and decrease exchange and only serve narrow special-interest groups. Neither would exist in a pure capitalist society.

9. **Social Security.** To libertarians, Social Security combines a compulsory savings program with a redistribution program—both of which they oppose. It is wrong to force people to save for old age (or anything else for that matter). How much one saves or doesn't save should be up to the individual. As to the redistributory aspect of Social Security, it is tantamount to theft for the government to reach into one person's pocket, take out money, and redistribute that money to someone else.

10. Welfare. Welfare is a forced redistribution program. In addition, in many instances, welfare programs produce outcomes contrary to the stated goals of the programs. For example, welfare often makes people more dependent on others and less likely to acquire work skills. Libertarians are in favor of voluntary charities.

A Critique of Libertarianism

The pure capitalism case, or libertarianism, has many critics. Here are some of the points the critics make:

1. Libertarians do not see the merit of using government's taxing, subsidy, and regulatory powers to adjust for third-party effects. In most exchanges, probably only two persons are affected—the person buying the good or service and the person selling the good or service. In some exchanges, however, there are *third-party effects,* whereby someone not involved in the exchange itself is nonetheless affected by it. Sometimes the third party is affected adversely by an exchange that others enter into: Say, company X produces steel that it sells to customers; in the process it generates pollution that harms people that live near the steel factory. And sometimes the third party is affected positively: Say, the university sells education to students; in the process it generates benefits for people who now reside in a community of well-educated individuals. Many economists argue that third-party effects should be taken into account, or adjusted for, and that government is the proper institution to do the adjusting—through regulation, taxes, subsidies, and so forth. For example, government might subsidize education so that the social benefits, not just the private benefits, are realized. In addition, sometimes the only way third-party effects *can* be adjusted for is through government. Thus, the choice is either letting government adjust or not adjusting at all.

2. Libertarians do not seriously consider complex exchanges. A simple exchange might be one person trading an apple for $1. A complex exchange may be millions of voters choosing a political candidate who has promised, if elected, to increase government spending on defense, education, or public assistance programs. The critics of libertarianism argue that some goods and services simply cannot be obtained through the free market, and therefore people naturally turn to the political "market" to obtain them. They criticize libertarians for not seeing that exchange comes in different varieties. Many libertarians would maintain that a complex exchange is not really an exchange at all. What about the person who votes against the candidate who is elected and raises spending on defense? Libertarians might question whether this voter is benefiting from the so-called complex exchange. If not, then it is not clear an exchange has taken place.

The words of economist James Buchanan are relevant here:

> Politics is a structure of complex exchange among individuals, a structure within which persons seek to secure collectively their own privately defined objectives that cannot be efficiently secured through simple market exchanges. . . . In the market, individuals exchange apples for oranges; in politics, individuals exchange agreed-on shares in contributions toward the costs of that which is commonly desired, from the services of the local fire station to that of the judge.[1]

3. Libertarians do not see the stabilizing effects of government monetary and fiscal policies. Most libertarians will say that they do not see the stabilizing effects of government monetary and fiscal policies because there are no stabilizing effects

[1]James Buchanan, "The Constitution of Economic Policy," *American Economic Review* 77 (June 1987): 244.

to see. The critics argue otherwise, saying that since the economy does not always self-equilibrate at full-employment output, government management policies have a role to play.

KARL MARX (1818–83)

Karl Marx has played a major part in the development of socialist thought. Here we present a few of his major ideas.

The Basics of Marx's Thought

Few economists have had as much influence on the world as Karl Marx. In turn, Marx was influenced by the economist David Ricardo and the philosopher Georg Hegel, among others, in particular, by Ricardo's discussion of the labor theory of value and Hegel's dialectic.

Labor Theory of Value
Holds that the value of all commodities is equal to the value of the labor used in producing them.

The Labor Theory of Value.   The **labor theory of value** holds that all value in produced goods is derived from direct and indirect (or embodied) labor. A man or woman working on a factory line is an example of direct labor. A machine, made by a man or woman, is an example of indirect, or embodied, labor.

Marx argued that the value of a commodity is determined by the *socially necessary labor time* embodied in the commodity. This is the sum of the direct and indirect (or embodied) labor necessary to produce socially desired commodities. (By using the adjective *socially,* Marx was able to differentiate between those goods that were genuinely desired by people—like shoes, coats, and houses—and those that were not—like sand castles on the beach.)

For example, if it takes 5 hours of socially necessary labor time to produce X and 10 hours to produce Y, then Y will be twice as valuable as X. Marx realized that labor was not all of equal quality, but he believed that skilled labor could be calculated as some multiple of unskilled labor.

Marx maintained that the labor, or labor power, capitalists purchase is itself a commodity, and thus its value (like that of commodities) is determined by labor time. Also, the value of labor power tends toward a subsistence wage, that is, the *labor time* necessary for the worker to earn the necessities consumed by the worker and his or her family.

Consider an example from Marx's time. Suppose a worker needs 2 shillings a day to subsist. Furthermore, suppose it takes 4 labor hours to produce the gold that is in 2 shillings. This means that the worker needs to work 4 hours to earn 2 shillings. Two shillings is the value of labor power—it is what workers would be paid for a day's work. But here is the sticking point: The workday is longer than 4 hours. It is 10 hours. In this case, the worker works a 10-hour day to earn 2 shillings (which is equal to 4 hours labor time), and the value produced by the worker in the 6 remaining hours is **surplus value** that the capitalist exploits from the worker.

Surplus Value
In Marxist terminology, the difference between the total value of production and the subsistence wages paid to workers.

Question:

Why couldn't the worker simply refuse to work more than 4 hours for 2 shillings? In short, why wouldn't the worker prevent the capitalist from exploiting him or her?

Answer:

Marx argued that capitalism creates a large *reserve army of the unemployed* and this excess supply of labor keeps wages at the subsistence level. For Marx, it was a matter of the worker working on the capitalist's terms or not working at all.

Dialectic. According to Hegel, knowledge and progress occur through a process of integrating opposing ideas or forces. An existing idea, or *thesis,* is at some point confronted with an opposing idea, *antithesis,* and there is a struggle of sorts. The outcome of the struggle is a *synthesis,* which in turn becomes the new thesis and the process starts again. Marx adapted Hegel's **dialectic** to explain the stages of economic development.

Marx on Economic Development

Marx criticized many of his economic predecessors and contemporaries for not understanding that capitalism had emerged as a specific economic system, or mode of production, and through the dialectical process would eventually evolve into a different economic system. According to Marx, there are six stages of economic development through which a nation would progress:

- *Primitive communism.* The first stage of economic development is characterized by common ownership of property, and people cooperate to earn a meager living from nature. People generally have to work all day simply to produce the bare necessities for survival. Under these conditions, there is no surplus value and thus no exploitation since both require workers to produce more than they need to consume for survival.
- *Slavery.* At some point, the productive capabilities of people rise to such an extent that they are able to produce more than they need to consume for survival. Now slavery becomes a possibility; some people exploit others and garner the surplus value. Once this occurs, class conflict arises.
- *Feudalism.* The economic actors in feudalism were lords and serfs, who, in Marx's view, had a relationship that was essentially the same as that between the slavemasters and slaves in the preceding stage of economic development. The serf was permitted to work a few days per week on the land allotted to him, but on other days he was required to till the lord's land.
- *Capitalism.* Marx both disliked capitalism and marveled at its ability to greatly increase productivity and output. According to Marx, the means of production became more concentrated under capitalism. For him, the relationship between capitalist and worker was essentially the same as the relationship between slavemaster and slave and between lord and serf in earlier stages of economic development. The capitalist appeared to pay the worker for all the hours that he or she worked, but in reality only paid for a few hours and appropriated the value produced in the remaining hours to himself. Marx predicted intense class struggles under capitalism between the capitalists, or *bourgeoisie,* and the workers, or *proletariat.* He believed that capitalists would increasingly exploit the workers in the search for higher profits.
- *Dictatorship of the proletariat, or socialism.* According to Marx, the intense class struggles under capitalism will eventually result in the state being used as an instrument of oppression by the capitalists against the workers. The workers will rise in revolt and overthrow the bourgeois state and establish in its place the dic-

Dialectic
The method of logic based on the principle that an idea or event (thesis) generates its opposite (antithesis), leading to a reconciliation of opposites (synthesis).

tatorship of the proletariat, in which the capital and land are owned by the proletarian government. Exploitation of the workers will cease.

■ *Pure communism.* The dictatorship of the proletariat eventually "withers away," only pure communism remains. In this stage of economic development, individuals produce according to their abilities and receive according to their needs. In pure communism, the highest stage of economic development, selfishness and greed are largely a thing of the past, and there is no need for a formal government apparatus.

The Critics of Marx

Here are some of the criticisms that have been levied against Marx's work:

1. The labor theory of value is faulty. Most contemporary economists agree that labor is not the sole source of value. They argue that land, capital, and entrepreneurship are independent factors of production and, like labor, are capable of creating value. Marxists sometimes retort that capital is ultimately created by labor, thus making it embodied labor. The critics agree that capital is *in part* past labor (and note that labor is paid its contribution to the production of capital), but they point out that capital is capable of creating value beyond the value of the labor employed to produce it.

2. There is no large reserve army of the unemployed. Marx maintained that capitalism produced a large reserve army of the unemployed that capitalists could use to hold wages down to a subsistence level. Massive unemployment has occurred under capitalism, but this has been the exception rather than the rule.

3. Most workers earn an above-subsistence wage. Here the critics argue that the competition for workers among business firms puts upward pressure on wages and causes firms to improve working conditions, shorten working hours, provide fringe benefits, and so forth.

4. Marxist revolutions have not appeared in the places Marx expected. Marx expected worker revolutions to appear in advanced capitalist nations where capitalism has had the longest time to develop, and the class conflict between capitalists and workers has had the longest time to intensify. According to Marx, countries such as Great Britain and the United States were far more likely to experience revolutions than countries such as Russia and China.

THE SOVIET ECONOMY: FROM COMMAND-ECONOMY SOCIALISM TO "IN TRANSITION"

■

Between 1985 and 1987, the Soviet economy evidenced growing problems: Growth rates were declining, there were few high-quality goods for consumers to buy, the scientific gap with the West was widening. In this environment, Soviet President Mikhail Gorbachev proposed two major reforms, which can be designated by the Russian terms *glasnost* and *perestroika*. **Glasnost** means greater openness in public discussions and the arts; **perestroika** means economic reform. The economic reforms are of particular interest to us.

The Soviet Union had been the primary example of a nation that practiced command-economy socialism. With the Gorbachev reforms, people began to wonder whether the Soviet Union would actually move away from command-economy socialism.

Glasnost
A Russian term popularly used to mean openness in public discussion and the arts.

Perestroika
A Russian term used to describe Soviet economic reform.

822

In August, 1991, communist hardliners waged a coup d'etat against Gorbachev. With Gorbachev under house arrest at his vacation home, Russian President and economic reform advocate, Boris Yeltsin, remained in the Russian republic's Parliament building and rallied large crowds to protest the military takeover. Coup leaders fled Moscow after they discovered that several military units would oppose the coup. Gorbachev was back in power in Moscow about 72 hours after he was first detained at his vacation home.

Immediately after the unsuccessful coup, Soviet President Gorbachev and Russian President Yeltsin forged a political alliance. Both men seemed committed to moving the Soviet economy away from command-economy socialism towards an economy where market forces and private property played a larger role than they had in the past. In the midst of their pursuit of economic reforms, many of the Soviet republics pushed for independence (independence was granted to the Baltic republics of Lithuania, Latvia, and Estonia in September, 1991), the Soviet economy witnessed an inflation rate of 250 percent, industrial production dropped substantially, and severe food shortages appeared imminent. So dire was the economic situation in the Soviet Union that many Soviet observers stated that another coup might be likely. This is the recent and fast-moving history of the Soviet Union.

We begin this section with a discussion of command-economy socialism, with particular reference to the Soviet economy. (In our description of the Soviet command economy, we continue to use the present tense, although events have already brought some changes.) We end with a discussion of the recent political and economic events in the Soviet Union—especially as they relate to the future of the Soviet economic system.

The Public and Private Sectors under Command-Economy Socialism

Under command-economy socialism, the private sector is very small; the public sector correspondingly large. This is simply another way of saying that most of what there is to be owned is owned by the central government—the state. For example, in the Soviet Union under command-economy socialism, the government owns and operates almost all the manufacturing, communication, transportation, and banking enterprises; wholesale and retail stores; and farms. A relatively few private farms (along with some garden plots), retail shops, and private personal services constitute the legal private sector. In addition to the legal private sector, command economies always have *black markets,* where goods are traded in violation of official regulations and prices. Still, the black market and the legal private sector together represent only a small percentage of the total economic activity in command economies.

Gosplan

In the Soviet Union under command-economy socialism, the central planning agency, or **Gosplan,** has the responsibility of drafting the economic plan for the Soviet economy. Gosplan does not, however, draft the economic plan without receiving input from the high Communist party officials in the Politburo (parliament), as well as supervision by the Council of Ministers, whose vice chairman is also the director of Gosplan.

Gosplan constructs two plans: a five-year (long-range) plan and a one-year (short-range) plan. The five-year plan allocates the nation's economic resources; it deter-

Gosplan
In the Soviet Union under command-economy socialism, the Soviet central planning agency that has the responsibility of drafting the economic plan for the nation.

mines how much goes to investment, how much to the military, how much to consumption, and so forth. The one-year plans are much more detailed than the five-year plans; they outline what each of the more than 200,000 Soviet enterprises under Gosplan's supervision is to produce, the amounts of labor and raw materials each will be allocated, the amount and type of machinery that will be installed, and so on.

To get a sense of how the process works, let's translate it to the American scene. If there were an American Gosplan, it would probably be located in Washington, D.C. The American Gosplan would then issue orders to General Motors, IBM, and other companies stating what each is to produce. For example, it might direct General Motors to produce 300,000 cars. In turn, Gosplan would direct the companies supplying General Motors to send so much steel, so much plastic, and so many tires to the company. It would also tell General Motors whether it could expect to have its factories updated, what type of new capital goods would be arriving, and other crucial information.

Allocating Resources: A Major Problem under Command-Economy Socialism

A planning agency's task is monumental; it must take the inputs of the economy and direct them into outputs in a manner consistent with the objectives set forth by the government leadership. This requires a careful balancing between output goals and available resources.

Suppose the planning agency sets as its annual goal the production of 100,000 units of X, 200,000 units of Y, and 300,000 units of Z. Next, it must allocate resources in such a way that it meets its goals. Suppose input W is necessary to the production of goods X, Y, and Z. The planning agency must then allocate input W so that 100,000 units of X, 200,000 units of Y, and 300,000 units of Z are produced. How will it know exactly how much input W to send to the enterprises producing goods X, Y, and Z? To know this, the planning agency needs to know how many units of W are required to make $1X$, $1Y$, and $1Z$.

Perhaps the planning agency thinks that 5 units of W are needed to make $1X$, 4 units of W are needed to make $1Y$, and 6 units of W are needed to make $1Z$. It therefore allocates 500,000 units of W to the enterprise producing good X ($5W$ for each of the required $100,000X$), 800,000 units of W to the enterprise producing good Y ($4W$ for each of the required $200,000Y$), and 1,800,000 units of W to the enterprise producing good Z ($6W$ for each of the required $300,000Z$). Although this sounds simple enough, several problems can easily arise.

First, the planning agency might incorrectly estimate the number of units of W that are required to make $1X$, $1Y$, and $1Z$. It could, say, overestimate the number of units of W required to produce good X and underestimate the number of units of W required to produce good Z. If this happens, then too many units of W will be sent to one enterprise and too few units of W will be sent to another.

Second, the number of units of input W required to make $1X$, $1Y$, and $1Z$ is likely to change over time. The quality of input W might fall so that more units will be needed to make $1X$. Will the planning agency know about this right away and adjust accordingly?

Third, the enterprise making W might require inputs from the enterprise that produces X before it can produce and ship W. Consider an enterprise that produces trucks. To produce trucks, the enterprise requires oil to generate the energy to run its plants. But, in turn, the enterprise producing oil needs trucks to move the oil to the truck factory. In such a situation, where one enterprise's production depends on another's, a failure by one enterprise to meet its production goals can make it impossible for other enterprises to meet their production goals, too.

Question:

First, if a U.S. enterprise fails to produce as expected, can't this make it impossible for other enterprises to meet their production goals, just as in the Soviet Union? After all, if firm X needs what firm Y produces and firm Y needs what firm Z produces, a slip-up by firm Z can prevent firms X and Y from producing as many units of their goods as they might want.

Answer:

Certainly, in the United States, one firm might be dependent on receiving supplies from another firm, but if it doesn't receive its supplies, it is more likely than its Soviet counterpart to locate substitute inputs. In the Soviet Union, if an enterprise doesn't receive the necessary inputs to make good X, the directors of the enterprise really have no incentive to locate substitute inputs. It is not the job of the directors of the enterprise to solve economic problems like this; it is the job of the planning agency. In the United States, however, the managers and owners of the business firm have an incentive to find substitute inputs because less output often means fewer dollars in their pockets.

The Case against Central Economic Planning

One of the major differences between individuals who favor pure capitalism and those who favor command-economy socialism is the issue of economic planning. The former are against central economic planning, and the latter are for it.

Critics advance two major arguments against central economic planning. First, economic plans, made by economic planners, cannot take into account as much relevant information as a market does; therefore, economic plans cannot coordinate economic activity or satisfy consumer demand as well as market forces. Consider an economic planning board, composed of 30 to 40 persons, that must decide how many houses, apartment buildings, buses, cars, and pizza parlors should be built within the next year. Where would the planners start? Would they know about people's changing demands for houses, apartment buildings, and the rest? Critics of economic planning argue that they would not. At best, the planners would be making a guess about what goods and services consumers would demand and how much they would buy at different prices. If they guess wrong, say the critics, resources will be wasted and demands will go unfulfilled. Private individuals, guided by rising and falling prices and by the desire to earn profits, are better at satisfying consumer demand. Economic planners risk little themselves when they draw up economic plans for others to follow (they don't put *their* money on the line), and therefore aren't as likely to avoid costly economic mistakes as are risk-taking entrepreneurs in a free market.

Second, economic planners mistakenly believe that the plans they construct will be followed by the members of society. Relevant here is Adam Smith's description of the economic planner or, as he called him, "the man of system":

> The man of system . . . seems to imagine that he can arrange the different members of a great society with as much ease as the hand arranges the different pieces upon a chess-

board. He does not consider that the pieces upon the chess-board have no other principle of motion beside that which the hand impresses upon them; but that, in the great chess-board of human society, every single piece has a principle of motion of its own, altogether different from that which the legislature might choose to impress upon it. If those two principles coincide and act in the same direction, the game of human society will go on easily and harmoniously, and is very likely to be happy and successful. If they are the opposite or different, the game will go on miserably, and human society must be at all times in the highest degree of disorder.[2]

Question:

Everybody uses plans. A person makes plans for his or her life, which include going to college, getting a job, and so forth. A business might draw up a plan for the next five years. If individuals and firms plan, why not societies? What do the critics of central economic planning say to this?

Answer:

They say that there is a major difference between the plan an individual or business firm makes and an economic plan for all of society. First, if an individual or a firm makes a plan that fails, only the individual or the firm suffers. For the most part, the rest of society is unaffected. This is not the case if a central economic plan (for all of society) fails. One mistake here can have major consequences for many people.

Second, if one person makes a personal plan, this does not prohibit others from making and following their own plans. But an economic plan that encompasses all of society just might do that. For example, a young woman with computer skills living in one part of a command-economy nation may want to move to another part. But whether she can realize her plan depends on whether her plan is consistent with the economic plan set down by the central authorities. It may be that the economic plan calls for technological development in the area of the country where the young woman lives and that she will be required to continue to live and work there.

The Next Step: Supply and Demand

As we have seen, a planning agency determines the aggregate quantity of goods in a command economy; that is, how many radios, television sets, cars, refrigerators, toasters, and so forth will be provided. This is the supply side of the market. As we know, though, there is also a demand side to every market, and supply and demand together determine price.

Besides determining the supply of a particular good, the Soviet central planners under command-economy socialism also set its price. For example, they might decide that 11 million toasters will be produced this year and that each will sell for a price of 25 rubles. Unless 25 rubles is the equilibrium price, though, there will be either a surplus or a shortage of toasters. Exhibit 38–2 illustrates what happens when the price for toasters is set below the equilibrium price. A shortage of toasters results. In a market system, the price of toasters would be bid up to the equilibrium price, and the quantity demanded of toasters would equal the quantity supplied. But in the Soviet Union under command-economy socialism, it is illegal

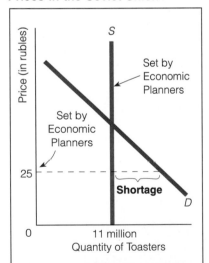

EXHIBIT 38–2
Prices in the Soviet Union

Here is an example where the wrong price is set. Planners set the ruble price for toasters too low; as a result, there is a shortage, and toasters are rationed by some combination of ruble price and waiting in line.

[2]Adam Smith, *The Theory of Moral Sentiments* (Oxford: Oxford University Press, 1976), p. 234.

to bid up the ruble price of a good. So, instead, toasters are rationed by some combination of ruble price and waiting in line (that is, the rationing device, first-come-first-served).

Western travelers to the Soviet Union have observed long lines in front of some stores and no people at all in front of other stores. What accounts for this? Some prices are set below the equilibrium price, producing shortages and long lines of people, and some prices are set above the equilibrium price, producing surpluses and relatively empty stores. As long as price is centrally imposed, shortages or surpluses are likely to result. It would be most unusual if the planners could correctly guess the equilibrium price.

The Soviet Union in Transition

Currently, the Soviet Union is in transition. We describe some of the historical events of this transition period.

Gorbachev's Goal.   In the late-1980s, Gorbachev's stated goal was to shift the Soviet Union from an overly centralized command system of management to a more flexible system incorporating some decentralization and choice. His desire was to increase efficiency and productivity by loosening the bureaucratic stranglehold on the economy. Most Western observers believed this meant that the Soviet leader wanted his country to adopt some market practices. Specifically, Gorbachev was proposing (a) the modernization of industry, (b) worker incentives, (c) a move towards the freer operation of supply and demand forces, and (d) more decentralized decision making.

Opposition to Reform.   According to Soviet economist G. Povov, two main groups have opposed economic reform in the Soviet Union. First, there are the managers of state enterprises that have done well under the old system, satisfying their supervisors by using political skills they have cultivated over the years. Operating under the dictates of the marketplace would undermine their security and force them into new patterns of behavior. Second are the numerous workers who oppose economic reform because, under the old system, they are paid and guaranteed a job irrespective of the quality of their work.

Gorbachev's Problem.   Gorbachev probably knew that the road to economic reform would not be easy. If the Soviet citizen was to accept the greater emphasis on supply and demand forces (especially when this meant he would have to pay higher prices for some goods), reduced job security, and the demand for harder and higher-quality work, then he had to see that he would get something for all this. Many Soviet citizens thought the reward would be higher pay and more consumer goods to buy. Without these two as the "carrot" to entice the Soviet citizens onward down the road of economic reform, the road for Gorbachev and his supporters was bound to be bumpy.

Eastern Europe.   Nineteen eighty-nine (1989) was a revolutionary year. It was the year the Berlin Wall came down. One after the other, the nations of Eastern Europe toppled their communist governments. The new leaders of these countries proclaimed their intent to achieve political and economic freedom for their people (in varying degrees). Some commentators said that the upheavals in Eastern Europe could not have occurred had not Gorbachev earlier introduced glasnost and perestroika in the Soviet Union and had he not tacitly acceded to the desires of the peoples of Eastern Europe to free themselves from oppressive communist regimes.

Bad Economic News.   In 1990, Soviet real GNP fell 6.4 percent and in 1991 it fell 17 percent. The inflation rate was 10 percent in 1990, and it had risen to 250 percent in 1991. When Soviet citizens were asked in a 1991 poll what the Soviet Union had to offer its citizens, 65 percent of the persons polled responded: "Shortages, waiting in lines, and a miserable existence."

We Ask Five Economists A Question.   In early 1991, *before* the unsuccessful coup against Mikhail Gorbachev, we asked five well-known economists this question: **With recent economic and political changes in the Soviet Union and Eastern Europe, some people are suggesting this is an end of an era. Any thoughts on the subject?** This is what they had to say:

- **Lester Thurow.** The post-World War II era is over. Capitalism beat communism. A new, as yet unnamed, era has begun. It will feature a contest between individualistic Anglo-Saxon capitalism and a more communitarian form of capitalism found in Germany and Japan.
- **Gordon Tullock.** The world is not so much entering a new era as going back to an older one. Before 1914, there was no communism in the world. We had a set of nation states who frequently had bad relations with each other or had wars, but there was no crusading economic religion in existence which was attempting to change the world in its own direction. That period, retrospectively, was a good one, but not a period of perfect peace or total prosperity. That is what we seem to be entering into provided that Gorbachev's reforms are successful.
- **John Kenneth Galbraith.** I think they will move [toward a market system] but I also think the passage is much more difficult than we had imagined. It is difficult essentially because of the lack of institutions and to some extent the lack of motivation. I believe the lack of motivation comes from having a history of relatively leisurely living.
- **Milton Friedman.** The world is entering a new era but it is much too early to know how it will turn out. One thing is clear: communism in the Stalinist version is dead. But it is not clear that private free markets will emerge in Eastern Europe. That remains to be seen.
- **James M. Bhuchanan.** The century-long ideological conflict between socialism and the market is no longer present, but there is no rebirth of laissez-faire. I find it hard to predict what will indeed emerge.

The Political and Economic Environment Shortly *Before* the (Unsuccessful) August 1991 Coup d'Etat.   As we said earlier, there was an unsuccessful coup d'etat against Mikhail Gorbachev in August, 1991. The political and economic environment before the coup is best described as chaotic and uncertain. On the political front, several of the republics of the Soviet Union were vigorously pushing for independence. The hardliners in the Kremlin argued that the U.S.S.R. would have to be preserved, no matter the cost. Also, the hardliners could not forgive Gorbachev for introducing glasnost and perestroika. On the other hand, the democrats and reformers wanted independence for the republics pursuing this goal, and they were angry at Gorbachev for not working hard enough for political liberalization and economic reform. The leader of the political liberals and economic reformers was the president of the largest republic in the Soviet Union (Russia), Boris Yeltsin.

On the economic front, the Soviet Union was witnessing high inflation, a severe drop in GNP, and a huge budget deficit. Many of the Soviet citizens were squarely behind greater political freedom, but their current experience with what they perceived as economic reform seemed less than favorable.

The Coup d'Etat and Yeltsin.   In a matter of a few days, the hardliners coup d'etat against Milkhail Gorbachev had ended. Gorbachev returned to Moscow from his vacation home where he had been under house arrest. The man of the hour was not Gorbachev, however, but Boris Yeltsin, who had rallied the forces of liberalism and economic reform against the coup leaders.

The Political and Economic Environment Shortly *After* the August 1991 Coup d'Etat.   Shortly after his return to Moscow, Gorbachev and Yeltsin forged a political alliance. The coup had been defeated and it seemed as if the victorious forces of political liberalism and economic reform had been finally thrust to center stage. In this environment, three of the (then) 15 republics of the Soviet Union were granted independence—Estonia, Latvia, and Lithuania. In this environment, Gorbachev no longer had to perform the political tightrope walk that he once performed between hardliners and reformers. But still the problems of the economy loomed large. There was both talk and some action among the remaining 12 republics to form a "common market" similar to that of the Economic Community (EC). The debate in the Soviet Union was waged between those who wanted to push hard and fast for radical economic change—which included selling state assets, strict fiscal and monetary discipline, private ownership of property on a wide scale, the decentralization of almost all government functions, freeing up most prices, and delegating responsibility for key economic affairs to the republics—and those who wanted a much more moderate and slower approach.

Yeltsin Proposes Commonwealth of Independent States: No More Soviet Union.   In the midst of economic chaos in the Soviet Union, and Gorbachev's plea to maintain some solidarity within the Soviet state, Boris Yeltsin proposed a commonwealth of independent states with no central government. On Wednesday, December 11, 1991, Yeltsin won a decisive victory for his plan by persuading top military commanders that a post-Soviet commonwealth was the way to proceed. (Yeltsin also promised to raise all military salaries by 90%, effective January 1, 1992.) Under Yeltsin's commonwealth plan both Gorbachev's position as Soviet president, and the Soviet Union as we have come to know it, would perish. The move to create a commonwealth of independent states also coincided with Yeltsin's plan to move quickly toward a market economy.

What's Ahead?

Will the land mass we have known as the Soviet Union continue to be a union, or will it be a commonwealth of independent states? Will it join the ranks of market economies? In answer to the second question, we know that in the face of massive economic woes—high inflation, low production—it has made a first attempt. But the pace at which it will move toward privatization, free prices, and decentralization is unknown. Economic hardship, currently being felt by the Soviet citizenry, is often the soil in which radical changes can be made. Whether the radical changes will be back towards command-economy socialism—perhaps as a result of a successful coup in the future—or towards a market economy and a commonwealth, we don't know for sure. At minimum, the drama being played out continues to be worth watching, as its process and outcome will influence world events for years to come.

THE PEOPLE'S REPUBLIC OF CHINA

After the Communist (Maoist) takeover in 1949, the Chinese economy, using the Soviet economic system as a model, put command-economy socialism into effect, although Chinese economic planning was less centralized than Soviet planning.

In 1958, Mao Tse-tung instituted an economic plan known as the *Great Leap Forward,* which called for the development of heavy industry, a dramatic increase in output, and a more intensive use of labor. The plan was largely a failure. Goods were produced that no one wanted, large-scale projects (such as irrigation) were poorly planned, people were transferred from rural areas to the cities, and goods such as steel produced by unskilled workers in primitive work environments were of low quality. In Hunan province alone, 5,376 collectives were combined into 208 large people's communes with an average of 8,000 households in each. National income fell dramatically.

The next major Maoist attempt at national reconstruction was the *Cultural Revolution,* which began in 1966. This radical left movement aimed at remaking Chinese society in general and at eliminating all foreign influences from the country in particular. During the Cultural Revolution, teashops and private theaters were shut down; hand holding and kite flying were forbidden; the National Gallery of Fine Arts was closed, as were radio and television stations, newspapers, and magazines; and libraries were ransacked and books burned. (Mao disliked formal education. He once said, "The more books one reads, the stupider one becomes.") This was not an environment in which economic development could flourish. National income fell once again during the Cultural Revolution. Mao's death on September 9, 1976, ended the Cultural Revolution and opened the way for change.

The economic changes in China today are generally attributed to China's leader, Deng Xiaoping, who came to power shortly after Mao's death. These changes are examined next.

Bao gan dao hu

Bao gan dao hu means "contracting all decisions to the household." It is the essence of China's economic reforms in rural areas. China's collective farms are currently operated by households under the following system: (1) The government gives collectives specific production quotas that they must meet. (2) The government buys the quota-procured output at a fixed price. (3) Although the state owns the farmland, it is divided into small plots that are farmed by the households; households are allowed to contract with the collective to produce a share of the quota. (4) Once the households have met their quota-procurement responsibilities, they can produce and sell in the free market any output they want. These new agricultural reforms have led to a rise in agricultural output. For example, between 1978 and 1984 (a peak year), grain production increased 34 percent to 400 million tons. For a short while, China was a grain exporter instead of an importer.

A Shaky Free Market. Saying that China has adopted some free market practices does not mean that a free market practice put into effect today will not be abandoned tomorrow. For example, Hong Kong buys many of its pigs from Guangdong province in China. A few years ago, an increase in the demand for pigs in Hong Kong raised the price of pigs in Guangdong. Farmers in Hunan, the province north of Guangdong, saw the higher prices for pigs in Guangdong and started to ship their pigs there. As a result, the supply of pigs in Hunan decreased, and the price of pigs in Hunan increased. The provincial government in Hunan responded to

PART XI
ECONOMIC GROWTH, DEVELOPMENT,
AND ALTERNATIVE ECONOMIC
SYSTEMS

830

the higher prices by banning the export of pigs raised in Hunan. When the press criticized this policy, the provincial government repealed its ban on exports and imposed an export tax on pigs instead. This policy had basically the same effect as the ban. Such interventions by provincial governments are thought to hamper the efficiency of the Chinese agricultural sector.

Unleashing Industry. In 1978, Zhao Ziyang, the first secretary of the Communist party in Sichuan province, ordered that six Sichuan enterprises be partly freed from the central planning system. These enterprises, like the agricultural collectives, were first obligated to meet a state procurement target, after which they could produce according to the dictates of the marketplace. Since 1978, a few thousand enterprises have been allowed to operate under the same conditions as the original six Sichuan enterprises. In 1985, a truck-producing enterprise in China sold 55,000 of the 91,500 trucks it produced to the government and sold the remainder on the free market.

Leasing Bankrupt State-Owned Enterprises. A few state-owned enterprises that were on the brink of bankruptcy have been leased to private citizens. In many cases, these private citizens have turned the enterprises around and have been able to keep some of the profit for their efforts.

Evading the system. In China, large, well-managed enterprises are often required to meet larger production quotas than small, inefficient firms. Some commentators have noted that such a system actually penalizes the large, well-managed firms since they have to allocate many of their resources to fulfill government plans and thus have little left over to produce goods that can be sold on the free market. To get around this, many large, well-managed firms have either tried to hide some of their productive capacity (to look smaller) or to disguise their relative efficiency in production by failing to meet some contracts. (The reasoning here is that if government believes the enterprise is small and inefficient, it will look elsewhere to meet its production quotas, leaving the enterprise to produce for the market.)

Tian An Men Square, June 1989

Perhaps because of their new-found economic freedoms, and partly because of successes experienced by citizens of Eastern European nations, many Chinese began to demand greater political freedom. This desire for greater freedom coalesced in the mass rallies in Tian An Men Square in June 1989. Hundreds of thousands of demonstrators stood in the square and demanded (very moderate) political reforms. The Chinese government asked the demonstrators to leave, but they would not. Finally, the government ordered the army to disperse the protestors. Many hundreds of people were killed, scores more injured, as horrified viewers all over the world watched the carnage on their television screens.

What Next?

China has entered on a path of economic reform in the face of a resistance to political reforms. Whether reactionary politics will stifle economic reform, or economic reform will moderate reactionary politics, few people, if any, know at this time.

   In March 1991, China's premier Li Peng, in a speech before the National People's Congress (China's legislature), said that China will continue to use central planning through the year 2000 and that enterprises will gradually be pushed into a market environment. Li stressed that as China cautiously moves forward with economic reforms, the Communist Party would not relax its hold on power.

THE JAPANESE ECONOMY

Japan is a country the size of Montana, with a population of 124 million people in 1991. It is also a country with the second largest market economy in the world (after the United States). In this section, we discuss the Japanese economy; in particular, the ways in which it differs from the U.S. economy.[3]

Savings

As we discussed in Chapter 37, there is a link between *non*consumption, or saving, and capital formation. As the savings rate increases, capital formation increases, and so does economic growth. For example, during the period 1961–90, the Japanese average annual growth rate in real GNP was approximately 6 percent, whereas during the same period in the United States, the average annual growth rate in real GNP was 3.3 percent. At these rates, the Japanese economy would double in size every 12 years, whereas the U.S. economy would double in size every 22 years.

Japan has a relatively high savings rate. To illustrate, savings as a percentage of disposable (after-tax) income has been around 5 percent in the United States in recent years, but it has been noticeably higher in Japan. There are probably a number of reasons for this.

1. Homebuyers are required to make a minimum downpayment of 40 percent of the purchase price of the home they buy which, since land is relatively scarce, is priced relatively high. As a consequence, households are required to save a large percentage of their income.
2. Social security benefits are relatively low and retirement age is rather young (55 to 60). Workers therefore must save for their old age.
3. It is a practice in Japanese firms to set a relatively low wage rate and offer large bonuses (based on profits) twice a year.
4. Japan's tax system allows substantial exemptions on interest income, thus stimulating saving.

Labor Market Considerations

Between 1962 and 1989, the average annual unemployment rate in the United States was 6.0 percent. In Japan, it was 1.8 percent.[4] During this period, Japan was consistently able to hold its unemployment rate below that of the United States, and without greater inflation.

---

[3]Much of the discussion in this section comes from Andrew Zimbalist, Howard J. Sherman, and Stuart Brown, *Comparing Economic Systems: A Political-Economic Approach* (San Diego: Harcourt Brace Jovanovich, 1989).

[4]It is natural to ask whether the Japanese define and measure unemployment as it is done in the United States. The answer is that there are minor methodological differences. However, a study by the Bureau of Labor Statistics reports that if Japan were to use the U.S. definition and measurement, its unemployment rate would nevertheless be unchanged: the upward and downward biases would cancel each other. Also, a study released by the Japanese embassy in Washington concluded that minor methodological differences lower the measured unemployment rate in Japan by only two-tenths of one percentage point.

Why has the Japanese unemployment rate consistently been lower than the U.S. unemployment rate? On the macro level, rapid economic growth, which Japan has had, brings with it a high demand for labor. On the micro level, the Japanese attribute it to lifetime employment and union–management cooperation, which we discuss next.

Lifetime Employment. Lifetime employment refers to the institutional setup in Japan where a person is guaranteed a job with a specific company until retirement. Lifetime employment does not cover all workers at all companies, nor does it always cover all workers at a given company. Still, it is a major feature of the Japanese economy.

There are some disadvantages to lifetime employment: It results in too many employees working in a company during an economic downturn and the retention of (sometimes) less than efficient workers. The advantages include lower worker turnover (which results in lower job training expenses), less worker resistance to technological change, and enhancement of worker loyalty to the firm.

Union–Management Cooperation. Approximately one-third of the Japanese labor force is unionized; moreover, Japanese unions and management commonly share the same goals and means to accomplish them. The founding slogan of the Nissan Company labor union was "Those who truly love their union, love their company." Some commentators argue that in Japan unions and management get along better than, say, U.S. unions and U.S. management, because Japanese management tries to cultivate a "family feeling" and "sense of loyalty" among workers. Several ways it does this is by offering lifetime employment, having a more equal distribution of income between managers and workers than in the United States (the gap between top management salaries in Toyota and worker salaries is less than the gap between top management salaries at General Motors and worker salaries), offering pay bonuses to workers, and regularly consulting with workers on how the company should be run.

Economic Policy-Making in Japan

In Japan, economic policy making, especially industrial policy making, is more in the hands of professional bureaucrats than the legislature. Two of the major economic bodies in the professional bureaucracy include the Ministry of Finance (MOF) and the Ministry of International Trade and Industry (MITI). One of the major duties of the MOF is to encourage banks to increase or decrease their lending to specific industries, largely identified by MITI.

MITI is the organization in Japan that largely forges Japan's **industrial policy.** Japanese industrial policy focuses on "watering the green spots": aiding those industries that are most likely to be successful in the world marketplace. The idea behind MITI "is that the private sector alone has insufficient vision, coordination, resources, and risk-bearing ability to conduct its affairs in an optimal manner. To alleviate bottlenecks, to avert overproduction, to anticipate market shifts, to develop and deploy unchartered technology, the government is needed to assist in the sharing of information, pooling of resources, and overall collaboration of efforts. As a result of the successful implementation of this approach, MITI has referred to the Japanese system as a *plan-oriented market economy.*"[5]

The powers MITI has at its disposal to aid and guide certain industries are numerous. A few include (1) designating certain regions as industrial parks and

Industrial Policy
In Japan, the policy of "watering the green spots," or aiding those industries that are most likely to be successful in the world marketplace.

[5]Zimbalist, Sherman, and Brown, p. 52.

providing an infrastructure for the parks; (2) imposing trade barriers to protect firms; and (3) coordinating research efforts among firms in an industry.

The degree to which MITI has aided Japanese economic growth is controversial. Some economists maintain that MITI too often gets in the way of good ideas. For example, it mistakenly tried to discourage Japanese car manufacturers from competing in the world automobile market in the 1960s.

Others state that MITI has greatly benefitted the Japanese economy. For example, a key success seems to be in the semiconductor industry, an industry largely dominated by U.S. firms until MITI encouraged and aided Japanese firms. Currently, the Japanese supply almost 90 percent of the international semiconductor market.

Question:

Will the U.S. economy become more like the Japanese economy in the near future, or will the Japanese economy become more like the U.S. economy?

Answer:

That is hard to say. Critics of industrial policy in the U.S. believe that over time government policies are turned to the advantage of powerful interest groups and may actually retard economic performance instead of improve it. This fear is a powerful barrier to adopting MITI-type policies in the United States. It remains to be seen whether industrial policy will have these harmful effects in Japan as time passes. It is probably too early to say much more than this.

Economic Realities and Economic Systems

■ The following hold for all economic systems: scarcity, opportunity cost (no free lunch), the need for a rationing device, the law of demand, and rational self-interested behavior. In addition, all economic systems must answer the following questions: What goods will be produced? How will the goods be produced? For whom will the goods be produced?

Pure Capitalism

■ Pure capitalism is an economic system characterized by private ownership of the factors of production, market allocation of resources, and decentralized decision making; most economic activities take place in the private sector, and government plays a small role or no role at all in the economy. The advocates of pure capitalism are often called libertarians.

■ Libertarians maintain that in a pure capitalist economy, none of the following would exist: government-granted professional licenses, minimum wage laws, only one firm that delivers first-class mail, restraints on price, discretionary fiscal and monetary policies, the Federal Reserve, antitrust policy, quotas, and tariffs, and compulsory saving or redistribution programs. Libertarians generally argue that whatever the government does, the private sector can do better and that some things the government does shouldn't be done and wouldn't be done by the private sector.

■ The critics of libertarianism state that libertarians (1) do not see the merit of sometimes allowing government to adjust for third-party effects through taxes, subsidies, and regulations; (2) do not seriously consider complex exchanges, and (3) do not see the stabilizing effects of government monetary and fiscal policies.

Karl Marx

■ Two major intellectual strands in Marx's thinking are the labor theory of value and the dialectical process. Marx argued that (1) the value of a commodity is determined by the *socially necessary labor time* embodied in it, and (2) history could be interpreted in terms of the dialectic, in which two opposing forces or ideas (the thesis and antithesis) form a synthesis that becomes the new thesis, thereby starting the process all over.

■ Marx identified the stages of economic development as primitive communism, slavery, feudalism, capitalism, the dictatorship of the proletariat, and pure communism.

■ The critics of Marx argue that the labor theory of value is faulty; there is no large reserve army of the unemployed as Marx predicted; contrary to Marx, most workers earn above-subsistence wages; and Marxist revolutions have not appeared in the places Marx expected.

The Soviet Economy: From Command-Economy Socialism to "In Transition"

■ Under command-economy socialism, the private sector is very small; the public sector correspondingly large.

■ Command economies make use of central planning agencies whose job it is to allocate the nation's resources. The critics of central planning argue that economic planners cannot take into account as much relevant information as a market does; therefore, economic plans cannot coordinate economic activity or satisfy consumer demand as well as market forces. Secondly, economic planners mistakenly believe that the plans they construct will be followed by the members of society.

■ Planning agencies in command economies set the prices of goods and services. Since planners rarely set prices at their equilibrium levels (because it is unlikely they could know what the equilibrium prices are without allowing the forces of supply and demand to operate), command economies commonly experience surpluses and shortages.

■ Currently the Soviet economy is in transition. Soviet President Mikhail Gorbachev's stated goal is to shift the Soviet Union from an overly centralized command system of management to a more flexible system incorporating some decentralization and choice. Russian President Boris Yeltsin has played a major part in spearheading the move towards an economy where market forces and private property play a major role. As of this writing (December, 1991), the Soviet economy is experiencing major economic problems: high inflation and sharply declining real GNP. In this setting, it is difficult to tell what will happen next. Some observers believe there may be a return to command-economy socialism and political repression; others believe that while the transition to an economy where market forces and private property play a major role will be arduous that nonetheless it will continue.

The Chinese Economy

■ After the Communist (Maoist) takeover in 1949, the Chinese economy, using the Soviet economic system as a model, put command-economy socialism into effect.

■ In 1958, Mao Tse-tung instituted an economic plan known as the Great Leap Forward. The next major Maoist attempt at national reconstruction was the Cultural Revolution, which began in 1966. Mao died in 1976.

■ Currently the Chinese economy is experimenting with some economic reforms, mainly focused on implementing a few modified market practices.

■ Perhaps because of their new-found economic freedoms, many Chinese began to demand greater political freedom. This resulted in mass rallies in Tian An Men Square in June 1989.

The Japanese Economy

■ Japan has a relatively high savings rate. Savings as a percentage of disposable (after-tax) income has been around 5 percent in the United States in recent years, but it has been noticeably higher in Japan.

■ Between 1962 and 1989, the average annual unemployment rate in the United States was 6.0 percent; in Japan, it was 1.8 percent.

■ Lifetime employment, which does not cover all Japanese workers at all companies, is a major feature of the Japanese economy.

■ MITI, the organization in Japan that largely forges Japan's industrial policy, has certain powers. A few include (1) designating certain regions as industrial parks and providing an infrastructure for the parks; (2) imposing trade barriers to protect firms; and (3) coordinating research efforts among firms in an industry.

Key Terms and Concepts

Mixed Capitalism	Decentralized Socialism	Glasnost
Pure Capitalism	Labor Theory of Value	Perestroika
Command-Economy Socialism	Dialectic	Gosplan
	Surplus Value	Industrial Policy

QUESTIONS AND PROBLEMS

1. Choose one of the fundamental economic realities that both the United States and the Soviet Union (under command-economy socialism) face, and explain the different ways by which the two economies would deal with it.

2. Socialists in the Soviet Union have remarked, in the past, that at least their economic plans maintain full employment, whereas capitalism cannot. What is the likely libertarian response?

3. Some people argue that capitalism and socialism are usually evaluated only on economic grounds, where capitalism has a clear advantage. But in order to evaluate the two economic systems evenhandedly, both should be evaluated on other factors as well—justice, fairness, the happiness of the people living under both systems, the crime rate, the standard of living of those at the bottom of the economic ladder, and much more. Do you think this is the proper way to proceed?

4. The *convergence hypothesis,* first proposed by a Soviet economist, suggests that over time the capitalist economies will become increasingly socialistic and the socialist economies will become increasingly capitalistic. Do you believe the convergence hypothesis has merit? What real-world evidence can you cite to prove or disprove the hypothesis?

5. Predict how mixed capitalism, pure capitalism, and command-economy socialism would each deal with the problem of pollution.

6. What are some of the advantages of industrial policy? the disadvantages?

Glossary

Absolute Advantage The situation where a country can produce more of a good than another country can produce with the same quantity of resources.

Absolute Price The price of a good in money terms.

Abstraction The process (used in building a theory) of focusing on a limited number of variables to explain or predict an event.

Accounting Profit The difference between total revenue and explicit costs.

Activists Persons who argue that monetary and fiscal policies should be deliberately used to smooth out the business cycle.

Adaptive Expectations Expectations that individuals form from past experience and modify slowly as the present and the future become the past (as time passes).

Aggregate Demand (*AD*) Curve A curve that shows the quantity demand of real GNP at different price levels, *ceteris paribus.*

Antitrust Law Legislation passed for the stated purpose of controlling monopoly power and preserving and promoting competition.

Appreciation An increase in the value of one currency relative to other currencies.

Arbitrage Buying a good in a market where its price is low, and selling the good in another market where its price is higher.

Assets Anything of value to which the firm has a legal claim.

Attainable Region Includes those points on and below the production possibilities frontier.

Automatic Fiscal Policy Changes in government expenditures or taxes that occur automatically without (additional) congressional action.

Average Fixed Cost Total fixed cost divided by quantity of output: $AFC = TFC/Q.$

Average-Marginal Rule When the marginal magnitude is above the average magnitude, the average magnitude rises; when the marginal magnitude is below the average magnitude, the average magnitude falls.

Average Total Cost (Unit Cost) Total cost divided by quantity of output: $ATC = TC/Q.$

Average Variable Cost Total variable cost divided by quantity of output: $AVC = TVC/Q.$

Bad Anything from which individuals receive disutility or dissatisfaction.

Balanced Budget Government expenditures equal tax receipts.

Balanced Budget Theorem A change in real GNP is equal to the change in government spending when government spending and taxes change by the same dollar amount and in the same direction.

Balance of Payments A periodic statement (usually annual) of the money value of all transactions between residents of one country and residents of all other countries.

Balance Sheet An accounting of the assets, liabilities, and net worth of a business firm.

Barter Exchanging goods and services for other goods and services without the use of money.

Base Year The year chosen as a point of reference or comparison for prices in other years; a benchmark year.

Black Market An illegal market. There are two varieties: one in which illegal goods are bought and sold and one in which goods are bought and sold at illegal prices.

Board of Governors The governing body of the Federal Reserve System.

Bond An IOU statement that promises to pay a certain sum of money (the principal) at maturity and also to pay periodic fixed sums until that date.

Budget Constraint All the combinations or bundles of two goods a person can purchase given a certain money income and prices for the two goods.

Budget Deficit Occurs when government expenditures (*G*) are greater than tax receipts (*T*): $G > T.$

Budget Surplus Occurs when government expenditures (*G*) are less than tax receipts (*T*): $G < T.$

Business Cycle Recurrent swings (up and down) in real GNP.

Business Firm An entity that employs factors of production (resources) and produces goods and services to be sold to consumers, other firms, or the government.

Capital Produced goods that can be used as inputs for further production, such as machinery, tools, computers, trucks, buildings, and factories.

Capital Account Includes all payments related to the purchase and sale of assets and to borrowing and lending activities. Components include outflow of U.S. capital and inflow of foreign capital.

Capital Account Balance The summary statistic for the outflow of U.S. capital and the inflow of foreign capital. It is equal to the difference between the outflow of U.S. capital and the inflow of foreign capital.

Capital Consumption Allowance or Depreciation The estimated amount of capital goods used up in production through natural wear, obsolescence, and accidental destruction.

G–1

Capture Hypothesis Holds that no matter what the motive for the initial regulation and the establishment of the regulatory agency, eventually the agency will be "captured" (controlled) by the special interests of the industry that is being regulated.

Cartel An organization of firms that reduces output and increases price in an effort to increase joint profits.

Cartel Theory In this theory of oligopoly, oligopolistic firms act as if there were only one firm in the industry.

Cash Leakage Occurs when funds are held as currency instead of being deposited into a checking account.

Ceteris Paribus The Latin term meaning "all other things held constant."

Choice The act of selecting among restricted alternatives.

Closed Economy An economy that does not trade goods and services with other nations.

Closed Shop An organization in which an employee must belong to the union before he or she can be hired.

Coase Theorem In the case of trivial or zero transaction costs, the property rights assignment does not matter to the resource allocative outcome.

Collective Bargaining The process whereby wage rates and other issues are determined by a union bargaining with management on behalf of all union members.

Command-Economy Socialism An economic system characterized by government ownership of the non-labor factors of production, government allocation of resources, and centralized decision making; most economic activities take place in the public sector, and government plays a very large role in the economy.

Commercial Banks Privately owned, profit-seeking institutions that offer a wide range of services (checking accounts, savings accounts, loans) to customers.

Comparative Advantage The situation where a country can produce a good at lower opportunity cost than another country.

Complements Two goods that are used jointly in consumption. With complements, the demand for one rises as the price of the other falls (or the demand for one falls as the price of the other rises).

Complete Crowding Out The decrease in one or more components of private spending completely offsets the increase in government spending.

Concentration Ratio The percentage of industry sales (or assets, output, labor force, or some other factor) accounted for by x-number of firms in the industry.

Constant-Cost Industry An industry in which average total costs do not change as (industry) output increases or decreases, as firms enter or exit the industry, respectively.

Constant Returns to Scale Exist when inputs are increased by some percentage and output increases by an equal percentage, causing unit costs to remain constant.

Consumer Equilibrium Occurs when the consumer has spent all income and the marginal utilities per dollar spent on each good purchased are equal: $MU_A/P_A = MU_B/P_B = MU_C/P_C = \ldots = MU_Z/P_Z$, where the letters $A–Z$ represent all the goods a person buys.

Consumer Price Index The most widely cited index number for the price level; the weighted average of prices of a specific set of goods and services purchased by a typical household.

Consumers' Surplus The difference between the price buyers pay for a good and the maximum or highest price they would have paid for the good. It is a dollar measure of the benefit gained by being able to purchase a unit of a good for less than one is willing to pay for it.

Consumption Household spending on consumer goods.

Contestable Market A market in which entry is easy and exit is costless, new firms can produce the product at the same cost as current firms, and exiting firms can easily dispose of their fixed assets by selling them.

Continued Inflation A continued increase in the price level.

Contractionary Fiscal Policy Fiscal policy designed to decrease aggregate demand or aggregate supply.

Corporation A legal entity that can conduct business in its own name the way an individual does; ownership of the corporation resides with stockholders who have limited liability in the debts of the corporation.

Coupon Rate The percentage of the face value of the bond that is paid out regularly (usually quarterly or annually) to the holder of the bond.

Craft (Trade) Union A union whose membership is made up of individuals who practice the same craft or trade.

Credit In the balance of payments, any transaction that either supplies a foreign currency or creates a demand for the nation's currency in the foreign exchange market.

Credit Market A market that channels funds from savers (lenders) to borrowers.

Cross Elasticity of Demand Measures the responsiveness in quantity demanded of one good to changes in the price of another good.

Crowding Out The decrease in private expenditures that occurs as a consequence of increased government spending or of the financing needs of the deficit.

Currency Includes coins and paper money.

Current Account Includes all payments related to the purchase and sale of goods and services. Components of the account include exports, imports, and net unilateral transfers abroad.

Current Account Balance The summary statistic for exports of goods and services, imports of goods and services, and net unilateral transfers.

Cyclical Unemployment Rate The difference between the unemployment rate and the natural unemployment rate.

Debit In the balance of payments, any transaction that either supplies the nation's currency or creates a demand for foreign currency in the foreign exchange market.

Decentralized Socialism An economic system characterized by government ownership of the non-labor factors of production, largely market allocation of resources, and decentralized decision making; most economic activities take place in the public sector, and government plays a major overseer role in the economy.

Decreasing-Cost Industry An industry in which average total costs decrease as output increases and increase as output decreases, as firms enter and exit the industry, respectively.

Demand The willingness and ability of buyers to purchase different quantities of a good at different prices during a specific time period.

Demand Curve The graphical representation of the law of demand.

Demand Curve for Money (Balances) Represents the inverse relationship between the quantity demanded of money balances and the price of holding money balances.

Demand Deposits A deposit of funds that can be withdrawn without restrictions and is transferable by check.

Demand Schedule The numerical tabulation of the quantity demanded of a good at different prices.

Dependency Ratio The number of children under a certain age plus the number of the elderly (aged 65 and over) divided by the total population.

Depreciation A decrease in the value of one currency relative to other currencies.

Derived Demand Demand that is the result of some other demand. For example, factor demand is the result of the demand for the products that the factors go to produce.

Devaluation An official governmental act that changes the exchange rate by lowering the official price of a currency.

Dialectic The method of logic based on the principle that an idea or event (thesis) generates its opposite (antithesis), leading to a reconciliation of opposites (synthesis).

Diamond–Water Paradox The observation that those things that have the greatest value in use sometimes have little value in exchange and those things that have little value in use sometimes have the greatest value in exchange.

Directly Related Two variables are directly related if they move in the same direction.

Discount Rate The interest rate the Fed charges depository institutions that borrow reserves from it.

Discretionary Fiscal Policy Deliberate changes of government expenditures and taxes to achieve particular economic objectives.

Diseconomies of Scale Exist when inputs are increased by some percentage and output increases by a smaller percentage, causing unit costs to rise.

Disequilibrium A state of either surplus or shortage in a market.

Disequilibrium Price A price other than equilibrium price. A price at which quantity demanded does not equal quantity supplied.

Disposable Income (DI) That portion of personal income that can be used for consumption or saving. It is equal to personal income minus personal taxes (especially income taxes).

Disutility The dissatisfaction one receives (from the consumption of a bad).

Dividends A share of profits distributed to stockholders.

Double Coincidence of Wants In a barter economy, a requirement that must be met before a trade can be made. It specifies that a trader must find another trader who is willing to trade what the first trader wants and at the same time wants what the first trader has.

Double Counting Counting a good more than once when computing GNP.

Dumping The sale of goods abroad at a price below their cost and below the price charged in the domestic markets.

Economics The science of scarcity: the science of how individuals and societies deal with the fact that wants are greater than the limited resources available to satisfy those wants.

Economic Analysis The process of applying economic tools and the economic way of thinking to real-world problems.

Economic Good A scarce good. A good where the amount available is less than people would want if it were given away at zero price.

Economic or Monopoly Rent A payment in excess of opportunity cost.

Economic Problem The fact that there are not enough resources to produce enough goods to satisfy peoples' unlimited wants.

Economic Profit The difference between total revenue and total (opportunity) cost, including both its explicit and implicit components.

Economic Rent Payment in excess of opportunity costs.

Economies of Scale Exist when inputs are increased by some percentage and output increases by a greater percentage, causing unit costs to fall.

Efficiency In terms of production, the condition where the maximum output is produced with given resources and technology. Efficiency implies the impossibility of gains in one area without losses in another.

Efficiency Criterion Addresses the question of whether an alternative arrangement exists that can make at least one person better off without making anyone else worse off.

Efficiency Wage Models These models hold that it is sometimes in the best interest of firms to pay their employees higher than equilibrium wage rates.

Elastic Demand The percentage change in quantity demanded is greater than the percentage change in price. Quantity demanded changes proportionately more than price changes.

Elasticity of Demand for Labor Percentage change in the quantity demanded of labor divided by the percentage change in the wage rate.

Employee Association An organization whose members belong to a particular profession.

Employment Rate The percentage of the noninstitutional adult civilian population that is employed: Employment rate = number of persons employed/number of persons in the noninstitutional adult civilian population.

Entrepreneurship The particular talent that some people have for organizing the resources of land, labor, and capital into the production of goods, seeking new business opportunities, and developing new ways of doing things.

Equation of Exchange An identity stating that the money supply times velocity must be equal to the price level times real GNP.

Equilibrium Equilibrium means "at rest." Equilibrium is the price–quantity combination in a market from which there is no tendency for buyers or sellers to move away. Graphically, equilibrium is the intersection point of the supply and demand curves.

Equilibrium Price (Market-clearing Price) The price at which quantity demanded of the good equals quantity supplied.

Equilibrium Quantity The quantity that corresponds to equilibrium price. The quantity at which the amount of the good buyers are willing and able to buy equals the amount sellers are willing and able to sell, and both equal the amount actually bought and sold.

Excess Capacity Theorem States that a monopolistic competitor in equilibrium produces an output smaller than the one that would minimize its costs of production.

Excess Reserves Any reserves held beyond the required amount. The difference between total reserves and required reserves.

Exchange rate The price of one currency in terms of another currency; for example, 1 dollar = 2 marks.

Excludability A good is excludable if it is possible, or not prohibitively costly, to exclude someone from receiving the benefits of the good once it has been produced.

Expansionary Fiscal Policy Fiscal policy designed to increase aggregate demand or aggregate supply.

Expectations Effect The increase in the nominal interest rate due to a higher expected inflation rate.

Explicit Cost A cost that is incurred when an actual (monetary) payment is made.

Exports Total foreign spending on domestic (U.S.) goods.

Externality A side effect of an action that affects the well-being of third parties.

Ex Ante Distribution (of Income) The before-tax-and-transfer-payment distribution of income.

Ex Ante Real Interest Rate The nominal interest rate minus the expected inflation rate.

Ex Post Distribution (of Income) The after-tax-and-transfer-payment distribution of income.

Ex Post Real Interest Rate The nominal interest rate minus the actual inflation rate.

Face Value (Par Value) Dollar amount specified on the bond.

Factor (or Resource) Markets Markets where the factors of production or resources are bought and sold.

Factor Price Searcher A firm that drives up factor price if it buys an additional factor unit. It faces an upward-sloping supply curve of factors.

Factor Price Taker A firm that can buy all of a factor it wants at the equilibrium price. It faces a horizontal (flat, perfectly elastic) supply curve of factors.

Fallacy of Composition The erroneous view that what is good or true for the individual is necessarily good or true for the group.

Federal Funds Market A market where banks lend reserves to one another, usually for short periods.

Federal Funds Rate The interest rate in the federal funds market; the interest rate banks charge one another to borrow reserves.

Federal Open Market Committee (FOMC) The 12-member policy-making group within the Fed. This committee has the authority to conduct open market operations.

Federal Reserve Notes Paper money issued by the Fed.

Final Good A good in the hands of its final user.

Fine-tuning The (usually frequent) use of discretionary monetary and fiscal policies to counteract even small undesirable movements in economic activity.

Fiscal Policy Changes in government expenditures and taxation in an effort to achieve particular macroeconomic goals, such as low unemployment, stable prices, economic growth, and so on.

Fixed Costs Costs that do not vary with output.

Fixed Exchange Rate System The system where a nation's currency is set at a fixed rate relative to all other currencies, and central banks intervene in the foreign exchange market to maintain the fixed rate.

Fixed Input An input whose quantity cannot be changed as output changes in the short run.

Fixed Investment Business purchases of capital goods, such as machinery and factories, and consumer purchases of new residential housing.

Flexible Exchange Rate System The system whereby exchange rates are determined by the forces of supply and demand for a currency.

Flow Variable A variable that can only be meaningfully measured over a period of time. GNP is a flow variable.

Foreign Exchange Market The market in which currencies of different countries are exchanged.

Fractional Reserve Banking A banking arrangement that allows banks to hold reserves equal to only a fraction of their deposit liabilities.

Free Good A good where the amount available is greater than the amount people want at zero price.

Free Rider Anyone who receives the benefits of a good without paying for it.

Frictional Unemployment The unemployment due to the natural "frictions" of the economy, caused by changing market conditions and represented by qualified individuals with transferable skills who change jobs.

Full Employment The condition that exists when the unemployment rate is equal to the natural unemployment rate.

Fungibility A term that is Latin in origin, meaning "such that any unit is substitutable for another." Fungibility means substitutable.

Game Theory A mathematical technique used to analyze the behavior of decision makers who try to reach an optimal position for themselves through game playing or the use of strategic behavior, are fully aware of the interactive nature of the process at hand, and anticipate the moves of other decision makers.

Gini Coefficient A measurement of the degree of inequality in the income distribution.

Glasnost A Russian term popularly used to mean openness in public discussion and the arts.

GNP Deflator The weighted average of prices of all goods and services produced in an economy.

Gold Standard The monetary arrangement whereby a nation backs its paper money totally or partially with gold.

Good Anything from which individuals receive utility or satisfaction.

Gosplan The Soviet central planning agency (under command-economy socialism) that has the responsibility of drafting the economic plan for the nation.

Government Bureaucrat An unelected person who works in a government bureau and is assigned a special task that relates to a law or program passed by the legislature.

Government Expenditures, or Government Spending The total dollar amounts spent by federal, state, and local governments on final goods and services.

Gross National Product (GNP) The total market value of all final goods and services produced annually in an economy.

Gross Private Domestic Investment, or Investment The sum of all purchases of newly produced capital goods plus changes in business inventories. It also includes expenditures on new residential housing.

Guaranteed Income Level Income level below which people are not allowed to fall.

Herfindahl Index Measures the degree of concentration in an industry. It is equal to the sum of the squares of the market shares of each firm in the industry.

Human Capital Education, development of skills, and anything else that is particular to the individual and increases his or her productivity.

Implicit Cost A cost that represents the value of resources used in production for which no actual (monetary) payment is made.

Implicit Marginal Tax Rate The rate at which the negative income tax payment, or any cash grant or subsidy, is reduced as earned income rises.

Imports Total domestic (U.S.) spending on foreign goods.

Income Effect (Micro) That portion of the change in the quantity demanded of a good that is attributable to a change in real income (brought about by a change in absolute price).

Income Effect (Macro) The increase in the real and nominal interest rates brought on by an increase in GNP.

Income Elastic The percentage change in quantity demanded of a good is greater than the percentage change in income.

Income Elasticity of Demand Measures the responsiveness of quantity demanded to changes in income.

Income Inelastic The percentage change in quantity demanded of a good is less than the percentage change in income.

Income Unit Elastic The percentage change in quantity demanded of a good is equal to the percentage change in income.

Incomplete Crowding Out The decrease in one or more components of private spending only partially offsets the increase in government spending.

Increasing-Cost Industry An industry in which average total costs increase as output increases and decrease as output decreases, as firms enter and exit the industry, respectively.

Independent Two variables are independent if as one changes, the other does not.

Indifference Curve A curve that shows all the bundles of two goods that give an individual equal total utility.

Indifference Curve Map Represents a number of indifference curves for a given individual with reference to two goods.

Indifference Set Group of bundles of two goods that give an individual equal total utility.

Industrial Policy In Japan, the policy of "watering the green spots," or aiding those industries that are most likely to be successful in the world marketplace.

Industrial Union A union whose membership is made up of individuals who work in the same firm or industry but do not all practice the same craft or trade.

Inefficiency In terms of production, the condition where less than the maximum output is produced with given resources and technology. Inefficiency implies the possibility of gains in one area without losses in another.

Inelastic Demand The percentage change in quantity demanded is less than the percentage change in price. Quantity demanded changes proportionately less than price changes.

Inferior Good A good the demand for which falls (rises) as income rises (falls).

Inflation An increase in the price level.

Inflationary Gap The condition where the real GNP the economy is producing is greater than the natural real GNP, and the unemployment rate that exists is less than the natural unemployment rate.

Inflation Rate The annual percentage change in some price index—such as the CPI or GNP deflator.

Injection Any expenditure on (U.S.) goods and services besides consumption expenditures is considered an injection. In short, any nonconsumption expenditure.

Inside Information Information that is not yet public; it is known only to a small group of people called insiders.

Interest Rate Effect The changes in household and business buying as the interest rate changes.

Intermediate Good A good that is an input in the production of a final good.

Internalizing Externalities An externality is *internalized* if the person(s) or group that generated the externality incorporate into their own private or *internal* cost–benefit calculations the external benefits (in the case of a positive externality) or the external costs (in the case of a negative externality) that third parties bear.

International Monetary Fund (IMF) An international organization created by the Bretton Woods system to oversee the international monetary system. Although the Bretton Woods system no longer exists, the IMF does. It does not control the world's money supply, but it does hold currency reserves for member nations and makes loans to central banks.

International Trade Effect The change in foreign sector spending as the price level changes.

Interpersonal Utility Comparison Comparing the utility one person receives from a good, service, or activity with the utility another person receives from the same good, service, or activity.

Inventory Investment Changes in the stock of unsold goods.

Inversely Related Two variables are inversely related if they move in opposite directions.

In-Kind Transfer Payments Transfer payments, such as food stamps, medical assistance, and subsidized housing, that are made in a specific good or service.

J-Curve The curve that shows a short-run worsening in the trade deficit after a currency depreciation, followed later by an improvement.

Junk Bonds Risky bonds that offer high coupon rates.

Kinked Demand Curve Theory A theory of oligopoly that assumes that if a single firm in the industry cuts price, other firms will do likewise, but if it raises price, other firms will not follow suit. The theory predicts price stickiness or rigidity.

Labor The physical and mental talents people contribute to the production process.

Labor Theory of Value Holds that the value of all commodities is equal to the value of the labor used in producing them.

Laffer Curve The curve, named after Arthur Laffer, that shows the relationship between tax rates and tax revenues. According to the Laffer curve, as tax rates rise from zero, tax revenues rise, reach a maximum at some point, and then fall with further increases in tax rates.

Land All natural resources, such as minerals, forests, water, and unimproved land.

Law of Demand As the price of a good rises, the quantity demanded of the good falls, and as the price of a good falls, the quantity demanded of the good rises, *ceteris paribus*.

Law of Diminishing Marginal Returns As ever-larger amounts of a variable input are combined with fixed inputs, eventually the marginal physical product of the variable input will decline.

Law of Diminishing Marginal Utility The marginal utility gained by consuming equal successive units of a good will decline as the amount consumed increases.

Law of Increasing Opportunity Costs As more of a good is produced, the higher the opportunity costs of producing that good.

Law of Supply As the price of a good rises, the quantity supplied of the good rises, and as the price of a good falls, the quantity supplied of the good falls, *ceteris paribus*.

Leakage An outflow or withdrawal of expenditures from the spending stream. Any part of income that does not go to purchase (U.S.) goods and services is considered a leakage.

Least-Cost Rule Specifies the combination of factors that minimizes costs. This requires that the following condition be met: $MPP_1/P_1 = MPP_2/P_2 = \ldots = MPP_n/P_n$, where the numbers stand for the different factors.

Less-Developed Country (LDC) A country with a low per-capita GNP.

Liabilities A debt of the business firm.

Limited Liability A legal term that signifies that the owners (stockholders) of a corporation cannot be sued for the corporation's failure to pay its debts.

Limited Partnership A form of business that is organized as a partnership, but which gives some of the partners the legal protection of limited liability.

Liquid Asset An asset that can easily and quickly be turned into cash. Some assets are more liquid than others; that is, assets differ as to the degree of liquidity.

Liquidity Effect The decrease in the real and nominal interest rates due to an increase in the supply of loanable funds.

Liquidity Trap The horizontal portion of the demand curve for money.

Loanable Funds Funds that someone borrows and another person lends, for which the borrower pays an interest rate to the lender.

Logrolling The exchange of votes to gain support for legislation.

Long Run A period of time in which all inputs can be varied (no inputs are fixed).

Long-Run Aggregate Supply Curve The long-run aggregate supply curve shows the real GNP the economy is prepared to supply at different price levels, assuming wage rates and all other input prices have fully adjusted to eliminate a recessionary or inflationary gap.

Long-Run Average Total Cost (*LRATC*) Curve A curve that shows the lowest (unit) cost at which the firm can produce any given level of output.

Long-Run Competitive Equilibrium The condition where $P = MC = SRATC = LRATC$. There are zero economic profits, firms are producing the quantity of output at which price is equal to marginal cost, and no firm has an incentive to change its plant size.

Long-Run Equilibrium The condition that exists in the economy when the real GNP being produced equals the natural real GNP and the unemployment rate that exists equals the natural unemployment rate. In long-run equilibrium, the quantity demanded of real GNP equals the (long-run) quantity supplied of real GNP. This condition is met at the intersection of the aggregate demand curve and the long-run aggregate supply curve.

Long-Run Industry Supply Curve Graphic representation of the quantities of output that the industry is prepared to supply at different prices after the entry and exit of firms is completed.

Lorenz Curve A graph of the income distribution. It expresses the relationship between cumulative percentage of families and cumulative percentage of income.

Macroeconomics The branch of economics that deals with human behavior and choices as they relate to highly aggregated markets (such as the goods and services market) or the entire economy.

Managed Float A managed flexible exchange rate system, under which nations now and then intervene to adjust their official reserve holdings to moderate major swings in exchange rates; this is today's international monetary system.

Managerial Coordination The process in which managers direct employees to perform certain tasks.

Marginal Analysis Weighing additional benefits of a change against the additional costs of a change with respect to current conditions.

Marginal Cost The change in total cost or total variable cost that results from a change in output: $MC = \Delta TC/\Delta Q = \Delta TVC/\Delta Q$.

Marginal Factor Cost The additional cost incurred by employing an additional factor unit.

Marginal Physical Product The change in output that results from changing the variable input by one unit, holding all other inputs fixed.

Marginal Productivity Theory States that firms in competitive or perfect product and factor markets pay factors their marginal revenue products.

Marginal Rate of Substitution The amount of one good an individual is willing to give up to obtain an additional unit of another good and maintain equal total utility.

Marginal Revenue The change in total revenue that results from selling one additional unit of output.

Marginal Revenue Product (*MRP*) The additional revenue generated by employing an additional factor unit.

Marginal Tax Rate The change in a person's tax payment divided by a change in the person's taxable income: Δtax payment/Δtaxable income.

Marginal Utility The additional utility a person receives from consuming an additional unit of a particular good.

Market Any arrangement by which people exchange goods and services.

Market Coordination The process in which individuals perform tasks, such as producing certain quantities of goods, based on changes in the market forces such as supply, demand, and price.

Market Failure A situation in which the market does not provide the ideal or optimal amount of a particular good.

Market Structure The particular environment a firm finds itself in, the characteristics of which influence the firm's pricing and output decisions.

Median Voter Model Suggests that politicians in a two-person political race will move towards matching the preferences of the median voter (that is, that person's preferences which are at the center, or in the middle, of the political spectrum).

Medium of Exchange Anything that is generally acceptable in exchange for goods and services. A function of money.

Merchandise Trade Balance The difference between the value of merchandise exports and the value of merchandise imports.

Merchandise Trade Deficit The situation where the value of merchandise exports is less than the value of merchandise imports.

Merchandise Trade Surplus The situation where the value of merchandise exports is greater than the value of merchandise imports.

Microeconomics The branch of economics that deals with human behavior and choices as they relate to relatively small units—the individual, the firm, the industry, the single market.

Minimum Efficient Scale The lowest output level at which average total costs are minimized.

Mixed Capitalism An economic system characterized by largely private ownership of the factors of production, market allocation of resources, and decentralized decision making; most economic activities take place in the private sector in this system, but government plays a substantial economic and regulatory role.

Monetary Base The sum of reserves and currency outside banks.

Monetary Policy The deliberate control of the money supply and credit conditions in an effort to achieve particular macroeconomic goals, such as low unemployment, stable prices, economic growth, and so on.

Monetary Rule Describes monetary policy that is based on a predetermined steady growth rate in the money supply.

Monetary Wealth The value of a person's monetary assets. *Wealth,* as distinguished from *monetary wealth,* refers to the value of all assets owned, both monetary and nonmonetary. In short, a person's wealth equals his or her monetary wealth (such as $1,000 cash) plus nonmonetary wealth (a car or a house).

Money Any good that is widely accepted for purposes of exchange.

Money Demand Line The graphical representation of the direct relationship between the quantity demanded of money and GNP.

(Money) Income The current-dollar amount of a person's income.

Money Market Accounts Accounts with banks (called money market deposit accounts, MMDA) or mutual fund companies (called money market mutual fund accounts, MMMF) that pay interest and offer limited check-writing privileges.

Money Multiplier Measures actual change in the money supply for a dollar change in the monetary base.

Monitor Person in a business firm who coordinates team production and reduces shirking.

Monopolistic Competition A theory of market structure based on three assumptions: many sellers and buyers, firms producing and selling slightly differentiated products, and easy entry and exit.

Monopoly A theory of market structure based on three assumptions: There is one seller, it sells a product for which no close substitutes exist, and there are extremely high barriers to entry.

Monopsony A single buyer in a factor market.

M1 Includes currency held outside banks + demand deposits + other checkable deposits + traveler's checks.

M2 Includes M1 + small-denomination time deposits + savings deposits + money market accounts + overnight repurchase agreements + overnight Eurodollar deposits.

National Debt The total sum of what the federal government owes its creditors.

National Income The sum of the payments to suppliers of the factors of production. It is equal to the compensation of employees + proprietors' income + corporate profits + rental income of persons + net interest.

Natural Monopoly The condition where economies of scale are so pronounced in an industry that only one firm can survive; an industry in which it is not economical to have more than one firm providing a good.

Natural Rate Hypothesis The idea that in the long run, unemployment is at its natural rate. Within the Phillips curve framework, the natural rate hypothesis specifies that there is a long-run Phillips curve, which is vertical at the natural rate of unemployment.

Natural Real GNP The real GNP that is being produced at the natural unemployment rate.

Natural Unemployment Rate Unemployment caused by frictional and structural factors in the economy. Natural unemployment rate = frictional unemployment rate + structural unemployment rate. For some economists, this is the unemployment rate toward which the economy tends to return; it is the long-run average unemployment rate.

Negative Externality Exists when a person's or group's actions cause a cost (adverse side effect) to be felt by others.

Net Exports Exports − imports.

Net National Product (NNP) GNP minus the capital consumption allowance.

Net Taxes Taxes minus transfer payments.

Net Worth (Equity or Capital Stock) Value of the business firm to its owners; it is determined by subtracting liabilities from assets.

Nominal GNP The value of final goods and services produced in a given year in that year's prevailing market prices. The terms GNP, nominal GNP, and current-dollar GNP are used interchangeably.

Nominal Interest Rate The interest rate actually charged (or paid); the market interest rate. Nominal interest rate = real interest rate + expected inflation rate.

Nonactivists Persons who argue against the deliberate use of discretionary fiscal and monetary policies. They believe in a permanent, stable, rule-oriented monetary and fiscal framework.

Nonexcludability A good is nonexcludable if it is impossible, or prohibitively costly, to exclude someone from receiving the benefits of the good once it has been produced.

Nonprofit Firms Firms in which there are no residual claimants; any revenues over costs must be plowed back into the operation of the firm so that "what comes in" equals "what goes out."

Nonrivalrous in Consumption A good is nonrivalrous in consumption if its consumption by one person does not reduce its consumption by others.

Normal Good A good the demand for which rises (falls) as income rises (falls).

Normal Profit Zero economic profit. A firm that earns normal profit is earning revenues equal to its total opportunity costs. This is the level of profit necessary to keep resources employed in that particular firm.

Normative Economics The study of "what should be" in economic matters.

Oligopoly A theory of market structure based on three assumptions: few sellers and many buyers, firms producing either homogeneous or differentiated products, and significant barriers to entry.

One-Shot Inflation A one-time increase in the price level. An increase in the price level that does not continue.

Open Economy An economy that trades goods and services with other nations.

Open Market Operations The buying and selling of government securities by the Fed.

Opportunity Cost The most highly valued opportunity or alternative forfeited when a choice is made.

Overnight Eurodollar Deposits Dollar-denominated deposits in banks outside the United States.

Overnight Repurchase Agreements An agreement by a financial institution to sell short-term securities to its customers, combined with an agreement to repurchase them at a higher price at a specified future date.

Overvaluation A currency is overvalued if its price in terms of other currencies is above the equilibrium price.

Own Price The price of a good. For example, if the price of oranges is $1, this is (its) own price.

Parity Price Ratio A ratio of an index of prices that farmers receive to an index of prices that farmers pay.

Partnership A form of business that is owned by two or more co-owners (partners) who share any profits the business earns; each of the partners is legally responsible for all debts incurred by the firm.

Perestroika A Russian term used to describe Soviet economic reform.

Perfect Competition A theory of market structure based on four assumptions: there are many sellers and buyers, sellers sell a homogeneous good, buyers and sellers have all relevant information, and there is easy entry into and exit from the market.

Perfect Price Discrimination Occurs when the seller charges the highest price each consumer would be willing to pay for the product rather than go without it.

Perfectly Elastic Demand A small percentage change in price brings about an extremely large percentage change in quantity demanded (from buying all to buying nothing).

Perfectly Inelastic Demand Quantity demanded does not change as price changes.

Personal Income (PI) The amount of income that individuals actually receive. It is equal to national income minus undistributed corporate profits, social insurance taxes, and corporate profits taxes, plus transfer payments.

Per-Capita Real Economic Growth An increase from one period to the next in per-capita real GNP, which is real GNP divided by population.

Phillips Curve A curve that originally showed the relationship between wage inflation and unemployment. Now it more often shows the relationship between price inflation and unemployment.

Policy Ineffectiveness Proposition (PIP) If (1) a policy change is correctly *anticipated*, (2) individuals form their expectations rationally, and (3) wages and prices are flexible, then neither fiscal policy nor monetary policy is effective at meeting macroeconomic goals.

Positive Economics The study of "what is" in economic matters.

Positive Externality Exists when a person's or group's actions cause a benefit (beneficial side effect) to be felt by others.

Positive Rate of Time Preference Preference for earlier availability of goods over later availability of goods. A person's rate of time preference equals the percentage increase in future consumption that the person needs to obtain before he or she will sacrifice some amount of present consumption.

Poverty Income Threshold (Poverty Line) Income level below which people are considered to be living in poverty.

Present Value The current worth of some future dollar amount of income or receipts.

Price Ceiling A government-mandated maximum price above which legal trades cannot be made.

Price Discrimination Occurs when the seller charges different prices for the product it sells, and the price differences do not reflect cost differences.

Price Elasticity of Demand Measures the responsiveness of quantity demanded to changes in price.

Price Elasticity of Supply Measures the responsiveness of quantity supplied to changes in price.

Price Floor A government-mandated minimum price below which legal trades cannot be made.

Price Index A measure of the price level.

Price Leadership Theory In this theory of oligopoly, the dominant firm in the industry determines price, and all other firms take their price as given.

Price Level The weighted average of the prices of all goods and services.

Price Searcher A seller that has the ability to control to some degree the price of the product it sells.

Price Support The minimum price government determines farmers will receive for their products. Not all agricultural products have price supports.

Price Taker A seller that does not have the ability to control the price of the product it sells; it takes the price determined in the market.

Producers' Surplus The difference between the price sellers receive for a good and the minimum or lowest price for which they would have sold the good. It is a dollar measure of the benefit gained by being able to sell a unit of output for more than one is willing to sell it.

Product Markets Markets where goods and services are bought and sold.

Product Price Searcher A firm that faces a downward-sloping demand curve for the product it sells. It sells fewer units at higher prices than lower prices. The monopoly, monopolistic competitive, and oligopoly firms are product price searchers.

Product Price Taker A firm that faces a horizontal demand curve for the product it sells. It can sell as many units of its good as it wants without affecting price. The perfectly competitive firm is a product price taker.

Production Possibilities Frontier Represents the possible combinations of two goods that an economy can produce in a certain period of time, under the conditions of a given state of technology, no unemployed resources, and efficient production.

Profit The difference between total revenue and total cost.

Profit-maximization Rule Profit is maximized by producing the quantity of output at which $MR = MC$.

Proprietorship A form of business that is owned by one individual who makes all the business decisions, receives the entire profits, and is legally responsible for the debts of the firm.

Public Choice The branch of economics that deals with the application of economic principles and tools to public-sector decision making.

Public Employee Union A union whose membership is made up of individuals who work for the local, state, or federal government.

Public Franchise A right granted to a firm by government that permits the firm to provide a particular good or service and excludes all others from doing the same.

Public Good A good provided to one person that gives benefits to more than one person; it is characterized by non-rivalry in consumption and nonexcludability.

Public Interest Theory of Regulation Holds that regulators are seeking to do, and will do through regulation, what is in the best interest of the public or society at large.

Purchasing Power The quantity of goods and services that can be purchased with a unit of money. Purchasing power and the price level are inversely related: As the price level goes up (down), purchasing power goes down (up).

Purchasing Power Parity (PPP) Theory States that exchange rates between any two currencies will adjust to reflect changes in the relative price levels of the two countries.

Pure Capitalism An economic system characterized by private ownership of the factors of production, market allocation of resources, and decentralized decision making; most economic activities take place in the private sector, and government plays a small role or no role at all in the economy.

Pure Economic Rent A category of economic rent where the payment is to a factor that is in fixed supply, implying that it has zero opportunity costs.

Quota A legal limit on the amount of a good that may be imported.

Ratex Short for rational expectations.

Rational Expectations Expectations that individuals form based on past experience and also on their predictions about the effects of present and future policy actions and events.

Rational Ignorance The state of not acquiring information because the costs of acquiring the information are greater than the benefits.

Rationing Device Something that is used to decide who gets what of available goods and resources. Price is a rationing device.

Real Balance Effect The change in the purchasing power of dollar-denominated assets that results from a change in the price level.

Real Business Cycle Theory The theory that business cycle contractions are generally brought about by aggregate supply changes that reduce the economy's capacity to produce.

Real Economic Growth An increase from one period to the next in real GNP.

Real GNP The value of the entire output produced annually in an economy, adjusted for price changes. It also can be defined as GNP (gross national product) valued in prices prevailing in the base year.

Real Income Income adjusted for price changes. A person has more (less) real income as the price of a good falls (rises), *ceteris paribus.*

Real Interest Rate The nominal interest rate adjusted for expected inflation; that is, the nominal interest rate minus the expected inflation rate.

Recession A decline in real GNP that lasts for two consecutive quarters (six months) or more.

Recessionary Gap The condition where the real GNP the economy is producing is less than the natural real GNP, and the unemployment rate that exists is greater than the natural unemployment rate.

Regulatory Lag The period between the time when a natural monopoly's costs change and the time when the regulatory agency adjusts prices for the natural monopoly.

Relative Price The price of a good in terms of another good.

Rent Seeking Actions of individuals and groups who spend resources to influence public policy in the hope of redistributing (transferring) income to themselves from others.

Required-Reserve Ratio (*r*) A percentage of each dollar deposited that must be held on reserve (at the Fed or in the bank's vault).

Required Reserves The minimum amount of reserves a bank must hold against its deposits as mandated by the Fed.

Reserve Requirement The rule that specifies the amount of reserves a bank must hold to back up deposits.

Reserves The sum of bank deposits at the Fed and vault cash.

Residual Claimants Persons who share in the profits of a business firm.

Resource Allocative Efficiency The situation that exists when firms produce the quantity of output for which price equals marginal cost.

Revaluation An official governmental act that changes the exchange rate by raising the official price of a currency.

Right-to-Work Laws Laws that make it illegal to require union membership for purposes of employment.

Rivalrous in Consumption A good is rivalrous in consumption if its consumption by one person reduces its consumption by others.

Roundabout Method of Production The production of capital goods that enhance productive capabilities and ultimately bring about increased consumption.

Satisficing Behavior Behavior directed to meeting some satisfactory (not maximum) profit target.

Savings Deposit A type of time deposit. In principle (though not always in practice), the depositor can be required to give advance written notice prior to withdrawal.

Scarcity The condition where our wants are greater than the limited resources available to satisfy those wants.

Screening The process used by employers to increase the probability of choosing "good" employees based on certain criteria.

Second-Degree Price Discrimination Occurs when the seller charges a uniform price per unit for one specific quantity, a lower price for an additional quantity, and so on.

Separation of Ownership from Control (or Management) Refers to the division of interests between owners and managers that may occur in large business firms.

(Shares of) Stock A claim on the assets of a corporation that gives the purchaser a share of the ownership of the corporation.

Shirking Behavior descriptive of a person who is putting forth less than the agreed-to effort when doing a job.

Shortage (Excess Demand) A condition in which quantity demanded is greater than quantity supplied. Shortages only occur at prices below equilibrium price.

Short Run A period of time in which some inputs are fixed.

Short-Run Aggregate Supply (SRAS) Curve Shows the real GNP producers will offer for sale at different price levels, *ceteris paribus.*

Short-Run Equilibrium In the economy, the condition that exists when the quantity demanded of real GNP equals the (short-run) quantity supplied of real GNP. This condition is met where the aggregate demand curve intersects the short-run aggregate supply curve.

Short-Run Industry (Market) Supply Curve The horizontal summation of all existing firms' short-run supply curves.

Short-Run (Firm) Supply Curve The portion of the firm's marginal cost curve that lies above the average variable cost curve.

Simple Deposit Multiplier The reciprocal of the required-reserve ratio, $1/r$.

Simple Quantity Theory of Money The theory that assumes that V and Q are constant and predicts that changes in M lead to strictly proportional changes in P.

Slope The ratio of the change in the variable on the vertical axis to the change in the variable on the horizontal axis.

Socially Optimal Output The output level at which all benefits (external as well as private) and all costs (external as well as private) have been taken into account and adjusted for.

Special Drawing Right An international money, created by the IMF, in the form of bookkeeping entries; like gold and currencies, they can be used by nations to settle international accounts.

Special-Interest Groups Subsets of the general population that hold (usually) intense preferences for or against a particular government service, activity, or policy. Often special-interest groups gain from public policies that may not be in accord with the interests of the general public.

Stagflation The simultaneous occurrence of high rates of inflation and unemployment.

Stock Variable A variable that can be meaningfully measured at a moment in time. For example, the nation's money supply is a stock variable.

Store of Value The ability of an item to hold value over time. A function of money.

Strike The situation where union employees refuse to work at a certain wage or under certain conditions.

Structural Unemployment Unemployment due to structural changes in the economy that eliminate some jobs and create others for which the unemployed are unqualified.

Substitutes Two goods that satisfy similar needs or desires. With substitutes, the demand for one rises as the price of the other rises (or the demand for one falls as the price of the other falls).

Substitution Effect That portion of the change in the quantity demanded of a good that is attributable to a change in its relative price.

Sunk Cost A cost incurred in the past that cannot be changed by current decisions and therefore cannot be recovered.

Supply The willingness and ability of sellers to produce and offer to sell different quantities of a good at different prices during a specific time period.

Supply Schedule The numerical tabulation of the quantity supplied of a good at different prices.

Surplus (Excess Supply) A condition in which quantity supplied is greater than quantity demanded. Surpluses only occur at prices above equilibrium price.

Surplus Value In Marxist terminology, the difference between the total value of production and the subsistence wages paid to workers.

T-Account A simplified balance sheet that shows the changes in a bank's assets and liabilities.

Target Price A guaranteed price; if the market price is below the target price, the farmer receives a deficiency payment equal to the difference between the market price and the target price.

Tariff A tax on imports.

Tax Base When referring to income taxes, the total amount of taxable income. The (average) tax rate × tax base = tax revenues.

Technology The body of skills and knowledge concerning the use of resources in production. An advance in technology commonly refers to the ability to produce more output with a fixed amount of resources or the ability to produce the same output with fewer resources.

The Federal Reserve System (the Fed) The central bank of the United States.

Theory An abstract representation of the real world designed with the intent to better understand that world.

Third-Degree Price Discrimination Occurs when the seller charges different prices in different markets, or charges a different price to different segments of the buying population.

Tie-in Sale A sale whereby one good can be purchased only if another good is also purchased.

Time Deposits Interest-earning deposits that have a stated maturity date and carry penalties for early withdrawal.

Total Cost The sum of fixed and variable costs.

Total Revenue Price times quantity sold.

Total Utility The total satisfaction a person receives from consuming a particular quantity of a good.

Trade Deficit The situation where the value of exports is less than the value of imports.

Trade-off A situation in which the attainment of something desirable necessarily implies the loss of something else desirable.

Transaction Costs The costs associated with the time and effort needed to search out, negotiate, and consummate an exchange.

Transfer Payments Payments that are not made in return for goods and services currently supplied.

Transitivity The principle whereby if A is preferred to B, and B is preferred to C, then A is preferred to C.

Transmission Mechanism The routes or channels that ripple effects created in the money market travel to affect the goods and services market (represented by the aggregate demand and aggregate supply curves in the AD–AS framework).

Trust A combination of firms that come together to act as a monopolist.

Unattainable Region Includes those points above the production possibilities frontier.

Underground Economy Unreported exchanges that take place outside the normal recorded market channels. Some underground activities deal with illegal goods; others deal with legal goods and tax evasion.

Undervaluation A currency is undervalued if its price in terms of other currencies is below the equilibrium price.

Unemployment Rate The percentage of the civilian labor force that is unemployed: Unemployment rate = number of unemployed persons/number of persons in the civilian labor force.

Union Shop An organization in which a worker is not required to be a member of the union to be hired, but must become a member within a certain period of time after being employed.

Unit Elastic Demand The percentage change in quantity demanded is equal to the percentage change in price. Quantity demanded changes proportionately to price changes.

Unit of Account A common measurement in which relative values are expressed. A function of money.

Unlimited Liability A legal term that signifies that the personal assets of the owner(s) of a firm may be used to pay off the debts of the firm.

(Upward-sloping) Supply Curve The graphical representation of the law of supply.

U.S. Treasury Securities Bonds and bondlike securities issued by the U.S. Treasury when it borrows.

Util An artificial construct used to measure utility.

Utility The satisfaction one receives from the consumption of a good.

Value Marginal Product (*VMP*) The price of the good multiplied by the marginal physical product of the factor: $VMP = P \times MPP$. For a product price taker, $P = MR$, and thus $MRP = VMP$. For a product price searcher, $P > MR$, and $VMP > MRP$.

Variable Costs Costs that vary with output.

Variable Input An input whose quantity can be changed as output changes in the short run.

Veil of Ignorance The imaginary veil or curtain behind which a person does not know his or her position in the income distribution.

Velocity The average number of times a dollar is spent to buy final goods and services in a year.

Vicious Circle of Poverty The idea that countries are poor because they do not save (and invest) and that they cannot save (and invest) because they are poor.

"Voluntary" Export Restraint (VER) An agreement between two countries in which the exporting country "voluntarily" agrees to limit its exports to the importing country.

Wage Discrimination The situation that exists when individuals of equal ability and productivity (as measured by their contribution to output) are paid different wage rates.

Welfare Cost of Monopoly The net value (value to buyers over and above costs to suppliers) of the difference between the monopoly quantity of output (where $P > MC$) and the competitive quantity of output (where $P = MC$).

Welfare Cost Triangle A diagram of the welfare cost to society associated with monopoly.

X-Inefficiency The increase in costs and organizational slack in a monopoly resulting from the lack of competitive pressure to push costs down to their lowest possible level.

The Federal Budget, National Debt, Money Supply, Prices and Interest Rates

YEAR	FEDERAL BUDGET SURPLUS or DEFICIT (−) (billions of dollars)	NATIONAL DEBT (billions of dollars)	M1 MONEY SUPPLY (billions of dollars)	PERCENT CHANGE IN M1 FROM PREVIOUS YEAR	M2 MONEY SUPPLY (billions of dollars)	PERCENT CHANGE IN M2 FROM PREVIOUS YEAR	GNP DEFLATOR (1982=100)	CONSUMER PRICE INDEX (CPI) (1982–84=100)	INTEREST RATE ON 3-MONTH U.S. TREASURY BILLS (annual percent)
1929	1.2	16.9	—	—	—	—	14.6	—	—
1933	−1.3	22.5	—	—	—	—	11.2	—	.52
1939	−2.2	48.2	—	—	—	—	12.7	13.9	.02
1940	−1.3	50.7	—	—	—	—	13.0	14.0	.01
1941	−5.1	57.5	—	—	—	—	13.8	14.7	.10
1942	−33.1	79.2	—	—	—	—	14.7	16.3	.33
1943	−46.6	142.6	—	—	—	—	15.1	17.3	.37
1944	−54.5	204.1	—	—	—	—	15.3	17.6	.37
1945	−42.1	260.1	—	—	—	—	15.7	18.0	.37
1946	3.5	271.0	—	—	—	—	19.4	19.5	.37
1947	13.4	257.1	—	—	—	—	22.1	22.3	.59
1948	8.3	252.0	—	—	—	—	23.6	24.1	1.04
1949	−2.6	252.6	—	—	—	—	23.5	23.8	1.10
1950	9.2	256.9	—	—	—	—	23.9	24.1	1.22
1951	6.5	255.3	—	—	—	—	25.1	26.0	1.55
1952	−3.7	259.1	—	—	—	—	25.5	26.5	1.77
1953	−7.1	266.0	—	—	—	—	25.9	26.7	1.93
1954	−6.0	270.8	—	—	—	—	26.3	26.9	.95
1955	4.4	274.4	—	—	—	—	27.2	26.8	1.75
1956	6.1	272.7	—	—	—	—	28.1	27.2	2.66
1957	2.3	272.3	—	—	—	—	29.1	28.1	3.27
1958	−10.3	279.7	—	—	—	—	29.7	28.9	1.84
1959	−1.1	287.5	140.0	—	297.8	—	30.4	29.1	3.40
1960	3.0	290.5	140.7	0.5	312.3	4.9	30.9	29.6	2.93
1961	−3.9	292.6	145.2	3.2	335.5	7.4	31.2	29.9	2.38
1962	−4.2	302.9	147.9	1.8	362.7	8.1	31.9	30.2	2.78
1963	.3	310.3	153.4	3.7	393.2	8.4	32.4	30.6	3.16
1964	−3.3	316.1	160.4	4.6	424.8	8.0	32.9	31.0	3.55
1965	.5	322.3	167.9	4.7	459.4	8.1	33.8	31.5	3.95
1966	−1.8	328.5	172.1	2.5	480.0	4.5	35.0	32.4	4.88
1967	−13.2	340.4	183.3	6.5	524.3	9.2	35.9	33.4	4.32
1968	−6.0	368.7	197.5	7.7	566.3	8.0	37.7	34.8	5.34
1969	8.4	365.8	204.0	3.3	589.5	4.1	39.8	36.7	6.68
1970	−12.4	380.9	214.5	5.1	628.2	6.6	42.0	38.8	6.46
1971	−22.0	408.2	228.4	6.5	712.7	13.5	44.4	40.5	4.35
1972	−16.8	435.9	249.3	9.1	805.1	13.0	46.5	41.8	4.07
1973	−5.6	466.3	262.9	5.5	861.0	6.9	49.5	44.4	7.04
1974	−11.6	483.9	274.4	4.4	908.5	5.5	54.0	49.3	7.89
1975	−69.4	541.9	287.6	4.8	1,023.2	12.6	59.3	53.8	5.84
1976	−53.5	629.0	306.4	6.5	1,163.7	13.7	63.1	56.9	4.99
1977	−46.0	706.4	331.3	8.1	1,286.7	10.6	67.3	60.6	5.26
1978	−29.3	776.6	358.5	8.2	1,389.0	7.9	72.2	65.2	7.22
1979	−16.1	828.9	382.9	6.8	1,497.1	7.8	78.6	72.6	10.04
1980	−61.3	908.5	408.9	6.8	1,629.9	8.9	85.7	82.4	11.51
1981	−63.8	994.3	436.5	6.7	1,793.5	10.0	94.0	90.9	14.03
1982	−145.9	1,136.8	474.5	8.7	1,953.1	8.9	100.0	96.5	10.69
1983	−176.0	1,371.2	521.2	9.8	2,186.5	11.9	103.9	99.6	8.63
1984	−169.6	1,564.1	552.1	5.9	2,371.6	8.5	107.7	103.9	9.58
1985	−196.0	1,817.0	620.1	12.3	2,570.6	8.4	110.9	107.6	7.48
1986	−206.9	2,120.1	724.7	16.9	2,814.2	9.5	113.8	109.6	5.98
1987	−158.2	2,345.6	750.4	3.5	2,913.2	3.5	117.4	113.6	5.82
1988	−141.7	2,600.8	787.5	4.9	3,072.4	5.5	121.3	118.3	6.69
1989	−134.3	2,867.5	794.8	0.9	3,221.6	4.9	126.3	124.0	8.12
1990	−161.3	3,206.3	825.5	3.8	3,323.3	3.2	131.5	130.7	7.51

SOURCE: Council of Economic Advisers, *Economic Report of the President, 1991* (Washington, D.C.: U.S. Government Printing Office, 1991).